Ethnographi

Blackwell Anthologies in Social and Cultural Anthropology

Series Editor: Parker Shipton, Boston University

Drawing from some of the most significant scholarly work of the nineteenth and twentieth centuries, the *Blackwell Anthologies in Social and Cultural Anthropology* series offers a comprehensive and unique perspective on the ever-changing field of anthropology. It represents both a collection of classic readers and an exciting challenge to the norms that have shaped this discipline over the past century.

Each edited volume is devoted to a traditional subdiscipline of the field such as the anthropology of religion, linguistic anthropology, or medical anthropology; and provides a foundation in the canonical readings of the selected area. Aware that such subdisciplinary definitions are still widely recognized and useful – but increasingly problematic – these volumes are crafted to include a rare and invaluable perspective on social and cultural anthropology at the onset of the twenty-first century. Each text provides a selection of classic readings together with contemporary works that underscore the artificiality of subdisciplinary definitions and point students, researchers, and general readers in the new directions in which anthropology is moving.

Series Advisory Editorial Board:

1. *Linguistic Anthropology: A Reader, 2nd Edition*
   Edited by Alessandro Duranti
2. *A Reader in the Anthropology of Religion, 2nd Edition*
   Edited by Michael Lambek
3. *The Anthropology of Politics: A Reader in Ethnography, Theory, and Critique*
   Edited by Joan Vincent
4. *Kinship and Family: An Anthropological Reader*
   Edited by Robert Parkin and Linda Stone
5. *Law and Anthropology: A Reader*
   Edited by Sally Falk Moore
6. *The Anthropology of Development and Globalization: From Classical Political Economy to Contemporary Neoliberalism*
   Edited by Marc Edelman and Angelique Haugerud
7. *The Anthropology of Art: A Reader*
   Edited by Howard Morphy and Morgan Perkins
8. *Feminist Anthropology: A Reader*
   Edited by Ellen Lewin
9. *Ethnographic Fieldwork: An Anthropological Reader, 2nd Edition*
   Edited by Antonius C. G. M. Robben and Jeffrey A. Sluka
10. *Environmental Anthropology*
    Edited by Michael R. Dove and Carol Carpenter
11. *Anthropology and Child Development: A Cross-Cultural Reader*
    Edited by Robert A. LeVine and Rebecca S. New
12. *Foundations of Anthropological Theory: From Classical Antiquity to Early Modern Europe*
    Edited by Robert Launay
13. *Psychological Anthropology: A Reader on Self in Culture*
    Edited by Robert A. LeVine
14. *A Reader in Medical Anthropology: Theoretical Trajectories, Emergent Realities*
    Edited by Byron J. Good, Michael M. J. Fischer, Sarah S. Willen, and Mary-Jo DelVecchio Good
15. *Sexualities in Anthropology*
    Edited by Andrew Lyons and Harriet Lyons

Ethnographic Fieldwork

An Anthropological Reader

Edited by

Antonius C. G. M. Robben
and Jeffrey A. Sluka

Second Edition

WILEY-BLACKWELL

A John Wiley & Sons, Ltd., Publication

Library of Congress Cataloging-in-Publication Data

Ethnographic fieldwork : an anthropological reader / edited by
Antonius C. G. M. Robben and Jeffrey A. Sluka. – 2nd ed.
p.   cm. – (Blackwell anthologies in social and cultural anthropology)
Includes bibliographical references and index.
ISBN 978-0-470-65715-7 (pbk. : alk. paper)
1. Ethnology–Fieldwork. I. Robben, Antonius C. G. M. II. Sluka, Jeffrey A.
GN346.E675 2011
305.80072′3–dc23
2011023517

A catalogue record for this book is available from the British Library.

Set in 9/11pt Sabon by SPi Publisher Services, Pondicherry, India

Printed and bound in Singapore by Markono Print Media Pte Ltd

2   2013

Contents

About the Editors

Antonius C. G. M. Robben is Professor of Anthropology at Utrecht University, the Netherlands, and past President of the Netherlands Society of Anthropology. He is the author of *Sons of the Sea Goddess: Economic Practice and Discursive Conflict in Brazil* (1989) and *Political Violence and Trauma in Argentina* (2005), which received an award from the American Anthropological Association. He is the editor of more than half a dozen books, including *Fieldwork under Fire: Contemporary Studies of Violence and Survival* (with Carolyn Nordstrom, 1995) and *Iraq at a Distance: What Anthropologists Can Teach Us About the War* (2010).

Jeffrey A. Sluka is Associate Professor of Social Anthropology at Massey University, New Zealand. He is past Chair of the Association of Social Anthropologists of Aotearoa/New Zealand, a Fellow of the American Anthropological Association, author of *Hearts and Minds, Water and Fish: Popular Support for the IRA and INLA in a Northern Irish Ghetto* (1989), and editor of *Death Squad: The Anthropology of State Terror* (2000).

Editors' Acknowledgments

The staff in Malden, Massachusetts, has been superb as always during the production of the second edition of *Ethnographic Fieldwork*. The customer survey commissioned by Wiley-Blackwell was helpful for the revision, and so were the many suggestions volunteered by colleagues and users of the first edition. We want to express our gratitude to senior editor Rosalie Robertson and Anthropology and Linguistics book editor Julia Kirk for their enthusiasm and professionalism. The request for the last-minute addition to the selection of texts was honored with unusual flexibility, even though the production was already in full swing. They demonstrate that a large press and personal attention to authors can go together. Finally, we want to thank Sarah Dancy for the superb and smooth copy-editing as the book's project manager.

Acknowledgments to Sources

The editors and publishers gratefully acknowledge the permission granted to reproduce the copyright material in this book:

1   Joseph-Marie Degérando, pp. 61–70, 101–104 from *The Observation of Savage Peoples*, trans. F. C. T. Moore. London: Routledge & Kegan Paul, 1969[1800]. Copyright © F. C. T. Moore.

2   Franz Boas, "The Methods of Ethnology," pp. 311–321 from *American Anthropologist* 22(4), Oct.–Dec. 1920.

3   Bronislaw Malinowski, "Subject, Method and Scope," pp. 4–25 from *Argonauts of the Western Pacific*. Prospect Heights, IL: Waveland Press, 1984[1922].

4   Hortense Powdermaker, "A Woman Going Native," pp. 108–119, 183–187, 188–190, 196, 197–198 from *Stranger and Friend: The Way of an Anthropologist*. London: Secker & Warburg, 1967. Copyright © 1966 by Hortense Powdermaker. Reprinted by permission of W. W. Norton & Co., Inc.

5   Roschanack Shaery-Eisenlohr, "Fixing and Negotiating Identities in the Field: The Case of Lebanese Shiites," pp. 31–46 from *Women Fielding Danger: Negotiating Ethnographic Identities in Field Research*, ed. Martha K. Huggins and Marie-Louise Glebbeek. Lanham: Rowman & Littlefield, 2009.

6   Walter L. Williams, "Being Gay and Doing Fieldwork," pp. 70–85 *from Out in the Field: Reflections of Lesbian and Gay Anthropologists*, ed. Ellen Lewin and William L. Leap. Urbana: University of Illinois Press, 1996.

7   Paul Spencer, "Automythologies and the Reconstruction of Ageing," pp. 50–63 from *Anthropology and Autobiography*, ed. Judith Okely and Helen Callaway. London: Routledge, 1992.

8   Charles Wagley, "Champukwi of the Village of the Tapirs," pp. 398–415 from *In the Company of Man: Twenty Portraits of Anthropological Informants*, ed. Joseph B. Casagrande. New York: Harper & Row, 1960. Copyright © 1960 by Joseph B. Casagrande.

9 Gerald D. Berreman, "Behind Many Masks: Ethnography and Impression Management," pp. xvii–lvii plus selected bibliography from *Hindus of the Himalayas: Ethnography and Change*, 2nd edn. Berkeley: University of California Press, 1972. Copyright © 1963, 1972 by The Regents of the University of California. This material appeared originally, in a slightly different form, as Monograph No. 4 of the Society for Applied Anthropology, 1962. Reprinted by permission of the Society for Applied Anthropology.

10 Antonius C. G. M. Robben, "The Politics of Truth and Emotion among Victims and Perpetrators of Violence," pp. 81–103 from *Fieldwork under Fire: Contemporary Studies of Violence and Survival*, ed. Carolyn Nordstrom and Antonius C. G. M. Robben. Berkeley: University of California Press, 1995.

11 Vine Deloria, Jr., "Custer Died for Your Sins," pp. 130–137 from *To See Ourselves: Anthropology and Modern Social Issues*, ed. Thomas Weaver. Glenview, IL: Scott, Foresman & Co., 1973. Reprinted with permission of Scribner, an imprint of Simon & Schuster Adult Publishing Group, from *Custer Died for Your Sins* by Vine Deloria, Jr. Copyright © 1969 by Vine Deloria, Jr.; copyright renewed © 1997 by Vine Deloria, Jr.

12 Cecil King, "Here Come the Anthros," pp. 115–119 from *Indians and Anthropologists: Vine Deloria, Jr, and the Critique of Anthropology*, ed. Thomas Biolsi and Larry J. Zimmerman. Tucson: University of Arizona Press, 1997. Copyright © 1977 by The Arizona Board of Regents. Reprinted by permission of Arizona Press.

13 Ofra Greenberg, "When They Read What the Papers Say We Wrote," pp. 107–118 plus relevant bibliography from *When They Read What We Write: The Politics of Ethnography*, ed. Caroline B. Brettell. Westport, CN: Bergin & Garvey, 1993. Copyright © 1993, 1996 by Caroline B. Brettell. Reprinted by permission of Greenwood Publishing Group, Inc., Westport, CT.

14 Nancy Scheper-Hughes, "Ire in Ireland," pp. 117–40 from *Ethnography* 1(1), 2000. This article is drawn from the preface and epilogue of Nancy Scheper-Hughes's 20th anniversary updated and expanded edition of *Saints, Scholars and Schizophrenics: Mental Illness in Rural Ireland*, University of California Press (2001). Copyright © 2001 by The Regents of the University of California. Reprinted by permission of the University of California Press.

15 June Nash, "Ethnology in a Revolutionary Setting," pp. 148–165, plus references pp. 165–166, from *Ethics and Anthropology: Dilemmas in Fieldwork*, ed. Michael A. Rynkiewich and James P. Spradley. New York: John Wiley & Sons, 1976. Copyright © 1976 by John Wiley & Sons, Inc. Reprinted by permission of John Wiley & Sons, Inc.

16 Neil L. Whitehead, "The Ethnographer's Tale," pp. 1–2, 11–40 from *Dark Shamans: Kanaimà and the Poetics of Violent Death*. Durham: Duke University Press, 2002.

17 Cynthia Keppley Mahmood, "Anthropology from the Bones: A Memoir of Fieldwork, Survival, and Commitment," pp. 1–11 from *Anthropology and Humanism* 33(1 & 2), 2008.

18 Jeffrey A. Sluka, "Reflections on Managing Danger in Fieldwork: Dangerous Anthropology in Belfast," pp. 276–294 from *Fieldwork under Fire: Contemporary*

Studies of Violence and Survival, ed. Carolyn Nordstrom and Antonius C. G. M. Robben. Berkeley: University of California Press, 1995. Copyright © 1995 by The Regents of the University of California. Reprinted by permission of the University of California Press.

19   Irving Louis Horowitz, "The Life and Death of Project Camelot," pp. 138–148 from *To See Ourselves: Anthropology and Modern Social Issues*, ed. Thomas Weaver. Glencoe, IL: Scott, Foresman & Co., 1973. Copyright © 1965 by Transaction Publishers. This material originally appeared in *Society* magazine (December, 1965) by Transaction, Inc. Reprinted by permission of Transaction Publishers.

20   Philippe Bourgois, "Confronting the Ethics of Ethnography: Lessons From Fieldwork in Central America," pp. 110–126 from *Decolonizing Anthropology: Moving Further Toward an Anthropology for Liberation*, ed. Faye V. Harrison. Washington, DC: American Anthropological Association, 1991. Copyright © 1991 by the American Anthropological Association. Reprinted by permission of the author and the American Anthropological Association. Not for sale or further reproduction.

21   Gerald D. Berreman, "Ethics versus 'Realism' in Anthropology," pp. 38–71 from *Ethics and the Profession of Anthropology: Dialogue for a New Era*, ed. Carolyn Fluehr-Lobban. Philadelphia: University of Pennsylvania Press, 1991. Copyright © 1991 by the University of Pennsylvania Press. Reprinted by permission of the University of Pennsylvania Press.

22   Jeffrey David Ehrenreich, "Worms, Witchcraft and Wild Incantations: The Case of the Chicken Soup Cure," pp. 137–141 from *Anthropological Quarterly* 69(3), 1996.

23   "Code of Ethics of the American Anthropological Association," Washington, DC, 1998. Copyright © 1998 by the American Anthropological Association. Reprinted by permission of the American Anthropological Association.

24   Akhil Gupta and James Ferguson, "Beyond 'Culture': Space, Identity, and the Politics of Difference," pp. 6–20 plus relevant references pp. 21–23, from *Cultural Anthropology* 7(1), 1992. Copyright © 1992 by the American Anthropological Association. Reprinted by permission of the Copyright Clearance Center on behalf of the American Anthropological Association.

25   David B. Edwards, "Afghanistan, Ethnography, and the New World Order," pp. 345–360 from *Cultural Anthropology* 9(3), 1994. Copyright © 1994 by the American Anthropological Association. Reprinted by permission of the Copyright Clearance Center on behalf of the American Anthropological Association.

26   Ulf Hannerz, "Being There … and There … and There! Reflections on Multi-Site Ethnography," pp. 201–216 from *Ethnography* 4(2), 2003. Copyright © 2003 by SAGE Publications (London, Thousands Oaks, CA and New Delhi). Reprinted by permission of the author and Sage Publications Ltd.

27   Matsutake Worlds Research Group, "A New Form of Collaboration in Cultural Anthropology: Matsutake Worlds," pp. 380–403 from *American Ethnologist* 36(2), 2009.

28   Gregory Bateson and Margaret Mead, pp. xi–xvi, 13–17, 49–51, 84–88, plates 15, 16, and 17 from *Balinese Character: A Photographic Analysis*. New York: New York Academy of Sciences, 1942. Copyright © 1942 by The New York Academy of Sciences. Reprinted by permission of Blackwell Publishing on behalf of The New York Academy of Sciences and the Institute for Intercultural Studies.

29   Paul Stoller and Cheryl Olkes, "The Taste of Ethnographic Things," pp. 15–34 plus relevant references from *The Taste of Ethnographic Things: The Senses in Anthropology*. Philadelphia: University of Pennsylvania Press, 1989. Copyright © 1989 by the University of Pennsylvania Press. Reprinted by permission of the University of Pennsylvania Press.

30   Steven Feld, "Dialogic Editing: Interpreting How Kaluli Read *Sound and Sentiment*," pp. 190–210 from *Cultural Anthropology* 2(2), 1987. Copyright © 1987 by the American Anthropological Association. Reprinted by permission of the Copyright Clearance Center on behalf of the American Anthropological Association.

31   Kathryn Linn Geurts, "On Rocks, Walks, and Talks in West Africa: Cultural Categories and an Anthropology of the Senses," pp. 178–198 from *Ethos* 30(3), 2002.

32   Paul Rabinow, "Fieldwork and Friendship in Morocco," pp. 142–162 from *Reflections on Fieldwork in Morocco*. Berkeley: University of California Press, 1977. Copyright © 1997 by The Regents of the University of California. Reprinted by permission of the University of California Press.

33   Jeanne Favret-Saada, "The Way Things Are Said," pp. 3–12, 16–24 plus relevant references from *Deadly Words: Witchcraft in the Bocage*, trans. Catherine Cullen. Cambridge: Cambridge University Press, 1980[1977]. English translation © Maison des Sciences de l'homme and Cambridge University Press, 1980. Originally published in French as *Les mots, la mort, les sorts*. © Éditions Gallimard, Paris, 1977. Reprinted by permission of Cambridge University Press and Éditions Gallimard.

34   Thomas Csordas, "Transmutation of Sensibilities: Empathy, Intuition, Revelation," pp. 106–116 from *The Shadow Side of Fieldwork: Exploring the Blurred Borders between Ethnography and Life*, ed. Athena McLean and Annette Leibing. Malden: Blackwell, 2007.

35   Vincent Crapanzano, "'At the Heart of the Discipline': Critical Reflections on Fieldwork," pp. 55–78 from *Emotions in the Field: The Psychology and Anthropology of Fieldwork Experience*, ed. James Davies and Dimitrina Spencer. Stanford: Stanford University Press, 2010.

36   Margaret Mead, "Introduction – 1942," pp. 3–14 from *And Keep Your Powder Dry: An Anthropologist Looks at the American Character*. London: Ronald Whiting & Wheaton, 1967[1942]. (Reissued New York: Berghahn, 2000.)

37   Monique Skidmore, "Scholarship, Advocacy, and the Politics of Engagement in Burma (Myanmar)," pp. 42–59 from *Engaged Observer: Anthropology, Advocacy, and Activism*, ed. Victoria Sanford and Asale Angel-Ajani. New Brunswick: Rutgers University Press, 2008.

38   Roberto J. González, "'Human Terrain': Past, Present and Future Applications," pp. 21–26 from *Anthropology Today* 24(1), 2008.

39   Nikolas Kosmatopoulos, "The Gaza Freedom Flotilla: Ethnographic Notes on 'Othering Violence'," pp. 26–29 from *Anthropology Today* 26(4), 2010.

Part VI Introduction Fieldwork Ethics. Cartoon on p. 299: DOONESBURY © 1986 G. B. Trudeau. Reprinted with permission of UNIVERSAL PRESS SYNDICATE. All rights reserved.

Every effort has been made to trace copyright holders and to obtain their permission for the use of copyright material. The publisher apologizes for any errors or omissions in the above list and would be grateful if notified of any corrections that should be incorporated in future reprints or editions of this book.

Fieldwork in Cultural Anthropology: An Introduction

Jeffrey A. Sluka and
Antonius C. G. M. Robben

To understand a strange society, the anthropologist has traditionally immersed himself in it, learning, as far as possible, to think, see, feel, and sometimes act as a member of its culture and at the same time as a trained anthropologist from another culture. This is the heart of the participant observation method – involvement and detachment. Its practice is both an art and a science. Involvement is necessary to understand the psychological realities of a culture, that is, its meanings for the indigenous members. Detachment is necessary to construct the abstract reality: a network of social relations, including the rules and how they function – not necessarily real to the people studied. Field work is a deeply human as well as a scientific experience and a detailed knowledge of both aspects is an important source of data in itself, and necessary for any comparative study of methodology. (Powdermaker 1966:9)

For graduate students preparing for their first field trip, field work represents mystery, opportunity, and excitement. Field work is also a trial through battle in a war for which the novice has little preparation. The student knows that this is a challenge he will have to face, a major rite de passage *that will provide him with the opportunity to prove his ability, courage, and temperamental suitability for the profession. He knows that, in doing field work and in working with the ethnographic data he will collect, a number of transformations will occur. ... Much like the rites of passage of many primitive societies, success*

Ethnographic Fieldwork: An Anthropological Reader, Second Edition. Edited by
Antonius C. G. M. Robben and Jeffrey A. Sluka.
Editorial material and organization © 2012 John Wiley & Sons, Inc.
Published 2012 by John Wiley & Sons, Inc.

in field work is more a function of personality ability than of previous training in specific techniques. Success in field work proclaims manhood and generates a major transformation: a student of culture becomes an anthropologist.
(Freilich 1970:16)

Fieldwork is *the central activity of anthropology.* (Howell 1990:4)

One of the most enduring, perhaps the *most enduring, metaphors, or "keywords" ... in modern anthropology is "fieldwork" ... "fieldwork" is – it goes without saying, and thus must be said – the* sine qua non *of modern anthropology, the ritual initiation experience in the discipline.* (Berger 1993:174)

The tradition of fieldwork, and a conceptual repertoire derived from deep immersion in local ways of life, has been the source of anthropology's strength.
(Keesing and Strathern 1998:7)

These opening quotes, spanning the last half of the twentieth century, amply demonstrate the enduring central place of fieldwork in cultural anthropology. Every discipline has its own particularity in methods of gathering data. In cultural anthropology it is fieldwork based on participant observation, which hinges on the dynamic and contradictory synthesis of subjective insider and objective outsider. As an insider, the fieldworker learns what behavior means to the people themselves. As an outsider, the fieldworker observes, experiences, and makes comparisons in ways that insiders can or would not. As Gupta and Ferguson (1997) have observed, in anthropology "the field" represents a site, method, and location, and nearly every professional anthropologist has undertaken fieldwork, which is still viewed as the characteristic rite of passage into professional status in the discipline. Anthropologists "pioneered" ethnographic fieldwork, and cultural or social anthropology remains the only social science that relies on fieldwork based on participant observation as its central method. One of the main developments in cultural anthropology since the 1960s has been an increasing readiness of anthropologists to talk candidly about their experiences in the field, their relationships with informants, and the contexts in which they gathered their material. While in the past some dismissed these reflections on fieldwork as self-indulgent "navel-gazing," it is now generally accepted that they have made an important contribution to the discipline, because we can better understand and evaluate an ethnographic text if we know something about the writer, the experiences upon which the text is based, and the circumstances of its production. Furthermore, these reflections turn anthropologists into better fieldworkers by making them aware of their own practices, emotions, biases, and experiences.

Today, "the field" has broadened to include everywhere there are human beings, and every imaginable human group and context has become an actual or potential research site. Cultural anthropologists are conducting fieldwork in institutional and many other settings, with "little people" (dwarves), perpetrators and survivors of violence in war zones, elderly patients in hospices, HIV patients, firefighters, drug dealers, political militants, new religious movements, motor-home nomads, Olympic athletes, poker players, and modern Japanese geishas. Reports on fieldwork are a regular feature in *Anthropology News*, the newsletter of the American Anthropological Association. For example, the May 2005 issue highlighted the expanding "new venues" of fieldwork. Edward Bruner (2005) reported on fieldwork traveling with tourists and visiting tourist destinations; Linda Scarangella (2005) discussed fieldwork at the Buffalo Bill's Wild West Show attraction at Euro Disney; and Jonathan Marion (2005) described multi-site fieldwork with ballroom dancers at their studios and competitions. And when we say that every *imaginable* human context can be a potential fieldwork site, we mean it literally, since there is already a speculative "space" or "extraterrestrial" anthropology preparing for future fieldwork on space stations, space craft, and proposed human settlements on the Moon, Mars, and beyond, including the possibility of fieldwork with intelligent nonhuman extraterrestrials (cf. Maruyama 1975).

In the new millennium, fieldwork has become even more central to the discipline, to the extent that there are claims that it is the *only* common ground that holds it together. While this would seem to be an exaggeration, since fieldwork is only one of several key shared "paradigmatic" elements (described below) that have always distinguished the anthropological perspective, it again stresses the importance of fieldwork in the discipline today, and helps establish the *raison d'être* for this Reader.

Today, there is a vast and ever expanding literature on the practical experience of fieldwork, covering many disciplines and a wide range of field situations in most parts of the world. Learning how to conduct research based on participant observation has become a priority for scholars in an expanding number of disciplines beyond anthropology and sociology, including folklore, economics, psychology, geography, history, education, social work, nursing, and development studies, all of which have now published their own texts on fieldwork methods and edited volumes of fieldwork accounts (e.g., Jackson 1987; Devereux and Hoddinott 1992; Jackson and Ives 1996; Lareau and Shultz 1996; Delamont 2001; Scheyvens and Storey 2003; Fife 2005; Westbrook 2008). Along with dozens of books and edited volumes, there are hundreds if not thousands of articles on fieldwork in journals and other publications. Evidence of the emerging cross-disciplinary "trendiness" of fieldwork is the publication between 1999 and 2005 of five separate major multi-volume sets on ethnographic fieldwork, totaling 21 volumes (Bryman and Burgess 1999; Schensul and LeCompte 1999; Bryman 2001; Denzin and Lincoln 2001; Pole 2005).

Beginning in the 1960s, a steadily increasing flow of edited volumes of fieldwork accounts began to emerge, and in the 1970s so too did book-length monographs centering on particular anthropologists' fieldwork experiences and edited volumes on anthropological fieldwork. In cultural anthropology there are now numerous publications on nearly every imaginable aspect of fieldwork, including *ethics and fieldwork* (e.g., Rynkiewich and Spradley 1976; Appell 1978; Fluehr-Lobban 2002; Caplan 2003; Armbruster and Laerke 2008); *semiotics and fieldwork* (Manning 1987); the *psychology of fieldwork* (e.g., Wengle 1988; Hunt 1989); *fieldnotes* (Sanjek 1990; Emerson et al. 1995); *women in the field* (e.g., Golde 1970; Roberts 1981; Cesara 1982; Altorki and El-Solh 1988;

Marcus 1993; Yu 1997; Huggins and Glebbeek 2009); *feminist issues in fieldwork* (e.g., Wolf 1995); *sex and gender in fieldwork* (e.g., Whitehead and Conaway 1986); *intimacy and erotic subjectivity in fieldwork* (e.g., Kulick and Willson 1995; Markowitz and Ashkenazi 1999; Wolcott 2002); *gay and lesbian anthropologists in the field* (e.g., Lewin and Leap 1996); *fieldwork and globalization* (e.g., Robbins and Bamford 1997); *occupational safety and health in fieldwork* (e.g., Howell 1990); *violence and fieldwork* (Lee 1995; Nordstrom and Robben 1995; Greenhouse et al. 2002); *long-term fieldwork* (e.g., Foster et al. 1979; Kemper and Royce 2002); *fieldwork and friendship* (e.g., Powdermaker 1966; Chiñas 1992; Kumar 1992; Grindal and Salamone 1995; Ridler 1996); *emotions and fieldwork* (e.g., Kleinman and Copp 1993; Spencer and Davies 2010); *fieldwork and locality* (Gupta and Ferguson 1997; Coleman and Collins 2006); *engaged fieldwork* (Eriksen 2006; Sanford and Angel-Ajani 2006); and even *virtual fieldwork* (Hine 2000; Kozinets 2010). There are *humorous accounts of fieldwork* (e.g., Barley 1983, 1985, 1988; Borgerhoff Mulder and Logsdon 1996); books and volumes on fieldwork in particular countries (e.g., for Japan, see Hendry 1999; Bester et al. 2003) and most regions of the world (e.g., for the Pacific, see DeVita 1988; for the Caribbean, see Taylor 2010), and even explorations of the relationship between fieldwork conducted by sociocultural anthropologists, biological anthropologists, and primatologists (MacClancy and Fuentes 2010). In fact, so much has been written about fieldwork that by 1988 Gravel and Ridinger could publish an annotated bibliography of just *anthropological* fieldwork that already included 700 entries, and that number has probably more than doubled since then. Of particular value has been the publication of a large number of reflexive personal accounts of field experiences (see Appendices 2 and 3).

The articles in this collection have been selected from among this wealth of publications because they have a well-earned place in the "intellectual baggage" of most experienced fieldworkers in the discipline, and deserve to be passed on to a new generation. This Reader is intended to help facilitate this goal by providing students with an historical, methodological, ethical, reflexive, and stylistic context to fieldwork, and is ideally suited to be read in conjunction with a text on formal research methods (see Appendix 4) and an ethnography which includes a reflexive account of the fieldwork on which it is based (see Appendix 3). The articles present qualitative, subjective, and reflexive perspectives on fieldwork, and by reading them students can develop their knowledge and appreciation of the perspectives, approaches, methods, problems, experiences, and ethics involved in anthropological fieldwork. The Reader aims to provide students with a good sense of classical and contemporary reflections on fieldwork, the tensions between self and other, the relationships between anthropologists and research participants, conflicts and ethical problems, various types of ethnographic research, and different styles of writing about fieldwork. It is about *fieldwork* in general rather than formal "fieldwork methods," because the intention is not only to highlight the central role of fieldwork in anthropology, but also to explore its wider significance to the discipline.

Here, we provide a basic introduction to fieldwork from the perspective of cultural anthropology, including how it fits into the disciplinary paradigm and has been defined. It includes, furthermore, an overview of the history of fieldwork, a review of fieldwork in the postmodern era, a discussion of culture shock and the taboo against "going native," a general literature review and many suggestions and references for further reading and exploration of this topic, and, finally, a description of the construction and structure of the reader itself.

Fieldwork in the Anthropological Paradigm

Fieldwork represents one of the fundamental or "paradigmatic" elements of anthropology as an academic discipline. Thomas Kuhn (1962) argued that a paradigm was a conceptual model of an academic discipline, the learning of which represented the socialization process through which students are prepared for membership in a scientific or academic discipline. The basic paradigm of anthropology, outlined below, shows where fieldwork "fits in" or integrates with the rest of the core elements that define the discipline:

1 *Culture*: The core concept of cultural anthropology.
2 *Fieldwork*: The primary method of cultural anthropology. Long-term *fieldwork* based on participant observation. A "field" as opposed to "laboratory" science.
3 *Cross-cultural comparative perspective*: A scientific approach in anthropology, looking for regularities, patterns, generalizations, "rules" or "laws" concerning human and social behavior. Macro-analysis. Generalizing.
4 *Ethnography*: A case-study approach. In-depth study of the culture of a people, group, or community. Microanalysis. Particularizing.
5 *Holistic perspective*: Looks at human beings from all perspectives, stresses the interrelationships among different aspects of life, and asserts that any culture has to be understood not only in its local manifestation, but in relation to the wider global context in which it occurs.
6 *Eclectic approach*: Eclectic means "to pick and choose," in this case both topics and theories. There is a very wide variety of interests and no dominant theoretical model.
7 *Humanistic perspective*: "Humanism" focuses on people, with the applied aim of reducing suffering and improving the human condition. Referred to as "the Enlightenment vision." Includes anthropology as a form of cultural critique and advocacy.
8 *Scientific approach*: Empiricism and the scientific method. "Science" refers to the observation, identification, description, experimental investigation, and theoretical explanation of natural phenomena. Based on direct experience and observation.
9 *Combined subjective/objective perspective*: Equally interested in the subjective, participant's, actor's, or "emic" perspective and the objective, observer's, anthropologist's, or "etic" perspective.

These nine elements are *interrelated* – for example, one can see how fieldwork is affected by each of the other eight elements – and one of the central characteristics of the anthropological paradigm is that it sets up, and is based upon, a series of conceptual and theoretical oppositions, including:

Ethnography (microanalysis) / Cross-cultural comparison (macroanalysis)
Differences (particularizing) / Similarities (generalizing)
Synchronic (the "ethnographic present") / Diachronic (long-term)
Humanism / Science
Participant (subjective) / Observer (objective)

Since the earliest days of the discipline, it has been a fundamental theoretical tenet that the dynamic tension created by these oppositions has been the well-spring or fundamental source of the "anthropological imagination," and produces a unique perspective and important insights distinct from any other social science perspective.

Humanistic and Scientific Approaches: Fieldwork as Both Art and Science

> Anthropology is the most humanistic of the sciences and the most scientific of the humanities. (Alfred L. Kroeber 1876–1960; date of quotation unknown)

Traditionally, the self-image of anthropologists has been that of humanists and scientists, and they did not see any necessary contradiction between the two approaches. Eric Wolf is famous for his assertion that anthropology is a "bridging" discipline between the sciences and the humanities, and for his observation, after Kroeber, that anthropology has been "a bond between subject matters … in part history, part literature; in part natural science, part social science; it strives to study men from within and without … the most scientific of the humanities, the most humanist of the sciences" (1964:88). This conception of the dual nature of anthropology was described by Hortense Powdermaker in her classic fieldwork account, *Stranger and Friend*, in these terms:

> There are some anthropologists who rather arbitrarily reserve the label "scientific" for nonhumanistic studies. A scientific attitude ignores no level of understanding. … If the dual nature of anthropology – an art and a science, a humanistic science – is accepted, there is no reason why each cannot be expanded. The inherent ambiguities of this approach are only a reflection of those which exist in life itself. (1966:306)

And this idea has been explored more recently by Arnd Schneider and Christopher Wright in *Between Art and Anthropology: Contemporary Ethnographic Practice* (2010).

Humanities–sciences continuum in anthropological fieldwork

Humanities – Fieldwork as an art form	*Sciences – Fieldwork as a scientific method*
Humanistic	Scientific
Qualitative	Quantitative
Subjective	Objective
Participant (emic)	Observer (etic)
Postmodernism	Positivism/empiricism

This point is stressed here because, as stated above, this Reader is about *fieldwork in its most general sense*, rather than formal "fieldwork methods," because the practice of fieldwork has proven to be as much an art as a science. If anthropologists are "scientific instruments" they are also human ones, and successful fieldwork requires both well-developed research skills and interpersonal relations skills. This has long been recognized in the discipline. For example, in the 1960s Powdermaker observed: "In addition to a capacity for open involvements and for becoming detached from them, personal qualities such as kindness, patience, tact, endurance, and the ability to 'take' both loneliness and ambiguity are helpful. Other idiosyncratic characteristics may be useful in one field situation and not in another" (1969:420). Similarly, Seymour-Smith refers to "the imaginative leap involved in coming to terms with an alien culture or way of life" (1986b:429). Can a formal methods approach teach or train aspiring fieldworkers qualitative cognitive and interpersonal skills – Powdermaker's "idiosyncratic characteristics" – such as how to be kind, tactful, and empathetic, how to be accepted and get along with people who are different from you, or how to make the "imaginative leaps" Seymour-Smith says are required for successful fieldwork? This is not to say that training in formal methods is not useful, but only that it is incomplete.

Fieldwork Defined

A good way to introduce fieldwork is to begin by considering how it has generally been defined in the discipline. This can be done by reviewing some of the most popular definitions as presented in (1) the *International Encyclopedia of the Social Sciences*, (2) a popular introductory anthropology text, and (3) a leading anthropology dictionary. These also show how the definition of fieldwork has gradually changed, with the inclusion of new concerns and ideas about ethics, politics, reflexivity, collaboration, and reciprocity.

"Field work," from the International Encyclopedia of the Social Sciences (1969)

Hortense Powdermaker's entry provides a classic definition of fieldwork which draws upon her *Stranger and Friend: The Way of an Anthropologist* (1966), probably the most widely read book-length study of anthropological fieldwork, which discusses the mistakes, successes, and complex emotions of conducting research in Melanesia, Northern Rhodesia, and the USA:

> Field work is the study of people and of their culture in their natural habitat. Anthropological field work has been characterized by the prolonged residence of the investigator, his participation in and observation of the society, and his attempt to understand the inside view of the native peoples and to achieve the holistic view of a social scientist. … The publication of Malinowski's *Argonauts of the Western Pacific* in 1922 revealed the great potentialities of field work. This study of Trobriand Islanders, among whom Malinowski had lived for almost three years, set new standards for field workers which continue to operate. Field work came to mean immersion in a tribal society – learning, as far as possible, to speak, think, see, feel, and act as a member of its culture and, at the same time, as a trained anthropologist from a different culture. (Powdermaker 1969:418)

Powdermaker went on to discuss preparation for and starting fieldwork; the advantages and disadvantages of solo, family, and team research; approval and cooperation of authorities; gaining the good will and consent of research participants; the first steps of the fieldwork process; participation in the culture; objectivity; and the influence of the theoretical orientation of the field worker.

Powdermaker concluded by identifying an emerging interest in "the field worker as an individual": "A quite new development, not yet strong enough to be called a trend, is the recognition that the field worker is himself an inherent part of the situation studied and that his personal as well as his scientific reactions are an important part of the research process" (1969:422). She argued that anthropology has failed to grasp the scientific importance of the ethnographer's social role and personal characteristics, while giving short shrift to chance, mistakes, fieldwork's trial-and-error approach, and the interpersonal dynamic with the people under study. In the following decade, this "emerging interest" would evolve into the full-fledged "reflexive trend," one of the most significant modern developments in the anthropological approach to fieldwork of which *Writing Culture* (Clifford and Marcus 1986) is generally regarded as the most influential text (see Beteille and Madan 1975; Rabinow 1977; Ruby 1982).

"Fieldwork," from Cultural Anthropology:
A Contemporary Perspective *(1998)*

In the third edition of their popular introductory cultural anthropology textbook, Roger Keesing and Andrew Strathern define fieldwork as follows:

> For most anthropologists, the immediate problems of understanding and the sources of data come from what has come to be known as *fieldwork*: intimate participation in a community and observation of modes of behavior and the organization of social life. The process of recording and interpreting another people's way of life is called *ethnography*.
>
> Whether the setting is city, town, village, or jungle hamlet, the mode of anthropological research is in many important respects the same. Most essentially, it entails a deep immersion into the life of a people. Instead of studying large samples of people, the anthropologist enters as fully as possible into the everyday life of a community, neighborhood, or group. ... One learns by participant observation, by living as well as viewing the new patterns of life. Successful fieldwork is seldom possible in a period much shorter than a year, especially where a new language and culture must be learned. Ideally, the researcher stays a good deal longer, sometimes on several successive field trips. The value of fieldwork sustained over a long period is beginning to come clearly into view. Sustained and deep research yields insights into a culture, and into the processes of continuity and change, scarcely attainable any other way. (1998:7–9)

In their definition, Keesing and Strathern stress that fieldwork is a two-sided encounter between research participants and ethical researchers:

> Consider the encounter from the other side. A people's lives are interrupted by a strange foreigner, often with a family, who moves into the community .... This person seldom fits the types of foreigners the people have learned to deal with previously – missionaries, traders, government officers, politicians, or whatever. The newcomer is insatiably curious

about things private, sacred, and personal, for reasons and motives that are incomprehensible. The person must be accorded a role of some sort; clumsy efforts to speak, bad manners, and intrusions into daily life must be tolerated. All this attention may be flattering, but it may breed suspicion, hostility, and jealousy. In a less isolated and more sophisticated community, "being studied" may smack of condescension and may offend pride, not arouse it.

On the anthropologist's side, ethical problems loom large. Should one try to protect the identity of the community and its people by disguising names and places? Can one intervene in matters of custom and health? Can one betray the confidence of one's informants in some grave violation of the law? (1998:8–9)

Finally, Keesing and Strathern draw attention to the gap between the data described in fieldnotes and the lived experiences, sounds, smells, and scenes that cannot be captured in writing but are sedimented in the unconscious. Their use of the term "unconscious" is somewhat misleading, because it suggests that the fieldworker is unaware of these impressions, but Keesing and Strathern are right in arguing that the anthropologist draws upon an unpronounced background understanding that is larger than the fieldnotes, and gives the ethnography a richness which could not have been obtained any other way than through an extended immersion in the field. Sensorial fieldwork (see Part VIII) is an ethnographic approach that makes such influences conscious and the subject of systematic study.

Keesing and Strathern conclude their brief introductory discussion of fieldwork by observing that anthropology has retained its "humanistic vision" because it remains based on the fundamental intimacy of face-to-face research (1998:10).

"Fieldwork," from the Dictionary of Anthropology (1986)

Charlotte Seymour-Smith defines fieldwork in this way:

> fieldwork. Research undertaken by the anthropologist or ethnologist in a given ethnographic area or community. Such an ethnographic area in modern anthropology is not necessarily limited to the traditional tribal or peasant community, and may embrace studies of urban, industrial or other settings which the anthropologist selects for the purposes of intensive research. The anthropological perspective has similarly been employed in the study of subcultures and in institutional research within modern industrial society. So, while it was once true to say that anthropology was the study of people considered to be primitive, of exotic and little-known tribal cultures, and of peasant communities, modern anthropological research can no longer be defined by this criterion and must be defined instead by the application of its distinctive methods of fieldwork and analysis. In many cases, however, disciplinary boundaries become blurred in the study of modern industrial and urban society, due to the emergence of novel theoretical and methodological syntheses resulting from interdisciplinary collaboration and interchange. (1986a:117)

Seymour-Smith then focuses on ethical and political issues in fieldwork, and suggests that anthropologists might offer "to perform some useful or valued service in return for the collaboration he or she requires" (1986a:117). This call for reciprocity as an ethical requirement of fieldwork is a modern one, and Seymour-Smith notes that anthropologists are increasingly asked to legitimate their research before the communities under study, national politicians, administrators, and intellectuals, while being summoned to share the results and produce tangible benefits.

Seymour-Smith's discussion incorporates the emergence of the "reflexive trend" in cultural anthropology, and recognizes the beginnings of new forms of fieldwork with built-in reciprocity then emerging as a response to the ethical issues and criticisms of anthropology raised by research participants – the ethnographic "other" – that exploded in the discipline during the 1960s and 1970s. Reflexive anthropology turns the fieldworker's ongoing negotiation of his or her professional role into an object of study, analyzes the power relations involved, and questions the nature of participant observation.

Seymour-Smith also discusses the issue of neutrality, observing that "he or she may not always be able to conserve neutrality or may under certain circumstances feel that neutrality is not an ethically acceptable position" (1986a:118), and addresses the emerging politics of modern fieldwork:

> In many Third World nations, intellectuals and representatives of indigenous peoples and other oppressed or subordinate groups share the general view of western anthropology either as a form of espionage or an account of "folklore" and exotic customs perpetuating a totally false image of their national reality and the real problems of their minority groups. Anthropologists also enjoy a poor reputation for ethical behavior, and have been criticized principally for their lack of commitment to the welfare of the people they study, and the failure to share the results of their research .... It is natural enough for people who observe the anthropologist, comparatively wealthy by local standards and apparently free to pursue the line of research he or she chooses, to resent what they regard as the exploitation of the local community for the purposes of advancing his or her own career at home, placing the goals of his or her individual research project over and above any commitment to the aspirations and basic needs of the local population. And it is only to be expected that communities and peoples of the Third World will come more and more to reject this type of investigation and demand that the anthropologist contribute something in return for his or her presence. (1986a:118)

Thus, by the time this article was written in the mid-1980s, the trends in concern for ethics, criticism by research participants, neutrality, and reflexivity in cultural anthropology, which emerged in the 1960s and 1970s, were continuing, and there were new concerns with collaboration, reciprocity, and the politics of fieldwork.

An Historical Outline of Fieldwork

> The way to do fieldwork is never to come up for air until it is all over. (Margaret Mead 1901–78; source unknown)

In *Doing Fieldwork: Warnings and Advice* (1971:21–41), Rosalie Wax provided an excellent thumbnail sketch of the history of fieldwork. The following historical outline of the evolution of fieldwork is an elaborated and updated synopsis of Wax's history (cf. Urry 1984 for another useful history of fieldwork).

Wax began by observing: "Descriptive reporting of the customs, inclinations, and accomplishments of foreign peoples is almost as old as writing itself" (1971:21). Herodotus wrote accounts of the Persians and Scythians for the Greeks, and the

Romans continued this practice. With the rise of the Islamic empires, they too began to write descriptions of the foreign peoples they encountered. The first Europeans to collect and record ethnographic data about foreign peoples were Catholic missionaries and frontier merchants. During the last quarter of the nineteenth century, the rapid growth and spread of European and American colonialism and imperialism produced an explosion of ethnographic "fieldwork" and descriptive accounts of the new peoples and cultures encountered during this process. This resulted from the fact that "a good many literate and reasonably well-educated men – governmental officials, administrators, missionaries, and political exiles – were obliged to spend many years and sometimes most of their lives living and working with an alien or "backward" people" (1971:23). Many of them learned to speak the native languages and produced excellent field descriptions. In the latter part of the nineteenth century, social research involving the direct observation of groups of people in the researcher's *own* society began to be practiced in Britain and France (the roots of "sociological" fieldwork as opposed to "anthropological" fieldwork with other cultures or peoples).

Wax (1971:28) notes that among the eighteenth- and nineteenth-century philosophers identified as the "pioneers" or "fathers" of anthropology, sociology, and ethnography – such as Saint-Simon, Hume, Elliot Smith, Maine, Bachofen, McLennan, Tylor, and Morgan – only Morgan did what could be called genuine fieldwork. Instead, the others relied on secondhand reports and sources. When, in the late 1890s and early 1900s, some British anthropologists – Haddon, Seligman, Rivers, and Radcliffe-Brown – broke with the earlier academic tradition of working only from derived sources and went into the field to obtain data at first hand, they seem to have carried on their investigations more like natural scientists than the fieldworking officials or missionaries from whom the historical theorists had obtained their data. Their funds were meager, their time short, and they were in a hurry. Consequently, they made surveys, looked for and collected interesting or relevant specimens, observed native ceremonies, and questioned native informants as best they could. They were unable to reside near or with an alien people for long enough to observe or participate in the ongoing cultural and social events, even had this method of doing fieldwork occurred to them. And when Boas and his first students and research assistants began their fieldwork among the Indians of North America, they usually proceeded in much the same fashion (Wax 1971:30).

Boas's influence and the American fieldwork tradition

Franz Boas is renowned as a fieldworker, and considered the "father" of fieldwork in American cultural anthropology. However:

The fact is that Boas and his students did not customarily spend a great deal of their time in the field learning the native language and observing and taking part in native life. The kind of data they desired did not require this, and, besides, their funds rarely permitted them a field trip of more than a few weeks or, at most, a few [usually the summer] months. What most of them did was try to locate as rapidly as possible a competent informant who was fluent in English and the native language, knew the old stories and customs, and was willing to dictate and translate texts .... It is not surprising that the two hardships about which they complain most frequently in their letters are

(1) wasting valuable time trying to find or keep a good informant or interpreter and (2) writer's cramp. They were, of course, interested in observing and recording traditional ceremonies and in watching traditional craftsmen at their work. But most of them did not really try to do fieldwork in the style in which it was subsequently done by the British social anthropologists, and they did not, except for rare exceptions, become even moderately fluent in the native language. (Wax 1971:32)

Wax mentions further that Boas made 13 field trips during his lifetime, many of them less than two months long, to 40 different sites along the northwest coast. Boas complained in his letters home about the discomforts of fieldwork and the reluctant cooperation of the Indians, yet kept returning to the field because he believed in the utmost importance of collecting firsthand data. Only a few of his students or those who worked in his tradition wrote anything about how they did their fieldwork. Lowie's 1959 autobiography, written just before but published after his death, disclosed the serious difficulties of his first field trip, while a posthumously published collection of Ruth Benedict's articles and letters contains some material on her fieldwork (Mead 1959). They and their generation were reluctant to report openly about any fieldwork problems, afraid to tarnish the reputation of this young science.

Malinowski's influence and the British fieldwork tradition

Bronislaw Malinowski was the first professional anthropologist to describe what intensive fieldwork was really like, and how he obtained his data by living amidst the Trobriand people to observe their daily lives. His description, published in 1922 as the Introduction to his classic ethnography *Argonauts of the Western Pacific*, is one of the earliest, most widely read, and most influential accounts of fieldwork in anthropology, and is included in this Reader (see Chapter 3). Malinowski suggested that all ethnographic studies should include an account of the research methods and conditions "so that at a glance the reader could estimate with precision the degree of the writer's personal acquaintance with the facts which he describes, and form an idea under what conditions information had been obtained from the natives" (1922:3).

Malinowski is renowned for identifying what he termed "the proper conditions" or "secrets" of effective ethnographic fieldwork. He advocated living among the people under study and remaining far from Westerners. He emphasized the need for clear scientific objectives, a thorough methodology to obtain results, and the use of special data-gathering methods. Finally, he stressed that a fieldworker should stick his nose into all ongoing affairs, even at the risk of offending local etiquette, to discover how the people thought, behaved, and saw the world. Malinowski hoped thus to "grasp the native's point of view" as complementary to the more objective observer's perspective (1922:25).

Inspired by Malinowski's enthusiasm for this "new method," some of his and Radcliffe-Brown's students went into the field and followed this procedure. They and the students they trained produced many of the most valuable and influential ethnographies that emerged in the first half of the twentieth century. However, once again, only a few of these highly trained and experienced fieldworkers wrote anything about their experiences or methods. The most notable are the writings of

Evans-Pritchard, Bohannan, and Powdermaker (see Appendix 5 on early and classic accounts of fieldwork). In 1940, Evans-Pritchard published a short but excellent description of the difficulties he experienced doing fieldwork among the Nuer in the early 1930s. In 1954, Laura Bohannan, under the pseudonym Elenore Bowen Smith, published a fictionalized account of fieldwork in Africa which was a pastiche composed of the stories of several people and numerous field trips. And in 1966, Hortense Powdermaker, who had studied with Malinowski in the 1920s, published a detailed account of her fieldwork in four locations. In assessing what she had learned, Powdermaker (1966:287) concluded that the most important conditions for good communication between research participants and fieldworkers are physical proximity of the fieldworker to the people studied, sound knowledge of their language, and a high degree of psychological and emotional involvement. Powdermaker identified the ability to become totally involved and yet to observe with complete detachment, continually to "step in and out" of other cultures, as the key to successful fieldwork. She achieved this ideal to varying degrees in the societies in which she worked (Ellen 1984:97).

The influence of the "Chicago School"

During the 1920s and 1930s, sociologists at the University of Chicago, primarily influenced by the work of social psychologist George Herbert Mead, exerted a considerable influence on the development of sociology and anthropology. Led by Herbert Blumer, William Thomas, Robert Park, Albion Small, Charles Horton Cooley, Florian Znaniecki, and Louis Wirth, they came to be known collectively as the "Chicago School" and represented the first major attempt to conduct systematic ethnographic fieldwork – particularly "community studies" – in urban environments, beginning with Chicago and then spreading to other cities. The sociologists of the Chicago School produced ethnographic monographs about things like Jewish ghettos, taxi-dance halls, professional thieves, hobos, boy's gangs, and the like. They encouraged their students to do fieldwork, and reconceptualized their methodology around "participant observation." By focusing on participant observation, the Chicago sociologists "emphasized their linkage to the tradition of ethnographic fieldwork from Malinowski onward ... Like Malinowski, they wish[ed] to pitch their tents among the dwellings of the natives (even if these be drug addicts, mental patients, medical students, or rabbis)" (Wax 1971:40).

Common Subjective Aspects of Fieldwork

In its broader conception, fieldwork in cultural anthropology is characterized by a number of typical subjective or personal experiences. These are usually elided in formal methods texts, but are explored more fully in many reflexive accounts of fieldwork, and frequently arise as topics of discussion in anthropology methods courses. As several of the "pithy quotes" which open this introduction allude to, fieldwork is frequently described as "the professional ethnographer's necessary initiation – variously referred to as a puberty rite, ritual ordeal, or *rite de passage*" (Tedlock 1991:70).

Going native

Barbara Tedlock has observed that the "gone native" fieldworker is one of the archetypes of "the mythic history of anthropology" (1991:69), and Katherine Ewing has noted that:

> The idea of "GOING NATIVE" is one of the few taboos remaining within anthropology. Considered antithetical to the social scientist's stance of objectivity and standing as a professional, *going native* has traditionally been a term of derision among anthropologists. Despite an array of challenges to notions of objectivity, the taboo remains in place and continues to carry a heavy affective load. (1994:571)

Powdermaker included a section on "Going Native" in *Stranger and Friend* (1966:115–119), and Thomas Barfield states:

> [T]he lore about "going native," that quintessentially anthropological occupational hazard (albeit almost apocryphal), illustrates the advantages and perils of fieldwork. Participating too much results in one's going native; participating too little turns one into a superficial, ethnocentric, survey-wielding, number-crunching social scientist with, some say, zero insight into the people studied. (1997:190)

"Going native" is such a central idea in the anthropological tradition of fieldwork that it is not surprising that writer Susanna Kaysen includes it in her novel about an anthropology graduate student doing PhD fieldwork in the Faroe Islands:

> Going bush. Like many anthropological ideas, this one had been born in jungles and savannahs and gave off a tropical scent. Some old-timers called it "troppo," an occupational hazard that began with lassitude and ended by destroying your objectivity. Stories that went, "when we got there, two years later, he was living in a hut with three wives." The trouble was, anthropologists were supposed to be living in huts. The three wives were optional but not exceptional. The line between observer and participant is so fine as to defy detection much of the time. It started easily enough. When members of "your" tribe are going on a journey or planning to get married, they slaughter a chicken and read the blood for omens. They offer to read omens for you before your trip back down the river for supplies. What harm can it do? It will certainly give you a better sense of their worldview, and it might give you a little useful information. Pretty soon you have recourse to chicken slaughter every time you have to make a decision. (1990:192–193)

While only a very small number of anthropologists have actually "gone native" in the sense of giving up anthropology altogether to fully join the people they study, the *idea* has a much larger significance in the culture of fieldwork. Perhaps the most widely read example of an anthropologist accused of being at least a borderline case of going native is the experience of Kenneth Good, the author of *Into the Heart: An Amazonian Love Story* (1991). The subtitle of the American edition – *One Man's Pursuit of Love and Knowledge Among the Yanomama* – gives even more emphasis to the impression that there is more to fieldwork than just being a scientific method of gathering data. Good first contacted the Yanomama in 1975 while doing fieldwork for his doctorate. He was supposed to stay with them for 15 months, but ended up living with them for more than six years, spread over a 15-year period. Eventually, the tribe offered him a wife, Yarima, whom he married. He later took her back with him to New Jersey, where she lived as a "housewife" for four years and had three children. But eventually, Yarima found she could not live in New Jersey; she divorced Good, and left her children there to return to the forest.

Good reflected, in what has been described by reviewers (see Amazon.com) as "a fantastic love story," that "in my wildest dreams it had never occurred to me to marry an Indian woman in the Amazon jungle. I was from suburban Philadelphia. I had no intention of going native" (1991:122). Nonetheless:

> Down deep, all I really did want was to find some way to make a living and to get back into the jungle. Not only to study the Indians – I already had enough data for three books – but to live with them. More especially, to live with Yarima. That was what I had come to, after all these years of struggling to fit into the Yanomama world, to speak their language fluently, to grasp their way of life from the inside. My original purpose – to observe and analyze this people as an anthropological researcher – had slowly merged with something far more personal. (1991:145)

In the postmodern era, reflection on the meaning of "going native" has evolved and generated new debates and insights. Where in the past it was a criticism to say an anthropologist had "gone native," today an increasing number of anthropologists, having taken on board the postmodern critique of empiricism and objectivity, advocate rather than criticize the breaking down of the traditional barriers that separate the observer from the observed, and many – including "native anthropologists" – do fieldwork "at home" in their own culture (cf. Pink 2000). Tedlock suggests:

> What seems to lie behind the belief that "going native" poses a serious danger to the fieldworker is the logical construction of the relationship between objectivity and subjectivity, between scientist and native, between Self and Other, as an unbridgeable opposition. The implication is that a subject's way of knowing is incompatible with the scientist's way of knowing and that the domain of objectivity is the sole property of the outsider. Several fieldworkers have rejected this sharp analytical distinction between Self and Other. (1991:71)

This gives a new and interesting twist: are anthropologists who are "natives" of the culture they study immune from, or even more at risk of, the danger of "going native," or do they have an advantage because of their deeper level of participation? Ewing suggests that the taboo against going native is a result of the adoption of the scientific model's commitment to objectivity, but also represents a hegemonic Western practice aimed at control or domination, which has a deleterious effect because, in order to preserve a stance of what they imagine to be scientific objectivity and detachment, an ethnographer "may place the act of observing and recording between himself or herself and others" (Ewing 1994:571).

While participation in the culture under study is encouraged, researchers in the field are usually considered to have gone too far – "gone native" – if it comes to constitute a threat to their professional identity. Ewing has explored her experience with this anthropological taboo, describing her deep participation during fieldwork to the point of "belief" or "going native." She recounts how, during her fieldwork in

Pakistan, she was the recipient of a dream sent by a Sufi saint, who had earlier told her that he would come to her while she was sleeping. Her initial reaction was rejection of the veracity of the experience, which she attributed to her "internalization of the anthropological taboo against going native, a reaction that I suspect is shared by many anthropologists under similar circumstances and that shapes the ethnographic project" (1994:574). She "marveled aloud about the power of suggestion," but finally, before the end of her fieldwork, she chose to visit a Sufi saint "and, for once, to approach the whole encounter as a personal experience rather than as anthropological research" (1994:574–575).

Other anthropologists have also pushed the limits of "going native." For example:

> Ethnographers who have learned not only the language but also appropriate behavior (including nonverbal communication codes) have been transformed, sometimes quite radically, by their fieldwork experience ... David Hayano ... became so immersed in the subculture of California poker players that "within several years I had virtually become one of the people I wanted to study!" Liza Crihfield Dalby not only took on the social role of a geisha during her fieldwork in Japan, but she also claims to have *become* one in both body and spirit. Her assertion that she learned to think and behave as a geisha suggests the "gone native" archetype of the anthropological imagination. (Tedlock 1991:70)

Similarly, Edie Turner (1999) has recounted her extraordinary experience while observing a ritual practiced by the Ndembu in Zambia. She reported that a "medicine man" named Singleton and his supporters were making a collective effort to draw out an afflicting spirit or *ihamba* from a woman named Meru:

> I felt the spiritual motion, a tangible feeling of breakthrough going through the whole group. Then it was that Meru fell – the spirit event first and the action afterwards. I was clapping and singing with the others like one possessed, while the drums bellowed, and Singleton pressed Meru's back ... Meru's face in a grin of tranced passion, her back quivering rapidly. Suddenly Meru raised her arm, stretched it in liberation, and I saw with my own eyes a large thing emerging out of the flesh of her back. This thing was a big gray blob about 6 inches across, a gray opaque plasma-like object appearing as a sphere. I was amazed – delighted. I still laugh with glee at the realization of having seen it, the *ihamba*, and so big! We were all one in triumph. The gray thing was actually out there, visible and you could see Singleton's hands working and scrubbing on Meru's back – and then the thing was there no more. Singleton had it in his pouch, pressing it in his other hand as well. The receiving can was ready; he transferred whatever it was into the can and capped a castor oil leaf and bark lid over it. It was done. (1999:46)

Did Turner "go native," hallucinate, or actually experience what she believes she did?

These anthropologists did not really "go native," because they never abandoned their anthropological identities. But they were prepared to break the traditional taboo against "going native," and in doing so pushed the boundaries of the self/other dichotomy in anthropological fieldwork.

Culture shock

The common experience of culture shock as a consequence of fieldwork in a foreign culture or context is one of the oldest themes in cultural anthropology. Virtually all fieldworkers have experienced culture shock in varying degrees. This shared subjective experience provides one of the most fundamental bonds that unite anthropologists and the discipline, and it is probably the emotional experience of culture shock that in the main leads to the characterization of fieldwork as a rite of passage. Somewhat surprisingly, in her entry for "field work" in the *International Encyclopedia of the Social Sciences*, Powdermaker dismissed culture shock on entering the field, but warned of it on *returning home* from the field:

> Despite its reputation, the so-called culture shock is not often one of the problems of a trained anthropologist [because] he arrives with a general knowledge of the people and their culture through having immersed himself in the literature ... Culture shock is more likely to be experienced when he returns to his own modern urban society after an extended period in a tribal one. (1969:420–421)

But in the entry for "fieldwork" in her *Dictionary of Anthropology*, Seymour-Smith identifies culture shock as a characteristic difficulty of fieldwork, commenting that "This state of disorientation is perhaps necessary, and is in the long term a productive one, since like a rite of passage it prepares the ethnographer for the imaginative leap involved in coming to terms with an alien culture or way of life" (1986a:117). In many reflexive accounts of fieldwork, cultural anthropologists have commented on their experience of culture shock and adjustment, and it emerges that one very common or shared response to culture shock in the early phase of fieldwork is withdrawal from contact with the locals and escapism into reading novels, etc.

In the late 1950s, culture shock was first defined by anthropologist Kalervo Oberg as "the anxiety that results from losing familiar signs and symbols of social intercourse" (1960:177). In a comprehensive analysis, he argued that culture shock was a natural part of the process of adjustment to a new culture which leads eventually to cultural awareness. Oberg identified the signs of culture shock as homesickness, withdrawal, chauvinistic excesses, stereotyping of locals, need for excessive amounts of sleep, marital stress, loss of ability to work effectively, compulsive eating or drinking, unexplainable fits of weeping, irritability, psychosomatic illness, boredom, exaggerated cleanliness, and family tension and conflict. From these observations, Oberg (1974) developed a normative six-month model of the process of cultural adjustment, and made practical recommendations for dealing with culture shock, including learning more about the place and its people, refraining from criticizing the host culture, finding a friend, keeping a sense of humor, avoiding self-pity, getting enough rest, maintaining a healthy diet, getting enough exercise, keeping a sense of adventure, using friends and family for support, asking for help when needed, keeping involved with others and avoiding withdrawal, developing new interests and skills, and recording experiences, insights, and frustrations in a journal.

Postmodernism and Fieldwork

All variants of fieldwork have been thoroughly scrutinized and criticized since the mid-1970s. Hyper-positivist fieldwork methods are under fire from postmodernism ... Another source of critique is postcolonial studies, which deconstruct how a hegemonic Western social science such as anthropology fashions its particular alterity ... *Some anthropologists have found traditional anthropological fieldwork so problematic that they advocate cultural history approaches.* (Barfield 1997:190; emphasis added)

The 1970s and 1980s saw the emergence of postmodern perspectives and increasing debate and eclecticism in cultural anthropology. A heightened awareness of the relationship between power and the construction of knowledge produced a new concern with reflexivity – a "reflexive trend" – and new forms of fieldwork relations and ethnographic writing emerged. There was an increasing trend toward doing fieldwork "at home"; the emergence of interpretive or hermeneutic approaches; the development of feminist anthropology; a growing engagement with indigenous scholars; the emergence of autoethnography, narrative ethnography, indigenous anthropology, and new life-history approaches such as "testimonio"; and new practices of writing, communicating, and reading ethnographic accounts as "texts." This last development included a literary turn:

> Declared to be fictions "in the sense of something made or fashioned" (Clifford [in Clifford and Marcus] 1986:6), ethnographies, according to those who advocate this position, are partial or selective truths. They should be approached as texts whose style, rhetoric, and narrative structure can be subjected to the same kind of criticisms to which other works of literature are subjected. Writing about culture raises questions about modes of representation, about objectivity and accountability, relativism and ethnocentrism, science and truth. Textualists urge ethnographers to experiment with new forms of writing that are dialectical, dialogic, or polyphonic rather than analytic, authoritative, and univocal. Indeed, the omniscient "I know because I was there" voice of the post-Malinowskian participant-observer is perceived as a trope that is no longer acceptable in a postcolonial world. (Brettell 1993:2)

At a more general level, these trends reinvigorated debate and controversy between protagonists of the universal and relativist, objectivist and subjectivist, scientific and humanistic positions, and were mainly a response to two key developments in the 1960s – the theoretical critique of "neutrality," "objectivity," "truth," and "reality" in empiricism, and the political critique of the discipline's historical relationship with Western imperialism and colonialism. These developments included processes of "decolonization" (Harrison 1991) and the "reinvention" (Hymes 1969) of anthropology, and addressed the politics of the discipline, including such critical issues as the relationship between anthropology and imperialism, academic colonialism, sexism, and issues involved in applied, action, and partisan research (Huizer and Mannheim 1979). One aspect of reflexive postmodern anthropology was a renewed and invigorated interest in the process by which data are gathered – the fieldwork experience.

The postmodern critique of fieldwork

During the postmodern turn in cultural anthropology, some anthropologists, sensitized by the writings of Michel Foucault on power and knowledge, harshly criticized anthropological fieldwork as a kind of invasive, disciplinary "panopticon" – a type of prison building designed by the philosopher Jeremy Bentham in 1791 to allow a guard to observe all prisoners without them being able to tell if they were being observed or not, thus conveying a "sentiment of an invisible omniscience." The anthropological interview was criticized as being similar to the medieval inquisitional confession through which church examiners extracted "truth" from their native and "heretical" peasant parishioners. Finally, they criticized anthropological observation as a hostile act that reduces our subjects to mere "objects" of our scientific gaze. Consequently, some postmodern anthropologists gave up fieldwork and the practice of descriptive ethnography altogether.

As a result of this at times ruthless critique and autocritique of anthropology from historical, political, gender, and postmodern perspectives, even the basic conceptions of the "field" and "fieldwork" – perhaps the most fundamental bases of the anthropological approach – were and are still now being critiqued and contested. An example of the most radical form of postmodern critique is Roger Berger's article "From Text to (Field)work and Back Again: Theorizing a Post(modern)-Ethnography" (1993), in which he argues:

> The "field" is not just produced by the discipline. The ethnographic "field" is also a cultural construct, a disciplinary epiphenomenon, a discursive effect, part of the discursive formation that is anthropology. Without anthropology there is no "field," no "object" of study, *and* without the power to create "fields" there is no anthropology. Indeed, the "field" is a fundamental part of what Foucault terms "the production of truth through power." It is not just the "theoretical framework" that produces ethnographic facts but disciplinary power that enables the production of a "field" in which a conceptual framework can produce "facts." Our normative sense of the "field" functions to hide the power that produces the "field." To put it another way, the "field" is the hidden configuration of western hegemonic power. (1993:178)

The conclusion is that, since "fieldwork" is fundamentally an act of domination and control, and the "field" represents "the dominated bodies of the colonized" (Berger 1993:176), the decolonization of the discipline requires that these be abandoned and new approaches developed.

The postmodern turn

While few cultural anthropologists have abandoned fieldwork, this autocriticism stimulated an experimental era, which continues today, in which new conceptions and ways of doing fieldwork have developed. For example, some postmodern anthropologists see themselves as *artisans* fashioning ethnographies by forming communities and making conversations (Gudeman and Rivera 1995). In *The Art of Fieldwork* (2004), Harry Wolcott advocates approaching fieldwork as an art method; in *Person to Person: Fieldwork, Dialogue, and the Hermeneutic Method* (1996), Barry Michrina and CherylAnne Richards present a "step-by-step" guide for a "dialogical hermeneutic" approach to fieldwork; and volumes such as *Things as They Are: New Directions in Phenomenological Anthropology* (1996), edited by Michael Jackson, *Shifting Contexts: Transformations in Anthropological Knowledge* (1995), edited by Marilyn Strathern, and *Constructing the Field: Ethnographic Fieldwork in the Contemporary World* (2000), edited by Vered Amit, present a wide range of "experimental" articles exploring new ways of approaching ethnographic research.

The "new ethnography" that has emerged in the past few decades incorporates three interlocking concerns. First, an increased awareness of "multi-vocality" (multiple voices representing multiple interests or "realities"), which has raised issues of signature, authority, and advocacy. Second, a growing number of works concerned with the ethnographic encounter, with cross-cultural communication, and with making explicit the ways in which fieldwork is conducted and research participants are incorporated into the account. Third, an increased regard for the context and praxis of writing and reading ethnographic "texts." For example, one aspect of the postmodern turn is the "revolution" in readership; today, the ethnographic "other" is nearly always literate and can read and respond to – particularly criticize – what anthropologists write about them. As Driessen has observed: "The traditional dichotomy of the ethnographer who looks, listens, writes and reads, versus the native who talks and tries to figure out what the behavior and questions of the anthropologist mean, has largely collapsed" (1993:3). Thus, the elements of contemporary ethnography include experimental form and method, reflexivity on the part of the ethnographer, collaboration and multiple authorship, and the details of fieldwork dialogue and experience.

Narrative ethnography

Modern ethnographers have sought to increase the voice of the "other" through more active involvement of research participants in the co-production of ethnographic accounts, narratives, or texts. This is done by extensive direct quotes, co-authorship, and collaboration with research participants. As Tedlock has observed, beginning in the 1970s, "there was a shift in emphasis from participant observation to the observation of participation" (1991:78), entailing "a representational transformation" in which both the fieldworker and "other" are "presented together within a single narrative ethnography, focused on the character and process of the ethnographic dialogue" (1991:69). Narrative ethnography became a creative intermingling of lived experiences, field data, methodological reflections, and cultural analysis by a situated and self-conscious narrator. Tedlock argues that the development of this new "narrative ethnography" is driven by:

> a new breed of ethnographer who is passionately interested in the co-production of ethnographic knowledge, created and represented in the only way it can be, within an interactive Self/Other [epistemological] dialogue. These new ethnographers – many of whom are themselves subaltern because of their class, gender, or ethnicity – cannot be neatly tucked away or pigeonholed within any of the four historical archetypes [of] the amateur observer, the armchair anthropologist, the professional ethnographer, or the "gone native" fieldworker. Rather they, or we, combine elements from all four of these categories. Thus, for example we embrace the designation "amateur," since it derives from the Latin *amatus*, the past participle of *amare*, "to love," and we are passionately engaged with our endeavor. We accept the "armchair" designation because we have a serious concern with both reading and critiquing the work of other ethnographers in order to try to change past colonialist practices. We insist that we are "professional," because of the seriousness of our field preparation and engagement, and also because of our attention to issues of representation in our own work. Finally, to the extent that fieldwork is not simply a union card but the center of our intellectual and emotional lives, we are, if not "gone native," at least becoming bicultural. (Tedlock 1991:82)

Testimonio

One of the most important forms of narrative ethnography is the emergence of "*testimonio*" or testimonial narrative – a first-person account of a real situation that involves repression, marginalization, and violence, intended to function as a narrative that bears witness to and denounces human rights abuses. Such narratives, most coming out of Latin America since the 1970s, have been intended as a way to give voice to the voiceless. The most widely known example is the autobiographical *I, Rigoberta Menchú: An Indian Woman in Guatemala* (1984), which begins with this paragraph:

> My name is Rigoberta Menchú. I'm twenty three years old. This is my testimony. I didn't learn it from a book and I didn't learn it alone. I'd like to stress that it's not only *my* life, it's also the testimony of my people. It's hard for me to remember everything that's happened to me in my life since there have been many bad times but, yes, moments of joy as well. The important thing is that what has happened to me has happened to many other people too: My story is the story of all poor Guatemalans. My personal experience is the reality of a whole people. (1984:1)

John Beverley has defined *testimonio* and elaborated on its various approaches:

> By *testimonio* I mean a novel or novella-length narrative in book or pamphlet form, told in the first person by a narrator who is also a real protagonist or witness of the event he or she recounts, and whose unit of narration is usually a "life" or a significant life experience. *Testimonio* may include, but is not subsumed under, any of the following categories, some of which are conventionally considered literature, others not: autobiography, autobiographical novel, oral history, memoir, confession, diary, interview, eyewitness report, life history, *novella-testimonio*, nonfiction novel, or "factographic" literature … This situation of narration in *testimonio* has to involve an urgency to communicate, a problem of repression, poverty, subalternity, imprisonment, struggle for survival, and so on. (1996:24–25)

In the context of Latin America, *testimonio* developed as an important medium through which subalterns finally found a literary voice of their own. First and foremost, it is considered to be a tactic for empowerment and survival, in which the subaltern brings the existence of oppressive and repressive conditions to the attention of the world to bring about social and political change. Thus, for the work that has been publicized through her *testimonio*, Rigoberta Menchú was awarded the Nobel Peace Prize in 1992. *Testimonio* represents a, to some controversial (see Stoll 2000), form of experimental ethnography, based on a new approach to fieldwork and a new relationship between the anthropologist and the "other" (Beverley 2004).

Reciprocity, collaboration, and partnership

Another development in postmodern fieldwork, or another approach to the "new ethnography," is an increased commitment to reciprocity and collaborative research. The traditional purpose of fieldwork was to collect ethnographic data, and this position was summarized by Powdermaker in the 1960s, when she asserted: "The anthropologist is not primarily interested in helping his informants, although he may do so inadvertently. His motivation is to secure data" (1966:296). However, as noted above, by the mid-1980s there was an increasing commitment to *reciprocity* – to providing something useful back to research participants for their collaboration – as an ethical requirement of fieldwork. This led to the emergence of a new type of applied anthropology, in which serving the local community and collecting ethnographic data are equally important, and "the researchers are concerned with conducting research in a team effort that benefits the local people as well as themselves" (Kuhlmann 1992:275). In particular, this has been evidenced in the development of new approaches to ethnographic fieldwork such as collaborative research and research partnerships (see Clifford 1980; Kennedy 1995) in work with both groups (e.g., Kuhlmann 1992) and individuals (e.g., Marcus and Mascarenhas 2005).

In an article on collaborative research conducted with members of the Kickapoo tribe of Oklahoma, Annette Kuhlmann states: "[T]he goals of this approach include community participation, collaboration of the participants on all aspects of the project, reciprocal learning processes, and respect for the community's sense of tribal privacy in regard to publications" (1992:274). Kuhlmann worked with tribal members to develop books on Kickapoo history for classroom use. Traditionally, the Kickapoo related their past by passing on stories about events that happened to individuals and the tribe. Through interviews conducted by trained tribal members, these detailed and sometimes humorous life histories and stories were recorded from elders and put into history texts in a way that reflected this tradition.

Kuhlmann identifies the basic elements of participatory research. One approach is to look to enhance research that people may already be doing themselves. The orientation of this collaborative research

> entails an attitude on the part of the outside professionals that their work and their relationships with the local members are governed by a commitment to the people, to work *with* them, i.e., not for them and not about them ... This emphasis distinguishes collaborative research from other applied approaches in which the academic works *for* a specific employer, such as the federal government, another organization, or the tribe. Employer–employee relationships imply a hierarchy that the collaborative researchers strive to replace with reciprocity in learning in the context of mutually designed projects. (1992:277)

In collaborative research, the participants attempt to work together as equals, and this teamwork includes every aspect of the project – planning, implementation, problem solving, and evaluation.

Similarly, new approaches to fieldwork based on reciprocity and collaboration have emerged that emphasize *partnership*. This approach has been particularly developed by feminist anthropologists, and an increasing number of fieldworkers are choosing to enter into explicit research partnerships with individuals and groups. Research partnerships between anthropologists and the people with whom they work have already taken a variety of forms (e.g., see Shostak 1981), but generally it involves "partnerships between trained researchers and community members who are not trained in social research but who are interested in doing research into their own community" (Park 1992:581).

One of the best examples that has revealed some of the basic elements of partnership-based research is a project on the place of alcohol in the lives of New Zealand women, based on partnerships between anthropologists and Samoan, Cook Islands,

Maori, and Lesbian women (Park 1992:581). Julie Park observes that, as in business, research partnerships are negotiated relationships; the partnership does not necessarily have to be equal, but is one of joint engagement based on negotiation (1992:582). She argues that in order to be nonexploitative, research relationships not only have to be open to people's experiences and voices, but have to return to the participants appropriate and accessible research-based information as part of an empowering process (1992:583). Skills and resources should be shared, and just as in other forms of participatory research, in partnership-based fieldwork it is essential to work in close cooperation with members of the group, including seeking their active involvement in planning, research, and analysis of the project.

In 2006, George Marcus founded the Center for Ethnography at the University of California, Irvine, to develop new ethnographic research methodologies based on two assumptions: that the field site is no longer the only place for data gathering and the fieldworker is no more the single producer of such knowledge. Research projects should become open-ended productions, with colleagues working in ethnographic design studios and in dialogue with different audiences, even though the fieldwork will still be carried out by one or two anthropologists. The research results are discussed during the ongoing fieldwork through seminars and workshops (para-sites), where the ethnographer enters into a critical reflection through a dialogue with supervisors, colleagues, and research participants. Collaboration in a broad sense is the key to this innovative conceptualization of fieldwork. Anthropologists do not only conduct fieldwork with the assistance of local participants but are informed by a heterogeneous collection of interlocutors, such as colleagues, experts, activists, and policy and opinion makers (Rabinow et al. 2008; Faubion and Marcus 2009).

Contemporary Fieldwork in Cultural Anthropology

Without the continued grounding in the empirical that scientific aspects of our tradition provide, our interpretive efforts may float off into literary criticism and into particularistic forms of history. Without the interpretive tradition, the scientific tradition that grounds us will never get off the ground (Rappaport 1994:76).

The compassionate turn and emergence of "engaged fieldwork"

At the beginning of the twenty-first century, after more than three decades of intense postmodernist critique, cultural anthropology passed through another shift in its relation to fieldwork. In the mid-1990s, there arose a growing opposition to the destructive cynicism and negativism of the most extreme forms of postmodern critique, because few anthropologists accepted the radical proposition that fieldwork is inherently a form of imperialism, oppression, and control, which must be abandoned altogether. If modernism (empiricism) represented anthropology's original thesis characterized by a preoccupation with how to analyze and represent cultures, and the "postmodern turn" was its antithesis with an emphasis on the reflexive ethnographer, then lately we have seen a synthesis of these perspectives in the reassessment of the relation between anthropologists and the peoples they study. The discipline is in the middle of a period of soul-searching about the morality of fieldwork relations and the ethico-political implications of ethnography. One of the best examples of this critical stance toward a self-absorbed anthropology is the work of Nancy Scheper-Hughes, who has written:

> I am weary of these postmodernist critiques, and, given the perilous times in which we and our subjects live, I am inclined toward compromise, the practice of a "good enough" ethnography. While the anthropologist is always a necessarily flawed and biased instrument of cultural translation, like every other craftsperson we can do the best we can with the limited resources we have at hand: our ability to listen and to observe carefully and with empathy and compassion. (1995:417–418)

Most anthropologists today would agree with Scheper-Hughes's conviction that, rather than a "hostile gaze," anthropological fieldwork can be "an opportunity for self-expression. Seeing, listening, touching, recording can be, if done with care and sensitivity, acts of solidarity. Above all, they are the work of recognition. Not to look, not to touch, not to record can be the hostile act, an act of indifference and of turning away" (1995:418). In the unfolding "compassionate turn," there is a growing acknowledgment that – like all academic disciplines – cultural anthropology was, is, and will always be flawed or imperfect, and that vigorous internal debate and criticism are "normal" and beneficial. While recognizing that at any given time we are limited by the current state of knowledge and theory, we remain committed to fieldwork as our primary method, and still aspire to the production or creation of "good enough" or approximately right ethnography capable of presenting "adequate explanations" of human and social behavior which are "adequate to the times we live in" (Becker 1993).

An awareness of the moral and ethico-political dimensions of fieldwork has drawn anthropologists to the study of violence, genocide, suffering, trauma, resilience, healing, and reconstruction (e.g., Scheper-Hughes 1993; Das 1995; Daniel 1996; Mahmood 1996; Kleinman et al. 1997; Nordstrom 1997; Sluka 2000; Farmer 2003; Sanford 2003; Hinton 2005; Robben 2005). The opening phrases of the influential collection *Social Suffering* (Kleinman et al. 1997) address several major dimensions of this "compassionate turn":

> Social suffering … brings into a single space an assemblage of human problems that have their origins and consequences in the devastating injuries that social forces can inflict on human experience. Social suffering results from what political, economic, and institutional power does to people and, reciprocally, from how these forms of power themselves influence responses to social problems. Included under the category of social suffering are conditions that are usually divided among separate fields, conditions that simultaneously involve health, welfare, legal, moral, and religious issues. They destabilize established categories. For example, the trauma, pain, and disorders to which atrocity gives rise are health conditions; yet they are also political and cultural matters. (1997:ix)

The shift from a solipsistic postmodern anthropology to the study of the real suffering of real people carries multiple consequences for fieldwork. The multilayered and multidimensional complexity of research themes such as genocide, social suffering, cultural trauma, and social reconstruction requires a holistic approach that, after a long detour, reconnects fieldwork to the tradition of Boas and Malinowski. Yet, unlike these founding fathers, contemporary anthropologists have acquired enough academic confidence to draw freely on other disciplines. The "compassionate turn" makes anthropologists also re-emphasize the importance of empathy, not as a methodological technique to adopt the "native point of view," but as an epistemological approach. Compassionate empathy makes the fieldworker and the research participant share a subjective space, implicating them in each other's lives and in the production of ethnographic knowledge. This approach carries a political responsibility which is not a return to the action anthropology of the 1970s but, rather, a form of social advocacy delivered mostly from the steps of the academy and only rarely engaged directly in the field. Robert Borofsky's (2004) agenda for an anthropological outreach to the world is the public face of this compassionate fieldwork:

> Public anthropology demonstrates the ability of anthropology and anthropologists to effectively address problems beyond the discipline – illuminating the larger social issues of our times as well as encouraging broad, public conversations about them with the explicit goal of fostering social change. It affirms our responsibility, as scholars and citizens, to meaningfully contribute to communities beyond the academy – both local and global – that make the study of anthropology possible. (Borofsky 2004)

Public anthropology sees ethnographers as witnesses, instead of dispassionate observers or political activists, who connect their readers to the world's trouble spots and sensitize them to the suffering and struggles of disprivileged human beings. It wants to generate public discussion, influence opinion, and engage politicians and policymakers critically to achieve genuine social change without, however, becoming involved in its realization.

In 2001, Borofsky established the non-profit Center for Public Anthropology in order to encourage scholars to address public problems in public ways, which then collaborated with University of California Press to develop a new public anthropology book series which has already published 21 outstanding volumes, the latest being Philippe Bourgois and Jeff Schonberg's *Righteous Dopefiend* (2009), which describes the survival strategies and intimate lives of drug addicts. Journals have also been responsive to the development of public anthropology. In 2010, *American Anthropologist* introduced a Public Anthropology Reviews section to appreciate the depth, diversity, and significance of anthropological engagement with broad and varied publics, and *Anthropology Now* introduced a "Findings" column to highlight work that contributes directly to public debate about contemporary social and political problems.

In recent years, particularly since the first edition of this Reader was published, this trend has solidified into a growing interest in and new commitment to *politically engaged fieldwork*. In 1995, Nancy Scheper-Hughes published an inspirational article, "The Primacy of the Ethical: Propositions for a Militant Anthropology," which caught the mood of many in the discipline. She stated that if anthropology "is to be worth anything at all, [it] must be ethically grounded," and was one of the first to "attempt to imagine what forms a politically committed and morally engaged anthropology might take" (1995:409). While noting that such an idea or approach might strike many anthropologists "as unsavory, tainted, even frightening" (1995:415), she nonetheless made a strong rallying call for a new generation of "barefoot anthropologists" to act as "alarmists and shock troopers" by producing "politically complicated and morally demanding texts and images capable of sinking through the layers of acceptance, complicity and bad faith that allow the suffering and the deaths to continue without even the pained cry of recognition of Conrad's evil protagonist, Kurtz: 'The horror! The Horror!'" (1995:416). This call was influential in the emergence of a new interest in public or engaged fieldwork which seeks to critically engage a wider readership and the multiple urgent crises facing humankind today, as evidenced in the publication of Roberto González's edited volume, *Anthropology in the Public Sphere: Speaking Out on War, Peace, and American Power*, in 2004; Thomas Eriksen's *Engaging Anthropology: The Case for a Public Presence* and Victoria Sanford and Asale Angel-Ajani's volume, *Engaged Observer: Anthropology, Advocacy, and Activism*, in 2006; Heidi Armbruster and Anna Laerke's volume, *Taking Sides: Politics, and Fieldwork in Anthropology*, in 2008; *The Counter-counterinsurgency Handbook*, by the Network of Concerned Anthropologists (NCA), and David Vine's *Island of Shame: The Secret History of the US Military Base on Diego Garcia*, in 2009.

Anthropology in the Public Sphere presents more than 50 short, mostly media essays by leading anthropologists addressing the central political conflicts of our times and the serious repercussions of US involvement in the Third World. Eriksen introduces *Engaging Anthropology* by observing that, though the discipline is "exceptionally relevant as a tool for understanding the contemporary world, yet it is absent from nearly every important public debate" (2006:ix). He argues that anthropologists have failed to "build bridges connecting them with the concerns of non-specialists" and rarely "aimed at engaging a wider readership" (2006:ix). While Eriksen writes primarily about anthropology, he aims for a multidisciplinary audience and suggests several already proven approaches for communicating or engaging with a wider audience, including:

Defamiliarization (e.g., Daniel Miller's *A Theory of Shopping*, 1998)
The Cultural Autocritique (e.g., Margaret Mead's *Coming of Age in Samoa*, 1928)
The Riddle (e.g., Marvin Harris's *Cannibals and Kings*, 1978)
The Personal Journey (e.g., Claude Lévi-Strauss's *Tristes Tropiques*, 1955)
The Intervention (e.g., Ashley Montagu's *Man's Most Dangerous Myth: The Fallacy of Race*, 1942)
The Essay (e.g., Mary Douglas's *Purity and Danger*, 1966)
The Biography (e.g., Marjorie Shostak's *Nisa: The Life and Words of a !Kung Woman*, 1981)

In *Engaged Observer*, Sanford and Angel-Ajani present 12 case studies in the form of reflexive accounts of anthropology directly engaged with human suffering in Guatemala, Burma, Italy, Palestine, Colombia, Mexico, El Salvador, and with postwar cultures and HIV/AIDS sufferers. The contributors "meditate on truth, the contract of testimony, the politics of memory, and the moral imperative to witness and listen" (Sanford 2006:8), and the volume challenges anthropology particularly, but the social sciences generally, to become critically engaged with the multiple crises facing humankind today. The case studies present models for conducting engaged research which aids participants, and identify the contradictions and challenges of doing so.

The main point is that *engaged anthropology should be a political anthropology of advocacy and activism*; in a foreword Philippe Bourgois states: "This volume challenges anthropology, the social sciences – and anyone who reads university press books – to engage critically with the urgent crises faced by the socially vulnerable under the global lie of democracy and neoliberal prosperity in the 2000s" (2006:ix). In *Taking Sides*, contributors stress that anthropologists and other social scientists must be ethically and politically committed to the people they study. The contributors represent a new generation of scholars engaged with contemporary global movements for social justice and peace, and the volume shows the limits of some aspects of post-modern reflexivity, moves political contexts to the fore, and illustrates how anthropology can move beyond critical analysis to praxis. The contributors stress the virtues of politically engaged fieldwork, invite readers to reflect critically on what it means to be a scholar in today's conflict- and crisis-ridden world, and reflect on their efforts to try to integrate their research with their understanding of social science, politics, and ethics, and what political commitment means in practice and fieldwork.

Today, engaged fieldwork is being conducted on a widening range of pressing human and political issues, from counterinsurgency (NCA 2009, Kelly et al. 2010) and the "war against terrorism" (Robben 2010) to the militarization of contemporary American society (González 2010). This new approach to fieldwork is explored in Part X, the final section of this second edition.

"Being there"

The postmodern critique of fieldwork and its compassionate and engaged reaction have stimulated new conceptions of what constitutes "the field" and ethnography. This process continues today. People like James Fernandez (1985:19) argued two decades ago that fieldwork is mainly what anthropology is all about, and that the essential characteristic of fieldwork is "being there." This is particularly reflected in two recent books on fieldwork – *Being There: The Necessity of Fieldwork* (Bradford 1998) and *Being There: Fieldwork in Anthropology* (Watson 1999). But the very "what, where, and when" of fieldwork has shifted. For example, Deborah D'Amico-Samuels (1991:69) has questioned both the geographical and the temporal construction of the traditional division between "home" being here and "the field" being there, between where we write and publish and where we do our fieldwork, and explored "where does the field begin and end, if ever?" Does fieldwork end when we "leave the field," and what does "leave the field" mean in a high-tech, postmodern, and globalized world where even research participants in the remotest areas are accessible by telephone? D'Amico-Samuels argues that the notion of being "back from the field" implies an artificial separation in the ethnographic process, with unfortunate consequences. She concludes that today "the field is everywhere," and there is no division between home and the field because both exist in the same holistic context of globalized power relations (1991:83).

Traditionally, fieldwork ended when one returned from the field to analyze and write up the research results. However, in contemporary cultural anthropology, when researchers more frequently conduct *long-term* or diachronic fieldwork in the same location over many years and several field trips, and where the physical distance between "home" and "the field" is largely ameliorated by instantaneous means of electronic mass communication, this simple dichotomy between being "in the field" and then leaving no longer holds sway. Today, many anthropologists consider that, in a sense, they never really leave the field entirely, and thus their fieldwork never really ends. For example, in 1994 one of Jeffrey Sluka's key research participants in Belfast, the leader of a nationalist paramilitary group, was killed. Within a few hours of his death Sluka received a phone call from other research participants, and they spoke for nearly two hours about what had happened. This discussion was predicated on fieldwork-based relations, was the same as a research interview, and the notes Sluka wrote were indistinguishable from "fieldnotes." But there was an immense physical distance between them: Sluka was at "home" and the research participants were "in the field." But while Sluka was on the phone, was he not essentially "in the field," and was this not a form of attenuated "fieldwork"? (See Sunderland 1999 for a discussion of "fieldwork and the phone.")

Cultural anthropologists are increasingly exploring the implications for long-term fieldwork marked by the presence of the ethnographer at discrete periods over their life history and intellectual thought. For example, Anthony Cohen, who conducted fieldwork over 19 years in Whalsay, has observed that during this time there was "continuous change: in the field; in the discipline; to the author himself; and in his view of the discipline, the field, and his earlier analysis of his data" (1992:339). He referred to "that mental notebook which is never closed and which certainly does not recognize the geographical and cultural limits and specificities of our putative fields" (1992:339), called attention to "anthropologists' compulsion to carry 'their' field with them mentally, long after they have left it physically" (1992:344), and introduced the idea of "post-fieldwork fieldwork":

> We bring to the analysis of our fieldnotes [and headnotes] continuously accumulating experience extraneous to the circumstances in which they were written. "In this sense," says Ottenberg, "the field experience does not stop. Things that I once read in my fieldnotes in one way, I now read in another." Hastrup makes a similar point: "The past is not past in anthropology." It is precisely this process of rereading that I refer to by the phrase, "post-fieldwork fieldwork." (1992:345)

The war on terror, launched in 2001, has also affected the Malinowskian fieldwork practice by precipitating another period in the history of anthropology in which regions and countries have become inaccessible to fieldworkers. World War II prevented anthropologists from traveling to large parts of the world. British and American anthropologists developed indirect research methods to help the Allied war effort through national character analyses about Germany, Italy, Japan, and their occupied territories. This approach became known as "the study of culture at a distance," which received a new political relevance when China and the Soviet Union closed their doors because of the Cold War. Ruth Benedict founded the Columbia University Research in Contemporary Cultures program in 1946, with funding from the Office of Naval Research, to analyze "the cultural regularities in the characters of individuals who are members of societies which are inaccessible to direct observation" (Mead 1953:3). In the late 1960s, Kathleen Gough made an ardent plea for the critical study at a distance of dictatorial communist and capitalist regimes as well as

Third World countries where fieldwork was impossible because of revolutionary and anti-colonial insurgencies. Gough (1968:407) criticized the role of anthropologists enlisted in the Cold War and the Vietnam War, and emphasized that the indirect studies should be conducted "with the ultimate economic and spiritual welfare of our informants and of the international community, rather than the short run military or industrial profits of the Western nations, before us." Only a handful of anthropologists were able to carry out fieldwork in communist countries in the 1980s, through scientific exchange programs with Western countries. The end of the Cold War in 1989 opened the borders worldwide to ethnographic fieldwork, only to close again in 2001 – and especially 2003 – with the wars in Afghanistan and Iraq. Fieldwork has become difficult, if not impossible, in certain Muslim countries since then, and the employment of anthropologists in the war on terror has led to a general suspicion of anthropologists.

In response to this new period of ethnographic enclosure, Antonius Robben has called for ethnographic imagination at a distance to study inaccessible research settings through indirect means, and then to deepen the analysis through a systematic comparison with similar sites and issues examined through in-depth fieldwork. This approach was employed in 2006 by a group of anthropologists to understand the plight of the Iraqi people during the Iraq War at a time when not even foreign war correspondents dared to enter the street without military protection (Robben 2010).

Today, a common pattern of fieldwork for cultural anthropologists is one year of PhD fieldwork followed by a series of shorter trips, frequently three months in duration (over a summer break) or sometimes six months in duration (a semester sabbatical), over the course of an academic career. Some do considerably more fieldwork, but some do considerably less. It is increasingly difficult for graduate students to get funding for a year's fieldwork, or for faculty to take that long off as research leave. That is, economics often dictates the kind of fieldwork anthropologists do, and the tendency has been toward the development of more cost-efficient (i.e., cheaper) alternatives to long-term fieldwork. One result is that today much fieldwork resembles more the Boasian/American tradition than the Malinowskian/British one – namely, shorter periods working with one or a few key "research participants," rather than extended participant observation of a whole community for one or two years.

In cultural anthropology, the process of critiquing, refining, and redefining ethnography and fieldwork continues. Today, the "best practice" of fieldwork is *ethically grounded*, with free and informed consent of research participants. It is *participatory*, shaped with the active *collaboration* of research "participants" rather than "subjects," and conducted with their needs in mind. That is, *reciprocity* – giving something back to the community which they deem to be of use to them – is built into it by design. Increasingly, it also seeks to both address the most pressing human needs and issues, and to reach wider cross-disciplinary and public audiences. The new research orientations in fieldwork that began to emerge in the late 1980s and 1990s, such as *narrative ethnography* and *testimonio*, and the compassionate turn and emergence of public anthropology and politically engaged fieldwork in the first decade of the twenty-first century, are examples of the application and evolution of these themes.

The Construction and Organization of the
Second Edition of the Reader

That charming and intelligent Austrian-American anthropologist Paul Radin has said that no one quite knows how one goes about fieldwork. Perhaps we should leave the question with that sort of answer. But when I was a serious young student in London I thought I would try to get a few tips from experienced fieldworkers before setting out for Central Africa. I first sought advice from Westermarck. All I got from him was "don't converse with an informant for more than twenty minutes because if you aren't bored by that time he will be." Very good advice, even if somewhat inadequate. I sought instruction from Haddon, a man foremost in field-research. He told me that it was really all quite simple; one should always behave as a gentleman. Also very good advice. My teacher, Seligman told me to take ten grains of quinine every night and to keep off women. The famous Egyptologist, Sir Flinders Petrie, just told me not to bother about drinking dirty water as one soon became immune to it. Finally, I asked Malinowski and was told not to be a bloody fool. So there is no clear answer, much will depend on the man, on the society he is to study, and the conditions in which he is to make it. (Evans-Pritchard 1973:1)

So why this Reader about fieldwork rather than about methods? Should we not just improve our data-collection techniques and leave all talk about fieldwork to after dinner conversations or one-liners to reassure anxious students? In fact, our mentor Gerald Berreman told us when we were close to embarking on our doctoral fieldwork that what we had to do was "hang out" in cafés and on street corners. Yet, there is more here than meets the eye. Beneath the seemingly common-sense remarks by Berreman and by Evans-Pritchard's teachers, there are hints at the complexities of fieldwork relations and rapport (don't talk too long with an informant; keep off women; hang out), ethics (behave like a gentleman), conflicts, hazards, and danger in fieldwork (take quinine; don't worry about dirty water), and fieldwork identity (don't be a fool).

We therefore believe that the technicalities of field interviews or organizing field notes are not the problem, to mention two common concerns among students, but what goes on in the relation between ethnographer and research participants, and how to interpret fieldnotes. Insight in the interview experience and the epistemology of fieldnotes, rather than the technique, leads to better interviewers and better data. There are no recipes for gathering ethnographic data, just as there are no formulas for designing a groundbreaking experiment in nuclear physics. Instead, a better understanding of the experience of conducting fieldwork will heighten the anthropologist's sensitivity to the research process and enhance access to rewarding data rather than rely solely on trodden paths led by a singular concern with methods. This is not to say that anthropologists should not train themselves thoroughly in fieldwork methods – we have added an appendix with extensive bibliographic references to ethnographic data-gathering techniques for the interested reader (see Appendix 1) – but we are convinced that a sophisticated understanding of the fieldwork experience will make better fieldworkers and yield more profound and groundbreaking ethnographies.

Given the great many books and articles available on ethnographic fieldwork, several choices had to be made for this Reader. One, the selection concentrates on those texts which we believe to have continued relevance in the discipline and should be part of the background knowledge of every undergraduate and graduate student in cultural anthropology. Two, the selection aims to provide readers with a good sense of the breadth, variation, and complexity of the fieldwork experience. We have therefore not restricted this anthology to discussions of data-gathering proper, but extended it to include issues of professional identity, fieldwork relations, ethics, and the practice of ethnographic writing. Three, since much has been written about a great number of topics, we have been forced to choose from several equally superb articles on the same subject. Style, accessibility, imagination, innovation, and personal preference were considered in selecting one text over another.

Since publication of the Reader's first edition in 2007, evidence of the continuously expanding cross-disciplinary trendiness of fieldwork as a central method not just in cultural anthropology across the social sciences is found in the following 20 major publications:

1   *Improvising Theory: Process and Temporality in Ethnographic Fieldwork* (Cerwonka and Malkki 2007)
2   *Fieldwork Connections: The Fabric of Ethnographic Collaboration in China and America* (Harrell et al. 2007)
3   *The Shadow Side of Fieldwork: Exploring the Blurred Borders between Ethnography and Life* (McLean and Leibing 2007)
4   *Taking Sides: Ethics, Politics & Fieldwork in Anthropology* (Armbruster and Laerke 2008)
5   *Knowing How to Know: Fieldwork and the Ethnographic Present* (Halstead et al. 2008)
6   *Fieldwork Is Not What It Used to Be: Learning Anthropology's Method in a Time of Transition* (Faubion and Marcus 2009)
7   *Women Fielding Danger: Negotiating Ethnographic Identities in Field Research* (Huggins and Glebbeek 2009)
8   *Ethnographic Practice in the Present* (Melhuus et al. 2009)
9   *Ethnographic Fieldwork: A Beginner's Guide* (Blommaert and Dong 2010)
10 *Emotions in the Field: The Psychology and Anthropology of Fieldwork Experience* (Spencer and Davies 2010)
11 *Essentials of Field Relationships* (Kaler and Beres 2010)
12 *Netnography: Doing Ethnographic Research Online* (Kozinets 2010)
13 *Centralizing Fieldwork: Critical Perspectives from Primatology, Biological and Social Anthropology* (MacClancy and Fuentes 2010)
14 *Being Ethnographic: A Guide to the Theory and Practice of Ethnography* (Madden 2010)
15 *Out of the Study and Into the Field: Ethnographic Theory and Practice in French Anthropology* (Parkin and de Salles 2010)
16 *Between Art and Anthropology: Contemporary Ethnographic Practice* (Schneider and Wright 2010)
17 *Anthropological Fieldwork: A Relational Process* (Spencer and Davies 2010)
18 *Fieldwork Identities in the Caribbean* (Taylor 2010)
19 *Anthropologists in the Securityscape: Ethics, Practices, and Professional Identity* (Albro et al. 2011)
20 *Anthropological Practice: Fieldwork and the Ethnographic Method* (Okely 2011)

The rapidly expanding literature on fieldwork has necessitated a rethink of the Reader, and this second edition has provided a welcome opportunity to make appropriate updates and revisions in response. In making decisions about what new articles should be added, and hence, regretfully, which previously used ones must by necessity be lost, we have had recourse to the reviews of the first edition and a user feedback survey conducted by Wiley-Blackwell, and sought feedback and consulted widely with colleagues in making difficult choices about what revisions should be made. Besides updating references and the entries in the Appendices, with regard to articles, 15 from the first edition have been replaced with 16 new ones; and with regard to sections, we have replaced the entire final section in the first edition on "Fictive Fieldwork" with a new one on "Engaged Fieldwork," reflecting the development of this important new approach in recent years. It is with great regret that we lose the fictive fiction section: while it was important for conveying the wider significance of the idea of "fieldwork" in contemporary society and culture, feedback suggests it was the least useful to readers and most infrequently selected as assigned reading by those who used the first edition as a textbook. Nonetheless, the practice of anthropologists and ethnographers exploring and experimenting with different literary styles and writing fiction to help readers share in the ethnographic encounter, which makes fieldwork such a singular experience, appears to be thriving, with continued strong support by the Society for the Anthropology of Humanism. Also, we note the publication of another outstanding fieldwork novel, the appropriately titled *Fieldwork: A Novel*, by Mischa Berlinski (2008) which, like Susanna Kaysen's *Far Afield* (1994), amply demonstrates the emerging power of fiction to convey ethnographic truths through the trope of the "fieldwork adventure." We would like to remind readers that the articles on fictive fieldwork in the first edition are, of course, still available, and encourage you not to forget this wider perspective on the significance or "meaning" of fieldwork today.

The Reader is divided into ten parts, each representing a major subfield or theme in **ethnographic fieldwork** in cultural anthropology:

I   **Beginnings**   Ethnographic fieldwork had been carried out in various guises and forms at the turn of the nineteenth century, but Bronislaw Malinowski is generally considered the first "founding father" of extended, first-hand fieldwork in anthropology.

II   **Fieldwork Identity**   Self-reflection on research experiences has been more prominent in anthropology than in any other scholarly discipline. The long-term immersion in other societies and cultures, the status as foreigners and "others," the interactive research methods, and the nature of fieldwork as a professional rite of passage with often far-reaching effects on the self, have made fieldwork identity of great concern, and some authors argue that the anthropologist's identity has a decisive influence on the data gathered.

III   **Fieldwork Relations and Rapport**   The success of ethnographic fieldwork is in large measure determined by the ability to establish good rapport and develop meaningful relations with research participants. These relations range from friendship to hostility, and may be influenced by ethnicity, religion, class, gender, and age.

IV   **The "Other" Talks Back**   Access to schooling and the dissemination of anthropological writings have turned once illiterate "informants" into avid critics of their ethnographers. Such "talking back" has made anthropologists aware of their conduct as researchers, led to soul-searching about their writings, and enhanced the quality of ethnographic research.

V   **Fieldwork Conflicts, Hazards, and Dangers**   Fieldwork is not free of tensions, dilemmas, conflicts, hazards, and dangers, and even lethal hostility. Awareness of such risks is of life-saving importance to students embarking on their first fieldwork experience, and research troubles, even failures, are a source of ethnographic knowledge in themselves.

VI   **Ethics**   The relational nature of fieldwork addressed in Part III, the conflicts described in Part IV, and the changing relation between anthropologists and their research participants referred to in Part V have made contemporary fieldwork morally and ethically more complex. A grasp of the ethical implications of fieldwork is indispensable before students can develop their first research design.

VII   **Single and Multi-Sited Fieldwork**   Long-term, face-to-face, empirical research in a small community has been the enduring hallmark of anthropological fieldwork. However, in the past 15 years, there has been an increase in multi-sited and multi-authored fieldwork because of a growing interdisciplinary interest among anthropologists and forces of globalization which impinge on even the remotest community. Multi-sited fieldwork is not only concerned with different locales, but also involves widely varying topics such as bodies, imaginary beings, the internet, and the scientific enterprise itself.

VIII   **Sensorial Fieldwork**   Fieldwork is mostly based on verbal exchanges and yields generally a written narrative of research results. Still, attention to sight, sound, smell, and taste have also produced fascinating interpretations of culture.

IX   **Reflexive Ethnography**   The ethnographic turn of the 1970s heightened anthropology's awareness of the epistemology of the fieldwork encounter. Ethnographers' crucial role in dialogic data collection gave them a central place in anthropological writings. Reflexivity has enriched fieldwork by making ethnographers pay much closer attention to the interactional processes through which knowledge is acquired, learned, and transmitted, as well as the interpersonal emotions experienced during fieldwork.

X   **Engaged Fieldwork**   The emergence of compassionate and public anthropology approaches to fieldwork beginning in the 1990s coalesced in the development of ethically, morally, and politically engaged forms of fieldwork in the first decade of this century. However, that all is not well with the epistemology of fieldwork was revealed by the re-emergence of mission-related counterinsurgency research by social scientists deployed in US Army Human Terrain Teams in the wars in Iraq and Afghanistan, which has raised serious issues and generated great controversy and renewed debate about the ethics, practice, and praxis of fieldwork today.

With this introduction and structure in mind, welcome to the second edition of the Reader, and best wishes for success in fieldwork.

REFERENCES

This list includes works referred to in the Appendices
Adams, Richard and Jack Preiss, eds.
    1960   *Human Organization Research: Field Relations and Techniques.* Homewood, IL: Dorsey Press.
Agar, Michael H.
    1980   *The Professional Stranger: An Informal Introduction to Ethnography.* New York: Academic Press.

Agar, Michael H.
    1985   *Speaking of Ethnography*. London: Sage.
Albro, Robert, George Marcus, Laura MacNamara, and Monica Schoch-Spana, eds.
    2011   *Anthropologists in the Securityscape: Ethics, Practices, and Professional Identity*. Walnut Creek, CA: Left Coast Press.
Alland, Alexander, Jr.
    1975   *When the Spider Danced: Notes from an African Village*. Garden City, NY: Doubleday.
Altorki, Soraya and Camillia Fawzi El-Solh, eds.
    1988   *Arab Women in the Field: Studying Your Own Culture*. Syracuse, NY: Syracuse University Press.
Alvesson, Mats and Kaj Sköldberg
    2001   *Reflexive Methodology: New Vistas for Qualitative Research*. London: Sage.
Amit, Vered, ed.
    2000   *Constructing the Field: Ethnographic Fieldwork in the Contemporary World*. London: Routledge.
Anderson, Barbara Gallatin
    1990   *First Fieldwork: The Misadventures of an Anthropologist*. Prospect Heights, IL: Waveland.
Anderson, Barbara Gallatin
    1999   *Around the World in 30 Years: Life as a Cultural Anthropologist*. Prospect Heights, IL: Waveland.
Angrosino, Michael V., ed.
    2002   *Doing Cultural Anthropology*. Prospect Heights, IL: Waveland.
Angrosino, Michael V., ed.
    2005   *Projects in Ethnographic Research*. Long Grove, IL: Waveland.
Appell, G. N., ed.
    1978   *Ethical Dilemmas in Anthropological Inquiry: A Case Book*. Los Angeles: Crossroads.
Armbruster, Heidi and Anne Laerke, eds.
    2008   *Taking Sides: Ethics, Politics, and Fieldwork in Anthropology*. New York: Berghahn.
Atkinson, Paul, A. J. Coffey, S. Delamont, J. Lofland, and L. Lofland, eds.
    2001   *Handbook of Ethnography*. Newbury Park: Sage.
Barbash, Ilisa and Lucien Taylor
    1997   *Cross-Cultural Filmmaking: A Handbook for Making Documentary and Ethnographic Films and Videos*. Berkeley: University of California Press.
Barfield, Thomas, ed.
    1997   Fieldwork. In: *The Dictionary of Anthropology*. Thomas Barfield, ed., pp. 188–190. Oxford: Blackwell.
Barley, Nigel
    1983   *The Innocent Anthropologist: Notes From a Mud Hut*. Harmondsworth: Penguin.
Barley, Nigel
    1985   *A Plague of Caterpillars: A Return to the African Bush*. London: Viking.
Barley, Nigel
    1988   *Not a Hazardous Sport*. London: Penguin.
Becker, Howard S.
    1993   Theory: The Necessary Evil. In: *Theory and Concepts in Qualitative Research: Perspectives from the Field*. D. Flinders and G. Mills, eds., pp. 218–229. New York: Teachers College Press.
Bell, Colin and Howard Newby, eds.
    1977   *Doing Sociological Research*. London: George Allen and Unwin.

Bell, Colin and Helen Roberts, eds.
 1984   *Social Researching: Politics, Problems, Practice*. London: Routledge & Kegan Paul.
Berg, Bruce L.
 2003   *Qualitative Research Methods for the Social Sciences*. 5th edn. Boston: Allyn and Bacon.
Berger, Roger
 1993   From Text to (Field)work and Back Again: Theorizing a Post(modern) Ethnography. *Anthropological Quarterly* 66(4):174–186.
Berlinski, Mischa
 2008   *Fieldwork: A Novel*. New York: Picador.
Bernard, H. Russell
 2003   *Research Methods in Anthropology: Qualitative and Quantitative Approaches*. 3rd edn. Thousand Oaks, CA: Sage.
Berreman, Gerald D.
 1963   *Hindus of the Himalayas*. Berkeley: University of California Press.
Bester, Theodore, Patricia G. Steinhoff, and Victoria Lyon Bester, eds.
 2003   *Doing Fieldwork in Japan*. Honolulu: University of Hawaii Press.
Beteille, Andre and T. N. Madan, eds.
 1975   *Encounter and Experience: Personal Accounts of Fieldwork*. Delhi: Vikas.
Beverley, John
 1996   The Margin at the Center: On *Testimonio*. In: *The Real Thing: Testimonial Discourse and Latin America*. Georg Gugelberger, ed., pp. 23–41. Durham, NC: Duke University Press.
Beverley, John
 2004   *Testimonio: On The Politics of Truth*. Minneapolis: University of Minnesota Press.
Blommaert, Jan and Jie Dong
 2010   *Ethnographic Fieldwork: A Beginner's Guide*. Tonowanda, NY: Multilingual Matters.
Bogden, R. and S. Taylor
 1975   *Introduction to Qualitative Research Methods*. New York: Wiley.
Borgerhoff Mulder, Monique and Wendy Logsdon, eds.
 1996   *I've Been Gone Far Too Long: Field Trip Fiascoes and Expedition Disasters*. Oakland, CA: RDR Books.
Borofsky, Robert
 2004   Conceptualizing Public Anthropology. Electronic document, http://www.publican-thropology.org/Defining/definingpa.htm, accessed April 11, 2007.
Bourgois, Philippe
 2006   Foreword: Anthropology in the Global State of Emergency. In: *Engaged Observer: Anthropology, Advocacy, and Activism*. V. Sanford and A. Angel-Ajani, eds., pp. ix–xii. New Brunswick, NJ: Rutgers University Press.
Bourgois, Philippe and Jeffrey Schonberg
 2009   *Righteous Dopefiend*. Berkeley: University of California Press.
Bradford, Daniel
 1998   *Being There: The Necessity of Fieldwork*. Washington, DC: Smithsonian Institution Press.
Brettell, Caroline B.
 1993   Introduction: Fieldwork, Text and Audience. In: *When They Read What We Write: The Politics of Ethnography*. Caroline B. Brettell, ed., pp. 1–24. Westport, CT: Bergin and Garvey.
Briggs, Jean
 1970   *Never in Anger: Portrait of an Eskimo Family*. Cambridge, MA: Harvard University Press.

Bruner, Edward
    2005   Tourism Fieldwork. *Anthropology News*, May 5, pp. 16, 19.
Bryman, Alan, ed.
    2001   *Ethnography*. 4 vols. London: Sage.
Bryman, Alan and Robert G. Burgess, eds.
    1999   *Qualitative Research*. 4 vols. London: Sage.
Caplan, Pat, ed.
    2003   *The Ethics of Anthropology: Debates and Dilemmas*. New York: Routledge.
Casagrande, Joseph B., ed.
    1960   *In the Company of Man: Twenty Portraits of Anthropological Informants*. New York: Harper and Row.
Cerwonka, Allaine and Liisa Malkki
    2007   *Improvising Theory: Process and Temporality in Ethnographic Fieldwork*. Chicago: University of Chicago Press.
Cesara, Manda (a pseudonym for Karla Poewe)
    1982   *Reflections of a Woman Anthropologist: No Hiding Place*. London: Academic Press.
Chagnon, Napoleon
    1974   *Studying the Yanomamö*. New York: Holt, Rinehart and Winston.
Chiñas, Beverly Newbold
    1992   *La Zandunga: Of Fieldwork and Friendship in Southern Mexico*. Prospect Heights, IL: Waveland.
Clifford, James
    1980   Fieldwork, Reciprocity and the Making of Ethnographic Texts. *Man* 3:518–532.
Clifford, James and George E. Marcus, eds.
    1986   *Writing Culture: The Poetics and Politics of Ethnography*. Berkeley: University of California Press.
Cohen, Anthony P.
    1992   Post-Fieldwork Fieldwork. *Journal of Anthropological Research* 48(4):339–354.
Coleman, Simon and Peter Collins, eds.
    2006   *Locating the Field: Space, Place and Context in Anthropology*. Oxford: Berg.
Crane, Julia and Michael Angrosino, eds.
    1992   *Field Projects in Anthropology: A Student Handbook*. Prospect Heights, IL: Waveland.
Crapanzano, Vincent
    1980   *Tuhami: Portrait of a Moroccan*. Chicago: University of Chicago Press.
D'Amico-Samuels, Deborah
    1991   Undoing Fieldwork: Personal, Political, Theoretical and Methodological Implications. In: *Decolonizing Anthropology*. Faye Harrison, ed., pp. 68–87. Washington, DC: Association of Black Anthropologists, American Anthropological Association.
Daniel, E. Valentine
    1996   *Charred Lullabies: Chapters in an Anthropography of Violence*. Princeton: Princeton University Press.
Das, Veena
    1995   *Critical Events: An Anthropological Perspective on Modern India*. Delhi: Oxford University Press.
Delamont, Sara
    2001   *Fieldwork in Educational Settings*. 2nd edn. New York: Routledge.
Denzin, Norman K. and Yvonna S. Lincoln, eds.
    2001   *The American Tradition in Qualitative Research*. 4 vols. London: Sage.
Denzin, Norman K. and Yvonna S. Lincoln, eds.
    2005   *Handbook of Qualitative Research*. 3rd edn. Thousand Oaks, CA: Sage.

De Soto, Hermine and Nora Dudwick
   2000   *Fieldwork Dilemmas: Anthropologists in Postsocialist Societies*. Madison: University of Wisconsin Press.
Devereux, George
   1968   *From Anxiety to Method in the Social Sciences*. The Hague: Mouton.
Devereux, Stephen and John Hoddinott, eds.
   1992   *Fieldwork in Developing Countries*. New York: Harvester Wheatsheaf.
DeVita, Philip R., ed.
   1988   *The Humbled Anthropologist: Tales From the Pacific*. Belmont: Wadsworth.
DeVita, Philip R., ed.
   1992   *The Naked Anthropologist: Tales From Around the World*. Belmont, CA: Wadsworth.
DeVita, Philip R.
   2000   *Stumbling Towards Truth: Anthropologists at Work*. Prospect Heights, IL: Waveland.
DeWalt, Kathleen and Billie DeWalt
   2002   *Participant Observation*. Walnut Creek, CA: AltaMira.
Dobert, Marion L.
   1982   *Ethnographic Research*. London: Praeger.
Donner, Florinda
   1982   *Shabono: A True Adventure in the Remote and Magical Heart of the South American Jungle*. London: Triad/Paladin.
Douglas, Jack, ed.
   1972   *Research on Deviance*. New York: Random House.
Douglas, Mary
   1966   *Purity and Danger*. London: Routledge & Kegan Paul.
Driessen, Henk, ed.
   1993   *The Politics of Ethnographic Reading and Writing: Confrontations of Western and Indigenous Views*. Saarbrücken: Breitenbach.
Dumont, Jean-Paul
   1978   *The Headman and I: Ambiguity and Ambivalence in the Fieldwork Experience*. Austin: University of Texas Press.
Edgerton, Robert B. and L. L. Langness
   1974   *Methods and Styles in the Study of Cultures*. San Francisco, CA: Chandler and Sharp.
Ellen, R. F., ed.
   1984   *Ethnographic Research: A Guide to General Conduct*. London: Academic Press.
Ellis, Carolyn
   2004   *The Ethnographic I: A Methodological Novel about Autoethnography*. Walnut Creek, CA: AltaMira Press.
Emerson, Robert M., Rachel I. Fretz, and Linda L. Shaw
   1995   *Writing Ethnographic Fieldnotes*. Chicago: University of Chicago Press.
Epstein, A. L., ed.
   1967   *The Craft of Social Anthropology*. London: Tavistock.
Eriksen, Thomas Hyland
   2006   *Engaging Anthropology: The Case for a Public Presence*. Oxford: Berg.
Evans-Pritchard, E. E.
   1940   *The Nuer*. Oxford: Oxford University Press.
Evans-Pritchard, E. E.
   1973   Some Reminiscences and Reflections on Fieldwork. *Journal of the Anthropological Society of Oxford* 4:1–12.
Ewing, Katherine P.
   1994   Dreams from a Saint: Anthropological Atheism and the Temptation to Believe. *American Anthropologist* 96(3):571–583.

Farmer, Paul
    2003 *Pathologies of Power: Structural Violence and the Assault on Health and Human Rights*. Berkeley: University of California Press.
Faubion, James and George E. Marcus, eds.
    2009 *Fieldwork Is Not What It Used to Be: Learning Anthropology's Method in a Time of Transition*. Ithaca, NY: Cornell University Press.
Fernandez, James
    1985 Exploded Worlds: Text as a Metaphor for Ethnography (and Vice Versa). *Dialectical Anthropology* 10:15–26.
Fetterman, David M.
    1992 *Ethnography: Step-by-Step*. Newbury Park: Sage.
Fife, Wayne
    2005 *Doing Fieldwork: Ethnographic Methods for Research in Developing Countries and Beyond*. New York: Palgrave Macmillan.
Fluehr-Lobban, Carolyn, ed.
    2002 *Ethics and the Profession of Anthropology*. 2nd edn. Walnut Creek, CA: AltaMira.
Foster, George, T. Scudder, E. Colson, and R. Kemper, eds.
    1979 *Long-Term Field Research in Social Anthropology*. New York: Academic Press.
Freilich, Morris, ed.
    1970 *Marginal Natives: Anthropologists at Work*. New York: Harper and Row.
Friedrichs, Jürgen and Harmut Ludtke
    1975 *Participant Observation: Theory and Practice*. London: Saxon.
Georges, Robert A. and Michael O. Jones
    1980 *People Studying People: The Human Element in Fieldwork*. Berkeley: University of California Press.
Glazer, Myron
    1972 *The Research Adventure: Promise and Problems in Fieldwork*. New York: Random House.
Golde, Peggy, ed.
    1970 *Women in the Field: Anthropological Experiences*. Chicago: Aldine.
González, Roberto, ed.
    2004 *Anthropologists in the Public Sphere: Speaking Out on War, Peace, and American Power*. Austin: University of Texas Press.
González, Roberto
    2010 *Militarizing Culture: Essays on the Warfare State*. Walnut Creek, CA: Left Coast Press.
Good, Kenneth
    1991 *Into the Heart: An Amazonian Love Story*. London: Penguin.
Gough, Kathleen
    1968 New Proposals for Anthropologists. *Current Anthropology* 9(5):403–435.
Gravel, Pierre B. and Robert M. Ridinger
    1988 *Anthropological Fieldwork: An Annotated Bibliography*. New York: Garland.
Greenhouse, Carol J., Elizabeth Mertz, and Kay B. Warren, eds.
    2002 *Ethnography in Unstable Places: Everyday Lives in Contexts of Dramatic Political Change*. Durham, NC: Duke University Press.
Greenway, J.
    1972 *Down among the Wild Men: the Narrative Journal of Fifteen Years Pursuing the Old Stone Age Aborigines of Australia's Western Desert*. Boston: Little, Brown.
Grindal, Bruce and Frank Salamone, eds.
    1995 *Bridges to Humanity: Narratives on Anthropology and Friendship*. Prospect Heights, IL: Waveland.

Gudeman, Stephen and Alberto Rivera
1995 From Car to House (*Del coche a la casa*). *American Anthropologist* 97(2):242–250.

Gupta, Akhil and James Ferguson
1997 Discipline and Practice: "The Field" as Site, Method, and Location in Anthropology. In: *Anthropological Locations: Boundaries and Grounds of a Field Science*. G. Gupta and J. Ferguson, eds., pp. 1–46. Berkeley: University of California Press.

Halstead, Narmala, Eric Hirsch, and Judith Okley
2008 *Knowing How to Know: Fieldwork and the Ethnographic Present*. Bremen: Edition Temmen.

Hammersley, Martyn and Paul Atkinson
1995 *Ethnography: Principles and Practice*. 2nd edn. London: Tavistock.

Hammond, Phillip E., ed.
1964 *Sociologists at Work: Essays on the Craft of Social Research*. New York: Basic Books.

Harrell, Strevan, Ma Lunzy, and Bamo Ayi
2007 *Fieldwork Connections: The Fabric of Ethnographic Collaboration in China and America*. Seattle: University of Washington Press.

Harris, Marvin
1978 *Cannibals and Kings: The Origins of Culture*. Glasgow: Fontana.

Harrison, Faye, ed.
1991 *Decolonizing Anthropology*. Washington, DC: Association of Black Anthropologists, American Anthropological Association.

Hayano, D. M.
1990 *Road Through the Rain Forest: Living Anthropology in Highland Papua New Guinea*. Prospect Heights, IL: Waveland.

Heider, Karl G.
1976 *Ethnographic Film*. Austin: University of Texas Press.

Hendry, Joy
1999 *An Anthropologist in Japan: Glimpses of Life in the Field*. Routledge: New York.

Henry, Frances and Satish Saberal, eds.
1969 *Stress and Response in Fieldwork*. New York: Holt, Rinehart and Winston.

Hern, John
1996 *Co-operative Inquiry: Research Into the Human Condition*. London: Sage.

Hine, Christine
2000 *Virtual Ethnography*. New York: Sage.

Hinton, Alexander Laban
2005 *Why Did They Kill? Cambodia in the Shadow of Genocide*. Berkeley: University of California Press.

Hirabayashi, Lane Ryo
2001 *The Politics of Fieldwork: Research From an American Concentration Camp*. Tucson: University of Arizona Press.

Hobbs, Dick and Tim May, eds.
1993 *Interpreting the Field: Accounts of Ethnography*. Melbourne: Oxford University Press.

Holstein, James and Jaber Gubrium
1995 *The Active Interview*. Newbury Park: Sage.

Honigmann, John, ed.
1973 *Handbook of Social and Cultural Anthropology*. Chicago: Rand McNally.

Howell, Nancy
1990 *Surviving Fieldwork. Report of the Advisory Panel on Health and Safety in Fieldwork*. Washington, DC: American Anthropological Association.

Howes, David, ed.
　1991　*The Varieties of Sensory Experience: A Sourcebook in the Anthropology of the Senses*. Toronto: University of Toronto Press.
Huggins, Martha and Marie-Louise Glebbeek, eds.
　2009　*Women Fielding Danger: Negotiating Ethnographic Identities in Field Research*. Lanham, MD: Rowman and Littlefield.
Huizer, Gerrit and Bruce Mannheim, eds.
　1979　*The Politics of Anthropology: From Colonialism and Sexism to a View from Below*. The Hague: Mouton.
Hume, Lynne and Jane Mulcock, eds.
　2004　*Anthropologists in the Field: Cases in Participant-Observation*. New York: Columbia University Press.
Hunt, Jennifer C.
　1989　*Psychoanalytic Aspects of Fieldwork*. Newbury Park: Sage.
Hymes, Dell, ed.
　1969　*Reinventing Anthropology*. New York: Pantheon.
Jackson, Bruce
　1987　*Fieldwork*. Urbana: University of Illinois Press.
Jackson, Bruce and Edward D. Ives, eds.
　1996　*The World Observed: Reflections on the Fieldwork Process*. Urbana: University of Illinois Press.
Jackson, Michael, ed.
　1996　*Things as They Are: New Directions in Phenomenological Anthropology*. Bloomington: University of Indiana Press.
Jongmans, D. G. and P. C. W. Gutkind, eds.
　1967　*Anthropologists in the Field*. Assen, Netherlands: Van Gorcum.
Jorgensen, Danny L.
　1989　*Participant Observation: A Methodology for Human Studies*. London: Sage.
Kaler, Amy and Melanie Beres
　2010　*Essentials of Field Relationships*. Walnut Creek, CA: Left Coast Press.
Kaysen, Susanna
　1990　*Far Afield*. New York: Vintage.
Keesing, Roger and Andrew Strathern
　1998　Fieldwork. In: *Cultural Anthropology: A Contemporary Perspective*. 3rd edn, pp. 7–10. Fort Worth, TX: Harcourt Brace.
Kelly, John, Beatrice Jauregui, Sean Mitchell, and Jeremy Walton, eds.
　2010　*Anthropology and Global Counterinsurgency*. Chicago: University of Chicago Press.
Kemper, Robert and Anya Peterson Royce, eds.
　2002　*Chronicling Cultures: Long-Term Field Research in Anthropology*. Walnut Creek, CA: AltaMira.
Kennedy, Elizabeth Lapovsky
　1995　In Pursuit of Connection: Reflections on Collaborative Work. *American Anthropologist* 97(1):26–33.
Kim, Choong Soon
　1977　*An Asian Anthropologist in the South: Field Experiences with Blacks, Indians and Whites*. Knoxville: University of Tennessee Press.
Kimball, Solon and William Partridge
　1979　*The Craft of Community Study: Fieldwork Dialogues*. Gainesville: University of Florida Press.

Kimball, Solon T. and James B. Watson, eds.
1972 *Crossing Cultural Boundaries: The Anthropological Experience.* San Francisco: Chandler.
Kleinman, Arthur, Veena Das, and Margaret Lock, eds.
1997 *Social Suffering.* Berkeley: University of California Press.
Kleinman, Sherryl and Martha Copp
1993 *Emotions and Fieldwork.* Thousand Oaks, CA: Sage.
Kottak, Conrad
1983 *Assault on Paradise.* New York: Random House.
Kozinets, Robert
2010 *Netnography: Doing Ethnographic Research Online.* Los Angeles: Sage.
Kuhlmann, Annette
1992 Collaborative Research Among the Kickapoo Tribe of Oklahoma. *Human Organization* 51(3):274–283.
Kuhn, Thomas
1962 *The Structure of Scientific Revolutions.* Chicago: University of Chicago Press.
Kulick, Don and Margaret Willson, eds.
1995 *Taboo: Sex, Identity and Erotic Subjectivity in Anthropological Fieldwork.* New York: Routledge.
Kumar, Nita
1992 *Friends, Brothers and Informants: Fieldwork Memories of Banaras.* Berkeley: University of California Press.
Lareau, Annette and Jeffrey Shultz, eds.
1996 *Journeys Through Ethnography: Realistic Accounts of Fieldwork.* Boulder, CO: Westview.
Lee, Raymond M.
1995 *Dangerous Fieldwork.* Thousand Oaks, CA: Sage.
Lévi-Strauss, Claude
1955 *Tristes Tropiques.* Harmondsworth: Penguin.
Lewin, Ellen and William Leap, eds.
1996 *Out in the Field: Reflections of Lesbian and Gay Anthropologists.* Urbana: University of Illinois Press.
Lowie, Robert E.
1959 *Robert E. Lowie, Ethnologist: A Personal Record.* Ann Arbor, MI: Books on Demand.
MacClancy, Jeremy and Agustin Fuentes, eds.
2010 *Centralizing Fieldwork: Critical Perspectives from Primatology, Biological and Social Anthropology.* New York: Berghahn.
Madden, Raymond
2010 *Being Ethnographic: A Guide to the Theory and Practice of Ethnography.* Newbury Park: Sage.
Mahmood, Cynthia
1996 *Fighting For Faith and Nation: Dialogues With Sikh Militants.* Philadelphia: University of Pennsylvania Press.
Malinowski, Bronislaw
1922 Introduction: The Subject, Method and Scope of This Inquiry. In: *Argonauts of the Western Pacific*, pp. 1–25. New York: Dutton.
Malinowski, Branislaw
1967 *A Diary in the Strict Sense of the Term.* London: Routledge & Kegan Paul.
Manning, Peter, ed.
1987 *Semiotics and Fieldwork.* Thousand Oaks, CA: Sage.

Marcus, George and Fernando Mascarenhas
   2005   *Ocasião: The Marquis and the Anthropologist, A Collaboration.* Walnut Creek, CA: AltaMira.
Marcus, Julie, ed.
   1993   *First in Their Field: Women and Australian Anthropology.* Melbourne: Melbourne University Press.
Marion, Jonathan
   2005   "Where" is "There"? *Anthropology News,* May 5, p. 18.
Markowitz, Fran and Michael Ashkenazi, eds.
   1999   *Sex, Sexuality, and the Anthropologist.* Urbana: University of Illinois Press.
Marriott, Alice
   1952   *Greener Fields: Experiences among the American Indians.* Garden City: Doubleday.
Maruyama, Magorath, Arthur Jenkins, and the American Anthropological Association
   1975   *Cultures Beyond Earth.* New York: Vintage.
Maybury-Lewis, David
   1965   *The Savage and the Innocent.* Cleveland: World Publishing.
McCall, G. J. and J. L. Simmons, eds.
   1969   *Issues in Participant Observation: A Text and Reader.* Reading, MA: Addison-Wesley.
McLean, Athena and Annette Leibing, eds.
   2007   *The Shadow Side of Fieldwork: Exploring the Blurred Borders between Ethnography and Life.* Hoboken, NJ: Wiley-Blackwell.
Mead, Margaret
   1928   *Coming of Age in Samoa.* Harmondsworth: Penguin.
Mead, Margaret
   1953   The Study of Culture at a Distance. In: *The Study of Culture at a Distance.* M. Mead and R. Métraux, eds., pp. 3–53. Chicago: University of Chicago Press.
Mead, Margaret
   1959   *An Anthropologist at Work: Writings of Ruth Benedict.* Boston: Houghton Mifflin.
Mead, Margaret
   1977   *Letters From the Field, 1927–75.* New York: Harper and Row.
Melhuus, Marit, John Mitchell, and Helena Wulff, eds.
   2009   *Ethnographic Practice in the Present.* Oxford: Praeger.
Menchú, Rigoberta with Elisabeth Burgos-Debray
   1984   *I, Rigoberta Menchú: An Indian Woman in Guatemala.* London: Verso.
Merriam, Alan P.
   1964   *The Anthropology of Music.* Evanston, IL: Northwestern University Press.
Messenger, John C.
   1991   *Inis Beag Revisited: The Anthropologist as Observant Participant.* Salem, WI: Sheffield Press.
Messerschmidt, Donald A., ed.
   1981   *Anthropologists at Home in North America: Methods and Issues in the Study of One's Own Society.* Cambridge: Cambridge University Press.
Michrina, Barry P. and CherylAnne Richards
   1996   *Person to Person: Fieldwork, Dialogue, and the Hermeneutic Method.* New York: State University of New York Press.
Miller, Daniel
   1998   *A Theory of Shopping.* Cambridge: Polity.
Mitchell, William E.
   1978   *The Bamboo Fire: An Anthropologist in New Guinea.* New York: Norton.
Montagu, Ashley
   1942   *Man's Most Dangerous Myth: The Fallacy of Race.* New York: Oxford University Press.

Myers, Helen, ed.
    1992   *Ethnomusicology: An Introduction*. London: Macmillan.
Narroll, Raoul and Ronald Cohen, eds.
    1970   *A Handbook of Methods in Cultural Anthropology*. Garden City, NY: Natural History Press.
NCA (Network of Concerned Anthropologists)
    2009   *The Countercounterinsurgency Handbook*. Chicago: Prickly Paradigm.
Nordstrom, Carolyn
    1997   *A Different Kind of War Story*. Philadelphia: University of Pennsylvania Press.
Nordstrom, Carolyn and Antonius C. G. M. Robben, eds.
    1995   *Fieldwork Under Fire: Contemporary Studies of Violence and Survival*. Berkeley: University of California Press.
Oberg, Kalervo
    1960   Culture Shock: Adjustment to New Cultural Environments. *Practical Anthropology* 7:177–182.
Oberg, Kalervo
    1974   *Culture Shock*. Indianapolis, IN: Bobbs-Merrill.
Okely, Judith
    2011   *Anthropological Practice: Fieldwork and the Ethnographic Method*. Oxford: Berg.
Park, Julie
    1992   Research Partnerships: A Discussion Paper Based on Case Studies from "The Place of Alcohol in the Lives of New Zealand Women Project." *Women's Studies International Forum* 15(5/6):581–591.
Parkin, Robert and Anne de Salles, eds.
    2010   *Out of the Study and Into the Field: Ethnographic Theory and Practice in French Anthropology*. New York: Berghahn.
Pelto, Pertti J. and Gretel H. Pelto
    1978   *Anthropological Research: The Structure of Inquiry*. 2nd edn. Cambridge: Cambridge University Press.
Perry, J., ed.
    1989   *Doing Fieldwork: Eight Personal Accounts of Social Research*. Geelong: Deakin University Press.
Piddington, Ralph
    1957   Methods of Field Work. In: *An Introduction to Social Anthropology*. Vol. 2, pp. 525–596. New York: Macmillan.
Pink, Sarah
    2000   "Informants" Who Come "Home." In: *Constructing the Field: Ethnographic Fieldwork in the Contemporary World*. Vered Amit, ed., pp. 96–119. New York: Routledge.
Pole, Christopher
    2005   *Fieldwork*. 4 vols. Newbury Park: Sage.
Polsky, Ned
    1967   *Hustlers, Beats, and Others*. Harmondsworth: Penguin.
Powdermaker, Hortense
    1966   *Stranger and Friend: The Way of an Anthropologist*. New York: Norton.
Powdermaker, Hortense
    1969   Field Work. In: *The International Encyclopedia of the Social Sciences*. D. Sills, ed., pp. 418–424. New York: Macmillan.
Punch, Maurice
    1986   *The Politics and Ethics of Fieldwork: Muddy Boots and Grubby Hands*. London: Sage.
Rabinow, Paul
    1977   *Reflections on Fieldwork in Morocco*. Berkeley: University of California Press.

Rabinow, Paul, George E. Marcus, James D. Faubion, and Tobias Rees
  2008   *Designs for an Anthropology of the Contemporary*. Durham, NC: Duke University Press.
Radcliffe-Brown, A. R.
  1966   *Methods in Social Anthropology*. Chicago: University of Chicago Press.
Radin, Paul
  1933   *The Method and Theory of Ethnology*. New York: McGraw-Hill.
Rappaport, Roy A.
  1994   Comment on "Cultural Anthropology's Future Agenda." *Anthropology Newsletter* 35(6):76.
Raybeck, Douglas
  1996   *Mad Dogs, Englishmen, and the Errant Anthropologist: Fieldwork in Malaysia*. Prospect Heights, IL: Waveland.
Read, Kenneth
  1966   *The High Valley*. London: George Allen and Unwin.
Read, Kenneth
  1986   *Return to the High Valley*. Berkeley: University of California Press.
Richards, Audrey I.
  1939   The Development of Field Work Methods in Social Anthropology. In: *The Study of Society*. F. C. Bartlett et al., eds., pp. 272–316. London: Routledge.
Ridler, Keith
  1996   If Not the Words: Shared Practical Activity and Friendship in Fieldwork. In: *Things as They Are: New Directions in Phenomenological Anthropology*. Michael Jackson, ed., pp. 238–258. Bloomington: Indiana University Press.
Robben, Antonius C. G. M.
  2005   *Political Violence and Trauma in Argentina*. Philadelphia: University of Pennsylvania Press.
Robben, Antonius C. G. M., ed.
  2010   *Iraq at a Distance: What Anthropologists Can Teach Us About the War*. Philadelphia: University of Pennsylvania Press.
Robbins, Joel and Sandra Bamford, eds.
  1997   Fieldwork Revisited: Changing Contexts of Ethnographic Practice in the Era of Globalization. Special Issue of *Anthropology and Humanism* 22(1).
Roberts, Helen, ed.
  1981   *Doing Feminist Research*. London: Routledge & Kegan Paul.
Rohner, Ronald
  1969   *The Ethnography of Franz Boas: Letters and Diaries of Franz Boas Written on the Northwest Coast from 1886 to 1931*. Chicago: University of Chicago Press.
Royal Anthropological Institute of Great Britain and Ireland
  1951   *Notes and Queries on Anthropology*. 6th edn. London: Routledge & Kegan Paul.
Rubinstein, Robert
  1991   *Fieldwork: The Correspondence of Robert Redfield and Sol Tax*. Boulder: Westview.
Ruby, Jack, ed.
  1982   *A Crack in the Mirror: Reflexive Perspectives in Anthropology*. Philadelphia: University of Pennsylvania Press.
Rynkiewich, Michael and James Spradley, eds.
  1976   *Ethics and Anthropology: Dilemmas in Fieldwork*. New York: John Wiley and Sons.
Sanford, Victoria
  2003   *Buried Secrets: Truth and Human Rights in Guatemala*. New York: Palgrave Macmillan.

Sanford, Victoria
  2006   Introduction. In: *Engaged Observer: Anthropology, Advocacy, and Activism*. V. Sanford and A. Angel-Ajani, eds., pp. 1–15. New Brunswick, NJ: Rutgers University Press.
Sanford, Victoria and Asale Angel-Ajani, eds.
  2006   *Engaged Observer: Anthropology, Advocacy, and Activism*. New Brunswick, CT: Rutgers University Press.
Sanjek, Roger, ed.
  1990   *Fieldnotes: The Making of Anthropology*. Ithaca, NY: Cornell University Press.
Scarangella, Linda
  2005   Fieldwork at Buffalo Bill's Wild West Show. *Anthropology News*, May 5, pp. 17, 19.
Schensul, Jean J. and Margaret D. LeCompte, eds.
  1999   *Ethnographer's Toolkit*. 7 vols. Walnut Creek, CA: AltaMira.
Scheper-Hughes, Nancy
  1993   *Death Without Weeping: The Violence of Everyday Life in Brazil*. Berkeley: University of California Press.
Scheper-Hughes, Nancy
  1995   The Primacy of the Ethical: Propositions for a Militant Anthropology. *Current Anthropology* 36(3):409–420.
Scheyvens, Regina and Donovan Storey, eds.
  2003   *Development Fieldwork: A Practical Guide*. Thousand Oaks, CA: Sage.
Schneider, Arnd and Christopher Wright, eds.
  2010   *Between Art and Anthropology: Contemporary Ethnographic Practice*. Oxford: Berg.
Seymour-Smith, Charlotte
  1986a   Fieldwork. In: *Dictionary of Anthropology*, pp. 117–118. Boston: Macmillan.
Seymour-Smith, Charlotte
  1986b   Participant Observation. In: *Dictionary of Anthropology*, p. 429. Boston: Macmillan.
Shaffir, William and Robert A. Stebbins, eds.
  1991   *Experiencing Fieldwork: An Inside View of Qualitative Research*. Newbury Park: Sage.
Shaffir, William, Robert Stebbins, and Allan Turowetz, eds.
  1980   *Fieldwork Experience: Qualitative Approaches to Social Research*. New York: St Martin's.
Shostak, Marjorie
  1981   *Nisa: The Life and Words of a !Kung Woman*. Cambridge, MA: Harvard University Press.
Slater, Mariam
  1976   *African Odyssey: An Anthropological Adventure*. New York: Doubleday.
Sluka, Jeffrey A.
  1989   *Hearts and Minds, Water and Fish: Popular Support for the IRA and INLA in a Northern Irish Ghetto*. Greenwich, CT: JAI Press.
Sluka, Jeffrey A., ed.
  2000   *Death Squad: The Anthropology of State Terror*. Philadelphia: University of Pennsylvania Press.
Smith, Carolyn D. and William Kornbluh, eds.
  1995   *The Field: Readings on the Field Research Experience*. 2nd edn. New York: Praeger.
Smith, Elenore Bowen (a pseudonym for Laura Bohannan)
  1954   *Return to Laughter*. Garden City: Natural History Press.
Spencer, Dimitrina and James Davies, eds.
  2010   *Emotions in the Field: The Psychology and Anthropology of Fieldwork Experience*. Stanford: Stanford University Press.

Spencer, Robert F., ed.
  1954   *Method and Perspective in Anthropology*. Minneapolis: University of Minnesota Press.
Spindler, George D., ed.
  1970   *Being an Anthropologist: Fieldwork in Eleven Cultures*. New York: Holt, Rinehart and Winston.
Spradley, James P.
  1979   *The Ethnographic Interview*. New York: Holt, Rinehart and Winston.
Spradley, James P.
  1980   *Participant Observation*. New York: Holt, Rinehart and Winston.
Srinivas, M. N., A. M. Shah, and E. A. Ramaswamy, eds.
  1979   *The Fieldworkers and the Field: Problems and Challenges in Sociological Investigation*. Delhi: Oxford University Press.
Stocking, George W., ed.
  1983   *Observers Observed: Essays on Ethnographic Fieldwork*. Madison: University of Wisconsin Press.
Stoll, David
  2000   *Rigoberta Menchú and the Story of All Poor Guatemalans*. New York: HarperCollins.
Stoller, Paul and Cheryl Olkes
  1987   *In Sorcery's Shadow: A Memoir of Apprenticeship Among the Songhay of Niger*. Chicago: University of Chicago Press.
Strathern, Marilyn, ed.
  1995   *Shifting Contexts: Transformations in Anthropological Knowledge*. London: Routledge.
Strauss, Anselm and Juliet M. Corbin
  1998   *Basics of Qualitative Research: Techniques and Procedures for Developing Grounded Theory*. 2nd edn. Newbury Park, CA: Sage.
Sunderland, P. L.
  1999   Fieldwork and the Phone. *Anthropological Quarterly* 72(3):105–117.
Taylor, Erin, ed.
  2010   *Fieldwork Identities in the Caribbean*. Coconut Creek, FL: Caribbean Studies Press.
Tedlock, Barbara
  1991   From Participant Observation to the Observation of Participation: The Emergence of Narrative Ethnography. *Journal of Anthropological Research* 47(1):69–94.
Thapan, Meenakshi, ed.
  1998   *Anthropological Journeys: Reflections on Fieldwork*. London: Sangam.
Turner, Edith
  1999   Relating Consciousness, Culture and the Social. *Anthropology Newsletter*, January, p. 46.
Urry, James
  1984   A History of Field Methods. In: *Ethnographic Research: A Guide to General Conduct*. R. F. Ellen, ed., pp. 35–61. London: Academic Press.
Van Maanen, John, ed.
  1983   *Qualitative Methodology*. London: Sage.
Vidich, Arthur J., Joseph Bensman, and Maurice R. Stein, eds.
  1964   *Reflections on Community Studies*. New York: John Wiley and Sons.
Vine, David
  2009   *Island of Shame: The Secret History of the US Military Base on Diego Garcia*. Princeton: Princeton University Press.

Ward, Martha C.
  1989 *Nest in the Wind: Adventures in Anthropology on a Tropical Island*. Prospect Heights, IL: Waveland.
Watson, C. W., ed.
  1999 *Being There: Fieldwork in Anthropology*. London: Pluto Press.
Watson, Lawrence C. and Maria-Barbara Watson-Franke
  1985 *Interpreting Life Histories: An Anthropological Inquiry*. New Brunswick, NJ: Rutgers University Press.
Wax, Rosalie
  1971 *Doing Fieldwork: Warnings and Advice*. Chicago: University of Chicago Press.
Weinberg, Darin, ed.
  2002 *Qualitative Research Methods*. Malden: Blackwell.
Wengle, John L.
  1988 *Ethnographers in the Field: The Psychology of Research*. Tuscaloosa: University of Alabama Press.
Werner, Oswald and Mark G. Schoepfle
  1987 *Systematic Fieldwork*. 2 vols. Beverly Hills, CA: Sage.
Westbrook, David A.
  2008 *Navigators of the Contemporary: Why Ethnography Matters*. Chicago: University of Chicago Press.
Whitehead, Tony and Mary Conaway, eds.
  1986 *Self, Sex, and Gender in Cross-Cultural Fieldwork*. Urbana: University of Illinois Press.
Whitman, Glenn
  2004 *Dialogue with the Past: Engaging Students and Meeting Standards through Oral History*. Walnut Creek, CA: AltaMira.
Whyte, William Foote
  1985 *Learning From the Field: A Guide From Experience*. New York: Holt, Rinehart and Winston.
Williams, Thomas R.
  1967 *Field Methods in the Study of Culture*. New York: Holt, Rinehart and Winston.
Wolcott, Harry F.
  2002 *Sneaky Kid and Its Aftermath: Ethics and Intimacy in Fieldwork*. Walnut Creek, CA: AltaMira.
Wolcott, Harry F.
  2004 *The Art of Fieldwork*. 2nd edn. Walnut Creek, CA: AltaMira.
Wolf, Diana Deere, ed.
  1995 *Feminist Dilemmas in Fieldwork*. Boulder, CO: Westview Press.
Wolf, Eric R.
  1964 *Anthropology, Humanistic Scholarship in America*. Englewood Cliffs: Prentice-Hall.
Wright, Richard and Dick Hobbs, eds.
  2005 *Handbook of Fieldwork*. Newbury Park: Sage.
Yow, Valerie Raleigh
  2005 *Recording Oral History: A Guide for the Humanities and Social Sciences*. 2nd edn. Walnut Creek, CA: AltaMira.
Yu, Pei-Lin
  1997 *Hungry Lightning: Notes of a Woman Anthropologist in Venezuela*. Albuquerque: University of New Mexico Press.

Part I

Beginnings

Introduction

Antonius C. G. M. Robben

Since antiquity the Western world has been curious about other cultures. The exploits of the Greeks and Romans in Europe, Africa, and Asia yielded descriptions of subjected populations and sparked philosophical reflections about the nature of society and humankind. This interest declined after the fall of the Roman Empire. Europe entered the Dark Ages and was beset by political fragmentation, economic decline, and foreign invasions. The Renaissance brought a new élan with the emergence of strong states, flourishing arts, technological innovations, commercial expansion, and a desire for learning and knowledge. Portuguese explorers and traders, Spanish conquerors and missionaries, Dutch merchants and sailors, European slaves of the Ottoman Empire, English captives of Native Americans, and so forth described the strange customs and mores of the people they met. Their observations emphasized the exotic and were often random.

The study of non-European cultures received a tremendous impulse from the rise of a humanist philosophy which exalted the dignity of Man, emphasized that people are natural beings, and propagated the study of nature by scholars. The more serious European students of foreign cultures began, from the sixteenth century onward, to call for the systematic collection of knowledge, a plea which had already been made in the fourteenth century by the Arab historian Ibn Khaldûn. Scientific expeditions were organized around the mid-eighteenth century which mapped the world's natural riches and legitimated imperialism (see Honigmann 1976; Malefijt 1976; Pratt 1992; Launay 2010). Of the numerous instructions that were produced over the centuries, one particularly influential and even visionary example has been selected here. In the year 1800, the young French philosopher Joseph-Marie Degérando

Ethnographic Fieldwork: An Anthropological Reader, Second Edition. Edited by
Antonius C. G. M. Robben and Jeffrey A. Sluka.
Editorial material and organization © 2012 John Wiley & Sons, Inc.
Published 2012 by John Wiley & Sons, Inc.

wrote a manual for a scientific expedition to Australia and South Asia led by Captain Baudin, entitled *Considerations on the Various Methods to Follow in the Observation of Savage Peoples*. These instructions served as a basis for the *General Instruction to Travelers*, published in 1840 by the Ethnological Society of Paris. This French guide, in turn, strongly influenced the 1841 British publication *Queries respecting the Human Race to be addressed to travellers and others*. The *Queries* developed in 1874 into the highly influential *Notes and Queries on Anthropology*, which guided numerous generations of anthropologists through fieldwork (RAI 1951; Urry 1972).

In the excerpt from *The Observation of Savage Peoples* (1969[1800]), Joseph-Marie Degérando gives a critique of the travel accounts by explorers and proposes a systematic study of simple societies for the edification of humankind. Explorers must become philosophical travelers who use scientific methods to know other people. Degérando wants the Science of Man to follow in the footsteps of natural science by emphasizing observation, analysis, and comparison. Simple societies are ideal study objects, so he argued, because crucial properties can be more easily isolated than in complex societies. Simple societies represent the original human society, and thus reflect our own distant past. Comparison will then yield a detailed cultural evolution through which all societies need to pass from savagery to civilization. Seventy-seven years later, the American anthropologist Lewis Henry Morgan (1985[1877]) believed he had discovered the principal stages of this evolutionary development.

The botanists, zoologists, geographers, and other natural scientists on Captain Baudin's mission may not have used Dégerando's manual, but one century later his instructions were to become the principal standards of ethnographic fieldwork. Dégerando found eight shortcomings in the descriptions and travelogues of the restless explorers, who were keener on discovering than carefully mapping new territories. His eight recommendations are remarkably current and, with some stretch of the imagination, will therefore be presented here in today's anthropological terms. One, ethnographers must study all facets of a society in a contextualized way, instead of just focusing on a few individuals or rituals. Two, ethnographers must make first-hand observations, obtain representative samples, and not rely on secondary accounts. Three, observations must be made in a systematic, unbiased, and holistic way, and be confirmed by informants. Four, conclusions must be based on thorough data collection and drawn inductively, not through deduction or analogy. Five, ethnographic accounts must approximate as closely as possible local meanings and understandings, instead of being presented in Western cultural terms. Six, ethnographers should not rely on first impressions, but should immerse themselves in the host society. Seven, a thorough knowledge of the native language is indispensable for trustworthy observations and conclusions. Finally, ethnographers should pay close attention to the historical origins and development of simple societies by studying their oral tradition. In sum, Degérando recommends ethnographers to conduct sustained research in the native language, establish rapport, use an emic approach, and see society from the native's point of view.

Unfortunately, Degérando's sound recommendations were heeded neither by Baudin's expedition nor by future travelers, who relied more on brief observations than on learning the local language, asking people about their culture, and becoming one of them. At best, they kept item lists which reaped what they sowed, providing nineteenth-century anthropologists with decontextualized answers that allowed comparative analyses which would feed into preconceived evolutionary notions. They lacked the lived experience, cultural knowledge, and local understandings which fascinated later generations of anthropologists, and did not conduct the long-term, systematic ethnographic studies propagated by Degérando and finally implemented to varying degrees by Franz Boas and Bronislaw Malinowski, the two most famous and influential forefathers of modern fieldwork.

The German-born Franz Boas was neither the first American scholar to systematically study local cultures – Henry Rowe Schoolcraft, Ely Parker, Putnam, and Lewis Henry Morgan had preceded him – nor America's first ethnographer – Frank Hamilton Cushing had already conducted more than two years of fieldwork among the Zuñi. But Boas was certainly the first American anthropologist to professionalize the awakening discipline, introduce an inductive analysis of culture, and instill ethnographic fieldwork as its principal research method. Boas held the first Chair in Anthropology, founded the first Department of Anthropology at Clark University in Worcester, Massachusetts, awarded the first PhD in anthropology at Clark, and trained the first generation of American anthropologists at Columbia University, including Alfred Kroeber, Margaret Mead, Robert Lowie, Ruth Bunzel, Edward Sapir, Paul Radin, and Ruth Benedict. As an ethnographer, Boas is best remembered for his fieldwork among Native Americans in British Columbia along the northwest coast (see Stocking 1974, 2001).

The selected article "The Methods of Ethnology" (Boas 1920) is a frontal attack on the evolutionary and diffusionist approaches that dominated European anthropology, and also influenced American scholars. Boas emphasizes the study of cultural change through meticulous ethnographic fieldwork with great attention to detail, before trying to answer larger questions about the long-term development of cultures and societies. In this sense, he agrees with Degérando's instructions, but not with his assumptions about social evolution. Boas also raises doubts about the older evolutionary notion that culture is determined by psychological needs and the, at the time novel, psychoanalytic explanation of culture as repressing destructive unconscious desires by channeling them into social institutions. The title of the article included here is somewhat deceptive, because Boas does not describe fieldwork methods per se but, rather, the object and nature of anthropological data collection. He makes three crucial points: (1) social and cultural phenomena are both cause and effect in a dynamic process of continuous change; (2) individuals shape and are shaped by their social environment; and (3) larger anthropological conclusions must be reached through induction.

The lasting contribution of Franz Boas to ethnographic fieldwork is his emphasis on the careful ethnographic study of societies undergoing rapid change without reducing cultures to evolutionary laws, psychological processes, or collections of traits acquired through migration and diffusion. His critique is epistemological rather than methodological because he is more concerned with the type of knowledge acceptable to the scientific study of culture than with how to acquire that knowledge. Boas leaves ethnographers in the dark about the practice and process of fieldwork. It was the Polish expatriate Bronislaw Malinowski who advanced the methodology of ethnographic investigation through his research among the Trobrianders of Melanesia. He reconciled Boas's desire for rigorous, detailed, and contextualized data collection with the earlier experience-rich accounts of explorers, missionaries, captives, and other amateur scribes of foreign culture, adding his own attention to local world-views. Malinowski thus became the great synthesizer of ethnographic fieldwork, who deeply influenced twentieth-century anthropological research methods.

The excerpt "Method and Scope of Anthropological Fieldwork" from Malinowski's seminal 1922 ethnography *Argonauts of the Western Pacific* (1984[1922]) is anthropology's most classic and enduring statement about ethnographic fieldwork. Malinowski begins this exposé by stating that even many years of residence among a population leave the untrained eye blind to local culture. Fieldworkers can accomplish much more in just a year, when they live amidst a population as one of them and pursue clear scientific objectives in a systematic, methodical and active way. Malinowski hammers on the importance of separating the wheat from the chaff by delineating the laws, regularities, social constitution, and "firm skeleton" of cultural phenomena in a holistic manner. This approach covers all cultural domains, the ordinary as well as the quaint, and technology as much as religion and kinship. The anatomy of rules and regularities is not apparent in nonliterate tribal societies and therefore has to be formulated inductively from observed behavior and actions. Still, the skeleton is bare without the flesh and blood of everyday reality with its intimate social life and excitement of feasts, rituals, and ceremonies. An ethnographer must not be satisfied with describing the structural features of culture, but must also have an eye for the "imponderabilia of actual life" discovered through close presence and participation. Malinowski advocates participant observation as a crucial method to obtain such inside perspective. Flesh, blood, and bones are inanimate without a spirit, so ethnographers must also study people's ideas, opinions, and world-views. How people feel and think in their own language as members of their community is crucial to complete the picture of the culture under study. According to Malinowski, anthropology's overarching aim is "to grasp the native's point of view," to see their world and their relation to life through the eyes of the local population. Thus, he sets a high standard for ethnographic fieldwork that relies on in situ research in the native language and from the native's perspective, while gathering data on the structure, practice, and world-view of society in a holistic fashion (see also Firth 1957; Young 1979, 2004).

With Malinowski, fieldwork had come of age, and his students, including Raymond Firth, Edward Evans-Pritchard, Meyer Fortes, Audrey Richards, Lucy Mair, Gregory Bateson, Edmund Leach, Max Gluckman, Hortense Powdermaker, and many others fanned out across the world to write their own ethnographies based on long-term research. Malinowski's fieldwork method remained hegemonic in anthropology, a true rite of passage for aspiring anthropologists, until the 1990s when encompassing processes of globalization raised the call for multi-sited fieldwork (see Part VII).

REFERENCES

Boas, Franz
  1920   The Methods of Ethnology. *American Anthropologist* 22(4):311–321.
Degérando, Joseph-Marie
  1969[1800]   *The Observation of Savage Peoples*. Trans. F. C. T. Moore. London: Routledge and Kegan Paul.

Firth, Raymond, ed.
  1957 *Man and Culture: An Evaluation of the Work of Bronislaw Malinowski.* London: Routledge and Kegan Paul.
Honigmann, John J.
  1976 *The Development of Anthropological Ideas.* Homewood, IL: The Dorsey Press.
Launay, Robert, ed.
  2010 *Foundations of Anthropological Theory: From Classical Antiquity to Early Modern Europe.* Malden, MA: Wiley-Blackwell.
Malefijt, Annemarie de Waal
  1976 *Images of Man: A History of Anthropological Thought.* New York: Alfred A. Knopf.
Malinowski, Bronislaw
  1984[1922] *Argonauts of the Western Pacific.* Prospect Heights, IL: Waveland Press.
Morgan, Lewis Henry
  1985[1877] *Ancient Society.* Tucson, AZ: University of Arizona Press.
Pratt, Mary Louise
  1992 *Imperial Eyes: Travel Writing and Transculturation.* London: Routledge.
RAI (Royal Anthropological Institute)
  1951 *Notes and Queries on Anthropology.* 6th edn. London: Routledge & Kegan Paul.
Stocking, Jr., George W., ed.
  1974 *The Shaping of American Anthropology, 1883–1911: A Franz Boas Reader.* New York: Basic Books.
Stocking, Jr., George W.
  2001 *Delimiting Anthropology: Occasional Essays and Reflections.* Madison, WI: University of Wisconsin Press.
Urry, James
  1972 Notes and Queries on Anthropology and the Development of Field Methods in British Anthropology, 1870–1920. *Proceedings of the Royal Anthropological Institute of Great Britain and Ireland,* pp. 45–57.
Young, Michael W.
  1979 *The Ethnography of Malinowski: The Trobriand Islands, 1915–18.* London: Routledge & Kegan Paul.
Young, Michael W.
  2004 *Malinowski: Odyssey of an Anthropologist, 1884–1920.* New Haven, CT: Yale University Press.

1

The Observation of Savage Peoples

Joseph-Marie Degérando

I Advertisement

These considerations are addressed to Captain BAUDIN, correspondent of the society, about to leave for his expedition of discovery, and to the various observers accompanying him; they are addressed also to Citizen LEVAILLANT, who is going to attempt a third expedition in the interior of Africa. Since it is possible that both have occasion to encounter peoples at very different degrees of civilization or barbarity, it seems the right course to provide for any hypothesis, and to make these CONSIDER-ATIONS so general that they can be applied to any society differing in its moral and political forms from those of Europe. The leading purpose has been to provide a complete framework comprising any point of view from which these societies can be envisaged by the philosopher. It has not been supposed that certain simple questions that can easily be foreseen should be omitted, when they were necessary to the completeness of the whole.

It seems astonishing that, in an age of egoism, it is so difficult to persuade man that of all studies, the most important is that of himself. This is because egoism, like all passions, is blind. The attention of the egoist is directed to the immediate needs of which his senses give notice, and cannot be raised to those reflective needs that reason discloses to us; his aim is satisfaction, not perfection. He considers only his individual self; his species is nothing to him. Perhaps he fears that in penetrating the mysteries of his being he will ensure his own abasement, blush at his discoveries, and meet his conscience.

True philosophy, always at one with moral science, tells a different tale. The source of useful illumination, we are told, like that of lasting content, is in ourselves. Our insight depends above all on the state of our faculties; but how can we bring our faculties to perfection if we do not know their nature and their laws? The elements of happiness are the moral sentiments; but how can we develop these

Joseph-Marie Degérando, pp. 61–70, 101–104 from *The Observation of Savage Peoples*, trans. F. C. T. Moore. London: Routledge & Kegan Paul, 1969[1800]. Copyright © F. C. T. Moore.

Ethnographic Fieldwork: An Anthropological Reader, Second Edition. Edited by Antonius C. G. M. Robben and Jeffrey A. Sluka.
Editorial material and organization © 2012 John Wiley & Sons, Inc.
Published 2012 by John Wiley & Sons, Inc.

sentiments without considering the principle of our affections, and the means of directing them? We become better by studying ourselves; the man who thoroughly knows himself is the wise man. Such reflection on the nature of his being brings a man to a better awareness of all the bonds that unite us to our fellows, to the re-discovery at the inner root of his existence of that identity of common life actuating us all, to feeling the full force of that fine maxim of the ancients: 'I am a man, and nothing human is alien to me.'

But what are the means of the proper study of man? Here the history of philosophy, and the common voice of learned men give reply. The time for systems is past. Weary of its centuries of vain agitation in vain theories, the pursuit of learning has settled at last on the way of observation. It has recognized nature as its true master. All its art is applied in listening carefully to that voice, and sometimes in asking it questions. The Science of Man too is a natural science, a science of observation, the most noble of all. What science does not aspire to be a natural science? Even art, which men sometimes contrast with nature, aims only to imitate her.

The method of observation has a sure procedure; it gathers facts to compare them, and compares them to know them better. The natural sciences are in a way no more than a series of comparisons. As each particular phenomenon is ordinarily the result of the combined action of several causes, it would be only a deep mystery for us if we considered it on its own: but if it is compared with analogous phenomena, they throw light each on the other. The particular action of each cause we see as distinct and independent, and general laws are the result. Good observation requires analysis; now, one carries out analysis in philosophy by comparisons, as in chemistry by the play of chemical affinities.

Man, as he appears to us in the individuals around us, is modified at the same time by a multitude of varying circumstances, by education, climate, political institutions, customs, established opinions, by the effects of imitation, by the influence of the factitious needs that he has created. Among so many diverse causes that unite to produce that great and interesting

effect, we can never disentangle the precise action that belongs to each, without finding terms of comparison to isolate man from the particular circumstances in which he is presented to us, and to lift from him those adventitious forms under which, as it were, art has hidden from our eyes the work of nature.

Now, of all the terms of comparison that we can choose, there is none more fascinating, more fruitful in useful trains of thought than that offered by savage peoples. Here we can remove first the variations pertaining to the climate, the organism, the habits of physical life, and we shall notice that among nations much less developed by the effect of moral institutions, these natural variations are bound to emerge much more prominently: being less distinguished by secondary circumstances, they must chiefly be so by the first and fundamental circumstances belonging to the very principle of existence. Here we shall be able to find the material needed to construct an exact scale of the various degrees of civilization, and to assign to each its characteristic properties; we shall come to know what needs, what ideas, what habits are produced in each era of human society. Here, since the development of passions and of intellectual faculties is much more limited, it will be much easier for us to penetrate their nature, and determine their fundamental laws. Here, since different generations have exercised only the slightest influence on each other, we shall in a way be taken back to the first periods of our own history; we shall be able to set up secure experiments on the origin and generation of ideas, on the formation and development of language, and on the relations between these two processes. The philosophical traveller, sailing to the ends of the earth, is in fact travelling in time; he is exploring the past; every step he makes is the passage of an age. Those unknown islands that he reaches are for him the cradle of human society. Those peoples whom our ignorant vanity scorns are displayed to him as ancient and majestic monuments of the origin of ages: monuments infinitely more worthy of our admiration and respect than those famous pyramids vaunted by the banks of the Nile. They witness only the frivolous ambition and the passing power of some

portance the study Man in neral.

Of the observation of savages in particular.

individuals whose names have scarcely come down to us; but the others recreate for us the state of our own ancestors, and the earliest history of the world.

And even should we not see in savage peoples a useful object of instruction for ourselves, would there not be enough high feelings of philanthropy to make us give a high importance to the contact that we can make with them? What more moving plan than that of re-establishing in such a way the august ties of universal society, of finding once more those former kinsmen separated by long exile from the rest of the common family, of offering a hand to them to raise them to a happier state! You who, led by a generous devotion on those far shores, will soon come near their lonely huts, go before them as the representatives of all humanity! Give them in that name the vow of brotherly alliance! Wipe from their minds the memory of cruel adventurers who sought to stay with them only to rob or bring them into slavery; go to them only to offer benefits. Bring them our arts, and not our corruption, the standard of our morality, and not the example of our vices, our sciences, and not our scepticism, the advantages of civilization, and not its abuses; conceal from them that in these countries too, though more enlightened, men destroy each other in combat, and degrade each other by their passions. Sitting near them, amid their lonely forests and on their unknown shores, speak to them only of peace, of unity, of useful work; tell them that, in those empires unknown to them, that you have left to visit them, there are men who pray for their happiness, who greet them as brothers, and who join with all their hearts in the generous intentions which lead you among them.

Faults in the observations made up to the present. In expressing here everything that we expect of your careful and laborious work, we are far from wishing to underestimate the many services done to society by the explorers who have gone before you. Had they merely prepared the way, by their brave undertakings, for those who were to follow them, and provided valuable guidance, by that alone they would have earned a great title to our gratitude. But they began to establish some communication with savage societies; they have reported to us various information on the customs and language of these peoples. It is merely that, divided by other concerns, and with a greater impetus to discover new countries than to study them, constantly moving when they should have stayed at rest, biased perhaps by those unjust prejudices that cast a slur in our eyes on savage societies, or at least, witness of our European indifference for them, they did not sufficiently devote themselves to bringing back exact and complete observations; they have met the invariable end of those who observe in a precipitate and superficial manner – their observations have been poor, and the imperfection of their reports has been the penalty of our carelessness.[1] Since man's curiosity is aroused more by the novelties that strike his senses than by any instruction that his reason may gather, it was thought far more worth while to bring back from these countries plants, animals and mineral substances, than observations on the phenomena of thought. So naturalists daily enriched their specimen cases with many genera, while philosophers spent time in vain disputes in their schools about the nature of man, instead of uniting to study him in the arena of the universe.

Let us review the main faults of the observations on savage man made by these explorers, and the gaps that they have left in their accounts. When we realize what they have not done, we shall see better what remains to be done.

The first fault that we notice in the *First fault.* observations of explorers on savages is their incompleteness; it was only to be expected, given the shortness of their stay, the division of their attention, and the absence of any regular tabulation of their findings. Sometimes, confining themselves to the study of some isolated individuals, they have given us no information on their social condition, and have thus deprived us of the means of estimating the influence which these social relations might have on individual faculties. Sometimes, pausing on the smallest details of the physical life of the savages, they have given us scarcely any details of their moral customs. Sometimes, describing the customs of grown men, they have failed to find out about the kind of education received in childhood and youth: and above all, preoccupied almost entirely with the external and overt characteristics of a people, of its ceremonies and of its dress, they have generally taken too little care to be initiated in the far more important circumstances of its theoretical life, of its needs, its ideas, its passions, its knowledge, its laws. They have described forms rather than given instructive reports; they have marked certain effects, and explained scarcely any causes.

ond fault.   Further, such insufficient observations have not always been very certain or authentic, whether because they have sometimes been too particular, and explorers have wished to judge a society by a few of its members, a character by a few actions, or because they have sometimes confined themselves to hearsay, to the stories of the Savages whom they met, and who perhaps were not properly understood, perhaps not well-versed in what was asked, and perhaps had no interest in telling the truth, or at least in making it known in its entirety.

hird fault.   We should add that these observations have been badly ordered, and even in many cases quite without order. The explorers had not enough understood that there is a natural connection between the various facts that one gathers about the condition and character of societies, that this order is necessary to the precision of the individual facts, and that often some of them should serve as preparation for the others. We should study effects before trying to go back to first principles; observe individuals before trying to judge the society; become acquainted with domestic relations inside families before examining the political relations of society; and above all we should aim at full mutual understanding when we speak to men before basing certain conclusions on the accounts that we claim to have received.

urth fault.   Often explorers have based the accounts that they bring us on incorrect or at least on dubious hypotheses. For example, they habitually judge the customs of Savages by analogies drawn from our own customs, when in fact they are so little related to each other. Thus, given certain actions, they suppose certain opinions or needs because among us such actions ordinarily result from these needs or opinions. They make the Savage reason as we do, when the Savage does not himself explain to them his reasoning. So they often pronounce

excessively severe judgments on a society accused of cruelty, theft, licentiousness, and atheism. It were wiser to gather a large number of facts, before trying to explain them, and to allow hypothesis only after exhausting the light of experience.

    In the case of the accounts of explorers Fifth fault. there is another cause of uncertainty, a fault of language rather than of imperfect observation, namely that the terms used to pass on to us the results of their observations are often in our own language of vague and ill-determined meaning. Consequently, we are in danger of taking their accounts in a way which they did not intend. This happens particularly when they try to record the religious, moral, and political beliefs of a people. It happens too when instead of giving a detailed and circumstantial account of what they have actually seen, they limit themselves to summary descriptions of the impressions which they received, and of the general judgments which they inferred on the character of peoples. Yet this drawback could easily have been avoided by making it a policy either to describe things without judging them, or to choose expressions whose sense is more agreed, or to give a precise stipulation of the sense in which one intends their use.

    This is not the place to enumerate the Sixth inaccuracies springing from a lack of impartial- fault. ity in explorers, from prejudices imposed by their particular opinions, from the interests of vanity or the impulse of resentment. The character of the worthy men today devoting themselves to this noble undertaking is a sufficient guarantee that such a stamp will never shape their accounts. But explorers with the purest and most honest intentions have often been led into error about the character of peoples by the behaviour they meet with. They have inferred too lightly from the circumstances of their reception, conclusions about the absolute and ordinary character of the men among whom they have penetrated. They have failed to consider sufficiently that their presence was bound to be a natural source of fear, defiance, and reserve; that reasons of policy might exaggerate this unusual circumspection; that the memory of former attacks might have left dark prejudices in the mind of such peoples;

that a community might be gentle and sociable, and yet believe itself in a state of natural war with strangers whose intentions are unknown; and finally that for a just estimate of the character of a tribe, one should first leave time for the reactions of astonishment, terror, and anxiety bound to arise in the beginning to be dispelled, and secondly one should be able to be initiated into the ordinary relations which the members of the community have with each other.

Seventh fault.

But of all the regrets left by the accounts of the explorers who went before you, the strongest is their failure to tell us of the language of the peoples visited. In the first place, the scanty information which they do give lacks precision and exactness, whether because they fail to record how they went about questioning the Savages, or because they themselves have often taken little care to pose the questions properly. The demonstrative and natural gestures which they have used to ask the Savages the names of objects were often themselves liable to considerable uncertainty; one cannot know if those who were questioned understood the gestures in the same way as the explorers who were using them, and so whether they were giving proper replies to their questions. Further, to provide us with some useful and positive ideas of the idioms of savage peoples, it was wrong for explorers to limit themselves as they did to taking at random names of various objects with scarcely any relation between them; at least a family of analogous ideas should have been followed up, when it was impossible to make a record of the whole language, so that some judgment could be made on the generation of terms, and on the relations between them; it was not enough to be content with some detached words; but it would have been sensible to record whole sentences to give some idea of the construction of discourse. Further, one should have discovered whether these words were simple, or composite, as their length would often lead us to suppose; whether they were qualified by any articles or particles; and finally whether they were inflected or remained in the absolute, and whether they were liable to any kind of grammatical laws.

Eighth fault.

Failing to acquaint themselves thoroughly with the idiom of savage peoples, explorers have been powerless to draw on perhaps the most interesting ideas that could have been available. They have been unable to pass on the traditions that such peoples may preserve of their origin, of the changes that they have undergone, and of the various details of their history; traditions which perhaps would have thrown great light on the important question of how the world was peopled, and on the various causes of the present state of these societies. They have been unable to explain the significance of a mass of ceremonies and customs which are probably no more than allegorical; they have given us bizarre descriptions which tickle the idle curiosity of the many, but which offer no useful instruction to the philosophically minded. Lacking the means to carry on connected conversation with such peoples, they have been able to form only very hazardous and vague ideas of their opinions and notions; finally, they have been unable to provide us with these data, as revealing as they are abundant, that the language of a society presents on its way of seeing and feeling, and on the most intimate and essential features of its character.

The main object, therefore, that should today occupy the attention and zeal of a truly philosophical traveller would be the careful gathering of all means that might assist him to penetrate the thought of the peoples among whom he would be situated, and to account for the order of their actions and relationships. This is not only because such study is in itself the most important of all, it is also because it must stand as a necessary preliminary and introduction to all the others. It is a delusion to suppose that one can properly observe a people whom one cannot understand and with whom one cannot converse. The first means to the proper knowledge of the Savages, is to become after a fashion like one of them; and it is by learning their language that we shall become their fellow citizens.

But if there is a marked lack of good methods even for learning well the languages of neighbouring civilized nations; if this study often requires much time and effort, what position shall we be in for learning the idioms of savage tribes, when there is no dictionary, no spokesman to translate to us, and no shared habits and common associations of ideas as in

Observati to make. I Signs of Savages.

the case of the former languages, through which explanations can be made? Let us not hesitate to say that the art of properly studying these languages, if it could be reduced to rules, would be one of the master-works of philosophy; it can be the result only of long meditation on the origin of ideas. We shall confine ourselves here to making some general remarks; the reflective thought of the enlightened men to whom we address them will assure their development, and direct their application.

The most important thing to observe in the study of the signs of Savages, is the order of the enquiry.

[...]

Conclusion We are aware that the totality of problems here posed for the explorer's wisdom calls for a huge amount of work, whether because of the number and the very importance of the questions, or the detailed and painstaking observations that each one demands. We are aware that this work is surrounded by all kinds of difficulties, and that one must expect to meet great obstacles in the first relations that one wishes to establish with the Savages. For these peoples cannot penetrate the real intentions of those who approach them, they cannot easily distinguish their friends from their enemies, and those who bring help, from those who come to invade their territory. But we may rightly expect anything of the patience, the perseverance, and the heroic courage of the travellers to whom today we bid farewell; we are assured of it by their personal character, by the intentions animating them, by the dazzling proofs which they have already vouchsafed. Oh! What have they not already done for science, what noble course have they not already run! It was worthy of them still to defer its term, and to go on to complete so fine a work! Estimable men, as we salute you here on the eve of a departure soon to come, as we see you tear yourselves from your land, your family, and your friends, and leap beyond the limits of the civilized world; as we dwell on the thought of the fatigues, the privations and the dangers which await you, and of that long exile to which you have voluntarily condemned yourselves, our souls cannot resist a deep emotion, and the movement of sensibility in us

is joined to the respect which we owe to so noble an undertaking. But our thought is settled in advance on the term of that undertaking; and dwelling on this prospect, all our feelings are mixed in that of admiration and enthusiasm. Illustrious messengers of philosophy, peaceful heroes, the conquests which you are going to add to the domain of science have more brilliance and value in our eyes than victories bought by the blood of men! All generous hearts, all friends of humanity join in your sublime mission; there is in this place more than one heart which envies you, which groans in secret that inflexible duties keep him on these shores, who would put his glory in following your path and your example. Our prayers at least will follow you across the Ocean, or in the lap of the desert; our thoughts will often be with you, when below the equator, or near the pole, you gather in silence precious treasures for enlightenment. We shall say to each other: 'On this day, at this hour, they are landing perhaps on an unknown land, they are perhaps penetrating to the heart of a new people, perhaps they are resting in the shade of antique forests from their long sufferings; perhaps they are beginning to enter into relations with a barbarous people, to eliminate its unsociable suspicions, to inspire in it a curiosity to know our ways and a desire to imitate them, and perhaps they are laying the foundations of a new Europe.' Oh! who will tell in fact all the possible or probable results which may spring one day from these fine undertakings? I speak here not only of our fuller specimen cases, our more accurate and extensive maps, of our increased knowledge of the physical and moral history of the world, of the name of France taken to unknown shores! Think of the other bewitching prospects still offered to the reeling imagination! Trade extended by new relations; the navy brought to perfection by greater experience; journeys made easier by discoveries; our political grandeur increased by new colonies or new alliances! Who can tell? Perhaps whole nations civilized, receiving from civilization the power to multiply themselves, and associate themselves with us by the ties of a vast confederation; perhaps broader and more useful careers open to human ambition, talent and industry; these peoples of Europe, daily contesting at the cost of their blood some narrow strip of land, expanding at pleasure in more beautiful terrain; perhaps a new world forming itself at the extremities of the earth; the whole globe covered with happier and wiser inhabitants, more equally provided for, more closely joined, society raising itself to more rapid progress by greater competition and reaching perhaps by these unexpected changes that perfection on which our prayers call, but to which our enlightenment, our methods, and our books, contribute so little! ... Vain chimerae perhaps; but chimerae to which our long unhappiness, our sad dissensions, and the sight of our corruption, yet give so much charm! ... At least it is certain that these brave enterprises, directed to the most obscure parts of the Universe, lay up for posterity a new future, and that it is only for the wisdom of our descendants to gather the abundant fruits of this course that you are going to open. See how much the discoveries of Columbus changed the face of society, and what amazing destinies bore that fragile vessel to which he trusted himself! It is true, this grand revolution has not all been to our advantage, still less to that of the peoples to whom it has given us access. But Columbus put

in the New World only greedy conquerors; and you are proceeding towards the peoples of the South only as pacifiers and friends. The cruel adventurers of Spain brought only destruction before them, and you will spread only good deeds. They served but the passions of a few men, and you aspire only to the good of all, to the glory of being of use! This glory, the sweetest, the truest, or rather the only true glory, awaits you, encompasses you already; you will know all its brilliance on that day of triumph and joy on which, returning to your country, welcomed amid our delight, you will arrive in our walls, loaded with the most precious spoils, and bearers of happy tidings of our brothers scattered in the uttermost confines of the Universe.

NOTE

1 It is unnecessary to give warning that the critical reflections that we are making on the accounts of explorers are levelled at the usual run of these accounts, and consequently admit notable exceptions. Far be it from us to wish a lessening of the admiration due to men like Cook, Bougainville and others. In this respect, you will have preceded us: it has been your first concern to study their writings.

2

The Methods of Ethnology

Franz Boas

During the last ten years the methods of inquiry into the historical development of civilization have undergone remarkable changes. During the second half of the last century evolutionary thought held almost complete sway and investigators like Spencer, Morgan, Tylor, Lubbock, to mention only a few, were under the spell of the idea of a general, uniform evolution of culture in which all parts of mankind participated. The newer development goes back in part to the influence of Ratzel whose geographical training impressed him with the importance of diffusion and migration. The problem of diffusion was taken up in detail particularly in America, but was applied in a much wider sense by Foy and Graebner, and finally seized upon in a still wider application by Elliot Smith and Rivers, so that at the present time, at least among certain groups of investigators in England and also in Germany, ethnological research is based on the concept of migration and dissemination rather than upon that of evolution.

A critical study of these two directions of inquiry shows that each is founded on the application of one fundamental hypothesis. The evolutionary point of view presupposes that the course of historical changes in the cultural life of mankind follows definite laws which are applicable everywhere, and which bring it about that cultural development is, in its main lines, the same among all races and all peoples. This idea is clearly expressed by Tylor in the introductory pages of his classic work "Primitive Culture." As soon as we admit that the hypothesis of a uniform evolution has to be proved before it can be accepted, the whole structure loses its foundation. It is true that there are indications of parallelism of development in different parts of the world, and that similar customs are found in the most diverse and widely separated parts of the globe. The occurrence of these similarities which are distributed so irregularly that they cannot readily be explained on the basis of diffusion, is one of the foundations of the evolutionary hypothesis, as it was the foundation of Bastian's psychologizing treatment of cultural phenomena. On the other hand, it may be recognized that the hypothesis implies the thought that

Franz Boas, "The Methods of Ethnology," pp. 311–321 from *American Anthropologist* 22(4), Oct.–Dec. 1920.

our modern Western European civilization represents the highest cultural development towards which all other more primitive cultural types tend, and that, therefore, retrospectively, we construct an orthogenetic development towards our own modern civilization. It is clear that if we admit that there may be different ultimate and coexisting types of civilization, the hypothesis of one single general line of development cannot be maintained.

Opposed to these assumptions is the modern tendency to deny the existence of a general evolutionary scheme which would represent the history of the cultural development the world over. The hypothesis that there are inner causes which bring about similarities of development in remote parts of the globe is rejected and in its place it is assumed that identity of development in two different parts of the globe must always be due to migration and diffusion. On this basis historical contact is demanded for enormously large areas. The theory demands a high degree of stability of cultural traits such as is apparently observed in many primitive tribes, and it is furthermore based on the supposed correlation between a number of diverse and mutually independent cultural traits which reappear in the same combinations in distant parts of the world. In this sense, modern investigation takes up anew Gerland's theory of the persistence of a number of cultural traits which were developed in one center and carried by man in his migrations from continent to continent.

It seems to me that if the hypothetical foundations of these two extreme forms of ethnological research are broadly stated as I have tried to do here, it is at once clear that the correctness of the assumptions has not been demonstrated, but that arbitrarily the one or the other has been selected for the purpose of obtaining a consistent picture of cultural development. These methods are essentially forms of classification of the static phenomena of culture according to two distinct principles, and interpretations of these classifications as of historical significance, without, however, any attempt to prove that this interpretation is justifiable. To give an example: It is observed that in most parts of the world there are

resemblances between decorative forms that are representative and others that are more or less geometrical. According to the evolutionary point of view, their development is explained in the following manner: the decorative forms are arranged in such order that the most representative forms are placed at the beginning. The other forms are so placed that they show a gradual transition from representative forms to purely conventional geometric forms, and this order is then interpreted as meaning that geometric designs originated from representative designs which gradually degenerated. This method has been pursued, for instance, by Putnam, Stolpe, Balfour, and Haddon, and by Verworn and, in his earlier writings, by von den Steinen. While I do not mean to deny that this development may have occurred, it would be rash to generalize and to claim that in every case the classification which has been made according to a definite principle represents an historical development. The order might as well be reversed and we might begin with a simple geometric element which, by the addition of new traits, might be developed into a representative design, and we might claim that this order represents an historical sequence. Both of these possibilities were considered by Holmes as early as 1885. Neither the one nor the other theory can be established without actual historical proof.

The opposite attitude, namely, origin through diffusion, is exhibited in Heinrich Schurtz's attempt to connect the decorative art of Northwest America with that of Melanesia. The simple fact that in these areas elements occur that may be interpreted as eyes, induced him to assume that both have a common origin, without allowing for the possibility that the pattern in the two areas – each of which shows highly distinctive characteristics – may have developed from independent sources. In this attempt Schurtz followed Ratzel who had already tried to establish connections between Melanesia and Northwest America on the basis of other cultural features.

While ethnographical research based on these two fundamental hypotheses seems to characterize the general tendency of European thought, a different method is at present pursued by the majority of American anthropologists. The difference between the two directions of study may perhaps best be summarized by the statement that American scholars are primarily interested in the dynamic phenomena of cultural change, and try to elucidate cultural history by the application of the results of their studies; and that they relegate the solution of the ultimate question of the relative importance of parallelism of cultural development in distant areas, as against worldwide diffusion, and stability of cultural traits over long periods to a future time when the actual conditions of cultural change are better known. The American ethnological methods are analogous to those of European, particularly of Scandinavian, archaeology, and of the researches into the prehistoric period of the eastern Mediterranean area.

It may seem to the distant observer that American students are engaged in a mass of detailed investigations without much bearing upon the solution of the ultimate problems of a philosophic history of human civilization. I think this interpretation of the American attitude would be unjust because the ultimate questions are as near to our hearts as they are to those of other scholars, only we do not hope to be able to solve an intricate historical problem by a formula.

First of all, the whole problem of cultural history appears to us as a historical problem. In order to understand history it is necessary to know not only how things are, but how they have come to be. In the domain of ethnology, where, for most parts of the world, no historical facts are available except those that may be revealed by archaeological study, all evidence of change can be inferred only by indirect methods. Their character is represented in the researches of students of comparative philology. The method is based on the comparison of static phenomena combined with the study of their distribution. What can be done by this method is well illustrated by Dr Lowie's investigations of the military societies of the Plains Indians, or by the modern investigation of American mythology. It is, of course, true that we can never hope to obtain incontrovertible data relating to the chronological sequence of events, but certain general broad

outlines can be ascertained with a high degree of probability, even of certainty.

As soon as these methods are applied, primitive society loses the appearance of absolute stability which is conveyed to the student who sees a certain people only at a certain given time. All cultural forms rather appear in a constant state of flux and subject to fundamental modifications.

It is intelligible why in our studies the problem of dissemination should take a prominent position. It is much easier to prove dissemination than to follow up developments due to inner forces, and the data for such a study are obtained with much greater difficulty. They may, however, be observed in every phenomenon of acculturation in which foreign elements are remodeled according to the patterns prevalent in their new environment, and they may be found in the peculiar local developments of widely spread ideas and activities. The reason why the study of inner development has not been taken up energetically, is not due to the fact that from a theoretical point of view it is unimportant, it is rather due to the inherent methodological difficulties. It may perhaps be recognized that in recent years attention is being drawn to this problem, as is manifested by the investigations on the processes of acculturation and of the interdependence of cultural activities which are attracting the attention of many investigators.

The further pursuit of these inquiries emphasizes the importance of a feature which is common to all historic phenomena. While in natural sciences we are accustomed to consider a given number of causes and to study their effects, in historical happenings we are compelled to consider every phenomenon not only as effect but also as cause. This is true even in the particular application of the laws of physical nature, as, for instance, in the study of astronomy in which the position of certain heavenly bodies at a given moment may be considered as the effect of gravitation, while, at the same time, their particular arrangement in space determines future changes. This relation appears much more clearly in the history of human civilization. To give an example: a surplus of food supply is liable to bring about an increase of population and an increase of leisure, which gives opportunity for occupations that are not absolutely necessary for the needs of every day life. In turn the increase of population and of leisure, which may be applied to new inventions, give rise to a greater food supply and to a further increase in the amount of leisure, so that a cumulative effect results.

Similar considerations may be made in regard to the important problem of the relation of the individual to society, a problem that has to be considered whenever we study the dynamic conditions of change. The activities of the individual are determined to a great extent by his social environment, but in turn his own activities influence the society in which he lives, and may bring about modifications in its form. Obviously, this problem is one of the most important ones to be taken up in a study of cultural changes. It is also beginning to attract the attention of students who are no longer satisfied with the systematic enumeration of standardized beliefs and customs of a tribe, but who begin to be interested in the question of the way in which the individual reacts to his whole social environment, and to the differences of opinion and of mode of action that occur in primitive society and which are the causes of far-reaching changes.

In short then, the method which we try to develop is based on a study of the dynamic changes in society that may be observed at the present time. We refrain from the attempt to solve the fundamental problem of the general development of civilization until we have been able to unravel the processes that are going on under our eyes.

Certain general conclusions may be drawn from this study even now. First of all, the history of human civilization does not appear to us as determined entirely by psychological necessity that leads to a uniform evolution the world over. We rather see that each cultural group has its own unique history, dependent partly upon the peculiar inner development of the social group, and partly upon the foreign influences to which it has been subjected. There have been processes of gradual differentiation as well as processes of leveling down differences between neighboring cultural centers, but it would be quite impossible to understand, on the basis of a single evolutionary scheme, what happened to any particular people. An example of the contrast between the two points of view is clearly indicated by a comparison of the treatment of Zuñi civilization by Frank Hamilton Cushing on the one hand, on the other by modern students, particularly by Elsie Clews Parsons, A. L. Kroeber and Leslie Spier. Cushing believed that it was possible to explain Zuñi culture entirely on the basis of the reaction of the Zuñi mind to its geographical environment, and that the whole of Zuñi culture could be explained as the development which followed necessarily from the position in which the people were placed. Cushing's keen insight into the Indian mind and his thorough knowledge of the most intimate life of the people gave great plausibility to his interpretations. On the other hand, Dr Parsons' studies prove conclusively the deep influence which Spanish ideas have had upon Zuñi culture, and, together with Professor Kroeber's investigations, give us one of the best examples of acculturation that have come to our notice. The psychological explanation is entirely misleading, notwithstanding its plausibility, and the historical study shows us an entirely different picture, in which the unique combination of ancient traits (which in themselves are undoubtedly complex) and of European influences, have brought about the present condition.

Studies of the dynamics of primitive life also show that an assumption of long continued stability such as is demanded by Elliot Smith is without any foundation in fact. Wherever primitive conditions have been studied in detail, they can be proved to be in a state of flux, and it would seem that there is a close parallelism between the history of language and the history of general cultural development. Periods of stability are followed by periods of rapid change. It is exceedingly improbable that any customs of primitive people should be preserved unchanged for thousands of years. Furthermore, the phenomena of acculturation prove that a transfer of customs from one region into another without concomitant changes due to acculturation, are very rare. It is, therefore, very unlikely that ancient Mediterranean customs could be found at the present time practically unchanged in different parts of the globe, as Elliot Smith's theory demands.

While on the whole the unique historical character of cultural growth in each area stands out as a salient element in the history of cultural development, we may recognize at the same time that certain typical parallelisms do occur. We are, however, not so much inclined to look for these similarities in detailed customs but rather in certain dynamic conditions which are due to social or psychological causes that are liable to lead to similar results. The example of the relation between food supply and population to which I referred before may serve as an example. Another type of example is presented in those cases in which a certain problem confronting man may be solved by a limited number of methods only. When we find, for instance, marriage as a universal institution, it may be recognized that marriage is possible only between a number of men and a number of women; a number of men and one woman; a number of women and one man; or one man and one woman. As a matter of fact, all these forms are found the world over and it is, therefore, not surprising that analogous forms should have been adopted quite independently in different parts of the world, and, considering both the general economic conditions of mankind and the character of sexual instinct in the higher animals, it also does not seem surprising that group marriage and polyandrous marriages should be comparatively speaking rare. Similar considerations may also be made in regard to the philosophical views held by mankind. In short, if we look for laws, the laws relate to the effects of physiological, psychological, and social conditions, not to sequences of cultural achievement.

In some cases a regular sequence of these may accompany the development of the psychological or social status. This is illustrated by the sequence of industrial inventions in the Old World and in America, which I consider as independent. A period of food gathering and of the use of stone was followed by the invention of agriculture, of pottery and finally of the use of metals. Obviously, this order is based on the increased amount of time given by mankind to the use of natural products, of tools and

utensils, and to the variations that developed with it. Although in this case parallelism seems to exist on the two continents, it would be futile to try to follow out the order in detail. As a matter of fact, it does not apply to other inventions. The domestication of animals, which, in the Old World must have been an early achievement, was very late in the New World, where domesticated animals, except the dog, hardly existed at all at the time of discovery. A slight beginning had been made in Peru with the domestication of the llama, and birds were kept in various parts of the continent.

A similar consideration may be made in regard to the development of rationalism. It seems to be one of the fundamental characteristics of the development of mankind that activities which have developed unconsciously are gradually made the subject of reasoning. We may observe this process everywhere. It appears, perhaps, most clearly in the history of science which has gradually extended the scope of its inquiry over an ever-widening field and which has raised into consciousness human activities that are automatically performed in the life of the individual and of society.

I have not heretofore referred to another aspect of modern ethnology which is connected with the growth of psycho-analysis. Sigmund Freud has attempted to show that primitive thought is in many respects analogous to those forms of individual psychic activity which he has explored by his psycho-analytical methods. In many respects his attempts are similar to the interpretation of mythology by symbolists like Stucken. Rivers has taken hold of Freud's suggestion as well as of the interpretations of Graebner and Elliot Smith, and we find, therefore, in his new writings a peculiar disconnected application of a psychologizing attitude and the application of the theory of ancient transmission.

While I believe some of the ideas underlying Freud's psycho-analytic studies may be fruitfully applied to ethnological problems, it does not seem to me that the one-sided exploitation of this method will advance our understanding of the development of human society. It is certainly true that the influence of impressions received during the first few years of life have been entirely underestimated and that the social behavior of man depends to a great extent upon the earliest habits which are established before the time when connected memory begins, and that many so-called racial or hereditary traits are to be considered rather as a result of early exposure to a certain form of social conditions. Most of these habits do not rise into consciousness and are, therefore, broken with difficulty only. Much of the difference in the behavior of adult male and female may go back to this cause. If, however, we try to apply the whole theory of the influence of suppressed desires to the activities of man living under different social forms, I think we extend beyond their legitimate limits the inferences that may be drawn from the observation of normal and abnormal individual psychology. Many other factors are of greater importance. To give an example: The phenomena of language show clearly that conditions quite different from those to which psycho-analysts direct their attention determine the mental behavior of man. The general concepts underlying language are entirely unknown to most people. They do not rise into consciousness until the scientific study of grammar begins. Nevertheless, the categories of language compel us to see the world arranged in certain definite conceptual groups which, on account of our lack of knowledge of linguistic processes, are taken as objective categories and which, therefore, impose themselves upon the form of our thoughts. It is not known what the origin of these categories may be, but it seems quite certain that they have nothing to do with the phenomena which are the subject of psycho-analytic study.

The applicability of the psycho-analytic theory of symbolism is also open to the greatest doubt. We should remember that symbolic interpretation has occupied a prominent position in the philosophy of all times. It is present not only in primitive life, but the history of philosophy and of theology abounds in examples of a high development of symbolism, the type of which depends upon the general mental attitude of the philosopher who develops it. The theologians who interpreted the Bible on the basis of religious symbolism were no less certain of the correctness of their views, than the psycho-analysts are of their interpretations of thought and conduct based on sexual symbolism. The results of a symbolic interpretation depend primarily upon the subjective attitude of the investigator who arranges phenomena according to his leading concept. In order to prove the applicability of the symbolism of psycho-analysis, it would be necessary to show that a symbolic interpretation from other entirely different points of view would not be equally plausible, and that explanations that leave out symbolic significance or reduce it to a minimum, would not be adequate.

While, therefore, we may welcome the application of every advance in the method of psychological investigation, we cannot accept as an advance in ethnological method the crude transfer of a novel, one-sided method of psychological investigation of the individual to social phenomena the origin of which can be shown to be historically determined and to be subject to influences that are not at all comparable to those that control the psychology of the individual.

3

Method and Scope of Anthropological Fieldwork

Bronislaw Malinowski

[...]

III

Imagine yourself suddenly set down surrounded by all your gear, alone on a tropical beach close to a native village, while the launch or dinghy which has brought you sails away out of sight. Since you take up your abode in the compound of some neighbouring white man, trader or missionary, you have nothing to do, but to start at once on your ethnographic work. Imagine further that you are a beginner, without previous experience, with nothing to guide you and no one to help you. For the white man is temporarily absent, or else unable or unwilling to waste any of his time on you. This exactly describes my first initiation into fieldwork on the south coast of New Guinea. I well remember the long visits I paid to the villages during the first weeks; the feeling of hopelessness and despair after many obstinate but futile attempts had entirely failed to bring me into real touch with the natives, or supply me with any material. I had periods of despondency, when I buried myself in the reading of novels, as a man might take to drink in a fit of tropical depression and boredom.

Imagine yourself then, making your first entry into the village, alone or in company with your white cicerone. Some natives flock round you, especially if they smell tobacco. Others, the more dignified and elderly, remain seated where they are. Your white companion has his routine way of treating the natives, and he neither understands, nor is very much concerned with the manner in which you, as an ethnographer, will have to approach them. The first visit leaves you with a hopeful feeling that when you return alone, things will be easier. Such was my hope at least.

I came back duly, and soon gathered an audience around me. A few compliments in pidgin English on both sides, some tobacco changing hands, induced an atmosphere of mutual amiability. I tried then to proceed to business. First, to begin with subjects which

Bronislaw Malinowski, "Subject, Method and Scope," pp. 4–25 from *Argonauts of the Western Pacific*. Prospect Heights, IL: Waveland Press, 1984[1922].

Ethnographic Fieldwork: An Anthropological Reader, Second Edition. Edited by Antonius C. G. M. Robben and Jeffrey A. Sluka.
Editorial material and organization © 2012 John Wiley & Sons, Inc.
Published 2012 by John Wiley & Sons, Inc.

might arouse no suspicion, I started to "do" technology. A few natives were engaged in manufacturing some object or other. It was easy to look at it and obtain the names of the tools, and even some technical expressions about the proceedings, but there the matter ended. It must be borne in mind that pidgin English is a very imperfect instrument for expressing one's ideas, and that before one gets a good training in framing questions and understanding answers one has the uncomfortable feeling that free communication in it with the natives will never be attained; and I was quite unable to enter into any more detailed or explicit conversation with them at first. I knew well that the best remedy for this was to collect concrete data, and accordingly I took a village census, wrote down genealogies, drew up plans and collected the terms of kinship. But all this remained dead material, which led no further into the understanding of real native mentality or behaviour, since I could neither procure a good native interpretation of any of these items, nor get what could be called the hang of tribal life. As to obtaining their ideas about religion, and magic, their beliefs in sorcery and spirits, nothing was forthcoming except a few superficial items of folk-lore, mangled by being forced into pidgin English.

Information which I received from some white residents in the district, valuable as it was in itself, was more discouraging than anything else with regard to my own work. Here were men who had lived for years in the place with constant opportunities of observing the natives and communicating with them, and who yet hardly knew one thing about them really well. How could I therefore in a few months or a year, hope to overtake and go beyond them? Moreover, the manner in which my white informants spoke about the natives and put their views was, naturally, that of untrained minds, unaccustomed to formulate their thoughts with any degree of consistency and precision. And they were for the most part, naturally enough, full of the biassed and pre-judged opinions inevitable in the average practical man, whether administrator, missionary, or trader, yet so strongly repulsive to a mind striving after the objective, scientific view of things. The habit of treating with a self-satisfied frivolity what is really serious to the ethnographer; the cheap rating of what to him is a scientific treasure, that is to say, the native's cultural and mental peculiarities and independence – these features, so well known in the inferior amateur's writing, I found in the tone of the majority of white residents.[1]

Indeed, in my first piece of Ethnographic research on the South coast, it was not until I was alone in the district that I began to make some headway; and, at any rate, I found out where lay the secret of effective fieldwork. What is then this ethnographer's magic, by which he is able to evoke the real spirit of the natives, the true picture of tribal life? As usual, success can only be obtained by a patient and systematic application of a number of rules of common sense and well-known scientific principles, and not by the discovery of any marvellous short-cut leading to the desired results without effort or trouble. The principles of method can be grouped under three main headings; first of all, naturally, the student must possess real scientific aims, and know the values and criteria of modern ethnography. Secondly, he ought to put himself in good conditions of work, that is, in the main, to live without other white men, right among the natives. Finally, he has to apply a number of special methods of collecting, manipulating and fixing his evidence. A few words must be said about these foundation stones of fieldwork, beginning with the second as the most elementary.

IV

Proper conditions for ethnographic work

These, as said, consist mainly in cutting oneself off from the company of other white men, and remaining in as close contact with the natives as possible, which really can only be achieved by camping right in their villages. It is very nice to have a base in a white man's compound for the stores, and to know there is a refuge there in times of sickness and surfeit of native. But it must be far enough away not to become a permanent milieu in which you live and from which you emerge at fixed hours only to "do the village." It should not even be near enough to fly to at any moment for recreation. For the native is not the natural companion for a white man, and after you have been working with him for several hours, seeing how he does his gardens, or letting him tell you items of folk-lore, or discussing his customs, you will naturally hanker after the company of your own kind. But if you are alone in a village beyond reach of this, you go for a solitary walk for an hour or so, return again and then quite naturally seek out the natives' society, this time as a relief from loneliness, just as you would any other companionship. And by means of this natural intercourse, you learn to know him, and you become familiar with his customs and beliefs far better than when he is a paid, and often bored, informant.

There is all the difference between a spo-radic plunging into the company of natives, and being really in contact with them. What does this latter mean? On the Ethnographer's side, it means that his life in the village, which at first is a strange, sometimes unpleasant, sometimes intensely interesting adventure, soon adopts quite a natural course very much in harmony with his surroundings.

Soon after I had established myself in Omarakana (Trobriand Islands), I began to take part, in a way, in the village life, to look forward to the important or festive events, to take personal interest in the gossip and the developments of the small village occurrences; to wake up every morning to a day, presenting itself to me more or less as it does to the native. I would get out from under my mosquito net, to find around me the village life beginning to stir, or the people well advanced in their work-ing day according to the hour and also to the season, for they get up and begin their labours early or late, as work presses. As I went on my morning walk through the village, I could see intimate details of family life, of toilet, cook-ing, taking of meals; I could see the arrange-ments for the day's work, people starting on their errands, or groups of men and women busy at some manufacturing tasks. Quarrels, jokes, family scenes, events usually trivial, sometimes dramatic but always significant, formed the atmosphere of my daily life, as well

as of theirs. It must be remembered that as the natives saw me constantly every day, they ceased to be interested or alarmed, or made self-conscious by my presence, and I ceased to be a disturbing element in the tribal life which I was to study, altering it by my very approach, as always happens with a new-comer to every savage community. In fact, as they knew that I would thrust my nose into everything, even where a well-mannered native would not dream of intruding, they finished by regarding me as part and parcel of their life, a necessary evil or nuisance, mitigated by donations of tobacco.

Later on in the day, whatever happened was within easy reach, and there was no possibility of its escaping my notice. Alarms about the sorcerer's approach in the evening, one or two big, really important quarrels and rifts within the community, cases of illness, attempted cures and deaths, magical rites which had to be performed, all these I had not to pursue, fearful of missing them, but they took place under my very eyes, at my own doorstep, so to speak. And it must be emphasised whenever anything dramatic or important occurs it is essential to investigate it at the very moment of happening, because the natives cannot but talk about it, are too excited to be reticent, and too interested to be mentally lazy in supplying details. Also, over and over again, I committed breaches of etiquette, which the natives, familiar enough with me, were not slow in pointing out. I had to learn how to behave, and to a certain extent, I acquired "the feeling" for native good and bad manners. With this, and with the capacity of enjoying their company and sharing some of their games and amusements, I began to feel that I was indeed in touch with the natives, and this is certainly the preliminary condition of being able to carry on successful fieldwork.

V

But the Ethnographer has not only to spread his nets in the right place, and wait for what will fall into them. He must be an active huntsman, and drive his quarry into them and follow it up to its most inaccessible lairs. And that leads us to the more active methods of pursuing ethnographic evidence. It has been mentioned at the end of Division III that the Ethnographer has to be inspired by the knowledge of the most modern results of scientific study, by its principles and aims. I shall not enlarge upon this subject, except by way of one remark, to avoid the possibility of misunderstanding. Good training in theory, and acquaintance with its latest results, is not identical with being burdened with "preconceived ideas." If a man sets out on an expedition, determined to prove certain hypotheses, if he is incapable of changing his views constantly and casting them off ungrudgingly under the pressure of evidence, needless to say his work will be worthless. But the more problems he brings with him into the field, the more he is in the habit of moulding his theories according to facts, and of seeing facts in their bearing upon theory, the better he is equipped for the work. Preconceived ideas are pernicious in any scientific work, but foreshadowed problems are the main endowment of a scientific thinker, and these problems are first revealed to the observer by his theoretical studies.

In Ethnology the early efforts of Bastian, Tylor, Morgan, the German Völkerpsychologen have remoulded the older crude information of travellers, missionaries, etc., and have shown us the importance of applying deeper conceptions and discarding crude and misleading ones.[2]

The concept of animism superseded that of "fetichism" or "devil-worship," both meaningless terms. The understanding of the classificatory systems of relationship paved the way for the brilliant, modern researches on native sociology in the fieldwork of the Cambridge school. The psychological analysis of the German thinkers has brought forth an abundant crop of most valuable information in the results obtained by the recent German expeditions to Africa, South America and the Pacific, while the theoretical works of Frazer, Durkheim and others have already, and will no doubt still for a long time inspire fieldworkers and lead them to new results. The fieldworker relies entirely upon inspiration from theory. Of course he may be also a theoretical thinker and worker, and there he can draw on himself for

stimulus. But the two functions are separate, and in actual research they have to be separated both in time and conditions of work.

As always happens when scientific interest turns towards and begins to labour on a field so far only prospected by the curiosity of amateurs, Ethnology has introduced law and order into what seemed chaotic and freakish. It has transformed for us the sensational, wild and unaccountable world of "savages" into a number of well ordered communities, governed by law, behaving and thinking according to consistent principles. The word "savage," whatever association it might have had originally, connotes ideas of boundless liberty, of irregularity, of something extremely and extraordinarily quaint. In popular thinking, we imagine that the natives live on the bosom of Nature, more or less as they can and like, the prey of irregular, phantasmagoric beliefs and apprehensions. Modern science, on the contrary, shows that their social institutions have a very definite organisation, that they are governed by authority, law and order in their public and personal relations, while the latter are, besides, under the control of extremely complex ties of kinship and clanship. Indeed, we see them entangled in a mesh of duties, functions and privileges which correspond to an elaborate tribal, communal and kinship organisation. Their beliefs and practices do not by any means lack consistency of a certain type, and their knowledge of the outer world is sufficient to guide them in many of their strenuous enterprises and activities. Their artistic productions again lack neither meaning nor beauty.

It is a very far cry from the famous answer given long ago by a representative authority who, asked, what are the manners and customs of the natives, answered, "Customs none, manners beastly," to the position of the modern Ethnographer! This latter, with his tables of kinship terms, genealogies, maps, plans and diagrams, proves the existence of an extensive and big organisation, shows the constitution of the tribe, of the clan, of the family; and he gives us a picture of the natives subjected to a strict code of behaviour and good manners, to which in comparison the life at the Court of Versailles or Escurial was free and easy.[3]

Thus the first and basic ideal of ethnographic fieldwork is to give a clear and firm outline of the social constitution, and disentangle the laws and regularities of all cultural phenomena from the irrelevances. The firm skeleton of the tribal life has to be first ascertained. This ideal imposes in the first place the fundamental obligation of giving a complete survey of the phenomena, and not of picking out the sensational, the singular, still less the funny and quaint. The time when we could tolerate accounts presenting us the native as a distorted, childish caricature of a human being are gone. This picture is false, and like many other falsehoods, it has been killed by Science. The field Ethnographer has seriously and soberly to cover the full extent of the phenomena in each aspect of tribal culture studied, making no difference between what is commonplace, or drab, or ordinary, and what strikes him as astonishing and out-of-the-way. At the same time, the whole area of tribal culture *in all its aspects* has to be gone over in research. The consistency, the law and order which obtain within each aspect make also for joining them into one coherent whole.

An Ethnographer who sets out to study only religion, or only technology, or only social organisation cuts out an artificial field for inquiry, and he will be seriously handicapped in his work.

VI

Having settled this very general rule, let us descend to more detailed consideration of method. The Ethnographer has in the field, according to what has just been said, the duty before him of drawing up all the rules and regularities of tribal life; all that is permanent and fixed; of giving an anatomy of their culture, of depicting the constitution of their society. But these things, though crystallised and set, are nowhere *formulated*. There is no written or explicitly expressed code of laws, and their whole tribal tradition, the whole structure of their society, are embodied in the most elusive of all materials; the human being. But not even in human mind or memory are these laws to be found definitely formulated.

The natives obey the forces and commands of the tribal code, but they do not comprehend them; exactly as they obey their instincts and their impulses, but could not lay down a single law of psychology. The regularities in native institutions are an automatic result of the interaction of the mental forces of tradition, and of the material conditions of environment. Exactly as a humble member of any modern institution, whether it be the state, or the church, or the army, is *of* it and *in* it, but has no vision of the resulting integral action of the whole, still less could furnish any account of its organisation, so it would be futile to attempt questioning a native in abstract, sociological terms. The difference is that, in our society, every institution has its intelligent members, its historians, and its archives and documents, whereas in a native society there are none of these. After this is realised an expedient has to be found to overcome this difficulty. This expedient for an Ethnographer consists in collecting concrete data of evidence, and drawing the general inferences for himself. This seems obvious on the face of it, but was not found out or at least practised in Ethnography till fieldwork was taken up by men of science. Moreover, in giving it practical effect, it is neither easy to devise the concrete applications of this method, nor to carry them out systematically and consistently.

Though we cannot ask a native about abstract, general rules, we can always enquire how a given case would be treated. Thus for instance, in asking how they would treat crime, or punish it, it would be vain to put to a native a sweeping question such as, "How do you treat and punish a criminal?" for even words could not be found to express it in native, or in pidgin. But an imaginary case, or still better, a real occurrence, will stimulate a native to express his opinion and to supply plentiful information. A real case indeed will start the natives on a wave of discussion, evoke expressions of indignation, show them taking sides – all of which talk will probably contain a wealth of definite views, of moral censures, as well as reveal the social mechanism set in motion by the crime committed. From there, it will be easy to lead them on to speak of other similar cases, to remember other actual occurrences or to discuss them in all their implications and aspects. From this material, which ought to cover the widest possible range of facts, the inference is obtained by simple induction. The *scientific* treatment differs from that of good common sense, first in that a student will extend the completeness and minuteness of survey much further and in a pedantically systematic and methodical manner; and secondly, in that the scientifically trained mind, will push the inquiry along really relevant lines, and towards aims possessing real importance. Indeed, the object of scientific training is to provide the empirical investigator with a *mental chart*, in accordance with which he can take his bearings and lay his course.

To return to our example, a number of definite cases discussed will reveal to the Ethnographer the social machinery for punishment. This is one part, one aspect of tribal authority. Imagine further that by a similar method of inference from definite data, he arrives at understanding leadership in war, in economic enterprise, in tribal festivities – there he has at once all the data necessary to answer the questions about tribal government and social authority. In actual fieldwork, the comparison of such data, the attempt to piece them together, will often reveal rifts and gaps in the information which lead on to further investigations.

From my own experience, I can say that, very often, a problem seemed settled, everything fixed and clear, till I began to write down a short preliminary sketch of my results. And only then, did I see the enormous deficiencies, which would show me where lay new problems, and lead me on to new work. In fact, I spent a few months between my first and second expeditions, and over a year between that and the subsequent one, in going over all my material, and making parts of it almost ready for publication each time, though each time I knew I would have to re-write it. Such cross-fertilisation of constructive work and observation, I found most valuable, and I do not think I could have made real headway without it. I give this bit of my own history merely to show that what has been said so far is not only an empty programme, but the result of personal experience. In this volume, the description is given of a big institution connected with ever so many associated activities, and presenting many aspects. To anyone who reflects on the subject, it will be clear that the information about a phenomenon of such high complexity and of so many ramifications, could not be obtained with any degree of exactitude and completeness, without a constant interplay of constructive attempts and empirical checking. In fact, I have written up an outline of the Kula institution at least half a dozen times while in the field and in the intervals between my expeditions. Each time, new problems and difficulties presented themselves.

The collecting of concrete data over a wide range of facts is thus one of the main points of field method. The obligation is not to enumerate a few examples only, but to exhaust as far as possible all the cases within reach; and, on this search for cases, the investigator will score most whose mental chart is clearest. But, whenever the material of the search allows it, this mental chart ought to be transformed into a real one; it ought to materialise into a diagram, a plan, an exhaustive, synoptic table of cases. Long since, in all tolerably good modern books on natives, we expect to find a full list or table of kinship terms, which includes all the data relative to it, and does not just pick out a few strange and anomalous relationships or expressions. In the investigation of kinship, the following up of one relation after another in concrete cases leads naturally to the construction of genealogical tables. Practised already by the best early writers, such as Munzinger, and, if I remember rightly, Kubary, this method has been developed to its fullest extent in the works of Dr. Rivers. Again, studying the concrete data of economic transactions, in order to trace the history of a valuable object, and to gauge the nature of its circulation, the principle of completeness and thoroughness would lead to construct tables of transactions, such as we find in the work of Professor Seligman. It is in following Professor Seligman's example in this matter that I was able to settle certain of the more difficult and detailed rules of the Kula. The method of reducing information, if possible, into charts or synoptic tables ought to be extended to the study of practically all aspects of native life. All types of economic transactions may be studied by following up connected, actual cases, and putting them into a synoptic chart; again, a table ought to be drawn up of all the gifts and presents customary in a given society, a table including the sociological, ceremonial, and economic definition of every item. Also, systems of magic, connected series of ceremonies, types of legal acts, all could be charted, allowing each entry to be synoptically defined under a number of headings. Besides this, of course, the genealogical census of every community, studied more in detail, extensive maps, plans and diagrams, illustrating ownership in garden land, hunting and fishing privileges, etc., serve as the more fundamental documents of ethnographic research.

A genealogy is nothing else but a synoptic chart of a number of connected relations of kinship. Its value as an instrument of research consists in that it allows the investigator to put questions which he formulates to himself *in abstracto*, but can put concretely to the native informant. As a document, its value consists in that it gives a number of authenticated data, presented in their natural grouping. A synoptic chart of magic fulfils the same function. As an instrument of research, I have used it in order to ascertain, for instance, the ideas about the nature of magical power. With a chart before me, I could easily and conveniently go over one item after the other, and note down the relevant practices and beliefs contained in each of them. The answer to my abstract problem could then be obtained by drawing a general inference from all the cases ... I cannot enter further into the discussion of this question, which would need further distinctions, such as between a chart of concrete, actual data, such as is a genealogy, and a chart summarising the outlines of a custom or belief, as a chart of a magical system would be.

Returning once more to the question of methodological candour ... I wish to point out here, that the procedure of concrete and tabularised presentation of data ought to be applied first to the Ethnographer's own credentials. That is, an Ethnographer, who wishes to be trusted, must show clearly and concisely, in a tabularised form, which are his own direct observations, and which the indirect information that form the bases of his account.

The Table will serve as an example of this procedure and help the reader of this book to form an idea of the trustworthiness of any statement he is specially anxious to check. With the help of this Table and the many references scattered throughout the text, as to how, under what circumstances, and with what degree of accuracy I arrived at a given item of knowledge, there will, I hope remain no obscurity whatever as to the sources of the book.

To summarise the first, cardinal point of method, I may say each phenomenon ought to be studied through the broadest range possible of its concrete manifestations; each studied by an exhaustive survey of detailed examples. If possible, the results ought to be tabulated into some sort of synoptic chart, both to be used as an instrument of study, and to be presented as an ethnological document. With the help of such documents and such study of actualities the clear outline of the framework of the natives' culture in the widest sense of the word, and the constitution of their society, can be presented. This method could be called *the method of statistic documentation by concrete evidence*.

VII

Needless to add, in this respect, the scientific fieldwork is far above even the best amateur productions. There is, however, one point in which the latter often excel. This is, in the presentation of intimate touches of native life, in bringing home to us these aspects of it with which one is made familiar only through being in close contact with the natives, one way or the other, for a long period of time. In certain results of scientific work – especially that which has been called "survey work" – we are given an excellent skeleton, so to speak, of the tribal constitution, but it lacks flesh and blood. We learn much about the framework of their society, but within it, we cannot perceive or imagine the realities of human life, the even flow of everyday events, the occasional ripples of excitement over a feast, or ceremony, or some singular occurrence. In working out the rules and regularities of native custom, and in obtaining a precise formula for them from the collection of data and native statements, we find that this very precision is foreign to real life, which never adheres rigidly to any rules. It must be supplemented by the observation of the manner in which a given custom is carried out, of the behaviour of the natives in obeying the rules so exactly formulated by the ethnographer, of the very exceptions which in sociological phenomena almost always occur.

If all the conclusions are solely based on the statements of informants, or deduced from objective documents, it is of course impossible to supplement them in actually observed data of real behaviour. And that is the reason why certain works of amateur residents of long standing, such as educated traders and planters, medical men and officials, and last, but not least, the few intelligent and unbiassed missionaries to whom Ethnography owes so much, surpass in plasticity and in vividness most of the purely scientific accounts. But if the specialised fieldworker can adopt the conditions of living described above, he is in a far better position to be really in touch with the natives than any other white resident. For none of them lives right in a native village, except for very short periods, and everyone has his own business, which takes up a considerable part of his time. Moreover, if, like a trader or a missionary or an official he enters into active relations with the native, if he has to transform or influence or make use of him, this makes a real, unbiassed, impartial observation impossible, and precludes all-round sincerity, at least in the case of the missionaries and officials.

Living in the village with no other business but to follow native life, one sees the customs, ceremonies and transactions over and over again, one has examples of their beliefs as they are actually lived through, and the full body and blood of actual native life fills out soon the skeleton of abstract constructions. That is the reason why, working under such conditions as previously described, the Ethnographer is enabled to add something essential to the bare outline of tribal constitution, and to supplement it by all the details of behaviour, setting and small incident. He is able in each case to state whether an act is public or private; how a public assembly behaves, and what it looks like; he can judge whether an event is ordinary or an exciting and singular one; whether natives bring to it a great deal of sincere and earnest spirit, or perform it in fun; whether they do it in a perfunctory manner, or with zeal and deliberation.

In other words, there is a series of phenomena of great importance which cannot possibly be recorded by questioning or computing documents, but have to be observed in their full actuality. Let us call them *the imponderabilia of actual life*. Here belong such things as the routine of a man's working day, the details of his care of the body, of the manner of taking food and preparing it; the tone of conversational and social life around the village fires, the existence of strong friendships or hostilities, and of passing sympathies and dislikes between people; the subtle yet unmistakable manner in which personal vanities and ambitions are reflected in the behaviour of the individual and in the emotional reactions of those who surround him. All these facts can and ought to be scientifically formulated and recorded, but it is necessary that this be done, not by a superficial registration of details, as is usually done by untrained observers, but with an effort at penetrating the mental attitude expressed in them. And that is the reason why the work of scientifically trained observers, once seriously applied to the study of this aspect, will, I believe, yield results of surpassing value. So far, it has been done only by amateurs, and therefore done, on the whole, indifferently.

Indeed, if we remember that these imponderable yet all important facts of actual life are part of the real substance of the social fabric, that in them are spun the innumerable threads which keep together the family, the clan, the village community, the tribe – their significance becomes clear. The more crystallised bonds of social grouping, such as the definite ritual, the economic and legal duties, the obligations, the ceremonial gifts and formal marks of regard, though equally important for the student, are certainly felt less strongly by the individual who has to fulfil them. Applying this to ourselves, we all know that "family life" means for us, first and foremost, the atmosphere of home, all the innumerable small acts and attentions in which are expressed the affection, the mutual interest, the little preferences, and the little antipathies which constitute intimacy. That we may inherit from this person, that we shall have to walk after the hearse of the other, though sociologically these facts belong to the definition of "family" and "family life," in personal perspective of what family truly is to us, they normally stand very much in the background.

Exactly the same applies to a native community, and if the Ethnographer wants to bring their real life home to his readers, he must on no account neglect this. Neither aspect, the intimate, as little as the legal, ought to be glossed over. Yet as a rule in ethnographic accounts we have not both but either the one or the other – and, so far, the intimate one has hardly ever been properly treated. In all social relations besides the family ties, even those between mere tribesmen and, beyond that, between hostile or friendly members of different tribes, meeting on any sort of social business, there is this intimate side, expressed by the typical details of intercourse, the tone of their behaviour in the presence of one another. This side is different from the definite, crystallised legal frame of the relationship, and it has to be studied and stated in its own right.

In the same way, in studying the conspicuous acts of tribal life, such as ceremonies, rites, festivities, etc., the details and tone of behaviour ought to be given, besides the bare outline of events. The importance of this may be exemplified by one instance. Much has been said and written about survival. Yet the survival character of an act is expressed in nothing so well as in the concomitant behaviour, in the way in which it is carried out. Take any example from our own culture, whether it be the pomp and pageantry of a state ceremony, or a picturesque custom kept up by street urchins, its "outline" will not tell you whether the rite flourishes still with full vigour in the hearts of those who perform it or assist at the performance or whether they regard it as almost a dead thing, kept alive for tradition's sake. But observe and fix the data of their behaviour, and at once the degree of vitality of the act will become clear. There is no doubt, from all points of sociological, or psychological analysis, and in any question of theory, the manner and type of behaviour

observed in the performance of an act is of the highest importance. Indeed behaviour is a fact, a relevant fact, and one that can be recorded. And foolish indeed and short-sighted would be the man of science who would pass by a whole class of phenomena, ready to be garnered, and leave them to waste, even though he did not see at the moment to what theoretical use they might be put!

As to the actual method of observing and recording in fieldwork these *imponderabilia of actual life and of typical behaviour*, there is no doubt that the personal equation of the observer comes in here more prominently, than in the collection of crystallised, ethnographic data. But here also the main endeavour must be to let facts speak for themselves. If in making a daily round of the village, certain small incidents, characteristic forms of taking food, of conversing, of doing work are found occurring over and over again, they should be noted down at once. It is also important that this work of collecting and fixing impressions should begin early in the course of working out a district.

Because certain subtle peculiarities, which make an impression as long as they are novel, cease to be noticed as soon as they become familiar. Others again can only be perceived with a better knowledge of the local conditions. An ethnographic diary, carried on systematically throughout the course of one's work in a district would be the ideal instrument for this sort of study. And if, side by side with the normal and typical, the ethnographer carefully notes the slight, or the more pronounced deviations from it, he will be able to indicate the two extremes within which the normal moves.

In observing ceremonies or other tribal events ... it is necessary, not only to note down those occurrences and details which are prescribed by tradition and custom to be the essential course of the act, but also the Ethnographer ought to record carefully and precisely, one after the other, the actions of the actors and of the spectators. Forgetting for a moment that he knows and understands the structure of this ceremony, the main dogmatic ideas underlying it, he might try to find himself only in the midst of an assembly of human beings, who behave seriously or jocularly, with earnest concentration or with bored frivolity, who are either in the same mood as he finds them every day, or else are screwed up to a high pitch of excitement, and so on and so on. With his attention constantly directed to this aspect of tribal life, with the constant endeavour to fix it, to express it in terms of actual fact, a good deal of reliable and expressive material finds its way into his notes. He will be able to "set" the act into its proper place in tribal life, that is to show whether it is exceptional or commonplace, one in which the natives behave ordinarily, or one in which their whole behaviour is transformed. And he will also be able to bring all this home to his readers in a clear, convincing manner.

Again, in this type of work, it is good for the Ethnographer sometimes to put aside camera, note book and pencil, and to join in himself in what is going on. He can take part in the natives' games, he can follow them on their visits and walks, sit down and listen and share in their conversations. I am not certain if this is equally easy for everyone – perhaps the Slavonic nature is more plastic and more naturally savage than that of Western Europeans – but though the degree of success varies, the attempt is possible for everyone. Out of such plunges into the life of the natives – and I made them frequently not only for study's sake but because everyone needs human company – I have carried away a distinct feeling that their behaviour, their manner of being, in all sorts of tribal transactions, became more transparent and easily understandable than it had been before. All these methodological remarks, the reader will find again illustrated in the following chapters.

VIII

Finally, let us pass to the third and last aim of scientific fieldwork, to the last type of phenomenon which ought to be recorded in order to give a full and adequate picture of native culture. Besides the firm outline of tribal constitution and crystallised cultural items which form the skeleton, besides the data of daily life and ordinary behaviour, which are, so

to speak, its flesh and blood, there is still to be recorded the spirit – the natives' views and opinions and utterances. For, in every act of tribal life, there is, first, the routine prescribed by custom and tradition, then there is the manner in which it is carried out, and lastly there is the commentary to it, contained in the natives' mind. A man who submits to various customary obligations, who follows a traditional course of action, does it impelled by certain motives, to the accompaniment of certain feelings, guided by certain ideas. These ideas, feelings, and impulses are moulded and conditioned by the culture in which we find them, and are therefore an ethnic peculiarity of the given society. An attempt must be made therefore, to study and record them.

But is this possible? Are these subjective states not too elusive and shapeless? And, even granted that people usually do feel or think or experience certain psychological states in association with the performance of customary acts, the majority of them surely are not able to formulate these states, to put them into words. This latter point must certainly be granted, and it is perhaps the real Gordian knot in the study of the facts of social psychology. Without trying to cut or untie this knot, that is to solve the problem theoretically, or to enter further into the field of general methodology, I shall make directly for the question of practical means to overcome some of the difficulties involved.

First of all, it has to be laid down that we have to study here stereotyped manners of thinking and feeling. As sociologists, we are not interested in what A or B may feel *qua* individuals, in the accidental course of their own personal experiences – we are interested only in what they feel and think *qua* members of a given community. Now in this capacity, their mental states receive a certain stamp, become stereotyped by the institutions in which they live, by the influence of tradition and folk-lore, by the very vehicle of thought, that is by language. The social and cultural environment in which they move forces them to think and feel in a definite manner. Thus, a man who lives in a polyandrous community cannot experience the same feelings of jealousy, as a strict monogynist, though he might have the elements of them. A man who lives within the sphere of the Kula cannot become permanently and sentimentally attached to certain of his possessions, in spite of the fact that he values them most of all. These examples are crude, but better ones will be found in the text of this book.

So, the third commandment of fieldwork runs: Find out the typical ways of thinking and feeling, corresponding to the institutions and culture of a given community, and formulate the results in the most convincing manner. What will be the method of procedure? The best ethnographical writers – here again the Cambridge school with Haddon, Rivers, and Seligman rank first among English Ethnographers – have always tried to quote *verbatim* statements of crucial importance. They also adduce terms of native classification; sociological, psychological and industrial *termini technici*, and have rendered the verbal contour of native thought as precisely as possible. One step further in this line can be made by the Ethnographer, who acquires a knowledge of the native language and can use it as an instrument of inquiry. In working in the Kiriwinian language, I found still some difficulty in writing down the statement directly in translation which at first I used to do in the act of taking notes. The translation often robbed the text of all its significant characteristics – rubbed off all its points – so that gradually I was led to note down certain important phrases just as they were spoken, in the native tongue. As my knowledge of the language progressed, I put down more and more in Kiriwinian, till at last I found myself writing exclusively in that language, rapidly taking notes, word for word, of each statement. No sooner had I arrived at this point, than I recognised that I was thus acquiring at the same time an abundant linguistic material, and a series of ethnographic documents which ought to be reproduced as I had fixed them, besides being utilised in the writing up of my account.[4] This *corpus inscriptionum Kiriwiniensium* can be utilised, not only by myself, but by all those who, through their better penetration and ability of interpreting them, may find points which escape my attention, very much as the other *corpora* form the basis for the various interpretations of ancient and prehistoric cultures; only, these ethnographic inscriptions are all decipherable and clear, have been almost all translated fully and unambiguously, and have been provided with native cross-commentaries or *scholia* obtained from living sources.

No more need be said on this subject here ... The *Corpus* will of course be published separately at a later date.

IX

Our considerations thus indicate that the goal of ethnographic fieldwork must be approached through three avenues:

1 *The organisation of the tribe, and the anatomy of its culture* must be recorded in firm, clear outline. The method of *concrete, statistical documentation* is the means through which such an outline has to be given.
2 Within this frame, the *imponderabilia of actual life*, and the *type of behaviour* have to be filled in. They have to be collected through minute, detailed observations, in the form of some sort of ethnographic diary, made possible by close contact with native life.
3 A collection of ethnographic statements, characteristic narratives, typical utterances, items of folk-lore and magical formulæ has to be given as a *corpus inscriptionum*, as documents of native mentality.

These three lines of approach lead to the final goal, of which an Ethnographer should never lose sight. This goal is, briefly, to grasp the native's point of view, his relation to life, to realise *his* vision of *his* world. We have to study man, and we must study what concerns him most intimately, that is, the hold which life has on him. In each culture, the values are slightly different; people aspire after different aims, follow different impulses, yearn after a different form of happiness. In each culture, we find different institutions in which man pursues his life-interest, different customs by which he satisfies his aspirations, different codes of law and morality which reward his virtues or punish his defections. To study the institutions, customs, and codes or to study the behaviour and mentality without the subjective desire of feeling by what these people live, of realising the substance of their happiness – is, in my opinion, to miss the greatest reward which we can hope to obtain from the study of man.

These generalities the reader will find illustrated in the following chapters. We shall see there the savage striving to satisfy certain aspirations, to attain his type of value, to follow his line of social ambition. We shall see him led on to perilous and difficult enterprises by a tradition of magical and heroical exploits, shall see him following the lure of his own romance. Perhaps as we read the account of these remote customs there may emerge a feeling of solidarity with the endeavours and ambitions of these natives. Perhaps man's mentality will be revealed to us, and brought near, along some lines which we never have followed before. Perhaps through realising human nature in a shape very distant and foreign to us, we shall have some light shed on our own. In this, and in this case only, we shall be justified in feeling that it has been worth our while to understand these natives, their institutions and customs, and that we have gathered some profit from the Kula.

NOTES

1 I may note at once that there were a few delightful exceptions to that, to mention only my friends Billy Hancock in the Trobriands; M. Raffael Brudo, another pearl trader; and the missionary, Mr M. K. Gilmour.

2 According to a useful habit of the terminology of science, I use the word Ethnography for the empirical and descriptive results of the science of Man, and the word Ethnology for speculative and comparative theories.

3 The legendary "early authority" who found the natives only beastly and without customs is left behind by a modern writer, who, speaking about the Southern Massim with whom he lived and worked "in close contact" for many years, says: – "...We teach lawless men to become obedient, inhuman men to love, and savage men to change." And again: – "Guided in his conduct by nothing but his instincts and propensities,

and governed by his unchecked passions. ..." "Lawless, inhuman and savage!" A grosser misstatement of the real state of things could not be invented by anyone wishing to parody the Missionary point of view. Quoted from the Rev. C. W. Abel, of the London Missionary Society, "Savage Life in New Guinea," no date.

4 It was soon after I had adopted this course that I received a letter from Dr A. H. Gardiner, the well-known Egyptologist, urging me to do this very thing. From his point of view as archæologist, he naturally saw the enormous possibilities for an Ethnographer of obtaining a similar body of written sources as have been preserved to us from ancient cultures, plus the possibility of illuminating them by personal knowledge of the full life of that culture.

REFERENCES

CHRONOLOGICAL LIST OF KULA EVENTS WITNESSED BY THE WRITER

First Expedition, August 1914–March, 1915.

March 1915 In the village of Dikoyas (Woodlark Island) a few ceremonial offerings seen. Preliminary information obtained.

Second Expedition, May 1915–May, 1916.

June 1915 A Kabigidoya visit arrives from Vakuta to Kiriwina. Its anchoring at Kavataria witnessed and the men seen at Omarakana, where information collected.

July 1915 Several parties from Kitava land on the beach of Kaulukuba. The men examined in Omarakana. Much information collected in that period.

September 1915 Unsuccessful attempt to sail to Kitava with To'uluwa, the chief of Omarakana.

October–November 1915 Departure noticed of three expeditions from Kiriwina to Kitava. Each time To'uluwa brings home a haul of *mwali* (armshells).

November, 1915–March 1916 Preparations for a big overseas expedition from Kiriwina to the Marshall Bennett Islands. Construction of a canoe; renovating of another; sail making in Omarakana; launching; *tasasoria* on the beach of Kaulukuba. At the same time, information is being obtained about these and the associated subjects. Some magical texts of canoe building and Kula magic obtained.

Third Expedition, October 1917–October, 1918.

November, 1917–December 1917   Inland Kula; some data obtained in Tukwaukwa.

December–February 1918   Parties from Kitava arrive in Wawela. Collection of information about the *yoyova*. Magic and spells of Kaygau obtained.

March 1918   Preparations in Sanaroa; preparations in the Amphletts; the Dobuan fleet arrives in the Amphletts. The *uvalaku* expedition from Dobu followed to Boyowa.

April 1918   Their arrival; their reception in Sinaketa; the Kula transactions; the big intertribal gathering. Some magical formulæ obtained.

May 1918   Party from Kitava seen in Vakuta.

June, July 1918   Information about Kula magic and customs checked and amplified in Omarakana, especially with regard to its Eastern branches.

August, September 1918   Magical texts obtained in Sinaketa.

October 1918   Information obtained from a number of natives in Dobu and Southern Massim district (examined in Samarai).

Part II
Fieldwork Identity

Introduction

Antonius C. G. M. Robben

Bronislaw Malinowski was sensitive to the social life on Kiriwina Island, but did not critically examine his own role and feelings toward the Trobrianders, even though his loneliness filters through the opening sentence of the excerpt from his "Method and Scope of Ethnographic Fieldwork" (Chapter 3). He had written an intimate diary about his depressions and his chagrin at the local population, but these revelations only became available after his death (Malinowski 1967). His student Hortense Powdermaker was among the first to openly reveal the personal hardships, role conflicts, and identity crises of fieldworkers. Laura Bohannan had preceded Powdermaker with *Return to Laughter* by more than a decade, but she had published under a pseudonym and written in a popularizing style (Bowen 1964). Bohannan and Powdermaker initiated a trend of self-reflection on the practice of fieldwork that became more prominent in anthropology than in any other scholarly discipline. The lengthy immersion in foreign cultures, the status of ethnographers as outsiders, the interactive anthropological research methods in general and participant observation in particular, and the nature of fieldwork as a professional rite of passage with often far-reaching effects on the self, made the concern for identity during fieldwork of great and enduring importance since the 1960s.

Hortense Powdermaker carried out her first fieldwork in 1929–30 among the Lesu on the island of New Ireland in Melanesia. In the excerpt "A Woman Going Native," taken from her book *Stranger and Friend: The Way of an Anthropologist* (1967), Powdermaker demonstrates how her gender and ethnic status influenced her research. Melanesian societies enforce a rather strict division between men and women into different social domains, and she therefore drifted naturally to those roles occupied by women in Lesu society: working in the taro gardens, preparing food, carrying and

Ethnographic Fieldwork: An Anthropological Reader, Second Edition. Edited by
Antonius C. G. M. Robben and Jeffrey A. Sluka.
Editorial material and organization © 2012 John Wiley & Sons, Inc.
Published 2012 by John Wiley & Sons, Inc.

delivering babies, and dancing at women's feasts. Her research among men carried more restrictions because of her female status. It consisted mostly of ethnographic interviews, even though she participated in fishing expeditions, feasts, and mortuary rituals whenever invited. Fortunately, Powdermaker was not fully categorized as a woman by the Lesu and was therefore able to cross gender boundaries with relative ease. Still, this gender neutrality carried the cost of not being confided in by either men or women. Only after throwing herself wholeheartedly into a dance during the incorporation ritual of boys who had been initiated into manhood did Powdermaker become accepted by the women, and, for the duration of the ceremony, she was treated by men with the same symbolic gender hostility as Lesu women. Such treatment, however benign, cannot but raise the awareness of anthropologists about the impact of gender on their data collection and research results. Powdermaker concludes that female anthropologists seem to have easier access to both sexes than male anthropologists, whose contact with women is often regarded as threatening by men. Yet, Gregory (1984) has argued the contrary, while Golde (1986) has pointed out that once a female anthropologist has been accepted into a society, she is expected to conform to prevailing gender roles and has less freedom to move around at will than men in comparable situations (see Wolf (1996) for a feminist critique of fieldwork).

After completing her research among the Lesu, Hortense Powdermaker returned to the United States and conducted fieldwork on African Americans in Mississippi between 1932 and 1934. She traced this interest to her student days when she rode a crowded streetcar on a blistering hot day in Baltimore. A white woman complained to her about the foul air around the sweaty African American workers. Powdermaker noticed the same odor, took a few steps toward the white workers, discovered that they smelled just as much of perspiration, and finally realized that in fact she herself reeked equally badly after spending the day working on her summer job at the playground (Powdermaker 1967:132). This anecdote reveals Powdermaker's anthropological intuition, even before her formal training: she noticed a racial remark, tested its validity, ascertained it to be unfounded, and then reflected on her similar personal state.

Powdermaker concealed her Jewish identity in the Mississippi Bible Belt community and tried to establish a good rapport with black and white. This was a time of strong racial segregation, when the lynchings of African Americans were common and the Ku Klux Klan was strong. Understandably, Powdermaker had to walk a fine line between the white and black neighborhoods in the town she called Indianola. Her confrontation with the exploitation of African American fellow-citizens, the racism of the white inhabitants, and the fear between both groups made her conscious of her own status as a white Jewish woman in a segregated American society. She also began to doubt whether she would have behaved differently toward African Americans had she been born in Indianola, hemmed in by social taboos and racial stereotypes. She entered an identity crisis as she shuttled back and forth between blacks and whites, adopting as if through osmosis some of the qualities of each group. Just as she had straddled the gender gap among the Lesu, she crossed the color barrier as if belonging to both segregated communities.

Powdermaker went through another serious crisis when a lynching party set out to hunt down an African American accused of raping a white woman. Feeling powerless, she decided to retreat in her role as the neutral observer trying to make sense of her fellow human beings. This distancing must have been a form of self-protection against the racial discrimination and the blatant social disparity she was seeing. Her ethnographic initiation on New Ireland allowed her to cope with her ambiguous social role in Mississippi, distance herself by assuming a professional attitude, and overcome her depressions, fears, and anxieties.

Powdermaker's fieldwork crises revolved mainly around gender and ethnic identity. Roschanack Shaery-Eisenlohr (2009) demonstrates in her essay, "Fixing and Negotiating Identities in the Field: The Case of Lebanese Shiites," that many more identities may come into play, and that the conflicting interpretations of those identities by informants greatly enhance fieldwork's interactional complexity. Shaery-Eisenlohr investigated the everyday and official constructions of Shiite political and national identity in Lebanon within the context of the complicated transnational relation between Lebanese Shiites and the Iranian government. She focused in particular on the two principal Shiite politico-religious parties, Hezbollah and AMAL (Afwaj al-Muqawama al-Lubnaniyya), and interviewed many middle-aged Lebanese and Iranian Shiite men (Shaery-Eisenlohr 2008).

Shaery-Eisenlohr regards herself as a secular diasporic Iranian woman. She was born in Germany to Iranian parents, spent her childhood in Iran, returned to Germany as a teenager, and moved to the United States with her German husband to pursue a doctorate in Near Eastern studies. She considered this multiple identity as self-evident, but her interviewees reduced her to the status of an Iranian Shiite woman, and ignored her formative diasporic experiences. Shaery-Eisenlohr's constructivist conceptualization of identity as being layered, flexible, and ever-changing clashed with her interlocutors' essentialist notion of identity as static, fixed, singular, and categorical. These two understandings are, however, not necessarily contradictory. Ewing (1990:251) has argued that people often experience their selves as a seamless whole at any particular time, but that they "can be observed to project multiple, inconsistent self-representations that are context-dependent and may shift rapidly." Precisely for this reason Shaery-Eisenlohr's multilayered self-representation resulted in many conflicting identity constructions by her interlocutors, who perceived her alternately as an upper-class Iranian Shiite, an exiled royalist who supported the Pahlevi monarchy deposed by the 1979 Islamic revolution of Ayatollah Khomeini, a radical militant who opposed the theocracy of ayatollahs, an Armenian Iranian, an Iranian Zoroastrian, an Iranian Baha'i, a CIA spy, a Westernized secular reformist, a Shiite woman who refused to wear a head scarf (hijab), a childless married woman, or a professional woman conducting research without her husband's presence. AMAL party leaders looked favorably upon some of these identities, which were disapproved of by her Hezbollah interlocutors, and vice versa. At the same time, the male interviewees privileged either her gender, religious, or ethnic identity, but all men and women emphasized her marital status in negative or positive ways. Shaery-Eisenlohr concludes that the confusion among her interlocutors about her identity, and her efforts at negotiating other representations, complicated fieldwork, but also yielded new insights into the politico-religious and national identity construction among Lebanese Shiites and their imagination of Iran and its influence on Lebanon.

Manda Cesara (1982) was the first anthropologist to address at length her sexual feelings and affairs in the field, albeit under a pseudonym. Few fieldworkers have followed in her steps, while the male heterosexual anthropological commu-nity has concealed the sexist, racist, and colonialist biases hiding behind much anthropological discourse about sexuality, according to Kulick (1995). Several collections on fieldwork and sexuality have appeared, nevertheless, especially by gay and lesbian anthropologists (Kulick and Willson 1995; Lewin and Leap 1996). The issue of sexual identity is of particular relevance to them as members of a group stigmatized in many societies. The question whether homosexual anthropologists should reveal their sexual identity in a largely heterosexual world is a matter of debate. Concealment versus openness is of a different relevance when studying neutral or homosexual topics, and the merits of either strategy are highly dependent on the host culture, as some may be hostile while others will be indifferent or sympathetic to the forthright fieldworker. In the excerpt "Being Gay and Doing Fieldwork" (1996), Walter Williams addresses the advantages of being a gay anthropologist, even though he is quick to add that managing this sexual identity is seldom the researcher's chief concern but rather attending to the everyday, mundane problems and hazards of fieldwork such as illnesses, accidents, and finding suitable housing, safe food, and good means of communication.

Williams's long-term study of gay men in nonhomophobic cultures originated in his political involvement in emancipatory African American and American Indian movements, and began with a personal fascination with two-spirited North American Indian men and women who identify with the opposite gender, also known as berdaches. He conducted ethnographic fieldwork in an Omaha reservation, and was only able to establish a good working relation with a local berdache when he became open about his gay identity. Determined to salvage still existing benign cultural attitudes toward homosexuality in an increasingly intolerant world, Williams embarked on a comparative study of two-spirited men through fieldwork among the Lakota, Crow, Cheyenne, and Navaho, and finally the Mayas. He emphasizes that his openness about being gay was not the main reason for his good rapport during these field visits, but, before anything else, his treatment of people with honesty, respect, trust, earnestness, and empathy.

Ethical concerns about the inequality of intimate relations in the field have made teachers urge students to refrain from sexual engagements with research collaborators. Aside from the fact that such sexual encounters will inevitably take place, two far more interesting issues are to what extent they affect the interpretation of research data, and whether the fieldworker's sexual subjectivity influences the data-gathering process. Williams approves of intimate involvements as long as the relationships are based on mutual consent and realistic expectations about the future. In his case, such relationships helped raise empathy for local gays who were often regarded as outsiders and of lower status, and yielded unique research data unavailable to heterosexual anthropologists. Williams thus demonstrates that what was true for the social identities of Powdermaker and Shaery-Eisenlohr in the field – ethnic, religious, political, gender, marital – is also true for sexual identity: namely, that researchers who can appeal to group membership obtain other data than those who are on the outside.

The three essays about fieldwork identity discussed so far, as well as the texts in Part IX, *Reflexive Ethnography*, show that empathy is a crucial intersubjective dimension of the field encounter, requiring dialogue to adjust and readjust mutual impressions (Hollan 2008). They also reveal that fieldworkers understand themselves by mentally observing their own social position and selfhood through autoethnography and by assuming the perspective of others (Ellis 2004; Reed-Danahay 1997; Collins and Gallinat 2010). Empathy contributes therefore to the ongoing construction and representation of self. Paul Spencer (1992) argues, in his essay

"Automythologies and the Reconstruction of Ageing," that people tend to fashion coherent self-representations that change over time. He demonstrates in an exegesis of two autobiographical anecdotes, one by a Maasai elder and another by himself, that narrators use exaggeration, hyperbole, and distortion to construct a self-image in harmony with their world-view and stage of life. They emphasize aspects that serve to captivate and convince not only their audiences but also themselves. From an anthropological perspective, personal anecdotes can reveal the narrator's biography, his or her social and historical context, and life's maturation process.

The Maasai elder Masiani told the story of how he had confronted and outsmarted several peers who wanted to punish him for his role in a drunken fight. The anecdote was implausible and incongruous, according to other Maasai, but still made sense to Spencer within Masiani's biography and the larger Maasai history. The boisterous account purveyed an image of the Maasai as a proud, independent people, Masiani's dilemma of defending himself and his cattle while upholding the disciplinary practices of his age-mates by accepting the fine, and his torn emotions over the declining power and authority of his ageing peer group. Spencer's personal anecdote concerns an awkward chance meeting with several Englishmen as he was conducting fieldwork among the Samburu and Rendille in Kenya. The discrepancies between his narrative and the published account by one of the Englishmen, years later, lead to a revealing analysis of various life crises that made Spencer doubt his Christian faith during adolescence and become disenchanted with British imperialism when the United Kingdom tried to prevent Egypt's nationalization of the Suez Canal in 1956, which drove him to anthropology, and made him immerse himself in Samburu culture and avoid expatriates in Kenya, thus explaining his anecdotal diffidence toward the English travelers. His field research among the Samburu became as much a scholarly endeavor as an emotional detour by way of the Samburu's clinging to the certainties of cultural tradition that reconnected Spencer with the inner need for an integrated self, and raised a better understanding of his personal turmoil through an identification with the rebellious Samburu youths, and the awareness of his repeated restructuring of past selves and past histories as he grew older.

These four contributions show that fieldwork is not a detached activity carried out by an objective observer, but that subjective experiences and selfhood are part and parcel of fieldwork. The ethnographer's multiple social identities and his or her dynamic self may be liabilities, but they are also research assets. Anthropologists may use their gender, sexual orientation, religion, nationality, age, marital status, and self-representations to obtain data that are unavailable to those with different person-hoods (Whitehead and Conaway 1986; Okely and Callaway 1992; Taylor 2010; see Cohen 1994 and Battaglia 1995 for a theoretical development of the concept of self). Fieldwork involves a negotiation between ethnographers and research collaborators in which their selves, identities, and social constitutions come into play.

The anthropological attention to the self in fieldwork has been broadened since the early 2000s with a concern for power and subjectivity. Power relations produce and are produced by social practices and social categorizations, such as race, gender, class, and age, that shape a person's self. How people act is influenced by individual constitutions, whether these are intentions, feelings, or unconscious desires, and by the sociocultural forces and formations that fashion them (Holland and Leander 2004; Ortner 2005). Subjectivity is then situated at the intersection of self, emotion, and power, referring "to the shared inner life of the subject and particularly to the emotional experience of a political subject" (Luhrmann 2006:356). In this way, the study of people's subjectivity returns to Malinowski (1984[1922]:517), who called upon fieldworkers to assume the native's point of view, "and through his eyes to look at the outer world and feel ourselves what it must feel to *him* to be himself."

Subjectivity becomes most visible when people's inner states collide with structural formations, social hierarchies, and institutional frameworks. Much ethnographic work on subjectivity has focused therefore on the powerless and the downtrodden bowing but not breaking under the weight of all too powerful forces (see Das et al. 2001; Biehl 2005; Biehl et al. 2007). Yet, anthropologists are not immune to such forces and may be affected in the field by violence and exploitation, as shown in Part V, *Fieldwork Conflicts, Hazards, and Dangers*. Anthropologists are acting subjects who can influence, and are influenced by, the social and political realities they study. The subjectivity of ethnographers deserves therefore equal attention as their fieldwork identity.

REFERENCES

Battaglia, Debbora, ed.
  1995   *Rhetorics of Self-Making*. Berkeley: University of California Press.
Biehl, João
  2005   *Vita: Life in a Zone of Social Abandonment*. Berkeley: University of California Press.
Biehl, João, Byron Good, and Arthur Kleinman, eds.
  2007   *Subjectivity: Ethnographic Investigations*. Berkeley: University of California Press.
Bowen, Elenore Smith (a pseudonym for Laura Bohannan)
  1964   *Return to Laughter: An Anthropological Novel*. Garden City, NY: Natural History Library.
Cesara, Manda (pseudonym for Karla Poewe)
  1982   *Reflections of a Woman Anthropologist: No Hiding Place*. London: Academic Press.
Cohen, Anthony P.
  1994   *Self Consciousness: An Alternative Anthropology of Identity*. London: Routledge.
Collins, Peter and Anselma Gallinat, eds.
  2010   *The Ethnographic Self as Resource: Writing Memory and Experience into Ethnography*. London: Berghahn.
Das, Veena, Arthur Kleinman, Margaret Lock, Mamphela Ramphele, and Pamela Reynolds, eds.
  2001   *Remaking a World: Violence, Social Suffering, and Recovery*. Berkeley: University of California Press.
Ellis, Carolyn
  2004   *The Ethnographic I: A Methodological Novel about Autoethnography*. Walnut Creek, CA: AltaMira Press.
Ewing, Katherine P.
  1990   The Illusion of Wholeness: Culture, Self, and the Experience of Inconsistency. *Ethos* 18(3):251–78.
Golde, Peggy
  1986   Introduction. In: *Women in the Field: Anthropological Experiences*. 2nd edn. Peggy Golde, ed., pp. 1–15. Berkeley: University of California Press.
Gregory, James R.
  1984   The Myth of the Male Ethnographer and the Woman's World. *American Anthropologist* 86(2):316–327.
Hollan, Douglas
  2008   Being There: On the Imaginative Aspects of Understanding Others and Being Understood. *Ethos* 36(4):475–489.

Holland, Dorothy and Kevin Leander
   2004   Ethnographic Studies of Positioning and Subjectivity: An Introduction. *Ethos* 32(2):127–139.
Kulick, Don
   1995   Introduction: The Sexual Life of Anthropologists: Erotic Subjectivity and Ethnographic Work. In: *Taboo: Sex, Identity, and Erotic Subjectivity in Anthropological Fieldwork*. Don Kulick and Margaret Willson, eds., pp. 1–28. London: Routledge.
Kulick, Don and Margaret Willson, eds.
   1995   *Taboo: Sex, Identity, and Erotic Subjectivity in Anthropological Fieldwork*. London: Routledge.
Lewin, Ellen and William L. Leap, eds.
   1996   *Out in the Field: Reflections of Lesbian and Gay Anthropologists*. Urbana: University of Illinois Press.
Luhrmann, T. M.
   2006   Subjectivity. *Anthropological Theory* 6(3):345–361.
Malinowski, Bronislaw
   1967   *A Diary in the Strict Sense of the Term*. London: Routledge & Kegan Paul.
Malinowski, Bronislaw
   1984[1922]   *Argonauts of the Western Pacific*. Prospect Heights, IL: Waveland Press.
Okely, Judith and Helen Callaway, eds.
   1992   *Anthropology and Autobiography*. London: Routledge.
Ortner, Sherry
   2005   Subjectivity and Cultural Critique. *Anthropological Theory* 5(1):31–52.
Powdermaker, Hortense
   1967   *Stranger and Friend: The Way of an Anthropologist*. London: Secker and Warburg.
Reed-Danahay, Deborah E., ed.
   1997   *Auto/Ethnography: Rewriting the Self and the Social*. Oxford: Berg.
Shaery-Eisenlohr, Roschanack
   2008   *Shi'ite Lebanon: Transnational Religion and the Making of National Identities*. New York: Columbia University Press.
Shaery-Eisenlohr, Roschanack
   2009   Fixing and Negotiating Identities in the Field: The Case of Lebanese Shiites. In: *Women Fielding Danger: Negotiating Ethnographic Identities in Field Research*. Martha K. Huggins and Marie-Louise Glebbeek, eds., pp. 31–46. Lanham, MD: Rowman & Littlefield Publishers.
Spencer, Paul
   1992   Automythologies and the Reconstruction of Ageing. In: *Anthropology and Autobiography*. Judith Okely and Helen Callaway, eds., pp. 50–63. London: Routledge.
Taylor, Erin B., ed.
   2010   *Fieldwork Identities in the Caribbean*. Coconut Creek, FL: Caribbean Studies Press.
Whitehead, Tony Larry and Mary Ellen Conaway, eds.
   1986   *Self, Sex, and Gender in Cross-Cultural Fieldwork*. Urbana, IL: University of Illinois Press.
Williams, Walter L.
   1996   Being Gay and Doing Fieldwork. In: *Out in the Field: Reflections of Lesbian and Gay Anthropologists*. Ellen Lewin and William L. Leap, eds., pp. 70–85. Urbana, IL: University of Illinois Press.
Wolf, Diane L., ed.
   1996   *Feminist Dilemmas in Fieldwork*. Boulder, CO: Westview Press.

4

A Woman Going Native

Hortense Powdermaker

X   A Woman Alone in the Field

In casual daily life I was much more with the women than with the men; the sexes were quite separate in their social and economic life. I often sat with the women of my hamlet and of neighboring ones, watching them scrape the taro, the staple of their diet, and prepare it for baking between hot stones. Notes on the different ways of preparing taro became so voluminous that I sometimes thought of writing a Melanesian cook book. I was apparently compulsive about writing everything down, but I justified the fullness of the cooking notes by saying that they illustrated Melanesian ingenuity and diversity with limited resources. More important than the cooking notes were my observations on the relationships of the women with their daughters and with each other; listening to the good-humored gossip provided many clues for further questions and added subtlety to my understanding.

Pulong, whom I saw daily, was in the middle stage of her pregnancy, and I could observe her customs such as not eating a certain fish believed to "fight" an embryo in the stomach. Full details about pregnancy customs and taboos came later and gradually. When I first asked Pulong if there was any way of preventing pregnancy, she said she did not understand and looked vague. It seemed evident that she did not want to talk about the subject. Somewhat later, she and my adopted "mother" and a clan "sister" brought me leaves that they said would produce an abortion if chewed in the early stages of pregnancy. I put them carefully in a botanical press for identification when I returned home.

It was taken for granted that I should go to all the women's feasts in or near Lesu. The morning of a feast was usually spent in preparing the food; then came the dances, distribution of food, and speeches. At one such feast in a nearby village to celebrate the birth

Hortense Powdermaker, "A Woman Going Native," pp. 108–119, 183–187, 188–190, 196, 197–198 from *Stranger and Friend: The Way of an Anthropologist*. London: Secker & Warburg, 1967. Copyright © 1966 by Hortense Powdermaker. Reprinted by permission of W. W. Norton & Co., Inc.

Ethnographic Fieldwork: An Anthropological Reader, Second Edition. Edited by Antonius C. G. M. Robben and Jeffrey A. Sluka.
Editorial material and organization © 2012 John Wiley & Sons, Inc.
Published 2012 by John Wiley & Sons, Inc.

of a baby, the hundred or so women were in a particularly gay mood, which I enjoyed. One woman, a born jester, who was not dancing because her relationship to the newborn baby precluded it, grabbed the drum and began doing amusing antics. It was like an impromptu skit and all the onlookers laughed loudly. Encouraged, she continued. Then came the distribution of bundles of baked taro, most of it to be carried home, and the women's speeches praising the ability of their respective husbands as providers of food. However, one complained that her husband was lazy and did not bring her fish often enough. In the late afternoon, my Lesu friends and I trudged home. A basket of food and sometimes a baby was on each woman's back (except mine), and although we were all tired after a long day, a pleasant, relaxed feeling pervaded the small group.

As I ate my dinner that night and thought about the day's events, I felt happy to be working in a functioning traditional culture rather than one in which the anthropologist has to get most of his data about tribal life from the reminiscences of the elders. Sometimes I asked for details of a ritual in advance of its performance; when it took place, some differences usually showed up, even though the customary pattern was followed. After one rather important ceremony, I made this point to an informant who had given me particularly full details in advance. He looked at me as if I was either stupid or naïve (or both), and asked if I didn't know that nothing ever took place *exactly* as it was supposed to. Nor can generalizations by Melanesians, or anyone else, include all the specific details of actual happenings.

Although it would not have been considered appropriate for me to be with the men in their casual social life as I was with the women, it was understood that I must observe and learn about men's economic and ritual life, which was apart from the women's. I worked on my veranda with individual men as informants and as teachers of the native language. I did not go to men's feasts and other rites unless I was invited, but I was invited to everything. When the men were having a feast, usually in the cemetery, two elders called for me and escorted me there. I sat on one side, apart from the men, and munched a banana as I recorded

what was said or done. Later I went over the notes with one or two of the men who had been present. One morning, although I arose very early – before dawn – to go to a men's feast in a neighboring village, I was still eating my breakfast when the Lesu men were ready to leave. Without saying anything to me, they detailed one man to wait. The sun was just rising when he and I started our walk to Ambwa, about three miles away.

I had to go to all feasts for the same reason that my presence was required at every mortuary rite. But no law of diminishing returns operated for the feasts, since the events they celebrated were so varied: birth, bestowal of name on a newborn baby, appearance of his first tooth, early betrothal, first menstruation, initiation of boys, marriage, completion of any work, death, and practically every other event – small or big – in life. Through these feasts I gained not only a knowledge of the normal round of life, but I saw also the economic system functioning. It was evident from the speeches and from my informants that the exchange of bundles of baked food was by no means casual, but followed a rather rigid system of reciprocal gifts. I heard praise for those who were generous and gossip about those who were slow to make gifts in return for those taken. As I typed my notes and mulled over them, I thought that perhaps I would organize all my data around feasts. An article on them, rather than a book, did eventually emerge after I left the field. There, I found it difficult to think in terms of articles, because I was always trying to relate one aspect of the culture to everything else.

I was more selective in going to other activities. I could not afford the time to go regularly with the women to their gardens. They left in the early morning and did not return until midafternoon. But I did go often enough to observe the various stages of their work. Fortunately, there was no feeling that my presence was necessary at all gardening activities. It was the same situation with the men's fishing. I waded into the shallow water by the beach and watched the different forms of fishing: with spears, nets, traps, and hooks. But I was content with seeing each kind of operation once or twice and discussing details of it afterwards with informants. Later, I wrote down the magical spells connected with gardening and with fishing.

I was lucky that during my stay the initiation rites for eight boys from Lesu and from two neighboring villages took place. (They did not occur every year, but only when the number of boys reaching puberty was sufficient to justify the elaborate rites.) Less than a month after I settled in Lesu, the women began practicing a dance each evening. An elderly man was teaching them, but it was taboo for other men to see the rehearsals, although they would see the dance at the ritual.

I sat watching the women practice. The moon was new and delicate, the sea dark and noisy, and the singing women moved in a circle around a fire with slow dancing steps. They asked me to join them, but I was too self-conscious. I sat watching and held one of the babies. But each night, as the music and formal steps became more and more monotonous, lasting until midnight, I became increasingly bored. I had to force myself to stay awake.

Finally, one evening, I gathered my courage and began dancing. My place in the circle was between Pulong and an important old woman in her clan. The old women danced with more vivacity than the young ones; the gayest woman of the village was a grandmother. Good-natured laughter greeted my mistakes, which were carefully corrected. The steps were not difficult and I soon caught on to them. No longer were the evenings monotonous. Every night, as the moon became fuller, I danced. But, somehow, I did not think ahead to the night of the big rites.

Finally it came. That morning, Pulong and several other women came over and presented me with a shell arm band and a *kepkep*, a tortoise-shell breast ornament, and asked that I wear their favorite dress – a pink and white striped cotton. I gulped, and said I was not going to dance; I would just observe. But why, they asked in astonishment, had I been practicing every night? I could not explain that I had started because I was bored and that now I felt too self-conscious to participate in rites which I knew would be attended by thousands of natives from all over the island and nearby islands. Soon I saw that I had to dance. A refusal now would be a rejection.

All day there was an increasing "before the ball" excitement. Hair was colored with bright dyes and bodies of men were ornamented. The tinsel trimming which I had brought with me was in demand by the women dancers, who wound it around their hair. At sunset my dancing companions assembled at my house and we walked together up to the far end of the village. Like the other women, I had a yellow flower behind my ear; the *kepkep* strung on a piece of vine hung from my neck; shell bracelets were on my left arm just above the elbow. I wore the pink and white striped dress. I was excited and nervous.

When we arrived, about two thousand Melanesians from all over New Ireland and neighboring islands were sitting around the fires. We took our places and watched the dances, which went on continuously all night long in an open clearing before an intently absorbed audience. Most of the men's dances were dramatic, often acting out a story such as the killing of a crocodile. Masks were elaborate; dancing was strenuous and the drums beat vigorously. The women wore no masks and their dances, which alternated with the men's, were far less elaborate and formed abstract patterns of lines, squares, and circles. Young men held burning torches near the dancers, so that all could see them.

I was unable to pay much attention. Consumed with self-consciousness, I imagined my family and friends sitting in the background and muttering in disapproving tone, "Hortense, dancing with the savages!" How could I get up before all these people of the Stone Age and dance with them? I prayed for an earthquake – the island was volcanic. But the earth was still, and all too soon it was our turn to dance. I wondered if I would not collapse on my way to the open clearing which served as the stage. But there I was in my proper place in the circle; the drums began; I danced. Something happened. I forgot myself and was one with the dancers. Under the full moon and for the brief time of the dance, I ceased to be an anthropologist from a modern society. I danced. When it was over I realized that, for this short period, I had been emotionally part of the rite. Then out came my notebook.

In the early morning the boys were circumcised inside the enclosure. I was invited to watch the operation, but decided not to. Nor had I gone into the enclosure during the preceding few weeks when the boys were confined there. The normal social separation between the men and women was intensified during the initiation of the boys. The mothers (real and classificatory) openly expressed their sorrow at losing their sons who would now join the adult men. The women wept (not ritual wailing) when the boys went into the enclosure for the operation, and began a dance which expressed their feelings. Men ran out from the enclosure and engaged in a spirited fight with the women. They threw stones and coconut shells at each other and exchanged jeering talk. Since I had been identified with the women, even to the extent of dancing with them, it seemed unwise in the hostile atmosphere between the sexes to swerve suddenly from the women's group to the men's. Or, perhaps, I was unable to switch my identifications so quickly.

Later in the morning the piles of food (contributed by the clans of boys who had been circumcised) were given to the dancers. A particularly large pile was put in front of me and a speech was made praising my dancing and expressing appreciation. From then on the quality of my relationships with the women was different. I had their confidence as I had not had it before. They came of their own accord to visit me and talked intimately about their lives. I secured eight quite long detailed life histories. My relationships with the men were also subtly strengthened. The formal escort to their feasts continued as before, but there was a greater sense of ease between us and they gave me freely any data I asked for. I was glad for many reasons that I had not given in to my self-consciousness. Thinking about it, I was amused to realize that all the things white people had tried to make me fear – snakes, sharks, crocodiles, rape – had not caused me anxiety. Nor had the expedition taken any particular courage. As one of my friends remarked, I had the courage of a fool who did not know what she was getting into. But to dance with the women at the initiation rites – that had taken courage.

A woman alone in the field has certain advantages. Social separation between the sexes is strict in all tribal societies. Male anthropologists say it is difficult for them to be alone with native women, because the men (and the women, too) suspect their intentions. When traders and other white men have had contact with native peoples, they frequently have had sexual relations with the women, with or without their consent. No precedent existed, at least in Melanesia when I was there, for a white woman to live alone in a native village. We could establish our own patterns, and obviously these large strong Melanesians could not be afraid of me. (The gun which Radcliffe-Brown had insisted I take with me for protection remained hidden in the bottom of a trunk.) My relations with the women were more chummy than with the men, and data from the former were more intimate. But the men completely understood that I had to find out as much as possible about all sides of life and, very definitely, did not want the masculine side omitted. It was the men, not I, who suggested escorting me to all their feasts. My impression is that fieldwork may be a bit easier for a woman anthropologist alone than for a man alone.

Being alone for a male or female anthropologist gives a greater intensity to the whole field experience than living with company, and frequently provides more intimate data because the fieldworker is thrown upon the natives for companionship. On the other hand, it has the disadvantage of loneliness, and, perhaps, getting "fed-up" more often. A mate and children reduce the loneliness, and they may be of help in securing data from their own sex and age groups. Children are often an entering wedge into the study of family life. A team of colleagues, particularly from different disciplines, makes possible a many-sided approach to complex problems and offers the stimulation of exchange of ideas while in the field. A disadvantage of the family and team is that they may make relationships with natives more difficult. One member may be quickly accepted and the other disliked. It is usually easier for people to relate to one stranger than to several. The initial pattern in participant observation was the lone anthropologist. Today the family and team are becoming more common.

XI   "Going Native?"

Although I had enjoyed those brief moments of feeling at one with the women dancers at the initiation rites and although I was fairly involved in this Stone-Age society, I never fooled myself that I had "gone native." I participated rather freely, but remained an anthropologist.

While I did fit, to a considerable degree, within the Melanesian social system, small incidents sometimes brought out a sense of my difference. When I admired the beauty of the night, my friends looked at me as if I were quite strange. They appeared to take the scenery for granted, and I never heard them comment on its beauty. When I was trying to find out about the inheritance of personal property, I naturally asked everyone the same question: who would inherit upon death their *tsera* (native shell currency), their *kepkep* (tortoise-shell breast ornament), and other small personal possessions. My informants apparently compared notes, for after a while one man wanted to know why I asked everyone the same question. Did I not know, he asked, that there was only one custom of inheritance? His question came at the end of a long day's work and I was too tired to explain the concept of a sample. I contented myself (and presumably him) with saying that asking the same question of many persons was one of the strange customs of my people, thinking to myself of social scientists. On the other hand, it was I who thought it a strange custom when an old man told me while I was doing his genealogy that he had strangled his father and mother when both of them were old, ill, and wanting to die. I looked at the man's kindly face and wondered how he could have done it. I realized in a few minutes that his attitude might be called realistic and mine sentimental, and I did not like the latter label.

Sometimes a crisis brought out a latent conflict between the roles of being in and being out of the society. My good friend Pulong was ill and no one knew whether she would live or die. In the early morning, before daybreak, she gave birth prematurely to her baby, born dead, and her own life appeared to be in danger. All day women of her clan were in her mother's house (where she had gone when the birth pains had started), giving her native medicine, performing magic to cure, and tending her. Ongus, her husband, sat on a log outside the house. (Because the illness was connected with childbirth, he could not go into the house.) He sat, with his back to the house, his shoulders bowed – a lonely, tragic figure. His large, beautifully proportioned body and its attitude of tragedy made me think of a Rodin statue and of one of Michaelangelo's figures on the ceiling of the Sistine Chapel.

Psychologically, I was not at ease. I walked in and out of the house where Pulong lay, but I could do nothing. Obviously I knew too little of medicine to administer anything from my kit. Pulong was my best friend among the women and a very good informant; personal sorrow was mingled with fear of scientific loss. My sense of helplessness was difficult to take. Inanely I remarked to Ongus that I hoped Pulong would be better soon; he replied gravely that he did not know. Even before he answered, I knew my remark was silly. I sat around the bed with the women, went back to my house, wrote up everything, wandered back to Pulong's bed again. The fact that I was getting good data did not take away my restlessness. I felt all wrong during this crisis: outside it, though emotionally involved.

Living in a culture not my own suddenly seemed unnatural. It was as if the group had withdrawn into itself, and I was left outside. Pulong recovered; the normal daily life was resumed and I lost this feeling. But during Pulong's illness and in similar emergencies, I knew that no matter how intimate and friendly I was with the natives, I was never truly a part of their lives.

Another crisis occurred when I was in Logagon for *Malanggan* rites. On the afternoon of the second day there, my Lesu friends, a large number of whom were at Logagon, were extremely cool to me; they were polite, but the easy friendliness had disappeared. I was puzzled and concerned. I tried to think of something I might have done to offend them, but could recall nothing. Then the rites began and, as usual, I took notes; but I worried about what had caused the strange unfriendliness.

That night, Kuserek told me the reason. The Lesu people felt that I had betrayed their confidence by reporting a case of sickness to a government medical patrol.

Earlier that day, two Lesu men, arriving for the rites, had stopped at my house to chat. Giving me news from Lesu, they mentioned that Mimis, a young girl, had been afflicted with the "big sickness." An epidemic causing the death or paralysis of natives had begun to sweep the island. The people called it the "big sickness."[1] Seven people had died of it in a village six miles from Lesu. Before I left for Logagon there were no cases in Lesu. Naturally, I was worried about its spread to Lesu. While I wondered what to do, a medical patrol from Kavieng drove down the road in a lorry. I dashed out of the house, yelling at them to stop. Finally they heard me and I told them about the sick girl in Lesu. They said they were going all the way to the southern end of the island, and would stop in Lesu on their way back and take the girl to the Kavieng hospital, if she were still alive. I walked back to the house, relieved that I had been able to report the sick girl to a medical patrol.

But my Lesu friends had a very different impression of this incident, which they had witnessed. For them, the Kavieng hospital was only a place in which death occurred, and if they were going to die, they preferred to do so in their own home. (Ill people were so far advanced in their sickness when they entered the hospital that they usually did die there.) By reporting the sick girl to the patrol, I was sending her to die in Kavieng, far from relatives.

Stunned by this version of the affair, I immediately went over to where a group of Lesu men, many of them trusted friends and informants, were sitting, and began to explain. They listened politely, said nothing, and turned the conversation to a different topic. Feeling helpless, I decided to let the matter drop for a few days. Everyone was busy with the rites, and I went about taking notes, wondering when I should try to reopen the subject. Then one evening when I was with Ongus and a few people whom I thought had trusted me, I began again. I gave the facts simply and clearly: the horrors of the "big sickness" and the seven deaths in a nearby village, all of which they knew. I said that I was concerned that the people of Lesu did not die in the same manner; that I did not know whether Mimis would live or die in the Kavieng hospital, but her absence from the village would at least prevent other Lesu people from catching the "big sickness" from her. I explained as well as I could the meaning of contagion. All this I repeated several times. The men listened and apparently understood the general point. The former friendliness returned.

The climax came several months later. Mimis returned from the Kavieng hospital, well, except for a slight limp. At a small feast to honor her homecoming I smiled inwardly when speeches were made stressing that I was responsible for her being alive.

An incident which might have been interpreted by outsiders to mean that the Lesu people thought I was one of them occurred when I was feeling a bit indisposed and tired, although not sick. I decided to take the day off. Kuserek dragged my cot out to the veranda and I lay on it, alternating reading with sleeping. In the late afternoon, Ongus came over and said that he was very sorry to hear of my illness and my approaching death. Startled, I hastily told him that I was not going to die. But he insisted the end was near. The cry of a certain bird, believed to be an omen of death, had been heard in the village, and the meaning was evident. Ongus then assured me that I did not have to worry. Since my own relatives were far away, "my" clan would take the responsibility for providing the proper mortuary rites. I got up immediately and walked about the village so that everyone could see that I was decidedly alive, and not begin preparation for my mortuary ritual. The attitudes of Ongus and of "my" clan did not mean that they regarded me as one of them, but rather that to them it was unthinkable for any human being not to have the proper rites after death. My new friends liked me, knew that my real relatives were far away, and therefore planned to do the "honors."

It never occurred to me or to the Melanesians that I was going "native." Understanding between people is, usually, a two-way process. I had told my Melanesian friends something about my family and explained my customs as those of my society; and they knew the function of my living in Lesu – to understand their society. Beyond our differences in culture, they seemed to perceive and understand me as a human being in much the same way that I perceived them as human beings. Preliterate people are usually able to size up an anthropologist as a person, understand his role, and become his friends if they like him, though his skin is of a different color and he comes from a strange culture. Likewise, they quickly spot the phoniness of an anthropologist who thinks or pretends that he is really one of them.

Long after I left Lesu, I was told about a couple – both anthropologists – who had worked among an Indian tribe in South America. The wife decided she wanted to "go native" and left her husband for a short time to live with an Indian family. She slept in their house, dressed as they did, ate the same food, and, in general, tried to live the native life. At the end of an agreed-upon period, her husband and his colleague called for her. As she climbed into their truck with a sigh of relief, her Indian host winked broadly at her husband. He and his family had been humoring her play-acting.

[...]

XVIII White Society

My life was not segregated, but it was compartmentalized into Negro and white spheres. Living in a white boarding house gave me a base in the white community. My fellow boarders and I ate three meals a day together, and in addition to good food, I absorbed local news and gossip and was continuously aware of the behavior and attitudes of a half-dozen white people. On the other hand, I paid the price of being unable to get away from the research.

The boarders and my landlady seemed to accept me even though they knew I broke the social title taboo. Mrs Wilson phoned occasionally, usually at meal time, since she knew I was apt to be home then. The phone was in the hall and conversations could be heard anywhere on the first floor. Whoever answered the phone would call out to me, "Annie's on the phone." I knew Mrs Wilson had heard the "Annie" and I began, "Good morning, Mrs Wilson." I could feel the strained

silence at the table in the next room. Our phone conversations were brief, making an appointment or changing the time for one. My fellow boarders had all told me that "Annie knew her place" and this belief probably kept them from being more disturbed by my calling her "Mrs."

Knowledge of the white people I obtained in different ways: systematic interviewing, considerable informal participation, and an attitude questionnaire administered toward the end of the study. My original plan had called for studying only the behavior and attitudes of white people in their relations with Negroes. But I soon realized that it was not possible to understand these relations without knowing more about the class system and the traditions and history of white society. It never occurred to me not to expand the study, within the limits of the available time.

Planters were systematically interviewed. The sample included those with "mean" and "good" reputations, solvent and insolvent; many were owners of the plantations on which I had interviewed sharecroppers and renters. Interviews with the planters were almost always by appointment; I did not write during them, but always immediately afterwards, as was my custom with Negroes. The frankness of the "mean" planters surprised me. One opened his books and, boastingly, showed how he cheated his sharecroppers. He admired his own cleverness, and was apparently so much a part of his social milieu that he was unaware of, or unconcerned about, other values. However, other planters rationalized their behavior with the commonly-held belief that a "nigger" had to be kept in debt or on a subsistence level in order to get him to work. Whatever the planter said, I maintained the "poker face" of an interviewer, and expressed only interest which was real, and an assumed naïveté.

Before coming south I had known that Negroes had no political or legal rights. But the total absence of economic rights was a minor shock. I had not before known of such a society. Tribal societies had their well-defined rules and customs of reciprocity. The Middle Ages, of which the South reminded me in some ways, had an established system of duties and responsibilities between lords and serfs. But the rules on which the sharecropping system was based were broken more often than followed.

Much of my data and understanding of the white people came from a seemingly casual social participation with the middle-aged and older people in Indianola. I did not participate in the parties of young unmarried people, because I could not take the heavy consumption of corn liquor, and going to them would also have necessitated a boy-friend, which, as already indicated, would have been disastrous to working with Negroes.

I was invited to white people's homes, and used the occasions to direct the conversation along the lines of my sociological interests. Sometimes useful information came up spontaneously. Each social visit or any encounter giving data was written up as soon as I was back in my room. Women invited me to afternoon bridge parties; since I did not know how to play bridge, I dropped in on a party now and then for sociability in the late afternoon when refreshments were being served. More rewarding for data were an afternoon visit or lunch with a woman alone, and dinner or supper with a family. When I dined at a white person's home, I usually knew the servant who waited on the table. We exchanged only a quick knowing look. I may have interviewed her, had refreshments in her home, or been with her on some other social occasion. I could trust her and she could trust me not to reveal our relationship. I was often amazed at the freedom with which my white host and hostess talked in front of their Negro servant. It was as if she did not really exist. The Negroes' awareness of the realities of white society was no accident.

White people talked freely about themselves, including their feelings and attitudes towards Negroes. Revealing also were their frank opinions about white neighbors and friends. Planters were described as "mean" or "good" to their sharecroppers; these evaluations usually agreed with those given by Negroes. The "mean," as well as the "good," planter might be an elder in the church, and this situation was regarded as normal. My host and hostess did not seem to notice, or did not care, that I said little and never expressed an opinion. They were pleased – and, perhaps, flattered – that I was genuinely interested in what they had to say.

Conversation about family background was always a source of data. Almost everyone boasted about having an ancestor who had been a Colonel in the Confederate Army, and tried to give an impression of being descended from men who had big plantations with a large number of slaves. Common sense told me that the Confederate Army must have had more privates than Colonels; reading had informed me that in the whole pre-Civil War South, not more than 25 per cent of the people had owned any slaves and the majority of these had owned but one or two. Only about 6 per cent had as many as twenty slaves. Since Mississippi was settled late, the percentages were probably even smaller in that state.

The pretenses to an aristocratic background, which could also be called fantasies or lies, were significant data on cultural values in the community. Lies frequently reveal much about the values of a society, even when the fieldworker can not check on them. The situation in Mississippi, in which it happened to be possible to distinguish between the equally important lie and fact disclosed two related points: the absence of a middle-class tradition, and the white people's burden in carrying a tradition that did not belong to them.

Having perceived these points in listening to fantasies about family background, I gained evidence of them in other places. For instance, the whites talked condescendingly about a planter from Ohio who was openly a middle-class farmer and without pretense to a higher social background. His late father, he said, had been a dirt farmer in Ohio. When I interviewed this midwestern immigrant to Mississippi, he was in overalls, doing manual work. This was completely atypical for a white planter. The man from Ohio owned one of the few solvent plantations in the county; he had a good reputation among the Negroes and his sharecroppers were busy all year long, rather than only during the short planting and picking seasons. He planted other crops besides cotton, and had an extensive and profitable peach orchard. As I had a cup of coffee with him and his wife at the end of the interview, he mentioned that he had little in common with his fellow planters and his wife said she had almost no contact with their wives.

White women as well as men thought all manual work beneath them. Some who were hard up during the depression and were even on Federal relief employed a Negro laundress. The traditional American middle-class tradition of the virtue of hard work and its function in "getting ahead" was absent from this Mississippi community in the mid-thirties. However, it was not beneath a white woman's dignity to run her household and be a skilled cook. Women of the pre-Civil War aristocracy had run large plantations and taught house slaves their skills. The Negroes' term "strainers," for most middle-class whites, was sociologically apt. While it is not difficult to understand why people want to pretend to a background to which culture gives a higher prestige than their own, it is almost axiomatic that this situation produces anxieties, as in cases of Jews denying their backgrounds, Negroes passing for whites, and so forth.

Conversation and behavior revealed that the white people in this middle-class community also had a heavy burden of anxiety or guilt, or both, in reference to the Negroes. No household was without its gun. The whites seemed to live in fear of the tables being turned. I was advised to carry a gun in my car as I drove alone at night "across the tracks." When I laughingly mentioned my total ignorance of firearms and said that I was more afraid of them than of people, I was considered courageous. Some women, particularly those who took their religion seriously, expressed in hesitant manner the contradictions they felt between their Christian beliefs and the accepted code of behavior towards Negroes. Their obvious guilt was, I think, somewhat allayed by my not being interested in assessing blame. I can think of no worse technique for getting data than making an informant feel guilty.

[...]

As I mingled with the white people, with values so different from my own, I was surprised at my tolerance and, even more, at my liking some individuals. I remembered that when I was working in the labor movement, I thought that anyone who did not believe in trade unions as the hope of society was beyond the pale of my liking or even socially recognizing. In Mississippi, I wondered if I would have been different from the other whites, if I had been born in this community and had never left it. I had learned through breaking the taboo on social titles for Negroes how difficult it was to go beyond the group uniformity and consensus. As I tried to understand the historical and social situation which had produced these white people, I occasionally wondered about my new self; anthropology had become part of my personality. But my values remained as strong as ever and the effort to understand people with an opposing code did not mean that I condoned it.

Instead, I felt compassionate. The whites seemed to be worse off psychologically in many ways than the Negroes, and I sometimes felt that if, Heaven forbid, I had to live in Mississippi, I would prefer to be a Negro. The oppressed group were sure God was on their side and sure of their eventual victory, and had a sense of satisfaction in successfully disguising their real attitudes and fooling the whites. Many of the dominant group felt either guilt or hypocrisy, or both, and fear. The initial resistance of the leading white citizens in Indianola to my study clearly indicated fear of what I might find out, and was in sharp contrast to the attitudes of Negroes who wanted me to learn the truth. Then, too, the area for reality thinking was larger among the Negroes than for the whites. The former knew well their own group and the whites, both of whom they regarded as ordinary human beings – good and bad. The white man's knowledge of Negroes was limited to opposing stereotypes: a child-like person always enjoying life or a potentially dangerous sub-human type.

However, my compassionate attitude towards whites was severely jolted late one afternoon when I ran into a crowd of about twenty-five rough-looking white men with dogs on a country road. They separated to let me drive by. I stopped for a couple of minutes and found out what I had immediately suspected. They were out to "get a nigger" who, they said, had raped a white woman in a neighboring county. He was supposed to have fled into Sunflower County. Shaken, I drove on. I knew the Negro would be lynched if caught. The would-be lynchers belonged to the poor-white group so easily distinguishable by their clothes and their red-tanned necks. Their faces, now transformed with brutality and hate, were frightening.

I could make only a pretense at eating supper when I returned to the boarding house. My fellow boarders had heard of the alleged crime, and were unconcerned about the possibility of lynching. It was too bad, they said, but after all, it was in the next county, and Negroes had to be taught a lesson once in a while, otherwise no white woman would be safe. That night I could not sleep. I felt I had to do something to prevent a possible lynching. I saw myself as a kind of Joan of Arc on a white horse. But what could I do? I knew that an appeal to police or other authorities was useless. The Negro and the white men hunting him lived in a county where I knew no one. By morning I had not thought of anything I could do to help the Negro. At breakfast I saw the local paper with a headlined story about the "sex crime."

But at least I could function as an anthropologist. The Negroes in Indianola stayed indoors and there was no need to study their attitudes. But I could study the middle-class whites who would not have participated in a lynching, although they condoned it. During the next couple of days I walked around the white section of town, sat in drug stores drinking Cokes with men and women, visited people I knew, listening all the time to what they had to say about the impending lynching. The story was almost always the same: no one believed in lynching, but what could one do with these "sex-crazed niggers." Only one person – a woman – wondered if the Negro was really guilty. She was a deeply religious middle-aged housewife whose family background was a bit higher in terms of education and wealth than the norm in Indianola.

The Negro man escaped to another state, and was not caught. The excitement died down. Whispers and rumors circulated that he had committed no crime, but had attempted to get back some money owed him by a white man, who happened at the time to be accompanied by a girl friend. The story of the Negro's attempted rape of her had been spread by this man.

I felt I had won my spurs as a fieldworker. I had interviewed, observed, and gotten data in a situation which had deeply disturbed me.

[...]

The constant participation and observation among Negroes and whites had its costs, too. Occasionally I wondered who I was, as I passed back and forth between the two groups. When I inadvertently "passed" for Negro, I would return to the boarding house and look in the mirror, wondering if the color of my skin had changed. There was always some tension in the situation for me. I never was sure that something terrible, or at least disastrous for my fieldwork, might not happen as Mr Smith had predicted. But I evidently managed fairly well; I do not remember having any even minor illness when I was in Mississippi.

[...]

Occasionally in Indianola, I was tired and depressed and wondered why I had come there. I remember one hot August night when the damp heat seemed to close in on me. It was more oppressive than the nights in Lesu, where cool sea breezes filtered through the thatched roof. I lay bathed in perspiration, although hardly making any movement. I asked myself, "Why do I have to suffer this heat?" The next day as I was getting some interesting data, I had the answer: I enjoyed fieldwork more than any other. It was a form of experiencing life, of stepping beyond the boundaries of my background and society and of making the latter more intelligible.

In the discussion of the Mississippi fieldwork, I have occasionally touched on some of the differences and similarities with the Lesu experience, in terms of method and techniques. Here, I would like to emphasize a few major points. The culture of Lesu was sufficiently strange and esoteric for me to be really outside of my society. Although the standards of living in Lesu were decidedly lower than in Mississippi, neither Melanesians nor I regarded this or any other aspect of their social organization as social problems – in the colloquial sense of presenting situations for which change was desirable. (Today, after the long contact with Japanese and Americans, as well as Australians, the situation might be quite different.) In Mississippi, it was impossible to escape the inherent social problems. Inevitably, I viewed the mores, behavior, and attitudes of Negroes and whites from the background of the larger American culture in which I had been reared and in terms of my personal values. Yet, I did manage to acquire a considerable social distance from the Mississippi community. Seeing it in historical perspective and as a kind of anachronism was helpful. The previous experience of being involved and detached in Lesu was invaluable. Finally, my identification with both racial groups and with the different classes in each gave me a measure of objectivity.

Of necessity, my roles in the biracial situation and power structure of the deep South were more complex than in Lesu. In the latter place, I occasionally was naïve; in Mississippi, I had sometimes to pretend to a naïveté. In Lesu, I had no anxiety about unknown dangers (once I got over my initial panic). As far as was necessary, I followed the Melanesian taboos, and when I broke them, such as going to a men's ritual feast, it was done at their invitation, with their help and with the approval of the community. In Mississippi, I had to break some taboos of the white power structure openly, and some secretly, never knowing what might happen in either case. "Carrying" two groups mutually hostile and fearful was far more difficult than

the clear-cut role in Lesu. My involvement in the two situations was quite different. No matter how high the level of my empathy with the people of Lesu, I never wondered if I was a Melanesian or a Caucasian, a member of the stone-age society or of my own. As already mentioned, in Mississippi, there were times, when passing back and forth between the two groups, being identified with each and occasionally mistaken for a Negro, that I wondered what group I really belonged to. Psychologically, I did belong to both, which in some cultures other than Mississippi would create no problems.

For all the differences between Lesu and Mississippi, many similarities existed. I was not only accepted in each place, but my presence and the study eventually taken for granted. In both the culture seeped into my bones, as I went over and over again to Melanesian feasts and to Mississippi churches, participated in the daily lives of Melanesians and Negroes, interviewed many people, and became close friends with a few.

NOTE

1 Unfortunately, I neglected to get its technical name and in my notes used the pidgin English, "big sickness." It seemed similar to polio.

5

Fixing and Negotiating Identities in the Field: The Case of Lebanese Shiites

Roschanack Shaery-Eisenlohr

Political Identities and Identity Designations: A Project in Motion

The larger study for which this research was conducted[1] explored the variety of ways that dominant Lebanese Shiite political parties and groups have constructed their national and political identities and positioned themselves in terms of the Lebanese nation, all within the context of the varying relationships of these groups with Iran since the 1970s. As a Western-educated secular Shiite woman of Iranian parentage, I quickly discovered that during thirteen months of field research in Beirut Lebanon, exploring the larger issue of Lebanese male politico-religious and national identity involved taking account of how my inter-locutors' identities, and their perceptions of what seemed to them to be my identities, interacted with my own definitions and presentations of these. In the process of

conducting this research, I began to realize that how differently politically situated interlocutors made sense of me and my background revealed much information relevant to my research. First, a male Lebanese Shiite interlocutor's positioning of my identity – politically, ideo-logically, religiously, and according to gender – suggested ways that Lebanese Shiites of various political shadings conceptualized their own politico-religious and national belonging. Second, by positioning me in various ways in terms of past and present Iranian politics, Lebanese Shiite interlocutors often quite clearly indicated how they defined their own relations with Iran in both political and cultural terms.

This chapter, which focuses on the research dynamics that grew out of the interactions between self-defined and ascribed identities, will illustrate that what could have been per-ceived as a stumbling block to the successful unfolding of an interview, in fact disclosed much about "transnationalism, Shi'ism, and the Lebanese State. Of course, such knowledge

Roschanack Shaery-Eisenlohr, "Fixing and Negotiating Identities in the Field: The Case of Lebanese Shiites," pp. 31–46 from *Women Fielding Danger: Negotiating Ethnographic Identities in Field Research*, ed. Martha K. Huggins and Marie-Louise Glebbeek. Lanham: Rowman & Littlefield, 2009.

Ethnographic Fieldwork: An Anthropological Reader, Second Edition. Edited by Antonius C. G. M. Robben and Jeffrey A. Sluka.
Editorial material and organization © 2012 John Wiley & Sons, Inc.
Published 2012 by John Wiley & Sons, Inc.

was not always obtained in the manner that I initially expected. I was not quite prepared for much that happened during an interview, particularly having an interlocutor's *assumptions* about my identity and the political allegiances they saw as associated with that assumed identity intrude into the research process. Especially at the beginning of my research, my impression management – which, according to Erving Goffman, inescapably shapes interpersonal interaction in both research as well as everyday life[2] – was informed by worries that certain identity subtexts were negatively shaping and complicating my conversations and interviews with male Lebanese interlocutors.

Undaunted, I began my research on the roles of national and transnational contexts in shaping Lebanese Shiite identity constructions with the objective of describing Lebanon's politico-religious terrain, especially in its relationship to modern Iranian politics. This meant understanding Lebanon's two important Shiite movements-turned-political parties and their relationships to the Iranian state. Each of these politico-religious groups – AMAL and Hezbollah – has a markedly different relationship to Islam and to Iranian politics, with implications for how they position themselves in Lebanon – politically, religiously, and socially.

This chapter, which focuses on identity building and dynamics in the interview phase of my research, is divided into six parts and a conclusion. The first part introduces the main Shiite actors in Lebanon's political landscape; their ideas and politico-religious beliefs became part of our interview identity dynamics. In the second and third sections, I lay out my own biography and its impact on locating interlocutors. The chapter's next three parts describe the dynamics of interviewing and negotiating self-defined and ascribed identities. In the conclusion, I explore the outcomes of shifting identities within my Lebanese research setting.

The Political Parties

The Afwaj al-Muqawama al-Lubnaniyya (AMAL) political party, currently led by the speaker of the Lebanese parliament Nabih Berri, was organized in 1974 by Musa Sadr, the Iranian-born Lebanese Shiite leader. Founded just one year before the 1975 Lebanese civil war, AMAL was the first Lebanese Shiite militia organization. After the success of the Iranian revolution in Iran, AMAL members rejected Ayatollah Khomeini's concept of the jurisprudential model of political rule (*wilayat al-faqih*); Khomeini's objective was to establish an Iranian-based hegemony over Shiites the world over. In 1982, Lebanon's AMAL Party broke off relations with the Iranian government, with this policy holding until the mid-1990s and resuming officially after the election of Iranian president Muhammad Khatami in 1997. The new president wanted state-to-state relations between Iran and Lebanon, and improved relations with all religious groups in Lebanon.

The second Lebanese Shiite political party, Hezbollah, established in 1982, emerged out of groups disaffected with AMAL politics. Those who formed Hezbollah favored the Shiite Islamist politics of postrevolutionary Iran; their political position to confront the occupying Israeli army by military means was particularly enhanced after the 1982 Israeli invasion of Lebanon. Through ideological and financial support from the Iranian ruling religious elite, Hezbollah is currently competing with AMAL over leadership of Lebanon's Shiite community. Hezbollah maintains close ties with Iran's religious elite, which the Western media often refers to as the Iranian government's conservative wing. Hezbollah and the religious elite in Iran place major importance on the Palestinian cause, defining themselves as staunch supporters of the Palestinians, especially those affiliated with Hamas, the Palestinian Islamist party. Lebanon's Hezbollah considers itself as "the guardian of authentic Shi'ism," excluding the AMAL party just the same from its "circle of Islamists." AMAL, often dubbed by Western media as a "secular" Shiite party, is religious in its outlook but imagines its politics as more moderate and thus fitting more into the realities of multisectarian Lebanon. AMAL does not maintain close ties to the religious elite in Iran.

Another set of important Lebanese actors, although not a political party, is the Lebanese Shiite followers of Sayyid Muhammad Husayn Fadlallah (b. 1936), a Lebanese Shiite religious scholar who considers himself a "source of emulation" (*mut'a*) for Shiite Muslims the world over. Fadlallah was widely considered the spiritual leader of Hezbollah until relations between Sayyid Fadlallah and the Iranian ruling elite darkened in 1995 as a result of power struggles over Fadlallah's claim that he ranked among the Islamic world's supreme Shiite leaders (*mut'a*). Such a claim placed Fadlallah in direct conflict with Iran's ruling religious elite.

Situating Researcher's Biography

Because my own background played a major role in the research process, it requires further explanation. Born in Germany into an Iranian family, I lived in Germany until I was three years old. In 1974 my family moved back to Iran, a few years before the 1978 Iranian revolution. Our family again returned to Germany in 1986, in the middle of the Iran-Iraq War. After receiving my master's degree in Germany, where I am a citizen, and marrying a German national, I left Germany in 1995 with my husband for the United States. There I began graduate studies in Near Eastern languages and civilizations at the University of Chicago. During the twelve years that I have lived in the United States, I have traveled to Lebanon for research, maintaining the United States as my residence.

I grew up in an upper-middle-class Iranian family, where Shiite religiosity played a minor role. Shiite practice was characteristic of my father's family, while being largely absent among relatives on my mother's side. Having spent most of my life outside of Iran, I define myself as a diasporic Iranian, an Iranian living outside of Iran who nonetheless feels a deep commitment toward Iran and maintains ties to that country. I acknowledge that the years spent in Germany and the United States have shaped my identity such that it would be difficult to call myself "an Iranian" without further explaining the ways in which I see myself as Iranian. The importance of this for my fieldwork is that, during my research in Lebanon, my hyphenated Iranian background seemed often unacceptable to my Lebanese interlocutors.

Locating Interlocutors

My research included both ethnographic work – participant observation and semistructured interviews – and archival research. This chapter focuses on the ethnographic dimensions of my research in Beirut, Lebanon, during the period from April 2002 to May 2003.

I conducted more than fifty interviews with various Lebanese and Iranian Shiite ethnic leaders in Lebanon and took part in Shiite rituals and visited Shiite-run schools. The research objectives of this fieldwork were twofold: to study the tensions between official political representations of Shiite identity production and Iran's role in such productions and to document the "unofficial" everyday ways that Shiites position themselves within the Lebanese national context and vis-à-vis the Iranian government.

My interviewees in Lebanon were primarily men above forty, many of whom had been in the Lebanese AMAL and Hezbollah militia during Lebanon's 1975–1990 civil war and who had not only participated in combat against other Lebanese sectarian groups but also against other Lebanese Shiite groups. In particular, Hezbollah and AMAL had fought intensely for two years, from 1988 to 1990, over leadership of the Lebanese Shiite community and over Iran's role in Lebanon and in the Lebanese Shiite community. Many of my interlocutors had done battle for access to and control of Lebanese state institutions.

My principal research associate during fieldwork was a Lebanese Shiite woman who had spent three years in Iran and also spoke Persian fluently. Her father, among the first group of Shiites to leave Lebanon for Iran after the 1979 revolution, was well connected politically in Lebanon. Furthermore, my research associate's husband – also well connected politically – was a high-ranking member of Lebanon's AMAL political party. Due to the important political background of my research associate's father and husband, and because of her own activities in the AMAL movement, my research partner was invaluable to the success of my project. I expected that her connections to a wide range of Shiite personalities in Lebanon would result in a steady stream of interviewees, and I was not disappointed.

Unsurprisingly, the research questions that I hoped to pursue with interlocutors – such as transnational relations between Iranians and Lebanese – was a sensitive topic to many Shiites. As in the United States, transnational connections between Iranians and Lebanese are generally designated as "terrorist networks." It increased the reluctance of Lebanese Shiites to discuss Iranian Lebanese relations with me that I was affiliated with an educational institution inside the United States: Some potential interlocutors assumed that I was carrying out intelligence work. Given this background, I found the generosity and eagerness of my research associate to help me with the research absolutely striking. Asking about her enthusiasm for the research project, my research associate set aside politics and relied on our intersecting personal biographies: "I lived in Iran and I like Iranians a lot, and then [it is also because] you are Shiite. I felt close to you the first time I saw you; the questions in your research have been central to my life, I lived in the middle of it all."

Performing and Negotiating Identities

In the first few months of research in Lebanon, while my research associate and I were still primarily establishing contacts, I noticed that one interlocutor would introduce me to another one as a *Bahitha Iraniyya* – a female Iranian researcher. Such an introduction conveyed the impression that I had come to Lebanon *from Iran* to conduct research. However, before describing the research itself to a potential interviewee, I would explain my ethnic and national background: that I am of Iranian parentage and have lived in Germany and the United States, and am now affiliated with the University of Chicago. This introduction complete, I was immediately struck by how little interest prospective interlocutors showed in my "German" or "American" background and how much they focused on my "Iranianness." I recognized very early that presenting my complex and layered identities made little sense to most of my interlocutors. In the eyes of Lebanese Shiites, I was an "upper-class Iranian woman," a designation that had

emerged from two facts about my biography: I was studying in the West and I did not observe *hijab* – the latter, a cultural and religious expectation about modest dress that includes using a head scarf to cover the head and neck.

The combination of these two visible realities of my identity was interpreted by most interlocutors as a sign of my political opposition to the current Iranian regime, a position often associated with the wealthy "Iranian royalists" now living in the United States. These two assumed facts about my personal, political, and social identities influenced the dynamics of my research in major ways. Most important, I felt that what I believed to be the subtleties of my identity were back-staged and stereotyped: I was seen as "an Iranian woman," not as I saw myself, a German or American woman. If I presented myself as "a German Iranian," many interlocutors assumed that I was "ashamed" of my Iranian Muslim parentage. In the end, due to my national and cross-national background, and because of my being an unveiled Shiite woman, I could not escape being associated, at best, with Iran's reformists and, at worst, with the U.S. government – presumably one of its spies. In either case, I could count on interviews sometimes becoming overtly politicized.

For example, after interviewing several Hezbollah members, I noticed that our conversations had resembled the debates in Iran between conservative and reformist political camps. My interview questions – such as "What books do you use in your [Hezbollah] schools?" or "Why have you chosen these books and not others?" – were usually interpreted as attacks on politically and religiously conservative Iranian ideologies. Such interpretations often resulted in my interlocutors' expounding at length about what they viewed as the faults of the Iranian reformist movement associated with President Khatami. When visiting one Hezbollah-run educational institution in Beirut, I asked about the number of their schools in other parts of Lebanon; the school director responded: "Are you upset that Iran sends money to Lebanon? If Iranians like you get to power in Iran, there will be no support for other Muslims outside of Iran because your identity is not based on religion but on secular values." The school director was assuming that

I was a supporter of the reformist movement in Iran, which he labeled negatively as "holding secular values" – equating secularism with "godlessness." In the school director's mind, this favored "nationalist" ideologies that would create an obstacle for pan-Islamic mobilization.

I had to address the dynamic of distrust that was sometimes created by some of my interlocutors' assumptions about my political and social identities if an interview was to proceed. In the case of the previous interlocutor, I responded that I did not think of Iranian reformists as "secularists," explaining that I had not lived in Iran for a long time and did not associate with any political group inside or outside of Iran. Sometimes this explanation eased tensions, while other interviewees still could not imagine that I did not maintain ties to the Iranian government, considering how important Lebanese Shiites were to Iran's foreign policy. With the motives for my research in question, along with the disconnect between interlocutors' assumptions about my identity and my own self-assumed identities, I tried other strategies for getting around interlocutors' skepticism, some of which I will describe in the section "Mediating Stumbling Blocks." Yet, however, it remained a distinct challenge to interview those Hezbollah members who had strongly negative views about diasporic Iranians. Those holding such views are generally suspicious of Iranians from "the West," and particularly of a Shiite woman who does not respect *hijab*.

Yet another source of suspicion about me and my research grew out of the circumstance that Lebanese Shiites very rarely get to know Iranian nationals personally. Daily encounters with Shiite taxi drivers (*servis*) underscored this fact: When the drivers asked me where I was from, and I replied, "I am an Iranian (*iraniyya*)," many of these taxi drivers assuming that I had said, "I am an Armenian (*armaniyya*)." This confusion of identities most certainly was not solely the result of my accented Arabic; it is equally probable that Lebanese cab drivers had difficulties imagining an Iranian woman without the *hijab*, thus assuming that she must be an Armenian Christian. Because I was violating the taxi drivers' images of Iranian women's

"proper" dress, they "heard" me say, "I am an Armenian," since an Iranian woman would not be in public without a head covering. The background of this is that most Lebanese derive their knowledge about Iran and Iranians from television, mainly from the Hezbollah television station al-Manar. This station's reporting is highly selective, presenting Iran as a successful Islamic government, where all women observe full *hijab* voluntarily. Al-Manar omits the struggles and diversity in Iranian views on religion and *hijab*. In any case, a day rarely passed without someone – on a Beirut street, in a social situation, during research – commenting about my identity. Some Lebanese Shiites speculated that I was an Armenian Iranian, others thought that I was an Iranian Zoroastrian or Baha'i. An unveiled Iranian Shiite woman was a conundrum to those whose primary knowledge of Iranian Shiites, and of Iranian Shiite women, had come from one-dimensional television news and feature film portrayals.

As for research among members of Lebanon's AMAL political party, these actors portrayed their activities in Lebanon as "moderate," explaining that they are "just like" the reformist movement in Iran. AMAL interlocutors took me for an upper-class "L.A. royalist" – a large proportion of Iranians in the United States reside in the greater Los Angeles area. AMAL members interpreted my "diasporic background" as evidence that their own critical views of postrevolutionary Iranian politics – which they began to share with me after a while – had been right. Assuming that my family had left Iran after the revolution because of the disagreeable political atmosphere there meant that their party's policy toward the Iranian government and their own judgment about its faults had been right. Being critical of Iranian religious conservatives, the AMAL interlocutors felt quite comfortable criticizing Iran and expressing their frustrations about what they saw as "Iran's hegemonic attempts in Lebanon."

However, some AMAL interlocutors associated me with Iran's 1980s military involvement in Lebanon. Their frustrations with the Iranian government were couched in pointed comments targeted at me: "*You* killed many of us during the war," referring to the fighting between AMAL and Hezbollah in the final stages of the 1988–1990 Lebanese civil war. Still attempting to locate me politically, after many meetings with AMAL interlocutors, they began to ask whether I was related to any members of the Iranian liberation movement – an Iranian anti-shah opposition movement active in the 1970s that operated mainly outside of Iran. Some of this movement's activists had been based in Lebanon. These questions became a turning point in my interviews with AMAL interlocutors, who generally became more open to my questions after locating me politically in a manner that squared my identity and past with their own and with their party's political worldview.

My meetings and interviews with AMAL members helped my research immensely: I became able to glimpse beyond official party rhetoric – that AMAL and the Iranian government have reestablished good relations – and understand how AMAL members construct their differences with Iranian Shiites and create a Lebanese Shiite religious "authenticity" that is directly connected to the history of Iranian-AMAL relations. My research associate, who arranged many of these meetings and attended some of them as well, was of immense help. She participated in some interviews and would introduce, from the position of an AMAL party member herself, her impressions of Iranians. The ensuing dialogue between my associate and an interviewee often enabled me to understand the ideas and practices through which AMAL members construct a Lebanese Shiite identity and see Iran through that lens.

Being Shiite and Female

I discovered in the process of research that interlocutors had two principal reactions to what they perceived as my gendered identities. On one hand, there were those pro-Iranian ruling clerical elite Shiites for whom my gender came before all else, shaping the interview process and their responses. These interlocutors saw me as a woman first and, based on what this meant to them, had trouble recognizing me as a professional researcher and scholar.

This included primarily (but not exclusively) Hezbollah interlocutors. On the other hand, some interviewees placed my nationality and ethnicity above gender, resulting in their seeing my being in Lebanon as an opportunity for them to give voice to their frustrations about Iran's political intentions and projects in Lebanon. Many AMAL interlocutors acted along these lines.

No matter what the political stripe of a Shiite interviewee, these interlocutors had questions about my marital status. I cannot recollect one interview, whether formal or a more informal extended conversation, in which the issue of my marital status did not come up. On the one hand, while many interlocutors seemed reassured when I told them that I was married, just as many were visibly troubled by the fact that my husband – at least those who believed I actually had one – was not with me during most of my fieldwork in Lebanon. Shiite women would show two kinds of reactions toward me, both related to my most important role as wife and mother: I was asked whether I was not worried that – considering that I did not have a child at the time – my husband would leave me and marry another woman[3]; or whether my work was worth the trouble that living far away from one's spouse could cause. At the same time, some Shiite women actually compared their lives unfavorably to mine, saying how much they would have enjoyed studying or researching, if only their husbands had allowed it. They thought I was lucky to be married to a European who was supportive of what was important to me. In their view, no Lebanese husband would have allowed me to conduct research in a foreign country, mostly on my own.

That I did not have children at an age many considered "overripe," and that I was in the field alone, and that my husband was European, seemed to make it acceptable for some male interlocutors to flirt with me. For example, one male Shiite interlocutor remarked: "You have beautiful Persian eyes," in response to an interview question I had just asked him. Another interlocutor – being interviewed about Iranian politics and the Lebanese AMAL Party – responded: "We won the war against Iran in 1990, [but] I am not sure I will win against you."

Such sexualizing comments also occurred in response to my questions about an interlocutor's family background, to which one interviewee responded: "Why don't *you* have children at your age, and how come your husband allows you to come to Lebanon?"

Being childless and in the field without my European husband also increased interlocutors' suspicions about the political motives behind my research. Distrust was in their faces and expressed directly. Some of them would ask, "Who gave you this research topic?" "Who has given you these questions to ask?" "Why are you interested in this topic?" "Who is your adviser?" "Why are you doing research in Lebanon?" and "Is your husband Lebanese?" Interestingly, such interlocutors' questions – besides indicating suspicion about the ends to which my research might be put – also questioned my research competence: What kind of researcher cannot come up with a research topic, develop acceptable research questions, and have sophisticated research interests? I presumably needed a strong other – an adviser, for example – to imagine, plan, and carry out research.

In another focus on my gender over my researcher status, almost as frequently as interlocutors asked about my marital status, they questioned me about children. For example, within the first five minutes after I introduced myself and explained my research project to a prospective interlocutor, once the interviewee had gotten beyond my marital status, he would then ask if I had children – more specifically, "How many children do you have?" After saying that I had no children, this person would then question why I was *still* childless, "considering your age"; this would be followed by a question about "the number of years that you have been married." Seeing the confusion and disappointment in these interlocutors' faces and in their tone of voice, I then explained that "my studies are important to me" and that having children now could put an end to my research and to my education. I then assured interviewees that I was "planning to have children later on." Unsatisfied with this explanation, some interlocutors recommended a doctor who could help me with the "medical problems" that were causing my "childlessness."

Some would even suggest that I divorce my husband and marry a Lebanese Shiite man because, as they explained, Lebanese Shiite men were the most virile (fertile) among all Lebanese men. These interlocutors often had either themselves or a relative in mind who would guarantee my having children.

Perhaps because of interlocutors' insistent focus on aspects of my gender identity that seemed unrelated, at least in my mind, to my research project, I often felt that I was not taken seriously as a researcher. Would these questions have been so common if I had been a Shiite man? I often recognized that my interviewees, who were mainly middle-aged men, seemed amused when I interviewed them about political questions. To these interlocutors, a "young Iranian woman" asking about powerful issues that had crucially shaped their identities and were important to their political lives seemed like entertainment. Politics, I realized from these interlocutors' responses (or nonresponses), was not an acceptable domain for a young woman. In Lebanon, women have rarely held political posts, and, as politicians' wives, women mainly carry out charity activities. Within such a gendered framework, it is highly uncommon for a young Shiite woman from the Middle East to study Lebanese-Iranian politics. There is no easy category into which interlocutors can place such a woman.

Without doubt, ethnic and religious markers profoundly shaped my interactions with interlocutors. In particular, being an Iranian Shiite established many Lebanese Shiites' expectations about me as a woman, especially among Hezbollah members, whose idealized image of Iran's Islamic Republic led them to conceive all Iranians as practicing Muslims. By necessity, Muslims had an obligation to be a moral and religious example to Shiites around the world. Accordingly, therefore, my appearance as an Iranian woman without the *hijab* raised serious questions. Among some Hezbollah my failure to wear *hijab* dominated interviews and led to discussions about my political sympathies regarding Iran – which they assumed were with the religious reformists there.

Even Lebanese Shiites not associated with Hezbollah were surprised that a woman with an Iranian background did not wear *hijab*, had a secular outlook, and was married to a European. However, at the same time, one aspect of my image was clear: An Iranian Shiite by background, I could not be correctly classified as a foreigner, yet at the same time I did not fit stereotyped expectations for a Shiite woman. I continued to ask myself throughout the field research whether this was an asset or an obstacle: Did it help or hinder my research that I was an "outsider"? The answer to this question certainly had implications for my research. Surely, my cultural knowledge of Shiism, which made many interviewees view me as an "insider," was an asset, since it triggered discussions about how certain Shiite rituals are performed in Lebanon and how they differ in Iran. These conversations were part of most of my informal meetings with Lebanese Shiites, and, while not "officially" about the topic of my research, such discussions helped establish rapport with interlocutors, but also enabled me to learn more about the role of everyday practices in marking the differences between Lebanese and Iranian Shiites.

By engaging in informal conversations that revealed my cultural knowledge of Shiism, I began to discover issues directly related to the subject of my research. Although my research was not initially about gender and its relationship to constructions of nationalism, I was pleasantly surprised that my being an Iranian woman triggered discussions about the differences between Iranian and Lebanese Shiite women. Most of the Lebanese male interlocutors explained that Iranian women were "dominant and aggressive" and Iranian men "submissive" to their wives. The interlocutors usually then added that, in contrast, Lebanese women are feminine – "more feminine" than Iranian women.

It also complicated my research that interlocutors wanted to be sure that I write "positively" about Shiism and Lebanese Shiites. Their message, whether direct or indirect, was that, as a Shiite woman, it was my obligation to stand by my community and defend it against hostile Western stereotyping. They would advise me at length about subjects they thought important for me to include in my dissertation. As a woman culturally familiar with the politeness codes, I sat silently and listened to interlocutors' expositions. I knew that any

overt move to return to what I judged to be my research interests would likely have been considered rude and evidence of a lack of respect for their concerns and for "my religious community." In a few cases, I interrupted an interlocutor as politely as I could to ask for more details or moved too quickly to the next question. Interlocutors' reactions to this were mixed. Some insisted that what they were telling me was more important than the questions I wanted to ask. Others answered the next question that I asked and then quickly returned to what they had been saying before the interruption. In those cases where I listened silently throughout an interview, I felt ill at ease: Some interlocutors gave me the impression that, as they saw it, I knew nothing about Lebanese Shiite politics, especially as a woman, and was in need of an education and lengthy lectures. In fact, what they shared with me is common knowledge among scholars of Shiism and of Lebanese Shiites. At the same time, sitting silently as an interlocutor answered a series of questions made me wonder if the interlocutor thought that I agreed with his political opinions and ideologies. Often I did not, but in only a few cases did I voice my opinion.

Especially after interviews with Hezbollah interlocutors, I was conflicted about whether I had conducted a successful interview. I had made a decision at the beginning of my research to cover my hair out of respect for religious figures or when going to Hezbollah or AMAL institutions. I decided not to cover my head when conducting interviews outside the setting of such institutions, except in encounters with religious dignitaries. Yet I could not help but wonder, had I worn the *hijab* for the sake of an interview, would the interview have been more productive? The fact that interviews with Hezbollah members usually became polemical – a fact in part influenced by these interlocutors' interpretation of my politics as contrary to theirs, and in part due to my being a Muslim woman without *hijab* – made me continually question my not having covered my head for research. I was also troubled by doubts about whether it had been a waste of time for me to discuss and try to rectify with Hezbollah interlocutors the erroneous images that they had about my politics. I must admit that before every interview – and up to the end of my research – such questions continued to dog me.

Mediating Stumbling Blocks

In the process of conducting research, one of my best strategies seemed to be to establish a joking relationship with interviewees. This seemed to neutralize somewhat a research terrain that could easily become a minefield due to the assumed and real politics between Iran and Lebanon, and between Iranian and Lebanese Shiites, and as a result of Lebanese Shiite perceptions of me as a woman, of my politics relative to theirs, of my religious identifications, and of my politics in relation to Iran's Islamic Republic. For example, when interlocutors explicitly associated me negatively with the Iranian reformist movement or with the exiled Iranian "royalists," I would jokingly say that I planned to become the next president in Iran and would make sure to keep their politico-religious interests in mind if they helped me with my project. Sometimes jokes helped to create the desired impression that I was interested in collecting material for my dissertation and without any political project of my own.

However, humor was not always positive in an interview. In one case, an interviewee turned a serious question of mine into a joke, which threatened to derail the interview. I was interested in the debates about temporary marriage (*muta'*) in Lebanon, a permissible practice according to Shiite jurisprudence. I wanted to know whether this practice had changed since the Iranian revolution. When I brought up this subject, interlocutors had two reactions: One was for interlocutors to respond to questions about "temporary marriage" as if my question reflected a desire on my part: "Why are you interested in this topic? Are you interested in such an arrangement?" Although these interlocutors presented their response as a joke, their response in fact created an uncomfortable atmosphere that needed to be reoriented. I often found it impossible to reorient the discussion after such a "humorous" frame break by a male interlocutor. A situation had been created with the capacity to shut down any real discussion about temporary

marriage and potentially even produce an embarrassing break in the interview itself. In another set of reactions to my questions about "temporary marriage," some interlocutors saw my questions as patently unacceptable: "You should not write about this since it gives a bad impression of Shiites." Such interlocutors refused to respond to questions about "temporary marriage."

Most commonly, the religious and ethnic markers of my identity created tensions during research, with interlocutors often slipping between being too familiar, based on their readings of my questionable "insider" female status – "You have beautiful Persian eyes" – or too distant, based on their designations of my somewhat-more-questionable "outsider" status – "Why do you sit like a European woman?" or "Why are you so aggressive?" Both sets of interlocutor responses were more likely to occur after questions asked "too directly" or when I "pushed" an interlocutor "too hard" about something that he seemed to want to avoid answering. For example, once when I tried to edge a particular interlocutor toward a specific topic that he did not consider relevant or was simply unwilling to talk about, my behavior was labeled "pushy and aggressive." In such cases, the sense of solidarity that was based on shared religion suddenly disappeared, and I became "like a European." My interlocutors often considered me "one of them" if I agreed to let them direct the topics and steer our conversation without interrupting.

I came to see that the borders were quite fluid between what an interlocutor was willing or not willing to reveal. In one case, I was struck by how generously one person shared details about topics that he considered secret, while another time, that same person would behave suspiciously and distance himself from a question dealing with things that were already well known. For example, one Hezbollah interlocutor denied that Iran had played any role in the creation of the Hezbollah Party, even though Iran's involvement in the founding of Hezbollah is well known. Then, to my surprise, during a subsequent interview this interlocutor spoke very freely and critically about the Iranian government and offered his negative impressions of Iran.

Conclusion

At the beginning of my research I was sometimes disappointed that interlocutors had, as I then felt, disclosed relatively little about Iranian-Lebanese Shiite relations. As interviews progressed, I began to realize that the ways my own background was interpreted by an interlocutor enabled me to learn much about the two central and interrelated objectives of my larger research project. First, the positioning of my identity and nationally, politically, ideologically, and religiously by Lebanese Shiite interlocutors, helped me understand how various Lebanese Shiite groups conceptualized their own politico-religious and national identities. For example, Hezbollah's association with Iran's religious ruling elite and Hezbollah assumptions that Iranian reformists were secular and as such were undermining politico-religious Shia traditions and political objectives, showed how Hezbollah constructs religious authenticity and differentiates out its political opponents. For them, as a woman, I had a particular duty to give an exemplary moral image of the nation I was seen to represent. For Hezbollah associates, this was inseparable from the wearing of proper *hijab*, while for AMAL supporters my lack of *hijab* was read as a distancing from the ruling circles of the Islamic Republic, and therefore a sign of moral superiority in itself.

Second, by positioning me in terms of past and present Iranian politics, each set of actors (e.g., Hezbollah and AMAL) among the Lebanese Shiite interlocutors expressed how they imagined the dynamics of such transnational networks with Iran. For example, many Lebanese Shiites asked me about my views on the Iranian revolution, on Iranian president Muhammad Khatami, and how I defined my own identity as an Iranian. With respect to the latter question, when I responded that my many years in Germany, and later in the United States, had shaped my sense of "national belonging" and my politics, I was sometimes interrupted with, "Why are you ashamed of being a Shiite and an Iranian?" I tried to explain that seeing myself as a secular Shiite woman with ties to several countries did not mean that I was ashamed of either the

Iranian or the Shiite side of myself. Linking my apparent neglect of religious identity to the idea that I was ashamed of it was directly related to these Lebanese Shiite interlocutors' experience in Lebanon, where Shiites are labeled as low-class, backward, and often excessively religious. Shame was not a category that I associated with my Shiite identity. The distinction in the Iranian context while I was growing up there was between secular and religious Shiites, not between backward Shiites and modern non-Shiites.

However, most of my interlocutors rejected this explanation, reaffirming that my sense of "belonging" – my identity – had to be defined in terms of my (rigidly prescribed) political and religious loyalties. Rather than seeing a person's identity as layered, flexible, and changing, most interlocutors tended to understand identity as categorical and fixed in ways that positioned a person as either congruent with their identity or in stark opposition to it, a way of positioning of identities that was specifically related to how sectarian identities in Lebanon are powerfully institutionalized, leaving very little room for public negotiation of ethno-religious belonging. This is illustrated by the questions of a Lebanese Shiite friend, followed by my responses to her, and her interpretations of those responses:

> My friend asked:
> —— "What is the name of your father?"
> —— "Where was he born?"
> —— "What is his religion?"
> I replied:
> —— "My father's name is Muhammad Mehdi."
> —— "He was born in Iran."
> —— "He is a Shiite."
> My friend responded:
> —— "So that is who you are [an Iranian Shiite]. What is then all this fuss (*fawda*) about your German and your American identity?"

This exchange suggests that, for this Shiite friend, in any ranking of my possible identities, my categorical status as Iranian and Shiite trumps all other possible images of myself, including my gender and my roots in the West.[4] It also shows the importance of patrilinear genealogy. For example, in Lebanon, citizenship is transmitted through the father's line of descent and mediated through the religious community.

In other words, as a Lebanese living in Lebanon, one is identified with the religious community of the father and obtains citizenship though him. While such ascriptions of belonging, in their various forms, often complicated my conversations and interviews, especially because my background as an Iranian Shiite provoked doubts about my ultimate research motives, as I have said, such doubts also provoked discussions about Iran's role in Lebanon and therefore helped me understand interlocutors' images of Iran. In the end, a question about how Lebanese Shiites imagined Iran, which was not initially included among the foci of my research, emerged as a serendipitous, valuable finding. I embraced the opportunity to write about the intersections between religious and national identities and how these, in case of Iranian-Lebanese networks, played out in one research setting. Thus, the very thing that I had initially considered least important to the success or failure of my research – interlocutors' designations of my layered identities and my own definition of self – opened an important page for me in an often unelaborated aspect of field research methods.

NOTES

1 Shaery-Eisenlohr 2008.
2 See Goffman 1995 [1959].
3 For a somewhat similar experience and type of questions regarding marital status and children during fieldwork, see Fawzi El-Solh 1988.

4 This is evocative of Lila Abu-Lughod's (1986) report of how her fieldwork was crucially supported by her Arab father's personal introduction to the Bedouin community she studied, as subsequently her Egyptian Bedouin interlocutors preferred to highlight her Arab descent and identity over the American dimensions of her background during her research and residence among them.

REFERENCES

Abu-Lughod, Lila
   (1986)   *Veiled Sentiments: Honor and Poetry in a Bedouin Society*. Berkeley and Los Angeles: University of California Press.
Fawzi El-Solh, Camillia
   (1988)   "Gender, Class, and Origin: Aspects of Role During Fieldwork in Arab Society." In *Arab Women in the Field: Studying Your Own Society*, edited by Soraya Altorki and Camillia Fawzi El-Solh, 91–114. Syracuse, NY: Syracuse University Press.
Goffman, Erving
   (1995 [1959])   "On Face-Work: An Analysis of Ritual Elements in Social Interaction." In *Language, Culture and Society*, edited by Ben Blount. Prospect Heights, IL: Waveland Press.
Shaery-Eisenlohr, Roschanack
   (2008)   *Shiite Lebanon: Transnational Religion and the Making of National Identities*. New York: Columbia University Press.

6

Being Gay and Doing Fieldwork

Walter L. Williams

While writing this essay I am in Rarotonga, in the South Pacific, and the problems of doing fieldwork are immediately apparent. As I type these words I have to shoo away the chickens, which seem attracted to the peck-peck-peck sound of my portable laptop computer. This is the first time I have brought a computer along on fieldwork, and the manual does not explain how to keep insects out of it. Sometimes I think I have inserted a misplaced comma, only to realize it is a tiny ant on the screen. At night the huge roaches here insist on crawling all over everything. They are not shy at all and seem to realize that I will not smush them as they wander across the keyboard. I hope none will be inside my portable printer as I try to print out the finished product. Last night I was reluctantly forced to do battle with the biggest spider I have ever seen, which had settled on my bed.

The point of this introduction is to say that being gay is only one potential issue involved in living in a fieldwork setting. In my experience doing fieldwork on numerous Indian reservations, in a Maya village in Yucatan, among Native Alaskans, in Java, and most recently among Polynesians, I have found that my gayness is much less of a problem than the common obstacles facing most fieldworkers. Sanitation, deciding what local foods and drinks I can safely consume, money transfers, diarrhea, snarling dogs, allergies, finding a suitable place to live, arranging to keep in touch with my parents (who worry about me constantly, even though I assure them I am much safer in these villages than I am back home in Los Angeles) – these are the kind of daily issues to which one has to adjust when arriving at a new locale. They must be attended to before one can even begin to think about one's interactions with the local people.

In terms of personal interactions, the most immediate issues are being misunderstood and possibly offending someone while trying to speak a foreign language (or even in English), violating some cultural style that makes one

Walter L. Williams, "Being Gay and Doing Fieldwork," pp. 70–85 from *Out in the Field: Reflections of Lesbian and Gay Anthropologists*, ed. Ellen Lewin and William L. Leap. Urbana: University of Illinois Press, 1996.

Ethnographic Fieldwork: An Anthropological Reader, Second Edition. Edited by
Antonius C. G. M. Robben and Jeffrey A. Sluka.
Editorial material and organization © 2012 John Wiley & Sons, Inc.
Published 2012 by John Wiley & Sons, Inc.

appear foolish or uncouth, and deciding what to share or hoard among the few (and usually absolutely necessary) material possessions one brings along to the field. In addition to all this, I now have to worry about voltage regulators, finding a dependable source of electricity, and what to do if my computer malfunctions.

Yet despite these petty problems of day-to-day living, I would not once think of trading my experiences as a fieldworker with those of any other profession. I consider my times doing fieldwork to be among the happiest years of my life. I do not think I would have had the fascinating experiences that I feel blessed to have had if I had not gone out to live among people of quite different cultures. One gains daily insight in the continuing education that is lived experience and feels enriched by the wealth of experiences one would not have in one's native society.

Because some of the other essays in this book cogently address some of the problems facing lesbian and gay anthropologists in the field, I want to focus on the advantages gained by being open about one's affectional orientation. While just being uncloseted is no guarantee that doors are automatically opened in every research situation, it can provide positive benefits. I would like to use my personal history of research to show how I happened upon my research topics. From the beginnings of my academic career, I structured my research around questions that are important to me. Many anthropologists do this, of course, but it strikes me as odd that some ethnographers don't seem to have any particular personal motivation for doing what they do. My suspicion is that those anthropologists who have personal motivations make better ethnographers.

In my case, my initial fieldwork, among the Eastern Cherokees, was partly motivated by my desire to learn about my family heritage due to childhood memories of my Cherokee great-great grandmother, who died when I was six. That research led to my first book (Williams 1979). My next books, although based more on library research than on fieldwork, were a result of my personal involvement in (and political commitment to) the 1960s' Pan-African black pride movement

and the 1970s' American Indian activism (Williams 1982, 1984).

It was in terms of my gayness, however, that I was led to my next experience with fieldwork. The late 1970s was when I began coming to terms with my homosexuality, and a turning point for my personal development was reading Jonathan Katz's *Gay American History* (1976). A whole section of that book consisted of documents relating to the Native American two-spirit alternative gender role and to the attempts of European imperialists to wipe out culturally accepted "sodomy" among Native Americans. In all of the anthropology classes I had taken, I had never once heard mention of such traditions. My anger at this denial of knowledge – information I desperately needed at that stage in my life – helped me determine to publicize this subject so that gays and lesbians in the future would not feel the isolation I had felt.

Even before I was openly gay at my university, I began to incorporate mention of the two-spirit roles into the class I was teaching on American Indian ethnohistory. In 1980 I received a Woodrow Wilson Foundation grant to do research at the UCLA American Indian Studies Center on ways to improve Indian legal status. After quickly writing a couple of essays on that topic I devoted the bulk of my grant time to research on two-spirit traditions.

I had decided that, having devoted years of my life to helping racial minorities overcome prejudice and mistreatment, it was time for me to devote my energies to helping my own gay minority. I clearly would not have undertaken this research had I not by that time developed a positive gay identity. Yet this was a case where my interests would not be in conflict, because I felt that by doing research on two-spirit traditions, I would also be helping contemporary Native Americans recapture part of their cultural heritage. I dedicated my energies especially to those young gay and lesbian native people, on reservations or in urban areas, who might never have heard of the two-spirit idea. The 1970s had been a time of cultural renaissance among Indian people, and I felt that gay and lesbian Indians deserved to participate in this renaissance of their heritage as well.

Because I was lucky enough to be in Los Angeles, I had access to the library of ONE Institute of Homophile Studies and to the International Gay and Lesbian Archives. Dorr Legg, Harry Hay, and Jim Kepner, truly pioneering heroes of the homophile movement of the 1950s, encouraged me and kindly provided additional sources. The most valuable anthropological writing they gave me was the path-breaking essay by Sue-Ellen Jacobs (1968). Armed with these leads, I began traveling to different archives, scouring obscure sources to see if I could find other mention of "berdaches" or "sodomy." My coming out in the profession consisted of a paper I presented on two-spirited people at the 1980 American Society for Ethnohistory annual meeting.

By 1982 I decided that, to pursue this topic, fieldwork with Native American traditionalists who were still following their aboriginal religions needed to be done. I was not confident of my ability to do such fieldwork because I did not have any prior experience among Western Indians, where knowledge of two-spirit roles was most likely to be remembered, Nevertheless, Sue-Ellen Jacobs and Harry Hay encouraged me to go ahead. I decided that if I did not pursue this fieldwork, it would not likely get done. After all, I at least had a background in American Indian studies and had fieldwork experience living as part of an Indian community. I realized I could probably not get a grant to do research on homosexuality, but I had a sabbatical due me, and I could choose whatever subject I wanted. Having the advantage of being tenured at my university due to my previous publications, I realized I was at that time one of a very few uncloseted gay scholars who had enough income and job security to conduct this research.

I felt lucky to know that the cultures that were my research specialty had a heritage of acceptance of same-sex eroticism. Still, I surmised that the impact of a century or more of Westernization and Christianity could not have failed to make such subjects sensitive. I hoped that, as I traveled to the Plains, I could locate a reservation where traditionalist elders might agree to talk to me about two-spirited people they remembered from their youth. The first reservation I went to in 1982 was the Omaha reservation. I had read century-old written documents about androgynous "mex-oga" being highly respected. When I asked local people for someone who could talk to me about the old Omaha traditions, I was referred to the tribal historian. He was a kindly gentleman who seemed to take an immediate liking to me. Yet, after long discussions on Omaha history, when I finally got up nerve enough to ask about the term *mex-oga*, his demeanor suddenly changed. His eyes narrowed, and he took on a hostile look as he demanded abruptly, "Why do you want to know about that?"

My heart raced as I nervously thought about how to respond. In near panic I visualized this man making sure I was immediately kicked off the reservation – or worse. Finally, not knowing what else to say, I decided to be honest. I summoned every bit of out-of-the-closet gay pride that I had picked up from gay activist political activities over the past few years and responded. Although my interests were about Omaha traditions in general, I explained, I had a personal interest in this particular subject because I am homosexual and wanted to see if the mex-oga tradition had anything to do with homosexuality as the written documents suggested.

As soon as I said this, the man relaxed and smiled warmly. I will never forget his next words: "We don't talk about me-xo-ga [which I had mispronounced] to outsiders, but I appreciate your honesty. I'll tell you. Me-xo-ga is the same thing as gay; it's just like in California." After that, we relaxed and began an even closer interaction. It was as if, knowing something deeply personal about me, this man found it easier to reveal his sacred tribal traditions. This was to be my first experience in coming out as openly gay to informants. I can say that in virtually all such experiences during the last ten years I have received a positive (or at the least, neutral) response. In my opinion, many lesbian and gay ethnographers have been unnecessarily closeted and overly cautious during their fieldwork, and I am dismayed that even some of those who are open about themselves at their university have so little self-esteem that they will lie to their informants. This statement, of course, ignores the fact that being openly gay or lesbian might have negative consequences in some situations, but in most instances an attempt to hide or deny one's sexuality results in a less trusting and information-sharing relationship with informants.

My experience on the Omaha reservation was also the first time I noticed that elderly Indian traditionalists prefer to use the term *gay* rather than *homosexual*. To them, focus on the sexual inclinations of the person is less important than what they call the person's "spirit." It took me a long time to realize, in many conversations with traditionalist Indians, that what they mean by spirit is close to what Westerners might call a person's basic character. Because of my informants' emphasis, my initial focus on homosexual behavior shifted to the spiritual and religious aspects of two-spirit traditions. That is why I ultimately titled my book *The Spirit and the Flesh* (1986).

When the Omaha historian became satisfied that I did not intend to approach his tribal traditions in a disrespectful manner, he did something even more surprising. He took me to meet a sixty-two-year-old male who is identified by his reservation community, and who identifies himself, as me-xo-ga. After I identified myself as gay, that man agreed to talk with me about his life. He said he would not have opened up if I had been the typical heterosexual anthropologist. He was the first two-spirited person I interviewed. In that experience, as with numerous others since then, I feel that I have had an enormous advantage in doing my fieldwork by being openly gay. Of course, a shared sexual orientation is not enough by itself to guarantee continued good relations with others (either crossculturally or among persons of similar cultural backgrounds), but it does help open many doors that might otherwise remain closed.

What I have said certainly depends on my choice of subject matter and fieldwork locations. I have consciously searched out cultures that have a tradition of acceptance of same-sex eroticism. Since 1982 I have resolved to do a different kind of fieldwork. Rather than living on one Indian reservation for a year and doing the usual community study

that ethnographers regularly do, I decided that my community of study would be two-spirited people themselves. Although an intensive community study focusing on such persons' interactions within that community is without doubt of value, the notion that two-spirit traditions have completely disappeared is so widespread among anthropologists that I decided it was more important for me to do a comparative study of these unique individuals on several reservations. I also think my prowess for exploring new locales and subjects is my strongest talent, whereas other ethnographers are more skilled in doing intensive analysis of one locale over a longer period. Both kinds of researchers are necessary to gain greater cross-cultural understanding.

After staying for a time with my initial Omaha informant, he sent his nephew to accompany me to the Rosebud Sioux reservation and to introduce me to *winkte*, two-spirits among the Lakota. After more experiences living at Rosebud and doing life history interviews and additional interviews with their relatives and neighbors, they referred me to other *winktes* on the Pine Ridge Sioux reservation. And from there, those *winktes* referred me to others they knew on the Crow and Northern Cheyenne reservations. And so it went, as I worked my way across the Plains.

I ended up observing, and eventually participating in, traditional religious ceremonies to which I am sure I would never have been invited had I not established a personal gay-to-gay (or two-spirit to two-spirit) relationship with my native informants. I was warned by whites in South Dakota that a white man would not be safe living on a reservation, especially in Pine Ridge, yet I never experienced hostility. I believe my acceptance in the community was because of my association with *winktes*. Traditionalist Lakotas are somewhat afraid of the spiritual power of *winktes*, which provides them and their consorts with a convenient form of protection. Being openly gay thus provided me an advantage in this fieldwork situation.

Although personal involvement was not my motivation for undertaking this research, one of my informants and I became very close as he went with me in doing my interviewing and

I accompanied him in his Lakota religion ceremonial activities. We went everywhere together, and his religious intensity opened up a whole new realm of spiritual concern in my personal life. He is without a doubt the most spiritual person I have ever met, and I consider my interaction with him to be a turning point in my life. Shortly before I was scheduled to leave his reservation, he surprised me by proposing that I become his husband and live with him on his reservation. I had known of his sexual attraction to me because I had previously gently deflected his initiatives for sexual involvement, yet I considered him more as my teacher than as my husband.

I explained that I had to return to my teaching job after my sabbatical year was over. He responded that I could quit my job and he would support me. He said that I would not have to worry about anything, because I could move into his house and he would provide us a good living. I could, he said, focus on my writing and would not have to worry about teaching at a university. I thanked him for the offer but told him I could not give up my academic career. Besides, I needed to pursue research on two-spirited people among other groups of Native Americans beyond the Plains.

By the end of 1982 I traveled down to the Navajo reservation and did additional research and interviewing. I was amazed to find that Navajo traditionalists were even more respectful of "nadleh" than the Plains tribes had been of their two-spirits. But I found the Arizona winter unexpectedly harsh and decided I could depend on several excellent published sources on the Navajo nadleh. So, in the spirit of Joseph Campbell, who said the highest life course is to be attained by following your own personal bliss, in January 1983 I took off for Mexico. In my library research I had run across a few sixteenth-century sources by Spanish conquistadores complaining about how the Mayas in particular were "addicted to sodomy," and another later letter claiming that the Catholic missionaries and Spanish government officials had successfully wiped out such vices among the Indians (quoted in Williams 1986:135–40). My previous research led me to distrust that claim.

Armed with nothing more than those few four-hundred-year-old references, and knowing no one, I headed for Mayan villages in Yucatan. Although I had not one personal contact, my positive experiences on the Plains during my 1982 fieldwork led me to approach the task with anticipation. I spent my first weeks in Yucatan touring through the magnificent Mayan archaeological sites of Uxmal, Chichen Itza, Tulum, and other ruins. Whenever I asked my Mayan tour guides about homosexuality, they uniformly replied in a noncondemnatory, accepting way. Within a couple of weeks I had not only made contact with a group of Maya "homosexuales" but also was developing a circle of friends.

I found the Mayas to be among the most friendly and attractive people I have ever met. One, whose nickname was "El Sexy," took a particular liking to me. He lived with his mother, who took me under her wing and was soon cooking delicious meals for me. They both became committed to the importance of a book being written on this topic. El Sexy helped me meet other "homosexuales" to interview and was a joyful companion as I did my study. He felt pleased that his and other homosexuals' lives and viewpoints were going to be included in a book. He also used me as a status symbol in his pueblo. One day, as we were riding in my automobile, he got great enjoyment from the fact that a boy publicly called out to him, "El Sexy, I see you have found your husband!" This humorous reference to me was not in any way derogatory, but merely a relaxed kidding that reflected the general knowledge of his attraction to men (Williams 1986:143–44).

While I feel positively about all my fieldwork locations, and each group of people has left its own unique imprint on my education and personal life, I left Yucatan very reluctantly. I think the Mayas are my favorite people of all. Their friendly and open demeanor, as well as their whole joyful approach to life, impressed me deeply.

Again, I want to emphasize that being openly gay is not by itself sufficient to ensure a good fieldwork experience. What is most necessary is to treat people with respect, caring, and earnestness and to interact with them on a human-to-human basis. Without this, no amount of fieldwork training or sophisticated research methodology will allow one to establish and maintain a positive relationship of any kind. Being open about oneself is necessary before one can establish a genuinely trusting and sharing interaction with people. As Stephen O. Murray and others in this volume rightly point out, we still cannot assume from personal experiences that what we are told or observe is the kind of behavior that actually occurs among people of the studied culture. But we cannot gain much valid knowledge without these conversations and observations.

After returning from Yucatan, going back to teaching and staying busy writing my fieldnotes and publishing my research, my next fieldwork was in 1987 and 1988. I had written a number of grant proposals to do research on homosexuality cross-culturally, but all of them had been rejected. Finally I managed to get funding by – once again – writing a grant for a different topic. This time I won a Fulbright Scholar Award to Indonesia. My Fulbright research proposal was to do life history interviewing of Javanese elders, with a special focus on gender. On the way to Indonesia, I took the opportunity to stop over in Bangkok and did some interviewing of Thai gay activists (Williams 1990). My experience has been that I have managed to do fieldwork on gay topics by getting grants on other subjects, and then doing my gay research in addition to the research I did for my grant. The only time I have received a grant specifically on homosexuality research was in 1989, when I won a small travel grant from the Institute for the Study of Women and Men at my university to go to Alaska to do research on homosexuality among Aleuts and Yupiks. In the case of my Indonesian work, I published a book of Javanese life histories (Williams 1991) and am still working on other publications specifically focused on homosexuality in Java (see, for example, Williams 1992a).

This process is not something I complain about; lesbian and gay ethnographers just have to work twice as hard to get more research done while in the field. In addition, although I think it is important for openly gay and lesbian

scholars to publish articles and books on homosexuality, it is also important for us to publish general ethnographies that include homosexuality as just one among many socially accepted aspects of particular cultures. This is what I tried to do in my *Javanese Lives* (1991:180–90, 210, 230n2).

Anthropologists can perform valuable documentation for the effort to overcome homophobia by pointing out to readers that same-sex eroticism is a fact of life in human societies around the world. It is thus doubly important that we focus upon cultures that are not inflicted with antihomosexual prejudices. We need to highlight the benefits that societies gain by not harboring such prejudices. This cross-cultural perspective can become an important part of the effort to reduce homophobia in American society (Williams 1992b).

I have written elsewhere (Williams 1990: 126) about the great need for openly gay and lesbian ethnographers to investigate nonhomophobic cultures before their accepting values are destroyed by rampaging Westernization. In every area of the world in which I have traveled I have found it alarming the extent to which fundamentalist Christian groups are exporting homophobia. Barraged with American missionaries, movies, television, literature, and outdated psychoanalytic theories of sexual deviance (that are still being propounded by many Western-educated teachers), many cultures are rapidly changing their attitudes toward sexuality. If we do not gather this research soon, it will be too late to learn about the vast array of differing institutionalized forms of same-sex eroticism.

We desperately need a more complete database for a broader understanding of human sexuality. Given the almost complete ignorance of female-female sexuality in non-Western cultures, I think the highest research priority is for lesbian scholars to undertake this work. As a male interviewer, I was painfully aware of my inability to get women to open up on this issue, and even my male informants usually knew very little on the subject. In *The Spirit and the Flesh*, I could only depend on the few historical documents and few publications on the subject by women scholars. In Java, I was not able to locate even one lesbian who would agree to be anonymously interviewed. I anxiously await the publication of more studies like Jennifer Robertson's (1992) fascinating ethnography of a female theater troupe in Japan.

It is not that sensitive heterosexuals lack the ability to do research on homosexuality; indeed, non-gay anthropologists such as Serena Nanda (1990) have made important contributions to the study of sexual variance. But it is still clear that openly lesbian ethnographers have an advantage in doing field research on female sexuality and openly gay ethnographers have an advantage in doing research on male-male eroticism. Peter Jackson (1989) suggested that gay people have a significant advantage over other foreigners in being able to integrate themselves quickly into a local culture. Because native homosexuals often see themselves as different, sometimes as outsiders in their own culture, they are likely to feel an immediate identity with others they perceive to be "like themselves" – even if those persons are from a different culture. I have certainly found that to be the case in my research.

Jim Wafer, an openly gay ethnographer in Brazil, pointed out several advantages to his being open about his sexuality among his informants. In the first place, his native lover provided many contacts and opened many doors. Because he had a personal relationship with the ethnographer and was committed to the project, this lover had additional motivation to make sure that what was written was accurate. Beyond that, Wafer pointed out, because their relationship was known and accepted in the community, it gave Wafer a "quasi-insider status. ... It meant, for example, that I was regarded as 'accounted for' within the kinship system ... [which] meant that I was less a threat than I might otherwise have been" (1990).

Anthropologists often verbalize an expectation that single fieldworkers who go into the field should refrain from any sexual activity in their fieldwork community. This expectation appears rather strange to the people of sexually free cultures, with anthropologists being pitied for denying themselves one of the basic necessities of life. Beyond the question of one's personal happiness, sexual involvement might also yield important research findings.

For example, one gay male ethnographer (who shall remain nameless for purposes of this essay) has verbally spoken informally of his experience in a non-Western fieldwork setting where he lived for over a year as an openly gay man. It was not hard for him to come out to people because soon after meeting they would often ask him if he were married. When he replied that he was not married, they frequently asked "Why not?" He then simply responded that he preferred loving men. That response was greeted with an accepting understanding of his sexual inclinations, but many local people still could not understand why he did not marry a woman and continue his sexual activities with males as well.

Later, when word got around the community that he enjoyed sex with males, a number of local men (mid-teen to late-thirties) made sexual advances toward him. Not wishing to remain celibate for a year, he responded positively. Yet because he did not wish to impose his foreign sexual styles, he always let them take the initiative in bed. After several encounters he saw the pattern: erotic inter-action between males in that culture involved only interfemoral friction. That is, one partner would lie down on his back or front, rub spit or lotion between his legs at the crotch, and cross his legs at the ankle. The other would lubricate his penis and stick it between the legs of the other. According to this anthropologist, "having his legs crossed at the ankle made all the difference, and it felt great – just like intercourse." Yet this was not intercourse, but "outercourse," a method of sexual interaction that does not lend itself to the transmission of most sexually transmitted diseases (including HIV). If he had not actually experienced the feeling of this type of interfemoral friction, with legs crossed at the ankle, he would not have thought to ask about the particulars of male-male sexual interaction and would have missed its safe-sex implications.

Prompted by this testimony of direct experience, I began to reexamine the literature and found mention of such interfemoral sexual methods being the standard form of male-male sexuality in many societies (ancient Greece, southern Africa, Morocco, some areas of Polynesia). With that anthropologist's encouragement, I hope to publish this data later as a contribution to safe-sex literature. By gathering information about varieties of sexual practices around the world, anthropologists in the age of AIDS can make important contributions in helping people expand their range of sexual practices to less dangerous noninsertive forms of expression. What more valuable application of applied anthropology could be more evident, if we will only drop our Western anti-sexual prudery? As Ralph Bolton (1991) has rightly pointed out, this is a high-priority, even "urgent," agenda for ethnographic research in the 1990s.

In nonhomophobic cultures a researcher can, by being open about his or her sexuality, be accepted by the local community and can gain access to people for interviewing. Over and over in my research, from Alaska to Java, informants have told me that they would never discuss such topics with a heterosexual. Native Americans in particular have reported feeling violated many times when things they told to white researchers were made fun of and written about in a disrespectful manner. By being personally involved in this subject, a researcher is better able to understand the issues facing informants and is more likely to be able to put data in their proper social context.

Yet it is not enough that a person simply be lesbian or gay and expect instant acceptance. I recognize that informants would not have continued to talk and interact with me had they not felt comfortable with me on an individual level. We must critically examine reports of nonacceptance by white anthropologists who feel that native people are summarily excluding them because of their race. Individual factors of personal interaction may more likely be the cause of such native nonacceptance. For example, in 1992 I was invited to speak at the annual gathering of the Two-Spirited People of the First Nations, which was held in an isolated rural area of British Columbia. A number of non-Indian gays and lesbians attended this gathering, which was organized by lesbian and gay American Indians and Arctic natives. Native people in attendance reacted to the non-Indians quite differently. Those non-Indians who came on their own as single persons were treated rather coolly by the native people in attendance. However, those non-Indians who were there as lovers and partners of natives were treated warmly, like they were "part of the family."

Native American gay people, like many other people I have encountered in Asia and the Pacific, seem to trust the judgment of their native friends. If a non-native outsider is a good enough person for a native person to enjoy being in a relationship with, then the others will accept that person's conclusion that such an outsider should be brought into the group. Otherwise, many of them will keep their distance. Given this situation, involvement of a fieldworker in an emotional personal relationship with a local native person can (besides its reward of personal happiness) also contribute to more effective interaction with the community within which one is living. I am not advocating that lesbian and gay anthropologists go out into the field with a cynical plan to locate a local mate in order to accomplish their fieldwork; such a plot would be exploitative in the extreme. What I am suggesting is that a prohibition on genuinely loving relationships is unrealistic and hypocritical. If a fieldworker and a local person are attracted to each other and the local person understands the realities of the field-worker's situation (the anthropologist is honest about how long she or he will be resident there, and that the information gathered will likely be published), then such a genuinely felt emotional bond can be a positive experience for all concerned.

A fieldworker with a personal involvement in the subject of study, moreover, has an added incentive to persevere when problems arise (like a lack of funding). A lesbian or gay fieldworker can more easily avoid false information, which might be given to a heterosexual researcher because informants are well aware of Western anti-gay prejudices. As I found from the help I received from gay archival organizations, an openly gay researcher is also able to draw upon specialized sources and unpublished documents which might be withheld from a non-gay researcher.

Conversely, another factor to consider is the disadvantage of lesbian and gay ethnographers trying to remain closeted. Frank Proschan reported the difficulties in his fieldwork with a Cambodian community in trying to hide his homosexuality. His informants could not account for his asexuality: "As a result of my own evasiveness and their sensitive avoidance of potentially embarrassing questions, I remained a riddle to the people with whom I worked" (1990:59). He realized that he came across to his informants as a naive, asexual, childlike eunuch (61). Moreover (he learned years later) his informants had not told him of certain things about Cambodian sexual variance, simply because they were uncertain how he would react to them: "As long as I presented myself as a riddle, leaving any sexual identity undefined and unsaid, my Cambodian friends consistently left anything with explicit sexual content unsaid in my presence – silence begetting silence" (62–63).

Anthropologists are beginning to write about the intersubjective relations connecting fieldworkers to informants, yet the subject of sexuality – certainly one of the most important aspects of human behavior – remains practically unanalyzed in print. Anthropologists have incorporated the worst aspects of Victorian prudery in avoiding an honest assessment of their sexual behaviors in the field. Gay and lesbian anthropologists, by questioning sexual boundaries and social roles, seem ideally positioned to lead anthropologists into a new honesty and openness about sexual interactions in the field, just as they freely write about other forms of daily interaction. Bolton (1991:138) has pointed out that after sexual intimacy people often open up and speak honestly and profoundly about their lives.

By living as part of a community as openly gay people, if that community is not inflicted with the kind of rampant homophobia seen in the West (and all too often reflected in anthropologists' writings), then we can truly offer an honest account of our participant-observation in that community. This is not by any means to suggest sexual irresponsibility on the part of the fieldworker (especially in this age of AIDS), which will exploit or harm informants. Just as there is a difference between an intimate union and a rape, fieldworkers must learn to assess sexual interactions in a more realistic and sophisticated manner.

What is most important, I have found, is that being an effective fieldworker requires honesty with my informants as well as with my readers. If I wish to remain credible, I must inform my informants exactly what kind of information I am interested in, and that my intention is to publish a book on the information gathered. When doing interviews with informants, if at all possible I try to conduct the interview with no one else present. I assure them that I will protect their privacy by not using their real name in order to get them to speak frankly and candidly about their experiences. I emphasize the need for us to know more about the lives of gay people (or using whatever term is locally appropriate) in different cultures around the world, and then after the interview is completed I may tell them about my findings in other cultures if they are interested.

My research entails interviewing informants about their most intimate experiences and feelings. What I find is that if a person reveals a particularly personal detail, it helps for me to throw in some intimate detail about my own experiences. This simple act makes the interview less of a one-sided probing of informant by researcher and more of an exchange of information among equals. That, ultimately, is what anthropology really is all about: to establish an appreciation for human diversity and an empathy with other individuals across the boundaries of culture.

I certainly recognize my weaknesses as an ethnographer, but I also see that I have been able to get data in interviews that others have not. I do not exactly know what I do that seems to get people to open up about themselves. There is something intangible involved, something no amount of training in field-methods classes can impart, that promotes a deep person-to-person interaction between the interviewer and the interviewee. My experience convinces me that the most important factor in successful fieldwork is the ability to empathize with others on a soul-to-soul level. Given the paucity of unbiased data on homosexuality in non-Western cultures and the demonstrated incompetence of most heterosexual anthropologists in gathering such data, I want to do everything I can to encourage more lesbian and gay male researchers to go out into the field and gather information about the subject before it disappears.

Other chapters in this volume have focused on the problems that might be encountered in fieldwork. Although lesbian and gay fieldworkers should certainly be aware of such problems, I agreed to write this essay to provide an example that might help to inspire young anthropologists to embark on additional such research. My general approach to life is to accentuate the positive, and I find many academics so overwhelmingly pessimistic and critical that they unwittingly discourage others. I think ethnographic knowledge is important, and I take my role seriously as a mentor in encouraging other researchers. I have presented my experiences here not to glorify myself but in the hope that such knowledge may be of help to encourage others to accomplish better ethnography in the future.

REFERENCES

Bolton, Ralph
  1991 "Mapping Terra Incognita: Sex Research for AIDS Prevention: An Urgent Agenda for the 1990s." In *The Time of AIDS*, ed. G. Herdt and S. Lindenbaum, 124–58. Newbury Park: Sage.
Jackson, Peter
  1989 *Male Homosexuality in Thailand*. Elmhurst: Global.
Jacobs, Sue-Ellen
  1968 "Berdache: A Brief Review of the Literature." *Colorado Anthropologist* 1(1): 25–40.
Katz, Jonathan
  1976 *Gay American History*. New York: Crowell.
Nanda, Serena
  1990 *Neither Man nor Woman: The Hijra of India*. Belmont, Calif.: Wadsworth.

Proschan, Frank
  1990 "How is a Folklorist Like a Riddle?" *Southern Folklore* 47(1): 57–66.
Robertson, Jennifer
  1992 "The Politics of Androgyny in Japan: Sexuality and Subversion in the Theater and Beyond." *American Ethnologist* 19(3): 419–42.
Wafer, Jim
  1990 "Identity Management in the Textual Field." Paper presented at the annual meeting of the American Anthropological Association, New Orleans.
Williams, Walter L.
  1979 *Southeastern Indians since the Removal Era*. Athens: University of Georgia Press.
Williams, Walter L.
  1982 *Black Americans and the Evangelization of Africa*. Madison: University of Wisconsin Press.
Williams, Walter L.
  1984 *Indian Leadership*. Manhattan, Kans.: Sunflower University Press.
Williams, Walter L.
  1986 *The Spirit and the Flesh: Sexual Diversity in American Indian Culture*. Boston: Beacon Press. 2d ed. 1992.
Williams, Walter L.
  1990 "Male Homosexuality in Thailand." *Journal of Homosexuality* 19(4): 126–38.
Williams, Walter L.
  1991 *Javanese Lives: Women and Men in Modern Indonesian Society*. New Brunswick, N.J.: Rutgers University Press.
Williams, Walter L.
  1992a "Gay Self-Respect in Indonesia: The Life History of a Chinese Man from Central Java." In *Oceanic Homosexualities*, ed. Stephen O. Murray et al. New York: Garland Publishing.
Williams, Walter L.
  1992b "Benefits for Nonhomophobic Societies: An Anthropological Perspective." In *Homophobia: How We All Pay the Price*, ed. W. Blumenfeld, 258–74. Boston: Beacon Press.

7

Automythologies and the Reconstruction of Ageing

Paul Spencer

In this chapter, I wish to consider personal anecdotes, told and elaborated before an audience, as a form of structured autobiography. Erving Goffman (1969: 28–40) has drawn attention to the element of performance in such presentations, with role play and the manipulation of reality to create an effect. In this way a contrived self-image is built up which inadvertently may even captivate the teller, hence my title. The aim here is to discern the relevance of exaggeration in recalling episodes of one's past for an insight into autobiography, and ultimately even the record of history itself. Both history and biography are concerned with processes in time and are bound up with the life courses of individuals. Autobiography gives a uniquely personal insight into the process of history, but may view the memories of earlier times through the distorting lenses of later life, and these in turn are moulded in part by the social construction of ageing.

To illustrate this, I have chosen two autobiographical anecdotes that relate in the first instance to the self-image built up by a colourful Maasai elder. The second is of a misencounter of my own during my first spell of field-work, narrated years later. Each can be viewed in its historical context and both are shown in the concluding section to relate to the interpretation of maturation and ageing in the relevant culture.

The Maasai Who Would Not Grow Old

Popular accounts of the Maasai give a larger than life portrayal of a proud, tradition-bound people who once dominated a whole region of East Africa. While these accounts are open to question, the larger than life aspect at least is fostered by the Maasai themselves who remain convinced of their stature. This is not only for the benefit of tourists, but is found also in remoter areas where it is the tourists who are the spectacle, and even today when there is a new status quo in Kenya with the Maasai

Paul Spencer, "Automythologies and the Reconstruction of Ageing," pp. 50–63 from *Anthropology and Autobiography*, ed. Judith Okely and Helen Callaway. London: Routledge, 1992.

Ethnographic Fieldwork: An Anthropological Reader, Second Edition. Edited by Antonius C. G. M. Robben and Jeffrey A. Sluka.
Editorial material and organization © 2012 John Wiley & Sons, Inc.
Published 2012 by John Wiley & Sons, Inc.

officially relegated to little more than an extension of the game parks.

While working among the Maasai, much of the information I collected, even from the most reliable informants, was dogged by this element of exaggeration. Collecting autobiographical accounts, then, had its dangers, especially when the informant projected his own role prominently. In one respect, however, any autobiography was a valuable resource. The Maasai are a semi-nomadic people, and no one with whom I had close contact early in my stay was still living with the same neighbours a year later, and many were no longer even in the same neighbourhood. Nomadism creates a situation in which a community study extended over time, comparable with Turner's Ndembu (1957) or Middleton's Lugbara (1960), is not feasible for the anthropologist. For the actors, on the other hand, there is a lifetime experience of an extended community. They see themselves over the years as itinerant members of a much larger slice of their society, making visits as well as moving with their herds, and constantly re-establishing social contacts that have lapsed in the course of migration. Autobiographical accounts provide an introduction to this wider community, albeit coloured and distorted by tricks of the memory and trips of the ego.

In Matapato in 1976, this dual aspect of autobiography was vividly illustrated by 'Masiani', an elderly Maasai who as an informant was not particularly interested or well informed. He was deaf, self-centred and impetuous, but also generous and a lively raconteur. His flamboyant narratives of his various encounters with other Maasai could hold an audience, giving the impression of a spirited young man (moran/warrior) who had never quite settled down to the more subtle ways of elderhood. I managed to collect enough of these anecdotes to piece together his life story over a period of historical change. This was complemented by rather different interpretations of some of the same events and of his character by his age mates and members of his family. An intriguing aspect of his self-centred perspective was his inability to fit together the two ends of his experience of the tense father-son relationship, first as a truculent boy and later as an overbearing patriarch.

When collecting his fragmented account, the strong element of exaggeration reminded me of The Life of Benvenuto Cellini (Cust 1935). As a Renaissance 'lie', Cellini's autobiography gives a vivid picture of the ethos of his times. Similarly, Masiani's colourful account was a Maasai 'lie', and the licence he assumed in his actions and recounting is a feature of Maasai society which increases with age. On his own terms, Masiani's self-portrayal provided an ideal type, riddled with Maasai clichés, and as much a truth of Maasai ideals as a distortion of biographical and historical detail.

Take, for instance, the incident when Masiani was punished by his age-set for being involved in a drunken brawl. He drew blood by retaliating against an age mate who had attacked him. This was a ritually dangerous offence for an established elder, and Masiani had to make reparation even though he claimed to be the innocent victim of the attack.

The elders of my age-set told me to give the man I had fought a sheep so that he could drink the liquid fat and we could become friends. But I refused: "I wont give anything to that man who throttled me until I wet myself and beat me until he thought I was dead", I said. I had many sheep, but I had none I was prepared to give that man. So they went round calling one another [to mount an age-set posse to punish Masiani's disobedience]. One night I could hear them yelping not far away. I had a quiver with poisoned arrows, so I went out of my village determined to shoot them as they approached. Another young man of our family came with me and told me not to shoot. The posse came and settled down to a discussion. We both lurked in the darkness to overhear what they said. They were as far away from us as that thorn-fence over there. One said: "Oye ... let's not rush in and grab his cattle: let us be careful in punishing this elder". And another said: "No. Let's rush in and beat him". And a third said: "He should not be rushed or beaten. We must get him carefully". My young friend then turned to me and whispered: "You said just now that you would shoot them all; but do you want to shoot men like that who are shooting away from you [and advising restraint]? Wouldn't that be bad?" And I said: "It would be bad. Let's forget about shooting at them". So we got up and walked slowly towards the discussion. And addressing these elders, I said: "Oye ... don't again suggest that you should rush in and grab my cattle". And they replied: "Forget it, for we are not going to rush in". And I went on: "When I overheard that you wanted to rush in and grab my cattle – I didn't beat that man recently nearly as hard as I would have beaten you, the one who made that suggestion. And you are that man's brother, you goodfornothing (*laka iposo*)!" So they came and grabbed two of my cattle: a heifer and an ox ... I did get that ox back again though. It had been placed by the elders in another herd and one day it strayed. So I stole it back and drove it away. I then swapped it for a white heifer elsewhere, and drove that one back to my own herd. The man who was looking after the ox came to search for it, but he never knew that it was me who had taken it, getting my own ox back.

The incongruity of this account is that Masiani was not just an implacable rebel. He was well connected within his own age-set and popular for his loyalty and the colour he brought to their ageing reputation. The whole episode – taking up his bow against his age mates, haranguing them, and then recovering his ox after it had strayed – overstretches credibility, as do many of his other stories. His excessive rashness at each stage, the coincidence of the stray ox combined with the incompetence of the herder simply does not ring true. Taken as a fantasy surrounding Masiani's punishment, on the other hand, the account seems to portray his feelings quite vividly: the urge to defend his herd; the voice of caution from a younger kinsman whom he was not obliged to obey; the desire to rise above his punishment by first boasting over the heads of his age mates and then staging an audacious counter-theft; and implicitly his ultimate loyalty to his age-set in submitting at least to the minimum fine of just one heifer. These expressions of the ambivalence that surrounds the defence of a man's own domestic interests as against his submission to age-set discipline would be perfectly intelligible to a Maasai audience. The tension between these two types of involvement alters in the course of the life span and is expressed in their ideology and in various Maasai stereotypes

(Spencer 1988: 225–6). Masiani's audacity may have been largely that he was prepared to fantasise in public what others would have felt in private. Rising in his own estimation above his adversaries, he also tried to show that he was prepared always to defer to higher Maasai ideals. At worst, he paid for his excesses by having little personal influence in the local political scene, but he still carried weight as a virile member of a dwindling age-set who refused to bow to old age. What he sometimes lacked in personal dignity, his age-set gained in popular acclaim placing them above trivial conformity. Their occasional flamboyant excesses displayed the irrepressible spirit of younger men, and to this extent old age itself had to be respected not only as the ultimate achievement, but also for its own irrepressibility. Historically, it was a period when ultimate power was felt to have slipped into the hands of younger men encouraged for the first time by an alien black administration. Against this trend within the local community, older men could retain their prestige so long as they could hold an audience with stories that glamorised their role and responses within Maasai tradition. Beyond the flamboyance of the performer, the element of exaggeration becomes intelligible in the wider context (q.v. Gulliver 1963: 38–9; Spencer 1988: 216–19).

It is perhaps significant that the setting for this episode was not, for instance, Samburu. The Samburu are up-country cousins of the Maasai and generally less competitive (Spencer 1988: 250). I suspect that a Samburu Masiani would have projected his fantasies and tales on to some peripheral third party, identifying himself as story-teller with the conformist majority. The struggle for power between senior age-sets was altogether weaker among the Samburu and to this extent, older men were in a more secure position than among the Maasai. Such accounts as I collected from older Samburu were essentially oral histories rather than self-centred fantasies.

The Apparition in the Bush

Masiani's account opens up the disquieting question of the extent to which all our

Goffmanesque presentations of ourselves – even to ourselves – contain an element of autobiographical distortion, giving coherence and meaning to our being. Given that any anthropological account is inevitably reflexive and indirectly autobiographical, this in turn throws doubt on the anthropologist's own judgement. To what extent, in other words, are my own accounts of the peoples of the Maasai region distorted by unresolved dilemmas of my own past and present? To what extent do I too respond to my perceived audience, and possibly in different ways on different occasions? Let me try to unravel this.

Writing about such peoples as the Maasai for an unknown reader, I feel obliged to be largely impersonal and essentially serious. Yarning about field-work with friends on the other hand, I find myself frequently resorting to personal anecdotes, rather like Masiani, and not altogether aware of the extent to which the retelling of these stories takes on new complexions in the effort to gain an effect or to hold an audience. The frequent theme of such stories is the incongruity of the encounter between two cultures wrapped up in a joke.

Take, for instance, my recollection of an episode that I have retold on a number of occasions. This concerns a time when I had just acquired a Land Rover, and I then ended my first long stint of fieldwork among the Samburu with a trip to their close allies, the Rendille. There I was faced once again with a new language and an unfamiliar culture. I simply did not have the energy to start all over again; and this made me realise that I needed a break. A motor road nearby led me to hanker for a dose of English culture, to be able to relax with others in my own language, and to indulge in some privacy. I had been struggling with these feelings for several days, when my lethargic research efforts with some Rendille elders were interrupted by an apparition. A boat had suddenly appeared, perhaps 40 feet long, sailing majestically above the sparse bush cover. I could not have dreamed up a more incongruous diversion. Even the elders seemed disconcerted. Then as we looked, the boat came to an abrupt halt. That day was clearly not destined for untangling Rendille kinship organisation. I ran towards the boat, half expecting to discover

some uncharted lake, but at least certain that any vessel that had run aground in the middle of this remote wilderness was in trouble or lost. This was the excuse I needed to get away from the Rendille and even to grapple with a western problem in English. I arrived at the roadside to find not just a stranded boat, but a line of stationary trucks with the boat perched on top of one of them. There was no lake and no sign of trouble, just some heavy vehicles and, beside them on the roadside, a huddle of Europeans looking at a map. This was my cue. Even if I could not help them unground a shipwreck, at least I could make out that I knew the area – and in English. 'Can I help?', I asked. They looked up with mild surprise and then down towards my feet. One of them said 'No thank you', and they turned back to their map. I too looked down and realised that I was wearing a well-seasoned blanket, a pair of sandals made from car tyres, and clutching a stick and a notebook. Had I been a Samburu – or if they had been Samburu – I would simply have stayed where I was and looked on. As it was, they were of my own kind and I wanted to escape. In desperation, I looked at my left wrist, as if wearing a watch that would remind me of an urgent appointment. 'Good heavens!', I said, 'I must be going! Bye bye'. They looked up again and said 'Goodbye', and then returned to their map. I turned and fled into the cover of the bush. That, then, was my slice of English culture for the present.

Years later, I came across an account by Hilary Ruben portraying an aspect of Africa that was fast disappearing. She and her family were members of this amphibious expedition and she gives a diverging account of the same incident. Possibly for effect, the encounter appears to be cited more than one hundred miles further north in an even more remote part.

One day ... a fantastic apparition appeared in the midst of all that nothingness: a white man, wearing shorts and shirt [sic] and a pair of thonged sandals [sic] like the nomads. He walked like a nomad too, with the same long [sic], springy gait. He smiled, waved [sic?], enquired whether everything was all right, and before we had time to catch our breaths and ask whence he came and whither he was going, passed on. Mad dogs and Englishmen, I muttered ... Months afterwards, we were to discover that this man was an anthropologist living mostly with the Samburu, and partly with the Rendille. It was in fact Paul Spencer ... (Ruben 1972: 160–1)

The two accounts are sufficiently similar to identify the same event, but they differ enough to raise questions. I am now unconvinced by at least one detail of my own version: it is altogether unlikely that I would have been wearing a blanket in the heat of Rendille country; a cloth just possibly, but even this would have been unlikely at this early stage of my research among them. Somehow over the years, the elaborations of this story seem to have taken over from the reality of the encounter. In my mind's eye, I do not see Hilary Ruben or her two daughters, but only a group of men, studiously trying not to look at me. The story has become part of my self-image. Even in writing about it now, I wanted to substitute a cloth for the (less plausible) blanket, missing and yet affectingly demonstrating the point I wish to make. I am equally unconvinced concerning minor details in the other account. Each version gives a different slant on this fleeting encounter. The normal view of the English meeting in remote Africa is of a spontaneous warmth that would be inconceivable anywhere in England. And yet here, in an unusually remote area, the very unexpectedness of the encounter appears to have led to a very English reserve on both sides. In my own account, they did not respond to my overture, and in Ruben's account I did not even give them a chance. Exaggerations in each of our anecdotes apart, we appear to have revealed – or rather concealed – something of our national character to each other. We had brought the stiff upper lip with us to Africa, barely camouflaged by brief pleasantries.

A feature of this self-portrayal (but not necessarily of the encounter itself) was that I was setting myself apart from the very people whose company I was seeking, as if unable to resolve the gulf between the two cultures. In elaborating the story – inventing the worn blanket for instance – I suspect that I was trying to insinuate how far I had gone to incorporate myself into Samburu/Rendille society, contrasting it with the world of maps, expeditions and affluence. This may well have been a pose, but it was in tune with my feelings of ambivalence towards my Englishness at this time.

The period was in the wake of the Suez crisis, which even today is remembered by many as a watershed between two eras of British policy. It was an episode that had split the nation (and my own family for that matter) between the believers in British imperialism and those embittered by the hypocrisy of an outdated paternalism towards the Third World. Decolonisation was already in progress, but after Suez a veil of disinformation had been swept to one side and the moral issue seemed to resolve from a matter of dignified enlightenment to one of naked self-interest. Having already launched on my own anthropological career in a mood of benign and innocent optimism, I now found myself ashamed of my nationality and irritated that the evidence of Suez had somehow become blurred once the issue ceased to be news. What had been a myth of my own schooling had been exposed and yet remained intact. The believers for the time being – my own kith and kin – could continue to believe. The episode had no direct effect on my approach to research, but it clarified the moral issue. In Kenya, I avoided those who represented in my mind the ultra-believers: the white settlers. In elaborating on my encounter with the convoy in the bush, clothed like a local (according to my story) and unable to make contact with those who spoke my native language, I was implicitly identifying myself with the exploited. Carrying the symbol of my profession – my anthropologist's notebook – I was at the same time legitimising my position there. Wrapping this up as a joke was, of course, a useful way of holding an audience, but it also permitted a certain licence to emphasise the gap between cultures and possibly to exaggerate my own isolation somewhere between them. The breakdown of communication within the society I had left less than a year before was replicated by a comedy of misencounter in the bush.

Adolescence and the Bottomless Pit

If the elaborations of this incident bore on my response to the Suez crisis, then this in turn evoked memories of my childhood at a deeper level. The Suez crisis can now be seen as a telling episode in the history of changing attitudes towards decolonisation, exposing the ugly side of ideas that so many of us had grown up with. Seen retrospectively, history and growing up were entwined, and the uniqueness of my experience was in part the uniqueness of the time in which I lived. As a child I had unquestioningly accepted the supremacy of British Empire, along with the sanctity of the family and the unambiguous truth of Christianity. My growing up in a time when each of these was put to the test was experienced as a series of painful episodes, each leaving me more uncertain than the last, and each perhaps priming me towards a value-free discipline, such as anthropology. What had once been an ideological commitment, pieced together in the comfortable certainty of my childhood, was exposed step by step as a self-deception, piercing the fragile shell of my innocence. For me personally, the Suez crisis in the mid 1950s was not a major watershed, but it hurt and left me angry precisely because it exposed my own gullibility and replicated the truths behind diplomatic lies that I had faced in the late 1940s, splitting the family in new ways.

The earlier period of disillusionment occurred during the years of adolescence, dulled by the absence of my father at home and the drabness of an undistinguished boarding school in Yorkshire. The transition at the age of thirteen from a southern background to the north was itself unnerving. The revelation of my parents' divorce two years later came as a blow that took years to come to terms with. In the late 1940s, divorce rates were climbing steeply, but within the cocoon of a prudish school that upheld Christian values, divorce was regarded as an outrage. With a sense of utter shame, I kept this family development from my schoolfriends, hiding it like some inner deformity. At home during the holidays, it was a topic that we simply did not discuss or admit to neighbours. We continued to live as we had before as though nothing had happened. If we had only discussed it among ourselves, then we might have come to terms with it and worked the grief out of our systems. As it was, there was an unresolved feeling of unreality about home. I was surprised that I had always accepted my father's absence as quite normal. Why had I never sought an explanation or even toyed with the most obvious one? It was as if my whole childhood had been a facade, undermined by an ugly truth that had been so well concealed that I did not even think of asking the most obvious questions.

My education had encouraged me to ask questions and yet at the same time to accept some basic dogmas. To question these dogmas was to lay bare a bottomless pit. Now, with no certainty to draw round me and a sense of divine injustice, I felt cheated and the questions started to flow. If there was no room for divorce in my religion, then somehow I did not belong. It was in this spirit of niggling doubt that the firmly held beliefs I had grown up with started to crumble. Within a year, what had been an unquestioning faith simply evaporated before my gaze. Belief gave way to immovable disbelief. At first, it was as if I had woken up from the comfort of a dream to find myself involved in a nightmare. My faith – whatever that had been – was destroyed and I was terrified. There was no one up there and nowhere to go after this life had run its course. Why should there be? I had discovered the fragility of my own mortality. The great cosmic mystery now shifted from the uncertainties of death and afterlife to the inscrutable fact of life itself. All I could rely on was the unique sense of my own existence to shield me from oblivion.

Once again, I felt that the facts had always been there, and yet my whole upbringing, as in the case of my family background, had blinded me to them. The facade of family unity seemed replicated at a higher level by an empty facade of religious belief in a society of half-believers. It was my own way of adjusting to a new set of values and to what has, after all, become a commonplace experience in the post-war decades. I was just one of many who encountered and had to accommodate a major historical trend in their own private way. Disenchantment with the assumptions that have surrounded childhood and schooling is perhaps a very general aspect of attaining adulthood, especially in times of change. To become an adult, one has to disengage from childhood. Autobiographical memory is then transformed into a kind of myth, rather like a Kuhnian paradigm. For me, this was the memory of a lifestyle infused with a set of beliefs that served to hold the family together but did not stand up to close scrutiny – or to being displaced by a new set of beliefs and perhaps a new myth. It was not so much the historical trend that was so shattering as the suddenness and stark intimacy of the realisation.

Other aspects of my world-view remained intact and I clung to these. I even assumed the basic integrity of the (southern) English way of life as something to which I could return after leaving school. Academically, my inclination was towards some unambitious scientific career, working among fellow beings, but concerned with inanimate problems associated with progress. However, at heart this vague notion of progress seemed part of the myth of my childhood. It did not answer the desire to recreate some kind of order, some meaning out of life itself, and it was this that gripped my need for understanding and pointed the only way out of my mental confusion. From a wholly uninformed start, the foundations had been laid for a search that was to be realised years later when I first came across social anthropology, which seemed to promise some insight into the fundamentals of human existence, and second the Samburu. These discoveries in themselves entailed a random element of chance. But the way in which I responded to each in turn seems to make sense in terms of my curiosity for understanding things that appeared hidden from me. Changing the course of my career, prior to the vociferous 1960s, was also a silent form of protest against a system that rang hollow and seemed based on half-truths and self-deception, especially after the Suez crisis.

To express this in Bernsteinian terms, it was as if my education encouraged an elaborated mode of thought along channels bounded by restricted dogma that ranged from Christian values to the mindless conformism of my own peer group. Once the dogma had been breached at one point, nowhere was it sacrosanct. An unrestricted elaborated mode of thought spiralled out of control, and life itself lost meaning.

If, as I have suggested, the dilemma of my youth had been the impasse of a search for answers in an endlessly elaborated mode of thought with no fundamentals of faith, then the highly traditionalist Samburu seem an odd object of study and my enchantment with them as a people even odder. Here, I wish to argue that the erratic course that led me eventually to the Samburu somehow offered a way forward; but I was not exactly aware of it at the time and have never quite been able to spell it out clearly. The impasse of one extreme and a sceptical view of progress led me stumbling towards a people who embraced the opposite extreme, whose resilient traditionalism was highly restrictive. From a family background that had seemed to evaporate inexplicably, I was heading towards a kinship system that had a benign halo of certainty and encompassed almost endless ramifications that I could explore at length. Emotionally, as I learned to accommodate this system and taking my adoption into a particular family seriously, it was like re-entering the primitive world of childhood. I had to be eased out of my bewilderment, not by my own ill-formulated questions, but by the questions that Samburu repeatedly asked me and that I in turn had to learn to turn back on them. Reflexivity was a term I had not then heard of, but the principle was inherent in any attempt to enter an exotic culture, to master the language and make conversation – any conversation – on topics that emerged from the context of the moment. The luxury of selecting my own topics had to wait until I could reformulate them.

Like so many others who have had dealings with the Samburu, I was wholly captivated by them. At times, I felt thoroughly drawn towards them and wanted to stay almost indefinitely. At other moments in the still of the night, I would sense the faint and solemn ticking of a clock, reminding me of the one at home during my childhood, and the ticking would then fade as I listened. Why my childhood? Or was this fantasy somehow bound up with the make-believe watch that beamed me away in my joke? Was it reminding me that life's opportunities were ticking away? Whatever my feelings for the Samburu or private misbeliefs, I could not completely rid myself of an inner Protestant ethic that always reminded me to use my time and to work to my open-ended brief. I had to separate my personal involvement from the task of research. Only by completing this research, ultimately as an outsider, could I justify the whole exercise to everyone concerned, including myself and including the Samburu, whose future was by no means certain in an independent Kenya. I had to transform my involvement with them into an involvement with a model about them as an outsider and disbeliever, aware of the contradictions within their system and of wider issues when viewed from outside. Again this was experienced as a very personal problem and yet is common for the anthropologist, whose attempts to empathise in order to analyse entails a moral dilemma. This stems at least in part from the fact that anthropological fieldwork in practice can never be value-free any more than it can be an emotionless experience, for it lies at the interface between two cultures rather like my joke.

In writing up this research as a thesis (1965), some aspects had a certain autobiographical relevance at one stage removed. These included: the angry reaction of youths (*moran*) to the narrow constraints of their upbringing; the ritualised nature of knowledge in manipulating the young; aspects of religious conversion in the course of socialisation; and tensions between the nineteenth-century middle-class family and boarding schools which I compared with the Samburu age system. I do not wish to dwell on these here since there were other equally important themes that were less autobiographical. To the extent that this study might now be seen as functionalist, I would question a widespread view that this approach represented a pre-reflexive phase in anthropology and was unsuspectingly caught up in a colonialist mode of thought (Asad 1973: 18). A more valid criticism of studies such as *The Samburu* is that they reflect too

close an identification with a widespread African sense of tradition and too little an awareness of processes of change. In other words, they are *too* reflexive at the expense of the historical context. Certainly, Evans-Pritchard as my supervisor was more concerned that my thesis should reflect my own personal experience of the Samburu than that it should embody a watertight argument. Today, this advice sounds surprisingly modern, reflexive and unfunctionalist (q.v. Pocock 1961: 72).

Yet it remains that the principal thrust of my research was to construct a meaningful whole out of the premises of Samburu society in order to demonstrate to myself that this could be done. Piecing together a self-contained argument out of fragmented field data was like piecing together a fragmented past. If order could be made out of chaos, then as a matter of faith other things could make sense. If this was a functionalist stance, then at least it echoed the self-awareness of such peoples as the Samburu for whom the concept of tradition was strong and implied no change. The warmth that they exuded was one of absolute certainty in their way of life within an unquestioned system of beliefs. There was a sense of wholeness, of wholesome integrity shared by nearly everyone, that I needed to replicate in my writing. It was the anthropology of Durkheim with collective representations, collective sentiments and a collective life in which society itself rode above the fragile dilemmas of the individual.

There was, need I say, a strong element of transference in my attachment to the Samburu, which built up as my relationship to one clan became firmer and more secure. Correspondingly, writing this up entailed an element of counter-transference with all the difficulties of disentangling myself from an emotional experience. Or a better metaphor perhaps would be that I had fallen in love: not with any individual, but with an idea that I associated with a community at large and the way of life of a people who had cast their charm over me. Writing this up was not so much a falling out of love, or grief at the loss of a loved object. It was more a matter of consummation, a necessary fulfilment of the relationship I had formed and of the conditions on which that relationship was based. The whole experience had been contrived, and yet its creative potential had led me towards a sense of completeness. I would suggest that this total experience was not idiosyncratic, but must be very common in the early careers of social anthropologists, and highly pertinent to any volume on their autobiographies.

Conclusion: Clinging to Youth, Disengaging from Childhood and the Autobiographical Reconstruction of History

Let me conclude by returning to Masiani's autobiographical encounter as compared with my own, each of us concerned with ambivalent views of our own society. Both were narratives in which the author presented himself presenting himself to his own culture, stepping into a realm of partial fantasy. The contrast between Masiani's account and my own stilted attempt here seems to be broadly the contrast between restricted and elaborated modes of thought: an older man conforming to an acceptable stereotype and a younger man out on a limb.

However, the Maasai are restricted only up to a point, since as I have noted, there is a competitive edge to their society that is generally lacking among the Samburu. Masiani's brand of nonconformity set out to stir a receptive audience. He emerges as a Maasai, competitive and thrusting among his peers, but perhaps a little more so than normal, as if to test the system to its limit and reassure himself of his position. The flavour of his account was not just his own irascibility, but also his faith in the certainty and strength of Maasai society. His reminiscences generally, and his boasts, were tinged with Maasai ideals. In the above episode, as elsewhere, he was using the latitude permitted an elder in late middle age to project himself as an undaunted spirit, clinging to youth with all the bravado of a committed *moran*, while maintaining his claim to seniority and respect as the occasion demanded. In a highly age-conscious society and within the restrictions

of Maasai convention, he was playing with his age to an extent not permitted to younger men.

In my own joke, I seem to have been projecting myself as a serious-minded research student who had lost contact with his own culture. In emphasising the unbridgable gap, I was implying how far I had gone in identifying myself with the Samburu, and perhaps gave the impression that living among them was an end in itself. But in making this a joke of my past self, I had clearly come back among friends and the end lay in my research. In an odd sort of way, preparing my thesis was a replication of the joke, reliving episodes of my life among the Samburu and Rendille, identifying with them in an attempt to understand; and yet now in the telling, slanting this experience as a bridge across the gap between their cultures and ours for the benefit of my audience: the hypothetical western reader in my mind's eye. The flavour of the joke was only made explicit in a brief preface: 'By adopting me into their numbers.... accepting me.... as a *moran* ... Time meant something quite different; and under this spell, three years of my life slipped past unnoticed' (1965: xiv). Note again the element of fantasy in expressing my enchantment: it was after all largely an adoption on terms of my own choosing; and what about the breaks in my fieldwork, what about that inner ticking reminding me of the seconds – and years – slipping away? Wrapped up in a joke or tucked away in a preface, I was projecting this whole episode of my career into a timeless limbo, suspended between a troubled youth and settling down. In a sense, like Masiani, I too was playing with my perception of ageing. Implicitly, I seem to have been viewing my development with its liminal period of separation as a rite of transition that had its counterpart among my Samburu peers: bush-loving *moran* in their twenties, socially suspended between childhood and elderhood (1965: 140, 162, 259–60). Once I had completed my thesis, I could settle down to whatever lay ahead. This left me apprehensive of the future, but with a sense of completion in respect of the past and a renewed confidence. Disengaging successfully from the Samburu had a therapeutic effect. It replicated and in some ways marked the end of disengagement from my childhood. At that point I determined to leave anthropology.

Perhaps it is in the nature of autobiographies to end inconclusively in mid-stream (*vide* Cellini). There is, however, a tail-piece here which bears on a broader issue. If, as I have suggested, my own experience as a novice anthropologist probably parallels that of others, then extrapolating the point, to what extent does fantasy infect the perception of our careers subsequently? How far does the recent popular history of anthropology echo real shifts in approach and genuinely new insights? Or how far is there an element of autobiographical fiction in all this, a self-deluding myth coined by a whole generation of scholars swept along by fashionable claims? This is not to deny the development of the subject with the accumulation of ethnographies and scholarship, and shifts of interest and opportunity. But it is to follow the argument posed by Malcolm Crick in this volume that the outpouring of anthropological concern for the 'self', reflexivity and related concepts are not as new as we often suppose, but have always been a necessary part of anthropology. This is to imply that many of us do not read (or re-read) earlier texts with the same reflexive care that we claim for our field studies. And if we misperceive the recent history of our subject, we are misrepresenting to ourselves our own pasts. A collective myth infiltrates our clouded memories and autobiographical self-regard. We often suggest that as students, we were swept along by prevailing fashions and the misperceptions of our mentors, but who are the mentors now?

The implication is oddly reminiscent of some biographical commentaries on Malinowski and Radcliffe-Brown (to name but two), who are now seen to have cultivated their own images as our hero ancestors, manipulating the historical record in the course of establishing their careers (Kuper 1973: 34–7; Langham 1981: 244–300). From Malinowski especially, we have inherited a discipline with a polemic touch of messianism (or indeed of Masiani); and as Crick notes,

the claims and expectations of something new outstrip the record of history and trigger polemic responses. But this is the essence of myth and says something about the subject of anthropology and its excitement, in which our careers too are embroiled. The Malinowskian flame lures us like moths, and in the pursuit of changing fashions and a personal sense of achievement, we are all vulnerable.

This then raises the question, ironically: to the extent that we misconstrue the past – even our own pasts – is it because we too are caught up in the autobiographical restructuring of our ageing? Is this perpetual rearrangement of the anthropological scenario really a development of the discipline or is it in part a false time perspective, a construct of our developing careers as successive generations reach for the fruits of middle age? Who is maturing, the discipline or us? And how will our future biographers view this confusion of history and ageing? And what was I letting myself in for in my second conversion to anthropology after a lapse of nine years? Another worn blanket?

REFERENCES

Asad, T. (ed.)
(1973) *Anthropology and the Colonial Encounter*. London: Ithaca Press.
Cust, R. H. H.
(1935, trans.) *The Life of Benvenuto Cellini*. London: Navarre.
Goffman, E.
(1969) *The Presentation of Self in Everyday Life*. Harmondsworth: Penguin Books.
Gulliver, P. H.
(1963) *Social Control in an African Society*. London: Routledge & Kegan Paul.
Kuper, A.
(1973) *Anthropologists and Anthropology: The British School 1922–72*. London: Allen Lane.
Langham, I.
(1981) *The Building of British Social Anthropology*. Dordrecht: Reidel.
Middleton, J.
(1960) *Lugbara Religion*. London: Oxford University Press.

Pocock, D.
   (1961)   *Social Anthropology*. London: Sheed
   and Ward.
Ruben, H.
   (1972)   *African Harvest*. London: Harvill
   Press.
Spencer, P.
   (1965)   *The Samburu*. London: Routledge &
   Kegan Paul.

Spencer, P.
   (1988)   *The Maasai of Matapato*. Manchester:
   Manchester University Press.
Turner, V. W.
   (1957)   *Schism and Continuity in an African
   Society*. Manchester: Manchester University
   Press.

Part III

Fieldwork Relations and Rapport

Introduction

Jeffrey A. Sluka

The success of ethnographic fieldwork is in large measure determined by the ability to establish good rapport and develop meaningful relations with research participants. When fieldwork fails, it is generally due to a failure either to establish rapport and good relations or to maintain them over time. These relations range from friendship to hostility, and may be influenced by ethnicity, religion, class, gender, and age, and whether the researcher is alone or accompanied by family.

One of the main ways cultural anthropologists have established fieldwork relations is by the development of strong bonds of friendship with particular individuals who often become both key informants and research assistants. Making a friend has proven to be one of the main ways that anthropologists have been able to establish rapport during the early part of fieldwork, and Oberg (1974) has suggested that it is one of the best ways of countering culture shock. This idea is well established in the discipline, and was the central idea expressed in the title of Powdermaker's classic study of her fieldwork *Stranger and Friend* (1966). She believed that: "Whatever the degree of the field worker's participation in the whole society, friendships with a few people develop, and they help him to find a niche in the community. It is these friends who often become his best informants" (1966:420).

In the 1990s, interest in reflections on the nature and quality of field relations between researchers and informants grew, and the theme of fieldwork and friendship was explored in a number of important publications, including Beverly Chiñas' *La Zandunga: Of Fieldwork and Friendship in Southern Mexico* (1992), Nita Kumar's *Friends, Brothers, and Informants: Fieldwork Memories of Banaras* (1992), and Bruce Grindal and Frank Salamone's edited volume, *Bridges to Humanity:*

Ethnographic Fieldwork: An Anthropological Reader, Second Edition. Edited by
Antonius C. G. M. Robben and Jeffrey A. Sluka.
Editorial material and organization © 2012 John Wiley & Sons, Inc.
Published 2012 by John Wiley & Sons, Inc.

Narratives on Anthropology and Friendship (1995). In the second half of the 1990s, this interest in fieldwork relations began to extend to consideration of the question of sexual relationships in the field. In particular, this was explored in two edited volumes: Don Kulick and Margaret Willson's *Taboo: Sex, Identity and Erotic Subjectivity in Anthropological Fieldwork* (1995) and Fran Markowitz and Michael Ashkenazi's *Sex, Sexuality, and the Anthropologist* (1999). Sex as part of participant observation is both a methodological and an ethical issue. Traditionally, there was a strong taboo against ethnographers engaging in sex with research participants, because it was believed that it represented an unfair use of their position of power and an inappropriate practice on other grounds. However, intimacy helps break down the distinction between "self" and "other" and the cultural boundaries that obscure the common humanity of researchers and their informants, and consensual sex between adults can be seen not as a power relationship but, rather, as its opposite – the breaking down of hierarchy and establishment of equality between them.

The classic image of successful rapport and good fieldwork relations in cultural anthropology is that of the successful ethnographer who has been "adopted" or named by the tribe or people he or she studies (see Kan 2001), and less successful fieldwork relations were rarely discussed until the reflexive trend began to emerge in the 1970s. One of the first and best discussions of less-than-ideal field relations was presented by Jean Briggs (1977) in her honest account of her fieldwork with an Eskimo (Inuit) community in the Canadian Arctic. Briggs was "adopted" by the tribe, but failed to maintain rapport with them. In order to achieve acceptance, anthropologists must assume a role that is defined as believable and non-threatening in the eyes of the people with whom they wish to do research. Briggs found acceptance in the form of fictive kinship by playing the role of a daughter. While this was a classic means of achieving rapport and a working relationship with people, this case shows that it is not always ideal, and even fictive kinship roles can break down under the stress of relations between researchers and the "others" with whom they work.

In practice, Briggs found it impossible to reconcile the two roles and "be simultaneously a docile and helpful daughter and a conscientious anthropologist" (1977:65). She became insubordinate, disobedient, obstinate, and grumpy, expressed her anger, did not always help with the chores, and sometimes refused requests to share her possessions – pretty much violating most of the fundamental values of Inuit culture. Not surprisingly, the tribe found her behavior "completely incomprehensible" (1977:65). She grew "annoyed and frustrated" (1977:67) with them, and they with her, and their relationship erupted into open conflict. She went from being treated as a slow child to being treated as "an incorrigible offender, who had unfortunately to be endured but who could not be incorporated into the social life of the group" (1977:72). After several months of "uneasiness," the Inuit began to avoid her, and expressed their wish that she leave. Eventually, however, she was able to satisfactorily explain her behavior and achieved a rapprochement with them. Briggs concluded: "Although an anthropologist must have a recognized role or roles in order to make it possible to interact with him sensibly and predictably, nevertheless it will be evident from what I have described of my own case that the assignment of a role may create as many problems as it solves for both the anthropologist and his hosts" (1977:78).

Similarly, William and Margaret Rodman (1990) suffered a loss of rapport in their relationship with their research participants. While conducting fieldwork on the small South Pacific island of Ambae, Margaret contracted malaria and nearly died. The tribe insisted that her illness was caused by a *wande* or river spirit. In a "failure to believe," they chose not to rely on the local cures that their research participants insisted they use, and instead went to a hospital. This resulted in a falling out with the tribe, particularly the chief with whom they were living. They lost rapport and had to leave the field for health reasons, and thus ended their fieldwork on Ambae.

In this part of the Reader, we present three articles which illustrate and explore important dimensions of fieldwork relations and rapport: Charles Wagley's "Champukwi of the Village of the Tapirs" (1960), Gerald Berreman's "Behind Many Masks: Ethnography and Impression Management" (1972), and Antonius Robben's "The Politics of Truth and Emotion Among Victims and Perpetrators of Violence" (1995).

Published in 1960, Wagley's account of his fieldwork in 1939 in a small village of about 175 Tapirapé Indians in central Brazil comes from the first volume dedicated to exploring field relationships between anthropologists and key informants (Casagrande 1960). He chose his relationship with Champukwi for this article because he "became my best informant, and after a time, an inseparable companion" (1960:400), and "for the brief span of about a year, he was my most intimate friend" (1960:398). But their close association began to cause trouble, and they had a falling out. Champukwi was an inveterate Lothario who gave his paramours beads that Wagley had given him. This caused stress between him and Wagley because, "as people continued to criticize Champukwi, much of their criticism [revolved] around his relationship with me" (1960:408). Nonetheless, their relationship continued, and Champukwi gradually evolved from not only being a friend and anthropological informant, but also a field assistant. Wagley reflects:

> In the security of our studies and in the classroom, we claim that anthropology is a social science ... But, at its source, in the midst of the people with whom the anthropologist lives and works, field research involves the practice of an art in which emotions, subjective attitudes and reactions, and undoubtedly subconscious motivations participate ... Anthropological field research is a profoundly human endeavor ... the anthropologist almost inevitably is involved in a complex set of human relations among another people ... and each anthropologist is a distinctive personality and each undoubtedly handles in his own way his dual role as a sympathetic friend to key informants and as scientific observer of a society and culture which is not his own. (1960:414–415)

Wagley concludes with a deeply personal reflection on his relationship with this "key informant," which expresses the fundamentally human nature of the face-to-face encounter in ethnographic fieldwork: "To me, Champukwi was, above all, a friend whom I shall remember always with warm affection" (1960:415).

Gerald Berreman's "Behind Many Masks" was published as the prologue to his outstanding ethnography *Hindus of the Himalayas* (1972). In the Preface to the second edition, he states:

> I believe firmly that ethnography cannot be understood independently of the experience which produces it. Just as I felt obliged to be thorough and candid in presenting my

research findings, so I have felt obliged to be thorough and candid about how I did that research. If fault be found with the former, it is the result of the latter. Written from an "interactionist" perspective, "Behind Many Masks" emphasizes the problems for research generated by the conflicting interests of the various castes and by their divergent culture and lifestyles, because even in small and isolated Sirkanda, social heterogeneity loomed as a major obstacle to my rapport and my understanding, just as it does to the people's relationships with one another. (1972:vi–vii)

Berreman presents a case study and analysis of "some of the problems and consequences inherent in the interaction of ethnographer and subjects," particularly the differential effects of his identification with high- and low-status groups in the village (1972:xix).

As a result of the fact that Hindu villages in India are internally divided along caste, religious, and other lines, "acceptance by one element of the community does not imply acceptance by the whole community and it frequently, in fact, precludes it" (1972:xxii). Berreman was not "adopted" by the locals, but he describes how he was able to establish acceptance and rapport in the village, and is candid about the nature of this relationship:

Although I remained an alien and was never made to feel that my presence in the village was actively desired by most of its members, I was thereafter tolerated with considerable indulgence. I became established as a resident of Sirkanda, albeit a peculiar one, and no one tried to get me to leave. I have heard strangers … inquire of Sirkanda villagers as to my identity … and be left to ponder the succinct reply, "He lives here." (1972:xxvii)

At different times during his fieldwork, Berreman employed two interpreter assistants – a Brahmin who became ill four months into the research and a Muslim who replaced him. Berreman applies Erving Goffman's interactionist model of "impression management" to reflect on the implications for his research of the differences in status of these two assistants. Pronounced stratification in the village meant that there were many competing groups or "teams," including the ethnographer and his research assistants, the village as a whole, low-caste and low-status villagers, and high-caste villagers. Within these teams, there were divisions as well – for example, between different high-caste factions. Berreman found that his interaction with each of these teams was different, and the use of the two assistants had different effects when working with them.

Today, the communities with which cultural anthropologists do research are nearly always stratified, plural, and internally divided, and relations have to be maintained with different factions and interest groups who may be in conflict or competition with each other. Establishing acceptance and working relationships with both a community as a whole and the various factions within it is frequently a difficult goal to achieve.

This reality, of the competing interests of research participants, is also apparent in Antonius Robben's article "The Politics of Truth and Emotion among Victims and Perpetrators of Violence" (1995). Usually, cultural anthropologists do fieldwork with people they like, respect, or even admire, but Robben raises the issue of establishing research relationships with people you do not like and who you may even consider to be morally reprehensible. As a result of his fieldwork with both victims and perpetrators of violence during the "dirty war" in Argentina, Robben warns of the dangers of "ethnographic seduction," which he defines as "a complex dynamic of conscious moves and unconscious defenses that may arise in interviews with victims and perpetrators of violence" (1996:72) and which undermine critical detachment. Few anthropologists have had his experience: "There were days when I talked in the morning to a victim of political persecution and in the afternoon with a military officer who had been responsible for the repression. These days were stressful because they demanded radical swings in empathetic understanding" (1996:97).

Robben was already sensitive to the risks to objectivity in doing research with victims of state terror, aware that it is easy in face-to-face research to be "seduced" by their obvious emotion and suffering. But he did not anticipate that this would be a problem when "studying up" state terrorists. He found that it was. The general and other military officers treated him well and with respect, and stressed their class affinities with him (well educated, elite, bourgeois). Although his initial sympathy was greater with members of human rights organizations than with the armed forces, he soon met officers whose politics he detested but for whom he came to feel a personal liking.

Once sensitized to this, Robben then found that he also recognized it in his subsequent meetings with bishops, human rights activists, former guerrilla leaders, and victims of state terror, and that each group was seductive in its own way. He observes: "It is much easier to acknowledge manipulation by victimizers than by victims. We have more sympathy for unmasking abuses of power than doubting the words of their victims. I have the same sympathies" (1995:84). Robben argues that seduction "disarms our critical detachment and thus debilitates the gathering of cultural knowledge" (1995:86), and that "victims may be harmed and their testimonies discredited if we report their views naively and uncritically" (1995:84).

Robben's article not only exemplifies some of the problems of establishing rapport and fieldwork relations in contexts of political violence, state repression, and popular resistance, but also the expanding venues of fieldwork into war zones and sites of violent conflict (cf. Nordstrom and Robben 1995), where there are major divisions between the parties to the conflict, and it is almost impossible to establish and subsequently maintain research relationships with both at the same time.

REFERENCES

Berreman, Gerald D.
  1972   Behind Many Masks: Ethnography and Impression Management. In: *Hindus of the Himalayas: Ethnography and Change*. 2nd edn. Pp. xvii–lvii. Berkeley: University of California Press.
Briggs, Jean L.
  1977   Kapluna Daughter: Adopted by the Eskimo. In: *Conformity and Conflict*. J. Spradley and D. McCurdy, eds., pp. 61–79. Boston: Little, Brown.
Casagrande, Joseph, ed.
  1960   *In the Company of Man: Twenty Portraits of Anthropological Informants*. New York: Harper & Row.

Chiñas, Beverly Newbold
   1992   *La Zandunga: Of Fieldwork and Friendship in Southern Mexico*. Prospect Heights: Waveland.
Grindal, Bruce and Frank Salamone, eds.
   1995   *Bridges to Humanity: Narratives on Anthropology and Friendship*. Prospect Heights: Waveland.
Kan, Sergei, ed.
   2001   *Strangers to Relatives: The Adoption and Naming of Anthropologists in Native North America*. Lincoln: University of Nebraska Press.
Kulick, Don and Margaret Willson, eds.
   1995   *Taboo: Sex, Identity and Erotic Subjectivity in Anthropological Fieldwork*. New York: Routledge.
Kumar, Nita
   1992   *Friends, Brothers, and Informants: Fieldwork Memories of Banaras*. Berkeley: University of California Press.
Markowitz, Fran and Michael Ashkenazi, eds.
   1999   *Sex, Sexuality, and the Anthropologist*. Urbana: University of Illinois Press.
Nordstrom, Carolyn and Antonius C. G. M. Robben, eds.
   1995   *Fieldwork Under Fire: Contemporary Studies of Violence and Survival*. Berkeley: University of California Press.
Oberg, Kalervo
   1974   *Culture Shock*. Indianapolis: Bobbs-Merrill.
Powdermaker, Hortense
   1966   *Stranger and Friend: The Way of an Anthropologist*. New York: Norton.
Robben, Antonius C. G. M.
   1995   The Politics of Truth and Emotion Among Victims and Perpetrators of Violence. In: *Fieldwork under Fire*. Carolyn Nordstrom and Antonius C. G. M. Robben, eds., pp. 81–103. Berkeley: University of California Press.
Robben, Antonius C. G. M.
   1996   Ethnographic Seduction, Transference, and Resistance in Dialogues about Terror and Violence in Argentina. *Ethos* 24(1):71–106.
Rodman, William and Margaret Rodman
   1990   To Die on Ambae: On the Possibility of Doing Fieldwork Forever. In: *The Humbled Anthropologist: Tales From the Pacific*. Philip DeVita, ed., pp. 101–120. Belmont: Wadsworth.
Wagley, Charles
   1960   Champukwi of the Village of the Tapirs. In: *In the Company of Man: Twenty Portraits of Anthropological Informants*. Joseph Casagrande, ed., pp. 398–415. New York: Harper & Row.

8

Champukwi of the Village of the Tapirs

Charles Wagley

Champukwi was not the first person who came to mind when a contribution to this volume was considered. I thought of Gregorio Martin, a dignified and wise old Mayan Indian of Santiago Chimaltenango in Guatemala, who in 1937 had taught me the way of life of his people. I thought of Camirang, the dynamic young chieftain whom I had known in 1941 in a village of Tenetehara Indians along the Pindaré River in northeastern Brazil. I thought also of Nhunduca, a gifted and witty story-teller from a small Amazon community, who in 1948 introduced me to the rich folklore of the Amazon *caboclo* or peasant. But then, among all the people I had known in the various primitive and peasant cultures in which I have done ethnological research, I chose Champukwi, a man of no outstanding talent, yet talented all the same – a man of not the highest prestige in his society, yet admired by all. For the brief span of about a year he was my most intimate friend.

I knew Champukwi some 20 years ago when I lived in his small village of about 175 Tapirapé Indians in central Brazil. I must have seen him at once, for presents were distributed to the whole population on the day of my arrival in late April of 1939. But I did not distinguish Champukwi as an individual, nor did he, at first, stand out in any way from the other men of his village. His name does not appear in the notes taken during my first month among the Tapirapé.

For me, and even more for Valentim Gomes, the Brazilian frontiersman who was my companion and employee, the first weeks in the Village of the Tapirs, as the small settlement was known, were a period of grappling with a strange and often confusing world. The Tapirapé Indians lived between the Araguaia and Xingú Rivers, an area at that time almost entirely isolated from modern Brazil. They had been visited by only a few people from the "outside" – by one or two missionaries;

Charles Wagley, "Champukwi of the Village of the Tapirs," pp. 398–415 from *In the Company of Man: Twenty Portraits of Anthropological Informants*, ed. Joseph B. Casagrande. New York: Harper & Row, 1960. Copyright © 1960 by Joseph B. Casagrande.

Ethnographic Fieldwork: An Anthropological Reader, Second Edition. Edited by Antonius C. G. M. Robben and Jeffrey A. Sluka. Editorial material and organization © 2012 John Wiley & Sons, Inc. Published 2012 by John Wiley & Sons, Inc.

by Herbert Baldus, a German-Brazilian anthropologist; and by a few frontiersmen from the Araguaia River. The nearest Brazilian settlement to the Village of the Tapirs was Furo de Pedra, a town of 400–500 persons that lay some 300 miles away on the Araguaia River. Three Tapirapé youths had spent a few months at mission stations and thus spoke a rudimentary form of Portuguese, using a vocabulary limited to a few basic nouns and verbs. At first our main problem was communication, but these youths were able to help us. Aside from them, the only individuals we knew by name during the first two weeks were the "captains," the older men who were the heads of the six large haypile-like houses arranged in a circular village pattern. These, we later learned, were each occupied by a matrilocal extended family. But even the personal names – such as Oprunxui, Wantanamu, Kamanare, Mariapawungo, Okané, and the like – were then hard to remember, let alone pronounce.

During the first weeks in the Village of Tapirs, I began to study intensively the Tapirapé language, a language belonging to the widespread Tupí-Guaraní stock. Until I could use this language at least passably, I was limited to observing and recording only those forms of Tapirapé culture that the eye could see. Even these usually needed explaining. I visited the extensive Tapirapé gardens in which manioc, beans, peanuts, cotton, and other native American crops were grown. I watched the women fabricate flour from both poisonous and "sweet" varieties of manioc, and make pots out of clay. I watched the men weave baskets out of palm fiber and manufacture their bows and arrows as they sat in hammocks in the large palmthatched structure in the center of the village circle. This building was obviously the men's club, for no women ever entered. I rapidly became accustomed to nudity. The women wore nothing at all, and the men only a palm fiber band around the prepuce. But even nude women could be modestly seated, and the men were careful never to remove their palm band to expose the glans penis. Obvious also to the uninstructed eye was the fact that the Tapirapé expressed their personal vanity in the elaborate designs carefully painted on their bodies with *rucu* (red) and *genipa* (black).

These and many other overt aspects of Tapirapé culture could be recorded in notes and photographs while I studied their language.

The Tapirapé, a friendly and humorous people, seemed rather pleased with the curious strangers in their midst. They found our antics amusing; the gales of laughter that accompanied the conversations that we could hear but not understand seemed evoked by tales of our strange behavior. (It is so easy to presume that oneself is the subject of conversation when listening to a strange language.) Then, of course, our presence was materially valuable – for the salt, knives, needles, beads, mirrors, and other presents we brought were greatly appreciated. However, within a very short time some of these people began to emerge as individuals. Awanchowa, a small boy of about 6, followed me about and literally haunted our little house, staring at our large bag of salt which he ate with the same relish children in other cultures eat sweets. Then there was Tanui, a woman of middle age (whose hair was cropped short indicating that a near relative had recently died) who often brought us presents of food. Gradually most of the villagers emerged as distinctive personalities and among them was Champukwi. I cannot remember when I first came to know him as an individual, but his name begins to appear regularly in field notebooks about one month after our arrival. Soon, he became my best informant, and after a time, an inseparable companion.

In 1939 Champukwi must have been about 25 years of age. He was tall for a Tapirapé male, measuring perhaps about 5 feet 6 inches, strongly built but lean, and weighing, I should judge, about 150 lbs. Like all Tapirapé men he wore his hair in bangs across his forehead with a braided pigtail tied at the back of his neck. He was somewhat of a dandy, for his feet and the calves of his legs were painted bright red every evening with *rucu*. From time to time he painted an intricate design on his body, and he wore crocheted disc-like wrist ornaments of cotton string dyed red. He was obviously a man of some prestige among men of his age, for youths and younger men treated him with deference, always finding a seat for him on the bench that was built against one wall of our house. I soon learned that he, too, had spent a short period at a mission station several years earlier and that he knew a few words of Portuguese. He was married and had a daughter about 2 years of age. His wife, hardly attractive according to my American tastes, appeared to be somewhat older than he, and was pregnant when we first met.

Champukwi seemed more patient than other Tapirapé with my attempts to use his language and to seek information. He would repeat a word, a phrase, or a sentence several times so that I might write it down phonetically. He resorted to his meager Portuguese and even to mimicry to explain what was meant. His patience was of course requited by gifts of beads, hardware, and salt which I provided judiciously from time to time. After a few days, I began noting questions to be asked of Champukwi in the late afternoon when he now habitually visited our house. But this was the time that others also liked to visit. At this hour of the day our house was often crowded with men, women, children, and even pets – monkeys, parrots, and wild pigs – for which the Tapirapé along with other Brazilian tribes have an especial fondness. Such social gatherings were hardly conducive to the ethnological interview or even to the systematic recording of vocabulary. So I asked Champukwi if I might go with him to his garden. There, alternating between helping him cut brush from his garden site and sitting in the shade, I was able to conduct a kind of haphazard interview. Often, while he worked, I formulated questions in my halting Tapirapé and I was able by repetition to understand his answers. Although the Tapirapé villagers began to joke of Champukwi's new garden site as belonging to the two of us, these days were very valuable for my research.

Walking through the forest to and from Champukwi's garden, we often hunted for *jacu*, a large forest fowl rather like a chicken. I attemped to teach Champukwi how to use my .22 rifle, but he had difficulty understanding the gunsights and missed continually. He attempted to show me how to "see" the *jacu* hidden in the thick branches of the trees, but I seldom caught sight of the birds until they had flown. Thus, our complementary incapacities combined to make our hunting in the tropical forest quite unproductive, and in

disgust Champukwi often resorted to his bow and arrow. Only later in the year, after he had practiced a great deal by shooting at tin cans did Champukwi master the use of the rifle, and this new-found skill greatly added to his prestige among the Tapirapé.

My abiding friendship with Champukwi perhaps really began when I came down with malaria about six weeks after our arrival. During the first days of my illness, I was oblivious to my surroundings. I am told that while one *panché*, or medicine man, predicted my death, another tried to cure me by massage, by blowing tobacco smoke over my body, and by attempting to suck out the "object" that was causing the fever. Evidently his efforts – plus the atabrine tablets administered by Valentim Gomes – were successful, for my fever abated. I realized, however, that convalescence would be slow. Unable to leave the house for almost three weeks, I spent my days and evenings suspended in a large Brazilian hammock. In this state of enervation, I must have been the very picture of the languid white man in the tropics. Each late afternoon our house became a gathering place for the Tapirapé villagers, who came not only to visit with me (communication was still difficult) but also with each other, and to gaze upon the belongings of the *tori* (non-Indian). My illness proved to be a boon for ethnographic research. People were more patient with the sick anthropologist than with the well one. They told stories, not only for my benefit, but also to entertain each other. In attempting to explain to me about a mythological culture hero, a man would find himself telling a myth to the attending audience. Thus, I heard (and saw) Tapirapé stories told as they should be – as dramatic forms spoken with vivacity and replete with mimicry of the animals that are so often characters in these folktales. With my still imperfect knowledge of Tapirapé I inevitably lost the thread of the story and it had to be retold to me more slowly.

Champukwi was a frequent visitor during these days of my convalescence. He came each morning on the way to his garden and he became accustomed to drinking morning coffee with us. And, each late afternoon after he had returned from his garden, he came "to talk" – often slowly retelling the stories and incidents that I had difficulty understanding the evening before. Several days during this period he did not work in his garden but sat for two or three hours talking. He learned when he should pause or repeat a phrase or sentence in order that I might take notes. He came to understand what writing meant, discovering that what I wrote in my notebook I could repeat to him later. In time he appreciated the fact that I was not so much interested in learning the Tapirapé language as I was in comprehending the Tapirapé way of life. As so often is the case when a person understands and speaks a foreign language poorly, one communicates best with but a single person who is accustomed to one's mistakes and one's meager vocabulary. Thus, I could understand and make myself understood to Champukwi better than any other Tapirapé. Moreover, because he spent long hours in our house, he was learning Portuguese from Valentim Gomes, and this was an aid in helping me translate newly learned words and phrases in Tapirapé and even helped me understand his explanations of Tapirapé culture patterns. Champukwi thus consciously became my teacher, and others came to realize that he was teaching me. During the next two months we had daily sessions, some very brief and others lasting two or more hours.

In October of 1939, some six months after my arrival, I found it necessary to leave the Village of the Tapirs to go to Furo de Pedra for supplies and to collect mail that was held there for me. Valentim Gomes and I had come up the Tapirapé River, a tributary of the Araguaia, pulled by an outboard motor belonging to an anthropological colleague who had since returned to the United States. Now we had to paddle ourselves downstream. We could expect little help from the sluggish current and since the river was so low, it might be necessary to haul our canoe through shallows. Malaria had left me weak and I doubted that I was equal to this strenuous task. Several Tapirapé men, including Champukwi, were anxious to accompany us, but having Indians with us in Furo de Pedra was not advisable. First, they were susceptible to the common cold, which among relatively uncontaminated peoples such as these American aborigines often turns into a

serious, and even fatal, disease. Second, unaccustomed to clothes, money, many foods, and other Brazilian customs and forms of etiquette, they would be totally dependent upon us during our stay in this frontier community. Nevertheless, the temptation to have my best informant with me during the trip and during our stay in Furo de Pedra was great and so we agreed to take Champukwi.

The trip was made slowly. Two good frontiersmen in a light canoe could have made it in three days, but we took eight. Champukwi was of little help in the canoe; unlike the riverine tribes the Tapirapé are a forest people who know little about the water, and few of them had ever traveled by canoe. Champukwi was unusual in that he could swim. Although he had more endurance than I, his efforts at paddling endangered the equilibrium of our canoe. However, he could shoot fish with his bow and arrow. The dry season had driven game from the open savanna which borders the Tapirapé River so that we were able to kill deer, *mutum* (another species of large forest fowl), and a wild goose to supplement the less palatable fare we had brought with us. Each night we camped on a beach from which we were able to collect the eggs of a small turtle, the *tracaja*, that had been buried in the sand. Only the mosquitoes which swarmed during sundown and early evening marred our trip. The experience remains one of the most memorable of my life, a feeling that was shared, I believe, by Valentim Gomes and by Champukwi.

Champukwi adjusted to Furo de Pedra with amazing rapidity. His short visit as a youth to the mission station undoubtedly contributed to his quick adaptation although, to be sure, there were minor problems and incidents. The Brazilians of Furo de Pedra were accustomed to Indians, for nearby there was a village of semi-civilized Caraja Indians who frequently visited and traded in the settlement. Yet, Champukwi was a bit of a curiosity – the townspeople had seen only one other Tapirapé. The local Brazilians invited him into their homes and offered him coffee and sweets. Both Valentim Gomes and I watched over his movements with all the anxiety of overprotective parents for fear that he might be exposed to a respiratory infection (he did not contract any) or that the hospitality of the local Brazilians might persuade him to drink *cachaça* (sugar cane *aguardiente*). Alcoholic beverages were unknown to the Tapirapé who are unlike most South American groups in this respect. According to Champukwi's own report, he tried *cachaça* only once in Furo de Pedra and (quite normally) found it distasteful and unpleasant. Yet there were moments that were awkward at the time however humorous they seem in retrospect. One day when I bought several dozen oranges in the street, Champukwi calmly removed the trousers that had been provided for him and made a sack to carry home the oranges by tying up the legs. In Furo de Pedra, he often went nude in the house we had rented for our stay. Even the Brazilian woman who came to prepare our meals became more or less accustomed to his nakedness, but sometimes he forgot to dress before sallying forth into the street. The rural Brazilian diet, derived in large measure from native Indian foods, seemed to please Champukwi, but he could not be comfortable eating at the table. He preferred during meals to sit across the room on a low stool.

Champukwi's reaction to this rural form of Brazilian civilization was not childlike in any way. He in turn became an ethnologist. He wanted to see gardens that provided the food for so many people (Furo de Pedra had hardly more than 400 people at that time). He was fascinated by the sewing machines with which he saw the women working. He attended the Catholic ceremonies held in the little chapel. He saw pairs of men and women dance face to face in semblance of an intimate embrace. About these and other strange customs he had many questions. But like the inquisitive anthropologist who had come to live in his village, his own curiosity sometimes became obtrusive. He peered into the homes of people and sometimes entered uninvited. And he followed the Brazilian women to their rather isolated bathing spot in the Araguaia River to discover if there were any anatomical differences between these women and those in his village. He even made sexual advances to Brazilian women, actions which, if he had known, were very dangerous in view of the jealous zeal with which Brazilian males protect

the honor of their wives and daughters. On the whole, however, Champukwi became quite a favorite of the local Brazilians during his two week visit to Furo de Pedra. His Portuguese improved while he visited in their homes, and he collected simple presents, such as fish hooks, bottles, tin cans, and the like, to take home with him. Even during this short period away from the village, my work with him continued. He told me of antagonisms, gossip, and schisms in the Tapirapé village which he would have hesitated to relate on home grounds. He told me of adulterous affairs in process and of the growing determination among one group of kinsmen to assassinate Urukumu, the powerful medicine man, because they suspected him of performing death-dealing sorcery.

After two weeks in Furo de Pedra, I found that it would be necessary for Valentim Gomes and me to go to Rio de Janeiro. It was not possible for Champukwi to accompany us and so I arranged for two Brazilian frontiersmen to return him to a point on the Tapirapé River from which he could easily hike to his village in a day. Valentim and I then began our slow trip up the Araguaia River to the motor road and thence to Rio de Janeiro. Two months later, rid of malaria and with a new stock of supplies, we returned to spend the long rainy months from November until the end of May in the Village of the Tapirs. Champukwi was there to welcome us, and he came each day to help repair and enlarge our house. We easily fell into our former friendly relationship, now strengthened by the experience in common of the trip to Furo de Pedra and by the feeling which many anthropologists have shared with the people of their communities – that anyone who returns is an "old friend."

My return to the village that November marked, in a sense, the end of what might be called the first phase of my relationship with Champukwi as friend and as anthropological informant. During the course of at least 200 hours of conversation (many of which may be methodologically dignified as interviews), I had learned much about Champukwi as a person as well as about Tapirapé culture. I knew that as a small boy he had come from Fish Village, where his parents had died, to live in the Village of the Tapirs. He had lived with his father's younger brother, Kamaira, who was the leader of a large household. He even confided to me his boyhood name; Tapirapé change their names several times during their lifetimes and mention of a person's first childhood name, generally that of a fish, an animal, or simply descriptive of some personal characteristic, causes laughter among the audience and considerable embarrassment to the individual. I knew that Champukwi had been married before he took his current wife, and that his first wife had died in childbirth. He revealed that her kinsmen had gossiped that her death was caused by his lack of respect for the food taboos imposed upon an expectant father. This same set of taboos now bothered him again. A series of foods, mainly meats and particularly venison, is prohibited to fathers of infants and to husbands of pregnant women. On two excursions to the savanna (which abounds with deer) Champukwi had eaten venison. Moreover, since the Tapirapé identified cattle with deer, and thus beef with venison, he had broken the taboo several additional times by partaking also of this forbidden meat. The rather scrawny condition of his 2-year-old daughter, he feared, resulted from his faults. Just after our return to the village in early November, his wife gave birth to a second daughter. She had a difficult delivery, and he remembered his transgressions. Several village gossips, without knowing anything about his misdeeds, had nevertheless accused him of this breach of taboo.

Champukwi's home life was not a happy one. He was frequently in conflict with his second wife, who had, indeed, considerable basis for complaint. She could not claim that he was a poor provider, for Champukwi was a good hunter and a diligent gardener. But he confided to me that he did not find her attractive, or at least not as attractive as other women in the village. Champukwi had a lusty sense of humor and enjoyed joking with Valentim and me. In this mood he told of his many extramarital affairs, which were in truth but slightly concealed. I would in any event have heard of these liaisons; he gave his paramours beads which everyone in the village knew I had given him as presents. This practice caused trouble for the women because their husbands could readily identify the source of the gifts. It also created trouble for Champukwi at home. His wife complained of his affairs and on one occasion, according to Champukwi, she attacked him, grabbing him by his pigtail and squeezing his exposed testicles until he fell helpless into a hammock. On other occasions, she retaliated in a manner more usual for a Tapirapé woman – she simply refused to carry drinking water from the creek, to cook food for him, and to allow him to sleep in the hammock which she and Champukwi shared. For a Tapirapé man to carry drinking water, to cook, or to sleep on a mat is considered ridiculously funny. In other circumstances, Champukwi would have had to seek recourse with a female relative. However, to do so would be tantamount to a public announcement of his marital difficulties; the whole village would have known, to their considerable merriment and jest. But having *tori* friends in the village, Champukwi could come quietly to us at night to drink water, to ask for something to eat, and even to sleep in an extra hammock we had for visitors. His affairs were evidently extensive, for he once divided all of the adult women of the village into two categories – those "I know how to talk with" (i.e., to seduce) and those "I do not know how to talk with." There were many with whom he "could talk."

Unfortunately, by late November of 1939, I knew too much about Champukwi's affairs either for his comfort or for mine. His wife sometimes came to my house to ask if I knew where he had gone (I could generally guess), and once an irate husband even came to inquire of his whereabouts. His Don Juan activities had evidently increased. His friendship with me caused him trouble with other Tapirapé who were envious of the presents he received. The story was circulated that he had stolen a pair of scissors which, in fact, I had given to him. Moreover, several people caught colds, and he was accused of bringing the infection from Furo de Pedra (actually it was probably transmitted by the frontiersman who had helped transport us to the village in November). Champukwi sought revenge by cutting down one of the main supports of the men's house, which promptly caved in. No one died or was seriously injured and the destruction of the men's house was soon forgotten since it is normally rebuilt each year. However, people continued to criticize Champukwi, much of their criticism revolving around his relationship with me. There are no realms of esoteric secrets in Tapirapé culture (as there are in many cultures) that must not be revealed to an outsider; there is only the "secret" of the men from the women that the masked dancers are not supernatural beings but merely masquerading men, but I had been fully and openly brought into the "secret." I was, moreover, exceedingly careful in conversation never to refer to any bit of personal information that some informant, Champukwi or another, had told me. But rumors were rife in the small village – that I was angry and would soon leave (I was by then a valuable asset), that Champukwi told me lies about others, that I refused to give a bushknife to a household leader because Champukwi had urged me not to do so (I refused because I had already given him one bushknife), and the like.

Champukwi reacted moodily, often violently, to this situation. I could no longer count on his visits nor on our research interviews. He now visited us with a glum look on his face, and when he was not at once offered coffee, he left offended. But the very next day he might return, gay and joking, yet without his former patience for teaching or explaining Tapirapé culture. Once he returned tired from a hunting trip, and, irritated by his wife, he beat her with the flat side of his bushknife and marched off in anger, thoughtfully taking the family hammock and a basket of manioc flour, to sleep four nights in the forest near his garden. Soon afterwards, he left his wife to take the wife of a younger man. This did not become a major scandal in the village. After some tense yet calm words between the two men, it seemed clear that the young woman preferred Champukwi and the abandoned husband peacefully moved into the men's house. Champukwi's former wife and their two young daughters continued to live with her relatives as is the Tapirapé rule. But the switch of spouses caused tension between Champukwi and his former wife's kinsmen, and between Champukwi and the abandoned

husband's kinsmen; and, to multiply his woes, he now had a new set of in-laws to satisfy. For about a month thereafter I rarely saw Champukwi; he obviously avoided our house. When we met in the village or in the men's house, he simply said that he was busy repairing his house or hunting.

Discussing emotions with someone from a culture as widely different as Tapirapé is from my own was difficult, and the language barrier was still a real one. Although my Tapirapé vocabulary was increasing, it was hardly adequate to probe deeply into emotional responses; nor was Champukwi given to introspection. I shall probably never fully understand Champukwi's temporary rejection of me, but the cause was probably both sociological and psychological. First, his apparent influence with me and our close friendship had created antagonism on the part of other villagers. By rejecting the outsider, he now hoped to reinstate himself in his own society. A second, deeper and more personal reason, contributed to his rejection of me; he had told me too much about himself, and feared that he had lost face in the process. Also, it was obvious that I was growing less dependent upon him for knowledge as my facility with the language improved and my information about the culture grew. Finally, the rejection was not one-sided. Now additional informants were desirable for my research. Also, if I remember correctly (it is not stated in my notebooks), I was annoyed by Champukwi's neglect and disappointed by his lack of loyalty.

When the heavy rains of late December and January set in, we were all more or less confined to the village as the rivers and streams rose to flood the savanna. What had been brooks in the tropical forest became wide streams, difficult, and sometimes dangerous, to ford. It rained many hours each day. The Tapirapé women and children spent most of the time in their dwellings, and the men and older boys lounged in the men's house. Our house again became a meeting place. And as this was of course an opportune time for interviewing, I joined the men in their club or entertained visitors at home. I began to see more of Champukwi – first, in the men's house and then as he again became a regular visitor at our house. Now, he brought his new (and younger) wife with him. He liked to sit up with us late at night after the other Tapirapé visitors had retired to their dwellings or to the men's house for the night-long sings that are customary during the season of heavy rains. Under the light of our gasoline lamp, we again took up our study of Tapirapé culture. Not once did he mention his period of antagonism except to complain that the Tapirapé gossip too much.

Sometime late in January there began what might be considered the second phase of my relationship with Champukwi. Our friendship was no less intimate than before, but our conversations and more formal interviews were not now as frequent. During the next months, Champukwi became almost my assistant, an entrepreneur of Tapirapé culture. He continued to provide invaluable information, but when I became interested in a subject of which he knew little, he would recommend that I talk to someone else. Though he directed me to Urukumu on the subject of medicine men or shamans, Champukwi himself related dreams he had heard other shamans tell. He explained that he did not want to become a shaman himself, for he had seen grieved relatives beat out the brains of Tapirapé shamans whom they suspected of causing a death by sorcery. He was not certain, he said, whether such shamans had actually performed sorcery; but he reasoned that any shaman might come to such an end. Champukwi did have the frequent dreams that are indicative of one's powers to become a shaman and, in some of these dreams, he saw *anchunga*, the ghosts and supernaturals who are the aids of shamans. He had told only one or two of his kinsmen about this, and he did not want it to be known throughout the village lest there be pressure on him to train for shamanism.

Champukwi sketched for me the stories of Petura, the Tapirapé ancestral hero who stole fire from the King Vulture, daylight from the night owl, *genipa* (used for dye) from the monkeys, and other items for the Tapirapé. However, he persuaded Maeumi, an elder famous for his knowledge of mythology, to relate the details although he himself helped

considerably to clarify for me the meaning of native phrases and to make the stories told by Maeumi more fully understandable. Champukwi also forewarned me of events that I might want to witness, events that without his warning I might have missed. Such were the wrestling matches which took place upon the return of a hunting party between those men who went on the hunt and those who remained at home. He told me of a particularly handsome basket a man had made, which I might want to add to my collection for the Brazilian National Museum. He came to tell me that a young woman in a neighboring house was in labor, thus enabling me to get a photograph of the newborn infant being washed in the stream, and he urged the men to celebrate for my benefit a ceremony which might easily have been omitted. Champukwi was no longer merely an informant. He became a participant in ethnographic research although, of course, he never thought of it in these terms. He seemed somehow to understand the anthropologist's task in studying his culture, and in the process he gained considerable objectivity about his own way of life.

Yet it must be said that Champukwi did not seem to discredit the norms, institutions, and beliefs of his own people. Although he saw Valentim and me walk safely down the path through the forest late at night, he steadfastly refused to do the same; for the path was a favorite haunt of the lonely ghosts of deceased Tapirapé who might harm the living. He reasoned that the *tori* were probably immune to this danger. When he was ill, he took the pills we urged upon him but he also called in the shaman. His curiosity about airplanes, automobiles, and "gigantic canoes" (passenger boats) which he saw pictured in the magazines we had brought with us, was great; but he boasted that the Tapirapé could walk farther and faster than any *tori* or even the Caraja (who are a canoe people). In fact, his interest in, and enthusiasm for, certain Tapirapé activities seemed to be heightened by our presence. Almost all Tapirapé ceremonials involve choral singing and Champukwi was a singing leader of one of the sections of the men's societies. He was always pleased when we came to listen, particularly if we made the motions of joining in. He was an excellent wrestler in Tapirapé style, in which each opponent takes a firm grip on the pigtail of the other and attempts to throw him to the ground by tripping. Our wrestling match was brief although I was much taller than he; and his match with Valentim Gomes, who outweighed him by more than forty pounds, was a draw. Unlike so many who get a glimpse at a seemingly "superior" cultural world, Champukwi never became dissatisfied with his own way of life.

In June of 1940, my period of residence among the Tapirapé Indians ended. The waters on the savanna which had to be crossed afoot to get to the Tapirapé River where our canoe was moored had not completely receded. Many Tapirapé friends, among them Champukwi, offered to carry our baggage, made lighter after a final distribution of gifts, down to the river. The night before our departure a festival with the usual songfest was held to celebrate the final phase of a ceremony during which a youth, this time the nephew of Kamiraho, became a man. Some Brazilian tribes make this occasion an ordeal by such means as applying a frame of stinging wasps to the body of the novice, but it is characteristic of the Tapirapé that the "ordeal" consists only of decorating the youth with a headdress of magnificent red macaw feathers, painting his body elaborately, and making him the center of dancing and singing – although the youth must himself dance continuously for a day and a night. Champukwi led the singing most of the night, but at dawn he came to our house to supervise the packing of our belongings into the basket-like cases made of palm which are used for carrying loads of any kind. He divided the baggage among the younger men. Even some of the older household leaders decided to accompany us but they, of course, did not carry anything. Our trip was slow because everyone was tired after the all-night festival and because of the water through which we had to wade. At one point, rafts had to be made to transport our baggage across a still-swollen stream. Since the Tapirapé do not swim – or, like Champukwi, they swim but poorly – it was the job of the *tori* to swim and push the rafts. I had the honor of swimming

across the stream, pushing the respected chieftain, Kamiraho. (How he got back, I shall never know.) After a day and a half, we reached the landing on the Tapirapé River, and the next morning we embarked downriver. My last memory of Champukwi was of him standing on the bank waving in *tori* style until our boat made the curve of the river.

I did not return to visit the Tapirapé until 1953, but news of them came to me at intervals. Valentim Gomes returned to the region in 1941 as an officer of the Brazilian Indian Service, and his post was charged with the protection of the Tapirapé Indians. In his first year in this capacity, he wrote me: "I report that I was in the village of the Tapirapé on the 26th of July [1941]. They were in good health and there were plenty of garden products such as manioc, yams, peanuts, and the like. There were plenty of bananas. But I am sorry to say that after we left them, twenty-nine adults and a few children have died. Fifteen women and fourteen men died. Among those who died was Champukwi, the best informant in the village, and our best friend." Several slow exchanges of letters brought further details from Valentim. In some manner, perhaps through a visit from a Brazilian frontiersman, several Tapirapé had contracted common colds. Its fatalness to them is indicated by the name they give it – ó-ó (ó is the augmentative which might be translated as "big, big"). Since they have no knowledge of the process of contagion and have not acquired immunity to the common cold, the disease spread rapidly throughout the village. The Tapirapé realized, I knew, that colds and other diseases such as measles which they had suffered before, were derived from visitors. Yet they also believed that death resulted from evil magic or sorcery. Why do some people who are very sick from colds get well, they asked, while others who are no more ill, soon die? It is only because those who die are the victims of sorcery, they had explained to me. So, following many deaths, including that of a young man like Champukwi, who enjoyed prestige and had many kinsmen, I was not surprised to learn from Valentim Gomes that the powerful shaman, Urukumu, had been assassinated. As Champukwi had told me, suspicion of

Urukumu had already been growing even during my residence in the village. After the death of Champukwi, one of his many "brothers" (actually a cousin but called by the same term as brother in Tapirapé) had entered Urukumu's house late at night and clubbed him to death. To the Tapirapé, grief and anger are closely related emotions and there is one word, *iwúterahú*, that describes either or both states of mind. Thus in both word and deed grief can be quickly transformed into vengeful anger.

In 1953, when I returned to the Araguaia River, I found only fifty persons, the remnants of the Tapirapé tribe, settled under the protection of the Brazilian Indian Service in a small village near the mouth of the Tapirapé River. My old companion, Valentim Gomes, was the Indian officer in charge. The history of the intervening years had been a tragic story; the Tapirapé had suffered steady depopulation from imported diseases and they had been attacked by the warlike and hostile Kayapo tribe, who had burned their village and carried off several younger women. They had been forced to leave their own territory to seek the protection of the Indian Service, and then cattle ranchers encroached upon the Tapirapé savannas, once rich with game. Champukwi was but one of the many victims of this disintegration of Tapirapé society. Upon my arrival several of Champukwi's surviving relatives met me with the traditional "welcome of tears"; to the Tapirapé, such a return mixes emotions of joy at seeing an old friend with the sadness of the memory of those who have died during the interim. Both the sadness and the joy are expressed almost ritually by crying. People spoke sympathetically to me of the loss of my friend and they brought a young man, who had been but a small boy in 1940, but who was now known as Champukwi. This boy had visited for many months, and had even studied a little, with the Dominican missionaries on the lower Araguaia River; he therefore spoke Portuguese well. He remembered my friendship with his namesake and perhaps felt, as I did, some strange bond between us. So again for a few days the name of Champukwi was entered into my notebook as my source of information on Tapirapé culture.

In the security of our studies and in the classroom, we claim that anthropology is a social science in which regularities of human behavior and of social systems are studied. But, at its source, in the midst of the people with whom the anthropologist lives and works, field research involves the practice of an art in which emotions, subjective attitudes and reactions, and undoubtedly subconscious motivations participate. Of course, the well-trained anthropologist takes all possible precautions to be objective and to maintain a detached attitude. He gathers information from a "cross section" of the population – from a variety of informants selected for their different status positions in their society. He interviews, as far as is possible, men and women, young and old, rich and poor, individuals of high and low status, so that his picture of the culture may not be distorted. The anthropologist might (he seldom has done so) go so far as to keep a record of his subjective reactions in an attempt to achieve greater objectivity. Yet he is never the entirely detached observer he may fancy himself to be – nor am I sure that this should be so. Anthropological field research is a profoundly human endeavor. Faced over a long period by a number of individuals, some intelligent and some slow, some gay and some dour, some placid and some irritable, the anthropologist almost inevitably is involved in a complex set of human relations among another people just as he is by virtue of his membership in his own society. And each anthropologist is a distinctive personality and each undoubtedly handles in his own way his dual role as a sympathetic friend to key informants and as a scientific observer of a society and culture which is not his own. To me, Champukwi was, above all, a friend whom I shall remember always with warm affection.

9

Behind Many Masks: Ethnography and Impression Management

Gerald D. Berreman

Ethnographers have all too rarely made explicit the methods by which the information reported in their descriptive and analytical works was derived. Even less frequently have they attempted systematic descriptions of those aspects of the field experience which fall outside of a conventional definition of method, but which are crucial to the research and its results. The potential fieldworker in any given area often has to rely for advance information about many of the practical problems of his craft upon the occasional verbal anecdotes of his predecessors or the equally random remarks included in ethnographic prefaces. To the person facing fieldwork for the first time, the dearth of such information may appear to be the result of a conviction, among those who know, that experience can be the only teacher. Alternatively, he may suspect ethnographers of having established a conspiracy of silence on these matters. When he himself becomes a bona fide ethnographer he may join that

conspiracy inadvertently, or he may feel obligated to join it not only to protect the secrets of ethnography, but to protect himself. As a result of the rules of the game which kept others from communicating their experience to him, he may feel that his own difficulties of morale and rapport, his own compromises between the ideal and the necessary, were unique, and perhaps signs of weakness or incompetence. Consequently, these are concealed or minimized. More acceptable aspects of the field experience such as those relating to formal research methods, health hazards, transportation facilities and useful equipment suffice to answer the queries of the curious. This is in large measure a matter of maintaining the proper "front" (see below) before an audience made up not only of the uninitiated, but in many cases of other ethnographers as well.

As a result of this pattern "Elenore Bowen" shared the plight of many an anthropological

Gerald D. Berreman, "Behind Many Masks: Ethnography and Impression Management," pp. xvii–lvii plus selected bibliography from *Hindus of the Himalayas: Ethnography and Change*, 2nd edn. Berkeley: University of California Press, 1972. Copyright © 1963, 1972 by The Regents of the University of California. This material appeared originally, in a slightly different form, as Monograph No. 4 of the Society for Applied Anthropology, 1962. Reprinted by permission of the Society for Applied Anthropology.

Ethnographic Fieldwork: An Anthropological Reader, Second Edition. Edited by
Antonius C. G. M. Robben and Jeffrey A. Sluka.
Editorial material and organization © 2012 John Wiley & Sons, Inc.
Published 2012 by John Wiley & Sons, Inc.

neophyte when, according to her fictionalized account she arrived in West Africa girded for fieldwork with her professors' formulae for success:

Always walk in cheap tennis shoes; the water runs out more quickly, [and] You'll need more tables than you think. (Bowen, 1954, pp. 3–4)

This prologue is not an exposition of research methods or field techniques in the usual sense. It is a description of some aspects of my field research, analyzed from a particular point of view. As such, it is an attempt to portray some features of that human experience which is fieldwork, and some of the implications of its being human experience for ethnography as a scientific endeavor. It is not intended as a model for others to follow. It tells what happened, what I did, why I did it and with what apparent effect. As in all fieldwork, the choices were not always mine and the results were frequently unanticipated. But the choices and results have proved instructive. I hope that this account will add depth to the ethnographic study which follows by conveying the methods and circumstances which led to it.

Introduction

Every ethnographer, when he reaches the field, is faced immediately with accounting for himself before the people he proposes to learn to know. Only when this has been accomplished can he proceed to his avowed task of seeking to understand and interpret the way of life of those people. The second of these endeavors is more frequently discussed in anthropological literature than the first, although the success of the enterprise depends as largely upon one as the other. Both tasks, in common with all social interaction, involve the control and interpretation of impressions, in this case those conveyed by the ethnographer and his subjects to one another. Impressions are derived from a complex of observations and inferences drawn from what people do as well as what they say both in public, i.e., when they know they are being watched, and in private, i.e., when they think they are not being watched. Attempts to

convey a desired impression of one's self and to interpret accurately the behavior and attitudes of others are an inherent part of any social interaction, and they are crucial to ethnographic research.

My research in a tightly closed and highly stratified society can serve as a case study from which to analyze some of the problems and consequences inherent in the interaction of ethnographer and subjects. Special emphasis will be placed upon the differential effects of the ethnographer's identification with high-status and low-status groups in the community.

The Setting

The research upon which this account is based took place in and around Sirkanda, a peasant village of the lower Himalayas of North India. Its residents, like those of the entire lower Himalayan area from Kashmir through Nepal, are known as *Paharis* (of the mountains). The village is small, containing some 384 individuals during the year of my residence there in 1957–8, and it is relatively isolated, situated as it is in rugged hills accessible only on foot and nine miles from the nearest road and bus service.

Strangers in the area are few and readily identifiable by dress and speech. People who are so identified are avoided or discouraged from remaining long in the vicinity. To escape such a reception, a person must be able to identify himself as a member of a familiar group through kinship ties, caste (*jati*) ties and/or community affiliation. Since the first two are ascribed characteristics, the only hope an outsider has of achieving acceptance is by establishing residence and, through social interaction, acquiring the status of a community-dweller; a slow process at best.

The reluctance of Sirkanda villagers and their neighbors to accept strangers is attested to by the experience of those outsiders who have dealt with them. In 1957 a new teacher was assigned to the Sirkanda school. He was a Pahari from an area some fifty miles distant. Despite his Pahari background and consequent familiarity with the language and customs of the local people, he complained after four months in the village that his reception had been less than cordial:

> I have taught in several schools in the valley and people have always been friendly to me. They have invited me to their homes for meals, have sent gifts of grain and vegetables with their children, and have tried to make me feel at home. I have been here four months now with almost no social contact aside from my students. No one has asked me to eat with him; no one has sent me so much as a grain of millet; no one has asked me to sit and talk with him; no one has even asked me who I am or whether I have a family. They ignore me.

He fared better than the teacher in another village of the area who had to give up after three months during which he and his proposed school were totally boycotted.

Among the forestry officers whose duty it is to make periodic rounds in these hills, villagers' lack of hospitality is proverbial. They claim that here a man has to carry his own food, water, and bedroll because he cannot count on villagers to offer these necessities to him on his travels. Community development and establishment of credit cooperatives, two governmental programs in the area, have been unsuccessful largely because of their advocates' inability to establish rapport with the people. My assistant, who had worked for more than a year in an anthropological research project in a village of the plains, was constantly baffled at the reticence and lack of hospitality of villagers. As he said:

> In Kalapur, when you walked through the village, men would hail you and invite you to sit and talk with them. Whether or not they really wanted you to do so, they at least invited you out of common courtesy. Here they just go inside or turn their backs when they see you coming.

The reasons for such reticence are not far to seek. Contacts with outsiders have been limited largely to contacts with policemen and tax collectors – two of the lowest forms of life in the Pahari taxonomy. Such officials are despised and feared not only because they make trouble for villagers in the line of duty, but because they also extort bribes on the threat of causing further trouble and often seem to take advantage of their official positions to vent their aggressions on these vulnerable people. Since India's independence, spheres of governmental responsibility have extended to include stringent supervision of greatly extended national forest lands, rationing of certain goods, establishment of a variety of development programs, etc. The grounds for interfering in village affairs have multiplied as the variety of officials has proliferated. Any stranger, therefore, may be a government agent, and as such he is potentially troublesome and even dangerous.

Villagers' fears on this score are not groundless. Aside from the unjust exploitation which such agents are reputed to employ in their activities, there are many illegal or semilegal activities carried on by villagers which could be grounds for punishment and are easily used as grounds for extortion. In Sirkanda, national forest lands and products have been illegally appropriated by villagers, taxable land has been underreported, liquor is brewed and sold illicitly, women have been illegally sold, guns have gone unlicensed, adulterated milk is sold to outside merchants, children are often married below the legal age, men have fled the army or escaped from jail, property has been illegally acquired from fleeing Muslims at the time of partition. Any of these and similar real and imagined infractions may be objects of a stranger's curiosity and therefore are reasons for discouraging his presence in the village.

Paharis are thought by people of the plains to be ritually, spiritually, and morally inferior. They are suspected of witchcraft and evil magic. In addition they are considered naive bumpkins – the hillbilly stereotype of other cultures. Paharis try to avoid interaction with those who hold these stereotypes. Alien Brahmins may seek to discredit their Pahari counterparts by finding evidence of their unorthodoxy; alien traders may seek to relieve them of their hard-earned cash or produce by sharp business practices; scoundrels may seek to waylay or abduct village women; thieves may come to steal their worldly possessions;

lawyers or their cohorts may seek evidence for trumped-up legal proceedings which a poor Pahari could not hope to counteract in court; Christian missionaries may hope to infringe on their religious beliefs and practices. Strangers are therefore suspected of having ulterior motives even if they are not associated with the government.

The only way to feel sure that such dangers do not inhere in a person is to know who he is, and to know this he must fit somewhere into the known social system. Only then is he subject to effective local controls so that if he transgresses, or betrays a trust, he can be brought to account. The person who is beyond control is beyond trust and is best hurried on his way. This is, therefore, a relatively closed society. Interaction with strangers is kept to a minimum; the information furnished them is scanty and stereotyped. Access to such a society is difficult for an outsider.

Within this closed society there is rigid stratification into a number of hereditary, ranked, endogamous groups – castes – comprising two large divisions: the high or twice-born castes and the low or untouchable castes. The high castes, Rajputs and Brahmins, are land-owning agriculturalists who are dominant in numbers, comprising ninety per cent of the population. They are dominant in economic wherewithal, in that they own most of the land and animals, while the other castes depend on them for their livelihood. They are dominant in political power, for both traditional and new official means of control are in their hands. They dominate in ritual status as twice-born, ritually clean castes while all other castes are untouchable (*achut*). In most villages, as in Sirkanda, Rajputs outnumber Brahmins and so are locally dominant, but the ritual and social distance between them is not great and the economic difference is usually nil (Srinivas, 1959).

The low castes, whose members are artisans, are disadvantaged in each respect that the high castes are advantaged. They are dependent upon the high castes for their livelihood and are subject to the will of the high castes in almost every way. Ideally their relationship to the high castes is one of respect, deference, and obedience. In return high-caste members are supposed to be paternalistic. In practice there is a good deal of tension in the relationship, and it is held stable largely by considerations of relative power (Berreman, 1960a).

In addition there are nonhierarchical cleavages within the high castes and within the low castes based upon kinship ties (lineage and sib lines being paramount) and informal cliques and factions. As a result of these factors the community is divided within itself. While there is consensus on some things, there is disagreement on others. Acceptance by one element of the community does not imply acceptance by the whole community and it frequently, in fact, precludes it.

The Research

It was into this community that my interpreter-assistant and I walked, unannounced, one rainy day in September, 1957, hoping to engage in ethnographic research. On our initial visit we asked only to camp there while we visited a number of surrounding villages. We were introduced by a note from a non-Pahari wholesaler of the nearest market town who had long bought the surplus agricultural produce of villagers and had, as it turned out, through sharp practices of an obscure nature, acquired land in the village. He asked that the villagers treat the strangers as "our people" and extend all hospitality to them. As might have been expected, our benefactor was not beloved in the village and it was more in spite of his intercession than on account of it that we ultimately managed to do a year's research in the village.

The note was addressed to a high-caste man who proved to be one of the most suspicious people of the village; the head of a household recently victorious in a nine-year court battle over land brought against the household by virtually the entire village; the leader of a much-resented but powerful minority faction. That he gave us an unenthusiastic reception was a blow to our morale but probably a boon to our chances of being tolerated in the village.

The interpreter-assistant who accompanied me was a young Brahmin of plains origin who had previously worked in a similar capacity for a large research project carried out in the plains village of Kalapur. I shall hereafter refer to him as Sharma.

For the first three months of our stay in the village, most of our time was spent keeping house and attempting to establish rapport, both of which were carried out under trying circumstances.

According to their later reports to us, villagers at first assumed that we were missionaries, a species which had not previously invaded this locality but which was well known. Several villagers had sold milk in Mussoorie, a hill station sixteen miles distant that is frequented by missionaries. When we failed to meddle in religious matters or to show surprise at local rituals, this suspicion gradually faded. We had anticipated this interpretation of our motives and so were careful not to show undue interest in religion as a topic of conversation. We purposely used Hindu rather than areligious forms of greeting in our initial contacts to avoid being identified as missionaries. As a topic for polite and, we hoped, neutral conversation, we chose agriculture. It seemed timely too, as the fall harvest season began not long after our arrival in the village. Partly as a result of this choice of conversational fare, suspicion arose that we were government agents sent to reassess the land for taxation purposes, based on the greater-than-previously-reported productivity of the land. Alternatively, we were suspected of being investigators seeking to find the extent of land use in unauthorized areas following the nationalization of the surrounding uncultivated lands. My physical appearance was little comfort to villagers harboring these suspicions. One man commented that "Anyone can look like a foreigner if he wears the right clothes." Gradually these fears too disappeared, but others arose.

One person suggested that our genealogical inquiries might be preliminary to a military draft of the young men. The most steadfast opponent of our presence hinted darkly at the machinations of foreign spies – a vaguely understood but actively feared type of villain. Nearly four months had passed before overt suspicion of this sort was substantially dissipated, although, of course, some people had been convinced of the innocence of our motives relatively early and others remained suspicious throughout our stay.

One incident nearly four months after our first visit to the village proved to be a turning point in quelling overt opposition to our activities in the village. We were talking one afternoon to the local Brahmin priest. He had proved to be a reluctant informant, apparently because of his fear of alienating powerful and suspicious Rajputs whose caste-fellows outnumbered his own by more than thirty to one in the village (his was the only Brahmin household as compared to 37 Rajput households in Sirkanda), and in whose good graces it was necessary for him to remain for many reasons. However, he was basically friendly. Encouraged by our increasing rapport in the village at large, by his own feelings of affinity with my Brahmin assistant, Sharma, and by the privacy of his secluded threshing platform as a talking place, he had volunteered to discuss his family tree with us. Midway in our discussion, one of the most influential and hostile of the Rajputs came upon us – probably intentionally – and sat down with us. The Brahmin immediately became self-conscious and uncommunicative but it was too late to conceal the topic of our conversation. The Rajput soon interrupted, asking why the Brahmin was telling us these things and inquiring in a challenging way what possible use the information could be to an American scholar. He implied, with heavy irony, that we had ulterior motives. The interview was obviously ended and by this time a small crowd of onlookers had gathered. Since a satisfactory answer was evidently demanded and since most members of the audience were not among the people we knew best, I took the opportunity to answer fully.

I explained that prior to 1947, India had been a subject nation of little interest to the rest of the world. In the unlikely event that the United States or any other country wanted to negotiate regarding matters Indian, its representatives had merely to deal with the British who spoke for India. Indians were of no importance to us, for they were a subject people. They, in turn, had no need to know that America existed as, indeed, few did. Then in 1947, after a long struggle, India had become independent; a nation of proud people who handled their own affairs and participated in the United Nations and in all spheres of international relations on a par with Britain and the United States. Indians for the first time spoke for themselves. At once it became essential for Indians and Americans to know one another. Consequently India sent hundreds of students to America, among other places, and we sent students such as myself to India. We had worked at learning their language and we also wanted to learn their means of livelihood, social customs, religion, etc., so that we could deal with them intelligently and justly, just as their students were similarly studying in and about America. Fortunately I had an Indian acquaintance, then studying a rural community in Utah, whom I could cite as a case comparable to my own. I pointed out that Indian and American scholars had studied Indian cities, towns and villages of the plains so that their ways were well known, but that heretofore the five million Paharis – residents of some of the richest, most beautiful, historically and religiously most significant parts of India – had been overlooked. I emphasized that Paharis would play an increasing role in the development of India and that if they were to assume the responsibilities and derive the advantages available to them it was essential that they be better known to their countrymen and to the world. My research was billed as an effort in this direction.

I would like to be able to report that on the basis of this stirring speech I was borne aloft triumphantly through the village, thereafter being treated as a fellow villager by one and all. Needless to say, this did not happen. My questioner was, however, evidently favorably impressed, or at least felt compelled to act as though he were before the audience of his village-mates. He responded by saying that he would welcome me in his house any time and would discuss fully any matters of interest to me. He also offered to supply me with a number of artifacts to take to America as exhibits of Pahari ingenuity. I might add, anticlimactically, that in fact he never gave me information beyond his reactions to the weather, and that the Brahmin, evidently shaken by his

experience, was never again as informative as he had been immediately prior to this incident.

The Rajput challenger, however, ceased to be hostile whereas formerly he had been a focus of opposition to my presence. General rapport in the village improved markedly and the stigma attached to talking with me and my interpreter almost disappeared. One notable aftereffect was that my photographic opportunities, theretofore restricted to scenery, small children, and adolescent boys in self-conscious poses, suddenly expanded to include a wide range of economic, ritual, and social occasions as well as people of all castes, ages, and both sexes. Photography itself soon became a valuable means of obtaining rapport as photographs came into demand.

The degree to which I was allowed or requested to take photographs, in fact, proved to be a fairly accurate indicator of rapport. One of the more gratifying incidents of my research in Sirkanda occurred at an annual regional fair some eight months after the research had begun. Soon after I arrived at the fair a group of gaily dressed young women of various villages had agreed to be photographed when a Brahmin man, a stranger to me, stormed up and ordered them to refuse. An elderly and highly respected Rajput woman of Sirkanda had been watching the proceedings and was obviously irritated by the fact and manner of the intervention. She stepped to the center of the group of girls, eyeing the Brahmin evenly, and said, "Please take my photograph." I did so, the Brahmin left, and my photography was in demand exceeding the film supply throughout the fair.

The incident described above, in which the Rajput challenged my interviewing of the Brahmin priest, came out favorably partly because of the context in which it occurred. For one thing, it occurred late enough so that many people knew me and my assistant. Having no specific cause for doubting our motives, they were ready to believe us if we made a convincing case. Also, there was a sizeable audience to the event. My explanation was a response to a challenge by a high-status villager and the challenger accepted it gracefully. It was the first time that many of these people had been present when I talked at any length and my statement was put with a good deal of feeling, which fact they recognized. It was essentially an appeal for their confidence and cooperation in a task they knew was difficult and which I obviously considered important. They were not incapable of empathy. As one man had said earlier, "You may be a foreigner and we only poor villagers, but when we get to know you we will judge you as a man among other men; not as a foreigner." With time, most of the villagers demonstrated the validity of his comment by treating me as an individual on the basis of their experience with me, rather than as the stereotyped outsider or white man.

Most important, my statement placed the listeners in a position of accepting what I said or denying their own importance as people and as citizens – it appealed to their pride. They have strong inferiority feelings relative to non-Paharis which account in large measure for their hostility, and my presence as defined in this statement counteracted these feelings. It was especially effective in response to the Rajput who put the challenge; a man with an acute, and to many aggravating, need for public recognition of his importance. He had gained some eminence by opposing my work; he now evidently gained some by eliciting a full explanation from me and magnanimously accepting it.

Although I remained an alien and was never made to feel that my presence in the village was actively desired by most of its members, I was thereafter tolerated with considerable indulgence. I became established as a resident of Sirkanda, albeit a peculiar one, and no one tried to get me to leave. I have heard strangers en route to or from further mountain areas inquire of Sirkanda villagers as to my identity, presuming that I was out of earshot or could not understand, and be left to ponder the succinct reply, "He lives here."

Other, less spectacular rapport-inducing devices were employed. Unattached men in the village were considered, not unjustly in light of past experience and Pahari morality, a threat to village womanhood. This fear with regard to my assistant and myself was appreciably diminished when our wives and children visited the village and when a few villagers had been guests at our house in town where our families normally resided. We won some good will by providing a few simple remedies for common village ailments. One of the most effective means of attracting villagers to our abode in the village during this period was a battery radio which we brought in; the first to operate in this area. It was an endless source of diversion to villagers and attracted a regular audience, as well as being a focal attraction for visiting relatives and friends from other villages.

At first, reportedly, there had been considerable speculation in the village as to why two people of such conspicuously different backgrounds as Sharma and myself had appeared on the scene as a team if, as we claimed, we were not sent by the government or a missionary organization. The plausibility of our story was enhanced when Sharma made it clear to villagers that he was my bona fide employee who received payment in cash for his services.

Villagers never ceased to wonder, as I sometimes did myself, why I had chosen this particular area and village for my research. I explained this in terms of its relative accessibility for a hill area, the hospitality and perspicacity of Sirkanda people, the reputation Sirkanda had acquired in the area for being a "good village," and my own favorable impression of it based on familiarity with a number of similar villages. The most satisfactory explanation was that my presence there was largely chance, i.e., fate. Everyone agreed that this was the real reason. Villagers pointed out that when the potter makes a thousand identical cups, each has a unique destiny. Similarly, each man has a predetermined course of life and it was my fate to come to Sirkanda. When I gave an American coin to a villager, similar comment was precipitated. Of all the American coins only one was destined to rest in Sirkanda and this was it. What greater proof of the power of fate could there be than that the coin had, like myself, found its way to this small and remote village.

All of our claims of motive and status were put to the test by villagers once they realized that we planned to remain in Sirkanda and to associate with them. Sharma's claim to Brahmin status was carefully checked:

extensive inquiry was made about his family and their origins; his behavior was closely watched; his family home was inspected by villagers on trips to town. Only then were villagers satisfied that he was what he claimed to be. When all of the claims upon which they could check proved to be accurate, villagers were evidently encouraged to believe also those claims which could not be verified.

That suspicions as to our motives were eventually allayed did not mean we therefore could learn what we wanted to learn in the village. It meant only that villagers knew in a general way what they were willing to let us learn; what impressions they would like us to receive. The range of allowable knowledge was far greater than that granted a stranger, far less than that shared by villagers. Although at the time I did not realize it, we were to be told those things which would give a favorable impression to a trustworthy plains Brahmin. Other facts would be suppressed and, if discovered, would be discovered in spite of the villagers' best efforts at concealment, often as a result of conversation with some disaffected individual of low esteem in the village. Our informants were primarily high-caste villagers intent on impressing us with their near conformity to the standards of behavior and belief of high-caste plainsmen. Low-caste people were respectful and reticent before us, primarily, as it turned out, because one of us was a Brahmin and we were closely identified with the powerful high-caste villagers.

Three months were spent almost exclusively in building rapport, in establishing ourselves as trustworthy, harmless, sympathetic, and interested observers of village life. In this time we held countless conversations, most of them dealing with the weather and other timely and innocuous topics. A good deal of useful ethnographic information was acquired in the process, but in many areas its accuracy proved to be wanting. Better information was acquired by observation than by inquiry in this period. We found cause for satisfaction during this frustrating and, from the point of view of research results, relatively fruitless time in the fact that we were winning the confidence of a good many people which we hoped would pay off more tangibly later. When the last open

opponent of our endeavor evidently had been convinced of our purity of motive in the incident described above, we felt that we could begin our data collecting in earnest.

Until this time we had done all of our own housekeeping, cooking, dishwashing, carrying of water and firewood. These activities gave us opportunity to meet people in a natural setting and to be busy in a period when rapport was not good enough to allow us to devote full time to research. As rapport improved we found our household chores too time-consuming for optimal research. We attempted to find assistance in the village but, unable to do so, we added as a third member of our team a 17-year-old boy who was of low-caste plains origin but had lived most of his life in the hill station of Mussoorie and was conversant with Pahari ways and the Pahari language. His role was that of servant and he assumed full responsibility for our housekeeping in the village. His informal contacts with some of the younger villagers were a research asset and his low-caste origin was not overlooked in the village, but otherwise he had little direct effect on our relations with villagers. His contribution to the research was primarily in the extreme reliability of his work and his circumspection in relations with villagers.

At this point of apparent promise for productive research, Sharma, the interpreter-assistant, became ill and it was evident that he would be unable to return to our work in the village for some time. Under the circumstances this was a disheartening blow. It plunged my morale to its lowest ebb in the fifteen months of my stay in India, none of which could be described as exhilarating. I cannot here go into the details of the causes for this condition of morale: the pervasive health anxiety with which anyone is likely to be afflicted when he takes an 18-month-old child to the field in India, especially if, as in this case, he is away from and inaccessible to his family a good share of the time; the difficulties of maintaining a household in town and carrying on research in an isolated village; the constant and frustrating parrying with petty officials who are in positions to cause all kinds of difficulty and delay; the virtual lack of social contact outside of one's family, employees, and the villagers among whom one works; the feeling of being merely tolerated by those among whom one works and upon whom one is dependent for most of his social interaction. In such circumstances research is likely to become the primary motivating principle and its progress looms large in one's world view. Therefore, to lose an assistant whose presence I deemed essential to the research, when I was on the threshold of tangible progress after a long period of preparation, was a discouraging blow. I shall not soon forget the anxiety I felt during the five-hour trek to the village alone after learning of Sharma's illness and incapacity. To await his recovery would have been to waste the best months for research because his illness came at the beginning of the winter slack season when people would, for the first time since my arrival, have ample time to sit and talk. In two months the spring harvest and planting season would begin and many potential informants would be too busy and tired to talk.

After a period alone in the village, I realized that I could not work effectively without assistance because of my inadequate knowledge of the language. Although I dreaded the task of selecting and then introducing a new and inexperienced assistant into the village, this seemed to be a necessary step to preserve the continuity of the research. My hope and intention was to utilize a substitute only until Sharma would be able to work again. Not wishing to spend too much time looking for a substitute, and with qualified people extremely scarce, I employed with many misgivings and on a trial basis the first reasonably promising prospect who appeared. Happily, he proved to be an exceptionally able, willing, and interested worker. He differed from Sharma in at least three important respects: age, religion, and experience. Mohammed, as he will hereafter be called, was a middle-aged Muslim and a retired school teacher who had no familiarity with anthropological research.

These facts proved to have advantageous as well as disadvantageous aspects. I was able to guide him more easily in his work and to interact more directly with villagers than had been the case with Sharma simply because he realized his inexperience, accepted suggestions readily, and was interested in helping me to know and communicate directly with villagers, rather than in demonstrating his efficiency as a researcher and his indispensability as an interpreter. As a result of his age he received a certain amount of respect. As a Muslim he was able to establish excellent rapport with the low castes but not with the high or twice-born castes. Perhaps most importantly, he had no ego-involvement in the data. He was interested and objective in viewing the culture in which we were working, whereas Sharma had been self-conscious and anxious to avoid giving an unflattering view of Hinduism and of village life to an American in this unorthodox (to him often shockingly so) example of a Hindu village. Moreover, the Brahmin, almost inevitably, had his own status to maintain before the high castes of the village while the Muslim was under no such obligation.

Since it seemed probable that Sharma would return to work after a few weeks, I decided to make the best of the situation and utilize Mohammed in ways that would make the most use of his advantages and minimize his disadvantages, for he was strong where Sharma had been weak, and vice versa. While high-caste people were suspicious of Mohammed on the basis of his religion, low-caste people were more at ease in his presence than they had been with Sharma. Furthermore, low-caste people proved to be more informative than high-caste people on most subjects. I therefore planned to utilize this assistant to get data about low castes and from them to get as much general ethnographic data as possible. I was counting on the return of Sharma to enable me to return to the high castes and my original endeavor to secure information from and about them. However, after several weeks it became evident that Sharma could not return to work in the village. By then we were beginning to get a good deal of ethnographic material with the promise of much more. In addition to remarkably good rapport with the low castes (greater than that Sharma and I had had with anyone in the village) we were also winning the confidence of some high-caste people. In view of these circumstances I felt encouraged to continue with Mohammed and to broaden our contacts in the village in the remaining months of research.

I had not anticipated the full implications for research of the differences in status of my associates, Sharma and Mohammed. For example, villagers had early determined that Sharma neither ate meat nor drank liquor. As a result we were barely aware that these things were done by villagers. Not long after Mohammed's arrival villagers found that he indulged in both and that I could be induced to do so. Thereafter we became aware of frequent meat and liquor parties, often of an inter-caste nature. We found that these were important social occasions; occasions from which outsiders were usually rigidly excluded. Rapport increased notably when it became known that locally distilled liquor was occasionally served at our house. As rapport improved, we were more frequently included in such informal occasions. Our access to information of many kinds increased proportionately.

Mohammed's age put him virtually above the suspicion which Sharma had had to overcome regarding possible interest in local women. Mohammed's association with me in my by then generally trusted status, precluded undue suspicion of missionary intent or governmental affiliation. Probably his most important characteristic with regard to rapport was his religion. As a Muslim he was, like me, a ritually polluted individual, especially since he was assumed to have eaten beef. For most purposes he and I were untouchables, albeit respected for our presumed wealth and knowledge.

With this description as background, the differential effects which my association with these two men had on the research can be analyzed. In discussing this topic special attention will be given to the implications of the status of each of them for the impressions we gave to villagers and received from them. Some of the more general problems of research in a tightly closed and highly stratified system will also be considered.

Analysis

Erving Goffman, in *The Presentation of Self in Everyday Life*, has devised a description and analysis of social interaction in terms of the means by which people seek to control the impressions others receive of them. He has suggested that this "dramaturgical" approach is a widely applicable perspective for the analysis of social systems. In this scheme social interaction is analyzed "from the point of view of impression management."

> We find a team of performers who cooperate to present to an audience a given definition of the situation. This will include the conception of [one's] own team of [one's] audience and assumptions concerning the ethos that is to be maintained by rules of politeness and decorum. We often find a division into back region, where the performance of a routine is prepared, and front region, where the performance is presented. Access to these regions is controlled in order to prevent the audience from seeing backstage and to prevent outsiders from coming into a performance that is not addressed to them. Among members of the team we find that familiarity prevails, solidarity is likely to develop, and that secrets that could give the show away are shared and kept. (Goffman, 1959, p. 238)

The ethnographic research endeavor may be viewed as a system involving the social interaction of ethnographer and subjects. Considered as a basic feature of social interaction, therefore, impression management is of methodological as well as substantive significance to ethnographers.

The ethnographer comes to his subjects as an unknown, generally unexpected, and often unwanted intruder. Their impressions of him will determine the kinds and validity of data to which he will be able to gain access, and hence the degree of success of his work. The ethnographer and his subjects are both performers and audience to one another. They have to judge one another's motives and other attributes on the basis of short intensive contact and then decide what definition of themselves and the surrounding situation they want to project; what they will reveal and what they will conceal and how best to do it. Each will attempt to convey to the other the impression that will best serve his interests as he sees them.

The bases for evaluation by an audience are not entirely those which the performer intends or can control.

Knowing that the individual is likely to present himself in a light that is favorable to him, the [audience] may divide what they witness into two parts; a part that is relatively easy for the individual to manipulate at will, being chiefly his verbal assertions, and a part in regard to which he seems to have little concern or control, being chiefly derived from the expressions he gives off. The [audience] may then use what are considered to be the ungovernable aspects of his expressive behavior as a check upon the validity of what is conveyed by the governable aspects. (Goffman, 1959, p. 7)

In their awareness of this, performers attempt to keep the back region out of the range of the audience's perception; to control the performance insofar as possible, preferably to an extent unrealized by the audience. The audience will attempt to glimpse the back region in order to gain new insights into the nature of the performance and the performers.

An ethnographer is usually evaluated by himself and his colleagues on the basis of his insights into the back region of the performance of his subjects. His subjects are evaluated by their fellows on the basis of the degree to which they protect the secrets of their team and successfully project the image of the team that is acceptable to the group for front-region presentation. It is probably often thought that this presentation will also satisfy the ethnographer. The ethnographer is likely to evaluate his subjects on the amount of back-region information they reveal to him, while he is evaluated by them on his tact in not intruding unnecessarily into the back region and, as rapport improves, on his trustworthiness as one who will not reveal back-region secrets. These are likely to be mutually contradictory bases of evaluation. Rapport establishment is largely a matter of threading among them so as to win admittance to the back region of the subjects' performance without alienating them. This is sometimes sought through admission to the subjects' team; it is more often gained through acceptance as a neutral confidant.

The impressions that ethnographer and subjects seek to project to one another are, therefore, those felt to be favorable to the accomplishment of their respective goals: the ethnographer seeks access to back-region information; the subjects seek to protect their secrets since these represent a threat to the public image they wish to maintain. Neither can succeed perfectly.

Front and back regions

One must assume that the ethnographer's integrity as a scientist will insure the confidential nature of his findings about the individuals he studies. Those individuals, however, are unlikely to make such an assumption and, in fact, often make a contrary one. While I think it practically and ethically sound for the ethnographer to make known his intention to learn about the way of life of the people he plans to study, I believe it to be ethically unnecessary and methodologically unsound to make known his specific hypotheses, and in many cases even his areas of interest. To take his informants into his confidence regarding these may well preclude the possibility of acquiring much information essential to the main goal of understanding their way of life. I think here of my own interest in the highly charged sphere of inter-caste relations, where admission of the interest to certain persons or groups would have been inimical to the research effort.

Participant observation, as a form of social interaction, always involves impression management. Therefore, as a research technique it inevitably entails some secrecy and some dissimulation on the level of interpersonal relations. If the researcher feels morally constrained to avoid any form of dissimulation or secrecy he will have to forgo most of the insights that can be acquired through knowledge of those parts of his informants' lives that they attempt to conceal from him. With time, a researcher may be allowed to view parts of what was formerly the back region of his informants' performance, but few ethnographers can aspire to full acceptance into the informants' team in view of the temporary nature of their residence and their status as aliens. In a society where ascription is the only way to full acceptance, this is a virtual impossibility.

If the ethnographer does not gain access to back-region information he will have to content himself with an "official view" derived from public sources publicly approved, and his research interests will have to be sharply limited. An out for those sensitive on this point may be, of course, to do the research as it must be done but to use the findings only with the explicit approval of the subjects. In any case, the ethnographer will be presenting himself in certain ways to his informants during the research and concealing other aspects of himself from them. They will be doing the same. This is inherent in all social interaction.

Teams and roles

Impression management in ethnographic research is often an exhausting, nerve-wracking effort on both sides, especially in the early phases of contact. Ethnographers may recognize themselves and their informants in this description:

> Whether the character that is being presented is sober or carefree, of high station or low, the individual who performs the character will be seen for what he largely is, a solitary player involved in a harried concern for his production. Behind many masks and many characters, each performer tends to wear a single look, a naked unsocialized look, a look of concentration, a look of one who is privately engaged in a difficult and treacherous task. (Goffman, 1959, p. 235)

The task is especially difficult and treacherous when the cultural gap between participants and audience is great. Then the impression that a given action will convey cannot always be predicted; audience reaction is hard to read and performance significance is hard to judge. Misinterpretation occurs frequently and sometimes disastrously in such circumstances. Anyone who has been in an alien culture can cite *faux pas* resulting from such misinterpretation. Inadvertent disrespect is a common type. Although no vivid example occurred in the research being reported here, largely due to an exaggerated caution about this, the author experienced such a misinterpretation in the course of research among the Aleuts. He once amused local children by drawing cartoon faces on the steamy windows of the village store. These were seen by an adult who interpreted them as insulting caricatures of Aleuts, although they were in reality generalized cartoons, totally innocuous in intent, and he reacted bitterly. He saw them in the light of unhappy past experience with arrogant non-Aleuts. Strained relations resulting from this incident could well have halted research had it not occurred late in the research effort, after most villagers had been convinced of the ethnographer's good intentions and friendly attitude.

In a tightly closed and highly stratified society the difficulty of impression management is compounded. In a closed society the outsider may be prevented from viewing the activities of its members almost completely. The front region is small and admittance to any aspect of the performance is extremely difficult to obtain. Pronounced stratification makes for many teams, many performances, many back regions (one for each performance group, as well as for each audience), and considerable anxiety lest one group be indiscreet in revealing the "secrets" its members know of other groups.

In Sirkanda the ethnographic team consisted of the anthropologist, an interpreter-assistant and, as a peripheral member for part of the time, a houseboy. This was a team in that it constituted "a set of individuals whose intimate cooperation is required if a given projected definition of the situation is to be maintained" (Goffman, 1959, p. 104). Villagers considered it to be a team. In their eyes the actions of each member reflected on the others.

The ethnographer

The initial response to an ethnographer by his subjects is probably always an attempt to identify him in familiar terms; to identify him as the performer of a familiar role. The impressions he makes will determine how he is identified.

In Sirkanda several roles were known or known of, under which strangers might appear, and each – missionary, tax collector or other government agent, spy – was for a time attributed to our ethnographic team by some or all villagers as being our real, i.e., back-region role. None of these was a suitable role for accomplishing our purposes and it was only by consistently behaving in ways inconsistent with these roles that we ultimately established a novel role for ourselves: that of scholars eager to learn what knowledgeable villagers could teach us about Pahari culture. I drew heavily on the familiar role of student, and my associates on the familiar role of employee or "servant." Foreign origin was an important aspect of my status, for I was a "sahib" and an "untouchable"; a person of relative wealth and influence but of ritually impure origin and habits.

For me the former was a more distressing status than the latter, but an equally inevitable one. I was always referred to as "the sahib" by villagers, although I succeeded in getting them not to address me as such. Goffman comments on the differences between terms of address and terms of reference in this context noting that

... in the presence of the audience, the performers tend to use a favorable form of address to them.... Sometimes members of the audience are referred to [in their absence] not even by a slighting name but by a code title which assimilates them fully to an abstract category. (Goffman, 1959, pp. 172–3)

Perhaps the cruelest term of all is found in situations where an individual asks to be called by a familiar term to his face, and this is tolerantly done, but in his absence he is referred to by a formal term. (Ibid., p. 174)

Had I been alone in the village I would have had a relatively free hand in attempting to determine whom I associated with, so long as I did not infringe too freely on village backstage life or on matters of ritual purity. However, since I was in almost constant association with an assistant whose performance was closely tied to my own, my status and his were interdependent. The definition of ourselves which we cooperated in projecting had to correspond to known and observable facts and clues about ourselves and our purposes. Since to villagers my assistant was more conventional and hence comprehensible as a person than I, it was largely from him that impressions were derived which determined our status. It is for this reason that the characteristics of the interpreter-assistant were of crucial significance to the research effort.

The Brahmin assistant

Sharma, the Brahmin assistant, was able to establish himself before villagers as a friendly, tactful and trustworthy young man. As such he was well-liked by high-caste villagers and was respected by all. Once his plains Brahmin status had been verified, it affected the tenor of all his relationships, and consequently of the ethnographic team's relations with villagers. The effects of these relationships on the research derived from his own attempts at impression management as a performer before several audiences, and from the attempts by villagers to control his impressions of them.

Most importantly, Sharma was a Brahmin of the plains. As such, he felt obliged to convey an acceptable definition of himself in this role to the villagers among whom he worked and to the ethnographer for whom he worked. Before villagers he was obliged to refrain from extensive informal contacts with his caste inferiors. He was expected to refuse to participate in such defiling activities as consumption of meat and liquor, and was in general expected to exemplify the virtues of his status. He was, in this context, acting as the sole local representative of plains Brahmins, a group with which he was closely identified by himself and by villagers.

In the presence of the ethnographer he joined a larger team, or reference group, of high-caste Indian Hindus. In this role he wished to convey a definition of Hinduism that would reflect well on its practitioners in the eyes of the foreigner. When possible he demonstrated an enlightened, sophisticated, democratic Hinduism quite unlike that indigenous to the village. Since, as a Hindu, he considered himself a teammate of villagers, he felt obliged to convey to the ethnographer an impression of village affairs that was not too greatly at variance with the notion of Hinduism which he wished to convey. He was, therefore, reluctant to discuss matters which might contradict the impression he had fostered – especially high-caste religious practices and inter-caste relations, the areas of most flagrant deviation (from his point of view) from the Hindu ideal. He tended, probably unconsciously, to color his accounts and structure our interactions with villagers to bias the impressions I received in this direction. On behalf of the ethnographic team, he was intent upon winning the villagers' acceptance and confidence, a fact which colored his accounts of us to them. His skill at impression management was evidenced by the rapport he achieved with both the ethnographer and the villagers, and by the fact that I, as ethnographer, was largely unaware of his manipulation of impressions until later when I had access to information without his management.

The village team

Villagers, too, had particular definitions of themselves that they wished to convey to the ethnographic team determined, to a large extent, by their interpretation of the nature and motives of this team. With a Brahmin in an important position on the team, low-caste people were reluctant to have close contact with it. High-caste people, on the other hand, were eager to demonstrate the validity of their claims to high-caste status before this patently high-status outsider.

Pahari Brahmins and Rajputs (the high castes of this area) customarily do many things that are unacceptable in high-caste plains circles. As a result they are denied the esteem of such people. The appellations "Pahari Brahmin" and "Pahari Rajput" are often used in derision by people of the plains. Among other unorthodox activities, these Paharis sacrifice animals, eat meat, drink liquor, are unfamiliar with the scriptures, largely ignore the great gods of Hinduism, consult diviners and shamans, fail to observe many of the ceremonies and ritual restrictions deemed necessary by high-caste plainsmen, take a bride price in marriage, marry widows, are not infrequently polygynous (and in some areas are polyandrous), occasionally marry across caste lines, share wives among brothers, "sell" women to men of dubious character from the plains. In order favorably to impress a plains Brahmin they must conceal these activities insofar as possible, and this they indeed do.

Just as Sharma wished to convey an impression of enlightened Hinduism to the ethnographer, villagers wished to convey their idea of enlightened Hinduism to Sharma. The two aims were complementary. Both resulted in projection of an exaggerated impression of religious orthodoxy. This exaggeration of behavior, indicating adherence to the "officially accredited values of the society," is a feature characteristic of impression management before outsiders (cf. Goffman, 1959, p. 35).

Impression management of this kind is especially difficult when the intended audience, as in the case of the ethnographic team, has a known or suspected interest in the detection of back-region attitudes and behaviors, and when it is in intimate association with the performers.

Virtually the entire village of Sirkanda was at first a back region for the ethnographic team: a great deal of the conventional behavior therein was back-region behavior. Attempts were made by villagers to avoid "inopportune intrusions" which Goffman describes as follows:

> When an outsider accidentally enters a region in which a performance is being given, or when a member of the audience inadvertently enters the backstage, the intruder is likely to catch those present *flagrante delicto*. Through no one's intention, the person present in the region may find that they have patently been witnessed in activity that is quite incompatible with the impression that they are, for wider social reasons, under obligation to maintain to the intruder. (Goffman, 1959, p. 209)

When, for instance, an opportunity arose for the ethnographic team to move from a buffalo shed on the periphery of the village to a house in its center, villagers' desire to maintain a modicum of overt hospitality wavered before their covert alarm until an untouchable was induced to place an objection before the potential intruders. The objection had the desired effect although it was immediately repudiated by its high-caste instigators, who blamed it upon the irresponsible meddling of a mere untouchable. They thus assured the continued privacy of the village while maintaining their front of hospitality. The untouchable who voiced the objection had been coerced and bribed with liquor to do so. He later commented that villagers had said that people, and especially women, would be inhibited in the performance of their daily rounds if strangers were to be continuously in their midst; that is, the backstage would be exposed to the audience.

Before the ethnographic team the village at this time presented an apparently united front. Villagers of all castes cooperated not only in concealing things inimical to the high-caste performance, but also those thought to reflect adversely on the people as a whole. For example, an intra-caste dispute among untouchables came to a head at a high-caste wedding where the disputants were serving as musicians. While the disputants were presenting their case to an informal council of high-caste guests which had convened one afternoon, a heated argument erupted. It was suppressed and the council disbanded with the explicit warning that the ethnographer would hear and think ill of the village.

During this period of the research, untouchables were usually relegated to an unobtrusive secondary role, largely in the back region. With a Brahmin on the ethnographic team and with high-caste people as our associates, low-caste villagers were disinclined to associate with us, much less to reveal backstage information. We were in their view associates of the high-caste team and as such were people to be treated cautiously and respectfully. High-caste villagers could not reveal such information to us either because we were, in their view, members of the plains Brahmin team and a source of potential discredit to high-caste Paharis.

Ethnographic information that was acquired in this context was largely of a sort considered innocuous by villagers – observations about the weather and current events, agricultural techniques, etc. Much of it was distorted. For example, our initial genealogies omitted all reference to plural wives; accounts of marriage and other ritual events were sketchy and largely in conformance with the villagers' conception of plains orthodoxy. Some of the information was false. Most of it was inaccessible. The back region was large and carefully guarded. Yet relations between the ethnographic team and the village were relatively congenial.

The Muslim assistant

When after four months the Brahmin assistant was replaced by a Muslim, there were important consequences for the villagers' conception of the ethnographic team and consequently for their performance before that team. The progress and results of the research reflected these changes.

Mohammed, the Muslim assistant, was respected for his age and learning, liked for his congeniality and wit, but doomed to untouchable status by his religion. This did not disturb him. As an educated and not particularly religious Muslim he had little personal involvement in the caste hierarchy of the village and little vested interest in the ethnographer's impression of village Hinduism. As an individual he was objective and interested but concerned more with projecting to villagers a favorable view of the ethnographic team than any particular image of his personal status. As a performer he played a less prominent role than his predecessor. This was reflected in his interpreting. Sharma had preferred to interpret virtually all statements and to direct the course of conversation to keep from offending villagers (and embarrassing himself) by treading on dangerous ground. Mohammed was anxious that communication between ethnographer and subjects be as direct as possible; that conversation be as undirected as possible except when particular topics were being pursued. Consequently interpreting occurred only as necessary; ethnographer and subjects determined the direction of conversation.

As an audience, the Muslim's effect on the village performance was drastically different from the effect of the Brahmin. High-caste people did not wish to associate openly with a Muslim, for he was by definition ritually impure. He was in no sense their fellow team member as the Brahmin had been; he was in some respects almost as alien as was the ethnographer himself. Consequently, high-caste villagers' behavior became correct but distant: informal conversations and visitations decreased in frequency; the ethnographer was told in private by some high-caste villagers that they could no longer associate closely with him.

Low-caste people, on the other hand, became less inhibited than formerly was the case. When by experimentation they found that the Muslim was apparently oblivious to caste, these people began to be friendly. In the vacuum of social interaction left by withdrawal of the high castes, they were not rebuffed. The effect was circular and soon the ethnographer's dwelling became identified as primarily a low-caste area.

Not all high-caste people were alienated, but most preferred to talk in their own homes, with low castes excluded, rather than in the ethnographer's house. Some would visit the ethnographer only when they had been assured that no low-caste villagers would be present.

In these circumstances the village no longer presented the aspect of a unified team. Now it became clear that the village was divided. From the point of view of the high castes there were at least two teams: low and high castes. The former feared the power of the latter; the latter feared the revelation of back-region secrets that might be given by the former. From the point of view of low castes there seem to have been at least three teams: high castes, "our caste" and (other) low castes. High castes were feared and resented; other low castes were to some extent competitors for status before outsiders. Competition took the form of conflicting claims as to the type and nature of interaction with one another, each caste claiming to treat as inferiors (or sometimes as equals) others who, in turn, claimed equal or superior status. Actually, in the context of the closed village a good deal of interaction took place among low castes with few status considerations.

Low-caste teams

The position of low castes – the untouchables – was an interesting one relative to the village team and its performance. Untouchables were in a position such that they might easily admit an audience to backstage village secrets. They

were members of the village team perforce, but they were uneasy and not fully trusted members. Goffman has appropriately stated that:

> One overall objective of any team is to sustain the definition of the situation that its performance fosters. This will involve the over-communication of some facts and the under-communication of others. Given the fragility and the required expressive coherence of the reality that is dramatized by a performance, there are usually facts which, if attention is drawn to them during the performance, would discredit, disrupt, or make useless the impression that the performance fosters. These facts may be said to provide "destructive information." A basic problem for many performances, then, is that of information control; the audience must not acquire destructive information about the situation that is being defined for them. In other words, a team must be able to keep its secrets and have its secrets kept. (Goffman, 1959, p. 141)

In Sirkanda, low-caste people are in a position to know high-caste secrets because all villagers are in almost constant contact with one another; they have little privacy. Castes are not separated physically, socially, or ritually to the extent that they are in many areas. Low-caste and high-caste cultures, including back-region behavior, proved to be very similar among these hill people (cf. Berreman, 1960b). But, for low-caste people the back region – the part that is to be concealed – is much smaller than for high-caste people. They do not feel obligated to protect village secrets to the extent that high-caste people do simply because their prestige and position are not at stake. They do not share, or are not heavily committed to, the "common official values" which high-caste people affect before outsiders. High-caste men, for example, were careful to conceal the fact that, in this society, brothers have sexual access to one another's wives. However, a low-caste man who had listed for the ethnographer the name and village of origin of the women of his family, including his wife and his brothers' wives, was not embarrassed to remark, when asked which was his wife, that "They are all like wives to me." A more striking contrast was evidenced in attitudes toward village religious behavior. After some time, low-caste people encouraged the ethnographer to attend their household religious observances wherein possessed dancing and animal sacrifice occurred. High-caste villagers did not want the ethnographer to be present at their own performances of the same rituals. Some of them also objected to my presence at the low-caste functions and exerted pressure to have me excluded. The reason was apparently that high-caste people felt such behavior, if known outside, would jeopardize their claims to high status. High-caste people, recognizing that village culture was essentially the same in all castes and that I was aware of this, felt their position threatened by the performance of the low-castes. Low-caste people had no such status to maintain.

Low-caste people, unlike their high-caste village-mates, had little prestige at stake in outsiders' conceptions of the Pahari way of life. They were not competing with plains people for status nor seeking acceptance by them to the extent that the high castes were. People assume the worst about untouchables so they have little to gain by concealment. This is not to say that there is no particular definition of their situation that untouchables try to project, or that it takes no effort to perpetuate it; the lowest-status group in Sirkanda, for instance, has tried to suppress its reputation for prostitution by giving up some of the activities associated with it. But the range of such back-region secrets among low castes is limited in comparison to that among high castes. It does not extend to Pahari practices as such, but instead is limited primarily to those few practices crucial to their status competition with other low castes in the village and, even more importantly, to negative attitudes toward the high castes – attitudes which must be concealed in view of the power structure of the society.

Goffman notes that

> … to the degree that the teammates and their colleagues form a complete social community which offers each performer a place and a source of moral support …, to that degree it would seem that performers can protect themselves from doubt and guilt and practice any kind of deception. (Goffman, 1959, pp. 214–15)

It is because, in this highly stratified society, moral support and rewards are allotted on the basis of caste that high-caste performers cannot trust their low-caste colleagues to sustain the performance – to practice the deception – voluntarily. Low-caste people resent their inferior position and the disadvantages which inhere in it (cf. Berreman, 1960a). Not only are they uncommitted to the village performance which is largely a high-caste performance; they are in private often committed to discrediting some aspects of this performance. Both of these are facts of which the ethnographer must be aware. As a result of them, if low-caste members feel they can do so in safety, they are not reluctant to reveal information about village life which embarrasses high-caste villagers. They may also, of course, manufacture information intended to discredit their caste superiors, just as the latter may purposely purvey false information to justify their treatment of low castes. The ethnographer must be constantly alert to the likelihood of such deceptions, using cross checks, independent observation and the like for verification. Eventually he can identify reliable informants and the subjects upon which particular informants or categories of informants are likely to be unreliable.

That high-caste people recognize the vulnerability of their performance and are anxious about it is revealed in their suspicion and resentment of low-caste association with outsiders, such as the ethnographic team. Anyone who associates too freely with such outsiders is suspected of telling too much, but only low-caste villagers are suspected of telling those facts which will seriously jeopardize the status of the dominant high castes. The suspicion that low castes are not entirely to be trusted to keep up the front is therefore not paranoia on the part of those they may reveal; it is a real danger. On the other hand, high-caste members encourage association between strangers and low castes by sending the latter to appraise strangers who come to the village and, if possible, to send them on their way. By so doing high castes avoid the risks of being embarrassed or polluted by the aliens. At the same time they increase low-caste opportunities for outside contact, acquisition of new ideas, etc., and they thereby increase their own anxieties about low-caste behavior and attitudes. They are apparently more willing to face this anxiety than to risk initial personal contact with strangers. As a result, some low-caste people are more at ease with strangers and more knowledgeable about them and their thought patterns, than are most high-caste people.

Since they are not willing to extend to low castes the status, power, and material rewards which would bring them into the high-caste team or commit them to the high-caste performance, high castes rely heavily on threats of economic and physical sanctions to keep their subordinates in line and their secrets, which these people know, concealed from outsiders. To the extent that low-caste people do sustain the performance they are evidently responding to their fear of high-caste reprisals more than to an internalized commitment to the performance.

High-caste teams

Even high-caste villagers do not present a united front or consistent performance on all matters. Bride-price marriage, for example, is traditional in these hills and until recent times only poverty accounted for failure to pay for a bride. To high-caste people of the plains bride-price marriage is reprehensible; a dowry is always demanded. This attitude has had its effect in the hills so that Paharis, and especially those of high caste, not infrequently forgo the bride price in a wedding. There was an interesting division of expressed attitude among high-caste villagers in Sirkanda on this matter. Although there was no consistent difference among families in practice, some claimed that their families would never accept or demand a bride price while others claimed that their families would never give or take a bride without an accompanying bride price. I was unsuccessful in attempting to account for this difference in terms of the economic, educational, or other readily apparent characteristics of those concerned. I finally realized that it was largely a function of the relationship of the particular informant to me and my assistant and, more specifically, the impression the

informant wished to convey to us. Many wanted to convey a picture of plains orthodoxy and, not realizing that we knew otherwise, or hoping that we would think their families were exceptions, they tailored their accounts of the marriage transaction to fit this. A few, notably some of the older men of the Rajput landowning caste, wanted to convey their conception of the proper Pahari tradition, perhaps in view of the fact that they knew we were aware of their practice of bride-price marriage and that to conceal it was by then useless. They expressed disapproval of dowry marriage and disclaimed willingness to be parties to such arrangements. They explained that as Rajputs they would not take charity (as a Brahmin would) and would insist on paying for anything they got, including a wife; conversely they would require payment for their daughters, because one does not give charity to other Rajputs. Moreover, gift brides die young and do not produce heirs, they asserted. Some villagers were more frank than either of the above groups when they got to know us, and described quite freely the specific circumstances under which bride price and dowry were and were not included in recent marriage transactions.

On at least one occasion highly controversial information was revealed by a Rajput because of an erroneous assumption on his part that others in his caste had been telling the ethnographer the story in a manner uncomplimentary to himself. Early in the research I learned that the village had been riven by a legal battle over land begun some twenty years previously, and although I knew in a general way who and what was involved, I had not ascertained the details. One evening the proudest, most suspicious and tight-lipped of the members of the winning faction appeared unexpectedly at my house, lantern in hand, and without introduction proceeded to recount the nine-year legal battle blow-by-blow. He was evidently attempting to counteract information which he presumed the losing faction had given me. I was subsequently able to check his version with several other versions from both sides in order to reconstruct approximately the factors involved in this complex and emotionally loaded episode.

Thus, high-caste members are not entirely free of suspicion and doubt regarding the extent to which they can rely upon their teammates to sustain their performance. Even among high castes there are different performances which various groups try to project to one another and occasionally to outsiders. Lines of differential performance and impression management among them most often follow kin group and caste affiliation. These high-caste performance teams are usually factional groups in the village, competing and disputing with one another. They often attempt to disparage one another within the high-caste context by such means as questioning purity of ancestry. The head of the largest family in Sirkanda, a member of one of the two large Rajput sibs of the village, expressed doubt that the other large sib, to which his wife (the mother of his five adult sons) belonged, was actually and legitimately a Rajput sib. This was a recurrent theme. Often cleavages between high-caste groups involved long-standing disputes over land and/or women.

High-caste performance teams also differed from one another in the age, sex, education, and outside experience of their members. Groups so defined can be described as performance teams because they differ in the definitions of their own and the village situation which they attempt to project to various audiences. Rarely, however, do they desert the high-caste team before outsiders or low castes, the two most crucial audiences.

The same kinds of statements can be made about particular low castes, although the low castes as a group rarely cooperate to put on a team performance. Usually, each low caste sustains its own performance, attempting to substantiate its claims to status relative to other low castes adjacent in the hierarchy.

[...]

Data, secrets, and confidence

As rapport increased and back-region information accumulated it became possible for the ethnographic team to accomplish useful research on a broader scale – to understand formerly incomprehensible activities and attitudes; to relate previously disparate facts, to make more sensible inquiries, to cross-check and verify information. The effect was cumulative. As we learned more, more information became accessible. By being interested, uncritical, circumspect, and meticulous about maintaining their trust, we won villagers' confidence. For example, high-caste people who avoided close contact with Mohammed in the village visited his home in town and even ate with him, with the plea that he tell no one in the village. No one ever discovered these indiscretions, and those who committed them were not unappreciative. Contrary to villagers' early fears, no missionaries, policemen, tax officers, or other outsiders came to Sirkanda as a result of what we learned there. We tried to show our increasing knowledge in greater comprehension of our environment, rather than by repetition of items of information. As we learned more, concealment from us decreased because we were apparently already aware of, and largely indifferent to, many of the facts about which villagers were most self-conscious or secretive. We took for granted things some villagers supposed were "dark secrets" (i.e., things contrary to the impression they hoped to convey to us) and far from our knowledge (cf. Goffman, 1959, p. 141). When we had asked, in genealogical inquiry, what a man's wife's name was, we always got one name. When we later found that polygyny was not uncommon we asked first how many wives a man had and thereby got accurate information. Most villagers were unaware that our interests went beyond formal genealogical records, economic techniques and ritual observances. Many secrets were revealed largely because of the apparent casualness of our interest in them, and because villagers had become accustomed to our presence in the village so that we were not considered to be as critical an audience as had once been the case.

Some of the most revealing instances of social interaction occurred between people who were apparently oblivious to the fact that the ethnographer was present. Frequently this was a temporary lapse. A performance for the ethnographer would be abandoned as tension, conviviality, concentration on a topic of conversation, or some other intensification of interaction occurred among the participants. Such instances of preoccupation with one another were conspicuous by the fact that attitudes were expressed or information divulged that would normally be suppressed. The breach in the performance would sometimes be followed immediately, or after some time, by embarrassment, apology, or anxious efforts to counteract its presumed effect on the ethnographer's view of the village or of those involved in the incident. Minor instances of the same phenomenon were frequent sources of insight into the functioning of the society, and sources of confirmation or contradiction of informants' data.

The accuracy of information on back-region subjects could often be checked through informants who would not have intentionally revealed it, by bringing the subject up naturally in conversation as though it were a matter of general information. That is, it was defined by the ethnographer as no longer restricted to the back region of the performance to which he was audience.

Some "secrets," however, could not be adequately verified simply because to do so would precipitate difficulty for all concerned, especially for those who would be suspected of revealing the secrets. Such secrets ranged from gossip about various past transgressions and indiscretions by particular families or individuals, to the fact that villagers of all castes were reported to eat occasionally the flesh of animals such as deer and goats found freshly dead or killed in the forest. One low-caste man told me there were secrets he could not reveal until I had my pack on my back and was leaving the village permanently. He was afraid that some intimation of my knowledge might leak out and he would be punished as the only one who would have revealed the damaging information. After I had said my final farewells this man journeyed sixteen miles to my home in town, primarily, to be sure, to get some utensils I had offered him, but partly to tell me some incidents which he had been afraid to tell or even hint at during my residence in the village and which he would not tell in the presence of my assistant or any other person. These incidents had to do primarily with the sensitive area of inter-caste

and other illicit sexual behavior among powerful members of the community.

To this man, as well as to other low-caste friends, the ethnographer had become what Goffman refers to as a "confidant," one who is located outside of the team and who partici-pates "… only vicariously in back and front region activity" (Goffman, 1959, p. 159). In this role I had access to a range of information not often accessible to those who came from outside the group. Where group membership is by ascription this seems to be the only feasible role for which the ethnographer may strive.

Certain secrets remained too dark to be told even by those who trusted us most. The village remained a team, united in its performance, with regard to some practices or beliefs which were too damaging to all (or to certain powerful high-caste people) to permit their revelation to an outsider. Obviously, like the perfect crime, most of these remain unknown. Indications of a few of them were received, however. For example, one old dispute which resulted in a factional split among Rajputs would have escaped me had not an old man referred to it briefly, bitterly, and inadvertently. Despite my best efforts I learned nothing about it beyond his chance remark that it involved a man and woman of the disputing sibs seen talking and laughing together at the water source some generations ago. Even the most willing informants would only say that "Those people are all dead now so it doesn't matter."

I learned that some Paharis occasionally sacrifice a buffalo to their gods, but that this has never occurred in Sirkanda. I was convinced that this was the case when considerable inquiry and observation seemed to verify it. Then, shortly before my final departure, a dog deposited the embarrassing evidence of such a sacrifice – the neatly-severed head of a buffalo calf – on the main village trail shortly before I chanced by. Villagers of all castes refused to discuss the matter in which all were obviously implicated. My one opportunity for a candid explanation occurred at the moment of discovery when I asked a child at my heels which god the buffalo had been sacrificed to. A reply seemed imminent until his elder, a few steps back on the trail, caught up and silenced the discussion as well as all chance for future fruitful inquiry on the subject. Villagers thought that to plains people this would seem akin to cow-killing, the greatest sin of all, and so it had to be rigorously concealed.

The sacrifice had evidently occurred during my absence from the village.

> If an individual is to give expression to ideal standards during his performance, then he will have to forgo or conceal action which is inconsistent with these standards. When this inappropriate conduct is itself satisfying in some way, as is often the case, then one commonly finds it indulged in secretly, in this way the performer is able to forgo his cake and eat it too. (Goffman, 1959, p. 41)

It was six months after my arrival before animal sacrifices and attendant rituals were performed in my presence, although they had been performed in my absence or without my knowledge throughout my residence in the village. Likewise, it was not until after Sharma left that I witnessed drinking and meat-eating parties in the village.

Since I left the village for two or three days every week or so, there was an opportunity for essential and enjoyable back-region activity to be carried on quite freely in my absence, and this opportunity was not neglected. In fact, it probably made my research in the village much more bearable to villagers than if I had been there constantly. It was largely the threat to their privacy that motivated villagers to make sure that I did not take up residence in the center of the village (as described above), but continued instead to live on its periphery. No doubt one of the most anxiety-producing situations known to man is to make public that which he considers to be private, back-region behavior.

[...]

Impression management in pursuit of research

Finally, my own behavior was tailored for my village audience. I carefully and, I think successfully, concealed the range of my interests and their intensity in some matters – such as

inter-caste relations. I refrained from going where I was not wanted, even when I could have gone without being challenged and when I very much wanted to go. One instance occurred when I decided not to move into the proffered house in the center of the village. As another example, I never attended a village funeral. On the two occasions upon which I could have done so, I found that there was considerable anxiety lest my presence upset guests from other villages, though Sirkanda villagers claimed they would welcome my presence. There was evident relief when I stayed home.

In the village I concealed the extent of my note-taking, doing most of it at night or in private. I felt free to take notes openly before only a few key informants, and then only after I had known them for a considerable time. I recorded some kinds of detailed information, such as genealogies and crop yields, in the presence of all informants when I found that I could do so without inhibiting responses appreciably. This, too, took time and circumspection. Some subjects, such as ceremonial activities, could be freely recorded before some informants and not at all before others. I discarded my plans to use scheduled interviews and questionnaires because I thought they would do more harm in terms of rapport than good in terms of data collection, in view of village attitudes and my relationship with villagers. I never took photographs without permission. I concealed such alien practices as my use of toilet paper – a habit for which foreigners are frequently criticized in India. I took up smoking as a step to increase rapport. I simulated a liking for millet chapaties and the burning pepper and pumpkin or potato mixture which makes up much of the Pahari diet. Even more heroically, I concealed my distaste for the powerful home-distilled liquor, the consumption of which marked every party and celebration. Such dissimulations were aimed at improving rapport and they were worth the trouble. In this behavior a front was maintained in order to sustain a particular definition of my situation; a definition which I thought would increase my access to village backstage life, thereby contributing to the ultimate goal of understanding the lifeways of these people.

Conclusion

In such a society as this the ethnographer is inevitably an outsider and never becomes otherwise. He is judged by those among whom he works on the basis of his own characteristics and those of his associates. He becomes identified with those social groups among his subjects to which he gains access. The nature of his data is largely determined by his identity as seen by his subjects. Polite acceptance and even friendship do not always mean that access will be granted to the confidential regions of the life of those who extend it. The stranger will be excluded from a large and vital area if he is seen as one who will not safeguard secrets, and especially if he is identified as a member of one of those groups from which the secrets are being kept.

Sharma was a high-caste plainsman and consequently identified with very important groups in the village, groups rigorously excluded from large areas of the life of both high-caste and low-caste villagers. As such he could likely never have achieved the kind of relationship to villagers which would have resulted in access to much of the life of Sirkanda. Access to that information was essential to the ethnographer because it constituted a large proportion of all village attitudes and behaviors. Mohammed was able to gain substantial rapport with the low castes. In view of the attitudes of villagers and the social composition and power structure of the village, the low castes were the only feasible source of information which high-caste villagers considered to be embarrassing, damaging or secret. They were a reasonably satisfactory source of such information about the entire village because all castes were in such close contact that they had few secrets from one another and did not differ greatly in culture.

This is not to say that the information obtained was complete or totally accurate, but only to assert that it was much more so than would have been the case had Sharma been my assistant throughout the research.

Thus, there is more than one "team" which makes up Sirkanda; more than one definition of the village situation is presented or may be presented to the outsider. As the ethnographer gains access to information from people in different social groups and in different situations he is likely to become increasingly aware of this.

The question of whether the performance, definition or impression fostered by one group is more real or true than that put forth by another, or whether a planned impression is more or less true than the backstage behavior behind it, is not a fruitful one for argument. All are essential to an understanding of the social interaction being observed.

REFERENCES

Berreman, Gerald D.
    1960a "Caste in India and the United States." *American Journal of Sociology*, Vol. 66, pp. 120–7.
Berreman, Gerald D.
    1960b "Cultural Variability and Drift in the Himalayan Hills." *American Anthropologist*, Vol. 62, pp. 774–94.
Bowen, Elenore Smith (pseud.)
    1954 *Return to Laughter*. New York: Harper & Row.
Goffman, Erving
    1959 *The Presentation of Self in Everyday Life*. Garden City, NY: Doubleday.
Srinivas, M. N.
    1959 "The Dominant Caste in Rampura." *American Anthropologist*, Vol. 61, pp. 1–16.

10

The Politics of Truth and Emotion among Victims and Perpetrators of Violence

Antonius C. G. M. Robben

"Let me help you," he said, as he held up my coat. "Thank you very much," I said. My arms slipped effortlessly into the sleeves as he gently lifted the coat onto my shoulders. Before I could return the gesture, he had already put on his overcoat.

We passed through the dark corridors of the old palace, walked down the marble stairway, and left the Officers Club through the main entrance. "You know, Dr. Robben," he began, "I am a very religious man. And I know deep down in my heart that my conscience before God is clear." We turned the corner at the Café Petit Paris and continued along Santa Fé Avenue. I looked at him and tried to overstem the noise of the traffic: "Well, general, but there are many Argentines who ..." "Look out!" he yelled and stretched his right arm in front of me. A taxi nearly hit me as I was about to step on the pavement.

A few months later, on October 7, 1989, the general was released from criminal prosecution by a presidential decree (*indulto*).

He had been indicted for ordering the disappearance of Argentine citizens and for carrying the hierarchical responsibility for their rape and torture by the men under his command. The decree did not acquit him of the charges or exonerate his military honor but merely dismissed his court case and those of dozens of other high-ranking officers. The Argentine president, Carlos Menem, hoped that this decree would "close the wounds of the past" and contribute to a "national pacification, reconciliation, and unity" among a people divided by the violence and repression of the 1970s.

Six months earlier I had arrived in Buenos Aires to study whether or not these wounds were closing and how the Argentine people were coping with the tens of thousands of dead and disappeared in what the military had called the "dirty war" against the leftist insurgency.[1] If Argentine society was to be pacified, then the people had to reconcile themselves with each other and their past.

Antonius C. G. M. Robben, "The Politics of Truth and Emotion among Victims and Perpetrators of Violence," pp. 81–103 from *Fieldwork under Fire: Contemporary Studies of Violence and Survival*, ed. Carolyn Nordstrom and Antonius C. G. M. Robben. Berkeley: University of California Press, 1995.

Chapters of history cannot be turned by decree. Crucial to national reconciliation was how the Argentine people made sense of the years of intense political repression and violence during the 1976–1983 military dictatorship. At the time, most people had only a vague notion of the incipient civil war that waged during the first half of the 1970s. Many welcomed the coup d'état of March 1976 as necessary to end the country's political and economic chaos. Constitutional rights were suspended, the Congress was sent home, and the unions were placed under military guardianship. People were aware of the censorship of the mass media, the pervasive intelligence network of the security forces, and the many arrests that were made, often under the cover of darkness. They also heard about the worldwide denunciation of human rights violations in Argentina, but the military government was quite successful in convincing the many Argentines who had not been affected personally that these accusations were being orchestrated by the revolutionary Left at home and abroad. It was only after the 1982 defeat of the Argentine armed forces at the Falkland/ Malvinas Islands that the public learned of the extent and brutality of the political persecution during the dictatorship. The Argentine people wanted to know and understand what had happened. At the fall of the military regime in 1983, retired generals, former cabinet ministers, human rights activists, union leaders, bishops, and politicians were flooding the news media with their conflicting accounts and analyses. The protagonists of the years of repression had become the nation's historiographers.

The historical reconstruction of the 1970s became intensely contested during the decade following the turn to democracy, not only through conflicting discourse but also through controversial political actions, including one guerrilla attack on an army base, three amnesties, and five military mutinies, the last and most violent of which occurred during my field work. The adversary interpretations came principally from the armed forces, the former guerrilla organizations, the human rights groups, and the Roman Catholic church. The public discourse of the leaders of these four groups became the centerpiece of my research

on the contested historical reconstruction of the political violence of the 1970s. I was not interested in writing a history of the so-called dirty war. Instead, I focused on how that history was being remembered, contested, negotiated, and reconstructed in public by its protagonists. I told my interlocutors that I was not in Argentina to establish truth or guilt because that was the prerogative of Argentine society. I made it clear at the start of every interview that I wanted to talk to the principal political actors and understand their explanations of the recent past in a time when opinions and interpretations were still being formed and reformulated. I wanted them to explain their position, just as they had done previously in television and radio programs, newspaper articles, public speeches, and their numerous meetings with local reporters, foreign correspondents, diplomats, and international fact-finding delegations. I chose this approach to the conflicting discourse about the decades of political violence because the historical protagonists refused to enter into face-to-face debates with their former adversaries. Hence I interviewed them about the same principal historical events, contrasted their arguments and interpretations, and compared the opinions imparted to me with their other public pronouncements.

It was in my interviews with the Argentine military that I first realized the importance of seduction as a dimension of fieldwork. My military interlocutors must have known that the image I had received abroad – and which they reckoned was being confirmed in my talks with their political opponents – was one of officers torturing babies and ordering the disappearance of tens of thousands of innocent Argentine civilians. I had, of course, anticipated their denial of these serious accusations, but I did not expect to be meeting with military men who exuded great civility and displayed a considerable knowledge of literature, art, and classical music. The affability and chivalry of the officers clashed with the trial records I had read, affected my critical sensibility, and in the beginning led me astray from my research focus. It was only later that I realized that I had been engrossed in ethnographic seduction. This process of seduction and subsequent awareness repeated itself in my meetings with bishops, human rights activists, and former guerrilla leaders. Each group was seductive in its own way, and it was only after months of interviewing that I succeeded in recognizing the prevalent defenses and strategies and learned to distinguish seduction from good rapport.

I have chosen the word *seduction* to describe those personal defenses and social strategies because it means literally "to be led astray from an intended course."[2] Seduction is used here exclusively in its neutral meaning of being led astray unawares, not in its popular meaning of allurement and entrapment. I prefer seduction to other terms, such as concealment, manipulation, or deception, that carry negative overtones and suggest dishonesty or malintent. Seduction can be intentional but also unconscious and can be compared to the ways in which filmmakers, stage directors, artists, or writers succeed in totally absorbing the attention of their audiences.

I am aware of the risks of using the word *seduction* in the context of violence. The association of the words *victim* and *seduction* makes me vulnerable to the charge that I am implying that somehow the victim brought on himself or herself the pain that was inflicted, while the mere suggestion that victims of violence might mold what they tell us runs the danger that I will be accused of contributing to their victimization. Ultimately, it might make people question my moral standards. How can I place doubt on the horror stories I have been told and distrust their narrators? It is much easier to acknowledge manipulation by victimizers than by victims. We have more sympathy for unmasking abusers of power than doubting the words of their victims. I have the same sympathies. However, I also realize that in the end the victims may be harmed and their testimonies discredited if we report their views naively and uncritically. We need to analyze their accounts and be attentive to our own inhibitions, weaknesses, and biases, all to the benefit of a better understanding of both victim and victimizer. The ethnographic seduction by victims and perpetrators of violence will in this way become a font of instead of an obstruction to insight.[3]

This chapter focuses on the ethnographic encounter because the most common transmission of cultural knowledge in fieldwork takes place through open interviews with key informants. I will argue that seduction is a dimension of fieldwork that is especially prominent in research on violent political conflict because the interlocutors have great personal and political stakes in making the ethnographer adopt their interpretations. The importance of seduction is enhanced by the special circumstances of studying-up conflict. An anthropologist who wishes to understand a major armed conflict from the perspective of its principal protagonists cannot resort to participant observation in its traditional sense but is restricted to account interviews. These interviews may range from a unique half-hour meeting to a series of long conversations. It is during these face-to-face encounters that ethnographic understanding and inquiry are most vulnerable to seduction.

Empathy and Dehumanization

Ethnographic understanding through empathy and detachment has been generally accepted as a common dialectic in fieldwork. We must establish a good rapport with our interlocutors to grasp the world from their perspective, while a simultaneous reflective detachment as observers must objectify our perceptions and enhance our analytical insight.[4] "One of the most persistent problems we confront is how to so subject ourselves and yet maintain the degree of 'detachment' necessary for us to analyze our observations: in other words, to be anthropologists as well as participants" (Ellen 1984:227). Bronislaw Malinowski conceived of anthropological research in these terms, and it was to remain a canon of our profession until the 1960s when Clifford Geertz began to problematize fieldwork and ethnography with his notion of "thick description."

Geertz calls attention to the many-layered subjective construction of culture and argues for reproducing this complexity in the ethnographic text.[5] He notes that the relation between informant and field-worker is bespeckled with mutual misunderstandings, clientelistic interests, power games, and cultural proselytizing. These problems of cultural interpretation are of central concern to the ethnographer. Geertz (1973:15) proposes, therefore, the "thick description" of culture "cast in terms of the constructions we imagine" our interlocutors "to place upon what they live through, the formulae they use to define what happens to them." A question that arises immediately is whether people's constructions and formulas – not just their content – change under social tension and to what extent violent conflict will therefore affect the thick description of culture. This chapter will show that an examination in the field of the principal methodological and epistemological problems of conducting ethnographic research under violent conflict may yield significant insights about people's interpretation and construction of the conflict under study.

The problem of ethnographic seduction deserves attention because it subverts the *thick conversation* that precedes its description in ethnographic texts. We may become engulfed in seductive strategies or defenses that convince us of the thinness of social discourse. We believe ourselves to be seeing the world through our interlocutor's eyes. Yet these eyes are looking away from that which we think they are seeing. We have been led away from the depths of culture to its surface in an opaque intersubjective negotiation of cultural understanding.

This manipulation of appearances touches on the heart of seduction, so Jean Baudrillard (1990) tells us.[6] Appearance rests on a deep faith in the immediacy of our senses and emotions. Sight, sound, and feeling are intimately tied to our subjective experience of authenticity. Seduction wins us over through this pretense of real understanding. However, what is revealed to us is nothing more than a trompe l'oeil, and a surreal one at that. The ethnographic seduction trades our critical stance as observers for an illusion of congeniality with cultural insiders.[7] We no longer seek to grasp the native's point of view, but we believe, at least for the duration of the meeting, that we have become natives ourselves. We have become so enwrapped in the ethnographic

encounter that we are led astray from our research objectives, irrespective of the theoretical paradigm we are using and the anthropological understanding we are pursuing.

Problems of representation, intersubjectivity, polyphonic complexity, and the historicity of truth aside – all of which have already been discussed at length in anthropology – I am calling attention to the epistemological pitfalls of ethnographic seduction. Ethnographic seduction subverts our understanding of social and cultural phenomena by dissuading an inquiry beyond their appearance. The difficulty with ethnographic seduction is that we are not aware it is taking place. Unlike ethnographic anxiety, which according to George Devereux (1967:42–45) is produced by our repression of cultural experiences in the field that correspond to unconscious desires and wishes, ethnographic seduction puts the ethnographer often at ease. Repression makes the ethnographer "protect himself against anxiety by the omission, soft-pedalling, non-exploitation, misunderstanding, ambiguous description, over-exploitation or rearrangement of certain parts of his material" (ibid., 44). Seduction, instead, makes us feel that we have accomplished something profound in the encounter, that we have reached a deeper understanding and have somehow penetrated reality. We are in a state of well-being, and have a we-feeling with our informants that we mistakenly interpret as good rapport. It is only when we look back at our meeting and review the information gathered that we realize that we displayed a personal inhibition to break our rapport with critical questions. We realize that we have mistaken seduction for empathy.

If, on the one hand, seduction disarms our critical detachment and thus debilitates the gathering of cultural knowledge, then, on the other, our empathy in research on violent conflict may be hindered by our awareness of the protagonism of our interlocutor. Going one morning from an interview with a mother who had lost two sons during the first year of the dictatorship to a meeting with a general who might have ordered their disappearance, it became hard not to dehumanize them both. How can we engage in constructing an intersubjective understanding with a person who either has violated or transcended the humanity we are trying to understand?

At the early stages of my research I was confounded both by the veil of authenticity that shrouded the personal accounts of my interlocutors and by the public discourse that depicted military officers as beasts or saviors and human rights activists as subversives or saints. We may become so overwhelmed by the presence of political actors who have been dehumanized in society that we may also begin to see them only as saints and sinners or heroes and cowards. As I became more conscious of these public characterizations in Argentine society, I realized that this same process of dehumanization had contributed to the escalation of political violence in the 1970s, when political opponents became enemies and enemies were less than human, only fit for elimination.

Ethnographic seduction sidesteps empathy and detachment. The Socratic dialectic that brings us ever closer to the truth, the positivist model of an oscillation between inductive and deductive steps through which falsification becomes possible, and finally the hermeneutic model of a spiraling ascendance between whole and part that deepens understanding encompass epistemological approaches that become suspended by seduction. Ethnographic seduction reduces communication and knowledge to appearance.

The Management of Impression and Ambiguity

Around the same time that Geertz problematized ethnography, questions were raised about the ethics of covert fieldwork in Latin America and Southeast Asia. In the 1960s, anthropologists began to take a closer look at their research practices. This methodological reflection was greatly influenced by West Coast sociologists such as Herbert Blumer, Harold Garfinkel, Erving Goffman, Aaron V. Cicourel, and Harvey Sacks who inspired ethnographers to focus on the dramaturgical dimension of the relation between field-workers and their informants. Anthropologists could not routinely study the social and cultural conduct

of their subjects but had to realize that the actors might deliberately manipulate and obstruct the gathering of ethnographic knowledge. "The impressions that ethnographer and subjects seek to project to one another are ... those felt to be favorable to the accomplishment of their respective goals: the ethnographer seeks access to back-region information; the subjects seek to protect their secrets since these represent a threat to the public image they wish to maintain. Neither can succeed perfectly" (Berreman 1972:xxxiv).

The work of Goffman (1966, 1969) on impression management remains highly relevant for our understanding of the inter-actional processes that develop in ethnographic encounters.[8] Nevertheless, impression management encompasses only part of the much more comprehensive and complex dimension of ethnographic seduction. Ethnographer and interlocutor may try to protect their public image and try to gain access to each other's back stage, as Berreman explains, but which boundary should they protect and which region do they wish to enter? The ethnographer's definition of the secret knowledge of the interlocutor may not coincide with the respondent's perception. This misunderstanding provides opportunities not only for dramaturgical impression management but also for unintended and counteractive seduction. For example, victims of repression who assumed that I regarded the torture session as the most personal and therefore most valuable back region, assumed that this appraisal could enhance their credibility as a reliable source of information about the years of political violence. Even though many informants intended to tell about it, they still veiled their experiences to impel the inquisitive ethnographer to urge them to share their stories. The more persuasion that was needed, the more persuasive their accounts would be. A troubling similarity between interrogation and interview appeared which could not have escaped the attention of these victims of torture. But now, they had control over how and which valuable information they would give. Several interviewees were conscious of the manner in which this knowledge was imparted and therefore delayed its disclosure.

Others did not try to withhold their revelations, but the effect was the same: I stopped at the threshold of their back region. Why did I refuse to accept the valuable knowledge that was eventually offered?

Baudrillard (1990:83) has written that "to seduce is to appear weak." Certain interviewees did not try to dominate or overpower me but, instead, disarmed me by showing their vulnerabilities. In my interviews with victims of torture, I seldomly asked directly about the abuse they had been subjected to but usually concentrated on their interpretation of the political violence of the 1970s. Being used to journalists who invariably asked them to provide graphic descriptions, several expressed their surprise at my reluctance and volunteered to give me detailed accounts. I generally responded that such painful recollection was not necessary because I had already read their declarations to the courts. Maybe I wanted to spare them, but I probably also wanted to protect myself. Whatever my motives, this voluntary offering of very personal experiences enhanced in my eyes the credibility of the entire interview, whether justified or not. The ethnographic seduction operated through a partial revelation of a dark world that was not further explored but was taken at face value in the belief that such hidden knowledge could always be uncovered.

Rhetoric and Persuasion

Persuasion seems to be the counterpole of seduction. Seduction wins us over by appearance, persuasion by argument.[9] It is not appearance and emotion that seem at stake but reason. We are supposed to become persuaded by a clear exposition of hard evidence that moves us to reconsider our poorly informed opinions. But how is the proof presented to us? How is the evidence rhetorically couched? How is the information molded to make its greatest impact on us and divert us from the questions we want to examine in depth? Are the interlocutors always aware of the rhetorical dimension of their conversations?[10]

Plato and Aristotle made a distinction between dialectic reasoning based on logic and

rigorous proof, which would lead to truth, and rhetoric reasoning, which tried to persuade people by arousing their emotions. "Rhetoric is that part of any self-consciously calculated piece of communication which fails to meet a philosopher's standards of accuracy, coherence, and consistency, but is still necessary if the communication is to be fully successful" (Cole 1991:13). Our suspicion of rhetoric comes from a distrust of such manipulation of our emotions. We feel somehow robbed of the ability to weigh the pros and cons of an argument. Nevertheless, rhetorical and aesthetic modes of exposition are not only an inextricable part of scientific discourse (see Gilbert and Mulkay 1984; Gross 1990) but "potentially powerful resources for the advancement of the sciences: promotion of hypotheses by appeal to aesthetic criteria; jocular and satirical critique of standard and entrenched practices" (Jardine 1991:236). Rhetoric stirs us discursively with tropes, allegories, and modes of exposition. Like seduction, rhetoric may become a play of appearance that diverts us from our research objectives.

Most of my Argentine interlocutors were public figures with great conversational experience and finesse. I could therefore safely assume that they had become sensitized to the effectiveness of various rhetorical devices. Invariably there was an exchange of social courtesies to create a friendly atmosphere for what we perceived could become a weighty and possibly painful conversation. These courtesies failed to seduce because of their blatant transparency. Seduction does not work through openness but through secrecy and mystification. Hence the common ground that became established at the start of a conversation depended to a great extent on an acquaintance with each other's cultural identity. Many of my interviewees had visited Europe, expressed their love of seventeenth-century Dutch painting, their admiration of the canals and polders, or recalled with glee the title match victory of Argentina over the Dutch team at the 1978 World Championship soccer tournament in Buenos Aires, during the heydays of the military regime. They also interpreted my presentation of self, assessed my class background, and tried to detect my political ideology. My being Dutch yet living in the United States, my status as a university professor, and above all my access to their political adversaries were of great importance. I, in turn, would praise the friendliness of the Argentine people, the beauty of the countryside, and the architecture of the main avenues of Buenos Aires.

Aside from this obvious impression management, there was a seductive dimension to discourse that was much harder to isolate but that first became clear to me in my conversations with former *guerrilleros*. Many of them had been college students. They had perfected a sophisticated political discourse through innumerable discussions in cafés, prisons, hideouts, and foreign hotels. They would speak in the intellectual's tongue. Well versed in the jargon of sociology and political science, their historical interpretations had a truthful ring. It was difficult to distinguish their vocabulary and semantic constructions from my own.

It was tempting to become absorbed in this discourse. It had an emotional pull. It seduced me by an indescribable familiarity, by its allure of going to the heart of historical events together with their architects; all this set in the special atmosphere of the grand cafés of Buenos Aires with their dense cigarette smoke, the buzzing of voices, and the waiters swiftly maneuvering through the maze of wooden tables while carrying trays of small coffee cups. I felt that I could take my guard down in this environment and become absorbed in a close discussion in which I could share intellectual doubts and queries with people of my own generation. I felt that I could not afford such openness with the military, the clergy, or with human rights activists who might become offended by too penetrating questions and deny me another interview. What I did not realize was that by this openness I had also abandoned my critical detachment.

Unlike the pseudoacademic discourse of the revolutionary Left, which allowed me to retain many of my conceptual tools, my interviews with the other three groups obliged me to adapt my vocabulary. For example, human rights groups use the term "concentration camp" (*campo de concentración*) to describe the secret places where disappeared persons were held. This term conjures up images of the Second World War and, by extension, suggests that the Argentine military are Nazis at heart. The use of the term "concentration camp" in conversations with military officers would immediately brand me as a sympathizer of the human rights groups and thus hinder the exchange. I therefore used their own term, "detention center" (*centro de detención*). This neutral term was part of an objectifying vocabulary that gave a semantic rationality to the violent practices of the dirty war.

The discursive strategy of the military consisted of appealing both to my common sense and to the dispassionate logic of reason that is supposed to be the hallmark of any scientist. This discursive technique consisted of an outright dismissal of any major human rights violations without denying that they could have occurred. If this technique failed to have the intended effect on me, then they began to relativize the Argentine abuses by making a comparison with atrocities committed by the so-called civilized Western world. In an interview on June 26, 1989, I asked the general mentioned at the beginning of this article about the relevance of licit and illicit rules of engagement, as defined by international law, to the "dirty war strategy" employed by the Argentine military.

I say that when we go to war – and in a war I have to be willing to kill my enemy because otherwise there would be no war – when I am willing to kill my enemy I can kill him with an arrow, but if the other has a machine gun then the arrow will be of no use to me. I have to find a cannon. When the other has … [when] I have a cannon, the other will look for a larger cannon or an aircraft. When the other has an aircraft, I will have to try, try to take a missile, and so on. That is to say, war by itself is a social phenomenon…. What is licit and what is illicit, when war presupposes that I am going to kill my enemy? Now, the philosopher of war par excellence is [Carl von] Clausewitz. And he says that war is evidently a human phenomenon in which I try to impose my will on the enemy and I therefore resort to violence. Now, he talks about the tendency to go to extremes. He then says that he who tries to impose violence without any consideration will have an advantage over he who has consideration. Well then, what happens? When they talk to me about restrictions in warfare, these are lucubrations made by jurists. The nations have not respected them. For example, when they threw the nuclear bomb on Hiroshima and Nagasaki, this was forbidden according to the Geneva Convention. But who was to say to Mister Truman, "Mister Truman, this is forbidden. Why did you throw it? You come along, we are going to take you to the Nuremberg tribunal." No, because he won the war. Who was going to do it? Now, why did Mister Truman do it? Because he said, "Well, there will die 200,000 persons, but if we do not throw the bomb then 600,000 North Americans will die, or one million. Well then, between 200,000 Japanese and one million North Americans let 200,000 Japanese die," and he threw the bomb. Because the distinction between the licit and the illicit in warfare is absurd to me, because war presupposes from the start the use of violence – as Clausewitz says – and the use of violence without restraint till the objective is attained.

Other Argentine officers also referred frequently to the bombings of Hiroshima, Dresden, and Nagasaki and to the double standard of the "human rights prophets," the French, who collaborated with the Nazis during the Vichy government, tortured Algerian partisans, and in 1985 bombed a Greenpeace ship in New Zealand, yet who convicted in absentia the Argentine navy officer Alfredo Astiz for his alleged role in the disappearance of two French nuns who had collaborated with subversive organizations, so the Argentine military argued. When I objected that two wrongs do not make a right, that the comparisons do not hold, or that many of the offenses by Western nations were backed by written orders, the Argentine military appealed to the vicissitudes and unpredictabilities of warfare.

Such rational discourse may be highly persuasive from a logical point of view – especially when one has not yet found equally powerful counterarguments or succeeds in listening dispassionately to the rationalizations – but produces an uncomfortable tension with

one's emotional aversion to the consequences of warfare. Just as it is hard to reconcile our instantaneous repudiation of violent death with a military necessity to fire on people, so it becomes very difficult to stand one's moral ground in the face of these technorational arguments for human suffering. The barrage of sophisticated rationalizations of violence together with the argument that the use of force is the constitutional prerogative of the security forces are very hard to counter. My objections that the violence was disproportional, that more humane counterinsurgency methods could have been used, that the prisoners were not given due process, that these methods violated the very principles of civilization that the military professed to protect, and, finally, that what was justified as mere excesses of war were deliberate and planned violations to paralyze the political expression of the Argentine people were dismissed either as leftist propaganda or as a manifestation of my unfamiliarity with the practice of warfare.

Another discursive tactic was to sketch ominous scenarios of what would have happened if the Argentine military had not destroyed the insurgents root and branch. The grave situation in Peru during the late 1980s, when the Shining Path revolutionaries controlled large areas of the highlands, and had even succeeded in reaching the gates of Lima at the time of my fieldwork, was mentioned as a nightmare that had been prevented in Argentina through the resolute action of the armed forces. Finally, the fall of the Berlin wall and the subsequent disenchantment with communism in Eastern Europe were presented as arguments for the moral righteousness of the repression in Argentina during the 1970s.

The human rights activists and former guerrilleros could have equally made appeals to common sense, but many preferred to make an emotional plea to a moral sense of humanity and justice. How to respond to an indignant rejection of torture, to the kidnapping of babies for the benefit of childless military families, and to the extraction of money from desperate parents with misleading information about the whereabouts of their disappeared son? Rational arguments, such as those given to me by the military, justifying torture as a conventional practice in counterinsurgency warfare, as was the case in Algeria, South Africa, Vietnam, Indonesia, Northern Ireland, Spain, Peru, El Salvador, and many other countries, are impotent against the tears of the parents of a revolutionary who was abducted, tortured, and executed. I became virtually unable to penetrate this emotional shroud with questions that might be easily misperceived as apologetic, uncaring, cold, callous, and hurtful.[11] The more emotional the reaction, the greater my personal inhibition to discuss these issues further.

The following fragment from an interview with the father of a seventeen-year-old member of the outlawed Peronist Youth (Juventud Peronista) who disappeared in April 1976 demonstrates this inhibition, despite the encouragement of the interlocutor to proceed. After his son failed to arrive at a birthday party where he was expected, the father began a desperate search. He contacted an acquaintance who is a police officer, and they began to make inquiries at the precincts and hospitals of Buenos Aires, all to no avail. After several months, the father came into contact with a colonel in active duty through the mediation of a befriended retired first lieutenant. The following dialogue took place.

And he says, "Tell me what happened." So I told him what happened. And with all virulence, you looked at ... I looked at this man, but I tell you as I told you before, that I tried to see from all sides if I could find the point of the ... of the thread of..., to, to arrive at the thread or the needle in the haystack [*punta del ovillo*], trying to, to discover anything. After telling him everything, he says, "Good. Look, you have to do the following: you have to pretend as if your son has cancer." I was listening and saying to myself, What is he saying? [The colonel continues.] "Pretend that he has cancer and that they have ... that he is in an operating room and that there is a butcher and a doctor; pray that it will be the doctor who will be operating on him." And then I looked at, at the one with whom I had made a certain friendship, and he took hold of his head and covered his, his face. Because he must have said, he himself must have said, What is this sonofabitch saying? Because then

he realized that all his venom, his virulence came out of him [the colonel]. This man had stuck a dagger in my wound and had twisted it inside me. I say to him, "Pardon me," I say, "Sir, but do you know something?" I said this because of what he was telling me. "No, no, I am weighing the various possibilities [*hago una composición de lugar*] and I am making a supposition. I don't know anything of what might have ha –." And I say, "But how do you have the gall to ..." and because of my nerves the words couldn't come out, but I had wanted to say "You are a son of a thousand bitches." You see, tell him whichever barbarity. And then the other saw my condition because he thought that I was going to lose it.... I wanted to grab him by the throat and strangle him, but then anyone of those who were there would have taken their gun and killed me. There, for the first time in my life, the desire came over me to murder someone. I had been destroyed....

Something [my wife] didn't know. With the passage of time I have told her. These are unfortunate things that happen to you in life. And there, yes, it crossed my mind that yes, that day I could have ended up killing that man. I don't know what stopped me. Because I was desperate. But you cannot imagine how, with what satisfaction he said what he was telling me. And you should analyze that, that this man was in active service.

But I was unable to analyze. Exactly as he had tried to detect any sign in the face and words of the colonel that betrayed the tiniest bit of information about his son but became paralyzed by the cruel supposition, so I became unable to stand aside and observe. He had incorporated me into his torment, sometimes discursively placing me in his shoes and at other times highlighting the moments of his greatest anguish. I could have asked him about the place of the meeting, the spatial arrangement of the offices, which army regiment had been involved, whether he ever heard of the colonel again, how he knew that the man was a colonel and not an extortionist who would try to wrest money from him, whether he ever saw the first lieutenant again, and so on. But my mind went blank, and I could only share this man's sorrow in silence.

I intuitively hesitate to present this account as an example of rhetorical seduction because the term "seduction" immediately evokes the association of an intentional manipulation of truth for dishonest ends. This is not the case here. I do not have any reason to doubt that this dialogue – whatever the exact words – took place, and I believe even less that the narrative was consciously constructed. Still, I think that the term "rhetorical seduction" is appropriate here because the repeated telling of the same story has led to a formulation that has proven to be the most moving and therefore most persuasive.[12] The account affected my emotional state to such a degree that I was no longer able to see the discourse behind the conversation. I could not ask further questions but allowed my interlocutor to take me along on the incessant search for his son.

Sometimes, I would end an interview here, unable or unwilling to continue. At other times, I would gently relieve the tension by leading the conversation into neutral waters, discussing highly abstract concepts such as war, justice, or political freedom. Only a radical break with my emotions would allow me to regard the conversation once again as analyzable knowledge.

This example has demonstrated the emotional incorporation of the ethnographer in the ethnographic encounter, but this intersubjectivity also has a counterpart in the interlocutor's reactions. An Argentine anthropologist, who knew one of my interviewees, a former guerrillero, recounted to me one day his rendition of my meetings with him. He had told her that during a stirring moment of our conversation in which he was reflecting on the terrible waste of lives in the political struggle of the 1970s, he saw tears in my eyes. This intensified the awareness of his own tragedy and made him break down as well. At these moments of a complete collapse of the critical distance between two interlocutors, we lose all dimensions of the scientific enterprise. Overwhelmed by emotion we do not have the need for any explanation because we feel that all questions have already been answered. What else is there to ask? What else is there to tell? What more do we need to know? What more is there to know?

Secrecy and Truth

Any research on political violence runs into too many skeletons to handle, too many closets to inspect. Aside from deliberate lies, half-truths, and unfounded accusations – many of which are impossible to trace or verify – there is a lot of malicious gossip and character assassination. One way in which interlocutors try to add credibility to their charges is by means of a staged confession introduced by statements such as "Let me tell you a secret," or "I have never told this to anyone," or "I will tell you this, but you may not record it or write it down."

Secrecy seduces. The belief that the interlocutor is hiding a darker side is seductive because it teases the ethnographer to surrender. Only a surrender to the interlocutor's conditions of truth will yield the desired information. The remarks about secrecy made by my interlocutors served as a strategy to overpower my interpretive stance as an observer. It was an invitation to complicity. I do not want to exaggerate the political influence of social scientists, but most of my interlocutors were aware of the potential impact of an authoritative analysis of the last dictatorship. The impartiality of local scholars is called into question by most Argentines. They are accused of writing polemic books (*libros de combate*), polemic in its most literal sense: books for waging war. These books are believed to sacrifice scientific accuracy to political ends. Foreign authors are regarded as more neutral than national scholars, and some of them, such as Robert A. Potash (1969, 1980) and Alain Rouquié (1987a, 1987b), have become household names.

The political weight of my research became most apparent during my last interview with the general who had saved me from being run over by a taxi. Almost two months after the presidential decree that dismissed the court case against him, I met him again at the Officers Club. After a quarter of an hour I told him that I noticed a change in his demeanor. He was much more relaxed than during our last series of interviews. He laughed and said that four months ago he was in the middle of a political battle (*batalla politico*). "Now," he said, "everything is history, and eventually the Argentine people will realize that the military acted in a correct way." Comparing this last interview with our previous conversations, he had become almost aloof and seemed uninterested in persuading me of his rightness. His short answers were delivered in a casual and offhand manner. The political battle had ended. Had I been one of its foot soldiers? Had I been used as a sparring partner for a future crossfire examination by the public prosecutor, or had I been used as a gullible courier of the general's political message?

The question of truth does not receive much attention in the many books on fieldwork that have appeared in the last three decades.[13] In contrast, earlier generations of anthropologists were much more concerned about prying the truth out of their informants (see Rosaldo 1986). For instance, Marcel Griaule (1957) writes in his book on fieldwork: "The role of the person sniffing out social facts is often comparable to that of a detective or examining magistrate. The fact is the crime, the interlocutor the guilty party; all the society's members are accomplices" (quoted in Clifford 1983*b*: 138). S. F. Nadel, Griaule's contemporary, favored equally inquisitive methods: "In the case of interviews which bear on secret and forbidden topics, I have found it most profitable to stimulate the emotionality of a few chief informants to the extent of arousing almost violent disputes and controversies. The expression of doubt and disbelief on the part of the interviewer, or the arrangement of interviews with several informants, some of whom, owing to their social position, were certain to produce inaccurate information, easily induced the key informant to disregard his usual reluctance to speak openly, if only to confound his opponents and critics" (1939:323). Finally, a classic field guide recommends: "It is sometimes useful to pretend incredulity to induce further information" (RAI 1951:33).

James Clifford (1983*b*:143–144) has remarked, "By the late sixties the romantic mythology of fieldwork rapport had begun publicly to dissolve.... Geertz undermines the myth of ethnographic rapport before reinstating it in an ironic mode. Like Griaule he seems

to accept that all parties to the encounter recognize its elements of insincerity, hypocrisy, and self-deception." However, a major difference between the two authors is that Griaule was still hunting for undisputable truth. Geertz, instead, is representative of an entire generation of anthropologists who accompanied the interpretive turn of the 1960s and 1970s. Function and explanation were exchanged for meaning and understanding, and many anthropologists felt more identified with notions such as the definition of the situation and the social construction of reality than with a positivist belief in truth and method.[14]

Even though most anthropologists today feel much closer to Geertz than to Griaule and Nadel, our informants continue to think in terms of truth and falsehood. This issue becomes especially relevant in research on violence because the protagonists of major political conflicts are often accused of undermining the very foundation of society and of being responsible for the ensuing human suffering. The question of historical interpretation is of great political importance to them, and they will do their best to convince us of their rightness and to ignore dissenting views. We can, of course, not expect our interlocutors to incriminate themselves or recount their traumatic experiences with an anesthetized detachment but, instead, we should anticipate that they may consciously or unconsciously try to divert us from our investigative aims by disarming our critical gaze. In response to Geertz: not all Cretans may be liars, but some are, and some of them are seducers as well.

Having become temporarily disillusioned by the subtle strategies of persuasion of my Argentine interlocutors, I turned to the texts they had produced in the 1970s. This led to a search for secret army documents, intelligence reports, human rights pamphlets, and the clandestine publications of the revolutionary Left. I realized, of course, that these written sources were just as much discursive constructions as the spoken word of their authors. Nevertheless, the texts were concurrent with the historical events I was studying, and I could compare the oral accounts I had recorded of those actions, decisions, and events with contemporary clandestine, classified, and official sources. I hoped to puncture the appearances of my interlocutors, disentangle myself from their seduction, and reach back in time to the origin of their talk, the events, ideological articulations, power struggles, and armed confrontations. The anxiety of not being able to rely on oral history made me cling to contemporary inscriptions that at least had an appearance of authenticity.[15] I do not use "authenticity" here in the sense of true or real but rather as genuine to the interlocutor's own sense of truth and reality. "Authenticity relates to the corroborative support given an account ... by its internal consistency or cross-reference to other sources of information" (Brown and Sime 1981:161; see also Denzin 1970, on triangulation). An analysis of the interviews and a comparison with statements made during the time of repression allowed me to distance myself from the surface account that they tried to make me accept as the only true reality.

Clearly, the ethnographer of violence and political conflict may become encapsulated in the webs of seduction spun by his or her informants and interlocutors. Just as Lenin had inverted von Clausewitz's definition of war by stating that politics is the continuation of war by other means, so seduction became the continuation of Argentine politics after the turn to democracy in 1983.[16] Neither brute force nor coercion but the molding of appearances became the weapon of influential players in the Argentine polity. Ethnographic seduction was my personal experience with a national debate in Argentina among the adversarial protagonists of the decades of political violence.

But why resort to seduction? Those who dispute power and authority are aware of the importance of seduction. They realize that arguments alone do not persuade people, that charisma is the privilege of the gifted few, but that appearances are taken at face value by many. We as ethnographers are also subjects of seduction because our informants have a stake in making us adopt their truths. They perceive us as the harbingers of history. We will retell their stories and through our investiture as scientists provide these with the halo of objectivity that our academic stature entails.

What a weight on our shoulders; the weight to be the arbitrators of an absolute truth in which we have lost faith ourselves. What should we respond? That there is no truth? That truth is always historical? That their truth is not the truth of their opponents? That they have entrusted us with a Rankean authority in which we do not believe and which we do not want? That we cannot verify what they tell us? "But what are you saying?" they asked me. "How can you doubt the tears I have shed with you?" They reassure me. "You will be able to tell the truth about what really happened in Argentina." "We need foreign researchers like you who will be able to tell the truth that we cannot write." "Abroad, they can write a truth that nobody wants to publish here." They made appeals to my responsibility. "We need scientists like you whose books will allow the Argentine people to reach a reconciliation." They even tried to induce guilt. "I have told you my story so that you can write the truth." "Do not use the things I have told you against us." "Make sure that my story can never be used by those who killed my daughter."

Shredding Shrouds of Power

He had been on their hit list for more than three decades, old admiral Rojas; this diminutive man with his piercing eyes and hawkish nose. He and general Aramburu had been the strongmen of the revolution against Perón in 1955, and in 1956 he had personally signed the execution order of general Valle after his failed uprising against the military government. Aramburu had been kidnapped in 1970 and was executed by the Montoneros guerrilla organization. Rojas was to be next.

The two petty officers in the hallway asked me to open my briefcase. After examining its contents, one of them opened the elevator door and we stepped inside. We stopped at the fourth floor. He accompanied me to the door. The admiral invited me in with a jovial gesture. I sat down on the couch as he sank away in a large armchair. "I have a great many grandchildren," he began. "They often come to visit me and stay for lunch or dinner." Now I knew why there was a pile of heavy-metal records next to the turntable. The image of an 84-year-old admiral Rojas listening to AC/DC in the company of his teenage grandchildren was disarming. This had been one of the most influential men in Argentine politics in the 1950s, but the stack of heavy-metal records gave him away. These records revealed the transparency of power.

Because isn't power nothing but seduction; a mesmerizing play of brocaded clothes and ermine mantles; an enchanting appearance that obscures the seducer's vulnerability? Seeing the bearers of Argentine authority surrounded by the photographs of their children, smelling the food from their kitchens, and walking on the plush carpets of their apartments disintegrated power into human transience.

But, you may object, power rests on real force, and our ethnographic judgment should not be swayed by outward niceties and runaway emotions. I think you are right. One may become so familiar with the power holders – in the sense of convivial as well as knowledgeable – that it may obstruct one's perception of the authority vested in them. I therefore have to retrace my final steps and erase the imprint they have left. Seduction means after all, in a literal sense, "to be led astray from an intended course."

I went to Argentina to understand the contested historical reconstruction of the violence of the 1970s but soon became entangled in the rhetoric and seduction played upon me by its protagonists. Disillusioned, I sought refuge in the denuded truth of some "hard facts," only to discover that my understanding had run aground in the shallowness of the written word. I had to retrace my steps and stop where seduction, rhetoric, interpretation, and intersubjectivity suffused the ethnographic encounter. I could only subvert seduction by playing along with it and grasp its meaning from the inside. This experience made me sensitive to what many Argentines, especially those who had suffered the disappearance of a relative, had felt during the years of repression. The disappearance was a form of deceit in which all appearances were kept up; the appearance of justice, of innocence, and due process. Where people became surface manifestations. Where lives changed course surreptitiously. And where reappearance depended on a

gesture, on a nod of the head. It was in this clearing that I realized that ethnographic seduction crosscuts the interplay of empathy and detachment that sound fieldwork ordains. Standing in this clearing, it became finally possible to realize that the many directions I had been sent to were only intended to entice me away from where I was already standing.

NOTES

1 The research in Buenos Aires, Argentina, from April 1989 until August 1991 was made possible by grants from the National Science Foundation and the Harry Frank Guggenheim Foundation. I thank Adam Kuper, James McAllister, Carolyn Nordstrom, Frank Pieke, and Jan de Wolf for their thoughtful comments.
2 Devereux (1967:44–45) has used the term "seduction" in his discussion of countertransference reactions among anthropologists. However, he defines it not as conscious manipulation but as emotional allurement.
3 An additional danger of using the term "seduction" is that it might result in an unwelcome association with Freud's seduction theory. For all clarity, my use of the term stands clear from Freud's theory about hysteria and distances itself from the implied notions of the repression of sexual desire.
4 Rapport is generally regarded as essential to successful fieldwork, "simply because of the assumption that people talk better in a warm, friendly atmosphere, and the additional assumption that attitudes are somehow complex and hidden and a lot of talking is essential before the attitude is elicited" (Hyman 1954:22). The issue of rapport has been discussed with much greater depth in sociology than in anthropology, possibly because the methodological emphasis on participant observation makes anthropologists downplay the actual importance of interview situations for acquiring local knowledge. See, e.g., the discussion of rapport by Hyman (1954:153–170) and Turner and Martin (1984:262–278) and the critique by Cicourel (1964:82–86).
5 Despite this call for attention to the native tongue, Clifford (1983a, 1988:38–41) has argued that Geertz has always remained the authoritarian voice that arbitrated the

interpretational disputes among his informants. Clifford has emphasized the dialogic intersubjectivity of the ethnographic encounter with its polyphonic variations and discursive conflicts, as exemplified by Dwyer (1982) and Crapanzano (1980).

6 This chapter has drawn inspiration from Baudrillard's general statements about seduction but should not be taken as an application of his ideas (for a feminist critique, see Hunter 1989).

7 The opposite of the illusion of the cultural insider is the illusion of the objective investigator. "Methodological objectivism is a denial of the intersubjective or dialogical nature of fieldwork through which ethnographic understanding develops" (Obeyesekere 1990:227).

8 The account interview is not a context-free exchange of information but in the first place a social relationship with all its concomitant complexities (Brenner 1978, 1981). The impression management during my research in Argentina involved an array of stratagems. The location of the interview was chosen with the aim of exuding authority or familiarity. Some preferred their homes, while others invited me to the stately buildings of the church and the armed forces or the personalized offices of the human rights and former guerrilla organizations. Impression management also involved a manipulation of the senses. Dress, physical gestures, facial expressions, and ways of making eye contact and shaking hands are all part of a presentation of self that influences the social interaction between ethnographer and interlocutor (Agar 1980:54–62). For an analysis of the unique problems of female researchers who study the military, see Daniels 1967.

9 Simons (1976:134–138) distinguishes between co-active, combative, and expressive forms of persuasion. The co-active form attempts to bridge the psychological differences among interlocutors by stimulating the identification between speaker and audience. The combative form tries to persuade through coercion and intimidation. Combative approaches are most effective in situations of social conflict. Finally, there is an expressive approach that deliberately rejects the conscious manipulation of the audience but that hopes to raise people's consciousness through self-criticism and by openly sharing experiences. The co-active form of persuasion is the most versatile strategy because it can incorporate aspects of the other two forms.

10 Roloff (1980) analyzes aspects of rhetorical persuasion that remain hidden to both speaker and audience.

11 A scene from *Shoah* comes to mind in which Claude Lanzmann virtually coerces Abraham Bomba, a survivor of Treblinka, to recall his experiences: "AB: A friend of mine worked as a barber – he was a good barber in my hometown – when his wife and his sister came into the gas chamber.... I can't. It's too horrible. Please. CL: We have to do it. You know it. AB: I won't be able to do it. CL: You have to do it. I know it's very hard. I know and I apologize. AB: Don't make me go on please. CL: Please. We must go on" (Lanzmann 1985:117).

12 Part of the dialogue quoted here can be found in almost the exact same words in Cohen Salama (1992:230).

13 Historians and sociologists have paid more attention to deliberate distortion; see Dean and Whyte 1970; Ginzburg 1991; Gorden 1975:445–460; Henige 1982:58–59.

14 During the same period, there was also considerable interest in action research and Marxist and feminist analyses. These three approaches are at the opposite end of seduction because the ethnographer tries to seduce people into accepting his or her interpretation of social reality as the most objective and correct analysis. The language of oppression and exploitation is used as a powerful rhetoric of persuasion.

15 Devereux (1967:46) explains this "anxious clinging to 'hard' facts" as an expression of the ethnographer's fear that he or she is not properly understanding or communicating with the informants.

16 War, according to von Clausewitz (1984:87), is "a continuation of political activity by other means."

REFERENCES

Agar, Michael H.
    1980 *The Professional Stranger: An Informal Introduction to Ethnography*. New York: Academic Press.
Baudrillard, Jean
    1990 *Seduction*. New York: St. Martin's Press.
Berreman, Gerald D.
    1972 "Prologue: Behind Many Masks, Ethnography and Impression Management."

In *Hindus of the Himalayas: Ethnography and Change*, ed. Gerald Berreman, xvii–lvii. Berkeley, Los Angeles, and London: University of California Press.

Brenner, Michael
1978 "Interviewing: The Social Phenomenology of a Research Instrument." In *The Social Contexts of Method*, ed. Michael Brenner, Peter Marsh, and Marylin Brenner, 122–139. London: Croom Helm.

Brenner, Michael
1981 "Patterns of Social Structure in the Research Interview." In *Social Method and Social Life*, ed. Michael Brenner, 115–158. New York: Academic Press.

Brown, Jennifer, and Jonathan Sime
1981 "A Methodology for Accounts." In *Social Method and Social Life*, ed. Michael Brenner, 159–188. New York: Academic Press.

Cicourel, Aaron V.
1964 *Method and Measurement in Sociology*. New York: Free Press.

Clausewitz, Carl von
[1832] 1984 *On War*. Princeton: Princeton University Press.

Clifford, James
1983*a* "On Ethnographic Authority." *Representations* 1(2):118–146.

Clifford, James
1983*b* "Power and Dialogue in Ethnography: Marcel Griaule's Initiation." In *Observers Observed: Essays on Ethnographic Fieldwork*, ed. George W. Stocking, 121–156. Madison: University of Wisconsin Press.

Clifford, James
1988 *The Predicament of Culture: Twentieth-Century Ethnography, Literature, and Art*. Cambridge: Harvard University Press.

Cohen Salama, Mauricio
1992 *Tumbas anónimas: Informe sobre la identificación de restos de víctimas de la represión ilegal*. Buenos Aires: Catálogos Editora.

Cole, Thomas
1991 *The Origins of Rhetoric in Ancient Greece*. Baltimore: Johns Hopkins University Press.

Crapanzano, Vincent
1980 *Tuhami: Portrait of a Moroccan*. Chicago: University of Chicago Press.

Daniels, Arlene Kaplan
1967 "The Low-Caste Stranger in Social Research." In *Ethics, Politics, and Social Research*, ed. Gideon Sjoberg, 267–296. Cambridge: Schenkman.

Dean, John P., and William Foote Whyte
1970 "How Do You Know if the Informant Is Telling the Truth?" In *Elite and Specialized Interviewing*, ed. Lewis Anthony Dexter, 119–131. Evanston: Northwestern University Press.

Denzin, Norman K., ed.
1970 *Sociological Methods: A Sourcebook*. Chicago: Aldine.

Devereux, George
1967 *From Anxiety to Method in the Behavioral Sciences*. The Hague: Mouton.

Dwyer, Kevin
1982 *Moroccan Dialogues: Anthropology in Question*. Baltimore: Johns Hopkins University Press.

Ellen, R. E, ed.
1984 *Ethnographic Research: A Guide to General Conduct*. London: Academic Press.

Geertz, Clifford
1973 *The Interpretation of Cultures*. New York: Basic Books.

Gilbert, G. Nigel, and Michael Mulkay
1984 *Opening Pandora's Box: A Sociological Analysis of Scientists' Discourse*. Cambridge: Cambridge University Press.

Ginzburg, Carlo
1991 "Checking the Evidence: The Judge and the Historian." *Critical Inquiry* 18(1):179–92.

Goffman, Erving
1966 *Behavior in Public Places: Notes on the Social Organization of Gatherings*. New York: Free Press.

Goffman, Erving
1969 *The Presentation of Self in Everyday Life*. London: Allen Lane.

Gorden, Raymond L.
1975 *Interviewing: Strategy, Techniques, and Tactics*. Homewood, Ill.: Dorsey Press.

Griaule, Marcel
1957 *Méthode de l'Ethnographie*. Paris: Presses Universitaires de France.

Gross, Alan G.
1990 *The Rhetoric of Science*. Cambridge: Harvard University Press.

Henige, David
1982 *Oral Historiography*. London: Longman.

Hunter, Dianne, ed.
1989 *Seduction and Theory: Readings of Gender, Representation, and Rhetoric*. Urbana: University of Illinois Press.

Hyman, Herbert H., et al.
1954 *Interviewing in Social Research.* Chicago: University of Chicago Press.

Jardine, Nicholas
1991 *The Scenes of Inquiry: On the Reality of Questions in the Sciences.* Oxford: Clarendon Press.

Lanzmann, Claude
1985 *Shoah: An Oral History of the Holocaust.* New York: Pantheon Books.

Nadel, S. F.
1939 "The Interview Technique in Social Anthropology." In *The Study of Society: Methods and Problems,* ed. F. C. Bartlett et al., 317–327. London: Kegan Paul, Trench, Trubner.

Obeyesekere, Gananath
1990 *The Work of Culture: Symbolic Transformation in Psychoanalysis and Anthropology.* Chicago: University of Chicago Press.

Potash, Robert A.
1969 *The Army and Politics in Argentina, 1928–1945: Yrigoyen to Perón.* Stanford: Stanford University Press.

Potash, Robert A.
1980 *The Army and Politics in Argentina, 1945–1962: Perón to Frondizi.* Stanford: Stanford University Press.

RAI (Royal Anthropological Institute)
1951 *Notes and Queries on Anthropology.* 6th ed. London: Routledge and Kegan Paul.

Roloff, Michael E.
1980 "Self-Awareness and the Persuasion Process: Do We Really Know What We're Doing?" In *Persuasion: New Directions in Theory and Research,* ed. Michael E. Roloff and Gerald R. Miller, 29–66. Beverly Hills, Calif.: Sage Publications.

Rosaldo, Renato
1986 "From the Door of His Tent: The Fieldworker and the Inquisitor." In *Writing Culture: The Poetics and Politics of Ethnography,* ed. James Clifford and George E. Marcus, 77–97. Berkeley, Los Angeles, and London: University of California Press.

Rouquié, Alain
1987a *Poder Militar y Sociedad Política en la Argentina I – hasta 1943.* Buenos Aires: Emecé Editores.

Rouquié, Alain
1987b *Poder Militar y Sociedad Política en la Argentina II: 1943–1973.* Buenos Aires: Emecé Editores.

Simons, Herbert W.
1976 *Persuasion: Understanding, Practice, and Analysis.* Reading, Mass.: Addison-Wesley.

Turner, Charles E., and Elizabeth Martin, eds.
1984 *Surveying Subjective Phenomena.* Vol. 1. New York: Russell Sage Foundation.

Part IV
The "Other" Talks Back

Introduction

Jeffrey A. Sluka

Access to schooling and the dissemination of anthropological writings have turned once illiterate "informants" into avid critics of their ethnographers. Such "talking back" has made anthropologists aware of their conduct as researchers, led to soul-searching about their writings, and enhanced the quality of ethnographic research. In Part IV of this Reader, we present critical views of anthropology expressed by "others," including a native academic (Vine Deloria, Jr.), an indigenous research subject (Cecil King), and two case studies of ethnographers who faced the wrath of research communities that responded powerfully and negatively to newspaper representations of their work (Ofra Greenberg and Nancy Scheper-Hughes).

Today, many cultural anthropologists have had this experience with the press as a mediator of their texts, and this is recognized in Caroline Brettell's edited volume *When They Read What We Write: The Politics of Ethnography* (1993). The volume's contributors present many and varied examples of the "other" talking back, challenging, and criticizing ethnographic works. In her excellent introduction, Brettell observes that ethnographers "cannot control how what they put into print is read, let alone how it is publicly presented" (1993:17). She describes how anthropologists have responded to criticisms of their writing, and notes that the "others" who "talk back" to anthropologists generally include three groups of people:

1 Research participants or those about whom an ethnography is written, including both those who have read it and those who have only heard about it second hand or read representations of it in newspapers.

Ethnographic Fieldwork: An Anthropological Reader, Second Edition. Edited by
Antonius C. G. M. Robben and Jeffrey A. Sluka.
Editorial material and organization © 2012 John Wiley & Sons, Inc.
Published 2012 by John Wiley & Sons, Inc.

2 Indigenous or native scholars, particularly anthropologists, in the country where
   an ethnography is set.
3 Journalists or other members of the press and media who write reviews of ethnographic writing.

Brettell also highlights Renato Rosaldo's identification of three forms of reactions
by anthropologists when challenged by "native" readers (1993:20–21). First, the
"Chicken Little Reaction" – they either retreat into hopelessness for the future of
ethnography, or defend their interpretations and reject the validity of the response.
Second, the "Two Worlds Reaction" – they emphasize that anthropologists and
research participants speak two languages, that of science on the one hand and of
everyday life on the other, and that "never the twain shall meet." Third, the "One
Conversation Reaction" – they emphasize the new insights that can result from listening to native responses, and argue that these often outweigh any misunderstandings. This reaction usually involves incorporating these responses into the original
text, frequently as an appendix in a subsequent edition, or presenting them in other
publications – as the selected readings by Greenberg and Scheper-Hughes represent.
Brettell also presents Rosaldo's conclusion:

> We should take the criticism of our subjects in much the same way that we take those
> of our colleagues. Not unlike other ethnographers, so-called natives can be insightful,
> sociologically correct, axe-grinding, self-interested, or mistaken. They do know their
> own cultures, and rather than being ruled out of court, their criticism should be listened
> to and taken into account, to be accepted, rejected, or modified, as we reformulate our
> analysis. (Cited in Brettell 1993:16)

In 1969, Vine Deloria, Jr., a Standing Rock Sioux law student at the University of
Colorado, published his controversial book *Custer Died for Your Sins: An Indian
Manifesto*, in which he severely criticized anthropologists for the way they conducted
their research with Native Americans. The best-known part of the book is Chapter 4,
"Anthropologists and Other Friends," on which the selection for this Reader was
based. It is among the most vehement of criticisms of anthropologists yet written,
and begins with the memorable but scathing line, "Into each life, it is said, some rain
must fall ... But Indians have been cursed above all other people in history. Indians
have anthropologists" (1973:131). While Deloria's caricature of anthropologists is
unfair because he overlooks the positive relationships that anthropologists have had
with Native Americans, he nevertheless makes important points that have not only
been supported by many other Native Americans and anthropologists as well, but
are typical of those made by a growing number of Third and Fourth World critics on
other continents, which also began to emerge at about the same time.

Despite the humor of his caricature of anthropologists, the message is very serious:
anthropologists have been a curse on Native Americans; they treat people as objects
for observation, experimentation, manipulation, and "eventual extinction" (1973:132);
and they are a greater threat to their existence than the US Cavalry ever was. In the
book-length version, Deloria adds: "Thus has it ever been with anthropologists. In
believing they could find the key to man's behavior, they have, like the churches,
become forerunners of destruction" (1988:100). He concludes by warning
anthropologists that "a new day is coming," and he advises us "to get down off [our]

thrones of authority and ... begin helping Indian tribes instead of preying on them" (1973:137). In particular, Deloria insisted that the "compilation of useless knowledge for knowledge's sake should be utterly rejected by the Indian people. We should not be objects of observation for those who do nothing to help us" (1973:136). Instead, he called for a new relationship between anthropologists and Native Americans based on reciprocity and Indian needs, and a redistribution of power in research relationships.

How Deloria's message has been interpreted and misinterpreted is explored in Thomas Biolsi and Larry Zimmerman's edited volume, *Indians and Anthropologists: Vine Deloria, Jr., and the Critique of Anthropology* (1997). In their introduction to the volume, Biolsi and Zimmerman observe that long before most anthropologists had heard of Michel Foucault or Pierre Bourdieu:

> Deloria had put his finger directly on what would later be called discursive formations, symbolic capital, and the micropolitics of the academy. Deloria asked, regarding Indian peoples, "Why should we continue to be the private zoos for anthropologists? Why should tribes have to compete with scholars for funds when the scholarly productions are so useless and irrelevant to real life?" (1997:4)

While part of Deloria's agenda was an attempt to deter anthropologists from further "meddling" with Native American communities, he did not reject the value of anthropology – only how anthropologists had acted; he respected anthropological research as long as it was put at the service of Indian communities; and he had a major impact on the discipline as a whole. In "Growing Up on Deloria," Elizabeth Grobsmith (1997) discusses the impact his work had on a generation of anthropologists:

> He [imposed] a test on us – a new standard, which those of us who would persevere had to meet. *Custer Died for Your Sins* became our primer for how not to behave, conjuring up the ultimate image of the tiresome meddler we dreaded and desperately hoped to avoid. It made us defensive, in the true sense of the term: we continually had to defend and justify our existence and practice self-reflection and introspection – tasks of self-evaluation critical to good social science. We would not advocate outside control or be party to schemes of exploitation, top-down development, or paternalistic imposition; rather, we applauded ... self-determination policies and attitudes ... and saw our role as facilitating indigenously defined agendas. (1997:36–37)

Grobsmith argues this led to "a different breed of researchers" and helped moved us toward research relationships based on mutual reward or reciprocity (1997:47).

Deloria's and King's articles in this Reader represent typical examples of the growing wave of criticism from Third and Fourth World research participants that led to the "reinvention" and "decolonization" of anthropology in the postmodern era. The publication of Deloria's book in 1969 inaugurated a new period in relations between American Indian people and anthropologists, and Deloria and King are typical of many other indigenous scholars around the world who have also articulated grave concerns about how anthropologists have represented them.

Cecil King's short article is in the spirit of Deloria and other indigenous critics of anthropology, and is the only entry in this Reader that is not by an anthropologist. We have included it because, in a section devoted to "the other talks back," we thought we should include at least one unmitigated example. King, a member of the Odawa people from Manitoulin Island, Ontario, and Professor of Education and Director of the Ontario Aboriginal Teacher Education Program at Queen's University, expresses the all-too-common refrain about anthropologists:

> We, as Indian people, have welcomed strangers into our midst. We have welcomed all who came with intellectual curiosity or in the guise of the informed student. We have honored those whom we have seen grow in their knowledge and understanding of our ways. But unfortunately, many times we have been betrayed. Our honored guests have shown themselves to be no more than peeping toms, rank opportunists, interested in furthering their own careers by trading in our sacred traditions. Many of our people have felt anger at the way our communities have been cheated, held up to ridicule, and our customs sensationalized. Singer Floyd Westerman (Dakota), for example, expressed his anger in his 1969 recording "Here Come the Anthros." (1997:115)

Like other indigenous voices "speaking back" to anthropologists, King combines his criticism with a demand for reciprocity – a call for anthropologists to "become instrumental to our ambitions, our categories of importance" (1997:117) – with a demand for a redistribution of power in the traditional (empiricist) research relationship:

> We want to escape from the zoo. We want to be consulted and respected as not only human beings, at the very least, but as independent nations with the right to determine what transpires within our boundaries. We want to say who comes to our world, what they should see, hear, and take away. *Most important, we want to appraise, critique, and censure what they feel they have a right to say about us.* (1997:118; emphasis added)

After the publication in 1989 of Ofra Greenberg's ethnography on an Israeli border community, where she had lived and conducted research for five years, a journalist wrote a review for a small local newspaper which, Greenberg says, "grossly distorted facts and displayed a complete misunderstanding of the book's contents. According to this journalist, the people of Kiryat Shmona were depicted by me in a venomous manner, as being cruel and generally obnoxious" (1993:108). The review took some quotes from the book out of context, distorted others and made some up, and portrayed the anthropologist

> as an arrogant, privileged individual who observes the "natives" from a superior viewpoint, "like the traditional European anthropologists who investigated the native Africans, and who enjoys describing their backward and cruel world." She emphasized my affiliation with the veteran sector of Israeli society, my European origins, my secularity, and my academic education, and underscored the extent to which these attributes make me quite different from the people I studied. It was thus easy to characterize me as a European colonialist, invading the lives of the natives out of sheer curiosity. (1993:109)

When the review came to the attention of the people of Kiryat Shmona, they reacted angrily, even though they had not actually seen or read the book. There was a public furor, and Greenberg was criticized in the local newspaper and received numerous complaints and other negative reactions. In the article reproduced in this Reader, she describes and analyzes the community's reactions to the book – or, more accurately, the newspaper review of it – stressing the role of the press in mediating the reading of her book and defining the anthropologist/ethnographer as a foreigner and outsider.

Greenberg was accused of superiority and condescension. Community people who read the newspaper review but not the book itself felt compelled to respond, and politicians took advantage of the situation to advance their own agendas. In her article, Greenberg emphasizes the multiplicity of responses that emerge from a diverse group of readers, especially when they are responding not to the actual text but to its (mis)representation in the press. The reactions were both direct and indirect, and both critical and supportive. She received phone calls and letters, both negative and positive, and wrote a letter to the newspaper countering the original article. The controversy was picked up by a national newspaper, and Greenberg had to defend herself in the press at that level as well.

Greenberg's main point is that the newspapers played the leading role in shaping the public response to the book – in "influencing what happens when the people we write about read what we write" (1993:117). While a few people did read the book in order to form their own opinion, "the great majority of the public relied solely on information gathered from newspapers and formed their opinions on that basis" (1993:114). This is of critical importance, because it suggests that even today, when research participants themselves are nearly always literate, they still relatively rarely actually read what anthropologists write about them, and they are far more likely to gain their knowledge of what has been written about them from media reports of it. It seems ironic that most of Kiryat Shmona's residents "would not have learned about the book's publication had it not been for the appearance of the [newspaper] article" (1993:116).

Like Greenberg's case, the furor over Nancy Scheper-Hughes's ethnography about mental health in an Irish village was sparked by an article published in a newspaper. Scheper-Hughes conducted fieldwork in "Ballybran" in 1974, and in 1979 published her award-winning ethnography *Saints, Scholars, and Schizophrenics: Mental Illness in Rural Ireland*. In 1980, Michael Viney, a columnist from the *Irish Times*, visited "Ballybran" and wrote an article about the local anger he experienced in reaction to the book: "[S]ince the publication last year, two or three copies of the book have been passing from house to house, hurt and anger flaring up like a gunpowder trail. The preface begs pardon 'for exposing the darker and weaker side of their venerable culture.' It seems unlikely to be granted" (Viney 1980:12). Like Greenberg, Scheper-Hughes responded by writing a "Reply to 'Ballybran'" (1981) for the *Irish Times*, defending her book. While she accepted that it may have caused a "diffuse and collective hurt experienced by members of a community that may view itself as betrayed," she denied that it should have caused individual hurt because she had only betrayed commonly known "community secrets" and no personal or family ones. Nonetheless, Scheper-Hughes exposed what people of "Ballybran" preferred not to have been exposed, and, in their words, "created a public shame" (1981:9–10).

In 1999, Scheper-Hughes finally returned to "Ballybran," 20 years after the book had been published, and attempted to reconcile herself with the community by apologizing for any unintentional hurt given. But in this she failed; the trip ended with her "expulsion" from the village, and she concludes that she had created a new category of "unwanted people" in the village – "that new species of traitor and friend, the anthropologist" (1995:136).

Brettell's conclusions concerning fieldwork, text, and audience – or "when they read what we write" – provide a succinct summary of the situation today: it is inevitable that anthropological texts will be read, in one way or another, by those in the community studied; these are the greatest critics, followed by those closely associated or identified with those people – native scholars and other elites (1993:22). Issues of identity and representation will always be at stake, and anthropologists today are aware that the texts they write will increasingly be read and contested. Drawing attention to the politics of ethnographic writing, particularly the impact of the audience (readers) on both the anthropologist and the text, has raised theoretical, ethical, and practical questions for anthropologists, who will increasingly be confronted by research participants who read and react. Consideration of cases of when "the other talks back" have helped us to move toward increased sensitivity and "new ways to involve our ethnographic subjects in their self-representation" (Brettell 1993:22).

REFERENCES

Biolsi, Thomas and Larry Zimmerman, eds.
1997   *Indians and Anthropologists: Vine Deloria, Jr., and the Critique of Anthropology.* Tucson: University of Arizona Press.
Brettell, Caroline B.
1993   Introduction: Fieldwork, Text, and Audience. In: *When They Read What We Write: The Politics of Ethnography.* Caroline B. Brettell, ed., pp. 1–24. Westport, CT: Bergin & Garvey.
Deloria, Jr., Vine
1973   Custer Died for Your Sins. In: *To See Ourselves: Anthropology and Modern Social Issues.* Thomas Weaver, ed., pp. 130–137. New York: Macmillan.
Deloria, Jr., Vine
1988   *Custer Died for Your Sins: An Indian Manifesto.* 2nd edn. Norman: University of Oklahoma Press.
Greenberg, Ofra
1993   When They Read What the Papers Say We Wrote. In: *When They Read What We Write: The Politics of Ethnography.* Caroline B. Brettell, ed., pp. 107–118. Westport, CT: Bergin & Garvey.
Grobsmith, Elizabeth
1997   Growing Up on Deloria: The Impact of His Work on a New Generation of Anthropologists. In: *Indians and Anthropologists: Vine Deloria, Jr., and the Critique of Anthropology.* Thomas Biolsi and Larry Zimmerman, eds., pp. 35–49. Tucson: University of Arizona Press.
King, Cecil
1997   Here Come the Anthros. In: *Indians and Anthropologists: Vine Deloria Jr., and the Critique of Anthropology.* Thomas Biolsi and Larry Zimmerman, eds., pp. 115–119. Tucson: University of Arizona Press.
Scheper-Hughes, Nancy
1981   Reply to "Ballybran." *Irish Times*, February 21, pp. 9–10.
Scheper-Hughes, Nancy
1995   Ire in Ireland. *Ethnography* 1(1):117–140.
Viney, Michael
1980   Geared for a Gale. *Irish Times*, September 24, p. 12.

11

Custer Died for Your Sins

Vine Deloria, Jr.

Into each life, it is said, some rain must fall. Some people have bad horoscopes; others take tips on the stock market. McNamara created the TFX and the Edsel. American politics has George Wallace. But Indians have been cursed above all other people in history. Indians have anthropologists.

Every summer when school is out, a stream of immigrants heads into Indian country. The Oregon Trail was never as heavily populated as Route 66 and Highway 18 in the summertime. From every rock and cranny in the East, *they* emerge, as if responding to some primeval migratory longing, and flock to the reservations. They are the anthropologists – the most prominent members of the scholarly community that infests the land of the free and the homes of the braves. Their origin is a mystery hidden in the historical mists. Indians are certain that all ancient societies of the Near East had anthropologists at one time, because all those societies are now defunct. They are equally certain that Columbus brought

anthropologists on his ships when he came to the New World. How else could he have made so many wrong deductions about where he was? While their origins are uncertain, anthropologists can readily be identified on the reservations. Go into any crowd of people. Pick out a tall, gaunt white man wearing Bermuda shorts, a World War Two Army Air Corps flying jacket, an Australian bush hat and tennis shoes and packing a large knapsack incorrectly strapped on his back. He will invariably have a thin, sexy wife with stringy hair, an IQ of 191 and a vocabulary in which even the prepositions have 11 syllables. And he usually has a camera, tape recorder, telescope, and life jacket all hanging from his elongated frame.

This odd creature comes to Indian reservations to make *observations*. During the winter, these observations will become books by which future anthropologists will be trained, so that they can come out to reservations years from now and verify the

Vine Deloria, Jr., "Custer Died for Your Sins," pp. 130–137 from *To See Ourselves: Anthropology and Modern Social Issues*, ed. Thomas Weaver. Glenview, IL: Scott, Foresman & Co., 1973. Reprinted with permission of Scribner, an imprint of Simon & Schuster Adult Publishing Group, from *Custer Died for Your Sins* by Vine Deloria, Jr. Copyright © 1969 by Vine Deloria, Jr.; copyright renewed © 1997 by Vine Deloria, Jr.

Ethnographic Fieldwork: An Anthropological Reader, Second Edition. Edited by
Antonius C. G. M. Robben and Jeffrey A. Sluka.
Editorial material and organization © 2012 John Wiley & Sons, Inc.
Published 2012 by John Wiley & Sons, Inc.

observations in more books, summaries of which then appear in the scholarly journals and serve as a catalyst to inspire yet other anthropologists to make the great pilgrimage the following summer. And so on.

The summaries, meanwhile, are condensed. Some condensations are sent to Government agencies as reports justifying the previous summer's research. Others are sent to foundations, in an effort to finance the following summer's expedition West. The reports are spread through the Government agencies and foundations all winter. The only problem is that no one has time to read them. So $5,000-a-year secretaries are assigned to decode them. Since these secretaries cannot comprehend complex theories, they reduce the reports to the best slogans possible. The slogans become conference themes in the early spring, when the anthropological expeditions are being planned. They then turn into battle cries of opposing groups of anthropologists who chance to meet on the reservations the following summer.

Each summer there is a new battle cry, which inspires new insights into the nature of the "Indian problem." One summer Indians will be greeted with the joyful cry "Indians are bilingual!" The following summer this great truth will be expanded to "Indians are not only bilingual, they are *bicultural*!" Biculturality creates great problems for the opposing anthropological camp. For two summers, they have been bested in sloganeering and their funds are running low. So the opposing school of thought breaks into the clear faster than Gale Sayers. "Indians," the losing anthros cry, "are a *folk* people!" The tide of battle turns and a balance, so dearly sought by Mother Nature, is finally achieved. Thus go the anthropological wars, testing whether this school or that school can long endure. The battlefields, unfortunately, are the lives of Indian people.

The anthro is usually devoted to *pure research*. A 1969 thesis restating a proposition of 1773, complete with footnotes to all material published between 1773 and 1969, is pure research. There are, however, anthropologists who are not clever at collecting footnotes. They depend on their field observations and write long, adventurous narratives in which their personal observations are used to verify their

suspicions. Their reports, books and articles are called *applied research*. The difference, then, between pure and applied research is primarily one of footnotes. Pure has many footnotes, applied has few footnotes. Relevancy to subject matter is not discussed in polite company.

Anthropologists came to Indian country only after the tribes had agreed to live on reservations and had given up their warlike ways. Had the tribes been given a choice of fighting the cavalry or the anthropologists, there is little doubt as to who they would have chosen. In a crisis situation, men always attack the biggest threat to their existence. A warrior killed in battle could always go to the happy hunting grounds. But where does an Indian laid low by an anthro go? To the library?

The fundamental thesis of the anthropologist is that people are objects for observation. It then follows that people are considered objects for experimentation, for manipulation, and for eventual extinction. The anthropologist thus furnishes the justification for treating Indian people like so many chessmen, available for anyone to play with. The mass production of useless knowledge by anthropologists attempting to capture real Indians in a network of theories has contributed substantially to the invisibility of Indian people today. After all, who can believe in the actual existence of a food-gathering, berrypicking, seminomadic, fire-worshiping, high-plains-and-mountain-dwelling, horse-riding, canoe-toting, bead-using, pottery-making, ribbon-coveting, wickiup-sheltered people who began flourishing when Alfred Frump mentioned them in 1803 in *Our Feathered Friends*?

Not even Indians can see themselves as this type of creature – who, to anthropologists, is the "real" Indian. Indian people begin to feel that they are merely shadows of a mythical super-Indian. Many Indians, in fact, have come to parrot the ideas of anthropologists, because it appears that they know everything about Indian communities. Thus, many ideas that pass for Indian thinking are in reality theories originally advanced by anthropologists and echoed by Indian people in an attempt to communicate the real situation. Many anthros reinforce this sense of inadequacy in order to further influence the Indian people.

Since 1955, there have been a number of workshops conducted in Indian country as a device for training "young Indian leaders." Churches, white Indian-interest groups, colleges, and, finally, poverty programs have each gone the workshop route as the most feasible means for introducing new ideas to younger Indians, so as to create leaders. The tragic nature of the workshops is apparent when one examines their history. One core group of anthropologists has institutionalized the workshop and the courses taught in it. Trudging valiantly from workshop to workshop, from state to state, college to college, tribe to tribe, these noble spirits have served as the catalyst for the creation of workshops that are identical in purpose and content and often in the student-body itself.

The anthropological message to young Indians has not varied a jot or a tittle in ten years. It is the same message these anthros learned as fuzzy-cheeked graduate students in the post-War years – Indians are a folk people, whites are an urban people, and never the twain shall meet. Derived from this basic premise are all the other sterling insights: Indians are between two cultures, Indians are bicultural, Indians have lost their identity, and Indians are warriors. These theories, propounded every year with deadening regularity and an overtone of Sinaitic authority, have become a major mental block in the development of young Indian people. For these slogans have come to be excuses for Indian failures. They are crutches by which young Indians have avoided the arduous task of thinking out the implications of the status of Indian people in the modern world.

If there is one single cause that has importance today for Indian people, it is tribalism. Against all odds, Indians have retained title to some 53,000,000 acres of land, worth about three and a half billion dollars. Approximately half of the country's 1,000,000 Indians relate meaningfully to this land, either by living and working on it or by frequently visiting it. If Indians fully recaptured the idea that they are tribes communally in possession of this land, they would realize that they are not truly impoverished. But the creation of modern tribalism has been stifled by a ready acceptance of the Indians-are-a-folk-people premise of the anthropologists. This premise implies a drastic split between folk and urban cultures, in which the folk peoples have two prime characteristics: They dance and they are desperately poor. Creative thought in Indian affairs has not, therefore, come from the younger Indians who have grown up reading and talking to anthropologists. Rather, it has come from the older generation that believes in tribalism – and that the youngsters mistakenly insist has been brainwashed by Government schools.

Because other groups have been spurred on by their younger generations, Indians have come to believe that, through education, a new generation of leaders will arise to solve the pressing contemporary problems. Tribal leaders have been taught to accept this thesis by the scholarly community in its annual invasion of the reservations. Bureau of Indian Affairs educators harp continuously on this theme. Wherever authority raises its head in Indian country, this thesis is its message. The facts prove the opposite, however. Relatively untouched by anthropologists, educators, and scholars are the Apache tribes of the Southwest. The Mescalero, San Carlos, White Mountain, and Jicarilla Apaches have very few young people in college, compared with other tribes. They have even fewer people in the annual workshop orgy during the summers. If ever there was a distinction between folk and urban, this group of Indians characterizes it.

The Apaches see themselves, however, as neither folk nor urban but *tribal*. There is little sense of a lost identity. Apaches could not care less about the anthropological dilemmas that worry other tribes. Instead, they continue to work on massive plans for development that they themselves have created. Tribal identity is assumed, not defined, by these reservation people. Freedom to choose from a wide variety of paths of progress is a characteristic of the Apaches; they don't worry about what type of Indianism is real. Above all, they cannot be ego-fed by abstract theories and, hence, unwittingly manipulated.

With many young people from other tribes, the situation is quite different. Some young Indians attend workshops over and over again. Folk theories pronounced by authoritative anthropologists become opportunities to escape responsibility. If, by definition, the Indian is hopelessly caught between two cultures, why struggle? Why not blame all one's lack of success on this tremendous gulf between two opposing cultures? Workshops have become, therefore, summer retreats for nonthought rather than strategy sessions for leadership. Therein lies the Indian's sin against the anthropologist. Only those anthropologists who appear to boost Indian ego and expound theories dear to the hearts of workshop Indians are invited to teach at workshops. They become human recordings of social confusion and are played and replayed each summer, to the delight of a people who refuse to move on into the real world.

The workshop anthro is thus a unique creature, partially self-created and partially supported by the refusal of Indian young people to consider their problems in their own context. The normal process of maturing has been confused with cultural difference. So maturation is cast aside in favor of cult recitation of great truths that appear to explain the immaturity of young people.

While the anthro is thus, in a sense, the victim of the Indians, he should, nevertheless, recognize the role he has been asked to play and refuse to play it. Instead, the temptation to appear relevant to a generation of young Indians has clouded his sense of proportion. Workshop anthros often ask Indians of tender age to give their authoritative answers to problems that an entire generation of Indians is just now beginning to solve. Where the answer to reservation health problems may be adequate housing in areas where there has never been adequate housing, young Indians are shaped in their thinking processes to consider vague doctrines on the nature of man and his society.

It is preposterous that a teen-aged Indian should become an instant authority, equal in status to the PhD interrogating him. Yet the very human desire is to play that game every summer, for the status acquired in the game is heady. And since answers can be given only in the vocabulary created by the PhD, the entire leadership-training process internalizes itself and has no outlet beyond the immediate group. Real problems, superimposed on the ordinary problems of maturing, thus become insoluble

burdens that crush people of great leadership potential.

Let us take some specific examples. One workshop discussed the thesis that Indians were in a terrible crisis. They were, in the words of friendly anthro guides, "between two worlds." People between two worlds, the students were told, "drank." For the anthropologist, it was a valid explanation of drinking on the reservation. For the young Indians, it was an authoritative definition of their role as Indians. Real Indians, they began to think, drank; and their task was to become real Indians, for only in that way could they recreate the glories of the past. So they *drank*. I've lost some good friends who drank too much.

Abstract theories create abstract action. Lumping together the variety of tribal problems and seeking the demonic principle at work that is destroying Indian people may be intellectually satisfying, but it does not change the situation. By concentrating on great abstractions, anthropologists have unintentionally removed many young Indians from the world of real problems to the lands of make-believe.

As an example of a real problem, the Pyramid Lake Paiutes and the Gila River Pima and Maricopa are poor because they have been systematically cheated out of their water rights, and on desert reservations, water is the single most important factor in life. No matter how many worlds Indians straddle, the Plains Indians have an inadequate land base that continues to shrink because of land sales. Straddling worlds is irrelevant to straddling small pieces of land and trying to earn a living.

Along the Missouri River, the Sioux used to live in comparative peace and harmony. Although land allotments were small, families were able to achieve a fair standard of living through a combination of gardening and livestock raising and supplemental work. Little cash income was required, because the basic necessities of food, shelter, and community life were provided. After World War Two, anthropologists came to call. They were horrified that the Indians didn't carry on their old customs, such as dancing, feasts, and giveaways. In fact, the people did keep up a substantial number of customs, but they had been transposed into church gatherings, participation in the county fairs, and tribal celebrations, particularly fairs and rodeos. The people did Indian dances. But they didn't do them all the time.

Suddenly, the Sioux were presented with an authority figure who bemoaned the fact that whenever he visited the reservations, the Sioux were not out dancing in the manner of their ancestors. Today, the summers are taken up with one great orgy of dancing and celebrating, as each small community of Indians sponsors a weekend powwow for the people in the surrounding communities. Gone are the little gardens that used to provide fresh vegetables in the summer and canned goods in the winter. Gone are the chickens that provided eggs and Sunday dinners. In the winter, the situation becomes critical for families who spent the summer dancing. While the poverty programs have done much to counteract the situation, few Indians recognize that the condition was artificial from start to finish. The people were innocently led astray, and even the anthropologists did not realize what had happened.

One example: The Oglala Sioux are perhaps the most well known of the Sioux bands. Among their past leaders were Red Cloud, the only Indian who ever defeated the United States in a war, and Crazy Horse, most revered of the Sioux war chiefs. The Oglala were, and perhaps still are, the meanest group of Indians ever assembled. They would take after a cavalry troop just to see if their bowstrings were taut enough. When they had settled on the reservation, the Oglala made a fairly smooth transition to the new life. They had good herds of cattle, they settled along the numerous creeks that cross the reservation, and they created a very strong community spirit. The Episcopalians and the Roman Catholics had the missionary franchise on the reservation and the tribe was pretty evenly split between the two. In the Episcopal Church, at least, the congregations were fairly self-governing and stable.

But over the years, the Oglala Sioux have had a number of problems. Their population has grown faster than their means of support. The Government allowed white farmers to come into the eastern part of the reservation and create a county, with the best farmlands owned or operated by whites. The reservation was allotted – taken out of the collective hands of the tribe and parceled out to individuals – and when ownership became too complicated, control of the land passed out of Indian hands. The Government displaced a number of families during World War Two by taking a part of the reservation for use as a bombing range to train crews for combat. Only last year was this land returned to tribal and individual use.

The tribe became a favorite subject for anthropological study quite early, because of its romantic past. Theories arose attempting to explain the apparent lack of progress of the Oglala Sioux. The true issue – white control of the reservation – was overlooked completely. Instead, every conceivable intangible cultural distinction was used to explain the lack of economic, social, and educational progress of a people who were, to all intents and purposes, absentee landlords because of the Government policy of leasing their lands to whites.

One study advanced the startling proposition that Indians with many cattle were, on the average, better off than Indians without cattle. Cattle Indians, it seems, had more capital and income than did noncattle Indians. Surprise! The study had innumerable charts and graphs that demonstrated this great truth beyond the doubt of a reasonably prudent man. Studies of this type were common but unexciting. They lacked that certain flair of insight so beloved by anthropologists. Then one day a famous anthropologist advanced the theory, probably valid at the time and in the manner in which he advanced it, that the Oglala were "warriors without weapons."

The chase was on. Before the ink had dried on the scholarly journals, anthropologists from every library stack in the nation converged on the Oglala Sioux to test this new theory. Outfitting anthropological expeditions became the number-one industry of the small off-reservation Nebraska towns south of Pine Ridge. Surely, supplying the Third Crusade to the Holy Land was a minor feat compared with the task of keeping the anthropologists at Pine Ridge.

Every conceivable difference between the Oglala Sioux and the folks at Bar Harbor was attributed to the quaint warrior tradition of the Oglala Sioux. From lack of roads to unshined shoes, Sioux problems were generated, so the anthros discovered, by the refusal of the white man to recognize the great desire of the Oglala to go to war. Why expect an Oglala to become a small businessman, when he was only waiting for that wagon train to come around the bend? The very real and human problems of the reservation were considered to be merely by-products of the failure of a warrior people to become domesticated. The fairly respectable thesis of past exploits in war, perhaps romanticized for morale purposes, became a spiritual force all its own. Some Indians, in a tongue-in-cheek manner for which Indians are justly famous, suggested that a subsidized wagon train be run through the reservation each morning at nine o'clock and the reservation people paid a minimum wage for attacking it.

By outlining this problem, I am not deriding the Sioux. I lived on that reservation for 18 years and know many of the problems from which it suffers. How, I ask, can the Oglala Sioux make any headway in education when their lack of education is ascribed to a desire to go to war? Would not, perhaps, an incredibly low per-capita income, virtually nonexistent housing, extremely inadequate roads, and domination by white farmers and ranchers make some difference? If the little Sioux boy or girl had no breakfast, had to walk miles to a small school, and had no decent clothes nor place to study in a one-room log cabin, should the level of education be comparable with that of Scarsdale High?

What use would roads, houses, schools, businesses, and income be to a people who, everyone expected, would soon depart on the warpath? I would submit that a great deal of the lack of progress at Pine Ridge is occasioned by people who believe they are helping the Oglala when they insist on seeing, in the life of the people of that reservation, only those things they want to see. Real problems and real people become invisible before the great romantic and nonsensical notion that the Sioux yearn for the days of Crazy Horse and Red Cloud and will do nothing until those days return.

The question of the Oglala Sioux is one that plagues every Indian tribe in the nation, if it will closely examine itself. Tribes have been defined; the definition has been completely explored; test scores have been advanced promoting and deriding the thesis; and, finally, the conclusion has been reached: Indians must be redefined in terms that white men will accept, even if that means re-Indianizing them according to the white man's idea of what they were like in the past and should logically become in the future.

What, I ask, would a school board in Moline, Illinois – or Skokie, even – do if the scholarly community tried to reorient its educational system to conform with outmoded ideas of Sweden in the glory days of Gustavus Adolphus? Would they be expected to sing "*Ein' feste Burg*" and charge out of the mists at the Roman Catholics to save the Reformation every morning as school began? Or the Irish – would they submit to a group of Indians coming to Boston and telling them to dress in green and hunt leprechauns?

Consider the implications of theories put forward to solve the problem of poverty among the blacks. Several years ago, the word went forth that black poverty was due to the disintegration of the black family, that the black father no longer had a prominent place in the home. How incredibly shortsighted that thesis was. How typically Anglo-Saxon! How in the world could there have been a black family if people were sold like cattle for 200 years, if there were large plantations that served merely as farms to breed more slaves, if white owners systematically ravaged black women? When did the black family unit ever become integrated? Herein lies a trap into which many Americans have fallen: Once a problem is defined and understood by a significant number of people who have some relation to it, the fallacy goes, the problem ceases to exist. The rest of America had better beware of having quaint mores that attract anthropologists, or it will soon become a victim of the conceptual prison into which blacks and Indians, among others, have been thrown. One day you may find yourself cataloged – perhaps as a credit-card-carrying, turnpike-commuting, condominium-dwelling, fraternity-joining, church-going, sports-watching, time-purchase-buying, television-watching, magazine-subscribing, politically inert transmigrated urbanite who, through the phenomenon of the second car and the shopping center, has become a golf-playing, wife-swapping, etc., etc., etc., suburbanite. Or have you already been characterized – and caricatured – in ways that struck you as absurd? If so, you will understand what has been happening to Indians for a long, long time.

In defense of the anthropologists, it must be recognized that those who do not publish perish. Those who do not bring in a substantial sum of research money soon slide down the scale of university approval. What university is not equally balanced between the actual education of its students and a multitude of small bureaus, projects, institutes, and programs that are designed to harvest grants for the university?

The effect of anthropologists on Indians should be clear. Compilation of useless knowledge for knowledge's sake should be utterly rejected by the Indian people. We should not be objects of observation for those who do nothing to help us. During the critical days of 1954, when the Senate was pushing for termination of all Indian rights, not one scholar, anthropologist, sociologist, historian, or economist came forward to support the tribes against the detrimental policy. Why didn't the academic community march to the side of the tribes? Certainly the past few years have shown how much influence academe can exert when it feels compelled to enlist in a cause. Is Vietnam any more crucial to the moral stance of America than the great debt owed to the Indian tribes?

Perhaps we should suspect the motives of members of the academic community. They have the Indian field well defined and under control. Their concern is not the ultimate policy that will affect the Indian people, but merely the creation of new slogans and doctrines by which they can climb the university totem pole. Reduction of people to statistics for purposes of observation appears to be inconsequential to the anthropologist when compared with the immediate benefits he can derive – the acquisition of further prestige and the chance to appear as the high priest of American society, orienting and manipulating to his heart's desire.

Roger Jourdain, chairman of the Red Lake Chippewa tribe of Minnesota, casually had the anthropologists escorted from his reservation a couple of years ago. This was the tip of the iceberg. If only more Indians had the insight of Jourdain. Why should we continue to provide private zoos for anthropologists? Why should tribes have to compete with scholars for funds, when their scholarly productions are so useless and irrelevant to life?

Several years ago, an anthropologist stated that over a period of some 20 years he had spent, from all sources, close to $10,000,000 studying a tribe of fewer than 1000 people. Imagine what that amount of money would have meant to that group of people had it been invested in buildings and businesses. There would have been no problems to study.

I sometimes think that Indian tribes could improve relations between themselves and the anthropologists by adopting the following policy: Each anthro desiring to study a tribe should be made to apply to the tribal council for permission to do his study. He would be given such permission only if he raised as a contribution to the tribal budget an amount of money equal to the amount he proposed to spend on his study. Anthropologists would thus become productive members of Indian society, instead of ideological vultures.

This proposal was discussed at one time in Indian circles. It blew no small number of anthro minds. Irrational shrieks of "academic freedom" rose like rockets from launching pads. The very idea of putting a tax on useless information was intolerable to the anthropologists we talked with. But the question is very simple. Are the anthros concerned about freedom – or license? Academic freedom certainly does not imply that one group of people has to become chessmen for another group of people. Why should Indian communities be subjected to prying non-Indians any more than other communities? Should any group have a franchise to stick its nose into someone else's business?

I don't think my proposal ever will be accepted. It contradicts the anthropologists' self-image much too strongly. What is more likely is that Indians will continue to allow their communities to be turned inside out until they come to realize the damage that is being done to them. Then they will seal up the reservations and no further knowledge – useless or otherwise – will be created. This may be the best course. Once, at a Congressional hearing, someone asked Alex Chasing Hawk, a council member of the Cheyenne Sioux for 30 years, "Just what do you Indians want?" Alex replied, "A leave-us-alone law."

The primary goal and need of Indians today is not for someone to study us, feel sorry for us, identify with us, or claim descent from Pocahontas to make us feel better. Nor do we need to be classified as semiwhite and have programs made to bleach us further. Nor do we need further studies to see if we are "feasible." We need, instead, a new policy from Congress that acknowledges our intelligence, and our dignity.

In its simplest form, such a policy would give a tribe the amount of money now being spent in the area on Federal schools and other services. With this block grant, the tribe itself would communally establish and run its own schools and hospitals and police and fire departments – and, in time, its own income-producing endeavors, whether in industry or agriculture. The tribe would not be taxed until enough capital had accumulated so that individual Indians were getting fat dividends.

Many tribes are beginning to acquire the skills necessary for this sort of independence, but the odds are long: An Indian district at Pine Ridge was excited recently about the possibility of running its own schools, and a bond issue was put before them that would have made it possible for them to do so. In the meantime, however, anthropologists visiting the community convinced its people that they were culturally unprepared to assume this sort of responsibility; so the tribe voted down the bond issue. Three universities have sent teams to the area to discover why the issue was defeated. The teams are planning to spend more on their studies than the bond issue would have cost.

I would expect an instant rebuttal by the anthros. They will say that my sentiments do not represent the views of all Indians – and they are right, they have brainwashed many of my brothers. But a new day is coming. Until then, it would be wise for anthropologists to climb down from their thrones of authority and pure research and begin helping Indian tribes instead of preying on them. For the wheel of karma grinds slowly, but it does grind fine. And it makes a complete circle.

12

Here Come the Anthros

Cecil King

N'dahwemahdik giye n'weehkahnisidok g'dahnamikohnim meenwa dush g'meegetch-iwinim geeweekomiyek monpee nongo weenashamigabwitohnigok djigeegidotamah manda enjimowndjidihying. -N'geekahwe bigossehnimah dush Wo kinah gego netawtot, weebi-weedji-yawyung, weemeezhiyung nihb-wakahwin meenwa dash nah gihnihgehnnah n'dahkidowinan djiminokahgohwing, mee gahzhi bigossehndahmah ... My sisters and my brothers I greet you and also I thank you for inviting me to speak to the topic at hand. As I was preparing my thoughts, I begged the Maker of all things to be among us, to give us some wisdom and also maybe to make my works be as a medicine for us all – those were my thoughts.

We, as Indian people, have welcomed strangers into our midst. We have welcomed all who came with intellectual curiosity or in the guise of the informed student. We have honored those whom we have seen grow in their knowledge and understanding of our ways.

But unfortunately, many times we have been betrayed. Our honored guests have shown themselves to be no more than peeping toms, rank opportunists, interested in furthering their own careers by trading in our sacred traditions. Many of our people have felt anger at the way our communities have been cheated, held up to ridicule, and our customs sensationalized. Singer Floyd Westerman (Dakota), for example, expressed this anger in his 1969 recording of "Here Come the Anthros."

We have been observed, noted, taped, and videoed. Our behaviors have been recorded in every possible way known to Western science, and I suppose we could learn to live with this if we had not become imprisoned in the anthropologists' words. The language that anthropologists use to explain us traps us in linguistic cages because we must explain our ways through alien hypothetical constructs and theoretical frameworks. Our *ezhibemah-dizowin* must be described as material culture, economics, politics, or religion. We must

Ethnographic Fieldwork: An Anthropological Reader, Second Edition. Edited by Antonius C. G. M. Robben and Jeffrey A. Sluka.
Editorial material and organization © 2012 John Wiley & Sons, Inc.
Published 2012 by John Wiley & Sons, Inc.

segment, fragment, fracture, and pigeonhole that which we hold sacred. The pipe, *d'opwahganinan*, becomes a sacred artifact, a religious symbol, a political instrument, a mnemonic device, an icon.

We have to describe our essence, *d'ochichaugwunan*, to fit academic conceptual packages, and we have become prisoners of what academics have done to our words to verify their words. We want to be given the time, money, luxury, and security of academic credibility to define our own constructs from within our own languages and our own worlds and in our own time.

We struggle as contemporary Indian, Metis, and Inuit peoples to unlock the classificatory chains choking our dynamic languages and growing, changing lives. How can we learn how our language is structured, how our world of languages was created, if we still must parse, analyze, and chop them up to fit the grammar of other languages? How can we define who we are, what we see, and what we think when the public, politicians, and policy makers have accepted the prepackaged images of who we are, as created by anthropologists?

I am an Odawa. I speak Odawa, but anthropologists have preferred to say I speak Ojibwe. My language is an Algonquin language, I am told, and it is structured by describing things as animate or inanimate, so I am told. English definitions of the terms "animate" and "inanimate" lead people to think of things being alive or not alive. Is this how our language is structured? I think not. In Odawa all so-called inanimate things could not be said to be dead. Does animate then mean having or possessing a soul? Is this a sufficient explanation? I think not. Is the animate-inanimate dichotomy helpful in describing the structure of my language? I think that it is limiting, if not wrong outright. For in Odawa anything at some time can be animate. The state of inanimateness is not the denial or negation of animateness as death is the negation of the state of aliveness. Nor can something have a soul and then not have a soul and then acquire a soul again. In Odawa the concept of animateness is limitless. It can be altered by the mood of the moment, the mood of the speaker, the context, the use, the

circumstances, the very cosmos of our totality. English terms imprison our understanding of our own linguistic concepts.

Having to define ourselves from the start with inappropriate English terms is not sufficient for our understanding. It is confining, and it is wrong. It seems that we must first defend ourselves against scholarly categories. We must find a way to break out of these cages. That takes a lot of unnecessary, unproductive time and energy and money.

In the last twenty years, Indian, Metis, and Inuit peoples have moved from reservations and isolated communities into places of greater visibility, but they are seen through the images built out of anthropological studies of them. We have been defined as "poor folks," members of a "minority" or "less sophisticated cultures"; we have been called "tribal," "underdeveloped," "nomadic," "less fully evolved." Therefore, real Indians are poor. You have provided us with the cop-outs: "Indian time" if we are late, "It's not the Indian way" if we don't want to do something. Employers have acquired cop-outs for not hiring Indians: Indians don't like competition, Indians don't like to work inside, Indians like seasonal employment. Teachers excuse the lack of Indian graduates. Indians themselves find excuses for their lack of employment, education, or dignity.

Now, we as Indian, Metis, and Inuit people want self-determination. We want self-government. When will anthropologists become instrumental to our ambitions, our categories of importance? How helpful is it to be called tribal or primitive when we are trying to negotiate with national and provincial governments as equal nations? Anthropological terms make us and our people invisible. The real people and the real problems disappear under the new rhetoric. Indian, Metis, and Inuit problems defined incorrectly lead to inappropriate solutions, irrelevant programs, and the reinforcement of the status quo. The real problems remain unresolved, and the Indian, Metis, and Inuit are again redefined.

The cumulative effects of all this are now evident. We have been redefined so many times we no longer quite know who we are. Our original words are obscured by the layers upon layers of others' definitions laid on top of them.

We want to come back to our own words, our own meanings, our own definitions of ourselves, and our own world. Now scholars debate among themselves the ethics to be used in working in our communities and homes. It is as if they are organizing the feeding schedule at the zoo. We want to escape from the zoo. We want to be consulted and respected as not only human beings, at the very least, but as independent nations with the right to determine what transpires within our boundaries. We want to say who comes to our world, what they should see, hear, and take away. Most important, we want to appraise, critique, and censure what they feel they have a right to say about us.

We acknowledge, with gratitude, the attempts by the National Endowment for the Humanities and the American Anthropological Association to regulate researchers by guidelines or codes of ethics. However, for most of us, these efforts are part of the problem. For we must ask: Whose ethics? In this era of aboriginal self-government, it is not for the outsider to set the rules of conduct on our lands and in our communities. It is our right and responsibility as aboriginal nations to do that. It is the right and responsibility of researchers to respect and comply with our standards. The dictates of Western science and the standards of behavior enshrined by associations of researchers dedicated to the advancement of social science may or may not be compatible with the code of ethics of our aboriginal communities.

Creative approaches must be discussed and debated by aboriginal communities, academic institutions, and individual researchers to reach a working relationship that neither constricts the advancement of knowledge nor denigrates the aboriginal communities' legitimate authority over the integrity of their own intellectual traditions.

Let me close with a story. I had a dream that all the peoples of the world were together in one place. The place was cold. Everyone was shivering. I looked for a fire to warm myself. None was to be found. Then someone said that in the middle of the gathering of Indians, what was left of the fire had been found. It was a very, very small flame. All the Indians were alerted that the slightest rush of air or the smallest movement could put the fire out, and the fire would be lost to humankind. All the Indians banded together to protect the flame. They were working to quicken the fragile, feeble flame. The Indians were adding minuscule shavings from small pieces of wood to feed it.

Suddenly, throughout the other peoples, the whisper was heard: The Indians have a fire. There was a crush of bodies stampeding to the place where the flame was held. I pushed to the edge of the Indian circle to stop those coming to the flame so that it would not be smothered. The other people became abusive, saying that they were cold too and it was our responsibility to share the flame with them. I replied, "It is our responsibility to preserve the flame for humanity, and at the moment it is too weak to be shared, but if we all are still and respect the flame it will grow and thrive in the caring hands of those who hold it. In time we can all warm ourselves at the fire. But now we have to nurture the flame or we will all lose the gift."

Those are my words. *Meegwetch.*

13

When They Read What the Papers Say We Wrote

Ofra Greenberg

In October 1989 my book *A Development Town Visited* was published in Israel (in Hebrew). The book contains an account of my experiences in Kiryat Shmona, a community where I lived and conducted research for five years. Kiryat Shmona was founded on Israel's northern border in 1950, largely as a result of a government policy promoting the geographical distribution of the population. It was settled by new immigrants from North Africa, Iraq, and Hungary, and was given the status of "development town" on the strength of its location and the composition of its population. This entitled both the municipality and its citizens to various government dispensations.

Within a few years, most of the inhabitants of European origin (Ashkenazis) had moved to the center of the country. By the 1980s, 90 percent of the population of 15,000 was of oriental origin, characterized by a low educational level (half the population had only an elementary education), negligible professional training, and low average income. During the period under study, families there were receiving welfare support at a rate 50 percent above the national average, partly a result of the high proportion of families with four or more children. Most of the inhabitants defined themselves as being religious, or at least as adhering to Jewish tradition.

At the outset of my research I was interested in the utilization of traditional medicine by immigrants from oriental countries. While attempting to investigate the extent and nature of this activity, I also looked into the characteristics and quality of the established medical services. Since Kiryat Shmona is situated far from the center of the country and has a predominantly low-income population, modern, private medicine was all but nonexistent. Virtually all medical services were provided by Kupat Holim, a medical insurance organization belonging to the labor federation.

I discovered early on that a large segment of the population was utilizing the services of

Ofra Greenberg, "When They Read What the Papers Say We Wrote," pp. 107–118 plus relevant bibliography from *When They Read What We Write: The Politics of Ethnography*, ed. Caroline B. Brettell. Westport, CN: Bergin & Garvey, 1993. Copyright © 1993, 1996 by Caroline B. Brettell. Reprinted by permission of Greenwood Publishing Group, Inc, Westport, CT.

Ethnographic Fieldwork: An Anthropological Reader, Second Edition. Edited by Antonius C. G. M. Robben and Jeffrey A. Sluka.
Editorial material and organization © 2012 John Wiley & Sons, Inc.
Published 2012 by John Wiley & Sons, Inc.

practitioners of traditional medicine. Residing in the town were several folk healers who employed a variety of techniques which included charms and combinations of herbs. They treated a diversity of physical, emotional, and social complaints. A considerable proportion of their patients simultaneously sought help from conventional physicians for ailments beyond the scope of the folk healers, such as heart problems or cancer. Some were treated by both folk and conventional medicine for the same complaint (e.g., depression, infertility), with the conventional practitioners utterly unaware that their patients were receiving treatment from folk healers. Use of folk medicine was concealed from establishment figures such as teachers, nurses, and social workers, since patients were apprehensive of their hostile and dismissive attitude toward such "primitive methods."

In due course, I broadened the scope of my observation to include the operation of the other social services, in particular the welfare and educational agencies. The findings revealed a predominantly passive population supported by a variety of social services. Moreover, this population demanded greater practical and financial support from the services than that provided for by the formal regulations and criteria (e.g., a demand for a full subsidy for children attending a summer camp rather than the 75 percent subsidy that had been offered). By contrast, in the realm of folk medicine – a sphere of activity whose existence is not recognized by the authorities – people acted independently, with initiative and even mutual assistance.

After the publication of my book I was interviewed by a young journalist from a small left-wing newspaper. Her review grossly distorted facts and displayed a complete misunderstanding of the book's contents. According to this journalist, the people of Kiryat Shmona were depicted by me in a venomous manner, as being cruel and generally obnoxious. I quote from her article:

Upon reading the book, only a masochist would want to visit the place. Kiryat Shmona, according to Greenberg's description, is a horrible town. The residents' outlook on life and their attitudes are fundamentally flawed, they are selfish and evil, public office holders are corrupt, the doctors and teachers are the worst imaginable.... During the five years she spent in Kiryat Shmona, Greenberg found innumerable negative traits among the town's residents, which she proceeds to enumerate one by one. First and foremost is the irritating tendency to change one's place of work. As if possessed, they leap this way and that, until at times it seems as though all of Kiryat Shmona is in a mad spin. (*Hotam*, November 10, 1989, p. 8)

She continues: "They don't know how to organize their meals or their lives so as to ensure that all the family is satisfied and healthy." In support of each such claim a quote is produced from the book, removed from its context and often distorted, as in the following phrase: "the greengrocer, a cunning and avaricious young man." This did not appear in the book, and neither did the following supposed quote: "The shoppers slice the cheese themselves with their filthy hands."

This journalist referred to a 1949 newspaper report about North African immigrants. (I have not checked its authenticity.) This report claimed that "we have here a people primitive in the extreme; their level of education is pitifully low, and worst of all, they are unable to absorb anything of intellectual value." She then added her own observation: "Forty years on, Greenberg does the same thing, the only difference being that she cloaks her argument in rational explanations." Purporting to quote from her interview with me, the journalist records a question she did not ask, and an answer I did not give: "One gathers from reading the book that the residents are worse than the establishment?" ... "That is what happens during the initial period there, they behave atrociously towards outsiders." ... "It seems that you have difficulty accepting the residents of Kiryat Shmona because you feel superior to them."

In her article, the journalist somehow connected the presentation of "the bad people of Kiryat Shmona" with the analysis of weakening family commitment. She is scornful of my analysis of the effect of social factors on the behavior of the members of the community, maintaining that I am suggesting that their inhuman behavior stems from their evil character. In fact, my analysis of the disappearance of family commitment does not imply any criticism of the local people. In the book I present in a neutral way the social conditions (in particular the proliferation of welfare services) that induce the general passivity of town residents toward their lives, expressed here in the evasion of family responsibilities and the expectation that the authorities will intervene. This pattern of behavior constitutes a surprising finding, considering that we are dealing with a traditional community characterized by binding family ties in its country of origin and during the initial period of settlement in Israel.

The journalist concluded her review by portraying me as an arrogant, privileged individual who observes the "natives" from a superior viewpoint, "like the traditional European anthropologist who investigated the native Africans, and who enjoys describing their backward and cruel world." She emphasized my affiliation with the veteran sector of Israeli society, my European origins, my secularity, and my academic education, and underscored the extent to which these attributes make me quite different from the people I studied. It was thus easy to characterize me as a European colonialist, invading the lives of the natives out of sheer curiosity.

This newspaper article was soon brought to the attention of the people of Kiryat Shmona, and they reacted angrily. I was attacked in the local newspaper and received several telephone complaints. In fact, the furor in the town eventually caught the attention of the national radio. A publication that would otherwise have reached only a circumscribed and mainly professional readership became, with the help of media exposure, a news item broadcast throughout the country. The controversy died down only when the editor of the local newspaper curtailed the publication of further letters. However, it had gone on long enough in print to ensure that almost everyone in the town had heard about the issue.

In this chapter I describe and analyze the reactions of the investigated population to the book's contents, paying particular attention to the role of the press in mediating the reading of my ethnography as well as in defining me, a native anthropologist, as a foreigner and an outsider.[1]

How the Community Responded

Direct responses

The stream of reactions was not monolithic. People responded differently to the publication, in general according to their position in society. In addition to the townfolk, responses came from friends and acquaintances, from public figures and politicians, and from professionals. Some responses were direct and others were indirect. The first direct response came through a phone call from an indignant acquaintance from Kiryat Shmona. Born in the town, she worked for the welfare services with senior citizens. "Ofra, what have you done to us?" she exclaimed. "How could you sling mud at us like that, after we accepted you so warmly?" I was surprised and embarrassed. Although the journalist had promised to send me a copy of the article as soon as it appeared, she had failed to do so. I did not know how to reply to this caller. Once I had managed to obtain a copy of the newspaper from friends living on a nearby kibbutz, I was appalled by what I read.

Some days later, the local Kiryat Shmona paper, *Maida Shmona*, printed an article written by the leader of the municipal opposition. This man also had an administrative position in the academic institution where I had taught, and he knew me personally. In the article he wrote: "Ofra, or rather Dr. Ofra Greenberg, who honored us by her presence, resided in Kiryat Shmona ... and collected incriminatory material about the locals ... the measure of evil, contempt, hatred, and in particular racism exhibited by one person towards an entire population, is equivalent to a lethal dose of cyanide." Later in his article, he admitted not having read the book, claiming, "The [newspaper] article is good enough for me."

From this point onwards, the episode rapidly developed into a full-scale public furor. People used different mechanisms to direct their criticisms at me. Personal acquaintances used the telephone. A friend who lived in the vicinity of Kiryat Shmona and who had worked with me at the local college was among the first to call. I explained the distortion in the newspaper account and suggested that she read the book, which she promised to do. She advised me to reply to a letter in the local paper, as silence on my part would be regarded as an admission of guilt. I took her advice and my letter appeared. It elicited no direct response.

Several other people called to express their support. These included a secretary at my former college who had spoken to the friend mentioned above; a former student who asked me to send him the book (unavailable in Kiryat Shmona); a volunteer teacher; and a former local journalist who had since moved to Jerusalem. The latter told me that after receiving a copy of *Maida Shmona* from his brother, he had immediately bought the book and read it in a day. He was calling to convey his support, as he could imagine how hurt I must feel. In his opinion, the book portrayed a true, if in part painful, picture of the place. He found in it considerable affection for the local people, and considered the "review" to be blatantly unfair both to the book and to me. He also mentioned that he had persuaded his brother to read the book, and his brother subsequently wrote a letter of support that was published in a different local paper.

In addition to telephone calls, I also received a number of letters, including one from the chief rabbi of Kiryat Shmona, with whom I was personally acquainted. He wrote with sympathy and support that "it is sufficient to photocopy the book's pages, conveying their love; there is no simpler or more relevant evidence. To my mind, the article in the newspaper … was an expression of the feeling that 'an outsider cannot understand us,' and A.'s aggressive review was a faithful expression of Kiryat Shmona's complexity, which you have portrayed with a craftsman's hand."

I received another letter from a member of Parliament who had lived in Kiryat Shmona for a while and to whom I had sent a copy of my book. He wrote: "A wave of memories swamped me upon reading the book, and the characters you describe so well – with sympathy, understanding, compassion and warmth – appeared before me again…. I believe that this little book,

which contains so much warmth and beauty, will find a path to the hearts of Kiryat Shmona's people." This member of Parliament, an active and well-known public figure in Israel, also wrote to the national newspaper.

My husband telephoned two or three friends who worked in the public service in Kiryat Shmona (the director of the urban renewal project, the coordinator of programs at the local community center) to enquire about their opinions. They reported that they had found it very difficult to accept the article in *Maida Shmona*, and that they wished to read the book. Once they had done so (I sent copies), they called back, expressing support and inviting us to visit them. They added that many people in Kiryat Shmona were now hostile toward me. The community center coordinator told us that there had been a number of lively discussions about the book among center employees. After people had read it a staff meeting was devoted to further debate about it.

Indirect reports

News of reactions reached me indirectly as well as directly. From a neighbor whose brother lives in Kiryat Shmona I received a report of the uproar that broke out after the local publication. The brother added that he would advise me to keep well away from the town. A friend who works near Kiryat Shmona, and who comes into contact with town residents, told of their anger and of the reaction of one man to a suggestion that he read the book. "I've read the article, and that's good enough for me." Another friend who teaches in the Department of Social Work at Haifa University reported a furious outburst from a student from Kiryat Shmona when my book was mentioned during a lesson. She had not read the book.

There were also responses in the local press. The first letter came from a lawyer, a Kiryat Shmona resident of many years' standing who was also a personal acquaintance of mine. He asked me to send him the book and wrote to the paper after he had read it. I quote from his published letter at length.

The reader will find a serious, balanced and fair work of research into the structure of Kiryat

Shmona's community, and the institutions that are supposed to serve this community. The author does not refrain from criticism, but likewise does not fail to record the positive aspects of this community. If the research is not entirely objective, this is due to the sense of pain born of love, which is evident in the book.

A copy of Ofra's book is to be found in the library of the college at which A. works, but he has not bothered to read it, preferring to criticize the book, and what is more, also the author (whom he knew personally during her five year stay in Kiryat Shmona), on the strength of a tendentious publication in the supplement "Hotam." This was A.'s first "foul." His second mistake was in failing to elicit the author's response. These two transgressions led A. to produce an amazing collection of unfounded and malicious slander, to which the term "character assassination" may be applied as an understatement.

No less serious than the damage caused by A.'s slanderous attack is the general outlook from which it derives. Unfortunately, this outlook is not peculiar to him … and is shared by most of those who represent and form public opinion in Kiryat Shmona. According to this outlook, mere residence in the town endows its inhabitants with rights devoid of obligations; the residents, and in particular their leaders, are above all criticism. Should the mirror reflect an ugly image, or the thermometer indicate the existence of a disease, they must be broken! (November 20, 1989, p. 20)

The local paper published three other responses, two of which expressed support from people who had read the book, while the other, from someone who read only the article, was angrily antagonistic. I received a long letter in favor of my book and castigating A.'s behavior, which the editor of *Maida Shmona* chose not to publish on the grounds of lack of space.

How the National Newspaper Responded

The discussion in the national newspaper *Hotam* was of a more academic and professional nature than that in the local paper *Maida Shmona*. In one camp were the author, a member of

Parliament, a university anthropology lecturer, and the publisher's editor, all of whom criticized the journalist's abuse of press freedom in the form of distortion of the facts. The respondents were the journalist and the editor of *Hotam*.

Whereas the correspondence in the local paper revealed emotions such as anger and hurt, and dwelt upon personal and emotive issues, such as the author's character and qualifications and the accuracy of descriptions of the town, the discussion in *Hotam* focused on general questions, such as the role of the press, or the anthropologist, as a detached and balanced observer. For example, the university anthropology lecturer wrote:

The contents, style, and spirit [of the article] constitute, in my opinion, a crass and disgraceful exploitation of the sacrosanct ideal of press freedom, in the name of which such an article can be published…. This is not merely a matter of quoting out of context, or of sarcastic comments with no basis whatsoever in the book, but mainly of the selective and tendentious manner in which the journalist has chosen to convey her own messages…. Finally, as a social anthropologist, I protest at the irreversible damage caused by the journalist to the reputation of the discipline…. The residents of Kiryat Shmona and of other development towns may, with justification, regard your article as an incitement to a renewal of inter-ethnic conflict. Had Ms. X done justice to the book, she may have discerned its constructive aspects, and by so doing may have encouraged political and social action designed to further the welfare and interests of the residents, who are deprived by the establishment and paid venomous and hypocritical lip-service by the media, of the sort exemplified by the article. (*Hotam*, December 1, 1989)

The journalist replied by alleging that the chapter containing descriptions of interesting and sympathetic characters had been added under pressure from the publisher (a complete fabrication), and that the complaint about quoting out of context was a routine and devious defense.

Finally, the publisher's editor responded by claiming that what infuriated him about the article was "not only its distortion of the book's contents, but also the malice evident between the lines.... The journalist from *Hotam* has missed the point of the book. She makes only brief mention of the governing institutions' responsibility for Kiryat Shmona's condition. Ironically, the establishment and its failings are let off extremely lightly by the crusading journalist" (*Hotam*, December 1, 1989).

Making Sense of the Responses

Perhaps the most interesting aspect of the reaction of members of the community where the research was conducted is that it was by no means monolithic. People both accepted and rejected the contents of the publication as well as the choice of action taken (or not taken) by government agencies as a result of the conclusions drawn. Their position was influenced by a number of factors including their public role, their level of education, issues of self-image, and their personal acquaintance with the researcher.

Certain local politicians used the event to further their own interests, that is, to achieve popularity by identifying with the "humiliated" public and by berating the "stranger." For example, the mayor of the town, who had his eye on a career in Parliament, added his comment to the original article when approached by the journalist. His reaction was given without reading the book and without checking her version with me. Quoting a Hebrew idiom, he spoke of the good people of the town being maligned by career-minded outsiders who "spat in the well from which they had drunk."[2]

The leader of the municipal opposition, an ambitious contender for the mayorship, also made no attempt to clarify the facts with me. His theme was ethnic prejudice and the lack of integrity on the part of educated Ashkenazis like myself. This theme, a recurring one in Israeli party politics, has been successfully invoked by the major right-wing party to win the votes of oriental Jews. Vidich and Bensman (1958b:4) observe that in Western society no reaction is to be expected when the ethnography deals with marginal or minority groups. In Israel, however, the poor and uneducated oriental population is somehow protected from public criticism, which can easily be construed by interested politicians as ethnic or even racial prejudice.

A few people read the book in order to form their own opinion, but the great majority of the public relied solely on information gathered from newspapers and formed their opinions on that basis. It appears that the higher a person's level of education, the greater was his ability and inclination to examine the facts independently (in this case by reading the book). The more educated individuals in the community were less likely to accept the newspaper account as the truth and more likely to take action beyond the confines of their immediate surroundings – by writing to the local or national press, for example.

There is a powerful relationship between self-esteem and a tendency to defend oneself and protest against criticism. In Israel, the correlation between oriental ethnic origin, low educational level, and low income has given rise to a paternalistic attitude on the part of the establishment toward the oriental communities. One of the by-products of this attitude has been low self-esteem among many of the uneducated oriental Jews who have no confidence in their ability to exert influence and to bring about change, and who therefore took no action with regard to my book even when they could have responded. This pattern of inactivity was evident in many aspects of life, some of which are discussed in *A Development Town Visited*. The general lack of active response upon reading the article in the local paper is symptomatic of this syndrome.[3]

On the other hand, when those suffering from low self-esteem imagine that their weakness is being pointed out, they are apt to react strongly. In the development town under discussion, many of the public officeholders had little formal education. The leader of the municipal opposition, who held a senior administrative position in the college although lacking a complete academic education, was quick to ridicule my doctor's title as well as my discipline as part of his defense of himself and his community.

While responses differed depending on factors such as public role and level of education, there were nevertheless a few issues around which objections were fairly uniform. One of these was my discussion of family ties and obligations. Not every issue will arouse the same intensity of objection, and they will vary from one culture to the next. In Israel, the family is clearly a sensitive topic.[4]

The role of the family in the national myth has, over the years, undergone several changes that have been bound up with the complex pattern of relationships between Ashkenazi and oriental Israelis. In the initial period of statehood, emphasis was placed by official ideology on the individual's commitment to society, whereas the importance of family attachment was considerably muted.

Later years brought with them a change in official attitudes toward the culture of oriental Jews in general, and toward the place of the family in that culture in particular. This change was due to complex sociopolitical processes. An accumulation of sociological knowledge stressed the importance of social continuity for the successful absorption and social adaptation of immigrants, and explained the central role played by the stability of the community and the family in the process of social integration. In a parallel development, political changes brought the "attitude toward oriental Jews" to the forefront of party political struggles, with the main right-wing party successfully turning it into a major election issue. The primary argument was that the time had come to respect once again the neglected honor of oriental Jews by, among other means, fostering their special culture, and by respecting their traditions.

As a result, there has been a revival in the value attached to the family. Whereas during the early years an effort was made to "modernize" the oriental Jews, recent years have seen a glorification of the "good qualities" of oriental ethnic groups (as a result of both social consciousness and political manipulation). Among the components that form this romantic-nostalgic idealization is the extended, warm, supportive family. This image plays its part in the newly acquired ethnic pride among some of the orientals. To question its validity in public discussion is unacceptable, although in private many orientals admit that reality falls far short of the ideal type. Nevertheless,

a description perceived to be critical of an important component of the recently established community pride (in this case also ethnic pride) causes an emotion-laden response.

As Brettell points out in the introduction to this volume, sensitivity on the part of an investigated community to its public image has been noted by other anthropologists following reactions to the publication of their research. Scheper-Hughes, for example, reports that people do not object to the distortion of reality, but rather to seeing it in print. They are willing to accept her writing about them – even if it is critical – as long as it is not widely published, even though this is intended to benefit them.[5] Conversely, criticism of public institutions such as schools or a health clinic is readily accepted because responsibility is easily assigned to outsiders, in particular to government offices and officials. It is, in short, the violation of self-image, that brings about the stormiest reactions.

Conclusion:
The Press as Mediator

Newspapers played a leading role in shaping the response to the publication of *A Development Town Visited*. Most of Kiryat Shmona's residents would not have heard about the book's publication had it not been for the appearance of the article. Without the journalist's subjective and tendentious interpretation there would have been no public outcry.[6]

Anthropological literature provides us with several examples of the manner in which the press magnifies the resonance of a research report, selectively publishing certain sections in an endeavor to provoke the interest of readers. Renato Rosaldo (1989:63) describes the reactions to his research among the Ilongot in the Philippines, while Gmelch (1992) had a similar experience in Ireland. The account extensively reported in the introduction to the present volume of the Italian media representation of Schneider's work strikes a familiar note, as does Wrobel's (1979) account of his treatment by the Detroit press.[7]

The conflict between the anthropologist and the journalist arises out of a discrepancy of interests and a different professional ethic. First, the journalist is guided by a goal of drawing maximum attention to his product. In some cases this is achieved by distorting the facts in order to create a more sensational effect. Second, his professional ethic allows him to make value judgments on the material he presents. Some journalistic ideologies (e.g., "new journalism" [DeFleur and Dennis 1981]) go so far as to encourage the journalist to express his own subjective opinions. Many journalists thus find it difficult to understand the complex approach of the anthropologist, who can respect the people he or she researches while at the same time describing and analyzing their behavior from a neutral perspective. The anthropologist does not make judgments, whereas the journalist in many cases does. The work of the anthropologist is thus evaluated according to journalistic criteria. This results in misunderstanding.

The press is often perceived by the public as a representative of society and its product as a reliable reflection of reality. The question of whether a certain event really did take place (in our case, whether the book actually contains derogatory material) becomes largely irrelevant. Most people will not bother to read the original book or article, as they "know what is written there already." The information that sticks is that put out by the media.

The media's version of the "truth" becomes the issue under discussion as the publication galvanizes an aggregation of individuals into a community under attack, seeking to defend its honor. The debate takes on a life of its own beyond the control of the ethnographer, and around issues (in this case the role of the family in Israel and the status of various ethnic groups) that may not even have been central in the original text.

What happened after the publication of *A Development Town Visited* is yet another instance of how the press shapes reality. As early as the 1920s Lippmann (1922) was aware of the communication media's ability to create their own version of reality. Consequently, people do not react to objective reality, but to an environment perceived through the media. More recently, theoreticians (including neo-Marxists) have discussed the "constructing of reality." According to them, the mass communication media necessarily present a nonobjective picture of reality and thus affect the moral and ideological perception of what is "really going on." For example, if a certain unusual phenomenon is presented from the conservative viewpoint of social consensus, the coverage will tend, indirectly, to denigrate the deviant phenomenon, thereby affirming the existing consensus (Cohen 1972). This "spiral of silence" theory (Noelle-Neumann 1974) maintains that the communication media not only form the image of reality, but actually intervene to play a part in forming reality itself by urging people to action or to passivity on the strength of distorted information. They thus bring about a result that would otherwise not have occurred (for example, people who do not bother to vote because they have been led by the press to believe that theirs is a lost cause). The press, in short, is a powerful factor influencing what happens when the people we write about read what we write.

NOTES

1 It would be possible to expand the discussion of the responses by including readers from outside the community, such as friends and fellow professionals. Here I focus primarily on the community in which the research was conducted and its variety of responses.

2 Criticism of me as a stranger and an outsider, although I am an indigenous anthropologist with shared citizenship, religion, and language, was very powerful. I was defined as an outsider because it was then easier to oppose my analysis, and to define it as emanating from ulterior motives for personal advancement. Evans-Pritchard (1968:173–4) describes the role of the mediator among the Nuer. This role is performed by a person belonging to one certain lineage who derives his authority from being an "outsider" (belonging to a specific lineage). To the outside observer, the mediator seems hardly to differ from other Nuer people, but from within he is an outsider. I find my position as "stranger" to be quite similar.

3 It is interesting to note that none of the town's inhabitants wrote to the national newspaper, although several had promised to do so. The sense of social distance proved decisive; the

townfolk did not feel sufficiently at ease or confident to contact the strange, "far-away" newspaper.

4 I had been apprehensive about objections that readers might voice with regard to my presentation of this topic, but I never imagined the intensity of the reactions. It must, however, be emphasized once more that the majority of those reacting in this manner had read only the commentary mediated by the press.

I admit to having had some misgivings about writing on the subject of a lack of family commitment, knowing that this would be a sensitive issue in Jewish culture in general, and among oriental Jews in particular. I was naive enough to believe that anyone reading the sociological explanations of this process would not regard my presentation of the phenomenon as an allocation of blame. Whereas the press's distortions came as a complete surprise, I could have foreseen that most of the local people would not read the book, but would merely seek a short summary of its contents, and would therefore have taken offense in any case. I was consciously thinking of a specific readership, made up of professionals and a slightly wider circle of interested general readers.

5 As an aside, I must admit to harboring some faint hope that the contents of the book would gain the attention of public authorities, who would then amend their policies in such a way as to bring about changes in phenomena such as apathy and lack of commitment. Unfortunately, I can report no such change of policy. What remains is the sense of humiliation and betrayal among residents.

6 Unless a local politician had learned of the book's publication, bothered to read it, and then used it to further his aims, I consider this an unlikely possibility.

7 I find a good deal of similarity between my experience and that of Wrobel, beginning with the quotes taken out of context, which lead the innocent reader to believe that the author was "blaming the victim," and continuing with the way in which other communications media took up and broadcast the issue. His reactions to the publication are also familiar, including the use of personal contacts to get friends from the community he researched to read the book, thereby gaining their understanding and moral support.

REFERENCES

Cohen, Stanley
  1972 *Folk Devils and Moral Panics*. London: McGibbon & Kee.
Evans-Pritchard, E. E.
  1968 (1940) *The Nuer*. Oxford: Clarendon Press.
Gmelch, Sharon
  1992 "From Beginning to End: An Irish Life History." *Journal of Narrative and Life History* 2 (1):29–38.
Lippmann, Walter
  1965 (1922) *Public Opinion*. New York: Free Press.
Noelle-Neumann, Elisabeth
  1974 "The Spiral of Silence: A Theory of Public Opinion." *Journal of Communication* 24 (1):43–51.
Rosaldo, Renato
  1989 *Culture and Truth: The Remaking of Social Analysis*. Boston: Beacon Press.
Vidich, Arthur J., and Joseph Bensman
  1958 "Freedom and Responsibility in Research: Comments." *Human Organization* 17 (4): 1–7.
Wrobel, Paul
  1979 *Our Way: Family, Parish and Neighborhood in a Polish-American Community*. Notre Dame: University of Notre Dame Press.

14

Ire in Ireland

Nancy Scheper-Hughes

Fulingeann fuil fuil I ngorta
ach Ni fhuilingeann fuil fuil a dortadh
[A man can tolerate his own blood starving to death, but he won't tolerate his blood
attacked by a stranger] (local proverb)

'A Hundred Thousand Welcomes' (Board Failte, *Irish Tourist Board*)

'Well, I am sorry to tell you, Nancy, but you are not welcome. No you are not. Have they let you a place to stay down in the village?' I was standing awkwardly in the once familiar doorway of 'Martin's' sturdy country house in a ruggedly beautiful mountain hamlet of An Clochan, a bachelor's outpost of some nine or ten vestigial farm households. Once, we had been good neighbors. During the summer of 1974, Martin had warded off the suspicions and dire warnings of his wary older sisters and had befriended us so far as to feel out my political sympathies toward various activities of the local IRA in which he and his extended family were involved. 'Ah, I should have listened to Aine', Martin said.

Over the past quarter of a century, some memories in An Clochan were engraved in stone like the family names of the Moriartys and the O'Neills carved over the smallest village shops in West Kerry signifying that *this* public house, *this* name, *this* family are forever. And what was remembered in this instance was a slight (in village terms, a slander) committed by me against the good name of the community. Ever the proud nationalist, Martin warned me to stay clear of village institutions: 'You'll not be expecting any mail while you are here', he said rather ominously.

Martin still cut a dashing, if compact, figure, now sporting a pair of gold wire-rimmed designer eye glasses and dressed on that

Nancy Scheper-Hughes, "Ire in Ireland," pp. 117–40 from *Ethnography* 1(1), 2000. This article is drawn from the preface and epilogue of Nancy Scheper-Hughes's 20th anniversary updated and expanded edition of *Saints, Scholars and Schizophrenics: Mental Illness in Rural Ireland*, University of California Press (2001). Copyright © 2001 by The Regents of the University of California. Reprinted by permission of the University of California Press.

Ethnographic Fieldwork: An Anthropological Reader, Second Edition. Edited by
Antonius C. G. M. Robben and Jeffrey A. Sluka.
Editorial material and organization © 2012 John Wiley & Sons, Inc.
Published 2012 by John Wiley & Sons, Inc.

afternoon in an impeccably starched white shirt. A shiny new sedan was parked outside his door. Martin's bachelor household, shared on the odd weekend with an older sister who works in the city, had clearly prospered over the past 2 decades. But all traces of active engagement with the land are gone. There was no sign of the haying that should have been going on during those precious few warm and sunny days in mid-June. No symmetrical mound of soft, boggy turf stood in front of the farm house. A quick side-long glance to the right showed the barn standing empty and swept clean. Above all, the neat row of newly laundered clothing strung across the outdoor line included no work-a-day overalls or denim shirts. What was once an active and viable farm had become a gentlemanly country home, a far cry from the days of Martin's youth when his beloved 'Da', the patriarch of a large household, rose early on winter mornings and went down to the sea to gather crannach, dilisk, carageen and other native edible seaweeds, half-freezing in his shirt-tails and warming himself by beating his sturdy arms across his chest. This, mind you, accomplished before the *real* work day of the farm had begun.

When Martin was still a very young man an older and more robust brother was sent off to America to make room for Martin, one of the younger and more vulnerable sons, to take up the family farm. Although primogeniture was then still customary, the father-patriarch had the freedom to choose his primary heir among his sons, according to his perceptions of his sons' skills, personalities, aptitudes and needs, as well as his and his wife's needs as they grew older. And the Da had settled upon Martin. But during the man's life-time, farming ceased being an enviable way of life and sibling jealousy had turned to sympathy toward those who were left behind to till the small 'rock farms' of An Clochan. And Martin's diasporic siblings had fared exceedingly well, numbering among them college teachers and clergy.[1]

Aine, the older sister, scowling while drying a plate and peering over Martin's shoulder, came out of the back of the house to give me a scolding: 'Who made you such an authority? You weren't such a grand person when you and your family came to live in our bungalow.

You could hardly control your own children. Why don't you go home and write about your own troubles. God knows, you've got plenty of them, with school children shooting each other and US planes bombing hospitals in Kosovo. Why pick on us?'

Martin interjected: 'Admit it. You wrote a book to please yourself at our expense. *You ran us down, girl, you ran us down.* You call what you do a science?' And before I could deny that I did, he continued, 'A science, to be sure, the science of scandals. We warn our village children before they go off to the university in Cork or Dublin to beware books about Ireland written by strangers.' Seeing that his words had found their mark and tears were coursing freely down my cheeks, Martin softened his stance a bit, but not his sister who roundly rejected my apologies: 'You say you are sorry, but we don't believe it. Those are crocodile tears! You are just crying for yourself.'

Breaking the mood, Martin turned to my adult son, Nate, who was busy trying to hide himself in a thick hedge near the barn. Martin's words were soft and courtly: 'You are a fine looking lad to be sure, Nate, and I'm sorry to be talking to your mother like this in your presence.' Then, he returned his gaze to me: 'Sure, nobody's perfect, nobody's a saint. We all have our weaknesses. But you never wrote about our strengths. You never said what a beautiful and a safe place our village is. You never wrote about the vast sweep of the eye that the village offers over the sea and up to Conor Pass. You said nothing about our fine musicians and poets, and our step dancers who move through the air with the grace of a silk thread. And we are not such a backwater today. There are many educated people among us. You wrote about our troubles, all right, but not about our strengths. What about the friendliness of neighbors? What about our love for Mother Ireland and our proud work of defending it?' When I protested that I could not have written about those radical activities for fear of reprisals from outside against the village, Martin replied: 'Ah, you were only protecting yourself.' 'Is there *anything* I can do?' I asked. 'You should have thought about that before. Look, girl, the fact is that ya *just didn't give us credit.*'

Homecoming

Twenty-five years had elapsed since a young and somewhat brash anthropologist and her off-beat, counter-cultural family – shaggy-haired, gentle 'hippie' husband and their three rambunctious babies and toddlers – stumbled somewhat dazed and almost by default into the relatively isolated, rugged mountain community of 'Ballybran' just over the spectacularly beautiful Conor Pass through the Slieve Mish mountains past the Maharees and nestled on the shores of Brandon Bay, a cul de sac on the eastern end of the Dingle Peninsula in West Kerry.

It was late spring 1974 and we had reached the end of the line, figuratively *and* literally. We had spent several weeks in a rented car canvassing villages in West Kerry and West Cork in search of an Irish-speaking (though bilingual) community kind enough to accept our presence for a year of live-in fieldwork. We would begin our tentative inquiries about securing housing with the local post mistress or the resident curate or parish priest only to be told that people living in this or that community would not much fancy being observed by a live-in stranger. Ethnographic fieldwork was still a new and alien concept for a country people known both for their spectacular hospitality and for their fierce family loyalty and privacy. Tourists who came and went for the brief salmon-fishing season on the Dingle Peninsula were one thing, and bothersome enough in their own way, but a resident writer-anthropologist was something else again. In a country dedicated both to the banning of books *and* to revering the written word, any writer learns to tread lightly and to have a quick exit plan.

On arriving for the first time in 'Ballybran' I introduced myself and my family to the young curate of the spectacularly beautiful 'half-parish' with some trepidation. My official documents failed to dazzle this down-to-earth curate. What *did* make a difference were letters from our local university chaplain vouching that Michael and I were 'good enough' Catholics, if perhaps a bit wayward in our post-Vatican II enthusiasms for the transformation of Mother Church, and an almost illegible note from an older friend and informal mentor, the late Canon Law scholar, David Daube, stating that we were trustworthy and decent people. And so, ironically, with the sponsorship and blessing of the same Irish Catholic Church that I would take to task in the pages of my book, we settled into Ballybran a few weeks before the feast of Corpus Christi in June 1974 and we stayed until late spring the following year.

A Fine Touch of Irish Madness

I arrived in Ballybran with a starting set of altogether alien and 'outsider' questions. Why did the Irish claim the highest rates of hospitalized mental illness in the world? Why was schizophrenia the primary diagnosis used in mental hospitals there? I believed that by studying 'madness' I could learn something about the nature of Irish society and culture as a whole. Deeply influenced by the early writings of Michel Foucault, I believed that a society revealed itself most in the phenomena it excludes, rejects and confines. Irish madness, I hypothesized, could be seen as a projection of specifically Irish conflicts and themes.

What was going on in remote, supposedly bucolic, western Ireland that was over-producing so many young psychiatric cases? Who were the likely candidates for mental hospital? What were the events that led up to a psychiatric crisis? Did the Irish actually have *more* mental illness than elsewhere, or were they simply more likely to label a village non-conformist as mad? Was the straight and narrow of Irish country life so rigid that it led to a straitjacket for some? What was going on in Irish farm families, and in the public spaces of village life, schools, pubs and church?

The book that emerged, *Saints, Scholars and Schizophrenics: Mental Illness in Rural Ireland* (1979), was a blend of old and new approaches: child rearing and adult personality, TAT tests, and reflexive/interpretive anthropology. Theoretically eclectic, it applied insights from Freud, Erikson, Durkheim, Gregory Bateson, R. D. Laing, and Michel Foucault to a tiny population of Irish-speaking farmers, shepherds and fishermen. Using the heterodox field methods of a qualitative and interpretive ethnographer, I amassed a great deal of circumstantial evidence supporting the pathogenicity of certain aspects of rural Irish social relations, especially those between the sexes and between parents and children. Rural Ireland, I concluded, was a place where it was difficult to be 'sane' and where 'normal' villagers could appear more 'deviant' than those institutionalized in the County Kerry mental hospital.

Madness was, I argued, a social script and there were appropriate and inappropriate ways of 'going' and 'being' mad in rural Ireland. Extreme eccentricity was allowable, even coddled, if it could pass as harmless 'foolery' or if it came wrapped in the mantle of Irish spirituality. 'Mihal, bless him, hasn't been quite right since the death of his mother, but what harm if he sits up all night in the barn singing to the cows?' Mihal would never see the walls of St Finian's madhouse. But there would be no excuses made for Seamus, the reluctant 44-year-old bachelor who expressed *his* frustration at a parish dance by leaping to the stage and drunkenly exposing himself to a crowd of village girls. He, of course, was quite mad.

Central to my thesis was the image of a dying and anomic rural Ireland resulting from the cumulative effects of British colonization, the Great Famine (1845–9), and various 20th-century development and 'modernization' schemes that tied the economy of rural western Ireland to Great Britain and then, with Ireland's belated entry into the European Community in 1973, to western Europe, as a whole. Throughout the process, the final vestiges of a subsistence-based peasant economy were destroyed to make way for capitalist modes and relations of production. The symptoms of malaise that I was observing in the mid-1970s were many: population decline in the coastal western villages resulting from out-migration and permanent celibacy; widespread welfare dependency of young, displaced farmers, shepherds and fishermen; depression, alcoholism and episodes of madness pushing up the Irish psychiatric hospitalization rates into first place worldwide.

Beneath the quaint thatched roofs and between the thick, clay walls of the rural farm households what was going on was an extraordinary emotional drama of labeling and denial that allowed some Irish country children (especially daughters and first-born sons) to achieve full adult status, education and eventual emancipation from the family, while consigning other children (especially latter-born sons) to the status of the 'leftover', worthless and pathetic *'aindeiseoir'* of the family. Every rural family seemed to have its high-achieving first-born pet sons and its under-achieving, last-born backward and painfully shy bachelors and its hopeless and stigmatized black sheep. Parental aspirations for achievement and status rested with the first-born, and everything was sacrificed to improve his life chances. In the 'old days' when farming was still a valued and productive way of life, he would have inherited the farm. But with Ireland's entry into the European Economic Community, the prized first-born was being reared for export, for emigration.

The rural Irish parents were faced with a new problem: how to keep back at least one son for the farm and to care for them in their old age. The task involves a certain amount of psychological violence: a cutting down to size and a crippling of the aspirations of the designated farm heir. In collaboration with village teachers, shopkeepers and the parish priest, farm parents tended to create a 'sacrificial child', oddly enough not in the form of the disinherited and dispossessed child, but in the more lethal and ambiguous form of the farm heir. From the time of his birth the heir is labeled 'the left over', 'the last of the litter', 'the scraping of the pot', 'the runt', 'the old cow's calf', a child who could never survive beyond the tolerant and familial confines of the village. 'Blessed are the meek', it is written, 'for they shall inherit the earth' ... and with it (I wanted to add) a life of involuntary celibacy, poverty, obedience and self-negating service to the old ones.

Through shaming and ridicule the farm heir eventually grows to fit his reduced role and life chances, and he comes to think of himself as only good enough for the farm and for the village, places generally thought of as not very good at all. Often enough the boy is able to make the necessary accommodations to his role. I have always been struck, even early in my anthropological career, by the enormous resilience and elasticity of the human spirit despite the violence that culture and society so often visit upon it. And there *were*, at least in the case of rural Ireland, some compensations and rewards: the boy who stays behind is praised as the dutiful, loyal, 'saint' of a son.

Some farm heirs never adjusted to the demands made of them and they aged poorly, becoming angry, isolated, bitter individuals, cut off from the flow of human life. Some became the depressed and alcoholic bachelor farmers who populated the several pubs that cater to a population of just 400 and some villagers. Others became eccentric hermits, and still others who deviated too far from the straight and narrow of village life became psychiatric patients at St Finian's Mental Hospital in Killarney. Many of these men were preoccupied with paranoid fears of bodily encroachment or obsessed with unfulfilled sexual and generative needs and fantasies.

Why didn't they escape? Some would have if they could, but too often they conceded to the prevailing view of themselves as incomplete men, lacking something, a bit too soft. To his face I've heard it said of a dedicated stay-at-home son: 'Sure our Paddy is a big old slob of a man, soft and sentimental, full of *dutcas*' (i.e. referring to warm, almost maternal, fellow feeling) while the man in question would nod his head in agreement. Hence, the rural Irish 'double bind' – two contradictory injunctions – on the one hand: 'You're worthless, you can't live beyond the farm; sure, if you had any guts you would have been out of here years ago', and, on the other: 'We need you – you're all we have; how could you even think of leaving your poor old Da? You're the last hope we have!' A third injunction prevented any escape from the horns of the dilemma: Stay, but you are forever a boy-o; leave, but you are guilty of filial disloyalty. A powerful ideology in the form of a puritanical and authoritarian version of Catholicism bolstered the symbolic violence contained in the exploitative social and family systems.

I had reinterpreted Gregory Bateson's (Bateson et al., 1963) double-bind hypothesis of schizophrenia within a larger social context to show that not only individual families, but entire communities can participate in patterns of distorted communication that can harm the individual while rescuing the social system. Scapegoating, collusions, family myths, and 'bad faith relations' are found not only in dis-eased or 'weak' families but in vulnerable communities as well. Social and economic situations can be double-binding, so that hard pressed farm families are forced to engage in unfair tactics for self-preservation at the expense of the designated child, and the whole community can come to accept and reinforce such distorted 'family myths'. It was not my intention to 'blame' village parents, but rather to shed light on an aspect of the rural Irish collective unconscious so that, once recognized, the emancipation and liberation of the generative scapegoat – the 'good, stay-at-home' son – might be possible.

The 'Native' Reaction: Ethnography on the Couch

Ironically, no sooner was I notified in early 1980 that I was to receive the Margaret Mead Award from the Society for Applied Anthropology, honoring a book that 'communicated anthropological ideas and concepts to a broadly concerned public', than *Saints, Scholars and Schizophrenics* became embroiled in a large and lively trans-Atlantic controversy. The first critics of the book suggested that 'Ballybran' did not exist at all, and that it represents a 'composite', made up of bits and pieces of dozens of rural communities, both real and imagined. But in the fall of 1980 a columnist from the *Irish Times*, Michael Viney, headed out along the Dingle Peninsula, peddling his 10-speed mountain bicycle, buffeted by awesome gale winds and pelting sheets of rain in search of what he later described in one of his columns as the 'mythical valley of Ballybran'.

After a few false starts and cases of mistaken identity, Viney (1980) rejoiced on finally reaching his desired goal as he slipped inside the snug materiality of Peg's Pub. 'Yes', said the publican identifying herself, 'I was one [in the book] who didn't believe in sociological statistics!' 'Mrs Scheper-Hughes had sat here often', Viney mused with a pint of Guinness in his hand, 'as I was doing now, with the rain hosing down from the mountains beyond the open door.' In a subsequent column (1983), Viney pictured himself as he thought the anthropologist might have seen him:

> Sometimes – cycling over the hill to the post office, past the rusty, crumpled bracken and the lichen-crusted walls – I look down at the little houses (which are for my writerly purposes crouched in Atlantic mist) and wonder what the anthropologist would make of our community (or indeed, of *me*, a squinting, unkempt figure in black oilskins and dripping cap, alienated, irretrievably from his own urban peer group, the epitome of *anomie* on wheels). Would she decide that our remote half-parish ... have a whole new perspective on [its] right or ability to exist?'

Both the scholarly and the popular Irish and Irish-American communities were up in arms. The approach I was developing – a form of cultural critique – was seen as 'biased' and ethnocentric. Admittedly, my approach deviated from the usual anthropological manners which determined that we describe only what was 'good' and 'right' about a given society and culture. One was *not* to use anthropology in order to diagnose the ailing parts of the social body as a cultural pathologist of sorts. Why, I was asked, did my description of unhappy and conflict-ridden rural life depart so radically from Conrad Arensberg's (1937) classic and almost loving portrait of *The Irish Countryman*? In part, perhaps, because my ethnography was told, not from the perspective of the old men seated comfortably at the pub and at the hub of Irish country life, but from the perspective of their thwarted middle-aged sons. These were the 'young lads' and boy-os who would have to wait until their 50s, if lucky, to come of age and into their own, and even then they would have to wait, hand and foot, on the old ones who had retired to the 'west room' of the household and who, unlike their fathers before them, would most likely never marry, given the demographic imbalance [village girls had long since begun to desert the village lured by the promise of relative freedom that out-migration

represented] or have a family and therefore a power base of their own.

Saints, Scholars and Schizophrenics offered a counter-hegemonic view of Irish country life, but one that struck some sensibilities as 'anti-Irish', 'anti-Catholic', or 'anti-clerical'.[2] In her incisive review of my book for the progressive Catholic journal, *Commonweal*, Sidney Callahan (1979: 311) charged me with religious bias suggesting that I was 'strangely insensitive to the religious idealism of the people' and that 'my hostility to the sexual repressiveness of Irish Jansenism, a hostility always to be encouraged [presumably by secular humanists such as myself], had made [me] tone deaf in [my] interpretation of religious phenomena.' Where I had seen needless self-sacrifice, Callahan questioned whether some 'repressions weren't worth the price' and she suggested that 'wit, learning, music, the work ethic, and altruistic sacrifice for family and high ideals' might also flourish in Ireland exactly because sex, aggression, and individualism were so severely curtailed. If the rural Irish values of self-discipline and mortification of the flesh contribute to the isolation, celibacy, depression, madness and alcoholism of bachelor farmers, they might also account for the extremely low incidence in the Republic of Ireland of physical assault, rape, adultery and divorce.

Another Irish-American critic, Eileen Kane (1982), described *Saints* as 'unethical' in its violation of the 'privacy' of the community and its right to maintain its 'community secrets'. These refer to the 'best-kept and worst kept secrets' (Bourdieu, 1977: 173), the ones that everyone in the community must keep in order to ensure the complicity of all in the collective forms of bad faith that make social life possible, such as, in this instance, the symbolic violence against the farm heir masquerading as concern and generosity toward the poor, inept last born sons of the village. In my various responses I denied that anthropologists had a responsibility to honor *community* secrets, especially those protecting what Sartre (1956) meant by 'bad faith' relations.

In *From Anxiety to Method*, George Devereux (1977) observed that in the field, as on the couch, the dynamics of transference and counter-transference can shape the ethnographer's perceptions and the resulting analysis. Indeed, the field can loom as a large Rorschach test for the naive anthropologist. Lacking sufficient critical distance and reflexive insight, the result can be distortion in the form of glaring omissions, editing, ambiguous descriptions and so forth. Ethnographers may use the field to work out their own neurotic conflicts and anxieties about attachment, power, authority, sanity, gender or sexuality. Here, confrontation and projection, rather than avoidance and denial, can lead to distortion in the form of a highly subjective interpretation that does violence to the natives' own understanding of the meaning of their culture and social relations.

From time to time, Devereux cautioned, the ethnographer should pause to analyse the nature of the object relations in the field and at home throughout the process of data analysis and writing. The goal of such ethnological self-analysis was to expose and to strip away the layers of subjectivity and bias that get in the way and distort the perception of an objective ethnographic reality. To the end Devereux remained an empiricist dedicated to a belief in the perfectibility of objective anthropological facts, data and interpretation.

In the aftermath of the Irish controversy, I found Devereux's solution less than satisfying. For, as I saw it, the real dilemma and contradiction was this: How can we know what we know other than by filtering experience through the highly subjective categories of thinking and feeling that represent our own particular ways of being – such as the American Catholic-school-trained, rebellious though still ambivalently Catholic, post-Freudian, neo-Marxist, feminist woman I was in my initial encounter with the villagers of Ballybran.

Both the danger *and the value* of anthropology lie in the clash and collision of cultures and interpretations as the anthropologist meets her subjects in a spirit of open engagement, frankness and receptivity. There was, I concluded, no 'politically correct' way of doing anthropology. Anthropology is by nature intrusive and it entails a certain amount of symbolic and interpretive violence to the 'native' peoples' own intuitive, though still partial, understanding of their part of the world. The question then

becomes an ethical one: What are the proper relations between the anthropologist and her subjects? To whom does she owe her loyalties, and how can these be met in the course of ethnographic fieldwork and writing, especially within the problematic domain of psychological and psychiatric anthropology where the focus on disease and distress, difference and marginality, over-determine a critical view.

Getting Over: Crediting An Clochan

Over the past two decades, 'Ballybran' has been host to a small but steady stream of anthropologists and sociologists from Europe and North America – little red paperback of *Saints, Scholars and Schizophrenics* in hand – searching among the dispersed mountain hamlets for some of the key protagonists of the book. And so, the drama of hide-and-seek played between villagers and their various defenders, unabashed curiosity seekers and global interlocutors continues to this day.

Today, of course, neither 'Ballybran', anthropology, nor the ethnographer are what they were in the mid-1970s. The Ballybran that I describe here is barely recognizable. The last of the real thatched farm houses have been razed and modern suburban ranch style homes have appeared in their place. The only 'thatched cottage' in evidence is Nellie Brick's former tea-rashers-butter-and-bread shop now being renovated as a snug and romantic pub for the pleasure of tourists. The interior is rustic English countryside and the thatch has been imported from Poland. But the thatchers, at least, are from Killarney even if they learned their 'traditional' trade courtesy of a development grant from the European Union. Still, the thatch smells as sweet and inviting as ever, and some kind soul had thought to stick a cardboard sign on a window sill indicating 'Nellie's window', the vantage point from which the wonderful old wag had once kept tabs on the village world.

Still, were I to be writing the book for the first time and with hindsight, of course there are things I would do differently. I would be inclined to avoid the 'cute' and 'conventional' use of pseudonyms. Nor would I attempt to scramble certain identifying features of the individuals portrayed on the naive assumption that these masks and disguises could not be rather easily de-coded by villagers themselves. I have come to see that the time-honored practice of bestowing anonymity on 'our' communities and informants fools few and protects no one – save, perhaps, the anthropologist's own skin. And I fear that the practice makes rogues of us all – too free with our pens, with the government of our tongues, and with our loose translations and interpretations of village life.

Anonymity makes us unmindful that we owe our anthropological subjects the same degree of courtesy, empathy and friendship in writing as we generally extend to them face to face in the field where they are not our 'subjects' but our boon companions without whom we quite literally could not survive. Sacrificing anonymity means we may have to write less poignant, more circumspect ethnographies, a high price for any writer to pay. But our version of the Hippocratic oath – to do no harm, in so far as possible, to our informants – would seem to demand this. Additionally, a hermeneutics of (self-) doubt could temper our brutally frank sketches of other people's lives as we see them, close-up but always from the outside looking in and 'through a glass darkly'.

As for the selectivity of my observations, what I had left out and what I might have said about An Clochan in the mid-1970s was that the village offered an extraordinary glimpse of a closed corporate rural community in which social hierarchy and social difference were successfully curtailed, where 'putting on airs' was spurned in the interests of *communitas* and where, despite the general rule of farm family patriarchy, girls were reared to be high achievers, women did *not* have to marry, and single women could raise sheep, drive cows, manage a village pub, run a primary or secondary school, scold the local gombeen man, or boss the local curate till he 'cried uncle' and gave in on a particular theological or political point. Rural women could choose to marry young or they could wait and marry late in life and then marry men much younger than themselves. Alternatively, especially in a family of

daughters, they could refuse several marriage proposals in order to remain at home and inherit their father's fields and his favorite pipe or their father's pub and his celebrated goat-skin drum. Moreover, married women kept their maiden names *and* their pre-marital social and self identities.

Perhaps nowhere else in the world were women so free to walk country roads at night without fear of either physical assault or malicious gossip. Nowhere else have I seen women and men banter with each other in public without every source of humor reduced to a double-entendre. And nowhere else were bachelors and spinsters accepted as normal and unremarkable members of society, able to lead autonomous, if lonely, lives. No eyebrows were raised at the bachelor who not only planted and harvested but also cooked his own spuds, who not only raised his own sheep but was quite capable of knitting his own socks and sweater. How distant this was from Ivan Illich's (1982: 67) description of the woeful state of bachelors in those parts of traditional Europe more characterized by gender 'complementarity':

You could recognize the bachelor from afar by his stench and gloomy looks…. Solitary men left no sheets or shirts when they died…. A man without a wife, sister, mother, or daughter had no way to make, wash, and mend his clothes; it was impossible for him to keep chickens or to milk a goat.

In An Clochan at the time of my study social life was not confined to couples. Dress for both sexes was casual and the sturdy figure ahead of you on the road wrapped in layers of trousers, woolen vests, long coat and shod in muddy green Wellington boots, and waving a stick, was just as likely to be that of a woman 'driving' her small herd of cows. I may have misread important aspects of social life in a community where *gender* and *sibling* bonding was as or more important than the sexual or the erotic bond. If marital relations were problematic it was in part because marriage interrupted and intruded upon other competing and equally valued affections and loyalties. Surely any anthropologist practicing today would not wish to suggest a hierarchy of appropriate affections such that life-long friendships, brotherly and sisterly in nature, would somehow count for less than conjugal relations.

If psychiatric hospitalization rates were high, rape and sexual assault were unknown at that same time. Theft was so rare that one definition of an eccentric was a person who was overly preoccupied about the safety of his property, while a case of 'paranoid schizophrenia' could be diagnosed on the grounds of having accused one's neighbors of wanting to steal one's sheep or cows or having shifted the stone boundaries that mark off one field from another. And 'Brendan the rapist' who I interviewed at the county mental hospital in Killarney had sinned only in his thoughts and was by his own account a virgin, unlucky in sex. So, as a young married woman in An Clochan, I could hail a ride on the back of Morris's motorbike without any hint of scandal, just as I could sit and talk with the local curate over a mid-morning cup of tea in his living room with the priest still in his pajamas.

House-keeping, gardening and meal-preparation were kept to a minimum, thus freeing both women and men for other voluntary activities and a good deal of leisure time that was spent in fostering friendship and conviviality – for men in one of several village pubs, at local sheep fares and regional markets, and for women in shops, church and school related activities, and for older women and widows in house calls to friends and far-out kin. There was time out for story-telling and time out for play. There was time to gather around deaths, wakes and funerals – a full day was given over for the funerals of each of the 38 villagers who died during 1974–5. Everyone had radios and some owned televisions, but most people still preferred 'live entertainment' and they gathered frequently, especially during the winter, at pubs, church halls and in each other's homes to entertain themselves with their own music, singing, step-dancing, and poetry recitation. Both young and old, male and female, were encouraged to develop their own repertoire of songs, recitations, or 'steps' which they could be called on to perform at the drop of a hat. Though the shyness

and modesty of bachelors could be heart-breaking, the institutionalized pattern of 'coaxing' could bring even the most reluctant fisherman or shepherd to perform his 'party piece' and shine before his peers.

The ethic of modesty and deference assured that no one singer ever stood out or sought undue attention. Meanwhile, the reciprocal call and response mode – 'Sing us a song, Paddy'; 'Oh, I couldn't', etc. – allowed for the limited expression of praise and appreciation which could always destabilize into 'codding' – 'Sure, he's the best singer in the village'. Together these promoted a strong sense of community solidarity at the expense of the individual, aimed as they were at suppressing any hint of unseemly arrogance or self-importance. In other words, social equality was fostered through the very same witty games of 'codding', 'giving the mickey' and 'having a crack' which I had described in *Saints and Scholars* as having a decidedly adverse effect on the more psychologically vulnerable individuals who were less able to evaluate and respond appropriately to the 'double-binding' messages they carried. To wit: refuse the praise and you are putting a damper on the high spirits of your companions; accept the praise and you appear the fool for taking it seriously.

Gregory Bateson, who had developed the 'double bind' theory of schizophrenia that I used in my book, understood that human communication patterns were extremely complex and that some double-binding injunctions were damaging to certain individuals while some were beneficial, even therapeutic to others. The verbal duels and interactional challenges so characteristic of rural Irish wit may have contributed to the cognitive dissonance suffered by Irish schizophrenics unable to differentiate literal from metaphorical truth. But just as surely these communication patterns contributed to the development of Ireland's long tradition of saints, poets and scholars as well.

So, while I told the anecdote about the cruel codding in the pub of a shy bachelor who was teased unmercifully about his inability to speak to me without stammering, I failed to tell the anecdote about the day of our leave-taking from the village when I saw out my front window the very same painfully shy man standing under a tree at the bottom of the little path that led up to our cottage. I wondered what he was doing there, 'loitering' for such a long time. I went about my packing and house-cleaning, but each time I passed the window I saw him standing there, so still, hardly changing his posture. Finally, after a few hours, it occurred to me that perhaps he was waiting for me to come down the path on my way to the village after an errand. So, I packed up the babies into strollers and backpacks and we made our way down the path as if on our way to the village post office. As I came close to Paddy, I shyly lifted a finger and crooked my neck at him in the traditional, understated Kerryman greeting at which Paddy came forward and put out his hand which I clasped in both of mine as he said: 'You're leaving us. I just wished ... wanted ... well ... God bless you, Mum. And God bless Michael and the wee ones, too.' In all my many comings and goings as an anthropologist, there was no goodbye that I have held as dear over the many years as this one which had been wrested from the giver with so much difficulty.

The supreme irony is that the anthropologist who has always been in search of a relatively classless, genderless, egalitarian society, had stumbled on to one early in her career without ever recognizing it as such or singing its praises in this regard. This village egalitarianism was expressed as well in the painful decisions that had to be made about inheritance, the argument that was so central to my thesis. While these decisions never came easily to either generation, parents or children, in the end they were decided with a strong commitment to fairness and with attention to correcting the unwitting losses experienced by one sibling at the hands of the other. Unlike rural English patterns of primogeniture based on a 'winner takes all' model, Irish farm families always strived to settle each of their 'disinherited' sons and daughters with some kind of life security – whether through carefully sought after connections with potential patrons in commerce and the trades in the next town (see Arensberg, 1937) or through the Catholic Church and its extensive web of educational and social welfare institutions, or

through helpful relatives and former neighbors abroad – so that virtually no 'disinherited' Irish child was sent out into the world to 'seek their fortune' alone as had so many generations of 'disinherited' rural English children (*see* Birdwell-Pheasant, 1998). Consequently, the 'traveling' and diasporic Irish, including over the generations a great many from the little parish of An Clochan, have contributed, disproportionately, to the culture and civilization of the larger English-speaking world (see Hout, 1989: chapter 5; Keneally, 1998). For all these reasons and for whatever it could possibly matter now – all credit to An Clochan.

Crediting Ethnography

To begin with, I wanted that truth to life to possess a concrete reliability, and I rejoiced most when the poem seemed most direct, an up front representation of the world it stood in for or stood up for or stood its ground against. (Heaney, 1995:12)

At the heart of the anthropological method is the practice of witnessing, which requires an engaged immersion over time in the lived worlds of our anthropological subjects. Like poetry, ethnography is an act of translation and the kind of 'truth' that it produces is necessarily deeply subjective, resulting from the collision between two worlds and two cultures. And so, the question often posed to anthropologist-ethnographers about the dangers of 'losing one's objectivity' in the field is really quite beside the point. Our task requires of us only a highly disciplined subjectivity. There are scientific methods and models appropriate to other ways of doing anthropological research, but ethnography, as I understand it, is not a science.

Very much like the poet who decides to enter another oeuvre for the purpose of translation – Seamus Heaney, for example, describing his entering the poetry of Dante[3] – the anthropologist sees something in another world that intrigues them. It can be as simple as 'Oh, I like that! Let me see if I can't understand how that particular mode of being and thinking and feeling and sensing the world works, the sense it makes, the logic and the illogic of it, the pragmatics and the poetics of that other way of life.' And so we think, 'Yes, I'll go there for a while and see if I can't come back with a narrative, a natural history, a thick description – call it what you will – that will enrich our ways of understanding the world'. Like any other form of 'translation' ethnography has a predatory and writerly motive to it. It is not done 'for nothing' in a totally disinterested way. It is *for* something, often it is to help us understand something – whether it is about schizophrenia as a projection of cultural themes or about ways of solving perennial human dilemmas around the reproduction of bodies and families and homes and farms.

In referring to his own long-term project of translating the Beowulf, Seamus Heaney (1999) drew on a generative metaphor based on the Viking relationship between England and Ireland, distinguishing between the historical period known as the Viking raids and the period known as the settlement. The raid, he said, is a very good motive for poetic translation. The poet can raid Italian or German poetry and come back with a kind of 'booty' called 'imitations' of Homer or Virgil, for example. Or, alternatively – as Heaney did with the Beowulf translation – the poet can approach the translation through 'settlement', that is, entering the oeuvre, 'colonizing' it, taking it over for one's artistic purposes. In settling in with the work, you stay with it a long time, identify with it in an imaginative way. You change it and it changes you.

Similarly, there are 'raiding' and 'settlement' ways of doing the work of anthropological translation, although granted both these metaphors play on our discipline's worst nightmares. Neither raiders nor settlers have much currency in the parts of the post-colonial world where most of us still work. In our vocabulary, 'raiding' is what Margaret Mead sometimes did – going in and after a culture in order to raid an idea, a practice that could be useful to young mothers in Boston or to adolescents in Los Angeles. Another form of raiding is the kind of 'quick and dirty' research we sometimes conduct with a specific goal, such as evaluating an AIDS prevention program in Botswana or a child survival program in Northeast Brazil for a governmental or international agency. Quick and dirty – a raid, if you will – but necessary at times and valuable in its own right.

And, then, there is ethnography and participant observation – the settlement metaphor par excellence. Here we enter, settle down, and try to stay for as long as people will tolerate our presence. As 'travelling people' we are at the mercy of those who agree to take us in as much as they are at our mercy in the ways we represent them after the living-in and living-with is over. Anthropologists are a restless and nomadic tribe, hunters and gatherers of human values. Often we are motivated by our own sense of estrangement from the society and culture into which we were existentially thrown. I went to rural Ireland, in no small part, in search of better ways to live and I found these especially among some of the old ones with whom I spent the greater part of my days and long winter evenings in An Clochan and who, perhaps, biased me toward an overly critical view of village life in the mid-1970s.

Rabbit Run: Taking Leave

The fateful visit with Martin spelled the beginning of the end of my return to An Clochan. By the next day I was beginning to feel the weight of social censure closing in, not so much on me personally, as on those in the village who had taken me in – in the village vernacular who had 'fed me and kept me' – or had taken me under their wing. When S., for example, arrived to meet me for breakfast the next morning, she was in a state of considerable agitation. She had not slept well the previous night. 'I was awakened', she said, 'by a terrible nightmare. Oh, it was an awful sensation, as if my house was being invaded by a dark force, an ill-wind, or an alien invader.' She looked hesitantly to me for a clue to her ominous dream. I replied only that houses were often symbols of the body and of the self and left it at that.

But that night it was my turn to be awakened by a ghostly visitation, a hooded creature who pointed a long skinny finger over and beyond my head and toward the sea. Like Scrooge, I was happy to find myself unchanged in the morning and I suppressed the urge to hug the wooden bedstead promising: 'I am *not* the woman I was, I am not the woman I was'. But I knew this to be untrue in certain fundamental ways. And I took out my little notebook – the one that would ultimately prove to be my undoing – and jotted down a few ragged thoughts.

Shaken, I continued my daily rounds of the village, by now heavy of heart, and uncertain of step. I waved to a solitary hay-maker, the first one I'd seen in several days. He did not recognize me and he stopped to take a break. Making small talk I asked why the man took such care in making several small little hay cocks rather than larger haystacks. 'Because the hay is much sweeter this way and it pleases the animals more', he replied, tipping his cap as I walked along. After the visit with Martin I began to walk the country roads with my head bowed, practicing a government of my eyes so as not to elicit an automatic greeting from those who might later regret it. And I took to announcing myself at the open door of older friends and acquaintances: 'It's Crom Dubh, the crooked one, come back to An Clochan.' Indeed, I *was* beginning to feel very much like Crom Dubh, the pagan force and alter-ego of the village who epitomized everything dark, hidden, secret, and overgrown, tangled among the brambles of the old graveyard – everything that needed to be resisted. My presence was a daily reminder – 'salt in the wound' said one villager – of everything they would like to hide, deny and secret away.

In fact, however, most villagers did not avoid me. Many fell back into the old habit of telling me poignant stories and catching me up on people, events and changes in the parish. At times there seemed to be a pressure, even a hunger to speak. Kathleen shook her head one evening: 'You are like the village analyst and we are all on the couch. We can't seem to stop ourselves from talking.' It made no difference that I was not back looking for secrets, for there was simply no way of escaping them. Since I had no other reason for being in the village except to visit with people, my presence became something of an obstacle, even to myself. In this small world, words were as dangerous as hand grenades or bullets, as

much for those who gave as for those who received them.

An older couple took the risk of going about with me in public at considerable social risk to themselves. It was, they said, the Christian thing to do, and never mind what others thought or said. Aiden even appointed himself my colleague in arms and after an afternoon of making house calls together, he commented wearily: 'Ah, but this fieldwork is tiring'. But as the situation grew more prickly I asked the new priest of An Clochan to help me call a parish meeting so that I could apologize in general terms for any pain I caused the community and so that villagers who wished could collectively express their anger. Then, I hoped, naively perhaps, we could clear the air and move forward. I explained how difficult it was to try to do this work of repentance and explanation door to door. The priest was unsure, however. 'Will you be up for it?' he mused. 'And will *they* be up for it? Is this drawing too much attention to an old hurt? Should you apologize? Would this be a good thing?' The good priest promised to mull it over with a few confidants in the community and he promised to get back in touch with me. 'But come to Mass this Sunday', he urged. When, a few days later, I approached the Communion line, Father M. held the Host up high and looked about him reciting my name very loudly, indeed: 'Nancy, receive the body and blood of Christ'. But after Mass he said that a parish meeting would be too risky and that I should just continue as I was doing, making my rounds, door to door, the best I could. As I walked home alone from Mass I wondered how much longer I should stay.

The 'drumming' out of the village, when it came, was swift. There were warning signs a few days before that trouble was brewing. Conversation would suddenly stop when I entered a pub, and I would smile weakly and turn on my heels. During an afternoon drive I was taken past a few sites that had been subject to local harassment, including car and house bombings. No one had ever been hurt in these attacks, but the damage to property was considerable and the message conveyed was clear. The parish was controlled, in part, by threats and intimidation by a small but active group of local cultural nationalists. Among the kinds of people 'unwanted' in the village were British landowners, suspected homosexuals, purported drug dealers, 'gombeen men' (local petty capitalists who bought up old farms) and me, that new species of traitor and friend, the anthropologist.

My local friends were shaken by the tide of rejection, and they were understandably conflicted by divided loyalties. On the last evening of my stay in An Clochan I returned to my B&B filled with stories to share. It had been a good day and I had managed to make contact with some dear old acquaintances. My flagging spirits were on the rebound. But as I popped my head into the kitchen to tell B. that I'd be down for tea in a few minutes, she turned from the stove with a face that was flushed by more than the gas burners. 'I have some terrible news', she blurted. 'Is something wrong at home?' I asked, clutching at my throat. 'Did something happen to Michael or one of the children?' 'No, no, not that. But, Nancy, you have to leave. Right now. This evening. You can't eat here. You can't sleep here anymore.'

'Did I do something wrong?' I asked. 'Did I offend someone in the village today?' It was evening, I was dog-tired, and my feet were sore. I had no transportation. Was it even possible to call up a taxi from distant Tralee at this hour? 'Is there anyone else who can put you up tonight?', B. asked. 'Let me think', I said stupidly, 'while I go upstairs to pack.' In the little attic room I moved slowly as in a dream, folding my few things into the suitcase pulled out from under the bed. I hadn't eaten since morning and I had missed dinner the evening before. So I was hungry as well as tired. But where could I go? Who would be safe from whatever intimidation B. had gotten? And what was she told? 'Get that woman out of here immediately before someone gets hurt'? I sat on the edge of the narrow bed and jotted down a few thoughts to clear my head. But they were so scrambled I tore out the page, crumpled it into a small wad, and tossed it carelessly into the waste-paper basket.

Outside night was falling. The closest home where I thought I might be able to stay was a mile away and I walked there quickly. My reception was kind but wary, and my new friend let me know, at last, that indeed the community as a whole had closed down where I was concerned. 'It's not fair', he said, 'But I can't not tell you that it hasn't happened. It's really not very good right now for *anyone* to be seen with you.' Nonetheless, he kindly insisted that I spend the night, or even the week, if I wished. He refused, he said, to be intimidated. 'Well, I'll go back and get my bags, but I will only stay until morning. And I'm so sorry for putting you in this situation.' 'It's only a book', he said. 'And people here will tell you on the side that it has made them rethink a thing or two, for example, about how to raise and treat one's children.' And he laughed. 'The young mothers, here, they now go all out of the way to nurse their babies, and they are forever hugging them. Just to show you, I sometimes think.'

By the time I walked back to my 'guest' house to pick up my bags, my older friend and village sponsor was already waiting for me in the parlor.

'Where have you been? We've been worried. We've worked out a solution', he said glumly. 'You can spend your last night here – I'll see to it that no one blames B. – and I'll be back to fetch you first thing in the morning. Be completely ready. I'll carry you as far as Limerick and from there you'll take the bus to Dublin. No, don't argue; I insist. We can at least see you off to the next county. And we can use the extra time to talk.'

The next morning as I crept quietly down the creaking stairs I found a good strong bowl of tea and a plate of toast waiting for me in the 'guest room'. Ah, I thought, it's the *Lon na Bais*, the custom of the last meal that was left out just before an old one dies.[4] The family of the house had gathered around the long table in the kitchen for a breakfast that was taken in almost monastic silence. I tried to be equally silent in the next room. In taking my leave finally from B. she confronted me with my crime: 'All that time you spent in your room upstairs. You weren't just reading – you were writing! You left a trail in the wastepaper basket. People *said* you were writing. They saw you scribbling into your note book outside the pub in Brandon.' 'I won't deny it', I said. 'But was it such a grave sin? I needed to write my way through my own confusion and loneliness.' Then, B. gave me a quick hug and whispered in my ear, 'I'm so sorry for this. Ignore them. Keep up the good work.'

Then, the *Lon na Bais* ritual continued as my village mentor took me on our final rounds together of the village, this time to feast my eyes for the last time. Like a local funeral procession, he drove me slowly past all the sites that were dearest to me. 'Take a good look', he said. 'There's your Brandon Head. And there's your creamery, what's left of it. And here is your primary school. In a few hours the children will be lining up to march inside. And here's your Peg's pub, your Tailor Dean's house, and your old widow Bridge's cottage overgrown with brambles.' Then, as we turned the final curve past the abandoned little hamlet of Ballydubh, with the village almost out of sight, he forced me to turn around and take in the full sweep of the mountains and the sea. 'And there', he said, 'is your An Clochan. You had best say good-bye, now.'

In the end perhaps we deserve each other – well matched and well met, tougher than nails, both of us. Proud and stubborn, too. *Unrepentant* meets *Unforgiving*. So, in a way villagers were right to say 'We don't believe you are *really* sorry.' In their view this would mean nothing less than a renunciation of self and of my vexed profession, a move I could not take. *Saints* was written from a particular perspective at a particular moment in time and by a particular sort of anthropologist-ethnographer. And time, as they say, is a great healer. There is no such thing as everlasting ire anymore than there is undying love. Anything can change. A sense of proportion and a sense of humor may eventually replace injured pride. And in the meantime, as the Tailor of Ballybran would have said, 'just leave that there.' The next 25 years may pass even more swiftly than the last. And, God willing, by then *both* Crom Dubh and I will have found a way to return to 'our' village.

NOTES

1   Michael Hout's (1989) excellent quantitative study of social mobility and industrialization in Ireland between 1959 and 1973 indicated that the 'excess' sons of rural farm families did well and better in the Irish cities to which they migrated than the urban-born children of the Irish working classes.

2   The debate swirled around the following: Sidney Callahan, 'An Anthropologist in Ireland', *Commonweal*, 25 May 1979, 310–11; Michael Viney, 'Geared for a Gale', *The Irish Times*, 24 September 1980; Nancy Scheper-Hughes, 'Reply to Viney and to Ballybran', *The Irish Times*, 21 February 1981; Eileen Kane, 'Cui Bono? Do Aon Duine?', *RAIN* 51, August 1982; Nancy Scheper-Hughes, 'Ballybran – Reply to Eileen Kane', *RAIN*, no. 51, August 1982; John Messenger, 'Reply to Kane', *RAIN*, No. 52, October 1982; Eileen Kane, 'Reply to Scheper-Hughes', *RAIN*, no. 52, October 1982; P. Nixon and P. Buckley, 'Reply to Kane', *RAIN*, no. 54, February 1983; Eileen Kane, John Blacking, M. McCann and G. McFarlane, 'Social Anthropology in Ireland – A Response', *RAIN*, No. 54, February 1983; Michael Viney, 'The Yank in the Corner: Why the Ethics of Anthropology are a Concern for Rural Ireland', *The Irish Times*, 6 August 1983; Nancy Scheper-Hughes, 'From Anxiety to Analysis: Rethinking Irish Sexuality and Sex Roles', *Journal of Women's Studies* 10, 1983: 147–60.

3   This section was inspired by a discussion between Seamus Heaney and Robert Haas on 'the art of translating poetry' at the University of California, Berkeley, on 9 February 1999.

4   According to tradition in West Kerry, the 'old ones' are expected to sense the approach of death, which was often personified as in the saying, 'Death hasn't left Cork on its way to meet me yet!', or 'He has struck me. I feel his blow in my heart.' Many an older villager would tell with great satisfaction of the moment his old mother or father took to bed and sent for the priest with the words, 'Today is my dying day' or 'Sure, I won't last the night'. A more discreet way of signaling that death was near was to ask for the final meal, what the old ones called the *Lon na Bais*. 'Auntie' Anne explained it as follows:

One morning, about two weeks after I had returned from America, my father called me to his bedside and he asked me to bring him a large bowl of tea and two thick slices of fresh baked bread. 'Father', says I, 'you must be mistaken. Our people haven't used bowls for more than a century.

You must mean a large cup of tea.' 'It's a bowl I want', he replied. I offered him some cognac to ease the pain, but he stopped me saying, 'No, my daughter, I have no more use for that – I had plenty enough when I was a boy. But today I am going to see my God.' So I did bring him the tea and the toast and I laid it next to his bed, but he never touched any of it. He just sat up in bed, smiling at it, anxiously waiting. He died that night.... Wasn't that a beautiful death? It was what the old folks called the *Lon na Bais*, the death meal.'

REFERENCES

Arensberg, Conrad
    1937   *The Irish Countryman*. Garden City, NJ: Natural History Press.
Bateson, Gregory et al.
    1963   'A Note on the Double Bind', *Family Process* 2: 154–61.
Birdwell-Pheasant, Donna
    1998   'Family Systems and the Foundations of Class in Ireland and England', *The History of the Family* 3(1): 17–34.
Bourdieu, Pierre
    1977   *Outline of a Theory of Practice*. Cambridge: Cambridge University Press.
Callahan, Sidney
    1979   'An Anthropologist in Ireland'. *Commonweal*, 25 May: 310–11.
Devereux, George
    1977   *From Anxiety to Method in the Behavioral Sciences*. New York: Humanities.
Foucault, Michel
    1967   *Madness and Civilization*. New York: Mentor.
Heaney, Seamus
    1995   *Crediting Poetry* (The Nobel Lecture). Loughcrew, County Meath: The Gallery Press.
Heaney, Seamus
    1999   'The Art of Translating Poetry', Public Lecture at the Berkeley Art Museum, University of California, Berkeley, 9 February.
Hout, Michael
    1989   *Following in Father's Footsteps: Social Mobility in Ireland*. Cambridge, MA: Harvard University Press.
Illich, Ivan
    1982   *Gender*. New York: Pantheon.
Kane, Eileen
    1982   'Cui Bono? Do Aon Duine?' *RAIN* 51 (August): 12.
Keneally, Thomas
    1998   *The Great Shame and the Triumph of the Irish in the English Speaking World*. New York: Doubleday.
Sartre, Jean-Paul
    1956   *Being and Nothingness*. London: Methuen.
Viney, Michael
    1980   'Geared for a Gale', *The Irish Times* 24 September.
Viney, Michael
    1983   'The Yank in the Corner: Why the Ethics of Anthropology are a Concern for Rural Ireland', *The Irish Times* 6 August.

Part V
Fieldwork Conflicts, Hazards, and Dangers

Introduction

Jeffrey A. Sluka

Fieldwork is not free of tensions, dilemmas, conflicts, hazards, dangers, and even lethal hostility. Awareness of such risks is of life-saving importance to students embarking on their first fieldwork experience, and research troubles, even failures, are a source of ethnographic knowledge in themselves. In this part of the Reader, these concerns are exemplified and addressed in June Nash's account of her experience of living through a strike in a Bolivian mining community, where she was forced to take sides with the strikers against the government at considerable personal and professional risk; Neil Whitehead's harrowing account of his fieldwork in Guyana on the homicidal assault sorcery of "dark shaman," referred to as *kanaimà*; Cynthia Mahmood's shocking but inspirational account of being sexually assaulted for political motives during fieldwork in India; and Jeffrey Sluka's article on managing danger in fieldwork based on his research on the conflict in Northern Ireland. The articles by Mahmood and Sluka reflect the increasing amount of fieldwork conducted by anthropologists working in war zones and other sites of sociopolitical unrest and violence. Sluka's article comes from *Fieldwork Under Fire: Contemporary Studies of Violence and Survival* (Nordstrom and Robben 1995), a collection of essays that explore the dynamics of sociopolitical violence, written by anthropologists who have conducted fieldwork with victims, perpetrators, and survivors in war zones and other sites of conflict. The main concerns addressed by the volume are the distinct research problems and experiences of ethnographers who study situations of violence, and the theoretical issues that emerge from studying topics that involve personal danger (Nordstrom and Robben 1995:4).

Ethnographic Fieldwork: An Anthropological Reader, Second Edition. Edited by
Antonius C. G. M. Robben and Jeffrey A. Sluka.
Editorial material and organization © 2012 John Wiley & Sons, Inc.
Published 2012 by John Wiley & Sons, Inc.

In 1990, Nancy Howell published the first comprehensive study of occupational safety and health in anthropology, *Surviving Fieldwork*, looking at "the fieldwork of anthropology, the risks that are taken, and the prices that are paid for doing fieldwork in the ways we do" (1990:1). This showed that anthropology can be dangerous and that hundreds of anthropologists have failed to protect themselves from dangers and been victims or casualties of fieldwork. Field accidents and illnesses are a serious component of professional work in anthropology. From snakebites and truck crashes to severe sunburn and diarrhea, fieldwork is regularly interrupted by crises and problems. Few fieldworkers escape harm entirely. Many are hospitalized, lose fieldwork time, or suffer long-term or permanent disabilities, and at least 60 people died from fieldwork mishaps during the 1980s alone.

Howell's study details the threats to health and safety experienced by anthropologists in the field presented by humans and animals, exposure, injury, accidents, parasitic, infectious, and degenerative diseases, mental health and illness, families in the field, and practicing medicine in the field, and provides advice on how to make fieldwork safer. In particular, with regard to "Human Hazards of Fieldwork," Howell notes that "many anthropologists suffer interpersonal attacks during the course of their fieldwork" (1990:89), including assault; rape and attempted rape; murder, suicide, and other mysterious deaths; political hazards, such as arrest and suspicion of spying; and political turmoil, such as military attack, factional conflict, hostage-taking, and assassination. Many of these human and nonhuman hazards are exemplified in the readings selected for this part of the Reader.

June Nash's fieldwork in a Bolivian tin-mining community in the early 1970s led to the publication of her outstanding ethnography, *We Eat the Mines and the Mines Eat Us: Dependency and Exploitation in Bolivian Tin Mines* (1979). In "Ethnology in a Revolutionary Setting," she recounts some of the difficulties, suspicions, and dangers she experienced while conducting her fieldwork, during a time of industrial unrest and political disorder. Nash was one of the first modern anthropologists to seriously address the issue of neutrality in fieldwork, and she concluded:

> In Bolivia it was not possible to choose the role of an impartial observer and still work in the tin mining community ... The polarization of the class struggle made it necessary to take sides or to be cast by them on one side or the other. In a revolutionary situation, no neutrals are allowed. (1976:150)

In her research, the support and approval she received from the mine management aroused suspicions among the workers; when a state security agent investigated her work, she began to worry about the danger her notes and tapes could bring to her informants, and she eventually had to respond to the growing suspicions that she was a CIA agent. These difficulties threatened her ability to continue her research and her personal safety. In the end, Nash was able to maintain relations with the mine management, the union, the tin mines, and the political authorities all at the same time, and convince the community she was neither a CIA agent nor a threat. She concludes that, in revolutionary or violent settings, the traditional scientific attitude of impersonal objectivity is inappropriate and that, "We can no longer retreat to the deceptive pose of neutrality" (1976:164).

"The Ethnographer's Tale" is the first chapter in Neil Whitehead's outstanding ethnography *Dark Shamans: Kanaimá and the Poetics of Violent Death* (2002), in which he describes the dangerous and frightening aspects of the fieldwork on which the book is based. In 1992, Whitehead went to Guyana to conduct a survey of archeological sites, but found his research redirected into what would prove to be a decade of work, including several field trips to Guyana which resulted in the publication of his book. During his fieldwork, Whitehead faced hostility and many harrowing threats and hazards, and he fell so desperately ill – probably as a result of either intentional food poisoning or black witchcraft – that he suffered greatly and very nearly died.

Whitehead describes how his research was not just influenced by the active participation of Patamuna individuals, but became shaped by *their* priorities. Virtually on arrival, he came under strong pressure from local people who had their own agendas to research *kanaimà* instead. They impressed on him that *kanaimàs* are "real people who do real killing of specific identifiable individuals" (2002:17), and a serious issue in their lives for which they wanted to recruit his help in bringing to the attention of the world. While conducting his survey, Whitehead was directed to a putative "burial" site, where he touched a clay pot while photographing it. He notes: "This act came to define my identity to many Patamuna in many ways. Indeed, I believe I was to some degree manipulated into this 'archaeological discovery'" (2002:19). His companions suggested the object was something *kanaimà*, and many villagers interpreted it as an excellent development which would enable him "to let everyone know the truth of these *kanaimàs*" (2002:18). But then he was served a meal prepared by a woman, who spoke of *kanaimà* as she cooked, and within a few minutes of eating he fell so ill the villagers feared he would die. They suggested that by "troubling" the vessel Whitehead had invited the enmity of *kanaimà*, and he unexpectedly found himself in the role of ethnographer and "impressed by the sophistication of Patamuna in exploiting the interests of outsiders for their own benefit" (2002:25).

In subsequent field trips Whitehead collected oral histories and interviewed both relatives of *kanaimà* victims and practitioners themselves, during which he frequently felt exposed and uncertain about whether he might be inviting attacks on himself and those who helped him. Eventually, local people suggested that he was "becoming involved in an active contest between the *kanaimàs* and those who would 'expose' them" (2002:26), frequently warned, "to the effect that I had 'gone too far,' that I should not have troubled such things" (2002:30), and finally admonished him strongly, "to now desist as 'bad things were happening'" (2002:31). Whitehead experienced many strange and scary incidents and hostility from some locals, and is concerned that his interest in shamanic warfare may have been responsible for someone's death – the ritual shamanic assassination of a particular *kanaimà* – because its "occasion was so conveniently timed to satisfy and so closely tied to my interest in such shamanic warfare" (2002:36). Of course, this implies that if a *kanaimà* was killed, so too could Whitehead have been. While Whitehead's fieldwork was "fraught with difficulty, if not outright danger" (2002:40), it resulted in a brilliant ethnography, presenting a "distinct and new view of *kanaimà* as a shamanic practice" (2002:40).

In 2008, Cynthia Mahmood published "Anthropology from the Bones: A Memoir of Fieldwork, Survival, and Commitment," a deeply personal and disturbing, but also moving and ultimately inspiring, account of how she was beaten up and raped by a gang of hired thugs or rogue police while conducting fieldwork in India in 1992, in an apparent attempt to prevent her from doing research on Sikh and Kashmiri militancy. Howell's survey showed that 2 percent of all fieldworkers and 7 percent of the women in her study reported incidents of rape (1990:93), but she warned that this is a "touchy subject" that was certainly underreported in her sample, and, as Winkler has observed, "few people have placed in writing the hideous description of a rape attack. To write these words is to relive the pain – in full" (1995:157). Mahmood does so honestly and graphically, and warns that "those who actually try to study 'the wrong' topics – the silenced, the tabooed, the dangerous topics that challenge the power holders of the world – may find out just what it takes to be a truly independent scholar" (2008:5).

When she originally went to India, Mahmood intended to study tribal development, and "had no stake in any religious or political controversies. But when others chose to use their very bodies as weapons, insulting my own at its very core, this ethnography became a very intimate matter indeed. The question is, what does one do with that deeply, literally visceral violent memory" (2008:9–10). She chose to use that "shattering intersection to begin a new journey" into her authoritative work on political violence in India. As Nordstrom and Robben have commented, "[v]ery few turn their personal tragedies into research" (1995:18), but this is precisely what Mahmood did. She totally subverted her attackers' intentions by doing exactly what they apparently most feared and acted in order to prevent – namely, publish brilliant ethnographic studies presenting the "tabooed" perspectives and experiences of Punjabi Sikhs and Kashmiri Muslims, and one of the finest ethnographies of political violence ever written (Mahmood 1996).

In the same year that Howell published *Surviving Fieldwork*, I published the first article specifically on managing danger in fieldwork as a methodological and subjective issue (Sluka 1990); since then, others, particularly sociologists, have addressed this issue as well (Lee 1995; Lee-Treweek and Linkogle 2000; Huggins and Glebbeek 2009). The selection taken for this Reader is an updated and elaborated version of that 1990 original article, incorporating subsequent fieldwork I conducted on the conflict in Northern Ireland. I begin by observing that "anthropological fieldwork is more dangerous today than it was in the past," and "few anthropologists will be able to avoid conflict situations and instances of sociopolitical violence in the course of their professional lives" (1995:276). I argue that while special ethnographic methodological, theoretical, and ethical sensitivities are required when working on and in sites of sociopolitical conflict and violence, these dangers can be mediated through foresight and planning. I present a reflexive account of my fieldwork with Irish nationalist militants, and make practical recommendations on how to enhance personal safety when conducting ethnographic research in dangerous or violent social contexts. These recommendations are intended as a starting point from which others considering fieldwork in dangerous contexts can map out their own strategies for conducting it as safely as possible.

One of the most important conclusions is that one of the main sources of danger for anthropologists in the field is the nearly universal suspicion that they may be spies. This is an old concern in the discipline that goes back at least as far as the Franz Boas "Scientists as Spies" controversy in 1919. I note that:

> Because the most common suspicion that research participants have about anthropologists is that they are spies, and it is difficult to find an anthropologist who

has done fieldwork who has not encountered this suspicion, this danger deserves special mention. Being defined as a spy [let alone actually being one, since death is the usual wartime penalty for spies] is inherently dangerous and the link between anthropology and war-related research has exacerbated this danger. Anthropologists have been involved in war-related, particularly counterinsurgency, research, others have had their research used or "applied" by governments, militaries, and intelligence agencies to help plan military operations, and spies or intelligence agents of various sorts have used the cover that they were anthropologists. As a result, people in many parts of the world have come increasingly to believe that anthropologists, even those engaged in "innocent" (or in Boas' terms "honest") research, are actually or potentially dangerous to them. Many nations and peoples are therefore justifiably suspicious of anthropologists and will not allow them to do research, and fieldwork has become more dangerous today than it was in the past. (1995:283)

In her occupational safety and health report Howell highlighted the danger that being suspected of acting as a spy has represented for many anthropologists; in her article Nash describes how she faced and overcame a serious threat of just this sort; and in my article I recount being asked to prove I was not a spy when I arrived in the field in Belfast.

This issue is of particular contemporary relevance, because in 2005 the already considerable danger represented by anthropologists under suspicion of being spies was exacerbated by the establishment of a CIA scheme to sponsor trainee spies through American university courses. In the aftermath of the September 11, 2001 terrorist attacks in the United States, the Pat Roberts Intelligence Scholars Program was launched to improve US intelligence-gathering capabilities. Armed with $4 million in scholarships, it pays anthropology and other students, whose names are not disclosed, up to $50,000 a year to use their postgraduate training and fieldwork to gather political and cultural details on other countries, and after graduation they are expected to work directly for the CIA (Price 2005). This development was met with anger and concern among US and British anthropologists; in particular, John Gledhill, President of Britain's Association of Social Anthropologists, called the scholarships ethically dangerous and divisive, and warned that they could foster suspicion within universities worldwide and cause problems in the field (BBC 2005).

In 1919, Franz Boas, who for two decades had dominated American anthropology, was formally censured by the American Anthropological Association (AAA) for publishing a letter in *The Nation* condemning anthropologists who used their profession as a cover for spying during World War I:

Sir: In his war address to congress, President Wilson dwelt at great length on the theory that only autocracies maintain spies; that these are not needed in democracies. At the time that the President made this statement, the Government of the United States had in its employ spies of unknown number … The point against which I wish to enter a vigorous protest is that a number of men who follow science as their profession, men whom I refuse to designate any longer as scientists, have prostituted science by using it as a cover for their activities as spies.

A soldier whose business is murder as a fine art, a diplomat whose calling is based on deception and secretiveness, a politician whose very life consists in compromise with his conscience, a business man whose aim is personal profit within the limits allowed by a lenient law – such may be excused if they set patriotic devotion above common everyday decency and perform services as spies. They merely accept the code of morality to which modern society still conforms. Not so the scientist. The very essence of his life is the service of truth … [Any person] who uses science as a cover for political spying, who demeans himself to pose before a foreign government as an investigator and asks for assistance in his alleged researches in order to carry on, under this cloak, his political machinations, prostitutes science in an unpardonable way and forfeits the right to be classed as a scientist.

By accident incontrovertible proof has come to my hands that at least four men who carry on anthropological work, while employed as government agents, introduced themselves to foreign governments as representatives of scientific institutions in the United States, and as sent out for the purpose of carrying on scientific researches. They have not only shaken the belief in the truthfulness of science, but they have also done the greatest possible disservice to scientific inquiry. In consequence of their acts every nation will look with distrust upon the visiting foreign investigator who wants to do honest work, suspecting sinister designs. Such action has raised a new barrier against the development of international friendly cooperation. (1973:51–52)

It is ironic that in 2005, at the same time in history when the AAA membership was voting overwhelmingly in favor of a resolution to rescind Boas's censure in 1919 for condemning anthropologists who served as spies, the largest ever government-sponsored program of recruiting anthropologists as spies emerged. This disturbing development promises to exacerbate the already considerable difficulties and dangers all fieldworkers face of being suspected of being spies, particularly CIA agents. It represents a serious threat both to anthropologists' ability to gain access to fieldwork sites, because it undermines our ability to gain the trust, rapport, and consent of research participants, and to their "occupational safety and health" in the field.

REFERENCES

BBC (British Broadcasting Corporation)
   2005   Fears Over CIA "University Spies." *BBC News World Edition*, June 2. http://news.bbc.co.uk/2/hi/uk_news/education/4603271.stm.
Boas, Franz
   1973   Scientists as Spies. In: *To See Ourselves: Anthropology and Modern Social Issues.* Thomas Weaver, ed., pp. 51–52. Glenview, IL: Scott, Foresman & Co.
Howell, Nancy
   1990   *Surviving Fieldwork: A Report of the Advisory Panel on Health and Safety in Fieldwork.* Washington, DC: American Anthropological Association.
Huggins, Martha and Marie-Louise Glebbeek, eds.
   2009   *Women Fielding Danger: Negotiating Ethnographic Identities in Field Research.* Lanham, MD: Rowman & Littlefield.
Lee, Raymond
   1995   *Dangerous Fieldwork.* Thousand Oaks, CA: Sage.
Lee-Treweek, Geraldine and Stephanie Linkogle, eds.
   2000   *Danger in the Field: Risk and Ethics in Social Research.* London: Routledge.
Mahmood, Cynthia Keppley
   1996   *Fighting for Faith and Nation: Dialogues With Sikh Militants.* Philadelphia: University of Pennsylvania Press.

Mahmood, Cynthia Keppley
  2008   Anthropology from the Bones: A Memoir of Fieldwork, Survival, and Commitment. *Anthropology and Humanism* 33(1/2):1–11.
Nash, June
  1976   Ethnology in a Revolutionary Setting. In: *Ethics and Anthropology: Dilemmas in Fieldwork*. Michael Rynkiewich and James Spradley, eds., pp. 148–166. New York: John Wiley & Sons.
Nash, June
  1979   *We Eat the Mines and the Mines Eat Us: Dependency and Exploitation in Bolivian Tin Mines*. New York: Columbia University Press.
Nordstrom, Carolyn and Antonius C. G. M. Robben, eds.
  1995   *Fieldwork Under Fire: Contemporary Studies of Violence and Survival*. Berkeley: University of California Press.
Price, David
  2005   The CIA's Campus Spies. *Counterpunch*. March 12–13. http://www.counterpunch.org/price03122005.html.
Sluka, Jeffrey
  1990   Participant Observation in Violent Social Contexts: Managing Danger in Fieldwork. *Human Organization* 49(2):114–126.
Sluka, Jeffrey
  1995   Reflections on Managing Danger in Fieldwork: Dangerous Anthropology in Belfast. In: *Fieldwork Under Fire: Contemporary Studies of Violence and Survival*. Carolyn Nordstrom and Antonius C. G. M. Robben, eds., pp. 276–294. Berkeley: University of California Press.
Whitehead, Neil
  2002   The Ethnographer's Tale. In: *Dark Shamans: Kanaimá and the Poetics of Violent Death*, pp. 1–7, 11–40. Durham, NC: Duke University Press.
Winkler, Cathy
  1995   Ethnography of the Ethnographer. In: *Fieldwork Under Fire: Contemporary Studies of Violence and Survival*. Carolyn Nordstrom and Antonius C. G. M. Robben, eds., pp. 155–183. Berkeley: University of California Press.

15

Ethnology in a
Revolutionary Setting

June Nash

There is a growing gulf between the anthropologist's two roles, that of field researcher and that of analyst. In the first role, we share the lives of the people we study and identify with them in the conflicts they face (Gough, 1968:4; Henry, 1966) as we "try the intimate experience of another upon ourselves to test our hypotheses" (paraphrasing Lévi-Strauss, 1969:51). In the second, we must objectify and distill our experiences. Ever since we discovered that secrecy was a defense against the dominant culture, we have been increasingly aware that our data may be used against those whose lives we have shared. In the period of decolonization, as Maquet (1964:48) has shown, the anthropologist has come to be classified with the enemy. Even where national independence is established, our material can be and is being used to counter popular uprisings. The people we study are often cut off from the data we publish by a language or literacy block. Without our

knowledge, our material may be fed directly to the "man in the field with the civic action program; working with a military establishment ... the person in psychological operations who has the basic fundamental studies that give him understanding of the masses" (in the words of Dante B. Fascell, chairman of the House of Representatives Subcommittee on Inter-American Affairs; see US Government, 1969). Since we have no official audience with statesmen or policy makers, we do not know how or whether our publications influence policies that will affect the lives of the people we study. Lacking control over the product of our research, we have lost the basis for social responsibility.

The issues raised by Project Camelot and the publication of the Thailand counter-insurgency research reveal the need to set ethical standards within the profession (Jorgensen, 1971, Wolf and Jorgensen, 1970). Berreman (1968) has gone beyond the issue of

Ethnographic Fieldwork: An Anthropological Reader, Second Edition. Edited by Antonius C. G. M. Robben and Jeffrey A. Sluka.
Editorial material and organization © 2012 John Wiley & Sons, Inc.
Published 2012 by John Wiley & Sons, Inc.

professional standards to signal the danger of leaving the use of our data to others: "politicians and journalists," "madmen and scoundrels," as well as "statesmen and benefactors." Stavenhagen (1971) has called for "decolonizing the profession."

In order to work out an understanding of the role we can begin to play, we need accounts of concrete field experiences such as those that Maquet (1964), Henry (1966), and Jones (1971) have given us. This report provides a comparative instance based on my recent field experience in the revolutionary setting of Bolivia. In my previous fieldwork with the Maya of Chiapas, Mexico, the impact of modern change was only indirectly felt. The old power structure of curers and diviners who controlled the supernatural was breaking down, and men who had been protectors of the community were being killed as witches. Hostility was turned inward, as a rising incidence of homicide within the community indicated. The defensive insulation of the community against the outside world protected me from the kinds of issues that arise in studying groups in the mainstream of change. People did not involve me in the witchcraft conflict that was the central struggle in their lives.

In Bolivia it was not possible to choose the role of an impartial observer and still work in the tin mining community of Oruro, where I had gone to study ideology and social change. The miners, who spoke Quechua and or Aymara as well as Spanish, had entered the modern industrial sphere and were demanding power in it. The polarization of the class struggle made it necessary to take sides or to be cast by them on one side or the other. In a revolutionary situation, no neutrals are allowed.

In the 146 years since Bolivia's independence, there have been 186 uprisings, resulting in more than 150 changes of government. Only one of these movements resulted in the formation of a legitimized, democratically elected succession of leaders seeking structural changes that would warrant its being called a revolution: the uprising of the National Revolutionary Movement (MNR) on April 9, 1952, when the people fought for the right to seat president-elect Victor Paz Estenssoro after

he had been refused power by the oligarchy of tin barons. Eventually Paz lost the confidence of the masses who had supported him as he turned to a false "development" based on loans and increasing external control. In the convulsive spring (our fall) of 1964, workers' strikes and student protest led to his withdrawal. Under the banner of the "revolution of reconstruction," Rene Barrientos Ortuno, a general who had become Paz's vice-president under pressure from the army, took advantage of the rebellion. Reneging on the promises he had made to labor, he instituted four years of the worst repression Bolivia had suffered since the days of the "Butcher" Mamerto Urriolagoitia, installed in the presidency by the tin oligarchy in 1948.

When I arrived in La Paz in July 1967, Che Guevara was still fighting in the tropics of Santa Cruz. Barrientos's troops had massacred 87 men, women, and children in Siglo XX Catavi on June 23. The massacre was precipitated by the Congress of Miners' Unions planned for the following day and was possibly an attempt to discourage workers from supporting Che Guevara's guerrilla movement. I took a bus to the old mining center of Oruro, where I found the San José mine paralyzed by the reorganization of the mines according to plans proposed by the Inter-American Development Bank as a condition of its loan to the Nationalized Mining Corporation of Bolivia. The corporation had just fired over 200 women who had worked in the concentration of metals and replaced them with men and machines. I spoke to only a few people on my first visit, a teacher in the company school, who sympathized with the workers and told me some of their problems; a woman in *chola* dress (the sign of transition from an Indian culture to urban life) selling candy and fruit punch to miners as they came off their shift; and a gatekeeper who was no longer able to work inside the mines due to silicosis, the "professional illness" of miners, but all of them spoke bitterly of the government and the nationalized administration. I read the writing on the walls of all the company buildings calling for the "fight against imperialism" and "death to the military assassins and parasites," signed with the initials of the various political parties and union federations. In large red letters, dripping from the hastily executed inscription, the word LIBERACION dominated the walls of the company store. It was as though the cry of the French Revolution for "liberty, equality, and fraternity" had been reduced to its minimal demand – liberty to work out their own destiny. I was determined to return to this place that revealed, even in such a short visit, the turbulence of a society holding on to a precarious niche in an industrial empire at the same time as it was trying to come to grips with an imposed system of exploitation.

I returned to Bolivia for a summer field session in June 1969 to study the ideology of tin-miners. Barrientos had died in an air crash two months before, and his vice-president, Luis Adolfo Siles Salinas, had scheduled an election for May, 1970. Most of the mines were running, as they had for several years, at a loss, decapitalized by inefficient management and the transfer of capital into military equipment. Pensioned workers were not receiving subsistence checks that, even when they arrived, could not cover food costs. Government-employed teachers had not been paid for months. Union leaders were in hiding or exile, and "yellow" unions were serving as spies for the management. Mining police received more pay than miners. Their job was to catch *jucos*, usually employed miners, who entered deserted shafts at night and "stole" what they considered to be their national riches. Many of the older engineers felt that productivity would increase and costs decrease if the police were fired and the company bought the metal the *jucos* extracted.

I spent an afternoon in the local office of the mine management, waiting for permission from La Paz to go ahead with my study. I had already spoken to some of the officials in La Paz, but the administrator of the San José mines wanted direct communication from them. When the assistant to the manager of industrial relations finally received a telegram approving the project, he went far beyond what I had requested in the way of cooperation and arranged for me to conduct interviews in the anteroom of his office. Furthermore, he ordered the superintendent of mines to send

miners to be interviewed when they finished work. I felt I couldn't refuse without arousing suspicion, so I started interviews on work conditions under these trying circumstances, where the assistant manager could hear everything that was said and where the men, tired after a day's work, were compelled to talk with a strange *gringa*.

One of the first miners I interviewed demanded that I explain what my study was about before he replied to my questions. I liked his forthright attitude and explained in detail. He seemed satisfied and spoke with interest and involvement. Another of the interviewees who impressed me in these early interviews was a watchman who, like all the others working in nonskilled jobs at the surface, could no longer work inside the mine because of silicosis. Since his duties were not pressing, he came by twice in the following week. He was more relaxed when I asked questions about ritual and folklore than when I questioned him about conditions in the mine. Once he brought up the massacres that had taken place in the mines, his tone turned from bitterness to compassion for the dead and he wept as he spoke of the massacre of December 21, 1942 in Siglo XX Catavi. Tears came to my eyes as he spoke of "our history" and of how Maria Barzola, a woman worker in the concentration of metal had seized the Bolivian flag during the march to the administrative offices to demand "more daily bread" and had been shot along with other men, women, and children by the soldiers called to the defense of the mine. Soon after that he and some of the other miners I had met in the course of my interviews invited me to their homes, and I could avoid the restrictive atmosphere of the administrative office. I think I had passed some kind of test that allowed me to go beyond a barrier to communication, a barrier that might never have been withdrawn, if I had remained a "stranger" (however desirable some ethnologists believe this to be [cf. Jarvie 1969]).

I was visiting in the mine one day when I heard that an agent of the Department of Criminal Investigation (DIC) had come to investigate what I was doing. When I returned to the house where I rented rooms, I found all my notes and tapes removed. I later learned that my student had taken them in a laundry sack to a friend's house in the mining community, but I had a few bad hours reflecting on the danger my notes could bring to my informants. The agent returned, and (remembering U Nu's "tension-releasing lunches" with his cabinet from my Burmese days of fieldwork), I invited him for breakfast the following day. That afternoon I received a call from one of my miner friends, who had begun an autobiography. He had heard the DIC was after me and was curious to know what had happened. I assured him that I would not let the DIC see any of his work, and said that I would burn it first if there was any danger. He protested against such drastic action; it made me feel good that he had confidence in me and was committed to the work we were doing. That evening we gave all the notes to a student who was traveling to La Paz retaining only a few myths and folk tales to show the DIC. The agent arrived promptly the following morning and waited for us to return from the anniversary mass of a friend's deceased mother. After we had chatted about folklore and rituals, he went on to tell us about his student days at the University of Wisconsin, where he said he had a scholarship to study "counterinsurgency," and about his friendship with an American CIA agent working in Oruro. Then he left, after asking only to see our passports, although on the previous day he had demanded that we show him all our notes.

Political campaigns for a presidential election were underway when I left Bolivia in September. The Mayor of La Paz, Armando Escobar Uria, was gaining popularity as a candidate. I was not surprised to read shortly after that Alfredo Ovando, who had helped Barrientos attain power and who had little reason to believe that he could win a democratic election, had seized power on September 26. Desiring to outdo Siles, who had been promising to revise the oil code to increase the national share of the wealth of the American holdings in Santa Cruz, he nationalized the oil company. Economically, it would have been preferable to await the installation of a gas line to Argentina's markets, but the move was dictated by the political urgency of stabilizing a weak military coup. Yielding to pressure

from intellectuals and workers, Ovando freed some of the jailed union directors, who returned to work in the mines. When I returned to Bolivia in January, 1970, I sensed the uncertainty that Ovando's moves had created among the miners. Some called for a position of *acerquismo*, getting closer to the center of power, by supporting Ovando and trying to influence policy. Others distrusted the attempts of what they felt was an opportunistic regime, still dominated by the military, to gain support among the masses. Wages and contracts cut in half by Barrientos in 1965 in a "temporary" austerity measure, remained at the same low level, a little under a dollar a day.

Labor had begun to rebuild its shattered organization. I visited the new secretary-general and presented my credentials and plan for a study of the mining community. (I had avoided the former representative because of the low esteem the miners had for him and their suspicion that he was a spy for management.) In April I attended a weeklong congress of the Federation of Mine Workers' Unions at Siglo XX Catavi, where old leaders and new gathered for the first time in five years to plan a program of action and elect a directorate. I was permitted to attend all of the sessions and to tape record the proceedings, except for those of the political commission. The regular attendance of myself and two assistants became something of a joke. It seemed too obvious a stunt for the CIA to pull – having a "blond" *gringa* sitting in front of a nearly all-male audience with a large paisley-covered tape recorder. For those with lingering doubts about my presence, it might even have been appealing that they had their own specially assigned agent bugging them. I felt that immediate feedback was essential to justify my presence to the miners, and so I wrote some of my impressions in an article published in *Temas Sociales* entitled "El XIVe Congreso y Después." In the months that followed, the union leadership concentrated on regaining the ground lost in the Barrientos period. The directors formulated a plan for reinstating wages at the pre-Barrientos level without producing inflation that had crippled the MNR government before currency stabilization in 1956. Their plan involved eliminating many of the bureaucratic and technical posts that had accumulated as the army invaded the administration and abolishing the mining police. Only one strike was called, and that was to demand replacements for machinery and tools in the mines. By the fall (our spring) of 1970, Ovando's government was beginning to swing farther to the right. The promised wage increase was not forthcoming and increased expenditures were made for armaments. One of the few left-of-center critics in the government, Marcelo Quiroga Santa Cruz, resigned from the Ministry of Mines and Petroleum in protest on May 18th. It wasn't just protest directly on miners' wages but on a whole swing to the right. He later revealed Ovando's intention of replacing all the civilian ministers with military men (*Presencia*, July 7, 1970). The only other civilian minister of the left, Kidrich Bailey, was forced to resign soon after. The union leaders alerted the workers to this swing to the right in the cabinet and called for an antiimperialist demonstration.

In the middle of July university students sent out a call to mobilize the National Army of Liberation, the guerrilla movement left over from the Che Guevara period, in Teoponte, and scores of students went there in the guise of literacy brigades. The 68 guerrillas were quickly defeated. As they were surrendering to the army, they were shot. Prisoners, some of them wounded, were killed with machine gun fire and hand grenades. Ovando refused to hand over the bodies of the victims to their families, perhaps, as rumor had it, because the thoroughly destroyed bodies revealed the brutality of the military operation. Not only relatives of the dead and political sympathizers, but many of the Bolivian people were outraged by this callous behavior. Other sectors of the middle class were alienated by Ovando's imprisonment and expulsion of priests in the middle of September.

A series of demonstrations in La Paz by university students protesting the government's bizarre handling of the dead guerrillas culminated in a march on September 21, the Day of Students. Usually a day for celebration of youth, when students crown their queens and dance, that year it was a day for rebellion against a regime that was falling into the old

pattern of ineptness and repression of the resulting discontent. Union directors joined the students in a symbolic funeral of the dead guerrillas. Although the miners had rejected the movement when it was active, they proclaimed its martyrs when they were no longer a threat to their trade union aims. The streets for blocks around the university were still filled with the tear gas used to break up the demonstration when I passed by several hours later. My taxi driver said bitterly, "Each one of those bombs costs us $U.S. 10, and look what they do with them!" As I waited to meet a foundation representative in the lobby of one of the few luxury hotels in La Paz, I was appalled to overhear some of my compatriots, attending a medical convention, joking about this latest of Bolivia's revolutions. I wondered how anyone could laugh at people prepared to die rather than continue selling their lives everyday in a market over which they had no control.

The weeks following were a time of near anarchy. Ovando's government had lost its legitimacy. The big question was: When will it end?

The union in San José and other mining centers built up its antiimperialist campaign in these weeks of guerrilla action and student protest. The campaign came to focus more and more on *Yanqui* imperialism. Finally, I became the target. On October 3, Doris Widerkehr, who was beginning her dissertation research, went to tape a union meeting, as we had been doing for a special study of the rhetoric of worker organizations. She came back shaken and upset. One of the former leaders, who was himself accused by some of being a CIA agent had asked why we were allowed to tape the sessions and why we were doing the study. (Since I had had several conversations with him about the work we were doing, this seemed a tactic for diverting suspicion from himself.) The question had opened a general discussion of our role in the mining center. Three strangers from Argentina, one of whom claimed to be an anthropologist had said that they never used tape recorders in their work and that furthermore anthropologists need only 3 months for a field study and we had already been there 10 months. Doris had been asked to leave.

We discussed the events of the meeting with my compadre, a retired miner, during lunch. He advised me not to get angry when eating because the bile would burst and I might die. I tried to control my anger until the afternoon, when I went to see the secretary-general. Fortunately he was not there. Since I had not yet worked out a plan of action, I then went to see another of my compadres, who was a delegate with the union. He consulted with a compadre who had many years of experience in labor struggles, and they decided that I should draft a letter explaining my problem and methods of investigation in detail and distribute copies to all the delegates as well as to the secretary-general, asking for an audience at the next meeting. I had, of course, discussed my work with the union before and had given the secretary-general copies of the articles I had published in Spanish, but changes in the union and in the political scene seemed to have made a reevaluation necessary. The strategy they outlined for me was to involve all of the men responsible for the operation of the union in the discourse, avoiding personal commitments to a single individual, who could then be suspected of being in complicity with me. I drafted the letter and revised it in accordance with comments from my compadre. The following day I passed out copies of the letter to the delegates as they were leaving a meeting concerned with an attempted coup in La Paz. The coup had begun on the morning of October 4, while Ovando was in Santa Cruz, with a radio-broadcast mandate signed by 64 officers calling for his renunciation of the presidency.

The following seven days have been called "The Week of the Generals" (Samuel Mendoza, *Presencia*, November 15, 1970). In the course of the week, six presidents entered and left the "Burned Palace." The contest became something like a football game between sectors of the armed forces, with the people listening to the radio with consternation, dismay, and a wild sense of the absurd as generals kicked the football of power from one to another.

Because I had not yet cleared up the question of whether I was an agent for the CIA, I did not go out except for brief trips to the plaza to see if any of the student demonstrations announced on the radio were taking place. A new group of DIC agents had taken possession of one of the benches in the plaza. I discovered their identity when I was about to take a photograph of soldiers massing near the Cathedral to block a scheduled student demonstration and one of the plainclothes agents rushed over to stop me, saying I had no right to photograph secret agents.

On Monday, October 5, as a result of the only "election" in two years, held in the Miraflores barracks, officers of the army called for Ovando (who had by now returned to the Palace) to renounce the presidency "for having defrauded the hopes of the people." General Rogelio Miranda, who had led the coup could not muster strong support even within the army, so he named a triumvirate to take control. Students and workers rallied behind General Juan José Torres, as the least imperialist, least Fascist, and least reactionary of the lot, to oppose the trio. When a strike was threatened for the following day, the tide turned against the triumvirate. Torres was proclaimed president on the afternoon of October 6. He promised to form a government based on *campesinos* (agricultural workers), miners and factory workers, and university students, with the support of the army, the various ministries to be divided among these four sectors of the population. The representatives of the Bolivian Workers' Central (COB) at first rejected the plan of coparticipation, on the basis of their experience with the MNR government and criticism of the compromises resulting from that episode, but later agreed to accept the posts of Housing, Mines, and Labor. Torres's attempts to find a popular base for his new government threatened a rebellion if labor were to have as much participation in government as Torres had promised them. Fearing the seizure of power by the rightist wing, the Political Command of the COB agreed to leave the new president at liberty to choose his cabinet without including them.

Meanwhile, Doris and I had made preparations in case of an attack on the Anglo-American-owned apartment building in which we lived. I took my daughter to stay at the house of a friend. We took suitcases of notes to the house of another friend and copies to still another. Then we shuttered the windows and listened to the radio. That night it looked as though the crisis was over, and we celebrated the assignment of ministerial posts assigned to labor leaders, some of whom we knew.

The Workers' Central of the Department of Oruro had planned a strike and an anti-fascist demonstration in Oruro on October 7, with participation by miners from other centers as well as San José. From the window of a dentist's office that morning, I watched a crowd of young men converging on the offices of the DIC. The guards ran up to the roof with machine guns, but they did not fire on the crowd below, whether because of cowardice or good judgment I do not know. The youths came out carrying rifles. (We later discovered that the guns had no firing pins, but they looked menacing at the time.) Not far away, students were assaulting the U.S. Information Service building, where the doors of the library were bombed open and books and materials carried off or burned.

When I returned home, our cook told me that she had just bought a can of oil in the market when one of her neighbors pointed a rifle at her and tried to seize it. He did not recognize her until she screamed, "Don Roberto, what are you doing?" and then he let go of the can. Shortly after, one of the university students came with news of the assault on the USIS. He brought tear gas bombs and a vomit bomb, plainly marked US Army, that he had liberated from the DIC office and gave them to us in case the Anglo-American school, as the only symbol of US imperialism left, should be the next target. I was beginning to get irritated at some of the "revolutionary" tactics of the mob, and I didn't want to leave without at least some show of resistance. I felt that, while I had to demonstrate that not all Americans were imperialists, I also had to make them realize that not all actions in the name of revolution were revolutionary.

There was nothing to do but sit in the shuttered living room listening to the transistor radio, with the bombs close at hand. Radio Universidad announced the arrival of truckloads of miners from Machacamarca. Others from Catavi and Siglo XX were expected to join them for the afternoon demonstration.

Suddenly a volley of shots was fired into the unarmed crowd in front of the central barracks. Whether it was triggered when civilians approached the door of the barracks, as some said or when a woman, hit by an orange peel thrown at the guards, screamed, is not verified. For the next eight hours there ensued a useless battle with random sniping, resulting in about 20 deaths and 100 injuries. Between desperate calls for a return to sanity radio announcers broadcast the lists of wounded and dead.

The teenage son of a miner came to visit us. He wanted to go out in the streets to see what was happening, but I made him help me bake a cake. When it was done, I wanted to invite Doris, who lived across the street, to join us for tea, but the moment we opened the door a volley of bullets from a sniper sitting on a nearby hill discouraged us. I made the teenager stay overnight for fear that he would be shot going home to the mine. In the morning his parents arrived looking for him. As I had feared they had thought he was in the hospital or the morgue and had made the rounds early in the morning and seen the dead and suffering. However, they agreed that the precaution had been worth their night of anxiety. In the afternoon of the following day, we went to the wake of eight students and youths in the university auditorium and then to the mine office, where three workers who had died were on view. Thousands came to pay their last respects and then attended the mass funeral on the following day. The speakers tried to make of the deaths a noble sacrifice for the revolution, but the people knew that they were due to nothing more than the stupidity and ineptness of the command of the armed forces.

In the following days people waited and watched the new officials. The DIC office was still occupied by students, who had put a likeness of Che Guevara in guerrilla fatigues on the pillar in the entryway. They soon acquired a reputation of being as arbitrary in their handling of cases as their predecessors. One of the miners told us that a fight had broken out in his family and everyone was detained in the cold cells without cots or plumbing facilities, even his 15-year-old daughter (who, as a minor, should not have been imprisoned). In a country that lives with the constant expectation of revolution, there is little preparation for a successful outcome. During this period, there was relative freedom of expression in the press and on the radio. Union leadership was given full liberty to pursue the plans for the restitution of wages. There was no evidence of restraint or recrimination against any of the combatants.

A week after my accusation, I went to ask the secretary-general for time to explain my work to the delegates. He agreed to give me some time in the next meeting. In my presentation, I stressed that the tape recorder was a tool to get more accurate data and not an instrument of espionage. One of the delegates told me that the suspicion had arisen when I had lent the tape recorder to one of the delegates to a COB conference. Though the title of the tape on the machine had been erased, the tape itself had not and it contained accusations by one of the members against some of the directors. The delegate had played the tape for the other delegates to the conference and let it be known that it was mine. I was dismayed at what I had let happen after all my care, and assured them it was an error of stupidity and not evil intention. They seemed prepared to believe this. Despite their hatred of the CIA, they had a very high regard for the agency's performance, and this blunder did not fit the image. I felt that they had accepted my continued stay in the community when the directorate's intellectual advised me how I could improve and amplify the study by investigating work conditions of the women on the slag pile.

The episode, although disturbing and threatening the very possibility of continuing my work, yielded some ethnographic benefits. Enemies of the leadership became friendly to me when I was cast as an enemy of their enemy. They told me of the leaders' attempts to gain favor with the administration and described the circle of *llunkus*, men who curry favor with those in power, that surrounded each of them. They spoke more frankly of their own fear of being deceived by their leaders, the ever-present fear of the powerless. I learned of the corrupt union leader's technique of taking issues from the management, and introducing them as union demands, such as constructing additions to social service buildings (projects that meant a lot of graft). I discovered that I had been under almost constant surveillance by a neighbor whose husband worked in the mine, and that her report of my visitors' being only workers from the rank and file reassured the people that my interest in the mine stemmed from genuine sympathy. In the week of my own "suspension" I came to understand more fully the insecurity that robs working people of their revolutionary zeal.

Several days after my meeting with the union delegates, I saw the jeep station wagon put at the disposal of the union by the company raising a cloud of dust behind me as I walked down the road. Still not sure how they had taken my defense, I jumped into the ditch to avoid being run down; much to my surprise, the driver pulled up to me and the secretary-general asked me if I would like a ride. I was too overcome to think of an excuse, so I agreed, but I recovered my defense enough to decline a drink of chicha (the fermented drink of the workers). At that point I was afraid of being seen with him and his *llunkus*. The next time I showed up at a union meeting, two of my compadres came over and greeted me, using the formal address of *comadre*, thus establishing the relationship publicly. Later, when a newcomer who was trying to gain footing in the union tried to intercept my taking a photograph of two children listening in to the discussion at a meeting, two other friends came over and asked him what he thought he was doing. After the meeting a man invited me to be comadre of the soccer team. I could hardly refuse, although it meant buying socks for the 13 members.

Torres visited the San José mines in December, just after the announcement that the wage raises would go into effect in January. The crowd of 200 or so miners who came to the stadium to listen to him applauded his speech but saved most of their *vivas* for the working class and the martyrs of the union struggles. The president called for confidence in his government and the good will of the armed forces, and he pleaded for peace to work out a program for economic improvement. "You have fought enough," he told the miners, "in the war of Nancahuasu and when Maria Barzola marched and sacrificed her life asking for more bread for the workers"; the miners responded with a call for arms for the workers. Miners have learned that the words of presidents have little value unless they have confidence enough in the workers to give them weapons.

I left in December feeling somewhat optimistic about the future of the mines. When I returned in July, 1971, to make a film based on the miner's autobiography mentioned earlier, there was a new secretary-general, formerly a leader in Siglo XX who had been jailed during Barrientos's term of office. When he had been elected in December, one of the superintendents expressed relief that he had won over the more Marxist-revolutionary candidates, since he had a good reputation as a foreman concerned with production. He had already aroused some criticism from the rank and file for getting employment in the mines for members of his extended kin group. Furthermore, newspaper articles implicated him in the torture and slaying of a union leader during Ovando's period of office. The last thing he needed was a *gringa* working in the mines. He agreed to let me show the Super-8 film we had made the year before. I had looked forward to this as an opportunity of telling people in the mining community about the 16-mm film we proposed to do. When I arrived at the union hall, the order to permit the showing of the film had not been given. I sensed that I was going to have some opposition from official union sources in making the film and continuing my work, although my friends and compadres were cooperative throughout.

There had been a marked shift to the left in the Torres government. Two or more attempted coups in January (one by Hugo Banzer, who was to carry out the successful coup in August) had been put down with the help of miners. The right was on the defensive or in flight. The Popular Assembly, a kind of forum of union leaders, *campesinos*, and left politicians, opened in June. Ideologies and programs of the left were aired in what *Presencia* (August 6, 1971) referred to lyrically as a "symphony for the revolution." The main business of the Assembly became the working out of the details of coparticipation of workers in the

administration of mines and factories. Workers in the mining center were doubtful about the program, since they felt that in the coparticipation phase of the MNR regime the union leadership had lost its revolutionary aims as it learned to participate in the spoils of the company. At an August meeting in San José mine, the director was unable to secure a quorum, and those present began to whistle and protest that the leaders had not come to advise them about the plan for coparticipation. The director turned to me and ordered me to go, thereby diverting the workers from their protest and eliminating a witness of the breakup of the meeting for lack of a quorum. After the meeting, rank-and-file members told me resentfully that they were again being used as "steps" in the rise of opportunistic labor leaders.

During July and August there were invasions of agricultural and business enterprises. Miners seized private holdings in Colquecharca, Postosi, and Catavi. Peasants seized the homes of the *hacendados* (estate owners) for whom they worked. Some of the presses and radio stations were taken over by the men who worked in them or by popular pressure groups and were turned into cooperatives. There was an air of apprehensiveness and expectation; people stood in their doorways, watching to see the next development, just as they did in the week of Carnival waiting for the dancers to come in. When I went to the University of Oruro's library on the morning of August 7, pensioned miners who had been on a hunger strike to gain their subsistence money surged into the building, which had once been the residence of a tin baron. As the men and women pressed into the main hall of the baroque mansion, shorter than I by a head, stunted by years of malnutrition and shaken with the racking cough of silicosis, I felt the full impact of the revolutionary pressures in an economy hedged in by foreign powers that did not have to yield to their demands.

In the early days of August, rumors of military plots originating in Santa Cruz led to the demand for arms for the people to "defend their revolution and take positive steps toward socialism" (*Presencia*, August 8, 1971). On August 14, union directors in Santa Cruz advised Torres of subversion in their capital.

Torres failed to act, but the military began to prepare themselves; on August 16, students in the military college were assigned to the central barracks without any official explanation. The union leaders of Santa Cruz sent more urgent messages, and both union leaders and the Popular Assembly in Cochabamba asked for arms for the workers. On August 20, Hugo Banzer and 38 coconspirators were imprisoned. After a day of demonstrations in favor of his release, Banzer was set free and began to mobilize rebel forces.

In Oruro, miners were mobilizing from Siglo XX, Catavi, Huanuni, and Santa Fe to fight the rebels. On the morning of the 10th, union leaders of San José called for a work stoppage and a united demonstration of miners from the other centers. The call was broadcast on the union radio until 11 A.M. At 11:20 A.M. 14 truckloads of miners arrived in Oruro. The union leaders were no longer to be found. The mayor and government leaders had left their posts. At 12:45 P.M., the military guard of Oruro yielded to the insurgents. The demonstration was called off. On the following day, reinforcements arrived from Santa Cruz by air. Radio Pio XII, the Oblate mission station in Siglo XX, called for a withdrawal of miners still in the area to prevent bloodshed. At midnight the radio broadcast a speech, said to be by Victor Paz Estenssoro (whose MNR party, along with the Social Phalanx of Bolivia [FSB], was behind the rebellion), calling for their dispersal. (Those familiar with his voice say that it was difficult to recognize it because of the poor transcription.) Some of the miners left the city in response to his plea.

The miners were still under contradictory orders from their leaders on the following day. Over 1500 miners from Siglo XX and Huanuni, resolved to take the Oruro airport and hold it against the insurgents, were repelled by heavily armed forces, and 8 were killed. According to 2 miners taken prisoner, their leaders had told them that they would be joined by military forces under the command of President Torres (*Presencia*, August 23, 1971). The prisoners reported that the directors of the union escaped in some of the vehicles, leaving the dead and wounded without help (*Patria*, September 22, 1971).

The 280-day presidency of Juan José Torres ended after 3 days of fighting in the capital cities of Santa Cruz, Oruro, Cochabamba, and La Paz departments. Torres had given the country over nine months of freedom – freedom for workers to reorganize the unions, for students to march in protest against imperialism, and for politicians of the right as well as of the left to formulate positions and seek alliances. For some, this freedom meant only anarchy, but in a country that had lived in a state of dependency and subjugation to outside economic and political interests, it was a time to assess who Bolivians were as a people and where they were going.

Throughout his term, there had been persistent rumors of intervention by the United States. That the US Embassy knew that a coup was about to take place is established by the warning to stock up on food supplies 48 hours before the coup in La Paz, reported by Cuban correspondent Ernesto Gonzales Bermejo. Reports indicate that Torres had himself reserved 60 places for exiles in the Chilean Embassy. The reported association of Major Robert J. Lundin with Banzer prior to and during the coup (*Washington Post* on August 29, 1971) has been denied as having had a serious impact on the movement of the rebels in Santa Cruz by General Remberto Iriarte (*Presencia*, August 31, 1971), but those who were in Bolivia during the coup attest to the importance of a network of radio communication linking the activities of rebels and demoralized government armed forces.

Despite the US denial of military involvement, officials did not conceal their satisfaction at the success of the coup (*Presencia*, August 30, 1971). The financial support immediately offered the Banzer government indicated to Bolivians which side the United States was on. On August 28, *Presencia* reported a US loan of $2,500,000 for cotton agriculture. On September 7, *Presencia* announced in large headlines US offers of $100,000,000 credit with $3,000,000 earmarked for construction of three new markets. The Bank of America announced a $12,000,000 loan to the Nationalized Mining Corporation of Bolivia September 11, 1971. Victor Siracusa, US Ambassador, promised special financing to

Bolivia that would offset any problems with the proposed law restricting imports (*Presencia*, September 14, 1971). Brazil and Argentina added to US promises loans totaling $10,000,000.

The new government is relying on military strength to hold on to what it has gained. The university and mines were occupied by troops until September. Recently armed tanks were delivered to Oruro, where the barracks are situated right next to the mining encampment. The two parties that backed the rebellion, the Social Phalanx of Bolivia and the National Revolutionary Movement, still maintain an uncertain alliance, but the old left-of-center supporters of the latter have urged Paz Estenssoro to denounce the government of Banzer for its treatment of students during the raid on the University of San Andres.

Reading the newspaper reports of the aftermath of the coup, I felt that I was back in 1954 in Guatemala, when Castillo Armas entered the country with 200 rebel troops equipped by the United Fruit Company and backed by promises of support from the US government. I was living in an Indian town in the western highlands and saw trucks loading campesinos with nothing more than machetes to "defend their revolution" the night that Jack Purifoy, special representative of the US government, maneuvered the ouster of President Arbenz. The coup also has a parallel in the US invasion of the Dominican Republic, when President Johnson sent in Marines to take back control from a government considered too far left.

Recalling the consequences of our intervention in these countries, I began to reflect on the role we social scientists are called on to play. Do anthropologists go to these countries just to write epitaphs for the movements that are cut down when they go beyond the limits the US government sets for them? Those of us who are concerned with the welfare of the people we study must reveal what we know about the US involvement and what it means to them. In the months I worked in Oruro, I came to realize the CIA symbolized the American presence in Bolivia. Their agents act in secrecy and are protected by the State Department, while we, as American citizens, must bear the burden of guilt for their actions. It seems a

corollary of this that we must dedicate ourselves to eradicating their influence on our government's policy.

The role of the participant-observer in a revolutionary setting has a special dynamic. Just by being there, threatening the existing role-structure and hovering in the conflict of identity, I became an instrument in the research. The attacks directed against me gave information of the inner conflicts of a people who had suffered "in their very flesh" the presence of the United States and the abhorred CIA agents. In evaluating my own role in the community, I realized that the CIA agent is not entirely different from the witch in the Maya community. The difference was that, while I despised the activities of the CIA of my own country, I felt neutral about witches in another country, and while I became one of the targets of accusation in Bolivia my cultural distance protected me from becoming part of the witch hunt in the Maya community. This breakdown of my carefully cultivated "cultural relativist" position forced me to realize that it was premised on a colonialist attitude. I did not judge the witchcraft institutions because I felt removed from and impervious to them. In Bolivia I was no longer able to maintain this pose, because the CIA agents and I were part of the same historical continuum. I realized more fully the implications of Maquet's (1964) rejection of the scientific attitude of impersonal objectivity as inappropriate for the kind of research in which we by our very presences are instruments of that research. The world is no longer our laboratory, as Berreman has remarked (1971:100), but a community in which we are coparticipants with our informants.

Anthropologists are now at the crossroads in defining a participation-observer perspective more adequate to the load that revolutionary stress is putting on their role in the field. We must begin to specify the "degree of indeterminancy" (Heisenberg, quoted in Mannheim, 1936) arising from our own perspective. We can no longer retreat into the deceptive pose of neutrality (Henry, 1966). Science advances only by honest declaration of the convictions that influence our data gathering and analysis. It is a paradox that the physical sciences cast aside the pose of neutrality decades before the social sciences, with their presumably greater humanitarian orientation. In Bolivia I became convinced that part of our professional task as anthropologists is to attack the multifarious ways in which the US State Department operates to destroy the independence movements of the countries that supply it with raw materials. Lévi-Strauss (1969:52) announced prematurely that "our science arrived at maturity the day that Western man began to see that he would never understand himself as long as there was a single race or people on the surface of the earth that he treated as an object." We have yet to reach the goal he envisioned of becoming "an enterprise reviewing and atoning for the Renaissance, in order to spread humanism to all humanity".

REFERENCES

Berreman, Gerald D.
1968 "Is Anthropology Alive?," *Current Anthropology*, 9:391–6.
Berreman, Gerald D.
1971 "The Greening of the American Anthropological Association: Address to the Council," American Anthropological Association, 69th Meeting, San Diego, November 19, 1970, *Critical Anthropology*, 2(1):100–4.
Gough, Kathleen
1968 "New Proposals for Anthropologists," *Current Anthropology*, 9:403–7.

Henry, Frances
1966 "The Role of a Fieldworker in an Explosive Political Situation," *Current Anthropology*, 7:552–8.
Jarvie, I. C.
1969 "The Problem of Ethical Integrity in Participant-Observation," *Current Anthropology*, 10:505–9.
Jones, Delmos J.
1971 "Social Responsibility and the Belief in Basic Research: An Example from Thailand," *Current Anthropology*, 12:347–50.
Jorgensen, Joseph G.
1971 "On Ethics and Anthropology," *Current Anthropology*, 12: 321–35.
Lévi-Strauss, Claude
1969 *The Scope of Anthropology*. Bungay, Suffolk: Grossman.
Mannheim, Karl
1936 *Ideology and Utopia*. New York: Harcourt, Brace.
Maquet, Jacques
1964 "Objectivity in Anthropology," *Current Anthropology*, 5:47–55.
Stavenhagen, Rodolfo
1971 "Decolonizing Applied Social Science," *Human Organization*, 30:333–57.
US Government Printing Office, Washington, DC
1969 Hearings before the Subcommittee on Inter-American Affairs of the Committee on Foreign Affairs, House of Representatives.
Wolf, Eric and Joseph G. Jorgensen
1970 "Anthropology on the Warpath in Thailand," *New York Review of Books*, November 19, pp. 26–35.

16

The Ethnographer's Tale

Neil L. Whitehead

Introduction

The term *kanaimà* refers both to a mode of ritual mutilation and killing and to its practitioners. The term also can allude to a more diffuse idea of active spiritual malignancy, in existence from the beginning of time, that consumes the assassins. This book is about those killers and the reasons they give for their actions. It is also about their victims.

Kanaimà as an ethnographic issue is complex to research because it is a discourse that operates at a number of levels, referring simultaneously to the dynamics of the spirit world, physical aggression by individuals, the tensions and jealousies between villagers and family members, and the suspicions of distant enemies and outsiders. This means that any ethnography of kanaimà necessarily involves a broad appreciation of cultural life and social organization, not least because one of kanaimà's key characteristics is that it is regional, not just local, in its practice. It is therefore part of the cultural repertoire of a number of Amerindian groups, and is known of and suffered by their closest neighbors as well. As a result, one is simultaneously dealing with convincing case histories, wild rumors, considered attributions of blame, false accusations, ungrounded gossip, and justified suspicion.

This pervasive and profound discourse of kanaimà is a central ethnographic fact of the lives of the people of the Guyana Highlands. Both dramatizing the human condition and indicating its futility, kanaimà is a daily subject of conversation and closely influences the decisions that people make with its vision of a cosmos filled with predatory gods and spirits whose violent hungers are sated by humans. Decisions to go to the farm, to make a journey with someone else or not, to carry a gun or not, to pass by the spirit abode of a famed killer, or to walk by a longer route are thus woven into the texture of everyday life, influencing its practical aspects as much as the ideational. For those that participate in this discourse there is also the distant but steady drum-beat of the killings that are the

Neil L. Whitehead, "The Ethnographer's Tale," pp. 1–2, 11–40 from *Dark Shamans: Kanaimà and the Poetics of Violent Death*. Durham: Duke University Press, 2002.

Ethnographic Fieldwork: An Anthropological Reader, Second Edition. Edited by Antonius C. G. M. Robben and Jeffrey A. Sluka.
Editorial material and organization © 2012 John Wiley & Sons, Inc.
Published 2012 by John Wiley & Sons, Inc.

discursive proof of the malign nature of the cosmos and the enmity of others.

For these reasons the following study examines the discourse of kanaimà as well as the histories of the killings. This is not just for the good theoretical reason that acts and ideas cannot properly be treated as separate realms, but also because our notions of causality and facticity are challenged by the nature of kanaimà. Such has been the case in the study of magical and spiritual phenomena worldwide, particularly where the possibility of dark shamanism, "witchcraft," and assault sorcery is under discussion. While this is not a unique problem, however, this book is not about the philosophy of causation or the conceptual conflicts between "science" and "magic" but about the way in which such issues are woven into the fabric of everyday life; that is, this book looks at the poetics of kanaimà and the violent, mutilating death it envisages. This poetic is neither a system of empirical observation nor a fanciful embellishment of the inexplicable – it is both. The term *poetic*, in this sense, suggests that the meaning of violent death cannot be entirely understood by reference to biological origins, sociological functions, or material and ecological necessities but must also be appreciated as a fundamental and complex cultural expression. Such cultural expression itself, if it is to be understood, must necessarily involve competence in the manipulation of signs and symbols. Any particular act of manipulation – that is, any given cultural performance – is therefore akin to the poetical in that it involves discursive forms of allusion and implication that are highly specialized, albeit rarely textual. In short, I am not concerned with the formal properties of signs, symbols, and rituals – semiotics – but how those signs are used performatively through time – poetics.
[...]

The Ethnographer's Tale

As I got off the plane in Paramakatoi in 1992, I had not a thought of kanaimà in mind. The purpose of my journey was to make, in collaboration with the Walter Roth Museum of Anthropology, a preliminary survey of archaeological sites, in particular cave occupation sites, urn burials, and old villages. I hoped with that survey to begin to counter the exceptionally negative view that the region was sparsely populated and devoid of cultural time-depth, a view that had been promulgated in the archaeological literature outside of Guyana. I was accompanied by a Lokono man from the Mahaica River who was a highly experienced field archaeologist. He had been through the region a couple of years previously and had already examined the kinds of sites – old villages, burials, battle sites – that we were now interested in documenting as systematically as we could. We planned to walk out from Paramakatoi, south toward the Ireng River, then follow the north bank of the Ireng to Puwa village, turn north to Kurukabaru and then south again to Kato, where we would be able to catch a flight to Georgetown. Logistically and physically this was a difficult itinerary since we would have to carry most of what we needed over a terrain that features numerous mountains covered in dense tropical forest alternating with savannas. However, with the aid of various Patamuna who were enthusiastically behind the project, it seemed feasible to accomplish within the six to eight weeks we had planned to be away.

I want to emphasize the active participation of Patamuna individuals, both at the outset of this project and in subsequent ethnographic investigations. I do so to indicate not only their interest in my work but also the way in which my research was shaped by their priorities. While this may sound ideal, it meant that my research risked becoming partisan as it became more closely identified with the interests and ambitions of certain individuals, albeit that they were legitimate leaders of the community. This is not to suggest that there can be any "unpositioned" viewpoint; clearly any researcher is necessarily part of one kind of social network and therefore not another. However, the public authority of the individuals involved – or, later, their lack of it – became a particularly significant factor in the history of my fieldwork in the Pakaraimas between 1992 and 1997. It also fundamentally influenced my ability to gain otherwise relatively obscure, and even dangerous, knowledge.

Although this was not my first visit, Guyana had been relatively off-limits to anthropologists and most outsiders during the years of the People's National Congress government. Policies of self-reliance and an understandable antipathy to intellectual colonization by the United States and United Kingdom meant that foreign researchers were often judged superfluous. However, the Walter Roth Museum, under the directorship of Denis Williams, provided invaluable support for my field trips into the Pakaraimas, and without that assistance it is doubtful I could have worked in Guyana at all. I was therefore doubly pleased to not just be in Guyana but to have the opportunity to reach an interior region that was largely unknown in recent archaeology or ethnography.

Unknown to me at the moment the plane touched down, but soon apparent, the kanaimà would come to dominate that trip's research, as well as subsequent fieldwork in the region. Within thirty minutes of landing, we were visited by the Nurse for Paramakatoi, who politely listened to our plans, then launched into a startling account of what we "should really be investigating" – the kanaimà, especially because of the interest (not all of it favorable) that the earlier work of my Lokono companion had aroused.

It is hard now to reconstruct how much I knew or had heard of kanaimà before that moment, as it has come to dominate my thoughts over nearly the whole of the last decade. However, being reasonably well read in the anthropological and historical literature of northeastern South America, I had certainly heard the term. I had also at some point read Walter Roth's classic synthesis of materials on the kanaimà and so vaguely recalled kanaimà as some peculiar revenge cult that was probably in substance a colonially projected idea of native savagery. I had even referred to Brett's account of an "unappeased" kanaimà in a publication on Karinya warfare, but only as a possible example of the results of colonial suppression of warfare in the nineteenth century (Whitehead 1990b). I was therefore intrigued and surprised to find kanaimà being almost the first topic of conversation, since

I had assumed that the phenomenon had simply faded away, which had seemed to be the implication of Roth's account. I could not have been more wrong.

The sequence of my own intellectual interest in kanaimà seems, as an anthropological issue and category of ethnographic description, to closely reproduce the history of anthropological debate about "cannibalism." As will become evident, nonnative ideas about kanaimà, as with cannibalism more widely, cannot be taken as simply reflecting impartial results of an encounter with some objectively present form of native savagery or exoticism. Rather, our interest in the savagery of others, in particular when it appears to take the form of cannibalism, clearly has served an ideological purpose in both politically justifying and morally enabling violent conquest and occupation of native South America (Arens 1979; Hulme 1986, 2000; Hulme and Whitehead 1992; Whitehead 1988, 1995a, 1995c). Nonetheless, ideological agendas aside, some cultural practices are undeniably challenging to interpret, in that they apparently give meaning and value to acts that we might abhor or simply deny as "real." However, this lack of "reality" often reflects our own lack of understanding, and what we actually mean is that those acts are "incomprehensible."

Kanaimà perfectly instantiates such a category, for the term invokes truly strange and troubling acts. In both the colonial literature and native oral testimony, kanaimà refers to the killing of an individual by violent mutilation of, in particular, the mouth and anus, into which are inserted various objects. The killers are then enjoined to return to the dead body of the victim in order to drink the juices of putrefaction.

> The ... victim will first become aware of an impending attack when the *Kanaimàs* approach his house by night, or on lonely forest trails [*asanda*], making a characteristic whistling noise.... a direct physical attack might come at any point, even years thereafter, for during this period of stalking the victim is assessed as to their likely resistance and their suitability as "food." ... In some attacks the victims may have minor bones broken,

especially fingers, and joints dislocated, especially the shoulder, while the neck may also be manipulated to induce spinal injury and back pain. This kind of attack is generally considered to be a preliminary to actual death and mutilation; ... fatal attack will certainly follow but, informants stress, many months, or even a year or two, later. When a fatal physical attack is intended, victims are always struck from behind and physically restrained.... A variety of procedures, intended to produce a lingering death, are then enacted. The victim has their tongue pierced with the fangs of a snake, is turned over and either an iguana or an armadillo tail is inserted into their rectum so that the anal muscles can be stripped out through repeated rubbing. Then, pressing on the victim's stomach, a section of the sphincter muscle is forced out and cut. Finally, the victim's body is rubbed down with astringent plants ... and a thin flexed twig is forced into the rectum, so that it opens the anal tract. Packets of herbs are then rammed in as deeply as possible. This is said to begin a process of auto-digestion, creating the special aroma of *Kanaimà* enchantment, rotting pineapple.... As a result of the completion of these procedures, the victim is unable to speak or to take any sustenance by mouth. Bowel control is lost and the clinical cause of death becomes acute dehydration through diarrhoea.... the *Kanaimàs* will try and discover the burial place of their victim and await the onset of putrefaction in the corpse that usually occurs within three days.... [When] the grave site is discovered, a stick is inserted through the ground directly into the cadaver, then the stick is retracted and the *maba* (honey-like) juices sucked off.... If the corpse is indeed sufficiently "sweet," it will be partially disinterred in order to recover bone material and, ideally, a section of the anal tract. The use of previous victim's body parts is necessary to facilitate the location and killing of the next victim. (Whitehead 2001b)

One can readily appreciate, then, how issues of "representing others" are brought forcibly to mind by apparently "objectively encountering" such a ritual complex not as a textual remnant from colonial days but as the earnest testimony of living individuals. Moreover, I was to learn that the idea of kanaimà exercises a constant and intense influence over the cultural imagination of the Patamuna and their neighbors, the Akawaio and Makushi. However, my initial reactions to the Nurse were to try to fold her testimony into that more general discourse on "witchcraft" and to see her declarations as a performance of Patamuna alterity and desire to differentiate and distance themselves from others, especially white anthropologists.

However, the Nurse's – and later other's – absolute insistence on the physical reality of kanaimà, coupled with her sophisticated acknowledgment of its wider discursive properties, was unsettling; it challenged me to truly confront a kind of cultural difference that it had been easy to assume had been eroded by the long histories of colonial contact in this region, even if the Patamuna had not been in the forefront of that process. Indeed, I found that my hesitation to immediately acknowledge the reality of kanaimà put me alongside the British missionaries who had, according to the Nurse, assumed that kanaimà was just part of the "superstitious nonsense" cooked up by "primitive" peoples. The missionaries, lacking cultural competence, simply dismissed kanaimà as some kind of spirit, an example of Wittgenstein's observation that "Wherever our language leads us to believe there is a body, but no body exists, there is a spirit" (1953, 1:36).

Nonetheless, if I had not then encountered something more "real" than "just talk," presumably I, too, would have remained within the standard view of the anthropological literature, that is, that whatever may have been true in the past, accusations of kanaimà exemplified the social functions of belief in witchcraft as a mechanism for community inclusion/ exclusion. So they may be, but that by no means exhausts the matter – and not just because such a discourse might serve as a rich realm of cultural performance and signification, but because people actually die in ways consistent with the notion of kanaimà attack. I have never witnessed such an attack, nor have I attempted to do so, even though the lack of eyewitness accounts has rightly been adduced as an ethnographic weakness in anthropological discussions of cannibalism. Nonetheless, a moment's reflection should indicate that to witness physical violence is in itself extremely dangerous and necessarily entails complex ethical judgments as to how (and whether) such events should be described or published. Yet it is equally clear that the only difference between my position and that of the missionaries would be a willingness to take seriously what was so evidently being impressed on me – that kanaimàs are real people who do real killing of specific and identifiable individuals.

We were due to leave Paramakatoi early the day after next in order to keep to our itinerary, and though I made copious notes of that first conversation, I did not yet seriously entertain deviating from our original plan. So we walked from Paramakatoi, which is on a small savanna at the top of a mountain at the end of the Yawong River valley, down into the valley to search for our chief Patamuna collaborator, whom I call "Waiking." It was on this day that archaeology and kanaimà came together in a startling way. We learned that, at the head of the valley, there was a small cave, Kuyali'yen (Macaw Cave), in which an urn burial had recently been found. This was exactly the kind of information we had hoped to gather, and it immediately justified our decision to organize the research in a way that directly involved Patamuna. To have uncovered this site through physical survey would have been much more time-consuming and uncertain. We decided to visit the site immediately so that we could walk out of the valley, as planned, the following day.

When I first saw the "burial" I was disappointed as it was evident that the "burial" vessel was very small, not nearly large enough to contain a complete human set of remains. It was accompanied by a small *tumi* (offering bowl). It had not been my intention to collect archaeological materials; we not only wished to be alert to Patamuna sensitivities about the handling of ancestral remains, but we were also in no position to carry heavy and fragile ceramics for the remaining six weeks. However, what happened next was to become, both in my mind and that of others, a defining moment: as the Patamuna with us would not "trouble" the pot in any way, my Lokono companion moved the pot to the cave mouth where I could photograph it – and where I, too, without thinking, touched it.

This act came to define my identity to many Patamuna in many ways. Indeed, I believe I was to some degree manipulated into this "archaeological discovery," since I was not the first non-Patamuna to see it. It also transpired that the reasons for showing it to me were substantially more connected with contemporary conflicts than with the archaeological past, for the pot was in fact a ritual vessel still being used by a kanaimà, as was evident from the contents of the pot – it contained human skeletal and tissue material that appeared, and was later verified to be, very recent indeed, not at all archaeological. As yet, though, none of this was apparent.

At the time, and despite the obviously ethnographic nature of the context, we nonetheless had given an archaeological commitment to the Walter Roth Museum, which we honored by measuring and photographing the pot and, unfortunately, by removing a sample of the bone material to determine its age. I say "unfortunately" because this act, as far as can be said with certainty, may have been the immediate reason for an apparent attempt to poison me. The less-than-favorable light in which the earlier archaeological survey was held by some Patamuna thus came to have a real and definite consequence.

On our way back from the cave, my Patamuna companions suggested that this was something "kanaimà" and that we should return via the benab of an individual whom I call "Pirai." At that moment, I presumed that this was because Pirai was living the closest to the cave, but it transpired that he had a much more substantive connection with the vessel. I could not follow the initial part of the conversation with Pirai on arriving at his benab, but it was obvious that he was very excited and upset about something, and the word *kanaimà* occurred a number of times. We climbed back up the bump to Paramakatoi to find that news of the "discovery" was already in the village and that, in the opinion of those villagers who spoke to me about it, it was an excellent development and should enable the museum "to let everyone know the truth of those kanaimàs." But, whatever the intriguing ethnographic aspects, the implications of the ritual vessel seemed to be something I could better pursue on a subsequent visit and that anyway might not please the museum, on which I was reliant for future permissions to work anthropologically in the interior. All that was changed dramatically by the events that followed.

We were lodged at the boarding school for the duration of our visit, since it was still the Christmas vacation and the children had returned to their home villages. We also had use of the refectory, and while we were starting to prepare some food that evening, a Makushi woman came in and offered to cook for us. As she did so she started to talk animatedly about kanaimà, although we had not raised the topic, but neither of us spoke Makushi and her English was fragmented. I must confess that I had had quite enough of the topic for one day and was more concerned with how I was going to physically meet the challenges of six weeks of hard trekking. I knew that, among other things, eating properly was a basic rule, and I wished that she would simply serve up the rations that we had given her to prepare. The food was execrable. Although it was simply rice and a few dried shrimp, she had managed to make it taste absolutely horrible. My Lokono companion suggested that it was just the *casareep* (manioc juice) that she had used to flavor the dried shrimp and that I was being a typical "white boy" in my excessive delicacy of taste. But I had eaten casareep before and so just concluded that she was a lousy chef.

I have no proof otherwise and make no accusations, but I started feeling extremely ill within a few minutes of finishing that meal, and the symptoms got steadily and acutely worse during the next few days. I was quite unable to sleep that night because of a high temperature and incessant vomiting. I was feeling very weak by sunrise when, nevertheless, we set off back down the Yawong valley to rendezvous with Waiking. Thinking that my illness was a reaction to some form of food poisoning, I ignored my physical state as well as I could. However, in the general conversation we had while redistributing our loads at Waiking's house, the matter of my "illness" came up, as the *droghers* (carriers) were concerned about taking me into the bush while in such a condition. When I jokingly blamed the poor culinary arts of the Makushi woman, someone, I don't recall whom, remarked that to have let her cook for us was "a stupid thing to do, boy. Don't you know she lives by Pirai?" Of course we hadn't known, but with that strange luminosity that comes with feverish thought, I suddenly appreciated that what was being suggested was not poisoning *by* my food but *of* my food.

During that day my condition got worse and worse until, when we were almost at the summit of Aluatatupu on the other side of the Yawong valley, I collapsed with severe retching and stomach cramps. I had never ever lain down on the forest floor before, for the obvious reason that it is home to many voracious biting insects, but neither can I recall having felt quite so grim, even though I have had malaria, hepatitis, and pneumonia, as well as "normal" food poisoning. My companions carried me to the summit, about a half mile farther on. I was laid down and I cried by the waters of Akaikalakparu. In the crossing place of this creek is a small, submerged stone; carved on it is the face of a *totopù* (spirit guardian) who died right there, from exhaustion, as he couldn't make it down into the valley. We eyed each other balefully.

Everyone was thoroughly alarmed at the prospect of having me die, for it was acknowledged that even Patamuna could simply "fall down on the line [asanda]," that a fear of "not making it" would kill you as certainly as any accident or other misfortune. Of course, the Patamuna regularly walked this route and could easily make the next village, Taruka, from Paramakatoi. However, as the petroglyph of the to-topù's face at Akaikalakparu suggested, longer journeys were always a challenge for small parties or lone individuals, given the food shortages that could occur if the bumps weren't walked in sufficient time. It was not that people had no food, or indeed would refuse to share it if someone were desperate, but there was not necessarily enough food to buy or trade, and what there was had become extremely expensive due to the mining activities throughout the region. We had planned to reach Taruka in one day and Monkey Mountain in one or two days after that and so had only minimal rations with us. These were immediately exhausted by meals that night and the next morning. I slept for a few hours and actually felt better, if weak, the next day. My load was distributed among the others: Waiking; his brother, Yabiku; and Hashiro, my Lokono companion.

It took us all of that day to reach Taruka. On the line we had another uncanny experience when Pirai passed us in the company of two adolescent boys. What was peculiar was that he, as well as his companions, simply refused to address anyone. They emerged right behind us on the trail as we stopped by a creek to drink, and while Pirai made eye contact with us all, he responded neither to greetings nor to the insults shouted after him as he proceeded up the mountain trail. When we finally arrived at Taruka we were greeted politely and offered bowls of *cassiri* (manioc beer), but only one of my companions accepted, which I knew to be a real breach of etiquette. Taruka was a Makushi village at that time, and the conviction that the Makushi were kanaimàs was certainly part of Patamuna ethnic prejudices, but refusal of cassiri seemed to imply a very particular judgment about this village. Perhaps unsurprisingly, then, no one had food to sell us. This was a serious matter, as we had no food left and the only place to buy it would be Monkey Mountain, which we could clearly see some twenty miles away toward the Brazilian border.

We were stuck. We could not go on, or at least I couldn't, because I could hardly walk to the latrine, let alone Monkey Mountain, and my symptoms now became far worse, developing into a constant diarrhea and nausea. All that night I had to keep leaving the house we were lodged in. On one occasion I staggered some twenty yards from the house, squatted, and looked out over the savanna toward Siparuni mountain. The moon was bright, and as I tried to enjoy the beauty of the scene I saw in the distance some movement that appeared to be two distinct figures moving along the ground toward me. My first thought was that they were dogs, but as they turned to flank me they appeared instead to have the shape of anteaters because of the elongated head and tail. As I pulled up my pants, I looked away, then could not find the figures again when I looked back. Although that seemed odd,

I reflected that, all other things considered, perhaps this was to be taken seriously. I would not recount this incident at all were it not for the unpleasant effect it had on everyone else, who immediately took the distant figures to have been kanaimàs and who were now convinced that the interest of the kanaimàs was centered on us. It was rather unsettling to be sick, to be a long walk from the next village, and to feel menaced by something I could not easily understand or explain away.

The next morning it had become vital that we either try to go on or go back, and we were fortunate that someone did finally sell us three eggs and some pieces of *tasso* (dried meat). We were not technically starving as yet. It was fortunate also that Waiking had been able to persuade someone to fetch a horse, Sharon, so that I could be carried down the trail to Monkey Mountain. Since everyone was now weak and tired from hunger, our progress was slow. Although I do not think we ate the whole of that day either, we did occasionally find wild cashew trees in fruit, which inhibited my diarrhea. As we finally reached Monkey Mountain early the next morning, we passed the remains of a crashed aircraft, a token of the mining frontier, once used by a Brazilian diamond trader who had been flown in to buy up stones. In Monkey Mountain we were able to purchase food, and we also met Johnny Roth, the great-grandson of Walter Roth. Having eaten at last, everyone was feeling better, including myself, and we planned to continue toward Puwa with a good store of rations. It was not to be.

I have taken some pains to depict the palette of events and ideas from which each of us constructed our pictures of what happened next, and I am not suggesting that we were necessarily all in perfect accord. I can therefore only speak to my impressions, but that certainly does not exclude suggesting the motivations present in others – that being the essence of any attempt at anthropological explanation or cultural interpretation. The pervasive nature of kanaimà as a cultural discourse and the manner in which I had entered into it – by inviting enmity as a result of "troubling" the vessel in Kuyali'yen – entailed certain consequences that were beyond my control.

I was lying in my hammock while the others had gone to the shop at Monkey Mountain, when, to my surprise, one of the youths who had been with Pirai on the line into Monkey Mountain appeared in the doorway. He said not a word at first and didn't respond to my questions. He then began to speak rapidly but deliberately in Patamuna, which I couldn't clearly follow. Waiking, Yabiku, and Hashiro saw the youth as they returned and they let out a loud shout, at which he bolted off. When I explained what had happened they suggested that he had been sent to "check you out" and that he had been threatening me. Whether or not this was the case, and I certainly don't like to think it was so, this at least suggested that we should abandon our original itinerary. It had been a key aspect of the project that it should be done with Patamuna cooperation and, although I was receiving support from some of them, it seemed that my presence was simply not welcome to others among them. Since this was actually the inference of my Patamuna companions, I also took this to mean that persisting at this point was likely to be a cause of further trouble for them.

In retrospect it is clear that tension was building with Pirai and that Hashiro and I were unwittingly increasing that tension, since we must have seemed intent on uncovering kanaimà pots as much as burials. Nonetheless, we all had the sense that we were being forced to give up something that was important and useful. Waiking and others in Paramakatoi, such as the Nurse, believed that a key aspect of future political and economic opportunities for the Patamuna was to possess a recognizable and distinct external ethnic identity. Archaeology and ethnography were seen as part of the means by which that could be achieved. In addition the Walter Roth Museum itself had been making a series of efforts to more adequately inform the Guyanese about the interior populations. The aim was to establish the antiquity of the Amerindian presence in Guyana through excavation and also to document the little-known highland peoples through broad archaeological and/or ethnographic surveys, such as the one we were conducting, as well as through longer term fieldwork.

At that moment it seemed to me that the best way to return to this survey, or another project in Paramakatoi, would be to leave now before the suspicions of kanaimà grew out of hand and something worse happened. In any case I was still very ill. I discussed the possibility of leaving with both Hashiro and Waiking, and we agreed that we should do so but that we would return and make the kanaimà itself the focus of investigation – not least because it was evident that the ritual vessel we had disturbed was very significant. To answer why that should be and to find further physical evidence of kanaimà activity seemed feasible, if risky, given our own direct encounters with those held to be kanaimà. Moreover, to leave and then return, rather than continue on, seemed preferable at that point, not just because I was very sick but also because it would allow us to plan properly and let things calm down a bit. In addition, Waiking was adamant that it would be possible to interview piya on the matter, since there was a general feeling that the "work of the kanaimà had to be better known," and setting up those interviews would take time. The Nurse's testimony was further evidence of this appeal for openness about ritual practice, and I was intrigued to find myself already cast in the role of "ethnographer." Usually an ethnographer is expected to justify and explain that role as a precondition of extended research. So I was very impressed by the sophistication of Patamuna in exploiting the interest of outsiders for their own benefit. In fact, I came to understand that this theme had been very deeply inscribed on their historical consciousness, as the "fetching" of both alleluia and various missionaries into Paramakatoi, which I discuss later, clearly showed. In this sense it was not me as such but the need for a certain kind of external connection that made me appropriate and useful in the political aims of Patamuna.

So that was it. We used the police radio at Monkey Mountain to contact the bush-pilot Derek Leung who extracted Hashiro and myself the following morning. We had promised Waiking that we would return at a future date.

Once in Georgetown we decided to utilize the remaining weeks with a survey of archaeological sites on the Berbice River which proved to be highly productive. But with time and distance I found myself more and more intrigued by what had "really happened" in Paramakatoi, and the kanaimà remained for me a continual topic of conversation, reflection, and inquiry. I had felt a bit better when I returned to Georgetown, with only intermittent fever, vomiting, and diarrhea, but I became alarmed again when I started urinating blood after a couple of days in Berbice. I had now begun to be persuaded that whatever the cause of my sickness it was not routine, as the symptoms did not match readily with any particular cause. Hashiro then had the suggestion that I fight "fire with fire" by consulting someone on the Berbice who had knowledge of bush-medicine. This we did and I swallowed what I was given. I stopped passing blood.

It was only then that Hashiro told me something which he had not previously mentioned – his own father had been killed by kanaimàs. According to Hashiro, his father was working as a woodcutter at the time and had gone upriver to Mahaica, only stopping at St Cuthbert's, where they lived, to collect pineapples. He returned unusually late, around 6:30 P.M., saying he couldn't remember why or what had happened. His wife began to worry about him, but he bathed as usual. He then started feeling very sick and from then on his condition deteriorated rapidly. Despite seeking medical help in Georgetown the very next day and being given a clean bill of health and a release form, he died suddenly on the third day. As he was being prepared for burial the family noticed finger marks and bruising on his arms and back. For the family this was evidence of the *yawáho* (kanaimà) but they insisted that this was actually a case of an attack gone wrong, in that the man who claimed the killing had mistakenly identified Hashiro's father as the intended victim. According to Hashiro, they also pointed to the fact that the killing was "not done that way," implying that the attackers had actually realized their misidentification and had therefore stopped short of enacting the full kanaimà ritual. However, Hashiro further surprised me by making an explicit connection between his own earlier work in the Paramakatoi region, the possibility that his father's death might have

been intended for himself, and the menacing circumstances we had just encountered. In short, Hashiro felt that I was becoming involved in an active contest between the kanaimàs and those who would "expose" them.

I was not able to return to Paramakatoi until 1995 as I had accepted a post in the United States, at the University of Wisconsin. The demands of migrating from England to a new country with a wife and two small children, none of whom had visited the United States before, had meant I could not visit South America in 1993. Prior to this, on my return from Paramakatoi in 1992, my father had been diagnosed with inoperable colorectal cancer, on top of which my maternal uncle died just before Christmas of that year. I will say that this deeply affected me, as the loss of a father in particular would affect anyone, but that it also affected my view of the events in Guyana. In that time of stress it was hard not to recall that Hashiro's father had been "mistakenly" killed for his son and to not let form the idea that the anal wounding of the typical kanaimà victim was somehow being recalled and reduplicated, first in the rectal pain I had suffered as a consequence of being continually sick, and then in the fatal rot that was eating away my father's insides. He did not go quietly into that long night, and my family situation meant that it fell to me to nurse him in his last weeks of life in the spring of 1994. Again, then, I was unable to return to Paramakatoi, although I had kept the connection with Waiking active with the help of the museum and Hashiro.

In 1995, however, I was able to plan my return to Paramakatoi for the summer months. By that time, having had many reasons to contemplate the cultural forms of death and dying, I was also resentful and angry toward those who, it seemed, had tried to poison me – for on my return to Guyana I found that this was the story being told. This story was heard not just in Paramakatoi, where anthropologist Duncan Kilgour had recorded it in 1994, but it also had spread right across the highland region to Lethem and eventually even as far as Dominica in the Caribbean. My return to Paramakatoi was thus considered highly significant, both because it signaled a refusal to be intimidated by the possibility of kanaimà and because I could be of definite use as an ethnographic recorder. In fact, it was my work on historical themes that proved the most important, as the textual recording of oral history was, for the Patamuna in Paramakatoi, the principal benefit of my presence. The investigation of kanaimà was certainly a secondary consideration for some Patamuna and was therefore always going to be the more provocative and divisive subject of research. However, there was also strong support for bringing kanaimà "into the open," to publish accounts of their practices, to "collect" their ritual equipment, and to interview avowed kanaimàs directly so that their "reality" could finally be established in the minds of outsiders and so that their violent criminality, as it was then pictured, might somehow be curbed.

During 1995 I collected both oral histories about the Patamuna generally and about Paramakatoi in particular (Whitehead 1996c). I was also able to interview piya on the subject of kanaimà and, eventually, a powerful kanaimà himself. The centerpiece of the oral historical materials was undoubtedly the testimony on warfare, alleluia, and the arrival of the missionaries; such testimony was given in rather a formal way. I was not encouraged to ask questions as such, but rather to be as faithful a recorder as possible. Testimony was always given in Patamuna, tape-recorded, then translated and transcribed into English by myself and an English-speaking Patamuna. The Patamuna also insisted on the adoption of particular spellings for Patamuna words, since they felt that misspelling was a particularly damaging form of misrepresentation by outsiders, given their overall commitment to resisting language loss.

As a result of achieving the aims of addressing Patamuna wishes for a record of key events in the history of both Paramakatoi and the initial occupation of the Yawong Valley by the Patamuna ancestors, I then received full support for researching the issue of kanaimà. The key interviews with piya and kanaimà occurred during my 1995 research trip. Without the assistance of Waiking, the initial interviews could not have been easily achieved, but once I had identified the key

kanaimà, I then made independent approaches. These interviews were hard to broker, but the lure of money and the sense that, whether or not they granted interviews, I was going to say or do something which might affect them did encourage some kanaimàs to speak with me. This in turn built a momentum such that more senior kanaimàs, their ritual tutors, finally also agreed to speak directly with me. I avoided Pirai, however, because of a suspicion that he was behind the problems I had experienced in 1992. The younger kanaimàs were often braggarts and sometimes really quite ignorant of ritual matters, but they did allow me to form a picture of possible motivations for becoming involved in kanaimà practices. The older kanaimàs were much more intimidating, less given to freely explaining their motives or procedures, and physically wasted in appearance. Interviews with piya were also complex to arrange and conduct but were not tinged with the same air of menace. The most forthcoming of the older kanaimàs, whom I call "Emewari," probably supplied the bulk of the information I had from these sources, and other interviews were really confirmations (or not) of what he said. The other key interview was with a piya who is known widely across the region, and it was he who made a shamanic attack on a kanaimà while I was present, though I think not at my behest.

The interview with Emewari was of course invaluable, not just for the detailed information he gave but also because the conviction that kanaimà lacked "reality" had arisen in part from the absence of anyone avowing to be a killer. I should note that Emewari asked for, and got, a considerable sum of money for information on the kanaimà. Although I was initially suspicious of the fact that such knowledge would be "for sale" at all, I found that for the kanaimà, as for the piya, material rewards serve as tokens of spiritual eminence and power. I would also add that, as with all the other avowed killers I have encountered, Emewari had a marked tendency to boast about what he could achieve. Since most avowed killers admit to no specific killing and allusions to killing are often given metaphorically – as when it is said "we tied a cow" to mean "trussed up a victim" – it is perhaps unsurprising, then, that Emewari was extremely difficult to interpret, speaking of certain events through allusions to individuals I could not identify and using words that were not of Patamuna origin. Although I had linguistic assistance from a Patamuna, who I cannot name for obvious reasons, the results of this much-anticipated encounter were still frustratingly incomplete – one always thinks of the best questions only with hindsight. However, what I did understand was illuminating, even if still somewhat inconclusive [...].

As mentioned, I was able to supplement this interview by seeking out alleged kanaimàs in more distant villages, and even in Georgetown, the capital of Guyana. None of these individuals would admit to any specific incidence of violence, but most were grimly keen to "educate" me in generalities. For this, I had to play my role as one who was morbidly fascinated with kanaimà and with "manly" violence more generally, and who was quite ready to recount my own "experiences" of inflicting pain and violence in return for theirs. The catalog of violence in and by Western cultures from which I could draw such "experiences" is sufficiently replete and shocking to have made kanaimà appear quite tame at times. In particular, I remember that tales of Nazi atrocities and the refinements of modern "antipersonnel" armaments, such as the Claymore mine, particularly captured the imagination of one of these individuals.

The reasons that these interviews were possible at all were, I believe, closely connected to the political positioning that was going on in Paramakatoi in 1995 with regard to promised, or at least rumored, development schemes. I think the Patamuna felt that, if it were to be the subject of an ethnography, kanaimà would no longer be merely a "cultural problem" for the Patamuna but could be repositioned as a political and law enforcement "problem" for the government. As various interest groups vied for the scarce resources of the Guyanese state, the issue of kanaimà, it was supposed, would politically dramatize the situation of the Patamuna and therefore encourage attention to their overall situation.

Operating on a subtler level were the more local conflicts that led some individuals to see my "research" as a way of getting back at

those boasting of their kanaimà connections or knowledge. If such supposedly "secret" knowledge could be made available to all, through writing about it and publishing the results, then the "real story" of kanaimàs could be told and their influence undermined. It is certainly the case that the very vagueness, yet pervasiveness, of the presence of kanaimà allows it to assume a central place in indigenous imagination. Given this, the kind of "documentation" that outsiders are particularly good at producing serves to make exact and particular what otherwise can be elusive and uncertain. In this sense kanaimà is a joint and mutual cultural production not just by practitioners but by victims, bystanders, and outsiders, as well.

Nonetheless, community support resulted in interviews not only with avowed kanaimàs but also with many of the victims' families, as well as with piya who had experienced spirit battles with kanaimàs. The atmosphere in Paramakatoi, however, began to intensify as more people learned that we had been "troubling" kanaimà and, worst of all, had recovered some ritual paraphernalia used by a killer. As a result I received a very alarming note from Waiking, warning me off further inquiry into the topic and withdrawing his hitherto vital assistance and protection. This was quite understandable under the circumstances, but it left me feeling very exposed and uncertain – perhaps I had been too successful and thus was inviting attacks on those who had helped me, or even on myself?

Such thoughts were not dispelled by the various warnings I then began to receive, sometimes from individuals with whom I had never spoken, warnings to the effect that I had "gone too far," that I should not have troubled such things. It was therefore particularly unsettling to be visited, on three successive nights, by an unidentified person(s). I was lodged in Paramakatoi in a four-room concrete building next to the clinic. The windows had firmly locking shutters, and the only door was also secured by a strong lock, although there were, of course, gaps in the fit of both windows and doors. I was alone, since only other visitors would sleep there. Although I had assumed that, whatever the case in 1992, the passage of time and my apparent ability to culturally negotiate interviews with kanaimàs had rendered me irrelevant or external to the politics of ritual assassination, those illusions were ended over those three nights. Each night, I would clearly hear the approach of one person, maybe more, followed by the sound of a deliberate scratching at the doorframe and windows. I would call out but receive no reply. Then, once again, I would hear scratching that moved in a circle round the building, ending back at the doorway each time. I might have taken this as a (not very funny) prank by the young men had it not been that on each occasion I found afterward a *yamaliwok* (coral snake) somewhere in the house.

I would have been much happier to think of these incidents as coincidence and overactive imagination – and I admit that my imagination had been put into overdrive by that point. However, the very unwelcome news soon came that "Bishop," held to be the most adept kanaimà from the Kopinan River, had already left there five days before to come over and "check me." The bearer of these tidings was particularly alarmed because that meant that he must already be "in the bush outside PK [Paramakatoi]," as he had not come into the village. I was also visited by one of my most knowledgeable informants, whom I call "Acoori," as well as by the village *Tushau* (chief), who both warned me quite strongly to now desist as "bad things were happening."

With only about ten days left in my planned time in the Paramakatoi region, I decided that this was definitely the moment to go, but only after having first promised to return when the oral historical materials were in a published form. Around that time, I also began to get high fevers in the night, which I could not separate in my imagination from the alleged presence of Bishop and the unsettling events around my own house. In fact these fevers continued for about two months after my return to the United States. The doctors were unable to identify a cause as such, but while investigating all possible angles they discovered that I had incurable hepatitis C, probably contracted from contact with a large amount of infected human blood when I went to the aid of someone accidentally who had severed

an artery with a cutlass while working on his *mùloka* (farm). So it felt as if the kanaimàs had gotten me anyway!

The Walter Roth Museum responded magnificently to both the historical materials and the desire of Patamuna leaders to see them published. Denis Williams suggested that I put the materials into order and that the museum would then print them up in pamphlet form for distribution as widely as possible among the Patamuna villages. The result was published in 1996, and I returned in 1997 to carry the 5,000 pamphlets up to Paramakatoi and help with their distribution.

When I returned to Paramakatoi in the summer of 1997, various Patamuna expressed a great deal of satisfaction with the outcome of my previous visit and held a parade and ceremony to hand over the "little history" that had been made. At this point I also hoped to be able to reinterview some people as, inevitably, there were many aspects to kanaimà magic and ritual that remained obscure. However, interest and support for this had waned, and those who had previously supported the research were now quite hostile to me. I found out that the reasons for this were threefold. First, a strong suspicion had developed that all along I had only been trying to initiate myself as a kanaimà. This threw me somewhat, as quite the opposite had always been the basis of our collaboration, but it was sufficient indication that I should not look to the same set of individuals for more assistance with this. Nonetheless, I very much needed to dispel this suspicion, which had been "proven" by a sequence of deaths that had occurred since my last visit, among them the wife of Pirai and the father of the family that lived next to him. I countered that the deaths of my uncle and father were equal proof that I was not the origin of the "magical death" sent against them. In addition, some argued that the white man was probably trying to steal kanaimà, just like he stole cocaine from the Amerindians, and that he would put kanaimà to use against the Amerindians, just as he had done with cocaine. On this occasion I countered that the white man had no need of kanaimà, that the whole of the Yawong valley could be made a desert if the white man called in an airstrike, so that we had no need of kanaimà. I don't know how convincing this ultimately was, but it abated talk of my "becoming kanaimà." Connected to their suspicions was also the charge that I had stirred up trouble between Paramakatoi and neighboring villages by having published, in the oral history pamphlet, Patamuna accounts of warfare that featured a well-known raid by the Kopinan on Paramakatoi. Unfortunately my protestations that I had only faithfully done what I had been asked to do could not overturn the impression that this might be another example of my "kanaimà-like" propensities for conflict.

A second reason for hostility was the emergence of a new antipathy to external researchers in general and the threat that such researchers might steal from or otherwise exploit indigenous people for their cultural knowledge. The figure of the ethnobotanist, I must say, rather than the ethnographer was the chief villain of the piece. The debate around intellectual property rights, quite rightly, had become a big issue with all the Amerindian people in Guyana, but the effect for me was to have to continually explain why the notion that I could "make millions" from my research was unfair, if not entirely inaccurate in relative terms. Clearly I was better off materially than all the Patamuna, so I could certainly pay them for assistance at a rate that reflected that relative wealth, but unfortunately not at the level that the rhetoric of the foreign nongovernmental organizations suggested.

A third reason for encountering new difficulties may have stemmed from the "magical force" of the pamphlet itself. By this I mean that the mere fact of the pamphlet, whatever its particular contents, stimulated excitement because of an association, initiated in alleluia shamanism, between texts and divine power. Alleluia thus comprises both alleluia'san and *iwepyatàsak* (prophets) and, as will later become clear, such prophetism has often been evidenced through the possession of special texts. That may also be the reason why I was told that both the pamphlet and my presence had been prophesied. Either way, that was not a recommendation for those already becoming ill-disposed to the research.

Given these obstacles, the opportunity to interview kanaimàs further seemed unlikely, if not foolish. I therefore decided to examine the relationship between kanaimà and alleluia more closely, since it had struck me that there was perhaps a ritual and a historical connection. I also knew that alleluia had gone "underground" in Paramakatoi after the arrival of the Pilgrim Holiness missionaries but was not by any means extirpated. Unfortunately, those who had formerly assisted me were not only now reluctant to speak out about kanaimà but also showed a similar disinterest in discussing alleluia. I therefore got to know Alfred Edwin one of the still-practicing alleluia singers, and his son, Roger. From Alfred, and with the translation assistance of Roger, I recorded both alleluia songs and a whole series of mythic tales and historical accounts. In particular Alfred guided us to many of the alleluia places in the Yawong valley that had fallen into disuse. This was the happiest of times, and the materials we gathered will certainly be the subject of further publication, but the practice of alleluia also carries political implications. Neither did we ignore the subject of kanaimà, and it was precisely the disinterest of my earlier collaborators that now encouraged other Patamuna to relate their experiences and even act them out.

These changing orientations of my research directly replicated some of the social and political divisions in Paramakatoi itself. No longer being exclusively involved with one extended family, I was now able to be much more involved with others, like the Edwins. They did not have a high status in Paramakatoi, and this was partly connected to their obdurate practice of alleluia. Alfred's brother, Roy, is a lay pastor in the village and therefore gave up being an alleluia singer against Alfred's wishes, evidence that even close family ties were affected by decisions to abandon, or not, the practice of alleluia. Roger wanted his father's songs to be heard again in the village and to have a film record made of the event. The idea thus evolved that I would sponsor an alleluia event that would enable Alfred to sing alleluia in Paramakatoi for the first time since the 1960s. Roger therefore spent an enormous amount of time and effort to build an "Alleluia House" as a venue for this rather subversive event, which was simultaneously a snub to those who had withdrawn their support for my researches. The resulting event was filmed, but what the film cannot adequately communicate was the background conflicts that were played out that day and night.

People began assembling at the Alleluia House the day before the singing was to begin, and I was surprised to see that people had traveled up from as far as Lethem to join in the event. This did not mean that all who had come had come to see it succeed, and my heart fell when a group from Lethem wired a boom box to a car battery and started playing Brazilian samba and passing out bottles of rum. Given the sacral nature of alleluia, such behavior would ruin the possibility of the event vindicating alleluia in Paramakatoi. The next day was to be the commencement of the alleluia singing, but the following morning the samba party was still in full swing. A showdown had to be engineered to eject the interlopers, if not quiet them. As the day wore on, more and more people from Paramakatoi arrived at Roger's place, and it became clear from the reactions of the crowd, that the "moral majority" was definitely in favor of hearing "real" alleluia, and the loutish elements were quickly quelled.

So it was that the first alleluia songs were heard in Paramakatoi for over forty years, and I can only say that it was a true privilege to have been there. Indeed, those who had abandoned me so suddenly were now insisting that I return with video equipment as soon as possible in order to record "proper" alleluia. These same individuals had boycotted Roger's event, considering it too much of a "spree" (drinking party), just as the outsiders from Lethem had wanted. Indeed, the disruption by the outsiders from Lethem may have been directly encouraged by these individuals, since a younger brother of one was prominent in the attempt to wreck the event.

This was the closing scene from that 1997 trip, and I returned to Georgetown and again received the enthusiastic support of the Walter Roth Museum for a publication containing all the materials on alleluia and kanaimà I had just gathered, which would then be distributed among Patamuna villages, as had happened

with my first set of materials. But I should have known that such things cannot be easily repeated. Even as I was rushing to complete the manuscript for the museum back in the United States, Denis Williams, the director of the museum, was dying of what had become symbolically potent to me: colorectal cancer. While Williams did review and approve my manuscript before he died, which was a comfort to me, he was not always an easy person and was therefore a controversial figure in Guyanese political life. The Ministry of Culture, which took over the administration of the museum after Denis died, saw only a minimal academic product in my manuscript and so declined to publish the work, even though the galleys were already at the printer. Unlike Denis, the ministry saw no political value in the production and donation of this text to the Patamuna. The Patamuna themselves, I later learned, had come to suspect the museum of selling the earlier work at a great profit, since there was a nominal cover charge for tourists or visitors who purchased a copy at the museum itself.

On top of this I was given a final "sign" that the project, so precipitously begun in 1992, was probably at an end. Derek Leung – the bush-pilot without whom not only my fieldwork but more important the daily life of the people in Paramakatoi would have been infinitely more difficult, for want of emergency medical assistance and supplies of gasoline, tools, and the like – was killed. His plane lost instrumentation just outside Mahdia, his base of operations, and, according to air-traffic control, his last words were, in that inimitable terseness that was his hallmark, "Ooooh fuck." The logistical and political obstacles to my return seemed insurmountable, and the writing of this book is partly a symptom of that frustration.

The way in which ethnographers might become enmeshed in the beliefs and desires of those they study has been addressed before in the anthropological literature, and the book that I read in 1995 that seemed best to provide an analogy with my own situation was Paul Stoller's and Cheryl Olkes's (1987) account of their time with Songhay sorcerers in the Republic of Niger. What struck me about the account was that, in seeking to understand Songhay sorcery more closely, Stoller was sucked in as an unknowing agent of sorcery, even to the extent of possibly having been responsible for someone's death. This story is still, strangely, something of a comfort, as I remain anxious as to the reason for the shamanic assassination of a particular kanaimà, since its occasion was so conveniently timed to satisfy and so closely tied to my intense interest in such shamanic warfare, as I discuss later.

In South American ethnology in general, the topic of violent and aggressive shamanism has rarely been broached, and I made a point of canvasing colleagues as to whether or not they had had any similar experiences, or even experience of killing shamanism at all. I was surprised, and somewhat relieved, to find that this phenomenon was more common than I had thought, though it was not part of my colleagues' research projects at the time. Darell Posey, an anthropologist of the Kayapó, wrote the following to me in 1996: "I REALLY enjoyed our brief encounter in Madison. Your research is certainly interesting and, well, frightening. I have seen so much of this stuff up close and from around the edges … and, frankly, one of the reasons I left the Kayapó was that I was learning too much about these things. The other dimensions (death-shamanism) have a physical component, but the visible is only the mask."

Terry Roopnaraine, a fellow anthropologist born in Guyana, wrote to me in June 1997, just after my departure from that country. He had returned from the Pomeroon, where he had decided to make inquiries about kanaima, being intrigued and perhaps a little skeptical of my reports from Paramakatoi since he had himself done his doctoral research in Monkey Mountain:

This is pretty much everything I have on kanaima. I believe that there is more information to be had, but frankly I got too nervous to pursue the matter. As I said on the phone, I had three successive nights of identical nightmares. For about a week, I was very edgy and quick-tempered. All in all, I had the feeling that there was something awful crawling in my head. Sometimes, for no apparent reason, all the hair on my arms would stand up. On a couple of occasions, I just started crying, apropos of nothing. So I am sorry, but I am very reluctant to continue these inquiries in the field. There are some things best left alone. I was getting genuinely worried about you in the Pakaraimas, and I am very glad you're OK.

Terry expressed well the emotional state that dealing with kanaimà generates, and certainly a daily focus on kanaimà meant I often felt I was just "getting through it." Both Darrell and Terry were also right to raise the possibility that such things might be better left alone, but, as I related, the intensity with which an investigation of kanaimà was initially supported and the genuinely affecting stories of those who had suffered from their attacks had caused me to persist. Of course, these were not the only reasons; no academic can help being seduced by the prospect of discovering what has previously been secreted or hidden, of making that original contribution to the ethnographic literature of the region, so I suppose that motive must have been in there, too, crowded out though it was at the time by the sheer vividness and immediacy of kanaimà violence. I also think that a certain anger, connected to my grief after the death of my father, was focused into my research on kanaimà and that such anger led me to persist in the face of difficult or trying circumstances.

Despite my personal rage, there has also been a wider mythopoetic dimension to my experiences, in that they at times seem to uncannily recapitulate the experiences of other outsiders who encounter kanaimà. Graham Burnett (2000, 183–89) provides a nice discussion of the reactions of various nineteenth-century travelers to the "demon landscape" of the interior of Guyana, pointing out how the discovery and desecration of native spirit places, as well as their occasional defacement, served to enable the possession of that landscape through a mapping and surveying that exorcized the genius loci. In a less literally geographical sense, ethnography also, through its explanations, undoubtedly robs cultures of some of the force of their performative expression. In this sense, knowledge itself becomes colonial (Whitehead 1995b). However, as Burnett also notes, the very "recognition of the hallucinatory power of the landscape placed the explorer at risk; it was a short step from empathy to the kind of collapse – the 'going native' (or mad) – that disqualified the explorer," and also the ethnographer, no doubt.

In the hallucinatory landscape of kanaimà, tales or allegations of whites poisoned or killed by the kanaimà are of particular interest for the way in which they reveal the nature of kanaimà as a cultural discourse. As such, kanaimà is not just directed toward other Amerindian groups, nor only toward co-villagers, but also toward the agents of eighteenth- and nineteenth-century "colonial" and twentieth-century "modernizing" development. The colonial development of the interior, principally under the Dutch, was intended to occur through trade for forest products, which included slaves. By 1750 it was already apparent that such trade had indeed had a considerable effect on the peoples of the interior, particularly in the Essequibo – Rupununi – Rio Branco corridor. In his report of that year to the Dutch West India Company, the colony's *commandeur*, Storm van's Gravesande, noted that the traders "act so badly towards the natives that several have already been murdered by the latter; others get poisoned and expose the Colony to danger of war with the savage tribes" (Harris and Villiers 1911, 260). Van's Gravesande also noted that the trade in "red slaves" from the upper Essequibo region was "fairly large" and that some of the traders "do not hesitate even to go with some tribes to make war upon others … and selling them as slaves, and abusing Indian women. Hence it was that in the year 1747 the rovers G. Goritz and H. Bannink were murdered by the Indians [in upper Essequibo], some others poisoned, and others forced to flee" (Harris and Villiers 1911, 269).

Colonial development under the British administration of the nineteenth century was at best "absent minded" (Rivière 1995) and so largely devolved into the missionary effort that I describe later. At the forefront of evangelical progress in the highlands was the British missionary Thomas Youd. His case is examined more fully below, but the tale of his poisoning by kanaimàs has become notorious.

Although there are reasons to question the accuracy of this tale, its place in the discourse of kanaimà is undeniable. Lesser known in twentieth-century literature but equivalent to the case of Youd was that of one Pastor Davis. Theodor Koch-Grüneberg described Davis as having died in a village by Roraima "from a hemorrhage, as it was described, and was buried here" and indicated that it was a killing enacted by Patamuna or Makushi kanaimàs (1979, 1:103, 109, 114; 3:186).

Either way, the notion of the susceptibility of whites to death by kanaimà is not just a particular claim about the forensic causes of death in any given instance but a wider attempt to bring whites within native categories in a way that renders them less powerful and threatening. This is how I have come to understand the "legend" of my own poisoning by kanaimàs, as well as that of other whites, about which I was carefully and deliberately informed. In particular, the case of Bengi, eventually shotgunned in the late 1960s, was related to me on a number of occasions by different persons, so as to firmly impress it on my thinking, as a relatively recent example of how avaricious whites might fall victim to shamanic attack. Bengi and his brother were known as practicing kanaimàs who went to work for a white man in a *balata*-bleeding (rubber-gathering) operation on the Siparuni. However, the white man got angry because he thought they were being lazy. They in turn demanded a payment of cigarettes, but when the confrontation ended, they were smiling. Everyone in the balata camp wondered if the white man would try to chase them out of the camp, and everyone thought that since he had a concrete house that could be closed up tight he was safe. But it is said that Bengi and his brother must have gotten into the white man's house, because they left the next morning and he was sick on waking. He died within a week. Clearly other forms of assault sorcery are not being distinguished from specifically kanaimà attack in the way these events are narrated, but the point for those who recount this incident is to suggest the susceptibility of whites to Amerindian occult forces.

The cultural contextualization of specific histories like these thus allows us to see that such multiple versions erode the authority of the idea of History itself. How can we say "what happened" if the cultural meanings of a story (*histoire*) diverge in such a way as to appropriate the key events, which are registered in all versions but in culturally specific ways? Probably only by counting all versions as relevant and legitimate historiographical expressions. As a result, whatever such kanaimà deaths may have involved, including the clear possibility that they were not examples of ritual violence, they should not be interpreted as we once thought they might be, as opportunities for the destruction of the Mythical by the Historical. This was the notion that drove the colonial occupation and exorcism of the "demon landscape" in the nineteenth century.

A more adequate response, in the light of nearly a hundred years of ethnographic engagements, must be to recognize the discursive origins of apparently empirical claims and that the proof of such claims is established by reference to the discourse from which they emerge, not by a suprahistorical procedure in factual verification. In one sense it really does not matter if I, or anyone else, was clinically poisoned – it is the claims made to that effect that are anthropologically significant for our understanding of the histories and historicities of others. As with Hugh Goodwin's death on the Orinoco in the sixteenth century, or the death of Captain Cook which has exercised the anthropological imagination more widely, the "apotheosis" of whites in the cosmologies of others, their relevance to the cultural discourses of history, reflects not their historical importance as we understand it but precisely an attempt to negate that potential. The effort, then, to disprove or prove kanaimà deaths becomes the vehicle for the colonization of the historical experience of others by bringing it within an external model of historiography. It remains important to ethnographers to know who did or didn't die and how, but our knowledge of the cultural plurality of notions of death, individuality, and agency also teaches us the limits of our own notion of history.

The purpose of this chapter has been, among other things, to illustrate the entanglements that fieldwork involves, the ethical duties we have to our informants, and the unforeseen consequences of close ethnographic engagement. My experience is not presented as an example of how those difficulties might be avoided, but rather to suggest that, even with the best of intentions, they are inevitable. At the same time, if the classic injunction of ethnographic fieldwork – to be a participant observer – is not to be taken as a mere tautology, then it must mean that our manner of "participation" should be no less an object of our theoretical and methodological reflection than the issues of "observation" that have been the focus of discussion since the early 1990s.

In the case of the kanaimà, participation has, of course, been fraught with difficulty, if not outright danger, but it has resulted, I believe, in a distinct and new view of kanaimà as a shamanic practice. Moreover, in negotiating the sometimes contradictory and shifting attitudes and statements that are made with regard to kanaimà, it becomes apparent that its "reality" as conceived of within an empiricist and rationalist tradition of thought is quite different from its "reality" for those who live kanaima and its consequences. This is why the matter must be approached as a form of discourse whose practice is simultaneously and in varying degrees verbal, emotional, psychological, sociological, and cultural – in a word, *real*. Kanaimà, therefore, is not just a matter of "forensic" evidence, although the following chapters certainly contain such evidence, since it is certainly the more culturally satisfying to minds trained in the traditions of rational empiricism. Nonetheless, as I will attempt to show, kanaimà is much more than the poisoned and mutilated bodies it produces.

REFERENCES

Arens, William
    1979 *The Man-eating Myth*. New York: Oxford University Press.
Burnett, D. Graham
    2000 *Masters of All They Surveyed: Exploration, Geography, and the British El Dorado*. Chicago: Chicago University Press.

Harris, Charles and Villiers, John
1911 *Storm Van's Gravesande: The Rise of British Guiana*. London: Hakluyt Society.
Hulme, Peter
1986 *Colonial Encounters: Europe and the Native Caribbean, 1492-1797*. London: Routledge.
Hulme, Peter and Whitehead, Neil, eds.
1992 *Wild Majesty: Encounters with Caribs from Columbus to the Present Day: An Anthology*. Oxford: Oxford University Press.
Koch-Gruneberg, Theodore
1979[1924] *Del Roraima al Orinoco*. Translated from the German by Frederica de Ritter. 3 vols. Caracas: Ediciones del Banko Central de Venezuela.
Riviere, Peter
1995 *Absent Minded Imperialism: Britain and the Expansion of Empire in Nineteenth-Century Brazil*. London: I. B. Tauris and Company.
Roth, Walter E.
1924 *An Introductory Study of the Arts, Crafts, and Customs of the Guiana Indians*. 38th annual report of the Bureau of American Ethnology, 1916–17. Washington: Smithsonian Institution.
Stoller, Paul and Olkes, Cheryl
1987 *In Sorceries Shadow*. Chicago: Chicago University Press.
Whitehead, Neil
1988 *Lords of the Tiger-Spirit: A History of the Caribs in Colonial Venezuela and Guyana, 1498–1820*. Dordrecht-Providence: Foris Publications.

Whitehead, Neil
1990b The Snake Warriors – Sons of the Tiger's Teeth: A Descriptive Analysis of Carib Warfare: 1500–1820. In: *The Anthropology of War*. Jonathan Haas, ed., pp. 146–170. Cambridge: Cambridge University Press.
Whitehead, Neil
1995a Ethnic Plurality and Cultural Continuity in the Native Caribbean: Remarks and Uncertainties as to Data and Theory. In: *Wolves from the Sea: Readings in the Archaeology and Anthropology of the Island Carib*. Neil Whitehead, ed., pp. 91–112. Leiden: KITLV Press.
Whitehead, Neil
1995b The Historical Anthropology of Text: The Interpretation of Ralegh's *Discoverie*. *Current Anthropology* 36:53–74.
Whitehead, Neil
1995c *Wolves from the Sea: Readings in the Archaeology and Anthropology of the Island Carib*. Leiden: KITLV Press.
Whitehead, Neil
1996c *An Oral History of the Patamona, Yawong Valley, Guyana*. Georgetown, Guyana: Walter Roth Museum.
Whitehead, Neil
2001b Kanaima: Shamanism and Ritual Death in the Pakaraima Mountains, Guyana. In: *Beyond the Visible and the Material*. Laura Rival and Neil Whitehead, eds., pp. 235–246. Oxford: Oxford University Press.
Wittgenstein, Ludwig
1953 *Philosophical Investigations*. Oxford: Blackwell.

17

Anthropology from the Bones: A Memoir of Fieldwork, Survival, and Commitment

Cynthia Keppley Mahmood

"It's not an interesting subject," said my colleague, an anthropologist at a research institute in north central India. He was referring to the Sikh separatist insurgency then at its peak in the northwestern region of Punjab. I was puzzled by his answer.

"Not interesting?" I queried. Horrifying, maybe; tabooed, maybe; frightening, maybe; all kinds of other adjectives could be applied to the uprising that claimed tens of thousands of lives in the name of a sovereign state for the Sikhs, but "not interesting" was hardly an expected answer. Not least, from a fellow anthropologist.

"No, not at all," came the firm dismissal. "You don't want to inquire about that. It's not a point with any research potential. We should continue with tribal development. That's what you came here for, isn't it?"

You don't want to read the rest of this story. Not if you want to avoid confronting the utter disgrace of a world in which some people think they can threaten, pummel, and punish scholars into studying "the right" topics. Not if you want to believe that knowledge is found in ivory towers and quiet libraries, that it comes without pain, that it is always welcome.

I had gone to this undeveloped region of India to study tribal issues, and that's what we did. My associate clearly did not want to approach the topic of Punjab, and there were, after all, so many other "interesting" things to study in this vast nation. Interesting and safe, my memory adds parenthetically.

When the tribal project was finished, I mentioned Punjab once again. It was 1992, and the newspapers were aflame with news of the northwest. In avowedly secular India, a religious minority had spawned a sovereignty movement so strong that it was seen as threatening the very unity of the nation. This Sikh uprising inspired further separatist unrest to the north in Kashmir, among the Muslims. A heavy crackdown in both states by the central government was prompting criticism of human rights abuses from every major international watchdog organization. An observer of India could hardly deem all this "uninteresting."

Cynthia Keppley Mahmood, "Anthropology from the Bones: A Memoir of Fieldwork, Survival, and Commitment," pp. 1–11 from *Anthropology and Humanism* 33(1 & 2), 2008.

"Might not one consider a study of the situation in Punjab," I prompted again, "when the tribal work is concluded?" There was nothing partisan, merely neutral, in my proposition. But my interlocutor returned my query with silence. I could understand it, because for him as an Indian it might well be problematic to show too much interest in security-sensitive topics. For me it could be different. No one really grasped what was going on with the Sikhs, for example. To say that they were "terrorists" didn't begin to unpack the massive alienation of the Sikh population from the India they had opted to join in 1948. But I remained puzzled by the overwhelmingly "bad press" the Sikh separatist movement had gotten. There appeared to be no sympathetic voices anywhere. Something told me there must be a story behind that ... my anthropologist's nose told me that such 100 percent agreement on a subject spelled ideology, not ground-level truth. The success of the Sikh guerilla fighters meant that somebody supported them. That was why I brought up the subject, here, far away from the actual conflict in Punjab.

That evening, as I was returning from dinner, something happened that changed my personal and professional life forever. It was quieter than usual for this bustling, even raucous, area of the town. Twilight had fallen, shadows lengthening into darkness where alleyways twisted between buildings, but it was light enough on the major street where I walked. Thinking about the article I was working on, and feeling replete with a lovely vegetarian meal, I hummed a bit as I neared the last corner on the way home.

Suddenly I had a vague sense that something was wrong. I was walking alongside a low wall marking the boundary between the street and the city's maidan, the grassy parade ground from British times, when I saw a small group of men walking in my direction across the field. There was nothing particularly wrong with that, but something clicked in my mind that they were striding a little bit too purposefully. It wasn't a typically Indian way of walking, in the dusk of a warm evening. Brushing this idea aside, I continued on my path, looking ahead.

But when the group passed behind me, one of them, to my horror, leapt forward, grabbed me around the waist, and hauled me over the wall into the maidan. It happened so fast, as they say, I couldn't think. It took me a moment to even realize what had happened. Before I knew it I was being pulled across the grass, stumbling, half-running, now grabbed by a second man, deeper into the darkness of the maidan. My adrenaline was shooting up, every warning I'd received about street gangs in India whipping through my mind. I fumblingly reached inside my bag when we stopped running. My hand came out with some bills and coins, probably more than these men had seen in a long time, and spilled them onto the grass.

"Take this money," I gasped. "Here, take my passport." I reached into my shirt to pull out my "secure" wallet. "American."

A US passport was worth a lot on the black market, and I fully expected my assailants to scramble for the money and passport, and evaporate into the night. These gangs did such things for money. This was India's poorest state, with roving bands of unemployed youths. Typically, they weren't serial murderers. If you weren't involved in their local caste wars and it wasn't a communal confrontation, what they wanted was money. I knew all this from books and magazines and newspapers. I ticked through the facts in my mind as I stood there, agonizingly waiting for the thugs to reach for the bills, the passport, the coins.

But to my horror, the crumpled bills I dredged out of my bag fell to the ground unheeded. One of the men grabbed my passport roughly out of my hand, held it to the light, and spat on it vehemently. For good measure he stomped on some of the currency that now lay in the grass, grinding it down with the worn black heel of his shoe. I saw that the fellow next to him was barefoot, and one of the others wore flip-flops. My mind now started mentally checking off these details, click-clicking, ticking, as my fear rose like a gorge in my throat.

Was this really a street gang, or what?

A hand was on my wrist. Whump! I was flat on the ground. No time to do anything, breathless from the impact of my back hitting the field.

"What do you want?" I was saying. Was I shouting, screaming, or whimpering? Or speaking serenely? My voice sounded oddly calm to my ears. The men were hugely tall from my vantage point; hulking shadows, faces swathed in cloths. Only then did I notice that all of them were carrying *lathis*, Indian police batons. What could that mean?

As I inhaled, the air carried the scent of rotten tangerines. Someone must have thrown fruit here on the maidan, I thought, as people occasionally did with the remnants of family picnics or workers' lunches. I almost gagged on the smell; it enveloped all of me and went straight down my throat to my stomach.

The black-shoe man kicked me in the side just as the barefoot man put his dirty foot over my nose and mouth. Now I really will throw up, I thought. *Who are these men? Are they thugs? Could they be police?* I wondered as my eyes roamed wildly around, like they do in movies. For some crazy reason I tried to look straight at the barefoot man high above my face. I tried not to let my eyes roam wildly. I concentrated on that.

"Bitch! Whore!" – and a string of Punjabi curses followed. Unindividuated members of the band I couldn't distinguish were swearing and hitting my legs and lower body with their lathis. Intermittently, black-shoe man was leaning over to spit in my face, that part not covered by the other guy's foot, choking me with its pollution and filth. He pushed his accomplice's foot out of the way at one point to obtain a wider target.

"Stop! Stop!" I half sobbed, though my mind insisted I was in control. "I am an American scholar. You won't get away with this." I said it but it sounded ridiculous – asserting US power from my position lying flat down in a maidan in Patna, surrounded by big men with sticks. Before I could register this half-thought, I felt my *salwar* ripping. A hand was on my breast, pinching my right nipple. It hurt! Jesus, it hurt!

I saw the glint of a knife. It was held in a large dark hand down near my waist, pulling up the silky cloth of my *kameez*. Thank God, I thought, they are not going to kill me. They are only cutting the *nala* to get my pants down to rape me. I calmed my mind. If they had

wanted to kill me they would have done so already, I thought. They didn't take my money, I thought. They have a different aim in mind.

So quickly does the mind change gears, it thinks of rape as "only" – they are "only" going to rape me. At least their aim is not murder.

As my salwar was pulled off and my breasts were fondled by multiple hands, I continued, disembodied, to think clearly. They want to humiliate me or scare me. I can survive. I will live through this experience and go on. My thoughts were hovering above my body thinking themselves through rationally.

One of the men had put my hand on his penis, kneeling by my side. It was horrible, gross! A sausagelike thing. Repulsive thing. Vomit thing. Stinking bowel movement of a thing. Shouldn't I fight back? I barely formed this thought in my mind when twist! My hand snapped his organ around, a loud wail from his masked mouth! No registration of triumph though. The knife at my wrist. Slash, slash, blood. I see the blood dripping, even in the dark. I smell my own blood over the smell of the rotten tangerines.

I cannot fight back, not against this. I should survive, only survive.

Oh! I hadn't noticed. Black-shoe man is raping me.

The stars are very bright. Odd, even with the city lights you can see the stars. I wonder if people at home are looking at these same stars. Of course! Silly me. It's daytime there.

My thoughts, above, focus on daytime, nighttime, the rotation of the earth.

There are, amazingly, many stones in the maidan, despite its grassy appearance. The stones are getting into my hair. I'll have to wash it before the trip home. What kind of shampoo will I use? A supermarket array of shampoo brands flash through my mind. Herbal Essence. Pantene Pro-V. More Value for Your Money. A Fresh Scent.

It's a different man now. I can't feel him. He smells like garlic. Horrible. Throw up! No, pay attention. Pay attention to when he gets up. When he gets up, jump up somehow. Jump up and run away.

My thoughts tell me to gather my strength, jump up, and run away.

I try to hold on to my thoughts of plans, but they fly away like butterflies. I try to catch them but the fragile wings tear. They are off and away, up into the night.

Bushy eyebrows. I force myself to see, to pay attention. The man is sweating. Mumbling curses. How can I jump up? My legs have been beaten. My side hurts. I am bleeding. Rape man pushes on. Can I stick my thumb into his eye, as I've been told Special Forces do, to kill someone? I realize somebody else is standing on my hand. The nonbleeding hand.

Blood and tangerines, semen, sweat. Inhale the solid miasma of degradation, get it past your nose and mouth, get that into your lungs, let it rip into your soul.

With a groan he is done. Somewhere, people are clapping. I hear a motorcycle nearby. Now! I think. I don't know how but somehow I am up, running with bent knees and twisted ankles but running, toward the sound of the motorcycle. RUN! My thoughts tell me, my brain screams.

Men are laughing behind me, and their laughter feels like knives. I don't know if I am crying or screaming or if my mouth is open but utterly soundless, but I do know that I am away.

I run and stumble and run and run. It is like a dream where you can't run, but I am running. I look down and see that my legs are moving. "Help me," I croak to motorcycle man. "Help me, help me," I plead to utter-stranger man, and fall onto the back of the motorcycle.

My thoughts are back in my brain now.

My thoughts, my brain, my body, we are one filthy, humiliated, angry whole now. I finally start to cry, weeping onto the shoulders of kind-Samaritan man, bumping over the rotting streets of the city on a sputtering moped.

You do not want to know that this has happened, of course. You do not want to envision it. You do not want to read about the stones in my hair and the smell of the rotten tangerines. You do not want to imagine a woman you know as respectable and dignified clinging, weeping, to a total stranger in a north Indian night. Discreetly, I have admitted to a few privileged friends and colleagues that, yes, I was assaulted, but it was a long time ago, and I am alright now. Such admissions, legs held

firmly together, avoid confronting the utter disgrace of a world in which some people think they can threaten, pummel, and punish scholars into studying "the right" topics. We don't want to throw that into the faces of polite academia. We want to believe we choose our research topics freely and follow our conclusions where they lead.

Those who actually try to study "the wrong" topics – the silenced, the tabooed, the dangerous topics that challenge the power holders of the world – may find out just what it takes to be a truly independent scholar. But it is important not to hide the price some scholars pay for that in the interests of conventional good manners. That way leads to a trivializing of what scholarship – the pursuit of truth – actually is. Pursuing the truth is a highly political endeavor! It is not the way of safety, of security, of sweet dreams, and comfortable retirements. It is a jihad.

You do not want to know the nightmares I wake up trembling from, years later, the gripping, contorting, wringing headaches that plague me continuously, the PTSD symptoms that do not leave despite therapy and medication and time. I don't thrust such things before you, not in regular discourse. Not too many people know about "what happened to me." After all, I don't want to be viewed as a victim, as some sort of permanent cripple. What happened impels me, though, to push forward rudely with other things people do not want to know but need to see.

Now, remember those Sikhs in Punjab? They were the people my colleague at the institute found so "uninteresting" that he dissuaded me from thinking about studying them. After I was assaulted (oh! that word covers a universe! an epoch!) I gradually came to learn that the entire episode had been set up to scare me into avoiding the topic of Punjab and the Sikh insurgency. Why else would my assailants have refused my money, my passport? I hypothesized. Spat on me, insulted me? And yet, they didn't simply kidnap or kill me either. The more I thought about the whole thing the more I came to the conclusion that this was an attempt to scare. And in light of that theory, other things fell into place. Slowly an explanation evolved that fit pieces into the puzzle.

The person I had met for dinner was a well-known senior scholar of Marxist orientation who had written provocative analyses of the then-current Ayodhya controversy and, in the process, boldly critiqued the Hindu majoritarian nationalism that enflamed minority passions among Sikhs, Muslims, tribals, and others. I had been warned by my colleagues and hosts not to meet this respected academic, this senior scholar, and out of deference to them I had waited until our joint project on tribal development was nearly completed before deciding that, as a free agent, I could and should go ahead and seek out a conversation with him. I did so by accepting a dinner invitation that evening, in a public place, on the way back from which I was so purposefully attacked.

When I had stumbled back to the institute that awful night, bruised and battered, my colleagues had proven unsympathetic. I was advised not to go to the police, because that could result in problems for our research project and potential future permits. Besides, everyone knew that police were corrupt and women could face even more problems with them. The matter could even become an international incident. But these were pragmatic concerns. Stranger still was the overall mood of "we told you so" that greeted me when I explained what had just happened. My hosts advised me to listen to their guidelines next time. If I hadn't taken time away from our current project to meet with dubious individuals concerned with "uninteresting" subjects, none of this would have happened. Instead of being comforted, I got more warnings: maybe you've learned your lesson now, maybe now you will stick with the projects approved by this institute.

I was reminded, then, of other oddities about the trip that I had brushed aside at the time: the reluctance of my all-Hindu, all-male colleagues to trust me with a map of the border-area tribal region we were investigating; the insistence that I drop my married (Muslim) name and go back to my (Germanic) maiden name; the intellectual disagreements we had over whether the tribals should be classed as Hindus or as "animists" for the Indian census. This latter was an important political question, bearing as it does on the figures of just how extensive the "Hindu majority" in India really is, and invoking incendiary calls for *hindutva* (loosely translated, "Hinduness" or "the Hindu way") as a defining feature of the Indian nation. I had assessed the groups we investigated as clearly animist, whereas my colleagues uniformly classed them as Hindu. (We listed them as Hindu, with the majority, but I wrote a politely dissenting article.)

The clarion call to *hindutva* by Hindu nationalist organizations, who in 1992, were just leading the march to tear down the mosque at Ayodhya on grounds that an ancient Hindu temple lay beneath, was the same call that prompted Sikhs – over on the other side of the subcontinent – to fear for their place in ostensibly secular India. Muslims in Kashmir, Nagas in the Northwest, Christians in the south, Dalits ("untouchables") everywhere; these were the non-Hindu communities becoming restive over the rise in "muscular Hinduism" (Hansen 1999; Jaffrelot 1996, 2007). These tensions have only increased since the time of this incident in 1992, so that by now, in 2008, we see violence in all the peripheral areas of India where Hindus and non-Hindus bump up against each other in India's jostling democracy.

The Hindu right is sophisticated enough to fight one battle in its political war in the meadows of higher education. Although pogroms have occurred out in the streets against Sikhs or Muslims, the world inside the ivy-covered walls is not immune. We would do well to remind ourselves time and again that, as Salman Rushdie commented in 1984 regarding the Jonah-in-the-whale tale, there are no more whales in which to remain insulated, not for the arts nor for academia (Rushdie 1991). In 2004, a group of slogan-chanting Hindus looted the Bhandarkar Oriental Institute, where James Laine, a scholar whose book excited some controversy, had done his research. A Hindu mob nabbed and tarred the face of the Indian historical researcher he had acknowledged in the volume. Wendy Doniger, Paul Courtright, and David White have also been among those academics who have been targeted by the Hindu right because of their intellectual work on the religion. Doniger, a senior scholar of the Hindu tradition, regularly receives death threats; a letter-writing campaign tried to prevent another young scholar's tenure at Rice.

It is probably difficult for readers without a background in India to imagine the venomous quality of these disputes over religion, which are tied to postcolonial identities and to the allocation of resources and rewards in post-independence India. The Sikhs who brandished the flag of their own homeland of "Khalistan" in 1992 were especially threatening because that was the height of the new Hindu nationalist drive to rebuild the Ram temple at Ayodhya, and coincidentally it was the peak of the armed Sikh insurgency in Punjab. At that historical moment, it seemed as if the Khalistani guerillas might even succeed in establishing a Sikh homeland, making that separatist movement the first to actually challenge the integrity of the Indian state. The Kashmiri insurgency followed the example of the Sikhs, and India fast became a "fearful state" (Ali 1993), responding to challenges with overpowering violence. Vigilante groups and civilian posses felt emboldened to defend the Indian motherland, in Punjab and Kashmir and in the "cow belt" – the Hindu heartland where I had just been assaulted. Few were prosecuted; indeed, many were cheered on by the media.

Indeed, India sees the threats posed by centrifugal tensions as so dangerous that it is willing to risk its reputation as "the world's largest democracy" to quash any potential revolutionary movements. International human rights groups have all criticized the ubiquitous use of torture and arbitrary detention by police and security forces in India, and, where separatist insurgency threatens, extrajudicial executions and disappearances as well. But sadly, even the marketplace of ideas is now constrained by the fearful Indian government. Although the Constitution provides for freedom of speech and expression, under the Official Secrets Act the government may prosecute anyone who publishes or communicates information that could be harmful to the state. A press council composed of journalists, publishers, academics, and politicians – which in the United States might be standing up for press and academic freedoms – in India sets a code of conduct to regulate and self-censor materials that might incite communal violence. The government bans books considered incendiary, bans films deemed offensive to "communal sentiment," and applies restrictions to the travel and activities of visiting scholars and experts. It has to approve all forms of seminars, conference, guest lectures, and collaborative research involving international scholars. The Informational Technology Act allows the government to limit access to the Internet if such access is deemed detrimental to national security, including allowing police to search the homes and offices of Internet users. The government itself is afraid of what ideas can do, and it is not surprising that the agenda of allowing only certain kinds of ideas a place would also be carried through to government think tanks, research institutes, and universities.

Back in 1992, I was only peripherally aware of rising tensions between Hindus and other religious groups, about which I unfortunately know so much now. That is to say, I knew about communal conflict in India, but imagined that because my studies were not directly impinging on these issues, I could pursue my work on tribal development in peace. Through gang rape, beatings, and broken bones, I learned differently. The books I had read had not made me understand the systemic quality of the silencing that goes on in a place dominated by fear, where state security has become synonymous with national identity. Even small comments, small gestures, small names, small dissents, blossomed into seemingly major potential threats.

Facing the ambiguity of not knowing whom to trust, in pain, humiliation, and frustration, I got to the airport the morning after I was assaulted for the first flight to Delhi and then home to the United States. There followed months of back-and-forth negotiations of who did and said what, and about which groups were ultimately responsible. There remained many basic ambiguities that were never resolved, ambiguities I later recognized as characteristic of the arenas of terror in which many of the people I now study (Sikhs, Muslims; Mahmood 1999) live themselves, never quite clear who is an ally and who is an enemy, perhaps doubting their own complicity in the suffering they endure. Did they bring it on themselves? (As so many say.) It took me years after that to sort through what I should have, could have, or might have done as a victim–survivor who is also a scholar. What was not a gray area for me was whether to continue to work in this region, on those topics. I had to. Every scar, as it faded, begged me to.

Since 1992, I did turn my scholarly attention to Punjab and I did learn a great deal about the Sikhs who are so "uninteresting" that their suffering goes ignored by the entire world – those Sikhs with their wounds of torture, their disappeared relatives, their raped women, and their secretly cremated remains. I studied the tabooed "Khalistanis" who definitely had more of a story behind them than the simple narrative of criminal–terrorist upheld by the Indian state and indeed the whole of the (non-Sikh) civilian population. Through face-to-face ethnography – looking into dragons, not domesticating or abominating them (following Geertz 1984) – I learned about the history of Sikh grievances, the theology of war and peace, and the dynamics of the widespread Sikh diaspora. I learned that Sikh militants did indeed kill and bomb and terrify – but Sikh civilians suffered and died. They were ashamed, and were scared, and their government did not protect them. The human rights abuses going on in Punjab were horrific: this in the land of Gandhi; this in "the world's largest democracy." These things are among those that people seem not to want to know about Sikhs and about Punjab, things that we must make them know anyway, I decided. Put that raw and burning flesh right out there in coarse exhibition, legs splayed open obscenely. Make it so people can't turn away. Make somebody look. Make somebody question. Why is a generation gone from the plains of Punjab?

Anyone who loves India should know what has happened in Punjab, I reasoned, because a tiny 2-percent minority like the Sikhs are the proverbial canary in the coal mine, the bellwether that can point to how the winds of Indian democracy are blowing. Are the rights of a small, dissenting minority protected? If not there, where? When we come to the much larger minority of Muslims? When we come to

the vast lowest level of the Indian pyramid, the Dalits? It troubled me that people in India viewed Sikhs as troublemakers, that they had no sympathizers, that even progressives didn't stand up against the nightmarish abuses of rights in Punjab.

You may not want to know what happened to me – me, a mere drop in the heaving oceans, a mote in the vast eye of God – but you damn well *will* know what happened to Harinder Singh and Mehtab Kaur and Pritpal Singh and Jatinder Singh Kahlon and Maninderpal Kaur and the Sikhs at the Golden Temple and the others in the distant villages, and those unnamed who went up in smoke, and those named but still missing. In pain I will put it right before you until you have to know and you have to ask why.

"Sikh Studies," a traditionally Orientalist field that has consciously steered clear of the topic of conflict in Punjab, even as tens of thousands of Sikhs perished, wants us to look at medieval religious texts while the heart of Sikhism is in flames. If we touch the fire, if then too we burn and say ouch! – then we are shunned. But then again, academia has never done well in perilous times. Raphael Lemkin, who coined the term *genocide*, was thought to be crazy when he pointed to the crimes of Nazi Germany, and academics have sadly been more complicit than protesting in mass killing campaigns from Rwanda to Bosnia. What's wrong with us? Not even in India, but internationally? In America, where we are "safe?" So few speak up. Like the tin man in the Wizard of Oz, do we simply have a deficit of heart?

You may not want to know about that young man, bound and gagged, dropped from a helicopter in Atlantic waves, or about the state that now shelters his killers. Do you want to see – or is it too "pornographic," as we say (no one living with violence considers such an argument) – the beheading of that journalist, the muffling of those children in improvised live graves? Is it not time to think more critically about our institutional discourse of "safety" and "risk assessment" and how it guides us securely away from the martyring truths that might really unseat the powerful and change the status quo? How it is part of the machine that keeps academia complicit in the silencing of abuses, the turning away from suffering?

We think of scholarship as a quietist occupation, but in this unjust world must it not be sometimes a militant one, as Scheper-Hughes so plaintively suggests (1995)? Is it not amazing that in this day and age serious scholars get death threats, major academic bodies ignore the human pathos at their very feet, and "terrorism experts" in academia and our governments may never have crossed the path of a person enmeshed in violence?

One may choose to be an "engaged anthropologist" as an intellectual matter; there are reasons enough as the 21st century dawns. I had gone to north–central India in 1992 to study tribal development needs as a scholar, an observer. I had no stake in any religious or political controversies. But when others chose to use their very bodies as weapons, insulting my own at its very core, this ethnography became a very intimate matter indeed. The question is, what does one do with that deeply, literally visceral violent memory? Use the healing of self to forget that unsought connection when my study of violence and my very being were suddenly thrown into one another on a maidan's grassy surface? Or, use that shattering intersection to begin a new journey, in which the bloody love of the other throws the anthropologist into the role of pilgrim – truthseeker – advocate, *from the bones?* Seek a new way to understand anthropology as a spiritual journey and a political commitment as well as a science, art, and profession?

It's past time, I think, that we talk to our students not only about safety but also about courage. We should ask them what they think it takes to be an anthropologist in this perilous world of ours – not GRE scores but character. *How will you stand up to it?* How will you pursue, teach, and write the truth in a world intent on masking it?

Sometimes people ask me, how can you continue to do this work, how can you continue to have hope? How can you, a teacher of peace studies, imagine that the Sikhs and Kashmiris, who have now suffered so much, will heal, will flourish, will give back to the world the spirituality and music and art and all of those things for which they were known,

"before?" How can you imagine that the Indian police and military, who have tortured and jailed and murdered, will become in the end human beings of peace and goodwill? How can you believe that militants who slaughter in the name of God or sovereignty will emerge as forgivers and reconcilers? Those who have become rapists or raped, is there hope for them, now?

I believe that a future of healing and peace is possible because I know that human beings are more resilient than we can ever imagine. I have bones that have been broken and have healed. I have wounds that have bled, have scarred over, and are barely visible now. I have memories that have haunted me but have faded, and new, better memories that have replaced them. I know that despite all my continuing personal demons, when a gentle, strong man holds me, I melt.

What other kinds of love are not possible?

What courage is not possible when the courage of people all around us wells up through drownings, beheadings, live burials, wells up again and again until we are tired of watching it on our televisions and reading it in our newspapers – and yet people still find the strength to resist, and resolve, and forge on ahead?

There are those who find peace unimaginable, so they warn of "uninteresting" topics. They send goons to scare off the inquisitive. They beat people with lathis to force them into cowardice. But we survivor–anthropologists are not afraid. We believe in the possibilities, find all human beings "of interest," and will not turn away.

NOTES

Acknowledgments. I dedicate this article to the graduate students of the Kroc Institute for International Peace Studies, Notre Dame, who, on the eve of their first fieldwork, gave me the strength to tell this long-muted story. Colleagues at the institute were the first to read and comment on drafts of this article: Martha Merritt, Scott Appleby, Larissa Fast, Anne Hayner, and Diane King, and I thank you for your early support. Anthropologists Agustin Fuentes, Daniel Lende,

Greg Downey, Eric Lindland, Jim Bellis, Debra MacDougall, Lisa Mitchell, Ian Kuijt, Kalyani Menon, and Patrick Gaffney provided critical feedback and encouragement to publish. Gratitude also goes to two anonymous readers at *Anthropology and Humanism*, who provided useful suggestions. None of the above should be held responsible for any of the contents or opinions in this piece, however, which are entirely my own.

[*Cynthia Mahmood did go on to become a leader in the academic study of violence and human rights in Punjab. She is the author of* Fighting for Faith and Nation: Dialogues with Sikh Militants *(1996);* The Guru's Gift: Exploring Gender Equality with North American Sikh Women *(Mahmood with Brady 2000);* A Sea of Orange: Writings on the Sikhs and India *(2001b), and many articles and book chapters on related topics. Mahmood also speaks and testifies publicly on terrorism, rights, and resistance in democracies such as India and the United States (see Mahmood 2001a). She founded and now directs the book series on "The Ethnography of Political Violence" at the University of Pennsylvania Press. Mahmood's current project is a book on state violence and historical silencing.*]

REFERENCES

Ali, S. Mahmud
1993   *The Fearful State: People, Power and Internal War in South Asia.* London: Zed Books.
Geertz, Clifford
1984   Anti Anti-Relativism. *American Anthropologist* 86(2):263–278.
Hansen, Thomas Blom
1999   *The Saffron Wave: Democracy and Hindu Nationalism in Modern India.* Princeton, NJ: Princeton University Press.
Jaffrelot, Christophe
1996   *The Hindu Nationalist Movement in India.* New York: Columbia University Press.
Jaffrelot, Christophe, ed.
2007   *Hindu Nationalism: A Reader.* Princeton: Princeton University Press.
Mahmood, Cynthia Keppley
1996   *Fighting for Faith and Nation: Dialogues with Sikh Militants.* Philadelphia: University of Pennsylvania Press.
Mahmood, Cynthia Keppley
1999   Trials by Fire: Dynamics of Terror in Punjab and Kashmir. *In Death Squad: The Anthropology of State Terror.* Jeffrey A. Sluka, ed. pp. 79–90. Philadelphia: University of Pennsylvania Press.
Mahmood, Cynthia Keppley
2001a   Myth, Terror and the Power of Ethnographic Praxis. *Journal of Contemporary Ethnography* 30(5):520–545.
Mahmood, Cynthia Keppley
2001b   *A Sea of Orange: Writings on the Sikhs and India.* Philadelphia, PA: XLibris.
Mahmood, Cynthia Keppley, with Stacy Brady
2000   *The Guru's Gift: Exploring Gender Equality with North American Sikh Women.* Mountain View, CA: Mayfield.
Rushdie, Salman
1991[1984]   Outside the Whale. *In Imaginary Homelands: Essays and Criticism 1981–1991.* pp. 87–102. London: Granta.
Scheper-Hughes, Nancy
1995   The Primacy of the Ethical: Propositions for a Militant Anthropology. *Current Anthropology* 36(3):409–420.

18

Reflections on Managing Danger in Fieldwork: Dangerous Anthropology in Belfast

Jeffrey A. Sluka

In many areas of the world, anthropological fieldwork is more dangerous today than it was in the past.[1] There are approximately 120 "armed conflicts" (euphemism for wars) in the world today (Nietschmann 1987), and given that about one-third of the world's countries are currently involved in warfare and about two-thirds of countries routinely resort to human rights abuses as normal aspects of their political process to control their populations, it is clear that few anthropologists will be able to avoid conflict situations and instances of socio-political violence in the course of their professional lives (Nordstrom and Martin 1992:15). While it has long been recognized that danger is probably inherent in anthropological fieldwork, it is only recently that the methodological and subjective issue of danger has been addressed directly and systematically. In 1986, Nancy Howell first called attention to the need to discuss the issue of danger in fieldwork in an unpublished paper, "Occupational Safety and Health in Anthropology." She noted that the personal dangers involved in doing fieldwork had largely been ignored, denied, or taken for granted and argued that this issue should be a major concern of anthropological fieldworkers. She also suggested that one of the professional associations should conduct a comprehensive survey of occupational safety and health in the discipline, and this idea was adopted by the American Anthropological Association (AAA). In 1990, the first publications directly dealing with danger in fieldwork emerged – an AAA special report titled *Surviving Fieldwork* (Howell 1990) and an article titled "Participant Observation in Violent Social Contexts" (Sluka 1990). This chapter presents an updated and revised version of my earlier article on managing danger, incorporating reflections on new fieldwork. I begin with a brief description of the research setting during my two periods of

Ethnographic Fieldwork: An Anthropological Reader, Second Edition. Edited by Antonius C. G. M. Robben and Jeffrey A. Sluka.
Editorial material and organization © 2012 John Wiley & Sons, Inc.
Published 2012 by John Wiley & Sons, Inc.

fieldwork in the Catholic-nationalist ghettos of Belfast, Northern Ireland, in 1981–2 and 1991 and then make some general comments and recommendations concerning the conduct of ethnographic research in dangerous or violent social contexts, deriving from these experiences and similar ones by other anthropologists.

While special ethnographic, methodological, theoretical, and ethical sensitivities are required when working on, and in, dangerous areas, to a substantial degree the dangers faced by anthropologists in their fieldwork can be mediated through foresight, planning, and skillful maneuver. While this chapter deals specifically with participant observation in countries characterized by political instability, conflict, and insurgency, much that is said is broadly applicable to generalized situations in which fieldworkers may be in physical danger from human sources (i.e., research participants, authorities, and others).[2]

Setting

In 1981–2, I conducted research in Divis Flats, a Catholic-nationalist ghetto on the lower Falls Road in Belfast. This research was based on participant observation and interviews with seventy-six families, and the monograph emerging from this was a study of the social dynamics of popular support for the Irish Republican Army (IRA) and Irish National Liberation Army (INLA) (Sluka 1989).[3] After nearly a decade, in July 1991, I returned to the Catholic-nationalist ghettos of Belfast for six months of fieldwork on "aspects of political culture in Northern Ireland." These "urban village" ghetto communities represent the major battlegrounds or "killing fields" of the war in Northern Ireland. For over twenty-three years, the residents of the Catholic-nationalist ghettos have been caught between the urban guerrilla warfare of the IRA and INLA and the counter-insurgency operations of the Security Forces. Since the beginning of the war in 1969, the British authorities have sought to contain repression and resistance within the Catholic ghettos of Belfast, Derry, Newry, and other towns and cities and in the rural border areas where Catholics are the majority population

(e.g., the so-called bandit country of south Armagh around Crossmaglen) (Rolston 1991). Counterinsurgency operations and the "dirty war" apparatus (Dillon 1990; Faligot 1983), coupled with the activities of pro-government death squads and sectarian attacks by Loyalist extremists, have created an unpredictable deployment of terror concentrated in these communities, with the result that every family or household can tell you about a relative, neighbor, or friend in jail or killed by the Security Forces or Loyalists. The Catholic ghettos are "killing fields" in the sense that they represent the major sites of violence, the battlegrounds where domination and resistance in general and the war in particular are concentrated, contained, and isolated. They are spaces of violence, death, and transformation that continually generate both recruits to the Republican paramilitaries and enough popular support and sympathy among the rest of the people to maintain the current struggle.

When I returned to Belfast in 1991, two things had occurred in the interim that directly affected this research. First, in 1986, a bloody internal feud split the INLA and led to the formation of a new, breakaway paramilitary organization calling itself the Irish People's Liberation Organization (IPLO). Second, in 1989, my book on popular support for the IRA and INLA in Divis Flats was published. I sent a copy of the book to friends in Belfast, who subsequently lent it to a number of people to read, including senior Republican activists. Because of the close association of the INLA, and now IPLO, with Divis Flats, I had contacts who advised me that if I ever returned to Belfast and wanted to meet the "High Command" of the IPLO, this could be arranged. Because this research was based on sabbatical leave, I was able to pursue an attempt at participatory research. I wanted to return to Belfast before I decided exactly what research I would engage in, and I wanted to find a subject that offered to be of mutual advantage to me and to the local community. I hoped local people in Belfast might suggest such a research topic.

When I arrived in Belfast I was introduced by friends, in a local pub, to, first, Martin "Rook" O'Prey, the local Belfast commander of the IPLO, and a few days later, the overall commander, Jimmy Brown. (I name these people here because they are now deceased and are publicly recognized as having held these positions in the IPLO at the time of their deaths.)[4] Brown told me that he had read my book and thought it was very good. He then shocked me by asking if I would be interested in writing a book about the IPLO. I said that might be possible, if we could agree on the precise conditions and expectations involved, and we arranged to meet a week later to talk about it. A few days before this meeting could take place, Rook O'Prey, who I had only just met, was assassinated by a Loyalist death squad in his home, one of the new houses built as part of redevelopment, at the bottom of Divis Tower and in plain sight of the army observation post on top. The meeting was postponed a week, and then I met with Brown and the new commander for Belfast.

These IPLO leaders told me that if I was interested in writing a book "like the first one" about their organization, they would "open all the doors" I needed to gather the information. The first thing I discussed with them was, did they know what an anthropologist was and understand what I would be doing? I said that as a social scientist I was committed to objectivity – that is, letting the evidence lead to the conclusions – and the politics of truth. I was willing to write an ethnography of the IPLO if I was allowed academic independence and freedom to write the truth as I saw it, as a result of my own research. The IPLO leaders agreed to this. They knew what an anthropologist was and wanted me to act as one because they believed that an independent academic study would carry more authority and could not be easily dismissed as propaganda. They said they would like to see a book that presented an inside or participant's view of the IPLO. They admitted that they hoped the book would do two things for them. First, because the IPLO lacked effective means of publicizing their perspective – for example, nothing like the weekly paper, *An Phoblacht/Republican News*, which presents the perspective of the Provisional Republican movement (Sinn Fein and the IRA) – the book would be a chance to present their perspective to the world and describe who they were, what they were doing,

and why they were doing it. Second, the book would humanize the people in the IPLO, which might serve as a partial antidote to the concerted propaganda campaign by the British authorities aimed at vilifying and dehumanizing them as an aspect of their counterinsurgency or "psychological warfare" operations.

The conditions we agreed on were that I would be allowed to talk to or interview any member I wished, and I could ask questions freely. The interviews would be completely open, and I was not required to submit a list of the questions or subjected to any other apparent monitoring or control practice. During the course of the research, I was never refused an answer to any question. (As with my previous research, I voluntarily chose not to ask about some things such as weapons, finance, and planned military operations, which I felt were unnecessary and potentially dangerous both to me and to other research participants.) I was free to do my anthropological "thing," with only two conditions. I promised that I would allow the IPLO to review the manuscript of the book before it was published. They would not have editorial control, but I agreed to two things. First, I would alter anything in the manuscript necessary to ensure the immediate security of any living member of the IPLO, for example, to protect anonymity of the research participants. Second, if there was anything else in the manuscript that we disagreed on, I would give them a right of response. That is, while I would not modify or delete my own independent conclusions and interpretations, I would include IPLO statements expressing their disagreement with my views wherever they felt it necessary. I thought this was fair, since it would leave readers of the book to judge for themselves whose view they gave more credence to. This struck me as an equitable and reciprocal research "bargain," in which both the researcher and participants stood to benefit, and believed that it did not compromise my professional ethics. It also represented, to the best of my knowledge, the most direct, open, and unimpeded access any researcher has yet been granted to a paramilitary organization in Northern Ireland. I decided to accept the IPLO's offer and approach the research as an experiment in liberation anthropology.

Over the next six months I researched and did fieldwork with the IPLO. This was based on interviews, library and archival research, and participant observation – as far as I thought this was practicable in the circumstances. I conducted formal interviews with fifteen members of the IPLO, selected to provide a representative cross-sample; I conducted interviews in Catholic-nationalist ghettos in Belfast, Derry, Newry, and Dublin, with men and women of all ranks and including both founding and new members. I spent considerable time "hanging out," traveling with, and talking informally with about two dozen other IPLO members and attended a number of IPLO-related social and political functions, such as the funeral and other events surrounding the death of Rook O'Prey.

With regard to the dangers inherent in such fieldwork, I handled or "managed" these much as I had during my first period of research in Belfast (see Sluka 1990). But this new research involved much more direct and intense interaction with guerrilla fighters than I had had in 1981–2, and it presented new problems and dangers. Because members of the IPLO are actively involved in a war, their lives are dangerous, and it is dangerous simply being with them. As with the IRA and INLA in my previous research, I never felt that I was in any danger from the IPLO. As before, my major concern was the authorities – particularly the army and police – and Loyalist paramilitaries, both of whom I believed represented more of a threat now than before because now I was directly researching a guerrilla organization. In particular, the fieldwork period was marked by a major increase in Loyalist violence, from which academics were not immune. In September 1991, Adrian Guelke, a lecturer in politics at the Queen's University of Belfast, was shot by a Loyalist death squad from the Ulster Freedom Fighters (UFF, generally acknowledged as a nom de guerre or front for the Ulster Defence Association). In the early hours of the morning, two or three masked gunmen entered his house and he was shot in the back at close range with a pistol as he lay sleeping with his wife. His life was saved when the automatic pistol used in the attack jammed. Guelke is a South African-born opponent of apartheid who has lived in Northern Ireland

since 1974. A distinguished academic, he had no connections with any paramilitary or political groups and was working on a book comparing political violence in South Africa, Israel, and Northern Ireland. The motives for the attack are not clear, and the Security Forces claim it was a case of mistaken identity, but Guelke believes that South African elements, who have links with the Loyalist paramilitaries, may have set him up.[5]

I tried to ameliorate these dangers in two ways. First, I tried to camouflage my research with the IPLO as best I could so that only they and a couple of close and trusted friends knew that I was doing it. I did research on two other projects at the same time (one on Republican martyrs and the other on the cultures of terror and resistance in Northern Ireland), and when asked about my research, I talked about these instead. Second, I tried to control and limit my contact with IPLO members. They were not the only people I spent my time with. In fact, most of my time was not spent with IPLO members, particularly in the first few months of the fieldwork, when I worked on other projects and did library and archival research on the history of the IPLO. Restricting interaction with research participants is not ideal in participant observation, but I believed it necessary for security reasons. As the research progressed, I spent increasingly more time with IPLO members, and the most intense period of interviewing and participant observation occurred during the last two months.

In the end, during the course of this fieldwork, I was not directly threatened in any way. While I was stopped by Security Forces patrols for identity checks twice while in the company of IPLO leaders, I was not approached by the army or police, and they never indicated to me that they were aware that I was conducting research with the IPLO. When asked by soldiers and police about my research, I told them I was studying political culture and did not mention the IPLO. On one occasion I crossed the border illegally with Jimmy Brown on a trip to Dublin. When I told him I was driving to Dublin with Jimmy, a trusted friend warned me that under no circumstances should I use the back roads to avoid the border checkpoints. He warned that if I ran into a

Security Forces patrol or SAS unit (the elite commando forces of the British army) on a deserted back road while alone in a car with the commander of the IPLO, I was likely to be shot dead. When Jimmy and I reached the border, I followed his directions and we used back roads to cross and avoid the checkpoint. I did so because I believed that he was in the best position to decide on the route we should take. I only did this once, and I probably would not do it again.

On one occasion I was participant observer during an IPLO operation, a propaganda exercise. This was a photo-shoot for publicity purposes, and an IPLO photographer was present. I was invited along because they figured I could take some photos of my own for the book. Six armed IPLO members in military uniform and wearing masks, dark glasses, and IPLO armbands emerged in Poleglass (a Catholic-nationalist ghetto on the outskirts of West Belfast) to set up a vehicle checkpoint. They stopped about half a dozen cars and then disappeared. The operation lasted only a few minutes but was probably the most dangerous thing I have ever done as an anthropologist. Armed guerrillas are usually shot on sight in Northern Ireland. For the IPLO to emerge in public in this way is to enter a combat situation. Because of the constant surveillance and patrolling of these districts by the Security Forces, such operations have to be planned very carefully, and there is always a distinct danger of encountering an army patrol or undercover unit or being observed by the surveillance helicopters constantly hovering overhead.

Another new problem I faced resulted from the fact that I taped the fifteen formal interviews. In my previous research I had not taped interviews, so the necessity of protecting tapes was a new experience. I tried to protect these in two ways. First, I tried to ensure there was nothing on them that would directly identify any individual, particularly the interviewee. Second, I hid them away from the house where I lived, so there was never more than one there at a time. Of course, these were not foolproof protections. I felt justified in making the tapes because I had formal agreements with the IPLO as an organization and the individuals

interviewed that I would try to use IPLO members' own words to present their views in the book. Because they were willing to accept the risk, and I believed I could protect the tapes and minimize that risk, I taped the interviews.

Reflections and Recommendations

What then are my recommendations to anthropologists considering fieldwork in dangerous or violent social contexts? Before you go to the field, try to evaluate as realistically as possible the degree of danger, and try to identify potential sources of danger. Decide if you are prepared to accept the risks involved, and if you are, consider both what sorts of actions you might take to ameliorate or manage them and what sorts of actions might exacerbate them. Give some thought to what an "acceptable level" of danger might be. I assume that most researchers are not prepared to give their lives for their research and would retreat to safer ground if a direct threat to life or limb arose. Recognize as well that you may have to terminate your research on your own initiative, or that the authorities or other "powers that be" may compel you to do so. Always have a plan of escape, a means of extricating yourself from the situation as quickly as possible, should the need arise.

Discuss the potential dangers with advisers and colleagues, and seek out people with direct experience in the area where you intend to do your research. If at all possible, try to go to the proposed field location for an exploratory visit before you commit yourself to doing research there. I was able to visit Belfast for two weeks during the summer prior to my arrival there for fieldwork.

Investigate your sources of funding. For example, Myron Glazer (1972:137), a sociologist who studied student politics in Chile, learned only after his return from the field that his funding came from a US Army-sponsored research group. Today, governments, militaries, and intelligence agencies are funding research both directly and indirectly through front organizations (e.g., right-wing think tanks). Ethical considerations aside, it can be dangerous to accept funding from agencies that one's research participants consider objectionable. Certainly, the danger of being defined as a spy is greatly exaggerated if one is funded by the military or the CIA. Know the origins of your funding, consider how people in your research area might view those origins, and be open with them about it.

Given that the people among whom anthropologists do their research have usually never had an anthropologist working in their midst, it should be kept in mind that they are naturally going to try to figure out what you are doing there. Usually, at least at first, they will define the anthropologist with reference to preexisting categories derived from experience with other strangers who have appeared in the community. Spy, journalist, policeman, tax collector, and missionary are common categories often mistakenly applied to anthropologists in the field. It is essential that researchers in the field make a substantial effort to counter these public definitions of themselves, a process entailing a conscious effort at impression management (Berreman 1962; Goffman 1959). It can be done by recognizing how people are likely to define you, avoiding acting in ways that might reinforce these suspicions, and being as honest and straightforward as possible about who you really are and what you are really doing.

Because the most common suspicion that research participants have about anthropologists is that they are spies, and it is difficult to find an anthropologist who has done fieldwork who has not encountered this suspicion, this danger deserves special mention. Being defined as a spy is inherently dangerous, and the link between anthropology and war-related research has exacerbated this danger (see Sluka 1990). Anthropologists have been involved in war-related, particularly counterinsurgency, research, others have had their research used or "applied" by governments, militaries, and intelligence agencies to help plan military operations, and spies or intelligence agents of various sorts have used the cover that they were anthropologists. As a result, people in many parts of the world have come increasingly to believe that anthropologists, even those engaged in "innocent" (or in Boas's [1973]

terms "honest") research, are actually or potentially dangerous to them. Many nations and peoples are therefore justifiably suspicious of anthropologists and will not allow them to do research, and fieldwork has become more dangerous today than it was in the past.

If you do not want to be defined as a spy, then do not be one or act like one. (See Glazer 1970 for a good account of dealing with research participants' suspicions that the researcher is a spy.) At first, I avoided asking questions about sensitive political topics. In a similar manner, anthropologists seeking to counter suspicions that they are missionaries would at first avoid asking questions about religion. The sociologist Ned Polsky (1967:126–7) suggests that a good rule of fieldwork in sensitive contexts is to "initially, keep your eyes and ears open but keep your mouth shut. At first try to ask no questions whatsoever. Before you can ask questions ... you should get the 'feel' of their world by extensive and attentive listening."

When you consider how your research participants are likely to define you, consider ways of not only countering these definitions but of also promoting one that will enhance your safety and your research. It is not enough to not be a threat to your research participants; act in such a way as to *be seen* not to be a threat. In my case, my association with the priest and the former IRA man was fortunate in this respect because once they accepted my explanations of what I was doing in Belfast, others found it easier to do so as well. Polsky (ibid., 129) refers to this cumulative effect as "snowballing"; "get an introduction to one [informant] who will vouch for you with others, who in turn will vouch for you with still others." He suggests that it is best to start at the top, with the most prestigious person in the group you are studying. He also suggests that answering research participants' questions frankly will help in this regard (ibid., 131). I suggest that it is important to give people as honest and complete a description of what you are doing as you can, particularly when they specifically ask for such an explanation.

However, people will develop their own explanations of what researchers are doing, and these are often much-simplified versions of the explanations given by the researchers themselves. It is very common for research participants to reduce the sometimes quite involved explanations given by researchers simply to the explanation that they are "writing a book" about the community or some aspect of it. For example, this was both William Foote Whyte's (1943:300) and my own experience. It is important to bear in mind that people may reduce your best and most complete explanations to much simpler, less accurate, and perhaps inaccurate ones. It can also be dangerous to give simplified explanations of what you are doing. For example, if you simply tell people that you are writing a book about them, when they learn specific details of what you are writing about, they may believe that you have misled them. They will naturally wonder why you would want to do so and wonder if you have some ulterior motive. Be honest and give as complete and accurate a description of what you are doing as you can, but recognize that people are going to interpret and possibly misinterpret this. Continuously monitor their definitions of you, as these may change over time, and view your efforts at impression management as an ongoing process.

That you should approach this as a conscious effort at impression management is not to suggest that this should be some sort of cold-blooded Machiavellian manipulative strategy. Like Polsky, I argue that it is important to be honest with people. This is imperative both ethically and with reference to managing danger. Being dishonest is more dangerous than being honest, because it creates the possibility of being caught out in a lie. By extension, acting ethically is also safer than acting unethically.[6] Be as honest and ethical as possible, bearing in mind that it is your research participants' definition of these things that you should seek to conform to rather than your own. Of course, this may raise other dangers, for example, when the definitions of what is ethical differ between the group studied and other groups in society, particularly between the group studied and the authorities.

Being honest is relatively simple as long as you have nothing to hide. This was not a problem during my first period of fieldwork,

but it became one during the second period because I needed to camouflage my research with the IPLO. I told the authorities vaguely that I was studying aspects of political culture; the IPLO and a few trusted friends knew I was working with the IPLO; and I told everyone else I was doing research on Republican martyrs and the cultures of terror and resistance. In most fieldwork situations today, marked as they are by conflict, it will probably prove to be impossible to be completely truthful with everyone. Nonetheless, it is a good danger management strategy to be as truthful as possible.

Along with honesty, flexibility can be important in danger management. Consider how far you are prepared to modify your interests, methods, and goals to adapt to dangerous contingencies that may arise. Doing research in a dangerous environment may produce situations in which researchers must consider modifying or perhaps even compromising their work. These are difficult decisions to make, and they may be fateful both for the research and for the researcher. Polsky discusses flexibility, summing it up in the comment that "a final rule is to have few unbreakable rules." He points out that you should revise your plans "according to the requirements of any particular situation" and recognize that you will probably encounter "unanticipated and ambiguous situations for which one has no clear behavioral plan at all" (1967:133).

While in the field, take precautions to secure your field notes and recordings. To do so is, of course, required to protect your research participants, but it may also be necessary to protect yourself. This issue is discussed by Jenkins (1984), who suggests that one should be selective in information gathering. He points out that some information should not be used at all and recommends that information of this sort should not be recorded. Some information is best kept only in one's head. When sensitive information is recorded, it is imperative to protect research participants' anonymity. Jenkins (ibid., 156) suggests that one carry around only the current day's notes, and it is probably advisable in some cases that you never have more than a few weeks' notes in your possession at any time while in the field. Your notes can be kept under lock and key, and arrangements can be made to periodically remove them from the field (perhaps by mailing them off or by depositing them in a safe deposit box).

Consider the possibility that some dangers may not end once you return from the field. There may be those at home who object to your research, and they may threaten you as well. (For example, I have been threatened by Loyalists since I left Belfast.) Also, consider the possibility that ethical and other considerations may mean that you will not be able to publish your findings.

If you intend to do research on political topics, particularly if you intend to do "partisan anthropology" or participate in political activities, it goes without saying that the dangers are correspondingly greater.[7] In reference to "partisan anthropology," the Association of Social Anthropologists' book on ethnographic research notes that "siding with a guerrilla movement ... can be dangerous to oneself as well as to one's objectivity" (Ellen 1984:80). It is interesting to note that the usual concern is not that such involvement may be dangerous but rather that it may not be "objective." It should be kept in mind that one does not actually have to be a member or supporter of a political organization to be at risk from their enemies. Association, even if purely "objective," can be dangerous in itself. In some cases the status of an outsider or "objective scientific observer" provides a degree of protection, but do not count on it. And if you are actually a participant, your status as a social scientist will probably offer you no protection at all.

One might think that neutrality is a good danger management strategy, but this is not always the case. For example, June Nash, in what is perhaps the best account by an anthropologist of managing dangers encountered while conducting fieldwork in a politically sensitive environment, notes,

In Bolivia it was not possible to choose the role of an impartial observer and still work in the tin mining community of Oruro, where I had gone to study ideology and social change.... The polarisation of the class struggle made it necessary to take sides or to be cast by them

on one side or the other. In a revolutionary situation, no neutrals are allowed. (1976:150)

By contrast, Frances Henry discusses research in a situation of conflict between the government and trade unions in Trinidad. She notes,

Commitment to the unions ... could conceivably have led to loss of freedom, detention, or, at the very least, deportation.... On the other hand, commitment to the government could have resulted in loss of rapport with union officials. Identification with either faction can lead to serious personal difficulties and it obviously limits one's research freedom. (1966:553)

Henry was able to establish rapport with both sides and discusses how she got around attempts to get her to abandon her neutrality. Basically, she did so by expressing "sympathy or agreement with persons on both sides" (ibid.). In face-to-face interactions with her research participants, she expressed sympathy with them, even though they had conflicting points of view. While Henry maintains that in fact she was "neutral," this was not the image she presented to her research participants. Rather, she misled her informants by presenting an image of being on their side when she knew that she was not. Besides the ethical questions this raises, Henry admits that this was dangerous, and I would not recommend it.

In some cases, professing neutrality may be a good danger management strategy; in others, it may not be. In some cases, you may want to tell some people that you are neutral and others that you are not. It may sound like a case of "situational ethics," but I had no qualms about telling British soldiers on the streets of Belfast who inquired as to my personal politics that I was a "neutral social scientist" while at the same time letting my research participants in the ghettos know that I sympathized with their situation.

When conducting research based on participant observation in communities involved in political conflicts, it is generally the case that, as Nash, myself, and many others have found, "no neutrals are allowed." As Glazer (1970:314) notes, "In times of heightened group antagonism there is little room for neutrality." This does not necessarily mean that you have to become a partisan. In my case, it was sufficient to communicate in various ways to people where my "sympathies" lay; that is, with them. Whether or not you take sides, those actively involved in the situation are going to define whose side they think you are on. They will act toward you on the basis of this definition, regardless of your professions of neutrality.

Gerrit Huizer (1973), a social psychologist who has done fieldwork in several Latin American countries, including El Salvador and Chile, provides illumination here. When he worked in a village in El Salvador, government officials often warned him of the "dangers" of living among the peasants. Despite these warnings, he chose not to carry a pistol like government officials did. Instead, he "relied mostly on the common human sympathy" he felt for the villagers. Basically, Huizer's approach to handling danger is to gain people's confidence by convincing them that you are "on their side." This is done by sincerely identifying with their interests, understanding and sympathizing with their problems and grievances, and showing them that you are willing to act accordingly (ibid., 21, 28). I think that this is quite the most common approach taken by anthropologists today, and it can be very effective as a danger-ameliorating approach to fieldwork.

When working in a community in which guerrilla organizations are present, you must learn to walk softly. Be sensitive to what sorts of questions may be asked and what sorts are taboo. For example, I found that it was all right to ask people what they thought of the IRA and INLA, if they did or did not support them and why, about the role the guerrillas played in the community, and about criticisms they had concerning them. But I did not ask questions about things like arms and explosives, or about who might be a guerrilla or actively involved with them. If you want to make direct contact with guerrillas, it is best to make it known that you are interested in this and then wait until they come (or do not come) to you. If you do make contact (which is illegal in most cases), you must be flexible and honest with them.

In situations in which insurgencies are going on, fieldworkers may have to deal with both the insurgents and the authorities combating them at the same time and this can be a very difficult task. Often, if you become associated with one, this alienates you from the other. In many field situations the authorities represent a significant source of danger. This warning is particularly true if you are studying or involved with political organizations. For example, Arnold Ap, an anthropologist in West Papua, was tortured and killed by the Indonesian army in 1984, as a result of his association with the Free Papua Movement (OPM). The army claimed that he was "a known OPM helper" (Osborne 1985:xiv). And in 1980, Miriam Daly, a lecturer at the Queen's University of Belfast, was assassinated, probably by intelligence agents, as a result of her involvement with the Irish Republican Socialist party (Faligot 1983:98).

Just as I found in my research, Polsky found that most of the risk in his fieldwork came from the authorities rather than from his research participants. He notes that "most of the danger for the fieldworker comes not from the cannibals and head-hunters but from the colonial officials" (1967:145). In his particular case, he found that most of the risk came from the police rather than from the "career criminals" that were his research participants.

> The criminologist studying uncaught criminals in the open finds sooner or later that law enforcers try to put him on the spot – because, unless he is a complete fool, he uncovers information that law enforcers would like to know, and, even if he is very skillful, he cannot always keep law enforcers from suspecting that he has such information. (Ibid.)

The dangers emanating from the authorities include the risks of intimidation, physical assaults, arrest, interrogation, torture, prosecution, imprisonment, and even execution or assassination. Other dangers include being defined as a guerrilla "sympathizer" or being accused of "giving aid and comfort to the enemy," as a result of which the authorities may revoke their permission for the research. These dangers should be recognized, and efforts should be made to reduce them. (See Carey 1972 for a good discussion of the legal risks faced by researchers in situations in which illegal activities occur.)

An associated phenomenon that can also generate danger is the fact that "people tend to associate the research that a researcher is conducting with the researcher himself" (Henslin 1972:55). As Henslin points out, if you do research on drug users or homosexuality, you may fall under suspicion of being a drug user or homosexual yourself. If you do research on a political movement, some, particularly those opposed to that movement, may believe that you are a partisan. The more political or controversial a subject one researches, the more likely one is to be suspected of bias or partisanship.

While you are in the field, do not grow complacent about the dangers you face, and do not treat the situation as a game or adventure. Do not ignore potential threats when they arise: they rarely just "go away" if you ignore them. For example, dangerous rumors may emerge at almost any time while in the field. Whether these rumors are true or false, they should be dealt with. If they are false, they should be publicly denied rather than ignored. If there is some truth to the rumors, work to convince people that you are not a threat, and if you are a direct threat, get out. James T. Carey (1972:86–7) discusses "handling damaging rumors" in fieldwork and makes some useful suggestions. Try to anticipate the circumstances under which dangerous or damaging rumors are likely to arise, and then limit your actual observations of activities and situations (e.g., illegal ones) that might lead to these circumstances. If and when such rumors do arise, try to get people who have vouched for you in the past to do so again.

Make a continuing effort to define and redefine risks and dangers in light of actual experiences, and work to reduce such dangers by improving old methods and developing new ones as your network of contacts and degree of experience expand over time. Managing the dangers inherent in fieldwork in a context like that of Belfast is not something that can be gotten out of the way in the first few weeks in the field and then dismissed as taken care of.

On the last day of my first period of research in Belfast, I was returning home to pack and found the street cordoned off by the army. They would not allow me to go down the street to my house because of the presence of a "suspect device." I argued with a sergeant about it, and he finally said in disgust that I could go to the house if I was prepared to take responsibility for the risk. It turned out that local children had taped some wire to a can of paint and rolled it under an army Land Rover as a prank.

With time, you may be able to successfully allay suspicions and reduce some of the dangers, but new ones will continue to arise. One need not be paranoid about the dangers involved in doing research in violent social contexts, but a good dose of realistic appreciation goes a long way. And, all in all, it is no doubt better to be a bit paranoid about such things than it is to be a bit complacent about them.

Finally, remember that while most dangers can be mediated at least to some degree by skillful maneuver, some dangers may be beyond management. For example, despite your best efforts at danger management, simple bad luck can sometimes result in the termination of the research, or worse yet the termination of the researcher. Researchers working in dangerous environments should, like professional gamblers, recognize that their enterprise is inherently a combination of both skill and luck (Ellen 1984:97). Good luck can sometimes help overcome a lack of skill, and well-developed skills can go far to help overcome the effects of bad luck. But sometimes no amount of skill will save one from a gross portion of bad luck. What distinguishes the professional from the amateur, in both gambling and anthropology, is the concerted effort always to maximize skillful handling of the situation, while recognizing that skill alone is no guarantee of success. Danger is not a purely "technical" problem and is never totally manageable.

It might seem that most of these recommendations amount to little more than common sense. They are by no means exhaustive, but I hope that they are thought provoking or "consciousness raising" and indicative of some of the problems involved in managing danger. They are intended to be a starting point from which those considering research in dangerous contexts can map out their own strategies for conducting fieldwork safely. It should go without saying that counting on people to rely on common sense is a wholly inadequate approach to almost anything. Certainly, it is not adequate for advisers to tell their students that they should use "common sense" while they are in the field, and leave it at that. The example of the anthropologist shot in Belfast is a case in point. Some might say that his mistake was simply that he did not use common sense. My point has been that such an analysis of these cases is an inadequate response.

Conclusion

These observations were made in reference to my experience in Northern Ireland, where a guerrilla war has been going on now for more than twenty-three years. As I said at the beginning, there are about 120 armed conflicts in the world today. There is an urgent need for research in all of the places where these conflicts are occurring, and many other violent or dangerous locations as well.

Fieldwork is possible even in the most dangerous contexts. Anthropologists should not select themselves out of research in such contexts on the basis of stereotypes, media images, or inadequate information concerning the dangers involved. And they should not select themselves out of such research because training in managing such dangers is not provided in anthropology. Many more anthropologists could and should do fieldwork in these areas. The dangers are often exaggerated, and in most cases they are not insurmountable.

The world is not becoming a safer place for the pursuit of anthropological fieldwork, but, perhaps for that very reason, there is more need now for such research than there has ever been before. We can meet this challenge, but we should do so rationally by considering the dangers as methodological issues in their own right. The intention of this chapter has been to further our consideration of danger as a methodological issue and contribute to developing

ways of minimizing risks and protecting anthropologists while they are in the field. It is not an exaggeration to say that this is, in fact, a matter of life and death.

NOTES

1 At least sixty anthropologists have died of "fieldwork mishaps" in the past decade (Howell 1990), and at least three have been killed "on the job" as a result of political violence. In 1982, Ruth First, a South African-born anthropologist and professor, was killed by a mail bomb in her office at Maputo University in Mozambique. "It is suspected that the bomb was sent by the South African secret service to end her effective political protests against apartheid" (ibid., 100). In 1984, the Melanesian anthropologist Arnold Ap was tortured and killed by the Indonesian army in West Papua, allegedly because of his association with the Free Papua Movement (OPM). In 1990, Myrna Mack, a Guatemalan anthropologist, was brutally assassinated as she was leaving the research center where she worked in that country. She had been studying the effects of the civil war on indigenous peoples. In February 1993, a former Guatemalan soldier was sentenced to twenty-five years in prison for her murder.

2 It should also be noted that Nancy Howell's *Surviving Fieldwork* is the first comprehensive study of "the risks that are taken, and the prices that are paid for doing fieldwork in the ways we do" (1990:1). It is intended to help fieldworkers anticipate the dangers they will face and prepare for preventing and responding to them. She shows that anthropology can be dangerous and that hundreds of anthropologists have failed to protect themselves from dangers and have been victims of fieldwork. She devotes a chapter specifically to human hazards of fieldwork, which includes descriptions and discussion of incidents involving arrest, military attack, suspicion of spying, living through political turmoil, factional conflict, and the taking of anthropologists as hostages in the field.

3 The risks and dangers of participant observation-based research in Belfast are described in

detail in my article on managing danger in fieldwork (Sluka 1990).

4   Seven months after completing this research, in August 1992, Jimmy Brown was shot dead in a feud within the IPLO. This feud ultimately led to the dissolution of the organization by the IRA in November of that year.

5   In 1989, three members of Ulster Resistance – a quasi-paramilitary loyalist group set up in 1985 – were charged in Paris with arms trafficking, receiving stolen goods, and conspiracy for the purpose of terrorism. They had been found in a hotel room with a mock-up of a Blowpipe shoulder-fired missile launcher, built by Protestant workers at the Shorts factory in East Belfast. With them were an American arms dealer with CIA links and a South African diplomat. Later, South Africa issued a statement rejecting allegations of links with Loyalist paramilitaries and denying they had supplied them with weapons. However, it is thought South Africans supplied Loyalists with their biggest-ever arms shipment in January 1988.

6   Conducting fieldwork in dangerous contexts raises very important ethical issues. I have struggled with these issues both personally and professionally for many years. I have chosen not to discuss the ethics of conducting research in dangerous contexts here because, in my opinion, that issue is more important than the issue of managing danger in fieldwork and therefore deserves a paper (or better yet, a book) devoted exclusively to it. Others may be of the opinion that it is inappropriate to discuss managing danger without discussing the larger issue of the ethics of conducting research in dangerous contexts. However, for the reason stated above, I have chosen to stick specifically to the topic of managing danger. The question, therefore, is, what is the relationship between ethics and managing danger?

7   The best contemporary example of drastic partisan anthropology is the case of the Dutch anthropologist Klaas de Jonge, who was involved in smuggling weapons and explosives for guerrillas of the African National Congress. To avoid arrest, he sought asylum in a Dutch embassy office in Pretoria, where he spent two years before being allowed to leave South Africa as part of a prisoner exchange in September 1987.

REFERENCES

Berreman, Gerald D.
1962   "Behind Many Masks: Ethnography and Impression Management." In *Hindus of the Himalayas*, by G. Berreman, xvii–lvii. Berkeley and Los Angeles: University of California Press.

Boas, Franz
1973   "Scientists as Spies." In *To See Ourselves: Anthropology and Modern Social Issues*, ed. Thomas Weaver, 51–2. Glencoe, Ill.: Scott, Foresman.

Carey, James T.
1972   "Problems of Access and Risk in Observing Drug Scenes." In *Research on Deviance*, ed. Jack Douglas, 71–92. New York: Random House.

Dillon, Martin
1990   *The Dirty War*. London: Arrow Books.

Ellen, Roy F., ed.
1984   *Ethnographic Research: A Guide to General Conduct*. London: Academic Press.

Faligot, Roger
1983   *Britain's Military Strategy in Northern Ireland: The Kitson Experiment*. London: Zed Press.

Glazer, Myron
1970   "Field Work in a Hostile Environment: A Chapter in the Sociology of Social Research in Chile." In *Student Politics in Chile*, ed. Frank Bonilla and Myron Glazer, 313–33. New York: Basic Books.

Glazer, Myron
1972   *The Research Adventure: Promise and Problems of Fieldwork*. New York: Random House.

Goffman, Erving
1959   *The Presentation of Self in Everyday Life*. New York: Anchor.

Henry, Frances
1966   "The Role of the Field Worker in an Explosive Political Situation." *Current Anthropology* 7, no. 5 (December): 552–9.

Henslin, James M.
1972   "Studying Deviance in Four Settings: Research Experiences with Cabbies, Suicides, Drug Users, and Abortionees." In *Research on Deviance*, ed. Jack Douglas, 35–70. New York: Random House.

Howell, Nancy
1986   "Occupational Safety and Health in Anthropology." Paper presented at the annual

meetings of the American Association of Practicing Anthropologists, 10 April, Albuquerque, New Mexico.

Howell, Nancy
1990 *Surviving Fieldwork*. Washington, DC: American Anthropological Association.

Huizer, Gerrit
1973 *Peasant Rebellion in Latin America*. Harmondsworth: Penguin. [Chapter 2, "A Field Experience in Central America," and chapter 3, "A Field Experience in Chile."]

Jenkins, Richard
1984 "Bringing It All Back Home: An Anthropologist in Belfast." In *Social Researching: Politics, Problems, Practice*, ed. Colin Bell and Helen Roberts, 147–63. London: Routledge and Kegan Paul.

Nash, June
1976 "Ethnology in a Revolutionary Setting." In *Ethics and Anthropology: Dilemmas in Fieldwork*, ed. Michael Rynkiewich and James Spradley, 148–66. New York: Wiley and Sons.

Nietschmann, Bernard
1987 "The Third World War." *Cultural Survival Quarterly* 11 (3): 1–16.

Nordstrom, Carolyn, and JoAnn Martin
1992 "The Culture of Conflict: Field Reality and Theory." In *The Paths to Domination, Resistance, and Terror*, ed. Carolyn Nordstrom and JoAnn Martin. Berkeley, Los Angeles, and Oxford: University of California Press.

Osborne, Robin
1985 *Indonesia's Secret War. The Guerrilla Struggle in Irian Jaya*. Sydney: Allen & Unwin.

Polsky, Ned
1967 *Hustlers, Beats and Others*. Harmondsworth: Penguin.

Rolston, Bill
1991 "Containment and Its Failure: The British State and the Control of Conflict in Northern Ireland." In *Western State Terrorism*, ed. Alexander George. Cambridge: Polity Press.

Sluka, Jeffrey A.
1989 *Hearts and Minds, Water and Fish: Popular Support for the IRA and INLA in a Northern Irish Ghetto*. Greenwich, Conn.: JAI Press.

Sluka, Jeffrey A.
1990 "Participant Observation in Violent Social Contexts." *Human Organization* 49 (2):114–26.

Whyte, William Foote
1943 *Street Corner Society*. Chicago: University of Chicago Press.

Part VI

Fieldwork Ethics

Introduction

Jeffrey A. Sluka

The relational nature of fieldwork addressed in Part III, the conflicts described in Part IV, and the changing relation between anthropologists and their research participants referred to in Part V have made contemporary fieldwork morally and ethically more complex. A grasp of the ethical implications of fieldwork is indispensable before students can develop their first research design. Part VI of this Reader deals with ethics in fieldwork. In making the selections for this part many difficult choices had to be made. We could simply have chosen exemplary case studies from the growing literature on ethical dilemmas faced by anthropologists in the field (e.g., Rynkiewich and Spradley 1976; Appell 1978; Ellen 1984; Cassell and Jacobs 1987; Caplan 2003; Fluehr-Lobban 2003b; Meskel and Pels 2005; Armbruster and Laerke 2008), or included something on the Tierney/Chagnon "Darkness in El Dorado" debate, which has been described as the greatest ethical debacle in the history of the discipline (see Tierney 2000; Borofsky 2005). In the end, we have chosen to focus more generally on how the concern with ethics emerged and has evolved in the discipline – that is, on the context of ethical thinking rather than particular case studies. Thus, we have chosen articles by Irving Horowitz (1973),

Ethnographic Fieldwork: An Anthropological Reader, Second Edition. Edited by
Antonius C. G. M. Robben and Jeffrey A. Sluka.
Editorial material and organization © 2012 John Wiley & Sons, Inc.
Published 2012 by John Wiley & Sons, Inc.

Philippe Bourgois (1991), and Gerald Berreman (1991), which provide the general history, context, and critique of the evolution of ethical codes in anthropology; Jeffrey Ehrenreich's case study of providing amateur medical care, which has been one of the classic or traditional ethical dilemmas in anthropological fieldwork; and finally the third, or most recent, Code of Ethics of the American Anthropological Association (AAA) adopted in 2009 (for the British code of ethics, see Association of Social Anthropologists 1999).

In the late 1960s and early 1970s, anthropologists first began seriously to discuss the ethical dilemmas faced by fieldworkers studying and living in a world rife with political turmoil, and the first code of ethics in anthropology emerged as a direct result of the protest against counterinsurgency research for the US government in Latin America and Southeast Asia. Leading anthropologists denounced the collaboration of anthropology with the counterinsurgency agencies of the US government – specifically Project Camelot in Latin America, Project Agile in Thailand, and the Himalayan Border Countries Project in India. In particular, the issues raised by Project Camelot and the publication of the Thailand counterinsurgency research (Wolf and Jorgensen 1970) launched the debate on ethics in anthropology, revealed the pressing need to set ethical standards within the profession, and led to the development and adoption of the AAA's "Principles of Professional Responsibility" (PPR) in 1971 (Fluehr-Lobban 2003a).

In the 1990s, there was renewed vigor in discussion and debate about ethics in anthropology, which led to the adoption of a new (critics such as Gerald Berreman would say eviscerated) code of ethics by the AAA in 1998. The impetus for this change was a general trend in the discipline toward "professionalism" and the changing employment market for anthropologists, with an increasing number employed outside academia in the private sector. Peter Pels (1999) has identified professionalization as a dominant trend in contemporary anthropology. He argues that the purpose of professional ethics codes is to guarantee the technical and moral quality of service rendered to clients and to help discipline members of the profession who fail to maintain what, in corporate-speak, would be termed "quality control." Professionalism seems to mean redefining anthropology as a form of employment like any other – simply a marketable research skill or commodity for sale in the marketplace. Thus, professionalization and corporatization are the same thing, and the second AAA code of ethics reflected those developments. This was a significant change, because the primary purpose of the original ethics code was first and foremost the protection from harm of research participants. The shift toward professionalism subverts this, with the result that harm or negative consequences to those researched are ameliorated by "competing" ethical obligations and responsibilities to employers and authorities, now referred to in corporate-speak as "clients" and "shareholders," whose interests are treated as equal to those of the people researched.

Pels (1999) observes that, in defining their professional interests and duties, anthropologists are now wavering between, on the one hand, responsibility to the people researched and, on the other, service to those who fund research and the authorities under whose jurisdiction those researched live. We now appear to be confused about who our "clients" are: those studied? ourselves? the authorities, funders, and sponsors? the public? And if all four, do we have equal ethical obligations to them all? In the original PPR, there was a clear hierarchical principle that helped to sort this conflict out – the interests of the research participants were treated as primary, since their cooperation can be obtained only on the basis of trust.

As noted, the first major debate about ethics in anthropology, which led to the adoption of the first code of ethics in the discipline, was sparked by the controversy generated about government-sponsored social science research for military and political purposes, which occurred as a result of Project Camelot. Project Camelot was a major research project conducted in 1964 into the causes of insurgency and potential revolution in Latin America, sponsored by the US Departments of Defense and State, which was terminated in its early stages as a result of the controversy it generated. In "The Life and Death of Project Camelot" (1973), Horowitz, who also edited a definitive volume on the controversy (1974), describes Project Camelot and recounts the history of the academic reactions to it which eventually led to its cancellation. Horowitz argues that the central issue concerns the dangers inherent in government-sponsored "mission-oriented" research motivated by political and military interests, especially when they are carried out in other nations, and that at the heart of the problem of Project Camelot is the question "What are and are not the legitimate functions of a scientist?" (1973:147).

The theme of Philippe Bourgois's article "Confronting the Ethics of Anthropology" is "the politics of ethics," and he presents a powerful critique of anthropological research ethics as embodied in the AAA code, based on his fieldwork experience in Central America. He begins by observing:

> The ethics of anthropological research are too complicated and important to be reduced to unambiguous absolutes or even perhaps to be clearly defined … The eminently political orientation of a supposed apolitical commitment to empirical research must be appreciated for its internal inconsistencies and ultimate ethical poverty. (1991:110)

In 1981, while in El Salvador exploring potential research sites, Bourgois was caught up with local villagers fleeing from a government counterinsurgency "search and destroy" operation that became a peasant massacre. He fled with them, and "for the next fourteen days, we stayed together running at night and hiding during the day" (1991:118). These military operations were supported by the Reagan administration's foreign policy, and when Bourgois returned to the United States he sought out the media and human rights lobbyists on Capital Hill to present his testimony to the public. But most significantly, he published a report critical of US policy, entitled "Running for My Life in El Salvador," in the *Washington Post* (February 14, 1982).

The academic reaction consisted of severe criticism of Bourgois's actions as being unethical, and this nearly ended his career in anthropology. In a telling footnote, he recounts:

> A church-based director of a human rights organization rebuked me when I explained to him the anthropological ethics which prevented me from showing members of US Congress photographs of peasant victims during my testimony on the military invasion: "For God's sake; what are you talking about! Testify as a human being then – not as an anthropologist." (1991:123)

Bourgois argues that the problem with anthropological ethics is that the boundaries of what is defined as ethical are too narrowly drawn and that ethics can be subject to rigid, righteous interpretations which place them at loggerheads with overarching human rights concerns. He asks: What are the limits of informed consent in research involving highly unequal power relations? Is the consent of the powerful required to do research with the powerless, or on the effects of powerlessness? Do we need the consent of repressive authorities in order to do research with those who are oppressed by them? How does one fulfill the obligation to obtain informed consent from the powerful, and respect their privacy and interests? He argues that it is very difficult, if not impossible, to satisfy the discipline-bound code of ethics if one does research on political topics such as marginalization and oppression, and that these unresolved questions reveal "that there is nothing apolitical about the North American commitment to relativism and to its methodologically defined body of ethics. Most dramatically, the ethic of informed consent as it is interpreted by human subjects review boards at ... universities implicitly reinforces the political status quo" (1991:120).

Bourgois concludes: "It would be dangerous and arrogant to think that there are definite answers to any of these ethical/moral questions. We need to discuss them and think about them in both practical and theoretical terms" (1991:122–123). It is also notable that this article was published in Faye Harrison's groundbreaking edited volume, *Decolonizing Anthropology*, published in 1991. At that time he could write that "few self-respecting anthropologists would condone the exercise of anthropology at the service of a world superpower or as a complement to espionage" (1991:111). However, as noted in the introduction to Part V, and as we shall see in Part X, this is being challenged and there are now anthropologists who are prepared to condone this in support of the "wars on terrorism" initiated by US President George W. Bush and UK Prime Minister Tony Blair in Iraq and Afghanistan. This has not only exacerbated the dangers and hazards of anthropological fieldwork, but reinforces the criticism that in the 1990s there was a shift to the right in the discipline, marked by the weakening of the AAA code of ethics, which represents a trend toward the "recolonization" of the discipline.

Gerald Berreman has been one of the leading actors and spokespersons involved in the dialogue over ethics during the past four or five decades. In "Ethics versus 'Realism' in Anthropology" (1991), he presents a strong defense of the preservation of the core features of the original code, the Principles of Professional Responsibility. Berreman was a member of the AAA Committee on Ethics during some of the most turbulent times in the history of the discipline, and was one of the drafters of the original PPR in 1971. He fears a neoliberal return to an immoral and instrumental interventionism. He describes what he sees as the evisceration of the original code of ethics, leading up to the adoption of the second code in 1998, and offers an excellent discussion of the issue of clandestine research, a subject which is of renewed relevance today during a "new era" in which much anthropological research is increasingly subject to contract-client restrictions.

Berreman's article is the most important and damning critique of the changes in the AAA code of ethics. These changes were driven by the interests of the growing number of anthropologists employed outside universities in the private sector, and the new code was partly intended to prevent the division of the profession into "academic" and "practicing" moieties. Berreman decries the shift away from idealism (and all notions of universal human rights, ethics, or morality are, by definition, idealistic) toward self-centered practicality, and he identifies four major removals that represent this shift: that paramount responsibility is to the people studied; the censuring of covert research; the principle of accountability for ethical violations; and the commitment to public duty rather than private interest. Berreman scathingly concludes that omitting these concerns results in

> not a code at all, but a mild statement of interest, and one conspicuously devoid of ethical content. It is, in fact, a license for unfettered free-enterprise research, advising and engineering disguised as anthropology with the intent of employing the ethical reputation of the discipline to enable and facilitate a wide range of mission-oriented activities, including those of dubious ethical and even egregiously unethical nature. (1991:52)

Many anthropologists, but particularly those in the Third World or Global South, share Berreman's view that such changes represent an "abject surrender of principle to a misguided practicality, a sacrifice of public interest to misperceived self-interest; replacing ethics with greed" (1991:57). Berreman coins the term "Reaganethics" to describe what he sees as the retreat away from more global, humanistic concerns, embodied in the original code of ethics, toward a greater concern with the protection and preservation of academic careers and reputations.

In "Worms, Witchcraft and Wild Incantations: The Case of the Chicken Soup Cure" (1996), Jeffrey Ehrenreich addresses the ethical dilemmas of practicing medicine without a license while in the field. While the practical issues of amateur doctoring are fairly common for anthropologists working in remote areas of the world, and this was one of the first ethical issues addressed in the discipline (e.g., McCurdy 1977), there are few discussions of the ethical issues entailed (for another example, see Pollock 1996). Ehrenreich and a colleague chose to operate a medical clinic while conducting fieldwork in Ecuador because their participants demanded it as a condition of the research, and because the ethnographers viewed it as a form of reciprocity in their relations with them. Ehrenreich reflects on the ethical dilemmas and consequences of having treated a dying Awá woman brought to them as a last resort. In order to get the woman to accept their western treatments, they were compelled to convince her in Awá cultural terms that they were powerful shamans who could lift the evil spell that she believed was the cause of her malady. Basically, they faked a shamanic ritual while administering their medical treatment. This worked and the woman was "cured" (she lived), but this act of "witch doctoring" in the field troubled Ehrenreich deeply and left him feeling "forever compromised" (1996:139). He had "done no harm" and saved a life. But his "fake doctoring" could be seen as dishonest, fraudulent, or manipulative. Did it respect his research participants' dignity, right to honesty, and even informed consent as expressed in ethics codes? To what degree was it a situational or "the ends justify the means" ethics, reflecting assumptions of power and superiority on the part of the ethnographers? Thus, Ehrenreich addresses not just the pragmatic ethics of practicing "bush medicine" while in the field, but also the ethics of honesty and deception in relations with research participants.

Regardless of the ongoing debates on issues surrounding research ethics, today anthropologists increasingly believe that solutions to ethical problems that arise during fieldwork should be found through a process of negotiation. The trend is toward ethical "contracts" or agreements worked out in the field with the research participants themselves. While codes of ethics provide useful guidelines, in the field ethical research relationships must be actively, if not creatively, negotiated, maintained, and adapted to the specifics of the situation or context.

REFERENCES

American Anthropological Association
    2009   *Code of Ethics of the American Anthropological Association*. Washington, DC: American Anthropological Association.
Appell, George N.
    1978   *Ethical Dilemmas in Anthropological Inquiry: A Case Book*. Los Angeles, CA: Crossroads Press.
Armbruster, Heidi and Anna Laerke, eds.
    2008   *Taking Sides: Ethics, Politics, and Fieldwork in Anthropology*. New York: Bergahn.
Association of Social Anthropologists
    1999   Ethical Guidelines for Good Research Practice. http://www.theasa.org/ethics/guidelines.shtml.
Berreman, Gerald D.
    1991   Ethics versus "Realism" in Anthropology. In: *Ethics and the Profession of Anthropology: Dialogue for a New Era*. Carolyn Fluehr-Lobban, ed., pp. 36–71. Philadelphia: University of Pennsylvania Press.
Borofsky, Robert, ed.
    2005   *Yanomami: The Fierce Controversy and What We Can Learn From It*. Berkeley: University of California Press.
Bourgois, Philippe
    1991   Confronting the Ethics of Ethnography: Lessons Learned From Fieldwork in Central America. In: *Decolonizing Anthropology: Moving Further Towards Anthropology for Liberation*. Faye Harrison, ed., pp. 110–126. Washington, DC: American Anthropological Association.
Caplan, Pat, ed.
    2003   *The Ethics of Anthropology: Debates and Dilemmas*. New York: Routledge.
Cassell, Joan and Sue-Ellen Jacobs, eds.,
    1987   *Handbook on Ethical Issues in Anthropology*. Washington, DC: American Anthropological Association.
Ehrenreich, Jeffrey D.
    1996   Worms, Witchcraft and Wild Incantations: The Case of the Chicken Soup Cure. *Anthropological Quarterly* 69(3):137–141.
Ellen, R. F., ed.
    1984   Ethics in Relation to Informants, the Profession and Governments. In: *Ethnographic Research: A Guide to General Conduct*, pp. 133–154. London: Academic Press.
Fluehr-Lobban, Carolyn
    2003a   Ethics and Professionalism: A Review of Issues and Principles Within Anthropology. In: *Ethics and the Profession of Anthropology*. 2nd edn. Carolyn Fluehr-Lobban, ed., pp. 13–35. Walnut Creek, CA: AltaMira Press.
Fluehr-Lobban, Carolyn, ed.
    2003b   *Ethics and the Profession of Anthropology: A Dialogue for Ethically Conscious Practice*. 2nd edn. Walnut Creek, CA: AltaMira Press.

Horowitz, Louis Irving
　1973　The Life and Death of Project Camelot. In: *To See Ourselves: Anthropology and Modern Social Issues*. Thomas Weaver, ed., pp. 138–148. Glenview, IL: Scott, Foresman & Co.

Horowitz, Louis Irving, ed.
　1974　*The Rise and Fall of Project Camelot*. Cambridge, MA: MIT Press.

McCurdy, David
　1977　The Medicine Man: Doctoring Informants. In: *Conformity and Conflict*. James Spradley and David McCurdy, eds., pp. 80–92. Boston: Little, Brown.

Meskel, Lynn and Peter Pels, eds.
　2005　*Embedding Ethics: Shifting Boundaries of the Anthropological Profession*. Oxford: Berg.

Pels, Peter
　1999　Professions of Duplexity: A Prehistory of Ethical Codes in Anthropology. *Current Anthropology* 40(2):101–114.

Pollock, Donald
　1996　Healing Dilemmas. *Anthropological Quarterly* 69(3):149–157.

Rynkiewich, Michael and James Spradley, eds.
　1976　*Ethics and Anthropology: Dilemmas in Fieldwork*. New York: John Wiley & Sons.

Tierney, Patrick
　2000　*Darkness in El Dorado: How Scientists and Journalists Devastated the Amazon*. New York: Norton.

Wolf, Eric R. and Joseph Jorgensen
　1970　Anthropology on the Warpath in Thailand. *The New York Review of Books*. November 19, pp. 26–35.

19

The Life and Death of Project Camelot

Irving Louis Horowitz

In June of this year [1965] – in the midst of the crisis over the Dominican Republic – the United States Ambassador to Chile sent an urgent and angry cable to the State Department. Ambassador Ralph Dungan was confronted with a growing outburst of anti-Americanism from Chilean newspapers and intellectuals. Further, left-wing members of the Chilean Senate had accused the United States of espionage.

The anti-American attacks that agitated Dungan had no direct connection with sending US troops to Santo Domingo. Their target was a mysterious and cloudy American research program called Project Camelot.

Dungan wanted to know from the State Department what Project Camelot was all about. Further, whatever Camelot was, he wanted it stopped because it was fast becoming a *cause célèbre* in Chile (as it soon would throughout capitals of Latin America and in Washington) and Dungan had not been told anything about it – even though it was sponsored by the US Army and involved the tinderbox subjects of counterrevolution and counterinsurgency in Latin America.

Within a few weeks Project Camelot created repercussions from Capitol Hill to the White House. Senator J. William Fulbright, chairman of the Foreign Relations Committee, registered his personal concern about such projects as Camelot because of their "reactionary, backward-looking policy opposed to change. Implicit in Camelot, as in the concept of 'counterinsurgency,' is an assumption that revolutionary movements are dangerous to the interests of the United States and that the United States must be prepared to assist, if not actually to participate in, measures to repress them."

By mid-June the State Department and Defense Department – which had created and funded Camelot – were in open contention over the project and the jurisdiction each

Irving Louis Horowitz, "The Life and Death of Project Camelot," pp. 138–148 from *To See Ourselves: Anthropology and Modern Social Issues*, ed. Thomas Weaver. Glencoe, IL: Scott, Foresman & Co., 1973. Copyright © 1965 by Transaction Publishers. This material originally appeared in *Society* magazine (December, 1965) by Transaction, Inc. Reprinted by permission of Transaction Publishers.

Ethnographic Fieldwork: An Anthropological Reader, Second Edition. Edited by Antonius C. G. M. Robben and Jeffrey A. Sluka.
Editorial material and organization © 2012 John Wiley & Sons, Inc.
Published 2012 by John Wiley & Sons, Inc.

department should have over certain foreign policy operations.

On July 8, Project Camelot was killed by Defense Secretary Robert McNamara's office which has a veto power over the military budget. The decision had been made under the President's direction.

On the same day, the director of Camelot's parent body, the Special Operations Research Organization, told a Congressional committee that the research project on revolution and counterinsurgency had taken its name from King Arthur's mythical domain because "It connotes the right sort of things – development of a stable society with peace and justice for all." Whatever Camelot's outcome, there should be no mistaking the deep sincerity behind this appeal for an applied social science pertinent to current policy.

However, Camelot left a horizon of disarray in its wake: an open dispute between State and Defense; fuel for the anti-American fires in Latin America; a cut in US Army research appropriations. In addition, serious and perhaps ominous implications for social science research, bordering on censorship, have been raised by the heated reaction of the executive branch of government.

Global Counterinsurgency

What was Project Camelot? Basically, it was a project for measuring and forecasting the causes of revolutions and insurgency in underdeveloped areas of the world. It also aimed to find ways of eliminating the causes, or coping with the revolutions and insurgencies. Camelot was sponsored by the US Army on a four to six million dollar contract, spaced out over three to four years, with the Special Operations Research Organization (SORO). This agency is nominally under the aegis of American University in Washington, DC, and does a variety of research for the Army. This includes making analytical surveys of foreign areas; keeping up-to-date information on the military, political, and social complexes of those areas; and maintaining a "rapid response" file for getting immediate information, upon Army request, on any situation deemed militarily important.

Latin America was the first area chosen for concentrated study, but countries on Camelot's four-year list included some in Asia, Africa, and Europe. In a working paper issued on December 5, 1964, at the request of the Office of the Chief of Research and Development, Department of the Army, it was recommended that "comparative historical studies" be made in these countries:

(Latin America) Argentina, Bolivia, Brazil, Colombia, Cuba, Dominican Republic, El Salvador, Guatemala, Mexico, Paraguay, Peru, Venezuela.
(Middle East) Egypt, Iran, Turkey.
(Far East) Korea, Indonesia, Malaysia, Thailand.
(Others) France, Greece, Nigeria.

"Survey research and other field studies" were recommended for Bolivia, Colombia, Ecuador, Paraguay, Peru, Venezuela, Iran, and Thailand. Preliminary consideration was also being given to a study of the separatist movement in French Canada. It, too, had a code name: Project Revolt.

In a recruiting letter sent to selected scholars all over the world at the end of 1964, Project Camelot's aims were defined as a study to "make it possible to predict and influence politically significant aspects of social change in the developing nations of the world." This would include devising procedures for "assessing the potential for internal war within national societies" and "identify(ing) with increased degrees of confidence, those actions which a government might take to relieve conditions which are assessed as giving rise to a potential for internal war." The letter further stated: "The US Army has an important mission in the positive and constructive aspects of nation-building in less developed countries as well as a responsibility to assist friendly governments in dealing with active insurgency problems." Such activities by the US Army were described as "insurgency prophylaxis" rather than the "sometimes misleading label of counterinsurgency."

Project Camelot was conceived in late 1963 by a group of high-ranking Army officers connected with the Army Research Office of the

Department of Defense. They were concerned about new types of warfare springing up around the world. Revolutions in Cuba and Yemen and insurgency movements in Vietnam and the Congo were a far cry from the battles of World War II and also different from the envisioned – and planned for – apocalypse of nuclear war. For the first time in modern warfare, military establishments were not in a position to use the immense arsenals at their disposal – but were, instead, compelled by force of a geopolitical stalemate to increasingly engage in primitive forms of armed combat. The questions of moment for the Army were: Why can't the "hardware" be used? And what alternatives can social science "software" provide?

A well-known Latin American area specialist, Rex Hopper, was chosen as director of Project Camelot. Hopper was a professor of sociology and chairman of the department at Brooklyn College. He had been to Latin America many times over a thirty-year span on research projects and lecture tours, including some under government sponsorship. He was highly recommended for the position by his professional associates in Washington and elsewhere. Hopper had a long-standing interest in problems of revolution and saw in this multi-million dollar contract the possible realization of a life-long scientific ambition.

The Chilean Debacle

How did this social science research project create a foreign policy furore? And, at another level, how did such high intentions result in so disastrous an outcome?

The answers involve a network spreading from a professor of anthropology at the University of Pittsburgh, to a professor of sociology at the University of Oslo, and yet a third professor of sociology at the University of Chile in Santiago, Chile. The "showdown" took place in Chile, first within the confines of the university, next on the floor of the Chilean Senate, then in the popular press of Santiago, and finally, behind US embassy walls.

It was ironic that Chile was the scene of wild newspaper tales of spying and academic

outrage at scholars being recruited for "spying missions." For the working papers of Project Camelot stipulated as a criterion for study that a country "should show promise of high pay-offs in terms of the kinds of data required." Chile did not meet these requirements – it is not on the preliminary list of nations specified as prospects.

How then did Chile become involved in Project Camelot's affairs? The answer requires consideration of the position of Hugo G. Nutini, assistant professor of anthropology at Pittsburgh, citizen of the United States and former citizen of Chile. His presence in Santiago as a self-identified Camelot representative triggered the climactic chain of events.

Nutini, who inquired about an appointment in Camelot's beginning stages, never was given a regular Camelot appointment. Because he was planning a trip to Chile in April of this year – on other academic business – he was asked to prepare a report concerning possibilities of cooperation from Chilean scholars. In general, it was the kind of survey which has mild results and a modest honorarium attached to it (Nutini was offered $750). But Nutini had an obviously different notion of his role. Despite the limitations and precautions which Rex Hopper placed on his trip, especially Hopper's insistence on its informal nature, Nutini managed to convey the impression of being an official of Project Camelot with the authority to make proposals to prospective Chilean participants. Here was an opportunity to link the country of his birth with the country of his choice.

At about the same time, Johan Galtung, a Norwegian sociologist famous for his research on conflict and conflict resolution in under-developed areas, especially in Latin America, entered the picture. Galtung, who was in Chile at the time and associated with the Latin American Faculty of Social Science (FLACSO), received an invitation to participate in a Camelot planning conference scheduled for Washington, DC, in August 1965. The fee to social scientists attending the conference would be $2,000 for four weeks. Galtung turned down the invitation. He gave several reasons. He could not accept the role of the US Army as a sponsoring agent in a study of counterinsurgency. He could not accept the notion of the Army as an agency of national development; he saw the Army as managing conflict and even promoting conflict. Finally, he could not accept the asymmetry of the project – he found it difficult to understand why there would be studies of counterinsurgency in Latin America, but no studies of "counter-intervention" (conditions under which Latin American nations might intervene in the affairs of the United States). Galtung was also deeply concerned about the possibility of European scholars being frozen out of Latin American studies by an inundation of sociologists from the United States. Furthermore, he expressed fears that the scale of Camelot honoraria would completely destroy the social science labor market in Latin America.

Galtung had spoken to others in Oslo, Santiago, and throughout Latin America about the project, and he had shown the memorandum of December 1964 to many of his colleagues.

Soon after Nutini arrived in Santiago, he had a conference with Vice-Chancellor Alvaro Bunster of the University of Chile to discuss the character of Project Camelot. Their second meeting, arranged by the vice-chancellor, was also attended by Professor Eduardo Fuenzalida, a sociologist. After a half-hour of exposition by Nutini, Fuenzalida asked him pointblank to specify the ultimate aims of the project, its sponsors, and its military implications. Before Nutini could reply, Professor Fuenzalida, apparently with some drama, pulled a copy of the December 4 circular letter from his briefcase and read a prepared Spanish translation. Simultaneously, the authorities at FLACSO turned over the matter to their associates in the Chilean Senate and in the left-wing Chilean press.

In Washington, under the political pressures of State Department officials and Congressional reaction, Project Camelot was halted in midstream, or more precisely, before it ever really got under way. When the ambassador's communication reached Washington, there was already considerable official ferment about Project Camelot. Senators Fulbright, Morse, and McCarthy soon asked for hearings by the Senate Foreign Relations Committee. Only an

agreement between Secretary of Defense McNamara and Secretary of State Rusk to settle their differences on future overseas research projects forestalled Senate action. But in the House of Representatives, a hearing was conducted by the Foreign Affairs Committee on July 8. The SORO director, Theodore Vallance, was questioned by committee members on the worth of Camelot and the matter of military intrusion into foreign policy areas.

That morning, even before Vallance was sworn in as a witness – and without his knowledge – the Defense Department issued a terse announcement terminating Project Camelot. President Johnson had decided the issue in favor of the State Department. In a memo to Secretary Rusk on August 5 the President stipulated that "no government sponsorship of foreign area research should be undertaken which in the judgment of the Secretary of State would adversely affect United States foreign relations."

The State Department has recently established machinery to screen and judge all federally-financed research projects overseas. The policy and research consequences of the Presidential directive will be discussed later.

What effect will the cancellation of Camelot have on the continuing rivalry between Defense and State departments for primacy in foreign policy? How will government sponsorship of future social science research be affected? And was Project Camelot a scholarly protective cover for US Army planning – or a legitimate research operation on a valid research subject independent of sponsorship?

Let us begin with a collective self-portrait of Camelot as the social scientists who directed the project perceived it. There seems to be general consensus on seven points.

First, the men who went to work for Camelot felt the need for a large-scale, "big picture" project in social science. They wanted to create a sociology of contemporary relevance which would not suffer from the parochial narrowness of vision to which their own professional backgrounds had generally conditioned them. Most of the men viewed Camelot as a bona fide opportunity to do fundamental research with relatively unlimited funds at their disposal. (No social science project ever before had up to $6,000,000 available.) Under such optimal conditions, these scholars tended not to look a gift horse in the mouth. As one of them put it, there was no desire to inquire too deeply as to the source of the funds or the ultimate purpose of the project.

Second, most social scientists affiliated with Camelot felt that there was actually more freedom to do fundamental research under military sponsorship than at a university or college. One man noted that during the 1950s there was far more freedom to do fundamental research in the RAND corporation (an Air Force research organization) than on any campus in America. Indeed, once the protective covering of RAND was adopted, it was almost viewed as a society of Platonist elites or "knowers" permitted to search for truth on behalf of the powerful. In a neoplatonic definition of their situation, the Camelot men hoped that their ideas would be taken seriously by the wielders of power (although, conversely, they were convinced that the armed forces would not accept their preliminary recommendations).

Third, many of the Camelot associates felt distinctly uncomfortable with military sponsorship, especially given the present United States military posture. But their reaction to this discomfort was that "the Army has to be educated." This view was sometimes cast in Freudian terms: the Army's bent toward violence ought to be sublimated. Underlying this theme was the notion of the armed forces as an agency for potential social good – the discipline and the order embodied by an army could be channeled into the process of economic and social development in the United States as well as in Latin America.

Fourth, there was a profound conviction in the perfectibility of mankind; particularly in the possibility of the military establishment performing a major role in the general process of growth. They sought to correct the intellectual paternalism and parochialism under which Pentagon generals, State Department diplomats, and Defense Department planners seemed to operate.

Fifth, a major long-range purpose of Camelot, at least for some of its policy-makers, was to prevent another revolutionary holocaust

on a grand scale, such as occurred in Cuba. At the very least, there was a shared belief that *Pax Americana* was severely threatened and its future could be bolstered.

Sixth, none of them viewed their role on the project as spying for the United States government, or for anyone else.

Seventh, the men on Project Camelot felt that they made heavy sacrifices for social science. Their personal and professional risks were much higher than those taken by university academics. Government work, while well-compensated, remains professionally marginal. It can be terminated abruptly (as indeed was the case) and its project directors are subject to a public scrutiny not customary behind the walls of ivy.

In the main, there was perhaps a keener desire on the part of the directing members of Camelot not to "sell out" than there is among social scientists with regular academic appointments. This concern with the ethics of social science research seemed to be due largely to daily confrontation of the problems of betrayal, treason, secrecy, and abuse of data, in a critical situation. In contrast, even though a university position may be created by federally-sponsored research, the connection with policy matters is often too remote to cause any *crise de conscience*.

The Insiders' Report

Were the men on Camelot critical of any aspects of the project?

Some had doubts from the outset about the character of the work they would be doing, and about the conditions under which it would be done. It was pointed out, for example, that the US Army tends to exercise a far more stringent intellectual control of research findings than does the US Air Force. As evidence for this, it was stated that SORO generally had fewer "free-wheeling" aspects to its research designs than did RAND (the Air Force-supported research organization). One critic inside SORO went so far as to say that he knew of no SORO research which had a "playful" or unregimented quality, such as one finds at RAND (where for example, computers are used to plan invasions but also to play chess). One staff member said that "the self-conscious seriousness gets to you after a while." "It was all grim stuff," said another.

Another line of criticism was that pressures on the "reformers" (as the men engaged in Camelot research spoke of themselves) to come up with ideas were much stronger than the pressures on the military to actually bring off any policy changes recommended. The social scientists were expected to be social reformers, while the military adjutants were expected to be conservative. It was further felt that the relationship between sponsors and researchers was not one of equals, but rather one of superordinate military needs and subordinate academic role. On the other hand, some officials were impressed by the disinterestedness of the military, and thought that far from exercising undue influence, the Army personnel were loath to offer opinions.

Another objection was that if one had to work on policy matters – if research is to have international ramifications – it might better be conducted under conventional State Department sponsorship. "After all," one man said, "they are at least nominally committed to civilian political norms." In other words, there was a considerable reluctance to believe that the Defense Department, despite its superior organization, greater financial affluence, and executive influence, would actually improve upon State Department styles of work, or accept recommendations at variance with Pentagon policies.

There seemed to be few, if any, expressions of disrespect for the intrinsic merit of the work contemplated by Camelot, or of disdain for policy-oriented work in general. The scholars engaged in the Camelot effort used two distinct vocabularies. The various Camelot documents reveal a military vocabulary provided with an array of military justification; often followed (within the same document) by a social science vocabulary offering social science justifications and rationalizations. The dilemma in the Camelot literature from the preliminary report issued in August 1964 until the more advanced document issued in April 1965, is the same: an incomplete amalgamation of the military and sociological vocabularies.

(At an early date the project had the code name SPEARPOINT.)

Policy Conflicts Over Camelot

The directors of SORO are concerned that the cancellation of Camelot might mean the end of SORO as well in a wholesale slash of research funds. For while over $1,000,000 was allotted to Camelot each year, the annual budget of SORO, its parent organization, is a good deal less. Although no such action has taken place, SORO's future is being examined. For example, the Senate and House Appropriations Committee blocked a move by the Army to transfer unused Camelot funds to SORO.

However, the end of Project Camelot does not necessarily imply the end of the Special Operations Research Office, nor does it imply an end to research designs which are similar in character to Project Camelot. In fact, the termination of the contract does not even imply an intellectual change of heart on the part of the originating sponsors or key figures of the project.

One of the characteristics of Project Camelot was the number of antagonistic forces it set in motion on grounds of strategy and timing rather than from what may be called considerations of scientific principles.

The State Department grounded its opposition to Camelot on the basis of the ultimate authority it has in the area of foreign affairs. There is no published report showing serious criticism of the projected research itself.

Congressional opposition seemed to be generated by a concern not to rock any foreign alliances, especially in Latin America. Again, there was no statement about the project's scientific or intellectual grounds.

A third group of skeptics, academic social scientists, generally thought that Project Camelot, and studies of the processes of revolution and war in general, were better left in the control of major university centers, and in this way, kept free of direct military supervision.

The Army, creator of the project, did nothing to contradict McNamara's order cancelling Project Camelot. Army influentials did not only feel that they had to execute the Defense Department's orders, but they are traditionally dubious of the value of "software" research to support "hardware" systems.

Let us take a closer look at each of these groups which voiced opposition to Project Camelot. A number of issues did not so much hinge upon, as swim about, Project Camelot. In particular, the "jurisdictional" dispute between Defense and State loomed largest.

State vs. defense

In substance, the debate between the Defense Department and the State Department is not unlike that between electricians and bricklayers in the construction of a new apartment house. What "union" is responsible for which processes? Less generously, the issue is: who controls what? At the policy level, Camelot was a tool tossed about in a larger power struggle which has been going on in government circles since the end of World War II, when the Defense Department emerged as a competitor for honors as the most powerful bureau of the administrative branch of government.

In some sense, the divisions between Defense and State are outcomes of the rise of ambiguous conflicts such as Korea and Vietnam, in contrast to the more precise and diplomatically controlled "classical" world wars. What are the lines dividing political policy from military posture? Who is the most important representative of the United States abroad: the ambassador or the military attaché in charge of the military mission? When soldiers from foreign lands are sent to the United States for political orientation, should such orientation be within the province of the State Department or of the Defense Department? When undercover activities are conducted, should the direction of such activities belong to military or political authorities? Each of these is a strategic question with little pragmatic or historic precedent. Each of these was entwined in the Project Camelot explosion.

It should be plain therefore that the State Department was not simply responding to the recommendations of Chilean left-wingers in urging the cancellation of Camelot. It merely employed the Chilean hostility to

"interventionist" projects as an opportunity to redefine the balance of forces and power with the Defense Department. What is clear from this resistance to such projects is not so much a defense of the sovereignty of the nations where ambassadors are stationed, as it is a contention that conventional political channels are sufficient to yield the information desired or deemed necessary.

Congress

In the main, congressional reaction seems to be that Project Camelot was bad because it rocked the diplomatic boat in a sensitive area. Underlying most congressional criticisms is the plain fact that most congressmen are more sympathetic to State Department control of foreign affairs than they are to Defense Department control. In other words, despite military sponsored world junkets, National Guard and State Guard pressures from the home State, and military training in the backgrounds of many congressmen, the sentiment for political rather than military control is greater. In addition, there is a mounting suspicion in Congress of varying kinds of behavioral science research stemming from hearings into such matters as wiretapping, uses of lie detectors, and truth-in-packaging.

Social scientists

One reason for the violent response to Project Camelot, especially among Latin American scholars, is its sponsorship by the Department of Defense. The fact is that Latin Americans have become quite accustomed to State Department involvements in the internal affairs of various nations. The Defense Department is a newcomer, a dangerous one, inside the Latin American orbit. The train of thought connected to its activities is in terms of international warfare, spying missions, military manipulations, etc. The State Department, for its part, is often a consultative party to shifts in government, and has played an enormous part in either fending off or bringing about *coups d'état*. This State Department role has by now been accepted and even taken for granted.

Not so the Defense Department's role. But it is interesting to conjecture on how matter-of-factly Camelot might have been accepted if it had State Department sponsorship.

Social scientists in the United States have, for the most part, been publicly silent on the matter of Camelot. The reasons for this are not hard to find. First, many "giants of the field" are involved in government contract work in one capacity or another. And few souls are in a position to tamper with the gods. Second, most information on Project Camelot has thus far been of a newspaper variety; and professional men are not in a habit of criticizing colleagues on the basis of such information. Third, many social scientists doubtless see nothing wrong or immoral in the Project Camelot designs. And they are therefore more likely to be either confused or angered at the Latin American response than at the directors of Project Camelot. (At the time of the blowup, Camelot people spoke about the "Chilean mess" rather than the "Camelot mess.")

The directors of Project Camelot did not "classify" research materials, so that there would be no stigma of secrecy. And they also tried to hire, and even hired away from academic positions, people well known and respected for their independence of mind. The difficulty is that even though the stigma of secrecy was formally erased, it remained in the attitudes of many of the employees and would-be employees of Project Camelot. They unfortunately thought in terms of secrecy, clearance, missions, and the rest of the professional nonsense that so powerfully afflicts the Washington scientific as well as political ambience.

Further, it is apparent that Project Camelot had much greater difficulty hiring a full-time staff of high professional competence, than in getting part-time, summertime, weekend, and sundry assistance. Few established figures in academic life were willing to surrender the advantages of their positions for the risks of the project.

One of the cloudiest aspects to Project Camelot is the role of American University. Its actual supervision of the contract appears to have begun and ended with the 25 percent overhead on those parts of the contract that a university receives on most federal grants.

Thus, while there can be no question as to the "concern and disappointment" of President Hurst R. Anderson of the American University over the demise of Project Camelot, the reasons for this regret do not seem to extend beyond the formal and the financial. No official at American University appears to have been willing to make any statement of responsibility, support, chagrin, opposition, or anything else related to the project. The issues are indeed momentous, and must be faced by all universities at which government sponsored research is conducted: the amount of control a university has over contract work; the role of university officials in the distribution of funds from grants; the relationships that ought to be established once a grant is issued. There is also a major question concerning project directors: are they members of the faculty, and if so, do they have necessary teaching responsibilities and opportunities for tenure as do other faculty members.

The difficulty with American University is that it seems to be remarkably unlike other universities in its permissiveness. The Special Operations Research Office received neither guidance nor support from university officials. From the outset, there seems to have been a "gentleman's agreement" not to inquire or interfere in Project Camelot, but simply to serve as some sort of camouflage. If American University were genuinely autonomous it might have been able to lend highly supportive aid to Project Camelot during the crisis months. As it is, American University maintained an official silence which preserved it from more congressional or executive criticism. This points up some serious flaws in its administrative and financial policies.

The relationship of Camelot to SORO represented a similarly muddled organizational picture. The director of Project Camelot was nominally autonomous and in charge of an organization surpassing in size and importance the overall SORO operation. Yet at the critical point the organizational blueprint served to protect SORO and sacrifice what nominally was its limb. That Camelot happened to be a vital organ may have hurt, especially when Congress blocked the transfer of unused Camelot funds to SORO.

Military

Military reaction to the cancellation of Camelot varied. It should be borne in mind that expenditures on Camelot were minimal in the Army's overall budget and most military leaders are skeptical, to begin with, about the worth of social science research. So there was no open protest about the demise of Camelot. Those officers who have a positive attitude toward social science materials, or are themselves trained in the social sciences, were dismayed. Some had hoped to find "software" alternatives to the "hardware systems" approach applied by the Secretary of Defense to every military-political contingency. These officers saw the attack on Camelot as a double attack – on their role as officers and on their professional standards. But the Army was so clearly treading in new waters that it could scarcely jeopardize the entire structure of military research to preserve one project. This very inability or impotence to preserve Camelot – a situation threatening to other governmental contracts with social scientists – no doubt impressed many armed forces officers.

The claim is made by the Camelot staff (and various military aides) that the critics of the project played into the hands of those sections of the military predisposed to veto any social science recommendations. Then why did the military offer such a huge support to a social science project to begin with? Because $6,000,000 is actually a trifling sum for the Army in an age of multi-billion dollar military establishment. The amount is significantly more important for the social sciences, where such contract awards remain relatively scarce. Thus, there were differing perspectives of the importance of Camelot: an Army view which considered the contract as one of several forms of "software" investment; a social science perception of Project Camelot as the equivalent of the Manhattan Project.

Was Project Camelot Workable?

While most public opposition to Project Camelot focused on its strategy and timing, a considerable amount of private opposition centered on more basic, though theoretical, questions: was Camelot scientifically feasible and ethically correct? No public document or statement contested the possibility that, given the successful completion of the data gathering, Camelot could have, indeed, established basic criteria for measuring the level and potential for internal war in a given nation. Thus, by never challenging the feasibility of the work, the political critics of Project Camelot were providing back-handed compliments to the efficacy of the project.

But much more than political considerations are involved. It is clear that some of the most critical problems presented by Project Camelot are scientific. Although for an extensive analysis of Camelot, the reader would, in fairness, have to be familiar with all of its documents, salient general criticisms can be made without a full reading.

The research design of Camelot was from the outset plagued by ambiguities. It was never quite settled whether the purpose was to study counterinsurgency possibilities, or the revolutionary process. Similarly, it was difficult to determine whether it was to be a study of comparative social structures, a set of case studies of single nations "in depth," or a study of social structure with particular emphasis on the military. In addition, there was a lack of treatment of what indicators were to be used, and whether a given social system in Nation A could be as stable in Nation B.

In one Camelot document there is a general critique of social science for failing to deal with social conflict and social control. While this in itself is admirable, the tenor and context of Camelot's documents make it plain that a "stable society" is considered the norm no less than the desired outcome. The "breakdown of social order" is spoken of accusatively. Stabilizing agencies in developing areas are presumed to be absent. There is no critique of US Army policy in developing areas because the Army is presumed to be a stabilizing agency. The research formulations always assume the legitimacy of Army tasks – "if the US Army is to perform effectively its parts in the US mission of counterinsurgency it must recognize that insurgency represents a breakdown of social order...." But such a proposition has never been doubted – by Army officials or anyone else. The issue is whether such breakdowns are in the nature of the existing system or a product of conspiratorial movements.

The use of hygienic language disguises the antirevolutionary assumptions under a cloud of powder puff declarations. For example, studies of Paraguay are recommended "because trends in this situation (the Stroessner regime) may also render it unique when analyzed in terms of the transition from 'dictatorship' to political stability." But to speak about changes from dictatorship to stability is an obvious ruse. In this case, it is a tactic to disguise the fact that Paraguay is one of the most vicious, undemocratic (and like most dictatorships, stable) societies in the Western Hemisphere.

These typify the sort of hygienic sociological premises that do not have scientific purposes. They illustrate the confusion of commitments within Project Camelot. Indeed the very absence of emotive words such as revolutionary masses, communism, socialism, and capitalism only serves to intensify the discomfort one must feel on examination of the documents – since the abstract vocabulary disguises, rather than resolves, the problems of international revolution. To have used clearly political rather than military language would not "justify" governmental support. Furthermore, shabby assumptions of academic conventionalism replaced innovative orientations. By adopting a systems approach, the problematic, open-ended aspects of the study of revolutions were largely omitted; and the design of the study became an oppressive curb on the study of the problems inspected.

This points up a critical implication for Camelot (as well as other projects). The importance of the subject being researched does not *per se* determine the importance of the project. A sociology of large-scale relevance and reference is all to the good. It is important that scholars be willing to risk something of their shaky reputations in helping resolve major world social problems. But it is no less urgent that in the process of addressing major problems, the autonomous character of the social science disciplines – their own criteria of worthwhile scholarship – should not be abandoned. Project Camelot lost sight of this "autonomous" social science character.

It never seemed to occur to its personnel to inquire into the desirability for successful revolution. This is just as solid a line of inquiry as the one stressed – the conditions under which revolutionary movements will be able to overthrow a government. Furthermore, they seem not to have thought about inquiring into the role of the United States in these countries. This points up the lack of symmetry. The problem should have been phrased to include the study of "us" as well as "them." It is not possible to make a decent analysis of a situation unless one takes into account the role of all the different people and groups involved in it; and there was no room in the design for such contingency analysis.

In discussing the policy impact on a social science research project, we should not overlook the difference between "contract" work and "grants." Project Camelot commenced with the US Army; that is to say, it was initiated for a practical purpose determined by the client. This differs markedly from the typical academic grant in that its sponsorship had "built-in" ends. The scholar usually *seeks* a grant; in this case the donor, the Army, promoted its own aims. In some measure, the hostility for Project Camelot may be an unconscious reflection of this distinction – a dim feeling that there was something "nonacademic," and certainly not disinterested, about Project Camelot, irrespective of the quality of the scholars associated with it.

The Ethics of Policy Research

The issue of "scientific rights" versus "social myths" is perennial. Some maintain that the scientist ought not penetrate beyond legally or morally sanctioned limits and others argue that such limits cannot exist for science. In treading on the sensitive issue of national sovereignty, Project Camelot reflects the generalized dilemma. In deference to intelligent researchers, in recognition of them as scholars, they should have been invited by Camelot to air their misgivings and qualms about government (and especially Army-sponsored) research – to declare their moral conscience. Instead, they were mistakenly approached as skillful, useful potential employees of a higher body, subject to an authority higher than their scientific calling.

What is central is not the political motives of the sponsor. For social scientists were not being enlisted in an intelligence system for "spying" purposes. But given their professional standing, their great sense of intellectual honor and pride, they could not be "employed" without proper deference for their stature. Professional authority should have prevailed from beginning to end with complete command of the right to thrash out the moral and political dilemmas as researchers saw them. The Army, however respectful and protective of free expression, was "hiring help" and not openly and honestly submitting a problem to the higher professional and scientific authority of social science.

The propriety of the Army to define and delimit all questions, which Camelot should have had a right to examine, was never placed in doubt. This is a tragic precedent; it reflects the arrogance of a consumer of intellectual merchandise. And this relationship of inequality corrupted the lines of authority, and profoundly limited the autonomy of the social scientists involved. It became clear that the social scientist savant was not so much functioning as an applied social scientist as he was supplying information to a powerful client.

The question of who sponsors research is not nearly so decisive as the question of ultimate use of such information. The sponsorship of a project, whether by the United States Army or by the Boy Scouts of America, is by itself neither good nor bad. Sponsorship is good or bad only insofar as the intended outcomes can be predetermined and the parameters of those intended outcomes tailored to the sponsor's expectations. Those social scientists critical of the project never really denied its freedom and independence, but questioned instead the purpose and character of its intended results.

It would be a gross oversimplification, if not an outright error, to assume that the theoretical problems of Project Camelot derive from any reactionary character of the project designers. The director went far and wide to select a group of men for the advisory board, the core planning group, the summer study group, and the various conference groupings, who in fact were more liberal in their orientations than any random sampling of the sociological profession would likely turn up.

However, in nearly every page of the various working papers, there are assertions which clearly derive from American military policy objectives rather than scientific method. The steady assumption that internal warfare is damaging disregards the possibility that a government may not be in a position to take actions either to relieve or improve mass conditions, or that such actions as are contemplated may be more concerned with reducing conflict than with improving conditions. The added statements about the United States Army and its "important mission in the positive and constructive aspects of nation building ..." assume the reality of such a function in an utterly unquestioning and unconvincing form. The first rule of the scientific game is not to make assumptions about friends and enemies in such a way as to promote the use of different criteria for the former and the latter.

The story of Project Camelot was not a confrontation of good versus evil. Obviously, not all men behaved with equal fidelity or with equal civility. Some men were weaker than others, some more callous, and some more stupid. But all of this is extrinsic to the heart of the problem of Camelot: What are and are not the legitimate functions of a scientist?

In conclusion, two important points must be clearly kept in mind and clearly apart. First, Project Camelot was intellectually, and from my own perspective, ideologically unsound. However, and more significantly, Camelot was not cancelled because of its faulty intellectual approaches. Instead, its cancellation came as an act of government censorship, and an expression of the contempt for social science so prevalent among those who need it most. Thus it was political expedience, rather than its lack of scientific merit, that led to the demise of Camelot because it threatened to rock State Department relations with Latin America.

Second, giving the State Department the right to screen and approve governmentfunded social science research projects on other countries, as the President has ordered, is a supreme act of censorship. Among the agencies that grant funds for such research are the National Institutes of Mental Health, the National Science Foundation, the National Aeronautics and Space Agency, and the Office of Education. Why should the State Department have veto power over the scientific pursuits of men and projects funded by these and other agencies in order to satisfy the policy needs – or policy failures – of the moment? President Johnson's directive is a gross violation of the autonomous nature of science.

We must be careful not to allow social science projects with which we may vociferously disagree on political and ideological grounds to be decimated or dismantled by government fiat. Across the ideological divide is a common social science understanding that the contemporary expression of reason in politics today is applied social science, and that the cancellation of Camelot, however pleasing it may be on political grounds to advocates of a civilian solution to Latin American affairs, represents a decisive setback for social science research.

20

Confronting the Ethics of Ethnography: Lessons From Fieldwork in Central America

Philippe Bourgois

North American Cultural Anthropology

The ethics of anthropological research are too complicated and important to be reduced to unambiguous absolutes or even perhaps to be clearly defined. The human tragedy and political dilemmas I encountered in my ethnographic fieldwork in Central America obliged me to confront the inadequacy and internal contradictions of current definitions of research ethics in North American anthropology. These ethical quandaries arise within the epistemological tension imposed by the US intellectual tradition of allegedly apolitical liberal relativism in opposition to engaged universalism. In Europe, Latin America, and elsewhere this intellectual dichotomy between science and politics is not as clearly drawn. Indeed, throughout much of the rest of the world, engaged scholarly analysis is not only

legitimate but part of the researcher's "social responsibility."

I am not proposing a systematic political economy of North American anthropological knowledge, but I do feel that the framing of ethical issues in cultural anthropology needs to be understood in the context of the history of the development of the discipline in the larger society. The eminently political orientation of a supposed apolitical commitment to empirical research must be appreciated for its internal inconsistencies and ultimate ethical poverty. Finally, the emergence in the late 1980s of the "post-modernist deconstructivist" focus on "culture-as-text" within symbolic anthropology as the most attractive theoretical tendency among US anthropologists needs to be placed in the problematic context of anthropological ethics in a politically polarized world.

In the late 1960s and early 1970s North American social scientists began discussing the

Ethnographic Fieldwork: An Anthropological Reader, Second Edition. Edited by Antonius C. G. M. Robben and Jeffrey A. Sluka.
Editorial material and organization © 2012 John Wiley & Sons, Inc.
Published 2012 by John Wiley & Sons, Inc.

ethical dilemmas faced by fieldworkers studying and living in a world rife with political turmoil. Several important edited volumes in anthropology were produced on the subject (cf. Weaver 1973; Huizer and Mannheim 1979; Hymes 1972) and major journals devoted considerable space to earnest – and at times polemical – debates by important figures in the discipline (cf. *Current Anthropology* 1968, 9(5):391–435; 1971, 12(3): 321–56).

In an important early volume a dozen anthropologists from around the world questioned the historical relationship between the development of the discipline in a functionalist theoretical framework in Great Britain and the political and economic realities of British colonial domination and indirect rule in Africa and elsewhere (Asad 1973). This critical reappraisal of the roots of the discipline was even prominently incorporated in a major cultural anthropology textbook in 1981 (Keesing 1981: 481–99). Respected anthropologists in North America have denounced the conscious and unconscious collaboration of anthropology with the counterinsurgency agencies of the US government – specifically Project Camelot in Latin America (Horowitz 1967), Project Agile in Thailand (Gough 1973; Jones 1971; Wolf and Jorgensen 1970), and the Himalayan Border Countries Project in India (Berreman 1973).[1]

The at times polemical debates of the late 1960s and early 1970s have injected an important self-consciousness among US anthropologists researching far from home. We have come a long way from our European forebears (especially the British) who flew into colonial war zones under the auspices of colonial offices to interview "natives" and write "how-to-administer-more-humanely" reports for government bureaucracies intent on increasing "administrative" efficiency and lowering costs. Today few self-respecting anthropologists would condone the exercise of anthropology at the service of a world superpower or as a complement to espionage. Significantly, however, during the 1980s and early 1990s, articles and volumes devoted primarily to the *politics of ethics* were relatively scarce with notable exceptions (Magubane and Faris 1985; Rebel 1989a, 1989b; Sanadjian 1990). Instead, most

ethnographers now include a discussion of the methodological and personal ethical dilemmas they faced during their fieldwork. Most recently, when the politics of ethics are referred to it is often in the style of the "reflexive poetics" of one of the post-modernist approaches, far removed from effective practice. In their deconstruction of domination the post-modernists risk trivializing the experience of oppression. At its worst this "poetics of politics" degenerates into what the late Robert F. Murphy (1990:331) satirized as "a kind of egghead rap-talk" or "thick writing."

The Discipline's Narrow Definition of Ethics

Traditionally our discipline cites a limited dimension of ethical dilemmas: We worry about whether or not our research subjects have truly consented in an "informed" manner to our study; we ponder over the honesty of our presentation of self; we condemn the distortion in the local economy caused by the resources we inject into it in the form of "informants'" gifts or wages; we are wary of the social disapproval foisted on our primary informants when they become the objects of envy or ridicule from the rest of the community because of the resources, prestige, or shame we bring them; we no longer steal ceremonial secrets unapologetically; we examine our emotions introspectively to control our ethnocentrism; we uphold cultural relativism and avoid unconsciously conveying disrespect for traditional institutions and values through our lifestyle; we preserve the anonymity of our research subjects and host communities; we feel guilty for violating the privacy of our informants and their culture; we worry about "scientific colonialism" and our "responsibility to the host community" (so we send extra copies of our publications to our research site); we do not take photographs indiscriminately and we do not tape record without obtaining prior permission; we discuss the pros and cons of consulting forbidden archives or quoting from personal diaries and letters; we question the ethics of accepting financial support from governments and politically biased institutions;

we worry about the potential misuse of our research material once it has been published in the public domain; and finally we take care not to jeopardize the access of future colleagues to our fieldwork site by our actions and publications.

These are indeed, all vitally important ethical issues that we must all confront during fieldwork and write-up. But why does the anthropological concern with ethics stop here? What about the larger moral and human dimensions of the political and economic structures ravaging most of the peoples that anthropologists have studied historically? With notable exceptions most North American anthropologists do not include the political or even the human rights dimension confronting the people they research in their discussion of "anthropological ethics." In fact the trend has been to avoid these issues by a theoretical focus on the meaning of signs and symbols outside of social context – what Roger Keesing (1987) has also criticized methodologically as the tendency to impose articulate but intensely subjective and exotic interpretations of religion, myth, and cosmology on the people we study; and what Hermann Rebel argues are the "tendencies in recent work by anthropologists ... to downplay the degradation and terror experienced by victims of exploitation and persecution" (1989a:117).

The problem with contemporary anthropological ethics is not merely that the boundaries of what is defined as ethical are too narrowly drawn, but more importantly, that ethics can be subject to rigid, righteous interpretations which place them at loggerheads with overarching human rights concerns. How does one investigate power relations and fulfill the researcher's obligations to obtain informed consent from the powerful? What about the right to privacy of absentee landlords as a social group? It is much more difficult – if not impossible – to satisfy the discipline-bound anthropological/methodological code of ethics if we attempt to research marginalization and oppression, than if we focus on the philosophical aesthetics of cosmology. Can we analyze the urgent problems faced by our research subjects and still obey our discipline's interpretation of methodological ethics?

A Moral Imperative to Anthropology

The simple solution so often adopted by anthropologists is to avoid examining unequal power relationships – and to orient their theoretical interests towards safer, more traditionally exotic focuses. In the late 1960s Eric Wolf (1972[1969]:261) admonished anthropology to avoid a "descent into triviality and irrelevance" by focusing on large-scale "problems of power."

A logistical imperative could also be advanced for why cultural anthropologists might want to assign priority to an analysis of power inequalities in their research. Unlike philosophers, literary critics, or art historians, we usually study living human beings. Furthermore we differentiate ourselves methodologically from other social science and humanities disciplines which also study humans through our technique of participant/observation fieldwork. We are not allowed to remain at our desks to pore over census tracts; we have to venture into everyday life not just to interview people but to actually participate in their daily life and to partake of their social and cultural reality. In the Third World, therefore, fieldwork offers a privileged arena for intensive contact with politically imposed human tragedy. Perhaps this methodological obligation to be participant/observers could inject a humanistic praxis into our research? Does social responsibility have to contradict our discipline's commitment to cultural relativism?

A moral argument for theoretical compassion does not stop at methodological praxis. We also have a historical responsibility to the particular types of research subjects selected by our forebears. Historically our discipline differentiated itself from sociology and other social sciences by focusing on the "distinctive other" (Hymes 1972:31). Since our inception we have had what Keesing (1987:161) calls a "predilection for the exotic" and what Sidney Mintz (1970:14) criticized as a "preoccupation with purity." We are most famous for having trekked deepest into the remotest corners of colonial territories to try to find people outside the reach of "civilization." We have unabashedly worshipped "the traditional" – so long as it is in a pristine vacuum. Over the past two decades we have begun to remedy our ahistorical, disarticulated focus on the particular. Ethnographies are increasingly situating our research in regional contexts. In fact, as Carol Smith (1984) notes in an article on the Maya in the Western Highlands of Guatemala, it has almost become fashionable for anthropologists to bemoan the myopic-community-study-in-a-vacuum focus of traditional anthropology.

Even when we succeed in finding a particularly remote cultural cranny where a "traditional" people has had only minimal contact with the outside world we can safely predict that these noble folk will sooner than later be sucked into the world economy in a traumatized manner. There is a good chance that their land and subsistence base will be stolen; their efforts at resistance will be met with violence, sometimes genocide; their entrance into the labor market will be in the most vulnerable niche; if they are hired by a multinational agro-export company – as they so often are – they will be systematically assigned to the labor gangs that spray venomous pesticides; if they work for a transnational subsidiary exploiting mineral resources – as they so often do – they will be sent to the bottom of the shafts to contract lung cancer – or worse. If they manage to maintain their ancestral lands, when they finally start to bring their produce to markets they will be obliged to sell at below subsistence prices; when they come into contact with the dominant ethnic groups and classes of their nation they will be ridiculed. In other words, with few exceptions, the traditional, noble, and "exotic" subjects of anthropology have today emerged as the most malnourished, politically repressed, economically exploited humans on earth. As a rule of thumb, the deeper, more traditional, and more "isolated" the people our forebears studied, the more traumatized their lifeways have become today.

Given that there is virtually no such thing as a traditional people disconnected from the outside world, then our "traditional" fieldwork sites should grant us privileged access to the massive sector of humanity pinned into the world economy's most vulnerable nexus. We have chosen to study the wretched of the earth. These are the individuals too often condemned to periodic famines, to below subsistence-level incorporation in flooded labor markets, to relocation, dislocation, or more simply extermination. Many of our discipline's former research subjects are fighting back in organized political movements; but as the Central American experience demonstrates, their struggles are prolonged, bloody, and often unsuccessful. Although as uninvited outsiders it might be naive and arrogant for us to think we have anything definitive to offer, we can still recognize the ethical challenge. Why do we avoid it?

In the early 1980s dissertations were written on the hermeneutics of shame among the Maya. But how can we understand the meaning of that important cultural construct if we ignore the tens of thousands of Maya massacred by the military at the same time, or the hundreds of thousands who migrate each year to harvest cotton, sugar cane, and coffee.

Even if there were no urgent human rights imperatives as in the case of the Maya; even if there was no extreme economic exploitation and subsistence dislocation; there is at least a scientific imperative to situate their "webs of significance" in the context of what they are really doing every day.

Compassion for the Fourth World – Only

The journals and books that regularly denounce ethnocide and genocide published by indigenous rights organizations – such as the IWGIA in Copenhagen, Survival International in England and France, or Cultural Survival in Cambridge, Massachusetts – are a welcome exception to the tendency for anthropologists to escape a human rights mandate. Significantly, however, often these organizations tend to legitimize their militance by purposefully narrowing their focus in the classically anthropological manner – in pursuit of the "noble savage." They prefer to denounce genocide when it also entails ethnocide.

In Central America this theoretical orientation is referred to as *indigenista* or "fourth worldist." Amerindian culture is seen in a manichean manner as the human ideal while Hispanic culture is treated as irrelevant at best. This *indigenista* tendency is most prevalent among North American anthropologists, and one can recognize its intellectual roots in the discipline's traditional focus on exotic, isolated community studies.

Although guided by a moral vision to denounce human rights abuse, fourth worldists tend to ignore international geo-political contexts because of their geographically and culturally reductionist theoretical focus. This leads to arbitrary compassion; for example, I published a brief account of the poisoning of Guaymi Indian banana workers who spray pesticides for the United Fruit Company in a special issue of a French fourth worldist journal documenting the human rights violations of indigenous peoples in Central America (Bourgois 1986). The editors would not have been interested in the article had the poisoned sprayers been Hispanic mestizoes rather than Amerindians. In fact they decided not to publish anything on massacres in the Salvadoran countryside because the peasants being killed were not Amerindians. Ironically only two generations ago most of the grandparents of these "Hispanic" Salvadoran rural dwellers currently being massacred were Pipils. They were forced to abandon their traditional language, dress, and indigenous culture when the government began systematically killing all indigenous peoples – between 18,000 and 30,000 individuals were massacred – following an Amerindian rebellion in 1932.

Fourth worldists provide vitally needed documentation of tragic human rights violations but they often fail to make common cause with human beings. They discriminate according to ethnicity, reproducing the traditional anthropological focus on the "exotic other" in a vacuum. This obscures their theoretical understanding of the structural roots of repression and exploitation by framing it exclusively in manichean culturalist terms.

Fieldwork in Central America

At war in Nicaragua's Moskitia

Let me document this critique in a classically anthropological manner – by drawing on my own fieldwork experience. My first stop in pursuit of a dissertation topic was Nicaragua in 1979 just after the overthrow of Somoza by the Sandinistas (Bourgois 1981). Like a good anthropologist, I went as far away from the capital city as possible into the Moskitia, the most remote corner of the only province where an indigenous population – the Miskitu – were said to have maintained organically their non-Hispanic culture. Their language, religious system, cultural identity, structure of land tenure, etc., was indeed distinct from the national Hispanic mainstream. Of course, the historical record reveals that there is nothing "traditional" or isolated about Amerindian culture in the Moskitia. The Miskitu emerged as a people distinct from their Sumu Amerindian neighbors in the 1600s through the colonial confrontation of the two great superpowers of the time – Spain and England. They allied themselves with British pirates – and later with Her Majesty herself – to fight off the Spanish conquerors. In the process they became the first indigenous people to obtain firearms. This enabled them to conquer all their aboriginal neighbors. They became warriors and economic middlemen selling Amerindian slaves and smuggled trade goods from the Central American mainland to British settlers in the Caribbean. Some of this historical legacy has been frozen linguistically – one-third of the words in their "traditional" language, for example, bear a relationship to English (Holm 1978).

Soon after I arrived in the heartland of Miskitu territory, the indigenous population began mobilizing to defend their historic rights to land and autonomy in a tragic alliance with the Central Intelligence Agency. "My" fieldwork village, accessible only by a full-day's journey upstream in a dug-out canoe, became the central arena of a bloody conflict against the central government. Although the underlying causes for this indigenous war were the historical structures of racism and marginalization of the region dating back to the colonial period, and repression by the central government during the contemporary period, the actual bloody logistics of the fighting was sponsored economically and was escalated militarily by the US government.

My theoretical training in anthropological approaches to political economy and history prepared me to deal with understanding who the Miskitu were – why there was nothing "traditional" about them – and why they might rise up in arms against their central government. I was completely unprepared, however, for what to do on the more important practical human level. Should I publish my material or would CIA analysts perusing academic journals seize upon my information to refine counterinsurgency operations the way monographs by unsuspecting – and not so unsuspecting – anthropologists working in Indochina were abused in Southeast Asia during the Vietnam War? (cf. discussion by Jones 1971 and the preface to Condominas 1977.) When I discussed these issues at professional societies in the US context I was "being political" or I was "outside the realm of anthropology." If I went to the media I was by definition no longer an academic researcher – or worse yet – I was a political activist posing as an anthropologist. If we are to be logically consistent to our discipline's position on honesty of self-presentation should we punish the closet human rights activists as firmly as we condemn the counterrevolutionary spy?

Peasant massacre in El Salvador

My next aborted fieldwork experience proved to be even more painful and even more "political." Having been a participant/observer among a people who went through an extraordinarily rapid political mobilization, I entered the robust, interdisciplinary debate on peasant political mobilization. Anthropology's tradition of participant/observation fieldwork encouraged me to try to live among radicalized peasants rather than limit myself to examining their vital statistics from the vantage point of historical archives or census tract statistics. Indeed, I felt this lack of fieldwork data to be a crucial limitation of much of the literature

published in political science, sociology, and history on peasant revolts.

With this in mind I went to explore the possibility of fieldwork in a Salvadoran refugee camp in Honduras (Bourgois 1982). My central ethical concern was that counterinsurgency experts would have access to my eventual publications and that I might unwittingly contribute to more efficient repression in the long run. I was also concerned lest I attract attention to refugee political leaders merely by being seen talking to them regularly. Because of these problems, I initially canceled my fieldwork plans, but on second thought I decided that the potential of the research warranted at least a preliminary feasibility investigation.

In my exploratory visits to the refugee camps, I was surprised to learn that the refugees desperately wanted foreigners to reside in the camps with them. They sought out my company because a foreign witness deters local military officials from engaging in random abuses. They assured me that far from placing them in danger, my physical presence granted them a measure of security. The church and United Nations organizations operating the camps were also interested in having an anthropologist present on a long-term basis. They pointed out that, as a full-time researcher, I would also be in an ideal position to document human rights abuses and to help receive civilians continuing to flee government search and destroy operations just across the border. In fact, all the human rights workers I spoke with urged me to stay and undertake my study in the camps.

This did not remedy the problem of the potential misuse of my published research. Several refugees suggested I cross the border into El Salvador and discuss this complicated issue with the fighters and sympathizers who remained in their home communities. (I think the refugees also hoped that a brief visit on my part would end my repeated uninformed questions on such obvious facts as the distance between their houses or the fertility of their fields.) Although CIA analysts probably collect most theoretical studies on peasant politicization in Central America, I thought one manner of reducing the practical counterinsurgency

value of such research would be to delay publication – aside from periodic human rights
reports – until the political and military situation had changed sufficiently to limit the applicability of my data. The theoretical questions I
would be exploring were already a part of the
rigorous scholarly debate on revolutionary
peasants in the social sciences. Was that entire
debate to be dropped from social science
research for fear of raising the analytic capabilities of the CIA?

To abbreviate a long story, a few days after
my arrival, while I was still debating this issue a
group of peasants planning to cross into El
Salvador a few hours later offered to let me
accompany them. I impetuously – in retrospect
unwisely – jumped at the opportunity. My intent
was to stay in El Salvador for only 48 hours. I
thought conversations with peasants and fighters in the war zone would help me come to a
final decision as to whether or not extended
fieldwork in the refugee camps in Honduras was
feasible and – more importantly – ethically
defensible.

My 48 hour visit to El Salvador was prolonged into a fourteen day nightmare when the
Salvadoran military launched a search and
destroy operation against the region. The government forces surrounded a 40 square kilom-
eter region (approximately a dozen hamlets)
and began systematically bombarding, mortar-
ing, and strafing the entire zone with airplanes,
Huey helicopters, and artillery. There were
approximately a thousand peasants living in
the area and only one or two hundred of these
had guns and probably less than a dozen were
formal members of the FMLN. The population
was composed of a typical cross-section of
peasants – the kind of people you would find
anywhere in rural Latin America if you circled
off 40 square kilometers: grandmothers,
grandfathers, young and middle-aged men and
women, pregnant mothers, suckling infants,
children etc…. We were all the target of the
Salvadoran air force and army. I gave the following oral account to a journalist shortly
after my return to the US:

When the bombardments and strafings began
we would take cover anywhere we could. I
was told to crouch beside a tree trunk and,

whatever I did, not to move. They'd shoot at
anything that moved. I remember inching
around a tree trunk to keep something solid
between me and the machine-gun fire of the
helicopters.

Sometimes the mortar shots came 10 times
in a row, and there's a tremendous sense of
panic when you hear them getting closer and
closer. I was told that when I heard a mortar
fired I should grit my teeth and keep my
mouth open to prevent my ear drums from
rupturing…. On the first four days, … about
15 men, women and children … were
wounded. Shrapnel was removed, and amputations were performed with absolutely no
pain medicine. (*Washington Post* February 14,
1982 pp. C1)

On the fourth night of the invasion we tried
to break through the government troops encir-
cling us. The plan was for the FMLN fighters
(i.e., younger peasants with guns and minimal
military training) to draw fire from a machine
gun nest set up by the government soldiers on
a knoll while the rest of us civilians tried to run
by unseen in the darkness of the night. Once
again, there were about a thousand of us all
ages, several pregnant, others sick, one blind,
and many under three years of age:

We were on a rocky path with a Salvadoran
gunpost off to our left. FMLN guerrillas, also
on our left and to the rear, drew fire while we
made a break for it. The babies the women
were carrying were shrieking at the noise
and, as soon as we got within earshot, the
Salvadoran forces turned their fire on us.

At this point, it was pandemonium.
Grenades were landing around us; machine
guns were firing; we were running. A little boy
about 20 yards ahead of me was blown in half
when a grenade landed on him. His body lay
in the middle of the path, so I had to run over
it to escape. (Ibid.)

I remember at one point being crouched
near a woman under cover of some bushes
when her baby began to cry. She waved at me
with her hand and whispered to me to run
away as fast as possible before the government
soldiers heard the noise. I obeyed, and sprint-
ing forward I heard machine gun bullets and

shrieks all around me. Mothers and infants made up the bulk of the casualties that night. Only a mother can carry her baby under fire because only a mother has a chance of preventing her suckling infant from crying. The Salvadoran military was shooting in the darkness into the sound of crying babies.

Six to seven hundred of us managed to sprint past the machine gun nest. For the next fourteen days, we stayed together running at night and hiding during the day:

> One of the major hazards we always faced was the noise of crying babies and the moans of the wounded, making the whole group vulnerable to detection. Rags were stuffed in the mouths of the wounded, so their cries would not be heard. The babies cried a lot because they were hungry; their mothers' milk had dried up.
>
> A young woman gave birth on the second night of our flight. She was up and running for her life the next day, along with the rest of us. Those of us who were young and healthy were lucky. It was the law of survival at its cruelest: the slow runners and the elderly were killed. (Ibid.)

At one point we crossed back through the villages we had fled out of:

> ... we were hit with the overpowering stench of decaying bodies. There were donkeys, pigs, horses, chickens – all dead. The soldiers had burned down as many of the houses as they could, ripped apart the granaries, it even looked as if they had tried to trample the fields. (Ibid.)

> ... [We] came upon the naked body of a middle-aged woman. Her clothes had been ripped off and apparently acid had been poured on her skin because it was bubbling off. The body had been left in a prominent position along the path, presumably to terrorize any survivors. (Bourgois 1982:21)

The academic reaction

That was the end of my fieldwork on ideology and material reality among revolutionary peasants. It was also almost the end of my anthropological career, after I sought out the media

and human rights lobbyists on Capitol Hill to present my testimony to the public. I had violated several of the anthropological/methodological ethics discussed earlier along with the specific duties of a graduate student to keep his/her academic advisors informed of a change in research plans. A strong argument was made to terminate me as a graduate student – and with abundant justification according to the anthropological ethics I had broken: I had crossed a border illegally thereby violating the laws of my host country government; I had not notified my dissertation committee of my decision to explore a new dangerous research site; I had notified the media and contacted human rights organizations thereby violating the right to privacy of my research subjects; I had potentially jeopardized the future opportunities of colleagues to research in Honduras and El Salvador by breaking immigration laws and calling attention to government repression in public forums.

Significantly, had I not gone to the media with my testimony of human rights violations anthropological ethics would not have been violated in as serious a manner. It would have remained a personal story between my committee and myself as an unsuccessful and reckless preliminary fieldwork exploration that had been decided against as too dangerous. By remaining silent I would not have violated anyone's rights to privacy nor have threatened my colleagues' access to the field, nor offended my host country government.

Of course my personal sense of moral responsibility obliged me to provide public testimony and I entered the media/political arena. I discovered that a North American anthropologist is not supposed to document human rights violations if it involves violating a host country government's laws or contravenes the informed consent and right to privacy of the parties involved. In other words, anthropology's ethics can be interpreted at loggerheads with humanity's common sense. I could have crossed into FMLN territory as a journalist or as a human rights activist but not as an anthropologist because access to the information I was seeking was only available by crossing a border illegally; publicizing that information also violated a people's right to privacy and informed consent. Subsequently, lobbying to change US foreign policy exacerbates these transgressions since political denunciation is not conduct befitting an anthropologist.

To reiterate, the problem is rooted in a specifically North American epistemology of relativism and "value-free science" which forbids engaged research and – when taken to its logical conclusion – denies absolute assertions including those of universal human rights. This alleged "apolitical" orientation expresses itself within US academia in a phobic relationship to the media and in a righteous condemnation of "political activism." In contrast to Europe – especially France – where political militance and an occasional *Op Ed* in *Le Monde* is a sign of academic prestige (Bourdieu 1984), in the US, newspaper editorials and magazine articles are often interpreted as an indication of lack of serious commitment to science. While we do have to be cautious of sacrificing analytical rigor by becoming too immersed in media presentations and political polemics are we supposed to keep our human rights denunciations out of the public domain in the name of anthropological ethics and scientific rigor?[2]

It is important that the discipline enforce the tenets of informed consent and respect for host country governments. Taken out of context, however, these academic requisites obscure the political and economic realities of the regions where we have traditionally been most active. A research project which investigates structures of inequality will have a hard time passing a human subjects review board if the canons of anthropological ethics are rigidly applied. Are we supposed to abandon controversial research? Most political economy studies can be defined as potentially unethical. A fieldworker cannot obtain important information on unequal power relations by strictly obeying the power structure's rules and laws (cf. Nader 1972:303ff). How does one obtain meaningful information on peasant/landlord relations if the landlord is required to provide truly informed consent? What are the limits to "informed consent" in settings of highly unequal power relations? Do we have to notify absentee landlords prior to interviewing sharecroppers on their estates? Are we allowed to obtain jobs in factories in order to document

union repression? Did I have an obligation to obtain informed consent from the Salvadoran government troops firing at us before photographing the children they wounded? Where does one draw the line? Does one abandon urgent research simply because a dictatorial host nation government does not want its repressive political system to be documented? How does one decide whether a host country government is sufficiently repressive to warrant breaking its laws? These unresolved questions reveal that there is nothing apolitical about the North American commitment to relativism and to its methodologically defined body of ethics. Most dramatically, the ethic of informed consent as it is interpreted by human subjects review boards at North American universities implicitly reinforces the political status quo. Understood in a real world context, the entire logic of anthropology's ethics is premised on a highly political assertion that unequal power relations are not particularly relevant to our research.

Informed consent: United Fruit Company versus banana workers

For my final dissertation fieldwork project, I purposefully selected a host country which was free of civil-political strife; nevertheless, the same ethical contradictions arose. I studied ethnic relations on a United Fruit Company banana plantation spanning the Costa Rica/Panama border (Bourgois 1988, 1989). My first obvious problem was that the transnational corporation had redefined the border, and the plantation's operations illegally straddled Panama and Costa Rica. My real host country "government," therefore, turned out to be the United Fruit Company – not Costa Rica or Panama. High level United Fruit Company officials considered my topic – "a history of the ethnicity of the population in the plantation region" – innocuously "anthropological" and ordered local plantation officials to graciously open their confidential files to me. I was even allowed to reside in workers' barracks for some 16 months. Had management's consent been truly informed and had the Company understood what a historical analysis of ethnicity in a plantation context would reveal, I would not have been allowed to document systematically the transnational's quasi-apartheid labor hierarchy; its ethnic discrimination on occupational safety issues; or its destruction of the union movement by ethnic recruitment etc. The head managers would not have toured me through their golf course, drunk whiskey with me, and made racist comments about their workers to me if they had really understood anthropological participant/ observation research technique. Although I was never overtly dishonest; and although I always precisely explained my research topic to everyone; they obviously did not understand my research implications or they would have run me out of the area and/or beaten me up.

In fact, participant/observation fieldwork by its very definition dangerously stretches the anthropological ethic of informed consent. We obviously have an obligation to let the people we are researching know that they are being studied and that a book and/or articles will eventually be written about them. Furthermore, we have to explain as precisely as possible the focus of our study. At the same time, we are taught in our courses preparatory to fieldwork that the gifted researcher must break the boundaries between outsider and insider. We are supposed to "build rapport" and develop such a level of trust and acceptance in our host societies that we do not distort social interaction. Anything less leads to the collection of skewed or superficial data. How can we reconcile effective participant/observation with truly "informed consent"? Is rapport building a covert way of saying "encourage people to forget that you arc constantly observing them and registering everything they are saying and doing"? Technically, to maintain truly informed consent we should interrupt controversial conversations and activities – Miranda act style – to remind everyone that everything they say or do may be recorded in fieldwork notes.

Experienced fieldworkers usually advise novice ethnographers not to take notes in public while undertaking fieldwork. Is that a false presentation of self? Is good participant-observation fieldwork inconsistent with anthropological ethics? Where do we draw the line? Are we allowed to research illegal operations? Do we systematically have to avoid frequenting the rich and powerful who regularly bend and break laws? Once again, these important ethical dilemmas become even more pronounced when we are focusing on conflict and unequal power relations.

Theoretical Context

I hope I have not raised these issues in too moralistic and righteous a tone. Anthropologists do not have to convert themselves into human rights activists and political cadre for "worthy" causes in order to remain ethical persons. Although perhaps another – arguably more consistent – way of reformulating anthropological ethics would be to require that our studies among the "poor and powerless" contribute to their empowerment. That would certainly be different from the current practice of requiring "ethical researchers" to obtain the informed consent of landlords and military bureaucracies. Nevertheless, this discussion of our human responsibility to our research subjects does not imply that we automatically have something concrete to offer in their struggles for survival or for political rights. We are outsiders; and we have a formidable capacity unwittingly by our mere presence to cause trouble or to complicate matters seriously.

Symbolic studies of all kinds are important for the vitality of anthropology just as is literary and artistic criticism, folklore, and philosophy for understanding the most important dimensions of humanity. From a more specifically political perspective, interpretative, post-modernist studies have potentially emancipating insights to offer us. They have identified axes of domination which have been inadequately worked out by Marxists. There have been many important exploratory articles dealing from a symbolic perspective with the meaning of violence and political repression (cf. Falla 1983; Taussig 1984). More squarely within the post-modernist movements, feminist theoreticians such as Donna Haraway (1988) with her call for "situated knowledges" have advocated politically committed research. There are also voices from inside anthropology calling colleagues to task for ignoring histories of explosively repressive status quos in pursuit of vigorously essentialist visions of isolated Indians (Starn 1991). Similarly, interpretive anthropologists and sociologists from historically dominated ethnic groups have challenged intellectuals to confront the content of racism in creative ways (Gilroy 1987, Limon 1989, Rosaldo 1990, Santamaria 1986).

Nevertheless, in our explosive real world context, practitioners of the post-modernist deconstructivist movements within anthropology can be more confident than can most political economy-oriented ethnographers that their publications will not cause absentee landlords to unleash the secret police on their respondents; nor are their future colleagues as likely to be barred by host governments because of how they interpreted the poetics of power. All of us, regardless of our theoretical orientation, need to reexamine the place of human concern in our pursuit of science among the starving and the persecuted. Let us not be political when we claim to be apolitical in the name of ethics; and vice versa let us not allow our "politics" to stagnate behind sensitive rhetoric.

It would be dangerous and arrogant to think that there are definite answers to any of these ethical/moral questions. We need to discuss them and think about them in both practical and theoretical terms. Meanwhile, however, as all of us (without exception) wallow in a phenomenological swamp of signs and symbols we should not forget that our "informants" continue to be crucified.

NOTES

1   By the time anthropologists mobilized effectively as a discipline to censure intelligence work, the US Defense Department had already successfully tapped anthropological expertise to refine counterinsurgency strategies in Indochina. The US military even started an "Ethnographic Study Series" and published a volume *Minority Groups in North Vietnam* which was "designed to be useful to military and other personnel who need a convenient compilation of basic facts about the social, economic, and political institutions and practices of minority groups in North Vietnam" (Kensington Office of the American Institutes

for Research 1972). Incidentally, the chapter on the "Meo" [Hmong] in this volume specifically notes that the "Meo ... make excellent guides" and "reliable porters, who can carry heavy loads (up to 50 kilograms) while maintaining a rapid gait" (Ibid.: 239).

2   A church-based director of a human rights organization rebuked me when I explained to him the anthropological ethics which prevented me from showing members of US Congress photographs of peasant victims during my testimony on the military invasion: "For God's sake; what are you talking about! Testify as a human being then – not as an anthropologist."

REFERENCES

Asad, Talal ed.
    1973   Anthropology and the Colonial Encounter. New York: Humanities Press.
Berreman, Gerald
    1973   Academic Colonialism: Not so Innocent Abroad. *In* To See Ourselves: Anthropology and Modern Social Issues. Thomas Weaver, ed. pp. 152–6. Glenview, IL: Scott, Foresman.
Bourdieu, Pierre
    1984   Homo Academicus. Paris: Minuit.
Bourgois, Philippe
    1981   Class, Ethnicity and the State Among the Miskitu Amerindians of Northeastern Nicaragua. Latin American Perspectives 8:22–39.
Bourgois, Philippe
    1982   What U.S. Foreign Policy Faces in Rural El Salvador: An Eyewitness Account. Monthly Review (May):14–30.
Bourgois, Philippe
    1986   Guaymi: Les Damnes de la Plantation. Ethnies 4/5, Fall/Autumn, pp. 43–5.
Bourgois, Philippe
    1988   Conjugated Oppression: Class and Ethnicity Among Kuna and Guaymi Banana Workers on a Corporate Plantation. American Ethnologist 15:2:328–48.
Bourgois, Philippe
    1989   Ethnicity at Work: Divided Labor on a Central American Banana Plantation. Baltimore: Johns Hopkins University Press.
Condominas, Georges
    1977[1957]   We Have Eaten the Forest; The Story of a Montagnard Village in the Central Highlands of Vietnam. Translated by Adrienne Foulke. New York: Hill and Wang.

Falla, Ricardo
1983 Voices of the Survivors: The Massacre at Finca San Francisco, Guatemala. Cambridge MA: Cultural Survival Occasional Publication, no. 10.

Gilroy, Paul
1987 There Ain't No Black in the Union Jack: The Cultural Politics of Race and Nation. London: Hutchinson.

Gough, Kathleen
1973 World Revolution and the Science of Man. pp. 156–65 in Weaver 1977.

Haraway, Donna
1988 Situated Knowledges: The Science Question in Feminism and the Privilege of Partial Perspective. Feminist Studies 14:3: 575–99.

Holm, John
1978 The Creole English of Nicaragua's Miskito Coast: Its Socio-Linguistic History and a Comparative Study of its Lexicon and Syntax. Unpublished PhD dissertation, University of London, Department of Linguistics.

Horowitz, Irving ed.
1967 The Rise and Fall of Project Camelot. Studies in the Relationship between Social Science and Practical Politics. Cambridge MA: MIT Press.

Huizer, Gerrit & Mannheim, Bruce, editors
1979 The Politics of Anthropology: From Colonialism & Sexism Toward a View from Below. Mouton de Gruyter.

Hymes, Dell
1972 Introduction: The Use of Anthropology: Critical, Political, Personal. pp. 3–79 in Hymes 1972.

Hymes, Dell ed.
1972 Reinventing Anthropology. New York: Pantheon.

Jones, Delmos
1971 Social Responsibility and the Belief in Basic Research: An Example from Thailand. Current Anthropology 12: 3:347–50.

Keesing, Roger
1981 Cultural Anthropology: A Contemporary Perspective. New York: Holt, Rinehart and Winston (second edition).

Keesing, Roger
1987 Anthropology as Interpretive Quest. Current Anthropology 28:2:161–76.

Kensington Office of the American Institutes for Research

1972 Minority Groups in North Vietnam, Ethnographic Study Series. Washington DC: US Government Printing Office.

Limon, Jose
1989 Carne, Carnales, and the Carnivalesque – Bakhtinian Batos, Disorder, and Narrative Discourse. American Ethnologist 16:3: 471–86.

Magubane, Bernard and James C. Faris
1985 On the Political Relevance of Anthropology. Dialectical Anthropology 9:1–4:91–104.

Mintz, Sidney
1970 Foreword. In Norman Whitten & John Szwed, eds. Afro-American Anthropology: Contemporary Perspectives. Norman Whitten & John Szwed, eds. pp. 1–16. New York: Free Press.

Murphy, Robert F.
1990 The Dialectics of Deeds and Words: Or Anti-the-Antis (and the Anti-Antis). Cultural Anthropology 5:3: 331–7.

Nader, Laura
1972 Up the Anthropologist – Perspectives Gained from Studying Up. pp. 284–344 In Reinventing Anthropology. Dell Hymes, ed. pp. 284–311. New York: Pantheon.

Polier, Nicole & William Roseberry
1989 Tristes Tropes: Post-Modern Anthropologists Encounter the Other and Discover Themselves. Economy and Society 18:2: 245–64.

Rebel, Hermann
1989a Cultural Hegemony and Class Experience: A Critical Reading of Recent Ethnological-Historical Approaches (Part One). American Ethnologist 16:1: 117–36.

Rebel, Hermann
1989b Cultural Hegemony and Class Experience: A Critical Reading of Recent Ethnological-Historical Approaches (Part Two). American Ethnologist 16:2:350–65.

Rosaldo, Renato
1990 Others of Invention: Ethnicity and Its Discontents. Voice Literary Supplement, February, pp. 27–9.

Sanadjian, Manuchehr
1990 From Participant to Partisan Observation: An Open End, Critique of Anthropology 10:1:113–35.

Santamaria, Ulysses
1986 L'Amérique Noire. Les Temps Modernes (Special Issue on Black America) 474:1–8.

Smith, Carol
1984 Local History in Global Context: Social and Economic Transitions in Western Guatemala. Comparative Studies in Society and History 26:1:193–228.

Starn
1991 Missing the Revolution: Anthropologists and the War in Peru. Cultural Anthropology 6:1:63–92.

Taussing, Michael
1984 Culture of Terror – Space of Death. Roger Casement's Putumayo Report and the Explanation of Torture, Comparative Studies in Society and History 26:3: 467–97.

Weaver, Thomas, ed.
1973 To See Ourselves: Anthropology and Modern Social Issues. Glenview IL: Scott, Foresman.

Wolf, Eric
1972 American Anthropologists and American Society. pp. 251–63 in Hymes 1972.

Wolf, Eric & Joseph Jorgensen
1970 Anthropology on the Warpath in Thailand. New York Review of Books, November 19, pp. 26–35.

21

Ethics versus "Realism" in Anthropology

Gerald D. Berreman

Introduction

At the annual meeting of the American Anthropological Association in December 1985, I participated as a representative of the Association's Committee on Ethics (COE) during the era in which its Principles of Professional Responsibility (PPR) – the official euphemism for our code of ethics – was drafted and adopted: 1969 to 1971. The situation at the time of that meeting was that a new, draft Code of Ethics (dCoE) had been placed before the membership in the October 1984 edition of the *Anthropology Newsletter*, fundamentally redefining and reformulating the concepts of ethics and responsibility in the profession to accord with what its authors said were the changed circumstances of the time. Discussion of the draft code was invited in the columns of the *Newsletter* and in an open forum, which had been held for the purpose at the 1984 annual meeting, with the goal of revising it and

bringing it to a vote in the fall of 1985. If adopted it was to supersede the PPR or, if a vote were to appear premature at that time, further discussion was to be scheduled before holding the vote. The latter course was followed (including the 1985 session, "Ethics, Professionalism and the Future of Anthropology," and a follow-up session at the 1986 meetings). My role in each was to put the draft code into historical context and give my response to it. This chapter is based on those two presentations. The vote, incidentally, was never held.

I will introduce the context for what I have to say simply by asserting that I believe humane ethics in research and scholarship to be practical necessities for anthropologists today, just as human rights and self-interest – social justice and survival – have become inseparable for people everywhere (Berreman 1980:12; cf. 1971c:398–9). Therefore, when I speak of ethics versus realism in anthropology I am not

Gerald D. Berreman, "Ethics versus 'Realism' in Anthropology," pp. 38–71 from *Ethics and the Profession of Anthropology: Dialogue for a New Era*, ed. Carolyn Fluehr-Lobban. Philadelphia: University of Pennsylvania Press, 1991. Copyright © 1991 by the University of Pennsylvania Press. Reprinted by permission of the University of Pennsylvania Press.

Ethnographic Fieldwork: An Anthropological Reader, Second Edition. Edited by Antonius C. G. M. Robben and Jeffrey A. Sluka.
Editorial material and organization © 2012 John Wiley & Sons, Inc.
Published 2012 by John Wiley & Sons, Inc.

referring to the "consummate realism" that
Ernest Becker called "instrumental utopianism" (1971:xi), and that both he and C. Wright
Mills before him advocated: the forthright
application of reason to the solution of human
problems. Rather, the "realism" I contrast
ironically with ethics is that referred to by
Mills (1963:402) as the boast of "crack-pot
realists," whom Becker called "hard-headed
realists," that is, "the militarists and other
bureaucrats ... [with] their age-old practical
nightmares" (Becker 1971:xi). That said, let
me proceed to some historical background
for the issues of ethics and "realism" in
anthropology today.

History: Anthropology and Ethics, 1919 to 1986

The first ethical issue to discernibly attract the
attention of the American Anthropological
Association was the brief and tragicomical
imbroglio of 1919 to 1920, wherein Franz
Boas, founder of our discipline in America,
became the only member of the association
ever to be censured and expelled (Stocking
1968:273). His offense was that he reported in
The Nation "incontrovertible proof," which
had "accidentally" come his way, that "at least
four" anthropologists had served as spies
under cover of scholarly research during
World War I (Boas 1919:729; see also AAA
1920:93–4).

The first serious systematic concern with
ethics as such in our profession came about
thirty years later, after World War II, when in
1948 the association adopted the "Resolution
of Freedom of Publication," urging "all sponsoring institutions to guarantee their research
scientists complete freedom to interpret and
publish their findings without censorship or
interference, provided that the interests of
[those] studied are protected" (AAA 1949:
370).[1] (That resolution should be borne in
mind, I think, as we consider the provisions of
the draft code.) But it took the infamous and
ill-fated Project Camelot, an American counterinsurgency research plan for Chile in 1965 –
more than fifteen years after the research
freedom resolution – to focus anthropological

attention squarely on the issues of ethics and
secrecy in research (Horowitz 1967). It was in
response to this that the Beals Committee
was appointed by the Executive Board of the
AAA in 1967, which then produced the
ground-breaking report entitled "Background
Information on Problems of Anthropological
Research and Ethics" (Beals et al. 1967:2–13).
As a result of this report, the membership of
the AAA voted adoption, in March 1967, of
the "Statement of Problems of Anthropological
Research and Ethics," based on that report. It
is still in effect and is part of the packet of
materials entitled *Professional Ethics* (1983),
that is available from the Executive Office of
the American Anthropological Association.
It comprises essentially a draft code of ethics
for the association and is a forerunner, both
in time and content, of the Principles of
Professional Responsibility.

At this point in the history of these matters,
we move into what for many members of the
association were the glory days (or the gory
days, depending upon one's social and political
viewpoint) of the late 1960s and early 1970s.
The virtuous and the villainous were unambiguously defined no matter which side one
was on, with few who were neutral or unde-
cided. To say that is not to belittle the struggle or its importance. It was the good fight and
the stakes were high. University and college
departments were politically and ethically
split (my own, for one), as was the profession.
Friendships were severed, even as others were
forged that would be strong and everlasting;
enemies were made, respect was won and lost,
principles were upheld and betrayed. The association was riven. The turmoil was perhaps
most vividly displayed during and following
the presidential election of 1970, wherein I, a
member of the Committee on Ethics (which
had confronted the Executive Board on issues
surrounding the PPR and the ethics of anthropologists' involvement in mission-oriented
activities in Southeast Asia, notably Thailand),
was nominated as a presidential candidate. It
was the first time that a nomination for association office had come from the electorate, as
provided in the constitution, in addition to
those candidates provided by the Committee
on Nominations (three in the case of the

presidency; *Newsletter*, 1970d:1). Shortly before the election, two of the three nominees of the committee withdrew their candidacies in favor of the third, considered the strongest of the three, in order to make it a two-person contest "because of the serious issues confronting the association and the introduction of a new nominee" (*Newsletter*, 1970e:1). The tactic evidently worked, as the committee's remaining candidate, Anthony Wallace, won by a margin of about two to one, although there is, of course, no way to know what might have been the outcome had all four candidates fulfilled the agreement upon which their acceptance of nomination was constitutionally predicated: that they would run and would serve if elected (*Newsletter*, 1971:1).[2]

In any case, in an effort to heal the wounds of these divisive events, at the annual meeting I was asked by the president, George Foster, to give a brief address to the council in my role as the defeated candidate and presumed spokesperson for the dissident minority. In view of the then-recent abolition of the presidential address, mine was the only address delivered before the council that year, an unusual parliamentary event, to say the least, and an opportunity I could hardly decline (Berreman 1971a; 1971b). I doubt that my talk did much to realize the hopes which motivated the request that I speak, but though it viewed the future of the association through what proved to have been a rather clouded crystal ball, it did gratify those who had supported my nomination for the values it represented. The tensions, disagreements, and divisions that surfaced in those days have diminished only slowly and uncertainly at best. The continuing controversy over the PPR, and the possibility of its replacement by the dCoE, are manifestations of that schism, and the heat of the continuing arguments reflects that of the Vietnam era, with some of the same cast of characters generating it. It is still a good fight and the stakes are still high, on both sides, but the substance of disagreement has clearly diminished within the profession, the arguments have become less dramatic, the membership less polarized, and the social and political context less conducive to clearcut definition and resolution of the issues. Nevertheless, they retain their vital, ultimate

importance to anthropology and will continue to trouble it as a discipline and a profession through periods of both apathy and concern.

I have gone through those now rare and yellowed documents, letters, telegrams, pronouncements, minutes of endless meetings, and recaptured some of the vitality I remember from that bygone era – the issues debated, the evidence cited, the strategies planned, the counterstrategies detected – and was reminded of the names and actions of coconspirators, adversaries, and commentators whom I had not seen or thought of for years, as well as those who are oft- and well-remembered. They are all there in the dusty files of the faithful and, no doubt, in those of the faithless as well. They await some energetic chronicler of our profession to bring them systematically to light as an exercise in the sociology (or anthropology) of knowledge, social change, and history.

At the time of these events, American military involvement in Vietnam, both directly and via Thailand, was heavy and rapidly escalating. Chad Gordon put it clearly in a memo to the Cambridge Project advisory board which objected to that involvement: "As the Defense Department's posture in the world becomes increasingly bizarre and dangerous, any participant in such projects will undoubtedly feel called upon to account for his action to colleagues, students and the wider public" (quoted by Coburn 1969:1253). Coburn adds, with renewed relevance today to the proposed dCoE, "It is this issue of accountability that troubles many" (ibid.).

Such concerns were widespread even as those, including anthropologists, whose actions inspired them were running amok with their involvement as advisers and contributors to military adventurism (Student Mobilization Committee 1970; Flanagan 1971).

Committee on Ethics and Principles of Professional Responsibility

At the end of 1968, the Executive Board of the AAA appointed an ad hoc Committee on Ethics, whose mission was "to consider questions of the role of the Association with regard to ethical conduct on the part of anthropologists," and to report the results of their deliberations to the Executive Board (*Newsletter*, 1969:3).

The ad hoc committee was composed of David Schneider, cochairman (University of Chicago), who played a key role in selecting his co-members, David Aberle, cochairman (University of British Columbia), Richard N. Adams (University of Texas), Joseph Jorgensen (University of Michigan), William Shack (University of Illinois, Chicago Circle), and Eric Wolf (University of Michigan). They met on 25–6 January 1969 and wrote a report which included a recommendation for an elected "Standing Committee on Ethics" of the association. Defining in detail the responsibilities of the proposed standing committee, the ad hoc committee outlined "the framework for the issues that the Committee on Ethics must consider." This constituted, in effect, a draft code of ethics for the AAA, and was published in the April 1969 issue of the *Newsletter* (compare: ad hoc Committee on Ethics, *Newsletter*, 1969:3–6, with Principles of Professional Responsibility, *Newsletter*, 1970f:14–16).

That draft code was perhaps too radical for the Executive Board in those turbulent times, for they tabled it and attended only to a second recommendation of the ad hoc committee, namely,

> IMMEDIATE election of an Ethics Committee DIRECTLY responsible to the electorate of Fellows (and of students enfranchised).... The Committee urged that the new, elected Committee ... be independent of the Board.... This recommendation was NOT accepted by the Board.... It agreed to hold an election for a pro tem Ethics Committee concurrent with the autumn [1969] election of the President-Elect and new members of the Executive Board. (*Newsletter*, 1969:3)

Thus, the two bodies agreed on the principle of an elected ethics committee, but disagreed on whether it should be responsible directly to the electorate or to the Executive Board. This difference of opinion remained a bone of contention for years because, once the elected Committee on Ethics was in place, it defined its responsibility as being directly to the membership of the association, which the Executive Board disputed.

The mission of the new committee was to include consideration of the advisability and nature of an ethics code. The elected committee would consist of nine elected members except that initially, for purposes of continuity, three would carry over for one year from the appointed ad hoc committee, while six would be elected (three allotted terms of three years and the other three, terms of two years). In addition there would be a member of the Executive Board to serve ex officio as a nonvoting liaison member of the committee. Those elected in the fall of 1969 were Norman Chance (University of Connecticut), Robert Ehrich (Brooklyn College, CUNY), Wayne Suttles (Portland State University), Terence Turner (University of Chicago), Oswald Werner (Northwestern University), and I (University of California, Berkeley). Those carried over from the ad hoc committee were Eric Wolf (chair), Joseph Jorgensen, and William Shack. David Aberle, who had been a member of the ad hoc committee, had in the meantime been elected to the Executive Board, which appointed him as liaison member to the pro tem committee.

The newly constituted committee met several times, working primarily toward the preparation of a code of ethics, which it submitted to the Executive Board in May 1970. The board promptly retitled it "Principles of Professional Responsibility" (to soften the blow for members who did not want anyone to subject them to the constraints a "code" seems to imply), and it was published in the November 1970 *Newsletter*, as cited above. After heated debate in the columns of the *Newsletter*, in committees, at annual meetings, in departments, and in private, and after many intervening crises in the Executive Board, the Committee on Ethics, the council, and within the membership, the principles were adopted by vote of the association in May 1971.

The PPR's initial year, spanning the period from its formulation to its adoption, was a stormy one, to say the least. On 30 March 1970, the Student Mobilization Committee to Stop the War in Vietnam (SMC) sent to a number of scholars, including some members of the Committee on Ethics of the AAA, as well as to people in other academic disciplines (primarily people involved in Asian studies of various sorts), materials indicating participation by scholars in what they regarded as clandestine, counterinsurgency research and other activities in Southeast Asia under sponsorship of various United States governmental agencies, including such mission-oriented ones as the Departments of Defense and State and special agencies within them. The SMC planned to release a report on these documents at a press conference they had called for 3 April at the Annual Meeting of the Association for Asian Studies, to be held in San Francisco during the first week of April 1970, and at another press conference scheduled simultaneously, or nearly so, in Washington, DC. The materials were minutes, letters, reports, financial accountings, publications, and similar contents of the files of an anthropology professor at a major West Coast university, copied by a student employee of the professor from files to which she had legitimate access in the course of her work. She had regarded their contents as alarming, and had taken the liberty of making copies for herself, which she then turned over to the Student Mobilization Committee. The SMC proceeded to publish them in the 2 April 1970 edition of *The Student Mobilizer*, under the edition title *Counterinsurgency Research on Campus Exposed*. At the press conferences arranged to announce these findings and distribute *The Student Mobilizer*, four of the scholars who had been sent advance copies of some of the documents issued statements condemning the work that had been exposed: Eric Wolf, Joseph Jorgensen, Marshall Sahlins (in Washington, DC), and I (in San Francisco). Later, others joined in condemning that which had been exposed, while still others condemned the exposure and those who participated in it and those who had decried the activities exposed. Some wrote of "liberated" documents; others of "purloined" ones. Controversy raged, charges and countercharges, insults and counterinsults were traded, lawsuits were threatened (though since no law had been broken, none was ever filed). For vivid and partisan accounts – and all were partisan in this matter, including

me – see "Anthropology on the Warpath in Thailand" (Wolf and Jorgensen 1970a:26–36) and "Anthropology on the Warpath: An Exchange" (Foster et al. 1971:43–6).

The Executive Board wrote a stinging (and, I would have to say, ill-informed) letter on 19 May 1970, reprimanding the Committee on Ethics and, specifically, Wolf and Jorgensen for their statements and actions (*Newsletter*, 1970b:1, 10). The letter included these remarks:

> The Board instructs the Ethics Committee to limit itself to its specific charge, narrowly interpreted, namely to present to the Board recommendations on its future role and functions, and to fulfill this charge without further collection of case materials or by any quasi-investigative activities.

It concluded that "the Board explicitly instructs the members of the Ethics Committee ... to make clear in individual statements that they do not speak for the Committee or the Association."[3] It was the alleged violation of this last after-the-fact instruction which evidently brought the wrath of the Board down on Wolf and Jorgensen for their joint statement on the SMC revelations, and exempted – at least from explicit condemnation – Sahlins and me. Sahlins was exempted because he was not on the committee, and I was because my statement was made as an Asianist scholar in the context of the Association for Asian Studies meetings, rather than as a member of the AAA ethics committee. Wolf and Jorgensen had identified themselves as members of the ethics committee and indicated their intent to bring "these serious matters" to the attention of the American Anthropological Association, but in no way did they imply that they were speaking *for* the Committee on Ethics. They responded quickly, strongly, and in detail in a letter dated 25 May 1970 to the president and president-elect of the association, the Executive Board (which includes those two officers), and the Committee on Ethics. They concluded the letter with their resignation from the committee, pointing out that

> In its Statement the Board wishes the Ethics Committee to limit itself to its specific charge, narrowly interpreted; but it is not equally

specific about its own intention to cope with the issues raised by an applied anthropology which has for its focal concern the internal security of the present Thailand government. In drawing attention to the action of particular members of the Ethics Committee, the Board evidently hoped to avert a threat to the internal harmony of our Association. In not applying themselves with equal diligence to an analysis of the issues which prompted these individual actions, the Board averts its eyes from the real sources of a danger which threatens not only the integrity of the Association, but the fate and welfare of the peoples among whom we work. In view of the failure of the Board to interpret its mandate to the Ethics Committee to include a concern of vital relevance to the profession, we ourselves fail to perceive how the Committee can "present to the Board recommendations on its future role and functions." We therefore tender our resignations as Chairman and Member of the Committee on Ethics. (Wolf and Jorgensen 1970b, which includes not only this letter, but the letter and other documents which the Executive Board found untenable)[4]

Within a week, David Aberle resigned as the board's liaison member on the Committee on Ethics (Aberle 1970:19), while Wolf and Jorgensen encouraged other members to remain on the committee to continue its work.

A month later, in response to demands from both sides of the controversy, David Schneider, then a member of the Executive Board, proposed that a committee be appointed to look into the entire issue, both the activities of the Committee on Ethics and those of anthropologists working in Thailand. Accordingly, the Executive Board quickly appointed the "Ad Hoc Committee to Evaluate the Controversy Concerning Anthropological Activities in Relation to Thailand," consisting of three members: Margaret Mead, chair (Columbia University and American Museum of Natural History); William Davenport (University of California, Santa Cruz); David Olmsted (University of California, Davis); and, as executive secretary, Ruth Freed (New York University and American Museum of Natural History). This ad hoc committee (often called the "Mead Committee") collected documents

from a variety of sources, many of them from the Committee on Ethics, and others from principals in the controversy and from other people knowledgeable about Thailand and the issues of the controversy. By this committee's account, "all members of the ad hoc committee and its Executive Secretary ... examined all of these materials in detail" and in the process "approximately 6000 pages were read, and many reread in order for the ad hoc committee to write this report" (Davenport et al. 1971:2). This achievement was the more remarkable in view of the fact that the committee's chairperson was for much of the year in the South Pacific. The six-page report that resulted was submitted to the Executive Board on 27 September 1971. It totally exonerated all members of the American Anthropological Association of any ethical wrongdoing in the context of this controversy: "1. No civilian member of the American Anthropological Association had contravened the principles laid down in the 1967 Statement on Problems of Anthropological Research and Ethics (Beals Report) in his or her work in Thailand" (Davenport et al. 1971:4). It went on to explain seeming offenses as merely misleading claims in research applications and reports made necessary by a climate where defense relevance was required in order to obtain government funding for research. As the committee put it, "The mislabeling or redirecting of scientific projects in order to obtain funds may have seemed necessary: it may also have prepared anthropologists ... to close their eyes to misuse of their data ... and ... talents" (ibid., 4). It was suggesting that "counterinsurgency" may have been merely a buzzword incorporated in applications and reports to release funds for the author's scholarly research, just as earlier buzzwords such as "community development" and "mental health" served this function.

At the same time, the Mead Committee reprimanded the members of the Committee on Ethics who, it said, "acted hastily, unfairly, and unwisely in making public statements ... without first having consulted the anthropologists named in the purloined documents which formed the basis of their charges, and without having obtained authorization from the Board" (ibid.). The Mead Report was presented to the Council of the AAA in New York at its annual meeting on 19 November 1971, where by vote of the assembled body, and over the vehement objections of its authors, it was divided into three substantive sections and presented for discussion preparatory to a vote on whether to accept or reject each of the sections: part 1 was primarily about the activities of anthropologists in Thailand; part 2 was primarily on the actions of the Committee on Ethics; and part 3 constituted proposed guidelines, recommendations, and resolutions.

The debate, before some four hundred members, focused on the exoneration of those who had been criticized for their work in Thailand. The atmosphere was tense in view of the demands of the chairperson of the ad hoc committee, on behalf of herself and the other authors, that the report not be put to a vote but simply be put in the record as submitted (for the handwriting was already on the wall), and the membership's determination, ratified in short order by its vote, to put each section to a vote. No doubt the most telling moments in the discussion of the report were when two members of the Committee on Ethics, responding to the assertion that no civilian member of the AAA had contravened the ethical principles of the association in their work in Thailand, read from two egregiously unethical projects in which civilian fellows of the association had been directly involved, as demonstrated in documents which the ad hoc committee had had in its hands, provided by the Committee on Ethics. The first was as follows, as reported in its author's own abstract of the project:

AD-468 413 Military Research and Development Center, Bangkok (Thailand) LOW ALTITUDE VISUAL SEARCH FOR INDIVIDUAL HUMAN TARGETS: FURTHER FIELD TESTING IN SOUTHEAST ASIA. By [an anthropologist] 15 June 65, 83 pp. Unclassified. Project description text:

This report is a detailed study of quantitative information on the ability of airborne observers to sight and identify single humans on the ground. The target background for most of the testing was rice paddy with scattered bushes and trees at the end of the dry season in Southeast Asia ... [etc., etc.].

The second item read to the membership consisted of excerpts from a forty-four-page proposal in which a fellow of the AAA was involved, titled "Counter-Insurgency in Thailand: The Impact of Economic, Social and Political Action Programs." This was a half-million-dollar social science research and development proposal submitted to the Advanced Research Projects Agency of the Department of Defense by the American Institutes for Research of Pittsburgh in 1967. After introducing the problem, to design preventive counterinsurgency measures for Thailand, and to "pave the way for the generalization of the methodology to other programs in other countries" (p. ii, see below), the proposal went on to state:

The struggle between an established government and insurgent forces involves three different types of operations: the first is to make inputs into the social system that will gain the active support of an ever-increasing proportion of the population. *Threats*, promises, ideological appeals, and tangible benefits are the kinds of inputs that are most frequently used. The second is to reduce or interdict the flow of the competing inputs being made by the opposing side by installing anti-infiltration devices, cutting communications lines, *assassinating key spokesmen, strengthening retaliatory mechanisms* and similar preventative measures. The third is to counteract or neutralize the political successes already achieved by groups committed to the "wrong" side. This typically involves *direct military* confrontation.

The social scientist can make significant contributions to the design of all three types of operations. (American Institutes for Research, 1967:1; all emphasis added)

The proposal continues in this vein for forty-four chilling pages. In the final paragraph of what is termed the "Operational Plan," we read the following: "The potential applicability of the findings in the United States will also receive special attention. In many of our key domestic programs, especially those directed at *disadvantaged sub-cultures*, the methodological problems are highly similar to those described in this proposal, and the application of the Thai findings at home constitutes a potentially most significant project contribution" (ibid., 34; emphasis added).

The proposal was accepted and funded, but its semiannual reports are classified, hence unavailable – for good reason, one suspects. (See Berreman 1981a:72–126, wherein many more examples of ethically questionable and untenable anthropological projects are itemized.)

In that great auditorium where over four hundred anthropologists were seated, there followed a deathly silence. No rebuttal was offered by the Mead Committee or from the membership. The votes were held on the three sections and the report was overwhelmingly rejected, section by section. The *Newsletter* of January 1972 reported it on page 1 under the headline "COUNCIL REJECTS THAI CONTROVERSY COMMITTEE'S REPORT." After introducing the account in general, the article proceeded: "The first part in this division [of the report for purposes of the vote] ... was rejected by a vote of 308 to 74. The second part was also rejected, 243 to 57. And a final motion to consider the issue of anthropologists' actions in Thailand unresolved and to reject the remainder of the report ... was carried by a vote of 214 to 14 as the clock move into Saturday and the Council dwindled away" (*Newsletter*, 1972:1).

In the same issue of the *Newsletter*, two letters were printed as "Replies to the Report of the Ad Hoc Committee to Evaluate the Thailand Controversy," both of which had been distributed to the council at its meeting. One, by Wolf and Jorgensen, gave point-by-point rebuttals to many of the ad hoc committee's assertions and concluded that "we are as much dismayed by the callousness of the report as by its factual and theoretical faults." The other letter was by May N. Diaz and Lucile F. Newman, who challenged the report and concluded that "anthropologists cannot serve both science and war" (ibid., 3–4).

That, then, is the context within which the Principles of Professional Responsibility originated and evolved. It is against this background that we must understand the emergence of the draft Code of Ethics, changes in the role and function of the Committee on Ethics, and even the reorganization of the American Anthropological Association. I think these three changes are symptomatic of common forces at work within the profession, common pressures from without, and common processes at work on the national and international levels. They comprise a shift away from idealism and toward self-interested practicality. It is to the demand for a new code of ethics as a symptom of these broader discontents, and to the implications of that demand and those discontents, that I now turn – or return.

The Draft Code of Ethics: Text and Context

The Principles of Professional Responsibility, having been adopted in 1971 and having served the profession adequately, if not remarkably, for some years as a cautionary and exemplary model more than as an enforcement mechanism or deterrent (although with the potential to serve those functions as well), gradually lost the attention of the membership it was designed to serve, as did the committee which was to sustain and implement it. There had been only three amendments to it since its adoption: one, in 1974, relating to plagiarism (*Newsletter*, 1974:9); and two in 1975, one requiring that informants be apprised of the fact that anonymity cannot be guaranteed against the possibility of accidental disclosure, and the other advising that exclusionary policies against colleagues on the basis of non-academic attributes and the transmittal of such irrelevant factors in personnel actions is unethical (*Newsletter*, 1975:1). The only overall revision as such was the removal of generic use of the masculine pronoun from the document in about 1976.

According to the October 1984 *Newsletter*, "by 1975, active concerns had surfaced about aspects of the PPR and the grievance procedures. The growing number of non-academically based anthropologists held that the PPR was based only on academic considerations ... Important inconsistencies and ambiguities were found in the various documents relating to ethics" (*Newsletter*, 1984:2). In short, and in currently popular jargon, the hegemony of academic anthropology, and especially of academic social and cultural anthropology, was challenged. The Executive Board asked the Committee on Ethics to consider these and related problems and to propose remedies. It did so, and its suggestions were circulated to committees and individuals in the association. In 1980, an ad hoc committee was appointed to prepare a new draft code. It was made up of Karl Heider, chair (University of South Carolina); Barry Bainton and Alice Brues (University of Colorado, Boulder); Jerald Milanich (University of Florida and Florida State Museum); and John Roberts (University of Pittsburgh). After the committee members had prepared the draft and it had been circulated, commented upon, and revised, it was finally considered by the Executive Board to be "ready to go to the membership" in 1982 (ibid.). However, in view of the fact that the association was in the throes of reorganization at that time – which process, like the proposed new code, was designed to facilitate and respond to changes in the profession and especially to its members' employment structure – it was thought the membership might be distracted from attending adequately to the ad hoc committee's proposals on ethics. Accordingly, it was decided that the proposed code would be withheld from the membership until the fall of 1984. Therefore, the draft Code of Ethics (dCoE) was first presented to the membership when it was published in the October 1984 *Newsletter* (ibid.).

An "open forum" on the proposed dCoE was held at the November 1984 annual meetings in Denver. These were also the first meetings of the AAA organized to reflect the reorganization of the association into its five major divisions, now merged with its previously "affiliated" societies. In spite of the chaotic novelty of these changes, there was a lively debate on the ethics proposal – a debate which was reviewed, with discussion invited, by President-elect Helm in the April *Newsletter* (Helm 1985:1). Thereafter, the *Newsletter* was sprinkled with letters and commentaries on the subject, displaying a variety of opinions and commitments, in the months leading to the 1985 annual meetings in Washington, DC, at which the session on "Ethics, Professionalism

and the Future of Anthropology" (where the contents of this chapter were originally presented) was held.

These events were in accord with the original declaration in the PPR that it would be "from time to time" scrutinized and revised as the membership of the AAA "sees fit or as circumstances dictate" (*Professional Ethics*, 1983:5).

The 1985 session on ethics was aimed at bringing out key facts, issues, and points of view surrounding the proposed changes in the ethical stance of the AAA in the context of scholarly presentations and intellectual discussion, not to exclude debate and commitment, but with the goal of providing more light than heat.

Ethics versus Practicality: An Interpretation

The remainder of this chapter will comprise my response to the status or condition of ethics in the AAA as it has emerged since 1985. It is an interpretation, therefore, rather than, as above, a historical review. One must be familiar with both the PPR and the dCoE to consider the matter fairly, which is why I have delved into history at such length and why, in addition, these two critical documents are reproduced in this volume.

There are four major changes proposed in the draft Code of Ethics – four deletions from the Principles of Professional Responsibility – which I regard as drastic. These four must be clearly stated and directly addressed in the implications they hold for anthropology and anthropologists to convey why I, and many others, regard the changes as pernicious.

First is the downgrading – the virtual elimination – of the primary and fundamental tenet of the Principles: "1. Relations with those studied: In research, anthropologists' paramount responsibility is to those they study."

Second is the elimination of secret and clandestine activity in anthropological endeavors as constituting violations of anthropological ethics.

Third is removal of the principle of accountability of the anthropologist for violations of ethical principles – removal of any mention of sanctions, or their legitimacy, to say nothing of eliminating all traces of mechanisms for enjoining adherence to ethical principles.

Fourth is deletion of anthropologists' positive responsibilities to society at large, their own and/or those they study: the responsibility to convey their findings and the implications thereof forthrightly to all concerned fully and publicly, to the best of their professional abilities.

I maintain that these omissions have resulted not in a code at all, but a mild statement of intent, and one conspicuously devoid of ethical content. It is in fact, I think, a license for unfettered free-enterprise research, advising and engineering disguised as anthropology, with the intent of employing the ethical reputation of the discipline to enable and facilitate a wide range of mission-oriented activities, including those of dubious ethical and even egregiously unethical nature.[5] To title the draft document "Code of Ethics" is to misrepresent it seriously. It might be better to adopt a title parallel to that of the PPR – this one: Principles of Professional Irresponsibility (PPI). To do so would serve the interests of candor and thereby make at least one contribution to ethics in the profession.

I will briefly discuss these four principles-by-omission, in reverse order.

Positive responsibilities in anthropology

To my mind the most insidious, because inconspicuous, deletion from the PPR in the dCoE is the issue of the positive responsibility of anthropologists to let it be known publicly what they have learned and what they believe its implications to be for all concerned. It is stated this way in the PPR:

2. Responsibility to the Public:
   d. .... Anthropologists bear a positive responsibility to speak out publicly, both individually and collectively, on what they know and what they believe as a result of their professional expertise gained in the study of human beings. That is, they bear a

professional responsibility to contribute to an "adequate definition of reality" [Mills 1963:611] upon which public opinion and public policy may be based.

That is, we acknowledge a responsibility to practice what C. Wright Mills (ibid., and 1959:178–9) called "the politics of truth" for, as he insisted, in the defining instance, truth *is* our politics and our responsibility (Mills 1963:611). If we do not fulfill this responsibility, we are nothing more than human engineers – hirelings in the service of any agency with any agenda that can buy our expertise, as some indeed became during the Vietnam War. This theme has pervaded virtually all discussions of ethics in our profession during the past twenty-five years (cf. Berreman 1968, 1981b).

Accountability

Now it is proposed that we adopt a code of ethics without accountability. In the dCoE there is no mechanism whatsoever by which individuals can be held to account for their actions, no matter how blatantly and destructively they flaunt their profession's ethical standards and regardless of how bland such standards may be.

Why? Do those who propose and endorse this deletion intend to leave open the opportunity to violate at will the very principles of ethical conduct upon which their profession has agreed? I hope not. Is the statement in the PPR too harsh, too constraining, too dangerous? I think not. Accountability is mentioned in the PPR only in its epilogue, where it is stated:

In the final analysis, anthropological research is a human undertaking, dependent upon choices for which the individual bears ethical as well as scientific responsibility. That responsibility is a human, not superhuman, responsibility. To err is human, to forgive humane. This statement of principles of professional responsibility is not designed to punish, but to provide guidelines which can minimize the occasions upon which there is a need to forgive. *When anthropologists, by their actions, jeopardize peoples studied, professional colleagues, students, or others, or if they otherwise betray their professional commitments, their colleagues may legitimately inquire into the propriety of those actions, and take such measures as lie within the legitimate power of their Association as the membership of the Association deems appropriate.* (*Professional Ethics*, 1983:2; emphasis added)

The italicized sentence is a statement of accountability and is the nearest thing in the PPR to a mechanism for its enforcement. Is it too threatening to the new anthropology, to practicing anthropology, to be incorporated into the proposed code? Does it go against the spirit and intent of the dCoE? I think so. It must be remembered that in the Vietnam anthropologist-warriors' case it was accountability that was the issue; it was accountability that was denied by one side and insisted upon by the other. Maybe *that* is the crux of the problem now; maybe *that* is what the draft code proposes to protect future warrior-anthropologists from. Perhaps now all's to be fair in love, war, and anthropology; maybe it is proposed that henceforth there is to be no more honor among anthropologists than has long been claimed to be among thieves. Are we witnessing an attempt to exempt us as scholars, as scientists, as anthropologists from the principle invoked by the United Nations at Nuremberg after World War II, which held accountable soldiers and bureaucrats who sought to evade being held responsible for their atrocities on the ground that they were only doing their jobs, for their country? Do the anthropologists protesting against accountability not protest too much? If so, again we must ask, why? If, as I prefer to believe is the case (because I am ever charitable in such matters), the aim is simply to forestall the possibility of an ethics witch-hunt, it is misguided – a clear case of the proposed cure being worse than the affliction. There is a striking lack of evidence to even suggest that the PPR is conducive to such an eventuality. In its twenty-year history, the Committee on Ethics has pursued only one case that I know of to the Executive Board, and *no* case went any further than that for, in the balance of power enacted into the "Rules and Procedures" (*Professional Ethics*, 1983:7–9), the Executive Board must agree

with the Committee on Ethics that there is a prima facie case of ethical violation for the matter to be pursued further. That has not, to my knowledge, ever occurred. But I believe that the possibility of censure or other measures of accountability within the association, however mild and symbolic, gives credibility to our claims to ethical standards and therefore has a salutary effect in their realization, which a purely and piously advisory "code" would not.

Secrecy and clandestine activity

We are urged to consider adoption of an ethics for anthropological endeavor which tolerates secret and clandestine activities or, as the president-elect suggested in 1985, which permits secret activity but prohibits that which is clandestine: perhaps she can explain it; I cannot:

> The PPR coupling of "clandestine and secret research" may constitute a *prima facie* condemnation of some anthropologists employed in non-academic settings. In this ... respect, it appears that the first step might be to set aside the pejorative concept "clandestine" from the consideration of ethical issues arising in employment and research – notably for government, business, industry and special interest groups – that may involve some form or degree of secrecy. (Helm 1985:13)

Yet again, why? Is it, as seems to be the argument, that although "secret" and "clandestine" mean the same they are after all necessary activities in the minds of some practicing anthropologists and "clandestine" *sounds* worse?

It should be noted that the repudiation of secret or clandestine activity in the name of anthropology has been the most long-standing and the most consistently, unequivocally enunciated of ethical principles embraced by American anthropologists. From our earliest expressions of ethical concern as an association and a profession, no secret or clandestine research, no secret reports, have been tolerated among us. In 1948, the association adopted a resolution on freedom of publication and protection of the interests of those studied.

It thereby anticipated the PPR by addressing two of its four key principles, now repudiated in the dCoE. That resolution forty years ago stated in part: "(1) that the AAA strongly urge[s] all sponsoring institutions to guarantee their research scientists complete freedom to interpret and publish their findings without censorship or interference; provided that (2) the interests of the persons and communities or other social groups studied are protected" (American Anthropological Association 1949:370). That resolution was reaffirmed by the association in its 1967 "Statement on Problems and Anthropological Research and Ethics," the introduction to which asserted that, "constraint, deception and secrecy have no place in science. Actions which compromise the intellectual integrity and autonomy of research scholars ... not only weaken those international understandings essential to our discipline, but in so doing they also threaten any contribution anthropology might make to our own society and to the general interests of human welfare" (*Professional Ethics*, 1983:3). The statement went on to quote and endorse the 1948 resolution quoted above and, in order "to extend and strengthen this resolution," added that,

> Except in the event of a declaration of war by Congress [*note*: there was no such declaration in the Vietnam War], academic institutions should not undertake activities or accept contracts in anthropology that are not related to their normal function of teaching, research and public service. They should not lend themselves to clandestine activities. We deplore unnecessary restrictive classifications of research reports ... and excessive security regulations imposed on participating academic personnel.
> 3. The best interests of scientific research are not served by the imposition of external restrictions. The review procedures instituted for foreign area research contracts by ... the Department of State ... offer a dangerous potential for censorship of research. Additional demands [for clearance and the like] ... are incompatible with effective anthropological research. (Ibid.)

There followed an unambiguous resolution passed at the annual meetings of the AAA in 1969, ratified by mail ballot in the spring of 1970: "Resolution 13 (Karen Sacks), Resolved that members of the AAA shall not engage in any secret or classified research" (*Newsletter*, 1970a; 1970c).

A year later, the issue of secrecy and clandestine activity was addressed directly by the membership of the AAA when it adopted the Principles of Professional Responsibility, which dealt with it in at least six places in the body of the principles and once in an appendix – an indication of the great importance such activity has continued to hold in our profession. It is worthwhile to extract and quote each of these treatments of the issue so that we are vividly reminded of the enormity of the deletion of this subject from the dCoE:

From the PPR:

1. Relations with those studied: ...
   g. In accordance with the Association's general position on clandestine and secret research, no reports should be provided to sponsors that are not also available to the general public and, where practicable, to the population studied.
2. Responsibility to the public:
   a. Anthropologists should not communicate findings secretly to some and withhold them from others.
3. Responsibility to the discipline:
   a. Anthropologists should undertake no secret research or any research whose results cannot be freely derived and publicly reported.
   b. Anthropologists should avoid even the appearance of engaging in clandestine research, by fully and freely disclosing the aims and sponsorship of all research.
5. Responsibility to sponsors:
   ... Anthropologists should be especially careful not to promise or imply acceptance of conditions contrary to their professional ethics or competing commitments. This requires that they require of sponsors full disclosure of the sources of funds, personnel, aims of the institution and the research project, and disposition of research results.

Anthropologists must retain the right to make all ethical decisions in their research. They should enter into no secret agreements with sponsors regarding research, results or reports.

6. Responsibility to one's own government and to host governments:

... [Anthropologists] should demand assurance that they will not be required to compromise their professional responsibilities and ethics as a condition of their permission to pursue research. Specifically, no secret research, no secret reports or debriefings of any kind should be agreed to or given. If these matters are clearly understood in advance, serious complications and misunderstandings can generally be avoided. (*Professional Ethics*, 1983:1–2)

Appendix C: A Note on "Clandestine"

The 1967 *Random House Dictionary of the English Language*, defines the term clandestine as follows:

characterized by, done for, or executed with secrecy or concealment, especially for purposes of subversion or deception; private or surreptitious.

The [Ethics] Committee construes these definitions to mean that the concealment of research goals from a subject population (including nonarticulation of such goals when they include potentially injurious consequences to the social, economic, cultural and/or physical well being of the population) or other forms of deception of the population with respect to the uses to which the researcher is aware the data he gathers will be put, regardless of whether or not the research program itself is kept secret or whether publications issuing from it are classified, properly falls within the meaning of the term "clandestine" and thus is in violation of the 1967 resolution ["Statement on Problems of Anthropological Research and Ethics"]. (Annual Report of the Committee on Ethics, September 1970, *Newsletter*, 1970f:16)

In thinking back to Helm's suggestion that *clandestine* be distinguished from *secret*, and the former be prohibited and the latter permitted, it seems that *secret* is to be the word for approved clandestinity; *clandestine* will be

the word for disapproved secrecy or, as she wrote, the "pejorative" word for secrecy. Whatever the terminology, it is clear that the draft code, in rescuing secret and clandestine activities from the list of unethical practices, is proposing that they be regarded as acceptable, necessary, even desirable (in the case of practicing anthropologists) items in the anthropological bag of methodological tricks. This I regard as abject surrender of principle to a misguided practicality; a sacrifice of public interest to misperceived self-interest: replacing ethics with greed.[6]

I had thought these matters through well before joining the Committee on Ethics or confronting the task of helping prepare a code of ethics. At the risk of offering a surfeit of my own opinions on the subject, I will offer some words of my own, presented in a paper for the presidential panel titled "The Funding of Asian Studies" at the Association for Asian Studies annual meeting in 1970 (the same meeting, incidentally, at which the Student Mobilization Committee held its press conference discussed above):

There is no scholarly activity any of us can do better in secret than in public. There is none we can pursue as well, in fact, because of the implicit but inevitable restraints secrecy places on scholarship. To do research in secret, or to report it in secret, is to invite suspicion, and legitimately so because secrecy is the hallmark of intrigue, not scholarship.... I believe that we should make freedom from secrecy an unalterable condition of our research. (Berreman 1971c:396)

So much for secret *and/or* clandestine activity as excusable, much less legitimate, by anthropologists, and so much for an ethics that permits it.

In the new, and otherwise satisfactory (to me) "Revised Principles of Professional Responsibility," prepared after this essay was initially written (published for discussion in the November 1989 issue of the *Anthropology Newsletter*; submitted for ratification to the membership, 15 March 1990), I am alarmed to note that the issue of secrecy is side-stepped. The word does not appear, nor is the matter addressed beyond a single passing mention of a commitment to "open inquiry." This strikes me as odd, to say the least, in view of the centrality of the issue throughout the history of discussions of anthropological ethics in this country. To tolerate secret research is to sacrifice the credibility of anthropology as a research discipline and a humane science.

Priority of the welfare of those studied in anthropology

Finally, I return to the first of these principles-in-absentia of the draft Code of Ethics, namely deletion from the code of the primary principle in the Principles of Professional Responsibility: that the welfare of those studied is the anthropologist's paramount responsibility. This was anticipated by a second resolution presented to the Council of the Association by Karen Sacks at the 1969 annual meetings, which was passed there and ratified in the spring of 1970:

> Resolution 14 (Karen Sacks),
> Resolved that fieldworkers shall not divulge any information orally or in writing, solicited by government officials, foundations, or corporation representatives about the people they study that compromises and/or endangers their well-being and cultural integrity. (*Newsletter*, 1970a; 1970c)

The Principles of Professional Responsibility stated this point unambiguously at the head of its list of principles. It is worthwhile to repeat a bit in order to remind ourselves:

> 1. Relations with those studied:
>   In research, anthropologists' paramount responsibility is to those they study. When there is a conflict of interest, these individuals must come first. Anthropologists must do everything in their power to protect the physical, social and psychological welfare and to honor the dignity and privacy of those studied. (*Professional Ethics*, 1983:1)

Contrast that statement with the ambiguous one in the dCoE (bearing in mind that it is perhaps the *least* ambiguous of all the provisions in that document):

> 1. Anthropologists must seriously consider their own moral responsibility for their acts when there is a risk that an individual, group or organization may be hurt, exploited, or jeopardized physically, legally, in reputation, or in self-esteem as a result of these acts. (*Newsletter*, 1984:2)

Witness the fact that the people we study would be dropped not only from the highest priority (which they held in the ethical obligations specified by the PPR), but would virtually be dropped out of the draft code altogether.[7] And note that people are to be put on a par with organizations. If one were studying the Ku Klux Klan, concern for the well-being of individual informants would evidently be reduced to par with that for the KKK as an organization (or that of the organization would be raised to parity with individuals, as proponents might prefer to put it).

A more fundamental question than the quality of the proposed substitute code is why the change has been proposed – what forces have led to it?

Reaganethics: The Temper of the Times

The history of the Committee on Ethics since 1971 has been one of rapid decline – *transformation* would be a more diplomatic word. It has evolved or devolved from a committee on ethics to essentially a grievance committee; from one concerned with ethical principles and practice to one devoted primarily to personnel matters: fairness in appointments and promotions, issues of plagiarism, priority of publication, and conflict of interest (e.g., AAA 1975:54–5). This parallels a shift in concern and involvement of faculty in a number of universities from issues of academic freedom to issues of privilege and tenure (as the respective academic senate committees are called on my campus), and a pervasive concern in our society with personal well-being at the expense of concern with broader principles of social justice.

I do not blame the members of the Association's Committee on Ethics for this situation. Those are the kinds of cases with which they have been saddled. The grievances are legitimate ones, but they should be the responsibility of a committee constituted for that purpose rather than of an ethics committee perverted to that purpose. The Committee on Ethics, which has evolved in this direction, was largely responsible for the draft code, with additional input from the significantly named "Committee on Anthropology and the Profession." The combination of an ethics committee concerned largely with professional grievances and a committee on anthropology as a profession (and, therefore, presumably focused primarily on nonacademic careers) not surprisingly proposed a code which was avowedly responsive to the "new realities" of a changing profession and, especially, as has been repeatedly asserted, to the circumstances of nonacademic anthropologists: those employed in government and in corporate and consultative agencies. But it was not only these two bodies that constructed the new code. According to the *Newsletter's* announcement of the draft code, "more than 60 members" of the association had already participated in composing the draft over a period of four years by the time it was first published in October 1984 (*Newsletter*, 1984:2). Everyone knows that a camel is a horse that was designed by a committee, as comedian Allan Sherman was wont to say, and this one was a super-committee. No wonder the result was a super-camel. The PPR was the result of a mere thirteen minds in over a year's time – a bit swaybacked and perhaps even of another color, but definitely the intended horse.

Alexander Leighton has quoted a saying popular in government circles during World War II that "the administrator uses social science the way a drunk uses a lamp post, for support rather than illumination" (Leighton 1949:128). The imperatives are different if one is providing policy support or if profits are the bottom line from a case in which one is seeking understanding. This is where the dCoE differs basically from the PPR, for the former is responsive to the needs of those who provide support; the latter to the needs of those who

provide illumination. The letters in the columns of our newsletter make vivid the circumstances and ideologies that underlie both the demand for and the resistance to a revised code. One complains that the PPR

> established a set of standards so narrowly focused on a single environment that it excluded ... those of us who have chosen to work outside the grove.... Many institutions of government are charged with delivering specific services. The anthropologist can in many cases contribute to making that delivery more effective and humane. But in order to do so ... he or she ... must play by the rules of the game....
>
> This is no less the case in the private sector where there are many organizations which exist to *sell* knowledge.... Thus, many of us are conducting research the results of which are proprietary ... they belong to the firm and are simply not available except at a price.
>
> In a similar vein the prohibition of secret research simply fails to take into account the realities of today's world ... . Anthropologists working in classified areas do so because they wish to influence national policy ... . I welcome a Code of Ethics which considers such work a matter of personal choice. (Downs 1985:2)

Another correspondence, from a different perspective, notes the increased population of anthropologists and the diminished availability of "'classic' fieldwork experience," which raises critical problems, especially as anthropologists get involved in "the commercial market, and when they begin to reassess their ethical codes." Now that government support is drying up, he continues,

> we must seriously question whether or not the accommodation of individual economic incentives and the priorities of employment constitute an admittedly painful but critical conflict of interest for assessing the ethical directions for anthropology. It is not an oversimplified analogy to note that the wilderness bears of North America have been reduced to garbage dump scavengers. What will a century of private marketing under such priorities do to the ideals and perspectives for the practice of anthropology?

... if anthropology does not begin to secure some long-term analysis and planning, its ethical heritage will not sustain itself. (Wyoch 1986:24)

American anthropology has had a tradition of ethical concern and social responsibility of which we can be proud. The revelation of mission-oriented, counterinsurgency, and classified research and consultation undertaken by anthropologists working in Southeast Asia during the Vietnam War does not necessarily contradict this assessment. Such activities may well have been exceptional in the profession. Also, we must avoid the temptation to castigate Southeast Asianist anthropologists as unusually insensitive to ethical issues. I do not think people with that regional specialization were more ready to sell out than others; only that they had unique opportunities and inducements to do so. Had American military adventurism been elsewhere, I am sure that some anthropologists would have stepped forward to do the dirty work there. But I believe such people are in a minority in our profession. The very fact that the ethical issues were raised, the unethical activities exposed and deplored, is evidence of the profession's social conscience. The involvement of anthropologists in deplorable activities was not unusually pervasive, only unusually forthrightly condemned in the discipline. Other social scientists were doubtless equally or more frequently and deeply involved – political scientists, for certain, perhaps psychologists, economists, sociologists, geographers – but their involvement may have been more taken for granted by their colleagues as acceptable professional behavior, for they were not called to account so forcefully, if at all. Thus, the very fact and manner of revelation of anthropologists' involvement reflects an alert professional conscience that is commendable.

On the other hand, we cannot afford to be too self-congratulatory, either. We have had a tradition as well of complicity in colonial and neocolonial activity (Asad 1973; Lewis 1973), of advising exploiters of people and expropriators of their resources. Those who disclaim this have to resort to generalized denial together with claims to extenuating values

and behaviors held to be traditional and pervasive in the profession that in fact may prove to have been more often implicit than explicitly manifest. For counterevidence they must rely on a very few individual and collective efforts in opposition to unethical activities, advocating and contributing to the cause of autonomy or emancipation of colonized and otherwise victimized peoples (Maybury-Lewis 1974). Nor can we deny the tendency in our association to overlook or sweep under the rug some of the most egregious of unethical involvements, while seeking to protect our collective reputation, as occurred in the instance described above of the expulsion of Boas by the council, replicated fifty years later by the effort of the Mead Committee to reprimand Wolf and Jorgensen – both instances comprising responses to courageous but potentially embarrassing revelations of unethical behavior by fellow anthropologists. On the positive side, we have the facts that the Mead Report was overwhelmingly rejected by the association and, of course, that the Principles of Professional Responsibility were enthusiastically adopted and seem still to be endorsed by an overwhelming majority of its members.

It is worth remembering, too, that for nearly two years (1972–4), there was a Committee on Potentially Harmful Effects of Anthropological Research (COPHEAR), appointed by the Executive Board at the direction of the membership as a result of a motion passed at the annual meeting of 1971 (AAA 1972:42; 1973:23, 62; 1974:72).[8] When that committee died on the vine in 1974, primarily for want of cooperation and success in collecting information sufficient to carry out its charge, there sprouted a proposal supported by many for a successor Committee on Ethnocide and Genocide to address some of the same issues but without limiting itself to anthropological culpability. This proposal was inexplicably dropped by the Executive Board shortly before the 1974 annual meetings. So far as I am aware, the important issues that it and COPHEAR were to have pursued have not been directly addressed in the association since then, but they did hold our attention for a time, and may again.

Meanwhile, such issues have been the focus of several organizations and collectivities of dedicated anthropologists operating on financial shoestrings outside of the framework of the association. Most notable among them are Cultural Survival, the International Work Group for Indigenous Affairs (IWGIA), and the currently inactive Anthropology Resource Center (ARC).[9] Probably the most useful source of information on these and others of the sort is in the appendix titled "Organizations and Periodicals" in the second edition (and, I understand, the forthcoming third edition) of John H. Bodley's *Victims of Progress* (Bodley 1982:217–20). As an example I would cite Shelton Davis and Robert Mathews (and their Anthropology Resource Center), who advocated and exemplified "public interest anthropology," which seems to be on a most positive track where ethical commitments and practicality are concerned:

Public-interest anthropology differs from traditional applied anthropology in what is considered the object of study, whose interests the researcher represents, and what the researcher does with the results of his or her work. Public interest anthropology grows out of the democratic traditions of citizen activism rather than the bureaucratic needs of management and control. It is based on the premise that social problems – war, poverty, racism, sexism, environmental degradation, misuse of technology – are deeply rooted in social structure, and the role of the intellectual is to work with citizens in promoting fundamental change. (Davis and Mathews 1979:5)

Closely related to their stance is that of those who use the term "liberation anthropology" (Huizer 1979; cf. Frank 1969) to describe their activist approach to helping achieve the emancipation and autonomy of indigenous and other oppressed peoples – in analogy to the "liberation theology" of certain Christian clergy and lay people in Latin America (Berryman 1987). Bodley (1982:191–216) has proposed a useful typology of activist anthropological approaches and those who employ them: the "Conservative-Humanitarian," the "Liberal-Political," and his own commitment, the "Primitivist-Environmentalist." I leave it to the interested reader to pursue the definitions and philosophies of these perspectives and their implications for, and illuminations of, the ethical practice of anthropology.

The recent impetus for redefinition of anthropological ethics comes clearly from those outside of academia who find the Principles of Professional Responsibility to be inconsistent with the demands of their employment. Often calling themselves "practicing anthropologists," they work primarily for corporations, government agencies, and other mission-oriented employers whose priorities, they point out, are not consistent with those confronted by scholar-anthropologists.[10] For them, anthropological ethics as heretofore defined are inconvenient, constraining, even threatening, both to their missions and to their careers. Corporate ends are profits; governmental goals are national political, and international geopolitical, advantage. Anthropologists have something of value to offer in the pursuit of these "real-world" ends, for they know about the peoples and cultures that will provide the work force and customers, the allies and adversaries. They know the populace that will decide the political and economic alignment of its government; who occupies the territory that contains the sought-after resources; and which will be the sites of the military bases and missile silos. As these corporate and national priorities become anthropologists' priorities, no wonder that the subjects of study no longer come first, that secrecy and even clandestinity are no longer condemned, that anthropologists become wary of being held accountable to their colleagues for the ethical practice of their profession, that they do not feel obliged to share with society as a whole the implications of their professional knowledge, and that they view the very concept of ethical standards with anxious skepticism. Anthropologists in these roles are agents of their employers, not advocates for those they study or for the principles of their profession.

It is scarcely surprising, then, that the draft code, arising as it did in response to these circumstances, devotes nine of its new provisions to matters of "professional relations" and only four to the people among whom anthropologists work, whether in practice or in research. This is a major reversal in direction from the focus of the Principles of Professional Responsibility.

Evidently, a code of ethics for the era of practicing anthropology must not subordinate the requirements of the marketplace and real-politik to mere adherence to principle. The question then is whether this draft code speaks for anthropologists as humane students and advocates of humankind, or as bureaucrats and human engineers. Are there to be two kinds of anthropologists, practicing and humanist; two kinds of ethics, practical and humane; two kinds of anthropology, laissez-faire and principled? I think we should resist such a division as unnatural, unnecessary, and counterproductive. Resistance to it is in the public interest, in our professional interest, and in our individual interests. The demands and opportunities of careers in anthropology, be they in practice or in academia, must not substitute for ethics.

To the extent that anthropologists can remain true to their principles while practicing their profession outside of the academy, I would urge them to follow their career preferences and opportunities. To the extent that they cannot, I believe they must curtail their career choices. There is no place anywhere for unprincipled anthropology or anthropologists.

Conclusion

In conclusion, let me emphasize that I am not opposed to revision of our code of ethics, the Principles of Professional Responsibility. I *am* opposed to the abandonment of the spirit of ethical practice of anthropology which it embodies, and the tenets which codify that spirit. Specifically, I am steadfastly opposed to compromise or elimination of what I believe to be the four fundamental principles of our ethics as anthropologists, all of which are prominent in the PPR and in the history of anthropology, and all of which are conspicuously absent from the draft Code of Ethics which was proposed to replace it. They are well worth repeating:

(1) That "anthropologists' paramount responsibility is to those they study" (PPR 1).

(2) That "anthropologists should undertake no secret research" (PPR 3a) and "should avoid even the appearance of engaging in clandestine research" (PPR 3b).

(3) That anthropologists are accountable for their professional actions: "when anthropologists ... betray their professional commitments [as set forth in the PPR] ... their colleagues may legitimately inquire into the propriety of those actions, and take such measures as lie within the legitimate powers of their Association as the membership deems appropriate" (PPR Epilogue).

(4) That anthropologists bear "the positive responsibility to speak out publicly ... on what they know and ... believe as a result of their professional expertise ... . That is, they bear a professional responsibility to contribute to 'an adequate definition of reality' upon which public opinion and public policy may be based" (PPR 2d).

I see the PPR as structurally analogous to the United States Bill of Rights or the Constitution as a whole: a basic document subject to review and revision by amendment proposed from the membership either directly or through its representatives on the Executive Board, when ratified by vote of the membership at large. But I believe it to be a drastic mistake for a committee to be appointed to create a substitute code, *in toto*, in response to what are said to be the changed realities of the moment – in this case, primarily changes in the anthropological marketplace. This is exactly what was done when the dCoE was proposed just ten years after the original code – the PPR – was drawn up and adopted. At this rate, our ethics would become simply fleeting reflections of the temper of the times, our code a weather vane shifting with every social and political wind, responsive to each economic fluctuation, political fad, or international spasm. If this were to happen, we would not be alone. As the editor of *New York* magazine wrote not long ago, "Ethics in America seem to have dropped to one of the lowest points in history," and "moral lapses blot American history ... . But," she went on to point out, "today's go-go ethics are in many ways new. For one thing, there's little doubt that idealism is in decline and cynicism on the rise" (Kanner 1986:9). Surely anthropologists, as students of humankind, as practitioners of what Eric Wolf (1964:88) called "the most scientific of the humanities, the most humanist of the sciences," are more principled than to jump on that bandwagon; surely our ethical commitments are more profound, independent, and stable than that; surely those among whom and in whose interests we work deserve better than that.

In short, I believe the draft Code of Ethics constituted an evisceration of the PPR and, as such, betrayed our ethical principles and was unworthy of our discipline and our profession. It proposed to sacrifice the nobility of the politics of truth for the perversity of realpolitik. It seems that the era of Reaganomics spawned the nightmare of Reaganethics. I trust that history will soon be enabled by our profession's collective decision to relegate this episode to the dustbin of other short-lived aberrations of the 1980s.

NOTES

1 The *Newsletter* of the American Anthropological Association (known at various times also as the *Fellow Newsletter* and *Anthropology Newsletter*), from its inception in 1960 until the present (and especially from 1967 when the "Correspondence" columns became a regular feature), and before that the *American Anthropologist*, are the best, and generally the only, sources for resolutions, votes, and debates. Some of these concerning the issues discussed in this essay have been brought together in Berreman 1973.

2 I can no longer refrain from noting that one of the two candidates who withdrew astounded me a couple of years later, when we were both on the Executive Board, by spontaneously announcing one evening, "I owe you an apology!" He went on to explain that this was because of his role in that maneuver when he acceded to an unexpected late-evening telephone request by the then president of the association to withdraw in favor of the strongest of the three candidates nominated by the Nominations Committee; he was asked, further, that he call the third candidate to persuade him

to do likewise, in order to save the presidency from the challenge of "the radicals." He professed having felt guilty ever since.

3 The Executive Board at the time consisted, I believe, of George M. Foster, president (University of California, Berkeley), Charles Wagley, president-elect (Columbia University), Dell Hymes (University of Pennsylvania), David Schneider (University of Chicago), David Aberle (University of British Columbia), Eugene Hammel (University of California, Berkeley), Cyril Belshaw (University of British Columbia), and James Gibbs (Stanford University).

4 Wolf and Jorgensen's observation that in condemning them, "the Board evidently hoped to avert a threat to the internal harmony [and, I would add, the reputation] of the Association," is astute. The action was in this respect reminiscent of the council's action in 1920, hastily condemning and expelling Boas without concerning itself at all with the situation he reported. Both of these instances anticipated the Ad Hoc Committee to Evaluate the Controversy Concerning Anthropological Activities in Relation to Thailand, which concluded its deliberations in 1971 by simply denouncing those who sounded the alarm and thereby threatened the internal harmony and public reputation of the association. The tendency in all three was to close the wagons in a circle to blindly fend off the attackers, principle be damned.

5 "'Free enterprise scholarship' … is scholarship which uses whatever resources are available by whoever has access to them, for immediate payoff without thought to consequences for others. This is a selfish, short-sighted and destructive posture" (my definition: Berreman 1971c: 398).

6 The Society for Applied Anthropology has made mention of secrecy-related issues in the 1963, 1973, and 1983 versions of its brief "Statement of Professional and Ethical Responsibilities," although only in 1973 was secrecy explicitly addressed: "2. We should not consent to employment in which our activities and/or scientific data remain permanently secret and inaccessible." That seems to have disappeared in the 1983 version, even as the dCoE of the AAA has jettisoned the issue as well (see: Society for Applied Anthropology 1963; 1973; 1983).

7 The quality of the prose in the draft code fell, relative to that in the PPR, as precipitously as its idealism. To confirm this, one need only compare the preambles to each of the two documents. Alternatively, one might read again the sentences quoted in the discussion above ... or any pair of paragraphs at random. Better yet, read the documents in their entirety with this in mind. I would recommend that the draft code be dropped for the dreadful precedent it provides for dull, turgid anthropological prose, if for no other reason.

8 COPHEAR first met in October 1972, and it existed through June 1974. Its members were: Stephen A. Barnett, chair (Princeton University), Norman A. Chance (University of Connecticut), Shepard Forman (University of Michigan), Sally Falk Moore (University of Southern California), Robert J. Smith (Cornell University), and I, liaison member of the Executive Board (University of California, Berkeley) (AAA 1973:23, 62; 1974:72).

Other commitments prevented Sally Falk Moore from serving during the second year of the committee's existence.

9 These three most prominent organizations and their publications are: (1) Anthropology Resource Center (ARC; currently inactive, but publications available through Cultural Survival, Inc.); publications: *ARC Newsletter; The Global Reporter;* a series of occasional special reports and monographs. (2) Cultural Survival, Inc., 11 Divinity Ave., Cambridge, MA 02138; publications: *Cultural Survival Quarterly* (newsletter); occasional papers and special reports. (Also distributor for other publications including those of Anthropology Resource Center.) (3) Although not an American publication, this one is so central to its American audience that I include it here also: International Work Group for Indigenous Affairs (IWGIA), Fiolstraeda 10, DK-1171 Copenhagen K, Denmark; publications: *IWGIA Newsletter; IWGIA Yearbook; IWGIA Documents* (monograph series).

10 For a broader spectrum of points of view than those described here, consult the quarterly journal *Practicing Anthropology: A Career Oriented Publication of the Society for Applied Anthropology* (Box 24083, Oklahoma City, OK 73214). Now in its eleventh year and volume, it began publication in October 1978.

REFERENCES

Aberle, David
1970 Correspondence: Ethics committee issues. *Newsletter* (AAA) 11(7):19.
American Anthropological Association
1920 Council meeting, 30 Dec., 4:45 p.m. *American Anthropologist* 22:93–4.
American Anthropological Association
1949 Resolution on freedom of publication. *American Anthropologist* 51:370.
American Anthropological Association
1971 Annual report 1970 and directory. April. Washington, DC: American Anthropological Association.
American Anthropological Association
1972 Annual report 1971. April. Washington, DC: American Anthropological Association.
American Anthropological Association
1973 Annual report 1972. Distinguished lecture, proceedings, directory 1973. Washington, DC: American Anthropological Association.
American Anthropological Association
1974 Annual report 1973. Distinguished lecture, proceedings, directory 1974. Washington, DC: American Anthropological Association.
American Anthropological Association
1975 Annual report 1974. Distinguished lecture, proceedings, directory 1975. Washington, DC: American Anthropological Association.
American Institutes for Research
1967 Counter-insurgency in Thailand: The impact of economic, social, and political action programs. (A research and development proposal submitted to the Advanced Research Projects Agency.) Pittsburgh: American Institutes for Research (AIR International). December.
Asad, Talal, ed.
1973 *Anthropology and the colonial encounter.* London: Ithaca Press.
Beals, Ralph L., and Executive Board of the American Anthropological Association
1967 Background information on problems of anthropological research and ethics. *Newsletter* (AAA) 8(1):2–13.
Becker, Ernest
1971 *The lost science of man.* New York: George Braziller.
Berreman, Gerald D.
1968 Is anthropology alive? Social responsibility in social anthropology. *Current Anthropology* 9(5):391–6.

Berreman, Gerald D.
1971a Berreman speech to council. *Newsletter* (AAA) 12(1):18–20.

Berreman, Gerald D.
1971b The Greening of the American Anthropological Association: Address to council, AAA, 69th Annual Meetings, San Diego, 19 Nov. 1970. *Critical Anthropology* (New York: New School for Social Research), Spring 1971:100–4.

Berreman, Gerald D.
1971c Ethics, responsibility and the funding of Asian research. *Journal of Asian Studies* 30(2):390–9.

Berreman, Gerald D.
1973 The social responsibility of the anthropologist, *and* anthropology and the Third World. In *To see ourselves: Anthropology and modern social issues*, ed. Thomas Weaver, 5–61; and 109–79, Glenview, IL: Scott, Foresman.

Berreman, Gerald D.
1980 Are human rights merely a politicized luxury in the world today? *Anthropology and Humanism Quarterly* 5(1):2–13.

Berreman, Gerald D.
1981a In pursuit of innocence abroad: Ethics and responsibility in cross-cultural research. In *The politics of truth: Essays in critical anthropology*, ed. Gerald D. Berreman, 72–126, New Delhi: South Asian Publishers.

Berreman, Gerald D.
1981b *The politics of truth: Essays in critical anthropology*. New Delhi: South Asian Publishers.

Berryman, Phillip
1987 *Liberation theology: The essential facts about the revolutionary movement in Latin America and beyond*. New York: Pantheon Books.

Boas, Franz
1919 Correspondence: Scientists as spies. *The Nation* 109:729.

Bodley, John H.
1982 *Victims of progress* (2nd edition). Palo Alto, CA: Mayfield Publishing.

Coburn, Judith
1969 Project Cambridge: Another showdown for social science? *Science* 166:1250–3.

Davenport, William, David Olmsted, Margaret Mead, and Ruth Freed
1971 Report of the Ad Hoc Committee to Evaluate the Controversy Concerning Anthropological Activities in Relation to Thailand, to the Executive Board of the American Anthropological Association. 27 Sept. Washington, DC: American Anthropological Association.

Davis, Shelton, and Robert Mathews
1979 Anthropology Resource Center: Public interest anthropology – beyond the bureaucratic ethos. *Practicing Anthropology* 1(3):5.

Downs, James F.
1985 Proposed code of ethics supported. *Newsletter* (AAA) 26(4):2.

Flanagan, Patrick
1971 Imperial anthropology in Thailand (AICD Occasional Paper No. 2). Sydney: K. J. Mcleod.

Foster, George M., Peter Hinton, A. J. F. Köbben, Eric Wolf, and Joseph Jorgensen
1971 Anthropology on the warpath: An exchange. *New York Review* 16(6):43–6.

Frank, Andre Gunder
1969 Liberal anthropology vs. liberation anthropology. In *Latin America: Underdevelopment or revolution*, Andre Gunder Frank, 137–45. New York: Monthly Review Press.

Heller, Scott
1988 From selling Rambo to supermarket studies, anthropologists are finding more nonacademic jobs. *The Chronicle of Higher Education*, 1 June: A24.

Helm, June
1985 Commentary: Ethical principles, discussion invited. *Newsletter* (AAA) 26(4):1, 13.

Horowitz, Irving Lewis, ed.
1967 *The rise and fall of Project Camelot: Studies in the relationship between social science and practical politics*. Cambridge, MA: MIT Press.

Huizer, Gerrit
1979 Anthropology and politics: From naiveté toward liberation? In *The politics of anthropology*, ed. Gerrit Huizer and Bruce Mannheim, 3–41. The Hague: Mouton.

Kanner, Barbara
1986 The ethics pendulum swings: Idealism's out, cynicism's in. *San Francisco Examiner-Chronicle* (This World section) 10 August: 9, 12. (First published in *New York* magazine.)

Leighton, Alexander
1949 *Human relations in a changing world: Observations on the use of the social sciences*. New York: E. P. Dutton.

Lewis, Diane
1973 Anthropology and colonialism. *Current Anthropology* 14(5):581–91.

Maybury-Lewis, David
    1974 Don't put the blame on the anthropologists. *New York Times* (Op-Ed section) 15 March: 13.
Mills, C. Wright
    1959 *The sociological imagination.* New York: Oxford University Press.
Mills, C. Wright
    1963 *Power, politics and people: The collected essays of C. Wright Mills,* ed. I. L. Horowitz. New York: Ballantine Books.
Newsletter (AAA)
    1969 Report of the ethics committee. 10(4):3–6.
Newsletter (AAA)
    1970a Resolutions to be ratified. 11(1):7.
Newsletter (AAA)
    1970b Board statement on ethics issue. 11(6):1, 10.
Newsletter (AAA)
    1970c Resolutions ratified. 11(6):1.
Newsletter (AAA)
    1970d Candidate information. 11(7):1.
Newsletter (AAA)
    1970e Spaulding and Spuhler withdraw candidacies for president-elect. 11(8):1.
Newsletter (AAA)
    1970f Annual report of the Committee on Ethics, September 1970. 11(9):10–16.
Newsletter (AAA)
    1971 Wallace voted president-elect. 12(1):1.
Newsletter (AAA)
    1972 Council rejects Thai controversy committee's report. 13(1):1.
Newsletter (AAA)
    1974 Council to vote on amendment to PPR. 15(7):9.
Newsletter (AAA)
    1975 COE proposes two additions to PPR. 16(2):1.
Newsletter (AAA)
    1984 For discussion: Proposed code of ethics would supersede Principles of Professional Responsibility. 25(7):2.

Newsletter (AAA)
    1989 Proposed draft revision of the Principles of Professional Responsibility 30(8): 22–3.
Professional Ethics (AAA)
    1983 Professional ethics: Statements and procedures of the American Anthropological Association. Washington, DC: American Anthropological Association.
Society for Applied Anthropology
    1963 Statement on ethics of the society for applied anthropology. *Human Organization* 22(4):237.
Society for Applied Anthropology
    1973 Statement on professional and ethical responsibilities. The Society for Applied Anthropology (circulated to the membership).
Society for Applied Anthropology
    1983 Proposed statement on professional and ethical responsibilities. The Society for Applied Anthropology (circulated to the membership).
Stocking, George W., Jr.
    1968 *Race, culture, and evolution: Essays in the history of anthropology.* New York: Free Press.
Student Mobilization Committee to End the War in Vietnam
    1970 Counterinsurgency research on campus exposed. *The Student Mobilizer* (April) 3(4).
Wolf, Eric R.
    1964 *Anthropology.* Englewood Cliffs, NJ: Prentice-Hall.
Wolf, Eric, and Joseph Jorgensen
    1970a Anthropology on the warpath in Thailand. *New York Review* 15(9):26–36.
Wolf, Eric, and Joseph Jorgensen
    1970b Correspondence: Ethics Committee issues. *Newsletter* (AAA) 11(7):2, 19.
Wyoch, Bruce
    1986 Anthropology: Corporate tribe or market commodity. *Newsletter* (AAA) 27(1):24.

22

Worms, Witchcraft and Wild Incantations: The Case of the Chicken Soup Cure

Jeffrey David Ehrenreich

… one cannot discuss lies merely by claiming that they don't matter. More often than not, they do matter, even where looked at in simple terms of harm and benefit.
                                    Sissela Bok 1978: 71

… What are the problems of practicing backwoods medicine? There are dangers to the patients in doing so. The medical establishment has a simple rule: First of all, do no harm. With the best of intentions, untrained medical care providers can allow their ambition to outrun their ability, and harm patients ….
                                    Nancy Howell 1990: 180

Introduction: Anthropologists, Medicine, and Fieldwork

Speaking philosophically about native American peoples, Vine Deloria, Jr., has remarked that "[i]nto each life … some rain must fall…. But Indians have been cursed above all other people in history. Indians have anthropologists" (1969: 78). Deloria's arguments directed at anthropologists, perhaps tongue in cheek, perhaps not, were essentially political, not ethical, in nature. Ethical questions concerning the process of doing anthropology, however, have become increasingly important as anthropologists have grown more critical and reflexive concerning the enterprise of fieldwork. The question of anthropologists' engaging in medical or health care delivery in the field and their presumed right to do so, along with corollary questions centered around where responsibility lies in the event some harm is done to "patients," seem to me to be, relatively speaking, a most urgent and neglected issue.

Nancy Howell has recently published a report through the American Anthropological Association entitled *Surviving fieldwork* (1990), in which she outlines some of the dangers incurred by anthropologists working

Jeffrey David Ehrenreich, "Worms, Witchcraft and Wild Incantations: The Case of the Chicken Soup Cure," pp. 137–141 from *Antropological Quarterly* 69(3), 1996.

Ethnographic Fieldwork: An Anthropological Reader, Second Edition. Edited by Antonius C. G. M. Robben and Jeffrey A. Sluka.
Editorial material and organization © 2012 John Wiley & Sons, Inc.
Published 2012 by John Wiley & Sons, Inc.

in the field (for example, snakebite, hepatitis, malaria, diarrhea, falling off a cliff, drowning, auto accidents). To state the obvious, fieldwork can indeed be dangerous to anthropologists, especially for ethnographers working in remote and isolated areas far from the facilities of "western medicine." Howell's superb report briefly addresses (pp. 176–181) the issue of "practicing medicine in the field," primarily from the vantage point of a sociological questionnaire survey conducted among a sample of anthropologists. Her report indicates, at least from an emic perspective, that anthropologists "frequently feel that they used their skill to save a life, and rarely feel that any mistake they made caused someone to get worse" (p. 180). Yet, as Howell also suggests, we must surely question whether some harm occasionally occurs when anthropologists engage in what might be labeled "witch doctoring" in the field. I am aware of no attempt on the part of anthropologists to address seriously or systematically questions of the dangers of ethnographic fieldwork to natives with reference to the common practice of "witch doctoring" by anthropologists. This article is about such issues in the broadest sense. More specifically, it is concerned with not only the everyday ethical dilemmas of practicing medicine in the field without license or training, but also with a case in which fake doctors commit yet another major sham among the Awá-Coaiquer of Ecuador.

Fieldwork and the Awá of Ecuador

The Awá are an egalitarian horticultural people located in the rain forest of the wet littoral coastal region of Ecuador (see Ehrenreich 1985, 1990; Kempf 1985). In our first moments among the Awá-Coaiquer during a preliminary trip in 1977 into their territory, the Awá made direct appeals for medical help from Judith Kempf and me. As we were trying to decide whether or not to work among them, the Awá were immediately establishing exactly what they wanted from us if we did. They were open to our living with them only if we could provide them with medical services and drugs. They had

previous experience with "western" medicine and care, and they were impressed.

Upon our return to do long-term fieldwork shortly thereafter, we set up a "clinic" in a section of the house that was to be the center of our activities in the widely dispersed Awá territory. Neither of us had any previous experience or training as doctors or nurses, except perhaps as children playing that time-honored game. We did, like other anthropologists before us, make real efforts before arriving in Ecuador to be as well informed as possible about doctoring in the field. To this end we consulted with medical doctors with relevant experience for their guidance and help. Kempf, in fact, had genuine research interests in health, botanical, and medical issues, while my own interests in "doctoring" were nil. I neither liked doctors very much (out of my personal fear and terror of them) nor did I feel especially comfortable medically or ethically in the role of delivering health care services to anyone in the field. From a "political" perspective, however, giving something back to the people with whom we worked seemed to us a responsible act. For better or worse, we were resigned to "practice medicine" among the Awá because they requested it. To this end, we brought to the field a Merck manual, eventually a copy of the book *Donde no hay doctor*, lots of aspirin and antibiotics, lots of vitamins (our standard placebo), and a full array of emergency pharmaceuticals and paraphernalia, ranging from thermometers to snake-bite kits. As with those proverbial boy scouts, we were prepared. For the record, our approach to medicine and "witch doctoring" in the field was simple: do as little as possible as infrequently as possible; be as conservative as possible; and never do anything that would cause harm. So much for our standards and credo.

With our guidelines in place, we proceeded as ethnographers and as witch doctors. In our "practice" we "treated" a full array of problems, ranging from headaches and stomachaches, colds, fevers, cuts, bruises, wounds, snakebites, skin rashes. We also took one woman to a hospital four travel days away and recommended that others make the same trip whenever we felt out of our depths medically, a fairly frequent occurrence.

Worms and Witchcraft

About a year into our fieldwork word came to Kempf and me that a woman named Rosa had been carried for five days on her husband Ishmael's back specifically to see us. She was very sick and, in fact, a number of people told us she was dying. According to our informants, all the traditional measures had already been taken – a number of *chutun* (shamanic curing) ceremonies had been held for her to rid her of chutun spirits (that is, the spirits that cause illness), and herbal remedies had been exhaustively tried, all to no avail. Up to this time those Awá who knew us best saw us as relatively powerful and effective "shamans" in their terms. The guarded use of antibiotics, aspirin, and other drugs had certainly enhanced our reputations. We were also "cheap." In fact, we charged nothing for our services, although people paid us anyway in the traditional way with the gift of plantains and carefully wrapped eggs. On these bases we were seen as Rosa's last realistic hope for survival, a last but slim hope at best.

At our house Rosa seemed to be in really dire shape. We unceremoniously gave her some milk and soup but she hardly ate anything. Tension was high and it was quickly decided that Rosa, who was frightened, should be moved to her son-in-law's house and that we would visit later with some medicines. When we arrived a little later in the day, Rosa was lying on the floor of the house whimpering. She had already vomited the little food we had given to her earlier.

Her husband Ishmael also told us that the chutun ceremonies held for her had failed to cure her and that a sorcerer or witch (*brujo*) was killing her through witchcraft. Some time back, Ishmael said, he was walking in the forest and came across a distant neighbor. The man was aggressive (*bravo*) with him and so Ishmael responded in kind. Later, the man had a similar run-in with Rosa. In simple social terms, from his own perspective Ishmael had broken the standard code of etiquette and proper Awá behavior. He now believed that this man was a witch and that he was killing Rosa in revenge for Ishmael's lack of manners (see Ehrenreich 1985, 1990;

and Kempf 1985 for further details concerning witchcraft among the Awá).

Rosa was now both sick and extremely frightened. Because the food we gave her had caused her to vomit, she was not feeling much trust towards us, and our presence was disquieting to her. Her fear and trembling were of real concern to us. We believed that, from our etic perspective, we could help her. From what we had observed and learned in our conversation with Ishmael, we believed that, whatever else was wrong, Rosa had a severe case of parasitic infection (probably round-worms) and that her loss of appetite was causing her steadily to starve herself to death. Notably, such illness was pervasive throughout the Awá population with whom we worked. In addition, her panic about being bewitched was compounding the situation. The notion that her death was impending, regardless of the supposed cause, was reinforced further by the fact that people had started to visit in order to say their last goodbyes to her. From this perspective the solution seemed clear to us – Rosa needed nutrition that she could hold down, medicines to purge the parasites from her body, and relief from the ordeal of being bewitched.

The solution, however, was complicated by the fact that, based on our interactions to that moment, Rosa did not believe we were shamans powerful enough to help her. Nor, for that matter, had we ever stepped out of the bounds of administering medicine in any but a western fashion. So she scornfully begged off our help. Kempf and I conferred and decided that the only way to get Rosa to take the medicines and (the proverbial) chicken soup (the nutrition we believed she needed) was to convince her that, in her terms, we really knew what we were doing. We needed to give the appearance of powerful shamans. We came to believe that we had to treat Rosa's worms, her starvation, and her beliefs and fears of witchcraft.

Wild Incantations and Chicken Soup

Kempf and I decided to ritualize our curing techniques in the hope that Rosa might be more cooperative and trusting. And thus, the show commenced. I thought some strange incantations might help us accomplish our goals, so I began to sing Hebrew prayers I remembered from my childhood. As I prepared chicken soup, the traditional cure-all of Jewish folklore, I sang: "*Baruch atah Adonai Eloheinu melech ha-olam, borei paree ha gafen.*" This, for those who are not familiar with Hebrew ritual, is the traditional blessing said over wine, not chicken soup.

In order to induce Rosa to eat, I sang another prayer recalled from my youth: "*Ma nishtanah halailah hazeh, mikol halailot; sheb'chol halailot anu ochlin, chametz u'matzah, halailah hazeh, kulo matzah....*" This passage is the first of the four questions asked at the Passover Seder before eating the ritual meal.

Kempf, herself a *shiksa*, made three tiny wooden crosses and placed them around the patient. In the days to follow she would burn the crosses, which had become receptacles for the evil causing illness, in order to symbolize the removal of Rosa's bewitchment. Kempf also set up a minialtar with the queen of hearts card as the centerpiece. The altar was placed in Rosa's line of vision. Kempf rubbed the card over Rosa's stomach as she comforted her in her pain.

For days we performed these mini-rites aimed at getting food and medicine into our reluctant patient. We were simultaneously concerned with saving Rosa's life and worried about any consequences of possible failure. Though not motivated by it, we were also conscious of the fact that our reputations as shamans and our position among the Awá would be considerably enhanced if we were successful.

There were certainly ironies in all this. As anthropologists among the Awá, we conjured up our own shunned heritages in order to succeed as witch doctors in the field. The religious training we had endured and rejected as children had turned out to be useful after all. The emptiness we had perceived in our own traditions did not prevent us from grasping the significance of ritualizing our secular cure in order to make it work. In a sense, the one fraud for me (western religion) became the foundation upon which our own

fraud had been constructed. To my mind, the chicken soup cure was duplicitous, and it left me feeling forever compromised.

Conclusions: "Witch Doctoring," Ethics, and Anthropology

What is it that is still so troubling to me? After all, the patient recovered. She believed she was fully cured of both the physical symptoms and the witchcraft which had brought her to the brink of death. She was even grudgingly grateful to Kempf and me for having saved her life. From a medical perspective we had done no harm and had undoubtedly saved a life. What harm, then, had been done?

From the moment we decided to put on a show for Rosa, we crossed what I believe to be a critically significant line in our activities as doctors in the field. Until then we had practiced medicine with the informed consent of our patients. They knew our limitations and no deception of any kind had occurred (notwithstanding the broader question of the right of any medically uncredentialed anthropologist to practice medicine in the field). But now we had manipulated the situation through a calculated sham in order to get an Awá patient to accept on false premises what we "knew" or thought to be the solution to her medical/spiritual problems. As all such rationalizations suggest, we had "done it for her own good." As philosopher Sissela Bok has suggested, "The paternalistic assumption of superiority to patients ... carries great dangers for physicians [and presumably witch doctors] themselves – it risks turning to contempt" (1978: 227).

The rationale that we saved a life is, of course, very powerful. Yet, how is this reasoning different from what fanatical missionaries claim for their enterprises? The evangelical who believes that only by the act of the conscious embrace of Jesus can the human soul be "saved," is, from this assumption, operating ethically for the obvious good of others when engaged in any acts of proselytizing. The reasoning offered by some missionaries that causing the death of indigenous tribal people via the introduction of disease in the material world is an acceptable price to pay if just one soul (convert) is "saved" is not essentially different from the argument that medically saving a life justifies paternalistic intervention accomplished via deceit. Such reasoning rests on assumptions of power and superiority veiled in self-conceit and arrogance. Notably, anthropologists, including myself, have argued vehemently against this kind of "the-end-justifies-the-means" ethics employed by missionaries, government officials, and even applied anthropologists. It is interesting that shortly after Ishmael and a cured Rosa left for home, an Awá man who had previously been disdainful of our presence in the area sent us a significant offering of food in order to stay in our favor. The message of our asserted "power" during the course of treating Rosa was surely not lost on him.

The case of the chicken soup cure was immediately understood and felt by me to be a major "transcendental" event of my fieldwork. Although I would act no differently if I had it to do again, my personal sense of compromise remains for me a particularly heavy personal burden. As in the case of a pacifist who is situationally forced to take a life for some greater good (for example, to save an innocent child's life or in self-defense), the justification itself does not ameliorate the impact on the principle now shattered, nor does it relieve the contradictions now created. It is not a question of guilt (personal or cultural) or a doubt about whether I was right to do what I did. When confronted with a situation in which I could either save a life or not act at all, I chose to act without hesitation, even as I was required to engage in a self-defined sham that violated my personal and professional code of ethics. My personal sense of humanity overrode my sense of professional purity and responsibility. However, I will always feel the loss of this ethical ideal which had always informed my work as an anthropologist. None of the reasoning offered from students and friends to whom I have told this story over the years has allowed me to differentiate my actions from those of other intruders – missionaries, government officials and politicians, land developers, colonists – who believe that they know what is best for members of other cultures such as the Awá, and that they therefore have the right to

act out of their own convictions. For all intents and purposes, I must admit that my actions finally were, no matter how justified, rationalized or humane, just like theirs. I must therefore reluctantly extend to them my understanding, if not my approval. I have also come to see – painful though the insight may be – that I am more like them than I would ever care to be.

In the summer of 1989, when I visited the Awá after a decade's absence, there was great disappointment that this time I had come with no medicines for them. Perhaps, in their terms, they believed that I had lost my medical or shamanic power through the years. In my terms, perhaps they were right.

NOTE

Acknowledgments The fieldwork for this article was supported by research grants from the Center for the Study of Man, Smithsonian Institution (1977–78) and the Instituto Otavaleño de Antropologia (1977–78). My thinking on the events described here was first stimulated during an NEH Research Seminar in which I participated, held at Cornell University in the summer of 1988, and directed by Sander L. Gilman. An earlier version of this work was then presented at the 89th American Anthropological Association Meetings, held in New Orleans, 1990, in a symposium entitled "The Anthropologist as Healer: Ethical Dilemmas of 'Witchdoctoring' Among the Indigenous Peoples of South America," which I organized. I want to thank Samual Stanley, Hernon Crespo-Toral, Plutarco Cisneros A., Judith Kempf, and Janet Chernela for their roles in my work with the Awá.

REFERENCES

Bok, Sissela
    1978 *Lying: Moral choice in public and private life*. New York: Vintage Books (Random House).
Deloria, Vine, Jr.
    1969 *Custer died for your sins: An Indian manifesto*. New York: The Macmillan Company.
Ehrenreich, Jeffrey David
    1985 Isolation, retreat, and secrecy: Dissembling behavior among the Coaiquer

Indians of Ecuador. In *Political anthropology in Ecuador: Perspectives from indigenous cultures*, ed. Jeffrey Ehrenreich. Albany NY: The Center for the Caribbean and Latin America of the State University of New York and the Society for Latin American Anthropology.

Ehrenreich, Jeffrey David
1990 Shame, witchcraft, and social control: The case of an Awá-Coaiquer interloper. *Cultural Anthropology* 5(3): 338–345.

Howell, Nancy
1990 *Surviving fieldwork: A report of the Advisory Panel on Health and Safety in Fieldwork, American Anthropological Association*. Special Publication of the American Anthropological Association, No. 26. Washington DC: American Anthropological Association.

Kempf, Judith
1985 The politics of curing among the Coaiquer Indians. In *Political anthropology in Ecuador: Perspectives from indigenous cultures*, ed. Jeffrey Ehrenreich. Albany NY: The Center for the Caribbean and Latin America of the State University of New York and the Society for Latin American Anthropology.

23

Code of Ethics (2009)

American Anthropological Association

I. Preamble

Anthropological researchers, teachers and practitioners are members of many different communities, each with its own moral rules or codes of ethics. Anthropologists have moral obligations as members of other groups, such as the family, religion, and community, as well as the profession. They also have obligations to the scholarly discipline, to the wider society and culture, and to the human species, other species, and the environment. Furthermore, fieldworkers may develop close relationships with persons or animals with whom they work, generating an additional level of ethical considerations.

In a field of such complex involvements and obligations, it is inevitable that misunderstandings, conflicts, and the need to make choices among apparently incompatible values will arise. Anthropologists are responsible for grappling with such difficulties and struggling to resolve them in ways compatible with the principles stated here. The purpose of this Code is to foster discussion and education. The American Anthropological Association (AAA) does not adjudicate claims for unethical behavior.

The principles and guidelines in this Code provide the anthropologist with tools to engage in developing and maintaining an ethical framework for all anthropological work.

II. Introduction

Anthropology is a multidisciplinary field of science and scholarship, which includes the study of all aspects of humankind – archaeological, biological, linguistic and sociocultural. Anthropology has roots in the natural and social sciences and in the humanities, ranging in approach from basic to applied research and to scholarly interpretation.

As the principal organization representing the breadth of anthropology, the American

Ethnographic Fieldwork: An Anthropological Reader, Second Edition. Edited by Antonius C. G. M. Robben and Jeffrey A. Sluka.
Editorial material and organization © 2012 John Wiley & Sons, Inc.
Published 2012 by John Wiley & Sons, Inc.

Anthropological Association (AAA) starts from the position that generating and appropriately utilizing knowledge (i.e., publishing, teaching, developing programs, and informing policy) of the peoples of the world, past and present, is a worthy goal; that the generation of anthropological knowledge is a dynamic process using many different and ever-evolving approaches; and that for moral and practical reasons, the generation and utilization of knowledge should be achieved in an ethical manner.

The mission of American Anthropological Association is to advance all aspects of anthropological research and to foster dissemination of anthropological knowledge through publications, teaching, public education, and application. An important part of that mission is to help educate AAA members about ethical obligations and challenges involved in the generation, dissemination, and utilization of anthropological knowledge.

The purpose of this Code is to provide AAA members and other interested persons with guidelines for making ethical choices in the conduct of their anthropological work. Because anthropologists can find themselves in complex situations and subject to more than one code of ethics, the AAA Code of Ethics provides a framework, not an ironclad formula, for making decisions. Persons using the Code as a guideline for making ethical choices or for teaching are encouraged to seek out illustrative examples and appropriate case studies to enrich their knowledge base.

Anthropologists have a duty to be informed about ethical codes relating to their work, and ought periodically to receive training on current research activities and ethical issues. In addition, departments offering anthropology degrees should include and require ethical training in their curriculums.

No code or set of guidelines can anticipate unique circumstances or direct actions in specific situations. The individual anthropologist must be willing to make carefully considered ethical choices and be prepared to make clear the assumptions, facts and issues on which those choices are based. These guidelines therefore address *general* contexts, priorities and relationships which should be considered in ethical decision making in anthropological work.

III. Research

In both proposing and carrying out research, anthropological researchers must be open about the purpose(s), potential impacts, and source(s) of support for research projects with funders, colleagues, persons studied or providing information, and with relevant parties affected by the research. Researchers must expect to utilize the results of their work in an appropriate fashion and disseminate the results through appropriate and timely activities. Research fulfilling these expectations is ethical, regardless of the source of funding (public or private) or purpose (i.e., "applied," "basic," "pure," or "proprietary").

Anthropological researchers should be alert to the danger of compromising anthropological ethics as a condition to engage in research, yet also be alert to proper demands of good citizenship or host-guest relations. Active contribution and leadership in seeking to shape public or private sector actions and policies may be as ethically justifiable as inaction, detachment, or noncooperation, depending on circumstances. Similar principles hold for anthropological researchers employed or otherwise affiliated with nonanthropological institutions, public institutions, or private enterprises.

A. Responsibility to people and animals with whom anthropological researchers work and whose lives and cultures they study

1. Anthropological researchers have primary ethical obligations to the people, species, and materials they study and to the people with whom they work. These obligations can supersede the goal of seeking new knowledge, and can lead to decisions not to undertake or to discontinue a research project when the primary obligation conflicts with other responsibilities, such as those owed to sponsors or clients. These ethical obligations include:

- To avoid harm or wrong, understanding that the development of knowledge can lead to change which may be positive or negative for the people or animals worked with or studied

- To respect the well-being of humans and nonhuman primates
- To work for the long-term conservation of the archaeological, fossil, and historical records
- To consult actively with the affected individuals or group(s), with the goal of establishing a working relationship that can be beneficial to all parties involved

2. In conducting and publishing their research, or otherwise disseminating their research results, anthropological researchers must ensure that they do not harm the safety, dignity, or privacy of the people with whom they work, conduct research, or perform other professional activities, or who might reasonably be thought to be affected by their research. Anthropological researchers working with animals must do everything in their power to ensure that the research does not harm the safety, psychological well-being or survival of the animals or species with which they work.

3. Anthropological researchers must determine in advance whether their hosts/providers of information wish to remain anonymous or receive recognition, and make every effort to comply with those wishes. Researchers must present to their research participants the possible impacts of the choices, and make clear that despite their best efforts, anonymity may be compromised or recognition fail to materialize.

4. Anthropological researchers should obtain in advance the informed consent of persons being studied, providing information, owning or controlling access to material being studied, or otherwise identified as having interests which might be impacted by the research. It is understood that the degree and breadth of informed consent required will depend on the nature of the project and may be affected by requirements of other codes, laws, and ethics of the country or community in which the research is pursued. Further, it is understood that the informed consent process is dynamic and continuous; the process should be initiated in the project design and continue through

implementation by way of dialogue and negotiation with those studied. Researchers are responsible for identifying and complying with the various informed consent codes, laws and regulations affecting their projects. Informed consent, for the purposes of this code, does not necessarily imply or require a particular written or signed form. It is the quality of the consent, not the format, that is relevant.

5. Anthropological researchers who have developed close and enduring relationships (i.e., covenantal relationships) with either individual persons providing information or with hosts must adhere to the obligations of openness and informed consent, while carefully and respectfully negotiating the limits of the relationship.

6. While anthropologists may gain personally from their work, they must not exploit individuals, groups, animals, or cultural or biological materials. They should recognize their debt to the societies in which they work and their obligation to reciprocate with people studied in appropriate ways.

B. Responsibility to scholarship and science

1. Anthropological researchers must expect to encounter ethical dilemmas at every stage of their work, and must make good-faith efforts to identify potential ethical claims and conflicts in advance when preparing proposals and as projects proceed. A section raising and responding to potential ethical issues should be part of every research proposal.

2. Anthropological researchers bear responsibility for the integrity and reputation of their discipline, of scholarship, and of science. Thus, anthropological researchers are subject to the general moral rules of scientific and scholarly conduct: they should not deceive or knowingly misrepresent (i.e., fabricate evidence, falsify, and plagiarize), or attempt to prevent reporting of misconduct, or obstruct the scientific/ scholarly research of others.

3. Anthropological researchers should do all they can to preserve opportunities for future fieldworkers to follow them to the field.

4. Anthropologists have a responsibility to be both honest and transparent with all stakeholders about the nature and intent of their research. They must not misrepresent their research goals, funding sources, activities, or findings. Anthropologists should never deceive the people they are studying regarding the sponsorship, goals, methods, products, or expected impacts of their work. Deliberately misrepresenting one's research goals and impact to research subjects is a clear violation of research ethics, as is conducting clandestine research.

5. Anthropological researchers should utilize the results of their work in an appropriate fashion, and whenever possible disseminate their findings to the scientific and scholarly community.

6. Anthropological researchers should seriously consider all reasonable requests for access to their data and other research materials for purposes of research. They should also make every effort to insure preservation of their fieldwork data for use by posterity.

C. Responsibility to the public

1. Anthropological researchers should make the results of their research appropriately available to sponsors, students, decision makers, and other nonanthropologists. In so doing, they must be truthful; they are not only responsible for the factual content of their statements but also must consider carefully the social and political implications of the information they disseminate. They must do everything in their power to insure that such information is well understood, properly contextualized, and responsibly utilized. They should make clear the empirical bases upon which their reports stand, be candid about their qualifications and philosophical or political biases, and recognize and make clear the limits of anthropological expertise. At the same time, they must be alert to possible harm their information may cause people with whom they work or colleagues.

2. In relation with his or her own government, host governments, or sponsors of research, an anthropologist should be honest and candid. Anthropologists must not compromise their professional responsibilities and

ethics and should not agree to conditions which inappropriately change the purpose, focus or intended outcomes of their research.

3. Anthropologists may choose to move beyond disseminating research results to a position of advocacy. This is an individual decision, but not an ethical responsibility.

IV. Teaching

Responsibility to students and trainees

While adhering to ethical and legal codes governing relations between teachers/mentors and students/trainees at their educational institutions or as members of wider organizations, anthropological teachers should be particularly sensitive to the ways such codes apply in their discipline (for example, when teaching involves close contact with students/trainees in field situations). Among the widely recognized precepts which anthropological teachers, like other teachers/mentors, should follow are:

1. Teachers/mentors should conduct their programs in ways that preclude discrimination on the basis of sex, marital status, "race," social class, political convictions, disability, religion, ethnic background, national origin, sexual orientation, age, or other criteria irrelevant to academic performance.

2. Teachers'/mentors' duties include continually striving to improve their teaching/training techniques; being available and responsive to student/trainee interests; counseling students/trainees realistically regarding career opportunities; conscientiously supervising, encouraging, and supporting students'/trainees' studies; being fair, prompt, and reliable in communicating evaluations; assisting students/trainees in securing research support; and helping students/trainees when they seek professional placement.

3. Teachers/mentors should impress upon students/trainees the ethical challenges involved in every phase of anthropological work; encourage them to reflect upon this and other codes; encourage dialogue with colleagues on

ethical issues; and discourage participation in ethically questionable projects.

4. Teachers/mentors should publicly acknowledge student/trainee assistance in research and preparation of their work; give appropriate credit for coauthorship to students/trainees; encourage publication of worthy student/trainee papers; and compensate students/trainees justly for their participation in all professional activities.

5. Teachers/mentors should beware of the exploitation and serious conflicts of interest which may result if they engage in sexual relations with students/trainees. They must avoid sexual liaisons with students/trainees for whose education and professional training they are in any way responsible.

V. Application

1. The same ethical guidelines apply to all anthropological work. That is, in both proposing and carrying out research, anthropologists must be open with funders, colleagues, persons studied or providing information, and relevant parties affected by the work about the purpose(s), potential impacts, and source(s) of support for the work. Applied anthropologists must intend and expect to utilize the results of their work appropriately (i.e., publication, teaching, program and policy development) within a reasonable time. In situations in which anthropological knowledge is applied, anthropologists bear the same responsibility to be open and candid about their skills and intentions, and monitor the effects of their work on all persons affected. Anthropologists may be involved in many types of work, frequently affecting individuals and groups with diverse and sometimes conflicting interests. The individual anthropologist must make carefully considered ethical choices and be prepared to make clear the assumptions, facts and issues on which those choices are based.

2. In all dealings with employers, persons hired to pursue anthropological research or apply anthropological knowledge should be honest about their qualifications, capabilities, and aims. Prior to making any professional commitments, they must review the purposes of prospective employers, taking into consideration the employer's past activities and future goals. In working for governmental agencies or private businesses, they should be especially careful not to promise or imply acceptance of conditions contrary to professional ethics or competing commitments.

3. Applied anthropologists, as any anthropologist, should be alert to the danger of compromising anthropological ethics as a condition for engaging in research or practice. They should also be alert to proper demands of hospitality, good citizenship and guest status. Proactive contribution and leadership in shaping public or private sector actions and policies may be as ethically justifiable as inaction, detachment, or noncooperation, depending on circumstances.

VI. Dissemination of Results

1. The results of anthropological research are complex, subject to multiple interpretations and susceptible to differing and unintended uses. Anthropologists have an ethical obligation to consider the potential impact of both their research and the communication or dissemination of the results of their research on all directly or indirectly involved.

2. Anthropologists should not withhold research results from research participants when those results are shared with others. There are specific and limited circumstances however, where disclosure restrictions are appropriate and ethical, particularly where those restrictions serve to protect the safety, dignity or privacy of participants, protect cultural heritage or tangible or intangible cultural or intellectual property.

3. Anthropologists must weigh the intended and potential uses of their work and the impact of its distribution in determining whether limited availability of results is warranted and ethical in any given instance.

VII.   Epilogue

Anthropological research, teaching, and application, like any human actions, pose choices for which anthropologists individually and collectively bear ethical responsibility. Since anthropologists are members of a variety of groups and subject to a variety of ethical codes, choices must sometimes be made not only between the varied obligations presented in this code but also between those of this code and those incurred in other statuses or roles. This statement does not dictate choice or propose sanctions. Rather, it is designed to promote discussion and provide general guidelines for ethically responsible decisions.

VIII.   Acknowledgments

This Code was drafted by the Commission to Review the AAA Statements on Ethics during the period January 1995-March 1997. The Commission members were James Peacock (Chair), Carolyn Fluehr-Lobban, Barbara Frankel, Kathleen Gibson, Janet Levy, and Murray Wax. In addition, the following individuals participated in the Commission meetings: philosopher Bernard Gert, anthropologists Cathleen Crain, Shirley Fiske, David Freyer, Felix Moos, Yolanda Moses, and Niel Tashima; and members of the American Sociological Association Committee on Ethics. Open hearings on the Code were held at the 1995 and 1996 annual meetings of the American Anthropological Association. The Commission solicited comments from all AAA Sections. The first draft of the AAA Code of Ethics was discussed at the May 1995 AAA Section Assembly meeting; the second draft was briefly discussed at the November 1996 meeting of the AAA Section Assembly.

The Final Report of the Commission was published in the September 1995 edition of the *Anthropology Newsletter* and on the AAA web site (http://www.aaanet.org). Drafts of the Code were published in the April 1996 and 1996 annual meeting edition of the *Anthropology Newsletter* and the AAA web site, and comments were solicited from the membership. The Commission considered all comments from the membership in formulating the final draft in February 1997. The Commission gratefully acknowledges the use of some language from the codes of ethics of the National Association for the Practice of Anthropology and the Society for American Archaeology.

Subsequent revisions to this Code were initiated by the passing of a resolution, offered by Terry Turner at the AAA Business Meeting held in November of 2007, directing the AAA Executive Board to restore certain sections of the 1971 version of the Code of Ethics. A related motion, introduced by John Kelly, directed the Executive Board to report to the membership a justification of its reasoning if a decision was made to not restore, in total, the language proposed in the Turner motion.

On January 20, 2008, the Executive Board tasked the Committee on Ethics, whose membership included Dena Plemmons (acting chair), Alec Barker, Katherine MacKinnon, Dhooleka Raj, K. Sivaramakrishnan and Steve Striffler, with drafting a revised ethics code that "incorporates the principles of the Turner motion while stipulating principles that identify when the ethical conduct of anthropology does and does not require specific forms of the circulation of knowledge." Six individuals (Jeffrey Altshul, Agustin Fuentes, Merrill Singer, David Price, Inga Treitler and Niel Tashima) were invited to advise the Committee in its deliberations.

On June 16, 2008, the Committee on Ethics issued its report to a newly formed subcommittee of the Executive Board created to deal with potential code revisions. The subcommittee (consisting of TJ Ferguson, Monica Heller, Tom Leatherman, Setha Low, Deborah Nichols, Gwen Mikell and Ed Liebow) examined the Committee on Ethics report and solicited the input of the Committee on Ethics; the Commission of the Engagement of Anthropology with the US Security and Intelligence Communities; the Committee on Practicing, Applied and Public Interest Anthropology; and the Network of Concerned Anthropologists, asking these groups to advise before making its own recommendations to the larger Executive Board. After examining the input of these groups, the EB subcommittee forwarded its recommendations to the entire Executive Board August 8.

Subsequent to these activities, AAA President Setha Low reached out to a number of stakeholders to solicit their input. On September 19, 2008, the Executive Board approved a final version of the Code of the Ethics.

Part VII

Multi-Sited Fieldwork

Introduction

Antonius C. G. M. Robben

Long-term, face-to-face, holistic ethnographic fieldwork on an island or in a small community has been the hallmark of anthropology, the model for graduate training, and the standard by which professional careers are still measured. This is not to say that anthropologists like Boas and Malinowski or Powdermaker and Mead were not aware that the people they studied were connected to their surrounding world through trade, travel, and power, but they were more interested in local than in translocal cultures and connections. This research focus was in part epistemological, in part methodological, and in part a reflection of the times. Prolonged fieldwork was to enhance the scientific rigor and improve the empirical basis of anthropology, a discipline that was struggling to become accepted in the academy during the early twentieth century. The world also looked different from how it does today. Certainly, people did not live in the splendid isolation which the early ethnographies seemed to suggest – a view that was thoroughly debunked by Eric Wolf (1982) in his anthropological world history – but travel, communication, and commerce did not yet have the vertiginous pace and transience of the late twentieth century which therefore became so conducive to multi-sited fieldwork.

Multi-sited fieldwork is not the same as fieldwork at multiple sites. The history of ethnographic fieldwork contains several examples of comparative research projects, such as Margaret Mead's (1935) study in three tribal cultures, and Robert Redfield's analysis (1941) of a rural–urban continuum in Mexico, but these comparative projects departed still from a bounded research universe, whether a region or a theme. Instead, translocal ethnographers go where their research takes them to create an emergent field and study object. The emphasis is on multiple connections rather

Ethnographic Fieldwork: An Anthropological Reader, Second Edition. Edited by
Antonius C. G. M. Robben and Jeffrey A. Sluka.
Editorial material and organization © 2012 John Wiley & Sons, Inc.
Published 2012 by John Wiley & Sons, Inc.

than multiple sites. As George Marcus has stated in an influential programmatic review article: "Multi-sited research is designed around chains, paths, threads, conjunctions, or juxtapositions of locations in which the ethnographer establishes some form of literal, physical presence, with an explicit, posited logic of association or connection among sites that in fact defines the argument of the ethnography" (1995:105). Marcus identifies seven modes or practices of constructing multi-sited ethnographies – namely, by following the paths and movements of people (e.g., foreign correspondents hopping from crisis to crisis), things (e.g., worldwide commodity flows or music styles), metaphors (e.g., the proliferation of discourse about the immune system from medicine to other domains), narratives (e.g., the spreading of myths and stories), biographies (e.g., life histories as journeys through social and spatial contexts), and conflicts (e.g., the transnational wanderings of refugees). Finally, Marcus identifies a type of multi-sited ethnography which focuses on a strategically situated (single-site) research object which unfolds an emerging world (e.g., the ongoing conversations about factory work among working-class boys at school). The selected contributions by David Edwards, Ulf Hannerz, and the Matsutake Worlds Research Group are exemplary multi-sited ethnographies situated around conflicts, people, and goods, but we begin with an important conceptual critique of traditional single-sited ethnographies by Akhil Gupta and James Ferguson.

In "Beyond 'Culture': Space, Identity, and the Politics of Difference," Gupta and Ferguson (1992) criticize the common presupposition that space, location, culture, society, and collective identity come together within one circumscribed complex, and that cultural difference implies the existence of identifiable boundaries, breaks, divisions, and discontinuities (see also Gupta and Ferguson 1997). This basic assumption raises questions about cultural differentiation within such allegedly bounded complexes, about the hybrid cultures of postcolonial societies, about the identity of groups of people (refugees, migrant workers, businessmen) who frequently cross borders, and about sociocultural change, power relations, and the construction of difference in border zones. These issues have become particularly pertinent since globalization processes accelerated after the fall of the Berlin Wall in 1989, ending the Warsaw Pact and ushering in the disintegration of the Soviet Union. People, products, and information crossed borders and flowed unimpeded throughout the world in the 1990s, only to be slowed down and increasingly monitored by states and world powers in the 2000s because of the so-called global war on terror that began after New York and Washington were struck by terrorist attacks on September 11, 2001. How are such geopolitical developments redrawing erased borders, interrupting communication networks in what Appadurai (2006:29) has called a "crisis of circulation," and reterritorializing the world? What are the implications for traditional ethnographic interests ranging from tribal societies to inner-city barrios? If borderlands do not only exist at the perimeter of states but are wreathed through and across countries, then who are its inhabitants, how do they give content and form to their hybridized identities, and what distinguishes them, if at all, from the rest of society?

Gupta and Ferguson advocate a fundamental rethinking of the spatialization of culture through the notion of cultural difference. Cultural difference presupposes a dichotomy between "us" and "them" which quickly evolves into "here" and "there," even when our sympathies lie with "the Other" living "elsewhere." Instead, anthropologists should examine the processes that produce or resurrect such differentiations in the first place, and be sensitive to the many interconnections, bridges, crossings, and shared spaces and histories that effectively undermine these dichotomies. In fact, so argue Gupta and Ferguson, borderlands are more representative of the globalized post-Cold War reality than stable, bounded states and communities. In many ways, we are all transworld transients without the stable identities we imagine to possess (see also Lovell 1998). We participate in assemblages of scapes or multiple grids that intersect at unexpected locations, with unexpected persons, and in unanticipated power fields. The challenge to ethnographic fieldwork is then how to account adequately for the numerous interconnections that fan out across the world from hitherto more easily bounded research sites. Multi-sited ethnography is presented as the answer.

In "Afghanistan, Ethnography, and the New World Order" (1994), David B. Edwards reveals the haphazard ways in which such multi-locale ethnographies become constituted. Anthropologists have always used a networking method for fieldwork in complex societies. This approach forced Edwards to follow his research participants around the world and into the virtual spaces of the internet. During the 1980s, he had set out to study an isolated mountain village in south-central Afghanistan, as so many anthropologists had done for decades all over the world, but he and the community became wrapped up in the liberation war of the *mujahidin* guerrilla forces against Afghanistan's communist government, the Afghan army, and Soviet troops. Edwards's emotional and professional involvement with the mountain villagers took him to locations in Afghanistan where the *mujahidin* were fighting, to the city of Peshawar and several refugee camps in Pakistan, to a heterogeneous group of refugees in Washington DC, and into two Afghan internet news groups.

Edwards grapples with the question of how to construct an ethnographic narrative that reflects the translocal qualities and reciprocal influences of these diverse field sites, and how to do justice to their intuitive connections and his in situ experiences. He is not looking for some overarching analytical structure or master narrative, even though that is generally regarded as what distinguishes anthropology from journalism, but he tries to find a style of ethnographic writing more congenial to his diverse research sites. The anonymous Afghan who posts a message on an electronic bulletin board seems to contrast sharply with the guerrilla commander visiting Washington, but are they really so different? Does Edwards know more about this *mujahid* than about the person who writes from a university-based email address in Europe? They are both political players out of place acting in foreign settings, yet connected and motivated by a deep attachment to Afghanistan. Edwards hopes to retain some of the vicissitudes and happenstance of a globalized reality by juxtaposing his heterogeneous fieldwork experiences rather randomly. His ethnography would have been different if he had been to other sites and encountered other players, but he still remains convinced that this and other translocal renditions would capture similar connections – connections unseen in single-sited fieldwork.

Ulf Hannerz illustrates, in "Being There … and There … and There! Reflections on Multi-Site Ethnography" (2003), the differences between single-sited and multi-sited fieldwork through his research about foreign correspondents, both the familiar faces on the evening news reporting from their permanent station in Moscow, Jerusalem, or Paris, and those roving reporters who show up near a natural disaster and reappear only days later at the edge of a mass grave or makeshift refugee camp (see also Hannerz 2004). After carrying out some preliminary research in New York, Hannerz decides upon Tokyo, Jerusalem, and Johannesburg as his principal sites, while realizing that he could equally well have chosen other places. Hannerz points out that this research perspective would better be labeled translocal than multi-sited, because it is not the different localities themselves but their interconnections that matter most.

Hannerz focuses on the national and international networks of foreign correspondents with local troubleshooters, who arrange cars, food, shelter, cameramen, and willing interviewees, and with translocal editors, bureau chiefs, and fellow-correspondents whom they meet at airports, offices, and television studios. He also pays attention to the collaboration between news agencies, and studies the career paths of reporters. Social networks and life histories are tried research instruments that continue to be important for multi-sited fieldwork, but they rely much less on face-to-face contacts, while the involvement in activity fields and social domains is much more diffuse than in single-sited research. Appadurai (1996) has used the term "scapes" to describe unique spheres of circulation (such as financescapes, mediascapes, and ethnoscapes) that resemble a collection of Venn diagrams. It is typical of such translocal scapes that the community of foreign correspondents cannot be grasped ethnographically and holistically as is common in single-sited fieldwork. Fleeting relations, short research periods, and a patchwork of field sites yield different outcomes in different configurations. This partiality is less worrisome than it seems, so argues Hannerz, because the constant flux of people, things, and ideas in our globalized world does, by itself, give rise to constantly changing hybrid realities instead of the apparent regularities and structures of more stable societies examined by early generations of anthropologists. Hannerz's conclusion that "ethnography is an art of the possible" (2003:213) is as much true for single-sited, traditional fieldwork as for multi-sited research, with the difference that translocal research topics are harder to pin down because of a greater variation in methods, informants, and locations.

The next logical step of multi-sited fieldwork has been taken by the Matsutake Worlds Research Group (2009), which consists of six anthropologists who examine the economic, political, global, botanical, and symbolic dimensions of the matsutake mushroom at multiple international locations. The demanding article, "A New Form of Collaboration in Cultural Anthropology: Matsutake Worlds," is a hybrid text that expresses the group's conscious avoidance of a shared theoretical perspective, a clear division of labor, and well-integrated outcomes – unlike research teams in the natural sciences or the multi-sited comparative anthropological projects of the 1950s and 1960s, in which a group of fieldworkers worked under the aegis and guidance of one or two senior scholars who set the research agenda and consolidated conclusions. This experiment in scientific collaboration hopes, according to the authors Tsing and Inoue, to maximize their diverse expertise while maintaining the unique interpretive perspective or empirical interests of each contributor. This research collaboration has four characteristics:

1 Research analyses are not integrated in a coherent synthesized whole but are dialectic and dialogic.

2 Research outcomes are multivocal but nevertheless encourage collaborators to rethink the basic assumptions of their disciplines and specializations.
3 The fieldwork is multi-sited and focuses on the connections that enable the flow of a particular commodity across localities.
4 A research design is not imposed on the research subject, but the subject informs and dynamically reshapes the design.

Matsutake mushrooms are highly valued in Japan because of their exquisite aroma. They are very expensive because of the small yields and their usage for bribes and ritual gifts. The mushrooms cannot be cultivated, but grow only in the wild at the roots of red pine trees. The availability of Japanese matsutake mushrooms declined in the 1970s as a result of the displacement of red pine trees by broadleaf trees. New reserves came to be exploited throughout the northern hemisphere. The Matsutake Worlds Research Group is interested in how globalization produced the intertwinement of vernacular and scientific knowledge about matsutake mushrooms, and how the picking, commerce, and consumption were constituted locally and globally. This interdependence makes the research group regard the matsutake mushroom as a field collaborator that operates in human–nonhuman interactions through aroma and smell, mushroom growth and global warming, and scientific efforts to cultivate these wild mushrooms.

Choy and Satsuka, writing under the pseudonym Mogu Mogu, employ the symbiotic relation between red pines and dendritic fungi that yields the mushrooms as both a metaphor of and perspective about the matsutake sociocultural complex, with its transnational commodity flows, national markets and local foragers, regional habitats and global climate changes, and the interpenetration of vernacular and scientific knowledge. Lieba Faier describes how Japanese mushroom pickers and traders are aware of the contingencies of global warming and bug infestation. They draw upon scientific knowledge to explain the presence of weevils, and employ extended weather forecasts to assess annual yields. Michael Hathaway follows one of the global flows of matsutake mushrooms to mainland China, and analyzes how the different ecological explanations among Japanese, Chinese, and American scientists are influencing and are influenced by local knowledge and practices intending to increase mushroom yields. He shows how the Chinese matsutake boom is affecting land tenure and livelihood strategies in Yunnan Province, and how the forest management is faced with conflicting Japanese and American scholarly recommendations. This collage of different research strands about the matsutake mushroom is an experimental attempt to combine multi-sited fieldwork and multi-authored ethnographies without sacrificing the unique skills and insights of each collaborator.

Marcus (2009) regards the alliance between an anthropologist and local research participants as another promising multi-sited collaborative strategy beyond the hegemonic Malinowskian approach to fieldwork as an extended in situ examination of people's everyday lives in a culturally distinct place. This approach combines the counterpart's perspective – thus retaining Malinowski's native point of view – with the anthropologist's interpretation of the same research universe (see Marcus and Mascarenhas 2005).

Multi-sited fieldwork has great appeal because research topics are not bound to particular places, seasons, communities, or people (see Rheingold 1993; Burawoy et al. 2000; Falzon 2009). Interviews, impressions, text analysis, photography, video, and the internet are therefore becoming important research tools. Ethnographers can combine short visits to particular locations with telephone conversations, observations in public spaces, joint trips with research participants, and so on. This exploratory freedom away from Malinowski's canon of a four-season fieldwork in one place is also opening up new areas of anthropological research about internet sites, hyperlinks, web spheres, news groups, mediated relations, virtual communities, and mobile phones that no longer require the ethnographer's physical presence in a field turned online (Baym 2000, 2010; Hine 2000, 2005). Questions about the mediated interactions of field relations, the translocal nature of the research space, the conceptualization of the local perspectives of research subjects, and fieldwork ethics in open media use need to be addressed to situate such virtual fieldwork in multi-sited ethnography.

REFERENCES

Appadurai, Arjun
  1996   *Modernity at Large*. Minneapolis: University of Minnesota Press.
Appadurai, Arjun
  2006   *Fear of Small Numbers: An Essay on the Geography of Anger*. Durham, NC: Duke University Press.
Baym, Nancy K.
  2000   *Tune In, Log On: Soaps, Fandom, and Online Community*. Thousand Oaks, CA: Sage.
Baym, Nancy K.
  2010   *Personal Connections in the Digital Age*. Cambridge: Polity.
Burawoy, Michael, Joseph A. Blum, Sheba George, Zsuzsa Gille, and Millie Thayer, eds.,
  2000   *Global Ethnography: Forces, Connections, and Imaginations in a Postmodern World*. Berkeley: University of California Press.
Edwards, David B.
  1994   Afghanistan, Ethnography, and the New World Order. *Cultural Anthropology* 9(3):345–360.
Falzon, Mark-Anthony, ed.
  2009   *Multi-Sited Ethnography: Theory, Praxis and Locality in Contemporary Ethnography*. Farnham, UK: Ashgate.
Gupta, Akhil and James Ferguson
  1992   Beyond "Culture": Space, Identity, and the Politics of Difference. *Cultural Anthropology* 7(1):6–23.
Gupta, Akhil and James Ferguson, eds.
  1997   *Anthropological Locations: Boundaries and Grounds of a Field Science*. Berkeley: University of California Press.
Hannerz, Ulf
  2003   Being There … and There … and There! Reflections on Multi-Site Ethnography. *Ethnography* 4(2):201–216.
Hannerz, Ulf
  2004   *Foreign News: Exploring the World of Foreign Correspondents*. Chicago: University of Chicago Press.
Hine, Christine
  2000   *Virtual Ethnography*. London: Sage.

Hine, Christine, ed.
    2005   *Virtual Methods: Issues in Social Research on the Internet.* Oxford: Berg.
Lovell, Nadia, ed.
    1998   *Locality and Belonging.* London: Routledge.
Marcus, George E.
    1995   Ethnography in/of the World System: The Emergence of Multi-Sited Ethnography. *Annual Review of Anthropology* 24:95–117.
Marcus, George E.
    2009   Multi-Sited Ethnography: Notes and Queries. In: *Multi-Sited Ethnography: Theory, Praxis and Locality in Contemporary Ethnography.* Mark-Anthony Falzon, ed., pp. 181–196. Farnham, UK: Ashgate.
Marcus, George E. and Fernando Mascarenhas
    2005   *Ocasião: The Marquis and the Anthropologist, a Collaboration.* Walnut Creek, CA: AltaMira Press.
Matsutake Worlds Research Group
    2009   A New Form of Collaboration in Cultural Anthropology: Matsutake Worlds. *American Ethnologist* 36(2):380–403.
Mead, Margaret
    1935   *Sex and Temperament in Three Primitive Societies.* New York: W. Morrow & Company.
Redfield, Robert
    1941   *The Folk Culture of Yucatan.* Chicago: University of Chicago Press.
Rheingold, Howard
    1993   *The Virtual Community: Homesteading on the Electronic Frontier.* Reading, MA: Addison-Wesley.
Wolf, Eric R.
    1982   *Europe and the People Without History.* Berkeley: University of California Press.

24

Beyond "Culture": Space, Identity, and the Politics of Difference

Akhil Gupta and James Ferguson

For a subject whose central rite of passage is fieldwork, whose romance has rested on its exploration of the remote ("the *most* other of others" [Hannerz 1986:363]), whose critical function is seen to lie in its juxtaposition of radically different ways of being (located "elsewhere") with that of the anthropologists' own, usually Western, culture, there has been surprisingly little self-consciousness about the issue of space in anthropological theory. (Some notable exceptions are Appadurai [1986, 1988], Hannerz [1987], and Rosaldo [1988, 1989].) This collection of five ethnographic articles represents a modest attempt to deal with the issues of space and place, along with some necessarily related concerns such as those of location, displacement, community, and identity. In particular, we wish to explore how the renewed interest in theorizing space in postmodernist and feminist theory (Anzaldúa 1987; Baudrillard 1988; Deleuze and Guattari 1987; Foucault 1982; Jameson 1984; Kaplan 1987; Martin and Mohanty 1986) – embodied in such notions as surveillance, panopticism, simulacra, deterritorialization, postmodern hyperspace, borderlands, and marginality – forces us to reevaluate such central analytic concepts in anthropology as that of "culture" and, by extension, the idea of "cultural difference."

Representations of space in the social sciences are remarkably dependent on images of break, rupture, and disjunction. The distinctiveness of societies, nations, and cultures is based upon a seemingly unproblematic division of space, on the fact that they occupy "naturally" discontinuous spaces. The premise of discontinuity forms the starting point from which to theorize contact, conflict, and contradiction between cultures and societies. For example, the representation of the world as a collection of "countries," as in most world maps, sees it as an inherently fragmented space, divided by different colors into diverse

Ethnographic Fieldwork: An Anthropological Reader, Second Edition. Edited by Antonius C. G. M. Robben and Jeffrey A. Sluka.
Editorial material and organization © 2012 John Wiley & Sons, Inc.
Published 2012 by John Wiley & Sons, Inc.

national societies, each "rooted" in its proper place (cf. Malkki 1992). It is so taken for granted that each country embodies its own distinctive culture and society that the terms "society" and "culture" are routinely simply appended to the names of nation-states, as when a tourist visits India to understand "Indian culture" and "Indian society," or Thailand to experience "Thai culture," or the United States to get a whiff of "American culture."

Of course, the geographical territories that cultures and societies are believed to map onto do not have to be nations. We do, for example, have ideas about culture-areas that overlap several nation-states, or of multicultural nations. On a smaller scale, perhaps, are our disciplinary assumptions about the association of culturally unitary groups (tribes or peoples) with "their" territories: thus, "the Nuer" live in "Nuerland" and so forth. The clearest illustration of this kind of thinking are the classic "ethnographic maps" that purported to display the spatial distribution of peoples, tribes, and cultures. But in all these cases, space itself becomes a kind of neutral grid on which cultural difference, historical memory, and societal organization are inscribed. It is in this way that space functions as a central organizing principle in the social sciences at the same time that it disappears from analytical purview.

This assumed isomorphism of space, place, and culture results in some significant problems. First, there is the issue of those who inhabit the border, that "narrow strip along steep edges" (Anzaldúa 1987:3) of national boundaries. The fiction of cultures as discrete, object-like phenomena occupying discrete spaces becomes implausible for those who inhabit the borderlands. Related to border inhabitants are those who live a life of border crossings – migrant workers, nomads, and members of the transnational business and professional elite. What is "the culture" of farm workers who spend half a year in Mexico and half a year in the United States? Finally, there are those who cross borders more or less permanently – immigrants, refugees, exiles, and expatriates. In their case, the disjuncture of place and culture is especially clear: Khmer refugees in the United States take "Khmer culture" with them in the same complicated way

that Indian immigrants in England transport "Indian culture" to their new homeland.

A second set of problems raised by the implicit mapping of cultures onto places is to account for cultural differences *within* a locality. "Multiculturalism" is both a feeble acknowledgment of the fact that cultures have lost their moorings in definite places and an attempt to subsume this plurality of cultures within the framework of a national identity. Similarly, the idea of "subcultures" attempts to preserve the idea of distinct "cultures" while acknowledging the relation of different cultures to a dominant culture within the same geographical and territorial space. Conventional accounts of ethnicity, even when used to describe cultural differences in settings where people from different regions live side by side, rely on an unproblematic link between identity and place.[1] Although such concepts are suggestive because they endeavor to stretch the naturalized association of culture with place, they fail to interrogate this assumption in a truly fundamental manner. We need to ask how to deal with cultural difference while abandoning received ideas of (localized) culture.

Third, there is the important question of postcoloniality. To which places do the hybrid cultures of postcoloniality belong? Does the colonial encounter create a "new culture" in both the colonized and colonizing country, or does it destabilize the notion that nations and cultures are isomorphic? As discussed below, postcoloniality further problematizes the relationship between space and culture.

Last, and most important, challenging the ruptured landscape of independent nations and autonomous cultures raises the question of understanding social change and cultural transformation as situated within interconnected spaces. The presumption that spaces are autonomous has enabled the power of topography to conceal successfully the topography of power. The inherently fragmented space assumed in the definition of anthropology as the study of cultures (in the plural) may have been one of the reasons behind the long-standing failure to write anthropology's history as the biography of imperialism. For if one begins with the premise that spaces have *always* been hierarchically interconnected, instead of naturally disconnected, then cultural and social change becomes not a matter of cultural contact and articulation but one of rethinking difference *through* connection.

To illustrate, let us examine one powerful model of cultural change that attempts to relate dialectically the local to larger spatial arenas: articulation. Articulation models, whether they come from Marxist structuralism or from "moral economy," posit a primeval state of autonomy (usually labeled "precapitalist"), which is then violated by global capitalism. The result is that both local and larger spatial arenas are transformed, the local more than the global to be sure, but not necessarily in a predetermined direction. This notion of articulation allows one to explore the richly unintended consequences of, say, colonial capitalism, where loss occurs alongside invention. Yet, by taking a preexisting, localized "community" as a given starting point, it fails to examine sufficiently the processes (such as the structures of feeling that pervade the imagining of community) that go into the construction of space as place or locality in the first instance. In other words, instead of assuming the autonomy of the primeval community, we need to examine how it was formed *as a community* out of the interconnected space that always already existed. Colonialism, then, represents the displacement of one form of interconnection by another. This is not to deny that colonialism, or an expanding capitalism, does indeed have profoundly dislocating effects on existing societies. But by always foregrounding the spatial distribution of hierarchical power relations, we can better understand the process whereby a space achieves a distinctive *identity* as a place. Keeping in mind that notions of locality or community refer both to a demarcated physical space *and* to clusters of interaction, we can see that the identity of a place emerges by the intersection of its specific involvement in a system of hierarchically organized spaces with its cultural construction as a community or locality.

It is for this reason that what Jameson (1984) has dubbed "postmodern hyperspace" has so fundamentally challenged the convenient fiction that mapped cultures onto places and peoples. In the capitalist West, a Fordist regime of accumulation, emphasizing extremely large production facilities, a relatively stable work force, and the welfare state, combined to create urban "communities" whose outlines were most clearly visible in company towns (Davis 1984; Harvey 1989; Mandel 1975). The counterpart of this in the international arena was that multinational corporations, under the leadership of the United States, steadily exploited the raw materials, primary goods, and cheap labor of the independent nation-states of the postcolonial "Third World." Multilateral agencies and powerful Western states preached, and where necessary militarily enforced, the "laws" of the market to encourage the international flow of capital, while national immigration policies ensured that there would be no free (i.e., anarchic, disruptive) flow of labor to the high-wage islands in the capitalist core. Fordist patterns of accumulation have now been replaced by a regime of flexible accumulation – characterized by small-batch production, rapid shifts in product lines, extremely fast movements of capital to exploit the smallest differentials in labor and raw material costs – built on a more sophisticated communications and information network and better means of transporting goods and people. At the same time, the industrial production of culture, entertainment, and leisure that first achieved something approaching global distribution during the Fordist era led, paradoxically, to the invention of new forms of cultural difference and new forms of imagining community. Something like a transnational public sphere has certainly rendered any strictly bounded sense of community or locality obsolete. At the same time, it has enabled the creation of forms of solidarity and identity that do not rest on an appropriation of space where contiguity and face-to-face contact are paramount. In the pulverized space of postmodernity, space has not become irrelevant: it has been *reterritorialized* in a way that does not conform to the experience of space that characterized the era of high modernity. It is this that forces us to reconceptualize fundamentally the politics of community, solidarity, identity, and cultural difference.

Imagined Communities, Imagined Places

People have undoubtedly always been more mobile and identities less fixed than the static and typologizing approaches of classical anthropology would suggest. But today, the rapidly expanding and quickening mobility of people combines with the refusal of cultural products and practices to "stay put" to give a profound sense of a loss of territorial roots, of an erosion of the cultural distinctiveness of places, and of ferment in anthropological theory. The apparent deterritorialization of identity that accompanies such processes has made Clifford's question (1988:275) a key one for recent anthropological inquiry: "What does it mean, at the end of the twentieth century, to speak ... of a 'native land'? What processes rather than essences are involved in present experiences of cultural identity?"

Such questions are of course not wholly new, but issues of collective identity today do seem to take on a special character, when more and more of us live in what Said (1979:18) has called "a generalized condition of homelessness," a world where identities are increasingly coming to be, if not wholly deterritorialized, at least differently territorialized. Refugees, migrants, displaced and stateless peoples – these are perhaps the first to live out these realities in their most complete form, but the problem is more general. In a world of diaspora, transnational culture flows, and mass movements of populations, old-fashioned attempts to map the globe as a set of culture regions or homelands are bewildered by a dazzling array of postcolonial simulacra, doublings and redoublings, as India and Pakistan apparently reappear in postcolonial simulation in London, prerevolution Tehran rises from the ashes in Los Angeles, and a thousand similar cultural dreams are played out in urban and rural settings all across the globe. In this culture-play of diaspora, familiar lines between "here" and "there," center and periphery, colony and metropole become blurred.

Where "here" and "there" become blurred in this way, the cultural certainties and fixities of the metropole are upset as surely, if not in the same way, as those of the colonized periphery. In this sense, it is not only the displaced who experience a displacement (cf. Bhabha 1989:66). For even people remaining in familiar and ancestral places find the nature of their relation to place ineluctably changed, and the illusion of a natural and essential connection between the place and the culture broken. "Englishness," for instance, in contemporary, internationalized England is just as complicated and nearly as deterritorialized a notion as Palestinian-ness or Armenian-ness, since "England" ("the real England") refers less to a bounded place than to an imagined state of being or moral location. Consider, for instance, the following quote from a young white reggae fan in the ethnically chaotic neighborhood of Balsall Heath in Birmingham:

> there's no such thing as "England" any more ... welcome to India brothers! This is the Caribbean! ... Nigeria! ... There is no England, man. This is what is coming. Balsall Heath is the center of the melting pot, 'cos all I ever see when I go out is half-Arab, half-Pakistani, half-Jamaican, half-Scottish, half-Irish. I know 'cos I am [half Scottish/half Irish] ... who am I? ... Tell me who I belong to? They criticize me, the good old England. Alright, where do I belong? You know, I was brought up with blacks, Pakistanis, Africans, Asians, everything, you name it ... who do I belong to? ... I'm just a broad person. The earth is mine ... you know we was not born in Jamaica ... we was not born in "England." We were born here, man. It's our right. That's the way I see it. That's the way I deal with it. (Hebdige 1987:158–9)

The broad-minded acceptance of cosmopolitanism that seems to be implied here is perhaps more the exception than the rule, but there can be little doubt that the explosion of a culturally stable and unitary "England" into the cut-and-mix "here" of contemporary Balsall Heath is an example of a phenomenon that is real and spreading. It is clear that the erosion of such supposedly natural connections between peoples and places has not led to the modernist specter of global cultural homogenization (Clifford 1988). But "cultures" and "peoples," however persistent they may be, cease to be plausibly identifiable as spots on the map.

The irony of these times, however, is that as actual places and localities become ever more blurred and indeterminate, *ideas* of culturally and ethnically distinct places become perhaps even more salient. It is here that it becomes most visible how imagined communities (Anderson 1983) come to be attached to imagined places, as displaced peoples cluster around remembered or imagined homelands, places, or communities in a world that seems increasingly to deny such firm territorialized anchors in their actuality. The set of issues surrounding the construction of place and homeland by mobile and displaced people is addressed in different ways by a number of the articles in this issue.

Remembered places have often served as symbolic anchors of community for dispersed people. This has long been true of immigrants, who (as Leonard [1992] shows vividly) use memory of place to construct imaginatively their new lived world. "Homeland" in this way remains one of the most powerful unifying symbols for mobile and displaced peoples, though the relation to homeland may be very differently constructed in different settings (see Malkki 1992). Moreover, even in more completely deterritorialized times and settings – settings where "home" is not only distant, but also where the very notion of "home" as a durably fixed place is in doubt – aspects of our lives remain highly "localized" in a social sense, as Peters (1992) argues. We need to give up naive ideas of communities as literal entities (cf. Cohen 1985), but remain sensitive to the profound "bifocality" that characterizes locally lived lives in a globally interconnected world, and the powerful role of place in the "near view" of lived experience (Peters 1992).

The partial erosion of spatially bounded social worlds and the growing role of the imagination of places from a distance, however, themselves must be situated within the highly spatialized terms of a global capitalist economy. The special challenge here is to use a focus on the way space is imagined (but not *imaginary*!) as a way to explore the processes through which such conceptual processes of place making meet the changing global economic and political conditions of lived spaces – the relation, we could say, between place and space. As Ferguson (this issue) shows, important tensions may arise when places that have been imagined at a distance must become lived spaces. For places are always imagined in the context of political-economic determinations that have a logic of their own. Territoriality is thus reinscribed at just the point it threatens to be erased.

The idea that space is made meaningful is of course a familiar one to anthropologists; indeed, there is hardly an older or better established anthropological truth. East or West, inside or outside, left or right, mound or floodplain – from at least the time of Durkheim, anthropology has known that the experience of space is always socially constructed. The more urgent task, taken up by several articles in this issue, is to politicize this uncontestable observation. With meaning making understood as a practice, how are spatial meanings established? Who has the power to make places of spaces? Who contests this? What is at stake?

Such questions are particularly important where the meaningful association of places and peoples is concerned. As Malkki (1992) shows, two naturalisms must be challenged here. First is what we will call the ethnological habit of taking the association of a culturally unitary group (the "tribe" or "people") and "its" territory as natural, which is discussed in the previous section. A second, and closely related, naturalism is what we will call the national habit of taking the association of citizens of states and their territories as natural. Here the exemplary image is of the conventional world map of nation-states, through which school-children are taught such deceptively simple-sounding beliefs as that France is where the French live, America is where the Americans live, and so on. Even a casual observer, of course, knows that not only Americans live in America, and it is clear that the very question of what is a "real American" is largely up for grabs. But even anthropologists still talk of "American culture" with no clear understanding of what that means, because we assume a natural association of a culture ("American culture"), a people ("Americans"), and a place ("the United States of America"). Both the ethnological and the national naturalisms present associations of people and place as solid, commonsensical, and agreed-upon, when they are in fact contested, uncertain, and in flux.

Much recent work in anthropology and related fields has focused on the process through which such reified and naturalized national representations are constructed and maintained by states and national elites. (See, for instance, Anderson 1983; Handler 1988; Herzfeld 1987; Hobsbawm and Ranger 1983; Kapferer 1988; Wright 1985.) Borneman (1992) presents a case where state constructions of national territory are complicated by a very particular sort of displacement, as the territorial division and reformation of Germany following the Second World War made unavailable to the two states the claims to a territorially circumscribed home and culturally delineated nation that are usually so central to establish legitimacy. Neither could their citizens rely on such appeals in constructing their own identities. In forging national identities estranged in this way from both territory and culture, Borneman argues, the postwar German states and their citizens employed oppositional strategies, ultimately resulting in versions of the displaced and decentered identities that mark what is often called the postmodern condition.

Discussions of nationalism make it clear that states play a crucial role in the popular politics of place making and in the creation of naturalized links between places and peoples. But it is important to note that state ideologies are far from being the only point at which the imagination of place is politicized. Oppositional images of place have of course been extremely important in anticolonial nationalist movements, as well as in campaigns for self-determination and sovereignty on the part of ethnic counternations such as the Hutu (Malkki 1992), the Eritreans, and the Armenians. Bisharat (1992) traces some of the ways in which the imagining

of place has played into the Palestinian struggle, showing both how specific constructions of "homeland" have changed in response to political circumstances and how a deeply felt relation to "the land" continues to inform and inspire the Palestinian struggle for self-determination. Bisharat's article serves as a useful reminder, in the light of nationalism's often reactionary connotations in the Western world, of how often notions of home and "own place" have been empowering in anticolonial contexts.

Indeed, future observers of 20th-century revolutions will probably be struck by the difficulty of formulating large-scale political movements *without* reference to national homelands. Gupta (1992) discusses the difficulties raised in attempting to rally people around such a nonnational collectivity as the nonaligned movement; and he points out that similar problems are raised by the proletarian internationalist movement, since, "as generations of Marxists after Marx found out, it is one thing to liberate a nation, quite another to liberate the workers of the world" (Gupta 1992). Class-based internationalism's tendencies to nationalism (as in the history of the Second International, or that of the USSR), and to utopianism imagined in local rather than universal terms (as in Morris's *News from Nowhere* [1970], where "nowhere" [*utopia*] turns out to be a specifically English "somewhere"), show clearly the importance of attaching causes to places and the ubiquity of place making in collective political mobilization.

Such place making, however, need not be national in scale. One example of this is the way idealized notions of "the country" have been used in urban settings to construct critiques of industrial capitalism (cf. in Britain, Williams 1973; for Zambia, Ferguson 1992). Another case is the reworking of ideas of "home" and "community" by feminists like Martin and Mohanty (1986) and Kaplan (1987). Rofel (1992) gives another example in her treatment of the contested meanings of the spaces and local history of a Chinese factory. Her analysis shows both how specific factory locations acquired meanings over time and how these localized spatial meanings confounded the modernizing, panoptic designs of planners – indeed, how the durability of memory and localized meanings of sites and bodies calls into question the very idea of a universal, undifferentiated "modernity."

It must be noted that such popular politics of place can as easily be conservative as progressive. Often enough, as in the contemporary United States, the association of place with memory, loss, and nostalgia plays directly into the hands of reactionary popular movements. This is true not only of explicitly national images long associated with the Right, but also of imagined locales and nostalgic settings such as "small-town America" or "the frontier," which often play into and complement antifeminist idealizations of "the home" and "family."[2]

Space, Politics, and Anthropological Representation

Changing our conceptions of the relation between space and cultural difference offers a new perspective on recent debates surrounding issues of anthropological representation and writing. The new attention to representational practices has already led to more sophisticated understandings of processes of objectification and the construction of otherness in anthropological writing. However, with this said, it also seems to us that recent notions of "cultural critique" (Marcus and Fischer 1986) depend on a spatialized understanding of cultural difference that needs to be problematized.

The foundation of cultural critique – a dialogic relation with an "other" culture that yields a critical viewpoint on "our own culture" – assumes an already-existing world of many different, distinct "cultures," and an unproblematic distinction between "our own society" and an "other" society. As Marcus and Fischer put it, the purpose of cultural critique is "to generate critical questions from one society to probe the other" (1986:117); the goal is "to apply both the substantive results and the epistemological lessons learned from ethnography abroad to a renewal of the critical

function of anthropology as it is pursued in ethnographic projects at home" (1986:112).

Marcus and Fischer are sensitive to the fact that cultural difference is present "here at home," too, and that "the other" need not be exotic or far away to be other. But the fundamental conception of cultural critique as a relation between "different societies" ends up, perhaps against the authors' intentions, spatializing cultural difference in familiar ways, as ethnography becomes, as above, a link between an unproblematized "home" and "abroad." The anthropological relation is not simply with people who are different, but with "a different society," "a different culture," and thus, inevitably, a relation between "here" and "there." In all of this, the terms of the opposition ("here" and "there," "us" and "them," "our own" and "other" societies) are taken as received: the problem for anthropologists is to use our encounter with "them," "there," to construct a critique of "our own society," "here."

There are a number of problems with this way of conceptualizing the anthropological project. Perhaps the most obvious is the question of the identity of the "we" that keeps coming up in phrases such as "ourselves" and "our own society." Who is this "we"? If the answer is, as we fear, "the West," then we must ask precisely who is to be included and excluded from this club. Nor is the problem solved simply by substituting for "our own society," "the ethnographer's own society." For ethnographers, as for other natives, the postcolonial world is an interconnected social space; for many anthropologists – and perhaps especially for displaced Third World scholars – the identity of "one's own society" is an open question.

A second problem with the way cultural difference has been conceptualized within the "cultural critique" project is that, once excluded from that privileged domain "our own society," "the other" is subtly nativized – placed in a separate frame of analysis and "spatially incarcerated" (Appadurai 1988) in that "other place" that is proper to an "other culture." Cultural critique assumes an original separation, bridged at the initiation of the anthropological fieldworker.

The problematic is one of "contact": communication not within a shared social and economic world, but "across cultures" and "between societies."

As an alternative to this way of thinking about cultural difference, we want to problematize the unity of the "us" and the otherness of the "other," and question the radical separation between the two that makes the opposition possible in the first place. We are interested less in establishing a dialogic relation between geographically distinct societies than in exploring the processes of *production* of difference in a world of culturally, socially, and economically interconnected and interdependent spaces.

[...]

What is needed, then, is more than a ready ear and a deft editorial hand to capture and orchestrate the voices of "others"; what is needed is a willingness to interrogate, politically and historically, the apparent "given" of a world in the first place divided into "ourselves" and "others." A first step on this road is to move beyond naturalized conceptions of spatialized "cultures" and to explore instead the production of difference within common, shared, and connected spaces – "the San," for instance, not as "a people," "native" to the desert, but as a historically constituted and de-propertied category systematically relegated to the desert.

The move we are calling for, most generally, is away from seeing cultural difference as the correlate of a world of "peoples" whose separate histories wait to be bridged by the anthropologist and toward seeing it as a product of a shared historical process that differentiates the world as it connects it. For the proponents of "cultural critique," difference is taken as starting point, not as end product. Given a world of "different societies," they ask, how can we use experience in one to comment on another? But if we question a pre-given world of separate and discrete "peoples and cultures," and see instead a difference-producing set of relations, we turn from a project of juxtaposing preexisting differences to one of exploring the construction of differences in historical process.

In this perspective, power does not enter the anthropological picture only at the moment of representation, for the cultural distinctiveness that the anthropologist attempts to represent has always already been produced within a field of power relations. There is thus a politics of otherness that is not reducible to a politics of representation. Textual strategies can call attention to the politics of representation, but the issue of otherness itself is not really addressed by the devices of polyphonic textual construction or collaboration with informant-writers, as writers like Clifford and Crapanzano sometimes seem to suggest.

In addition to (not instead of!) textual experimentation, then, there is a need to address the issue of "the West" and its "others" in a way that acknowledges the extra-textual roots of the problem. For example, the area of immigration and immigration law is one practical area where the politics of space and the politics of otherness link up very directly. Indeed, if the separateness of separate places is not a natural given but an anthropological problem, it is remarkable how little anthropologists have had to say about the contemporary political issues connected with immigration in the United States.[3] If we accept a world of originally separate and culturally distinct places, then the question of immigration policy is just a question of how hard we should try to maintain this original order. In this perspective, immigration prohibitions are a relatively minor matter. Indeed, operating with a spatially naturalized understanding of cultural difference, uncontrolled immigration may even appear as a danger to anthropology, threatening to blur or erase the cultural distinctiveness of places that is our stock in trade. If, on the other hand, it is acknowledged that cultural difference is produced and maintained in a field of power relations in a world always already spatially interconnected, then the restriction of immigration becomes visible as one of the main means through which the disempowered are kept that way.

The enforced "difference" of places becomes, in this perspective, part and parcel of a global system of domination. The anthropological task of de-naturalizing cultural and spatial divisions at this point links up with the political task of combating a very literal "spatial incarceration of the native" (Appadurai 1988) within economic spaces zoned, as it were, for poverty. In this sense, changing the way we think about the relations of culture, power, and space opens the possibility of changing more than our texts. There is room, for instance, for a great deal more anthropological involvement, both theoretical and practical, with the politics of the US/Mexico border, with the political and organizing rights of immigrant workers, and with the appropriation of anthropological concepts of "culture" and "difference" into the repressive ideological apparatus of immigration law and the popular perceptions of "foreigners" and "aliens."

A certain unity of place and people has been long assumed in the anthropological concept of culture. But anthropological representations and immigration laws notwithstanding, "the native" is "spatially incarcerated" only in part. The ability of people to confound the established spatial orders, either through physical movement or through their own conceptual and political acts of re-imagination, means that space and place can never be "given," and that the process of their sociopolitical construction must always be considered. An anthropology whose objects are no longer conceived as automatically and naturally anchored in space will need to pay particular attention to the way spaces and places are made, imagined, contested, and enforced. In this sense, it is no paradox to say that questions of space and place are, in this deterritorialized age, more central to anthropological representation than ever.

Conclusion

In suggesting the requestioning of the spatial assumptions implicit in the most fundamental and seemingly innocuous concepts in the social sciences such as "culture," "society," "community," and "nation," we do not presume to lay out a detailed blueprint for an alternative conceptual apparatus. We do, however, wish to point out some promising directions for the future.

One extremely rich vein has been tapped by those attempting to theorize interstitiality and hybridity: in the postcolonial situation (Bhabha 1989; Hannerz 1987; Rushdie 1989); for people living on cultural and national borders (Anzaldúa 1987; Rosaldo 1987, 1988, 1989); for refugees and displaced peoples (Ghosh 1989; Malkki 1992); and in the case of migrants and workers (Leonard 1992). The "syncretic, adaptive politics and culture" of hybridity, Bhabha points out (1989:64), questions "the imperialist and colonialist notions of purity as much as it question[s] the nationalist notions." It remains to be seen what kind of politics are enabled by such a theorization of hybridity and to what extent it can do away with all claims to authenticity, to all forms of essentialism, strategic or otherwise (see especially Radhakrishnan 1987). Bhabha points to the troublesome connection between claims to purity and utopian teleology in describing how he came to the realization that

> the only place in the world to speak from was at a point whereby contradiction, antagonism, the hybridities of cultural influence, the boundaries of nations, were not sublated into some utopian sense of liberation or return. The place to speak from was through those incommensurable contradictions within which people survive, are politically active, and change. (1989:67)

The borderlands are just such a place of incommensurable contradictions. The term does not indicate a fixed topographical site between two other fixed locales (nations, societies, cultures), but an interstitial zone of displacement and deterritorialization that shapes the identity of the hybridized subject. Rather than dismissing them as insignificant, as marginal zones, thin slivers of land between stable places, we want to contend that the notion of borderlands is a more adequate conceptualization of the "normal" locale of the postmodern subject.

Another promising direction that takes us beyond culture as a spatially localized phenomenon is provided by the analysis of what is variously called "mass media," "public culture," and the "culture industry." (Especially influential here has been the journal, *Public Culture*.) Existing symbiotically with the commodity form, profoundly influencing even the remotest people that anthropologists have made such a fetish of studying, mass media pose the clearest challenge to orthodox notions of culture. National, regional, and village boundaries have, of course, never contained culture in the way that anthropological representations have often implied. However, the existence of a transnational public sphere means that the fiction that such boundaries enclose cultures and regulate cultural exchange can no longer be sustained.

The production and distribution of mass culture – films, television and radio programs, newspapers and wire services, recorded music, books, live concerts – is largely controlled by those notoriously placeless organizations, multinational corporations. The "public sphere" is therefore hardly "public" with respect to control over the representations that are circulated in it. Recent work in cultural studies has emphasized the dangers of reducing the reception of multinational cultural production to the passive act of consumption, leaving no room for the active creation by agents of disjunctures and dislocations between the flow of industrial commodities and cultural products. However, we worry at least as much about the opposite danger of *celebrating* the inventiveness of those "consumers" of the culture industry (especially on the periphery) who fashion something quite different out of products marketed to them, reinterpreting and remaking them, sometimes quite radically, and sometimes in a direction that promotes resistance rather than conformity. The danger here is the temptation to use scattered examples of the cultural flows dribbling from the "periphery" to the chief centers of the culture industry as a way of dismissing the "grand narrative" of capitalism (especially the "totalizing" narrative of late capitalism), and thus of evading the powerful political issues associated with Western global hegemony.

The reconceptualization of space implicit in theories of interstitiality and public culture has led to efforts to conceptualize cultural difference without invoking the orthodox idea of "culture." This is a yet largely unexplored and

underdeveloped area. We do, clearly, find the clustering of cultural practices that do not "belong" to a particular "people" or to a definite place. Jameson (1984) has attempted to capture the distinctiveness of these practices in the notion of a "cultural dominant," whereas Ferguson (1990) proposes an idea of "cultural style," which searches for a logic of surface practices without necessarily mapping such practices onto a "total way of life" encompassing values, beliefs, attitudes, et cetera, as in the usual concept of culture. We need to explore what Homi Bhabha calls "the uncanny of cultural difference."

[C]ultural difference becomes a problem not when you can point to the Hottentot Venus, or to the punk whose hair is six feet up in the air; it does not have that kind of fixable visibility. It is as the strangeness of the familiar that it becomes more problematic, both politically and conceptually ... when the problem of cultural difference is ourselves-as-others, others-as-ourselves, that borderline. (1989:72)

Why focus on that borderline? We have argued that deterritorialization has destabilized the fixity of "ourselves" and "others." But it has not thereby created subjects who are free-floating monads, despite what is sometimes implied by those eager to celebrate the freedom and playfulness of the post-modern condition. As Martin and Mohanty (1986:194) point out, indeterminacy, too, has its political limits, which follow from the denial of the critic's own location in multiple fields of power. Instead of stopping with the notion of deterritorialization, the pulverization of the space of high modernity, we need to theorize how space is being *re*territorialized in the contemporary world. We need to account sociologically for the fact that the "distance" between the rich in Bombay and the rich in London may be much shorter than that between different classes in "the same" city. Physical location and physical territory, for so long the *only* grid on which cultural difference could be mapped, need to be replaced by multiple grids that enable us to see that connection and contiguity – more generally the representation of territory – vary considerably by factors such as class, gender, race, and sexuality, and are differentially available to those in different locations in the field of power.

NOTES

1 This is obviously not true of the "new ethnicity" literature, of texts such as Anzaldúa (1987) and Radhakrishnan (1987).
2 See also Robertson (1988, 1991) on the politics of nostalgia and "native place-making" in Japan.
3 We are, of course, aware that a considerable amount of recent work in anthropology has centered on immigration. However, it seems to us that too much of this work remains at the level of describing and documenting patterns and trends of migration, often with a policy science focus. Such work is undoubtedly important, and often strategically effective in the formal political arena. Yet there remains the challenge of taking up the specifically *cultural* issues surrounding the mapping of otherness onto space, as we have suggested is necessary. One area where at least some anthropologists have taken such issues seriously is that of Mexican immigration to the United States (e.g., Alvarez 1987; Bustamante 1987; Chavez 1991; Kearney 1986, 1990; Kearney and Nagengast 1989; and Rouse 1991). Another example is Borneman (1986), which is noteworthy for showing the specific links between immigration law and homophobia, nationalism and sexuality, in the case of the Cuban "Marielito" immigrants to the United States.

REFERENCES

Alvarez, Robert R., Jr.
   1987 Familia: Migration and Adaptation in Baja and Alta California, 1800–1975. Berkeley: University of California Press.
Anderson, Benedict
   1983 Imagined Communities: Reflections on the Origin and Spread of Nationalism. London: Verso.
Anzaldúa, Gloria
   1987 Borderlands/La Frontera: The New Mestiza. San Francisco, Calif.: Spinsters/Aunt Lute.

Appadurai, Arjun
   1986 Theory in Anthropology: Center and Periphery. Comparative Studies in Society and History 28(1):356–61.
Appadurai, Arjun
   1988 Putting Hierarchy in its Place. Cultural Anthropology 3(1):36–49.
Baudrillard, Jean
   1988 Selected Writings. Stanford, Calif.: Stanford University Press.
Bhabha, Homi
   1989 Location, Intervention, Incommensurability: A Conversation with Homi Bhabha. Emergences 1(1):63–88.
Bisharat, George
   1992 Transformations in the Political Role and Social Identity of Palestinian Refugees in the West Bank. *In* Culture, Power, Place: Explorations in Critical Anthropology. Roger Rouse, James Ferguson, and Akhil Gupta, eds. Boulder, CO: Westview Press.
Borneman, John
   1986 Emigrés as Bullets/Immigration as Penetration: Perceptions of the Marielitos. Journal of Popular Culture 20(3):73–92.
Borneman, John
   1992 State, Territory and Identity Formation in Postwar Berlin 1945–1989. Cultural Anthropology 7(1):45–62.
Bustamante, Jorge
   1987 Mexican Immigration: A Domestic Issue or an International Reality? *In* Hispanic Migration and the United States: A Study in Politics. Gastón Fernández, Beverly Nagel, and León Narváez, eds. pp. 13–30. Bristol, Ind.: Wyndham Hall Press.
Chavez, Leo
   1991 Outside the Imagined Community: Undocumented Settlers and Experiences of Incorporation. American Ethnologist 18(2):257–78.
Clifford, James
   1988 The Predicament of Culture. Cambridge, Mass.: Harvard University Press.
Cohen, Anthony
   1985 The Symbolic Construction of Community. New York: Tavistock.
Davis, Mike
   1984 The Political Economy of Late-Imperial America. New Left Review 143:6–38.
Deleuze, Gilles, and Félix Guattari
   1987 A Thousand Plateaus: Capitalism and Schizophrenia. Minneapolis: University of Minnesota Press.

Ferguson, James
1990 Cultural Style as Inscription: Toward a Political Economy of the Styled Body. Paper presented at the meetings of the American Ethnological Society, Atlanta.

Ferguson, James
1992 The Country and the City on the Copperbelt. Cultural Anthropology 7(1): 80–92.

Foucault, Michel
1982 Power/Knowledge. New York: Pantheon.

Ghosh, Amitav
1989 The Shadow Lines. New York: Viking.

Gupta, Akhil
1992 The Song of the Nonaligned World: Transnational Identities and the Reinscription of Space in Late Capitalism. Cultural Anthropology 7(1):63–79.

Handler, Richard
1988 Nationalism and the Politics of Culture in Quebec. Madison: University of Wisconsin Press.

Hannerz, Ulf
1986 Theory in Anthropology: Small Is Beautiful, the Problem of Complex Cultures. Comparative Studies in Society and History 28(2):362–7.

Hannerz, Ulf
1987 The World in Creolization. Africa 57(4):546–59.

Harvey, David
1989 The Condition of Postmodernity: An Enquiry into the Origins of Cultural Change. New York: Blackwell.

Hebdige, Dick
1987 Cut 'n' Mix: Culture, Identity and Caribbean Music. London: Methuen.

Herzfeld, Michael
1987 Anthropology Through the Looking-Glass: Critical Ethnography in the Margins of Europe. New York: Cambridge University Press.

Hobsbawm, Eric, and Terrence Ranger, eds.
1983 The Invention of Tradition. New York: Cambridge University Press.

Jameson, Frederic
1984 Postmodernism, or the Cultural Logic of Late Capitalism. New Left Review 146:53–92.

Kapferer, Bruce
1988 Legends of People, Myths of State: Violence, Intolerance, and Political Culture in Sri Lanka and Australia. Washington, DC: Smithsonian Institution Press.

Kaplan, Caren
1987 Deterritorializations: The Rewriting of Home and Exile in Western Feminist Discourse. Cultural Critique 6:187–98.

Kearney, Michael
1986 From the Invisible Hand to Visible Feet: Anthropological Studies of Migration and Development. Annual Review of Anthropology 15:331–61.

Kearney, Michael
1990 Borders and Boundaries of State and Self at the End of Empire. Department of Anthropology, University of California, Riverside, unpublished MS.

Kearney, Michael, and Carol Nagengast
1989 Anthropological Perspectives on Transnational Communities in Rural California. Working Group on Farm Labor and Rural Poverty. Working Paper, 3. Davis, Calif.: California Institute for Rural Studies.

Leonard, Karen
1992 Finding One's Own Place: The Imposition of Asian Landscapes on Rural California. In Power, Place: Explorations in Critical Anthropology. Roger Rouse, James Ferguson, and Akhil Gupta, eds. Boulder, Colo.: Westview Press.

Malkki, Liisa
1992 National Geographic: The Rooting of Peoples and the Territorialization of National Identity among Scholars and Refugees. Cultural Anthropology 7(1):24–44.

Mandel, Ernest
1975 Late Capitalism. New York: Verso.

Marcus, George E., and Michael M.J. Fischer
1986 Anthropology as Cultural Critique: An Experimental Moment in the Human Sciences. Chicago, IL.: University of Chicago Press.

Martin, Biddy, and Chandra Talpade Mohanty
1986 Feminist Politics: What's Home Got to Do with It? In Feminist Studies/Critical Studies. Teresa de Lauretis, ed. pp. 191–212. Bloomington: Indiana University Press.

Morris, William
1970[1890] News from Nowhere. London: Routledge.

Peters, John
1992 Near-Sight and Far-Sight: Media, Place, and Culture. In Culture, Power, Place: Explorations in Critical Anthropology. Roger Rouse, James Ferguson, and Akhil Gupta, eds. Boulder, CO: Westview Press.

Radhakrishnan, R.
    1987 Ethnic Identity and Post-Structuralist
    Difference. Cultural Critique 6:199–220.
Robertson, Jennifer
    1988 Furusato Japan: The Culture and
    Politics of Nostalgia. Politics, Culture, and
    Society 1(4):494–518.
Robertson, Jennifer
    1991 Native and Newcomer: Making and
    Remaking a Japanese City. Berkeley: University
    of California Press.
Rofel, Lisa
    1992 Rethinking Modernity: Space and
    Factory Discipline in China. Cultural
    Anthropology 7(1):93–114.
Rosaldo, Renato
    1987 Politics, Patriarchs, and Laughter.
    Cultural Critique 6:65–86.
Rosaldo, Renato
    1988 Ideology, Place, and People Without
    Culture. Cultural Anthropology 3(1):77–87.

Rosaldo, Renato
    1989 Culture and Truth: The Remaking of
    Social Analysis. Boston, MA: Beacon Press.
Rouse, Roger
    1991 Mexican Migration and the Social
    Space of Post-Modernism. Diaspora 1(1):
    8–23.
Rushdie, Salman
    1989 The Satanic Verses. New York: Viking.
Said, Edward W.
    1979 Zionism from the Standpoint of Its
    Victims. Social Text 1:7–58.
Williams, Raymond
    1973 The Country and the City. New York:
    Oxford University Press.
Wright, Patrick
    1985 On Living in an Old Country: The
    National Past in Contemporary Britain.
    London: Verso.

25

Afghanistan, Ethnography, and the New World Order

David B. Edwards

Anthropologists do not usually – or at least they are not usually thought to – comment on global issues. The anthropological perspective is generally assumed to be a localized one. We are the resident observers of particular places, usually obscure ones, and until recently at least we have been relatively happy with our obscurity. Strange things happen, however. Events move beyond our control, and fieldwork sites that seem to be as remote and insignificant as any on the planet suddenly take on a global significance that forces the most nocturnal of researchers into the light. When I first decided to be an anthropologist, it was basically because I wanted an excuse to go back to Afghanistan to carry out a traditional sort of village study in some mountain community. I had worked for two years as an English teacher in Kabul in the mid-1970s, had fallen in love with the place, and it seemed that anthropology offered a way to spend more time in parts of the country I would otherwise not be able to visit. So, I started graduate

school, and in the meantime a revolution happened that changed my plans.

Afghanistan's obscurity may have been part of what appealed to me in the first place, but for the last ten years I have been trying to come to grips with its notoriety, its confusion, and its disparate energies. Since 1982, I have carried out fieldwork in a variety of places, including the city of Peshawar, Pakistan, and various refugee camps scattered around the Northwest Frontier Province. One summer, I also traveled inside Afghanistan to observe the operations of a group of *mujahidin*, and I have spent quite a bit of time among Afghan refugees in the Washington, DC, area. Finally, and most recently, I have been monitoring the activities of an Afghan computer newsgroup.

All of these experiences have collectively contributed to what I know about Afghans and Afghan culture, and I have found that this knowledge is not easily divisible. Though distant in space, the different contexts are not isolated from one another. What goes on inside

David B. Edwards, "Afghanistan, Ethnography, and the New World Order," pp. 345–360 from *Cultural Anthropology* 9(3), 1994. Copyright © 1994 by the American Anthropological Association. Reprinted by permission of the Copyright Clearance Center on behalf of the American Anthropological Association.

Ethnographic Fieldwork: An Anthropological Reader, Second Edition. Edited by Antonius C. G. M. Robben and Jeffrey A. Sluka.
Editorial material and organization © 2012 John Wiley & Sons, Inc.
Published 2012 by John Wiley & Sons, Inc.

Afghanistan affects what is happening in the camps, just as both of these situations influence (and are influenced by) the lives of Afghans in more distant locales. The various attempts I have made over the years to isolate single parts of this larger totality, so that I might be able to produce a more traditional sort of community study, have always been frustrating for me. In a sense that I did not recognize until recently, these attempts represented traumatic amputations of what I know and what I have experienced, and not surprisingly, they resulted in texts that have felt partial, incomplete, and vaguely untruthful. Somehow I have needed to find a mechanism that would reflect more closely the whole story as I understood it, a story that is not confined to any one point in time or space.

What follows is the partial product of recent attempts to address the problem of representing the spatially discontinuous and temporally disjointed nature of my fieldwork experience. In pursuing this end, I have been led to employ what might be called a contrapuntal, rather than a traditional, linear structure of exposition, and to move into and out of ethnographic place rather more freely than is usually done. The objective in employing this style of writing is not to develop any particular theoretical point. It is rather to pull together, in one place, experiences that are otherwise separate and distinct in time and space but that seem in some marginally inchoate way to need each other's company.

One effect of assembling these vignettes in one place is to transgress the normal conception of what constitutes "fieldwork." Traditionally framed as a *rite de passage* through which all anthropologists had to pass, the idea of fieldwork carried with it certain definite obligations, for instance that it be conducted over a calendar year and that it take place in an exotic locale in some sort of bounded community like a village or a hunter-gatherer settlement. This conception of fieldwork, as venerable as it might be, is no longer adequate to the reality of shifting boundaries and migrating cultures. People don't stay in one place any more – if they ever did – and the notion that the terms *culture, community,* and *place* are more or less synonymous cannot be sustained.

The good news in all this, I think, is that, despite the proliferation of media-driven consumerism crossing every mountain range and border on the planet, the monoculture of our nightmares does not seem to be developing. Cultural differences still abound, and cross-cultural contact appears to be accelerating the process of hybridization as much as it is that of homogenization. One result of this – for anthropologists at least – is that, while the distant cultures we have traditionally studied are no longer so easily isolable or exotic as they were in the past, those that are closer to home are also a great deal more strange and interesting than we ever imagined.

Paktia

It is a morning in May 1984. I have had my breakfast of bread and tea and am taking a morning walk through the tiny village of Serana, in the territory of the Zadran tribe in south-central Paktia Province, eastern Afghanistan. Paktia Province has long enjoyed the reputation of being the most fiercely independent region of Afghanistan. Time and again, the tribes of Paktia have poured out of the mountains to challenge the government of Kabul's right to rule. That is why I have come here – to see firsthand this *yaghistan* – this place of rebellion – but so far at least I have not met very many native Paktiawal. Most people have left the area, and I have seen only a handful of children and hardly any women at all since arriving.

It is cool in the mountains, cool enough that the few people I pass wear their shawls wrapped tightly around their shoulders. Climbing a short hill on the outskirts of the village, I see a mullah with a billowy white turban seated in the chair of a two-barrel Dashika antiaircraft gun. The Dashika is a Soviet design, but markings on the gun indicate that it is of Chinese manufacture. These guns are shiny and new and only recently arrived by camel caravan across the Pakistani frontier. The mullah is young – late-twenties – and he scans the sky for signs of Soviet MiGs. Only a few weeks before, mujahidin gunners had brought down a MiG-23 not too far from here, and there is fighting going on not too far away; so the mullah is keeping careful watch. As he does so, he listens to a cassette on his Japanese tape recorder of an Egyptian muezzin chanting verses from the Qur'an.

We continue on around the perimeter of the base, climbing as we do toward another antiaircraft gun emplacement located on a ridge overlooking Serana. When we reach the heights, we see another Afghan gunner manning a four-barrel Zigoyak gun, also Soviet-designed and Chinese-made, also recently arrived in the base. This is the largest-caliber gun in their arsenal, and the best gunners have been assigned to maintain and fire it. There are three gunners present, all ex-soldiers from the Afghan army. It is not surprising to find soldiers here. The area is overrun with them, and it seems that the majority of people I have talked with during my trip have been recruits and conscripts from distant parts of the country, who have taken refuge with the mujahidin after deserting from the army.

The soldier who is manning the Zigoyak when we arrive is a burly man. Like everyone else, he is bearded, but he has the additional distinguishing feature of tatooed dots across his face. He tells me that these are associated with his tribe – the Achakzais – in southern Qandahar Province. He is a friendly man, much friendlier than the mullah who had kept his cassette playing as we passed and stared vacantly at me as I took a photo of him. The Qandahari gunner is more affable and offers us tea in the Afghan refugee tent that stands off to the side of the gun emplacement.

He has been away from his home for two years now, ever since he was press-ganged into the army. Six months ago, he escaped, and he has been in Zadran ever since. He doesn't like it here. The Zadrans, he insists, are *vahshî*: wild, savage. You can't trust them. They are Muslims by day and thieves by night. At the same time, however, he also tells me that he intends to stay where he is for awhile. A mountain base like this one is relatively safe. Down in the plains, the government can capture you, and if they don't, you'll probably get killed by one of the parties. Perhaps one day this situation will change, but he will stay where he is for awhile. The roads are too unsafe to travel. The refugee camps in Pakistan are overcrowded, the

summers there unbearably hot, and the local officials always want bribes.

Later in the day, I meet another ex-soldier, a Persian-speaking Tajik from the Kohistan region just north of Kabul. He is a young man – not more than 22 or 23 – and boyishly handsome. Although he looks more like a teenager than a man, a man he must be since he served as a parachute commando in the army before deserting last year. Unlike most of the other mujahidin I have met, he has little time for Islam and openly admits to me that he had been a follower of a famous leftist guerrilla leader named Majid Kalakani who had been captured and killed by the government some years before. He talks proudly of his time with Kalakani and tells me of the American sniper rifle that he used to own. It had a scope on it, and once he killed four Soviet tankists as they drove in a convoy down the main road toward Kabul. The beauty of the American rifle, he says, is its small bullets and its silent action. This means that the tankist sitting in the turret could be quietly picked off while the tank was rumbling along the road. Only later did his comrades recognize that the man on top was dead, and by then the sniper was long gone.

It is early afternoon as we talk. The young Kohistani is guarding a Communist prisoner who was captured a few weeks ago during a surprise ambush of a wedding party in the nearby town of Gardez. It is the time of early afternoon prayers, and we are near the mosque. Several mullahs pass by, and each tells my companion in rough Persian to go to the mosque: "*Namaz bokhan* (Go pray)!" To each, he smiles and replies that he is on duty and can't leave his post. He tells me that he is tired of it here. Tired of the mullahs, tired of the tribes. In a month or so, he will leave Zadran and join Khalil, a Jamiat commander, whose base is in Kohistan. Things will be better there. He will be rid of these damn Pakhtuns and return to his own people.

The next morning, I head east with my companions. We are going back to Pakistan, and every hour or so, we pass another group of 10 and 20 mujahidin who are on their way back inside the country. Most are from nearby and have only another day or so to travel. Some are from the far north and will be on the road for the next two or three weeks. All are well armed. Most have AK-47s, and almost every group has at least one rocket-propelled grenade launcher, a weapon particularly useful for ambushes along the road. It is spring, and another season of killing is about to begin.

At the end of the second day, we near the base at Zhawar. It is our last stop before crossing the border. The path takes us along a high ridge that skirts a broad plain. To the north is the garrison town of Khost, and in the distance we can see tall plumes of dust rise up from the ground. Tanks are headed toward us. An operation is going on. The government is trying to retake a post about a mile ahead of us that the mujahidin had captured some weeks earlier. Overhead, a MiG appears. Small at first, it gets larger and larger as it approaches. I can see the bombs under its wings as it banks above us. The antiaircraft guns at Zhawar begin firing. The screaming of the jet is punctuated by the dull, jackhammer thud of the antiaircraft guns. I'm not sure, but I think I can hear an occasional and distant "ting, ting, ting," as the shells ricochet off the armored belly of the jet.

Ahead of us, off to the northeast, we can just make out Laizha, the base that is under attack, and we watch as the MiG levels off and releases its bombs. They twirl off the undercarriage, pirouette for a moment, then brown clouds of dust billow up, and a few seconds later, we hear the dull concussion of metal smashing stone. I can't help myself from thinking: it's just like the movies. Then I get scared, but when I look at my companions they are grinning. One of them shouts to me, "Turn on your tape recorder!" I fumble the machine out of my bag and push the record button. "Isn't it dangerous where we are?" I ask. The older and more experienced of my companions looks at me. "Yes, very!" he says and laughs. Somehow this relaxes me. There is no place to go anyway; so I turn back to watch the MiG and listen again to the antiaircraft guns beating their rhythm against the sky.

The Net

Last fall, the computer center at my college hooked me up to Internet, one feature of which is a bulletin board consisting of over two thousand news groups. I regularly monitor two of these two thousand groups: "Soc.Cul. Afghanistan" and "Soc.Religion.Islam". The first of these news groups is a bulletin board where Afghans and those interested in things Afghan can post messages to each other, and the second is a bulletin board that attracts messages for and by Muslims generally about issues having to do with their religion. Anyone who wants to send a message out for others to read and comment on writes up what he or she wants to say and then posts it to the bulletin board where it is available for inspection and comment until whoever manages the bulletin board decides to dump the existing postings to make space for new messages.

Those who contribute to Soc.Cul. Afghanistan and Soc.Religion.Islam are scattered rather widely over the globe, but it is difficult to know exactly how many people are out there, doing what I am, which is to say, reading other people's messages. I have to admit I am sometimes uncomfortable in this role, both because it feels rather like voyeurism and because it is strangely similar to anthropology. After all, isn't reading other people's messages what we do for a living? Only, in this case, there doesn't have to be even a pretense of reciprocity. I simply log on and click my mouse enough times to get me into the news group I want to monitor, and then I read. Since I sometimes go to my office early in the morning, I occasionally find myself staring at the screen in the twilight hours before dawn, which increases the sense that I am doing something illicit.

Eventually, I will start posting my own messages, but I haven't yet. Those who regularly post resent people like me. We are "lurkers." In the news groups I monitor, lurking takes on a political complexion, and I have sometimes come across messages warning against "foreign spies" who are out to subvert Islam and Afghanistan. My intentions seem innocent enough, to me at least, but I know that I would be included in that category. Occasionally, those who worry about foreign spies try to encode their messages, generally by transliterating Persian in English script. Some have even worked out complicated ways of combining the available character set symbols into visual approximations of the Persian script, but these systems are cumbersome, and everyone always ends up back in English.

I have only been monitoring these bulletin boards since November 1992; so I am not in a position to make great claims about what goes on these news groups. However, I have noticed certain persistent features that do stand out and are worth noting, such as the oft-expressed concern for "what kind of group we are going to be." One of the most charged issues related to this question has to do with who has the right to put their messages on the bulletin board, and I have encountered frequent complaints by regular contributors when Iranians, Pakistanis, and what are referred to by some as "Islamic fundamentalists" post to the Afghan group.

For many of the so-called fundamentalists, national boundaries are artificial distinctions, and they reflect this belief in their practice of dispatching their computer messages to multiple news groups on "the Net." Many Afghans resent these cross-postings, however, viewing them as violations of their community's boundaries. In the opinion of these Afghans, the practice of cross-posting computer messages replicates the problem that Afghans face in real life, for just as Arabs, Iranians, and Pakistanis intrude upon their news group, so, over the past 15 years, have they repeatedly interfered in Afghanistan's internal affairs.

Beyond this problem of who has the right to participate in the discourse of the news group, there are many other issues that come up on the Net that reflect the contemporary concerns not just of Afghans, but of Muslims more generally. Questions of this sort that I have noticed have included the following:

—Is it permissible to get married over the phone, and if so, how do the mullah and witnesses perform their roles?

—Does contemporary genetic science indicate that marriage to your first cousin increases risks of birth defects?

—What does Islam say about oral sex?

—Are there stipulations in Islam against investing in mutual funds and other current financial instruments?

—Should the beginning and end of the month of fasting be decided according to scientific measures now available, or by local observation, or by the calculations of Saudi officials in Mecca?

Although most of these issues are particular to the better-off immigrants coping with the modern diaspora, there are nevertheless striking similarities between these questions and those that arose in the mud-walled refugee camp where I worked. The refugee camp, like the Net, is an unprecedented place to be working out issues of identity and community, and consequently there are many matters that had previously been unproblematic that have come to take on major significance in the context of the camp. Should one arrange marriages with kinsmen who might be far away or with current neighbors from the camp? How are weddings to be celebrated in a time of jihad? Can people play music on their tape recorders? Who decides guilt and punishment when someone gets injured in a fight or accident? Who will contribute when the mosque roof gets washed out by winter rains? Since most people have to leave their compounds to defecate and there are so many people in camp, how is it going to be possible for women to go about their business without compromising purdah?

The problems that arise on the Net are obviously not the same as these questions, but there are still certain shared features. In both contexts, the usual diacritica of identity have been subjected to pressure and dislocation. In both places, strangers have come together out of common need and have been forced by circumstance to share an unaccustomed *space* in such a way that all can get along. To deal with this situation, new modes of communication and compromise have been developed, and in both contexts Islam has been critical to the effort.

When I lived in Afghanistan before the civil war, it was always my impression that Muslim identity was simply a fact of life and not a subject of contestation. The great majority of men (at least) went to the mosque, prayed, and – for the most part – seemed to accept the obligations imposed on them by religion as givens. Now, however, in contexts in which there are no givens, in which the most basic circumstances of everyday life are subject to flux and uncertainty, Islam has become the primary focus of concern. Although Islam too is subject to novel pressures, it appears to many people more stable than anything else around them. In a sea of uncertain choices, Islam is a life-ring that they can hang on to. But, of course, holding the rope at the other end are the political parties.

The belief of many Afghans that the political parties are manipulating Islam for their own purposes lends a strident political tone to almost every debate that takes place both on the Net and in the camp. However innocently a discussion begins, it always ends up enmeshed in politics. One example that comes to mind involves an American high school student who posted a message on the bulletin board asking for assistance with a homework assignment he was working on. The student seemed to want a thumbnail sketch of Afghan culture and history – presumably one he could copy directly into whatever social studies paper he was writing. However, what he actually got – whether he realized it or not – was much more revealing, for the posters who responded soon forgot about the student's inquiry and launched into a set of diatribes for and against the various Afghan political parties. Since the practice of the Net is for each poster to post his or her message interlinearly within that of the preceding poster, what one saw in following this debate was the gradual erosion of discourse as each new response was laid down on top of the previous one and the text as a whole became progressively more shrill, garbled, and incoherent.

The deterioration of discourse that one encounters graphically on the Net rather accurately approximates the general fracturing of Afghan society – inside and outside Afghanistan's borders – after more than fifteen years of war. At the same time, however, there are differences between the kinds of deterioration one finds inside Afghanistan or in the camps and in the further-flung diaspora of the Net. The bombs that I heard at a distance in Paktia were aimed at real people, and they did not discriminate whether those they struck were mujahidin or children. Likewise, when refugees crammed side by side in their squalid compounds were unable to resolve their disputes and the few avenues of mediation available to them proved unworkable, they usually ended up seeking redress in the old-fashioned way. Only

now, the instruments and protocols for seeking redress have changed. Automatic weapons are plentiful, and so too are silent, stealthy paybacks: bombs tossed into compounds, the use of hired gunmen to conceal responsibility, and the proliferation of street-corner kidnappings.

Debates on the Net sometimes aspire, in their rhetorical way, to the level of violence that exists "on the ground," but the fact that these debates have been adapted to the ether space of the computer distinguishes them both in their practice and in their outcome. In the camp, a dispute, whether engendered by a personal feud or an ideological disagreement, will often lead to bitterness and killing, but in ether space words that elsewhere provoke violence are articulated through glyphs and cursors, and no one gets hurt. Violence remains finally in the minds of the beholders, and the escalation of harms and consequences that develops in the course of a normal feud never takes place because of the faceless quality of communication on the Net.

The image that comes to mind when I think about this new technology is the old technology of the panopticon. The new reverses the old, however, for with the new technology one does not have a central controlling observer looking into each of the cells located on the outer ring of the circle. Rather, one finds that the panopticon has been inverted so that all of the inmates are now allowed to look inward toward the central, illuminated space of the Net. In this space, posters dream their dreams, vent their rage, and assume their roles. The antagonisms can be vicious here, but no one really knows who it is they are striking. No one suffers the consequences of their anger, and it is all ultimately rather futile. People have often noted the proliferation of simulated sex in the era of AIDS, but the Net reveals to us that there is also a kind of simulated politics in the age of the global diaspora.

DC

It is a Sunday in April 1991, and I am at a flea market in Georgetown. I have come to Washington, DC, to visit Shah Mahmood, my old research assistant who is now a political refugee in the States, and to interview a famous mujahidin commander who is staying with him. The day before we had conducted our interview, and today we are trying to sell a shipment of rugs that has been sent to Shah Mahmood by a friend in Pakistan. Every Sunday for the last few months, Shah Mahmood has been taking the rugs to the Sunday morning flea market in Georgetown where he hawks his wares. We are accompanied this day by the commander and another Afghan who shares Shah Mahmood's apartment in Northern Virginia. Unlike Shah Mahmood, this man is an illegal alien who has no papers and few prospects for attaining political asylum.

While we are at the flea market, an Afghan comes up to Shah Mahmood and the commander, and they embrace and chat for awhile. The man is rather chubby and wears an expensive leather coat and a rayon shirt, open at the neck. Next to Shah Mahmood, who is wearing khaki pants and a cotton sport shirt, and the commander, who wears a dark suit and white shirt, the man looks rather flashy, and his carriage is that of someone with a roll of bills in his pocket. The talk is friendly but stiff. After he leaves, Shah Mahmood tells me that this man is from the Surkh Rud district of Afghanistan, not far from where the commander lives. The commander is from the tribal areas in the mountains. This man is from the neighboring plains. His family is very wealthy, and for a long time they have had a variety of business ventures going on in Afghanistan and Pakistan. Now, they have come to the States and have managed to take control of a large percentage of the hot-dog carts operating in the capital district.

One of the secrets of their success, according to Shah Mahmood, is that they are able to hire other Afghans to operate the pushcarts at low salaries. Most of those they hire have recently arrived in the country, and many – like Shah Mahmood's roommate – are illegals. Shah Mahmood himself owned a cart for awhile, but not for long. Those with papers usually look elsewhere for work since the pushcart business doesn't pay well, requires long hours, and is thought of as rather demeaning. The job of choice for most refugees is driving a

taxi. That's considered the best, even though it is also difficult work and requires long hours if the driver is going to cover expenses and make any money. But, at least when you're driving a taxi, you're your own man. For Afghans, that's important.

Apparently, the businessman has been trying to see the commander for some time; so his visit to the flea market is not coincidental. The commander is famous, and the businessman wants to show his respect. The businessman may have commercial interests in the States now, but his base of operations is still the Afghan-Pakistan frontier. He knows that the commander is a man of influence back home and may be even more important in the future; so he has reason to want to cultivate their relationship. Before leaving, he has invited us to his home for dinner. We will go there after finishing up with the carpets.

The businessman's apartment is in a high-rise complex that Shah Mahmood says is called the "Watergate of the Pentagon." The complex looms over us as we approach, and the fact that we must pass through a security gate lets us know that we are going someplace very different from the dingy, low-rent apartment where Shah Mahmood currently resides. We park and enter one of the towers. A shiny elevator deposits us before tall mirrors on a long, carpeted corridor with threadbare pretensions to elegance. The hallway door opens to reveal a modern apartment unit: wall-to-wall carpeting, matching sofas upholstered in sleek black Naugahyde, a sliding door and balcony looking out over the exurban landscape of Northern Virginia. Straight ahead is the television and VCR in a black Plexiglas console. Around the corner to the right, I can make out a dining room table. In the same direction, I hear kitchen sounds – water running in a sink, dishes rattling – and also the high-pitched sound of small children playing and the hushed voice of a woman who remains unseen.

There are four men present when we arrive. We all greet, and then the men form a single line for prayers, facing the sliding glass door. It is an awkward space for this activity, and bodies inadvertently touch and jostle as the men kneel and rise and kneel again. It is the month of fasting; so, as soon as prayers are finished, all of the men immediately break fast with the sickly sweet juice that is favored for this occasion. Then, we are invited to eat. But not at the dining room table, which remains unused. Rather, we sit on the floor around a plastic sheet that has been placed between the sofas in the living room. It is a cramped space, but the food is good and abundant, and it is gone within minutes.

After the meal, the man we met at the flea market and his younger brother clear the dishes while the elder brother, who is around 45 or 50, sits in an armchair smoking a cigarette. Throughout the evening the younger brothers defer to this man, fetching matches, offering tea and sweets to the guests, and otherwise performing the standard services expected of younger brothers. Most of the conversation goes back and forth between the elder brother and the commander. The commander's opinion on the political situation is solicited, and he tells stories I have heard before about the fighting, the assassination attempts made against him, his wounds. There is a sense of resignation in the room. How many times have such stories been told? How many times have all of these people expressed the same opinions about the leaders and the parties? Their country is sunk in a quagmire, and no one has any idea how it might end. But, they are also not waiting to find out. The Surkh Rudis have their business and their green cards. They don't know it, but the commander has applied for his as well. I have promised to write a letter for him to INS. So have other Americans that the commander has met during his stay. He doesn't want to move here just yet, but everyone is trying to keep as many options open as possible. No one wants to be stuck in Pakistan for the rest of their lives.

After an hour or so, the conversation flags, and our host suggests that we watch a videotape made of his younger brother's wedding that was held in Peshawar the year before. The VCR is turned on, and all turn to watch as a static image of the Surkh Rudi businessman comes on the screen. This time, he is dressed in traditional Pakhtun clothing and wears around his neck a gaudy tinsel garland that droops almost to the floor. He is flanked by a number of other men in similar dress, and every minute or so someone new comes up to him. He rises, and they embrace. Some of the greeters carry garlands of the sort the bridegroom already has around his neck. These garlands are covered in rupee notes, and each greeter places his around the bridegroom's neck. There the garlands remain for a few seconds before a servant comes forward to take the topmost ones away.

The tape, it appears, will go on for hours. Occasionally, the camera pans over the room, but mostly it focuses on the bridegroom rising to greet his guests. There is nothing joyous or celebratory in any of this. None of those who greet the bridegroom look him in the eye or even smile. There are no jokes. No frivolity. It is entirely mechanical, and the camera has exposed that quality more vividly for me than reality ever managed to do. Strangely, it almost seems that there is more intimacy and liveliness in our gathering than at the wedding depicted on the screen, for while the guests on screen are mostly mute and expressionless, our hosts eagerly provide names, background information, and short anecdotes for virtually every guest who greets the bridegroom. This number includes prominent Afghans and Pakistanis. Some are older tribal chiefs dressed in traditional garb; others are sleek young sophisticates. All seem to be men of influence and power, and it is abundantly clear both that this family has a lot of important contacts and that they are extremely proud of this fact.

Most of the names that are mentioned mean little to me, however, and my attention begins to wander until I suddenly notice a lull in the conversation. A new face has appeared on the screen to greet the bridegroom, but for the first time our hosts have remained silent. No one says anything, and there is a palpable feeling of embarrassment that even I can sense despite my unfamiliarity with most of the personalities on the screen and my general obliviousness to the subtleties of the cultural performance I am witnessing. The tape continues, but the enthusiasm has dimmed. After a few minutes, Shah Mahmood begins to fidget and says something about my having to catch a train early in the morning. The intrusion is not unwelcome. The tape is turned off, and everyone stands, chatting and waiting for the appropriate moment to head toward the door.

The man we met at the flea market breaks off from the group and then a few minutes later brings his young son out from one of the bedrooms. He is a proud father, and the sight of the small boy reanimates the conversation. It occurs to me that it is very late for a child this age to be up, and then I realize that while we have been in the apartment, the domestic life of the family has been frozen. At least one woman has been in the kitchen the whole evening. Others (whose voices I have occasionally heard, usually scolding children) have been confined to the back bedrooms. Children have moved about, but the women, obedient to the laws of a distant homeland, have not. Custom and the configuration of the apartment have thus conspired to make their lives quite miserable, at least for this evening, and I'm sure there have been many others not unlike this one.

We embrace and say good-bye to our hosts at the door, but the middle brother, the one we first met that afternoon at the flea market, insists against our objections on escorting us downstairs. Again, there are embraces, and then Shah Mahmood gets behind the wheel of his car, a '76 Chevy Caprice Classic. Shah Mahmood's roommate, the illegal who operates the hot-dog cart, sits beside him, and the commander and I sit in the rear. As we make our way back through the maze of highways and strip malls, we talk about the gathering, and as usual, I go over all of the events and points of discussion that were unclear to me during the course of the evening. One thing that immediately comes to mind is the unnamed man in the videotape, and I ask why it was that everyone had stopped talking when he appeared.

The commander laughs and tells me that the man who had come on the screen was a well-known Communist from Surkh Rud and that he had been in a group of government security officers that the commander had captured in a big operation a few years ago. There had been over seventy men in the group, and the commander had tricked them into an ambush. Almost all of them had been executed, but he had allowed this man to be released because he came from a "good" family. He himself was no good, of course, but his people

were "pure"; so he let him go. Sometime later, the man had crossed the border and become a refugee in Pakistan. Now, he's doing business again. There is no outrage, or even disapproval, in the commander's voice when he tells me this, and he goes on to explain that the man's story is in no way unusual. Lots of refugees used to be Communists, he says, including many who now present themselves as pious Muslims. Before, they carried red banners through the streets of Kabul. Now, they wear beards and say their prayers five times a day. That's the kind of war this is. It's just that kind of war.

Orientations

In this essay, I have brought together incidents whose only apparent connection to one another is that they all involve Afghans as actors and me as witness to their actions. Why these particular moments? Why not others? I cannot say for certain. However, as I was mulling over what I should write about on the subject of "multiply-inflected cultural objects," these episodes struck me as somehow telling, and one reason for this is certainly that they all involve people who are not where they are supposed to be (or at least where they used to be). Whether it is the many mujahidin who have found their way to the mountains of Paktia from diverse regions of Afghanistan, or the graduate students on the Net at their various campuses, or the jihad commander in the high-rise apartment in Virginia, one thread running through each of these narratives is the common condition of coping in foreign places with unfamiliar people.

Another recurrent theme in these vignettes has to do with technology and the way in which technology mediates and transforms social and political relations. In Paktia, technology was represented principally by the multiple instruments of killing that were everywhere to be seen, but there were other sorts of technology present as well, such as the mini-tape recorder that helped to define my otherwise elusive identity to those I met and the portable radio/tape player that one of the gunners had beside him that allowed him to listen to recitations of the Qur'an, alongside broadcasts from Radio Moscow, the VOA, and the BBC. In the Net, we confront a revolutionary apparatus that makes possible interactive, unmediated communications between perfect strangers from around the globe; but, more dumbfounding than the wizardry of the technology itself is the speed with which the recombinant forms of a postmodern, postnational communicative medium have been harnessed to the ancient wagons of feud and faction. In the story of the jihad commander in Northern Virginia, we encounter the blankly staring presence of the videocassette recorder. Perhaps the most ubiquitous of all new technologies, the VCR has begun to radically reorder the protocols by which identity and community are imagined and managed in an increasingly scattered and globally decentered world.

Each of these themes can be seen in the stories I have told, but I want to reiterate a declaration made at the beginning of this essay, which is that my primary object in bringing these stories together is not to provide graphic illustrations for a particular theory or point of view. The choice of which stories to include here has been arrived at intuitively rather than analytically and has not been guided by any particular proposition. To the contrary, I simply wanted to write up accounts of several remembered incidents from the not-too-distant past, and along the way, I also decided to include a brief excursus into a current fascination – the Net – that seemed somehow to fit with the rest. As I read them now, what the memories I have included and the discussion of the Net all seem to share, to my mind at least, has less to do with definable issues like migration, dislocation, and technology, than with an essential ambiguity and estrangement that I discern in each. That, I suppose, is why they never got included in anything I had written before and why I wanted to put them together here – to make some sense of what was to me their abiding strangeness.

The trip to Paktia, for example, illustrates several obvious themes – the dislocation and realignment of ethnic groups in a time of war, the unanticipated role of the political party as safe haven in response to general upheaval – but it also seems to me to contain a more

enigmatic quality, as well, that is less easy to specify. I don't know if that quality has to do with the place itself or if it derives from my perception of it, for my memories of the events described have a timeless, floating quality to them that seems to increase with distance. The experience of war, like that of a natural disaster or of more mundane births and deaths, rests outside of ordinary time. And while these experiences can be hellish, they are also intensely memorable, though in ways that sometimes distort what actually happened. In moments of stress and uncertainty, time itself gets stretched in awkward directions, and when they are recalled as memory, the experienced events are sometimes darkly compressed, and other times bathed in a saturated, unnatural sort of light.

Should these qualities of perception and distortion be suppressed, or should we seek to reflect them in the texts we write? My answer is obviously that they constitute an important part of our experience, even if we do not know at first what they might signify. In this essay, I have tried to convey a sense of the tactile, if sometimes contorted, immediacy of remembered experience by using the first-person and the present tense. The present tense, in particular, is scorned these days as reminiscent of an older style of anthropological writing in which the author bolstered the authenticity of the finished account, along with his/her own authority, by constructing a false facade of realistic, "I-am-the-camera" details. The critique was a valid one, but the present tense remains a useful tool for representing the lived-experience of fieldwork – especially the contingent quality of events as they are apprehended on the run.

Although I understand them better now for having written them down and placed them together, the episodes and situations described here contain other ambiguities, as well, beyond those derived from the deformities of perception and memory. I have no idea, for instance, who my friend the commander really is or which of the things I heard from him are true. Nor can I say with any certainty what sort of negotiations were being transacted that evening in the Surkh Rudis' apartment or how deep was the play. I also can't say for sure what was going on up in the mountains of Paktia. Men from all parts of Afghanistan had been thrown together. That much I know, but what kind of place was it? Was it the forward outpost of a group of committed Muslim warriors – the kind so feared today in the West – or was it more like a small boat seeking a calm anchorage during a very rough night of storms? In the case of the Net, a different sort of uncertainty is present, an uncertainty and a sadness, for it seems to me that obscured beneath the tumult of scrolled postings and the blinking cacophony of interlaced diatribes is a silence that surrounds every individual who logs on. Underlying the diverse communities of interest that the Net makes possible is the specter of solitude – the loneliness of the darkened cell and the humming quiet of the illuminated screen.

We all want simple truths. We want mysteries that give way to our probings. We want situations that yield to analysis. We want tried-and-true concepts to mean what they always have and the assurance that design and method can ultimately win out over randomness and entropy. And maybe more than anything, we want stories that have clear morals, heroes, and villains who are what they appear to be, and endings that finally end. If recent events tell us anything, however, it is that such illusions are vain. The announcement of a new world order and of history's death was premature, and we have come to understand that whatever transient order had existed in world affairs was largely the result of the unnatural constraints that had been imposed upon them by superpower rivalry.

Ethnographers and ethnographic writing cannot change these facts, but they should at least strive to reflect them and resist the urge to impose an overarching order when such order is not what is most apparent. One implication of this assertion is that, just as anthropologists provide a space in their texts for analysis and interpretation, so should they leave room for strangeness and uncertainty and the stuff that troubles understanding. As they enlist theories and explanatory models to specific ends, so should they make it clear that their scope is finite and that at least some of the symmetries they perceive are produced by the theoretical

lenses they choose to wear. In coming to grips with the interconnected worlds we inhabit and chronicle, we must also think very carefully about the methodological practices we keep and the rhetorical ways in which we conceive and fashion the "data" of our research. Despite our best efforts to be truthful, traditional modes of organization and articulation can and often do lend to what we construe as "our research objects" a formal logic and coherence that bears little or no relationship to our original experience of those objects.

Recognizing this fact, I have tried to explore in this paper new ways of organizing and articulating my accounts of the people and places I study. What I have come up with is a more improvisational or aleatoric style of writing, the goal of which has been to convey a sense of the scattered and disjointed contexts in which I have conducted field research. In the process of putting together this text, however, I have also been faced with the fact that, however far-flung they might be, the social worlds I study nevertheless reveal between themselves certain patterns and processes despite the disjunctions and dislocations to which they are subject. While I have tried to see my fieldwork as experience rather than data collection and to avoid imposing an extraneous order upon the events I have witnessed, a certain kind of order has emerged nonetheless. Is it an order that resides out there, or has my anthropological training so conditioned me to see the world in certain ways that my own perception has become an extension of the discipline's priorities? I can't answer this question with any confidence, but I hope that I can at least contribute to the realization that such questions matter and to the experimentation that will be required for anthropologists to capture the sense and significance of the multiply-inflected, multiply-conflicted global cultures they presently confront.

Peshawar

Since I have stated a commitment to experience over theory and to ambiguity over certainty, I will conclude by recounting a final episode that (like so many stories coming out of a war zone) has the shadow of violence upon it. The incident took place one afternoon, not long before I left Peshawar, when an Afghan friend drove up to my house in a Suzuki pickup. He worked for one of the relief organizations, and he'd told me before that he'd be coming by. He had a passenger with him, a man of about 45, I would have guessed, but his grizzled beard made it difficult to guess his age with any precision. My friend had to help him get out because his eyes could no longer see. We sat down inside, and he told me his story, what there was to tell.

He'd been a village *mulla* before the war. For the last six years, he had been leading the life of a *mujahed*, living in the mountains, laying ambushes, leading prayers, traveling back and forth to Pakistan for supplies. One day, he was walking along a path and spied a book lying on the ground nearby. From the cover, he could tell it was a copy of the Qur'an. Normally, Afghans cover their Qur'ans with cloth and keep them in special niches in the walls of their homes. This one was soiled and abandoned. He opened it, and a bomb concealed within exploded in his face. That's why he'd been brought to me. My friend knew that I had a Pakistani friend who was a doctor. I'd called him, and my doctor friend had recommended a specialist with whom I made an appointment.

The man we went to see was about my age at the time. Early thirties. He'd gotten his medical education at Khyber Medical College in Peshawar and then went on to receive advanced training in eye surgery in London. The examination was brief. He shined a light into the mulla's eyes, peered through an instrument into each of the two scarred orbs, and then signaled me to come with him back to his office. There was nothing that could be done. Both eyes were destroyed. He shook his head. I can't remember exactly what he said, but it was something about the savagery of tribal people. It is difficult for us to understand them or their violence, he told me. They're just different from you and me, and by way of elaboration, he pulled out a handful of photographs. They showed a woman in traditional tribal dress. She looked like other Pakhtun women I had seen, except that her face was horribly disfigured.

The doctor explained that her husband had slashed her repeatedly with a knife for some perceived indiscretion. She probably should have died, her wounds were so severe, but some relatives had managed to get her out of the house and had taken her to the hospital. That's where the doctor had seen her. Because she had been cut around her eyes, as well as on other parts of her face, he had examined her, and later, when she was recovering and the scars were healing, he had taken these snapshots. As I looked at the photographs, he looked at me and smiled a dry, wry sort of smile. It was not a smile of amusement, but of identification. From the doctor's surname, I knew that he was himself a Pakhtun. His people had once been tribal people, and even now, he might have women in his own extended family who looked and dressed very much like the woman in the pictures. But now he was an educated man like myself, and these photographs seemed in some sad, horrible way to join us together, in testament to our common bond, our common civilization, and our common difference.

26

Being There ... and There ... and There! Reflections on Multi-Site Ethnography

Ulf Hannerz

In 1950, Professor Edward Evans-Pritchard, not yet 'Sir' but certainly a central figure in mid-century anthropology, gave a radio lecture on the BBC Third Programme where he outlined what an Oxford man (no doubt here about gender) would properly do to become an accomplished fieldworker in social anthropology. Having prepared himself meticulously for a couple of years, and if fortunate enough to get a research grant, the anthropologist-to-be would proceed to his chosen primitive society to spend there usually two years, preferably divided into two expeditions with a few months in between, if possible in a university department where he could think about his materials. In the field, Evans-Pritchard's anthropologist would throughout be in close contact with the people among whom he was working, he must communicate with them solely through their own language, and he must study their 'entire culture and social life'. For one thing, the long

period in the field would allow observations to be made at every season of the year. Having returned home, it would take the anthropologist at least another five years to publish the results of his research, so the study of a single society could be reckoned to require 10 years. And then, Evans-Pritchard concluded, a study of a second society was desirable – lest the anthropologist would think for the rest of his life in terms of a particular type of society (Evans-Pritchard, 1951: 64ff).

The idea of such a thorough, formative, exclusive engagement with a single field is of course at the base of the enduring power in anthropology of the prospect, or experience, or memory, or simply collectively both celebrated and mystified notion, of 'being there'.[1]

Something much like Evans-Pritchard's prescription has very long remained more or less the only fully publicly acknowledged model for fieldwork, and for becoming and being a real anthropologist. Perhaps, it works

Ulf Hannerz, "Being There ... and There ... and There! Reflections on Multi-Site Ethnography," pp. 201–216 from *Ethnography* 4(2), 2003. Copyright © 2003 by SAGE Publications (London, Thousands Oaks, CA and New Delhi). Reprinted by permission of the author and Sage Publications Ltd.

Ethnographic Fieldwork: An Anthropological Reader, Second Edition. Edited by Antonius C. G. M. Robben and Jeffrey A. Sluka.
Editorial material and organization © 2012 John Wiley & Sons, Inc.
Published 2012 by John Wiley & Sons, Inc.

with full force especially in the continued instruction of newcomers in the discipline – in many ways I conformed to it myself in my first field study, in an African American neighborhood in Washington, DC, although that was something quite different from Evans-Pritchard's classic 'primitive society'. Yet the hegemony of the model seems remarkable since it is fairly clear that a great many anthropologists, especially those no longer in the first phase of their careers, have long, but perhaps a bit more discreetly, been engaging in a greater variety of spatial and temporal practices as they have gone about their research. It may have been only Gupta and Ferguson's *Anthropological Locations* (1997) that really brought this variety entirely into the open. (I realize, certainly, that the power of the model has not been as strong among the ethnographically inclined in other disciplines, not so fully exposed to it, and obviously working under other conditions.)

So it may be, then, that when the conception of multi-site fieldwork – being there ... and there ... and there! – propagated most consistently by George Marcus (e.g. 1986, 1995), first gained wider recognition in anthropology in the later years of the 20th century, it was not really so entirely innovative. For one thing, in studies of migration, it was already becoming an established ideal to 'be there' at both points of departure and points of arrival (see e.g. Watson, 1977), thus working at least bilocally. Nor should we disregard the fact that the real pioneer of intensive anthropological fieldwork, Malinowski, was already going multilocal when he followed the Trobrianders along the Kula ring. Yet the very fact that this style of doing ethnography was given a label, and prominently advocated, and exemplified (if in large part by borrowing a case from journalism), and that this occurred much at the same time as ideas of place and the local were coming under increasing scrutiny in and out of anthropology, no doubt helped accelerate its recent spread, as a practice or as a topic of argument.

Whether due to convergent interests or mutual inspiration, a number of my colleagues in Stockholm and I were among those who fairly quickly saw possibilities in configuring our projects along multilocal lines. One of us studied the organizational culture of Apple Computer in Silicon Valley, at the European headquarters in Paris, and at the Stockholm regional office; another studied the occupational world of ballet dancers in New York, London, Frankfurt and Stockholm; a third connected to the Armenian diaspora across several continents; a fourth explored the emergent profession of interculturalists, what I have elsewhere a little facetiously referred to as the 'culture shock prevention industry'; and so on. We debated the characteristics of multilocal field studies fairly intensely among ourselves and with other colleagues, and a book some 10 of us put together on our projects and experiences, particularly for teaching purposes, may have been the first more extended treatment of the topic (Hannerz, 2001a). As far as I am concerned myself, perhaps lagging a little behind my more quickly-moving colleagues and graduate students, my involvement with multisite work has been primarily through a study of the work of news media foreign correspondents which I will draw on here.[2]

Among the Foreign Correspondents

The general background was that some 20–25 years ago I rather serendipitously drifted into the area which later came to be known as 'globalization' through a local study of a West African town, and then spent some time in large part thinking about the anthropology of the global ecumene in more conceptual and programmatic terms. By the time my itch to return to fieldwork combined with an actual opportunity to do so, several of us in Stockholm were concerned with 'globalization at work' – that is, responding to the fact that a large proportion of existing or emergent transnational connections are set up in occupational life. (This meant that we could also find food for thought in occupational ethnography outside anthropology, not least in the Chicago sociological tradition of Everett Hughes, Howard Becker and others.) More specifically, my own project could draw on the fact that I am a life-time news addict, and assumed as I began to think about it that if globalization

was also a matter of becoming more aware of
the world, and having more elaborated understandings of the world, 'foreign news' would
be a central source of such understandings.[3]
Perhaps most concretely, my curiosity fastened
on some of the reporting I was habitually
exposed to, for example when listening to the
morning news program on the radio while
having breakfast, and trying to wake up. There –
this would have been in the mid-1990s – a
familiar voice would report on street riots in
Karachi, or the latest triumph of the expanding
Taliban … and then sign off from Hong Kong.
There are people, then, such as 'Asia correspondents', or 'Africa correspondents'. These
are also people, clearly, engaged in an occupational practice of 'being there … and there …
and there' – and sometimes possibly even
appearing to be where they are not, if for
example they can make a Karachi street scene
come alive in their reporting even when they
quite clearly are at a desk thousands of miles
away from it. But just how do they do it?

I should say that as I was becoming seriously
attracted to the idea of doing something like
an ethnography of the social world of foreign
correspondents, I was still a bit ambivalent.
I found that on my shelves I already had some
number of the kind of autobiographies some
correspondents do, usually probably as their
careers begin approaching an end; and I had
seen most of those movies which over the years
have turned the foreign correspondent into a
kind of popular culture hero. As the saying
goes, 'anthropologists value studying what
they like and liking what they study'
(Nader, 1972: 303) – and I wondered whether
I would find foreign correspondents unap-
proachable, or perhaps arrogant prima donnas,
or just possibly too suspicious of an academic
who they might fear would always be inclined
to carping criticisms of their work.

As it turned out, I need not really have
worried. I did a series of pilot interviews in
New York during a period when I found myself
there as the field spouse of another multi-site
ethnographer, and the journalists I talked to
there, having made first contacts through
anthropologist mutual acquaintances, were
very hospitable and encouraging. (The only
thing I found a bit funny was that so many of

them were Pulitzer Prize winners.) And that is
how it continued to be. In the following
years I engaged in a series of conversations
with foreign correspondents and, sometimes,
strictly speaking, excorrespondents, mostly in
Jerusalem, Johannesburg and Tokyo, but also
in some number of other places including
New York and Los Angeles, where I seized
on the opportunity which some other kind of
trip provided, to add another handful of
interviews. Altogether, I talked to some 70
correspondents, and a few foreign news editors
offering the perspective from headquarters.

As I see it, an ethnography of foreign news
work of my kind can attempt to fill a noteworthy gap between two sets of representations of
international news. At least since the 1970s,
when a critical awareness grew of the communication imbalances in the world, it has been
recurrently noted that the apparatus of global
news flow is in large part controlled by what
we have described as either 'the West' or 'the
North' – the obvious examples of such domi-
nance have been major news agencies such as
Reuters or the Associated Press, with CNN
more recently added as another key symbol of
the apparatus. The other set of representations
I have in mind consists of those memoirs by the
newspeople themselves which I just referred to.
These tend to be quite individual-centered,
focusing on the authors as men and women of
action, facing all kinds of dangers as they
struggle to file their reports from the trouble
spots of the world.

The gap, then, is one between foreign
correspondents represented as puppets and as
heroes. In the heavily macro-oriented views of
media imperialism, the individuals who would
be its flesh-and-blood representatives at the
outer reaches of the newshandling apparatus
are hardly seen as anything other than
anonymous, exchangeable tools. In the autobiographical genre, in contrast, the individuals
tend to the strong, the wider structure of news
reporting not so noticeable.

Certainly my study of the foreign
correspondents reflects the asymmetry in the
global landscape of news. I deal mostly with
Europeans and Americans, reporting from
parts of the world which do not send out a
comparable number of correspondents of their

own to report from other places. In large part, this obviously matches the classic asymmetry of anthropology; and my choice of Jerusalem, Johannesburg and Tokyo as main field sites also reflects an interest in the way foreign correspondents, on a parallel track to ours, deal with issues of 'translating culture', of 'representing the other'. Apart from that, however, we face here once more the problem of striking a balance between structure and agency. What I have attempted to do in my study is to portray the networks of relationships more immediately surrounding the foreign correspondents, locally or translocally; the patterns of collaboration, competition and division of labor which organize their daily activities, formally or informally; and not least their room for maneuver and personal preferences in reporting. I have been curious about the partnerships which evolve between correspondents who prefer each other as company when going on reporting trips, and about the relationships between correspondents and local 'fixers', reminding me of the multifaceted links between anthropologists and their field assistants.

I have explored, too, the often obscure passages of news in roundabout ways between news agencies, electronic media and print media, which sometimes offer convenient shortcuts in correspondent work but which also generate tensions and now and then back-stage satirical comment about recycling and plagiarism. And not least have I been concerned with the implications of career patterns and with the spatial organization of foreign correspondence. How might it matter to reporting that some correspondents spend most of a life time in a single posting, while others are rotated every three years or so, between countries and continents? When large parts of the world get only brief visits by correspondents, described on such occasions as 'parachutists' or 'firemen', and only when there is a crisis to cover, how does this shape their and our view of these lands?

I am not going to devote my space here to any great extent, however, to discuss the specifics of my own project. I will rather try, against the background of this experience and that of some of my colleagues, to spell out a few of the issues which characteristically arise in multi-site ethnography, and ways in which it is likely to differ from the established model of anthropological field study, as I have let the latter be represented above by Evans-Pritchard and his half-century old formulation. For I believe that in arguments over the worth of multilocal work, it is not always made entirely transparent how it relates to the assumptions based on classic understandings of 'being there'.

Constituting the Multi-Site Field

In a way, one might argue, the term 'multilocal' is a little misleading, for what current multilocal projects have in common is that they draw on some problem, some formulation of a topic, which is significantly *trans*local, not to be confined within some single place. The sites are connected with one another in such ways that the relationships between them are as important for this formulation as the relationships within them; the fields are not some mere collection of local units. One must establish the translocal linkages, and the interconnections between those and whatever local bundles of relationships which are also part of the study.[4] In my foreign correspondent study, a major such linkage was obviously between the correspondents abroad and the editors at home. But then there was also the fact that the correspondents looked sideways, toward other news sites and postings, and sometimes moved on to these. They often knew colleagues in some number of other such sites, having been stationed in the same place some time earlier, or by meeting somewhere on one or more of those 'fireman' excursions which are a celebrated part of the public imagery of foreign correspondence, or by working for the same organization. In some loose sense, there is a world-wide 'community' of foreign correspondents, connected through local and long-distance ties.

These linkages make the multi-site study something different from a mere comparative study of localities (which in one classical mode of anthropological comparison was based precisely on the assumption that such linkages did not exist). Yet certainly comparisons are often built into multi-site research. My colleague Christina Garsten (1994), in her study of three sites within the transnational organization of Apple, was interested in comparing center and periphery within the corporation, as well as the way company culture in the offices was influenced by national cultures. As Helena Wulff (1998) studied the transnational ballet world she was similarly interested in national dance styles, but also in the differences between those companies in large part supported by the state and those working more entirely in the market. In my own study I could note the differences in foreign correspondent work between Jerusalem, where close at hand there was an almost constant stream of events commanding world attention; Tokyo, where it was a certain problem for correspondents that much of the time nothing really newsworthy seemed to happen; and Johannesburg, where designated 'Africa correspondents' based there would mostly travel to other parts of the continent when there was a war or a disaster to report on.

If we could make use of the possibilities for comparison, however, neither I nor my colleagues could claim to have an ethnographic grasp of the entire 'fields' which our chosen research topics may have seemed to suggest – and this tends to be in the nature of multi-site ethnography. It may be that in a migration study where all the migrants leave the same village and then turn up in the same proletarian neighborhood in a distant city, the potential and the actual combinations of sites are the same. On the other hand, a multinational corporation has many branches, ballet companies exist in a great many cities, a diaspora like that of the Armenians is widely dispersed, and foreign correspondents are based in major clusters in some 20–25 places around the world (disregarding here those temporary concentrations which result when the 'firemen' descend on a remote and otherwise mostly neglected locus of hard news). Consequently, multi-site ethnography almost always entails a selection of sites from among those many which could potentially be included. Evans-Pritchard may not actually have been everywhere in Azandeland or Nuer country, but this would hardly be as immediately obvious as the selectiveness, or incompleteness, of the multi-site study, where potential sites are clearly separate from one another.

The actual combination of sites included in a study may certainly have much to do with a research design which focuses on particular problems, or which seeks out particular opportunities for comparison. When I chose the somewhat exotic sites of Jerusalem, Johannesburg and Tokyo, it was because I was interested in reporting over cultural distances – I would have been less attracted by reporting between, say, Brussels and Stockholm, or between London and New York. Yet I wonder if it is not a recurrent characteristic of multi-site ethnography that site selections are to an extent made gradually and cumulatively, as new insights develop, as opportunities come into sight, and to some extent by chance. I had originally had in mind including India in my study, but then the first time I was planning to go a national election was called there, and while that could have been an attractive field experience, I suspected it would be a time when correspondents would have little time for me. Then the second time an ailment of my own made the streets of Delhi seem a less appealing prospect. To begin with, I had not expected to include Tokyo in my study, although it turned out to be a very good choice. But in no small part I went there because I had an invitation to a research workshop in Japan at a time when I could also stay on for some research.

Questions of Breadth and Relationships

Evans-Pritchard's anthropologist, again, would study the 'entire culture and social life' of the people assigned to him. Being around for at least a year, he could make observations during all seasons, and he would work in the local language (although it would probably be true that it was a language which in large part he had to learn during that year). And then, having spent, everything included, a decade of his life on that study, one could hope that there would also be time left for getting to know another people.

This is the kind of image of 'real' fieldwork which tends to worry current practitioners of, and commentators on, multi-site studies in anthropology. Compared to such standards, are these studies inevitably of dubious quality? If you are involved with two, three or even more places in much the same time span that classical anthropology would allow for one, which for various practical reasons may now be the case, what can you actually do? I do not want to assert that no problems of depth and breadth arise, that no dilemmas are inevitably there to be faced. Yet it is important that we realize how one site in a multi-site study now differs from the single site of that mid-20th century anthropologist.

I was in Jerusalem and Johannesburg and Tokyo, and more marginally in several other places, but I was clearly not trying to study the 'entire culture and social life' of these three cities. I was merely trying to get to know some number of the foreign newspeople stationed in them, and the local ecology of their activities. In fact, I was not trying hard to get to know these individuals particularly intimately either; what mattered to me about their childhood or family lives or personal interests was how these might affect their foreign correspondent work.

Anthropologists often take a rather romantic view of their fields and their relationships to people there. They find it difficult to describe their informants as informants because they would rather see them as friends, and they may be proud to announce that they have been adopted into families and kin groups – not only because it suggests something about their skills as fieldworkers, but also because it carries a moral value. They have surrendered to the field, and have been in a way absorbed by it. (Evans-Pritchard [1951: 79] shared similar sentiments: 'An anthropologist has failed unless, when he says goodbye to the natives, there is on both sides the sorrow of parting'.) Perhaps it is for similar reasons that I much prefer describing my encounters with correspondents as conversations, suggesting a more personal quality, rather than as interviews, although I certainly also want to convey the idea of only rather mildly structured exchanges, with room for spontaneous flow and unexpected turns.

There is no doubt a time factor involved in how relationships evolve. Yet I believe most multi-site studies really also have built-in assumptions about segmented lives, where some aspect (work, ethnicity or something else) is most central to the line of inquiry, and other aspects are less so. The ethnographer may be interested in the embeddedness of a particular line of belief or activity in a wider set of circumstances, but this hardly amounts to some holistic ambition. It is a pleasure if one discovers a kindred soul, but one keeps hardnosedly in mind what more precisely one is after, and what sorts of relationships are characteristic of the field itself, as one delineates it.

To some extent personalizing encounters in the modern, multi-site field comes not so much from deepening particular interactions as from the identification of common acquaintances – form placing the ethnographer in the trans-local network of relationships. Meeting with foreign correspondents, I have sensed that it is often appreciated when it turns out that I have also talked to friends and colleagues of theirs in some other part of the world; perhaps more recently than they have. Or even to their editor at home. As I have tried to include informants from the same news organization in different postings, to develop my understanding of its operations and as a kind of triangulation, such connections can be discovered fairly often and easily. It is a matter of establishing personal credentials.

Site Temporalities

Anthropology's classic image of fieldwork also includes an assumption about the durability of fields, and the involvement of 'natives' in them, relative to the length of the ethnographer's field stay. At least implicitly there is the notion that the ethnographer, alone a transient, has to develop in that year or two the understandings which match what the locals assemble during a life time. That year, moreover, covers the most predictable variation that one finds in local life: that of seasons.

Obviously the people we are concerned with in present day field studies tend mostly to be less dependent on seasons and their cycles of activity – on planting and harvesting, or on moving herds to greener pastures. But in addition, these people themselves often have other kinds of relationships to the site than that of real 'natives'. In Evans-Pritchard's time, the Azande and the Nuer among whom he mostly worked were pedestrians – in a lifetime they did not go all that far away. There may be some such people in Jerusalem, Johannesburg and Tokyo as well, but hardly among the foreign correspondents. And generally the people on whom we focus in multi-site field studies tend to be the more mobile ones, those who contribute most to turning the combinations of sites into coherent fields, and who also make the sites themselves, at least for the purposes of the studies, more like 'translocalities' (Appadurai, 1996). Some of the sites may even in themselves be short-lived phenomena. My Stockholm colleague Tommy Dahlén (1997), studying the making of the new interculturalist profession, found international conferences, including ritual events, workshops, exhibits and parties, central to his ethnography. And by the time his study was over, he had surely attended more of these conferences than most interculturalists. Such temporary sites – conferences, courses, festivals – are obviously important in much contemporary ethnography.

In some sites now, this goes to say, there are no real natives, or at any rate fewer of them, sharing a life-time's localized experience and collectivized understandings. There are more people who are, like the anthropologist, more like strangers. I find thought-provoking James Ferguson's (1999: 208) comment on what ethnography on the urban Zambian Copperbelt was like toward the end of the 20th century:

> Here there is much to be understood, but none of the participants in the scene can claim to understand it all or even take it all in. Everyone is a little confused (some more than others, to be sure), and everyone finds some things that seem clear and others that are unintelligible or only partially intelligible ... Anthropological understanding must take on a different character when to understand things like the natives is to miss most of what is going on.

This can be as true in single-site as in multi-site studies, but it problematizes the relationship between 'native' and ethnographer knowledge. Do things become easier for fieldworkers if their informants also find the world opaque, or more difficult as they have to understand not only the structure of knowledge such as it is, but also the nature and social organization of ignorance and misunderstandings? In any case, we sense that we have moved away from the classic fieldwork model.

Materials: Interviews, Observations, Etc.

Again, in my foreign correspondent project, interviews, be they long, informal and loosely ordered, were a large part of my field materials. I did sit in on a daily staff meeting of the foreign desk at one newspaper, and went on a reporting trip to the Palestinian West Bank with one correspondent. More materials of these and other kinds would no doubt have been of value, but for practical reasons I did not pursue some such possibilities, using the time at my disposal rather to ensure diversity through the interviews. (I tried to include different kinds of media, although with an emphasis on print correspondents, and I wanted to include a reasonably broad range of nationalities.) Also, as in Jerusalem, Johannesburg and Tokyo, and to a more limited extent in a couple of other places, I met with correspondents as they were immersed in the activities of a particular beat, and the interviews could be detailed and concrete.

Probably the time factor has a part in making many multi-site studies rather more dependent on interviews than single-site studies. If the researchers have to handle more places in the time classic fieldwork would devote to one, they may be more in a hurry. Language skills also probably play a part. In interviews, it is more likely that you can manage in one or two languages. My conversations with foreign correspondents were in English, except for those with fellow Scandinavians. In those sites, for many of the correspondents – particularly those who were expatriates, rotating between assignments – English was their working language as well.

George Marcus (1995: 101) concludes that most multi-sited field studies so far have been carried out in monolingual, mostly English-speaking settings.

This is surely not to say that multi-site ethnography must rely entirely on interviewing and informant work (in which case some might even feel that in the field phase, it is less than fully ethnographic – the ethnographic tendency may become more obvious in the style of writing); this still depends on the nature of research topics. Studying ballet companies, Helena Wulff could view performances and sit in on endless rehearsals. Although she could not very well 'participate' in the public performances, her own dance background meant that she still had a particular empathetic insight into the more practical, bodily aspects of dancing lives.

But then if pure observation, or participant observation, has a more limited part in some multi-site studies than in the classic model of anthropological fieldwork, it may not have so much to do with sheer multi-sitedness as with the fact that they tend to involve settings of modernity. There are surely a great many activities where it is worthwhile to be immediately present, even actively engaged, but also others which may be monotonous, isolated, and difficult to access. What do you do when 'your people' spend hours alone at a desk, perhaps concentrating on a computer screen?

At the same time, whatever you may now do along more classic ethnographic lines can be, often must be, combined with other kinds of sources and materials. Hugh Gusterson (1997: 116), moving on personally from an ethnography of one California nuclear weapons laboratory to a study of the entire American 'nuclear weapons community', and looking intermittently at the counterpart Russian community as well, describes contemporary ethnography as a matter of 'polymorphous engagements' – interacting with informants across a number of dispersed sites, but also doing fieldwork by telephone and email, collecting data eclectically in many different ways from a disparate array of sources, attending carefully to popular culture, and reading newspapers and official documents. Skills of synthesis may become more important than

ever. Certainly it is in considerable part relationships which are not, or at least not always, of a face-to-face nature which make the multi-site field cohere. Media, personal or impersonal, seem to leave their mark on most multi-site studies. Ulf Björklund (2001: 100), my colleague engaged in studying the Armenian diaspora, quotes an editor explaining that 'wherever in the world there are two dozen Armenians, they publish some kind of paper'. Helena Wulff describes the varied ways in which dance videos are used in the transnational dance community, including instruction as well as marketing. In my foreign correspondent study, the correspondents' reporting itself naturally makes up a large part of my materials, interweaving with my interviews. In the end, too, this means that Evans-Pritchard's words about the 'sorrow of parting' seem just a little less to the point. Just as their reporting could allow me to know at least something about them before meeting them in the flesh, so I could also to a degree keep track of them thereafter by following their reporting, from the sites where I met them or from elsewhere in the world, as I was back in Stockholm.

An Art of the Possible: Fitting Fieldwork into Lives

The pilot interviews apart, I began field studies for my foreign correspondent project in late 1996, and did the last interview in early 2000. In a way, then, I could seem to come close to Evans-Pritchard's five-year norm for a project, but that did not really include my preparatory work, nor time for writing up. On the other hand, I was not at all working full time on the project. In between, I was back in Stockholm engaged in teaching and administration, and also had a couple of brief but gratifying research fellowships elsewhere. But all the time, of course, I was following the reporting of foreign news.

Whether it is single-site or multi-site, I am convinced that much ethnographic work is now organized rather like that. Professional or domestic obligations make the possibility of simply taking off for a field for a continuous stretch of another year or two appear rather remote. For some that means never going to the field again, so there is no 'second society' experience of the kind which would supposedly broaden your intellectual horizons. But then ethnography is an art of the possible, and it may be better to have some of it than none at all. And so we do it now and then, fitting it into our lives when we have a chance.

Often, no doubt, this will be a matter of being there – and again! and again! – returning to a known although probably changing scene. Multi-site ethnography, however, may fit particularly well into that more drawn-out, off-and-on kind of scheduling, as the latter does not only allow us to think during times in between about the materials we have, but also about where to go next. It could just be rather impractical to move hurriedly directly from one field site to the next, according to a plan allowing for little alteration along the way.

Concluding one of his contributions to a recent British volume on anthropological fieldwork – Oxford-based, and thus also in a way updating the classic Evans-Pritchard model – detailing his own enduring East African commitment, David Parkin (2000: 107) notes that practical circumstances such as the growing number of anthropologists, and governmental financial restrictions on purely academic research, are factors which probably matter more to changes in styles of doing research than does intellectual debate; and he suggests that if more ethnographers now actually spread their fieldwork over many shorter periods than do it in the classic way of larger blocks of time, that is one such change. That sounds very likely, for again, ethnography is an art of the possible. Yet this is not to say that intellectual argument over changes and variations in the conduct of ethnography is useless. Perhaps these notes on experiences of multi-site fieldwork can contribute to such debate.

NOTES

1   'Being there' is, for one thing, the title of the first chapter in Clifford Geertz's (1988) study of anthropological writing, where another chapter is indeed devoted to Evans-Pritchard. It is also the title of another British

anthropologist, C.W. Watson's (1999) collection of accounts of fieldwork, half a century after Evans-Pritchard's statement. Paul Willis reminds me, moreover, that it is the title of a Peter Sellers movie.

2   The project has had the support of the Bank of Sweden Tercentenary Foundation. Previous writings resulting from it include Hannerz (1998a, 1998b, 1999, 2001b, 2002). The project was discussed in the Lewis Henry Morgan Lectures at the University of Rochester in November 2000, and a book will result from these lectures (Hannerz, forthcoming). I will also draw to a certain extent here on my discussion of multi-site ethnography in a more general handbook chapter on transnational research (Hannerz, 1998c).

3   As I soon learned, that was not self-evident – foreign correspondents have recently been inclined to think that international news reporting is under great pressure, perhaps particularly in the United States. As I write this, I come upon an item in what amounts to the gossip column of the *International Herald Tribune* (28 August 2002), according to which Dan Rather, CBS anchorman, tells *TV Guide* in an interview that less than a year after 11 September 2001, there is a new lack of emphasis on such reporting. 'The public has lost interest', Rather says. 'They'd much rather hear about the Robert Blake murder case or what is happening on Wall Street. A feeling is creeping back in that if you lead foreign, you die.'

4   Marcus (1995), in his discussion of this matter, has seen it in large part as a matter of choosing between, or making some combination among, six strategies: follow the people; follow the thing; follow the metaphor; follow the plot, story, or allegory; follow the life or biography; or follow the conflict.

REFERENCES

Appadurai, Arjun
   1996 *Modernity at Large*. Minneapolis: University of Minnesota Press.
Björklund, Ulf
   2001 'Att studera en diaspora: den armeniska förskingringen som fält', in Ulf Hannerz ed. *Flera fält i ett*, pp. 86–107. Stockholm: Carlssons.

Dahlén, Tommy
1997 *Among the Interculturalists*. Stockholm Studies in Social Anthropology 38. Stockholm: Almqvist & Wiksell International.

Evans-Pritchard, E.E.
1951 *Social Anthropology*. London: Cohen & West.

Ferguson, James
1999 *Expectations of Modernity*. Berkeley: University of California Press.

Garsten, Christina
1994 *Apple World*. Stockholm Studies in Social Anthropology 33. Stockholm: Almqvist & Wiksell International.

Geertz, Clifford
1988 *Works and Lives*. Stanford, CA: Stanford University Press.

Gupta, Akhil, and James Ferguson eds.
1997 *Anthropological Locations*. Berkeley: University of California Press.

Gusterson, Hugh
1997 'Studying Up Revisited', *Political and Legal Anthropology Review* 20(1): 114–19.

Hannerz, Ulf
1998a 'Of Correspondents and Collages', *Anthropological Journal on European Cultures* 7: 91–109.

Hannerz, Ulf
1998b 'Reporting from Jerusalem', *Cultural Anthropology* 13: 548–74.

Hannerz, Ulf
1998c 'Transnational Research', in H. Russell Bernard (ed.) *Handbook of Methods in Anthropology*. Walnut Creek, CA: Altamira Press.

Hannerz, Ulf
1999 'Studying Townspeople, Studying Foreign Correspondents: Experiences of Two Approaches to Africa', in H.P. Hahn and G. Spittler eds., *Afrika und die Globalisierung*, pp. 1–20. Hamburg: LIT Verlag.

Hannerz, Ulf ed.
2001a *Flera fält i ett*. Stockholm: Carlssons.

Hannerz, Ulf
2001b 'Dateline Tokyo: Telling the World about Japan', in Brian Moeran ed. *Asian Media Productions*, pp. 126–48. London: Curzon.

Hannerz, Ulf
2002 'Among the Foreign Correspondents: Reflections on Anthropological Styles and Audiences', *Ethnos* 67: 57–74.

Hannerz, Ulf
forthcoming *Foreign News*. Chicago, IL: University of Chicago Press.

Marcus, George E.
1986 'Contemporary Problems of Ethnography in the Modern World System', in James Clifford and George E. Marcus (eds) *Writing Culture*, pp. 165–93. Berkeley: University of California Press.

Marcus, George E.
1995 'Ethnography in/of the World System: The Emergence of Multi-Sited Ethnography', *Annual Review of Anthropology* 24: 95–117.

Nader, Laura
1972 'Up the Anthropologist – Perspectives Gained from Studying Up', in Dell Hymes (ed.) *Reinventing Anthropology*, pp. 284–311. New York: Pantheon.

Parkin, David
2000 'Templates, Evocations and the Long-term Fieldworker', in Paul Dresch, Wendy James and David Parkin eds., *Anthropologists in a Wider World*, pp. 91–107. Oxford: Berghahn.

Watson, C.W. ed.
1999 *Being There*. London: Pluto.

Watson, James L. ed.
1977 *Between Two Cultures*. Oxford: Blackwell.

Wulff, Helena
1998 *Ballet across Borders*. Oxford: Berg.

27

A New Form of Collaboration in Cultural Anthropology: Matsutake Worlds

Matsutake Worlds Research Group

Cultural anthropologists' interests in global and multisited phenomena require new kinds of ethnographic methods. In this report, we describe how collaboration can tackle a multi-faceted research topic without employing a preset division of specialized labor – a move that would automatically foreclose the singular gift of cultural anthropology: the sensitivity of the research question to the insights of fieldwork.[1]

Collaboration is made difficult by institutional requirements for junior scholars in social and cultural anthropology; universities have not been willing to recognize collaboration as, in itself, a contribution to knowledge. Collaborative research is often regarded as a poor substitute for the originality and rigor of single-author scholarship. Sometimes, of course, research collaborators do only play minor roles. In contrast, our project begins with the premise that every contributor should be able to draw the project into new and original directions; the project should continually shift because of its collaborative innovations. We offer this preliminary report not only to inspire other experimental collaborations but also to provoke institutional reform that might make collaboration more possible. At the very least, scholars at every rank deserve the right to explain the model of collaboration that inspires their research. The prevalent model, which splits the research contribution into fractions such that every collaborator dilutes the pool, is not a good representation of any research practice we know. In our project, every contributor reformulates the research, adding exponentially to its contribution. In this report, each participant offers a view of what working together makes possible. In offering this "research in progress," we hope to show the promise of collaborative experiments in cultural anthropology – and the concomitant need for institutional reform.

Matsutake Worlds Research Group, "A New Form of Collaboration in Cultural Anthropology: Matsutake Worlds," pp. 380–403 from *American Ethnologist* 36(2), 2009.

On Collaboration, by
Anna Tsing

Anthropologists are talking about collaboration. For many years, or so the story goes, cultural anthropology was the work of lone ethnographers. Lone ethnographers could be adventurers, philosophers, and creative geniuses all wrapped into one. There was – and is – something thrilling about this model, raising cultural anthropology above the imagined collective drudgery of other disciplines. The excitement of working alone is palpable, and calls to reform anthropology by making it more like normal science have had little resonance. But might there be creative and charismatic forms of collaboration capable of pushing forward the distinctive adventure of anthropology? Anthropologists are talking.

Various kinds of collaboration are being discussed. On the one hand, cultural anthropologists are newly interested in the often-unspoken collaborations of our work, such as the learning relationships we have in the field with our research subjects or the analytic circles at home through which we gain our categories and questions. Formal collaborations, particularly with scientists and activists, have pushed forward disciplinary agendas, training anthropologists in new habits of speaking and listening (see, e.g., Fortun 2001; Rabinow and Dan-Cohen 2006). On the other hand, new kinds of professional working relations among anthropologists are being discussed in which taken-for-granted material routines as well as philosophies of investigating, interpreting, and writing come under new scrutiny.

Even within the restricted universe of collaborations among anthropologists, arrangements are extraordinarily diverse. One way to plot such diversity might be to contrast big-science and intimate-authorship arrangements. In big science, collaboration is a guide as well as a method. This is because good research in big science should offer an object on which many researchers can agree. New methods and perspectives should not change the research object. Thus, collaboration is both a means and a goal. Common questions, goals, and methods

facilitate coordination among researchers and demonstrate the factual stability of the research object. Through collaboration, differences among researchers can be absorbed into the whole; ideally, the research object that emerges should have the multidimensionality of the collaborators' separate forms of expertise without taking up the jarring gaps across them that might interrupt its object status.

This model, which sets shared standards to ease collaboration, has a clear appeal. But it has worked poorly for cultural anthropologists because it gets in the way of ethnographic immersion. Ethnographic immersion requires the fieldworker to allow research objects to emerge from the events and contingencies of interactive field experience. Good fieldwork is supposed to change the fieldworker's research questions. Standardized questions, goals, and methods block this kind of ethnographic learning, in which goals and methods change in the research process. Jarring gaps are the stuff of ethnographic learning. Big science may be elegant, but it loses the point of ethnographic analysis.

At the other end of the range of collaborative anthropologies are those that look for a place in the tradition of creative individual authorship. Some – but not many – collaboratively written novels, artworks, and musical compositions exist. They are rare because creative authorship in collaboration is hard work. How might more than one person inhabit the space that Enlightenment legacies have given to the interior genius of the singular individual? Methods of collaboration are up for grabs. In some cases, the work requires a merging of creative personalities; in social science, one example is J. K. Gibson-Graham, the intellectual merging of Kathryn Gibson and Julie Graham (see Gibson-Graham 1996, 2006). In anthropology, the editorial collaborations that created and directed the subfield called "feminist anthropology" are examples.[2] Perhaps creative collaboration is associated with feminist scholarship in part because it requires a labor of emotional intimacy, entailing close hours and long years of negotiation and great care over procedural matters. Who takes the lead? Whose insights take precedence? Whose style works? These questions are never settled. When things go well, the experience is delightful; when disagreements arise, everyone feels crushed. This is because there is no easy complementarity among roles. No a priori standards set the frame. Questions, methods, and goals are worked out in the process. This open-endedness makes collaboration in creative authorship an intriguing – but also terrifying – possibility for ethnographic research and writing.

In practice, a good deal of heterogeneous territory lies between big science and creative authorship. The Matsutake Worlds Research Group is an experiment in making one piece of this territory livable. On the one hand, group members have separate and well-defined areas of expertise. In particular, we know different languages and have been trained in the literature on different world areas. Our project requires this combined expertise. Some of the time too we conduct fieldwork on our own or with collaborators from outside the project. Some of the time, we write alone or with just one selected coauthor. But we have tried, and are continuing to try, a variety of collaborative experiments that exceed both individual and big-science models. First, we have conducted overlapping and joint fieldwork. Not all our fieldwork has taken this form – but enough to consider what intersubjective immersion might mean. Second, we have worked to consider how to analyze data in tandem. And, third, we are involved in varied experiments in collaborative writing. These experiments push us beyond our training, requiring bravery – and opening new possibilities for the discipline of cultural anthropology. We call our process "strong collaboration," that is, a form of collaboration in which explicit attention to the process is part of the project.[3]

Our subject is an aromatic gourmet mushroom, a species cluster of the genus *Tricholoma*, commonly known as matsutake. Matsutake are much appreciated in Japan as well as in Korea, and they may be the world's most expensive mushrooms. Poetry has been written about this mushroom; in Japan it is a featured subject in anime cartoons, cooking shows, and traditional ceremonies for the autumn season. Until the 1970s, Japanese forests produced sufficient matsutake for domestic use, but

ecological changes since WWII have caused a sharp decline in the Japanese matsutake population. The decline corresponded with Japanese prosperity. Beginning in the 1980s, Japan began to import matsutake from forests around the northern hemisphere: North and South Korea, China, the United States, Canada, Morocco, Mexico, Bhutan, and, most recently, Sweden and Finland.

Despite strenuous efforts, matsutake has never been cultivated. To find matsutake, one must forage in forests, where the mushrooms emerge in association with particular host trees, mainly conifers. Once they are picked, they must be sent posthaste to Japan; there is little market for dried or preserved matsutake, because the mushroom loses its aroma if not consumed fresh. The matsutake trade requires efficient global connections, the space–time compression that scholars and pundits call "globalization." The trade also dips into the extraordinary diversity of foraging ecologies. Foraging and globalization are worlds apart in most social theory. Our team became fascinated by their combination in the matsutake commodity chain.

In central Japan, festive village auctions arrange picking rights. In the US Pacific Northwest, war-scarred Southeast Asian refugees camp out in national forests to forage. In British Columbia, Canada, First Nations claim the mushrooms. In southwest China, "matsutake mansions" are built as villages consolidate their forest boundaries.[4] Foraging and forest-management arrangements contrast; so too do both vernacular and scientific understandings of matsutake forest ecology. Our collaborative research investigates how knowledge and value are created both within and across these sites. For this task, we follow both commerce and science.

From the first, we have been intrigued by how both connections among and differences across national and regional formations of matsutake science and forest management emerge. Why, for example, do US forest managers urge less human impact on matsutake forests whereas Japanese forest managers arrange for more human impact (Tsing and Satsuka 2008)? To pursue questions about regional and national difference follows easily from the heritage of anthropology. Yet equally important is taking the knowledge claims of scientists – which focus on connection, not difference – at face value. To become interlocutors for scientists and forest managers, we work hard to train ourselves in mycology and forest ecology, as these disciplines teach us new ways to appreciate the mushrooms. The challenge is to follow cosmopolitan connections at the same time that we attend to gaps and awkward encounters. Our previous research hones our theoretical tools for this task (Choy 2005; Faier 2009; Hathaway 2006; Inoue 2006; Satsuka 2004; Tsing 2005).

Taking our responsibilities as fieldworkers seriously, we have tried to avoid building an analysis based only on superficial encounters. This is the nightmare possibility of multisited ethnography and one that collaboration can potentially address. Members of our team have language fluency in Japanese and Chinese and area-studies experience from earlier research in Japan, China, Canada, the United States, and Southeast Asia. But how were we to share these talents without dividing up the labor – and thus losing the gift of immersion fieldwork, the shifting research object? Our experiments began with overlapping fieldwork. We challenged each other's sensual experience of the field, soliciting continual reinterpretation and cascades of translation. None of us had done joint fieldwork before, and its pleasures were a revelation. We aimed not to cancel each other's peculiar appreciations, as in big-science collaborative syntheses but, rather, to heighten our differences as a source of questions. Faier named this strategy "echolocation," a term that stresses the importance of intersubjective perception in our collaborative process (Matsutake Worlds Research Group in press). After all, the aromatic matsutake teaches us to pay attention to the senses.

Matsutake remind us to smell out connections: Pickers sometimes locate the mushrooms, which may not break the ground's surface, through smell. Smell is our human reaction to chemicals released by the mushroom to attract its own harvesters, who spread its spores. Thinking through the notion of smell provided our team with another ground for experiment, one of analysis. We collectively imagined the mushroom itself as a collaborator. The shared sensitivity to chemicals of both humans and mushrooms, which might broadly be called "smell," bridges human–nonhuman differences. Smell signals multispecies connection from the mushroom's point of view as well as from the human's. What could be gained if we considered the problem of collaboration from the vantage point of mushrooms – or even wider collaborative commitments? This question enlivened one of our first writing experiments, a chapter for a book on multisited ethnography (Matsutake Worlds Research Group in press). The chapter was not intended to address the problem of smell but, rather, the problem of collaboration. But smell was the issue that sparked debate about collaboration in our group: Can humans and mushrooms really be collaborators? Might all knowledge, then, require collaboration? If so, what might we gain by making these necessary collaborations apparent? These questions continue to inform our discussions.

Writing together introduced its own challenges. We have been loath to merge our identities completely without the careful work of developing a common voice. Our first full-group experiment (Matsutake Worlds Research Group in press) offered a compromise: We each wrote a short signed essay and then sandwiched them all between an introduction and conclusion. When we read the resulting chapter as a whole, we were intrigued and surprised by the effect of multiple voices. Individual styles amplified the collective endeavor. Meanwhile, various subsets of the group have developed their own experiments, exemplified by Mogu Mogu's section in this report. The current report thus offers a second experiment, in which both individual and merged authorships are represented. As we develop voices for different texts and audiences, we plan more writing experiments.

The process is both difficult and fun. At its very best, collaboration can be exhilarating and a needed antidote to the lonely competition of the academy. However, the academy itself enforces that loneliness in its standards, and this has been our biggest challenge. Collaboration is difficult in cultural anthropology for material and symbolic reasons that have nothing to do with research, analysis, or writing per se. Institutional requirements get in the way. Although collaboration in big science is a recognized quantity, creative forms of collaboration are not valued in the academy. The accounting system of big science gives individual researchers only partial credit for collaborative work, yet creative collaboration takes much more effort than is required in single authorship. Junior scholars, in particular, feel constrained from trying collaborative experiments because of anxieties about promotion and tenure. Beyond the institution, the culture of academe molds all scholars through its standards. We learn to throw our ambition at individual advancement rather than imagining wider circles and more playful interconnections through which contributions might be made. We feel driven to market our ideas for their quick-sale appeal, not for their contribution to a slow collective project; we forget to ask how our work opens curiosity rather than admiration.

Might we devise a practice that has it both ways – that meets the demands of the academy at the same time that it builds a world worth living in? Might we use the heady rush of creativity and charisma, but plow it back into the scholarly process rather than toward the fetish of individual brilliance? Collaborative experiments, at their best, make the process more important than the race. Chewing into the filing systems of both auditing and one-upmanship, they open worm-sized breathing spaces within the corporate culture of the neoliberal academy.

Each section in this report addresses the possibilities of collaboration: between group members; between humans and nonhumans; and in making knowledge and social practice, more generally, both within and beyond the academy. Our group argues that formal experiments in collaboration allow scholars to consider already existing collaborative dynamics that we ignore to our peril. Tracking collaborations between scientists and mushrooms, or between mushroom pickers, buyers, and scientists from different parts of the world, or between anthropologists themselves also urges consideration of the ways knowledge emerges from social process. In each case, the findings of research reports are just

the fruiting body of a larger underground life process. It may be impossible to acknowledge all the mycelial threads that weave together below this tip, but it is important to follow at least a few. Thus, for example, the reader can follow our group discussions about multinational scientists and mushrooms in and out of the sections that follow. Some pieces of the story are not present here: Tsing's "Unruly Edges: Mushrooms as Companion Species" (in press b), written in dialogue with the work of Donna Haraway before the research collaboration began, opens the door to building social theory from mushrooms but is carried to startling new horizons by Mogu Mogu. Hathaway enlarges, through work on China, a more prosaic comparison of matsutake science in Japan and the United States begun in Tsing and Satsuka's "Diverging Understandings of Forest Management in Matsutake Science," written for *Economic Botany* (2008). Neither is the discussion limited to the ideas of members of the research group. We were pleased to find Timothy Ingold's (2006) references to mycelia as models for social theory. We are encouraged by Paul Stamets's (2005) confidence that mushrooms will save the world. Indeed, every scientist and mushroom picker we have spoken to exudes a sense of having found a hidden cache of wonderful knowledge: This enthusiasm breathes life into our analyses.

Mogu Mogu's "Mycorrhizal Translations, a Mushroom Manifesto" addresses the heart of our collective project by exploring translations of value. How might the nature of the mushroom itself shape human understandings of its value? Mycorrhiza are structures formed between fungi and tree roots; the authors argue that they form a useful image for social theory. In this realm of mycorrhizal relations, this section offers an intertwined authorial identity: It is jointly written by Choy and Satsuka, using the name Mogu Mogu. Even as a name, Mogu Mogu expresses the playful possibilities of collaboration. In Japanese, the term might be translated as "yum, yum," and in Chinese, *mogu* is a mushroom. Satsuka described the pleasures of collaboration here: "It was like jazz," she said, with insights flying back and forth in emergent, improvised rhythms. Mogu Mogu challenge us to open up our understandings of social theory, collaboration, and even love, to the rhythms and textures of interspecies life.

Our second section, "Weather and Bugs as Contingencies of Matsutake Connections," continues the theme of human–nonhuman relations with a meditation on the importance of contingency in vernacular evaluations of mushroom science. Faier interviewed matsutake pickers in rural Nagano, Japan, and was struck by their discussions of both unpredictable patterns of weather and insect infestations. Matsutake science in Japan has evolved in a layered historical conversation between cosmopolitan modern science, on the one hand, and practical village knowledge, on the other hand. Scientists have been attentive to village practices, and villagers have listened to scientists. Matsutake connoisseurs in Central Kiso offered their version of matsutake science to Faier: At the heart of the matter was indeterminacy. What might this interpretation mean for global scientific connections around matsutake? This question again refigures our group's collaborative research topic: the interplay of situated and traveling forms of knowledge and value.

The spread of matsutake commerce around the northern hemisphere has opened new centers of matsutake science and forest and business management. Hathaway takes readers to southwest China, where matsutake has become an important commodity – and an object of both research and policy. China's matsutake research, Hathaway shows, is ideally situated to address questions of post-colonial science, that is, science recognized as simultaneously universal and culturally located. Because matsutake is a relatively recent export commodity in southwest China, the emergence of both interconnection and specificity is still clear. Hathaway shows how the history of international conservation projects in southwest China shapes the possibilities of local expertise and policy. His discussion also illuminates how collaboration can lead to continually revitalized research trajectories. At the heart of his discussion is an implicit international dialogue involving Japanese, US, and Chinese researchers and forest managers.

Chinese science and forest management, Hathaway shows, emerges in the context of strikingly contrasting models developed in Japan, on the one hand, and the US Pacific Northwest, on the other hand. Our collaborative project – like that of the forest managers we study – engages multiple layers of this transnational dialogue.

Finally, Inoue returns the report to the question of collaboration. How does collaboration change the conditions of knowledge production? What tenets of modern knowledge will scholars be forced to reconsider?

Mycorrhizal Translations, a Mushroom Manifesto, by Mogu Mogu

Mogu mogu

mogu mogu
spores fly shiro abides
lines of love and value mushroom
yum yum[5]

The matsutake mushroom has been fetishized in Japan for its symbolic and material value as a rare delicacy. Its high price and the recent decline of the Japanese domestic harvest have stimulated a new transnational commodity chain in Korea, China, and the west coast of the United States and Canada. The Matsutake Worlds Research Group investigates the layers of transnational networks of commercial dealers and harvesters, scientists, forest administrators, amateur mushroom pickers, and food consumers through which matsutake is commoditized, transformed, studied, and consumed. This section represents an initial stage of concept work: a reflection on potential theoretical and methodological implications and the development of some working tools and concepts to instigate lines of ongoing research.

Rhizomes, fungi

Gilles Deleuze and Félix Guattari provoke readers in *A Thousand Plateaus* (1987) to approach the world from the point of view of a rhizome. Why do they care about rhizomes? For them, the rhizome serves less as a concept than as a poetics – a poetics of the ontology of multiplicity. It offers an ontology that refuses tree being, arborescent being, being as if there were a general, unifying force – a one – under which all phenomena are organized. The rhizome offers a way to talk about fields and lines of connecting, relating, interpenetrating, becoming, and transforming. One point is crucial: The rhizome not only refuses arborescent being but it also requires a nonarborescent analysis. Its organization – and the proper organization of thought – is emergent through the actualization of connections. The rhizome acts at times in Deleuze and Guattari's text as rhizomic plants such as strawberry, ginger, and bamboo do. At other times, it assumes other living forms – appearing as trees, wolves, ticks, and fungi.

We pursue the rhizome-as-fungus here at more length. Why? Because through the eyes of a fungus, we may attune our sense of the world's relations differently.[6] Modern human eyes are accustomed to apprehending a landscape through its trees, grasses, and flowers. Yet this habit reproduces an overlooked violence; one needs no other reminder than Tsing's (in press b) account of the scandalous victory of cereals that have domesticated human and nonhuman lives. Fungi slip from view, marginalized in the celebratory dioramas of sedentary agriculture.

Another look, however, reveals that the grassy victory is more superficial than it would at first appear. As we keep our eye on a fungus, and look through the fungus, we learn to see not only multiplicity but also diversities and incipient relations in the landscape more clearly and concretely. Fungi continue to act vitally in the connections that make up landscapes. Human beings' lots are cast with theirs.

The diversity of fungi

Mycologists categorize mushrooms according to the ways in which they take nutrition or how they relate to a host. They typically divide them into three types: saprobic, parasitic, and mycorrhizal. Saprobic mushrooms take nutrition from a dead body of plants, such as trees, logs, straw, or compost, or from other fungi and animals. Both parasitic and mycorrhizal mushrooms take nutrition from living organisms. Parasitic mushrooms harm the host plants, at times eventually killing them. In contrast, mycorrhizal mushrooms form a symbiotic relationship with the roots of trees. In fact, plants need symbiotic relationships with fungi to take nutrition from the soil. Most plants have fungi on the tips of their roots. The fungi break down soil components, effectively predigesting nutrients for the plants. In exchange, the plants supply nutrition produced by photosynthesis to the fungus. Mushrooms are the fruit bodies of some of these symbiotic fungi.

Most cultivated mushrooms, such as button, portobello, and shiitake are saprobes. Because they live with – or on – dead plants, humans can easily replicate their living conditions and produce them on a commercial scale. Most highly prized wild mushrooms, such as the truffle, porcini, chanterelle, and matsutake, are mycorrhizal. They dwell in and create the landscape in different ways.

Shiitakes are easy to understand because they act like timber. They are born into the commodity chain from dead trees through an inoculation technology that has been used for hundreds of years in China and Japan. Shiitake cultivators drill a series of holes into oak logs and place plugs with shiitake spawn in them. The logs are then stacked outdoors under canopies. After several months, shiitake mushrooms grow out of the inoculated logs. Increasingly, since the development of indoor sawdust cultivation in 1980s, outdoor log cultivation has declined in favor of indoor production. Humans can believe that shiitakes are domesticated. Little mystery surrounds their propagation.

The mycorrhizal relationship between a matsutake and its host, by contrast, is more complex. The matsutake produces a dense mycelial mass in its subterranean habitat. This mass is called "shiro," which in Japanese literally means the color white (白), a castle (城), or a place (代). If one scrapes the topsoil, one will see shiro as a white or pale gray soil between or around host trees. Shiro works like a fort around a castle: Matsutake is a weak competitor with other fungi and microorganisms. Matsutake avoid rich organic soil where others thrive. The shiro excludes mold and bacteria. Plant roots that try to penetrate the shiro from the outside turn rotten at the tips or make a U-turn away from the shiro. Within its colonized domain, the shiro can be compared to a seedbed for the matsutake mushrooms.

Matsutake mycelia mesh with the young growing roots of pine trees and create mycorrhiza. They cover the tips of fine pine roots, penetrate between cells in the roots, and form a structure known as a Hartig net, through which they exchange substances with pines. When a pine root grows thick, the growth of fine, lateral roots stops. The thick main roots do not create a mycorrhizal relationship with matsutake anymore. Matsutake–pine mycorrhiza are produced only temporarily, when the growing cycles of pine roots and matsutake mycelia match. The cooperation of entangled pine roots, matsutake mycelia, and other microbes secures food for the mushroom. Mycorrhiza in a shiro is a structure of symbiosis. It assembles life with other organisms and lets their fruit, the mushrooms, bloom.

Many aspects of this symbiotic relationship are still mysterious to humans and pose an exciting challenge for scientists and commercial engineers (Suzuki 2005; Yamada and Omasa 2003). Yet another challenge lies in assessing how porous the trophic categories themselves might be. Lu-Min Vaario and colleagues (2002) have broached the question, for instance, of whether a mycorrhizal mushroom might harbor saprobic potential.

A diagram as a map

The diagram in Figure 27.1 maps some of matsutake's mycorrhizal relations. Put your finger on it to trace them. Matsutake, trees, foresters, buyers, gatherers, industries, scientists, and eating – all nourish each other.

This diagram is a machine of abstraction. It flattens the multidimensionality of the landscape. It simplifies relationships so that one can clearly trace the generative interconnections of each actor. The diagram codifies action, helps the user to copy and repeat the action, and creates the desire to reproduce the effects. It is a tool for tracing actions in a closed terrain. It produces an expected effect.

Yet, if one sees this diagram through the eyes of fungus, it appears as a map. A map can also be a tool for abstraction, but it has two faces. One face of the map reifies objects in the landscape, strata, and territories. It flattens. But the other face of the map shows the line of flight, stimulates movement toward deterritorialization and destratification. It creates desire to connect different dimensions. The landscape pops up. It sparks imagination outside the closed terrain. It connects to the outside.

A spore flies and lands on the soil where microbes dwell. A mycelium reaches out and entangles itself with plant roots. It collaborates with microbes and diversifies itself into different strands. Fungus and microbes dissolve the soil and create new strata and a new landscape. A mushroom as a fruit body blooms as a product of these intra-species actions.[7]

Analytic advantages of mycorrhiza

Thinking mycorrhizally points us to landscapes and practices that thrive in the "gap" between what is taken as wild and what is taken as domesticated – the "seam" between supposed nature and culture. In doing so, it not only orients us to the subterranean processes that draw those gaps and seams into being but it also alerts us to others that might draw those edges differently.

Matsutake is commonly considered a wild mushroom, one that cannot be artificially cultivated. Yet Dr Makoto Ogawa (1991), a pioneering Japanese matsutake scientist, has cautioned that matsutake might be better described as an "unintentionally cultivated" mushroom.

In the main islands of the Japanese archipelago, matsutake mostly grow in red pine (Pinus densiflora) forests. Red pine is a pioneer species in plant succession. As a pioneer species, the red pine thrives in shallow soils where other plants cannot survive, such as mountain ridges with exposed rock. Matsutake particularly like thin red-pine forests; the mushrooms are usually observed in mountains that have either been

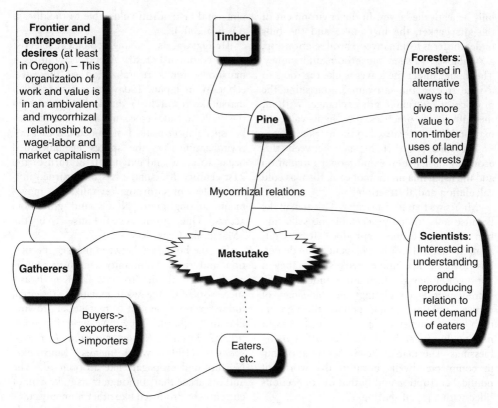

Figure 27.1 *Map*

cleared by foresters and farmers for wood use and shifting cultivation or that are in recovery.

The matsutake's favorite habitat in Japan is *satoyama*, an ecological network of low-altitude mountains, forest, and human dwellings. Throughout history, people have used satoyama for cutting firewood, collecting fallen leaves for fertilizer, making charcoal, and carving terraced paddies. Satoyama is a secondary natural environment, an ecology that includes human activities. A landscape of human intervention is necessary for the growth of the "wild" matsutake mushroom.

Matsutake mycorrhizal relationships: Three examples

Looking at the landscape through the matsutake's mycorrhizal relations tunes our senses to complex chemistries linking and forming different actors. Something unforeseen may pop up in the multinatural landscapes matsutake leads us to. Let us share with you three fruits of matsutake's relations with love, knowledge, and money.

Example 1: Mr Y. Mr Y is a quality-vegetable merchant in Kyoto. His store has been dealing quality matsutake since the 1880s. His idea of "commerce" tells of a gift exchange system in the heart of an urban capitalist center.[8] The joy of matsutake, Mr Y says, is not in the eating. It is about giving a gift. People do not buy top-end, expensive matsutake to eat by themselves. The matsutake is not like an ordinary commodity that a buyer consumes by her or himself. The matsutake functions as money. Mr Y explains that, actually, matsutake is often used as a bribe. When people give matsutake as a gift, they rest the mushrooms on a bed of *urajiro (Gleichenia japonica)* ferns in a basket, often placing some 10,000-yen bills beneath the leaves. In the environment of the gift basket, the matsutake and the bills under the ferns form a mycorrhizal relationship, a symbiosis between mushroom and money. The money under the leaves is like the roots of a pine tree in the satoyama, nourishing the practice of matsutake gift exchange. Without the gift-giving practices, the high value of matsutake is not realized in the market.

But there is a slight gap between this economy of matsutake and money circulation and the usual imagination of capitalism as cold calculation and abstraction.

Mr Y says that he is fascinated by matsutake because it is the only vegetable he sells that human beings cannot reproduce. It is a gift from the natural world, a blessing from deities. His love of matsutake evokes the ancient notion of money as a medium coming from the sacred world, circulating the blessings of deities, and connecting people through its mobility. Commerce can be greedy profit making, but it can be also an act of dispersing blessings. The matsutake–money relationship in commerce dwells both in the world of political corruption and in that of connections filled with a joy of sharing.

Example 2: Mushroom modernity. In 1868, the Meiji government was established, following the model of the modern nation-state. The Meiji government actively incorporated Western industrial technologies in hopes of strengthening the nation. During the modernization process, resource extraction was accelerated, massively transforming Japan's landscapes. Many mountains went bald. Matsutake flourished.

The 1960s saw the Japanese "fuel revolution." People turned from wood and charcoal fuels to propane and petroleum gas, even in rural areas. Satoyamas were abandoned. Red-pine forests were succeeded by broadleaf trees. The soil became too rich for matsutake mycelia to grow. With an urban economic boom, young people migrated from rural areas to the cities. The rural communities were left with old people and abandoned mountains. Around the same time, pine wilt disease caused by nematodes became a serious problem throughout Japan. Many red pines were killed. Dr Ogawa believes that the decline of mycorrhiza weakened the red

pines and made them vulnerable to the disease (Ogawa 2007).

Dr Ogawa, as a young ecological scientist in the National Forestry Agency, saw hope in matsutake for a revitalization of the rural economy in Japan. Today, he is retired from matsutake research. He grew disappointed in the ways matsutake became an object of market speculation instead of a medium of rural revitalization. Yet the spores he unleashed began to grow and extend at the turn of the 21st century. Matsutake has been turned into an emblem of satoyama revitalization movements among many NGOs and grassroots actors. One group even calls itself the "Matsutake Crusaders."

But the boundary between market speculation and rural community empowerment is murky. Dr Takashi Ito and Dr Koji Iwase, successors of Dr Ogawa in matsutake research, today promote the idea of matsutake growing like an "orchard." They have written a book titled *Matsutake: Kajuen kankaku de fuyasu sodateru* (1997), which means "Matsutake: Nurture and propagate like an orchard." The authors argue that, although matsutake cannot currently be produced like other humanly cultivated plants, it is possible to transform a whole mountain environment to make it suitable for matsutake production. As successors of Dr Ogawa, the authors express strong concern about the wellbeing of rural communities, but they beg the question of the different dynamics an "orchard" brings to the way satoyamas have been used (Tsing and Satsuka 2008).

Example 3: SEV. Our third example takes us from Japan to Oregon, to the relations matsutake's mycorrhizal relations themselves forge with efforts to imagine alternative forms of value. It takes us to an incubated thought, an article-spore. Five foresters set out in 2002 to compare the production and value of timber and of wild edible mushrooms in the Pacific Northwest. To do so, they used an economic instrument known as the Soil Expectation Value, or SEV. SEV estimates the net worth of a forest on a per-hectare basis. To be more accurate, it assesses the potential value of land in terms of the income that will accrue if the land is used for particular purposes. SEV is explicitly

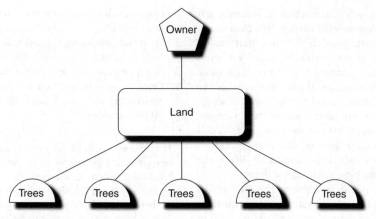

Figure 27.2   *Arborescent ownership*

an instrument of comparison, a technique for projecting two or more futures – two or more landscapes – in a common currency.

Now, translating land into SEV is relatively straightforward if one thinks about – and like – a tree.[9] In the world of timber trees, all expenses and returns are organized under the one – the one who owns the land – making the costs and returns straightforward to track. Costs – of planting, thinning, and harvesting – are relatively predictable as are yields. The SEV of trees is calculated as the delivered log price minus the harvest cost, wages and transportation costs, and other costs associated with harvesting and transporting the trees. The landowner captures all the return to the resource because property rights and markets are well defined (see Figure 27.2).

But things get tricky with matsutake and other wild edible mushrooms. Just as matsutake lead us to an appreciation of mycorrhizal relations and intra-active exchanges between (what become) trees and mushrooms, so too they lead us to a mycorrhizal system of value. For economic returns on the mushrooms do not flow to the one. They are distributed – between landowner and harvesters. The structure of distribution is not free or equal, but neither is it arborescent. With matsutake, the landowner captures a small fraction of the value – only the income, if any, from permit sales. How, then, will the foresters estimate the value of mushroom "production" (if one can

even call it "production" when speaking of "wild" mushrooms)? They must find the net return to the harvesters.

This presents a challenge for three reasons: (1) Property rights are not clearly defined, and public documentation of markets and prices for matsutake is poorer than it is for timber markets; (2) given a short growing season and unpredictable yields, the matsutake market is imperfect and volatile; and (3) information about harvesters' expenses and revenues is scarce.[10] Harvesters do not talk readily about how much they earn selling mushrooms or about how much they spend on food and gas. Harvesters compete with each other to gather the most and the best mushrooms. Secrecy and privacy rule the day, as harvesters guard knowledge of potential mother lodes.

Still, the foresters find a handful of harvesters willing to talk; and what they cannot gather in the wild, they fill in with the help of a former harvester's memoir, *Matsutake Mushroom: "White" Goldrush of the 1990s* (Guin 1997).

With this information, they reach a remarkable conclusion. Comparing SEVs for potential timber use and matsutake harvesting in the same forest, the tasty mushrooms' SEV eclipses that of trees. This is striking, because matsutake's brethren, chanterelle and morel, are not so lucky; they cannot generate comparable values – largely because they are not dear enough. They fetch less per pound, most likely because they lack the extraculinary relations with the monetarized circuits of Japanese gift and graft that nourish matsutake's cash value. It is this anticipated high value that makes buyers early in the commodity chain willing to pay more for matsutake. It is this high value that, in turn, nourishes the frontier spirit of the "white gold rush" and the imagination of a self-made fortune among the harvesters in Oregon, the willingness to assume the financial risks and hard labor involved in dedicating days to looking for mushrooms that barely break the surface of the pine-needle forest floor.

In this instance, within the controlled environment of the foresters' argument, trees lose the value game. Land utilized to nurture and harvest matsutake has the same SEV as, or a better one than, land planted with trees meant to be felled. Matsutake and their mycorrhizal relations with Oregon's pine trees thus cast a spore of thought for the foresters. With matsutake's aid, they can argue that land is worth more as a landscape than as land. Trees can be mycorrhizal partners – they can be something other than timber.

Thinking through matsutake's translation of forest values offers a possibility of a less clear-cut future. It does not mean thinking utopically, however, or generally, about fungi or value. Specificities matter. Chanterelles and morels, although equally mycorrhizal and equally delicious, cannot muster such value. This calculus, furthermore, works only within a specific regime of property ownership in Oregon.[11]

Instruments, love

Timber value exists in disavowal of trees' mycorrhizal needs, unless mycorrhizal mushrooms are instrumentalized as nutritional amendments for tree production (see Wang and Hall 2004). Matsutake and those who love them, however, turn the tables, instrumentalizing trees for mushrooms. By *love*, we mean something akin to what Dr Minoru Hamada means when he writes in his *Matsutake nikki* (Matsutake diary; 1974) of the possibility of a chemical love.

"When we analyze love as a scientific phenomenon," Hamada writes, "there emerge the following questions":

1 Is it an exclusive phenomenon among living organisms?
2 Is it an exclusive phenomenon among human beings?
3 Is it a phenomenon towards different sex?
4 Does it presuppose sexual maturity or sexual activity? Can you observe it among infants or elders?

The above questions all involve ambiguous categories ... all living forms are bipotential or bisexual ... often the actors of "love" are not perfectly male or female, they may be sterile, or there may be a better sexual partner. Even after a lover passes away, the feeling of love may remain or even become stronger. The object of love does not need to be a living organism. It is also hard to draw a boundary between "true love" and the love between a parent and a child, between friends, desire for a thing or work. [1974:185]

He defines love as follows: "positive and negative approach towards a variety of stimulation caused by a non-living being, a living being or a group of living beings. In other words, love is the whole process of movement stimulated to move toward a certain direction. Love is positive or negative action, that is, approach or estrangement. Once the movement is over, love is over" (Hamada 1974:185–186).

We leave unpacking the ethical possibilities of such a queer love for a later time. What lies immediately ahead is the practical task of tracing more of (and in more detail) the still-active pathways of movement that articulate matsutake with trees, forests, mountainsides, gifts, entrepreneurial dreams, rural development schemes, conservationists' hopes for viable timber alternatives, and more. Doing so requires us to think with, but also beyond, commodity chains and chains of translation, those chains whose successive links lend an object its material facticity in the world and that give it value. The lines cast by matsutake do not work only serially – they work in parallel or radially, refusing a single direction, cause, or logic. The practical conditions of matsutake's mycorrhizal life – in all the specific sites where matsutake thrive – call for a different calculus of nature, love, and value.

Weather and Bugs as Contingencies of Matsutake Connections, by Lieba Faier

What follows is a preliminary reflection on how two non-human forms – weather and bugs – figure in the ways that some matsutake pickers and traders in rural Japan talk about local and global science. My research centers on a region of mountain towns and villages in southwestern Nagano Prefecture that I call "Central Kiso." Central Kiso is not among those regions in Japan famous for matsutake; only a small quantity of these mushrooms are found there every year. Because the area is not at the center of matsutake culture in Japan, it is a good place to consider the relations between official and vernacular knowledges. My interest here is in how Central Kiso residents make sense of matsutake-related weather and bugs by mobilizing and embellishing scientific and local knowledges to accommodate local commitments and concerns.

Science studies challenge scholars to think of science as itself a kind of vernacular knowledge – a form of knowledge produced through social alliances and contingencies of practical method (e.g., Haraway 1989; Latour 1987; Traweek 1988). However, less attention has been paid to how scientific and technological knowledge is taken up outside official institutional sites, such as in conventionally "vernacular" spaces. This article joins science studies and scholars in other disciplines who have tried to pick up this dropped thread to understand the interplay of forms of knowledge through which nonscientists understand the natural world (see, e.g., Braun 2002; Cruikshank 2005; Haraway 1997; Mol 2002; Verran 2001; Whatmore 2002).

Matsutake are useful for thinking about such questions because understandings of them in Japan, including ecological understandings, have historically been forged in a dialogue between scientific and village knowledges. Scientists have long drawn on village knowledge and practices to learn about matsutake. In turn, rural residents consult the research of experts and listen to their advice to understand conditions of local matsutake growth.

Here I focus on the ways that Central Kiso residents' understandings of weather and bugs develop in dialogues across these vernacular and scientific traditions of knowledge making. I draw on the work of my collaborators in the Matsutake Worlds Research Group who are studying scientific forms of knowledge surrounding matsutake. Their studies have been exploring the cross-cultural dimensions of scientific knowledge about matsutake and the ways scientists account for relationships among fungi, trees, insects, people, and other forms of matter and life (see, e.g., Tsing and Satsuka 2008).

In conversation with this work, I have found that, when Central Kiso residents engaged with scientific discourse to make sense of weather and bugs, they articulated official understandings with vernacular ones to highlight their pride in the local landscape and their concerns regarding its future. One way they did this was by characterizing weather and bugs as contingencies of connections: dependent but not entirely predictable conditions that shape possibilities for, and forms of, matsutake-based connections on local, national, and global scales.

Let me first share two ethnographic sound bites that illustrate how weather and bugs figure as contingencies of connection for Central Kiso residents. I then discuss some of the ways these residents mobilized and embellished scientific knowledge about weather and bugs to make room for local concerns. I end by reflecting on some future considerations for our collaborative research.

First, then, let me tell you about Morikawa-san, the vice mayor of a small town in Central Kiso. Morikawa-san is known not only as a local *matsutake no meijin* (a matsutake expert or master) but also as a good marksman who once killed a bear. Referred to by other Central Kiso residents as a true "outdoorsman," Morikawa-san wears bolero neckties and hunts deer and wild boar. And he gathers all kinds of mountain vegetables and mushrooms from the mountains he owns, although matsutake is likely the most valuable of these species.

Morikawa-san agreed to take me up to one of his matsutake-gathering spots when I was visiting Central Kiso in October of 2005.

I was surprised when he picked me up for our appointment in a pale green, two-cylinder minicar (*minikā*), the kind of car usually driven by young housewives in the area. Morikawa's choice of transportation made sense to me once we started up the extremely narrow and at times (what felt like) nearly vertical dirt road that led to the top of the mountain where he gathers matsutake. Morikawa-san spoke to me in a local dialect that he moderated for my benefit. He explained that he had dug the road, which was just about a minicar's width across, three or four years earlier. The job had taken an entire year's worth of Saturdays and Sundays. He confirmed that he had bought the car specifically to use on the road.

As soon as I got into his car, Morikawa-san began to explain that there were not many matsutake this year, at least not in Central Kiso: "It didn't rain in May this year," he stressed.

You need rain in May and September.... If there isn't enough rain, the mushrooms won't grow. This May there was hardly any rain. And in September too, it didn't fall the 100 millimeters we get in the average year. It only rained one or two days this September. The mushrooms, they start to grow around the beginning of April. That's why you also need rain in April and May ... or the mushrooms won't grow well.... Last year [2004] there were lots of typhoons. They all came to Japan. And not just typhoons, there was lots of rain too in May, and even in June.... But this year none came through here.... We had lots of strong high pressure air in the skies [and he used words one often hears on weather reports to explain this]. Even if the typhoons came this way, it drove them all away. They slid right by. They all went to Taiwan and China.

As a result, Morikawa-san explained, whereas the previous year he had found more than 100 matsutake on his mountain, a relatively large number for him, this year he had found fewer than 30.

Morikawa-san also told me that in Japan matsutake first appeared each year in Nagano because it is so high above sea level. (This turns out not to be necessarily true, but

Morikawa-san's identification of the region in such terms offers a glimpse into how weather and matsutake figure in some of the ways locals imagine regional identity, a point to which I return below.) Morikawa-san mentioned that the matsutake season in Kiso ends early too, because the weather gets cold. He also said that the cold weather keeps away the *matsukuimushi* (pine weevils, lit. pine-eating bugs) that eat the trees under which matsutake grow and that are destroying the matsutake harvest in Tanba, a region near Kyoto famous for matsutake where Satsuka, Tsing, and Hathaway have conducted field-work. Morikawa-san explained, "The bugs that eat the trees can't survive in places that drop below five degrees Celsius. In Kiso, it drops below ten. They can't survive in a cold place like Kiso."

Morikawa-san had been gathering matsutake since he was a child. His grand-parents taught him to find the mushrooms in the mountains surrounding their home. His grandparents had gone up into the mountains to collect leaves to use for fertilizer. The resultant thinning of the mountain soil had encouraged the growth of matsutake, just as it exposed the mushroom caps to interested pickers. Morikawa-san told me that his grandparents had been poor in those days, so they had sold all the matsutake they had gathered. He told me that he never sells them now. Collecting them is primarily a hobby. He usually eats them with family and visiting friends and offers them as gifts to maintain social networks with people both within and outside the region. But, he qualified, he only gives them to friends if the mushrooms are not infested with *mushi* (bugs; in this case, fungus flies). According to Morikawa-san, whether they are infested depends on weather conditions that allow for many wild mush-rooms to grow. He explained, "If there are a lot of mushrooms around, the bugs that eat mushrooms [*kinoko o taberu mushi*] won't get to the matsutake. But if there aren't many mushrooms, they likely will." He pointed out that few other mushrooms were growing in the vicinity that year, suggesting that the matsutake on his mountain would likely be full of bugs. He showed me how he gently presses on a mushroom to see if it is soft and, thus, whether there are mushi in it. He was pleased that the one he tested was still firm.

Morikawa-san was not the only Central Kiso resident involved in matsutake picking and trading who spoke to me about a lack of rain in the region that year and about problems caused by mushroom bugs. Watanabeya-san, the energetic wife and manager of a produce market in town, also stressed the importance of the weather for her matsutake business and the ways that bugs affected local matsutake. I had asked her where she had purchased the matsutake sitting in decorative boxes near the front of her shop. She responded in rapid, percussive tones: "Oh no, I didn't buy them from anywhere, they're all from the mountains around here. Well," she backpedaled,

and I also sometimes buy some cheaper ones from China. I buy ones from places like China and Korea at the regional wholesale market, but really most of them are picked from the surrounding mountains. You see, when it comes to picking them, there are conditions. It depends on whether there is a lot of rain and the weather is good. There are times when it isn't. It's never the case that we don't find any matsutake. You see, we have *doyō* matsutake during the "dog days" of summer. There were a lot of *doyō* matsutake during that time this year. But those matsutake don't have much of a fragrance and have a lot of bugs. But if it's cool during that time of the summer, if we don't get such intense heat, you know, if it's like you're thinking, "Is it hot?" Well then the matsutake really come out. Years like that you can find matsutake all the way from June through October. In short, even if it rains in September, if it doesn't before then, forget it. If you get some rain in July and August, then the mushrooms will come out throughout the mountains. However, if it's just a little rain, then it won't be enough to get under the leaves below the trees and the mushrooms won't develop. But if there's a lot of rain, like really a downpour, then it gets under the leaves and the mushrooms will develop. But then if it's hot the mushrooms will rot. Then in the climate of early autumn, and through October, they'll grow.

Watanabeya-san never goes to pick matsutake herself, not even on the mountains her family owns. She told me she is too busy with her produce business. She buys matsutake from neighborhood people who pick them from the surrounding mountains. She explained that in the past, during years when the weather in Central Kiso was unfavorable for matsutake and there were not enough local mushrooms, she imported most of those she sold from China and Korea, and a few from another part of Japan. She also regularly buys cheaper matsutake from places like China and Korea at regional wholesale markets to sell to local inns that serve matsutake cuisine to visiting urban tourists, who have come to expect such delicacies in mountain resort regions. Weather patterns, both local ones and those in other parts of the world, such as China and Korea, affect where Watanabeya-san's matsutake come from, how much she pays for them, and how many she imports; they are part of what determines links between Central Kiso and other parts of Japan and the world in any given year. Watanabeya-san said that there had been many local mushrooms in 2004 (the year before we had our conversation and the year Morikawa-san mentioned as having seen many typhoons and much rain). That year, she claimed, she hardly imported any matsutake at all.

Neither Morikawa-san nor Watanabeya-san depends on matsutake for his or her livelihood. As I mentioned, although some matsutake can be found in Central Kiso, the harvest is not really large enough to make the region significant or famous as a matsutake region. And yet, both Morikawa-san and Watanabeya-san recounted with insistent detail the weather conditions necessary for matsutake to grow in the surrounding mountains and the problems with bugs that could threaten them. They could tell me what the weather and bug conditions were like this year and in past years, and the relationships between weather conditions and bugs to matsutake harvests and markets both locally and in other parts of the world.

As local residents such as Morikawa-san and Watanabeya-san discussed matsutake-related weather and bugs, they embellished scientific knowledge to accommodate local commitments. Consider Morikawa-san's discussion of the problems with matsukuimushi in Tanba. Scientists have argued that a nematode carried by the pine weevil is killing the pine trees under which matsutake grow in this and other parts of Japan (Suzuki 2004). As I mention above, when I asked Morikawa-san about Tanba, he responded immediately that the pine trees under which matsutake grow there are dying because they were blighted by matsukuimushi. Yet Morikawa-san and other local residents did not mention the nematodes when discussing matsukuimushi and their effects on matsutake harvests. Rather, they stressed that cold weather had thus far kept the matsukuimushi away from Central Kiso. Scientists have also found that pine weevils prefer warm, dry climates (Suzuki 2004). However, when local residents pointed this out, they were not aiming to contribute to generalizable scientific knowledge about these weevils. Rather, they were engaging discourses of local identity tied to the notion that Kiso is a "samui tokoro" [cold place], as local residents regularly described the mountainous region to me. When speaking of the region in this way, they often recited with pride a line from the *Kisobushi* (The Kiso Melody), a folk song about the Kiso region that is familiar throughout Japan: "Natsu demo samui" [Even summer is cold]. In this way, discussions about matsutake-related weather and bugs became opportunities for distinguishing the region and asserting local forms of identity and expertise.

Central Kiso residents also related scientific knowledge about matsutake to their concerns about the depressed local economy. These concerns often centered on the neglect of local forests and the aging of the local community caused by the increasing number of young people who have been moving to urban areas. Another longtime matsutake picker, Kawanishi-san, told me that matsutake harvests have been decreasing over the past several decades. "It's quite different than it was in the past," she told me. She explained that before gas usage was widespread, people went into the forests to get firewood for cooking and heating their homes. "Before, the forests were

always neat and clean [*kirei*] and the matsutake grew. Now people use gas so … you can't find many matsutake anymore." She and another longtime resident lamented that local forests were no longer being maintained. Gesturing to the effects of urban migration and the corresponding graying of the local population, they explained that those who knew how to care for forests were elderly and thus could no longer manage such work.

To counter the decline in the regional forestry economy, local residents had turned to domestic tourism. But these efforts have met with limited success and come with liabilities. Watanabeya-san and Kawanishi-san also explained that local people had started roping off their mountains so tourists and golfers could not selfishly enter and incorrectly pick mushrooms, damaging the fungi and, thus, future fruiting prospects. At his home, Morikawa-san showed me the "no trespassing" signs he had recently painted and planned to put up on his mountain. A couple of years later, as I walked through the region with local residents, I noticed such signs and barriers across the landscape.

Central Kiso residents thus rearticulated science through an appreciation of locality. In doing so, they highlighted what they experienced as the unpredictability of nature, which they understood as always already global. They knew that matsukuimushi were not indigenous to the region but that these weevils traveled and could always make a sudden local appearance. The larvae of local fungus flies too were unpredictable, their sporadic appearance in mushrooms dependent on the weather. And the weather also taunted local prediction. It seemed to be increasingly shaped by the traveling abstraction of global climate.

In fact, some local residents cited "global warming" *(chikyū ondanka)* as a factor affecting local matsutake harvests. They spoke about how rain and other weather patterns had become unpredictable in recent years, explaining, "Matsutake need rain, but because of global warming, the rain patterns have changed." Watanabeya-san also told me that global warming could be affecting the quality of mushrooms in the region. "It used to be cooler in the summers and we had matsutake from June through October. Now that it's warmer, if they come, they rot." The effects of global warming in the region meant fewer and poorer-quality matsutake. It also meant, as Morikawa-san suggested, that if the temperatures got warm enough, matsukuimushi might eventually come to the area.

For Central Kiso residents, then, discussions about how weather and bugs affected matsutake harvests provided opportunities for relating scientific knowledge to local forms of expertise in ways that centered on life in the region. When local residents discussed global warming, pine weevils in Tanba, and typhoons in China, they staked a place in a cosmopolitan scientific world. This was an appealing world to participate in; many local residents were self-conscious about seeming parochial because they lived in an economically depressed part of rural Japan that was often identified as remote and traditional. Yet they also recognized that "the global" played out in their lives in unpredictable – and not always beneficial – ways. Central Kiso residents often connected the local economy's problems with the importation of cheaper woods to Japan from other parts of the world and to the appeal of cities like Tokyo, which they viewed as more modern and cosmopolitan.

Homi Bhabha points out that *contingent* has two meanings: "[It] is contiguity, metonymy, the touching of spatial boundaries at a tangent, and, at the same time, the contingent is the temporality of the indeterminate and the undecidable" (1994:186). For Central Kiso residents, weather and bugs were contingencies of connection in two senses, then. First, they were contingencies that shaped the kinds of connections local residents could forge with people in other parts of the region, Japan, and the world. Weather patterns and bugs shaped how many matsutake were found locally, where imported ones came from, how much they sold for, and who consumed them. Second, weather and bugs were uncertain factors that reflected the ways that not only matsutake harvests but also everyday life in Central Kiso were impacted by forces outside the region – and in this sense they were viewed as beyond local residents' control. Although both Morikawa-san and

Watanabeya-san could cite in careful detail the weather conditions necessary for a good local matsutake harvest, they could not be sure from year to year whether local weather conditions would be auspicious or whether those in other parts of the world might be more so. They also could not predict whether local matsutake would be infested with bugs or whether matsukuimushi would eventually make their way to the region. In this way, weather and bugs were not unlike other things with links outside the region that residents viewed as potentially taking a toll on life inside it.

As a theory through which local and global natures are connected, this understanding of contingency is not limited in its application to Central Kiso. Indeed, it makes an important point about global connection and the nature of science. To the extent that communities like those in Central Kiso form relations with locally specific forms of nature, recognizing global ties means recognizing the ways that these local forms, and thus one's life and surroundings, are not entirely in one's control. This sense of local indeterminacy is a particular form of self-positioning. It is one that can be identified with the vernacular itself. To be outside official centers of power is to be caught in contingency – to be made to respond to its vagaries rather than being able to force a response from them. Consider, in contrast, how contingency works for those who view the world as if they were positioned above it. From such a perspective, one tends to see powers of prediction in the possibilities of global connection. Contingency becomes fodder for modeling and remaking the world, not for responding to it. For instance, global climate scientists take the global nature of climate as the key to forming predictive models. Global forest managers take the global nature of deforestation as the beginning of their mandates for sustainable management. Such understandings of contingency are only possible when one sees oneself as positioned in some sense outside of global nature so that its uncertainty becomes entirely available for analysis. However, from the perspective of practical local engagements such as those of Central Kiso residents, the existence of global ties increases the unpredictability of local outcomes in a precarious way that demands one always be prepared to flexibly respond.

Ethnographers need to appreciate these situated perspectives to understand life on earth. Too often, social analysts follow globally oriented science and approach the globe as a patterned and predictable whole. We overlook differences and participate in creating a myth of a homogeneous globe. Attending to contingency helps us see the possibilities of difference in interconnection.

Central Kiso residents' understanding of weather and bugs as contingencies of connection is useful for appreciating matsutake ecology and commerce around the world. It points us to the ways that the roles played by weather, bugs, and matsutake themselves are not fixed across the globe. The participation of these nonhuman forms takes culturally, historically, and geographically specific shapes. Their roles in matsutake exchange shift in different moments and create different configurations of social–natural relationships in different locales. These relationships themselves take on varying significance to different people and things in different sites where members of the Matsutake Worlds Research Group are conducting research – they are different for Hmong pickers in Oregon, scientists in Yunnan or Tsukuba, and pine trees and residents in Tanba or Central Kiso. A collaborative research project enables us to explore the overlaps and gaps among these relationships and the different roles nonhumans are playing in them in various places around the world. By doing so, we can learn something about the connections and disjunctions among human–nonhuman worlds across the globe and how global processes take shape at their interface. Paying attention to ways that people in places like rural Nagano invoke weather and bugs as contingencies of connection helps us build the theoretical vocabulary necessary to do this. It helps us grasp both the patterned and the unsystematic ways that nonhumans figure in global processes as they take shape through locally situated dialogues between scientific and vernacular knowledges.

Postcolonial Science Studies and the Making of Matsutake Science in China, by Michael Hathaway

Over the last few decades, scientists' claims that their knowledge is universal and culture free have come under scrutiny. Scholars have shown how scientists' assumptions and epistemologies not only impinge on the interpretation of their results but also shape their research interests, experimental design, and conceptions of knowledge and authority (Anderson and Adams 2007; Barnes and Edge 1982; Latour 1987; Pickering 1995; Shapin 1994). Science studies, a wide umbrella combining scholarship from historical, sociological, philosophical, and anthropological traditions, has tried to reveal the "cultural fingerprints" (Harding 1994) left behind on scientific data, theories, and methods. Recent work in postcolonial science studies contributes to a legacy of science studies that focused on Western contexts, with some notable exceptions (i.e., Needham 1954 and subsequent volumes in the *Science and Civilization in China* series). Studies of science in non-Western contexts have tended to treat colonialism as having hegemonic powers and as a "machine" that used Western science to dominate (McClellan and Regourd 2000; Osborne 2005). Recent scholarship challenges this proposition, however, by examining how "Western" and "non-Western" sciences were made through a "complex process of translation, appropriation and accommodation" (Bray 2007:440). This recent work explores how science circulates through multiple centers and localities and how it is transformed and taken up in social and political practices by diverse constituencies (Abraham 2000; Anderson 2002; Biermann 2001; Harding 1993; Hayden 2003; Hecht 2002; Helmreich 2005; Lowe 2006).

The Matsutake Worlds Research Group builds on post-colonial science studies to examine the transnational production, flow, and transformation of scientific knowledge in the contemporary world. Our research examines the role of a high-value gourmet mushroom, the matsutake, in motivating a diverse realm of scientific practices in different countries. We examine how mycologists (mushroom scientists) and forest ecologists in the United States and Japan conduct experiments in the lab and forest and how their data, findings, and assumptions have influenced the production of matsutake science in China. We are particularly interested in how matsutake research in China is shaping and being shaped by the regional mushroom economy. Matsutake has become important as an object of financial value and as a symbol of ecological health. We ask, How are these knowledges informed by and informing networks of trade, taxation, and the emerging economy of nature conservation efforts? How do debates about matsutake science and policy foster connections between disparate groups, such as forest ecologists, conservationists, and social-justice advocates?

In this section, I outline some of our initial research findings from the United States and Japan. Then, to provide ethnographic context for our future research in China, I draw from my previous fieldwork there on the politics of transnational nature conservation efforts, activities that were always motivated and justified by reference to science. Such conservation activities have gained increasing importance in debates over matsutake management.

Fieldwork in the United States and Japan provides a baseline for our research in China. In the United States, Tsing has begun to uncover the social and institutional networks that create, disseminate, and use scientific studies of matsutake. She has shown that the bulk of this scientific research emanates from a nexus between state agencies (such as the US Forest Service), private logging interests, environmental NGOs, and the public. US-based ecologists usually regard matsutake as a "wild resource" and consider human presence in the forest intrinsically harmful. In turn, their studies about the effects of human harvests are always compared to a baseline study of "nonintervention" (i.e., Luoma et al. 2006). Much research is focused on sustainable yield and is haunted by an intense concern with overharvesting. One of the few US researchers who worked with Japanese matsutake scientists declared that Japanese "forest management goals differ greatly" from those in the United States (Hosford et al. 1997:46; see Tsing and Satsuka 2008).

Our work in Japan, guided by Satsuka, follows a differing genealogy. We trace the research trajectories of several matsutake scientists, who navigate a complex realm of support from the academy, government, and private industry. Unlike the situation in the United States, private interests in Japan play a major role in funding scientific research on cultivating matsutake in the lab (a project that has yet to be successful) and increasing "wild" populations in the forest. Scientists operate from the notion that, without proper human stewardship, matsutake yields will decrease. Human presence in the forest does not threaten "wild" populations; rather, humans can help revitalize the "matsutake mountains" that were previously found throughout rural Japan. Thus, our comparative study reveals that Japanese and US matsutake research, despite frequent exchange at conferences and in scientific journals, emerges from fundamentally different notions of nature and the role of human action.

Our future work in southwest China's Yunnan Province will examine how Japanese and US mycological perspectives vie for authority. We anticipate we will find that neither perspective totally dominates but that Chinese scientists create their own novel formations in conversation with others. Debates about the management of matsutake now include many actors, including conservation biologists, social justice advocates, foresters, and others who produce, consume, disseminate, and transform scientific studies. Thus, matsutake provides an excellent opportunity to examine the changing politics of science. The emergence of matsutake science in China is deeply inflected by Yunnan's particular sociohistorical context, in particular, the history of debate and interaction between foreign conservation NGOs and Chinese scientists, officials, and villagers. Such relationships are shaping the social landscapes of livelihoods and policy and the material landscapes of actions such as logging, mining, farming, and conservation.

My previous fieldwork revealed how some of these relationships emerged in China. Before I turn to a discussion of the recent history of matsutake in Yunnan, I describe shifts in official national policy toward conservation during the 1980s and show how some Chinese experts played a major role in transforming the political terrain on which matsutake management is debated. This history is important for understanding the changing dynamics of power and authority among conservation organizations and how these dynamics impinge on contemporary debates about matsutake.

By the 1990s, the politics of nature in China, at least officially, was turning away from earlier models of "nature as natural resource base" and "nature as pollution sink" toward a concern for ecological sustainability. Previously, state reports on wild animal and plant populations often focused on increasing levels of production, in numbers of furs and pounds of dried herbs; there was little regard for ecological issues per se. Likewise, Chinese state representatives argued in global forums for the "right to pollute" as part of the country's necessary transition toward a more industrialized economy; environmental controls were often regarded as an unfair imposition by the Global North (see Economy 2004). However, China became an increasingly frequent signatory to international environmental treaties by the 1990s and expanded its creation of nature reserves and environmental laws.

At that time, there were also substantial changes in Yunnan, arguably the province with the most environmental activity and the richest matsutake habitat (Litzinger 2004). In the 1980s, when international conservation NGOs first carried out their projects in Yunnan, NGO staff often conceived of villagers as antagonists of the natural world. Villagers were depicted as "peasants," who, with little capacity to understand science, damaged the surrounding forests with unsustainable practices, such as slash-and-burn agriculture. Two decades later, such depictions were increasingly challenged by a handful of Chinese experts. These experts had already played a critical role as cultural brokers, helping foreign conservation NGOs get established in Yunnan.[12] Over time, these experts were no longer acting as mere technical helpmates for foreign NGOs but were increasingly entrenched in global flows of funding,

academic prestige, and connections. They used archives to show that certain practices (such as villagers clearing large amounts of land by slash-and-burn agriculture) that are now regarded as environmentally damaging were not carried out by villagers on their own terms but were promoted and orchestrated by the state itself. Experts also countered accusations of villager ignorance by carrying out fieldwork documenting "indigenous knowledge," including villagers' knowledge of matsutake ecology.

Because of the influences of these experts, powerful organizations such as the Nature Conservancy (TNC), likely the world's wealthiest conservation NGO, found that their ability to set the terms for conservation and science in Yunnan was diminished. In addition to the experts, other agents now vie to influence agendas previously left to specialized scientific committees (on this development in the United States, see McLain et al. 1998). In turn, questions about managing the matsutake economy are increasingly reflected through this dynamic between state agencies, Chinese experts, research institutes, and villagers.

Unlike the trade of tea and horses, which goes back centuries in Yunnan, the matsutake economy is relatively new, only beginning in earnest in the late 1980s. The sheer newness of matsutake allows us to trace more closely how it became a commodity in transition, an object of scientific inquiry, and a transnational object of desire and concern. Of the multiple stories about matsutake in Yunnan, one heard by a colleague in 1990 speaks to several concerns (Bob Anderson, personal communication, November 2007). In the late 1980s, several Japanese biologists came to northwest Yunnan to collect rare butterflies. They traveled to the most important and imposing mountain in the area, Jade Dragon Snow Mountain (Yulong Xueshan). The butterfly collectors explored the mountain for days and were able to find numerous interesting species. When they descended the slopes, however, local officials discovered that the butterfly collectors lacked the proper permits. When the officials searched the biologists' supplies, they found evidence of the true reason for the expedition: matsutake mushrooms. These entrepreneurs, posing as butterfly collectors, gained access to the mountain at a time when political prohibitions meant that many places in Yunnan were still closed to foreign tourists but potentially open to scientific exchange. In this account, those who appeared to be disinterested scientists were, in disguise, entrepreneurs.

This account of entrepreneurialism, therefore, speaks to a larger question that emerged during ethnographic fieldwork on foreign environmental NGOs in Yunnan: Why are foreigners interested in Chinese nature?[13] During field work, I was asked by villagers as well as officials, What are environmental NGOs doing here in Yunnan? What is in it for them? What do foreigners like the Americans or the Dutch want with Chinese nature? Will groups like TNC try to buy up land and turn it into a tourist destination? In contrast, the Japanese butterfly collectors-cum-entrepreneurs are more easily and satisfactorily understood by Chinese villagers and officials: They have come to make money. Unlike Western expectations that scientists' efforts are purely motivated by the quest for knowledge, the butterfly-collector story revealed an expectation that scientists, or those who claim to be disinterested scientists, have entrepreneurial aims. When TNC started not just to promote ecotourism writ large as a new part of Yunnan's economy but also to endorse particular ecotourist destinations, the move was seen as evidence by some Chinese that its aims were not just to save nature but to save it to make a profit. Although TNC and other NGOs fought fiercely to present themselves as disinterested parties that use objective science for conservation goals, their actions were often interpreted differently. Foreign NGOs' sudden interest in matsutake only furthered those suspicions.

After the Japanese showed the potential of matsutake as a commodity, it began to be incorporated into a shifting set of networks. In the early 1990s, much of the literature on matsutake collection was celebratory, exclaiming its potential to assist in "poverty alleviation," and no one seemed concerned about its ecological impact. At the time, conservation organizations also promoted the harvest, as it fit with trends to find "non-timber forest products" (NTFPs). This strategy was based on the notion that if villagers could profit from forest-dependent natural resources such as wild mushrooms, they would have an incentive to protect the forest. Although the initial notion behind NTFPs was that these products (e.g., mushrooms and flowers) were of low value, during years of good harvest and high prices, matsutake has, in fact, brought massive amounts of wealth to Yunnan. In 1997, the crop was worth $40 million. In 1997, the average per capita income was about $125 a year, so tales of finding $50 worth of mushrooms in one day meant that mushrooms represented fantastic opportunities and brought newfound wealth to many families.

The market was given an unintentional boost in 1998, when logging was banned in the headwaters of the Yangtze River. China implemented the ban after a massive and devastating flood of the Yangzte. The ban was based on the widespread assumption that upstream logging resulted in downstream flooding. This was the world's largest ban of its kind, and, in enacting it, China was likely influenced by neighboring Thailand, Vietnam, and Sri Lanka, countries that had earlier declared logging bans. Prior to the ban, logging was a key industry in this part of Yunnan, sometimes bringing in more than 80 percent of local government revenues. After the ban, illegal logging continued to a small degree, but legally sanctioned logging came to a virtual standstill. Local governments, as well as thousands of individuals supported by forestry, began to search for financial alternatives, and matsutake was already there, having been "found" by the Japanese almost ten years earlier. Yet, as matsutake has risen in economic importance, the politics and practices of matsutake collection have become increasingly connected to emerging networks of actors concerned with Yunnan's ecological landscape. Many of these actors have expressed fears about the mushroom's overall sustainability and made dire predictions about the ecological consequences of the harvest. Whereas initial reports celebrated matsutake wealth as a way to alleviate poverty, recent discourses pay more attention to its role in remaking social and natural landscapes.

As a direct form of landscape making, the matsutake harvest seems fairly insignificant. Unlike more intensive methods of land use, such as converting forested riparian habitat into permanent rice paddy, matsutake harvest per se does not seem to have significant effects on other species. As far as scientists know, matsutake is not a "keystone species," and so, even if it were to go extinct, it is hard to know what other species would be affected,[14] other than *Homo sapiens*, as thousands of people devote themselves, at least seasonally, to its harvest, purchase, resale, trucking, marketing, taxing, and monitoring. Rather, it is the wealth, or potential wealth, of the matsutake that has fostered changes in rural land tenure and affected other livelihood activities such as herding.

The rise of the matsutake market has strongly influenced village land tenure. Until the early 1980s, villages in China were often part of large-scale communes, which had started to form in the late 1950s and had no clearly defined boundaries. Currently there are no national or provincial regulations on the matsutake harvest, and, instead, the village has become the most critical site for organizing the harvest. The matsutake economy has provided a new incentive to create firm boundaries between village lands, especially as some villages with productive habitat try to exclude others (Yeh 2000).[15] In addition, the creation of a valuable resource also conjured new social relations within the village, sometimes promoting *communitas* but also presenting new challenges as residents devised ways to protect the harvest from each other through regulations, guards, rules, seasons, and social sanctions.

Indirectly, the matsutake harvest is affecting landscapes as it displaces other forms of livelihood, such as yak herding, which have been practiced for centuries, if not millennia. Yaks range over a huge swath of land, and their grazing changes the kinds of vegetation that survive. Under the new environmental mandates, herding is coming under increasing scrutiny too, especially in terms of concern about its impact on flora and soil. In particular, some worry that new tree seedlings, subsidized by the logging-ban policy, will be threatened by the grazing animals. Herders, who tend to favor meadows for grazing, often set small fires to encourage the growth of lush plants and burn back tree seedlings. Yet, grazing land is shrinking because laws that prohibit the use of fire are now

increasingly enforced. In response, some families have sold their yak herds and increasingly devote themselves to the seasonal matsutake harvest.

Concern about the ultimate sustainability of the matsutake harvest has become a major issue in Yunnan, not only among officials and conservationists but also for many harvesters. This concern has mainly focused on matsutake as a species in and of itself. Few studies have examined the possible effects of decreased populations on other plant and animal species or how matsutake harvesting techniques might affect other species. Historically, this turn to incorporate fungus within conservation plans is novel, as such plans rarely give fungus the same status as plants or animals. Matsutake has become a notable exception, as it was declared an endangered species in China in 2008. Just six years earlier, at an international meeting on endangered species, only a few countries had even considered including any mushrooms at all on this list. Two countries, Japan and China, rejected this possibility, saying that mushrooms should not be added, as they are not threatened by trade (Thomas 2005). Now, for reasons not totally clear, China has added matsutake to its list of endangered species. Its pronouncement is challenged by some who suggest that little scientific work backs up claims that matsutake is endangered in China (Arora 2008; Menzies and Li in press; Winkler 2004). The mushroom's new status will certainly increase governmental and scientific interest and actions. Contrary to expectations, this listing does not necessarily remove matsutake from the commodity chain and may, in fact, stimulate its consumption through increasing its value.

In conclusion, it is important to recognize that, although Chinese scientists draw from a rich set of domestic scientific traditions, they have also been informed by Japanese and US studies, among others. In our future work, we will explore how to trace or sort out these scientific genealogies. What might we be cautious of? Scholarly studies of science have moved away from more general observations about science as a universal set of social practices to examine nationally specific pedigrees and cultural frameworks. For example, scholars such as Donna Haraway (1989) and Sharon Traweek (1988) highlight notable differences between Japanese and US scientists in creating scientific knowledge about primatology and physics. Such scientists differ not only in terms of training and method but also, more fundamentally, in terms of epistemological foundations. Yet, in the case of mycology, as well as other sciences, we might become increasingly aware of the ways in which science is formed through transnational exchange. In China, scientists and other participants in debates about matsutake management draw on Japanese and US funds, collaboration, and studies to guide their own research and buttress their arguments.

Scientists might be some of the most respected agents in debates about forest management, but others are now playing influential roles. Some Chinese social activists are now concerned about trends to restrict and police the matsutake harvest in Yunnan, a policy informed by visions of local people's actions as environmentally damaging. Indeed, there are rumors that officials may decide to ban the use of rakes in forests because of fear that raking the forest duff (the loose layer of pine needles and leaves on the forest floor) will harm the growth of mushrooms. In the United States, there are also controversies about the ecological effects of raking; most scientists believe that it damages the forest ecology, and, because of this belief, raking has been banned on US Forest Service lands (Luoma et al. 2006). In Japan, however, removing the forest duff with rakes is seen as part of the difficult but necessary labor of matsutake stewardship. Such a ban in Yunnan would have serious social consequences for, unlike the situation in the United States or Japan, many rural people in Yunnan raise animals for food and cash, and they need the duff as bedding for these animals.

Although Yunnan seems to be moving toward a raking ban, a Japanese NGO called the "Matsutake Crusaders" will soon visit the province to promote its methods for increasing matsutake yields, including raking. Members of this group will likely arouse interest and provide a more public and visible perspective on human–matsutake relationships than the

biological studies undertaken by their compatriots. They will, in turn, likely foster more debate in Yunnan and add new twists to the changing world of matsutake science, as it continues to transform.

Studies of science-in-the-making need to attend to the larger social context in which scientists carry out their work, in this case how social-justice advocates, forest officials, and pastoralists play a role in the larger social terrain in which matsutake studies are conducted in Yunnan. At the same time, however, scholars need ways to focus their analytic vision on those social interactions that are particularly influential in the production and transformation of this knowledge. In other words, when widening the scope to trace the social networks involved in creating, debating, and supporting this knowledge, it is important not to assume rhizomelike equity but to examine how differently situated actors engage with a power-laden world. Scholars must examine how national context inflects scientific knowledge, without assuming that national boundaries are rigid. Such a stance encourages efforts to investigate the ways that methods and perspectives travel, to trace the social life of scientific facts and theories, and to consider how all of these, in the process, are transformed.

Collaboration and the Subject of Anthropology, by Miyako Inoue

Sociocultural anthropologists grow up professionally and live in a subdiscipline that envisions collaboration as a marked category, perhaps even a bit eccentric. That is, we are all trained and disciplined to think of scholarship as a normally individual, even isolated, enterprise. We know this is an abstraction, indeed, a distortion. We know that intellectual labor is social, as is all labor, and that "the individual" is a dramatically social production. We know that our work is enabled by means of intellectual production purchased with real capital – what we call "resources" in the university – and that it is rooted in social relations of intellectual production, even if those relations are not precisely capitalist (although they appear increasingly corporate, even neoliberal, to faculty members who are not professional administrators). We know that the concrete situations in which we conduct our research and write and publish are made possible by relations inside and outside the university that are shot through with power; that ideas are never freestanding but are always circulated through inescapably social, political, and material means of reproduction; and that everything we do as scholars and teachers is founded on particular conditions of possibility, in both the discursive and material–social meanings of that phrase (see, e.g., Field and Fox 2007; Fox 1991).

It gives one pause to consider the improbability of such a field as social-cultural anthropology as not only having been invented (Hymes 1999) but also institutionalized (Vincent 1994). My immediate point, however, is that a complex and largely stable – if continuously negotiated – academic division of labor has to exist for social-cultural anthropology to exist. Cultural anthropologists have to agree with sociologists, psychologists, political scientists, historians, and linguists – not to mention biological anthropologists and archaeologists as well as deans and provosts – on how to divide up and organize the world to study, write, and teach about it. This is never a matter of clean mutual exclusivity, because we always refer to other disciplines in what we do, if only by implication. A host of others are involved in our "individual" intellectual enterprises, and although we do not usually call that "collaboration," we need to start with recognition that we never work alone.

It is ironic that in a field that should perhaps know better – social-cultural anthropology, particularly in its critical and humanistic versions – we are less open to "collaboration" or to seeing our work as a social product than are the "harder" intellectual workers down the hall from us or in the building next to ours. Scientists, engineers, biological anthropologists, and archaeologists all regularly work in teams of specialists with affirmatively dovetailing, or better, synergistic, knowledges, and major funding agencies such as the National Science Foundation and National Institutes of Health regularly support anthropological research teams – teams that often include specialists from other disciplines: biology, geology, and so on. Corporate research and development is, of course, never based on a model of individual pursuit of knowledge but is always organized in teams of complementary specialists.

We should also remember that much of the foundational work of 20th-century social-cultural anthropology emerged in collaborative projects in the immediate postwar period. Recall area studies and community studies, including Julian Steward's Puerto Rico Project (1948–51; see Steward et al. 1956), the Harvard Modjukuto Project (1952–54) and Chiapas Project (1957–92; see Vogt 1978), and Sol Tax's Fox Project (1948–59), which left indelible marks on the discipline by funding and training numerous graduate students who later became prominent figures in the field and by creating protocols of ethnographic collaborative research, many of which involved multiple graduate students funded by the project and a handful of faculty members working together in one area or community. So where are we in terms of collaboration in the present? (I leave aside the question of collaboration with our "informants" or "research consultants" because that is another can of worms.) Are we just trying to catch up with everybody else, from industry employees to our colleagues in the sciences, or is collaboration for us something different? Are we simply recycling postwar large-scale area and community studies, which had their own, historically particular, social relations of intellectual production?

The Matsutake Worlds Research Project is situated in a twofold intellectual and historical context. First, it is in many ways informed by the new challenges wrought by reflexive and experimental critiques at the core of what has been called "the linguistic turn" in anthropology in the 1980s. Debates that were brought about by the publication of *Writing Culture* (Clifford and Marcus 1986), for example, directed both new and renewed attention reflexively back to our own research methods and practices. The recognition of the historical kinship of anthropology with colonialism and imperialism, the reflection of this link in the unequal distribution of power in the relationship between researcher and informant, and the inherently political nature of ethnographic writing as productive of – rather than transparently representing – our objects of knowledge, all put on the table, and demanded, new modes of ethnographic research and writing.

Second, the consequences of contemporary translocal political-economic processes ("globalization") have made it necessary either to develop new methodologies for spanning "scales" of analysis (but see below) or otherwise finding "phenomena of connection" (see again below) or to critically recover and adapt appropriate methodologies from our disciplinary ancestors. In practical terms, how could critical knowledge up to the job of making sense of our present world be based on the work of individual scholarly entrepreneurs?

The reflexive and experimental turn has also productively pushed us to find anthropological subjects beyond the "primitive" and "exotic" in geographically and culturally remote areas, to find them close to home in modern institutions and practices, as in medicine, science, and technology, and among national and transnational agents of governance, finance, and social movements (see, e.g., Holland et al. 2007; Rabinow et al. 2008). Working with scientists, activists, NGO workers, government officials, and other experts not only challenges the anthropologist's monopoly of knowledge production but also complicates her or his ethical, political, and intellectual standpoints and thus recasts the subject of ethnographic research. Furthermore, it brings us a sober realization that anthropological knowledge is contingent on, and contiguous with, the production of other forms of knowledge, outside of academic institutions. It would well seem that we have little alternative but to respond to the historically specific conjuncture of our contemporary situation by recourse to collaboration. For those of us in the Matsutake Worlds Research Group, collaboration was one inevitable and logical answer to the question of how anthropological research is possible in the actually existing world of the present.

We are mindful of four characteristics of the process of our collaboration. First, strong collaboration is dialectical, not synthetic.

There is more to strong – and critical – collaboration than is highlighted in the hard sciences and corporate research and development. The benefit traditionally imputed to research teams is the integration of complementary specializations, the holistic payoff that comes from dividing up the work into functional categories and assigning it to different team members. If a family physician is not sure how to interpret a particular set of symptoms, both she and the patient are better off relying on an appropriate specialist. This is, of course, a quintessentially Fordist model, or, deeper, the model at the origin of the capitalist industrial division of labor.

What we are trying to do here is different. True, we have all assumed "specialized" roles in this project. But the model is not based on the idea that we are intending to synthesize our separate, freestanding analyses into an organic, complementary whole. On the contrary, our works may show that there are views of our object that are not assimilable to others; we might have to be content with productive tensions among our conclusions. The analogy in politics is the recognition that a will to consensus is often a will to power in that somebody has to yield to others to arrive at "consensus." We are often better off agreeing to disagree. Although all of us are familiar with this model of working together, we should mark its distinction from the traditional understanding of collaboration. James Clifford (1997) has written wonderfully about the multivocality of collaboration between anthropologists and indigenous peoples; they do not arrive at synthesis and perhaps not even agreement other than to work together by representing their distinct standpoints (which, of course, in the dialectics of open dialogue, are unlikely to remain unchanged). We welcome the method of "looking several ways" (Clifford 2004) and see multivocality as a productive outcome of collaborations with each other.

This particular kind of productivity, and its consequences for the partitioning of knowledge, is the second characteristic of our collaborative process. Specialists on research teams recognize that value comes from interdisciplinary or interspecialty dialogue, but there is generally little sense that disciplines or specialties might change their basic relations with each other or undergo internal reorganization on the basis of dialogue. Our project opens that possibility. Although it is never comfortable – and certainly not "efficient" – to seriously rethink one's questions or assumptions in the midst of doing the work, we need to continually ask how our frameworks for the project are hierarchically related. My point is that a collaboration among critical scholars can be an opportunity to think deeply about core ideas in our discipline and our specialties within the discipline.

Third, we focus on connections across different geographical sites rather than complementarity across different specialties. Bringing supposedly different "cases" to the table is not new in anthropology, but we are not interested in conventional comparison. Rather, we see these sites as socially and materially connected by a commodity, that is, the matsutake. Marx's (1990) concepts of the "commodity" and "commodity fetishism" are useful guides. Marx was not interested in "comparing" the site of production of a commodity with the site of its consumption, as if they were two different "cases" in the Human Relations Area Files. His work guides us to trace concrete connections between production and consumption, what Lila Abu-Lughod (1991), after Eric Wolf (1982), has aptly called "phenomena of connection." We also recognize the continuity of what we are after in our project with the "commodity chain" approach. But it is collaborative ethnography that allows us to appreciate the extent to which such connections are far from pre-determined, but, in fact, are unpredictable and contingent. Faier refers to "contingencies of connection" to highlight the provisional nature of the local's "vernacular" knowledge to manage the unpredictability of the weather and bugs. Hathaway shows how the rise of "postcolonial science" and the production of scientific knowledge, in fact, hinge on the ongoing divergence and convergence of multiple national and transnational stakeholders.

Furthermore, such connections are not best understood in terms of the functional requirements of capitalism or an integrated world system. That is precisely how one should

not be trying to understand phenomena of connection. Localities – "places," as geographers call them – are sui generis; some of them are more powerful than others and have the ability to tie the others to them – and sometimes to remake the others – in ways the less powerful have little choice over. What are those ways that powerful places have at their disposal, and how do less powerful places respond? How do less powerful places get caught up with the more powerful places to begin with? Although it is possible for a single scholar to address these kinds of questions through multisited ethnography or the kind of magisterial historical work done by Sidney Mintz (1986), it is collaborative work that is most promising for most anthropologists.

Finally, we want to let the research subject (the matsutake) inform our research design. In other words, we aspire to mimic the matsutake's rhizomic sociality for our research strategy to envision the productive multiplicity that underwrites our collaboration, and to defy the impulse of centralizing and totalizing knowledge production.

NOTES

1   The Matsutake Worlds Research Group consists of Timothy Choy, Lieba Faier, Michael Hathaway, Miyako Inoue, Shiho Satsuka, and Anna Tsing. The sections of this report were born at a session of the 2007 Annual Meeting of the American Anthropological Association. Tsing presented a related talk, "Kinship and Science in the Genus *Tricholoma*," at a separate 2007 AAA session honoring the work of Marilyn Strathern.

2   A chain of coedited anthologies directed and marked the course of feminist anthropology from the 1970s to the turn of the 20th century. A full discussion and listing would require another article. However, for a taste of the enterprise, see Rosaldo and Lamphere 1974, McCormack and Strathern 1980, and Ginsburg and Tsing 1992.

3   Our term echoes Sandra G. Harding's (1995) "strong objectivity," in which attention to process is part of objective science. We acknowledge the feminist heritage of our methods. We elaborate on the idea of "strong

collaboration" in Matsutake Worlds Research Group in press.

4   See Saito and Mitsumata 2008 for a discussion of Japanese village auctions. See Yeh 2000 and Arora 2008 on matsutake in Yunnan, China. I am grateful to Charles Menzies for sharing information about matsutake and First Nations in British Columbia. Matsutake forests in the US Pacific Northwest have been a site of my own intensive fieldwork, conducted in collaboration with Hjorleifur Jonsson and University of California, Santa Cruz, undergraduates Lue Vang and David Pheng. A preliminary discussion of the matsutake commodity chain can be found in Tsing in press a.

5   Mogu Mogu represents Shiho Satsuka and Timothy Choy writing together. In Japanese, *mogu mogu* is an onomatopoeia for eating. In Cantonese and Mandarin, *mogu* refers to a mushroom.

6   Ingold (2006:13) also mentions that he prefers fungal mycelia over rhizomes to understand the web of relations among organisms.

7   *Intra-species* is meant to connote and connect with a sense of "intra-action," a term coined by Karen Michelle Barad (2007) to convey a world in which things in relation do not pre-exist their relation. The ontologies of the things themselves are at stake in their relating. See also Strathern 1988. Also see Isabelle Stengers's (2003) work using the concept of "intercapture," which builds on Deleuze and Guattari's (1987) discussion of the "double capture" of orchid and wasp.

8   Katherine Rupp (2003) observes a similar coexistence of reciprocal relations nourishing gift and market economies in Japan.

9   As Susan J. Alexander and colleagues put it:

The methods by which timber is measured, marketed, and sold make SEV calculations for timber rather straightforward ...

For trees, the delivered log price minus the harvest cost, wages and transportation costs, and other costs associated with harvesting and transporting the trees, equals the stumpage price, or the bid price in government timber sales. The landowner captures all the return to the resource because property rights and markets are well defined. The stumpage price minus the landowner's cost of administering the sale is the return to the resource. The return to the resource after each cutting cycle for all time, discounted back to the present, equals the SEV. [2002:131]

10 Alexander and colleagues explain:

For wild edible mushrooms, the return to the resource is the net return to the landowner along with the net return to the harvester. This is different than the return to the resource calculation for timber. As mentioned previously, the owner of trees captures all the return to the resource, because property rights and markets are well defined. Return to the resource for wild edible mushrooms, as with many other nontimber forest products, is harder to calculate in part because the landowner usually captures little to none of the value. Permit prices, if a permit is granted, are usually fixed and low and may or may not cover the cost to the landowner. Property rights are not clearly defined, and markets and prices are not publicly documented for these resources as they are for timber markets. The harvest of wild edible mushrooms is labor intensive, the unit value is often low, the season is short, and the economic risk is high. The harvester captures much of what little return to the resource there might be by doing the labor and taking the risk, and often makes little money. The market is imperfect. Because the landowner captures little or none of the return to the resource through administratively set permit prices, or no permit at all, the return to the resource for wild edible mushrooms is the sum of net return to the landowner through permit sales, along with net return to the harvester.

The net return to the landowner is usually permit fees minus administrative cost; in most cases, the harvester is not the landowner. The net return to the harvester includes subtracting both an estimate of personal costs (gas, food, etc.) and an estimated personal minimum wage from mushroom revenues, realized by selling mushrooms daily at buying sheds. Each of these cost and revenue estimates must be converted to costs and revenue per hectare, as for timber calculations. These calculations depend on information that ranges from good to nonexistent. [2002:132]

11 We have yet to explore, for instance, what instruments of valuation address problems

of comparison in certain satoyamas in Japan that are owned communally.

12 Elsewhere, I argue that so many international projects came to Yunnan not just because it has so much biological diversity but because Chinese experts made it into a compelling location for research, conferences, scientific tourism, and international projects interested in "cultural diversity" and "indigenous knowledge."

13 This account parallels insights by Joan Fujimura (2000) that reveal the vast efforts undertaken by certain leading scientists (in this case, genomics scientists) as entrepreneurs, trying to find and sustain support for their research from private and state sources.

14 Even so, recent research on its microbial actions underground is showing complex and still largely unknown interactions with other species.

15 Boundaries for family land allocations are also vague. Books in rural Yunnan that give the boundaries of such property (which families lease from the state for a set period of time) describe the land not precisely in terms of total area or exact distance but loosely in terms of its relative position between neighbors' lands.

REFERENCES

Abraham, Itty
2000 Landscape and Postcolonial Science. Contributions to Indian Sociology 34:163–187.

Abu-Lughod, Lila
1991 Writing against Culture. In Recapturing Anthropology: Working in the Present. Richard G. Fox, ed. pp. 137–162. Santa Fe: School of American Research Press.

Alexander, Susan J., David Pilz, Nancy S. Weber, Ed Brown, and Victoria A. Rockwell
2002 Mushrooms, Trees, and Money: Value Estimates of Commercial Mushrooms and Timber in the Pacific Northwest. Environmental Management 30(1):129–141.

Anderson, Warwick
2002 Introduction: Postcolonial Technoscience. Social Studies of Science 32:643–658.

Anderson, Warwick, and Vincanne Adams
2007 Pramoedya's Chickens: Postcolonial Studies of Technoscience. In The Science and Technology Studies Handbook. Edward J. Hackett, Olga Amsterdamska, Michael Lynch, and Judy Wajcman, eds. pp. 181–204. Cambridge, MA: MIT Press.

Arora, David
2008 The Houses That Matsutake Built. Economic Botany 63(4):278–290.

Barad, Karen Michelle
2007 Meeting the Universe Halfway: Quantum Physics and the Entanglement of Matter and Meaning. Durham, NC: Duke University Press.

Barnes, Barry, and David Edge, eds.
1982 Science in Context: Readings in the Sociology of Science. Cambridge: Open University Press.

Bhabha, Homi
1994 The Location of Culture. New York: Routledge.

Biermann, Frank
2001 Big Science. Small Impacts – in the South? The Influence of Global Environmental Assessments on Expert Communities in India. Global Environmental Change 11:297–309.

Braun, Bruce
2002 The Intemperate Rainforest: Nature, Culture, and Power on Canada's West Coast. Minneapolis: University of Minnesota Press.

Bray, Francesca
2007 Review of On Their Own Terms: Science in China and A Cultural History of Modern Science in China. British Journal for the History of Science 40:439–441.

Choy, Timothy K.
2005 Articulated Knowledges: Environmental Forms after Universality's Demise. American Anthropologist 107(1):5–18.

Clifford, James
1997 Routes: Travel and Translation in the Late Twentieth Century. Cambridge, MA: Harvard University Press.

Clifford, James
2004 Looking Several Ways: Anthropology and Native Heritage in Alaska. Current Anthropology 45(1):5–30.

Clifford, James, and George E. Marcus
1986 Writing Culture: The Poetics and Politics of Ethnography. Berkeley: University of California Press.

Cruikshank, Julie
2005 Do Glaciers Listen? Local Knowledge, Colonial Encounters, and Social Imagination. Vancouver: University of British Columbia Press.

Deleuze, Gilles, and Félix Guattari
  1987 A Thousand Plateaus: Capitalism and Schizophrenia. Minneapolis: University of Minnesota Press.
Economy, Elizabeth C.
  2004 The River Runs Black: The Environmental Challenge to China's Future. Ithaca, NY: Cornell University Press.
Faier, Lieba
  2009 Intimate Encounters: Filipina Women and the Remaking of Rural Japan. Berkeley: University of California Press.
Field, Les, and Richard G. Fox, eds.
  2007 Anthropology Put to Work. Oxford: Berg.
Fortun, Kim
  2001 Advocacy after Bhopal: Environmentalism, Disaster, New Global Orders. Chicago: University of Chicago Press.
Fox, Richard G.
  1991 Introduction: Working in the Present. In Recapturing Anthropology: Working in the Present. Richard G. Fox, ed. pp. 1–16. Santa Fe: School of American Research Press.
Fujimura, Joan
  2000 Transnational Genomics: Transgressing the Boundary between the "Modern/West" and the "Pre-Modern/East." In Doing Science + Culture. Roddy Reid, and Sharon Traweek, eds. pp. 71–94. New York: Routledge.
Gibson-Graham, J. K.
  1996 The End of Capitalism (As We Knew It): A Feminist Critique of Political Economy. Oxford: Blackwell.
Gibson-Graham, J. K.
  2006 A Postcapitalist Politics. Minneapolis: University of Minnesota Press.
Ginsburg, Faye, and Anna Tsing
  1992 Uncertain Terms: Negotiating Gender in American Culture. Boston: Beacon Press.
Guin, Jerry
  1997 Matsutake Mushroom: The White Goldrush of the 1990s: A Guide and Journal. Happy Camp, CA: Naturegraph.
Hamada, Minoru
  1974 Matsutake nikki (Matsutake diary). Kyoto: Hamada Sensei Teinen Taikan Kinen Jigyōkai, Kyoto University.
Haraway, Donna
  1989 Primate Visions: Gender, Race, and Nature in the World of Modern Science. New York: Routledge.
Haraway, Donna
  1997 Modest_Witness@Second_Millennium. FemaleMan©_Meets_Oncomouse™. New York: Routledge.
Harding, Sandra, ed.
  1993 The Racial Economy of Science: Toward a Democratic Future. Bloomington: Indiana University Press.
Harding, Sandra G.
  1994 Is Science Multicultural? Challenges, Resources, Opportunities, Uncertainties. Configurations 2:301–330.
Harding, Sandra G.
  1995 Strong Objectivity: A Response to the New Objectivity Question. Synthese 104(3):331–349.
Hathaway, Michael J.
  2006 Making Nature in Southwest China: Transnational Notions of Landscape and Ethnicity. Ph.D. dissertation, Department of Anthropology, University of Michigan.
Hayden, Cori
  2003 When Nature Goes Public: The Making and Unmaking of Bioprospecting in Mexico. Berkeley: University of California Press.
Hecht, Gabrielle
  2002 Rupture-Talk in the Nuclear Age: Conjugating Colonial Power in Africa. Social Studies of Science 32(5–6):691–727.
Helmreich, Stefan
  2005 How Scientists Think; About "Natives," for Example. A Problem of Taxonomy among Biologists of Alien Species in Hawaii. Journal of the Royal Anthropological Institute 11:107–128.
Holland, Dorothy, Donald M. Nonini, Catherine Lutz, Lesley Bartlett, Marla Frederick-McGlathery, Thaddeus C. Guldbrandsen, and Enrique G. Murillo Jr.
  2007 Local Democracy under Siege: Activism, Public Interests, and Private Politics. New York: New York University Press.
Hosford, David, David Pilz, Randy Molina, and Michael Amaranthus
  1997 Ecology and Management of the Commercially Harvested American Matsutake Mushroom. Darby, PA: Diane.
Hymes, Dell, ed.
  1999[1969] Reinventing Anthropology. Ann Arbor: University of Michigan Press.
Ingold, Timothy
  2006 Rethinking the Animate, Re-Animating Thought. Ethnos 71(1):9–20.

Inoue, Miyako
    2006 Vicarious Language: Gender and
    Linguistic Modernity in Japan. Berkeley:
    University of California Press.
Ito, Takeshi, and Koji Iwase
    1997 Matsutake: Kajuen kankaku de fuyasu
    sodateru (Matsutake: Nurture and propagate
    like an orchard). Tokyo: Nōsangyoson Bunka
    Kyōkai.
Latour, Bruno
    1987 Science in Action: How to Follow
    Scientists and Engineers through Society.
    Cambridge, MA: Harvard University Press.
Litzinger, Ralph
    2004 The Mobilization of Nature:
    Perspectives from North-West Yunnan. China
    Quarterly 178:488–504.
Lowe, Celia
    2006 Wild Profusion: Biodiversity Con-
    servation in an Indonesian Archipelago.
    Princeton: Princeton University Press.
Luoma, Daniel L., Joyce L. Eberhart,
    Richard Abbott, Andrew Moore, Michael
    P. Amaranthus, and David Pilz
    2006 Effects of Mushroom Harvest Tech-
    nique on Subsequent American Matsutake
    Production. Forest Ecology and Management
    236:65–75.
Marx, Karl
    1990 Capital, vol. I. B. Fowkes, trans.
    London: Penguin.
Matsutake Worlds Research Group
    (Timothy Choy, Lieba Faier, Michael
    Hathaway, Miyako Inoue, Shiho Satsuka, and
    Anna Tsing)
    In press Strong Collaboration as a Method for
    Multi-Sited Ethnography: On Mycorrhizal
    Relations. In Multi-Sited Ethnography:
    Theory, Praxis, and Locality in Contemporary
    Social Research. Mark Falzon, ed. London:
    Ashgate.
McClellan, James E., III, and François Regourd
    2000 The Colonial Machine: French Science
    and Colonization in the Ancien Regime. Osiris
    15:31–50.
McCormack, Carol and Marilyn Strathern, eds.
    1980 Nature, Culture, Gender. Cambridge:
    Cambridge University Press.
McLain, Rebecca, H. H. Christensen, and
    M. Shannon
    1998 When Amateurs Are the Experts:
    Amateur Mycologists and Wild Mushroom
    Politics in the Pacific Northwest, USA. Society
    and Natural Resources 11:615–626.

Menzies, Nick, and C. Li
    In press One Eye on the Forest, One Eye on
    the Market: Multi-Tiered Regulation of
    Matsutake Harvesting, Conservation and
    Trade in Northwestern Yunnan Province. In
    Wild Products Governance: Finding Policies
    That Work For Non-Timber Forest Products.
    Sarah A. Laird, Rebecca McLain, and Rachel
    P. Wynberg, eds. People and Plants
    International Conservation Series. London:
    Earthscan.
Mintz, Sidney
    1986 Sweetness and Power: The Place of
    Sugar in Modern History. New York:
    Penguin.
Mol, Annemarie
    2002 The Body Multiple: Ontology in
    Medical Practice. Durham, NC: Duke
    University Press.
Needham, Joseph
    1954 Science and Civilisation in China,
    vol. 1: Introductory Orientations. Cambridge:
    Cambridge University Press.
Ogawa, Makoto
    1991[1978] Matsutake no seibutsugaku
    (Biology of the matsutake mushroom). Tokyo:
    Tsukiji Shokan.
Ogawa, Makoto
    2007 Sumi to kinkon de yomigaeru matsu
    (Pines revive with charcoal and mycorrhiza).
    Tokyo: Tsukiji Shokan.
Osborne, Michael A.
    2005 Science and the French Empire. Isis
    96:80–87.
Pickering, Andrew
    1995 The Mangle of Practice: Time, Agency,
    and Science. Chicago: University of Chicago
    Press.
Rabinow, Paul, and Talia Dan-Cohen
    2006 A Machine to Make a Future: Biotech
    Chronicles. Princeton: Princeton University
    Press.
Rabinow, Paul, and George E. Marcus, with
    James Faubion and Tobias Rees
    2008 Designs for an Anthropology of the
    Contemporary. Durham, NC: Duke University
    Press.
Rosaldo, Michelle, and Louise Lamphere, eds.
    1974 Woman, Culture, and Society. Stanford:
    Stanford University Press.
Rupp, Katherine
    2003 Gift-Giving in Japan: Cash,
    Connections, Cosmologies. Stanford: Stanford
    University Press.

Saito, Haruo, and Gaku Mitsumata
  2008 Bidding Customs and Habitat Improvement for Matsutake (Tricholoma matsutake) in Japan. Economic Botany 62(3):257–268.
Satsuka, Shiho
  2004 Traveling Nature, Imagining the Globe: Japanese Tourism in the Canadian Rockies. Ph.D. dissertation, Department of Anthropology, University of California, Santa Cruz.
Shapin, Steven
  1994 A Social History of Truth. Chicago: University of Chicago Press.
Stamets, Paul
  2005 Mycelium Running: How Mushrooms Can Help Save the World. Berkeley, CA: Ten Speed Press.
Stengers, Isabelle
  2003 Cosmopolitiques. 2 vols. Paris: La Découverte.
Steward, Julian H., Robert A. Manners, Eric R. Wolf, Elena Padilla Seda, Sidney W. Mintz, and Raymond L. Scheele
  1956 The People of Puerto Rico. Urbana: University of Illinois Press.
Strathern, Marilyn
  1988 The Gender of the Gift: Problems with Women and Problems with Society in Melanesia. Berkeley: University of California Press.
Suzuki, Kazuo
  2004 Pine Wilt and the Pine Wood Nematode. In Encyclopedia of the Forest Sciences. J. Burley, J. Evans, and J. Youngquist, eds. pp. 773–777. Amsterdam: Elsevier Academic Press.
Suzuki, Kazuo
  2005 Gaiseikinkon kyoseikei no seiri seitai to matsutake no pazuru (Ectomycorrhizal ecophysiology and the puzzle of Tricholoma matsutake). Journal of the Japanese Forest Society (Nihon Shinrin Gakkaishi) 87(1):90–102.
Thomas, Peter
  2005 Mushrooms and the Future of CITES. Endangered Species Bulletin 30:24–25.
Traweek, Sharon
  1988 Beamtimes and Lifetimes: The World of High Energy Physicists. Cambridge, MA: Harvard University Press.
Tsing, Anna
  2005 Friction: An Ethnography of Global Connection. Princeton: Princeton University Press.
Tsing, Anna
  In press a Beyond Economic and Ecological Standardization. The Australian Journal of Anthropology.

Tsing, Anna
  In press b Unruly Edges: Mushrooms as Companion Species. In Thinking with Donna Haraway. Sharon Ghamari-Tabrizi, ed. Cambridge, MA: MIT Press.
Tsing, Anna, and Shiho Satsuka
  2008 Diverging Understandings of Forest Management in Matsutake Science. Economic Botany 62(3):244–253.
Vaario, Lu-Min, Alexis Guerin-Laguette, Norihisa Matsushita, Kazuo Suzuki, and Frédéric Lapeyrie
  2002 Saprobic Potential of Tricholoma Matsutake: Growth over Pine Bark Treated with Surfactants. Mycorrhiza 12(1):1–5.
Verran, Helen
  2001 Science and an African Logic. Chicago: University of Chicago Press.
Vincent, Joan
  1994[1990] Anthropology and Politics: Visions, Traditions, and Trends. Tucson: University of Arizona Press.
Vogt, Evon Z.
  1978 Bibliography of the Harvard Chiapas Project: The First Twenty Years, 1957–1977. Cambridge, MA: Peabody Museum of American Archaeology and Ethnology, Harvard University.
Wang, Yun, and Ian R. Hall
  2004 Edible Ectomycorrhizal Mushrooms: Challenges and Achievements. Canadian Journal of Botany/Revue Canadienne de Botanique 82:1063–1073.
Whatmore, Sarah
  2002 Hybrid Geographies: Natures, Cultures, Spaces. London: SAGE.
Winkler, Daniel
  2004 Matsutake Mycelium under Attack in Southwest China. How the Mushrooming Trade Mines Its Resource and How to Achieve Sustainability. Electronic document, http://www.danielwinkler.com/matsutake_conservation_in_sw_china.htm, accessed February 9, 2009.
Wolf, Eric
  1982 Europe and the People without History. Berkeley: University of California Press.
Yamada, Akiyoshi, and Masatake Omasa
  2003 Matsutake kenkyū no dōkō (Trends in Matsutake research). Sanrin 5:68–73.
Yeh, Emily T.
  2000 Forest Claims, Conflict and Commodification: The Political Ecology of Tibetan Mushroom-Harvesting Villages in Yunnan Province, China. China Quarterly 161:264–278.

Part VIII

Sensorial Fieldwork

Introduction

Antonius C. G. M. Robben

Ethnographic fieldwork is generally presented in a text, even though people's sensory experience of the world reaches far beyond verbal or written expression. This literary bias deserves to be complemented with other means of representation, such as photography, film, and sound recordings, and a much needed attention to people's entire sensorium. The cultural mediation of sensory perception is, as Herzfeld (2001:240–241) has explained, the principal premise of the anthropology of the senses. The sensorium is the proverbial hardware which needs cultural software to become meaningful to people and allow them to interact. How people look, talk, sound, smell, or touch can influence whether they are stigmatized or treated with respect, and whether they are identified with one social group, community, and class, or another, because "every domain of sensory experience is also an arena for structuring social roles and interactions" (Howes 2003:xi). Herzfeld encourages sensorial fieldworkers to make the study of the entire sensorium indispensable to other domains of ethnographic inquiry, such as economics or politics, in order to lift the anthropology of the senses out of its subdisciplinary isolation. Just as attention to gender and power is now part and parcel of most ethnographic work, so the entire range of senses should become of similar concern.

The Western classification of the senses into sight, touch, taste, smell, and hearing is not universal. For example, Javanese recognize talking as their fifth sense, not taste. Hausa emphasize sight as one sense, but have only one word for the remaining senses, while some cultures add clairvoyance as a sixth sense (Howes and Classen 1991:257–258). Likewise, Andaman Islanders perceive and organize time and space through an annual cycle of smells and a shifting olfactory landscape, while the

Ethnographic Fieldwork: An Anthropological Reader, Second Edition. Edited by
Antonius C. G. M. Robben and Jeffrey A. Sluka.
Editorial material and organization © 2012 John Wiley & Sons, Inc.
Published 2012 by John Wiley & Sons, Inc.

Amazonian Suyá classify their flora and fauna into olfactory classes (Seeger 1981; Classen et al. 1994:95–101). The sensory experience of the natural and social world passes through culture. The sensorium fuses physiology with culture in specific forms of classification, encoding, social practice, power, agency, and negotiation. Some anthropologists have proposed the writing of ethnographies which describe all sensory experiences, because people construct the world and relate to one another within an integrated sensorium (see Howes 1991, 2003). Furthermore, cultures may combine sensory perceptions in unique ways, and even individuals may do so when equipped with the synesthetic ability to taste, smell, or see sounds. The difficulty of conveying the senses in a written narrative has drawn anthropology to other media such as photography, filmmaking, and sound recording.

Photography and moving pictures were used by ethnographers soon after they were invented. George Catlin took what are believed to be the first ethnographic photographs, only six years after the daguerreotype was invented in 1839, and Bronislaw Malinowski and Claude Lévi-Strauss were avid photographers (Lévi-Strauss 1995; Young 1998; Prins 2004). The first ethnographic film was shot in 1895 by the French physician-turned-anthropologist Félix-Louis Regnault. Alfred Haddon used film as a recording device during the 1898 Torres Straits expedition, and so did Franz Boas among the Kwakiutl (De Brigard 1995). These ethnographers used pictures and film mainly for reasons of illustration. Gregory Bateson and Margaret Mead were perhaps the first to employ photography and film as scientific instruments to analyze and interpret cultures. They had been looking for ways to avoid the detachment of a too analytic etic approach and the inaccessibility of a too emphatic emic approach. Furthermore, they were struggling with the difficulties of expressing foreign cultural meanings, social practices, and intangible intracultural connections into a scientific (English) language. They took recourse to film and photography. The selection from their ground-breaking photo-ethnography *Balinese Character* (Bateson and Mead 1942) demonstrates that photographs can be more than an *aide-mémoire* for fieldworkers or a pictorial illustration for readers. Photographs become a primary causeway into Balinese culture and thus organize the data analysis, the written commentary, and the ethnographic interpretation.

The fieldwork approach consisted of the taking of notes by Margaret Mead and the recording on film by Gregory Bateson. This division of labor continued upon their return home: Mead wrote the ethnographic interpretation and Bateson the photoanalysis. Mead's so-called "running field notes" followed the flow of observation and included detailed cross-references to the stills or moving pictures taken by her husband. She also kept a diary to record the principal occurrences in the village, and showed the footage to the Balinese for further commentary (Jacknis 1988).

Visual anthropology took flight after *Balinese Character* with the photo-ethnography on mortuary rituals in rural Greece by Loring Danforth and Alexander Tsiaras (1982), and the ethnographic documentaries by filmmakers such as Robert Gardner, Timothy Asch, John Marshall, and Jean Rouch (see Edwards 1992; Hockings 1995; Rouch 2003). Anthropologists soon realized that the visual image is not an accurate registration of reality, as early practitioners believed, but that "raw" photos and footage, just like "raw" field notes, are constructions encapsulating the intention, agency, and objectives of the ethnographer, and thus subject to reinterpretation. The finished product is the outcome of an elaborate editing process informed by an eth-nographic understanding of the culture under study (Heider 1976; Scherer 1992).

Balinese Character was more than an experiment in ethnographic representation and analysis because of its attention to the senses (see also Pink 2006). Mead explains in the introduction that she and her husband were interested in how pre-contact Balinese culture (i.e., before the arrival of Buddhist, Hindu, Christian, and Islamic influences) was reproduced and visibly manifested in everyday life. Bateson and Mead were under the sway of the American culture-and-personality school, and they believed that the study of postures, gestures, and interpersonal communications could uncover sedimented cultural features about Balinese personality, character, and ethos. Their reference to a hyperthyroid epidemic among the population, as if shedding the foreign cultural veneer to reveal some sort of ground plan of Balinese culture, fits this assumption. The three series of photographs selected for this Reader demonstrate how learning in Balinese culture is visual rather than verbal, and kines-thetic (body learning) instead of disciplinary. Bateson and Mead pay much attention to the cultural significance of nonverbal cues, subtle gestures, postures, the bending of joints, and the touching and spatial projection of the body, thus including a large part of the Balinese sensorium in their ethnography.

In their article "The Taste of Ethnographic Things" (1989) taken from the simi-larly titled book by Stoller (1989), Paul Stoller and Cheryl Olkes show how a research interest in the senses opens up a whole new realm of anthropological understanding and interpretation. Something as seemingly trivial as serving bad sauce is full of cul-tural meaning and social relevance. In this way, Stoller criticizes the generalizing and objectifying aims of one particular approach in sensorial anthropology which removes the senses from people's daily experience, and situates them in a knowable social and cultural reality to develop a theory of the senses, of smell, sight, hearing, touch, and taste. After a deconstruction of taste in Western philosophy and anthro-pology, Stoller advocates a "tasteful ethnography" which focuses on subjectivity, sensuality, meaningfulness, authenticity, and dialogic and ironic qualities of taste. This mélange evokes the lived experience of taste, blending interpretation with description, evocation with insight, and representation with sensibility (see also Seremetakis 1994; Rasmussen 1999; Sutton 2001; Farquhar 2002).

Stoller and Olkes accomplish such tasteful ethnography by revealing the signifi-cance of being presented with foul-smelling and foul-tasting sauces by their Songhay hosts in Niger. Not poor culinary skill, but sibling rivalry, ethnic tension, distrust, resistance to paternal authority, social transgression, a violation of custom, jealousy, frustration, and unsatisfactory reciprocity were the backdrop of the bad sauces. Hospitality turned into hostility through shameful sauces. Thus, the ethnographers' palate disclosed a new understanding of Songhay representation of domestic and fraternal conflict.

In the 1980s, there was a major shift from the anthropology of music to musical anthropology, as Seeger (1987:xiii) has pointed out. The anthropology of music studied what music adds to an existing culture (see Merriam 1964), while musical anthropology examines how music creates culture and social life itself. Steven Feld has been at the forefront of this shift, and his work is of particular importance to sensorial anthropology because of his interest in sound rather than music.

In "Dialogic Editing: Interpreting How Kaluli Read *Sound and Sentiment*" (1987), Feld analyzes the reception of his ethnography *Sound and Sentiment* (1982) by the Kaluli people of Papua New Guinea. This fieldwork encounter involved "dialogic editing" in which informants reshape the ethnographer's interpretation of their culture in word, image, or sound. This fieldwork technique is particularly complex in a society like that of the Kaluli, which does not share our Western emphasis on the verbal expression of culture, but structures storytelling, aesthetics, and sentiment through song and sound. The Kaluli and Feld agreed on the central importance of natural and human sounds to Kaluli culture. Nevertheless, Feld organized his ethnography around the aesthetics of local sentiment in singing and weeping, even though the people themselves were more concerned with memorable personal experiences than with ethnographic analysis and generalization.

The translation of English into the Bosavi language spoken by the Kaluli was the first dialogic obstacle between Feld and his research participants, because the word "translation" has three local connotations: transformation ("turn around"), exposure ("turn over"), and meaning ("underneaths"). Feld renarrated his ethnography by revealing submerged layers of meaning, recounting stories, redescribing activities, and reassigning ethnographic illustrations to their original actors. These conversations also demonstrated that every ethnography is a narrative construction which may not coincide with how people sense and represent their culture. The anthropologist is faced with restrictions imposed by publishers and peers with regard to length, composition, subject matter, analysis, logic, generalization, and theorization that are irrelevant to the people described.

These representational problems are magnified for sensorial anthropology. How could an ethnography ever do justice to the cultural prominence of sound in Kaluli culture? The Kaluli criticized Feld's ethnographic selections and the omission of everyday sounds, such as rain, thunder, and the morning noises of the awakening village. Feld resorted therefore to CD recordings. However, reproducing sound as a cultural system on CD is just as complicated as producing an ethnography through words and musical scores. After his rewarding experience with dialogic editing, Feld added dialogic auditing to yield a mixture of sounds that tried to evoke within the span of one hour the Kaluli experience of their local universe (Feld and Brenneis 2005). Like Stoller's tasteful ethnography, this approach prompted Feld (1991) to make a recording which represented a 24-hour period in the Kaluli village.

Herzfeld (2001:241–242) has argued that the Cartesian bias of Western science, namely the separation of body (the sensorial domain) and mind (the ideational domain), is the principal obstacle to a mature anthropology of the senses. Western culture came to regard the mind as the seat of reason, and vision as its principal judge. Science became dominated by verbal and visual representation, while smell, touch, and taste were dismissed as too subjective. In "On Rocks, Walks, and Talks in West Africa: Cultural Categories and an Anthropology of the Senses" (2003), Kathryn Geurts writes that this Cartesian prejudice initially hindered her fieldwork among the Anlo-Ewe people of southeastern Ghana. She had difficulty grasping their sensorium because of her tendency to break down bodily experiences into distinct cognitive, physiological, affective, and ideational aspects. She employs the corporal sensation of driving her car over a rock in her compound as a heuristic tool to understand the Anlo-Ewe cultural model of linking feeling, sensation, disposition, and volition. This approach leads her to a deeper understanding of Anlo-Ewe epistemology and ways of knowing.

Western Cartesian epistemology distinguishes between inner subjective sensations or states, such as emotions, feelings, and bodily balance, and outer sensations that are noticed objectively through the five sense organs. The Anlo-Ewe epistemology does not make such differentiation, but encompasses emotions, dispositions, sense organ experiences, and corporal sensations into a whole called *seselelame*, or "feeling in the flesh," as well as "feeling through the body." This is not to say that the Anlo-Ewe do not have a notion of seeing or hearing, since they do recognize deafness and blindness, but they do not assign them the unique properties that Westerners do and regard the senses as both more pliable and more integrated with other experiences (Geurts 2002:209–213). In other words, the cultural category *seselelame* addresses cognitive, affective, perceptional, moral, sensorial, and intersubjective experiences into a synesthetic mode of attributing meaning to reality. For example, a persistent swaying or staggering gait (*lugulugu*) may cause irresponsible conduct and a poor unruly character, and vice versa. The kinesthesia might become embodied in the mind, disposition, morality, and even the person's profession. Another example is the "feeling in the mouth" (*sesetonume*), which is an Anlo-Ewe cultural category that interconnects such oral sensations as speech, eating, kissing, and breathing.

Sensorial fieldwork and the anthropology of the senses are examining the complexities of the sensorium through three major lines of inquiry. One approach concentrates on each of the five Western senses, as exemplified here by the work of Stoller and Olkes (1989) and Feld (1987). The ethnographer starts from a Western notion of one particular sense, assumes the local culture's sensorial perspective, and then follows the sensorial practices and perceptions into the culture under study. The second approach is multisensorial, and focuses on the local senses altogether and especially their connections within an integrated sensorium (Howes 2005). The analysis made by Geurts (2003) about the Anlo-Ewe epistemology, and the intertwinement of knowing and sensing, is illustrative. The third approach is interdisciplinary. Many scholars draw selectively on work in other disciplines, but some pursue a genuine interdisciplinary research agenda that combines anthropology with history, geography, sociology, psychology, neurology, linguistics, and the arts (Howes 2005; Drobnick 2006; Pink 2009; Porcello et al. 2010).

REFERENCES

Bateson, Gregory and Margaret Mead
    1942 *Balinese Character: A Photographic Analysis*. New York: New York Academy of Sciences.
Classen, Constance, David Howes, and Anthony Synnott
    1994 *Aroma: The Cultural History of Smell*. London: Routledge.
Danforth, Loring M. and Alexander Tsiaras
    1982 *The Death Rituals of Rural Greece*. Princeton: Princeton University Press.
De Brigard, Emilie
    1995 The History of Ethnographic Film. In: *Principles of Visual Anthropology*. 2nd edn. Paul Hockings, ed., pp. 13–43. Berlin: Mouton de Gruyter.

Drobnick, Jim, ed.
　　2006　*The Smell Culture Reader*. Oxford: Berg.
Edwards, Elizabeth, ed.
　　1992　*Anthropology and Photography 1860–1920*. New Haven, CT: Yale University Press.
Farquhar, Judith
　　2002　*Appetites: Food and Sex in Postsocialist China*. Durham, NC: Duke University Press.
Feld, Steven
　　1982　*Sound and Sentiment: Birds, Weeping, Poetics, and Song in Kaluli Expression*. Philadelphia: University of Pennsylvania Press.
Feld, Steven
　　1987　Dialogic Editing: Interpreting How Kaluli Read *Sound and Sentiment*. *Cultural Anthropology* 2(2):190–210.
Feld, Steven
　　1991　*Voices of the Rainforest: A Day in the Life of the Kaluli People*. CD. The World series. Mickey Hart, ed. Boston: Rykodisc.
Feld, Steven and Donald Brenneis
　　2005　Doing Anthropology in Sound. *American Ethnologist* 31(4):461–474.
Geurts, Kathryn Linn
　　2002　*Culture and the Senses: Ways of Knowing in an African Community*. Berkeley: University of California Press.
Geurts, Kathryn Linn
　　2003　On Rocks, Walks, and Talks in West Africa: Cultural Categories and an Anthropology of the Senses. *Ethos* 30(3):178–198.
Heider, Karl G.
　　1976　*Ethnographic Film*. Austin: University of Texas Press.
Herzfeld, Michael
　　2001　*Anthropology: Theoretical Practice in Culture and Society*. Malden, MA: Blackwell Publishers.
Hockings, Paul
　　1995　*Principles of Visual Anthropology*. 2nd edn. Berlin: Mouton de Gruyter.
Howes, David, ed.
　　1991　*The Varieties of Sensory Experience: A Sourcebook in the Anthropology of the Senses*. Toronto: University of Toronto Press.
Howes, David
　　2003　*Sensual Relations: Engaging the Senses in Culture and Social Theory*. Ann Arbor: University of Michigan Press.
Howes, David, ed.
　　2005　*Empire of the Senses: The Sensual Culture Reader*. Oxford: Berg.
Howes, David and Constance Classen
　　1991　Conclusion: Sounding Sensory Profiles. In: *The Varieties of Sensory Experience: A Sourcebook in the Anthropology of the Senses*. David Howes, ed., pp. 257–288. Toronto: University of Toronto Press.
Jacknis, Ira
　　1988　Margaret Mead and Gregory Bateson in Bali: Their Use of Photography and Film. *Cultural Anthropology* 3(2):160–177.
Lévi-Strauss, Claude
　　1995　*Saudades do Brasil: A Photographic Memoir*. Seattle: University of Washington Press.
Merriam, Alan P.
　　1964　*The Anthropology of Music*. Evanston, IL: Northwestern University Press.

Pink, Sarah
  2006 *The Future of Visual Anthropology: Engaging the Senses.* London: Routledge.
Pink, Sarah
  2009 *Doing Sensory Ethnography.* Los Angeles: Sage.
Porcello, Thomas, Louise Meintjes, Ana Maria Ochoa, and David W. Samuels
  2010 The Reorganization of the Sensory World. *Annual Review of Anthropology* 39:51–66.
Prins, Harold E. L.
  2004 Visual Anthropology. In: *A Companion to the Anthropology of American Indians.* Thomas Biolsi, ed., pp. 506–525. Malden, MA: Blackwell Publishing.
Rasmussen, Susan
  1999 Making Better "Scents" in Anthropology: Aroma in Tuareg Sociocultural Systems and the Shaping of Ethnography. *Anthropological Quarterly* 72(2):55–73.
Rouch, Jean
  2003 *Ciné-Ethnography.* Ed. and trans. Steven Feld. Minneapolis: University of Minnesota Press.
Scherer, Joanna C.
  1992 The Photographic Document: Photographs as Primary Data in Anthropological Enquiry. In: *Anthropology and Photography 1860–1920.* Elizabeth Edwards, ed., pp. 32–41. New Haven, CT: Yale University Press.
Seeger, Anthony
  1981 *Nature and Society in Central Brazil: The Suya Indians of Mato Grosso.* Cambridge, MA: Harvard University Press.
Seeger, Anthony
  1987 *Why Suyá Sing: A Musical Anthropology of an Amazonian People.* Cambridge, MA: Cambridge University Press.
Seremetakis, C. Nadia, ed.
  1994 *The Senses Still: Perception and Memory as Material Culture in Modernity.* Boulder, CO: Westview Press.
Stoller, Paul
  1989 *The Taste of Ethnographic Things: The Senses in Anthropology.* Philadelphia: University of Pennsylvania Press.
Stoller, Paul and Cheryl Olkes
  1989 The Taste of Ethnographic Things. In: *The Taste of Ethnographic Things: The Senses in Anthropology.* Paul Stoller, ed., pp. 15–34. Philadelphia: University of Pennsylvania Press.
Sutton, David E.
  2001 *Remembrance of Repasts: An Anthropology of Food and Memory.* Oxford: Berg.
Young, Michael W.
  1998 *Malinowski's Kiriwina: Fieldwork Photography 1915–1918.* Chicago: University of Chicago Press.

28

Balinese Character: A Photographic Analysis

Gregory Bateson and Margaret Mead

Introduction

The form of presentation used in this monograph is an experimental innovation. During the period from 1928 to 1936 we were separately engaged in efforts to translate aspects of culture never successfully recorded by the scientist, although often caught by the artist, into some form of communication sufficiently clear and sufficiently unequivocal to satisfy the requirements of scientific enquiry. "Coming of Age in Samoa," "Growing up in New Guinea," and "Sex and Temperament"[1] all attempted to communicate those intangible aspects of culture which had been vaguely referred to as its *ethos*. As no precise scientific vocabulary was available, the ordinary English words were used, with all their weight of culturally limited connotations, in an attempt to describe the way in which the emotional life of these various South Sea peoples was organized in culturally standardized forms. This method had many serious limitations: it transgressed the canons of precise and operational scientific exposition proper to science; it was far too dependent upon idiosyncratic factors of style and literary skill; it was difficult to duplicate; and it was difficult to evaluate.

Most serious of all, we know this about the relationship between culture and verbal concepts – that the words which one culture has invested with meaning are by the very accuracy of their cultural fit, singularly inappropriate as vehicles for precise comment upon another culture. Many anthropologists have been so impressed with this verbal inadequacy that they have attempted to sharpen their comment upon other cultures by very extensive borrowing from the native language. This procedure, however, in addition to being clumsy and forbidding, does not solve the problem, because the only method of translation available to make the native terms finally intelligible is still the use of our own culturally limited language.

Gregory Bateson and Margaret Mead, pp. xi–xvi, 13–17, 49–51, 84–88, plates 15, 16, and 17 from *Balinese Character: A Photographic Analysis*. New York: New York Academy of Sciences, 1942. Copyright © 1942 by The New York Academy of Sciences. Reprinted by permission of Blackwell Publishing on behalf of The New York Academy of Sciences and the Institute for Intercultural Studies.

Ethnographic Fieldwork: An Anthropological Reader, Second Edition. Edited by Antonius C. G. M. Robben and Jeffrey A. Sluka.
Editorial material and organization © 2012 John Wiley & Sons, Inc.
Published 2012 by John Wiley & Sons, Inc.

Attempts to substitute terms of cross-cultural validity, while they have been reasonably successful in the field of social organization, have proved exceedingly unsatisfactory when finer shades of cultural meaning were attempted.

Parallel with these attempts to rely upon ordinary English as a vehicle, the approach discussed in "Naven"[2] was being developed – an approach which sought to take the problem one step further by demonstrating how such categories as ethos, there defined as "a culturally standardized system of organization of the instincts and emotions of individuals," were not classifications of items of behavior but were abstractions which could be applied systematically to all items of behavior.

The first method has been criticized as journalistic – as an arbitrary selection of highly colored cases to illustrate types of behavior so alien to the reader that he continues to regard them as incredible. The second method was branded as too analytical – as neglecting the phenomena of a culture in order to intellectualize and schematize it. The first method was accused of being so synthetic that it became fiction, the second of being so analytic that it became disembodied methodological discussion.

We are attempting a new method of stating the intangible relationships among different types of culturally standardized behavior by placing side by side mutually relevant photographs. Pieces of behavior, spatially and contextually separated – a trance dancer being carried in procession, a man looking up at an aeroplane, a servant greeting his master in a play, the painting of a dream – may all be relevant to a single discussion; the same emotional thread may run through them. To present them together in words, it is necessary either to resort to devices which are inevitably literary, or to dissect the living scenes so that only desiccated items remain.

By the use of photographs, the wholeness of each piece of behavior can be preserved, while the special cross-referencing desired can be obtained by placing the series of photographs on the same page. It is possible to avoid the artificial construction of a scene at which a man, watching a dance, also looks up at an aeroplane and has a dream; it is also possible to avoid diagramming the single element in these scenes which we wish to stress – the importance of levels in Balinese inter-personal relationships – in such a way that the reality of the scenes themselves is destroyed.

This is not a book about Balinese custom, but about the Balinese – about the way in which they, as living persons, moving, standing, eating, sleeping, dancing, and going into trance, embody that abstraction which (after we have abstracted it) we technically call culture.

We are interested in the steps by which workers in a new science solve piecemeal their problems of description and analysis, and in the relationship between what we now say about Balinese culture, with these new techniques, and what we have said with more imperfect means of communication about other cultures. A particular method of presentation has therefore been agreed upon. Margaret Mead has written the introductory description of Balinese character, which is needed to orient the reader so that the plates may be meaningful. She has used here the same order of vocabulary and the same verbal devices which have been made to do service in earlier descriptions of other cultures. Gregory Bateson will apply to the behavior depicted in the photographs the same sort of verbal analysis which he applied to his records of Iatmul transvestitism in "Naven," and the reader will have the photographic presentation itself to unite and carry further these two partial methods of describing the ethos of the Balinese.

Former students of Bali have approached Balinese culture as peripheral to and derivative from the higher cultures of India, China, and Java, carefully identifying in Bali the reduced and residual forms of the heroes of the Ramajana or of the Hindoo pantheon, or of the characters of the Chinese theater. All those items of Balinese culture which could not be assimilated to this picture of Asiatic diffusion have been variously classified as "Polynesian," "Indonesian," "animistic," or "*Bali aga*" (a term which some Balinese have learned to use in contradistinction to "*Bali Hindoe*"). We, however, always approached the material from the opposite point of view; we assumed that Bali had a cultural base upon which various intrusive elements had been progressively grafted over the centuries, and that the more rewarding approach would be to study this base first. We accordingly selected for our primary study a mountain village, Bajoeng Gede, near Kintamani in the District of Bangli, where most of the conspicuous elements of the later, intrusive culture were lacking. In Bajoeng Gede one does not find use of Hindoo names for the Gods, the importance of color in relation to direction in offerings, cremation, caste, the taboo upon eating beef, or any relationship to a Brahman priestly household. Writing there was, but only a half-dozen semi-literate individuals who were barely able to keep records of attendance, fines, etc. The village boasted one calendrical expert who was skilled enough to advise the village officials on the intricacies of the calendar of multiple interlocking weeks and "months." Furthermore, Bajoeng Gede was ceremonially bare, even compared with other Balinese mountain villages. There was a minimum of that reduplication and over-elaboration of art and ceremonialism which is such a marked characteristic of Balinese culture. Reliance on the calendar and compli-cation of offerings and *rites de passage* were all reduced to a meager and skeletal minimum – a minimum which would nevertheless seem highly complex in comparison with most of the known cultures of the world. In this locality, it was possible in the course of a year to get a systematic understanding of the ground plan of the culture.

This undertaking was facilitated by two circumstances: the population of Bajoeng Gede suffered from a pronounced thyroid condition, with about 15 per cent of the population showing various degrees of simple goiter; and the whole population was markedly slow both in intellectual response and in speed of bodily movement. These circumstances, which are no doubt interrelated, provided us with a community in which the cultural emphases were schematically simplified, and upon our understanding of this base it was possible to graft – as the Balinese had before us – an understanding of the more complex versions of the same essential forms which we encountered on the plains. (It is important to remember that Hindoo culture came by way of Java, where the culture was related to that

of Bali, and that most of the elements probably reached Bali in a partially assimilated form, already somewhat adapted to Balinese emphases and social structures.)

After an initial two months of exploration and work on the language in Oeboed (district of Gianjar), we selected Bajoeng Gede, and we worked there with only a few short absences from June 1936 to June 1937 and intermittently till February 1938. In November 1936, we established a second camp in Bangli in a pal-ace built by a former Rajah, from which we were able during various short stays to participate in the family ceremonies of the ruling caste of Bangli. Finally in 1937, we built a pavilion in the courtyard of a Buddhistic Brahman family in the village of Batoean, from which position we participated in and studied Brahman family life, simultaneously collecting the work and studying the personality of the large group of Brahman and casteless painters in the school of art which had sprung up in Batoean during the last ten years.

Through Miss Belo's work in Sajan, a peasant plains village dominated by feudal Kesatrya nobles; Mrs Mershon's work in Sanoer, a coastal fishing village consisting mainly of Sivaistic Brahmans and casteless people; and from material provided by our Balinese secretary who came from a rising casteless family in Singaradja, the Dutch capital in North Bali, we were able to gather various sorts of comparative materials to round out the picture of Balinese culture which we had developed on the basis of observations in Bajoeng Gede. The discussions of Balinese culture in this book are based on these experiences, and on short excursions by ourselves and our collaborators to other villages and cities in Bali.

It is true that every village in Bali differs from every other in many conspicuous respects, and that there are even more striking differences between districts, so that no single concrete statement about Bali is true of all of Bali, and any negative statement about Bali must be made with the greatest caution. But through this diversity there runs a common ethos, whether one is observing the home of the highest caste, the Brahman, or of the simplest mountain peasant. The Brahman's greater ease, due to the fact that there are fewer of those who know much more than he, is but another version of the peasant's unwillingness to commit himself, of his "lest I err, being an illiterate man." The most conspicuous exceptions to this common ethos are the culture of the ruling caste, the Kesatryas, and the culture of North Bali which has been exposed to strong foreign influences during the last sixty years. In both of these groups may be found an emphasis upon the individual rather than upon his status, an element of social climbing and an uneasiness of tenure which contrast strongly with the rest of Bali. For this reason, reference to these two groups, except for occasional bits of ceremonial which they hold in common with the rest of Bali, has been excluded from this discussion.

In the Plates, each single illustration is dated and placed, and it is not safe to generalize from its detailed content for other parts of Bali. The form, however, the ethological emphasis which is implicit, may be taken to apply to all those parts of Bali of which we have any knowledge, except for North Bali, the Kesatryas, and the Vesias, a lower caste which mimics the Kesatryas and upon which we did very little work. These groups we explicitly exclude and we avoid all detailed negative statements as such statements are virtually impossible to make about a culture which has found it possible to combine such extraordinarily divergent content with such a consistent ethological emphasis. There is no apparent difference in the character structure of the people in villages where trance is shared by all and those in villages where no one ever goes into trance; people in villages where every other woman is believed to be a witch and those in villages where no one is believed to be a witch. In most of the cultures of which we have systematic knowledge, such matters are intricately and inextricably part of the personality of every participant member of the culture, but in Bali the same attitude of mind, the same system of posture and gesture, seems able to operate with these great contrasts in content with virtually no alteration in form. So also for climatic contrasts, and contrasts in wealth and poverty: the mountain people are dirtier, slower, and more suspicious than the plains people; the poor are more frightened than the rich, but the differences are in degree only; the same types of dirtiness, of suspicion, and anxiety are common at all levels.

This volume is in no sense a complete account of [Balinese] culture, even in its most general outlines. It is an attempt to present, at this time when scientific presentations are likely to be widely spaced, those aspects of our results and those methods of research which we have judged most likely to be of immediate use to other students. A less pregnant period of history might have dictated another choice of subject matter for our first presentation. Balinese culture, even that of Bajoeng Gede, is very rich and complex, and our two years' work, with two American collaborators and three Balinese secretaries, can only claim to be a "sampling" of the Balinese scene. We attempted to make systematic samples of village organization, calendrical ceremonial and *rites de passage*, trance, painting, carving, the shadow-play puppets, death rituals, and child behavior, so as to provide a series of cross-cutting pictures of the culture which could be fitted together and cross checked against each other. The discussion which follows is a synthetic statement based upon these various samples; the photographs are a carefully selected series, analyzed on the basis of the same sampling.

Finally a word about the relevance of such researches to the period of history in which we find ourselves. Balinese culture is in many ways less like our own than any other which has yet been recorded. It is also a culture in which the ordinary adjustment of the individual approximates in form the sort of maladjustment which, in our own cultural setting, we call schizoid. As the toll of dementia praecox among our own population continues to rise, it becomes increasingly important for us to know the bases in childhood experience which predispose to this condition, and we need to know how such predisposition can be culturally handled, so that it does not become maladjustment.

Meanwhile, we are faced with the problem of building a new world; we have to reorient the old values of many contrasting and contradictory cultural systems into a new form which will use but transcend them all, draw on their respective strengths and allow for their respective weaknesses. We have to build a culture richer and more rewarding than any that the world has ever seen. This can only be done through a disciplined science of human relations and such a science is built by drawing out from very detailed, concrete materials, such as these, the relevant abstractions – the vocabulary which will help us to plan an integrated world.

Notes on the Photographs and Captions

Taking the photographs

[...] We tried to use the still and the moving-picture cameras to get a record of Balinese behavior, and this is a very different matter from the preparation of "documentary" film or photographs. We tried to shoot what happened normally and spontaneously, rather than to decide upon the norms and then get Balinese to go through these behaviors in suitable lighting. We treated the cameras in the field as recording instruments, not as devices for illustrating our theses.

Four factors may be mentioned which contributed to diminish camera consciousness in our subjects:

A. The very large number of photographs taken. In two years we took about 25,000 Leica stills and about 22,000 feet of 16 mm. film, and it is almost impossible to maintain camera consciousness after the first dozen shots.

B. The fact that we never asked to take pictures, but just took them as a matter of routine, wearing or carrying the two cameras day in and day out, so that the photographer himself ceased to be camera conscious.

C. We habitually directed attention to our photographing of small babies, and the parents overlooked the fact that they also were included in the pictures (as even American parents will, in similar circumstances).

D. We occasionally used an angular view finder for shots when the subject might be expected to dislike being photographed at that particular moment.

We usually worked together, Margaret Mead keeping verbal notes on the behavior and Gregory Bateson moving around in and out of the scene with the two cameras. The verbal record included frequent notes on the time and occasional notes on the photographer's movements, such as the direction from which he was working and which instrument he was using. Whenever a new roll of film was inserted in the camera, the date and time of insertion were scribbled on the leader; and when the film was removed, the date and time were again recorded, so that the film could be accurately fitted to the notes.

For work of this sort it is essential to have at least two workers in close cooperation. The photographic sequence is almost valueless without a verbal account of what occurred, and it is not possible to take full notes while manipulating cameras. The photographer, with his eye glued to a view finder and moving about, gets a very imperfect view of what is actually happening, and Margaret Mead (who is able to write with only an occasional glance at her notebook) had a much fuller view of the scene than Gregory Bateson. She was able to do some very necessary directing of the photography, calling the photographer's attention to one or another child or to some special play which was beginning on the other side of the yard. Occasionally, when we were working on family scenes, we were accompanied by our native secretary, I Made Kaler. He would engage in ethnographic interviews with the parents, or take verbatim notes on the conversations.

In a great many instances, we created the *context* in which the notes and photographs were taken, e.g., by paying for the dance, or asking a mother to delay the bathing of her child until the sun was high, but this is very different from posing the photographs. Payment for theatrical performances is the economic base upon which the Balinese theater depends, and the extra emphasis given to the baby served to diminish the mother's awareness that she was to be photographed.

A visit "to photograph the baby being bathed" would last from fifteen minutes to two hours, and the greater part of the time after the bathing would be spent watching the family in a large variety of types of play and other behavior. In such a setting, a roll of Leica film (about 40 exposures) lasted from five to fifteen minutes.

Selection of photographs

Selection of data must occur in any scientific recording and exposition, but it is important that the principles of selection be stated. In the field, we were guided first by certain major assumptions, e.g., that parent-child relationships and relationships between siblings are likely to be more rewarding than agricultural techniques. We therefore selected especially contexts and sequences of this sort. We recorded as fully as possible what happened while we were in the houseyard, and it is so hard to predict behavior that it was scarcely possible to select particular postures or gestures for photographic recording. In general, we found that any attempt to select for special details was fatal, and that the best results were obtained when the photography was most rapid and almost random. [...]

One rather curious type of selection did occur. We were compelled to economize on motion-picture film, and disregarding the future difficulties of exposition, we assumed that the still photography and the motion-picture film *together* would constitute our record of behavior. We therefore reserved the motion-picture camera for the more active and interesting moments, and recorded the slower and less significant behaviors with the still camera. The present book is illustrated solely by photographs taken with the latter, and as a result, the book contains no photograph of a father suckling his child at the nipple, and the series of kris dancers leaves much to be desired.

After taking the photographs, a further selection occurred. On returning to America, we had the entire collection of 25,000 frames printed as diapositives on strips of positive film, and in planning this book we made a list of categories which we intended to illustrate – a list similar to, but not identical with, the grouping of the plates in the table of Contents.

We then projected all the diapositives, one by one, and wrote category cards for those which seemed to merit further consideration for inclusion in the book. We thus obtained a list of about 6,000 frames. Of these, we enlarged approximately the first 4,000 in chronological order, desisting at this point because time was short. From these 4,000, the majority of the prints reproduced here were selected, and we only drew upon the later negatives for a few special points which were not represented in the earlier series. The book thus contains a disproportionate number of photographs taken in the first three-quarters of our time in Bali.

The final choice of photographs for each plate was in terms of relevance, photographic quality, and size. In a number of cases, relevance to a problem is necessarily two-sided; there would be some photographs making one half of a psychological generalization, and others making a converse or obverse point. In these cases, we have tried to arrange the photographs so that most of the plate is occupied with the more typical aspect, while a statement of the obverse is given by one or two photographs at the bottom (usually in the right-hand corner) of the plate. In other cases, it has seemed worth-while to devote two plates to the contrasting aspects of the same generalization.

Conflict between scientific relevance and photographic merit has usually been easily settled in favor of the former, and a large number of pictures have been included in spite of photographic faults. Selection by size was more distressing. Each plate was to be reproduced as a unit and therefore we had the task of preparing prints which would fit together in laying out the plate. Working with this large collection of negatives, it was not possible to plan the lay-out in advance, and therefore, in the case of the more important photographs, two prints of different sizes were prepared. Even with this precaution, the purely physical problems of space and composition on the plate have eliminated a few photographs which we would have liked to include.

Learning (Plates 15 to 17)

When the Balinese baby is born, the midwife, even at the moment of lifting him in her arms, will put words in his mouth, commenting, "I am just a poor little newborn baby, and I don't know how to talk properly, but I am very grateful to you, honorable people, who have entered this pig sty of a house to see me born." And from that moment, all through babyhood, the child is fitted into a frame of behavior, of imputed speech and imputed thought and complex gesture, far beyond his skill and maturity. The first time that he answers "*Tiang*," the self-subordinating ego pronoun, to a stranger, he will be echoing a word that has already been said, on his behalf and in his hearing, hundreds of times. Where the American mother attempts to get the child to parrot simple courtesy phrases, the Balinese mother simply recites them, glibly, in the first person, and the child finally slips into speech, as into an old garment, worn before, but fitted on by another hand.

As with speech, so with posture and gesture. The right hand must be distinguished from the left; the right hand touches food, and the right thumb may be used in pointing; the left hand is the hand with which one cleanses oneself, or protects one's genitals in bathing, and must never be used to touch food, to point, or to receive a gift. But the Balinese mother or nurse carries a child, either in or out of a sling, on her left hip, thus leaving her own right hand free. In this position, the baby's *left* arm is free, while the right is frequently pinioned in against the breast, or at best extended behind the mother's back. Naturally, when a baby is offered a flower or a bit of cake, it reaches for it with the free left hand, and the mother or the child nurse invariably pulls the left hand back, extricates the baby's right hand – usually limp and motiveless under this interference with the free gesture – and extends the right hand to receive the gift. This training is begun long before the child is able to learn the distinction, begun in fact as soon as the child is able to grasp at a proffered object, and discontinued usually when the child is off the hip. A three-year-old may often err and receive a casual present in his left hand, with no more punishment than to have some older child or nearby adult shout "*Noenas!*" ("Ask!") which means "Cup the right hand in the left," but the baby of four months is permitted no such leeway.

Over and over again, the first spontaneous gesture is clipped off, and a passive, plastic gesture is substituted.

Meanwhile, the child in the sling, or supported lightly on the carrier's hip, has learned to accommodate itself passively to the carrier's movements; to sleep, with head swaying groggily from side to side, as the carrier pounds rice; or to hang limp on the hip of a small girl who is playing "crack-the-whip." Surrendering all autonomy, and passively following the words spoken in its name or the rhythm of the person who carries it or the hand which snatches its hand back from a spontaneous gesture, the child's body becomes more waxy and flexible as it grows older; and gestures which are all echoes of an experienced pattern replace such spontaneous gestures of infancy as the pounding of the child's silver bracelets on any convenient board. This accommodation to the movements of others, to cues that come from a pattern rather than from a desire, is facilitated by the extent to which a Balinese child is carried. There is a strong objection to letting a child be seen crawling – an animal activity – by any but the family intimates; and babies, even after they are able to crawl and toddle, are still carried most of the time. The position on the hip limits spontaneity to the arms and the carrier's repetitive interference with hand gestures reduces it there.

Even at its 105-day birthday, the infant is dressed in full adult costume. The infant boy is seated in a parent's arms, and a headcloth ten times too large for him is arranged at least for a moment on his head. The infant's hands are put through the gestures of prayer, of receiving holy water, and of wafting the essence of the holy offering toward himself. By the 210-day birthday, the child will repeat these gestures himself, sitting dreamily, after the ceremony, clasping and unclasping his tiny hands, and then speculatively examining them, finger by finger. At this age also, before he can walk, he will be taught simple hand dance gestures, first by manual manipulation, and later he will learn to follow visual cues, as the parent hums the familiar music and gestures before the baby's eyes with his own hand. This situation, the child dancing in the sustaining arm of the parent and that arm vibrating rhythmically to the music, becomes the prototype of Balinese learning in which as he grows older he will learn with his eyes and with his muscles. But the learning with the eyes is never separated from a sort of physical identification with the model. The baby girl climbs down off her mother's hip to lift a bit of an offering to her head, when her mother or elder sister does the same.

Learning to walk, learning the first appropriate gestures of playing musical instruments, learning to eat, and to dance are all accomplished with the teacher behind the pupil, conveying directly by pressure, and almost always with a minimum of words, the gesture to be performed. Under such a system of learning, one can only learn if one is completely relaxed and if will and consciousness as we understand those terms are almost in abeyance. The flexible body of the dancing pupil is twisted and turned in the teacher's hands; teacher and pupil go through the proper gesture, then suddenly the teacher springs aside, leaving the pupil to continue the pattern to which he has surrendered himself, sometimes with the teacher continuing it so that the pupil can watch him as he dances. Learning with the eyes flows directly from learning passively while one's own body is being manipulated by another.

The Balinese learn virtually nothing from verbal instruction and most Balinese adults are incapable of following out the three consecutive orders which we regard as the sign of a normal three-year-old intelligence. The only way in which it is possible to give complex verbal instructions is to pause after each detail and let the listener repeat the detail, feeling his way into the instruction. Thus all orders tend to have a pattern like this. "You know the box?" "What box?" "The black one." "What black one?" "The black one in the east corner of the kitchen." "In the east corner?" "Yes, the black one. Go and get it." "I should go and get the black box in the east corner of the kitchen?" "Yes." Only by such laborious assimilation of words into word gestures made by oneself, do words come to have any meaning for action.

This same peculiarity is found in the pattern of story telling. The Balinese story teller does not continue gaily along through a long take, as the story tellers of most cultures do, but he makes a simple statement, "There was once a princess," to which his auditors answer, "Where did she live?" or "What was her name?" and so on, until the narrative has been communicated in dialogue. A thread, even a simple verbal thread, in which one's body plays no role, has no continuous meaning.

There is rarely any discernible relationship between the conversation of a group of Balinese and the activity which they are performing. Words must be captured and repeated to have meaning for action, but there is no need at all to translate action into words. One might listen at a spy hole for an hour to a busy group, hearing every word spoken, and be no wiser in the end as to whether they were making offerings, or painting pictures, or cooking a meal. The occasional "Give me that!" is interspersed with bits of comic opera, skits and caricatures, songs and punning and repartee. As Americans doodle on a piece of paper while attending to the words of a lecture, so the Balinese doodles in words, while his body flawlessly and quickly attends to the job in hand.

All learning in Bali depends upon some measure of identification, and we may consider as prototype of such learning, the child's continuous adaptation to movements into which it is guided by the parent who holds it. Lacking such identification, no learning will occur, and this becomes specially conspicuous when one attempts to teach a Balinese some new foreign technique. Most Balinese will balk and make no attempt to copy a European, or perform any act, no matter how simple, which only a European has been seen to perform. But if once one can persuade one Balinese to master a European skill, then other Balinese of the same or superior caste position will learn it very quickly. So in training our Balinese secretaries, we had no difficulty because I Made Kaler, our secretary, educated in Java, believed that he could do what Europeans did, just as he could speak their language, sit on their chairs and handle their tools. Other Balinese boys, seeing Made Kaler use a typewriter, learned to type accurately and well in a few days.

This particularistic identification with the movement and skill of other bodies, socially comparable to one's own, has undoubtedly served as a conservative element in Bali, maintaining the division of labor between the sexes, and partially limiting certain skills, like writing, to the high castes. Only by invoking some such explanation can we understand the division of labor in Bali. The system works smoothly and accurately but with a total absence of sanctions. In the few cases of women who become scholars or musicians, or men who become skilled in weaving, no one even bothers to comment on the odd circumstance. And those who cross the sex division of labor are not penalized; they are not regarded as more or less masculine or feminine nor confused with the occasional transvestite, although the latter includes the occupations of the opposite sex in his transvestitism. But without sanctions, with freedom to embrace any occupation, ninety-nine out of a hundred Balinese adhere simply to the conventions that spinning, weaving, making most offerings, etc., are women's work, whereas carving, painting, music, making certain other offerings, etc., are men's work.

Combined with this kinaesthetic type of learning and with the continuous insistence upon levels and directions, there is a preoccupation with balance, which expressed itself in various ways. When the young male child is still learning to walk, loss of balance or any other failure evokes a regular response: he immediately clutches at his penis, and often, to be sure of balance, walks holding on to it. Little girls clasp their arms in front of them, and sometimes hold on to their heads. As they grow older, an increased sense of balance makes it possible to stand motionless for quite a long time on one foot; but dancing on one foot, playing too freely with a preciously achieved and highly developed balance is associated with witches and demons. Just as in witchcraft, right and left are reversed, so also in witchcraft, the decent boundaries of body posture are trespassed upon.

Balinese children, especially little Balinese girls, spend a great deal of time playing with the joints of their fingers, experimenting with bending them back until the finger lies almost parallel with the back of the hand. The more coordinated and disciplined the motion of the body becomes, the smaller the muscle groups with which a Balinese operates. Where an American or a New Guinea native will involve almost every muscle in his body to pick up a pin, the Balinese merely uses the muscles immediately relevant to the act, leaving the rest of the body undisturbed. Total involvement in any activity occurs in trance and in children's tantrums, but for the rest, an act is *not* performed by the whole body. The involved muscle does not draw all the others into a unified act, but smoothly and simply, a few small units are moved – the fingers alone, the hand and forearm alone, or the eyes alone, as in the characteristic Balinese habit of slewing the eyes to one side without turning the head.

NOTES

1 Mead, Margaret, William Morrow, 1928, William Morrow, 1930, William Morrow, 1935, respectively.
2 Bateson, Gregory. Cambridge, England, Cambridge University Press, 1936.

Plate 15   Visual and Kinaesthetic Learning I

An individual's character structure, his attitudes toward himself and his interpretations of experience are conditioned not only by what he learns, but also by the methods of his learning. If he is brought up in habits of rote learning, his character will be profoundly different from what would result from habits of learning by insight.

Among the Balinese, learning is very rarely dependent upon verbal teaching. Instead, the methods of learning are visual and kinaesthetic. The pupil either watches some other individual perform the act or he is made to perform the act by the teacher who holds his limbs and moves them correctly. During this process the pupil is entirely limp and appears to exhibit no resistant muscular tensions. A Balinese hand, if you hold it and manipulate the fingers, is perfectly limp like the hand of a monkey or of a corpse.

1, 2, and 3. Learning to carry on the head. These three photographs were all taken on the same occasion and show a girl (fig. 2) preparing to go home from a temple feast, carrying on her head the offerings which her family sent to the ceremony. Figs. 1 and 3 show two smaller girls imitating her and so beginning to participate in the ceremonial life of the village.
  Fig. 1, I Djani; fig. 2, I Maderi (unrelated); fig. 3, I Djana (younger sister of I Djani).
  Bajoeng Gede. June 23, 1937. 11 Z 30, 26, 33.

4 and 5. A father teaches his son to dance, humming a tune and posturing with his hand. In the first picture, the father shapes his facial expression to a typical dance smile and the son looks at the raised hand. In the second picture, the son tries to grasp the arm, and the father's expression becomes inter-personal instead of stylized.
  Nang Oera, the father; I Karba, the son, aged 265 days.
  Bajoeng Gede. Oct, 1, 1936, 2 U 30, 31.

6. The same father teaches his son to play the xylophone.
  Nang Oera; I Karba, aged 393 days.
  Bajoeng Gede. Feb. 5, 1937. 4 S 1.

7. A child nurse teaches the same baby to walk. She holds the baby by the upper part of the arms. There was no baby in her household and she spent a great part of her time looking after her father's step-brother's child. This photograph of learning to walk was taken five months later than the photographs of the same child learning to dance.
  I Djeben teaching I Karba, aged 414 days.
  Bajoeng Gede. March 26, 1937. 6 F 15.

8. Small high-caste boys learning to draw in the sand. The boy in the center was the most skilled and the others stopped their own drawing to watch him. All three boys show the typical Balinese high kinaesthetic awareness in the hands, and this is heightened by their using very small twigs for their drawing.
  I. B. Saboeh; I Dewa Moeklen; I Dewa Loepiah.
  Batoean. Oct. 5, 1937. 16 M 2.

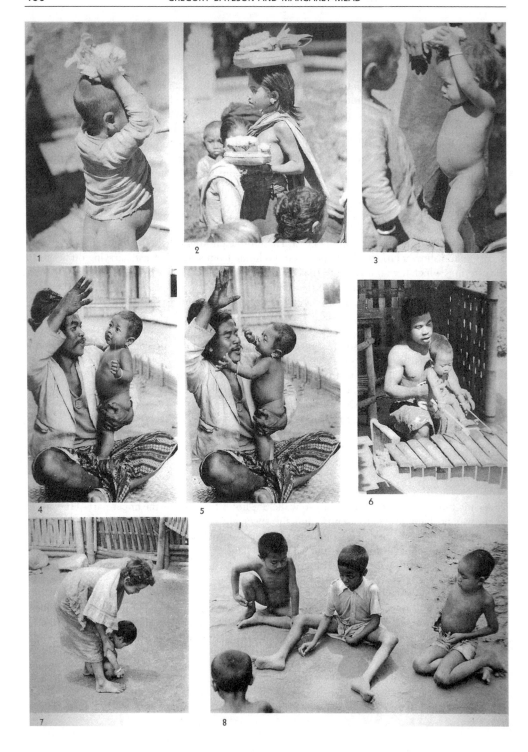

Plate 16 Visual and Kinaesthetic Learning II

Teaching by muscular rote in which the pupil is made to perform the correct movements is most strikingly developed in the dancing lesson.

Mario of Tabanan, the teacher in this sequence, is the dancer chiefly responsible for the evolution of the *kebiar* dance which has become very popular in Bali in the last twenty years. The dance is performed sitting in a square space surrounded by the instruments of the orchestra, but though the principal emphasis is upon the head and hands, the dance involves the whole body, and Mario has introduced a great deal of virtuosity into the difficult feat of rapid locomotion without rising from the sitting position. The chief faults in the pupil's dancing are that he dances only with his head and arms, and does not show the disharmonic tensions characteristic of the dance.

This sequence of photographs illustrates two essential points in Balinese character formation. From his dancing lesson, the pupil learns passivity, and he acquires a separate awareness in the different parts of the body.

1. The pupil dances alone while Mario watches in the background. Note the imperfect development of the pupil's finger posture.

2. Mario comes forward to show the pupil how it should be danced.

3. Mario urges the pupil to straighten up the small of his back. Note that this instruction is given by gesture rather than by words.

4. Mario's hand position and facial expression while demonstrating.

5. Mario takes the pupil by the wrists and swings him across the dancing space.

6. Mario makes his pupil dance correctly by holding his hands and forcing him to move as he should. Note that Mario is actually dancing in this photograph, and that he postures with his fingers even while holding the pupil's hands. The position of Mario's left elbow in these photographs is characteristic of the tensions developed in this dance.

7. Mario even assumes the conventional sweet impersonal smile of the dancer while he moves the pupil's arms and holds the pupil tightly between his knees to correct his tendency to bend the small of his back.

8. Mario again tries to correct the pupil's tendency to bend his back.
   I Mario of Tabanan teaching I Dewa P. Djaja of Kedere.
   Tabanan. Dec. 1, 1936. 3 O 11, 13, 14, 17, 21, 22, 23, 25.

Plate 17   Balance

Plates 15 and 16 taken together give us indications about the Balinese body image. We have, on the one hand, the fantasy of the inverted body with its head on the pubes; and on the other, the Balinese methods of learning through their muscles, the discrepant muscular tensions which are characteristic of their dancing, and the independent movement and posturing of the separate fingers in dance. We have, in fact, a double series of motifs – indications that the body is a single unit as perfectly integrated as any single organ, and contrasting indications that the body is made up of separate parts, each of which is as perfectly integrated as the whole.

This plate illustrates the motif of the perfectly integrated body image.

---

1 and 2.   A small boy learns to stand and walk. His father has set up for him in the houseyard a horizontal bamboo supported on two posts (*penegtegan*). The boy learns to walk by using this as a support.

The topology of this arrangement is the precise opposite of that of the play-pen of Western culture. The Western child is confined within restricting limits and would like to escape from them; the Balinese child is supported within a central area and is frightened of departure from this support. In fig. 2, when unsure of his balance, he holds onto his penis. This method of reassurance is common in Balinese baby boys.

I Karba, aged 414 days; I Kenjoen, his cousin, aged 317 days, behind him.

Bajoeng Gede. March 26, 1937. 6 F 20, 21.

3. A baby girl unsure of her balance. She clasps her hands in front of her abdomen.

I Kangoen.

Bajoeng Gede. April 21, 1937. 7 A 15.

4. A child nurse picks a baby from the ground. Note the straightness of the small of the back and the resulting emphasis on the buttocks.

I Njantel picks up I Karba; I Dani watches.

Bajoeng Gede. May 13, 1937. 8 U 30.

5. A girl stoops to pick up part of an offering. The flexibility of the body and the emphasis on the buttocks continue into later life, and occur even in those who are unusually heavily built.

I Teboes; I Tjerita behind her.

Bajoeng Gede. April 26, 1937. 7 H 18.

6. Decorative panel on a temple wall. This figure stands as one of a series of representations of transformed witches (*lejak*) and graveyard spirits (*tangan-tangan, njapoepoe*, etc., cf. Pl. 20, fig. 5).

Poera Dalem, Bangli. Nov. 23, 1936. 3 J 5.

7. A small boy scratches his leg. He was waiting in the road, uncertain whether his playmate was following. His natural movement is to raise his leg, rather than to stoop.

Bajoeng Gede. April 19, 1937. 6 W 19.

8 and 9. Paintings of a woman transforming herself into a witch (*anak mereh*). She goes out alone at night, sets up a little shrine and makes offerings on the ground to the demons. She dances before the shrine with her left foot on a fowl, and becomes transformed into supernatural size and shape. The fantasy that the body is as integrated as a single organ is here danced out in grotesque balance, and leads to a nightmare transformation or ecstatic dissociation of the personality. The drawings illustrate the close association between grotesque posture and the ecstasy of witchcraft (cf. figs. 6 and 7).

Paintings by I. B. Nj. Tjeta of Batoean.

Purchased Feb. 2, 1938. Reduced x 1/3 linear. Cat. Nos. 545 and 548.

29

The Taste of
Ethnographic Things

Paul Stoller and Cheryl Olkes

All meats that can endure it I like rare, and I like them high, even to the point of smelling bad in many cases.[1]

Montaigne

Like other peoples in Sahelian West Africa, the Songhay take great pride in their hospitality. "A guest is God in your house," goes the Songhay adage, and so when strangers are accepted as guests in most Songhay compounds they receive the best of what their hosts can afford to offer. The host displaces his own kin from one of his houses and gives it to the guest. He removes the mattress from his bed and gives it to the guest. And then he orders the kinswoman who prepares the family meals to make her best sauces for the guest.

In 1984 Paul Stoller, an anthropologist, and Cheryl Olkes, a sociologist, traveled to Niger to conduct a study of the medicinal properties of plants used in Songhay ethnomedicine. Since both Stoller and Olkes were seasoned

fieldworkers among the Songhay, they had experienced the pleasures of Songhay hospitality. And so when they came to the compound of Adamu Jenitongo, in Tillaberi, they were not surprised when Moussa, one of Adamu Jenitongo's sons, insisted that they stay in his mudbrick house. They were not surprised when Adamu Jenitongo, an old healer whom Stoller had known for fifteen years, gave them his best straw mattresses. "You will sleep well on these," he told them. They were not surprised when the old healer told Djebo, the wife of his younger son, Moru, to prepare fine sauces for them.

Stoller and Olkes had come to Tillaberi to discuss the medicinal properties of plants with Adamu Jenitongo, perhaps the most knowledgeable healer in all of western Niger. They planned to stay in Tillaberi for two weeks and then move on to Mehanna and Wanzerbé, two villages in which Stoller had won the confidence of healers. During the two weeks in Tillaberi, Stoller and Olkes ate a variety of

Paul Stoller and Cheryl Olkes, "The Taste of Ethnographic Things," pp. 15–34 plus relevant references from *The Taste of Ethnographic Things: The Senses in Anthropology.* Philadelphia: University of Pennsylvania Press, 1989. Copyright © 1989 by the University of Pennsylvania Press. Reprinted by permission of the University of Pennsylvania Press.

Ethnographic Fieldwork: An Anthropological Reader, Second Edition. Edited by Antonius C. G. M. Robben and Jeffrey A. Sluka.
Editorial material and organization © 2012 John Wiley & Sons, Inc.
Published 2012 by John Wiley & Sons, Inc.

foods and sauces. Some days they ate rice with black sauce (*hoy bi*) for lunch and rice with a tomato-based sauce flavored with red pepper and sorrel for dinner. Some days they ate rice cooked in a tomato sauce (*suruundu*) for lunch and millet paste with peanut sauce for dinner. All of these sauces contained meat, a rare ingredient in most Songhay meals. When Songhay entertain Europeans – Stoller and Olkes, for example – the staples of the diet do not change, but the quality of the sauces does. Europeans are guests in Songhay compounds; people do not prepare tasteless sauces for them!

People in the neighborhood had the same perception: "They have come to visit Adamu Jenitongo again. There will be good food in the compound." In good times a host spares no expense. In bad times Stoller and Olkes quietly slipped Adamu Jenitongo money so he could fulfill his ideal behavior.

The arrival of Stoller and Olkes in Tillaberi that year, in fact, was a bright beacon that attracted swarms of the "uninvited" in search of savory sauces. At lunch and dinner time visitors would arrive and linger, knowing full well that the head of a Songhay household is obliged to feed people who happen to show up at meal times.

The "men who came to dinner" were so many that poor Djebo had to double the amount of food she normally prepared. Djebo was a mediocre cook, but the uninvited guests didn't seem to mind as they stuffed their mouths with rice, meat, and sauce.

There was one particular guest, whom everyone called *Gao Boro* (literally "the man from Gao"), who unabashedly came to breakfast, lunch, and dinner every day of Stoller and Olkes' visit. This man, a refugee (or was it a fugitive?) from Gao, in the Republic of Mali, had been living hand-to-mouth in Tillaberi for four months. He had perfected a terrific rent scam to cut his expenses. In Tillaberi, landlords will let their properties to anyone who promises to pay the rent money at the end of the month. Paying at the end of the first month is a matter of Songhay honor. At the time of our visit, *Gao Boro* was on his third house. When a landlord would come for his money, *Gao Boro* would say he was broke. The owner would throw him out, and *Gao Boro* would find another

unsuspecting landlord. Stoller and Olkes soon realized the direct relationship between *Gao Boro*'s neighborliness – he lived 50 meters from Adamu Jenitongo's compound – and his ability to stretch his food budget.

Most people in the compound were reasonably happy with the food in 1984. Adamu Jenitongo's wives – Jemma and Hadjo – did complain about the toughness of the meat. So did Adamu Jenitongo. The problem, of course, was that Djebo refused to tenderize the meat – which had come from local stock – before cooking it in the sauce. Olkes suggested that Djebo marinate the meat. Djebo smiled at Olkes and ignored her advice. The toughness of the meat notwithstanding, everyone ate Djebo's sauces – until the last day of Stoller and Olkes' visit, when Djebo served bad sauce.

The last day in Tillaberi had been exhausting. Stoller had had two long sessions with Adamu Jenitongo during which they discussed the medicinal properties of plants and the Songhay philosophy of healing. Olkes had seen people in town and at the market. She had walked a good eight kilometers under the relentless Sahelian sun. At dusk, they each washed in the bath house: a three-foot-high square mudbrick enclosure equipped with a stool, a five-liter bucket, soap, and a plastic mug. Refreshed, they sat on one of their straw mattresses and waited for Djebo. Smiling, she brought them a large casserole of rice and a small one of sauce, set them at their feet, and gave them two spoons. When Stoller opened the small casserole, a sour odor overwhelmed them. Stoller saw the nightly procession of uninvited guests sauntering into the compound. Olkes wrinkled her nose.

"What is it?"

"It's *fukko hoy* [a sauce made by boiling the leaves of the fukko plant]," Stoller said.

"*Fukko hoy?*"

Stoller stirred the sauce with his spoon; it was meatless. "Shine your flashlight on the sauce, will you?" Stoller asked Olkes.

Olkes' flashlight revealed a viscous green liquid. "You can take the first taste," Olkes told Stoller.

"Wait a minute." Stoller picked up the small casserole and poured some of the *fukko hoy* over the rice. He put a spoonful of the rice and sauce into his mouth. "It's the worst damn sauce I've ever eaten," he told Olkes. "Straight *fukko hoy* seasoned with salt and nothing else!"

Olkes tasted the rice and sauce. "It's absolutely awful."

Like diplomats, Olkes and Stoller ate a little bit of the meal before pushing the casseroles away. Other people in the compound were less polite. Saying the sauce smelled and tasted like bird droppings, Moru, Djebo's husband, took his rice and sauce and dumped it in the compound garbage pit, a two-foot-deep hole about six feet in diameter that was littered with date palm pits, orange rinds, gristle, bones, and trash. "Let the goats eat this crap," he said.

Jemma, one of Adamu Jenitongo's two wives, said: "This sauce shames us. Djebo has brought great shame upon this compound." Hadjo, Adamu Jenitongo's other wife, echoed Jemma's comments. "How could anyone prepare so horrible a sauce for the guests in our compound?"

Gao Boro, the refugee-fugitive from Mali, arrived for his nightly "European" meal. He took one taste of the bad sauce, stood up and declared: "I refuse to eat sauce that is not fit for an animal. I'm going to Halidou's for *my* dinner tonight." From everyone's perspective, the bad sauce was in bad taste.

The Etiology of Bad Sauce

Djebo, a young Fulan (Peul) woman, came to live in Adamu Jenitongo's compound in the summer of 1982.[2] She had formed an attachment to Moru, a drummer in the possession cult, and had spent months following him to possession ceremonies. Eventually, she moved in with him – shameless behavior for a never-married 15-year-old girl. Still considered too young for marriage (most Songhay men do not marry until they are 30) 21-year-old Moru was a musician whose earnings were erratic. When he did have money it flew from his hands, which were always open to his "friends." Moru and Djebo brought much shame to Adamu Jenitongo's compound. Although first-time brides are not expected to be virgins, they are expected to avoid shaming their families. Adamu Jenitongo could have

asked Djebo to leave, but he did not. By the time Stoller arrived in December 1982, Djebo was visibly pregnant. Now, all the neighbors could see that Djebo and Moru had been living in sin. What to do? One option was abortion, a longstanding though unpopular Songhay practice. Another option was to send Djebo home to have her "fatherless" child, the usual Songhay practice. The final option was, of course, marriage. No one wanted an abortion. Moru wanted to marry his love. Adamu Jenitongo and his wives wanted the pregnant girl to return to her mother's compound.

During Stoller's visit, there were many arguments in the compound about Moru and Djebo.

"What would you do with her?" Adamu Jenitongo asked Stoller.

"You're asking me?"

"Moru should marry a Songhay woman," Adamu Jenitongo stated. "He should marry one of the girls from our home near Simiri. If he marries one of our people, everyone will be happy. Do you not agree?" he asked Stoller.

Concealing his uneasiness, Stoller said that he agreed.

Moru, who had been inside his hut, overheard the discussion between Stoller and his father and ran out to confront them.

"And what about me, Baba? Doesn't anyone ask me, Moru, about my feelings? I want Djebo. I want to marry her. I want her to have my child."

Adamu Jenitongo scoffed at Moru. "Marry her! First you bring this Fulan woman into my compound. Then you make her pregnant, and now you want to marry the worthless bitch." Adamu Jenitongo turned to Stoller. "What is this world coming to? The young people have no respect." He turned now to Moru. "You live in my household, you eat my food, you learn from me our heritage, but you have no heart and no mind. You are still a child."

Moru stormed off to his hut, fuming. Jemma, his mother, returned from the market with meat and spices. Hadjo, her co-wife, informed her of the most recent confrontation in the compound. Jemma looked at Stoller.

"Don't you think it is wrong for that worthless Fulan woman to be here? Look at her," she said loudly, pointing at the girl, who was sitting on the threshold of Moru's hut. "She's pregnant, but she's here with us. Pregnant women must live with their mothers so they give birth to healthy babies. Does that worthless Fulan do this? No! She sits here. She follows Moru to possession dances. Sometimes she walks for hours – she and the baby in her belly."

"Is this bad?" Stoller asked Jemma.

"They say that a mother who wanders with a baby in her belly will produce a monster child. That worthless Fulan is breeding a monster. I am certain of it."

"She should be with her mother," Hadjo reiterated.

During Stoller's visit there were also daily arguments between Jemma, Moru's mother, and Ramatu, Djebo's mother. On one occasion Ramatu attempted to drag her daughter back to her compound. Djebo broke her mother's grip and cursed her. Jemma cursed Djebo for cursing her mother. And Ramatu cursed Jemma for cursing her daughter. As the two older women traded ethnic slurs in Songhay, Fulan, and Hausa, a sobbing Djebo told Moru, her love, that she was walking into the bush to die. Since no one took Djebo at her word, they watched her walk toward the mountain. Ramatu returned to her compound, Jemma got back to her food preparations, and Moru went into his hut.

Two hours passed and Djebo had not returned. Moru entered Stoller's hut. "Should we go and look for her?"

"I think so, Moru."

Stoller and Moru left to search for Djebo. They returned with her two hours later. Everyone in the compound scolded the young girl.

"You are a hardheaded bitch," Jemma said.

"You are a worthless Fulan, who brings us heartache," Adamu Jenitongo said.

Djebo cried and Moru followed her into his hut.

When Stoller and Olkes returned to Adamu Jenitongo's compound in 1984, a child no more than a year and a half old waddled over to them. Laterite dust powdered her body. Mucus had caked on her upper lip.

"That's my daughter, Jamilla," Moru proclaimed.

Jamilla burst into tears when Olkes approached her.

"She's not used to white people," Jemma said.

"She's a monster child," Hadjo declared.

The term "monster child" swept Stoller back to his previous visit and the long discussions that had raged about women who wander when they are pregnant. Had the prediction come true?

"And no wonder," said Jemma, "with a mother who wandered the countryside with a child in her belly."

Moru told Stoller that he and Djebo were married shortly after his departure the previous year.

"And you didn't write?" Stoller joked.

Moru shrugged. Djebo pounded millet next to the compound's second mudbrick house, which Moru had built for his family. "Djebo," Moru called to his wife, "prepare a fine meal for them. They are tired from their trip, and we must honor them."

Adamu Jenitongo gave Djebo money and told her to go to the market and buy good spices and a good cut of meat. Djebo took the money and frowned. When she had left, Moussa (Adamu Jenitongo's other son), Jemma, and Moru complained about her. She was lazy. She was quarrelsome. They didn't trust her. She didn't know how to cook – probably because she hadn't listened to her mother long enough to learn. When she prepared meat it was so tough that even Moru couldn't chew it. The sauces were tasteless even though Adamu Jenitongo gave her money to buy the best spices. But no one had done anything to improve the domestic situation.

"Why don't you teach her how to cook?" Olkes asked.

"Hah," Jemma snorted. "She doesn't want to learn."

"Why don't you show her the right spices to buy?" Olkes persisted.

"She doesn't care. She doesn't care," Jemma answered.

Olkes felt sorry for Djebo. She was, after all, a teenager living among people who seemed set against her and who bore longstanding prejudice against her ethnic group. As the youngest affine in the compound, moreover,

Djebo was expected not only to cook, but to buy food in the market, take care of her infant, fetch water from a neighborhood pump, clean pots and pans, and do the laundry. From dawn to dusk, Djebo performed these tasks as Jemma and Hadjo sat in front of their huts and criticized her.

Olkes decided to befriend Djebo. She accompanied Djebo to the pump and to the market. On market day, Olkes bought Djebo a black shawl, the current rage in Tillaberi. For whatever reason – culture, age, or personality – Djebo did not respond to these overtures. She socialized outside of the compound and did not participate in the rambling conversations of the early evening.

One day before Stoller and Olkes' departure, Djebo prepared a wonderful sauce for the noon meal. She made a locust bean sauce flavored with peanut flour. Olkes and Stoller ate with abandon. When Djebo came to their house to collect the empty casseroles, Olkes complimented her on the meal.

Stoller raised his arms skyward and said: "Praise be to God."

Saying nothing, Djebo smiled and left their house. Thirty minutes later, Djebo returned to see Stoller and Olkes – her first social visit in two weeks. Saying little, she looked over their things. She opened the lid of their non-fat dry milk and tasted some. She touched their camera, and ran her fingers over their tape recorder. Olkes and Stoller had seen this kind of behavior before. A person in Niger rarely asks for money directly; rather, he or she lingers in the donor's house and says nothing. Djebo lingered in Stoller and Olkes' house for thirty minutes and left.

"Do you understand the reason for that scrumptious meal?" Olkes asked Stoller.

Stoller nodded. "She isn't satisfied with the black shawl?"

"I guess not."

"Damn her! We can't give her money. We have to give money to Adamu Jenitongo."

"She doesn't want to follow the rules of custom, does she?"

"I just bet that she has been pocketing some of the money given to her for food," Stoller said. "That's why the sauces have been mediocre."

That night Djebo's horrible *fukko hoy* expressed sensually her anger, an anger formed from a complex of circumstances. She wanted her sauce to be disgusting.

The Etiology of Taste

Djebo prepared a sauce to be rejected, cast away, spit out. Put another way, Djebo's sauce was the symbolic equivalent of vomit, something that our bodies reject. In the most literal sense Djebo's sauce was distasteful.

How does Djebo's sour sauce – her calculated distastefulness – fit with the conception of Taste in the Western philosophical tradition? In a word, it is different; it is non-theoretical.

One of the earliest writers on taste was Seneca. In his *Epistulae morales* he wrote that food not only nourishes our bodies, but also

> nourishes our higher nature, – we should see to it that whatever we have absorbed should not be allowed to remain unchanged, or it will be no part of us. We must digest it; otherwise it will merely enter memory and not the reasoning power. Let us loyally welcome such foods and make them our own, so that something that is one may be formed out of many elements.[3]

Seneca was among the first of the classical philosophers to write of judgment with digestive metaphors. "For Seneca, the proper digestion of received ideas both educates and is the result of an independent faculty of judgment, and this in turn is the precondition of right action."[4] These metaphors stem from the classical notion that the mouth and tongue enable us to "ingest" the outside world. Physical tasting is extended to mental tasting, the classical notion of judgment.[5]

In his *Critique of Judgment*, Kant rejects the classical notion that the faculty of taste can be extended to social, political, or scientific matters. In fact, he removes taste entirely from the domain of science, preferring to consider it a purely aesthetic sense.

> In order to distinguish whether anything is beautiful or not, we refer the representation,

not by the understanding to the object for cognition, but by imagination (perhaps in conjunction with the understanding) to the subject and its feeling of pleasure and pain. The judgment of taste is therefore not a judgment of cognition, and is consequently not logical but aesthetical, by which we understand that those determining grounds can be *no other than subjective*.[6]

Kant's passage suggests that the faculty of taste should be restricted to the apprehension of objects of beauty. Following the publication of the *Critique of Judgment* in 1790, taste was no longer considered an appropriate concept in the classically approved domains of politics, society and science – domains that were restricted to the logical, objective, and scientific reflection of the Enlightenment.

The etymology of taste in English

Raymond Williams writes that the word taste came into the English language around the thirteenth century, but that its earliest meaning was closer to "touch" or "feel."[7] "Taste" comes to us from the Old French *taster*, and from the Italian *tastare*, which translates to "feel, handle, or touch." "Good taast" in the sense of good understanding was recorded in 1425.[8] But the metaphoric extensions of the word became confused in the latter part of the seventeenth century and the eighteenth century, when it was associated with general rules. In English, then, the sensual aspects of taste were gradually replaced by the more general and rule-governed notion. Perhaps due to the Kantian influence, the meanings of *taste* and *good taste* are even today far removed from their sensual attributes. Djebo's sense of taste is sensual and subjective; Kant's sense of Taste is rarefied and objective.

The sensual tastes of Montaigne

Djebo's non-theoretical sense of taste is similar to Montaigne's. The final section of his *Essais*, entitled "Of Experience," is a compendium of Montaigne's physical tastes: what he likes to eat, how often he likes to eat, how much he

likes to eat. In this final book, Montaigne discusses his sleeping habits, his kidney stones, his medicines, his squeamishness, his hatred of sweets as a child and his love of sweets as an adult, his digestion, his indigestion, and even his bowel movements. On the subject of bowels, Montaigne also writes that "both Kings and philosophers defecate, and ladies too…. Wherefore I will say this about that action: that we should relegate it to certain prescribed nocturnal hours, and force and subject ourselves to them by habit, as I have done."[9] Montaigne's "father hated all kinds of sauces; I love them all. Eating too much bothers me; but I have as yet no really certain knowledge that any kind of food intrinsically disagrees with me."[10] Alas, Montaigne never ate Djebo's *fukko hoy*.

Derrida's dregs

Montaigne's sensuality has had a minimal influence on Western thought, however. More prevalent today are the rarefied Enlightenment metaphors of composition and construction. In Hegel's constructive system, for example, "the material of ideality is light and sound. Voice, in the relation to hearing (the most sublime sense), animates sound, permitting the passage from more sensible existence to the representational existence of the concept."[11] Sight and hearing are theoretical senses that represent the attempt of the Enlightenment philosophers to create from the chaos of appearances constructed systems of "reality," wherein one might Taste the Truth.

In sharp contrast to historical and modern masters of philosophy, Derrida stands for sensuality as opposed to rarefaction, for deconstructionism as opposed to constructionism, for decomposition as opposed to Taste. In *Of Grammatology* and in *Glas*, Derrida indicates a philosophical system based upon such non-theoretical senses as taste (also smell and touch) which depend upon a part of the body, the tongue, which is primary in speech production:

The dividing membrane which is called the soft palate, fixed by its upper edge to the border of the roof, *floats* freely, at its lower end, above the base of the tongue. Its two lateral sides (it is a quadrilateral) are called "pillars." In the middle of the floating end, at the entrance to the throat, hangs the fleshy appendage of the uvula, like a small grape. The text is spit out. It is like a discourse in which the unities model themselves after an excrement, a secretion. And because it has to do here with a glottic gesture, the tongue working on itself, *saliva* is the element which sticks the unities together.[12]

As Ulmer suggests, Derrida's texts condemn Hegel's assertion that odor and taste "are useless for artistic pleasure, given that esthetic contemplation requires objectivity without reference to desire or will, whereas 'things present themselves to smell only to the degree in which they are constituted by a process, in which they dissolve into the air with practical effects.'"[13] For Derrida there should be no separation of the intelligible from the sensible. Since Kant, he argues, Taste has been an objective, rarefied distancing from an object of art. Using the sensual Montaigne as one of his models, Derrida opposes *gustus* with disgust and taste with distaste. The key concept of Derrida's writing on taste is *le vomi*, "which explicitly engages not the 'objective' senses of hearing and sight, nor even touch, which Kant describes as 'mechanical,' all three of which involve perception of or at surfaces, but the 'subjective' or 'chemical' senses of taste and smell."[14] For Derrida, then, Djebo's *fukko hoy* should not only be spit out into an ethnographic text, but should be done so with sensual vividness, for Djebo's bad sauce is gloriously disgusting; it reeks with meaning.

Taste in anthropology

Beyond the sensual descriptions in anthropological cookbooks, most anthropologists have followed Hegel's lead in separating the intelligible from the sensible. This Hegelian tendency is evident from even a cursory examination of ethnographic writing. Like most writers, most ethnographers tacitly conform to a set of conventions that colleagues use to judge a work. Marcus and Cushman have suggested that conventions governing

ethnographic representation devolve from realism. They argue that realist ethnographic discourse seeks the reality of the whole of a given society, and that "realist ethnographies are written to allude to the whole by means of parts or foci of analytical attention which constantly evoke a social and cultural totality."[15] In an article in *L'Homme*, Stoller describes the philosophical development of realism in ethnography.[16] That development eventually resulted in a set of conventions that Marcus and Cushman have analyzed:

1 a narrative structure which devolves from cultural, functionalist, or structuralist analytical categories to achieve a total ethnography;
2 a third person narrative voice which distinguishes realist ethnographies from travel accounts;
3 a manner of presentation in which individuals among the people studied remain nameless, characterless;
4 a section of text, usually a Preface or Afterword, which describes the context of investigation;
5 a focus on everyday life contexts representing the Other's reality to justify the fit of the analytical framework to the ethnographic situation;
6 an assertion that the ethnography represents the native's point of view;
7 a generalizing style in which events are rarely described idiosyncratically, but as typical manifestations of marriage, kinship, ritual, etc.;
8 a use of jargon which signals that the text is, indeed, an ethnography as opposed to a travel account;
9 a reticence by authors to discuss their competence in the Other's language.[17]

While most ethnographers religiously followed these conventions of realist representation in the past, there are a growing number of scholars who are worried about the epistemological and political ramifications of ethnographic realism. Directly and indirectly, their ethnographic and theoretical writings reflect these philosophic issues.[18] Fabian writes of his concern about anthropology's intellectual imperialism: "Perhaps I failed to make it clear that I wanted language and communication to be understood as a kind of praxis in which the Knower cannot claim ascendency over the Known (nor, for that matter, one Knower over another). As I see it now, the anthropologist and his interlocuters only 'know' when they meet each other in one and the same contemporality."[19]

Although the new "experimental" works have been provocative, most of them consider typical anthropological subjects of study, albeit through partially altered conventions of representation. How could it be otherwise, when disciplinary constraints force most writers to concentrate on certain kinds of subjects: the theory of Taste instead of the taste of bad sauce, the theory of the family instead of texts that familiarize the reader with family members, the theory of experimental ethnography instead of experimental ethnographies. How can it be otherwise, when disciplinary constraints impose form and order on what is published. Take, for example, the *Abstracts of the Annual [Anthropology] Meetings*:

> Name, institution, and title of paper or film must precede narrative portion: Put last name first; use capital letters for author's last name and title of paper; do not include 'university' or 'college' with institution name given in parentheses.... Write the text in complete sentences. Use the present tense; use only third person.[20]

In addition, the American Anthropological Association gives prospective participants some useful tips on writing a "good abstract":

> A "good" abstract should be an informative summary of a longer work. It should state the central topic at the beginning; it should clearly indicate the nature and extent of the data on which it is based; it should outline the nature of the problem or issue and delineate the relevant scientific argument; and it should show how the content relates to the existing literature. Where helpful, citations may be used. The abstract must be typed *double spaced*, and it must fit *within* the box provided below.[21]

This prescription may be a fine model for terse scientific writing, but it discourages unconventionality in ethnographic writing with the message it sends to potential Annual Meeting participants: "We are a scientific organization. We sponsor scientific papers in our scientific program." Good or "beautiful" abstracts, in the sense of Kant and Hegel, are written in the present tense (the ethnographic present?) and in the third person (a marker of objectivity?) Even today, Hegel's *Esthetics* casts a long shadow over anthropological representation.

Despite the difficulties precipitated by a long entrenched philosophical tradition, it is altogether certain that the pioneering and courageous efforts of contemporary ethnographers have forced anthropologists to ponder the nature of both their scholarship and their being. But do these writers take us far enough? Are there other dimensions of ethnographic discourse, other conventions of representation which may carry anthropology deeper into the being of the others? Are there other modes of representation that better solve the fundamental problems of realist ethnographic representation: voice, authority, and authenticity?

Tasteful Ethnography

How does a piece of ethnographic writing get published? Here the digestive metaphors are particularly relevant. An author submits her or his manuscript to a publisher or to a journal. Editors ingest the manuscript. If the material falls within the conventions of representation of a discipline, the editors are likely to digest what they have taken in and the manuscript will eventually be published. If the material violates those conventions, the editors may well find the piece hard to swallow and the manuscript is returned to the author, a case of Derrida's *vomi*. Indeed, when editors write comments to authors of rejected (vomited) manuscripts, they often suggest how the author might transform his or her piece from disgusting vomit into digestible food for thought. Examples of these comments from Stoller's files illustrate how readers and editors reinforce conventional anthropological tastes.

Example 1 [Letter from acquisitions editor to Stoller]. I have just received two reviews of your manuscript, and I'm sorry to have to tell you that these have not been sufficiently encouraging for me to feel able to offer to consider the work further. Both reviewers thought that the script contained some interesting data, but felt that the theoretical argument was insufficiently well developed.

Example 2 [Comments from Stoller to anonymous author]. The author of this article suggests that anthropologists consider music more seriously, less tangentially, in their analyses of sociocultural systems. Merriman made more or less the same statement in his pioneering *Anthropology of Music* (1964), which the author unfortunately does not cite.... The author leads one to believe that we should consider the sociocultural aspects of music seriously. I fully agree. After reading the piece, however, I feel the author has fallen into the trap he/she says other anthropologists have fallen into. Music is not the central concern of this article; it is of secondary or perhaps tertiary importance when compared with the author's overriding concern with subsistence and the materialist perspective.... In short the author fails to highlight the importance of music in the cultural scheme of things....

Example 3 [Comments of Stoller to anonymous author]. In this piece the reader is treated to a plethora of excellent ethnography in which the author develops the sociological context of x's name change. But the author does not blend this rich material with other studies in Africa or elsewhere which are on similar topics.... What kind of contribution does this piece make to ethnological theory, method, compared to other works on the topic? ...

Example 4 [Reader's comments to Stoller]. I sympathize with the author's desire to go beyond the limits of positivism and enter into the mental set of the people he studies, though he might take note that this is the point of departure espoused by such diverse scholars as Boas, Malinowski, and Radin, among others. My objection to the work is not in his effort to seek an inside viewpoint, but in his failure to demonstrate its value, and, above all, in his failure to meet the canons of academic evidence. One must presume that the young man in his narrative was himself – but his

unwillingness to communicate in the scientific mode and to adhere to the Songhay rules, deprives us of direct evidence for this insight and makes us wonder at the source and character of his information.

Example 5 [Reader's comments to Stoller]. This is basically a suitable article for the ..., since it has an interesting and significant point to make concerning the need to recognize the importance of sound in many societies. I feel, however, that many readers would not be gripped enough at the beginning of the article [a narrative with dialogue] ... to see it through to the end.... My personal preference is for less humanistic and subjective language.

Example 6 [Reader's comments on Stoller's manuscript].... There is no question that the subject matter is important and underrepresented in the literature, or that the author has some very valuable field data in hand. It would be quite useful to have a good study of Songhay religion and culture.... While there is some interesting description of possession rituals, and of Songhay religion and history, if I have to judge it frankly I must say that at this point it is a half-baked manuscript.

The weakness of its theoretical grounding leads to the lack of any real integration of the descriptive material beyond the repeated (and ultimately somewhat boring) assertion that the cults are forms of cultural resistance.... I think there are two central points of weakness, which the author glides over at the beginning where he casually dismisses psychological and functional accounts: he shows no evidence of having read the work of Victor Turner ... and he shows no evidence of familiarity with the *recent* studies of the psychophysiology of trance which have made such rapid advances in our understanding of these phenomena....

And so it goes in the modern era of anthropology, an era that in many ways is past its shelflife.[22] One way of freeing ourselves from the constraints of Taste in Anthropology is to engage fully in a tasteful ethnography. Freed from the social, political, and epistemological constraints of realism, a tasteful ethnography would take us beyond the mind's eye and into the domain of the senses of smell and taste.

Such an excursion into sensuality would complement the rarefied Hegelian senses of sight and sound.

Tasteful fieldwork

In tasteful fieldwork, anthropologists would not only investigate kinship, exchange, and symbolism, but also describe with literary vividness the smells, tastes, and textures of the land, the people, and the food. Rather than looking for deep-seated hidden truths, the tasteful fieldworker understands, following Foucault, "that the deep hidden meaning, the unreachable heights of truth, the murky interiors of consciousness are all shams."[23] From the sensual tasteful vantage, the fieldworker investigates the life stories of individual Songhay, Nuer, or Trobrianders as opposed to totalized investigations of the Songhay, the Nuer, or the Trobriander. This recording of the complexities of the individual's social experience lends texture to the landscape of the fieldworker's notes. In this way, seemingly insignificant incidents as being served bad sauce become as important as sitting with a nameless informant and recording genealogies – data – that eventually become components in a system of kinship. In this way ethnographic research creates voice, authority, and an aura of authenticity.

Tasteful writing

There are probably many anthropologists who do engage in tasteful fieldwork. Despite their scientific objectives, they become sensually immersed in their field surroundings. These impressions, however, are usually cast aside – becoming vomit – in their published theoretical and ethnographic writings. Like Djebo's bad sauce, conventions of representation governing genre selection could be thrown into a trash pit.

Acknowledging the diverse collection of refuse, the tasteful writer uses the notion of melange as his or her guiding metaphor for producing tasteful ethnographic writing.

In Derrida's *Glas*, the writing on the pages is arranged in two columns. In the left-hand column is prose representing Hegel (rarefaction,

Taste, the Enlightenment and its theoretical senses). In the right-hand column, by contrast, is prose representing Genet (sensuality, taste, post-modernism and its non-theoretical senses). Within this revolutionary stylistics is a powerful indirect challenge to the fundamental metaphors of the Western philosophic tradition. Derrida's *Glas* is in bad Taste. But Derrida's bad Taste – his vomit – provides a point of reference for tasteful ethnographic writing that incorporates the non-theoretical senses.

Consider first an example from James Agee's *Let Us Now Praise Famous Men*, in which he describes the odors of a tenant farm house in Alabama.

These are its ingredients. The odor of pine lumber, wide thin cards of it, heated in the sun, in no way doubled or insulated, in closed and darkened air. The odor of woodsmoke, the fuel being again mainly pine, but in part also, hickory, oak and cedar. The odors of cooking. Among these, most strongly, the odors of fried salt pork and of fried and boiled pork lard, and second, the odor of cooked corn. The odors of sweat in many stages of age and freshness, this sweat being a distillation of pork, lard, corn, woodsmoke, pine and ammonia. The odors of sleep, of bedding and of breathing, for the ventilation is poor. The odors of all the dirt that in the course of time can accumulate in a quilt and mattress. Odors of staleness from clothes hung or stored away, not washed. I should further describe the odor of corn: in sweat, or on the teeth and the breath, when it is eaten as much as they eat it, it is of a particular sweet stuffy fetor, to which the nearest parallel is the odor of the yellow excrement of a baby....[24]

Consider next an example from John Chernoff's *African Rhythm and African Sensibility*, in which he describes how music and African social life interpenetrate.

At the beginning of each year the *harmattan* winds blow a fine dust from the Sahara Desert across the Sudan and over the coastal areas of the Gulf of Guinea. In Bamako, capital of Mali, you might observe the evening traffic as if through a reddish brown filter which softens and mutes the sights and sounds of the crowded streets. The atmosphere is tranquil, and standing on the long bridge over the Niger River, with cars passing just a few feet behind you, you might look at a lone fisherman in his graceful canoe and feel that only the lovely melodies of the harp-like *kora* could capture and convey the unity of the scene. At night the temperature drops until you might wonder why you ever thought you missed winter, and if by chance you found yourself in an isolated village at the right time and you looked up at the multitude of stars, you might hear the music of xylophones through the crisp air and believe that the clarity of the music was perhaps more than superficially appropriate to the stillness of the night.[25]

Consider finally an example from Lévi-Strauss's *Tristes tropiques*, "which, though it is very far from being a great anthropology book, or even an especially good one, is surely one of the finest books ever written by an anthropologist."[26] The example is an exegesis on the South American equivalent of bad sauce.

There had been no rain for five months and all the game had vanished. We were lucky if we managed to shoot an emaciated parrot or capture a large *tupinambis* lizard to boil in our rice, or managed to roast in their shells a land tortoise or an armadillo with black, oily flesh. More often than not, we had to be content with *xarque*, the same dried meat prepared months previously by a butcher in Cuiaba and the thick worm-infested layers of which we unrolled every morning in the sun, in order to make them less noxious, although they were usually in the same state the next day. Once, however, someone killed a wild pig; its lightly cooked flesh seemed to us more intoxicating than wine: each of us devoured more than a pound of it, and at that moment I understood the alleged gluttony of savages, which is mentioned by so many travellers as proof of their uncouthness. One only had to share their diet to experience similar pangs of hunger; to eat one's fill in such circumstances produces not merely a feeling of repletion but a positive sensation of bliss.[27]

These examples are only a slice of the life that lives in the tasteful ethnographies of Agee,

Chernoff, and Lévi-Strauss. In all the examples, the writers season their prose with the non-theoretical senses to evoke a world. Agee masterfully uses a melange of smells to evoke the habitus of southern tenant farmers – their fatty diet, their filthy clothes, their stuffy houses, their abject misery. In one smelly paragraph we have a memorable portrait of the lives of these people. Chernoff records the interpenetration of sound and sight in African social life. This paragraph evokes an African world in which "participatory" music gives shape to a people's system of values as well as to their manner of living-in-the-world. With Lévi-Strauss we come back to the sensual notion of taste. In one vivid paragraph he ruminates on the link between deprivation of diet and gluttony in the Amazon. Even European intellectuals can descend into gluttony!

Should this kind of writing be excised from the ethnographic manuscripts of the future? Aren't expositions on odors, sounds, and tastes extraneous to the ethnographic message? What can these details reveal about a sociocultural system? In terms of systematic analysis, these kinds of evocative details do not uncover a system of kinship or exchange or symbolism; hence Geertz's critique of *Tristes tropiques* as not even a good anthropology book. Tasteful anthropology books are analytic, theoretical, and ephemeral; tasteful ethnographies are descriptive, non-theoretical, and memorable. Writers of tasteful ethnographies mix an assortment of ingredients – dialogue, description, metaphor, metonomy, synecdoche, irony, smells, sights, and sounds – to create a narrative that savors the world of the Other. And just as Chernoff's drumming in Ghana once inspired members of an audience to say: "'Oh, the way you played! It moved me. It was sweet,'" so a well constructed narrative moves the listener or the reader to say: "Can I tell you a terrific story?" Indeed, there is life in the words of a good story; there is life in the prose of a tasteful ethnography.

In his monumental essay *L'Oeil et l'esprit*, Merleau-Ponty states that we lose much of the substance of life-in-the-world by thinking operationally, by defining rather than experiencing the reality of things.

Science manipulates things and gives up living in them. It makes its own limited models of things; operating upon these indices or variables to effect whatever transformations are permitted by their definition; it comes face to face with the real world only at rare intervals. Science is and always has been that admirably active, ingenious, and bold way of thinking whose fundamental bias is to treat everything as though it were an object-in-general – as though it meant nothing to us and yet was predestined for our own use.[28]

An ethnographic discourse that "comes face to face with the real world only at rare intervals" is usually so turgid that it is digestible by only a few dedicated specialists – a discourse that will soon be forgotten. A tasteful ethnographic discourse that takes the notion of melange as its foundation would encourage writers to blend the ingredients of a world so that bad sauces might be transformed into delicious prose.

One Month of Bad Sauce among the Songhay

Stoller returned to Songhay and Adamu Jenitongo's compound in June of 1987. Jamilla had died in 1985, having drowned in a garbage pit filled with water after a torrential rain. Soon thereafter Djebo was pregnant with Hamadu, who in 1987 was about 18 months old.

In 1984 Moussa, Adamu Jenitongo's elder son, worked as a tailor; his atelier was in his father's compound. But business was slack because the Jenitongo compound was far from the center of Tillaberi. In 1985 he found a suitable atelier in Baghdad, a bustling section of Tillaberi. Moussa would leave his father's compound early in the morning, return for lunch, and leave again to complete the afternoon tasks at his tailor shop. Since he soon had more work than he could handle himself, he hired an apprentice.

By the time Stoller arrived in June of 1987, Moussa was spending much of his time at his tailor shop. He took his lunches there; for dinner, he sometimes ate small meals at the Baghdad bars: steak and french fries, green beans, omelettes. After Stoller's arrival, to fulfill

the requirements of Songhay hospitality, Moussa made sure to return home to eat his meals.

The quality of the sauces hadn't changed. Djebo did not serve *fukko hoy*, but on occasion she refused to prepare meals, forcing Moussa, Stoller, and Adamu Jenitongo to eat meals of bread and sardines in soy oil.

"Things are better now that you have come," Moussa told Stoller. "Weeks go by and she doesn't prepare meals. Baba is old; he needs to eat better, but she doesn't care. My brother Moru doesn't care. And Baba, he chews kola and tobacco."

"Bad sauces are better than no sauces," Stoller said.

After one week of sauces the quality of which ranged from mediocre to bad, Stoller suffered a violent case of diarrhea. He quickly lost weight. Moussa suggested an alternative.

"Let's eat our lunches with Madame. She is an excellent cook." Madame was the daughter of Adamu Jenitongo's sister, Kedibo.

Moussa and Stoller began to eat lunch at Madame's house. The sauces were tasty: fine gombo, sesame, and squash sauces all of which were spiced delicately with permutations of garlic, ginger, locust bean, and hot pepper. Moussa and Stoller stuffed themselves, knowing that the evening fare would be much worse: tasteless rice paste drowned with watery tomato sauces all of which were spiced without imagination. There was millet in the compound, but Djebo refused to prepare it.

When it became apparent that Stoller was taking his meals at Madame's house, Djebo protested. Jemma, Djebo's mother-in-law, scowled.

"Why do you insist on your European sauces?" Jemma asked him. "Why don't you eat the sauces we prepare for you?"

Stoller did not respond directly; rather, he forced himself to eat two meals at lunch and one at dinner. Even with this increased consumption, Stoller lost more weight. His diarrhea continued.

Shamed by the bad sauces in his concession, Moussa confronted his younger brother Moru before an audience of visitors to the compound.

"How can anyone live in this compound with your lazy wife, who, when she lowers herself to prepare food for us, produces sauces that our chickens won't eat."

"Now hold on, older brother. How can you ..."

"Shut up, you ignorant peasant. I feel like a stranger in my own home. Why return to a place where I'm not wanted?"

Moru wagged his forefinger at Moussa. "You donkey. Worthless person. Come closer and insult my wife. I'll tear your eyes out. A man who doesn't even have a wife deserves to eat shit."

"Better to be single than to be a slave to a bitch," Moussa retorted. "I'll eat my sauces elsewhere."

Moru's wife and mother restrained him.

Stoller restrained Moussa.

Adamu Jenitongo called for peace. "We shame ourselves in front of strangers."

Moru and Moussa are half-brothers. In the Songhay language they are *bab'izey*, which has two translations: "half-brothers" and "rivals." In Songhay *bab'izey* frequently have relationships the major ingredient of which is jealousy and bad feelings built up over a lifetime. This problem has poisoned the relationships between Moru and Moussa. As men, they have very different kinds of temperaments. Moru is hot-headed and prone to verbal and even physical confrontation. Moussa is even-tempered and keeps his emotions more to himself. Moru is a musician who sometimes works as a laborer. Moussa is a tailor who works steadily. To add more salt to an open wound, both Moussa and Moru covet the powerful secrets of their father, one of the most powerful sorcerers (*sohanci*) in Niger.

In his old age Sohanci Adamu Jenitongo hinted that he would pass on his secrets to both Moussa and Moru. But only one of them would receive his chain of power and his sacred rings. To Moru, Jemma, and Djebo, the alliance of the younger son, it was painfully obvious that Adamu Jenitongo had chosen his eldest son Moussa to succeed him. Moussa had the relatively calm disposition required for receiving great power. Moussa also had powerful allies: Kedibo, Adamu Jenitongo's youngest sister, favored Moussa because Moussa's mother, Hadjo, was the sister of her late husband. Each time she visited her brother, Kedibo extolled the virtues of her "nephew."

Moussa's steady disposition and his strategic position in the family kinship network made Moru's situation hopeless. Being powerless to change the course of events, Moru, Djebo, and Jemma chose to make life miserable for Moussa, his mother Hadjo, and Adamu Jenitongo. As the recipient of power, Moussa would soon reap considerable social rewards. He would soon become the sohanci of Tillaberi; people would fear and respect him. Moru wanted the fear and respect that his older brother was soon to receive. Powerless, Moru, Jemma, and Djebo used sauce to express their frustrations. Moussa must eat bad sauces and suffer in exchange for his good fortune.

Sauce had again become the major ingredient in the stew of (Songhay) social relations, something which Montaigne had realized long before Djebo had produced her first (though certainly not her last) bowl of *fukko hoy*.

NOTES

1 Montaigne, [1580–8] 1943: 343.
2 The Songhay are a people of some 800,000 who live along the banks of the Niger River from as far north as Timbucktu, Mali, to as far south as Sansane-Hausa in the Republic of Niger. There are also some 2.5 million first-language Songhay speakers living in Mali, Niger, and northern Benin. These Songhay speakers, however, are members of other ethnic groups (Wogo, Kurtey, Zerma, Dendi) which have distinct social histories. Djebo's family is from Say, a town on the west bank of the Niger some 200 kilometers south of Tillaberi; it was the center of Fulan power in the nineteenth century.
3 Seneca, [63–5 ACE] 1962, Book 2: 281.
4 Kahn, 1980: 1271.
5 *Ibid.*: 1269.
6 Kant, [1790] 1966: 32.
7 Williams, 1976.
8 *Ibid.*: 264.
9 Montaigne, [1580–8] 1943: 320.
10 *Ibid.*: 345.
11 Ulmer, 1985: 52.
12 Derrida, 1974: 161.
13 Derrida, 1974: 109 as cited in Ulmer, 1985: 55.

14 Ulmer, 1985: 55.
15 Marcus and Cushman, 1982: 29.
16 Stoller 1984c: 102–3.
17 Marcus and Cushman, 1982: 31–6.
18 Some of the well-known contributions include Clifford, 1988; Crapanzano, 1980, 1985, 1987; Dumont, 1978; Dwyer, 1982; Marcus and Fischer, 1985; Rabinow, 1977; Stoller, 1984a, 1984b, 1986; Stoller and Olkes, 1987; Rose, 1987; Tyler, 1984, 1988.
19 Fabian, 1983: 164.
20 American Anthropological Association, 1984.
21 Ibid.: 2.
22 Jarvie, 1975.
23 Dryfus and Rabinow, 1982: 107.
24 Agee, 1941: 139–40.
25 Chernoff, 1979: 39.
26 Geertz, 1973: 347.
27 Lévi-Strauss, [1955] 1973: 362.
28 Merleau-Ponty, 1964: 159.

REFERENCES

Agee, J.
    1941 Let Us Now Praise Famous Men. Boston: Houghton-Mifflin.
American Anthropological Association
    1984 Title page and abstract for publication. Anthropology Newsletter 25 (1): 12D.
Chernoff, J. M.
    1979 African Rhythm and African Sensibility. Chicago: University of Chicago Press.
Clifford, J.
    1988 The Predicament of Culture. Cambridge, MA: Harvard University Press.
Crapanzano, V.
    1980 Tuhami: Portrait of a Moroccan. Chicago: University of Chicago Press.
Crapanzano, V.
    1985 Waiting: The Whites of South Africa. New York: Random House.
Crapanzano, V.
    1987 Editorial. Cultural Anthropology 2: 179–89.
Derrida, J.
    1974 Glas. Paris: Galilée.
Dryfus, H. and P. Rabinow
    1982 Michel Foucault: Beyond Structuralism and Hermeneutics. Chicago: University of Chicago Press.
Dumont, J.-P.
    1978 The Headman and I. Austin: University of Texas Press.
Dwyer, K.
    1982 Moroccan Dialogues. Baltimore: Johns Hopkins University Press.
Fabian, J.
    1983 Time and the Other. New York: Columbia University Press.
Geertz, C.
    1973 The Interpretation of Cultures. New York: Basic Books.
Jarvie, I. C.
    1975 Epistle to the Anthropologists. American Anthropologist 77: 253–67.
Kahn, V.
    1980 The sense of taste in Montaigne's essays. MLN 95: 1269–91.
Kant, I.
    [1790]1966 The Critique of Judgment. New York: Hafner Publishing Co.
Lévi-Strauss, C.
    [1955]1973 Tristes tropiques. J. and D. Weightman, transl. New York: Atheneum.
Marcus, G. E. and D. Cushman
    1982 Ethnographies as texts. Annual Reviews of Anthropology 11: 25–69.
Marcus, G. E. and M. Fischer
    1985 Anthropology as Cultural Critique. Chicago: University of Chicago Press.
Merleau-Ponty, M.
    1964 L'Oeil et l'esprit. Paris: Gallimard.
Montaigne, M. de.
    [1580–8]1943 Selected Essays. New York: Walter Black.
Rabinow, P.
    1977 Reflections on Fieldwork in Morocco. Berkeley: University of California Press.
Rose, D.
    1987 Black American Street Life: South Philadelphia, 1969–1971. Philadelphia: University of Pennsylvania Press.
Seneca [63–5 ACE]
    1962 Epistulae Morales. R. M. Grummere, transl. Cambridge, MA: Harvard University Press.
Stoller, P.
    1984a Horrific comedy: Cultural resistance and the Hauka movement in Niger. Ethos 12: 165–87.
Stoller, P.
    1984b Sound in Songhay cultural experience. American Ethnologist 11: 559–70.

Stoller, P.
1984c Eye, mind and word in anthropology. *L'Homme* 24: 91–114.

Stoller, P.
1986 The reconstruction of ethnography. In P. Chock and J. Wyman (eds.) *Discourse and the Social Life of Meaning*. Washington, DC: Smithsonian Institution Press: 51–74.

Stoller, P. and C. Olkes
1987 *In Sorcery's Shadow: A Memoir of Apprenticeship among the Songhay of Niger*. Chicago: University of Chicago Press.

Tyler, S.
1984 The vision quest in the West, or what the mind's eye sees. *Journal of Anthropological Research* 10: 23–41.

Tyler, S.
1988 *The Unspeakable*. Madison: University of Wisconsin Press.

Ulmer, G.
1985 *Applied Grammatology*. Baltimore: Johns Hopkins University Press.

Williams, R.
1976 *Keywords: A Vocabulary of Culture and Society*. New York: Oxford University Press.

30

Dialogic Editing: Interpreting How Kaluli Read *Sound and Sentiment*

Steven Feld

The word in language is half someone else's.
                              Mikhail Bakhtin

When the writer becomes the center of his attention, he becomes a nudnik. *And a* nudnik *who believes he's profound is even worse than just a plain* nudnik.
                              Isaac Bashevis Singer

An engaging dimension of current interpretive ethnography and its critical rhetoric is the concern to situate knowledge, power, authority, and representation in terms of the social construction of literary realism. Ethnographers today are reading, writing, and thinking more about the politics of ethnographic writing.[1] That is why I read Bakhtin; in his literary world, a dialogic imagination helps reposition ethnographic writing beyond its overt trajectories, and toward reflexive, critical readings. Yet I've had a tendency to *kvetch* about the very

literary genre and trend that I'm here to contribute to. I like the emphasis on a self-conscious, dialectical invention of culture, but I worry that the enterprise not devolve into an invention of the cult of the author. First-person narrative may be the fashionable way to write and critique ethnography these days, but that alone doesn't guarantee that the work is ethnographically insightful, self-conscious, or revelatory. That is why, in tandem, I read Singer; in his literary world, there is caution that first-person writing not pass as a ruse, that hermeneutic not pass for a mispronunciation of a *nom de plume*: Herman Nudnik.

A Context

This article opens to a fixed-in-print text to look at how a new set of readers – its original subjects – opened up and unfixed some of its

Steven Feld, "Dialogic Editing: Interpreting How Kaluli Read *Sound and Sentiment*," pp. 190–210 from *Cultural Anthropology* 2(2), 1987. Copyright © 1987 by the American Anthropological Association. Reprinted by permission of the Copyright Clearance Center on behalf of the American Anthropological Association.

meanings and repositioned its author's authority. I am the author, and the text is *Sound and Sentiment: Birds, Weeping, Poetics, and Song in Kaluli Expression* (1982), an ethnography about the Kaluli people of Bosavi, Papua New Guinea. While I have been stimulated in this endeavor by previous "afterword" essays in Papua New Guinea ethnographies – Bateson's for *Naven* (1958), Rappaport's for *Pigs for the Ancestors* (1984) – what follows was more directly inspired by a series of significant field experiences that positioned Kaluli and me in a more blatant subject-to-subject relationship.

In 1982 I returned to Papua New Guinea for a short summer field trip after an absence of five years. While I was back in Bosavi, my book was published; its arrival in the field, and my momentary fixation on it stimulated the Kaluli to ask about it, and stimulated me to attempt translating sections of it for discussion with them. This article reports on the form of ethnographic discourse that developed in these encounters.

The "dialogic" dimension here implicates what Kaluli and I say to, about, with, and through each other; with developing a juxtaposition of Kaluli voices and my own.[2] My focus on "editing" invokes a concern with authoritative representation; the power to control which voices talk when, how much, in what order, in what language. "Dialogic editing," then, is the impact of Kaluli voices on what I tell you about them in my voice; how their take on my take on them requires reframing and refocusing my account. This is the inevitable politics of writing culture, of producing selections and passing them off as authentic and genuine, and then confronting a recentered view of that selection process that both questions and comments upon the original frame and focus. In more direct terms, my aim here is to let some Kaluli voices get a few words in edgewise amongst my other readers and book reviewers.

My secondary title, "Interpreting How Kaluli Read *Sound and Sentiment*" is meant to implicate the work Kaluli helped me do in order to "write" them, and the work I had to do for them to "read" that writing. I want to suggest that this understanding is multiply textual, that Kaluli perceive the coherences and

contradictions in my representational work as being about me in similar ways to how I perceive the book to be written about them. I also want to suggest Kaluli perceive it as a story about themselves that they also have occasion to tell, a line I'll use to play off of Geertz's phrase situating culture as "a story they tell themselves about themselves" (1973:448). But Kaluli tellings are different from mine in arrangement, focus, intention, and style. I'd also suggest that my Kaluli readers realize as clearly as I do that all of our tellings elide and/ or condense certain scenarios while playing out others in detail; and that both kinds of tellings and tellers have a complicated cross-understanding of the way they speak and write with an acute awareness of different audiences.

A Text

Sound and Sentiment is an ethnography of sound as a cultural system, a book about natural and human sounds – birds, weeping, poetics, and song – and how they are meaningfully situated in the ethos, or emotional tone, of Kaluli expression. The form of the book originates with Kaluli ideas as they are packed into a myth about the origin of weeping, poetics, and song in the plaintive sound of a fruitdove, the *muni* bird. I present and unpack that myth, following its structure, with chapters on birds, weeping, poetics, and song that alternate structural and cognitive summaries with symbolic/performance case studies. In this fashion, the book continually moves back and forth between Kaluli idealizations, prescriptions, intentions, and actualizations, and these are played off each other by my juxtapositions of linguistic (from metalanguage to texts), musical (from form to performance), and cultural (from ideation to action) analyses.

As to what is "in" the book: Kaluli myths and cosmology portray birds and humans as transformations of each other in death and life, living in different planes of visible and nonvisible reality that in part "show through" to each other. Birds can "show through" by their sounds; Kaluli apprehend and relate bird sound categories to spirit attributions according to which ones "whistle," "say their names," "talk Kaluli," "cry," "sing," or "make a lot of noise." The explicit link between bird sound and human emotional expression is first formed in the arena of weeping. The descending four tones of the *muni* bird call create a melodic framework through which women's funerary wailing turns into wept song.

While the performance of this sung-texted-weeping evokes the image that, like the deceased, the weeper too has "become a bird," the switch from spontaneous to elaborately planned ritual expression hinges on poetics. Transforming the "hard words" of assertive discourse to the "bird sound words" of poetic song involves evocative linguistic strategies to speak "inside" the words, and to "turn them over" so they reveal new "underneaths." Song texts are organized by these devices to follow a "path" along a set of place-names; these evoke the pathos of experiences Kaluli share together at the places that they travel to or visit each day.

These poetic "bird sound words" are then melded with the musical material of bird sound, a melodic song scale again based on the tones of the *muni* bird call. A polysemous lexicon of water motion names the contours of song melody and creates a theoretical vocabulary for compositional and aesthetic discourse on song. To be deeply affective and to move members of an audience to tears, these "flowing" songs are then performed in a plaintive bird voice by a dancer costumed as a bird at a waterfall.

While these are some of the features detailed in the book, it is probably more to the point to say that my "topic" was the aesthetics of Kaluli emotion, or, put differently, the invention of sound as aesthetically organized sentiment. My work in *Sound and Sentiment* was to demonstrate how sound is constructed and interpreted as the embodiment of feelings; that is, as aesthetically affecting evocation in the Kaluli ritual performance of weeping and poetic song.

Readers and Readings

Let me now introduce some of my Kaluli readers and say something about how they read and about how they are positioned in relation to my ethnographic work. Virtually all Kaluli have seen books of some kind. (E. L.) Buck and Bambi Schieffelin (the researchers with whom I have worked in Bosavi over the last ten years) and I have always had a variety of books around the house, and Kaluli have had ample opportunities to watch us read. We also on occasion have read out loud to Kaluli and have shown them pictures and illustrations in books and magazines. Many Kaluli have gazed silently as we sat silently turning pages. A typical late afternoon interchange among Kaluli standing on our porches and looking in the windows might go like this: "What are they doing?" (interrupted by) "Nothing ... they're looking at books." Indeed, the word "book," which has the same phonological shape in English and *tok pisin*, the pidgin/creole lingua franca of urban Papua New Guinea (where it is spelled *buk*) is one of the few *tok pisin* words universally placed in the Kaluli loan-word lexicon at this juncture.

Other varieties of familiarity with books have developed through contact Kaluli have had with missionaries who have been in residence since 1971. The mission people have done a small amount of literacy work, and a local school now run by the provincial government exists at the mission station. There are books in the local school, and all Kaluli know that the missionaries have a master book of their beliefs, the Bible, that they intend to translate into the Kaluli language. Books are also not entirely the domain of whites: Kaluli have also been read to by other Papua New Guineans, for example, in church by Kaluli and other pastors, at the school by teachers, or in other situations by government workers.

Kaluli have also watched the Schieffelins and me type and write by hand, and they have asked why we do it. As an explanation we have all probably told them at one point or another that we write so that we can remember what they tell us, and make books about it that our own people can read. Moreover, writing and the handling of books is an activity clearly central to work we and Kaluli do together. When a missionary linguist went to Bosavi in 1964 to supervise the building of a local airstrip and to take a first crack at the language, he introduced the word "school" as the name for the activity that local people would do with him to teach their language. The word was turned into a verb, *sugul-a:la:ma,* "do school," and "doing school" is generically what Kaluli do when they work with us.[3] Part of school work is watching us *dogo:fwanalo,* "yellow skins," as Kaluli call us, write. One day Ayasilo: was helping Bambi Schieffelin and me recruit a new transcription assistant. "Doing school is very hard and goes slow," Ayasilo: explained to young Igale; "when you speak they write it and rub it out and keep writing it again." (The Kaluli verb for "etch" was semantically extended long ago to cover the activity of "writing.")

Young men like Ayasilo: and Igale are not typical Kaluli. Both have a Papua New Guinea school education, are among the five or six Kaluli we know who speak English with moderate conversational skill, and can read and write to a very modest extent in Kaluli, *tok pisin,* and English. Men of this sort have worked often with Bambi Schieffelin and me as linguistic transcription assistants. They have sophisticated senses of their own linguistic and cultural identities as well as substantial contact with outsiders and other Papua New Guineans.

Ayasilo: and Ho:nowo: were two young men in this category who read *Sound and Sentiment* with me at informal and formal school sessions. On occasion these men actually did read out loud directly from the book – passages that I selected for them, knowing that there would be relatively few difficult words or places with lists or diagrams full of Kaluli words. With these men I speak in a continual mixture of Kaluli and English.

At the other end of the spectrum of my readers were older Kaluli men. They typically have had no prolonged experience of the world beyond their immediate neighbors. What they know of the outside is what of it has been brought or narrated by younger Kaluli. With them I speak only in Kaluli. These men included Jubi, a Kaluli man of wisdom and knowledge in various realms of things traditional. Jubi was a particularly astute natural historian, and he lived through the whole sweep of contact experiences from the mid-1930s until the present. Jubi was someone with whom Buck Schieffelin and I had done substantial schooling during each of our previous field trips.

Somewhere in between these two poles were two other people. Gigio was in the same age range as the young men mentioned earlier, but he has never been to school. He is a nonliterate Kaluli speaker with several experiences in the 1970s on labor contracts in the Papua New Guinea world outside Bosavi, and thus has had substantial contacts with Europeans and with other Papua New Guineans with whom he can communicate in *tok pisin.*

As a young boy, Gigio started working as a cook for Buck Schieffelin in 1996, and has held a continually expanding version of that position during each of our field trips over the last 20 years. Gigio is in many ways our closest confidant, friend, and barometer of everyday meanings and events in Bosavi. He is someone we talk to each day about everything from the weather and local garden crops to the poetics of ceremonial songs and linguistic nuances of Kaluli speech. He is enormously intelligent, curious, and perhaps the most knowledgeable interpreter to other Kaluli about what the "yellow skins" are up to.

When I returned in 1982, I found that Gigio had married Faile; she joined him each evening with the cooking and washing work, and then often with the conversations that we typically had before we all went off to sleep. Some of the reading sessions with Gigio also included Faile, a monolingual Kaluli speaker with no experience outside of Bosavi. Gigio also helped me stage my most experimental attempt to hear Kaluli responses to *Sound and Sentiment,* by taking a tape recorder to the communal longhouse one night and there recording discussions he prompted about the book while I was away at my own house.

In summary, the diverse social positioning of these five readers couples with the general understanding of the book-as-work-and-object surveyed earlier to clarify the fact that the appearance of my book and the claim to Kaluli that I wrote it about them was not incomprehensible or bizarre. Now to turn to the substance of these casual and "doing school" readings and to some of the dialogues they animated.

Before translating from the English to Kaluli, I started the first sessions by letting my Kaluli readers handle and thumb through the

book. A substantial amount of time was thus
spent discussing the book as an object, especially the amount of and kinds of black and
white and color photographs, line drawings,
and print. Doing this, Ho:nowo: and Ayasilo:
noticed that there were two different kinds of
print, standard and italics, and they questioned
why this was so. That started the next dialogue
in motion.

I explained that at many places in the book
I told an idea first in the Kaluli language (italic
print) as they had helped me write or tran-
scribe it from conversation, texts, or songs.
Then I said the same thing in English (standard
print) so that my people would understand it.
I did not know a Kaluli term for "translate," so
I simply pointed to the italic writing and said
(in Kaluli), "Here it is written in Kaluli," then
pointing to the standard typeface below said,
"and then the same thing is written in English."
Ho:nowo: pointed and said (in Kaluli) "So
Kaluli language is written there, then turned
around in English language written there
below."

I then questioned him in English and Kaluli
about his use of this verb "turn around" for the
English word "translate," with two things in
mind. First, it is ironic that in *tok pisin* the
term for "translate" or "translator" is *turnim
tok*. (The term for the *tok pisin* verb "turn" is
not related and comes from English "about,"
namely, *baut, bautim*.) My immediate thought
was that Ho:nowo: had directly back-
translated this Kaluli verb from the *tok pisin*
idiom *turnim tok*, thereby coining a literalized
Kaluli verb for "translate."

But another piece of lexical evidence was
contradictory. The same Kaluli verb for "turn
around" is used in poetic metalanguage to
refer to a text copied in terms of major imagery
but reformulated with new place-names and
minor imagery. This kind of "turning around"
is a compositional strategy for recycling poignant poetic phrases while dressing them up
enough to have a fresh impact that bears the
mark of their singer/composer. What Kaluli
call a *gisalo nodolo:*, a "turned around *gisalo*
song," is one that has had the text reworked in
this way. One way to rework a *gisalo* text is to
switch back and forth between the use of the
Kaluli and Sonia languages. The latter is

known by few Kaluli speakers, and this kind of
textual "turning around" has the effect of
obfuscating the message, building the poetic
intensity until the idea is then again "turned
around" back into Kaluli. I was taught this
metalinguistic term and the strategy it labeled
in 1977 when I learned to compose *gisalo*, and
I noted it in the chapter on *gisalo* in my book
(1982:166). My teacher on that subject was
principally Jubi, an older Kaluli man; it is
highly doubtful he could have been aware of
the *tok pisin* term. Therefore I had been under
the impression that this "turn around" notion
was indeed an old Kaluli compositional term
related to nuances of linguistic similarity and
difference, or even code-switching per se in the
song context.

When I mentioned this, Ho:nowo: and
Ayasilo: both claimed that what Jubi had told
me was correct, that "turn around" was also
an old Kaluli way to talk about code-switching
or translation. They said they had not "turned"
this "turn around" term from *tok pisin* back to
Kaluli; that it was *Kaluli to hedele*, a "truly
Kaluli word," that is, not a loan-word or introduction from another language. Nevertheless,
there are a variety of ways that "turn around"
could have come from the *tok pisin* word
turnin tok in the last thirty years, and it is
doubtful whether we will ever really know the
solution to that lexical puzzle.[4]

But the real importance of "turning
around" Kaluli as the ethnographer's translation work comes by juxtaposition with the
next part of the story. During this discussion,
Ayasilo: and Ho:nowo: also noticed that there
was far more standard print than italic print in
the book. I explained that after I translate
from Kaluli to English, the book then uses
more English to tell the meaning of the translation. I should point out that having noticed
this difference, Ho:nowo: and Ayasilo: did not
question or contest why there was more
English than Kaluli. In fact, it made perfect
sense to them that a small bit of Kaluli would
have to be followed by a long stretch of
English, because even once the Kaluli is
directly translated ("turned around") they
assumed that it would take a long time to
reveal ("turn over") all the relevant meanings
("underneaths").

During this discussion I used the Kaluli word *hego:*, which means "underneath," for the English word "meaning." The phrase *hego: wido:* (or *wilo:*) means "showed the underneath."[5] The implication is to lay bare the meaning, to indicate what might not be literally evident, to show another side of the coin, or, literally following the idiom, to get under the surface of things. The notion that meanings are "underneath" surfaces is a rather fundamental Kaluli idea. Things are not simply what they appear to be; what is intended is always potentially far more than what is said or how it is said. In this context, the Kaluli metalinguistic label *bale to*, "turned over words," is quite apt to designate metaphors, obfuscations, allusions, connotations, lexical substitutes, and poetic devices (Feld 1982:138–44).

The everyday speech contrast of the two verbs *nodoma*, "turn around," and *balema*, "turn over," is revealing. One "turns around" objects with observably symmetrical, oppositional, or discrete planes; one "turns over" continuous multi-surfaced objects without them. Replacing one language with another is a "turning around" of discrete items by substitution. Getting to the "underneath" of what is implied is "turning over" words to rotate or shift their multifaceted figure and ground possibilities.

Ayasilo: and Ho:nowo: then told other Kaluli that this book for "yellow skins" is "turned around" and "turned over" Kaluli.[6] They said we ethnographers are *Kaluli to nodolesen kalu*, "Kaluli language turn around people," and *hego: widesen kalu*, "underneath shower people," whose books "turn around" Kaluli into English, and then "show the underneath" of the words. This rather clever image of the intricacies of ethnographic work fits, even if the notions of "turn around," "turn over," and "show the underneath" strike you more in the way of a kinky cross-language pun. After all, we may claim to benignly or sympathetically "translate" and "interpret" languages and meanings, but many of our critics claim that this amounts to little more than "ripping off" or "fucking over" the languages and peoples concerned.

Progressing to other readings, the tendency turned to more about the book's words rather than the nature of the book's work. Before discussing the details of some of these readings, a word about the general style of these dialogues is in order. The form often went like this familiar scenario: You begin to recount a story, and without your realizing it, the story is in fact one your partner has already heard. Perhaps you previously told it to them and forgot you did so. Perhaps it was told to them by another person. Perhaps that other teller first heard it from you. In any case they are hearing a familiar story, but being either polite, disinterested, or unable or unwilling to interrupt, they let you continue the tale without letting on that it is redundant for them. But at some point when you, the teller, pause or stumble for a word, your hearer provides it, and capitalizes on the opening to finish or close the interchange, or even fully situate the hearing as a second one.

Interactions like this constituted the most common form of my readings with Kaluli. Essentially I was providing foregroundings or anchors or scaffoldings to things they knew well; they would dive in and remind me of the workings and outcomes of it all, as if I were unaware of them, had forgotten them, or as if to remind me that we'd been over this ground before. Other times my translations might be slow or halting; a second spent stumbling around for a word or mispronouncing it is all it took to animate a Kaluli hearer.

Part of this was simply a matter of excitement and of Kaluli interactional styles, many of which seem governed by the maxim: Always maintain intensity; don't hold back. Kaluli interactions, with outsiders and Kaluli companions, often come across as animated, sharp, bubbly. This is a key feature of Kaluli assertion (E. L. Schieffelin 1967:118–26; B. B. Schieffelin 1979:141–3). Borrowing some hip-hop argot from Grandfmaster Blaster, many Kaluli don't hesitate to

> cap your rap,
> seal your deal,
> steal your meal
> while you spin your wheel

Indeed, it does not take long to figure out that Kaluli are quick to speak up and quicker to interrupt. You don't have to be like me,

Jewish and from the urban Northeast, to enjoy
and engage in Kaluli interactions, but I think it
helps, particularly in terms of interpreting the
subtleties of this lively interpersonal and verbal style as collaborative engagement rather
than pushy abrasiveness (a not-so-uncommon
attribution made both about Jews and Papua
New Guinea Highlanders).

In any case, a good amount of interruption,
side and splinter conversation, overlapped
speech, and direct or challenging polyphonic
discourse is common in Kaluli interaction,
whether light or heated. And in this marked
context I felt like I was often able to say no
more than a few words before Kaluli would
steal the moment, elaborate the tale, or provide
the punchline without any of the buildup.
Often I was left with the sense of "what you
meant to say was..." before I knew what hit
me.

Yet the form of these interchanges went
beyond the use of my utterances as precaden-
tial formulae, aide-mémoires, or Rorschach
stimuli for willing rap-cappers. The much more
interesting outcome of this was that even when
I was able to get a fair amount of my story told,
my Kaluli readers essentially reconstituted por-
tions or versions of source materials in my field
notes upon hearing them summarized, cap-
suled, or stripped of their situated details.
Kaluli took my stories and resituated them as
their own as they had once before. To do that,
they took every generality I offered and worked
it back to an instance, an experience, a remembered activity or action. In effect, they "turned
over" my story by providing recountings of the
stories that more typically are left behind in my
field notes, the stories I otherwise mined in
order to report Kaluli "underneaths" to my
own "yellow skin" constituency.

More pointedly, the abstracting, deperso-
nalizing, summarizing, and generalizing
moments that appear in my ethnography
unanchored to specific instances, attributions,
and intentions are the ones that Kaluli readers
most often responded to with a concretizing
and repersonalizing set of questions, side
comments, or interpretations. On the tapes
from the evening when Gigio took my tape
recorder to the longhouse, the most common
interjections are: "who said that?" and "who

told him that?" It was that desire to situate
knowledge and experience with specific actors,
agendas, and instances that was most on my
Kaluli readers' minds.

An example of this sort of contestation was
evidenced both in the readings of the chapter
on gisalo songs and the comments about that
chapter that Gigio recorded. That chapter contains a case history of a song sung through a
spirit medium during a seance. The medium
was a man from a distant community, and the
seance took place at Nageba:da:n, a community
an hour or so away from Sululib, our home.
Additionally, the initial transcriptions of the
songs were done with the help of Kulu, a young
man who was also from a distant community,
and most of the exegetic commentary,
responses, and ethnographic information that
went into my characterization came from
work I did with the medium and with people
from Nageba:da:n who were at the event. Few
people from Sululib experienced the event,
although many had heard the tape recordings.

The discussions then constantly involved
quizzing me about who told me what and, one
way or another, mildly challenged the authority involved. Direct and veiled accusations that
the medium was a fraud and that my transcription assistant was a Christian who didn't really
understand the "turned over words" of the
songs were mixed with queries as to whether
Buck and various people from Nageba:da:n
also agreed with what I said, and suggestions
that I really should have discussed a song sung
during a seance at Sululib by another medium
everyone (including Buck and me) knew was a
better performer.

Another example involved my characterization of male and female styles of weeping. The
second chapter of the book contains a metalinguistic, structural, and behavioral statement of
the dimensions of contrasts that differentiate
these styles. When we read this material, my
readers immediately complicated the generalizations I offered, largely related to events we
experienced together, as if to question my
memory. They recalled that most of my experiences of weeping derived from funerals that
took place when I initially arrived in Bosavi.
Hearing their comments was like reading my
field notes. In other words, they set their

explications in the context of specific events, actors, and actions, and constantly asked who had told me one thing or another. Field notes, of course, attend to such on-the-spot actions and situations in a way that pattern overviews typically do not.

The problem of compacting and compressing instances, structuralizing their form, and presenting them pulled away from the biographies and practices in which they were embedded is no minor problem in the critique of ethnographies. So how do we understand the obvious differences of the account and its readings? One way is to claim that they are fairly superficial. For example, there is always a difference in degrees of remove from situated experiences. And book work implicates style; the writer must select, edit, compress something. Investment and salience are also different; the ethnographer more typically accounts for self-investment and the reported investments of many Others rather than the single perspective of any one actor, any one Other. Different audiences also implicate different expectations.

An alternative is to suggest that Kaluli have given me a critique and lesson in poststructuralist method; that they have exposed a deep problem about (my) ethnography, and not a superficial one. A more cynical reaction would be to claim that all I have shown is that my Kaluli commentators are stuck in a world of the concrete (or stuck in the forest mud) and that this is precisely why an ethnographer is necessary – to tell "the point" of it all. Surely *Sound and Sentiment* is not intended as unmediated copy of "the native point of view." I think that few ethnographers these days would quibble with Geertz's (1976) assertion that ethnographies are supposed to be what we ethnographers think about things as much as they are supposed to be accounts of what we think the locals think they are doing.

Up against these possibilities, my own take on the interpretive moves of my readers is more local. I don't think that Kaluli readings of my ethnography are poststructuralist and praxis-centered, or that Kaluli are really "grounded," unable or unwilling to abstract what is going on in a way anything like mine. I also don't think that the issues here are easily resolved by just attributing them to differences

of writing and audience. Part of my reasoning turns on the next layer of readings.

When I was reading with Gigio and Faile from the material in my chapter on women's weeping and recounting there the weeping by Hane *sulo:* over the death of Bibiali at Aso:ndo:, Gigio quickly interrupted, giggling slightly, asking if I had told the story of my trip to Aso:ndo: to record the weeping and of my unexpected overnight stay there. I told him that I had not, and he was truly puzzled by that.

He then quickly began to recount in great detail how I had only been at Sululib for one month, how it was my first trip away from the village without Buck or Bambi, how I barely spoke Kaluli, how they had left me in the hands of a guy named Kogowe, instructing him to return with me the same day, how many people thought Kogowe was a bit flaky and unreliable, how everyone started speculating on why I wasn't home when it turned dark, how upset Bambi was that Kogowe might have gotten lost leading me back, how there was one really bad river bridge to cross on the way, how it had rained heavily all afternoon so maybe the river flooded or I slipped on a log and fell in, how Buck managed to gather up Hasele and Seyaka for the miserable task of walking with him through the forest at night, two-and-a-half hours from Sululib to Aso:ndo:, and how when they got there, they just found me resting comfortably by the fire with a mild stomach ache.

And Gigio went on to tell how we stayed up that night and listened to the tapes with the mourners at Aso:ndo:, and then walked back home the next morning at the crack of dawn, and how everyone playfully teased Kogowe about getting lost, while Kogowe kept protesting that after starting out in the heavy rain the new "yellow skin" kept falling down, stopping him in order to fix the plastic bags protecting the tape recorder case, and at each instance of a fall or stop turning yellower, as if he would puke any minute.

Gigio told this very dramatically and had Faile and me in stitches. But it was more than an amusing story about embarrassing moments in the lives of the "yellow skins." It was Gigio saying, on the "underneath": "This is what good stories are made of; so why didn't you tell it?" Here we were beyond the more typical routine of Kaluli hearers trying to position my account in terms of what other Kaluli speakers said, thought, or told me. Now I was hearing Gigio criticize me for not putting enough of myself in the book. I found this at once a recognition that Gigio read the book as *my* story as much as anyone else's, but also that the concern with positioned Kaluli speakers and their biographical accountability was no different for "yellow skins."

Later on there were a number of similar instances of asking why I didn't tell my stories. I couldn't say to Kaluli that I simply didn't tell my stories more because I often felt them to be unimportant sources for illuminating the Kaluli stories I was trying to tell. So I defended myself by reading with them certain sections of the book where I am more clearly situated in the story. But what was always at issue in these dialogues was the need for a personally situated point of view. My sense here is that Kaluli readings of *Sound and Sentiment* key closely on their sense of biographies, because biographies frame what is memorable about experiences. They extend that concern to all stories, tellers and tellings, even if they don't imagine that other meanings might be assigned to them beyond the ones they momentarily have at hand. I think Kaluli assume that what they find memorable about me is also something that I should be able to recognize. And it is perplexing that I might ignore such an obvious fact in the context of writing about events and times we shared.

One other Kaluli cultural framework helps make sense of this issue; namely, a clear model for this kind of storytelling is neither myth nor historical narrative, but song. There are two reasons for that. One is that Kaluli assume that I know what songs are about and how they are constructed. Another is that song poetics are the height of an aesthetic evocation of the meaning of shared experiences. Kaluli song poetics simultaneously reference abstract qualities and values, and personal situations and experiences, particularly poignant ones. Since the book so deeply concerned such questions, I found that as time and readings progressed, Kaluli seemed to absorb and respond to it as a

kind of meta-*gisalo* song, an evocation about evocation, a map of shared experiences about other maps of shared experiences.

In part, the book readings (particularly the chapters on poetics and song) were greeted like any Kaluli performance meant to move an audience, a performance intended to communicate to that audience the skill, care, and affective sensibilities of the composer/performer. And after the fact, I realized that during our reading sessions my companions frequently acted exactly the way Kaluli act at performances, rather than the way they act when we "do school." They often mixed side comments, wild interjections and exuberant chuckles, quiet clucks accompanied by downcast head turning (as if to say "this is heavy stuff"), feigned distraction and disinterest, intense concentration and engagement, and puns, put-ons and joking rounds playing off a passing verbal phrase or two.

As a matter of fact, there were instances in the readings of my chapter on *gisalo* songs when Gigio, Ho:nowo:, and Ayasilo: all went into silly mock weeping routines, as if both the recounting of a powerful song and my sung/spoken rendition of it had moved them to tears the way a real *gisalo* performance might well do. At one point I read Gigio the section recounting the time I composed a song about my loneliness over Buck and Bambi's departure, telling how it brought tears to his eyes. He playfully mocked weeping and limply fell over onto me, the way weepers at a ceremony throw their arms around the dancer they have just burned in retribution for a song that moved them to tears. Then he popped up and burst out laughing hysterically, exclaiming *Yagidi ni Sidif-o!*, as if to say "this is *too* much, Steve!"

What I think was going on there was the negotiation of a playful frame for a moment recalling shared experiences whose original experiential frames were emotionally highly charged. In a certain sense this was probably the most genuine and natural way for Gigio to take the book seriously, to communicate a positive and friendly aesthetic response to me, and to act perfectly Kaluli about the whole matter. In other words, Gigio knew that the way to greet my telling was not with a casual "that's good" or "yes, it was truly like that." Such responses would be distanced, impersonal, uncharacteristic of our relationship (and something that I would read as "informant behavior"). Gigio's manner of response was a way to say "we can laugh about the heaviness we shared." This Kaluli way to reaffirm the power of shared feelings and experiences is not uncommon; instances of mock weeping are often invoked to convey expressions of camaraderie and affection among young Kaluli men.

Another way to help illuminate the dynamics of Kaluli interpretive style here is to focus on the parts of *Sound and Sentiment* that seemed to be read most easily and successfully, and the ones that seemed to be most troublesome. Most successfully read were my telling of the *muni* bird myth, material in the chapter on birds, and much of the material in the chapter on song poetics. Less successful were some of the things in the chapters on weeping and song. This puzzled me because, with the exception of the ornithological materials, it reverses what I said earlier about a preference for the concrete. Indeed, the weeping and song chapters had the longest and most specifically situated case histories in them, whereas the myth and poetics materials were more often structurally compacted.

In the case of the weeping and song materials, which in the book include a full transcription, translation, involved case history, and explication for individual performances, the problems involved the nature of providing a context for a microanalysis, the nature of which item was selected for such intense treatment, and the fact that neither of these major case studies come from events that took place in my home village.

For example, with the *gisalo* song, Gigio was quick to remind me that it was an early one in a larger seance that included 13 songs. For Gigio this was not in fact the most memorable of all the songs. He was also right that a later song that also moved the same man to tears came at a more climactic moment in the overall seance, and that the later song was also longer, more poetically complicated, and moved several other people to tears as well. My real dilemma here was that Gigio was not only right about all of these things, but that

Aiba, the medium, Neono, a man who wept for both songs, and all the original consultants both from Nageba:da:n and Sululib told me exactly the same thing in 1977. I agreed then, and still do now, that the later song was more forceful (though no more typical of the genre) from musical-poetic-performative standpoints. But my choice of the song that appears in the book derived entirely from other considerations.

For example, the later song was almost one-and-a-half times as long as the earlier one, and involved linguistic, poetic, and pragmatic factors that would have required a much more extended discussion in the book. The multiplicity of agendas embodied in that song and the seance activity surrounding it meant that I could not have explained it clearly without discussing the larger event and its participants in greater detail. Also, I ran out of tape in the middle of that song, and the change of reels deletes about 30 seconds where I am not entirely sure of the text. Even though I worked with several people on that issue and have a pretty good idea of exactly what was included in the untaped verse, the situation was not ideal, because I wanted to publish the analyzed song on a record (as I have, Feld 1985) so that my readers could relate the performance to my description and analysis of it. Moreover, I was not really concerned with a discussion of the most powerful *gisalo* from this or any other single event, but simply with one that worked well to typify the style and the performance issues, and could accommodate my concern to integrate a case study into a larger sociomusical discussion of the genre.

Likewise, Gigio and Ho:nowo: were quick to point out that the *sa-ya:lab* weeping example that I picked for close scrutiny was done by a single woman. Indeed, *sa-ya:lab* are more typically wept by two to five women simultaneously. And there were other ways in which Hane sulo:'s long *sa-ya:lab* was not typical: it was more songlike than many, more poetically complicated, less ordinary, more profoundly moving. Here we have the inverse of the problem with the *gisalo* song selection. I picked what everyone agreed was the most forceful of the *sa-ya:lab* performances I had recorded for my case study only to be told (again, as I had been told before and knew well) that there were ways in which it was not entirely representative.

What I found interesting in these discussions was not that my readers were contesting my selection. Rather, it was that they were responding in real Kaluli style. Kaluli men seem to assume that whether or not they have anything substantial to say, or are explicitly asked their opinion, they are expected to have one, and expected to be ready with it and entirely up-front about asserting it. A premium is placed on having something to say, on saying it as a form of collaboration, and on engaging demonstratively. Talk is not only a primary measure of Kaluli social competence, but an arena for the display of intelligent interactive style, what Kaluli call *halaido*, "hardness" (Feld and B. B. Schieffelin 1982). If my readers were giving me "a hard time," it was in their cultural idiom, and not mine.

Gigio and Ho:nowo: never told me that I was "wrong," never proposed explicit changes, nor indicated that I should have said things differently. That would be too trivial a response and out of character. Their discussions opened issues rather than resolved them, and their comments were filled with sentences that opened or closed with classic Kaluli hedges, *hede ko:sega*, "true, but…" and *a:la:fo: ko:sega*, "like that, however…" The pragmatics of these very typical Kaluli phrases are complex, not just in terms of whether they open or close an utterance, but also in terms of how they work to always keep the conversation moving.

What Gigio and Ho:nowo: did say about my editorial policy was also very Kaluli; they occasionally responded to my assertions with a terse but semantically complicated Kaluli term, *ko:le*, "different." Sometimes this term can and should be taken at face value, a neutral and direct "oh, *that's* different." The term also can be distancing, carrying the sense of "well, OK, but that's *your* thing." It can also carry a very positive sense of different, a sort of "far out, I never saw it *that* way before." It can also imply a rather bland "different," carrying the sense of "I suppose you *could* see it that way." Or a more evaluatively suspect "that's *different*." Even when attending carefully to syntax, conversational context, intonation, and paralinguistics,

it is not easy to get a single semantic reading when Kaluli use this term. My intuition is that the term more often frames multiple or ambiguous attitudes rather than singular ones in any case. Here it seemed that Gigio and Ho:nowo: used it in virtually every way with me, creating a continually mixed feeling of acceptance and challenge.

As for the easier read sections, I went over all of the bird taxonomy, symbolism, and stories in real detail with Jubi. He was perhaps the best ornithologist in Bosavi, and had worked longest and hardest, at one point almost everyday for five straight months, with me on the bird materials originally. I was interested in his reading, and interested to see how similar or different his interpretations would be five years later. In about a week's time we went through the whole chapter; he corrected me on about four or five identifications that I had botched, elaborated others, insisted that I had "forgotten" certain things, but basically gave me the sense that my bird portrayal was fairly complete and accurate in terms of his knowledge and understanding.

It was clear, however, from Jubi and others, that I had not gone far enough in stating that classification of birds by sound was more typical of Kaluli everyday use and knowledge, and more salient than the detailed classification by beaks and feet to which I had devoted so much formal lexical attention. And if I had it to do over, I think that a restructuring of the way those two classifications are presented would be in order. Also, more attention to other bird myths would be in order, as I found that Jubi invoked them often, as he had done in the past, in order to explain the "underneaths" of bird colors, sounds, and behaviors. In any case, what was most successful here was the organization of the material in terms of metalinguistically and culturally focused Kaluli domains.

Similarly, what was successful to all my readers in the materials on poetics and song structure was the orderly presentation of things following the Kaluli metalinguistic demarcations. Like the ornithological materials, sections of the book framed by Kaluli domains led my readers to act as if my role in the presentation were more secretarial than "turn around"/"turn over." Set in that light, the isolated phrases from songs as examples were questioned less for being taken out of context. There were plenty of instances here that led me to feel justified in believing and stating that Kaluli can and do think quite abstractly and theoretically about song form, composition, and poetic construction as a kind of symbolic persuasion.

Dialogic Editing of Another Kind

I thought my most radical move in *Sound and Sentiment* consisted in simultaneously stressing the theoretical importance of sound (as distinct from music or language per se) and its situated importance in understanding how Kaluli constructed and interpreted their expressive modes. It turned out that this was read as rather less adventurous by both Gigio and Jubi. They were taken by how much time I had spent discussing a single song and a single weeping episode, but then how much less I had spent talking about the more mundane daily sounds – the ones that tell the weather, season of year, time of day. They asked why I told so much about birds but so little about frogs, about insects, different animals. They asked why I had told the *muni* bird myth and not told many others. They asked why I had not told about how all sounds in the forest are *mama*, "reflections" of what is unseen. I responded that I thought birds were most important; they had more stories, there were more of them, Kaluli *ane mama*, "gone reflections" (spirits of dead) more often show through as birds, and so on. They did not dispute this; they simply made it clear that every sound was a "voice in the forest" and that I should tell about them all.

The responses of Jubi and Gigio to the emphasis on weeping, poetics, and song, and to the ethnoliterary device of the case example made it clear to me that there was a gap between my emphasis on the meaning of Kaluli-performed human sounds and the kind of practical and affective everyday interaction with environmental sound that more deeply grounds the specific aesthetic and performative arenas that I focused upon.

My main response to this was to record more everyday sounds, usually on early morning and late afternoon treks each day in the surrounding bush with Jubi, and then to have playback sessions where I would let the tape recorder run and simply invite people to sit around and listen. I also stayed up all night on several occasions to record nighttime forest sounds, and tried to get Kaluli to identify and discuss all of them. What I was trying to do here was to create a pool of sensate material from which Kaluli and I could have different kinds of discussions from the ones we more typically had about linguistic, poetic, and musical material. My hope was that this kind of refocused activity could lead to better realizations about the nature of sound, particularly at the level of everyday Kaluli meanings and interpretations.

The dialogues that followed made it clear that the sociomusical metaphors I had earlier identified in discourse about human sound are thoroughly grounded in natural sounds. For example, *dulugu ganalan*, "lift-up-over-sounding," is an important concept in Kaluli song form and performance. It turns out to also be the most general term for natural sonic form. Unison or discretely bounded sounds nowhere appear in nature; all sounds are dense, multilayered, overlapping, alternating, and interlocking. The constantly changing figure and ground of this spatio-acoustic mosaic is a "lift-up-over-sounding" texture without gaps, pauses, or breaks.

This key image clarifies how the soundscape evokes "insides" and "underneaths" (*sa* and *hego:*) and "reflections" (*mama*). These notions involve perceptions, changes of focus and frame, motions of interpretive access to meanings packed into layers of sensation as they continually "lift-up-over" one another. It is not just that the forest is the abode of invisible spirits; it is that all sounds invite contemplation because their juxtaposition and constant refiguring make it possible to mildly or intensely interpret presences.

"Lift-up-over-sounding" sounds and textures disperse, pulse, rearrange. This constant motion is also an energy, a "hardness" that comes together and that "flows," remaining in one's thought and feelings. In song poetics, "making hard" (*halaido doma:ki*) is the image of competent formation; it is force, persuasion, the attainment of an energized evocative state. The holding power of that "hardened" state is its "flowing" (*a:ba:lan*), the sensation that sounds and feelings stay with you after they have been heard or performed.

What to do with these new understandings and new sounds? I had already produced two sampler phonograph discs illustrating all Kaluli song and instrumental styles (Feld 1981, 1985). The first of these contained an 8-minute-long unbroken stretch of Kaluli talking, singing, and whooping recorded during garden clearing work. But this brief attempt to place Kaluli soundmaking in the environmental context does not contain examples of the interplay of human and natural sounds (like singing and whistling with birds and insects) that I recorded in 1982. I decided that an extended version of this kind of recording would make it possible to illustrate the interaction of environmental sounds and Kaluli aesthetic sensibilities at the everyday, nonritual/ceremonial level. That led to the conception of *Voices in the Forest*, a tape recording depicting a day in the life of the Kaluli and their tropical rain forest home.[7] This tape attempts an editing dialogue with sounds in order to work more reflexively with Kaluli in a sensate idiom so naturally their own.

When fieldworkers make tape recordings and select a representative set of materials for publication or presentation, they generally follow certain realist conventions of sound as a mode of ethnographic representation. In these practices I think it fair to claim that the typical mode of tape editing and use is literal and descriptive; more important, bounded and discrete. The on/off switch or the fade up/fade down potentiometer of the tape machine marks a control over the finiteness of a recorded item. What comes in between the on and the off or the fade up and the fade down is itself expected to be whole, unmanipulated, unviolated. In other words, we expect a tape excerpt or a record band to be a true sonic index of the temporal stretch it occupies. Assurances that what we hear in that temporal stretch has not been spliced, cut, rearranged, altered, filtered, mixed, or otherwise edited are part of the guarantees of a recording's authenticity.

The kind of selection and editing necessary to construct *Voices in the Forest* is of a different sort. While it is a sound construction that is both narrative and realist in convention, it is closer in concept and execution to *musique concrète* than ethnomusicological tape display. Its form is accomplished by editing sounds. While it displays a concern with both ethnographic representativeness and audio accuracy, this concern is realized compositionally rather than literally. In this sense it owes much to R. Murray Schafer (1977) and the World Soundscape Project's concern that soundscape research be presented as musical composition.

To make *Voices in the Forest* I selected three hours of source material from about 60 hours of recordings made in 1976–7 and 1982.[8] The selected materials were arranged according to various graphs (again, modeled in part on Schafer's work) made in the field. These plot the pattern and interaction of daily human and natural sound cycles and have the names of the sound sources as well as Kaluli commentaries about them, noted at the time of recording or during playback sessions. These selections represent the typical cycle of sounds during a 24-hour period, patterned from a human point of view. In other words, the progression of sounds follows the progression of general Kaluli activities in the village and surrounding forest settings. The recording then attempts to present a participant's spatiotemporal ear-perspective.

Once the materials were arranged, no scissor cuts were made. Editing was accomplished by rerecording slices of the source material directly onto an eight-track recorder, using three sets of stereo tracks and two monaural ones. The eight tracks were then mixed down to two, continuously cross-fading to create the illusion of seamless narrative. In this way the sounds sampled from a 24-hour period are condensed to 30 minutes, beginning with the early morning hours, progressing through dawn in the village, morning and midday work in the forest, an afternoon rain storm back in the village, dusk and settling in for the night, and returning to the night and early morning hours.

As a sound object, *Voices in the Forest* is a mixed genre: experimental ethnography and musical composition. Its sources of inspiration include a variety of non-Kaluli notions that condition my perception of sound as an environmental sensorium. Nature recordings (like Jean-Claude Roché's extraordinary series *L'oiseau musicien*), environmental compositions (like R. Murray Schafer's *Music for Wilderness Lake*), and experiments in interspecies communication (like Jim Nollman's underwater guitar duos with dolphins) have all been interesting to me in this regard; they tell cultural stories about nature.

Voices in the Forest also tells this kind of story, using Kaluli directorial participation and my technical skills to complement each other. Here multitrack recording becomes the ethnoaesthetic means to achieve a Kaluli "lift-up-over-sounding" and "flowing" sound object full of "insides" and "underneaths" that speak to the "hardness" of Kaluli stylistic coherence, and to its "reflection" in my appreciation.

The main thing I have learned from the experience of recording the sounds, discussing them in the field, and editing *Voices in the Forest* is that for Kaluli, the nature of sounds is far more deeply grounded in the sounds of nature than I had previously realized. In other words, Kaluli culture rationalizes nature's sound as its own, then "turns it over" to project it in the form of what is "natural" and what is "human nature." This is the link between a perception of a sensate, lived-in world and the invention of an expressive sensibility. "Lift-up-over-sounding" sounds that "harden" and "flow," producing a sense of "insides," "underneaths," and "reflections" reproduce in Kaluli cultural form the sense that nature is natural, and that being Kaluli means being aesthetically "in it" and "of it." This is both the background and stage for Kaluli expressive styles, the natural condition and world-sense that makes it possible for bird sound, weeping, poetics, and song to be so inextricably linked, not just in mythic imagination and ritual performance, but throughout the forest and in the treetops at the same time.

While dialogic editing of the first kind mostly taught me how Kaluli felt the "underneath" of *Sound and Sentiment* needs more sentiment, the second kind made it possible for us to work together to "harden" the sound.

NOTES

1   Some of the recent literature that I have found stimulating in this regard includes Tedlock 1979, Clifford 1983, Marcus and Cushman 1982, and the essays in Clifford and Marcus 1986. My thoughts about the value of reflexive follow-up accounts and the dialectics of cultural invention were stimulated during fieldwork in 1982 by immediately prior readings of Dumont 1978, Rabinow 1977, and Wagner 1981.

2   "Dialogue is the fashionable metaphor for modernist concerns. The metaphor can illegitimately be taken too literally or hypostatized into philosophical abstraction. It can, however, also refer to the practical efforts to present multiple voices within a text, and to encourage readings from diverse perspectives. This is the sense in which we use dialogue" (Marcus and Fischer 1986:680). This is also the sense in which the notion of dialogue is employed in the present article.

3   The missionary-linguist was Murray Rule of the Unevangelized Field Museum (today, Asia Pacific Christian Mission); Rule 1964 is a first description of the Kaluli language. During an interview in November 1984, Rule told me that of all the people in Papua New Guinea he had worked with in his years of translation, he was most impressed with the intelligence and quickness of his Kaluli linguistic informants. He attributed this to "a definite gift for language that the Kaluli tribe must have received from the time of Babel." Minus biblical rationale, Rule's perception is not unique among both long- and short-term visitors to Bosavi.

The Kaluli *are* energetically verbal; the cultural focus on language skill as a social resource is a significant feature of Kaluli everyday life, and this is readily manifest in the adaptation of new words, lexical expansion and coinage, and interest in other languages, not to mention the more typical arenas (metalanguage, poetics, conversation, registers and styles, socialization, etc.). This verbal "high profile" is described in B. B. Schieffelin 1979, Feld and Schieffelin 1982.

4   What is clear is that in the last ten years a
    number of literal back-translations have come
    into Kaluli everyday use, sometimes standing
    alongside a Kaluli equivalent, sometimes intro-
    ducing a concept and coining a label. In 1984
    Bambi Schieffelin and I came upon several
    of these back translation uses, for example,
    tok pisin, stretim tok → Kaluli *di-galema:no:
    to.* Here the term for "settle a complaint"
    or "solve a discussion," literally "straighten
    (-ed, -ing) talk" is back-translated by the direct
    Kaluli terms for "straighten" and "talk."
5   Kaluli also use this "show" term as a metalin-
    guistic label to indicate what mothers do
    when teaching language to their children
    (B. B. Schieffelin 1979:105–6).
6   While the Kaluli generally interpret the Bible
    as an elaborate compendium of Christian
    "turned over words," my readers volunteered
    that missionary translation work is different
    from ours and is not "turned around" and
    "turned over" Kaluli.
7   *Voices in the Forest* was funded by the
    National Endowment for the Arts and the
    Satellite Program Development Fund of
    National Public Radio. The tape was copro-
    duced with Scott Sinkler, who was also the
    chief studio engineer. We thank the above
    agencies and Magnetik Recording Studios,
    Philadelphia, for their assistance. *Voices in the
    Forest* was aired in 1984 and 1985 on NPR,
    Pacifica, and independent stations in the USA,
    Europe, and the Pacific.
8   Stereo recordings were done with omnidirec-
    tional AKG condenser microphones in an
    X–Y configuration; monaural recordings,
    mostly of bird sounds, were made using a
    Gibson parabolic reflector. All were originally
    recorded on a Nagra IV-S at 7-1/2 or 15 ips.
    Sound pressure level readings in dB A, B, and
    C were taken at the time of each recording
    to insure proper volume level continuity
    throughout the studio rerecording and mix.

REFERENCES

Bakhtin, Mikhail
    1981   The   Dialogic   Imagination. Austin:
    University of Texas Press.
Bateson, Gregory
    1958   Naven. Stanford: Stanford University
    Press. [1936]

Clifford, James
    1983   On Ethnographic Authority. Represen-
    tations 1(2):118–46.
Clifford, James, and George Marcus, eds.
    1986   Writing   Culture: The   Poetics   and
    Politics of Ethnography. Berkeley: University of
    California Press.
Dumont, Jean-Paul
    1978   The   Headman and I: Ambiguity and
    Ambivalence in the Fieldworking Experience.
    Austin: University of Texas Press.
Feld, Steven
    1981   Music of the Kaluli. 12″ stereo disc
    with notes, map, photos. Boroko: Institute of
    Papua New Guinea Studies (IPNGS 001).
Feld, Steven
    1982   Sound and Sentiment: Birds, Weeping,
    Poetics and   Song   in Kaluli Expression.
    Philadelphia: University   of   Pennsylvania
    Press.
Feld, Steven
    1985   Kaluli Weeping and Song. 12″ stereo
    disc with notes (English and German), map,
    photos,   musical   transcriptions.   Kassel:
    Bärenreiter (Musicaphon/Music of Oceania,
    BM 30 SL 2702).
Feld, Steven, and Bambi B. Schieffelin
    1982   Hard Words: A Functional Basis for
    Kaluli Discourse. *In* Analyzing Discourse: Text
    and Talk (Georgetown University Roundtable
    on Languages and Linguistics, 1981). Deborah
    Tannen, ed. pp. 351–71. Washington, DC:
    Georgetown University Press.
Geertz, Clifford
    1973   Deep Play: Notes on the Balinese
    Cockfight. *In* The Interpretation of Cultures.
    pp. 412–53. New York: Basic Books.
Geertz, Clifford
    1976   From the Native's Point of View: On
    the Nature of Anthropological Understanding.
    In Meaning in Anthropology. Keith Basso
    and   Henry   Selby, eds. pp.   221–37.
    Albuquerque: University of New Mexico
    Press.
Marcus, George, and Dick Cushman
    1982   Ethnographies as Texts. Annual Review
    of Anthropology 11:25–69.
Marcus, George, and Michael Fischer
    1986   Anthropology   as   Cultural   Critique.
    Chicago: University of Chicago Press.
Rabinow, Paul
    1977   Reflections on Fieldwork in Morocco.
    Berkeley: University of California Press.

Rappaport, Roy
    1984 Pigs for the Ancestors. New Haven: Yale University Press. [1968]
Rule, Murray
    1964 Customs, Alphabet, and Grammar of the Kaluli People of Bosavi, Papua. [Typescript]
Schafer, R. Murray
    1977 The Tuning of the World. New York: Knopf.
Schieffelin, Bambi B.
    1979 How Kaluli Children Learn What to Say, What to Do, and How to Feel. Unpublished Ph.D. dissertation. Columbia University.

Schieffelin, Edward L.
    1976 The Sorrow of the Lonely and the Burning of the Dancers. New York: St Martin's Press.
Singer, Isaac Bashevis, and Richard Burgin
    1985 Conversations with Isaac Bashevis Singer. New York: Doubleday.
Tedlock, Dennis
    1979 The Analogical Tradition and the Emergence of a Dialogical Anthropology. Journal of Anthropological Research 35(4):387–400.
Wagner, Roy
    1981 The Invention of Culture. Chicago: University of Chicago Press.

31

On Rocks, Walks, and Talks in West Africa: Cultural Categories and an Anthropology of the Senses

Kathryn Linn Geurts

One day, in the middle of a nearly two-year stretch of fieldwork in southeastern Ghana, I drove my car over a rock in the center of the compound in which I lived. A jolt shot through my body as if I had been struck by lightning. Immediately upon entering the house, I told my husband about the experience. He laughed at me and stated, "I told you that rock was a *legba*!" I recorded this incident in my field notes but promptly repressed or forgot about it.

A month later, I was in Accra, visiting members of the extended family of Anlo-Ewe people in whose ancestral home we resided in the southern Volta Region. Somewhat out of the blue, Kodzo and Kwami observed that my husband and I had a habit of taking our car into the compound (as their brother had directed us to do), and they wondered if we had ever driven over that inconspicuous stone protruding out of the sand in front of Grandma's house. I was mortified by the question. I hesitated, but then admitted that I normally tried to avoid it but had recently run the right tire smack over the center of the

rock. I remembered the lightning bolt through my body; I remembered my friend Raphael telling me that Nyigbla, the god of war, never hesitated to strike mercilessly into a group of people holding a conversation, only to take out the single offending individual – bang, he was dead. While these thoughts were racing through my mind, Kodzo and Kwami had shifted to speaking in an animated tone (and in Ewe) and were trying to figure out to what extent I was culpable. Finally they turned to me and said, "Never mind. As for you, you didn't know what it was. Nothing needs to be done. But now that you know, just don't run over it again." I was not exactly clear on what I *now knew*, but when we left their house my husband said, "I told you that rock was a *legba*!"

I went to see Raphael the next day and told him everything. He said that the jolt of lightning I had felt was a clear instance of *seselelame* (an Anlo-Ewe term for "feeling in the body"), and he was startled by my (foolish, in his view) response, which was to ignore the feeling I experienced when driving over the stone.

Kathryn Linn Geurts. "On Rocks, Walks, and Talks in West Africa: Cultural Categories and an Anthropology of the Senses," pp. 178–198 from *Ethos* 30(3), 2002.

Ethnographic Fieldwork: An Anthropological Reader, Second Edition. Edited by Antonius C. G. M. Robben and Jeffrey A. Sluka.
Editorial material and organization © 2012 John Wiley & Sons, Inc.
Published 2012 by John Wiley & Sons, Inc.

I have puzzled over this incident for several years. It was one of those small moments of "aha" during fieldwork that nonetheless proves extremely difficult to write about. It provided insight into how Raphael, Kodzo, and Kwami (as well as other Anlo-Ewe people) might think and feel about certain experiences, but it seemed impossible to disentangle this event from issues of the supernatural and from problems of "observer subjectivity" (cf. Stein 2000:349) or questions about whether an ethnographer's feelings can be used as an index for what "the other" might be known to experience and perceive. Recently, however, ethnographers have begun to acknowledge their own "countertransference" and have begun to explore and make use of the notion that one's own "embodied feeling informs the researcher about deep elusive social realities" (Stein 2000:349). In this article I use some of my own experiences in tandem with those of Anlo people themselves, along with discussion of seselelame, to explore the nuances of this cultural category. I do this as a means of beginning to unpack their cultural model for immediate bodily experience, and to ask how sensory experience fits into a more general Anlo-Ewe understanding of *how we know what we know*. This unpacking is aimed at exploring the implications of cultural variation in sensory orders and sensory experience.

In the southeastern corner of Ghana, bordering Togo, lies a stretch of land surrounding the Keta Lagoon that is known as the Anlo homeland. Anlo is a dialect of the Ewe language and also refers to a subset of Ewe speakers who inhabit the southern portion of the Volta Region of Ghana. In addition, many Anlo and Ewe speakers reside in Accra as well as other areas in West Africa, and individual Ewe speakers and their families have also migrated to locations in Europe, North America, and elsewhere. The coastal area from Anyanui to Keta or Kedzi, and north of the lagoon to Anyako, is typically considered the heart of Anlo-land, and Anlo-Ewe speakers have inhabited this area for more than 300 years. Between 1992 and 1995, I spent approximately 20 months conducting ethnographic research among Anlo-Ewe people in both Accra and the Anlo homeland.

In addition to that initial period of fieldwork in Ghana during the mid-1990s, I have continued communicating with Anlo-Ewe people (some of them in Europe and the United States) about this topic of seselelame. So while my study includes the perspective of a wide range of Anlo-Ewe individuals, some of the most insightful and quote-worthy comments or reflections about seselelame (included in this article) have come from multilingual "informants" or people whom we would probably also have to say are "multicultural." It could be suggested that their exposure to cultural worlds beyond the Anlo-Ewe locale, and their fluency in both Ewe and English, might be a handicap or a source of contamination in our efforts to understand a cultural category such as seselelame. Instead of that view, however, I have chosen to listen closely to their thoughts about seselelame, as I think they are uniquely situated to reflect on the similarities and differences between a domain we think of as *sensing*, and their own historical category that they refer to as *seselelame*. The reasons why Raphael (mentioned in the anecdote recounted earlier and a key informant) was troubled by how I discounted sensations of immediate bodily disturbance when I ran the car tire over the rock will be explored as I describe a cultural category called *seselelame*.

Sensing and Epistemologies

In many Western epistemological traditions, a distinction is made between feeling (otherwise considered affect, sentiment, or emotion) and sensation (deemed physical stimulus from an extrasomatic object). In turn, the senses are usually defined in these traditions as the organs that provide us with information about the external world and that function to create representations in the mind. This means that hearing, sight, touch, taste, and smell are considered by many to be the only true senses, and they are treated as five distinct modes of experience.

In Anlo-Ewe cultural contexts in West Africa, however, a discrete category delineating these five sensory functions is not a tightly bounded or particularly meaningful way of classifying experience or theorizing about knowledge. Instead, in an Anlo-Ewe model, sensations caused by a stimulus from external objects are epistemologically related to sensations that stem from internal somatic modes (referred to in technical terms as *intero-receptors* or *interoceptors* that govern balance, movement, and proprioception), and they are also grouped or associated with affective states. Furthermore, sensations may also be linked to dispositional conditions and with vocational qualities inscribed within the self. In other words, Anlo cultural traditions do not seem to have a "theory of the senses," as we define this domain. But they do seem to have a coherent and fairly complex theory of inner states that links sensation to emotion, disposition, and vocation, and that many Anlo speakers refer to as *seselelame* (feeling in the body, flesh, or skin). Thus, while there are some striking similarities between a Western folk model and an Ewe folk model, there are also some intriguing differences. Here I will draw from the frameworks of cultural phenomenology and cultural psychology to elucidate the significance of *seselelame*.

A fundamental assumption in cultural psychology is that, as Markus et al. have suggested, "psychological processes are not just 'influenced' but are thoroughly culturally constituted, and as a consequence, psychological processes will vary with sociocultural context" (1996:859). While not denying that there may be certain psychic universals within the human species, cultural psychologists argue that general "psychologists may be prematurely settling on *one* psychology, that is, on one set of assumptions about what are the relevant or most important psychological states and processes, and on one set of generalizations about their nature and function" (Markus et al. 1996:858). The present article aims to address some of those sociohistorically constructed generalizations about the nature and boundaries of what we refer to as "the senses" and sensory experience, while simultaneously describing another cultural way of depicting how sensation relates to perception, meaning making, and bodily modes of knowing.

Within cultural psychology, studies of emotion provide an impetus for posing similar questions about the cultural grounding of sensation. For example, Richard Shweder asks, "What is the generic shape of the meaning system that defines an experience as an emotional experience (e.g., anger, sadness, or shame) rather than an experience of some other kind (e.g., muscle tension, fatigue, or emptiness)?" (1993:418). This can be transposed into an inquiry about the cultural psychology of the senses by exploring *the generic shape of the meaning system* that defines an experience as sensory. For example, why are balance and kinesthesia "sensory" in one cultural meaning system while classified as postural, locomotive, or motor skills in another? In addition, Shweder asks, "what is the role of everyday discourse and social interpretation in the activation of emotionalized and somatized meanings?" (1993:418). In terms of the senses, we can probe the same issue about how sensory meanings are socialized or acquired, and we can ask, What is the role of everyday practices and discourse in this process?

This article begins to address these questions by first examining the problem of cultural categories. What is deemed "sensory" in one meaning system does not necessarily translate directly into another cultural world, and this article works to elucidate the ways in which Anlo speakers conceptualize a range of immediate bodily experiences. In addition to outlining the general parameters of their particular cultural category of seselelame, thus, I will describe two specific dimensions of seselelame that fall outside the boundaries of a five-senses model: *azolizozo* or *azolime*, which denotes both a kinesthetic sense and the development of moral disposition; plus *sesetonume*, which refers to sensations related to speech as well as a more general category of "feeling in the mouth." Finally, I will revisit the event with which I opened the article and explore how the same object might be perceived as a stone by some while others perceive it as a spiritual guardian of thresholds – referred to as a *legba* in Anlo-Ewe worlds.

In a discussion of countertransference, Stein observed that "knowledge via the senses is especially powerful when it takes the observer by surprise. ... One knows not with disembodied thought, but with one's entire body – one's whole being" (Stein 2000:367). While I now agree with this notion of knowledge articulated by Stein, at the time I drove my tire over the stone I was in the habit of resisting most inclinations to attend to such direct sensory experiences. That is, my own socialization in mainly Euro-American contexts predisposed me to discounting direct experience. In addition, although anthropology claims participant-observation as its major methodological tool, the "participation" side of the equation is often suspect. In the minority still are ethnographers such as Paul Stoller who argue that the agency of the "sensuous scholar" is to be included (with its complexities and errors of judgment) and that our scholarship benefits from "lending one's body to the world" rather than aspiring to consume the knowledge of the world (Stoller 1997: prologue). There are days when I interpret my experience driving over the rock as a moment of grace, a moment of unmerited assistance in my task of understanding Anlo sensibilities, for I was living in a land where stones are often not what they seem. Here I will try to provide a taste of the ways in which living with Anlo-Ewe people and learning about seselelame opened the door to an ontological mode containing some subtle but interesting contrasts with a way of being steeped in a tradition that reifies a five-senses model.

Cultural Categories and the Domain of "Feeling in the Body"

In the 1920s, Diedrich Westermann compiled an Ewe-German dictionary that was subsequently translated into English, and the term sense was rendered in Ewe as *sidzenu* (Westermann 1973:214). When I first arrived in Anlo-land in the early to mid-1990s, I tried to use this term to refer to a domain of experience that includes hearing, touch, taste, smell, and sight but soon found myself in the middle of a massive problem of translation. *Sidzenu* did not mean that set of experiences, nor did it refer to an indigenous category of immediate bodily experiences that were

meaningful to the people with whom I worked. *Sidzenu* instead meant something along the lines of "thing recognized" (*dzesi:* to note, observe, recognize; *nu:* thing) and therefore implied a somewhat mentalistic and cognitive (rather than embodied) process or phenomenon. In addition, within the network of Anlo-speaking people with whom I worked, no one ever proposed or even passively agreed to the word *sidzenu* as a translation for the English word *sense*. I soon came to realize that one discrete lexical term for "the senses" did not seem to exist in the Anlo-Ewe language, and the problem of terminology and translation soon blossomed into an issue that centers around a much thornier problem of cultural categories and ways of organizing experience.

The absence of one clear term or an obvious category for what is commonly understood by many Westerners as "the senses" (hearing, touch, taste, smell, and sight) meant that interviews with a wide spectrum of Anlo speakers (from highly educated people who spoke both African and European languages, to individuals who had little exposure to either formal schooling or European languages) resulted in nearly as many configurations of sense-data as numbers of people interviewed. One informant suggested that senses could be called *nusenuwo* (*nu:* thing; *se:* to hear, feel; *nuwo:* things), which means roughly "things with which you can hear or feel things." Later he expanded the designation to *nutila nusenuwo* (*nuti:* exterior; *la:* flesh [*nutila:* human or animal body]; *nu:* thing; *se:* to hear; *nuwo:* things), which can be translated as "bodily phenomena with which you can hear (or feel, taste, smell, understand, and obey)." Sensing in general was also described as *nusiwo kpena de mia nuti hafi mienyaa nusi le dzodzom de mia dzi*, which can be translated as "things that help us to know what is happening (on) to us." Sensing was expressed by yet another Anlo person with the phrase *aleke nese le lame*, which means "how you feel within yourself" or "how you feel in your body." But the expression that seemed to be used most frequently was the very complicated and polysemous term *seselelame*.

Seselelame amounts to a culturally elaborated way in which many Anlo-Ewe people attend to and read their own bodies while simultaneously orienting themselves to objects, to the environment, and to the bodies of those around them. While it is difficult to make a direct translation into English of the term *seselelame*, since it refers to various kinds of sensory embodiment that do not fit neatly into Euro-American categories or words, we can think of it roughly in terms of "feeling in the body" or in terms of the literal translation of "feel-feel-at-flesh-inside." On one hand, it seems to refer to a specific sense or kind of physical sensation that we might call tingling in the skin (sometimes a symptom of impending illness), but in other instances it is used to describe sexual arousal or even heartache. In other contexts it refers to a kind of inspiration (to dance or to speak), but it can also be used to describe something akin to intuition (when unsure of exactly how you are coming by some information). Finally, it is also discussed as a generalized (almost synesthetic) "feeling through the body" and was proposed by some informants as a possible translation for the all-encompassing English term *sense*.

Seselelame is reminiscent of what Thomas Csordas has referred to as "somatic modes of attention" (1993). He uses this phrase to point us in the direction of "culturally elaborated ways of attending to and with one's body in surroundings that include the embodied presence of others" or "culturally *elaborated* attention *to* and *with* the body in the immediacy of an *intersubjective* milieu" (1993:138–139). Moreover, Csordas suggests that,

> Because we are not isolated subjectivities trapped within our bodies, but share an intersubjective milieu with others, we must also specify that a somatic mode of attention means not only attention to and with one's own body, but includes attention to the bodies of others. Our concern is the *cultural elaboration of sensory engagement*, not preoccupation with one's own body as an isolated phenomenon. (Csordas 1993:139, emphasis added)

Using the notion of "somatic modes of attention," how are we to understand an Anlo-Ewe phenomenon they call *seselelame*? Is it one sense or many? Is it the category of sensing in general or a specific sensory field? More fundamentally, is it even a "sense" at all, or is it better glossed as intuition, inspiration, emotion, or bodily knowing?

Here I would like to examine these questions in light of Csordas's discussion of the "poverty of our anthropological categories for going ... further in understanding what it is to attend to one's body in a mode such as that described above" (1993:147). He suggests that social scientists have a tendency to rely on the sole categories of "cognition" and "affect," even when these groupings fail to do justice to a great deal of embodied and intersubjective phenomena (Csordas 1993:147).[1] While Csordas is referring to the ethnographic descriptions he provided from Catholic Charismatic healers and Puerto Rican spiritist mediums, the point applies equally to this discussion of sensory perception and experience among Anlo-speaking people in that a phenomenon such as seselelame is both cognitive and affective – but cannot be confined to either of these categories as it encompasses or addresses even more varieties of experience. Following Csordas (1993:147), four additional categories of intuition, imagination, perception, and sensation will be used here to explore Anlo-Ewe accounts of seselelame.

We tend to think of perception as cognitive and sensation as physical, but seselelame seems to simultaneously transcend and bridge that supposed divide. In learning and employing the Ewe language, I usually translated the verb *se* or *sese* mainly as "hearing" or "feeling" (although in certain contexts it could be used to mean "tasting," "smelling," "understanding," "obeying," and also in reference to "knowing, hearing, or comprehending a language"). But an Ewe linguist recently suggested to me that *se* could actually be considered a basic perception verb, and he then translated the term *se-se-le-la-me* as "feel-feel-at-flesh-inside." So if *se* (in very broad terms) is "to perceive," we could also render *se-se-le-la-me* as "perceive-perceive-at-flesh-inside" – suggesting that seselelame then houses both the cognitive function of perception, as well as the somatic phenomenon of sensation (inside the flesh).

In addition, *seselelame* is also used in connection with certain emotional states. As one informant explained (in English): "You can feel happiness in your body, you can feel sorrow in your body, and you can feel other things, like cold. *Seselelame* describes all of these things because it is 'hearing or feeling in the body.' 'Mesi le lame' is what we say. So from that we just made a verbal noun: *seselelame*." And in a later part of the interview he referred to the experience of going to the theater: "You go and watch it, and you feel something inside. You hear music, see the actors act very well, and you feel something inside. You applaud, get up and dance, or shout something. That is a feeling and it comes through seselelame."

Another informant, Elaine, described the range of ways she thinks about experiences of seselelame in the following discussion.

seselelame can be a pain or a pleasure. I can feel pain in the body; I can enjoy another thing in the body. Somebody might be – excuse me – holding my breast and then I feel, you know, I enjoy it. So that's *seselelame*.... *Lame* is the flesh, in the body. "Lame vim": "I'm feeling pains in my body." Oh, "leke nye dokome dzidzo kpom": "I am happy." "Nye lame koe dzidzo kpom": "I am happy within myself." *Sese* is hearing – not hearing by the ear but a feeling type hearing.... Yes, *seselelame* means feeling in the body but *esia kple* means with the ear. Same spelling, same pronunciation, but different meaning. "Esia?" "Do you hear?" "Esi le lame?" "Do you feel it in your body?" ... Before you know that you are not well, you have to feel something in the *lame*.... You wake up and then you feel that, "Oh, I'm not fine." That means that you are feeling something inside you. "Seselelame deve. Nye meli nyuie egbe o. Seselelame ema." [Which means:] "There is an aching, painful feeling in my body. I'm not well, not feeling fine today. That (is that) feeling in my body." ... Sometimes you feel tiredness or a headache; you feel it through your body – *seselelame*. It's through the body that you know you're not fine.

These discussions reveal that painful and pleasurable sensations, emotional inspiration, and physiological indications of illness are all considered experiences that fall within a category of seselelame. They can often blend together in people's experience, or in their ideas about experience. So while different words might be employed in different Anlo-speaking contexts to distinguish certain phases of experience such as sensation, cognition, and imagination, attention to the connections seems to be valued, and *seselelame* is often used as the meta-term for many if not most of these inner states of being.

This point is illustrated in the following quote from an interview with Raphael in which he explained how seselelame, *sidzedze*, and *gomesese* are related (though slightly different) experiences or phenomena.

If you say *sidzedze* – in this case we are relating it to the various senses that we have mentioned in the Western sense [hearing, touch, taste, smell, and sight] – so if you say *sidzedzenu* we mean in effect that you have actually taken the thing to mind or you have actually observed the situation, analyzed it and realized that no, this is the thing.... In every level of the senses you can use it. Because it is like I said: You observe and then you analyze the situation with your brain to find out why that sensation, why that seselelame? [For example:] They say that this lady has been knocked down by a car. The man, her husband, is a good friend of mine. Your sense will tell you that you have to visit them and express sympathy. Your brain has quickly worked and actually told you your sympathy is called for at that point in time. So we would say you have realized it yourself. So it [seselelame] is just like sidzedzenu – it [sidzedzenu] is an advanced form of seselelame.... *Gomesese* is "•bderstanding" ... and is also not too different because when you have a sensation – some source of seselelame – you must analyze and understand what that thing can create within you or within the other inmates of the house. So it is a message, an external message, that you get and you have to – in a way – analyze it properly.

Raphael's explanation demonstrates the close links among sensation, perception, emotion, cognition, and so forth and indicates how seselelame is best understood utilizing numerous categories or analytic tools. Defying the divide between physical sensation and mental processes of perception, cognition, and imagination, seselelame is an indigenous category that bridges and transcends domains that in other cultural traditions might function as oppositions. Raphael also comments that one must analyze and imagine what the "messages" (messages that might otherwise be called sensations, emotions, and intuitions) create within you and within the other people in the house – revealing the intersubjective characteristic of seselelame or how it is a way of "attending to and with one's body in surroundings that include the embodied presence of others" (Csordas 1993:138–139).

One way to explore the kinds of phenomena that fall within the category of seselelame is to look at the larger class of words to which sense terms belong. As the Ewe language evolved from the closely related languages of Yoruba and Fon, there appears to have been an encoding of a perceived relationship among experiences of sensation, emotion, disposition, and vocation, such that sense words such as *hearing, tasting,* and *seeing* seem to belong to a larger class of words beginning with the prefix *nu-* (the morpheme *nu* meaning "object" or "thing").

For example, the following sensation terms begin with *nu-*: *nusese* (hearing), *nulele* (touching), *nukpokpo* (seeing), *nudodokpo* (tasting), and *nuvevesese* (smelling). In addition, some words denoting emotions or affective states begin with *nu-*, such as *nuxaxa* (grief, sorrow), *nugbenugbe* (pain, rage, being beside oneself with anger or joy), *nublanuikpokpo* (compassion, mercy, commiseration), and *nudzodzro* (longing, desirous, covetous). Furthermore, certain dispositional states attributed to persons also begin with *nu-*, for instance, *nuvowola* (a person who sins or commits evil), *nuvela* (a person who is economical or miserly), *nubiala* (a person who begs and asks for things), *nunyala* (a person who is wise and knowing), and *nublanuito* (a person who is deplorable, miserable, or unfortunate). Finally, many vocational descriptors also begin with *nu-*: *nufiala* (teacher), *nutula* (blacksmith), *nutola* (tailor), and *numela* (potter).

While this language analysis is meant to be suggestive rather than definitive, there seems to be a social interpretation implicit in this grouping, perhaps pointing to an archaic notion of links among sensing, affect, dispositions, and vocational qualities. In reflecting on these relationships, one informant suggested that he could "throw more light on the issue of disposition (a person's natural qualities of mind and character/tendency) and vocation" with some examination of "Anlo cultural logic" (Elvis Adikah, personal communication, August 10, 2001). He explained that "a unique but integral part of Anlo cultural philosophy is the belief not only in reincarnation but also destiny. It is believed that people were fated to have particular dispositions and sometimes even vocations. For instance, I know ... a good number of ... people who were believed to be the reincarnation of their grandparents."

He went on to explain that the way a family could determine the ancestor who was returning in their child was through:

> The manner of crying (when he was a child), resemblance, his gait (or style of walking), his birthmark, and even his disposition. It follows that many such ones have a predisposition to certain developments. In this respect, if the ancestor was a mild, boisterous, cranky, saintly, or mournful sort of person, [the reincarnated individual] is expected to be the same. And even sometimes his vocation, be it hunting, divination, blacksmithing, or fishing.... this philosophy is manifested in *Megbekpokpo na devi* and the *Dzonusasa* (i.e., a ritual marked with libations and tying *gblotsi* and *hloku* beads on the wrist of the infant believed to have reincarnated). Furthermore, a number of Anlo proverbs lend credence to the beliefs that people were fated to have particular dispositions or inclinations. (Elvis Adikah, personal communication, August 10, 2001)

Adikah offered two proverbs as examples. The first – "Akaga ledo megbea akoli (adukpo) o" – means, "A diseased vulture never parts company with the rubbish heap." He interpreted this to signify that "since fate (destiny) has decreed that a vulture should be a scavenger on a rubbish heap, so shall it come to pass even if the vulture is incapacitated by sickness. In the same way, if [an individual] is fated to have a mild or saintly disposition (azolime or *nonome*), or to be a blacksmith, so shall it be." The second proverb – "Menye tsimalemale tae adexe mumuna do o" – means, "The mudfish is odious by nature, but never because he does not bathe." He concluded with the reflection that "typical qualities and characteristics of a person" are the result of destiny, and "fate or destiny can be translated among Anlos as *Se* or *Ese*." In this notion of se we find both the roots of "feeling in the body" – seselelame – as well as the socioreligious phenomenon of destiny, fate, or reincarnated soul. This further reinforces the idea that there are links among the four domains of sensation, emotion, disposition, and vocation; or that in their social interpretations, bodily sensations and bodily ways of knowing link up to emotional or affective and dispositional dimensions of personality, and also connect with vocational issues, or the work in which a person is occupied or engaged.

Here we should return to one of the central questions posed at the beginning of the article, stemming from work on the cultural psychology of emotion (Shweder 1993:418): What is the general form of a meaning system that defines an experience as sensory rather than an experience of some other kind? Is sensing limited to *hearing* a sound, *seeing* a face, or *tasting* pepper? Or does sensing also encompass experiences such as balancing one's body as one sits on a stool, taking strides as one moves down the road, intuiting that some event is about to happen?

The notion of a five-senses model revolves around the external senses (hearing, touch, taste, smell, sight) and discounts our reading of internal feelings that arise from balance, kinesthesia, and proprioception. Furthermore, in this model the five senses are distinguished from emotion states such as anger, happiness, sadness, disgust, or surprise. When Anlo-Ewe people invoke the phrase or the term *seselelame* (feel-feel-at-flesh-inside), the experiences they include can range from physical sensations and emotional reactions to feelings they attribute to more generalized dispositions (often considered to be a condition or a result of se – destiny or fate). Their summary notion of this domain, seselelame, treats sensation, emotion, disposition, and vocation as a continuous

stream in a domain of bodily experience rather than as separate entities. There is an orientation toward integration in this model, which resists the separations and distinctions reified by a five senses approach. An ethnographic exploration of disposition and kinesthetic sensations, in the following section, will further develop this point.

Seselelame and the Way We Walk

Aaron and Kobla never seemed to go straight to the well when their mother sent them to fetch water. I often observed them "horsing around" as they made their way through the compound and out the gate to the community well in the village where we lived. One day, as I watched them running in circles, chasing each other, walking backwards, and swinging their buckets to and fro, I heard their mother shouting in a distressed voice something about how they were walking *lugulugu*. My ears perked up when I heard that adverb, *lugulugu*, as I had recently begun making a list of different kinds of walks or styles of comportment. I already knew that one could *zo kadzakadza* (walk like a lion),[2] or *zo minyaminya* (walk stealthily, as if eavesdropping), or *zo megbe-megbe* (walk backwards, leaving deceptive footprints). As Kobla's mother shouted at them from behind her kitchen wall, I watched them darting from one side of the compound to the other, swaying perilously on the outer edge of a foot, feigning to nearly fall down, and evidently imitating their mother's charge that they were moving lugulugu on their way to the well.

Many people considered azolizozo – movement, walking, or kinesthesia – to have sensorial qualities, and they wanted this phenomenon included in my writings about their sensorium. In addition, several informants had been insisting that I include "morality" among the senses that Anlo-Ewe people held dear. Morality had sensorial qualities, they explained, because of its close association between kinesthetic sensations (in azolizozo or movement) and dispositional feelings (in azolime or one's moral character). Both concepts share the root *zo* – to move or walk. Kobla and Aaron's mother's accusation of her sons' lugulugu approach to getting water from the well seemed like an opportune incident to probe for the logic behind these associations.

I began by asking Elaine, my research assistant, what *lugulugu* really meant. She explained that while a word such as *zo lugulugu* referred in the first instance to bodily motions such as swaying, tarrying, dawdling, or moving as if drunk, it could also be used to refer to a person's character. In response to a daughter's statement that "Kofi is the man I want to marry," Elaine explained that parents might discourage the young woman with the retort, "Tsyo! Ame lugulugu!" The expression reveals the parents' perception that Kofi was a lugulugu man: a person who did not simply move in a tarrying or dawdling fashion, but a person who was not serious – an aimless, irresponsible fellow.

So, were eight-year-old Kobla and ten-year-old Aaron already hopelessly lugulugu? I wondered if a person begins walking lugulugu first and then becomes a lugulugu person or vice versa? In response to my inquiries about this, Kobla and Aaron's mother (along with several other caregivers in our compound) made it clear that they had to be vigilant about the possibility of either. That is, a child could develop either a kind of lugulugu cognitive orientation or lugulugu somatic tendencies, but either way it would permeate other domains of personality. So in the process of fetching water from the well, when Aaron and Kobla were consistently "going this way and that," fooling around, distracting each other from the task, and stirring up trouble, the concern this evoked in their caregivers was that the phenomena that was embodied in these displays would begin to dominate their character. The logic expressed was that if you move in a lugulugu fashion you experience sensations of lugulugu-ness and begin thinking in a lugulugu way and become a lugulugu person, which is then evident to others from the way your lugulugu character is embodied in your lugulugu walk. Or, if you consistently think in a lugulugu way, you would also move in a lugulugu fashion and basically develop into a lugulugu person. Clearly, the specific

case of a kinesthetic phenomenon called *lugulugu* shows how analytic categories of language, cognition, sensation, perception, culture, and embodiment are not experienced in discrete stages at the phenomenal level or from the existential standpoint of being-in-the-world. Seselelame, I would suggest, as a model of how we process information, capitalizes on synesthetic modes of knowing.

The point is that in terms of a cultural logic found among many Anlo-speaking people, there is a clear connection or association between bodily sensations and who you are or who you become: Your character, your moral fortitude is embodied in the way you move, and the way you move embodies an essence of your nature. We should not mistake this consciousness as simply about people *seeing* the child walking lugulugu and thinking that he was wayward, but, rather, informants were quite clear about the sensations the child would experience in the body and then the imaginative structures that would develop in the mind and would be perceived by all involved as a culturally constituted and objectified phenomenon called *lugulugu*.

Perhaps we have a similar cultural logic in our own folk epistemology in Anglo-America. For example, in searching for a translation for *lugulugu*, the term *wishy-washy* comes to mind. Many English-speaking Americans probably believe that if a person feels wishy-washy day in and day out, then the person might actually carry himself with a wavering sort of comportment, and in general have an indecisive character. Intuitively, then, we can appreciate their concern. In Anlo-Ewe contexts, however, there is a striking elaboration of associations among movement, kinesthetic sensations, and moral character that deserves a closer look.

Onomatopoeia in Relation to Comportment and Gait

One notable feature of *lugulugu* – as well as other kinds of movement adverbs – is their typical reduplicated form. In addition, "walks" (which also index one's sense of morality) are symbolized with what Westermann described as "picture words (onomatopes), which attempt to express by their sound the impression conveyed by the senses" (1930:107). The Anlo-Ewe language therefore reflects the belief that movement, walking, or kinesthesia has a distinctively sensory quality. And this, I would suggest, helps to explain why azolizozo (movement) and azolime (dispositional feelings) fall into the cultural category of seselelame (feeling in the body) for so many Anlo-Ewe people.

Repetitive constructions or instances of reduplication are pervasive in the Ewe language (e.g., Ameka 1999; Ansre 1963; Sapir 1921:76–78; Westermann 1930). Ansre suggests (1963:128) that eight out of every 100 words spoken in Ewe are reduplicated terms, and in a much more recent study, Ameka indicates (1999:78) that Ansre's estimate about reduplication is probably too low. Furthermore, Samarin makes a fascinating observation that in the written version of a particular Ewe-language play there are few ideophones, but when he attended a performance, "the actors adlibbed by adding ideophones to the prepared script" (Samarin 1967:35). This undoubtedly added a sensory quality to the experience of the play that the performers felt moved to include.

In "The Power of Words in African Verbal Arts," Philip Peek suggests that "too often we have allowed our literate analytical heritage, recording methods, and concerns about texts and contexts to obscure the primacy of the oral nature of verbal art" (1981:42). He then argues that verbal art forms in African contexts should not be treated simply as "oral translations" we commit to paper. "We must continually remind ourselves of the limits of literacy and the hazards of exclusively literate scholarship. For many cultures that we seek to understand, hearing is believing" (Peek 1981:42–43). Samarin's experience of noting few ideophones in the written text, but then hearing many when the actors performed the play, is a good example of the difference between exploring certain characteristics of African languages in a literary venue and actually experiencing the speech itself. When one hears and experiences Anlo-Ewe speech, the significance of the sounds and tones of the language are readily apparent – as Samarin

implies. We will return to this point in a later discussion of "speech" as a sensory mode.

Ideophones have been described as "vivid vocal images or representations of visual, auditory and other sensory or mental experiences" (Cole 1955:370). They have also been defined as sensory nouns and as words that describe sound, color, smell, manner, appearance, state, action, or intensity (Cole 1955:370). Evans-Pritchard defined ideophones as "poetry in ordinary language" (1962:143). While not intending to take up the linguistic debate about what precisely the ideophone is or does, little disagreement exists over the notion that ideophones intend to evoke sensorially that which they represent. Indeed, when I witnessed Kobla and Aaron swaying and tarrying and swinging, and I heard their mother shouting "lugulugu," I experienced a very visceral (rather than merely intellectual) realization of what was going on – which takes us back to the issue of reduplication specifically in the arena of movement or "walks."[3]

Earlier I mentioned that while I was in the field I began to compile a set of Ewe terms indicating styles of comportment, and if we combine the number of "movement modes" that I noticed (Geurts in press) with a list prepared by Westermann (1930:107–109), it is fair to state that there are more than 50 terms in Ewe representing different kinesthetic styles – from zo bafobafo and zo bulabula to zo kodzokodzo and zo lumolumo (with the respective gloss for each being: the brisk movements made by a small man when he walks; walking without looking where one is going; walking with the body stooping forward; the hurried running of small animals, such as rats and mice [Westermann 1930:107–109]). The sheer number of ways one can talk about essentialized kinetic modes alerts us, on one level, to the significance of this domain in Ewe cultural worlds. The fact that many of these are reduplicated terms, onomatopes, or ideophones (see Westermann 1930:107) indicates a kind of "performative elaboration" (Csordas 1993:146) of the sensory dimension of azolizozo (movement) and azolime (moral essence). Or, as Sapir commented in relation to reduplication: "the process is generally employed, *with self-evident symbolism*, to indicate ... plurality, repetition, customary activity,... added intensity," and so forth (1921:76, emphasis added). And so, *with self-evident symbolism*, Ewe speakers refer to kinesthetic experiences, styles of comportment, or simply "the way you walk" with language and attitude that is saturated with sensory valuation.

Speech as a Sensory Field

If it is difficult for many Westerners to allow for movement or kinesthesia to be classified as like phenomena with hearing, touch, taste, sight, and smell; it is even more difficult for us to fathom adding "speech" to this domain. But many Anlo-Ewe speakers do include speech as a kind of "sense" or sensation, and here I will attempt to lay out their reasoning for such a categorization. First, just as sensing in their language is conceptualized with a more general term, *seselelame* (feeling in the body), speaking too falls within a broader category of experience they call *sesetonume*, which means "feeling in the mouth." This (sub)category includes sensations involved in eating, drinking, breathing, regulation of saliva, sexual exchanges, and also speech.

Because we tend to conceptualize speaking as an "active externalization of data" and we think of sensing as a passive receipt of stimulus from something outside our body, and because we think of speaking as learned and sensing as innate (Classen 1993:2–4), we tend to emphasize the distinctions between these bodily experiences. But Anlo speakers emphasize similarities and relationships in the experiences of speaking, eating, kissing, and so forth and call these all *sesetonume*: feeling in the mouth. An example of the links between speaking and a certain kind of illness may help to demonstrate further the sensorial aspects of speech.

While I was in Ghana, I attended about 15 births, and in this context I often witnessed the effects of something Anlo-speakers referred to by using the term *enu*, which translates as "mouth." In cases where labor pains were severe, when there was a delay in labor, or in the face of various complications during birth, the attending midwife usually sprayed the

woman's abdomen with saliva and brushed it with a twelve inch whisk, in an effort to discard the causes of enu. *Enu* is the term for a category of spiritual sicknesses (referred to as *gbogbomedo* and distinguished from *dotsoafe*, which are commonplace illnesses) that includes a host of afflictions to pregnant women and diseases that can kill children or render them deaf and dumb. The cause is deemed bad will or enmity among household members or kin. Contrary to what we might expect, however, it is not the meaning of the words expressing malice or malevolence that causes someone to fall ill but, rather, the sensory power contained in the sounds themselves.

The most common meaning of the word *enu* is simply "mouth," but it also refers to "opening, entrance, edge; contents, quantity; effect" (Westermann 1973:177). Pregnant women and other vulnerable adults can be seized with enu because of disrespectful, wicked, or evil things that pass through the mouths of people in the household. In fact, through sesetonume (feeling in the mouth) one can absorb one's own bad speech, and so speaking is believed to be one of the primary forces involved in the etiology of enu. Children, on the other hand, are not believed to contract enu from their own sesetonume, or feelings in the mouth, but rather through bodily absorption of the physical power of the words.

Stoller has pointed out that for the Songhay of Niger, as well as in many West African contexts, speech is believed to have a power or energy independent of its referential quality (1989:122). Words are not only information or knowledge but also sound, so in addition to their meaning, words have a physical force that operates not only at the site of the ear and mind but throughout the entire body. Peek has made a similar observation: "When we investigate beliefs concerning sound in African cultures, we find that human speech is frequently conceived as a tangible entity" and that "auditory space is perceived as a physical field" (1981:21). The Anlo term for speech and talking (*nufofo*) contains the morpheme *fo*, which means to strike, beat, blow – symbolizing the dynamic power ascribed to the words themselves. As a scholar of the neighboring Fon people has stated, "Critical to the activation potential of speech is both its transferential nature and its potent social and psychodynamic grounding" (Blier 1995:77). The "transferential nature" of nufofo (speaking) includes more than imparting meaning or "mental ideas," for in enu, speaking is one of the culprits in the transference of emotional and physiological disturbance, especially to children. In the presence of an acrimonious verbal exchange, it is not simply the meaning of the dialogue that causes children and pregnant women to fall sick but, rather, it is perceived as a phenomenon of seselelame (feeling in the body), and the animosity and rancor is transferred to their bodies in part through the striking action of the sound of speech itself. This reinforces the local cultural logic that "speech is irreversible; that is its fatality. What has been said cannot be unsaid, except by adding to it" (Blier 1995:76–77).

So it is not simply the hearing of an argument and the consequent psychological effect that is at stake here but, rather, the notion that once speech containing animus is externalized, adults can absorb their own anger through sesetonume (feeling in the mouth) and children absorb the rancor through seselelame (feeling in the body, flesh, or skin). Clearly, the proverb "Sticks and stones may break my bones, but words will never hurt me" would not ring true in this cultural setting. There is a level of direct experience and integration (in this cultural model of how experience occurs and how information is processed) that makes it somewhat different than what I earlier called the "five-senses model." That is to say, the five-senses model creates the illusion that we experience the world through distinct, separate modes of hearing, touch, taste, sight, and smell. It suggests to us that words can be experienced simply as meanings entering our minds through the ear, and it discounts the import of the sound itself. This is not to say that Euro-American English-speaking people do not pay attention to the tone of voice in which someone delivers a message but, rather, that our intellectual model for how we experience speech lacks the theory of sensory integration that we find in the Anlo-Ewe category of seselelame, which suggests that the word itself

(independent of a psychological processing of its meaning) has the sensory power to change a person's state of being.

Conclusion

Now that we have explored how *walks* and *talks* help further our understanding of Anlo-Ewe cultural categories and an anthropology of the senses, it is time to return to *rocks*, and to my experience of driving over the stone in the center of our compound. I recently came across several written versions of a trickster story called "Yiyi kple Kadzidoe" ("Spider and the Squirrel"). Both sources attribute this story to Ewe speakers, but it may be a tale that has circulated more generally throughout Africa. Nonetheless, in Ewe worlds Yiyi is the Trickster (Ananse in Ashanti contexts) who figures prominently in West African psychology and lore.

Joseph Bruchac recounted this story in the following way:

One year there is a great famine. Everyone goes out looking for food. As Yiyi walks along, he comes upon a stone with eyes. But he is so tired that he says nothing. He just sits down under a tree near the stone. An antelope comes along and sees the stone.

"It is a stone with eyes!" the antelope says. Then it falls down dead.

Interesting, Yiyi thinks. He drags the antelope home for dinner. Next day he goes back by the stone. A rabbit comes by.

"What is that?" says Yiyi, pointing at the stone.

"It is a stone with eyes," says the rabbit.

The rabbit falls down dead, too. Yiyi drags it home. From then on, every day, Yiyi goes out and sits by that stone.

One day, though, a squirrel is up in that tree. It sees what Yiyi is doing. It comes down the tree and walks by Yiyi.

"What is that?" says Yiyi, pointing at the stone.

"What is that?" says the squirrel.

"That there," says Yiyi.

"I don't see anything," says the squirrel.

"Are you blind?" says Yiyi, getting angry. "That!"

"What?" says the squirrel.

Yiyi says, "Can't you see? It is a stone with eyes."

Then Yiyi falls down dead.

(1997:21–22)

Earlier I mentioned that in Ewe worlds stones may not be what they seem. A legba, in fact, while it may appear to be a stone, is a spiritual guardian of thresholds. There are *legbawo* (plural form of *legba*) that have been constructed by humans, and these often have more distinctive shape to the face or body than did the one over which I drove the tire. But there are also legbawo that have been placed in their position not by humans but by spirits or gods, and these often merely resemble a rock.

Shweder makes a similar point about *weeds* in his effort to explain cultural psychology's concept of *intentional worlds*. He argues that "Because a weed is a weed is a weed, but only in some intentional world, there is no impersonal, neutral, 'objective,' 'scientific,' independent-of-human-response, botanical, genetic, or 'natural kind' definition of plants that we can specify *in the abstract* or *in general* which ones count as weeds" (Shweder 1991:75). His point is that "intentional things" have no identity or natural reality outside of our perceptions and designations of them as "weeds" or a "legba" or a "rock." He suggests that,

in some fascinating and important sense, the weeds in our gardens achieve their reality because we are implicated in their existence, and we achieve our reality, at least in part, by letting them become implicated in ours. Our identities interpenetrate and take each other into account. Without us nature knows little of the existence of weeds. (Shweder 1991:75)

How one responds to a particular plant – shall I eat it? sell it? burn it? use it as medicine? – is contingent upon sociocultural context and biosocialization. While all human groups experience and talk about "feeling in the body," the particular version that might cause a person to sense fear when driving over a stone is seselelame.

What do these examples then reveal about the *generic shape of the meaning system* that governs sensory experiences in Anlo-Ewe

worlds? Raphael made the point that "when you have a sensation – some source of seselelame – you must analyze and understand what that thing can create within you or within the other inmates of the house. It is a message ... and you have to analyze it properly." Seselelame, in certain ways, can be conceived of as a way of attending to and processing such "messages" – which include sensations, perceptions, intuitions, emotions, and even imaginations. It is, in the first instance, a category of "feelings within the body" – literally, "feel-feel-at-flesh-inside." But as Raphael makes clear, seselelame goes beyond pure physical sensation.

When I drove my tire over the legba in the center of our compound, I experienced a flood of sensations, emotions, and intuitions that I nonetheless ignored since my "cognitive system" concluded that it was simply a rock. Having been conditioned, throughout my life and in particular through my training as an academic, to dismiss such "feelings" as I had when running over the rock, I was able (or willing) to distinguish the different facets of the experience: (1) the sensation of the car tire in contact with an obstructing object, (2) the startle in my body or a physiological jolt, (3) the intuition that it was taboo in this cultural context to drive over this particular object, and (4) the cognitive conclusion that in the end it was only a rock. Raphael told me that my response was simply foolish. He wondered how I could receive so many "messages" about the significance of this event and still take such a materialist perspective – concluding that it was simply a rock. This would be like Kobla and Aaron's mother thinking, "Oh, it's just a walk," rather than knowing the connections between the sensations of lugulugu and the potential for her sons to turn into lugulugu boys.

In conclusion, *seselelame* represents a cultural meaning system in which bodily feeling is attended to as a source of vital information. Instead of concentrating on distinctions between sensations and emotions, and between intuition and cognition, these experiences (or processes) are often subsumed in one category called *seselelame*. Integration of processes is valued, so that a direct connection is perceived between ways of moving and sensations of motion with how one thinks and the kind of disposition one harbors as a core of one's moral character.

Antonio Damasio (1999) has described similar processes of subjective experiences among Western populations and has argued that there are clear links among bodily feelings, emotions, consciousness, and cognition. I want to make clear, therefore, that I am not suggesting that seselelame will be completely foreign or counterintuitive in relation to experiences that many Euro-Americans might have. But traditional models for *how we think about how we perceive* do indeed contain rather rigid distinctions between body and mind, between feeling and thought, and seselelame contains little of that dichotomous analysis.

"Probably every cultural category 'creates' an entity, in the sense that what is understood to be 'out there' is affected by the culturally based associations built into the category system" (D'Andrade 1984:91). While the five-senses model has been "created" as a cultural category through the process of more than two thousand years of Western tradition, in seselelame we are confronted with not only the nonuniversality of the five-senses model but with an Anlo theory of the nature of being and an Anlo theory of knowing that thoroughly and completely links knowledge and reason, along with the development of morality and identity, to the body and to *feelings in the flesh*.

NOTES

Acknowledgments. The research on which this article is based was funded by a Fulbright-Hays Doctoral Research Abroad Grant (#P022A30073) and the University of Pennsylvania Department of Anthropology. A National Institute of Mental Health postdoctoral research fellowship at the University of Chicago's Committee on Human Development, and a Weatherhead Residential Fellowship at the School of American Research, afforded me the time to reflect and write about the research. Names and descriptions of individuals in this article have been altered to conceal their actual identities, but I am grateful to numerous Anlo-Ewe colleagues for their insightful comments on various versions of this article.

1 For an exception to this, see D'Andrade 1987. This article uses perception, emotion, desire, beliefs and knowledge, intentions and resolutions in exploring a folk model of the mind, not limiting the analysis to the dichotomous categories of cognition and affect.

2 In Westermann's dictionary, *zɔ kadzakadza* is translated as "to walk awkwardly, clumsily." However, my informants adamantly disagreed with this gloss and explained that *zɔ kadzakadza* is "to walk like a lion." This seems to be reinforced by Westermann's translation of *akadza*, which is "readiness, as for a fight." Informants indicated that lions walk assertively, forcefully, majestically, even exhibiting an air of challenge (as if ready for a fight). In addition, the term *lion* in Ewe is *dzata*.

3 Here I invoke my own experience when hearing the word *lugulugu*, but Ewe speakers report that they themselves experience these reduplicated terms as both humorous and sensorially evocative. They state that they purposefully choose these kinds of terms when they want to drive home a point in a colorful way and summon *feelings* in their audience, in addition to images or thoughts.

REFERENCES

Ameka, Felix K.
  1999 The Typology and Semantics of Complex Nominal Duplication in Ewe. Anthropological Linguistics 41(1):75–106.
Ansre, Gilbert
  1963 Reduplication in Ewe. Journal of African Languages 2:128–132.
Blier, Suzanne Preston
  1995 African Vodun: Art, Psychology, and Power. Chicago: University of Chicago Press.
Bruchac, Joseph
  1997 Tell Me a Tale. New York: Harcourt Brace and Company.
Classen, Constance
  1993 Worlds of Sense: Exploring the Senses in History and across Cultures. London: Routledge.
Cole, Desmond T.
  1955 An Introduction to Tswana Grammar. London: Longmans Green.
Csordas, Thomas J.
  1993 Somatic Modes of Attention. Cultural Anthropology 8(2):135–156.

Damasio, Antonio
 1999   The Feeling of What Happens: Body
 and Emotion in the Making of Consciousness.
 San Diego: Harcourt.
D'Andrade, Roy
 1984   Cultural Meaning Systems. *In* Culture
 Theory. R. A. Shweder and R. A. LeVine, eds.
 pp. 88–119. New York: Cambridge University
 Press.
D'Andrade, Roy
 1987   A Folk Model of the Mind. *In* Cultural
 Models in Language and Thought. D. Holland
 and N. Quinn, eds. pp. 112–148. New York:
 Cambridge University Press.
Evans-Pritchard, E. E.
 1962   Ideophones in Zande. Sudan Notes and
 Records 43:143–146.
Geurts, Kathryn Linn
 In press   Culture and the Senses: Bodily Ways
 of Knowing in an African Community.
 Berkeley: University of California Press.
Markus, Hazel R., Shinobu Kitayama, and
 Rachel J. Heiman
 1996   Culture and "Basic" Psychological
 Principles. *In* Social Psychology: Handbook
 of Basic Principles. E. T. Higgens and
 A. W. Kruglanski, eds. pp. 857–913. New York:
 Guilford Press.
Peek, Philip M.
 1981   The Power of Words in African Verbal
 Arts. Journal of American Folklore 94(371):
 19–43.
Samarin, W. J.
 1967   Determining the Meanings of Ideophones.
 Journal of West African Languages 4(2): 35–41.

Sapir, Edward
 1921   Language: An Introduction to the Study
 of Speech. New York: Harcourt, Brace.
Shweder, Richard
 1991   Thinking through Cultures: Expeditions
 in Cultural Psychology. Cambridge, MA:
 Harvard University Press.
Shweder, Richard
 1993   The   Cultural   Psychology   of   the
 Emotions.   *In*   Handbook   of   Emotions.
 M. Lewis and J. Haviland, eds. pp. 417–431.
 New York: Guilford Press.
Stein, Howard F.
 2000   From Countertransference to Social
 Theory: A Study of Holocaust Thinking
 in   U.S.   Business   Dress.   Ethos   28(3):
 346–378.
Stoller, Paul
 1989   The Taste of Ethnographic Things:
 The Senses in Anthropology. Philadelphia:
 University of Pennsylvania Press.
Stoller, Paul
 1997   Sensuous   Scholarship.   Philadelphia:
 University of Pennsylvania Press.
Westermann, Diedrich
 1930   A   Study   of   the   Ewe   Language.
 A. L. Bickford-Smith, trans. London: Oxford
 University Press.
Westermann, Diedrich
 1973[1928]   Eweflala or Ewe-English Dictionary.
 Nendeln: Kraus-Thompson Organization, Kraus
 Reprint.

Part IX

Reflexive Ethnography

Introduction

Antonius C. G. M. Robben

Reflexive ethnography arose from a critique of existing fieldwork practices and forms of textual representation. Bronislaw Malinowski (see Chapter 3) had turned participant observation into the queen of anthropological field methods, and pioneered a combination of empathy and detachment, allowing an ethnographer to alternate the native's point of view with an objective stance. However, behind this seemingly controlled insider–outsider dialectic, there was continuous negotiation between fieldworker and informants about cultural representation which was shielded from readers by the ethnographer's rhetorical authority. Anthropologists did not pay attention to the power relation between fieldworker and informant, the intersubjective construction of field notes, and the translation of experience and dialogue into authoritative texts. These objectified ethnographies, so argues Clifford (1988), came under increasing attack in the 1960s because they ignored the voices of the informants and the subjective experiences of the fieldworkers. Influenced by a range of theories, notably hermeneutics, critical theory, feminist theory, ethnomethodology, and symbolic interactionism (see Alvesson and Sköldberg 2001), anthropologists began to emphasize the importance of meaning, interpretation, and intersubjectivity. An analogy was drawn between cultures and texts, because grasping the multiple meanings of actions and practices, just as understanding the many meanings of words and sentences, required interpretation. The most direct influence of this approach on ethnographic fieldwork and writing was a commitment to so-called thick description. Thick description involved an interpretation of the intertwined cultural constructions and social discourses of actors. This exegesis would result in a richly textured, multilayered,

Ethnographic Fieldwork: An Anthropological Reader, Second Edition. Edited by
Antonius C. G. M. Robben and Jeffrey A. Sluka.
Editorial material and organization © 2012 John Wiley & Sons, Inc.
Published 2012 by John Wiley & Sons, Inc.

and multi voiced ethnography (Geertz 1973). Such interpretation would be achieved methodologically by way of a hermeneutic circle in which understanding was advanced in circular, rather than linear, ways between part and whole, and back again. Clifford Geertz (1973) and David Schneider (1968) were at the forefront of this movement, which became known as interpretive anthropology, while the French philosopher Paul Ricoeur had an important theoretical impact (Ricoeur 1974; see also Rabinow and Sullivan 1979).

The postmodern turn of the 1970s heightened anthropology's awareness of the epistemology of fieldwork relations, the constitutive position of the researcher, and the prevalent styles of ethnographic writing. Reflexivity, i.e., the conscious self-examination of the ethnographer's interpretive presuppositions, enriched fieldwork by making anthropologists pay much closer attention to the intersubjective processes through which they acquired, shared, and transmitted knowledge. It implied a conscious reflection on the interpretive nature of fieldwork, the construction of ethnographic authority, the interdependence of ethnographer and informant, and the involvement of the ethnographer's self in fieldwork. Reflexivity also prompted an interest in narrative styles, because if ethnography was all about intercultural and intersubjective translation and construction, then form, style, and rhetoric were of central importance (see Dumont 1978; Ruby 1982; Clifford and Marcus 1986; Dwyer 1987; Geertz 1988; Trencher 2000). Concern for meaning, interpretation, subjectivity, intersubjectivity, thick description, dialogics, and polyphony found their way into standard fieldwork practice and social science methodology (Alvesson and Sköldberg 2001; for a critique, see Salzman 2002).

In "Fieldwork and Friendship in Morocco," from his book *Reflections on Fieldwork in Morocco* (1977), Paul Rabinow emphasizes that fieldwork is an intersubjective construction which relies heavily on the encounter between ethnographer and research participant. Anthropology is therefore an interpretive science which necessarily involves an unending search for meaning. Under the influence of his mentor Clifford Geertz, Rabinow regards culture as a heterogeneous web of meanings spun by people themselves, thus requiring interpretation and translation. Such translation is especially crucial during fieldwork in foreign cultures. Local people must first make sense of their own culture and then find the right discourse to explain it to a foreign ethnographer who lacks any lived experience in the community under study. Informants situated at the margins of society, as was the case for all but one of Rabinow's research participants, are ideal cultural interpreters because they have the ability to view several worlds from across the social fences that set them apart.

Rabinow describes Sefrou, an oasis market town in the Middle Atlas Mountains of Morocco, through a patchwork of fieldwork relations with a French expatriate, five Moroccans located at different places in Sefrou society, and his host ben Mohammed, who was positioned firmly in the local community. The book describes Rabinow's progressive involvement with these seven key persons from the foreign outsider Richard to the native insider ben Mohammed, from the social periphery to the social heart of Sefrou, without privileging the cultural understanding of any one of them. Each informant revealed unique aspects of Sefrou society because of his social position, opinions, and beliefs. Nonetheless, despite this diversity among his informants, Rabinow senses one fundamental divide between him and his Moroccan informants: the different pasts, historical traditions, and religious backgrounds. This awareness opened the way for a deeper intercultural reflection based on the acceptance of a fundamental cultural difference between the American ethnographer and the Moroccan research participants.

Jeanne Favret-Saada suggests, in "The Way Things Are Said," from her book *Deadly Words: Witchcraft in the Bocage* (1980[1977]), that only a complete surrender to the discourse of her interlocutors allowed her to understand witchcraft in western France. People in the Bocage suspect witchcraft after suffering a series of unusual misfortunes. The victim approaches doctors, therapists, priests, and eventually unwitchers, who, each from their own branch of knowledge, interpret the tragic events and recommend a cure. The unwitcher acknowledges witchcraft as the principal cause, traces the victim's soft spots, and identifies the witch through harmful words uttered in the past. The unwitcher turns those deadly words around, directs them against the witch, positions him- or herself between witch and victim, and seals the victim's weak spots.

Favret-Saada argues that the only way to understand witchcraft in the Bocage was to accept the position of an unwitcher. A detached objectivist stance (as taken by French folklorists), an apprenticeship (recommended by anthropologists), a verbal translation (employed by Rabinow), or even a dialogic exchange (practiced by Crapanzano 1980 and Dwyer 1987), would all fall short. Favret-Saada was faced with a body of literature that dismissed Bocage witchcraft as a superstitious belief, an exotic anachronism in modern France, an example of the peasants' pre-logical backwardness, and their inability to distinguish cause and effect. Evans-Pritchard's classic ethnography *Witchcraft, Oracles, and Magic among the Azande* (1968[1937]) comes to mind but, unlike Evans-Pritchard, Favret-Saada was not out to prove that the Bocage peasants were in full possession of their rational faculties, despite their belief in witchcraft. Instead, she argues, witchcraft did not exist in some esoteric knowledge or secret spells, but in the harmful words spoken by a witch or an unwitcher. There was no template beyond the words themselves. Words were power. Therefore, knowledge about witchcraft was powerful and could not be shared with a neutral, disinterested fieldworker because such knowledge implicated the researcher in the conflictive world itself. So, Favret-Saada had to demonstrate that she had been "caught" as either a bewitched victim or as an unwitcher to elicit the discourse of witchcraft victims and unwitchers.

Whereas Favret-Saada surrenders to Bocage culture, discourse, and practice to achieve an insider's perspective, in "Transmutation of Sensibilities: Empathy, Intuition, Revelation" (2007), Thomas Csordas reveals the shadow side of ethnographic immersion. The shadow side refers to field experiences, often mysterious, that cannot be situated in a larger ethnographic framework and are therefore left out and remain unspoken. Leibing and McLean (2007:3) distinguish two poles to the continuum of such residual experiences: a focus on uncanny personal experiences that give insight into social phenomena, or a focus on shadows encountered through the fieldworker's intersubjective negotiation with interlocutors. Csordas addresses the first approach by analyzing personal shadows that are entirely in tune with the field's cultural milieu and could have happened just as well to the people studied. He describes these unexpected moments as the transmutation of sensibilities to indicate the anthropological reflexivity embedded in these unexpected revelatory experiences.

In 1973, Csordas was conducting fieldwork among 30 members of a weekly prayer group living in the town where he had grown up. They wanted to start a healing ministry that would attend to sick people by the laying on of hands. The faithful belonged to the Catholic Charismatic Renewal movement, which believed that God could speak through the mouth and mind of the brethren. Suddenly, Csordas received a prophecy that cautioned the congregation about its plan. He shared this divine intervention with the priest, who merely acknowledged it. Csordas explains this experience as a combination of empathy for the group's authentic religiosity and his intuitive worries about the emotional costs of the healing mission, together with his thorough study of ritual speech, the immersion in prayer meetings, and the witnessing of prophecies revealed by charismatic believers.

The second example in which experiences were transmuted into a local cultural form occurred during a Night Way ritual at which masked Navajo dancers represent deities or *yei-bi-cheis*. Taking a drink from a wooden dipper, Csordas saw a deity reflected in the water. This revelation was not an hallucination. Csordas explains that he had been sensitized to this particular Navajo imagery because of his embodiment of Navajo performative conventions and dispositions. He would not have identified the same mirror image in another cultural setting as a Navajo deity, but as something entirely different.

The third example also took place among the Navajo, but this time at a prayer meeting of the Native American Church. Participants consume the hallucinogenic peyote cactus to communicate with the creator spirit. On the morning after one ceremony, as the mescaline was wearing off, Csordas felt an urge to drive to the gas station because his car was low on fuel. Once at the station, he decided to call his family. His wife picked up the phone and told him that their nine-year-old son had dreamt that his father was driving across an expanse of water with a group of people when he noticed that the car was running out of gas. The son then handed his father a gallon of gas. The concurrence of dream and real-life experience was brought about by Csordas's awareness of his son's unease with his field trips, and this feeling became couched in the idiom of the Navajo ritual. Csordas deduces from these three examples of fieldwork's shadow side that the intersubjectivity of empathy, the cultural connectedness of intuition, and uncanny revelations constitute the transmutation of sensibilities by fieldworkers who draw on the cultural performances and dispositions of their host cultures.

In his article, "'At the Heart of the Discipline': Critical Reflections on Fieldwork" (2010), Vincent Crapanzano reflects on the field encounter rather than participant observation. He is particularly interested in analyzing the intersubjective data-gathering process, drawing on his vast fieldwork experience among religious Haitian refugees in New York, white South African Pentecostalists awaiting the end of apartheid, the Navajos, Sufis in Morocco, born-again Christians in Los Angeles, and Algerian expatriates in France (for other studies attentive to the field encounter, see, in particular, Crapanzano 1972, 1980, 1985). Crapanzano formulates 12 generalizations about the complex internal dynamics of the ethnographic encounter. The gist is that the encounter between fieldworker and informant is a unique intersubjective engagement that waxes, wanes, and is reconstituted over time, and requires empathy and candidness by both interlocutors to be productive. The field encounter is at the same time complicated by the fieldworker's scientific desire for generalization, the prejudice of disciplinary premises, the disregard of external influences, the unawareness of unconscious cultural assumptions, and a lack of transparency about the ongoing discursive and interactional negotiation. These complications lead to misunderstandings, breakdowns in the dialogic flow, and accidental and contingent occurrences that can be troubling but also insightful.

Crapanzano does not conceive of the field encounter as a one-to-one relation or a purely dyadic or interpersonal negotiation between two interlocutors. Their exchanges are mediated by what he has termed the "Third" that defines the encounter's parameters, interpretive strategies, and modes of communication. This authoritative Third can refer to abstract conventions such as grammar or the law, to imagined figures such as spirits and gods, and to real persons such as fathers and mentors. The two interlocutors are influenced and formed by these multiple influences on their lives, and invoke them in the intersubjective negotiation process whose outcomes are gathered as data by the ethnographer.

Crapanzano also warns against reducing the field encounter to an I–other opposition. There are many distinctive qualities to the relation because the interlocutors can love, hate, seduce, idealize, persuade, derogate, anger, sadden, mistrust, dismiss, humiliate, and test one another. He illustrates how he had been put to the test during fieldwork when being obliged to drink a large amount of alcohol, building a long fence, eating unfamiliar food, and being challenged about his libido, language skills, and knowledge of the Bible. Informants used these tests as intersubjective strategies to obtain valuable information about him.

The analysis of fieldwork's psychodynamics by Csordas (2007) and Crapanzano (2010) manifests a shift from meaning to emotion in reflexive anthropology. In the 1950s and 1960s, Lévi-Strauss (1978[1955]), Bowen (1964), Powdermaker (1967), and Briggs (1970) had written about their personal emotions in the field, while Devereux (1967) had delineated the methodological implications. But Rosaldo's (1989) revealing self-analysis of the unsuspected anger and rage experienced after his wife's accidental fall to death while conducting fieldwork, and the accompanying ethnographic insight into the headhunting practices of bereaved Ilongot men in the Philippines, marked the beginning of a more sustained study of field emotions or emotional reflexivity (see, e.g., McLean and Leibing 2007; Borneman and Hammoudi 2009; Davies and Spencer 2010; Spencer and Davies 2010). This appreciation of the epistemology of personal and interpersonal emotions experienced during fieldwork has also renewed reflexive ethnography's interest in textual representation (for a critique, see Beatty 2010).

REFERENCES

Alvesson, Mats, and Kaj Sköldberg
 2001 *Reflexive Methodology: New Vistas for Qualitative Research*. London: Sage.
Beatty, Andrew
 2010 How Did It Feel for You? Emotion, Narrative, and the Limits of Ethnography. *American Anthropologist* 112(3):430–443.
Borneman, John and Abdellah Hammoudi, eds.
 2009 *Being There: The Fieldwork Encounter and the Making of Truth*. Berkeley: University of California Press.

Bowen, Elenore Smith (a pseudonym for Laura Bohannan)
  1964   *Return to Laughter: An Anthropological Novel*. Garden City, NY: Natural History
  Library.
Briggs, Jean L.
  1970   *Never in Anger: Portrait of an Eskimo Family*. Cambridge, MA: Harvard University
  Press.
Clifford, James
  1988   *The Predicament of Culture: Twentieth-Century Ethnography, Literature, and Art*.
  Cambridge, MA: Harvard University Press.
Clifford, James and George E. Marcus, eds.
  1986   *Writing Culture: The Poetics and Politics of Ethnography*. Berkeley: University of
  California Press.
Crapanzano, Vincent
  1972   *The Fifth World of Forster Bennett: Portrait of a Navajo*. New York: Viking Press.
Crapanzano, Vincent
  1980   *Tuhami: Portrait of a Moroccan*. Chicago: University of Chicago Press.
Crapanzano, Vincent
  1985   *Waiting: The Whites of South Africa*. New York: Random House.
Crapanzano, Vincent
  2010   "At the Heart of the Discipline": Critical Reflections on Fieldwork. In: *Emotions in
  the Field: The Psychology and Anthropology of Fieldwork Experience*. James Davies and
  Dimitrina Spencer, eds., pp. 55–78. Stanford: Stanford University Press.
Csordas, Thomas
  2007   Transmutation of Sensibilities: Empathy, Intuition, Revelation. In: *The Shadow Side
  of Fieldwork: Exploring the Blurred Borders between Ethnography and Life*. Athena
  McLean and Annette Leibing, eds., pp. 106–116. Malden, MA: Blackwell.
Davies, James and Dimitrina Spencer, eds.
  2010   *Emotions in the Field: The Psychology and Anthropology of Fieldwork Experience*.
  Stanford: Stanford University Press.
Devereux, George
  1967   *From Anxiety to Method in the Behavioral Sciences*. The Hague: Mouton.
Dumont, Jean-Paul
  1978   *The Headman and I: Ambiguity and Ambivalence in the Fieldworking Experience*.
  Austin: University of Texas Press.
Dwyer, Kevin
  1987[1982]   *Moroccan Dialogues: Anthropology in Question*. Prospect Heights, IL:
  Waveland Press.
Evans-Pritchard, E. E.
  1968[1937]   *Witchcraft, Oracles and Magic among the Azande*. Oxford: Clarendon Press.
Favret-Saada, Jeanne
  1980[1977]   *Deadly Words: Witchcraft in the Bocage*. Cambridge: Cambridge University
  Press.
Geertz, Clifford
  1973   *The Interpretation of Cultures*. New York: Basic Books.
Geertz, Clifford
  1988   *Works and Lives: The Anthropologist as Author*. Stanford: Stanford University
  Press.
Leibing, Annette and Athena McLean
  2007   "Learn to Value Your Shadow!" An Introduction to the Margins of Fieldwork. In:
  *The Shadow Side of Fieldwork: Exploring the Blurred Borders between Ethnography and
  Life*. Athena McLean and Annette Leibing, eds., pp. 1–28. Malden, MA: Blackwell.

Lévi-Strauss, Claude
1978[1955] *Tristes Tropiques*. New York: Atheneum.
McLean, Athena and Annette Leibing, eds.
2007 *The Shadow Side of Fieldwork: Exploring the Blurred Borders between Ethnography and Life*. Malden: Blackwell.
Powdermaker, Hortense
1967 *Stranger and Friend: The Way of an Anthropologist*. London: Secker and Warburg.
Rabinow, Paul
1977 *Reflections on Fieldwork in Morocco*. Berkeley: University of California Press.
Rabinow, Paul and William M. Sullivan, eds.
1979 *Interpretive Social Science: A Reader*. Berkeley: University of California Press.
Ricoeur, Paul
1974 *The Conflict of Interpretations: Essays in Hermeneutics*. Evanston, IL: Northwestern University Press.
Rosaldo, Renato
1989 *Culture and Truth: The Remaking of Social Analysis*. Boston, MA: Beacon Press.
Ruby, Jay, ed.
1982 *A Crack in the Mirror: Reflexive Perspectives in Anthropology*. Philadelphia: University of Pennsylvania Press.
Salzman, Philip Carl
2002 On Reflexivity. *American Anthropologist* 104(3):805–813.
Schneider, David M.
1968 *American Kinship: A Cultural Account*. Englewood Cliffs, NJ: Prentice-Hall.
Spencer, Dimitrina and James Davies, eds.
2010 *Anthropological Fieldwork: A Relational Process*. Cambridge: Cambridge Scholars Publishing.
Trencher, Susan R.
2000 *Mirrored Images: American Anthropology and American Culture, 1960–1980*. Westport, CN: Bergin and Garvey.

32

Fieldwork and Friendship in Morocco

Paul Rabinow

8 Friendship

Driss ben Mohammed, a jovial, portly, and even-tempered young man, had consistently refused to work as an informant. Over the course of my stay we had come to know each other casually, as time permitted, almost accidentally. Gradually, a certain trust had flowered between us. At its root, I think, was an awareness of our differences and a mutual respect.

Ben Mohammed was not afraid of me (as many other villagers were), nor did he have hesitations about associating with Europeans (although he had had almost no personal contact with them), nor did he seek to profit from my presence (he refused most gifts). Simply, he was my host and treated me with the respect which is supposed to be reserved for a guest, even one who stayed as long as I did.

To be friends, according to Aristotle, two people "must be mutually recognized as bearing goodwill and wishing well to each other ... either because of utility, pleasure, or good.... That type of friendship stemming from the good is best because ... that which is good without qualification is also pleasant, but such friendships require time and familiarity ... a wish for friendship may arise quickly but friendship does not."[1]

As time wore on and my friendship with ben Mohammed deepened, I was learning more and more from him. During the last months of fieldwork, when he was home from school and we could spend many of the hot hours together, the field experience, now nearing its completion, reached a new emotional and intellectual depth. Casually, without plan or schedule, just walking around the fields, ripe with grain or muddy from the irrigation water in the truck gardens, we had a meandering series of conversations. Ben Mohammed's initial refusal of informant status set up the possibility of another type of communication. But clearly our communication would not have been possible without those

Paul Rabinow, "Fieldwork and Friendship in Morocco," pp. 142–162 from *Reflections on Fieldwork in Morocco*. Berkeley: University of California Press, 1977. Copyright © 1997 by The Regents of the University of California. Reprinted by permission of the University of California Press.

Ethnographic Fieldwork: An Anthropological Reader, Second Edition. Edited by Antonius C. G. M. Robben and Jeffrey A. Sluka.
Editorial material and organization © 2012 John Wiley & Sons, Inc.
Published 2012 by John Wiley & Sons, Inc.

more regularized and disciplined relationships I had had with others. Partly in reaction to the professional situation, we had slipped into a more unguarded and relaxed course over the months.

Although we talked of many things, perhaps the most significant set of discussions turned on our relations to our separate traditions. It would have been almost impossible to have had such conversations with either Ali or Malik, enmeshed as they were in the web of their own local world. Nor, for that matter, would it have been possible with many of the Frenchified Moroccan intellectuals; half torn out of their own ill-understood traditions, and afflicted with a heightened and unhappy self-consciousness, they would be unable to bridge the gap either way. Ben Mohammed, in his own modest way, was also an intellectual, but he was one of those who still looked to Fez rather than Paris for his inspiration. This provided a crucial space between us.

The fundamental tenet of Islam, for ben Mohammed, was that all believers are equal before Allah, even though pride, egoism, and ignorance obscure this fact. Very, very, few people, in his view, actually believe in Islam. Most take only a "narrow" view: they think that if they merely follow the basic prescriptions then they are Muslims. Ben Mohammed emphatically disagreed. If belief in the equality among believers and in submission to Allah is not in your heart, and does not inform your actions, then prayer or even the pilgrimage to Mecca counts for nothing. *Niya*, or intention, is the key. You might be able to fool your neighbors by shallow adherence to externals, but you would not fool Allah. Today, for ben Mohammed, the true Muslim is mistrusted in the Islamic world. People interpret generosity and submission as weakness or foolishness. Boasting, hypocrisy, quarreling, and fighting prevail because people do not truly understand and accept the wisdom of Islam.

He brought up the example of Sidi Lahcen. Most of the saint's descendants knew little if anything about his teachings or his "path." They are ignorant. Yet they feel superior to other Muslims because they are descended from a famous saint and can lay claim to his *baraka*, to his holiness. But if they would read the books which their patron saint wrote, they would see that Sidi Lahcen himself fought against such vanity. He had preached submission to Allah alone. The only true nobles in Islam were those who lived exemplary lives and followed Allah. Sidi Lahcen's descendants, however, by relying on his spiritual strength, had lost their own. They think that their genealogical connections alone should command respect; Sidi Lahcen would have disagreed.

Ben Mohammed was striving, he said, to follow the path of Sidi Lahcen. But it posed specific problems for him. His father, whom he respected, vehemently opposed his "reformist" interpretations. This would not change ben Mohammed's personal beliefs, but it was his duty to respect those of his father. Ben Mohammed knew that his father, an old man set in his ways, was not about to alter his views. Actually, Sidi Lahcen himself had taken a parallel stance in his own age: popular religion was to be combatted in its excesses but tolerated for its piety.

For ben Mohammed the tensions of his world view turned on these two Moroccan alternatives. Morocco's future was far from bright. He would have great difficulty in finding the kind of work and life he desired. His expectations were geared to those of his country. But he also knew that the symbols and guides for the future would have to be drawn from Morocco's tradition. Moroccans could not ignore the West. This attitude required borrowing, integrating, and eliminating certain archaic and oppressive practices, but it did not mean merely imitating the West; and most important of all, it did not require the abandonment of Islam.

With most informants, I would have stopped at this point of generality. But with ben Mohammed I felt I could proceed further. Throughout my stay in Morocco I had noticed that black was negatively valued in a variety of ways. In the broadest terms, white was generally equated with good and black with evil. Malik in particular seemed consistently concerned about color distinctions and their symbolism. Black was bad, according to his view, a color worthy of a dog. The lighter you are the better you are, the more you shone in the eyes of Allah. Malik was joking one day about a very poor villager. He said the man was so poor he would have to marry a black. Malik's new-born daughter, he pointed out innumerable times, was very white. When I showed him pictures of America he always made a point of saying that he could not tell if the blacks were men or women. He had been very upset when he found out that one of his favorite songs on the radio was by a black group. After that, he was careful to find out the color of a singer before offering any opinions on the music. Malik was not at all timid about discussing this symbolism. He was quite sure of himself; his source of ultimate authority was the Koran.

Throughout my stay I had been the dutiful anthropologist and noted down his comments, refraining from publicly reacting. But toward the end I let myself be affected by them more, and they really began to rankle. I am light in complexion with blue eyes and light brown hair. I was tempted many times to ask Malik, who has a dark skin tone, kinky hair, and large lips, if he thought this made me superior to him, but I never did. There was no point in confronting him.

Ben Mohammed was a different story. When I finally approached him about my feelings on the matter, he was quite lucid. We were sitting on a hillside, under some fig trees, overlooking the Brueghelesque field below, amiably passing a hot, cloudless summer afternoon. I cautiously began to unburden myself about Malik. Again ben Mohammed straddled the cultural divide rather artfully. He fully agreed that the downgrading of blacks was a bad thing. It was incumbent on Muslims to fight racism in all its forms. There was no ambiguity on that point. But, such symbolism was indeed in the Koran. Most people rely on custom and not on their own intelligence. Malik was a peasant and could not be expected to know any better. He had been raised with these aphorisms, and lived with them, and he was not going to easily rid himself of such a bias.

He cautioned me, however, not to confuse Malik's views with the kind of racism he knew existed in America or Europe. Although Malik expressed anti-black sentiments, no Moroccan would ever keep someone out of a hotel or a job because of his skin color. Cultures were

different, ben Mohammed was saying. Even when they say the same thing, an expression can mean something entirely different when it is played out in society. Be careful about your judgments. I agreed.

Yet, there was one further question to ask: Are we all equal, ben Mohammed? Or are Muslims superior? He became flustered. Here there was no possibility of reformist interpretation or compromise. The answer was no, we are not equal. All Muslims, even the most unworthy and reprehensible, and we named a few we both knew, are superior to all non-Muslims. That was Allah's will. The division of the world into Muslim and non-Muslim was *the* fundamental cultural distinction, the Archimedean point from which all else turned. This was ultimately what separated us. But, as Aristotle points out, "in a friendship based on virtue, complaints do not arise, but the purpose of the doer is a sort of measure; for in purpose lies the essential element of virtue and character ... friendship asks a man to do what he can, not what is proportional to the merits of the case, since that can not always be done...."[2]

The lessons of tolerance and self-acceptance which ben Mohammed had been teaching me during the past months held sway. I had a strong sense of being American. I knew it was time to leave Morocco.

The "revolution" had occurred during my absence (1968–9). My friends from Chicago, many of them now living in New York, were fervently and unabashedly "political" when I returned. New York, where I had grown up, looked the same as when I had left it. But the city and my friends were now more impenetrable to me than ben Mohammed. The whole revery of future *communitas* which had sustained me through months of loneliness refused to actualize itself upon my return. I adopted a stance of passivity waiting for it to appear. Perhaps the most bizarre dimension of my return was the fact that my friends were now seemingly preoccupied with the Third World; at least the phrase had an obligatory place in their discourse. I had just been in the Third World with a vengeance. Yet this Third World which they so avidly portrayed bore no obvious relation to my experiences. Initially when I pointed this out, I was politely ignored. When I persisted it was suggested that I was perhaps a bit reactionary. The maze of slightly blurred nuance, that feeling of barely grasped meanings which had been my constant companion in Morocco overtook me once again. But now I was home.

Over the next several years other activities absorbed me, writing and teaching among them. Writing this book seems to have enabled me to go on to another type of fieldwork, to begin again on a different terrain.

Trinh Van Du entered the room carrying a dozen roses for our hostess. He was perhaps five feet tall and drew attention to this immediately by announcing that although he was thirty-three, Americans often mistook him for fifteen. The first hour or so of introductory chat was a bit stilted, but Du managed to include six or seven references to Ho Chi Minh along with the fact that he had been in the United States almost twelve years, doing odd jobs and teaching, for a time, at the Monterey Army language school. Things warmed up enormously when we switched from politics and credentials to language and culture. Yes, he would love to teach us Vietnamese and introduce us to Vietnamese literature, particularly poetry. The Hue dialect, his own, is the most poetic (as are its women), the Saigon dialect the most sing-song like Chinese, and the Hanoi the most precise and clear. But all Vietnamese read the same language and all love the *Tale of Kieu*. He would recite it for us in all three dialects and we would choose the one we liked best. Leaping up, filled with sparkle, yet almost solemn, he recited the first verses of the famous nineteenth-century poem, three times.

Conclusion

Culture is interpretation. The "facts" of anthropology, the material which the anthropologist has gone to the field to find, are already themselves interpretations. The baseline data is already culturally mediated by the people whose culture we, as anthropologists, have come to explore. Facts are made – the word comes from the Latin *factum*, "made" – and

the facts we interpret are made and remade. Therefore they cannot be collected as if they were rocks, picked up and put into cartons and shipped home to be analyzed in the laboratory.

Culture in all of its manifestations is overdetermined. It does not present itself neutrally or with one voice. Every cultural fact can be interpreted in many ways, both by the anthropologist and by his subjects. The scientific revolutions which established these parameters at the turn of the current century have been largely ignored in anthropology. Frederic Jameson's reference to the paradigm shift in linguistics applies to anthropology as well. He notes "a movement from a substantive way of thinking to a relational one.... Difficulties arose from terms which tried to name substances or objects ... while linguistics was a science characterized by the absence of such substances.... There are first of all points of view ... with whose help you then subsequently create your objects."[3]

The fact that all cultural facts are interpretations, and multivocal ones at that, is true both for the anthropologist and for his informant, the Other with whom he works. His informant – and the word is accurate – must interpret his own culture and that of the anthropologist. The same holds for the anthropologist. Both live in rich, partially integrated, ongoing life worlds. They are, however, not the same. Nor is there any mechanical and easy means of translation from one set of experiences to the other. That problem and the process of translation, therefore, become one of the central arts and crucial tasks of fieldwork. It should be clear that the view of the "primitive" as a creature living by rigid rules, in total harmony with his environment, and essentially not cursed with a glimmer of self-consciousness, is a set of complex cultural projections. There is no "primitive." There are other men, living other lives.

Anthropology is an interpretive science. Its object of study, humanity encountered as Other, is on the same epistemological level as it is. Both the anthropologist and his informants live in a culturally mediated world, caught up in "webs of signification" they themselves have spun. This is the ground of anthropology;

there is no privileged position, no absolute perspective, and no valid way to eliminate consciousness from our activities or those of others. This central fact can be avoided by pretending it does not exist. Both sides can be frozen. We can pretend that we are neutral scientists collecting unambiguous data and that the people we are studying are living amid various unconscious systems of determining forces of which they have no clue and to which only we have the key. But it is only pretense.

Anthropological facts are cross-cultural, because they are made across cultural boundaries. They exist as lived experience, but they are made into facts during the process of questioning, observing, and experiencing – which both the anthropologist and the people with whom he lives engage in. This means that the informant must first learn to explicate his own culture, to become self-conscious about it and begin to objectify his own life-world. He must then learn to "present" it to the anthropologist, to an outsider who by definition does not understand even the most obvious things. This presentation by the informant is defined, therefore, by being in a mode of externality. The informant is asked in innumerable ways to think about particular aspects of his own world, and he must then learn to construct ways to present this newly focused-on object to someone who is outside his culture, who shares few of his assumptions, and whose purpose and procedures are opaque. Thus when a Moroccan describes his lineage structure to an anthropologist, he must do several things. He must first become self-reflective and self-conscious about certain aspects of his life which he had previously taken largely for granted. Once he arrives at some understanding of what the anthropologist is driving at, thinks about that subject matter, and comes to a conclusion (all of which can occur in a matter of seconds, of course, and is not in itself a theoretical process), the informant must then figure out how to present this information to the anthropologist, an outsider who is by definition external to his usual life-world.

This creates the beginnings of a hybrid, cross-cultural object or product. During the period of fieldwork a system of shared symbols must be developed if this process of object formation – through self-reflection, self-objectification, presentation, and further explication – is to continue. Particularly in its early stages when there is little common experience, understanding, or language to fall back on, this is a very difficult and trying process; the ground is just not there. Things become more secure as this liminal world is mutually constructed but, by definition, it never really loses its quality of externality. This externality, however, is a moving ratio. It is external both for the anthropologist (it is not his own lifeworld) and for the informants, who gradually learn to inform. The present somewhat nasty connotations of the word do apply at times, but so does its older root sense "to give form to, to be the formative principle of, to animate." What is given form is this communication. The informant gives external form to his own experiences, by presenting them to meet the anthropologist's questions, to the extent that he can interpret them.

This informing, however, goes on not in a laboratory but in interpersonal interaction. It is intersubjective, between subjects. At best, it is partial and thin. The depth and scope of the culture that has been constructed is often woefully inadequate when measured against people interacting and carrying on their daily rounds in the everyday world. Anthropology is not a set of questionnaires which are handed over, filled out, and handed back. Most of the anthropologist's time is spent sitting around waiting for informants, doing errands, drinking tea, taking genealogies, mediating fights, being pestered for rides, and vainly attempting small talk – all in someone else's culture. The inadequacy of one's comprehension is incessantly brought to the surface and publicly displayed.

Interruptions and eruptions mock the fieldworker and his inquiry; more accurately, they may be said to inform his inquiry, to be an essential part of it. The constant breakdown, it seems to me, is not just an annoying accident but a core aspect of this type of inquiry. Later I became increasingly aware that these ruptures of communication were highly revealing, and often proved to be turning points. At the time, however, they seemed only to represent our frustration. Etymology comes to the rescue again: *e-ruption*, a breaking out, and *inter-ruption*, a breaking in, of this liminal culture through which we were trying to communicate.

Whenever these breaks occurred – and I have described several of the most important ones earlier – the cycle began again. This cross-cultural communication and interaction all took on a new content, often a new depth. The groundwork we had laid often seemed to fall away from under us and we scrambled somewhere else. More had been incorporated, more could be taken for granted, more could be shared. This is a moving ratio and one which never reaches identity, far from it. But there is movement, there is change, there is informing.

Fieldwork, then, is a process of intersubjective construction of liminal modes of communication. Intersubjective means literally more than one subject, but being situated neither quite here nor quite there, the subjects involved do not share a common set of assumptions, experiences, or traditions. Their construction is a public process. Most of this book has focused on these objects which my Moroccan friends and I constructed between us, over time, in order to communicate. That the communication was often painstaking and partial is a central theme. That it was not totally opaque is an equally important theme. It is the dialectic between these poles, ever repeated, never quite the same, which constitutes fieldwork.

Summing up, then, we can say the following.

The first person with whom I had any sustained contact was the Frenchman Maurice Richard. Staying at his hotel was an obligatory first step for Europeans entering into Sefrou (although recently the Moroccan government has opened a luxury hotel). Knowing that his clientele will not be with him long, Richard has developed a persona of cheerful good will, which becomes less and less convincing as he becomes more isolated. The contact with Richard was immediate. There was no language barrier. He was eager to talk. Being an outsider to all of the other Sefrou groups, he had interesting stereotypes of each, which he was more than willing to exchange for a receptive smile. His very accessibility, however, was also revealing of his limitations. He provided entry only to the past, to the last days of colonialism. He was located on the very edge of Sefrou society, its most external point. His corner was easily accessible, but it revealed only the fringes of Moroccan society. Although this subject provided ample material for an inquiry, and was in fact in the process of disappearing forever, my project led me in other directions.

Ibrahim was on the other side of the buffer zone between the French and the Moroccan societies. He had matured during the waning days of the Protectorate and made his career by artfully straddling the line between communities without any confusion as to which side of the line he was on. His speciality was presenting goods and services for external consumption. They were carefully packaged. He was a guide along the main thoroughfares of Sefrou society. His tour was quite helpful for understanding the Ville Nouvelle, but his aid stopped at the walls of the medina. Despite his caution, the first breakthroughs of Otherness occurred with Ibrahim. This professional of the external was, nonetheless, a Moroccan.

My guide through the medina of Sefrou and the transitional zones of Moroccan culture was Ali. My contact with him was the first major step toward a more intimate relationship with Sefrou. He was a floating figure within his own society, living a hand-to-mouth existence in the city. He was a patient, curious, highly imaginative, adventurous, sensuous, and relentlessly perceptive person. My orientation to Moroccan culture as immediacy, as lived experience, came from my friendship with Ali. He had rejected a certain way of life, but not other Moroccan alternatives. He was acerbic and direct in his criticisms of village ways, but they were insider's jibes.

Ali was also limited by his strengths. Because of his demeanor and antagonism he had almost become an outcast in the village. The insights and orientations which he continued to provide for me throughout the field experience were invaluable. He knowingly and adroitly used the villagers' inhibitions and vulnerabilities against them. Ali was an insider's outsider. His unique vantage point and provocative attitude periodically rescued me from impasses and collective resistance. Ali was, however, now outside village affairs, basically out of touch. He provided little help on the day-to-day level, but could be relied on for vital aid.

So, just as Richard was situated between the two French communities, and Ibrahim between the French and local Moroccan Ville Nouvelle groups, so Ali was situated between the floating population of the medina and his natal village of saint's descendants. All were marginal, all provided help in making transitions from group to group, site to site.

Within Sidi Lahcen itself, the situation became more tightly controlled. The community tacitly (and in some cases explicitly) attempted to situate the anthropologist and thereby control him. The first two young men with whom I worked exemplify this. Mekki, my first informant, literally pushed on me by the villagers, was from Ali's sub-lineage. Not being burdened with family or work obligations, he eagerly sought what to others was a mixed blessing. Unfortunately, he lacked both intelligence and the imaginative ability to objectify his own life-world and then present it to a foreigner. This was an insurmountable handicap. Rashid, my second informant, was everything that Mekki was not; that was his problem. He was imaginative, energetic, curious, intelligent, and was floating, like Ali, except that Rashid's experience was essentially limited to village life. He could have been and was (from time to time) an extremely important informant. But, again like Ali, he aroused strong community disapproval. Rashid's tongue was feared. Everyone, including his father, sought to silence him. Unsure about my presence in the village, they wanted some control over the information I was receiving. Rashid knew a great deal and was eager to convey it. As the Moroccan proverb goes, Those who have no shame, do as they please. And so those with no internal sense of appropriate behavior must be controlled by force. Rashid, unlike Ali, had no power base, no alternative cards to play. In general, he was forced to accede to the community's injunctions, yet he enjoyed violating them whenever the opportunity presented itself.

Malik offered an excellent compromise, both for me and for the community. I had forced my way into Sidi Lahcen, after all, and

the villagers feared that ultimately I had come to subvert their religion. Therefore, it was appropriate that the man who became my central informant was situated on the edge of the most respected of the saintly sub-lineages. This group had a very high rate of endogamous marriage. Malik's father, however, had married a woman not only from outside the sub-lineage but from outside the village. Consequently, as closely attached to this core group as he was emotionally, he was structurally somewhat on its edge, and he overcompensated for it.

He was the perfect representative of orthodoxy. He was proud of his tradition but he had failed to find a traditional role for himself. Impatient with the position of *fqi*, he was stymied in pursuing his own grandiose self-image. A conservative, he lacked institutions to defend. He proved to be the perfect community choice. The elders of his sub-lineage sanctioned his involvement and so did Sergeant Larawi, the most powerful man in the village. They knew they could trust Malik.

Malik, like Ibrahim, was self-controlled, orderly, and reserved. But unlike Ibrahim, he had not made a career of external relations. Malik had remained within the rural world. Malik would have liked to be the internal counterpart of Ibrahim. But no such role existed. He had to improvise as he went along. His "impression management," however, was in constant tension with the inputs of Ali, Rashid, and others. Malik attempted to steer cautiously around sensitive areas. Once challenged, he would yield, but after the early going, he would rarely initiate. As we proceeded, Malik became more dependent on me than I was on him. This helps explain his lack of sustained resistance on sensitive areas; Ibrahim, no doubt, would not have backed down so readily.

Many of the political dimensions of the informant relationship were obviated by Driss ben Mohammed's steadfast adherence to the role of host. This eventually established the grounds for a dialogue. Ben Mohammed was internal to the Moroccan tradition. He looked back to his forefather, the seventeenth-century saint, for guidance in the modern world. He maintained a belief in the ultimate and unconditional superiority of Islam.

This absolute difference which separated us was openly acknowledged only at the end of my stay. We had become friends, we had shown each other mutual respect and trust. The limits of the situation were not obscured for either of us. I was for him a rich member of a dominant civilization about which he had the profoundest reservations. To me, he was struggling to revive a cultural universe which I no longer inhabited and could not ultimately support. But our friendship tempered our differences. Here we had come full circle. There were now two subjects facing each other. Each was the product of an historical tradition which situated and conditioned him. Each was aware of a profound crisis within that tradition but still looked back to it for renewal and solace. We were profoundly Other to each other.

That I would journey to Morocco to confront Otherness and myself was typical of my culture (or the parts of it I could accept). That ben Mohammed would enter into this sort of dialogue without self-denigration was impressive. My restless and scientifically cloaked wanderings brought me to this mountain village in Morocco. Ben Mohammed sought the wisdom of the reformist saint, yet was willing, even eager, to tell me about him. Through mutual confrontation of our own situations we did establish contact. But this also highlighted our fundamental Otherness. What separated us was fundamentally our past. I could understand ben Mohammed only to the extent that he could understand me – that is to say, partially. He did not live in a crystalline world of immutable Otherness any more than I did. He grew up in an historical situation which provided him with meaningful but only partially satisfactory interpretations of his world, as did I. Our Otherness was not an ineffable essence, but rather the sum of different historical experiences. Different webs of signification separated us, but these webs were now at least partially intertwined. But a dialogue was only possible when we recognized our differences, when we remained critically loyal to the symbols which our traditions had given us. By so doing, we began a process of change.

NOTES

1 *Nicomachean Ethics*, Book VIII, Chapter 2, p. 1060 in *The Basic Works of Aristotle*, edited by Richard McKeon (Random House, New York, 1941).

2 *Nicomachean Ethics*, Book VIII, Chapter 13, p. 1075 in McKeon.

3 Frederic Jameson, *The Prison House of Language* (Princeton University Press, Princeton, 1972), p. 13.

33

The Way Things Are Said

Jeanne Favret-Saada

It seems that even the pure light of science requires, in order to shine, the darkness of ignorance.

Karl Marx (1856)

Take an ethnographer: she has chosen to investigate contemporary witchcraft in the Bocage[1] of Western France. She has already done some fieldwork; she has a basic academic training; she has published some papers on the logic of murder, violence and insurrection in an altogether different, tribal society. She is now working in France, to avoid having to learn yet another difficult language. Especially since in her view the symbolic shaping out of murder or aggression – the way things are said in the native culture – is as important as the functioning of political machinery.

The Mirror-Image of an Academic

Getting ready to leave for the field, she looks through the scientific (and not so scientific) literature on contemporary witchcraft: the writings of folklorists and psychiatrists, of occultists and journalists. This is what she finds: that peasants, who are 'credulous', 'backward' and impervious to 'cause or effect', blame their misfortune on the jealousy of a neighbour who has cast a spell on them; they go to an unwitcher[2] (usually described as a 'charlatan', now and again as 'naive') who protects them from their imaginary aggressor by performing 'secret' rituals which 'have no meaning', and 'come from another age'. The geographical and cultural 'isolation' of the

Jeanne Favret-Saada, "The Way Things Are Said," pp. 3–12, 16–24 plus relevant references from *Deadly Words: Witchcraft in the Bocage*, trans. Catherine Cullen. Cambridge: Cambridge University Press, 1980[1977]. English translation © Maison des Sciences de l'homme and Cambridge University Press, 1980. Originally published in French as *Les mots, la mort, les sorts*. © Éditions Gallimard, Paris, 1977. Reprinted by permission of Cambridge University Press and Éditions Gallimard.

Ethnographic Fieldwork: An Anthropological Reader, Second Edition. Edited by Antonius C. G. M. Robben and Jeffrey A. Sluka.
Editorial material and organization © 2012 John Wiley & Sons, Inc.
Published 2012 by John Wiley & Sons, Inc.

Bocage is partly responsible for the 'survival' of these 'beliefs' in our time.

If that is all there is to be said about witchcraft (and however much you try to find out from the books of folklorists or the reports of trials in the French press over the last ten years, you will learn no more), you may wonder why it seems to be such an obsession. To judge by the public's immense curiosity, the fascination produced by the very word 'witchcraft', the guaranteed success of anything written about it, one wonders what journalistic scoop could ever find a greater public.

Take an ethnographer. She has spent more than thirty months in the Bocage in Mayenne, studying witchcraft. 'How exciting, how thrilling, how extraordinary …!' 'Tell us all about the witches,' she is asked again and again when she gets back to the city. Just as one might say: tell us tales about ogres or wolves, about Little Red Riding Hood. Frighten us, but make it clear that it's only a story; or that they are just peasants: credulous, backward and marginal. Or alternatively: confirm that *out there* there are some people who can bend the laws of causality and morality, who can kill by magic and not be punished; but remember to end by saying that they do not really have that power: they only believe it because they are credulous, backward peasants … (see above).

No wonder that country people in the West are not in any hurry to step forward and be taken for idiots in the way that public opinion would have them be – whether in the scholarly version developed by folklorists, or in the equally hard faced popular version spread by the media.

To say that one is studying beliefs about witchcraft is automatically to deny them any truth: it is just a belief, it is not true. So folklorists never ask of country people: 'what are they trying to express by means of a witchcraft crisis?', but only 'what are they hiding from us?' They are led on by the idea of some healer's 'secret', some local trick, and describing it is enough to gratify academic curiosity. So witchcraft is no more than a body of empty recipes (boil an ox heart, prick it with a thousand pins, etc.)? Grant that sort of thing supernatural power? How gullible can you be?

Similarly, when the reporter, that hero of positivist discourse, goes along on behalf of a public assumed to be incredulous, and asks country people whether they 'still believe' in spells, the case is decided in advance: yes, people do still believe in spells, especially if you go to the Lower Berry or the Normandy Bocage. How convenient that there should be a district full of idiots, where the whole realm of the imaginary can be held in. But country people are not fools: they meet these advances with obstinate silence.

But even their silence about things to do with witchcraft, and more generally about anything to do with illness and death, is said to tell us about their status: 'their language is too simple', 'they are incapable of symbolizing', you won't get anything out of them because 'they don't talk': that is what I was told by the local scholarly élite. Why not say they are wild men of the woods, since they live in a 'bocage'; animals, even? 'Medicine is a veterinary art round here' a local psychiatrist once told me.

So all that was known about witchcraft is that it was unknowable: when I left for the field, knowledge of the subject boiled down to this. The first question I asked myself when I met the peasants, who were neither credulous nor backward, was: is witchcraft unknowable, or is it just that those who say this need to block out all knowledge about it in order to maintain their own intellectual coherence? Does the 'scholar' or the 'man of our own age' need to comfort himself with the myth of a credulous and backward peasant?

The social sciences aim to account for cultural differences. But can this be achieved by postulating the existence of a peasant who is denied all reality save that he is the mirror-image of an academic?

Whenever folklorists or reporters talk of witchcraft in the country, they always do so as if one were facing two incompatible physical theories: the pre-logical or medieval attitude of peasants, who wrongly attribute their misfortunes to imaginary witches; and ours, the attitude of educated people who know how to handle causal relations correctly. It is said or implied that peasants are incapable of this either because of ignorance or of backwardness. In this respect, the description given of the peasant and the *'pays'*, the canton, that determines him is governed by a peculiar set of terms which necessarily imply that he is incapable of grasping causal relations. Witchcraft is put forward as a nonsense theory which peasants can afford to adopt because it is the local theory. The folklorist's job is then to underline the difference between his own theory (which also happens to be a 'true' one) and the peasant's, which is only a belief.

But who can ignore the difficulties involved in postulating the coexistence of two incompatible physical theories which correspond to two ages of humankind? Do you really have to do thirty months of fieldwork to be in a position to say that country people are just as well able to cope with causal relations as anyone else, and to make the suggestion that witchcraft cannot be reduced to a physical theory, although it does indeed imply a certain kind of causality?

Words Spoken with Insistence

I began by studying the words used to express biological misfortunes, and used in ordinary conversation: about death, sterility, and illness in animals and humans. The first thing one notices is that they distinguish between ordinary misfortunes and their extraordinary repetition.

In the Bocage, as anywhere else in France, ordinary misfortunes are accepted as 'one-off'; so, a single illness, the loss of one animal, one bankruptcy, even one death, do not call for more than a single comment: *'the trouble with him is that he drinks too much'*; *'she had cancer of the kidneys'*; *'my cow was very old'*.

An onslaught by witchcraft, on the other hand, gives a pattern to misfortunes which are repeated and range over the persons and belongings of a bewitched couple: in succession, a heifer dies, the wife has a miscarriage, the child is covered in spots, the car runs into a ditch, the butter won't churn, the bread won't rise, the geese bolt, or the daughter they want to marry off goes into a decline ... Every morning, the couple ask anxiously: *'What on earth will happen next?'* And every time some misfortune occurs: always unexpected, always inexplicable.

When misfortunes occur like this in series, the countryman approaches qualified people with a double request: on the one hand for an interpretation, and on the other for a cure.

The doctors and vets answer him by denying the existence of any series: illnesses, deaths and mechanical breakdowns do not occur for the same reasons and are not treated in the same way. These people are the curators of objective knowledge about the body, and they can claim to pick off one by one the causes of the misfortunes: go and disinfect your stables, vaccinate your cows, send your wife to the gynaecologist, give your child milk with less fat in it, drink less alcohol ... But however effective each separate treatment may be, in the eyes of some peasants it is still incomplete, for it only affects the cause and not the origin of their troubles. The origin is always the evil nature of one or more witches who hunger after other people's misfortunes, and whose words, look and touch have supernatural power.

Faced with a bewitched, one can imagine that the priest is in a more awkward situation than the doctor, for evil, misfortune and the supernatural mean something to him. But what they mean has become singularly blurred by many centuries of theological brooding. The dividing line between the ranges of the natural and the supernatural has been fixed by Catholic orthodoxy; but the reasons given have scarcely been assimilated, especially since each late pronouncement does not categorically cancel former ones. So theological knowledge is no more unified in the mind of a country priest than it is in the body of doctrine.

Hearing the various stories told in his parish, the priest can choose between three different and mutually exclusive types of interpretation:

1   He can dismiss these misfortunes as part of the natural order, and so deny them any religious significance: by doing so he sides with medical ideology, and in effect says the bewitched are raving or superstitious people.
2   He can acknowledge that these misfortunes do pertain to the supernatural order,

but are an effect of divine love: so the bishop of Séez preaches 'good suffering' to a congregation of 'luckless' peasants. A universally aimed (Catholic) discourse can turn him who is 'luckless' into the most lucky. The man whom God loves best and so chastises, is only a victim in the eyes of the world. This reversal of appearances sometimes has its effect.

3 The priest can meet the peasant on his own ground and interpret his misfortunes as the work of the devil. He is permitted to do this by at least one branch or stratum of theology. He then has two alternatives.

He may consult, as he is supposed to, the diocesan exorcist, the official expert in diabolical matters appointed by the hierarchy. But in Western France, the priest knows very well that he is not likely to convince the expert, who has held this position for thirty years precisely because he is skeptical about the devil's interest in so-called 'simple' peasants: you have to be clever to interest the devil. So the diocesan exorcist, in the elitist style of any country priest who has risen in the Church or any peasant who has risen in society, offers the positivist interpretation. He refuses to give any religious meaning to the peasant's misfortune except by mentioning 'good suffering' or saying he will pray for him. Like the doctor, he refuses the peasant's request for a meaning by advising the man to consult a psychiatrist, to live a more balanced life, and to apply better the rules of the experimental method. The village priest knows in advance that to send a bewitched to the diocesan exorcist is to ask him to take his troubles elsewhere, and in effect to direct him to a doctor by way of the ecclesiastical hierarchy.

Alternatively, the priest comes and exorcises the farm and its inhabitants without consulting the hierarchy. As a more or less willing distributor of blessings and medals, holy water and salt, he plays the role in his parish of a small-scale unwitcher who protects people from evil spells without sending them back to the witch.

'If it's a small spell, it works': the series of misfortunes stops and everything returns to normal. It works, but the origin of the misfortune and its repetition are still not satisfactorily symbolized. For when the peasant talks about being bewitched to anyone who is willing to listen, what he wants acknowledged is this: if such repetitions occur, one must assume that somewhere someone wants them to. I shall show later that witchcraft consists in creating a misunderstanding about who it is that desires the misfortunes of the bewitched. Note here that the Church's rite merely clouds the issue by attributing the evil to some immaterial spirit included by half-hearted theology in a list of 'preternatural facts'. For the victim, the witch is some familiar person (a neighbour, for example) whose aims he can at least hope to discover.

If 'it doesn't work': if the priest 'isn't strong enough' because his parishioner is 'caught tight' in the spells, the bewitched is left with his question: why this series of events, and why in my home? What is at stake here, my sanity or my life? Am I mad, as the doctor says, or does someone have it in for me to the point of wanting me to die?

It is only at this point that the sufferer can choose to interpret his ills in the language of witchcraft. Some friend, or someone else who has noticed him moving deeper into misfortune and seen the ineffectiveness of approved learning makes the crucial diagnosis: 'Do you think there may be someone who wishes you ill?' This amounts to saying: 'you're not mad, I can see in you the signs of a similar crisis I once experienced, and which came to an end thanks to this unwitcher.'

The priest and the doctor have faded out long ago when the unwitcher is called. The unwitcher's task is first to authenticate his patient's sufferings and his feeling of being threatened in the flesh; second, it is to locate, by close examination, the patient's vulnerable spots. It is as if his own body and those of his family, his land and all his possessions make up a single surface full of holes, through which the witch's violence might break in at any moment. The unwitcher then clearly tells his client how long he still has to live if he stubbornly remains defenceless. He is a master of death; he can tell its date and how to postpone it. A professional in supernatural evil, he is prepared to return blow for blow against 'the person we suspect', the alleged witch, whose final identity is established only after an investigation, sometimes a long one. This is the inception of what can only be called a cure. The séances later are devoted to finding the gaps which still need sealing, as they are revealed day by day in the course of life.

When Words Wage War

In the project for my research I wrote that I wanted to study witchcraft practices in the Bocage. For more than a century, folklorists had been gorging themselves on them, and the time had come to understand them. In the field, however, all I came across was language. For many months, the only empirical facts I was able to record were words.

Today I would say that an attack of witchcraft can be summed up as follows: a set of words spoken in a crisis situation by someone who will later be designated as a witch are afterwards interpreted as having taken effect on the body and belongings of the persons spoken to, who will on that ground say he is bewitched. The unwitcher takes on himself these words originally spoken to his client, and turns them back on to their initial sender, the witch. Always the '*abnormal*' is said to have settled in after certain words have been uttered, and the situation persists without change until the unwitcher places himself like a screen between the sender and the receiver. Unwitching rituals – the actual 'practices' – are remarkably poor and contingent: this ritual or that, it makes no difference, any one will do. For if the ritual is upheld it is only through words and through the person who says them.

So perhaps, I was not entirely mistaken when I said I wanted to study practices: the act, in witchcraft, is the word.

That may seem an elementary statement, but it is full of implications. The first is this: until now, the work of ethnographers has relied on a convention (one too obvious to be stated) about the use of spoken words. For ethnography to be possible, it was necessary that the investigator and the 'native' should at least agree that speech has the function of conveying information. To be an ethnographer is first to record the utterances of appropriately

chosen native informants. How to establish this information-situation, the main source of the investigator's knowledge, how to choose one's informants, how to involve them in a regular working relationship ... the handbooks always insist on this truly fundamental point in fieldwork.

Now, witchcraft is spoken words; but these spoken words are power, and not knowledge or information.

To talk, in witchcraft, is never to inform. Or if information is given, it is so that the person who is to kill (the unwitcher) will know where to aim his blows. 'Informing' an ethnographer, that is, someone who claims to have no intention of using the information, but naïvely wants to know for the sake of knowing, is literally unthinkable. For a single word (and only a word) can tie or untie a fate, and whoever puts himself in a position to utter it is formidable. Knowing about spells brings money, brings more power and triggers terror: realities much more fascinating to an interlocutor than the innocent accumulation of scientific knowledge, writing a well-documented book, or getting an academic degree.

Similarly, it is unthinkable that people can talk for the sake of talking. Exchanging words just to show that one is with other people, to show one's wish to communicate, or what Malinowski called 'phatic communication' exists in the Bocage as it does anywhere else. But here it implies strictly political intentions: phatic communication is the expression of zero-aggressiveness; it conveys to one's interlocutor that one might launch a magic rocket at him, but that one chooses not to do so for the time being. It is conveying to him that this is not the time for a fight, but for a cease-fire. When interlocutors for whom witchcraft is involved talk about nothing (that is about anything except what really matters) it is to emphasize the violence of what is not being talked about. More fundamentally, it is to check that the circuit is functioning, and that a state of war does indeed hold between the opponents.

In short, there is no neutral position with spoken words: in witchcraft, words wage war. Anyone talking about it is a belligerent, the ethnographer like everyone else. There is no room for uninvolved observers.

When Evans-Pritchard, founder of the ethnography of witchcraft, studied the Zande, he made it his practice to interpret the events of his life by means of schemes about persecution, consulting oracles and submitting to their decisions: 'I was aided in my understanding of the feelings of the bewitched Azande', he says, 'by sharing their hopes and joys, apathy and sorrows [...]. In no department of their life was I more successful in "thinking black" or as it should more correctly be said "feeling black" than in the sphere of witchcraft. I, too, used to react to misfortunes in the idiom of witchcraft, and it was often an effort to check this lapse into unreason' (1937). But we learn from his book that actually the Zande had given him the position of 'Prince without portfolio', which is no slight consolation if one remembers that in Zande society, a prince can only be bewitched by another prince (a rather reassuring thought for an ethnographer established many miles from the court) and that by not giving him a portfolio, the Zande were exempting Evans-Pritchard from having to play the role, so important for the effectiveness of the cure, of symbolic guarantee of the return to order.

In other words, the ethnographer could not himself possibly be involved in a case of witchcraft.[3] In the Bocage, the situation happens to be less comfortable: nobody ever talks about witchcraft to gain knowledge, but to gain power. The same is true about asking questions. Before the ethnographer has uttered a single word, he is involved in the same power relationship as anyone else talking about it. Let him open his mouth, and his interlocutor immediately tries to identify his strategy, estimate his force, guess if he is a friend or foe, or if he is to be bought or destroyed. As with any other interlocutor, speaking to the ethnographer one is addressing either *a subject supposed to be able* (a witch, an unwitcher) *or unable* (a victim, a bewitched person).

It follows that wanting to know could only be – for me as for anyone else – in the name of a force which I claim to have or which my interlocutor credits me with. If I were not equipped to confront it, no one would believe I could survive unharmed, or even survive it at all.

'*Are you strong enough?*' I was often asked when I tried to establish an information-relationship, that is to get people who had experience of witch stories to tell me about them. A mere desire for information is the sign of a naïve or hypocritical person who must at once be frightened off. The effect that the person telling the story is trying to achieve is either to fascinate or to frighten: nobody would talk about it who did not hope to fascinate. If my interlocutor is successful, he says I have '*weak blood*' and advises me to change my course of research towards folk song or the ancient papegai festival. If he fears that he has not brought it off, he anxiously asks me how I can bear to hear such stories every day, and offers various assumptions: '*You've got strong blood*', or else '*you've got something*' (to protect yourself with). He then tries to identify my fetishes, to find out whether or not they are '*stronger*' than his own. Otherwise, he may identify me with a certain unwitcher who has just died, a double-edged compliment which I am bound to appreciate: to say that my '*hands tremble like Madame Marie's*' means that, like her, I'm '*quite strong*' – but also that in the end she met her master in witchcraft, and he did away with her quite recently.

As you can see, this is not exactly a standard situation, in which information is exchanged and where the ethnographer may hope to have neutral knowledge about the beliefs and practices of witchcraft conveyed to him. For he who succeeds in acquiring such knowledge gains power and must accept the effects of this power; the more one knows, the more one is a threat and the more one is magically threatened. So long as I claimed the usual status of an ethnographer, saying I wanted to know for the sake of knowing, my interlocutors were less eager to communicate their own knowledge than to test mine, to try to guess the necessarily magic use I intended to put it to, and to develop their force to the detriment of my own. I had to accept the logic of this totally combative situation and admit that it was absurd to continue to posit a neutral position which was neither admissible or even credible to anyone else. When total war is being waged with words, one must make up one's mind to engage in another kind of ethnography.[4]

[...]

A Name Added to a Position

In pursuing the ethnography of spells, the first point to grasp is being clear about whom each 'informant' thinks he is speaking to, since he utters such radically different discourses depending on the position he thinks his interlocutor holds. To someone who *'isn't caught'*, he will say: *'spells don't exist'*; *'they no longer exist'*; *'that was in the old days'*; *'they were true for our back people'*; *'they exist, but not here: go and look in Saint-Mars* (or Montjean, or Lassay: somewhere else …) *'over there, they're really backward'*; *'oh, spells! I don't hold with all that rot!'*. To someone who is *'caught'*, one speaks in a different way, depending on whether the person is given the position of bewitched or unwitcher. (No one talks to the alleged witch, but this very silence is in itself a whole discourse, the silent assertion of a fight to the death, which always has some effect.)

When an ethnographer works in an exotic field, he too has to take up some sort of stance. But common sense and the handbooks point out the virtues of distance and the advantages to be derived from the status of rich cannibal. To claim, on the other hand, that one wants to hear about peasant witchcraft yet remain alien to it is to condemn oneself to hearing only objectivist statements and to collecting fantastic anecdotes and for unwitching recipes – i.e. to accumulate statements which the stating subject formally disavows. So for the last hundred and fifty years, the native and the folklorist have been looking at themselves in a mirror each has held up to the other, without the folklorist apparently ever noticing the ironic complicity that this implies on the part of the native.

When I left for the Bocage, I was certainly in no better position than any of my predecessors, except that I thought their findings trivial compared with the reality at stake in a witchcraft attack. Within a few months I had myself done much the same collecting as they; it left me unsatisfied, and gave me no guidance about how to pursue my investigation. It would have been just as futile for me to try and win over the peasants with large-minded statements of good intention, since anyway, in matters of witchcraft, it is always the other person who decides how to interpret what you say. Just as a peasant must hear the words of the annunciator, if he is to confess that he is indeed bewitched, so it was my interlocutors who decided what my position was (*'caught'* or not, bewitched or unwitcher) by interpreting unguarded clues in my speech.[5]

I must point out that I knew nothing about this system of positions, and that the main part of my work has been to make it out little by little by going back over puzzling episodes. For several months my notes describe a number of situations in which my interlocutors placed me in this stance or that (*'not caught'*, *'caught'* – bewitched, *'caught'* – unwitcher) although at the time I did not see anything but a classic situation of ethnographic investigation, even if a somewhat difficult one because I was after something particularly secret.

I was probably not yet ready to maintain this speech process in the only way conceivable to my interlocutors: by accepting that being given such a stance committed me to utter my part in this discourse in the same way as they did. Of course this position existed before me and was acceptably occupied and maintained by others. But now I was the one being placed there, and my name was being attached to this position as well as to my particular personal existence.

Although I went through the whole experience in a state of some confusion, I can say today that it is actually patterned around a small number of characteristic situations in which my interlocutors required me to occupy a position that they indicated. They were conveying that they had no need of my ability to listen, for what mattered to them was not merely to be understood, or, in the language of communication-theory – they had no need for a decoder. In witchcraft, to receive messages obliges one to send out other, signed messages: it was time for me to speak.

For example, here are some instances of the manner in which I was put to the test: (1) the first time that the bewitched told me their own story (and not that of some hypothetical *'backward people'*), it was because they had identified me as the unwitcher who could get them out of their troubles. (2) A few months later, a peasant interpreted my '*weakness*', took on the role of annunciator of my state as a bewitched, and took me to his unwitcher to get me '*uncaught*'. (3) For more than two years, I subjected the events of my personal life to the interpretations of this unwitcher. (4) Several bewitched asked me to '*uncatch*' them. Although at this point I had become quite competent at handling magical discourse, I felt quite incapable of taking the speech-position upholding it, and I sent them on to my therapist. (5) Lastly, this unwitcher, with whom I had a complicated relationship (I was her client, agent, and guarantor of the truth of her words during the cures in which I was invited to participate) instructed me to bring her a healer who would relieve her of her bodily pains and to assist him in his task.

You could say, given the ideal assumption that I might have made my choice in full consciousness of the situation, that every time these were the alternatives: either I refused this assignment of my identity to a position and withdrew from the speech process pointing out that I was being mistaken for someone I was not (*I am not who you think I am*); or I agreed to occupy the position assigned to me, unless I could propose some other which I felt more able to occupy (*I am not where you think I am*). In the first case, I would have had to leave the Bocage, where I no longer had any place; in the second, the speech process would go on but I had to place myself in the position of subject of the enunciation.

It emerges from the asides of investigators that I was not the first person to be offered this alternative. Some folklorists, for example, tell of their amusement at having been invited, at one point or another, to act as unwitchers. This type of occurrence is worth looking into. Note in the first place, that it is out of the question for the investigator to be assigned the position of bewitched. He would have had to give some sign that he knows he is mortal, vulnerable or at least subject to desires – all things one can freely admit, but only to close relations and in confidence – certainly not to uneducated farmers and while practising one's profession. In the field, the investigator therefore routinely presents himself to his interlocutor as someone who does not lack anything: or to take up the expression I used above, he displays a continuous surface without holes in it. Everything in his behaviour suggests he is '*strong enough*'. This especially since he does not omit arguments likely to loosen their tongues: he may say he belongs to a local line of magic healers (he might claim, for example, that his maternal grandmother, who is still remembered in the area, '*passed the secret*' on to him); and in his conversations with 'informers', he shows he knows many unwitchment recipes, magic formulae and fantastic anecdotes. Without being conscious of it, the investigator has done everything necessary for his interlocutors to assign him the position of unwitcher. But if he is actually told this, and asked to perform, he is amused. He recounts this episode as if it were just an entertaining anecdote, and a particularly conclusive evidence of peasant gullibility, to a listener who is confidently assumed to feel equally superior. Indeed, there is cause to smile: there has been an error, a mistaken identity, the investigator was not the person he was thought to be.

But one may wonder who is more naïve, the peasant or the folklorist. The former cannot understand that one might collect formulae without putting them to any use, just for the sake of information; the latter judges that he has satisfied the demands of science by collecting information, without realizing he cannot do anything with it, neither science nor magic.

Not science: the folklorists failed to recognize the existence and role of the power of therapists in unwitching cures. They strained to find out what these therapists knew, and this in the particular form of secrets to be collected. In other words, whatever in their discourse most resembles an utterance, a statement which can stand on its own independent of the stating subject.

The content of the secret (the utterance) is for the most part neither here nor there: it does not matter whether one is told to pierce an ox heart, twist steel nails, or recite misappropriated Church prayers. Magicians know this, when they quietly say: '*to each one his secret*', and show themselves in no hurry to increase their knowledge. For what makes an unwitcher is his *'force'* and its links with a world of language (the very one which produced the content of the secret). The power of the magician, thus referred to a symbolic set, places him in the position of recognized avenger (and not, for example, of a criminal settling private scores), but on condition that he openly declares his readiness to assume this position.

Not magic: unwitching does not consist in uttering formulae or practising magic rituals. If they are to have any chance of being effective, a set of positions must first be established, by which someone who is not the magician places him in the position of subject supposed to be able; and the magician himself must acknowledge he is in it, and accept what this implies in terms of personal commitment to a discourse, and of assuming the effects of magic speech on his own body and so on.

So when the folklorist reacts to a request for unwitchment by laughing as if this were an inappropriate proposal, and excuses himself by saying he cannot do anything, or by sending the patient to his doctor, the peasant gathers that this academic does not want to commit his *'force'*, if he has any; or more likely, that he has no idea what *'force'* is or just how much is involved in speaking. The folklorist's mirth simply shows that he does not think he can cure anyone with magic formulae, and that for him such knowledge is pointless. And so it is, unless a subject agrees to become the support of these magic utterances and to proffer them in the name of his own *'force'* taken as part of a symbolic universe – i.e. to convert this knowledge into a power.

Taking One's Distances from Whom (or What)?

So one cannot study witchcraft without agreeing to take part in the situations where it manifests itself, and in the discourse expressing it. This entails certain limitations which will seem most unwelcome to those who favour an objectivizing ethnography.

1   You cannot verify any assertion: first because there is no position of impartial witness in this discourse. Second, because it is pointless to question outsiders: to be bewitched is to have stopped communicating with one's presumed witch as well as with anyone not involved in the crisis; so other villagers know almost nothing of the matter. Finally, it is inconceivable that an ethnographer to whom someone had spoken as to the legitimate occupier of one of the positions in the discourse might step outside it to investigate, and ask what is the truth behind this or that story.

2   You cannot hear both parties – the bewitched and their alleged witches – since they no longer communicate. Not only do they not talk to each other, they do not speak the same kind of language. If, exceptionally, it were ever possible to obtain both versions of the same story, they could not be set face to face, since witches always claim that they do not believe in spells, object to the discourse of witchcraft, and appeal to the language of positivism.[6] In any case, the bewitched prevent any such confrontation by warning the ethnographer to avoid meeting their aggressor, for fear of becoming his victim. To take no notice of this advice would be a sign either of disturbing masochism, or of a rash faith in the powers protecting you, or indeed of an intention to work some betrayal. Note that such daring would be just as disturbing to the 'witch', however imaginary he may be: knowing that the ethnographer sees people who call themselves his victims, he would, on receiving a visit from this stranger, see him as an unwitcher come to fight him. In time of war, nothing so resembles the characteristic weapons of the magician (words, look and touch) as an innocent 'how are you?' followed by a handshake.

3   One cannot investigate in one's own *'quartier'* [neighbourhood] so dreaded is the magic effectiveness of speech. The peasant thinks it wise to maintain a certain distance between the speaker and the listener, to prevent the latter from taking advantage of the situation. A serious crisis will never be taken to the local unwitcher. People prefer to choose their therapist

beyond some boundary (in a neighbouring diocese or *département*), in any case outside the network of acquaintanceship. For this reason, I never worked less than ten kilometres from where I was living. So in general, I remained unaware of the sociological context of witchcraft matters and especially of the particular positions of the opponents in the local struggles for prestige and power – and these usually constitute the subject-matter of ethnographic investigations into witchcraft.

4 One cannot set up any strategy of observation (even a 'participating' one) which keeps the agreed amount of distance that this implies. More generally, to claim an external position for oneself is to abandon hope of ever learning this discourse: first (remember) because those concerned react with silence or duplicity to anyone who claims to be outside. But more profoundly because any attempt at making things explicit comes up against a much more formidable barrier: that of the native's amnesia and his incapacity to formulate what must remain unsaid. These are the limits of what one can ask a willing informer (in so far as such persons exist in the Bocage), and they are soon reached.

To take one example: if you want to know the substance of a diviner's consultation, you can simply ask him what usually takes place in a séance, or what his clients consult him about. But you should not be surprised at trivial answers: *'They come because of illness, love affairs, animals, to recover money they have lost ...'* – 'And what about spells?' – *'That might be the case, but I don't deal with that'* will be the diviner's systematic reply. A barrier, then, of silence and duplicity: the diviner can only admit *'dealing with that'* in front of someone who puts forward a personal request for divination. About the séances, on the other hand, he claims he honestly has nothing more to impart than a few matters of technique: *'I begin with the game of piquet and go on to tarot cards.'* – 'But how do you guess their story?' – *'Well, I have the gift.'* Even when the ethnographer's questions are more subtle, they soon come up against the bounds of the

unstatable, represented here by the reference to a *'gift'*. Pressed to make himself more clear, the diviner can do no more than illustrate his statements by recounting the enigmatic circumstances in which, one day, a long time ago, when becoming a seer had not yet entered his head, a patient seeking for revelations sensed the *'gift'* in him, and announced it to the professional diviner who then initiated him.

If the ethnographer resorts to the patients, he obtains uniformly improbable statements: the diviner, he is told, *'reads me like an open book'*, or again, *'he's extraordinary, I never tell him anything and he knows everything'*. But if he has ever accompanied peasants to the diviner's and sat in the waiting room during the consultations, the ethnographer knows that they never stopped talking: it's just that, as after a hypnotic trance, they do not remember.

So the diviner and his client have a common 'misknowledge' which is not the same as the simple complicity of sharing a secret: no winning of trust will ever make the persons concerned capable of explaining what the terms *'gift'* and *'seeing everything'* really mean, because the whole institution of divination depends on the fact that they do not want to know anything about it.

For anyone who wants to understand the meaning of this discourse, there is no other solution but to practise it oneself, to become one's own informant, to penetrate one's own amnesia, and to try and make explicit what one finds unstatable in oneself. For it is difficult to see how the native could have any interest in the project of unveiling what can go on existing only if it remains veiled; or for what purpose he would give up the symbolic benefits of such important resources.

(I am well aware that there is a fundamental gulf between my present aims and those of my Bocage interlocutors. Until now, I have been content to state that the discourse of witchcraft is such that to gain access to it one must be in a position to sustain it oneself. And yet, it is one thing to have access to it – it was a memorable adventure which has marked me for my whole subsequent life – it is another thing to want to go on to develop its theory.)

If you want to listen to and understand a diviner, there is therefore no other solution but to become his client, i.e. to tell him your desire and ask him to interpret it.[7] Like any native – or any desiring subject – the investigator is bound on this occasion to be afflicted by misknowledge: so for several months, however carefully I tried to take notes after each divination séance, a certain part of the consultation, always the same, was censored by amnesia; similarly, when a seer, who I was hoping would teach me the everyday tricks of divination saw the '*gift*' in me and gave me her life-story for interpretation, claiming she had nothing to teach me that I did not already know, I could not help being amazed.

Persistent amnesia, dumbfoundedness, the inability to reflect when faced by the seemingly unstatable – i.e. a vague perception that *something in this cannot be coped with* – this was my ordinary lot during the adventure.[8] It may be wondered how, at a certain point, I managed to surmount this inability, that is, try to get it out in words, to convert an adventure into a theoretical project. But this question cannot be answered simply by invoking one's duty towards the demands of the scientific approach, or one's debt to the scholarly institution which acts as patron: if that respect applies, it is somewhere else and in another manner. To have been engaged in the discourse of witchcraft beyond what can be required of an ethnographer in the ordinary practice of her profession poses first the problem of motive; what could have been my own desire to know; why was I personally involved in the ambition to give a solid basis to the 'social sciences', and why, in the case of divination for example, was I not content to resolve the issue by invoking the concept of '*gift*', or, even sooner, by accepting the findings of the folklorists.

So the distance necessary if one is to be able to theorize does not have to be established between the ethnographer and his 'object', i.e. the native. But of all the snares which might imperil our work, there are two we had learnt to avoid like the plague: that of agreeing to 'participate' in the native discourse, and that of succumbing to the temptations of subjectivism. Not only could I not possibly avoid them; it is by means of them that I was able to work out

most of my ethnographic work. Whatever you may think of it, it must be granted that the masters' predictions do not always turn out to be true, which state that in such cases it becomes impossible to put any distance between oneself and the native or between oneself and oneself.

Anyway, I was never able to choose between subjectivism and the objective method as it was taught me, so long, that is, as I still wished to find an answer to my initial question – what are the people involved trying to shape out through a witchcraft crisis? Working in this way has at least preserved me from one limitation regularly met by the objectivizing ethnographer and which is never emphasized, since it is taken for granted: I mean the ethnographer's dependence on a finite *corpus* of empirical observations and native texts collected in the field. This kind of ethnography meets any new question with the answer that it is included, or not, in the *corpus*; it can be verified, or not, in the empirical data – and of anything not referred to in the *corpus*, nothing can be asserted. In my case, the fact that Bocage peasants forced me to come up with a number of statements in the same way as they did (i.e. to be an encoder) enabled me to break away from the limits of the *corpus*; or, and this comes to the same thing, to include my own discourse in it. For the sort of question posed by comparative grammarians, I was able to substitute that posed by transformationalists: can this utterance be produced or not? Hazarding my own words in the presence of native decoders, I became able to discriminate accepted from unacceptable meaning whatever the utterance and whether or not it was produced during my stay in the field. The limits of ordinary ethnography are those of its *corpus*. In the case of the ethnography I was practising, the problem was, each time, to evaluate correctly the limits of my position in speech. But my having occupied at one time or another all the positions in this discourse, knowingly or not, or willingly or not, at least enables me to have a view on everything that is statable.

It is now time to give a little information about the position of the witch. No one, in the

Bocage, calls himself a witch; it is not a position from which one can speak. A witch never admits his crimes, not even when he is delirious in a psychiatric hospital (this is considerably different from exotic witchcrafts). The witch is the person referred to by those who utter the discourse on witchcraft (bewitched and unwitchers), and he only figures in it as the subject of the statement. His victims claim that it is unnecessary for him to admit he is a witch, since his death speaks for him: everyone laughs at his funeral because he died in a significant way, carried off in only a few hours as a result of the diviner's curse, or neighing like the mare he had cast an evil spell on, and so on. This makes it highly unlikely that there are witches who actually cast evil spells, but this is surely not in the least necessary for the system to function.

NOTES

1   *Bocage*: countryside of Western France marked by intermingling patches of woodland and heath, small fields, tall hedgerows and orchards.
2   *Unwitcher*: The Bocage natives use the word *désorcelleur* rather than the more usual *désensorcelleur* [ensorceller = to bewitch]. I have translated it by *unwitcher* rather than *unbewitcher*. Similarly, *désorceller* is translated as *to unwitch* and *désorcellage* or *désorcellement* as *unwitching* or *unwitchment*.
3   He only recounts one incident (p. 460) in which the Zande were able to say he was bewitched.
4   It is not surprising that Clausewitz (1968) was an important point of reference at the beginning of my work: war as a supremely serious game, trying to dictate its laws to the enemy; as an extension of a duel on a wider scale and over a longer span; as a continuation of politics through other means, and so on. It was not always easy to decide which one was speaking: the discourse of war or the discourse of witchcraft, at least until I realized that it was meaningless to think of witchcraft in terms of the categories of game theory.
5   Anyone who called himself bewitched on his own authority would simply be thought mad: a warning to apprentice sorcerers who try to make peasants talk by simply declaring themselves '*caught*'.
6   A dodge which an Azande would never have imagined, since he can only choose between *witchcraft* and *sorcery*.
7   To consult without asking the seer to 'see' is futile, since the latter sees nothing and there is nothing for the ethnographer to understand.
8   I might just as well express it as 'can't be thought' or 'can't be said'; in talking of what 'can't be coped with', I am trying to point to an element of reality, that at some point escapes the grasp of language or symbolization.

REFERENCES

Clausewitz, K. von
1968   *On War*, edited with an introduction by A. Rapport, trans. J. S. Graham, Harmondsworth.
Evans-Pritchard, E. E.
1937   *Witchcraft, Oracles and Magic among the Azande*, Oxford.

34

Transmutation of Sensibilities: Empathy, Intuition, Revelation

Thomas J. Csordas

There are moments in the course of ethnographic work that occupy a particular position on the continuum between going native and feeling the absolute stranger. These moments occur on what the editors of this volume have called the "shadow side" of ethnography, and are quite different from moments of insight, apt translation, feeling at home, attaining to fluency, relaxed comfort, or true friendship with one's informants. They are moments that can best be described as the transmutation of sensibilities, when one has an unexpected and striking experience in a modality typical of the setting in which one is working. The experience is one that could have been experienced by an indigenous person in the sense of its form and its relevance to the immediate setting, but not in terms of its psycho-dynamic content or the dispositions upon which it is founded. This chapter describes three such moments that I have experienced, and examines the conjunction between existential and ethnographic significance to which they point.

* * * * *

Beginning in 1973 I began fieldwork in the Catholic Charismatic Renewal, a neo-Pentecostal movement within the Roman Catholic Church. One of the features of Charismatic ritual life that I found most intriguing was a system of genres of ritual language that included prayer, teaching, witnessing, and prophecy. Among these genres, prophecy was particularly potent in that it was understood as God speaking though the mind and mouth of the one gifted to deliver the utterance. It is a charism or gift of the Holy Spirit mentioned by St. Paul as among those granted to the apostles at Pentecost. In form, prophecy as I heard it in the 1970s and 1980s was often an elegant kind of inspired oral poetry produced in couplet form. In rhetorical effect it occasionally moved people to act in

Thomas J. Csordas, "Transmutation of Sensibilities: Empathy, Intuition, Revelation," pp. 106–116 from *The Shadow Side of Fieldwork: Exploring the Blurred Borders between Ethnography and Life*, ed. Athena McLean and Annette Leibing. Malden: Blackwell, 2007.

Ethnographic Fieldwork: An Anthropological Reader, Second Edition. Edited by Antonius C. G. M. Robben and Jeffrey A. Sluka.
Editorial material and organization © 2012 John Wiley & Sons, Inc.
Published 2012 by John Wiley & Sons, Inc.

certain ways or undertake certain projects that were highly consequential for their lives.

Charismatic prophecy is readily recognizable by prosodic features such as an authoritative vocal tone, and an opening formula of address such as "My children," and as a first person utterance in which the "I" is God. It articulates an identifiable vocabulary of motives and exhibits a repertoire of typical themes. The prophet is responsible for exercising "discernment" with respect to whether his or her inspiration is authentically from God as well as whether the message is intended for personal edification only or for the edification and exhortation of the larger group. In short, it is a full-fledged genre with conventions that can be assimilated by cultivated listening and that can be performed by all participants with appropriate legitimation from the community of devotees.

Soon after I began working in a Catholic Charismatic group in the city where I attended university as an undergraduate, I became aware that the movement had become widespread in the United States and had begun to expand abroad as well. I realized that if I were to claim to be studying the movement rather than a local instantiation of that movement my ethnography would necessarily be multi-sited. As I traveled among Charismatic communities I learned that various among them were allied into networks, were in regular contact with one another, and in symbolic terms tended to distinguish among themselves by adopting names that often reflected the notion that each community possessed a unique charism that it contributed to a "community of communities" just as within each community individual members were granted charisms that in their ensemble would contribute to the building of that community.

Small prayer groups sometimes aspired to grow into communities with a full complement of spiritual gifts, or at least to be able to develop a particular "ministry" in service to their own members and others who might seek their help or seek to join them, and by which they would be recognized among other groups. In the course of my travels, having spent time with a variety of groups over the course of several years, I visited the weekly prayer meeting of a small group of perhaps thirty members, coincidentally (perhaps) in the town where I had spent part of my childhood and adolescence. It became clear that the group had been prayerfully discussing whether to initiate a "healing ministry" which would become their defining activity. Such a healing ministry is one in which a team of people are chosen based on their perceived maturity and caring. They and other members pray to receive the charism of healing, and subsequently they can be approached by others for healing prayer and the laying on of hands. The prayer meeting itself was not an appropriate venue for discussion, but for "seeking the Lord's will" via prayer and openness to the divine response in prophecy.

At some point during the meeting, as I listened and observed the process of collective inspiration potentially giving birth to social form and practice, a brief sentence took form in my thoughts, or perhaps I could say that the following words came to me: "My children, be cautious." After perhaps a moment's lag time I did a mental double take, and said to myself, "O my God, I just got a prophecy." There was no mistaking the phenomenon, having studied it, listened to it, transcribed it, conducted interviews about it, read Charismatics' own manuals on how to recognize and use the gift. The words had emerged in thought spontaneously, fully formed and in effect with quotation marks already inscribed, though as I recall it the presentation was not in visual but in purely verbal form. It was more like the way a line of poetry or song lyric might come, visual only in the sense that it appealed to a disposition to commit such words to writing. This was my first encounter with the shadow side of ethnography.

What is required here is a precise phenomenological account of what happened to me in this instance, for it is perfectly inadequate to say that for a moment I was converted or that for a moment I went native. We would be getting closer by saying that my prophecy was an upwelling of empathy for their struggle, an authentic struggle to discern what they imagined as God's will for them as a group, a struggle to do the right things and provide service to their fellow Christians in a way for which they were best suited, a struggle to play their part in bringing about the kingdom of God, a struggle which I was able to recognize having observed others trying to create similar ministries, sometimes with greater resources. Associated with this empathy in a way that is critical and in need of further elaboration is a specific intuition about the circumstances under which this decision was being undertaken and the feeling of tension about something being at stake. Specifically, the intuition would be awareness of the risks involved based on ethnographic background knowledge of the stress and potential for "burnout" faced by those who placed themselves in the position of praying for the healing of others, others who could be emotionally quite needy and demanding. Risks, too, of "getting in over one's head," in situations where what was needed was a fully trained psychotherapist rather than a well-meaning layperson.

Still, empathy and intuition do not account for why my experience took the form of a prophecy. I have hinted at two possible idiosyncratic features that would incline the situation in that direction. The fact that it took place in my home town perhaps created an element of entitlement to speak authoritatively. The fact that I had some experience writing poetry and song lyrics and in addition studied the work of Alfred Lord on oral composition among folk poets perhaps created an element of subjective familiarity with the kind of genre conventions in question. However, the principal factor was that I had studied this genre of ritual speech and the system of genres in which it is embedded thoroughly enough so that, without being fully aware that this was taking place, I had both incorporated its performative conventions and inculcated within myself its performative dispositions. I am intentionally evoking language reminiscent of Bourdieu's discussion of habitus because it is only by immersion within a habitus that one can experience what I want to call the transmutation of sensibilities that occurred in my revelatory experience. That is, my upsurge of empathy and intuition was clothed in the immediacy of appropriate cultural form because I was immersed in the charismatic habitus. And by sensibilities I am not referring only to empathy

and intuition, but to language and expression as they are evoked in an intersubjective setting of bodily being in proximity to others who are simultaneously open to inspiration.

It is hardly relevant from this standpoint that I was not, nor could I be, actively engaged in the collective act of "seeking the Lord's will." What I will submit in evidence for my interpretation is the fact that my empathic/intuitive insight that took the form of revelation – that is, conformed to the genre conventions of prophecy – created a dilemma. Was I somehow obligated to pass on the message to the participants? The point is that I took this question quite seriously. It was not because I thought God was perhaps using me the non-believer as a messenger, though I have heard that possibility articulated. It was rather – again thinking retrospectively – that I respected the authenticity of inspiration, whether the source was actually the human imagination or misrepresented as divine intervention in human consciousness. The point is that the transmutation of sensibilities was sufficiently thorough that it made me actively question how to comport myself. So how did I handle it? The genre convention requiring discernment on the part of the prophet made it evident that a stranger, let alone a non-believer, should not speak out publicly without the most powerful sense of conviction. The question was whether to share the revelation with the priest who was leader of the group after the meeting. I did so, at the same time identifying myself as an anthropologist studying the Charismatic Renewal. He thanked me politely, and that was the end of the episode.

* * * * *

My second encounter with the shadow side of ethnography occurred more than twenty years later while I was participating in a Navajo Night Way ceremony. The Night Way is one of the crown jewels of the Navajo ritual system, a nine–night ceremony conducted during the winter months and featuring the appearance of troops of masked dancers representing the *yei-bi-cheis*, that is, the Navajo deities or Holy People. On the fourth and ninth nights of this ceremony ritual activities continue till dawn, with prayer, song, manipulation of ritual objects, and ministry to the patient – virtually every Navajo ceremony except those marking life cycle transitions is directed toward healing and has a patient.

Late on the fourth night of this particular ceremony, perhaps at four o'clock in the morning, a bucket of water was passed along with a wooden dipper for participants to take a drink. As is often the case in such situations, the passing of the water was not merely instrumental in the sense of recognition of the need to satisfy thirst, but was a ritual act involving the symbolic importance of water. The wooden dipper was hand carved such that the rounded bottom was not smooth but rugged from the action of the tool that had created its hollow. At the moment that I lifted the dipper to my mouth, light glinted off the wet and uneven inner surface of the dipper. I had two thoughts simultaneously as the light struck my eye. The first was that it appeared to have reflected from the lantern in the Hogan off my glasses and into the dipper. The second was that, for only an instant as the angle of the dipper and the reflected light changed with my movement, the reflection took the shape of a *yei-bi-chei*, specifically the hump-backed deity who is one of the participating gods in the Night Chant and who is related to the commonly depicted Kokopeli figure of the Pueblos.

We can consider this the apparition of a deity in the same sense as my Charismatic experience was an instance of prophecy. It was by no means a hallucination in the sense of an image suspended indeterminately in space, and neither was it an inward phenomenon like the prophecy (which as I noted emerged in consciousness as a line of poetry might). It appeared in concrete sensory form as a silhouette formed of light, although so instantaneously and briefly that it seems it could have passed unnoticed by me. I did notice it, however, again because of incorporated performative conventions and inculcated performative dispositions. To be more precise, I not so much recognized a form as endowed the shifting reflection with form. I in-formed it by means of a synthetic bodily act including not only the coalescence of a visual gestalt but the synchronization of lifting the water-filled dipper at a certain angle in relation to the lantern and in so doing performing a ritual act of the most minimal sort. I was rewarded with a revelation of the most minimal sort, just as my Charismatic prophecy was a minimal prophecy.

This time I felt no obligation to narrate the incident, although it can be considered important to share such information in Navajo ceremonialism since it may suggest some unanticipated ritual need to the chanter or indicate some danger to which the chanter must respond ceremonially. My motivation for telling the chanter what had happened was more to use the incident as a way to elicit a comment from him. I was interested in whether he would regard my experience as meaningful or epiphenomenal. In fact, he said "What you thought you saw is probably a sign that they're around [i.e., the yei-bi-cheis], intended to show someone who's not a believer that this is real." Note that in judging the apparition to be a sign from the deities he hedges by referring to what I "thought" I saw, and by saying that it was "probably" a sign. Yet later at end of the night's prayers he asked if I wanted to say anything, which I took as a cue to give a general thank-you speech to the healer and his team as well as the patient and his family for the privilege of participating and helping with the ceremony. In addition, however, the chanter prompted me to narrate the image for the edification of those in attendance, and pointedly stated in summary that "It wasn't just light reflected from your glasses."

Beyond this performative moment, my opening to the shadow side created a framework of intersubjectivity that was in turn grounds for an empathic bond that I had not anticipated. Later while we sat together eating at one of the tables in the large cook-tent set up to accommodate participants in the nine-night ceremony, he narrated an experience of his own in having direct contact with the Holy People. He began by noting that he built his house in 1960, and said that an event happened there in 1965. He was lying down on the couch, and though he thought he was awake at the time said he may have been asleep. He felt something on his toe, and saw one of the Holy People grabbing his toe and wiggling it, with all the holy paraphernalia spread out near the chanter's feet. He blinked and it was gone, but could still feel it on his toe. The touch of the deity, even in so peripheral a spot as the toe, and perhaps graciously on the toe so as not to overwhelm the mere mortal with too much bodily contact, was a profound and permanently remembered sign that he said really encouraged him in his ritual career.

I recognized this brief narrative as an ethnographic gift. The gift and its personal significance to me were enhanced by the gratification of hearing a narration of personal experience from a healer who was characteristically quite guarded in passing on any information the divulging of which might create a dangerous supernatural repercussion, a healer whom I had known for 15 years but who only now was exhibiting a degree of trust and recognition. Further, in narrating his experience of hierophany the chanter was acknowledging that my experience fell into the same category, and by reaching back to 1965 for his example he was acknowledging that such moments do not occur all that often.

I gave this as my second example not because it was more recent in my own experience but to preempt the inclination to account for my revelation in terms of suggestibility due to sleep deprivation during a long ceremony. I was not at all sleep deprived when I experienced Charismatic prophecy, and on the other hand the Navajo chanter who was my interlocutor in this instance also narrated an incident which took place on the border between sleep and waking. The altered state of consciousness is of no consequence in itself unless we consider it to be a preparation or enhancement of susceptibility to a disposition, convention, or sensibility rather than its creation.

In sum, my experience was constituted by a transmutation of sensibilities insofar as my sense of performative presence and power was spontaneously manifest in a culturally appropriate form. Although its subsequent narration created an intersubjective bond with my interlocutor the chanter, a bond that can be glossed as empathic, the revelation itself was not empathy. Transmutation of sensibilities can be a vehicle of empathy or intuition as in this or the Charismatic episode. But to say it is empathy for the ritual system and the performance

instead of reserving the term empathy for a bond with other persons would be an abuse of language. We are better off referring as I have done to the incorporation of performative conventions and inculcation of performative dispositions.

*****

My final bit of evidence also comes from Navajoland, but this time takes place not in a traditional Navajo ceremony but in a meeting of the Native American Church. Brought to the Navajo in the 1930s by members of Plains Indian tribes, the Native American Church has become an integral part of the religious landscape in the Navajo Nation. Its central ceremony, an all-night prayer meeting, has been adapted to Navajo sensibilities and is strongly oriented toward healing. Devotion is oriented toward a creator spirit sometimes assimilated to the Christian god, to whom access is granted through ritual ingestion of the peyote cactus. Peyote is at once a powerful medicine, a sacrament, and a spirit sometimes regarded as equivalent to Jesus. Chemically it includes a series of related alkaloids, the most significant of which in its effect is the hallucinogen mescaline. During peyote meetings the medicine is passed among participants several times during the night, often in both the forms of powder and tea. Proceedings are led by a healer called a road man whose function is to guide people along the "peyote road" of right living. A prayer meeting consists of alternating periods of song accompanied by rattle and drum, and periods of prayer until dawn when participants are fed a ritual meal and gradually allow the effects of the medicine to diminish so they can go about their everyday affairs.

My encounter with the shadow side took place not in the depths of the night's prayer and song, but after dawn when the sky had lightened. The morning hours after the ritual breakfast is served are typically spent lounging in the tepee, everyone tired from being awake all night but not yet able to sleep because of the peyote, joking and talking lazily as the effects of the medicine recede. On this particular morning at about 8:30 I left the tepee to go to the bathroom. While outside I recalled that my rented car was low on gas, and had the impulse to drive to the nearest gas station, which was nine miles down the road at the highway junction. As soon as I started the unfamiliar car the low fuel indicator light came on. It occurred to me that perhaps I should postpone this errand until later in the morning, when I had not only returned to a more accustomed perceptual state but had the opportunity to tell others where I was going. I remained anxious all the way to the gas station, mostly imagining how foolish I would appear to the others by driving off while the medicine was still affecting me, especially if I ran out of fuel and had to walk back.

I did arrive at the gas station without trouble. While filling the tank I noticed a pay telephone on the outside wall of the station, and decided to phone home to let my wife know I was all right after the all-night ceremony. The first thing she said upon answering the ring was that my son, who was 9 years old, had just told her his dream from the previous night. In the dream a group of people had gotten into our car and I was driving us all across a body of water to a place of freedom, where we would all have more space – apparently an underwater oasis with a swimming pool inside a bubble structure. In the dream I said we were low on fuel, and my son replied "Here, Dad, I have a gallon of gas, you can use this." I checked his container to make sure he really had gas (apparently as a dream father I did not fully trust that what he had was indeed gasoline), then put it in the tank and said "Now we can really travel." The cooccurrence of my son's experience and my own suggested that I had been the beneficiary of his dream gas in real time, and that this accounted for why I had successfully reached the gas station on an empty tank.

The impact on me of this dream narration would not have been as profound if I had not set off so impulsively without telling the others where I was going. When I rejoined them I narrated the incident to those present, and the healer's nephew translated for her into Navajo. As I spoke, it became narratively clear not only that my son's gallon is what allowed me to make it to the gas station, but that the water over which we were driving in his dream corresponded to the central symbolic role of water

in this healer's personal interpretation of the peyote religion. Moreover, the Navajo word for water is "*tooh*," and the Navajo word for gasoline is "*chidi bi tooh*," or "the car's water." In conversation, people often simply say "tooh" for both, and distinguish by context whether it means water or gas. The first thing the healer said in response to my narrative was "You better include this story in your book." The others said "Now you know for yourself how this medicine works. This is your story that you can tell."

In fact, the nature of the psychic connection between my son and me is that during that period he often felt quite unsettled when I was away traveling. To follow through on the notion of a transmutation of sensibilities, in this incident the medicine amplified and emphasized this connection in order to make a point to me. What can this mean in cultural and existential terms aside from the fact that I, like that other Thomas, am open to the persuasiveness of compelling evidence? As strong as it is, the peyote in itself does not account for the shadow side experience any more than sleep deprivation accounted for it in my second example. Again what is at issue are performative conventions and dispositions with respect to how to accommodate the effects of the medicine. This was eloquently put in two points made by one of the elders in this meeting as he spoke to me during a midnight break under the stars. In the first he analogized awareness of the peyote's effect to awareness of the wind: "How can you feel the wind is on you, the air moving against your body? How can you tell where it's coming from? How can you tell how the medicine is working, where it's coming from? It moves you." In the second he used the metaphor of peyote as a mirror: "The medicine is a mirror, it reflects what you do. If you want to be afraid it's afraid, if you want to be serious it's serious, if you want to joke around it jokes around, if you want to be macho it's macho. It matches you, your character."

These points, lessons really, capture both the alterity and identity of the sacred. In the first point, peyote is active and independent, like the wind blowing against a person, a sometimes subtle force that can be discerned and detected, and that moves one. It is an

Other with which one comes into relation, both external in its transcendence and internal as it is incorporated – the wind (*nilch'i*), in Navajo thinking, is not something inanimate or totally external, because the wind/air inhabits and animates us as humans, and therefore is continuous with us. In the second lesson the medicine is a function of the person as it corresponds with, responds to, is shaped by, and matches the person's character and intentions. This image also combines identity in the sense that it brings the true self to the fore, and alterity insofar as a reflection projects from and stands uncannily outside the self, indeed is perhaps the archetype of the alterity of the self. The sensibilities of alterity and identity outlined in these lessons are neither Navajo nor Anglo, but simply human, and for me their transmutation was literally a "change in form." That is, my incorporation of performative conventions and dispositions made possible a change of existential form and interpretive frame such that intuition and empathy as already constituted were amplified within a matrix of symbolic and personal connections that I would not otherwise have made.

*****

Anthropologists have a limited repertoire of ideas to discuss their personal encounters in the field. I will conclude by making several summary assertions about the usefulness of and interrelations among the principal terms I have evoked in my description of shadow side experiences. Empathy is a potentially valuable concept in this respect, since it can be a feeling in relation to a specific person, but also in relation to a way of life or mode of experience. But empathy is neither necessarily a personality trait, nor a learned/cultivated skill. It can also be a phenomenon of immersion in a cultural milieu.

Empathy is a specific case of intuition, one that has to do with feeling for and with another person. Intuition can be impersonal, both in the sense of not requiring a sense of caring for and in the sense that it can pertain to situations that do not involve other humans and may be about nature or inanimate objects. Empathy is eminently and perhaps obviously a phenomenon of intersubjectivity but, I would argue, so is intuition. This, pushing the argument, might even be said to be the case where intuition has to do with so-called inanimate objects.

Without adopting an overtly animist position, to the extent that even our inanimate objects participate in a world of human sensibilities, it is not going too far to invoke intersubjectivity in all instances of intuition insofar as intuition is constituted by immediate recognition of being enfolded in what Merleau-Ponty called the flesh of the world. This is perhaps easiest to see when the inanimate objects are elements of culture: artifacts, ideas, dispositions, modes of thought. Along these lines, empathy for a way of life is equivalent to intuition about a way of life, though intuition in this sense would have a more neutral evaluative valence than empathy. That is, empathy connotes fellow-feeling and kinship, being on the same side. Intuition can imply canny insight without precluding an underlying hostility.

When instances of intuition and/or empathy occur spontaneously, it is fair to call them revelation whether or not they occur within a ritual or religious setting. The instances I have recounted in this chapter were striking in part because of their spontaneity, and their spontaneity was in turn likely a product of the cross-cultural dynamics of the situations in which they took place. It is likely that the term transmutation of sensibilities describes the process of empathy, intuition, and revelation even in more mundane same-culture non-ritual settings. Nevertheless, the ensemble of performative conventions and dispositions that are brought into play to achieve the transmutation are more readily discerned in such instances as I have narrated here. And this is perhaps one of the services to ethnography that can be rendered by paying attention to its shadow side.

35

"At the Heart of the Discipline": Critical Reflections on Fieldwork

Vincent Crapanzano

"WE HAVE A JOB TO DO, SO LET'S GET ON WITH IT." These are the words of one of the most down-to-earth, most pragmatic anthropologists I have ever known. Mervin Meggitt and I were driving back to New York from Princeton, where I was teaching. Meggitt had given a talk there, and though I can no longer remember his subject, I remember our conversation vividly. He was describing how surprised he was when he came to the States by all the talk, the anguish, about fieldwork. "I never heard the word 'culture shock' in Australia." Culture shock was very much in fashion then, in the early seventies. It was with some impatience that Meggitt went on to say: "We have a job to do, so let's get on with it."

I remember thinking at the time how lucky Meggitt was. I was just beginning to write *Tuhami* and was struggling with the intricate dynamics of my encounter with a Moroccan tilemaker who believed himself to be married to a *jinniyya* – a she-demon (Crapanzano 1980). With some trepidation, I began to describe my project. Before I could finish, Meggitt interrupted: "I suppose it all depends on with whom you're working. The Aborigines and the Papuans are a very pragmatic people. The Moroccans don't seem to be." Clearly Meggitt had not read Geertz's "Islam Observed" (1968) or was simply dismissing Geertz's portrait of them as Wild West pragmatists. Meggitt had some unkind words to say about participant observation as well, but I don't remember exactly what he said.

I don't believe there was ever much fuss made about the nature of fieldwork, at least its psychological dimensions, in the United Kingdom. Nor was there in France. Nor, I believe, was there ever so much concern about methodology. This concern with methodology reflects the position of American anthropology in terms of its "sister" disciplines in the social and psychological sciences, which have elaborated methodologies that are themselves responses in part to the hegemonic position of the physical sciences and their methodologies.

Vincent Crapanzano, "'At the Heart of the Discipline': Critical Reflections on Fieldwork," pp. 55–78 from *Emotions in the Field: The Psychology and Anthropology of Fieldwork Experience*, ed. James Davies and Dimitrina Spencer. Stanford: Stanford University Press, 2010.

Ethnographic Fieldwork: An Anthropological Reader, Second Edition. Edited by Antonius C. G. M. Robben and Jeffrey A. Sluka.
Editorial material and organization © 2012 John Wiley & Sons, Inc.
Published 2012 by John Wiley & Sons, Inc.

It is also a response to the "scientific" criteria of granting agencies and in complex ways to American attitudes toward "hard" data, numbers, and literal meaning, all of which have influenced the American take on empiricism and positivism. It also reflects a particular epistemological stance that favors the universal, the general, over the particular. It accounts for an at times apologetic, at times defiant tone in anthropology's defense of itself. It may well account for American anthropologists' propensity to cling to one theoretical model or another, most often borrowed from other disciplines, with an intensity that borders at times on the religious, or at least the ideological. All of this affects the way American anthropologists have constructed and evaluated fieldwork.

I have stressed the "American" here and opposed it to the British and the French to call attention to important differences in national anthropological traditions. What I have to say about fieldwork reflects my training and my particular relationship to that tradition. Although I have attempted to preserve critical distance by assuming one external vantage point or another, I have to acknowledge that, even at a remove, my training echoes intellectually, stylistically, and emotionally in "my" research in often surprisingly uncritical, indeed unwitting, ways. "As a constraining conscience," I am tempted to add. I have placed "my" in "'my' research" in quotation marks to accent a propensity in anthropological research to take possession of that research's findings, often masking the complex interlocution at home and in the field which defines and gives direction to the research.

Fieldwork has been taken as the heart of the discipline, but it has not always had such a privileged position. In northern Europe, in Denmark until recently, fieldwork, as the task of the ethnographer, had a somewhat inferior status to interpretive and theoretical elaboration – the task of the ethnologist. Though it is at the heart of the discipline, it has, as Meggitt's words indicate, not received the critical reflection it deserves. To be sure, there has been a lot of talk about participant observation, but it is now recognized that "participant observation" does not adequately describe what occurs in the field. Its oxymoronic implication has been

belabored, but it does call attention to a particular demand in anthropological research: the need to be critically conscious of what one is doing as one does it. This reflective stance refers not only to whatever activities one is engaged in – watching a ritual, mending a fence, measuring a field – but to verbal exchanges as well.

***

I want to look at a range of encounters in the field, not only to illustrate this range but to suggest how these encounters influence the data collected and how those data are construed. Before proceeding, I want to make twelve general observations. They are abstract but will be filled in further on in this essay, when I discuss concrete field situations.

1. Every field encounter determines in part the way in which the data collected, including the encounter itself, is framed, interpreted, and generalized. We usually focus on what is in-frame – what transpires in the field – and ignore, misperceive, or devalue what is out-of-frame, outside the field experience itself. In so doing, we disturb the day-to-day experience of those with whom we work.

A First Corollary

However sensitive we are to our informants, we have to recognize that fieldwork is at some level always a violation. We are rather like uninvited guests who hopefully, once welcomed, behave with consideration and perhaps even offer our hosts something they value. We gain nothing by denying this violation: the inherent violence of field research.

2. Every field encounter, and every encounter in the field, is a unique encounter. But insofar as it is thought to lay bare social and cultural generalities, the immediacy of the encounter is torn asunder by a telos alien to most ordinary encounters that are the ethnographer's idealized object of study. In other words, the immediacy, the

spontaneity, the particularity of the encounter is corrupted by the generalizing goal of the anthropologist (and at times that of his informants). It is symptomatized. The ambiguity, the paradoxical nature of the ethnographic encounter, insinuates itself through all phases of research, analysis, interpretation, and textualization and the theory that is generated or implicated thereby. It demands – for lack of a better term – a deconstruction that assaults the normalized anthropological goal and produces defenses (denials) that are perhaps even more destructive of that goal or those goals (Devereux 1967).

3. Though the encounter influences the data, its influence is constrained both by psychological blinkers (blinders) and by the orientation – the conventions and assumptions – with which one approaches the encounter. In the words of Hans Georg Gadamer (1975), the encounter is influenced by preunderstanding and prejudice – the *Vorverständnis* and *Vorurteil* – with which one enters the field.

4. We tend to restrict these prejudices, this orientation, to those of our discipline. But in so doing, we may blind ourselves to the defensive structure, whatever its truth or efficacy, of these orientations. They may mask, for example, racialist assumptions that even if we are not racist affect how we construe the field situation.

5. There is in all fieldwork a struggle at both manifest and latent levels between openness to the new, to the exotic, to otherness and to our reductive loyalty to our orientations and prejudices. (I use "exotic" in a neutral but potent sense to refer to that which is foreign, unfamiliar, outside.) Our take on the data we collect is always a compromise between our acceptance of the risks posed by openness to the exotic and the comfort of reductive closure. It may be emotionally laden.

6. To be good fieldworkers – and none of us are always good fieldworkers – we require what Keats called negative capability – the ability to identify with a character (and, I would add, a point of view) without losing our own identity, our own point of view,

the confidence of our position. But I hasten to add, lest you remark on a contradiction between this Keatsian assertion and the stress I have given openness, that one's own point of view is subject to modification without crashing.

7. Thus far I have stressed the researcher as though he or she were operating singly in an exotic field. But clearly this is not the case, for fieldwork consists of encounters with others, who come to the encounter with their own prejudices and orientations, including the value they put on openness and closure. It is interpersonal, interlocutory – a mini-drama of plays of power, desire, and imagination.

Two Corollaries

The first is that the casting of the field encounter in terms of power and desire reflects a culture-specific orientation – what Joel Robbins (2006), following the theologian John Milbank's (1990) re-visioning of the social sciences, calls a social ontology of violence and conflict. Milbank urges, as we might expect, an ontology that gives central place to peace, charity, and reconciliation. Does an ontology of violence preclude one of peace, charity, and reconciliation?

The second corollary concerns that barbarous neologism *othering*. What is the attraction today of othering, otherness, the other? Yes, it is abstract enough to play an important (post-Hegelian) generalizing, indeed universalizing, role in the construction of our socio-logics. With this I have no quarrel, provided we recognize that its abstractness precludes, or at least facilitates the preclusion of, the recognition of more nuanced qualities of relationship – loving, hating, seductive, dismissive, idealizing, derogating. All of these relate "self" and "other" in subtly different ways that are of immense social and psychological importance. They may promote engagement, closeness, identification, fusion, and even possession or disengagement, distance, rejection, isolation, and solitude. Of course, their consideration raises a set of moral issues that, no less present, are not as salient when we refer simply to

othering, the dialectics of alterity, and otherness. We have to ask what we are excluding
from consideration. Are we attempting to
avoid the moral pressure of the intimate and
the particular? Or, in another way, the epipha-
nous quality of the particular and all it opens
up, including the aesthetic?

8. Fieldwork can produce deeply and
   sometimes troubling emotions in both the
   anthropologist and his or her informants,
   who, each in his or her own way, defend
   against them, say, through repression or
   by assuming a stoic stance. But fieldwork
   may also produce pleasurable emotions
   which we want, sometimes at our expense,
   to prolong. Here I want to stress that,
   though we in the West tend to locate emotions in the individual, not all societies
   conceive and experience them that way.
   They may understand them transaction-
   ally; the emotions may be thought to be
   shared or to hover as quasi objects in the
   between of an encounter. I myself have
   insisted on an interlocutory approach to
   emotions (Crapanzano 1992:229–238,
   1994; Rosenberg 1990). What becomes
   significant is the transfer of emotions from
   interlocutor to interlocutor and their
   dramatic progression (Crapanzano 1994).
9. Fieldwork extends over time. To say that
   the anthropologist is a participant observer
   in research that may extend over years,
   decades even, carries detemporalization
   and simplification to absurdity. Extended
   over time, fieldwork is subject to the conventional and contingent course of life, as
   it is subject to all the moods and feelings of
   the fieldworker and his or her informants.
   Given our particular chronotope, this temporal dimension is often spatialized and,
   as such, rendered static. We might, however, speak more dynamically of the centrifugal and the centripetal movement of
   the field experience.

Two Corollaries

The first concerns the importance of the contingent and accidental in fieldwork. I know of
no anthropologist who has not recounted the
contingencies that led him or her to settle in a
particular village, live with a certain family,
meet an especially insightful informant, or
discover an aspect of the society or culture
hitherto unknown to him or her. I myself could
give countless examples. We do depend on the
contingent from the moment we start our
research, and this dependency affects the way
we do our research. It may produce a particular
sense of time or progression: a fragile, at times
resigned, positive or negative, expectation
verging on the atomistic, infused – as troubling
as this may be – with a sense of fate or, less
systematically, with chance. It may promote
in reaction a strong sense of determination.

The second, related corollary concerns the
importance of breakdowns in the field. Not
only do they reveal responses that we might not
otherwise discover, but they also convert our
perspective and that of our informants from
one of unthinking engagement, being lost in the
flow of habitual activity, to a reflective, objectifying stance toward whatever has broken
down and its immediate surround. Heidegger
(1967:95 ff.) would understand this change as
a shift from the *Zuhanden* (ready-to-hand) to
the *Vorhanden* (presence-at-hand). I want to
stress the importance of breakdowns in conversation, many of which we understand in terms
of misunderstanding. These misunderstandings,
as dangerous as they may be, are one of the
principal ways to ethnographic discovery – that
is, if they are not ignored or dismissed. The
arrival of the anthropologist may itself be
understood as accidental by his or her informants and as a break – a breakdown – in their
routine life. They may conceive of the arrival as
fated, god-given, demonically inspired, or just a
product of chance. Obviously it will affect their
attitude toward the anthropologist.

10. For the anthropologist, the time of field-
    work is no doubt differently conceived
    and experienced than it is by his or her
    informants. To put it simply: the anthro-
    pologist's sense of time, marked as it is by
    a beginning and an ending – an arrival
    and a departure – is telic. It has a goal, in
    fact a moving goal: to come up with an
    array of findings that will eventually

become a text or texts of one sort or another that will make a contribution to the discipline, and ultimately (hopefully) to our understanding of being human. This goal, which is usually preformed (though expectably subject to change as the fieldwork progresses), affects the field experience in multiple ways. Among the most important of these is rendering it suspenseful and anxiety-provoking (Will I get the data?); curtailing time (Will I have sufficient time?); and extending time (I've got what I need, but I have to wait it out, don't I? Do I need more?). Often the goal leads to fishing for facts, which gives to the experience a staccato quality and in consequence a distortion of the shared experience of duration. It tests the anthropologist and his or her subjects' patience.

Two Corollaries

Note taking influences the progress of the field encounter by slowing it down, making it awkward, objectifying it, rendering it episodic and worthy of preservation. The notes extend the field experience in time as they reduce it by giving greater credence to the written word than to live – however, distorting – memory. As time goes on, the mnemonic force of the notes deadens even before its ultimate extinction with the demise of the note-taker. Under many circumstances, the privilege given (culturally) to the written word by the anthropologist clashes with that given to the spoken word, to the phatic dimension of interlocution, by the people under study. We might well consider King Ammon's (Thamus') response to Theuth's invention of writing in Plato's (1987:274d–e) *Phaedrus* as expressing one possible attitude toward the written and spoken word and memory. Socrates quotes the king: "If men learn this [the art of writing], it will implant forgetfulness in their souls: they will cease to exercise memory because they rely on that which is written, calling things to remembrance no longer from within themselves but by means of external marks: what you have discovered [writing] is a recipe not for memory,

but for reminder." The shift from memory to reminder would affect the anthropologist's experience of time both during and after fieldwork in ways radically different from that of those informants who do not share his or her faith in the written word. Audio and visual recordings are no less intrusive. Though they suggest greater accuracy than note-taking, they delimit the progression of field research. Recorded, they cannot capture the immediacy of contact of the spoken encounter: engaged co-presence (Traimond 2008). The foreknowledge of departure affects the anthropologist and his informants in different ways. It may be looked forward to or dreaded by both. It imposes a burden on the anthropologist. It may produce a *crise de conscience,* a sense of responsibility for real or imagined disruptions that his or her interventions have effected, and a constellation of feelings that arise from the knowledge that remediation will no longer be possible. I stress the negative here – regret – not because I want to deny the positive consequences of the presence of the anthropologist for the people studied – they may well be significant – but because most anthropologists with whom I have spoken describe their departures with regret, sorrow, and guilt. Frequently departure ends with a promise to return, which may well never be kept (as both parties suspect), and whose breach will color the aftermath of fieldwork for both the anthropologist and his or her subjects for years.

11. In field encounters, genre, convention, and style, the permissible and impermissible, what can and cannot be said and in what idiom are subject to complex negotiations. They open up imaginative horizons, as well as memories of the past, which may be received with enthusiasm or with fear and regret. To put it in language that is not usually used in discussing fieldwork, the anthropological encounter opens up transgressive possibilities that affect all parties to the encounter and the nature of the encounter in ways that extend beyond consciousness. The encounter demands a shift in perspective, or better, a continuing shift in perspective, by both the

researcher and his or her subjects (Bachnick 1986). I want, especially, to stress the negotiation of *a* perspective, which I liken to the editorial perspective that we adopt as we revise what we have written. Of course, what we are to write, what we write and have written, all figure in the maintenance of this perspective – its artifice. As the relationship between fieldwork and writing has been more than amply discussed by the writing anthropology school, I will not discuss it here.

One Corollary

We usually assume mimetic intention in what our informants tell us without recognizing that their intentions may be not mimetic but rhetorical, pragmatic, phatic, ironic, comic, or aesthetic. Our assumption rests, as I have often suggested (e.g., 1992:12–18), on the priority that we give to the semantic, the referential in our understanding of language usage, but it may be that in other linguistic communities, other linguistic *Einstellungen* are privileged. Where, for example, we assume that informants are describing their life-historical experience as it happened, leading us to phenomenological or experiential understanding, they may in fact be describing experiences that never occurred, or that occurred quite differently, in order to produce a desired effect in us or because they find those experiences aesthetically pleasing. These elaborations should not necessarily be understood in terms of fiction, for fiction itself is, conceptually, a product of our particular epistemological and axiological, indeed ontological, assumptions. It is by no means a universal category, as some of the writing culture proponents would have it. We have, I believe, at the earliest stage of fieldwork possible, to determine the prevailing take on language and by extension discourse and how that take affects what is said and interpreted.

12. In field encounters, particularly in their initial stages, the fieldworker and his or her informants are confronted with each other's opacity – with the inevitable fact

that we can never know what is going on in the mind of our interlocutors, in what I have called shadow dialogues, those inner conversations that accompany the mentation we have as we converse (1990). (We do have to recognize, however, that solipsism – the problem posed by other minds – supports our culturally and linguistically embedded philosophies in ways that may not be stressed or acknowledged in other societies.) Of course – I am not sure how to put it – this opacity is, in its deadness, its intransigence, alive; for whatever lies behind that opacity is, as we conceive of it, an active agent, capable of apprehending us not as we know ourselves to be but as we are assumed to be. It is not simply a mirroring, as complex as that may be, but an appraisal – a projective appraisal over which we have but scant control. We tend to figure this appraisal in visual terms – terms that may not be shared in other societies. As we see, we are seen. Inherent in the gaze, as the Lacanians insist, is the look – the gaze – of the other. The eye of the other, so it seems to be taken nowadays, by Foucault for example, is penetrating, controlling, alienating in its effect. But, we have to remind ourselves, it may also be reflective, loving, mysterious, an allure, charming in both its positive and its negative senses.

The "fact" of the opacity of those with whom we engage, the terrible loneliness that accompanies its recognition, our mistrust of the "charm" of the other's eye, are shunted aside in most conventional encounters. But anthropologists and often enough their informants do not have such conventional support, at least during the initial stages of research, because of the strangeness, the alien quality of their encounter. More important, the anthropological stance itself demands the preservation, to a surprising extent, of strangeness, alienation, what Brecht would call *Verfremdung* (1982:94–96, 143–145) and the Russian formalist Viktor Shklovsky, *ostranenie* and in consequence loneliness (1992). The absence of such conventions and our professional commitment to defamiliarization call attention to the illusions of knowing, of seeing through, and the fact, perhaps, of their possibility.

These observations certainly do not do justice to many recent attempts – and some older ones – to account for how the field experience affects the data we collect, its framing, and the range of acceptable interpretations. Many of these efforts understand this influence in psychological terms that stress subjectivity – subjective understanding – and the distortions to that subjectivity, that understanding, that arise out of the field situation in both conscious and unconscious ways (Wengle 1988). Reference is often made to transference and countertransference without regard, I have argued (1992:115–135; Hunt 1989:58; Ewing 1987), to the significant differences between a psychoanalytic session and a field encounter (Devereux 1951, 1967; Parin, Morgenthaler, and Parin-Matthèy 1966, 1971; Kracke 1987). I don't want to pursue these differences here other than to note that informants do not normally seek out the anthropologist the way patients do the psychoanalyst. They do not share the same intentions, frames of understanding, figurations of the anthropologist or psychoanalyst, and thus resistances. Usually the anthropologist and the therapist, even psychoanalytic anthropologists, do not have the same therapeutic or research goals and relations with those with whom they work. I do want to stress that there are two profoundly different understandings of transference and countertransference: in the first – the more typical in Anglo-American psychoanalysis – each party to the encounter responds, individually, to the encounter in terms of his or her biography; in the second – the French – the fact is stressed that both parties to the encounter are caught within an overriding transference relationship which governs the way in which transference and countertransference are experienced and interpreted. The emphasis here is on the intersubjective. I suggest that this second understanding of transference calls attention, analogically, to the way in which our engagements in the field – indeed, our interpretations – are governed by subsuming intersubjective, or, if you prefer, interpersonal relations, established – circularly – in the engagements themselves. Of particular significance in appraising field research are the ways we seek to escape this subsumption, this entrapment.

* * *

I want to turn now to certain of my field encounters to illustrate some of these points, especially those which I find worthy of elaboration, and to provide grounds for the beginning of their formalization. It's a tall order, and I will not be able to do justice to it in this essay, if ever I can. I apologize for using my own experiences. I do so neither out of egoism nor as confession, but because the consideration of field encounters requires intimate understanding. Of course, I can never have the critical distance necessary for the required objectivity, as "objectivity" has been conventionally stipulated. No matter. My lack of objectivity has itself to be seen as if not an objective fact, then a social fact or, as I prefer, a fertile fact in the manner in which Virginia Woolf understood it.

My first field experience, if it can be so called, was with Haitian refugees in New York City. It was part of a project for Margaret Mead's seminar on field methods at Columbia. Aside from being prayed for by several hundred people at a Seventh-day Adventist service – I'll have more to say about prayer later – I was forced into a drinking bout in which I consumed more than half a bottle of rum. It was a test – one I failed – and I was subjected to a lot of teasing, some of it good-natured and some of it, at least as I, humiliated, saw it at the time, malicious. I bring this first, initiatory experience up because it calls attention to two important relations one may have in the field: testing and humiliating.

Though humiliation plays an important role in many field encounters, I will only call attention to it, as responses to it vary significantly from person to person and situation to situation. It does reflect plays of power in the field situation. Testing, on the other hand, requires comment. A test is a way one's informant learns something about you. (I will restrict my discussion here to the anthropologist's being tested by the people under study.) It may involve physical prowess (as when, on the Navajo reservation, my stamina was carefully monitored as I helped build a thousand-foot fence); one's reaction to a food or practice that is assumed to be unpleasant or distasteful to outsiders; one's sexual capacity (so frequently challenged by Moroccan men); one's linguistic ability (often through punning); one's recollection of what one has been told (a prayer, the explication of a passage from the Bible); or what one really believes.

Sometimes one is immediately aware of the test and at others only later, upon reflection. When I was working with the Navajo, I was told, over the course of my brief stay, a set of stories, each of which I noted but did not link until long after I had left the reservation. The first of these was simply a joke: What is a Navajo family? It's a mother, a father, a bunch of kids, and an anthropologist. The second was about a psychologist who had visited the reservation a few months before my arrival and had paid the Indians a few dollars to tell him what they saw in a set of pictures he had shown them. It was, I believe, a thematic apperception test. He never told them why he was giving them the test or what it might mean. He simply left them hanging in the anxiety that such tests produce. Though they never quite put it this way, they inferred that the psychologist had stolen something – a secret – from them, but what it was, they did not know. Toward the end of my stay, the father of the family with whom I was living told me about a man – a drifter – who had arrived in the valley penniless one freezing winter day several years earlier. One of the valley families took him in, fed him, and befriended him. He spent the winter with them, and then in the spring, when it was warm, he raped and killed one of their daughters and stole what little money they had. I was asked by several other Navajos if I had been told the story. Clearly whether and when to tell it to me had been discussed. It was only when I read through my field notes, not even the first time, that I realized that each story was about a man who could have been me. Each, I believe, was about why the Navajo had been suspicious of me. Each marked a growing confidence in me. I was passing muster.

It is the testing of what one really believes that is most difficult to grapple with and leaves its mark, as a breakdown sometimes, on the course of fieldwork and its interpretation. Working on spirit possession among the Hamadsha, a popular Sufi confraternity in Morocco, I was asked one day what I thought of the *jnun*, the spirits. It was a general question asked by two young men whom I knew slightly. I sparred with them, saying such foolish things as "I find them interesting," "I find them dangerous." Quite rightly, none of my answers satisfied Moha and Driss. Finally, Driss asked if I thought the *jnun* existed (as if he and his friend hadn't suspected my disbelief). I was caught. If I said I did, they wouldn't believe me since *nasraniyya* – Europeans, Christians – do not believe in the *jnun*. If I said no, I might offend them and – more important – raise questions about why I was there asking about the spirits when I didn't believe in them. I would call attention to a hierarchical relationship, which I had done my best to counter, between Europeans and Moroccans. (The French protectorate had ended only a few years earlier.) What was I to say? Finally I admitted that I wasn't sure whether the *jnun* existed or not, quickly adding that I was deeply impressed by their power to strike and possess. Moha, who was more expressive than Driss, looked wounded; Driss said coldly, "We didn't think you did." I realized at that moment that most of the Moroccans with whom I was working were probably asking the same question and looking for signs of my belief or disbelief. I had to acknowledge a "display" quality – "we'll show you" – in some of the exorcisms I had witnessed. This seemed particularly true of one of the exorcists, Qandish, about whom I'll have more to say later. I had to concede that my stance might well have been experienced as objectifying, symptomizing, impersonal, put on, and insincere. I had to admit that my relations with many Moroccans were governed by my desire to avoid questions of my belief. Today, I recognize that I had rendered the role of belief rather more mechanical, more starkly factual, in my writings than it probably was. After this exchange, Driss and Moha avoided me, and when we finally met, they asked why I had been avoiding them. I didn't deny it. I said that I had felt uneasy, as I was sure they did, after our last conversation. Moha looked sheepish; Driss said nothing had changed, and the two of them walked off without another word.

None of the Moroccans ever tried to convert me. They preserved a distance when it came to their beliefs and practices. Though they sometimes told me about Europeans who had been possessed and cured by their healers, I did not find their stories a challenge to my presumed lack of belief or an admonishment. They assumed that *nasraniyya* were not usually subject to possession. Their attitude came as a relief – a relief I was to appreciate all the more when I worked with whites in apartheid South Africa, many of whom were participating in a revivalist movement, and with Christian fundamentalists in the United States (Crapanzano 1985, 2000).

The South African Pentecostalists made a concerted effort to convert me, my wife, and my eleven-year-old daughter (she had little patience with their attempts). The South Africans knew I was not a believer. They had been asking me about my beliefs – religious, social, racial, and political – since I first arrived. Indeed, the attitude of many of them was curiously ambivalent. I should note that I had less trouble in telling the South Africans that I was a non-believer than in telling the Moroccans that I did not believe in *jnun*. Does this have to do with my perception of their religious commitment? With the differing role of doubt in their respective faiths? With my greater familiarity with one culture than the other? With a propensity – an imperial propensity – to infantilize peoples from an exotic society? Imperial assumptions aside, infantilization of the people one works with, especially those from so-called simpler societies but others too, can be a defense against the challenges of the "exotic other" – a defense, I should add, that has received both institutional and ideological support from the way anthropology conceives of itself, the anthropologist, the informant, and the society under study. I would suggest, but cannot support this suggestion on firm grounds, that the founding and now tabooed notion of the primitive (not to mention the savage) that defined anthropology's constituted subject until rather more recently than most anthropologists like to admit is not without influence today in the constitution of the anthropologist's turf even when that turf, those subjects, come from "complex" societies.

Indeed, the very characterization of such societies as complex (however complex they may in fact be) evokes its opposite. My point here is that we, as individuals at least, should delve into those foundational assumptions of our discipline which have been set aside. Though silenced, the semantic, axiological, and emotional space that they occupy is never without effect. Indeed, as any rhetorician knows, the unsaid, the silenced, the paraleptic, can be more forceful than the said. I have made the same argument for anthropology's religious and romantic roots (Crapanzano 2004).

From the start, knowing that I had just come to South Africa, the South Africans asked me, nevertheless, what I thought of their country – as an expert, when clearly I wasn't – and took stock of what I said. It was as though I was affording them an external vantage point – an escape from the intensely involuted world in which they found themselves. Yet, though I tried to be as frank as I could about what I thought about apartheid without impeding my relations with them, they did not really trust me – some throughout my stay, others at its beginning. (Obviously what I said varied with their political position, but I tried to be as consistent as possible so that their gossip would not destroy my relations.) I was carefully watched by all the members of the community which I was studying (as well as by the Special Branch). Was I spending more time with the Afrikaners or the English speakers? The conservatives or the liberals? The Pentecostalists or the Anglicans? I was often warned about people I was interviewing. These warnings were not simply small-town gossip but a way in which the villagers were trying to convince me of their particular views. Persuasion, argument, dodging, and resistance were important undercurrents of my research there. Nearly all my informants aimed at some level to turn me into an apologist abroad for white South Africa. On a personal level, it was far more complicated, but generally I would argue that in attempting to persuade me of the validity of their views on apartheid, they sought transcending moral sustenance from me, an outsider, deemed, quite irresponsibly, to have the authority of an expert. The dynamics of the field situation revealed not only their moral ambivalence toward apartheid but also the way in which their "moral entrapment" led them to configure the outsider. Clearly it was not just the "good life" that led them to perpetuate apartheid, as many outsiders simplistically maintained, but also, perversely perhaps, the way in which their moral ambivalence often produced stubborn justifications for their position. It certainly points to the moral engagement sometimes demanded of the anthropologist and the consequent moral turbulence that can easily promote simplistic judgments, including those embedded in ethnographic description and interpretation.

The whites' witnessing my daughter, my wife, and me, however required by evangelical Christianity, can also be seen in terms of the persuasion demanded by their moral ambivalence. This is not the place to discuss the relationship between the two except to note their mutual displacement. Evangelical Christianity gave them certainty – the security of the Word, the promise of salvation, and an escape from moral, political, and other pressures that besieged them. It provided them with a transcending, if not transcendent, perspective which radically changed their relationship to their – crumbling – world. (Most of the villagers involved in the revivalist movement were what I [1985:210 and passim] have called the middling middle classes: those whites – English and Afrikaans speakers – who had no international connections to turn to in case of a bloodbath [a constant fear], no skills that could easily be transported to other countries, and insufficient wealth [if they could in fact export it] that would allow them to live independently. They were literally trapped in South Africa.) In many respects their evangelical Christianity resonated allegorically with the political situation in which they found themselves. Think only of the evangelicals' focus on the apocalypse, salvation, the Second Coming of Christ (in their understanding a deus-ex-machina figure), forgiveness of past sins, and a future orientation (Crapanzano 2000).

I found myself an inadvertent player in this allegory and a central figure of the evangelicals' proselytizing. Somehow – I have never

figured out exactly how – my conversion, the conversion of my family, outsiders as we were, would validate their spiritual (their otherworldly) stance and their political (their this-worldly) one. It was certainly clear that they put greater effort in trying to convert us than they did other villagers. In fact, as I was to learn, a group of women prayed for our salvation at a prayer meeting one morning, and Jesus instructed them to form three teams, each of which would be responsible for the conversion of one of us. As the fates, as God, the gods, would have it, ignorant of the meeting, I called one of the women who was responsible for my conversion for an appointment some twenty minutes after she returned home from the meeting. Their prayers had been heard. I had had a very interesting interview the week before with her – let me call her Pam – who was a Baptist and one of the leaders in the revivalist movement. I met her that afternoon. Before I could start the interview, Pam said, "Vincent, you've asked me a lot of questions. May I ask you one?" I agreed, and she asked me if I had been reborn. I said no, and she began to witness me – a witnessing that lasted more than four hours. I recorded it, but I have never dared listen to my recording. I do remember that I was caught between a barrage of questions about my spiritual life, my life in general, interrupted by quotations from the Bible, their explication with regard to my life, and prayers which I felt obliged to say *and* intense, embarrassing erotic feeling about Pam. She was in her late twenties, quite attractive, dressed like a Berkeley hippie from the sixties, who slid to the floor as she witnessed me, pressing her crotch against one of the legs of a coffee table. I never converted, though when I returned home, my wife asked me what was wrong. I had lost all color.

I have described this meeting in some detail, as I will return to it in my discussion of the dynamics of the field encounter. I have also been witnessed several times in my work with American Christian fundamentalists. They took different tacks. In one instance, a Mexican American evangelical bullied me, refusing to answer any of my questions because I could not possibly understand his answers until I was reborn. He tried to catch me up by angering me. (Certainly I was angered in other field situations that affected my research both positively and negatively. Anger, as Aristotle (1941:995–997 [Nic. Eth. Bk IV, Ch 5]) understood, can have a rhetorical function.) As I worked primarily with professors and master's students at Bible seminaries, mainly in Los Angeles, I adopted – we adopted – collegial relations, which precluded proselytizing, but underlying their patient answers to my questions was the certainty, I am sure, that I, an intellectual from New York, had been brought to them by Jesus. The book I was researching was simply his ploy. I found their knowing patience a burden. I used to joke that I was probably the only person in Los Angeles who looked forward to traffic jams as I drove from interview to interview. It gave me the time to come down.

I was reticent, non-confrontational, and hesitant to speak a language in which Jesus and the Bible predominated. I would like to say that my reticence was simply a way of avoiding being witnessed, but as secular as I am – I have had no religious training – I was moved by an awesome respect, a spiritual etiquette, that I found troubling. My first interviews were very difficult because I simply did not know the vocabulary of conservative evangelicalism. My knowledge of Protestantism was academic. I had studied the Reformation, read Luther, Calvin, and, of course, Weber and Troeltsch. I had even studied the philosophy of history with Paul Tillich, whose "godless theology" was anathema to the evangelicals. None of this prepared me for my meetings. Even after I had achieved some mastery of their language, I found it difficult to challenge them, however delicately, in their idiom. I felt constrained by it, hypocritical.

I do remember one meeting, however, in which I offered a critique of evangelical Christianity in its own idiom. I was interviewing an elderly professor of New Testament theology who had just completed an enormous commentary on Revelation. He was a gentle, understanding man, warm but not particularly charismatic, who had had to cancel our first appointment nearly a year earlier because of an emergency heart operation. I could not help thinking that his confrontation with death had

given him a wider perspective than most of his colleagues. I told him that one thing that troubled me about evangelical Christianity was its focus on Christ's Second Coming. It seemed to ignore His first coming and His message of love. The professor was startled by my observation. He remained silent for an inordinately long time. The room darkened for me; he suddenly seemed frail and very old – vulnerable. I regretted my question and was sure that I had hurt him deeply. Finally he spoke. "I've never thought of that. You may be right. I'll have to think about it." The room brightened; the professor lost his frailty, his vulnerability, and became a man of wisdom, spiritual wisdom (see Crapanzano 2006). Not only was I relieved by his answer but I felt open to him, as I believe he felt open to me. I have had a few similar experiences in the field, and far more in ordinary life. We may refer to them in Gadamer's terms as a blurring or blending of horizons, but Gadamer does not speak of the emotional impact of such moments. We may also speak of them in terms of a collapse of interlocutory distance.

* * *

I have touched on only a few modes of encounter in fieldwork, but I believe they are indicative of the rich texture of field experience and of some of the most important problems it poses. Obviously, there are many other emotional experiences beside being humiliated, tested, watched, persuaded, witnessed, prayed over, angered, morally engaged or entrapped, and caught within a seemingly shared subjectivity. These would include being sympathetic, loved, spurned, despised, mistrusted, feared, seduced, adopted, afraid, elated, euphoric, and saddened. They are all common experiences, and that is perhaps the most important characteristic of fieldwork: everydayness – the quotidian in the exotic. But this everydayness has at once to be guarded, experienced as it is, and yet, if only through reflection, defamiliarized. As fieldwork progresses, the balance between the two changes. At first, at least in exotic sites, the weight is on the unfamiliar, but with time the unfamiliar becomes familiar. *And* from an anthropological perspective, this familiarity, as necessary as it is ethnographically, is not without its dangers, ethnographically, for we risk losing track of what was once salient. Personally, I have found it far more difficult to render the familiar unfamiliar and yet maintain its familiarity than to render the unfamiliar familiar and yet maintain its unfamiliarity.

We have to take into account the trajectory of fieldwork and recognize our ever-shifting perspectives and the artifice of what I have called an editorial vantage point, an orientation that is at once outside – supported not only by our research but by other pertinent, and perhaps not so pertinent, episodes in our biographies, including our training and our relationships with our mentors and colleagues – and inside – sustained by the demands of the task we have set ourselves and those made by the people we study. Embedded, as we are, in the field situation, and removed, as we are, from it, we find any perspective unstable. Throughout our fieldwork, we are constantly negotiating our respective identities and our understanding of the situation in which we find ourselves. In *Tuhami* (1980) I focused on the way Tuhami and I negotiated the field experience over months: what was relevant, how it was expressed, who we each were and how we related to each other. As I reviewed the course of our exchanges, it became clear that our understanding of what we were doing shifted, at times dramatically, as when I decided to take a more active, therapeutic role and Tuhami, to whose desire I believed I was responding, acquiesced.

Such dramatic shifts need not, of course, be initiated by the anthropologist, as my encounter with Pam demonstrates. Against my will – my conscious will at least – Pam converted our research encounter, in which I was more or less in control, into a proselytizing one in which she – under the auspices of Jesus, as she would have understood it – was in control. I was, of course, caught by surprise and trapped by my desire to maintain good relations with her and the rest of her community and perhaps by curiosity, or even temptation. Pam had broken the idiosyncratic interview conventions that we had negotiated. (My use of "we" does not necessarily imply equal weight in these negotiations.) What rendered Pam's reformulation of our relationship unusual was her directness. In my experience, most shifts are less dramatic and far less self-conscious.

I would like to draw attention to another mode of dramatically breaking conventions, one which, I believe, will enable us to better understand the power of Pam's abrupt reformulation of our encounter – our relationship. You may recall that I mentioned Qandish, one of the Moroccan curers who liked to display the power of his exorcisms, you-better-believe-it style, not only to his followers but, quite consciously, to me as well. Qandish, one of the most brilliant men I have ever met, never allowed our encounters to become conventional (except, perhaps, in their unconventionality). I never knew what to expect. At one meeting, he would not say a word; he would simply tickle me or gently beat me with a switch he sometimes carried. At another he would be so talkative that I could never get in a question. On these occasions what he said sometimes made perfect sense and at other times no sense whatsoever. At still another time he would answer my questions with what seemed to me to be irrelevances, but when I went over my notes, I discovered that he actually had answered nearly all my questions but not directly after I had asked them. Qandish was very much a trickster, and he used his tricks not only in our encounters but in his cures. He achieved his cures, I believe, by creating a semantic vertigo in his patients, thereby heightening their suggestibility. When they had reached a level of hyper-suggestibility, he would issue instructions with full clarity. Though I never succumbed to his suggestions, I was dizzied in some of our meetings. I have noted similar, though less dramatic, techniques among other curers, shamans, an eccentric white South African Anglican priest, noted for his dramatic cures of alcoholics, and political protesters who, in the style of Vergès or Sandero Luminoso, exploited the unexpected and the non-conventional.

But to return to Pam – in a way her Jesus played in her witnessing a role not dissimilar to that of the anthropologist's mentor in the ethnographic encounter. They both give at least the illusion of authorizing the interventions we perform. In a number of papers (e.g., Crapanzano 1992:72, 88–90), I have argued that negotiations of interpersonal relations and their relevant context, indeed any negotiation, makes reference to what I have called the

Third. It is a function whose functionality is stable but whose definition is unstable, except in the most conventional encounters, since it shifts with the witting or usually unwitting appeals to it by all the parties to the encounter. I have suggested that this Third serves a meta-pragmatic function by authorizing various pragmatic or indexical maneuvers, which define the encounter, its relevant context, its personnel, its modes of communication, how that communication is to be taken, the appropriate etiquette, and thereby fitting interpretive strategies and their transgressive possibility. I have argued further that this function is conceptualized in terms of the law, grammar, or convention and embodied in authoritative figures like gods, totems, fathers, and even experts and their iconic materializations (images, statues, fetishes, masks, and actors who are identified with them in one way or another). I cannot do justice to my argument here, but I do want to make one important point: sometimes, particularly in explicit or even implicit hierarchical situations, the Third may be embodied – for the time being – in one of the parties to the encounter. The anthropologist? The informant? In complex encounters that have not yet become fully conventionalized through habit or repetition, like the ethnographic, the Third appealed to may be outside the encounter. Examples would be Pam's God or my mentor. In authorizing a particular framing of the situation and the conduct that follows therefrom, they may clash with each other. (Perhaps that is why I found my erotic desires so disturbing. They were not authorized.) In any case, I do not want to pit whoever my mentor was – I'm not even sure I ever had one – against God, giving our encounter a dramatically transcendent dimension it never had.

* * *

Thus far I have assumed that anthropological research is conducted, or assumed to be conducted, in ordinary times, but it can also be carried out in exceptional ones: after an earthquake, life-threatening inundations, fires, epidemics, polluting explosions, and – ever more common today – warfare, terrorism, and street violence. Though I have never done research in such exceptional circumstances,

except in South Africa, I have worked with many people who have experienced and suffered from violence. Fear was an ever-present undertone of my meetings with white South Africans who talked about current riots, violent protests, and ("necessary") police brutality and near-obsessively about the likelihood of a bloodbath when the "blacks" would finally rise up en masse. (I myself witnessed riots in Cape Town; I saw how a peaceful protest was nearly turned into a violent riot by the way the military police – their name tags removed – used ferocious dogs to threaten the protesters; and I had rocks thrown at my car as I drove past a "colored" hamlet on my way home one afternoon.) I often served as an external vantage point for whites, particularly when they speculated about their violent future, as, paradoxically, they tried to draw me into their own perspective. They were trapped, and I often felt ensnared by them. This was especially true when I told them how rocks had been thrown at me. Not only did they take what seemed to me to be vicarious pleasure in my experience, but they looked at it as a sort of initiation. "Now you know what our life is like," one man said and went on to describe how he had nearly been killed when this had happened to him. Our entrapment seemed to mirror one dimension of the larger political situation. Violence seemed the only way to break out. Needless to say, I was deeply disturbed – angered – by this feeling. At the end of a day's work I would collapse on my bed, fall into a syncope, and awake twenty or thirty minutes later in time for dinner. The effect of this situation lasted for some time, until I had finished writing *Waiting*, my book on white South Africans. Did writing serve as an exorcism?

These effects were, of course, in no way comparable to those experiences of anthropologists who, like Christopher Taylor, found themselves in the midst of violence. Taylor was doing fieldwork in Rwanda in 1994 when genocidal war broke out. He wrote:

It has taken me several years to move beyond the grief, the anger, and the bewilderment that I felt looking back on Rwanda when once again I set foot on American soil returning to

the cocoon of ignorant security and complacency that most of the country and elsewhere
in the West call "peace" and take as our God-
given right. Yet how often our peace seems
predicated on someone else's misery. (Taylor
1999:181)

Taylor was writing before September 11, 2001,
and the wars in Iraq and Afghanistan, but his
point is well taken even in these more turbulent times. Detecting anger – ironic anger – in
his words, I wonder if he or anyone else who
lived through such times can ever move
beyond. It is perhaps less a question of buried
traumata than the clarity of remembered
violence that persists.

It is not just the actual experience of violence
that has its effect on us but also descriptions of
the violence that our informants have suffered.
This is particularly true when they relive the
experience as they tell it. For the last several
years I have been working with the Harkis,
those Algerians who sided with the French during the Algerian war of independence, most of
whom were slaughtered immediately after the
war by the Algerian population at large. The
survivors were finally brought to France, where
some of them were incarcerated in camps for as
long as sixteen years. Listening to their stories
and those of their children has been deeply disturbing, not only in terms of their descriptions
of what they underwent but also in their
attempt to recruit me as a political advocate.
I resent their efforts to manipulate me as I
empathize with them. I feel at times helpless as
they relive their experiences, for there is nothing
I can do to alleviate their pain. I have found that
they resent emotional expressions of sympathy,
as they express themselves emotionally, if only
because my sympathy challenges their possession of those emotions and experiences around
which many of them have constructed, if not
their identity, then a partial identity. The paradoxical situation in which I find myself increases
my sense of helplessness before them and all the
emotions that stem from that helplessness. As I
have not witnessed what they describe, my
imagination is less constrained by reality. As the
Greek tragedians knew, the power of unseen
violence is far more effective than its depiction
onstage. I have come to believe that as our

explanations of violence have never been satisfactory, all we can do is describe it and its
effects. This of course is harrowing.

My aim in attempting to delineate some
aspects of the dynamic anatomy – or, better,
physiology – of the field situation has been to
call attention to the complex internal and
external plays of power and desire that constitute that situation. I have focused on the internal in this chapter, but it should be recognized
that the internal is encompassed by the external – that is, by the way in which anthropological research is framed and thereby situated
within a particular historical moment. Among
other things, we have to give critical recognition to the way in which such taken-for-
granted practices and their glosses as "research"
and "fieldwork" as well as their subject matter
constitute themselves and are constituted in
and through larger institutional structures, the
etiquette those institutions demand, the emotions they condone or censure, the interpretive
strategies they encourage or discourage, and
the transgressions they permit and forbid.
These institutional structures not only determine (within limits, to be sure, if only because
of the contingent and the foibles of human
freedom) the practices and their glosses and
evaluations but are evoked, performed, and
confirmed by these practices, glosses, and evaluations. They found a stratum of unwitting
responsiveness which at this particular historical moment we situate in the human psyche
and the "unconscious." The mini-dramas
of fieldwork are pragmatically and, more
important, meta-pragmatically constitutive. In
their particularity, in the absence of fixed
conventions, in the struggle to establish such
conventions, to permit meaningful communication and yet to preserve the uniqueness of
the ethnographic encounter, these mini-dramas
are disturbing insofar as they challenge the
taken-for-granted and its naturalization.

The danger is that we might lose sight of
the complexity of field research, ignore the
challenges it poses, and succumb to one
authoritative position or another – that is, to
accept uncritically whatever the fashionable
ideological or theoretical paradigm is. That
paradigm may afford understanding, at least
an illusion of understanding. I certainly do not

want to deny the possibility of understanding. It may facilitate the denial of the artifice of our position, its instability, its frailty, its situational particularity, and its contingency, promoting a social and cultural complacency that, in my view, sabotages the anthropological mission and the moral as well as the intellectual turbulence it must produce to be itself.

REFERENCES

Aristotle
    1941 "Nicomachean Ethics." In R. McKeon, ed., *The Basic Works of Aristotle*, 935–1112. New York: Random House.
Bachnick, J. M.
    1986 "Native Perspective of Distance and Anthropological Perspectives of Culture." *Anthropological Quarterly* 60:25–34.
Brecht, B.
    1982 *Brecht on Theater: The Development of an Aesthetic*. New York: Hill and Wang.
Crapanzano, V.
    1980 *Tuhami: Portrait of a Moroccan*. Chicago: University of Chicago Press.
Crapanzano, V.
    1985 *Waiting: The Whites of South Africa*. New York: Random House.
Crapanzano, V.
    1990 "Afterword." In M. Manganaro, ed., *Modernist Anthropology: From Fieldwork to Text*, 300–308. Princeton, NJ: Princeton University Press.
Crapanzano, V.
    1992 *Hermes' Dilemma and Hamlet's Desire: On the Epistemology of Interpretation*. Cambridge, MA: Harvard University Press.
Crapanzano, V.
    1994 "Kevin: On the Transfer of Emotion." *American Anthropologist* 96 (4): 866–885.
Crapanzano, V.
    2000 *Serving the Word: Literalism in America from the Pulpit to the Bench*. New York: New Press.
Crapanzano, V.
    2004 *Imaginative Horizons: An Essay in Literary Philosophical Anthropology*. Chicago: University of Chicago Press.
Crapanzano, V.
    2006 "The Scene." *Theoretical Anthropology* 6 (4): 27–45.

Danforth, L.
    1989 *Firewalking and Religious Healing: The Anastenaria of Greece and the American Firewalking Movement*. Princeton, NJ: Princeton University Press.
Derrida, J.
    1976 *Of Grammatology*. Trans. Gayatri Spivak. Baltimore: Johns Hopkins University Press.
Devereux, G.
    1967 *From Anxiety to Method in the Behavioral Sciences*. The Hague: Mouton.
Devereux, G.
    1969 *Reality and Dream: Psychotherapy of a Plains Indian*. New York: New York University Press.
Ewing, K. P.
    1987 "Clinical Psychoanalysis as an Ethnographic Tool." *Ethos* 15 (1): 16–33.
Gadamer, Hans-Georg
    1975 *Truth and Method*. New York: Crossroad.
Geertz, C.
    1968 *Islam Observed: Religious Development in Morocco and Indonesia*. New Haven, CT: Yale University Press.
Heidegger, M.
    1967 *Being and Time*. Trans. J. Macquarrie and E. Robinson. Oxford: Blackwell.
Kracke, W.
    1987 "Encounters with Other Cultures: Psychological and Epistemological Aspects." *Ethos* 15 (1): 58–82.
Lévi-Strauss, C.
    1984 *Tristes Tropiques*. Trans. J. and D. Weightman. New York: Atheneum.
Milbank, J.
    1990 *Theology and Social Theory: Beyond Secular Reason*. Oxford: Blackwell.
Parin, P., F. Morgenthaler, and G. Parin-Matthèy.
    1966 *Les blancs pensent trop: 13 entretiens psychanalytiques avec les Dogon*. Paris: Payot.
Parin, P.
    1971 *Fürchte deine Nächsten wie dich selbst: Psychoanalyse und Gesellschaft am Modell der Agni in Westafrika*. Frankfurt am Main: Suhrkamp.
Plato
    1987 *Phaedrus*. Trans. R. Hackforth. Cambridge: Cambridge University Press.
Robbins, Joel.
    2006 "Anthropology and Theology: An Awkward Relationship?" *Anthropological Quarterly* 79 (2): 285–294.

Rosenberg, D. V.
1990 "Language in the Discourse of the Emotions." In C. Lutz and L. Abu-Lughod, eds., *Language and the Politics of Emotion*, 162–185. Cambridge: Cambridge University Press.

Shklovsky, V.
1992 "Art as Technique." In H. Adams, ed., *Critical Theory since Plato*, 751–759. Rev. ed., Fort Worth: Harcourt Brace Jovanovich.

Taylor, C. C.
1999 *Sacrifice as Terror: The Rwandan Genocide of 1994*. New York: Oxford University Press.

Traimond, Bernard.
2008 *L'anthropologie à l'époque de l'enregistreur de paroles*. Bordeaux: William Blake and Co./Art and Arts.

Wengle, J. L.
1988 *Ethnographers in the Field: The Psychology of Research*. Tuscaloosa: University of Alabama Press.

Part X
Engaged Fieldwork

Introduction

Jeffrey A. Sluka

The emergence of compassionate and public anthropology approaches to fieldwork beginning in the 1990s coalesced in the development of ethically, morally, and politically engaged forms of fieldwork in the first decade of this century. However, that all is not well with the epistemology of fieldwork was revealed by the re-emergence of mission-related counterinsurgency research by social scientists deployed in US Army Human Terrain Teams in the wars in Iraq and Afghanistan, which has raised serious issues and generated great controversy and renewed debate about the ethics, practice, and praxis of fieldwork today. In the apparently permanent global "war on terrorism" there is a battle for the "hearts and minds" of anthropologists and a danger of recolonization of the discipline as an applied science of state control. As noted in the introduction to Part VI, the discipline first confronted the issue of anthropology in the service of counterinsurgency during the Vietnam War, which created great controversy and led directly to the adoption of the first code of anthropological ethics. In 1970, Eric Wolf and Joseph Jorgensen observed that "the old formula for successful counter-insurgency used to be ten troops for every guerrilla ... Now the formula is ten anthropologists for each guerrilla" (1970:32), and in 1976 June Nash reminded us that in the age of decolonization anthropologists came to be classified with the enemy and the discipline perceived as having served as "the handmaiden of colonialism and imperialism." As a consequence, for the next 30 years anthropologists considered involvement in counterinsurgency and other applied military research as ethically "taboo."

However, since the 9/11 terrorist attacks in the United States in 2001, there has been renewed debate within the discipline over what role anthropologists should

Ethnographic Fieldwork: An Anthropological Reader, Second Edition. Edited by
Antonius C. G. M. Robben and Jeffrey A. Sluka.
Editorial material and organization © 2012 John Wiley & Sons, Inc.
Published 2012 by John Wiley & Sons, Inc.

play in the wars in Iraq and Afghanistan. On one side are those who hold fast to the taboo against counterinsurgency research, and, on the other, are those, apparently only a few, who believe that in times of war American anthropologists have a patriotic duty to serve their government in the war effort, as many did during World War II, including leading anthropologists such as Margaret Mead, Ruth Benedict, and Clyde Kluckhohn. The issue of anthropologists doing "counter-terrorism" research, which is the same as counterinsurgency research, has taken on new urgency as the failure of the wars in Iraq and Afghanistan has become more apparent. By 2004, the US military was belatedly reassessing its tactics and calling for cultural knowledge of the adversary. It sponsored the Adversary Cultural Knowledge and National Security Conference, the first major Department of Defense (DOD) conference on the social sciences since 1962, and Project Camelot; also, as noted in the introduction to Part V, in 2005 the CIA launched the Pat Roberts Intelligence Scholars Program to sponsor trainee anthropologist-spies through American university courses.

Even more controversially, in 2006 the US Army initiated a new $60 million experimental counterinsurgency program called the Human Terrain System (HTS) which began to "embed" anthropologists and other social scientists with combat brigades in Iraq and Afghanistan to help them gather ethnographic intelligence (referred to as "conducting research") and understand local cultures better. The goal is to provide soldiers in the field with knowledge of the population and its culture in order to enhance operational effectiveness and reduce conflict between the military and the civilian population. The HTS program has generated great controversy among anthropologists, most of whom view it as fundamentally unethical, inherently harmful to those studied, and an attempt to "weaponize" the discipline (Price 2006). Many have criticized it as "mercenary anthropology" that exploits social science for political gain, warned that it will exacerbate the already considerable danger of anthropologists being viewed as intelligence agents or spies which nearly all anthropologists face in their fieldwork, and drawn a direct comparison with the infamous Phoenix Program and Project Camelot during the Vietnam War.

In October 2007, the Executive Board of the American Anthropological Association (AAA) formally opposed the program and denounced it as "an unacceptable application of anthropological expertise" which could lead to serious ethical problems, disgrace to anthropology as an academic discipline, restriction of future research opportunities, and increased risk of harm to both researchers and research participants. At the same time, "in response to concerns that such developments threaten the integrity of anthropology," the Network of Concerned Anthropologists (NCA) was formed and launched a "pledge of nonparticipation in counterinsurgency" campaign, which more than 1,000 anthropologists signed in the first few months (NCA 2007). Both the AAA and the NCA assert that counterinsurgency work in general, but in this case especially the HTS program, violates several core elements of the AAA ethics code, and in 2009 the code was revised directly in response to these developments.

Specifically, HT raises serious issues concerning potential harm to research participants and risk to researchers in the field, informed consent, public dissemination of research results, and preserving opportunities for further research by other academics: The HT system "is not compatible with any of these requirements because it does not provide meaningful informed consent; it endangers those studied; it generates knowledge that will disappear into Pentagon computers; and it increases the likelihood that other anthropologists will be perceived as spies and military operatives, thereby endangering the research, perhaps even the physical safety, of professional colleagues" (NCA 2007).

The seriousness of this issue has already been amply demonstrated in several important books. In 2009, the NCA published *The Counter-Counterinsurgency Handbook*, which presents a powerful critique of the US Army and Marine Corps *Counterinsurgency Field Manual* (2007) and strategies for resisting the deformation and exploitation of anthropology by the military. In 2009, George Lucas published *Anthropologists in Arms: The Ethics of Military Anthropology*, which traces the troubled history of social scientists' collaboration with military, security, and intelligence organizations, and analyses the moral and ethical debates provoked by the rise of military anthropology represented in the practice of embedding anthropologists with combat troops in Iraq and Afghanistan. Also in 2009, Roberto González published *American Counterinsurgency: Human Science and Human Terrain*, a devastating critique of the HTS program and dangers of social science subservient to counterinsurgency (see also González 2007). And in 2010, John Kelly et al. published an edited volume on *Anthropology and Global Counterinsurgency*, which investigates the history of counterinsurgency doctrine and practice, the debate over culture, knowledge, and conscience in counterinsurgency, and how anthropologists should respond to military overtures.

In the final part of this Reader we address the contradictory emergence of "engaged fieldwork" and militarized fieldwork by presenting Margaret Mead's (1942) historical account of how she reluctantly came to engage in war-related research for the US government during World War II; two examples of contemporary politically engaged fieldwork, by Monique Skidmore (2008) and Nikolas Kosmatopoulos (2010); and Roberto González's (2008) critical expose of the involvement of anthropologists and other social scientists with the HTS program. Involvement in counterinsurgency research is not a form of "engaged fieldwork," as its practitioners pretend, but rather its *antithesis*. As David Seddon (2010) has observed, it cannot be assumed that all "engaged anthropology" will be progressive and broadly supportive of the exploited and oppressed: "If 'taking sides' is unavoidable, and 'refusing to take sides' is also, in effect, a political decision in favor of the status quo, it is also possible for fieldwork to be used to 'investigate' (or 'spy' on) the poor and subaltern and see how better to manage exploitation and oppression." Historically as "the handmaiden of colonialism," anthropology provided knowledge "useful" to colonizing powers, and today "there is no rule to say that 'taking sides' necessarily implies taking one side rather than the other" and "the outcome is not inevitable." Those who choose involvement in counterinsurgency research in general and the HTS program in particular assert that *this* is a morally and politically legitimate form of "engaged fieldwork." However, because this contradicts the fundamental intention of engaged anthropology to function as a form of resistance to imperialism, domination, and exploitation, it should be considered its opposite. Mission-oriented fieldwork for the military is "anti-engaged fieldwork" because it is fundamentally *antiprogressive*, and assists rather than challenges domination and imperialism.

In *And Keep Your Powder Dry: An Anthropologist Looks at the American Character* (1965[1942]), Margaret Mead recounts how World War II compelled her (and others) to become involved in war-related research. She argues that scientists have a dual obligation to objectivity in their research and responsible participation in their society, that the situation represented such an extreme threat to the world that there was no choice but to become involved (or engaged), and that, in wartime,

> we have three courses – to retire into ivory towers, protect our scientific reputations, and wait, on the chance that peace will come without our help and leave us free again to back to our patient labors; or, we can do something non-anthropological, satisfy our patriotic consciences by becoming air-raid wardens, working in an area where no colleague will review our works. Or, we can say quite simply, with such knowledge and insights as we have, we will now do what we can, as anthropologists, to win the war. (1965[1942]:14)

The difference between then and now is that the war Mead was helping to fight was incontrovertibly a just war to prevent the destruction of democracy and the establishment of global totalitarianism, whereas the so-called "wars on terrorism" in Iraq and Afghanistan are clearly little more than the latest innings in the old "Great Game" of imperialism.

In "Scholarship, Advocacy, and the Politics of Engagement in Burma" (2008), Monique Skidmore presents a reflexive account of her fieldwork in a country ruled by a military dictatorship and characterized by extreme political violence from multiple pro- and anti-state forces, and where anthropologists are monitored and curtailed. She asserts that in Burma,

> There is urgent need to write about such violent events from the perspective of Burmese people caught up in the violence ... Not only are such histories of violence and suffering not being written but also the few attempts to document violence and human rights violations are often being subjected to a process of academic (and thus historical) denial and dismissal. (2008:44)

Skidmore describes the political situation in Burma, how she came to commit herself to engaged anthropology, and how she practices it in such a way that she is still able to get research visas and go there to conduct fieldwork. By typifying her research as studying fear, violence, and social suffering as opposed to repression and resistance per se, she is able to walk a fine line that allows her to continue with her research while conducting politically engaged anthropology that writes against state terror. Her fieldwork carries significant risks to herself and her informants, and "[k]nowing that such work is subversive, illegal, and dangerous has created a series of ethical and methodological dilemmas" (2008:46), which she addresses. She has chosen to take these risks because "[t]o gather data from the most disadvantaged sectors of Burmese society is, for me, an opportunity to give a voice to largely powerless people who have no recourse to justice and for whom universal human rights are incomprehensible, as they can never envisage how such rights would be accorded to them" (2008:47). Skidmore observes that the bonds formed between anthropologists and informants in such situations are stressed and "necessarily deep, as we are both in danger when we speak the truth to each other," and describes how they "often snap under the weight of fear and anxiety" (2008:49).

Skidmore draws inspiration from Michael Taussig's writings on the anthropology of violence and the creative potential of writing against terror, and reflects upon the decision to become an engaged anthropologist. She says that the question of whether or not she should is troubling to her, because "in such conditions of repression, terror, and civil war, there seems to me to be no ethical alternative to becoming engaged" (2008:54). Like other engaged anthropologists, she concludes that there is an ethical imperative to do so and that it would be unethical *not* to:

> How can anthropologists in particular (and academics in general) fail to engage with the fear, suffering, and hope that infuse our conversations with repressed people? How could one justify a research methodology or project in contemporary Burma, in which these turbulent lives are peripheral to the research questions at hand? Until such a time as Burmese people are free to write against the politics of forgetting, I will continue to write about Burmese repression ... To maintain a polysemous, multivalent rendering of accounts of violence, to juxtapose the absurdities of authoritarian rule, and to render the subjectivity of our informants in vivid detail is to remain true to Michael Taussig's vision of the essential possibility of creative disruption. (2008:56)

The core *ethos* and *eidos* of engaged anthropology is the conviction that it is driven by an ethical imperative not only to "avoid harm" but to intentionally work to try to "do some good" where it is needed.

In "'Human Terrain': Past, Present and Future Applications" (2008), Roberto González describes and critiques the origins and operations of the HTS counter-insurgency program. He observes that while it has been presented "as a kinder, gentler counterinsurgency," this is "completely unsupported by the evidence" (2008:21). He characterizes the program as reactionary, notes that the goal is population control, and argues that this "is more than a 'hearts-and-minds' approach, for the emphasis lies primarily on exploitation of 'tribal,' political, religious and psychological dynamics" (2008:22). He shows that it is the result of a "cultural turn" within the DOD, with a new emphasis on "cultural-centric warfare," understanding "adversary cultures," and recruiting cultural specialists – particularly anthropologists – to help in the wars in Iraq and Afghanistan. He also notes the dubious assertion by anthropologist Montgomery McFate, one of the principal architects of the HTS system, that "the national security structure needs to be infused with anthropology, a discipline invented to support war fighting in the tribal zone" (2005:43; see also Sluka 2010). González argues that "in unvarnished language, a fuller picture emerges: the goal of HTS data is to help 'win the "will and legitimacy" fights' (perhaps through propaganda), to 'surface the insurgent IED networks' (presumably for targeting), and to serve 'as an element of combat power' (i.e. as a weapon)" (2008:24).

González points out that military analysts draw explicit connections between HTS and the Phoenix Program during the Vietnam War, which used local information to help target suspects for incarceration, interrogation, or assassination, and "erased" more than 26,000 people in acts that amounted to war crimes (2008:25). He argues:

> To the extent that HTS peddles anthropological techniques and concepts in support of conquest and indirect rule, it deserves rejection. To the extent that HTS might be employed to collect intelligence or target suspected enemies for assassination, the program deserves elimination – and a period of sober reflection about the situation of American social science today. (2008:26)

Reminding us that, unfortunately, "scholars are not immune to nationalist and imperialist appeals in a highly militarized context" (2008:26), he concludes:

> In the future, historians may question why a small number of anthropologists – whose progressive 20th-century predecessors created the modern culture concept, critiqued Western ethnocentrism in its various guises and invented the teach-in – decided to enlist as embedded specialists in an open-ended war of dubious legality. They might wonder why these anthropologists began harvesting data on Iraqis and Afghans as a preferred method of perceived "real-world" engagement. They might ask why, at a time when majorities in the US, Iraq and Afghanistan called for the withdrawal of US troops this group of anthropologists supported an occupation resulting in hundreds of thousands of civilian deaths. (2008:26)

Engaged anthropologists believe that "seeing" or witnessing violence and then speaking and writing about it can be powerful tools of resistance and an ethically responsible way in which social scientists can respond to a world in crisis. In the final reading, "The Gaza Freedom Flotilla: Ethnographic Notes on 'Othering Violence'" (2010), Nikolas Kosmatopoulos presents a reflexive narrative account of the Israeli assault on the Gaza Freedom Flotilla, as witnessed by an anthropologist invited on board one of its ships.

On May 31, 2010, the Israeli military attacked six ships of the flotilla, carrying protestors and humanitarian aid, in international waters of the Mediterranean Sea. Organized by the Free Gaza Movement and Turkish Foundation for Human Rights and Freedoms and Humanitarian Relief, the flotilla intended to break the Israeli blockade of the Gaza Strip, and the participants expected to be attacked and possibly arrested. The ships were attacked and boarded by Israeli naval commandos and the "official" (Israeli) narrative is that on one ship clashes broke out when activists violently resisted, during which nine activists were killed and dozens more were wounded, including seven Israeli commandos; on three ships, activists resisted passively and were suppressed without deaths or severe injuries; and the final two ships were taken without incident. The activists were arrested and detained in Israel before being deported, but widespread international condemnation of the raid followed, Israel–Turkey relations were strained, and Israel subsequently eased its blockade.

Kosmatopoulos was formally invited to join the flotilla as an anthropologist, conduct fieldwork, and observe and witness what happened on the journey. The organizers also hoped that the fear of publicity might limit expected Israeli aggression. He argues that anthropologists should act as witnesses to events such as these, presents his experience as an example of this approach in practice, and concludes:

> The choice to be an outspoken participant-observer of Othering violence in my [capacity as] an anthropologist presented a difficult challenge and a step up from the already challenging exercise of participant-observation of a people in peacetime. Yet it is worthwhile, for it opens up novel spaces for reflection and research otherwise left to the sensationalist tendencies of journalism and the propaganda machinery of the state. (2010:29)

However, when Kosmatopoulos was arrested, all his research materials – including video footage, photos, interviews, and field notes – were confiscated and not returned when he was released. He states that the flotilla participants *expected* to be attacked and possibly arrested, but does not mention taking any extra precautions with sensitive research materials, and does not reflect on the possible repercussions of this confiscation by Israeli authorities.

These accounts of engaged fieldwork by Skidmore and Kosmatopoulos, and the article by González and those presented by the contributors to *Anthropologists in the Securityscape: Ethics, Practices, and Professional Identity* (Abro et al. 2011), highlight the challenging new questions and ethical issues arising in the development and praxis of engaged fieldwork both inside and outside state security institutions such as the military and intelligence communities.

REFERENCES

Abro, Robert, George Marcus, Laura MacNamara, and Monica Schoch-Spana, eds.
    2011 *Anthropologists in the Securityscape: Ethics, Practices, and Professional Identity*. Walnut Creek, CA: Left Coast Press.
González, Roberto J.
    2007 Towards a Mercenary Anthropology? *Anthropology Today* 23(3):14–18.
González, Roberto J.
    2008 "Human Terrain": Past, Present and Future Applications. *Anthropology Today* 24(1):21–26.
González, Roberto J.
    2009 *American Counterinsurgency: Human Science and Human Terrain*. Chicago: Prickly Paradigm.
Kelly, John, Beatrice Jauregui, Sean Mitchell, and Jeremy Walton, eds.
    2010 *Anthropology and Global Counterinsurgency*. Chicago: University of Chicago Press.
Kosmatopoulos, Nikolas
    2010 The Gaza Freedom Flotilla: Ethnographic Notes on "Othering Violence." *Anthropology Today* 26(4):26–29.
Lucas, George R., Jr.
    2009 *Anthropologists in Arms: The Ethics of Military Anthropology*. Lanham, MD: AltaMira Press/Rowman & Littlefield.
McFate, Montgomery
    2005 The Military Utility of Understanding Adversary Culture. *Joint Force Quarterly* 38:42–48.
Mead, Margaret
    1965[1942] Introduction – 1942. In: *And Keep Your Powder Dry: An Anthropologist Looks at the American Character*, pp. 3–14. London: Ronald Whiting & Wheaton.
Nash, June
    1976 Ethnology in a Revolutionary Setting. In: *Ethics and Anthropology*. Michael Rynkiewich and James Spradley, eds., pp. 148–166. New York: Wiley and Sons.
NCA (Network of Concerned Anthropologists)
    2007 The Network of Concerned Anthropologists Pledges to Boycott Counterinsurgency. *Anthropology News*, December, pp. 4–5.
NCA (Network of Concerned Anthropologists)
    2009 *The Counter-counterinsurgency Handbook*. Chicago: Prickly Paradigm.
Price, David
    2006 Resisting the Weaponization of Anthropology: American Anthropologists Stand Up Against Torture and the Occupation of Iraq. *Counterpunch*, November 20. http://www.counterpunch.org/price11202006.html.

Seddon, David
  2010   Starting at the Bottom. Review of *Taking Sides: Ethics, Politics and Fieldwork in Anthropology*, ed. H. Armbruster and A. Laerke. *International Socialism* 123. http://www.isj.org.uk/index.php4?id=569issue=123.
Skidmore, Monique
  2008   Scholarship, Advocacy, and the Politics of Engagement in Burma (Myanmar). In: *Engaged Observer: Anthropology, Advocacy, and Activism*. Victoria Sanford and Asale Angel-Ajani, eds., pp. 42–59. New Brunswick, CT: Rutgers University Press.
Sluka, Jeffrey
  2010   Curiouser and Curiouser: Montgomery McFate's Strange Interpretation of the Relationship Between Anthropology and Counterinsurgency. *PoLAR (Political and Legal Anthropology Review)* 33(S1):99–115.
US Army/US Marine Corps
  2007   *The US Army/Marine Corps Counterinsurgency Field Manual*. Chicago: University of Chicago Press.
Wolf, Eric and Joseph Jorgensen
  1970   Anthropology on the Warpath in Thailand. *New York Review of Books*, November 19, pp. 26–35.

36

Introduction – 1942

Margaret Mead

SIX TIMES[1] in the last seventeen years I have entered another culture, left behind me the speech, the food, the familiar postures of my own way of life, and sought to understand the pattern of life of another people. In 1939, I came home to a world on the brink of war, convinced that the next task was to apply what we knew, as best we could, to the problems of our own society. There was no more time to go far afield for the answers which lay crystallized in the way of life of distant, half-forgotten peoples who, for thousands of years, had been finding quite different and various answers to those problems which all human beings must solve if they are to continue to live together in groups. For a few short years the methods of anthropology had been used to explore social problems; and now, with such increased knowledge as the study of other cultures had given us, we had to tackle the enormous problem of a world on the verge of social self-consciousness, a world on the verge of a new period in history.

This did not mean that I, or any other anthropologist, was now to treat our own society exactly like a primitive society. The dispassionate study of culture, of the whole way of life of a people seen as a dynamic pattern, is dependent upon a degree of detachment which no one can attain concerning his own society and remain a normal, participant member of that society. My own culture, the language and gestures, the rituals and beliefs of Americans, will always be to me something more than materials for study, to be catalogued side by side with the practices of Samoans and Balinese. Where the Samoans and Balinese may have developed a pattern of life which disallows in cruelest fashion some special capacity of the human spirit, I can record that fact with clarity and a minimum of personal involvement. For my own culture, this cannot be. The obligation of the scientist to examine his material dispassionately is combined with the obligation of the citizen to participate responsibly in his society.[2] To the investigation

Margaret Mead, "Introduction – 1942," pp. 3–14 from *And Keep Your Powder Dry: An Anthropologist Looks at the American Character*. London: Ronald Whiting & Wheaton, 1967[1942]. (Reissued New York: Berghahn, 2000.)

Ethnographic Fieldwork: An Anthropological Reader, Second Edition. Edited by
Antonius C. G. M. Robben and Jeffrey A. Sluka.
Editorial material and organization © 2012 John Wiley & Sons, Inc.
Published 2012 by John Wiley & Sons, Inc.

of social materials to the end that we may know more, has to be added the organization of social materials that we may *do* more – here – now – in America towards fighting the war in a way that will leave us with the moral and physical resources to attack the problem of reorganizing the world.

Although the anthropologist never looks at his own culture and his own people with quite the clear, objective appraisal he is trained to give to South Sea Islanders and Indians, nevertheless, if those South Sea Islanders have been studied carefully enough, the anthropologist wears forever another set of lenses, a new set for each primitive culture which has been examined. With these lenses, acquired in the long months in which he minutely studied strange ways of life and held reflectively small wriggling babies – for the babies of each society wriggle in a slightly different way, and one learns from observing the differences – the anthropologist sees different things about the home culture from those things which others see who have never had to submit to this special discipline.

What the anthropologist sees is different from what the traveler sees. The American who has lived for many years in Paris or London, in Moscow, or Berlin, or Shanghai, comes back with freshened vision: notices how tight the Faculty wives' mouths are at the old university; how nervous the bridge club members are; how no one speaks to anyone else on a train in the East any more. Peculiarities in manners, which those who stay at home take for granted, show up when the eyes and ears of the returned traveler are turned upon them. Pearl Buck, returning to a world which she had dreamed of as a true democracy, saw, with a sharpness denied to most of those who have lived in America instead of having heard about America in China, how far from her dream – from our dream – we were. Men who fought in Spain, men who have gone through months of London in the blitz, or men who have seen the Russian front come back with eyes which see more clearly, more fiercely, than our own.

It is not these things that the anthropologist has to offer. The anthropologist is trained to see form where other people see concrete details, to think in terms which will bring

together a wedding in a cathedral and a ceremony on a small South Sea island, in which two middle-aged people with three children sit down and solemnly eat one chicken egg.[3] Seen in terms of the social history, both are marriages: both are socially-sanctioned ways of recognizing that two people, a man and a woman, now publicly assume complete responsibility for their children; although in one society the children are born before the ceremony, while in the other the ceremony must come first. Where the advocate of better housing worries about the moral effects of a whole family living in a trailer, the anthropologist knows that it is not the small space, nor the poor sanitation, which is crucial. The anthropologist has seen people live with complete dignity and morality under conditions which would make a modern trailer look like a palace, or even a share-cropper's cabin look like a substantial and prosperous dwelling. Behind the small space of the trailer and its possible effect upon the morals of adolescent children is seen a system of family relationships which depends upon privacy, upon doors and bathroom keys. People trained to depend upon such details of house construction to preserve incest taboos cannot do without them easily. So the anthropologist does not disagree with the housing expert, but the problem is seen in a different perspective against the background of shelter and tipi and pile house set in a shallow salt lagoon.

Speaking from a platform to a women's club, if one is merely an experienced speaker at women's clubs, one notices whether the audience is smartly dressed, and how smartly. If one is an American sociologist, one may add observations about the probable class level of the audience and the proportion of professional women – lawyers in sober suits seeking to tone down their sex, social workers in pleasant but serviceable headgear, civil servants with clothes that look like uniforms or clothes that aggressively do *not* look like uniforms. But I never completely lose a still further point of reference – the awareness that my audience wears clothes, and several layers of them; the consciousness that this is a great group of women of child-bearing age, and yet nowhere is there a baby crawling at its mother's feet or begging to be fed; the knowledge that, if there were a breast-fed baby in that audience, it would have to go hungry. I do not cease to observe whether this is a patriotic group of women, valiantly and self-consciously wearing last year's hats, or an afternoon group of women who are homemakers, or an evening group of women who, whether they are home-makers or not, don't do homemaking in the daytime – but this other consciousness: "These people are completely clothed," stays with me to widen my perspective.

In the chapters that follow, I do not present a study of America. This is not a *Middletown*[4] or a *Yankee City*[5] or a *Hollywood*,[6] although the detailed observation recorded in the pages of those books has been very valuable to me. This is not an indictment of America in the style of Grant Allen's *British Barbarians*,[7] in which the British are held up to ridicule because they have taboos and fetishes and totems. This is not an "Are We Civilized?" in which the random pieces of better behavior among primitive peoples the world over are cited to deflate our spurious complacency. This is not an attempt to take off Americans' clothes. I prefer Americans with clothes, just as much as I prefer South Sea Islanders without them. It is an attempt to say: In the last seventeen years I have been practicing a certain way of looking at peoples. I bring it – for what it is worth – to you, to us, at this moment when no American can escape the challenge to use what special or accidental skills he has.

A score of years ago, the British invented a special use for anthropologists as advisers to the government. In colonial countries, where a small colonial staff has to administer large areas filled with native people speaking diverse languages and practicing a large number of strange and diverse customs, there are always administrative problems: Why is there a sudden outbreak of headhunting in the gold-fields? Why have all the men in a certain area suddenly all gone away to work, or all refused to work? What will be the response of a tribe of two hundred fishing people if the government moves them to other land? How is it possible to stop a sudden messianic cult, which is sweeping from tribe to tribe making everyone

kill his pigs and neglect his gardens? These are recurrent situations, and some governments retained anthropologists to find immediate answers to these vexatious questions. Trained to get the outlines of a situation quickly in cultural terms, the anthropologist was asked to find the source of the trouble and to suggest satisfactory answers. His answers had to be within the rules of the colonial administration as set up: he couldn't recommend cannibalism as a substitute for headhunting. Education was too long a process. Some change had to be made quickly which would stop headhunting, yet leave the natives able to initiate their young men into manhood. He had to recommend something like pig-hunting; explaining, for instance, that for this given people, boys couldn't grow to full manhood without killing something, that this was a tribe which couldn't get on without some form of long pants.

So, in our own society at present, the anthropologist can comment on particular problems, based on a special type of experience. The war is putting new strains on men, women, and children;[8] on teachers;[9] on young people; on old people; on social workers; on factory owners; on farmers. The war is posing new problems for which there is desperate need of solutions. Most of the ideas in the chapters which follow were developed in answer to definite questions brought to me by groups of people hopeful that a different experience and training might throw light on their problems. The research, the detailed objective recording[10] of human behavior, which lies back of this discussion was not done in the United States, but in the South Seas. On the basis of that study I have looked at America; I have thought about Americans. I have offered certain diag-noses to Americans, who have found them, by virtue of their very strangeness, illuminating.

But one serious difficulty confronts the anthropologist. When writing about some strange South Sea culture, there is the persistent difficulty of translating strange native ideas into English, until one wishes passionately that it were possible to describe Samoa in Samoan and Arapesh in the Arapesh language. English words, no matter how skillfully used, do not convey accurately the meaning of a Balinese word like *tis*, which means not to be hot when it is hot, and not to be cold when it is cold. It's a lovely word, and it takes some fifteen English words to translate it even partially. But the anthropologist, writing about his own culture in his own language, suffers from the opposite difficulty. I wish to say different things from the things that have been said before, to look at America in a way that has not ever been attempted. But all the words are old; they have been used by novelists and journalists, by columnists and Fourth of July orators. It is extremely difficult to differentiate between a "glittering generality" and a careful statement arrived at by scientific means. Unless the reader follows the *kind* of reasoning, rather than the old familiar words in which the reasoning is perforce clothed, he is likely to turn away thinking, "Just some more remarks about the American way of life."

And there is an even more serious trap. As America has a moral culture – that is, a culture which accepts right and wrong as important – any discussion of Americans must simply bristle with words like *good* and *bad*. Any discussion of Samoans would bristle with terms for awkward and graceful, for ill bred and "becoming to those bred as chiefs." Any account of the Balinese would be filled with discussions of whether a given act would make people *paling*, the Balinese word for the state of not knowing where you are, what day it is, where the center of the island is, the caste of the person to whom you are talking, or being in trance or drunk. Similarly, when I talk about what Americans must do if they are to use the full resources of their character structure, I will be making highly technical statements, and they will often sound exactly like a Sunday-school lesson.

If I were writing about the way in which the Germans or the Japanese, the Burmese or the Javanese would have to act if they were to win the war, I would not need to use so many moral terms. For none of these peoples think of life in as habitually moral terms as do Americans. Only by remembering this, by pausing every time that a sentence in this book seems to sound like a Fourth of July sermon and realizing that Fourth of July sermons are, after all, what little Americans are made of – among other more temporary ingredients such as

Mickey Mouse and Superman – will it be possible for the reader to realize that this is a scientific discussion and that it sounds familiar, not because the points are old and familiar ones, but because it is expressed in the words and ideas of our culture with which we are all familiar. When automobiles replace outrigger canoes, apples replace mangosteens and papayas, and boxes of chocolates are substituted for octopus pudding as a suitable gift to take on a date, the whole incidental paraphernalia of strangeness which I could use to convey the cultures of other peoples is gone. Only by remembering that when I look at a box of chocolates I see it as just one item in one form of courtship – instead of a cigarette containing love magic, an octopus pudding, the heart of a coconut or a bunch of lotus stems in as many different systems of courtship – and that where I use the words *good* or *just* here, I might be using the words *status*, or the "*honor of the Emperor*," or "*keeping the world steady*," will it be possible for the reader to appreciate what I am trying to say, instead of being swamped by a barrage of old words, each one struggling to convey a new point of view.

If we were not at war, if the whole world were not at war, if every effort of each human being were not needed to ask the right questions so that we may find the right answers in time, I would not be writing this book. I would be on a ship, bound for some South Sea island to continue my study of rapidly vanishing primitive peoples in the belief that the knowledge thus accumulated would some day give us adequate guidance in building a good society. But even in a world relatively at peace, a world which gave a breathing spell for scientific work, I would have been bringing back whatever hints[11] and guesses seemed relevant to our own problems in need of solution. Now there is no longer time to go to any more islands, to study any more languages, to find any more cultures which might turn our traditional beliefs upside down. We are caught in a situation so dangerous, so pressing, that we must use what tools we have.

There are those social scientists who are unwilling to use tools which they know to be as clumsy, when measured against what we may some day develop, as a stone ax against an electric drill. They fear the fellow scientist who may review their work. The man who hit on the idea of a stone ax was free to use it because he could imagine nothing better. Because we know that we might have better tools and, in fact, are that much wiser than Stone Age man, there is no reason for us to become weaker because wiser, to be ashamed to use our stone axes. Nor need we wait passively for starvation and destruction, proud that we know that more precise tools of thought are available. Some of us feel that with every increase in knowledge – even with our wider vision of what Science may some day be – we should become stronger, not weaker; bolder, not more craven; freer to act.

Recently, I sat at a meeting to which a government official posed a question, a question for which there was insufficient data to give a full answer. At that meeting sat a nationally known psychologist. He objected: "We ought to do some research." The answer was: "You have a week in which to answer this question. Then *some* action will be taken." The nationally known psychologist sat up. "You mean we have to stick our necks out?" "Yes!" "Okay," and he squared his shoulders.

Anthropology was made for man; not man for anthropology. In peacetime we labor to increase anthropological knowledge, to construct a systematic picture of how human culture works, to provide the scientific basis for building an ever better world. In wartime we have three courses – to retire into ivory towers, protect our scientific reputations, and wait, on the chance that peace will come without our help and leave us free again to go back to our patient labors; or, we can do something non-anthropological, satisfy our patriotic consciences by becoming air-raid wardens, working in an area where no colleague will review our works. Or, we can say quite simply, with such knowledge and insights as we have, we will now do what we can, as anthropologists, to win the war. We can come out into the market place, work in the dust of the traveled road, laying aside the immunities of the ivory tower, and try to ask the right questions, secure in the faith that, whenever in all his history Man has asked the right question, he has found the answer.

NOTES

1　1925–26. Samoa (Auspices of National Research Council) 1928–29. Manus Tribe, Admiralty Islands, New Guinea (Auspices of Social Science Research Council)

　　1930. An American Indian Tribe (Auspices of Mrs. Elmhirst's Committee, American Museum of Natural History)

　　1931–33. New Guinea: Arapesh, Mundugumor, Tchambuli Tribes (Auspices of Voss Fund and South Seas Exploration Fund, American Museum of Natural History)

　　The following three trips were under the auspices of Voss Fund and South Seas Exploration Fund, American Museum of Natural History, in conjunction with Committee for Research in Dementia Praecox, 33rd Order of Masons, Scottish Rite Fund, and Social Science Research Council

　　1936–38. Bali

　　1938. New Guinea: Iatmul Tribe

　　1939. Short return visit to Bali

2　Mead, Margaret. On Behalf of the Sciences. *In* Symposium: "Toward an Honorable World." *Wilson College Bulletin*, Vol. 3, No. 4, pp. 19–29, 1940.

3　Loeb, Edwin M. Mentawei Social Organization. *American Anthropologist*, Vol. 30, No. 3, pp. 408–433, 1928.

4　Lynd, Robert S., and Helen M. Lynd. *Middletown: A Study in Contemporary American Culture*. New York, Harcourt, Brace, 1929. *Middletown in Transition: A Study in Cultural Conflicts*. New York, Harcourt, Brace, 1937.

5　Warner, W. Lloyd, and Paul S. Lunt. *The Social Life of a Modern Community*. (Yankee City Series, Vol. 1.) New Haven, Yale University Press, 1941.

6　Rosten, Leo C. *Hollywood: The Movie Colony; the Movie Makers*. New York, Harcourt, Brace, 1941.

7　Allen, Grant. *The British Barbarians: A Hill-Top Novel*. New York, Putnam's, 1895.

8　Mead, Margaret. War Need Not Mar Our Children. *The New York Times Magazine*, pp. 13, 34, February 15, 1942.

9　Mead, Margaret. Youth Would Be Valiant. *National Parent-Teacher*, Vol. 36, No. 2, pp. 14–16, 1941.

10　For an example of the type of detailed study of culture which provided the background for this study, see: Mead, Margaret. Living with the Natives in Melanesia. *Natural History*, Vol. 31, No. 1, pp. 62–74, 1931. More Comprehensive Field Methods. *American Anthropologist*, Vol. 35, No. 1, pp. 1–15, 1933. Kinship in the Admiralty Islands. Anthropological Papers of The American Museum of Natural History, Vol. 34, Pt. 2, pp. 138–358, New York, 1934. Native Languages as Field-Work Tools. *American Anthropologist*, Vol. 41, No. 2, pp. 189–205, 1939. The Mountain Arapesh. II. Supernaturalism. Anthropological Papers of The American Museum of Natural History, Vol. 37, Pt. 3, pp. 319–451, New York, 1940.

Bateson, Gregory, and Margaret Mead. *Balinese Character: A Photographic Analysis.* Special Publications of The New York Academy of Sciences, II. New York, 1942; reissued 1962.

11 Mead, Margaret. *From the South Seas (Containing Coming of Age in Samoa, Growing Up in New Guinea, and Sex and Temperament).* New York, Morrow, 1939. (See Introduction to book; also concluding chapter of each of the three parts.)

37

Scholarship, Advocacy, and the Politics of Engagement in Burma (Myanmar)

Monique Skidmore

April 26, 2005: A polythene bag is placed on the ground near a trash bin outside the Hla Bettman clothing shop in Mandalay's central Zeygyo market. It detonates at 4:15 in the afternoon, killing twenty-three-year-old Ma Moe Kyi from Sone Village, who was shopping at the clothing store, and an unidentified forty-five-year-old female market porter. Sixteen other people were injured, according to casualty figures given by staff at the Mandalay Hospital. The following day, Buddhist monks were asked to perform ceremonies designed to ward off evil spirits and the ghosts of those who had died in the explosion. Earlier that morning forty-four-year-old Khin Maung Lay had died from exposure to fumes inhaled while carrying injured people from the market. A week later, nineteen-year-old Myint Myint Aye, a worker in the Rising Sun textile store next door to the bombsite, also succumbed to her injuries in Mandalay Hospital (*Burma Issues* 2005; DVB 2005a, b, c, d; Myo Lwin 2005; *USA Today* 2005).

May 7, 2005: Eleven days later, on a busy Saturday afternoon, three bombs are detonated in Burma's capital city, Rangoon (Yangon). Two bombs targeted grocery shoppers; the other bomb was detonated at a Thai business expo taking place at the Yangon Convention Centers. Like the Mandalay market bombing, the fatalities and injuries that occurred at the Junction 8 and Dagon shopping centers had women and children as their main casualties. The bombs were detonated in five-minute intervals. Some have said that the terror campaign was executed with military precision.

The death count from these acts is impossible to know, as the military regime forbids medical staff from giving out information, and the regime's own figures are notoriously low. Official figures are 23 dead and 162 injured. The Thai prime minister, Thaksin Shinawatra, sent a C-130 military plane for the 122 Thai nationals attending the trade fair, and the Thai government reports at least 21 people died from these three bombings. Three Thais were

Monique Skidmore, "Scholarship, Advocacy, and the Politics of Engagement in Burma (Myanmar)," pp. 42–59 from *Engaged Observer: Anthropology, Advocacy, and Activism*, ed. Victoria Sanford and Asale Angel-Ajani. New Brunswick: Rutgers University Press, 2008.

Ethnographic Fieldwork: An Anthropological Reader, Second Edition. Edited by Antonius C. G. M. Robben and Jeffrey A. Sluka.
Editorial material and organization © 2012 John Wiley & Sons, Inc.
Published 2012 by John Wiley & Sons, Inc.

injured, and four Malaysians. One injured
Malaysian, Goh Cha Watt, was part of a
Lutheran Church group who were in Burma for
a week to visit an orphanage and set up a children's camp. The *Asia Times* reported eyewitness
accounts of the bombings and of Rangoon
General, Insein, and North Okkalapa hospitals
where injured people were initially treated:

> Within hours of the multiple bombing,
> witnesses at all three blast sites said they had
> seen dozens of casualties – many of them
> missing limbs or heads – and numerous black-
> ened corpses. An eyewitness who was at the
> General Hospital in Rangoon ... said the
> casualties overwhelmed the hospital's capacity
> and had to be laid on concrete floors. The
> witness, who asked not to be identified,
> reported seeing "nine or ten" people killed in
> the explosions who had been taken to the
> morgue, as well as many victims, including
> children and the elderly, who had lost body
> parts (*Asia Times* 2005).

Bombings are nothing new in Burma. There
are many each year; usually it's a hydropower
plant or a rail line being blown up, sometimes
it's a small explosion near a Western embassy
or a general's house, or even a military-built
new pagoda. No one pays them much attention
anymore. A few bombs have targeted the
generals and their families, but in the main
assassination attempts against members of the
ruling military council are rare. Until recently
there have been very few bombing campaigns
that targeted civilians. Almost unremarked
upon, a series of bomb blasts have occurred
in public areas in the past few months. For
example, on March 19, 2005, a bomb exploded
in the Panorama Hotel in Rangoon. Two days
earlier a bus was bombed in Rangoon and
an unexploded bomb was defused in a bus
terminal. In June of 2005, four bombs were
detonated close to Rangoon's central railway
station, as well as one in a French café near
Bogyoke Market, and one outside of the
Southern Division Court (*Irrawaddy* 2005a).
Bombers also targeted the Supreme Court in
Rangoon on March 22 (DVB 2005c).

Burmese activist groups correctly point out
that the kinds of civilians targeted are in general wealthy, and therefore have close links

with the military regime. Military sites have
also recently been targeted by bombers, and
the bus that was bombed was owned by
Myanmar Economic Holdings Limited, an
army-dominated company that owns much of
Burma's private enterprises (DVB 2005d). The
fact that military-owned sites or sites frequented
by the military were the main ones targeted
has prompted speculation among Rangoon
residents that the bombs were planted by
disgruntled former members of the military
intelligence branch, which was disbanded in
2004, and whose employees were jailed or fled
the country. The international media has
ignored scores of such bomb blasts in 2004
and 2005.

The military council, the State Peace and
Development Committee (SPDC), has accused
many expatriate groups, rebel armies, Western
organizations such as the CIA and political
opponents in-country of exploding the bombs.
In the first two weeks following the bombings,
most Rangoon residents reckoned that the
military regime had detonated the bombs in
order to be able to portray itself as a victim of
terrorism. Other rumors circulated in Rangoon
teashops suggesting that the regime committed
this violence to allow it to graciously hand
over its chairing of ASEAN (Association of
Southeast Asian Nations) later in the year to
another country, or perhaps to chair ASEAN
but to hold the meeting in Thailand, thus
diffusing American and European diplomatic
anger at ASEAN for allowing Burma to chair
the meeting.

Some of the bombings in the past year have
been the self-confessed work of Burma's own
terrorist organization, the Vigorous Burmese
Student Warriors (VSBW), and the military
junta were quick to blame this organization.
Following denial of the allegations by the
VSBW, the military regime continued to
deliberately conflate the aims and motivations
of armed and nonarmed political opponents.
In doing so it sought to remove suspicion from
the Burmese military, to inculcate a state of
vulnerability in the general populace, and to
justify its heightened security and surveillance
measures. Multiple forms of armed and nonarmed opposition and bombing campaigns
against the military rule are currently occurring

in Burma. The regime's obfuscation of this resistance, combined with the lack of attention paid by scholars to the violence that is occurring in Burma, has created a complex situation in need of analysis.

After the initial shock of the bombings, Burmese people were inundated with state propaganda vowing to find the culprits responsible for the carnage and offering a large reward for information leading to the arrest of the perpetrators. Teashop conversations vacillated between ongoing cynicism of the regime's words, and the beginning of doubts that the regime had truly committed this act against its own (urban) people. The rumor that the former prime minister and head of military intelligence Khin Nyunt was behind the bombing campaign, also circulated, as did various revenge scenarios meted out by his former intelligence operatives in hiding. There is an urgent need to write about such violent events from the perspective of Burmese people caught up in the violence, and within the context of the sociopolitical environment that has been created by the Burmese military regime. Not only are such histories of violence and suffering not being written but also the few attempts to document violence and human rights violations are often being subjected to a process of academic (and thus historical) denial and dismissal.

Burmese Scholarship

Anthropologists who work in Myanmar (Burma) are rare. It is not hard to be let into the country but it is difficult to be given permission by the Burmese military regime to stay there. International conferences about Burma are now held in Yangon (Rangoon), and the regime sends black saloon cars to ferry the conference speakers to and from their hotels. "Why do you go?" I ask the few anthropologists I know who attend these conferences. The answer is invariably, "Because it ensures our access and allows the regime to categorize us firmly as scholars and not journalists and activists." And that probably sums up why I've never gone to one of these in-country conferences.

It would be comforting for the regime to acknowledge that I am a scholar and to

continue to give me access to my field site. The trouble is, each time I think up a topic, I have to drastically censor myself. I would have to make no mention in my paper of the atrocities perpetrated by the regime, the ongoing civil war, and the suffering, fear, and injustice that envelop the nation. Do anthropologists have a moral duty to speak out publicly about such atrocities? The premise that one can choose to be an engaged anthropologist (or not) is troubling to me. I can see that for specialists of, say, lacquer ware and mulberry tree papermaking techniques, this may not be an issue. Similarly, for historians of precolonial Burma, there is no one to interview and no reason to go to Burma other than to view archival material. The problem is with speaking to the present, not the past.

Critiquing a recent article of mine about fear in Burma (Skidmore 2003a), a reviewer pointed out that I had become an activist-by-proxy. This comment made me truly reflect for the first time about why I had chosen Burma as a field site and why I work on violence and fear. I had ostensibly gone to Burma to research a medical anthropological topic, but at McGill University in the 1990s we were all aware that the medical is almost always political and the juridical, political, and medical arms of the state are sometimes inseparable. Social suffering was a theoretical paradigm I was eager to explore in Burma, but I had imagined my graduate work focusing upon help-seeking behaviors and forms of healing sought by the populace, and that this hoped-for healing would not necessarily differentiate between traumas of the mind and body.

It was evident to me upon arriving in Burma that the whole nation was in distress and engaged in help-seeking behavior. I remembered the Kleinmans' line about needing to attend to the concerns of our informants in their local moral worlds (Kleinman and Kleinman 1994). Suddenly, studying Burmese medicine and the occult just didn't seem enough when clear and planned resistance to military rule was being promulgated on the streets and in the teashops of the major cities. I decided to stay in the capital cities and document the resistance and fear that were overlaying so many thoughts and actions at the time. I wasn't sure where I was going with the project, but I knew instinctively that I was following the "cultural grain," something that Evans-Pritchard advocated many years ago (Evans-Pritchard quoted in Rozenberg 2005), a method only half-consciously passed on to each new generation of anthropology students.

What didn't occur to me as a graduate student was that concerns for social justice motivated my choice to study anthropology instead of medicine, and it undoubtedly, at least sub- or unconsciously, motivated me to choose field sites such as post-Pol Pot Cambodia (Skidmore 1995, 1996) and Burma. As I compiled literature reviews in preparation for that first long stint of fieldwork in Burma, I read avidly the brutal history of the nation and the complexities of the Burmese cultural and religious systems as well as the tortured past and present of Burma's political history and bloody civil war against the military regime. For years the Burmese nationalist movement had created the political momentum necessary for independence from Britain, and I read with horror the usurpation of the fledgling democratic government first by a hand grenade lobbed into the parliamentary cabinet room and several years later by the military coup of General Ne Win.

I approached the study of the suffering of the Burmese people from the perspective of an outsider who, over time, came to live in Burma in a mode similar to that of most Burmese people. That is to say, I became fearful of the military regime and I hid my thoughts, feelings, and actions from the gaze of the Office of the Chief of Military Intelligence. This was the point where the reviewer realized I had become an activist-by-proxy. I had not been able to admit this to myself until then. Given some time to think about it, I realized the consequences were different from those of being an anthropologist who approached Burma on a par with any other field site, collecting my data and pursuing methodologies as taught in fieldwork courses and textbooks. From that time onward I was able to examine my own motivations more clearly, and I made the conscious, and therefore frightening, decision to continue to work in Burma on issues of fear, violence, and suffering.

Knowing that such work is subversive, illegal, and dangerous for my informants has created a series of ethical and methodological dilemmas that I have written about elsewhere (Skidmore 2004, 2003b). It has also created a series of dilemmas in the way in which I write about suffering and fear. Burma studies in the fields of political science and international relations has, in recent years, become increasingly politicized. Political scientists have taken lucrative contracts to work for multinational organizations that have interests in Burma. Others have lobbied the U.S. government and the European Union to remove their sanctions banning business in Burma and Burmese exports. International conferences have occasionally been the scene of such public lobbying in the guise of scholarship, without the obvious conflicts of interest being declared. Several political scientists have argued that American sanctions prohibit them from gaining course materials necessary to teach about Burma. Both political scientists and international relations scholars and students have produced reports for international lending organizations that urge cooperation with the military regime (Taylor and Pedersen 2005). In their zeal to become "Burma experts," faculty at some universities have taken a pro-engagement stance toward the military regime (Bowring 2005), often in contravention to their own government's position of nonengagement with Burma.

The Burmese expatriate activist community has been damning in its condemnation of what it has labeled "pro-military scholarship" and in particular, against those political scientists and students known as the "Brussels Four" (*Irrawaddy* 2005b). To date, academics have rarely argued against such scholarship. My own ethnographic work about the subjectivities of Burmese people under dictatorship and the manifest social suffering occurring in Burma has become a target for a section of the Burma studies community. It has been described as "lurid," "emotive" and "full of dead facts" (Lambrecht and Mathieson 2005). The desire to be a "Burma expert" is leading some scholars and graduate students to a condemnation of ethnographic fieldwork as nonobjective and therefore inaccurate. There is much at stake here for such players. The international lecture and conference circuit is alluring to such authors, and discrediting in-country information creates the illusion that no one really knows what is occurring in Burma.

This kind of academic posturing does, to my mind, a great deal of violence to Burma and to Burmese people. To be an engaged anthropologist within the orbit of Burma studies is to be labeled a kind of fringe lunatic, the kind who would hang out with Burmese activists in Thailand and succumb to their emotional pleas for an end to the regime's rule. To gather data from the most disadvantaged sectors of Burmese society is, for me, an opportunity to give a voice to largely powerless people who have no recourse to justice and for whom universal human rights are incomprehensible, as they can never envisage how such rights would be accorded to them. But there is another reason to do ethnographic work in Burma, and that is to document the potential forms of political agency that exist in the various subjectivities that are created under authoritarianism. In this sense, being an engaged anthropologist is to advocate for the histories of terror and misery to be retained in the contemporary world. These alternate readings of political power, legitimacy, and moral authority have the power to puncture the hegemonic reading of past and present created by the military regime. They are not the political strategies documented by political scientists and international relations scholars, and they have no import on the global political stage. It seems important for some scholars to discredit the words, feelings, and actions of Burmese people, and it seems that to write about power in Burma is to be seen as a threat to such scholars: to be considered an activist and have a political agenda that interferes with some imagined view of objective fact gathering.

It is also worrying that scholars are choosing to interpret the war that has been waged by the Burmese military against its own populace since 1962 in terms of "security." The American government's belief in a "war on terror" has meant a reduction in the civil rights of people all over the world as governments have introduced legislation that allows increased powers of surveillance, arrest, and incarceration. The Burmese regime has sought to recast its attempt to permanently silence all those who resist its rule as a war on terror, one that requires the military to become engaged in securing the nation and its borders. Some scholars are borne along by the regime's tide of seemingly reasonable, pragmatic, long-term strategic planning goals, and choose not to investigate the means by which dissent is put down.

To many such scholars, the Burmese military regime is the only institution that emerged at the end of the 1950s with enough strength to pull the country together and form a government. The place of violence, of fear, of both genocidal and low-level intensity conflict is unwritten. The 2005 bombings of crowded public spaces will also be interpreted as a small part of the collateral damage involved in creating a unified country that can participate in international affairs and in the global economic and development marketplace.

The Ethics and Risks of Fieldwork in Burma

The perils of conducting ethnographic research in Burma on any issues that can somehow be regarded as political or "sensitive" are manifest. In 2002 I applied for my latest "official" research visa for 2002–2003, as I would not have been able to conduct fieldwork in rural areas of the country without permission. The visa was initially denied, even after I had used all of my previously successful networks and strategies for gaining a research permit. Finally the visa was signed by the former prime minister and chief of military intelligence, General Khin Nyunt. After signing my visa, Khin Nyunt warned me: "You are an angel of light come to help the Burmese people. You obviously have very high karma and your fate is linked with that of the nation. It would be a shame to lose that karma and go to hell from associating with negative political elements" (Khin Nyunt, personal communication 2002). Phone tapping, physical surveillance, luggage searches, and recourse to informants are ways in which the movements of anthropologists are monitored and curtailed in Burma. I was being warned off doing any of the things we both knew to be illegal in authoritarian Burma and, although phrased in a mild manner, it was a chilling reminder that fieldwork in Burma always carries significant risks to myself and my informants.

Government officials who read the signature on the research visa forms were incredulous. The letters to various government officials came in a manila folder with "Top Secret" stamped in the upper right-hand corner. No one could pronounce Khin Nyunt's name: it came out as a kind of squeak, the last part of the name seemingly swallowed. Eyes bulged with apprehension and several officials asked me about my personal connection to Khin Nyunt and my "real agenda." "Great," said my husband, when I told him about my day, "another ethical dilemma for you." And he was right. I was causing fear in people who were just trying to do their job. Every day, thousands of Burmese people weigh their involvement with the regime. By wanting to conduct research I had just made life more fearful for some people. There is no easy answer; I still don't know if I've made the right choice. In this particular case, I tried to minimize my contact with government officials.

Burmese people always carefully weigh their involvement with me. Khin Nyunt's belief that my fate is somehow intertwined with that of the nation is a statement that has also been made to me by medical, religious, and magical healers in the past decade. In my last period of prolonged fieldwork in Burma, I asked magical and religious healers if I could record our conversations. "Certainly," they invariably replied. "If you don't mind me recording you." Ancient tape players were used to record our conversation and at some point in the conversation I inevitably needed to provide my informants with batteries or tapes. When I asked for informed consent before interviewing these healers, I was almost always asked if I would use the knowledge passed on to me for good purposes, refrain from harming anyone armed with this knowledge, and if I had a pure heart. Continuously, Burmese people place upon my shoulders the burden of disseminating knowledge of their beliefs and life experiences in ways that are ethically appropriate and that contribute to a better future for Burma.

It's not an easy burden, and asking questions related to the political situation invariably causes some degree of fear. Knowing about people's political views and activities can occasion a variety of negative emotions and behaviors in my informants. A fellow anthropologist who works on Burma, Christina Fink, once told me that she remembers a meeting we had in Rangoon in 1996 when I expressed frustration at having to continuously tear up my field notes. Informants would spend a sleepless night tossing and turning before coming to my house at first light and demanding I destroy the notes I had made of our conversations. The bond formed between anthropologist and informant is necessarily deep, as we are both in danger when we speak the truth to each other. But this intensity exists only for that one issue; otherwise we know little about each other. In particular, Burmese people must trust that I will safely take my notes out of the country and that I will never identify them or put their family into jeopardy. Sometimes this causes a great deal of anxiety, especially when the cities are undergoing curfew or other heightened "security" measures.

Diplomats and Burmese people whom I had come to regard with great affection have accused me of being a spy. Many people have become so cynical under the current regime that they find it hard to envisage my motivations as being other than negative or egotistical. The affective milieu is one of heightened suspicion and sometimes paranoia, and gathering information in order to pass it on to political masters is a familiar norm. The bonds I form in the field (and attempt to reforge each year) often wither and snap under the weight of fear and anxiety that my leaving Burma occasions. Nightmares are created with my leaving the field, carrying the secrets of frightened people with me.

Subjectivity and Political Agency: Writing against Terror

To be an engaged scholar under conditions of authoritarianism and in a climate of fear is not an easy decision to make. As the mother of two young children, it is a decision I constantly reevaluate. It is not a decision I was aware of needing to make when I was in graduate school, but it is one that carries a weight of responsibility to oneself, one's family, and one's informants and their families. That responsibility begins with ensuring safety and ethical conduct, and ends with a commitment to portray the experiences of one's informants as powerfully as possible.

As Burma's ongoing bombing campaign shatters lives and instills fear in Burmese people who must constantly negotiate public spaces with a new feeling of vulnerability. I wonder how I can render a decade of witnessing suffering, misery, and terror in Burma in such a way that it will not become bound up in the chapter of Burma's history to be known as "attempts at resistance to military rule." Already some of my writings are glossed over by political scientists as being in-depth accounts of this specific moment and thus not representative of the ongoing nature of Burma's state of emergency. As an engaged anthropologist I seek to write not only against terror but also against the homogenizing weight of political forgetting.

The Burmese military regime has been writing propaganda, but it has also been writing violence, terror, and its own version of history into the very bodies of Burmese people since at least 1962. Burmese people respond by creating subjectivities under authoritarianism that hide political agency in a variety of forms. The regime is aware of the potential of some of these forms of subjectivity, and it attempts to crush the healers, teachers, and community leaders who advocate forms of subjectivity at odds with the regime's requirement of "disciplined democracy" from its "model citizens." In the following pages I describe some of these forms of subjectivity. In writing about the potential political agency embedded within them, I consciously write about the politics of everyday life in order to provide a different record from that created by successive military juntas. I also record these forms of subjectivity and political agency to deny nonengaged scholars the ability to dismiss the words and experiences of Burmese people. Both processes inscribe forgetting into the historical record, and both do violence to Burma and its people.

Following Benjamin (1983), Burmese forms of subjectivity, particularly those that lead to political agency, can constitute a potent weapon with which to pierce the future era of disciplined democracy and its associated linear historiographies. Such subjectivities are necessarily created within the framework of disciplined democracy. Forms of political agency arising from Burmese subjectivities are acknowledged by the military regime as requiring monitoring and, wherever possible, eradication. My argument here draws on Michael Taussig's writings on the anthropology of violence (Taussig 1980, 1987, 1991, 1992, 1997, 1999, 2003, 2004) and about the creative potential of writing against terror. I accordingly draw upon the forms of emergent subjectivity that Burmese people deploy to invest their repressive situations with hope and the possibility for change.

Domains in which memory can live and in which counterhegemonic subjectivities can be constituted and refined are actively crushed by the regime. The intelligence services, the Ministry of Information, the Department of Psychological Warfare, the Department of Propaganda, the Press Scrutiny Board, the system of reportage all the way from the Ten House Leader to the State Peace and Development Council, the parastatal organizations, the four-decade-long civil war, and the dominant political reportage of the generals versus a federal alliance of prodemocracy parties – all act to force narrative linearity upon history. This politics of forgetting attempts to channel the political agency and subjectivities of Burmese people.

For example, in the 1990s, the urban centers of Yangon (Rangoon) and Mandalay were transformed with the forcible removal of hundreds of thousands of residents to rice fields on the outskirts of the cities. The area became known as the "New Fields" (Allot 1994), and the residents began their new lives with virtually no compensation for the houses, apartment buildings, and businesses they left behind. The changes in living arrangements, quality of life, and economic prospects severely affected many families. Increased rates of sexual assault, commercial sex work, alcoholism, domestic abuse, and sexual barter (Skidmore 2003a) in the New Fields constitute evidence of the breakdown of many traditional social structures.

Residents were sundered from a Buddhist cosmology where they had lived close to main Buddhist infrastructures such as the pagoda complexes on Mandalay Hill and the Mandalay Fort and its surrounding monasteries and pilgrimage halls (Dhamma yon).

In the following fifteen years, garment factories opened and closed in industrial zones meant to employ these formerly urban workers. Hospitals, roads, and schools were opened or extended, and the markets in these townships have grown. Boom industries have developed in land speculation, money lending, gambling, and prostitution. In contrast to this reality, the history of this area, as written by the regime, is of a phenomenally successful "huts to high-rise" scheme, where urban residents are given modern accommodation and provided with employment opportunities and an ability to partake in the development of the nation (Skidmore 2004: 84–97). It is in the narrow lanes of these relocated townships that I first conducted ethnographic fieldwork and where I came to learn about a particular form of subjectivity and its radical political potential.

I already had an inkling that the regime was worried about forms of authority other than itself, and in particular, forms of charismatic authority. The demonization of Daw Aung San Suu Kyi in the regime's newspapers is unceasing, but it's not just prodemocracy politicians who are viewed as threatening, it is also charismatic religious leaders and healers. Burmese people need no reminding of this fact. Almost everyone in Rangoon can tell you about the well-known healer, Saya San, who led a peasant rebellion against the British in the 1930s (Herbert 1982). Rangoon landmarks memorialize key figures in the fight for independence in the 1940s and early 1950s, when fiery monks such as U Wizara rallied the population, in part through recourse to the Buddhist foundations of Burman culture. Army of God Twins, Johnny and Luther Htoo, led God's Army in southeastern Burma and were believed to create magical bullets that made themselves and their troops invincible (Ingram 2001). Religion and medicine are two areas of knowledge and praxis that the regime knows can lead Burmese subjects to collective political action.

Burmese beliefs in causality and order mean that things happen when a variety of necessary events and forces align to bring a particular path of possibility into existence. This tenet is one of a web of associated epistemological understandings of the structure of time, matter, and place that have pre-Buddhist antecedents. In the Burmese framework of existence, power is a property that moves through time and place and movement is rarely linear. All this means that Burmese people have an extremely strong belief in the miraculous. This belief forms the basis for the most potent types of political agency. When agents of the Burmese regime scurry from place to place removing statues of *weikza* (wizards), jailing mystics and those who practice both religion and medicine, the regime is acknowledging the power of the Burmese belief in the miraculous and its potential as a political threat to the state.

From the Burmese regime's perspective, the main problem with having a repressed populace who believe in the miraculous is that the linear narrative of state-making (that is, the belief in a forward-moving development into a peaceful, secure, prosperous, and modern nation) is at odds with the forms of temporality and causation that Burmese know to be true. A belief in the miraculous means that at any moment something totally unexpected can occur, and the path of the future will be changed. For the junta to convince Burmese people that they are going to rule in perpetuity and everyone ought to give up trying to resist them runs against popular wisdom. Burmese people know that power exists in many forms across various domains and that the military regime controls only one form of power in this particular moment.

Individual strategies for escaping from the oppressive present involve dissociation, both physical and mental, and are very common in Burma. The population of the central valleys and deltas hide their consciousness from the regime and wait out its ascendancy. State-making falters because for dissociative subjects, this form of being-in-the-world bears little similarity to the linear nature of the state's historical projects. Burmese see history as just another version or string of events that happened along one path of causality, making history a complex and contentious issue. In addition to the many histories of Burma's minority groups, alternate readings of history are also based upon an adherence to religious, cosmological, and occult time frames. These latter forms of temporality and causality are framed by the subjunctive mood, where different modes or levels of the present can fuse in particular moments to alter the course of the future.[1]

The strong belief in the miraculous is the most important example of the Burmese subjunctive mode. As the nation has become progressively impoverished, Burmese increasingly turn to the miraculous as a strategy for improving their daily lives. The construction of an ornate temple in Rangoon in which supernatural imagery is stressed is evidence of this phenomenon (Bekker 1989). *Dagò*, the manipulation of sacred power through objects associated with the Buddha (Kumada 2002), is also reported in times of political and economic crisis, as are increased encounters with Nat spirit mediums (Brac de la Perrière 2002) and ornate funerary and other rituals associated with the movement from one world to another (Robinne 2002). The creation of new Nat spirits, the reported thickening of the right side of Buddha images after the democracy leader, Aung San Suu Kyi, touched a particular Buddha image (Houtman 1999), and the reported appearances of a poltergeist at the site of the origin of the 1988 prodemocracy uprising (Leehey 2000) are small, everyday occurrences that reveal the deep Burmese belief and investment in the miraculous as a source of potential political and religious salvation. The millions of Burmese who have, since the failed democracy uprising, moved to meditation centers (Jordt 2001), monasteries and nunneries (Kawanami 2002), and semi-autonomous Buddhist areas such as that overseen by the late Thamanya Sayadaw (Tosa 2002; Rozenberg 2002) are further examples of the increasing disengagement that Burmese have with the world of authoritarian power. Instead, Burmese people have engaged in realms where forms of supernatural authority and power hold the potential for changes in the material and psychological conditions of one's daily life.

Waiting, wandering, denying, and forgetting – this is how the people of the New Fields characterize their lives and the strategies they enact to stay sane and ward off the feelings of rage, impotence, and despair. Many Burmese people whom I have spoken to in central Burma adopt a strategy of waiting, in which they describe their "minds" leaving temporarily, while waiting for change. In Burmese Buddhism the enduring part of consciousness that remains after death and moves through the cycle of reincarnation to its eventual release through enlightenment is conceived of as a butterfly spirit. These butterfly spirits are released by an oppressed populace out into the cosmos, where they congregate in various alternate dimensions and planes of reality. Burmese people suspend this-worldly history by allowing their butterfly spirits to inhabit nontemporal dimensions or realms. The mundane world (*loka*) is deferred as Burmese butterfly spirits wander through other subjective realities. They shelter in these domains, waiting for an end to military rule.

At the Rangoon Drug Rehabilitation Unit, I interviewed fifty men and boys being forcibly detoxified of heroin, methamphetamine, and barbiturate addiction. The young male heroin addicts tell me that they send their minds to the kinds of places that they see on television or read about in books; leisure and entertainment precincts that don't exist in Burma. Their minds sleepwalk through these pleasurable domains until withdrawal symptoms rouse them back to full consciousness in the mundane world. In a similar way, young women and girls working in the sex industry in the New Fields tell me that they send their minds flying to their mother's hearts when they are engaged in sexual intercourse. The dissociative strategy denies their mind to the men they service, while allowing them to provide money for themselves and their families, keeping all alive.

Unemployed housewives of the New Fields feel that they live each day the same as the last. They tell me of the many ways they refuse to live in this present reality. They concentrate on the minutiae of everyday life; their conversations skim along the surface of daily events and conditions; emotional life is kept deliberately shallow, and they refuse to remember the past or plan for the future; they refuse to listen to news and current affairs; and they invest their time and attention in escapist pursuits such as the video hut and participation in the monthly lottery draws (Skidmore 2003a, 2004). The nature of the subjunctive mood that blankets central Burma, with its chief characteristic of possibility and the potential for immediate transformation, makes waiting a positive strategy for both suffering and survival.

A reading of the violent past must thus include the subjunctive mode as a dimension of lives lived through conflict. As Arias (1997: 825) has written about Guatemala: "the enormous changes experienced in Guatemala in recent years ... force us to re-examine the inherent meaning of the space of subjectivity and the role of agency. In the end it is in these areas that systems of thought develop and knowledge that contributes to the renovation or restructuring of meaning emerges." He might also have added that it is in these spaces of subjectivity that forms of political agency may both arise and find shelter.

Engaged Anthropologist

I mentioned at the beginning of this chapter that the very question as to whether to be an engaged anthropologist (or not) is troubling to me. In such conditions of repression, terror, and civil war, there seems to me to be no ethical alternative to becoming engaged. This is especially true for anthropologists who take upon themselves the burden of conveying the most secret thoughts, fears, and experiences of our informants. This does not necessarily mean the kind of activism and advocacy on behalf of indigenous peoples that involves becoming engaged in the daily battles waged against an oppressive regime or system. This is the task of Burmese people, and the Burmese diaspora have been extraordinarily successful legal and cyber warriors (Danitz and Strobel 1999; Brooten 2004; Zarni 2005). Report upon report has been compiled by activist expatriate groups and by international human rights organizations about the atrocities perpetrated by the Burmese military regime against the people of eastern Burma (for example, SHRF and SWAN 2002; Apple and Martin 2003; WLB 2004). Thousands of stories of rape,

torture, and the death of babies, infants, girl children, men, and women lie between their pages, and yet the Burmese regime denies any wrongdoing or any violation of the Geneva Convention (Po Khwa 2002; AFP 2003). Even highly credible evidence of chemical weapons usage by the junta (Panter 2005) goes barely mentioned in the international press, and on such issues the Burmese scholarly community is completely silent.

Silence is a powerful force in the contemporary world. Mechanisms such as censorship and fear, and motivations like greed and a desire for power, fame, and wealth cause individuals, institutions, and companies to remain silent on the ongoing campaign of terror waged by the Burmese regime against its own people. Academic silence seems to me to be completely unacceptable and a form of complicity in the politics of forgetting pioneered by dictatorial regimes.

The funerals for the seventy people confirmed by the *Democratic Voice of Burma* killed in the three bomb blasts in Rangoon on May 7 (DVB 2005) have been anything but quiet. Hundreds of Burmese people have attended memorial services held at the Yea Way and Htein Pin cemeteries, and such funerals are loud in order to ward off green ghosts and malevolent spirits of the unquiet dead who died "green" or untimely deaths. Curiously, the Burmese ruling council has been silent on the issues of consolation and compensation for the families of the victims, fueling even more teashop speculation that the regime carried out the blasts against the economic interests of its in-house opponents.

The discrediting of in-country information as emotive, exaggerated, anecdotal, or nonverifiable makes the ongoing bombing campaign seemingly inexplicable; too many possible actors, too many potential motivations. The bombings are thus largely ignored because of the apparent paucity of information about them. Not enough is known about Burmese people's actions under authoritarianism, it is widely believed, for analysis to be made about such broad opposition.

How can anthropologists in particular (and academics in general) fail to engage with the fear, suffering, and hope that infuse our conversations with repressed people? How could one justify a research methodology or project in contemporary Burma in which these turbulent lives are peripheral to the research questions at hand? Until such time as Burmese people are free to write against the politics of forgetting, I will continue to write about Burmese repression and Burmese ways of understanding and acting upon the world with a sense of indeterminacy and in the subjunctive mode. To maintain a polysemous, multivalent rendering of accounts of violence, to juxtapose the absurdities of authoritarian rule, and to render the subjectivity of our informants in vivid detail is to remain true to Michael Taussig's vision of the essential possibility of creative disruption. Surely the spirits of the men, women and children whose bodies were recently buried at Yea Way and Htein Pin cemeteries are deserving of this relatively simple task from academics who make their lives and reputations from commenting upon, and working amid, other people's misery.

NOTE

1. The theory of subjunctivization describes how human beings understand the ruptures to temporality and their sense of normalcy at moments of crisis and rapid change. Victor Turner (1990: pp. 11–12) has described the "subjunctive mood" in the following way: "I sometimes talk about the ... 'subjunctive mood' of culture, the mood of maybe, might-be, as-if, hypothesis, fantasy, conjecture, desire ... a storehouse of possibilities, not by any means a random assemblage but a striving after new forms and structure." And as Edward Bruner (in Good and DelVecchio Good et al. 1994) notes, "to be in the subjunctive mode is to be ... trafficking in human possibilities rather than in settled certainties." Like chronic illness sufferers, frightened and repressed Burmese people leave the future unemplotted so as to admit the possibility of miraculous change. The subjunctive mode is the mode of Burma. To live with the unexpected, and with possibility, is the normal modus operandi of the entire nation. It is only when one is "beyond fear," for example in the darkest moments of terror or

despair, that one can no longer exist in a subjunctive mode (Skidmore 2003b).

REFERENCES

AFP (Agence-France Presse)
    2003 "Myanmar Rejects Latest U.S. Rape Accusation." *Agence-France Presse*, April 7.
Allot, Anna J.
    1994 *Inked Over, Ripped Out: Burmese Storytellers and the Censors*. Chiang Mai: Silkworm Books.
Apple, Betsy, and Veronika Martin
    2003 "No Safe Place: Burma's Army and the Rape of Ethnic Women." Refugees International, April, www.refugeesinternational.org/files/3023_file_no_safe_place.pdf.
Arias, Arturo
    1997 "Comment on Consciousness, Violence, and the Politics of Memory in Guatemala." CA Forum on Anthropology in Public. *Current Anthropology* 38.5 (December): 824–825.
Asia Times
    2005 "Junta Clamps down after Yangon Blasts." *Asia Times*, May 11.
Bekker, Sarah M.
    1989 "Changes and Continuities in Burmese Buddhism." In *Independent Burma at Forty Years: Six Assessments*, edited by Josef Silverstein. Ithaca: Cornell University Southeast Asia Program.
Benjamin, Walter
    1983 *Das Passagen Werk*. Frankfurt au Main: Suhrkamp.
Bowring, Philip
    2005 "Chances for Reform in Myanmar Are Slim." *International Herald Tribune*. New Features, April 5.
Brac de la Perrière, Bénédicte
    2002 "Transmission, Change and Reproduction in the Burmese Cult of the 37 Lords." Paper presented at Burma Studies Conference, Burma-Myanma(r) Research and Its Future. Gothenburg, Sweden, September 21–25.
Brooten, Lisa
    2004 "Human Rights Discourse and the Development of Democracy in a Multi-ethnic State." *Asian Journal of Communication* 14.2: 174–191.
Burma Issues
    2005 "Market Bomb Explosion Kills Two." *Burma Issues Weekly* 225 (April 21–27).

http://www.burmaissues.org/En/BIWeekly2005-04-27-225.html.

Danitz, Tiffany, and Warren P. Strobel
1999 "Networking Dissent: Cyber-Activists Use the Internet to Promote Democracy in Burma." *Virtual Diplomacy*. United States Institute of Peace, November 8. www.usip.org/virtualdiplomacy/publications/reports/vburma/vburma/vburma_intro.html.

DVB (*Democratic Voice of Burma*)
2005a "Bus Stop Bomb Spreads Fear in Burma's Capital." *Democratic Voice of Burma News*, March 18.

DVB
2005b "Another Bomb Blast in Burma's Capital." *Democratic Voice of Burma News*, March 22.

DVB
2005c "Bomb Blast in Mandalay Kills at Least Two." *Democratic Voice of Burma News*, April 26.

DVB
2005d "Burmese Authorities Invited Buddhist Monks to Ward Off Evil in Mandalay." *Democratic Voice of Burma News*, April 27.

DVB
2005e "Burma Mandalay Blast Claims Another Life." *Democratic Voice of Burma News*, May 2.

DVB
2005f "More than 70 People Killed in Rangoon Blasts, Not 19 as Claimed by Junta," *Democratic Voice of Burma News*, May 2.

Feldman, Allan
2004 "Memory Theatres, Virtual Witnessing, and the Trauma-Aesthetic." *Biography* 27.1: 163–202.

Good, Byron J., and Mary-Jo Delvecchio Good et al.
1994 "In the Subjunctive Mode: Epilepsy Narratives in Turkey." *Social Science and Medicine* 38.6 (March 15): 855–892.

Gutter, Paul
2001 "Law and Religion in Burma." *Legal Issues on Burma Journal* 8 (April): 1–18.

Hale, Charles R.
1997 "Consciousness, Violence, and the Politics of Memory in Guatemala." *Current Anthropology* 38.5 (December): 817–838.

Herbert, Patricia
1982 "The Hsaya San Rebellion (1930–1932). Reappraised." Melbourne: Monash University Centre for Southeast Asian Studies, Working Paper no. 27.

Houtman, Gustaaf
1999 *Mental Culture in Burmese Crisis Politics: Aung San Suu Kyi and the National League for Democracy*. Tokyo: Institute for the Study of Languages and Cultures of Asia and Africa, Tokyo University of Foreign Studies.

Ingram, Simon
2001 "God's Army Twins Captured." BBC News, January 17. www.news.bbc.co.uk/I/hi/world/asia-pacific/1121333.stm.

Irrawaddy
2005a "Death Toll Rising in Rangoon." *Irawaddy Online Edition*, May 8. http://www.irrawaddy.org/aviewer.asp?a = 4609.

Irrawaddy
2005b "Opposition groups scan 'Burma Day'." *Irawaddy Online Edition*, April 4. http://www.irrawaddy.org/aviewer.aspia = 4609.

Jordt, Ingrid
2001 "The Mass Lay Meditation Movement and State-Society Relations in Post-Independence Burma." Ph.D. dissertation, Harvard University.

Kawanami, Hiroko
2002 "Religious Ideology, Representation, and Social Realities: The Case of Burmese Buddhist Womanhood." Paper presented at Burma Studies Conference, Burma-Myanma(r) Research and Its Future. Gothenburg, Sweden, September 21–25.

Kleinman, Arthur, and Joan Kleinman
1994 "How Bodies Remember: Social Memory and Bodily Experience of Criticism, Resistance and Delegitimation Following China's Cultural Revolution." *New Literary History* 25.3 (Summer): 707–736.

Kumada, Naoko
2002 "Dago, Cosmogony, and Politics: Religion and Power in Burmese Society." Paper presented at Burma Studies Conference, Burma-Myanma(r) Research and Its Future. Gothenburg, Sweden, September 21–25.

Lambrecht, Curtis, and David Mathieson
2005 "Casting Light on Opacity: An Argument for a Grounded Political-Economy Approach to the Study of Burma." Paper presented at Australian National University, April 27.

Leehey, Jennifer
2000 "Censorship and the Burmese Political Imagination." Paper presented at Northern Illinois University, October.

Myo Lwin
2005 "Bomb at Mandalay Market Leaves Two Dead." *Myanmar Times and Weekly Review* 14.264 May 2–8.

Pandolfi, Mariella
1990 "Boundaries inside the Body: Women's Suffering in Southern Peasant Italy." *Culture, Medicine and Psychiatry* 14: 255–273.

Panter, Martin
2005 "Chemical Weapons Use by Myanmar Army." *Christian Solidarity Worldwide*, www.csw.org.uk.

Po Khwa
2002 "The Enemies of the People." *New Light of Myanmar*, September 12.

Redfield, Peter
2004 "A Few of His Favorite Things." *Anthropological Quarterly* 77.2 (Spring): 355–363.

Robben, Antonious C.G.M, and Marcelo Suárez-Orozco, eds.
2000 *Cultures under Siege: Collective Violence and Trauma*. Cambridge: Cambridge University Press.

Robinne, Françoise
2002 "Shamanistic Practice in a Kachin Village." Paper presented at Burma Studies Conference, Burma-Myanma(r) Research and Its Future. Gothenburg, Sweden, September 21–25.

Rozenberg, Guillaume
2002 "Reciprocity and Redistribution in the Quest for Sainthood. Burma." Paper presented at Burma Studies Conference, Burma-Myanma(r) Research and Its Future. Gothenburg, Sweden, September 21–25.

Rozenberg, Guillaume
2005 "Journey to the Land of the Cheaters." In *Burma at the Turn of the Twenty-First Century*, edited by M. Skidmore. Honolulu: University of Hawai'i Press.

Sartre, Jean-Paul
1972 *The Psychology of Imagination*. London: Methuen.

SHRF (Shan Human Rights Foundation) and SWAN (Shan Women's Action Network)
2002 "License to Rape: The Burmese Military Regime's Use of Sexual Violence in the Ongoing War in Shan State." May. www.shanland.org/HR/Publication/LtoR/license_to_rape.htm.

Skidmore, Monique
1995 "The Politics of Space and Form: Cultural Idioms of Resistance and Remembering." *Santé, Culture, Health* 10.1–2(Fall): 33–72.

Skidmore, Monique
1996 "In the Shade of the Bodhi Tree: Dhammayietra and the Re-awakening of Community in Cambodia." *Crossroads: An Interdisciplinary Journal of Southeast Asian Studies* 10.1: 1–32.

Skidmore, Monique
2003a "Behind Bamboo Fences: Forms of Violence against Women in Myanmar." In *Violence against Women in Asian Societies*, edited by L. Manderson and L. R. Bennett. London: RoutledgeCurzon.

Skidmore, Monique
2003b "Darker Than Midnight: Fear, Vulnerability and Terror-making in Urban Burma (Myanmar)." *American Ethnologist* 30.1: 5–21.

Skidmore, Monique
2004 *Karaoke Fascism: Burma and the Politics of Fear*. Philadelphia: University of Pennsylvania Press.

Taussig, Michael P.
1980 *The Devil and Commodity Fetishism*. Chapel Hill: University of North Carolina Press.

Taylor, Robert, and Morten Pedersen
2005 "Supporting Burma/Myanmar's National Reconciliation Process." Paper presented at the Burma Day conference. Brussels, April 5.

Taylor, Robert, and Morten Pedersen
1987 *Shamanism, Colonialism and the Wild Man: A Study in Terror and Healing*. Chicago: University of Chicago Press.

Taylor, Robert, and Morten Pedersen
1991 *The Nervous System*. New York: Routledge.

Taylor, Robert, and Morten Pedersen
1992 *Mimesis and Alterity: A Particular History of the Senses*. New York: Routledge.

Taylor, Robert, and Morten Pedersen
1997 *The Magic of the State*. New York: Routledge.

Taylor, Robert, and Morten Pedersen
1999 *Defacement: Public Secrecy and the Labor of the Negative*. Stanford: Stanford University Press.

Taylor, Robert, and Morten Pedersen
2003 *Law in a Lawless Land: Diary of a Limpieza*. New York: New Press.

Taylor, Robert, and Morten Pedersen
2004 *My Cocaine Museum*. Chicago: University of Chicago Press.

Tosa, Keiko
2002 "Weikza: The Case of Tamanya Tang Hsayadaw." Paper presented at Burma Studies

Conference, Burma-Myanma(r) Research and Its Future. Gothenburg, Sweden, September 21–25.

Turner, Victor
1990   "Are There Universals of Performance in Myth, Ritual and Drama?" In *By Means of Performance: Intercultural Studies of Theatre and Ritual*, edited by Richard Schechner and Willa Appel. Cambridge: Cambridge University Press.

United States of America Department of State, Bureau of Democracy, Human Rights and Labor
2005   *Burma: Country Reports on Human Rights Practice*-2004. February 28. http://www.state.gov/g/drl/rls/hrrpt/2004/41637.htm.

USA Today
2005   "Bomb Explodes in Myanmar, Killing Two and Wounding at Least 15." *USATODAY.com*. April 26. http://www.usatoday.com/news/world/2005-04-26-myanmar-blast_x.htm.

WLB (Women's League of Burma)
2004   "System of Impunity: Nationwide Patterns of Sexual Violence by the Military Regime's Army and Authorities in Burma." Women's League of Burma. September, www.womenofburma.org/Report/SYSTEM_OF_IMPUNITY.pdf.

Zarni
2005   "Trials of Total, and Pro-Boycott Burma Activism: Compiler's Note." Free Burma Coalition. http://freeburmacoalition.blogspot.com/2005/02/trials-of-toal-and-pro-boycott-burma.html.

38

"Human Terrain": Past, Present and Future Applications

Roberto J. González

Between July 2005 and August 2006, the US Army put together an experimental counter-insurgency programme called 'Human Terrain System' (HTS). The programme's building blocks are five-person teams ('Human Terrain Teams' or HTTs) assigned to brigade combat team headquarters in Iraq and Afghanistan, comprising regional studies experts and social scientists, some of whom are armed.[1]

This programme, which emerged as the result of the military's alleged interest in culture, has been uncritically portrayed in the media as saving lives, thanks to what appears to be an orchestrated Pentagon public relations campaign (e.g. Rohde 2007a, Peterson 2007, Mulrine 2007). Yet the way in which HTS has been packaged – as a kinder, gentler counter-insurgency – is completely unsupported by evidence. Despite HTS supporters' frequent claims that the programme has drastically reduced US 'kinetic operations' (military attacks) in Afghanistan, Pentagon officials have not responded to requests for data to back up such claims, and there has been no independent confirmation of these assertions. Indeed, there is no verifiable evidence that HTTs have saved a single life – American, Afghan, Iraqi or otherwise. According to Zenia Helbig (a former HTT member), an internal evaluation team that recently produced a positive report on HTS included evaluators with a vested interest in the programme.[2] It appears that HTS has two faces: one designed to rally public support for an increasingly unpopular war, and the other to collect intelligence to help salvage a failing occupation.

It is far more likely that HTS was created as an espionage programme. As the army launched HTS, some military analysts described it as 'a CORDS for the 21st century' (Kipp et al. 2006), in reference to Civil Operations Revolutionary Development Support, a Vietnam War-era counterinsurgency effort. CORDS gave birth to the infamous Phoenix Program, in which South Vietnamese officials and US agents gathered intelligence data to help target tens of thousands of people for 'neutralization' (incarceration or assassination), including

Roberto J. González, "'Human Terrain': Past, Present and Future Applications," pp. 21–26 from *Anthropology Today* 24(1), 2008.

many civilians (Valentine 1990). At the time, CORDS was publicly hailed as a humanitarian project for winning 'hearts and minds', while Phoenix simultaneously (and secretly) functioned as its paramilitary arm. This dubious history provides a critical reference point for understanding the potential uses of HTS.

It appears that the Pentagon has not released an official description of the HTS programme, and much remains unknown. Yet with a budget of approximately $60 million,[3] this may be the most expensive social science project in history. The programme deserves close scrutiny and critique, since HTS social scientists have discussed aspects of it in ways that do not square with military journals, job announcements and journalists' accounts. For example, some anthropologists involved in HTS have maintained that social scientists do not conceal their identities in Afghanistan, yet journalists have contradicted this claim (Rohde 2007b). In addition, HTS leaders have claimed that the data collected by HTS personnel is open and unclassified, yet James K. Greer (deputy director of HTS) has been quoted as saying: 'When a brigade plans and executes its operations, that planning and execution is, from an operational-security standpoint, classified. And so your ability to talk about it, or write an article about it, is restricted in certain ways' (Glenn 2007b). Such issues motivated a group of anthropologists – the Network of Concerned Anthropologists – to oppose involvement in counterinsurgency work and in direct combat support in summer 2007. In the light of the ethical concerns and potential conflicts articulated by these scholars, the American Anthropological Association (AAA) Executive Board issued a statement last November expressing disapproval of the programme (see González 2007).[4] At the 2007 AAA conference, members also adopted a non-binding resolution opposing certain kinds of secrecy in anthropological work – a resolution motivated by concerns about HTS.

The Origins of 'Human Terrain'

Recently defined as 'the social, ethnographic, cultural, economic, and political elements of the people among whom a force is operating ... defined and characterized by sociocultural, anthropologic, and ethnographic data' (Kipp et al. 2006: 9, 15), the concept of human terrain has become increasingly popular in US military circles.

Human terrain is often contrasted with geophysical terrain – a familiar concept for senior officers trained for conventional warfare against the Soviets. It implies that 21st-century warriors will fight 'population-centric' wars (Kilcullen 2007); therefore, the key to successful warfare is the control of *people*. This is more than a 'hearts-and-minds' approach, for the emphasis lies primarily on exploitation of 'tribal', political, religious and psychological dynamics: 'in Iraq, US and coalition forces must recognize and exploit the underlying tribal structure of the country; the power wielded by traditional authority figures; the use of Islam as a political ideology; the competing interests of the Shia, the Sunni, and the Kurds; the psychological effects of totalitarianism; and the divide between urban and rural' (McFate 2005a: 37).

Human terrain is not a new concept. Its reactionary roots stretch back 40 years, when it appeared in a report by the infamous US House Un-American Activities Committee about the perceived threat of Black Panthers and other militant groups. From the beginning, human terrain was linked to population control:

> Traditional guerrilla warfare ... [is] carried out by irregular forces, which just about always dispose of inferior weapons and logistical support in general, but which possess the ability to seize and retain the initiative through a superior control of the human terrain. This control may be the result of sheer nation-wide support for the guerrillas against a colonial or other occupying power of foreign origin; it may be the result of the ability of the guerrillas to inflict reprisals upon the population; and it can be because the guerrillas promise more to the population. (US HUAC 1968: 62)[5]

Human terrain appeared again in *The war for the cities* (1972) by Robert Moss, a right-wing journalist who in the 1970s edited

Challenges for DoD Investment
– What Have We Learned?

ADVANCED SYSTEMS AND CONCEPTS

Plan   Find   Fix   Track   Target   Engage   Assess

- **Need to 'Map the Human Terrain' across the Kill Chain**
  - Enables the entire Kill Chain for the GWOT
- **Target Detection may be Difficult and Require Non-Traditional Means**
- **Enemy Exists inside potentially High Collateral Damage Areas**
  - And ... in Denied Access Areas
- **Sometimes We ID the Enemy but ....**
  - ... do not have an adequate/appropriate Strike Solution in time
- **Mobile / Re-locatable Targets Remain a Problem!**
- **The Target Characteristics may Remain Unknown even at ... Time Over Target ... & "How Did We Do?"**
- **If Decision Timeline Varies and can be Long ... let's Enable the Rest of the Kill Chain to be Dynamically Responsive**

Figure 38.1 *Mapping the Human Terrain 'enables the entire kill chain', as asserted in this unclassified presentation by John Wilcox, Assistant Deputy Under Secretary of Defense (Precision Engagement) at the Precision Strike Winter Roundtable. 'Precision engagement – Strategic context for the Long War: Weapons technology blueprint for the future', 1 February 2007.*

Foreign Report, a journal affiliated with *The Economist*.[6] Like HUAC, Moss examined the threat of diverse 'urban guerrillas' including the Black Panthers, Students for Democratic Society, and Latin American insurgents. Human terrain appeared in reference to the latter: '[T]he failure of the rural guerrillas to enlist large-scale peasant backing in most areas also showed up in their distorted view of the political potential of the peasantry and their failure to study the human terrain ... Che Guevara's ill-conceived Bolivian campaign was the supreme example of these deficiencies' (Moss 1972: 154).

Contemporary human terrain studies date back seven years, when retired US Army Lieutenant Colonel Ralph Peters published 'The human terrain of urban operations' (2000). Peters has written more than 20 books, yet is more widely known as a neoconservative pundit.[7]

For years, Peters has espoused a bloody version of Huntington's 'clash of civilizations' thesis. He has argued that the US military will have to inflict 'a fair amount of killing' to promote economic interests and a 'cultural assault' aimed at recalcitrant populations:

There will be no peace ... The de facto role of the US armed forces will be to keep the world safe for our economy and open to our cultural assault. To those ends, we will do a fair amount of killing. We are building an information-based military to do that killing ... much of our military art will consist in knowing more about the enemy than he knows about himself, manipulating data for effectiveness and efficiency, and denying similar advantages to our opponents. (Peters 1997: 14)

Peters (2000: 4) has also argued that it is the 'human architecture' of a city, its 'human terrain ... the people, armed and dangerous, watching for exploitable opportunities, or begging to be protected, who will determine the success or failure of the intervention'. He describes a typology of cities ('hierarchical', 'multicultural' and 'tribal') and the challenges that each present to military forces operating there: 'the center of gravity in urban operations is never a presidential palace or a television studio or a bridge or a barracks. It is always human' (ibid.: 12).

As Peters' ideas began circulating among military analysts, others gradually adopted human terrain. Lieutenant Colonel Michael Morris (2005: 46) noted that the 'purpose of [al-Qaeda's] covert infrastructure [or "shadow government"] is to operationalize control of human terrain'. A year later, Lieutenant Colonel Richard McConnell and colleagues (2006: 11) suggested that US 'military transition teams' training Iraqi troops needed a better understanding of 'human terrain': 'you are not here to make this into an American unit – you are here to help this unit become the best Iraqi unit it can be'. Lieutenant Colonel Fred Renzi (2006: 16) made the case for 'ethnographic intelligence' to help understand *terra incognita* ... the *terra* in this case is the human terrain'.

Some CIA agents also appropriated the term. Henry Crumpton (2005: 170), leader of the CIA's Afghan campaign post-9/11, has written about agents working there during that period, including one 'who spoke Farsi/Dari, [and] was a cultural anthropologist intimately familiar with the tribes of the region ... These CIA officers needed to map the human terrain of their patch in Afghanistan, while understanding and contributing to the larger strategy.' In spite of Crumpton's use of the term, so far there is no indication of CIA involvement with HTS.

Pundits and think tanks have enthusiastically embraced 'human terrain'. Conservative columnist Max Boot (2005) wrote a commentary entitled 'Navigating the "human terrain"', in which he referred to the need for 'Americans who are familiar with foreign languages and cultures and proficient in such disciplines as intelligence collection and interrogation'. The RAND Corporation commissioned two counterinsurgency monographs advocating the importance of 'understanding the human terrain', though the emphasis is on information technologies and cognitive mapping rather than ethnographic expertise (Libicki et al. 2007, Gompert 2007).

Before examining the genesis of HTS, it is worth looking at '*human terrain*' from a linguistic perspective. The Sapir-Whorf hypothesis (which postulates that language influences the thought – and consequently actions – of its users) suggests that the term 'human terrain' will tend to have objectifying and dehumanizing effects. Consider the words of US Army Lieutenant Colonel Edward Villacres, who leads an HTT in Iraq: the team's objective is to 'help the brigade leadership understand the human dimension of the environment that they are working in, just like a map analyst would try to help them understand the bridges, and the rivers, and things like that' (Villacres 2007). The unusual juxtaposition of words portrays people as geographic space to be conquered – human beings as territory to be captured, as flesh-and-blood *terra nullius*. Much more serious is the way the term (like 'collateral damage' and 'enhanced interrogation') vividly illustrates George Orwell's (1946) notion of 'political language ... designed to make lies sound truthful and murder respectable'.

The Birth of HTS

How did 'human terrain' become a system? By 2006, desperation about mismanagement of the wars had set in among many military and intelligence officials. US casualties were mounting, Iraqi insurgent groups were becoming stronger, and Taliban fighters were regrouping. Some began seeking 'gentler' counterinsurgency tactics, according to an uncritical account prepared for the US Army War College's Strategic Studies Institute by anthropologist Sheila Miyoshi Jager:

> In sharp contrast to former Secretary of Defense Donald Rumsfeld's heavy-handed approach to counterinsurgency which emphasized aggressive military tactics, the post-Rumsfeld Pentagon has advocated a 'gentler' approach, emphasizing cultural knowledge and ethnographic intelligence ... This 'cultural turn' within DoD highlights efforts to understand adversary societies and to recruit 'practitioners' of culture, notably anthropologists, to help in the war effort in both Iraq and Afghanistan. (Jager 2007: v)

An early advocate was Major General Robert Scales, who told the US House Armed Services Committee that 'the British Army created a habit of "seconding" bright officers to various corners of the world so as to immerse them in the cultures of the Empire ... At the heart of a cultural-centric approach to future war would be a cadre of global scouts ... They should attend graduate schools in disciplines necessary to understand human behavior and cultural anthropology' (Scales 2004: 4–5). Backed up by Scales' ringing endorsement of imperialist strategy, the political groundwork was set for anthropological participation in 'cultural-centric' warfare.

Scales would need not wait long. In 2005, Montgomery McFate and Andrea Jackson published a pilot proposal for a Pentagon 'Office of Operational Cultural Knowledge' focused on 'human terrain' and consisting of social scientists with 'strong connections to the services and combatant commands' (McFate and Jackson 2005: 20). They would provide:

1 'on-the-ground ethnographic research (interviews and participant observation)' on the Middle East, Central Asia, etc.;
2 'predeployment and advanced cultural training ... [and] computer-based training on society and culture';
3 'sociocultural studies of areas of interest (such as North Korean culture and society, Iranian military culture, and so on)';
4 'cultural advisers for planning and operations to commanders on request' and 'lectures at military institutions';
5 'experimental sociocultural programs, such as the cultural preparation of the environment – a comprehensive and constantly updated database tool for use by operational commanders and planners' (ibid.: 20–21).

Initial costs for the first year were estimated at $6.5 million. The proposal was consistent with one of the authors' earlier provocative (if historically dubious) suggestions: 'the national security structure needs to be infused with anthropology, a discipline invented to support warfighting in the tribal zone' (McFate 2005b: 43).

Soon after, Jacob Kipp and colleagues from the army's Foreign Military Studies Office at Fort Leavenworth, Kansas outlined the 'Human Terrain System' to 'understand the people among whom our forces operate as well as the cultural characteristics and propensities of the enemies we now fight' (Kipp et al. 2006: 8). Captain Don Smith headed the implementation of HTS from July 2005 to August 2006, and the programme was housed in the Training and Doctrine Command at Fort Leavenworth (ibid.: 15). Each team would comprise an HTT leader (major or lieutenant colonel), a cultural analyst (civilian MA/PhD cultural anthropologist or sociologist), a regional studies analyst (civilian MA/PhD in area studies with area language fluency), an HT research manager (military intelligence background), and an HT analyst (military intelligence background).

In early 2007, BAE Systems began posting HTS job announcements on its company website; it was joined later by Wexford Group (CACI) and MTC Technologies. Before deployment, HTT members received military and weapons training, and in February 2007 the first team arrived in Afghanistan. The others deployed to Iraq in summer 2007.

Proponents insist that HTTs 'are extremely helpful in terms of giving commanders on the ground an understanding of the cultural patterns of interaction, the nuances of how to interact with those cultural groups on the ground'[8] – a dubious claim, since none of the PhD-qualified anthropologists working in HTTs have prior regional knowledge (Helbig 2007). However, HTTs are designed to collect regionally specific data on political leadership, kinship groups, economic systems and agricultural production. The data is to be sent to a central database accessible to other US government agencies: the CIA would be particularly interested (González 2007). Furthermore, 'databases will eventually be turned over to the new governments of Iraq and Afghanistan to enable them to more fully exercise sovereignty over their territory' (Kipp et al. 2006: 14). (It is worth remembering that CORDS officials hoped to ensure the South Vietnamese government's political stability through the Phoenix Program, though it was sometimes used as a mechanism for eliminating political opponents; see Valentine 1990.)

HTTs will supply brigade commanders with 'deliverables' including a 'user-friendly ethnographic and sociocultural database of the area of operations that can provide the commander data maps showing specific ethnographic or cultural features' (Kipp et al. 2006: 13). HTTs use Mapping Human Terrain (MAP-HT) software, 'an automated database and presentation tool that allows teams to gather, store, manipulate, and provide cultural data from hundreds of categories' (ibid.). According to the Secretary of Defense's budget, the goal is:

> to reduce IED [improvised explosive device] incidents via improved situational awareness of the human terrain by using 'green layer data/unclassified' information to understand key population points to win the 'will and legitimacy' fights and surface the insurgent IED networks ... [C]apability must be further developed to provide a means for commanders and their supporting operations sections to collect data on human terrain, create, store, and disseminate information from this data, and use the resulting information as an element of combat power.[9] (US OSD 2007: 18)

In unvarnished language, a fuller picture emerges: the goal of HTS data is to help 'win the "will and legitimacy" fights' (perhaps through propaganda), to 'surface the insurgent IED networks' (presumably for targeting), and to serve 'as an element of combat power' (i.e. as a weapon).

HTS supporters have equivocated when confronted with the question of whether such a database might be used to target Iraqis or Afghans. In a radio interview, an HTS architect stated: 'The intent of the programme is not to identify who the bad actors are out there. The military has an entire intelligence apparatus geared and designed to provide that information to them. That is not the information that they need from social scientists.' She claimed that HTT social scientists have 'a certain amount of discretion' with data, while providing no evidence that safeguards exist to prevent others from using it against informants. When asked about lack of independent oversight, she answered: 'We would like to set up a board of advisors. At the moment, however, this programme is proof of concept ... [I]t's not a

permanent programme. It's an experiment.' (Silverman 2007: 7).[10]

'Human Terrain' as Technological Fantasy

Pentagon budgets reflect an increasing commitment to so-called 'cultural knowledge' acquisition. Consequently, engineers, mathematicians and computer scientists have demonstrated acute interest in human terrain for modelling, simulation and gaming programs.

Among them is Barry Silverman, a University of Pennsylvania engineering professor who bluntly asks: 'Human terrain data: What should we do with it?' (Silverman 2007). Silverman has been at the forefront of efforts to develop computerized behaviour modelling programs designed to provide insight into the motivations of terrorists and their networks, and he hopes to integrate HTS data into these programs. According to one report, 'a Silverman simulation is an astoundingly sophisticated amalgamation of more than 100 models and theories from anthropology, psychology, and political science, combined with empirical data taken from medical and social science field research, surveys, and experiments' (Goldstein 2006: 30). The goal is to predict how various actors – 'a terrorist, a soldier, or an ordinary citizen' – might react to 'a gun pointed in the face, a piece of chocolate offered by a soldier ... [Silverman] is now simulating a small society of about 15,000 leader and follower agents organized into tribes, which squabble over resources' (ibid.).

At the heart of Silverman's simulations are 'performance moderator functions' representing 'physical stressors such as ambient temperature, hunger, and drug use; resources such as time, money, and skills; attitudes such as moral outlook, religious feelings, and political affiliations; and personality dispositions such as response to time pressure, workload, and anxiety' (ibid.).

Silverman makes grand claims about the potential utility of HTS data for human social profiling, though he has apparently not yet obtained any of it: 'the HT datasets are an invaluable resource that will permit us in the human behavior M&S [modelling and simulation] field to more realistically profile factions, and their leaders and followers'.

Similarly, a Dartmouth research team has created the Laboratory for Human Terrain, 'focused on the foundational science and technology for modeling, representing, inferring, and analyzing individual and organizational behaviors'.[11] It includes an engineer, a mathematician and a computer scientist who specialize in 'adversarial intent modeling, simulation, and prediction', 'dynamic social network analysis' and 'discovery of hidden relationships and organizations'. The Pentagon awarded a $250,000 grant to Eugene Santos to develop a 'Dynamic Adversarial Gaming Algorithm' (DAGA) for 'predicting how individuals or groups ... react to social, cultural, political, and economic interactions ... DAGA can evaluate how rhetoric from religious leaders combined with recent allied killing of radical military leaders, and perceptions of potential economic growth can cause shifts in support from moderate or radical leadership.'[12] The Dartmouth group uses the 'Adversary Intent Inferencing' (AII) model, a prototype of which was tested using scenarios replicating Gulf War battles (Santos and Zhua 2006: 13).

These programs are a small part of 'Human Social Culture Behavior Modeling', in which the goal is to 'build computer models ... [by] combining recent [insurgent] activity with cultural, political, and economic data about the region collected by DOD-funded anthropologists' – perhaps HTT personnel (Bhattacharjee 2007: 534).

Wired magazine's blog reports a boom in wartime simulation projects, including Purdue University's 'Synthetic Environment for Analysis and Simulation' which can 'gobble up breaking news, census data, economic indicators, and climactic events in the real word, along with proprietary information such as military intelligence. Iraq and Afghanistan computer models are the most highly developed and complex. Each has about five million individual nodes that represent entities such as hospitals, mosques, pipelines, and people' (Shachtman 2007). HTS data could conceivably be incorporated into this computer model.

The Air Force Research Lab has requested proposals for modelling programs, and suggests

that 'researchers should investigate cultural, motivational, historical, political, and economic data to determine if there are mathematical and statistical models that can be used to predict the formation of terrorist activities ... [the] goal is to determine sets of actions that can influence the root cause behaviors and cultivate a culture that does not support the development of criminal activity.'[13] The Navy has requested proposals for a 'Human, Social, and Culture Behavioral Modeling' simulation tool resembling a video game: 'We are looking for innovative ideas that explore and harness the power of "advanced" interactive multimedia computer games (e.g. "sim games") ... [incorporating] the best-practices of the videogame industry, including intuitive controls, storytelling, user-feedback ... scenario editing, and high quality graphics & sound.'[14]

These programs focus upon modelling and simulation, but it is not difficult to imagine that in the near future, agents might use cultural profiles for pre-emptive targeting of statistically probable (rather than actual) insurgents or extremists in Iraq, Afghanistan, Pakistan or other countries deemed to be terrorist havens.

Some Pentagon officials have already begun contemplating such applications. In February 2007, a dazzlingly illustrated PowerPoint presentation was released, which unambiguously stated a 'need to "Map the Human Terrain" across the kill chain – enables the entire kill chain for the GWOT [Global War on Terror]' (Figure 38.1).[15] The presentation (by Assistant Deputy Undersecretary of Defense James Wilcox) notes that '[s]ometimes we ID the enemy but ... do not have an adequate/appropriate Strike Solution in time', indicating that at least one senior Pentagon official sees such information as a potentially useful weapon.[16] Despite HTS proponents' claims that the programme will save lives, Pentagon officials are likely to use data in line with their own warfighting plans.

Human Terrain: Possible Futures

Examination of the information available, summarized above, reveals that HTS – and HTS data – may perform various functions simultaneously. Images of a 'gentler' counter-insurgency might serve as propaganda for US audiences opposed to military operations in Iraq and Afghanistan: propaganda that offers the apparently wonderful compromise of fighting a war that makes us feel good about ourselves. Public relations campaigns portraying HTT personnel as life-saving heroes might attract young scholars who want to do good, like the embedded administrators who served colonial interests. Information collected by HTTs might feed into a database accessible to the CIA, the Iraqi police or the Afghan military for strategic or tactical intelligence, or for use in targeting suspected insurgents for abduction or assassination. Agents might employ HTS data to design propaganda campaigns that exploit Iraqi or Afghan fears and vulnerabilities, or to co-opt local leaders into a system of indirect rule. Finally, HTS data might help create simulation and modelling programs which could conceivably be used for profiling imagined enemies by means of statistical probability. It is vital that we discuss ethical issues covering the range of possibilities.

As I noted in my introduction, some military analysts draw explicit connections between HTS and CORDS/Phoenix, which used local information to help target suspects for incarceration, interrogation or assassination (Kipp et al. 2006). Phoenix featured a computerized database:

Phoenix was enhanced with the advent of the Viet Cong Infrastructure Information System... [In January 1967] the Combined Intelligence Staff fed the names of 3000 VCI [Viet Cong 'infrastructure', including communist cadres and National Liberation Front members among others] (assembled by hand at area coverage desks) into the IBM 1401 computer at the Combined Intelligence Center's political order of battle section. At that point the era of the computerized blacklist began...VCIIS became the first of a series of computer programs designed to absolve the war effort of human error and war managers of individual responsibility. (Valentine 1990: 258–259)

Phoenix Program personnel collected a wealth of intelligence information, which was then passed on to 'analysts':

VCIIS compiled information ... on VCI boundaries, locations, structures, strengths, personalities, and activities ... [it] included summary data on each recorded VCI in the following categories: name and aliases; whether or not he or she was 'at large'; sex, birth date, and place of birth; area of operations; party position; source of information; arrest date; how neutralized; term of sentence; where detained; release date; and other biographical and statistical information, including photographs and fingerprints, if available ... Phoenix analysts [were able] instantly to access and cross-reference data, then decide who was to be erased. (ibid.: 259)

As a result, between 1967 and 1972 South Vietnamese officials, US advisors and mercenaries 'erased' more than 26,000 suspected members of the so-called Viet Cong 'infrastructure', including civilians (Valentine 1990) – acts that amounted to war crimes. Nowhere is this mentioned in Kipp's depiction of HTS as 'a CORDS for the 21st century', yet the historical record points to the potential dangers of computerized counterinsurgency databases.

The future of HTS is unclear. In February 2007, the army's Combined Arms Center issued a memo listing changes in military terminology to be adopted in the near future. It recommends that army personnel 'use "civil considerations" ... not "human terrain"' (US Army 2007: 1). It is uncertain whether this will have an effect on HTS, but it may signal awareness of the term's conceptual or public relations shortcomings.

Some are already calling for change. Credible accounts have emerged about difficulties plaguing HTS, including 'recruitment shortfalls', 'haphazard and often pointless' training, and a programme 'nearly paralyzed by organizational problems' (Glenn 2007a). Former HTT member Zenia Helbig has publicly criticized the programme, claiming that during four months of training, there was no discussion about informed consent or the potential harm that might befall Iraqis or Afghans. Furthermore, Helbig claims that 'HTS' greatest problem is its own desperation. The programme is desperate to hire anyone or anything that remotely falls into the category of "academic", "social science", "regional expert", or "PhD"', which has often resulted in gross incompetence (Helbig 2007). If such 'desperation' persists, it is conceivable that HTS might eventually wither, though there are indications that BAE Systems and other contractors will soon target students of political science and international relations for recruitment.[17] In the long run, HTS, HTTs, 'reachback research centers' and MAP-HT may turn out to be technological fantasies that were crushed soon after embedded social scientists' boots hit the ground.

In the future, historians may question why a small number of anthropologists – whose progressive 20th-century predecessors created the modern culture concept, critiqued Western ethnocentrism in its various guises and invented the teach-in – decided to enlist as embedded specialists in an open-ended war of dubious legality. They might wonder why these anthropologists began harvesting data on Iraqis and Afghans as a preferred method of practical 'real-world' engagement. They might ask why, at a time when majorities in the US, Iraq and Afghanistan called for the withdrawal of US troops, this group of anthropologists supported an occupation resulting in hundreds of thousands of civilian deaths. Economic incentives – approximately $250,000 for a year – and the results of decades of veneration of the military and those who support it – go some way toward explaining these phenomena. Scholars are not immune to nationalist and imperialist appeals in a highly militarized context.

Future historians might also be puzzled about some social scientists' failure to learn lessons from an earlier era: 'When we strip away the terminology of the behavioral sciences, we see revealed, in work such as this, the mentality of the colonial civil servant, persuaded of the benevolence of the mother country and the correctness of its vision of world order, and convinced that he understands the true interests of those backward peoples whose welfare he is to administer' (Chomsky 1969: 41). The fact that some social scientists have received HTS warmly reveals historical amnesia and a profound lack of imagination.

To the extent that HTS uses 'cultural knowledge' to create propaganda campaigns to win ' "will and legitimacy" fights', it deserves condemnation. To the extent that HTS peddles anthropological techniques and concepts in support of conquest and indirect rule, it deserves rejection. To the extent that HTS might be employed to collect intelligence or target suspected enemies for assassination, the programme deserves elimination – and a period of sober reflection about the situation of American social science today.

NOTES

I am grateful to David Price and four anonymous AT reviewers for commenting upon earlier drafts of this paper.

1 Currently, there are five HTTs in Iraq and one in Afghanistan. Central Command (CENTCOM) require 26 HTTs to be deployed. It is unclear whether other US government agencies have been involved in the design or implementation of the programme.
2 Zenia Helbig (personal communication, 6 December 2007).
3 According to *USA Today* (Jayson 2007), the initial cost of HTS was $20 million. According to the *New York Times* (Rohde 2007), the cost of HTS expansion will be $40 million. Together then, this will amount to $60 million.
4 AAA statement at http://www.aaanet.org/blog/resolution.htm. The Society for Applied Anthropology has equivocated on HTS: 'The SfAA is not a discipline-specific association and thus we do not feel equipped to decide whether there are particular aspects of the disciplines of "anthropology" and or "sociology" or of other disciplines which are violated by the participation of its members in the HTS [...] There is nothing in the SfAA Code of Ethics which is directly affected by the HTS' (Andreatta 2007: 2). SfAA's ethics code contradicts this claim.
5 HUAC suggested that urban unrest might require that the president declare an 'internal security emergency' which would enable a 1950 law authorizing detention of suspected spies or saboteurs. Much of the law was repealed in the 1970s, but some elements were restored in the Patriot Act.
6 *Foreign Report* 'specialize[d] in sensational rumors from the world's intelligence agencies' (Chomsky and Herman 1979: 173). One of Moss's books was reportedly funded by the CIA as pro-Pinochet propaganda in the 1970s (Landis 1985).

7   Peters (2006) suggests radically redrawing Middle East borders: Iraq would be partitioned into an 'Arab Shia state', 'Sunni Iraq' and 'free Kurdistan' (including eastern Turkey); 'free Baluchistan' would be carved from southeastern Iran and southwestern Pakistan; Afghanistan would absorb much of northwestern Pakistan; half of Saudi Arabia's territory would be distributed to Yemen, 'Greater Jordan' and a new 'Islamic sacred state'.

8   John Agoglia interview, *The Diane Rehm Show*, American University Radio, 10 October 2007.

9   'Green layer' data refers to information related to the general populations (as opposed to 'blue layer' [coalition forces] or 'red layer' [insurgents]) in occupied Iraq and Afghanistan. The Defense Secretary allocated $500,000 in 2007, $2.7 million in 2008, and $1.3 million in 2009 for MAP-HT. See http://www.dtic.mil/descriptivesum/Y2008/OSD/0603648D8Z.pdf (accessed 20 November 2007). MAP-HT software was developed by the Mitre Corporation, according to Zenia Helbig (personal communication, 6 December 2007).

10 Montgomery MeFate interview, *Here and Now*, National Public Radio, 12 October 2007.

11 See http://www.dartmouth.edu/~humanterrain/ (accessed 15 November 2007).

12 See http://www.dartmouth.edu/%7Ehuman terrain/Approach.html (accessed 15 November 2007).

13 US Air Force request for proposals posted at http://www.dodsbir.net/Topics/BasicTopics ResultsForm.asp?RanNo=8&bookmark= 32088&rec=1 (accessed 22 November 2007).

14 US Navy request for proposals posted at http://www.dodsbir.net/Topics/BasicTopics ResultsForm.asp?RanNo=10&bookmark =31858&rec=9 (accessed 22 November 2007).

15 See http://www.dtic. mil/ndia/2007psa_winter/ wilcox.pdf (accessed 20 November 2007).

16 For a similar depiction of how 'focusing on the "human terrain"' can help 'exploit vulnerabilities', see presentation by retired Colonel Greg Jannarone (US Air Force Behavioral Influences Analysis Center) at http://www.au.af.mil/bia/slides/bia_msn_ bfg.pdf (accessed 15 December 2007).

17 Zenia Helbig (personal communication, 6 December 2007). In the same communication, Helbig also noted that BAE Systems, responsible for HTT recruitment and training, was exceedingly inept and more concerned with maximizing profits than with meeting programme objectives. According to Helbig, BAE Systems was awarded the HTS contract through an 'omnibus' provision giving preferential consideration to existing contractors. If true, this would fit a decades-old pattern of a privatized Pentagon characterized by mismanagement, waste and war profiteering.

REFERENCES

Andreatta, S.
2007   Human Terrain/Department of Defense. *SfAA Newsletter* 18(4): 1–3.

Bhattacharjee, Y.
2007   Pentagon asks academics for help in understanding enemies. *Science* 316:534–535.

Boot, M.
2006   Navigating the 'human terrain'. *Los Angeles Times*, 7 December.

Chomsky, N.
1969   *American power and the new mandarins*. New York: Pantheon.

Chomsky, N., and Herman, E.
1979   *After the cataclysm*. Boston: South End Press.

Crumpton, H.
2005   Intelligence and homeland defense. In: Sims, J. and Gerber, B. (eds) *Transforming US intelligence*, pp. 162–179. Washington: Georgetown University Press.

Glenn, D.
2007a   Former Human Terrain System participant describes program in disarray. *Chronicle of Higher Education*, 5 December: 8.

Glenn, D.
2007b   Anthropologists vote to clamp down on secret scholarship. *Chronicle of Higher Education News Blog*, 1 December. http://chronicle.com/news/article/3532/anthropologists-vote-to-clamp-down-on-secret-scholarship

Goldstein, H.
2006   Modeling terrorists. *IEEE Spectrum*, 43(9):26–34.

Gompert, D.
2007   *Heads we win: Improving cognitive effectiveness in counterinsurgency*. Santa Monica: RAND Corporation.

González, R.J.
2007 Phoenix reborn? The rise of the 'Human Terrain System'. *Anthropology Today* 23(6): 21–22.
Helbig, Z.
2007 'Personal perspective on the Human Terrain System'. Unpublished manuscript. http://blog.wired.com/defense/files/aaa_helbig_hts.pdf
Jager, S.M.
2007 *On the uses of cultural knowledge.* Washington: Strategic Studies Institute.
Kilcullen, D.
2007 'Two schools of classical counterinsurgency'. *Small Wars Journal Blog*, 27 January. http://smallwarsjournal.com/blog/2007/01/two-schools-of-classical-count/
Kipp. J. et al.
2006 The Human Terrain System: A CORDS for the 21st century. *Military Review,* September-October.
Klein, J.
2007 When bad missions happen to good generals. *Time*, 22 January: 25.
Landis, F.
1985 Moscow rules Moss's mind. *Covert Action Information Bulletin* 24: 36–38.
Libicki, M. et al.
2007 *Byting back: Regaining information superiority against 21st century insurgents.* Santa Monica: RAND Corporation.
McConnell, R. et al.
2007 MiTT and its 'human terrain'. *Field Artillery*, January-February: 11–14.
McFate, M.
2005a Anthropology and counterinsurgency: The strange story of their curious relationship. *Military Review*, 85(2): 24–38.
McFate, M.
2005b The military utility of understanding adversary culture. *Joint Force Quarterly* 38: 42–48.
McFate, M.
2007 Building bridges or burning heretics? *Anthropology Today* 23(3):21.
McFate, M. and A. Jackson
2005 An organizational solution to DOD's cultural knowledge needs. *Military Review*, 85(4): 18–21.
Morris, M.
2005 Al Qaeda as insurgency. *Joint Force Quarterly* 39: 41–50.

Moss, R.
1972 *The war for the cities.* New York: Coward, McCann and Geoghegan.
Mulrine, A.
2007 Culture warriors. *US News and World Report*, 10 December: 34–37.
Orwell, G.
1946 Politics and the English language. In: Orwell, G. (ed.) *The Orwell Reader*, pp. 355–366. New York: Harcourt and Brace.
Peters, R.
1997 Constant conflict. *Parameters*. Summer: 4–14.
Peters, R.
2000 The human terrain of urban operations. *Proceedings* 30(1): 4–12.
Peters, R.
2006 Blood borders. *Armed Forces Journal*, June, http://www.afji. com/2006/06/1833899/.
Peterson, S.
2007 US Army's strategy in Afghanistan: Better anthropology. *Christian Science Monitor*, 7 September: 1.
Renzi, F.
2006 Terra incognita and the case for ethnographic intelligence. *Military Review*, 86(5): 16–23.
Rohde, D.
2007a Army enlists anthropology in war zones. *New York Times*, 5 October: AI, A6.
Rohde, D.
2007b Interview, *The Diane Rehm Show*, American University Radio, 10 October.
Santos, E, and Zhao, Q.
2006 Adversarial models for opponent intent inferencing. In: Kott, A. and McEneaney, W. (eds) *Adversarial reasoning*, pp. 1–20. Boca Raton: Chapman and Hall.
Scales, R.
2004 'Army transformation: Implications for the future'. Testimony before US House Armed Services Committee, 15 July. http://www.au.af.mil/au/awe/awegate/congress/04-07-15scales.pdf
Shachtman, N.
2007 'Sim Iraq' sent to battle zone. *Danger Room (Wired Blog)*, 19 November, http://blog.wired.com/defense/2007/11/mathematical-mo.html
Silverman, B.
2007 Human terrain data – What should we do with it? In: Henderson, S.G. et al. *Proceedings*

of 2007 Winter Simulation Conference. http:// repository.upenn.edu/cgi/viewcontent.cgi? article=1330&context=ese_papers

US Army Combined Arms Center
    2007 'Army doctrine update' (memo). http:// asc.army.mil/docs/transformation/Army_Doctrine_Update_FM501_ FM30.pdf

US House Un-American Activities Committee
    1968 *Guerrilla warfare advocates in the United States*, Washington: Government Printing Office.

US Office of Secretary of Defense
    2007 *OSD RDT&E Budget Item Justification.* Washington: Department of Defense.

Valentine, D.
    1990 *The Phoenix Program.* New York: Morrow.

Villacres, E.
    2007 Interview, The Drane Rehm Show, American University Radio, 10 October.

39

The Gaza Freedom Flotilla: Ethnographic Notes on "Othering Violence"

Nikolas Kosmatopoulos

On 25 May 2010, I embarked on the cargo ship *Eleftheri Mesogeios* ('Free Mediterranean' in Greek) along with 29 other passengers from Greece, Sweden, France, Germany, Egypt and Italy. The passenger list included journalists from Greece, Italy and Germany, as well as university professors, trade unionists and activists from Greece. The Swedes had succeeded in recruiting the globally renowned crime novelist Henning Mankell, a Swedish MP (of Turkish origin), and an Israeli Defence Force (IDF) veteran who now has Swedish nationality and a successful career as a musician/artist.

The ship set sail towards the besieged Gaza Strip with the aim of bringing this siege, which we believe to be both illegal and inhuman, to the forefront of the international agenda.[1] It was loaded with 2000 tonnes of humanitarian aid, including prefabricated houses, electric wheel-chairs, high-tech hospital equipment and medical supplies, donated by the people of Greece and Sweden to the people of Gaza. *Eleftheri Mesogeios* was part of the international humanitarian aid flotilla dubbed the 'Freedom Flotilla'.[2] The eight ships

(four passenger and four cargo vessels) that initially set sail for Gaza were carrying over 700 participants from 36 countries, and more than 10,000 tonnes of humanitarian aid (IHH 2010).

The steering committee of the 'Ship to Gaza-Greece' initiative[3] invited me to participate in the flotilla in my capacity as an anthropologist, to conduct fieldwork during the preparations and the journey. They hoped this would help offer an added dimension of witnessing to this journey. Publicity, along with political backing from MPs and grassroots campaigns, was the only defence against anticipated Israeli aggression, but the invitation was also a conscious choice that revealed a growing interest in anthropology among the flotilla organizers. Thus, since the participants had begun to regard themselves as a peculiar sort of maritime activist community, anthropological involvement was merely a matter of time.

I requested and was granted access to the ships, cargo, passengers and crew. In what follows, I describe my engagement with the initiative, as well as the events that unfolded

Nikolas Kosmatopoulos, "The Gaza Freedom Flotilla: Ethnographic Notes on 'Othering Violence'," pp. 26–29 from *Anthropology Today* 26(4), 2010.

Ethnographic Fieldwork: An Anthropological Reader, Second Edition. Edited by Antonius C. G. M. Robben and Jeffrey A. Sluka.
Editorial material and organization © 2012 John Wiley & Sons, Inc.
Published 2012 by John Wiley & Sons, Inc.

after the Freedom Flotilla was attacked by the Israeli navy. The Israeli authorities confiscated ships, cargo and all of our personal belongings, including expensive audio-visual equipment and data (footage, photos, interviews etc.), as well as my ethnographic field notes. This leaves me with little in terms of formal recordings of the event. As a recent experience still raw in memory, this narrative is necessarily a preliminary account of events unencumbered by much analysis. I hope to provide a more considered analytical account at a later date.

10–25 May 2010:
Preparing the 'Ship to Gaza'

I arrived in Athens on 10 May, and was immediately caught up in the myriad arrangements needed to prepare an old cargo vessel to traverse half the Mediterranean Sea. This was a major challenge – especially since none of us were particularly experienced in maritime expeditions of this kind: it involved a complex series of tasks which included co-ordinating with harbour workers, negotiating with inflexible port authorities, and acquiring highly specialized technical knowledge on everything from navigation to the storage of sensitive medical equipment.

Fascinated by the breadth of duties, I was keen to get involved in almost all the jobs required. I first joined the press team and the team of the 'digital ship', whose assignment was to digitally 'follow' the vessel en route to Gaza. I conducted semi-structured interviews with members of those teams and attended all the open meetings of the co-ordinating committee at Athens Polytechnic School, in a space provided free to the initiative by the School's Dean. Despite the enthusiasm with which I was welcomed as 'an anthropologist', I could not help but feel like a parachutist who had landed in new but highly charted territory. More often than not, my declared status as a *participant*, but still *observer*, demanded that I sit and write rather than stand and speak.

A shift in my engagement occurred on the night I was invited to visit 'the ship', which had just arrived from a secret location at the commercial port of Keratsini, in Piraeus. On board, my emotions were a mixture of fascination and alarm, feelings of intimacy yet also of alienation. I was overwhelmed by a sense of familiarity and impending danger. The industrial environment of the port, the gentle rocking of the ship, the anticipated geopolitical implications of that moment were as unsettling as they were appealing. Before the ship was to set sail, however, there was still much work to be completed. Over the next 10 days dozens of volunteers, including many Arab migrants and even a few Western visitors, painted cabins and decks, repaired mechanical parts, disposed of quantities of rust, debris and waste, cleaned, loaded the cargo, installed expensive radar and broadband connections, and last but not least, spent long nights guarding the cargo and ship against nasty surprises.

25–30 May: Crossing
the Mediterranean

On 25 May the port authorities inspect both the passenger ship *Sfendoni* and the cargo vessel *Eleftheri Mesogeios* before giving their final approval for departure from the port of Piraeus. Earlier that day the small passenger ship *Sfendoni* had been renamed *8000*, in an effort to raise awareness of the 8000 Palestinian prisoners held in Israeli jails.

Friends and family, and a sprinkling of journalists, bid us farewell. Not far from the port, an Egyptian grocer refuses payment for our hastily purchased supplies of water and juice. I speak to him in Arabic about the flotilla. He is excited, but sad that he can't join us; he calls us *manges* (the macho, honourable tough guys of old times, in Greek) and wishes us '*Allah ma'kon*' ('God be with you', in Arabic).

My investment of hard labour and sleepless nights in preparation meant that I regarded this ship as not only 'field' but also 'home' (Ferguson and Gupta 1997). My official initiation as a sailor was complete when I was allowed to steer the ship in open sea at night, when the captain and first mate were resting.

Our life at sea during the six-day trip on the Mediterranean was spiced with the compelling stories of expedition participants who had faced state aggression (Israeli or other) before, with personal dreams about settling down in Palestine (such as those of a Greek crew member whose English wife is treating children in Gaza), with lay military discussions about the possible scenarios of Israeli aggression, and last but not least, with heated debates on the hidden stashes of the Greek spirit *raki* on the ship. En route, I kept a small notebook in which I noted down incidents, statements, routes and interviews, all the while conscious of the risk of it being seized by the Israeli authorities. Almost all my questions, notes and remarks revolved around three spaces: the ship, the Gaza Strip and the Israeli prison.

The possibility that we might be attacked and imprisoned became almost a certainty when, south of Cyprus, we were informed that the Cypriot government had bowed to Israeli pressure and prohibited more than a dozen parliamentarians from joining us. As these politicians were regarded – along with journalists – as a protection against attacks by the Israeli Defence Force, this news was devastating. Many were convinced that we were about to be attacked.

30 May: The Attack

On 30 May, around midnight, and about 73 miles from the nearest coast, our ship receives orders to stop from the Israeli navy, followed by threats through the maritime radio channels. Soon after, *Eleftheri Mesogeios'* radar detects half a dozen ships in the vicinity. We draw closer to the other vessels of the flotilla almost instinctively.

31 May, 1.00 am. We hold an emergency meeting to allocate tasks in case of attack and to discuss basic forms of resistance and self-defence. The strategy is inspired by the dystopian symbolism of the siege on Gaza: a defence wire is rolled out around the ship to represent the embargo on Gaza through walls and barbed wire. Water pumps are prepared for use against the intruding navy, but this idea is immediately abandoned on the realization that the IDF will most likely respond with live ammunition.[4]

3.30 am. The Israeli warships begin to close in on us. They approach the passenger ships first. This move surprises us all for at least two reasons. First, there had been some propaganda alleging that our ships were carrying weapons,

so an attack on the cargo ships would be easier to defend in international forums. Second and most crucially, we knew that an attack on a 600-passenger ship in the middle of the night and in the middle of the sea would be likely to result in fatal casualties. What we didn't know, however, was that the IDF might have priorities other than the prevention of civilian deaths. In fact, the killings seemed a well-calculated move to convey the message that coming to Palestine involves great risk.

4.30 am. While many of the passengers on the *Mavi Marmara* are performing their morning prayers, a spectacular attack begins against the ship, which is sailing only half a mile away from us. Helicopters and speedboats attack from all sides with live ammunition, tear gas and stun grenades. Smoke appears from where commandoes have landed on the ship. The Greek representative on the *Mavi Marmara* calls by two-way radio to warn us that the IDF is using live ammunition. All other ships of the flotilla disappear from sight within the next half hour. They are all attacked and hijacked by the IDF.

5.30 am. We sail alone for an hour, approximately 80 miles from the coast. The warships can only be traced through our ship radars and the recurring threats over the radio. We expect the navy to emerge at any moment and soon after, a warship approaches, instructing us to stop the ship. The captain and leader of the mission reply with the same, repetitive message: 'This is a Greek ship on humanitarian mission, we are sailing in international waters, we don't obey orders from any foreign government, but only from the Greek government.' In response, the gunboat threatens us with sirens, flares, and verbal assaults. Three speedboats approach from the northeast, seeming to materialize from behind the rising sun.

5.45 am. We can see the commandos clearly now, dressed in black, completely masked and heavily armed. They throw grappling hooks with ladders onto both sides of our bow. We all gather around the bridge, to protect it. The soldiers are ungainly, taking at least 10 minutes to climb, assemble and advance towards us. Finally in formation, they order us to clear the way. We defy their order, stating in unison: 'You are illegal, you are attacking unarmed people, this is not your ship, we are carrying humanitarian aid.' They shoot two of our passengers with tasers and paintballs; they handcuff me and throw me to the floor. They grab the cameras from the journalists. Using force and weapons, they confine us all together in an open space below the bridge. Violent though they are, what disconcerts us most is that they seem inexperienced; we cannot anticipate their reactions.

7.00 am. They demand our passports. We refuse, saying that we will only give our passports to the police. 'We know our rights,' we repeat. They forcibly lead us one by one to the cabins below deck, where they continue to demand that we hand over our passports. Once in the cabins, we see that the soldiers have taken over our space and are sleeping in our beds. Later, they will open the fridge and consume our food. They confine us and a young female soldier begins to film us. We feel like animals in a cage. The Swedish writer puts his hand against the camera. The second time the 'filmmaker' attempts to record us, we shout to the camera: 'This is an act of piracy, we are held illegally by an army that attacked us in international waters.' The camera quickly turns away. We begin to suspect that the film might be made for the purposes not of reconnaissance, but of propaganda. Talking back to the camera defies and finally cancels the spectral violence that is being exercised upon us.

10.00 am. We struggle to keep awake, so that the filmmaker doesn't take us by surprise. We have already won some small battles (e.g. blocking filming, refusing to sign any documents) and this encourages us to discuss a response strategy against the Israeli authorities. I translate the suggestions from English to Greek, while Dror, our Swedish-Israeli colleague, informs us that a soldier has asked his colleague to record our discussion. We protest against this as immoral and unfair. We decide not to sign anything and to demand a lawyer and our respective ambassadors as soon as we arrive.

11.00 am-2.00 pm. Since my diary has been confiscated, I try to stay awake in order to find ways to remember every minute (impossible in such situations of utmost defencelessness). I look around me: people are tired, banging their heads against walls, since they are not allowed to use beds or mattresses. I persuade myself not to close my eyes, because I have to be able to recollect faces, movements, discussions, sentiments around me. Now memory has become a major battlefield. I take a pen and a small piece of paper and write a poem. It is a badly written poem, that only makes sense as the product of my struggle against exhaustion and fear. I compose rhymes in my head in order to stay awake, to keep alert. I feel I am not allowed to show fear, since many of my fellow captives consult with me about various orders or demands that we either refuse or negotiate with the masked men and women. We are allowed to go to the toilet, but only if escorted by a soldier. The door of the toilet must remain open. An officer pulls a laminated piece of paper out of his pocket. Over his shoulder, some of us are able to recognize names, photos and information about ourselves, which has been gathered long before our departure from Piraeus.

5.00 pm. We arrive at Ashdod, after 10 long hours captive at sea. Dozens of men and women in military uniform are standing on the quay. Spare clothes, notes, laptops, cameras and passports are all taken away from us and we are permitted to leave the ship, one by one, stripped of our belongings. They continue filming our every move: leaving the ship, entering the police car. Filming, body-searching and counting seem to preoccupy the Israeli authorities and we are thus counted, filmed and searched repeatedly. After the fourth thorough body search, a young officer stands in front of me in gloves and asks: 'Are you carrying any weapons?' I point with my index finger to my head, indicating that my mind, my memory, my motivations are the only weapons I carry.

7.00 pm. Uniformed personnel continue to count, film and body-search us inside a makeshift military compound. They ask us questions that remain unanswered; they threaten and try to intimidate us. Finally, we are charged with illegal entry. We are astonished, since we are there as the result of the crime of maritime hijacking perpetrated by those who charged us themselves. We are informed that we are going to be sent to jail. We are asked to sign a document that confirms that we illegally entered Israel. We keep on telling them that we were illegally and violently brought to Israel while heading to Gaza through international waters. Suddenly, amidst dozens of men in uniform a man falls to the floor with a bang. He is naked and bruised all over his body. The soldiers lift him up and force him to sit in a wheelchair. I realise that the man is Paul, the US activist aboard the *Sfendoni*. Paul is a non-violent activist. His only 'crime' is continually disobeying the orders of the Israeli police and army.

They move us away from him, bringing us before another officer who asks for our finger-prints. Yet another photo is taken. The soldiers say: 'Smile, you are in Israel.' The absurdity peaks. 'Either you give your finger, or we take it by force.' I ask to see the law. 'You can Google the law,' is the answer. The next passenger to give fingerprints is Vangelis, a senior member of the Greek mission. I am already behind the bars of the prison van when turmoil breaks out inside the compound. Dozens of men in uniform rush in, people scatter left and right. Vangelis is carried out and thrown to the floor. They beat him severely because he has refused to give his fingerprints. Two of his colleagues who protest, as well as the captain of *Sfendoni*, are likewise beaten and locked in isolation cells. They put us all in police vans behind bars and drive us for at least two hours.

31 May–5 June: Beer Sheeva Prison and Release

10.00 pm. Beer Sheeva prison, Section 5. We are the first inmates ever to be held in this section. Shaman, an Iraqi-Swedish fellow passenger, tells me that this one is 'at least clean'. 'At least?' He compares it to Abu Ghraib, where he spent eight months under Saddam Hussein. They film us again. They count us once more. The body searches seem never-ending. We are allocated our own gaol manager and given towels and toothbrushes. We are placed in cells, four to a cell. Our transformation into prisoners is now complete.

1 June, 6.00 am. The guards wake us up with heavy knocking on the cell doors. We come out to realize that during the night more inmates have arrived. They all come from different ships and everyone wants to know how the attack unfolded on the other ships. We are cut off from the outside world. No phone calls allowed, no lawyers, no embassy personnel.

12.00 am. We decide to form a 'prisoners' committee' to convey our demands to the prison authorities. The gaol manager announces to us that 'there are no demands, there are only requests.' As soon as we inform him that we have set up a committee that will represent all of us, we are ordered back to the cells for 'counting'. The counting lasts for hours. It is a bureaucratic punishment for our collective mobilization.

2 June, 12 pm. A group of well-dressed, middle-aged men and women arrive at the prison. We realize that these are the embassy staff and we all rush from the cells to meet them. They inform us of the global outcry against what some considered an Israeli act of state terrorism. This news gives us new hope. The situation gradually changes. The authorities can no longer force us to comply with their arbitrary decisions. We can feel solidarity building up on our side. We can sense the desire of the other side to be rid of us as soon as possible.

3 June, 6.00 am. I am woken by the prison guards' heavy knocking on the doors. Their nervousness suggests to us that today is going to be our last day in the prison. Indeed, during the night, all the Arab prisoners have been transferred to Jordan by bus. Now it is our turn. They call us one by one. We decide to leave en masse so that no one is left behind.

12.00 am. We are brought to the Ben-Gurion Airport amid continued tension. Prisoners talk back to the soldiers; the soldiers retaliate physically against their captives. They take us individually to a desk staffed by two officers, where we are supposed to sign a document that we willingly agree to deportation. We maintain our resistance against the Israeli absurdity.

7.00 pm. All the Greek citizens assemble in a room in Terminal 1 under constant police surveillance. They take us to the airport prison to meet the ambassador and two Israeli lawyers, whom we collectively hire for further legal action in Israel against the perpetrators of the attack.

Half of the passports, as well as all audio-visual equipment, photos, notebooks, tapes and personal items, remain unreturned to their owners.

Midnight. Three full days after our first encounter with the IDF, we board a military plane sent by the Greek government and return to Athens.

4 June, 2.00 am. On landing, government officials, press, family, friends and the general public greet us en masse. I cannot rid myself of the sense of absurdity. At dawn on 31 May, the Israeli navy launched what we experienced as a bloody military operation against the Freedom Flotilla in international waters almost 80 miles from the nearest coast. The damage now becomes more apparent to us: in the attack, nine passengers on the IHH ship *Mavi Marmara* were killed and more than 50 wounded.

5 June and after. Over the next few days media ask each participant to recount his/her experiences and counter the Israeli claims that the killings and attacks were 'self-defence'. In Europe, some media commentators coin ludicrous terms to describe us, such as 'peace terrorists' (Margolina 2010). We come to the bitter realization that another battle, for the 'facts', has only just begun. In press conferences, newspaper articles and TV appearances we are repeatedly confronted with accusations of terrorism and violence, as well as with the fabricated version of the events offered by the Israeli state machinery. Often, the feeling of alienation 'at home' is even greater than in prison. This is not to say that much public opinion and press coverage is not also overwhelmingly supportive.[5] After all, the facts told a clear story: military attack in international waters, nine activists shot and killed, only humanitarian cargo on board.

Concluding Remarks

The tragic events that unfolded around the Freedom Flotilla tell a compelling story of international solidarity in the face of our encounter with what we had experienced as brute state violence, marred only by ill-informed commentaries in the press 'at home'.

Each of the three spaces this story revolved around was transformed by Israeli authorities into a prison. Beer Sheeva prison was built on land initially allocated to the future Arab state of Palestine under the 1947 UN Partition Plan, but later seized by the Israeli army in the subsequent war and annexed to the Israeli state. Gaza was turned into a collective prison under the embargo imposed by the same army in June 2007, because the same state and her Western allies disapproved of the Palestinian people's freely elected choice of Hamas as their legitimate government. Finally, on the morning of 31 May 2010, the *Free Mediterranean* was paradoxically turned into a floating prison through what we considered an act of state terrorism undertaken by the same army, because they deemed a fleet of humanitarian aid ships in international waters a threat to national security.

Since this kind of violence creates prisons out of spaces of national liberation (Beer Sheeva), civic self-determination (Gaza) and international solidarity (*Eleftheri Mesogeios*), I propose to call it *Othering violence*. This is, to a great extent, the violence that characterizes our troubled times.

Moreover, our transformation into 'peace terrorists' by Israel and its apologists reminds me of the 'doubletalk' government propaganda George Orwell describes in *Nineteen eighty-four*, where the Ministry of Peace wages war, the Ministry of Truth lies, the Ministry of Love tortures and the Ministry of Plenty causes starvation. From my point of view, in order to excuse maritime piracy, a peaceful flotilla committed to non-violence needed to be framed first as a dangerous threat to Israel's national security and, under this pretext, to be assaulted in international waters and subsequently criminalized as the aggressors.

The choice to be an outspoken participant-observer of Othering violence in my immediate corporeality as an anthropologist represented a difficult challenge and a step up from the already challenging exercise of participant-observation of a people in peacetime. Yet it is worthwhile, for it opens up novel spaces for reflection and research otherwise left to the sensationalist tendencies of journalism and the propaganda machinery of states.[6]

When I refused to hand over my passport to these criminals in international waters, the masked soldiers grabbed and dragged me to the floor. In a moment of acute anxiety, I blurted out 'Stop, stop, I am a human being.' Instinctively, my appeal to our common humanity conveyed hope of surviving this kind of threat. Yet the threat to myself is dwarfed into insignificance by the threats millions of others experience on a daily basis all over the world, including Gaza, without unfortunately any witnesses to record them.

Acting as witness to events such as these, in our professional academic as well as in our personal capacity, could be a last line of defence against expanding Othering violence.

NOTES

I am grateful to Rana Boukarim, Michele Kayaleh and Shalini Randeria for reading and commenting on earlier drafts of this paper, and to the six anonymous AT reviewers. I would also like to thank Gustavo Barbosa and Elizabeth Frantz for inviting me to the SWANA seminar series at the London School of Economics to talk about my experience as an anthropologist with the Freedom Flotilla.

1 Hardly any ships have approached the port of Gaza since it was seized by the Israeli army in the 1967 war. The Israeli embargo on the Gaza Strip since the Hamas election victory in June 2007 includes fishing activity by Gazans more than three nautical miles from the coast, and any maritime traffic in and out of the port of Gaza. The list of Israeli-banned import goods includes spices, toys and musical instruments and much more.

2 Organized as a partnership of six organizations: The European Campaign to End the Siege on Gaza-Palestinian Diaspora, the Free Gaza Movement, the International Committee to End the Siege on Gaza, the Ship to Gaza-Sweden, the IHH Humanitarian Relief Foundation-Turkey, and the Ship to Gaza-Greece.

3 My relationship with members of that initiative goes back to the time of my fieldwork in Egypt in 2004, when we were all involved

in a road convoy to Gaza that was eventually blocked by the Egyptian military.

4 For a valuable one-hour-long video smuggled out of the Israeli Prison by Iara Lee, visit: www. culturesofresistance.org

5 The global outcry against the Israeli aggression was well documented and evident in media outlets such as *The Guardian, Le Monde, Der Spiegel, FAZ,* but also in a number of editorials in Israeli newspapers, such as that by Avneri (2010).

6 E.g. the 'Combating terrorism by countering radicalisation' research project (Keenan 2007), Human Terrain (González 2008) and Minerva (Lutz 2008).

REFERENCES

Avneri, U.
'Kill a Turk and rest'. http://www.avnery-news.co.il/english/index.html(accessed 5 June 2010).

Ferguson, J. and Gupta, A.
1997 Discipline and practice: 'The field' as site, method, and location in anthropology. In: Gupta, Akhil and Ferguson, James (eds), *Anthropological locations: Boundaries and grounds of a field science,* pp. 1–46. Berkeley: University of California Press.

González. R.J.
2008 Human Terrain: Past, present and future applications. *Anthropology Today* 24(1): 21–26.

Insani Yardim Vakfi (IHH)
2010 'Palestine our route humanitarian aid our load: Flotilla campaign summary report'. http://www.ihh.org.tr/insani-yardim-filosu-ozetraporu/en/ (accessed 11 July 2010).

Keenan, J.
2007 My country right or wrong. *Anthropology Today,* 23(1): 26–27.

Lutz, C.
2008 Selling ourselves? The perils of Pentagon funding of anthropology. *Anthropology Today,* 24(5): 1–3.

Margolina, Sonja.
Krieg ist Frieden: Wie Terroristen die Menschenrechte kapern (War is peace: How terrorists seize human rights). *Neue Zürcher Zeitung,* 17.06.2010.

Appendix 1: Key Ethnographic, Sociological, Qualitative, and Multidisciplinary Fieldwork Methods Texts (selected for relevance to anthropology; chronological, newest first)

- *Ethnographic Fieldwork: A Beginner's Guide* (2010), by Jan Blommaert and Jie Dong.
- *Essentials of Field Relationships* (2010), by Amy Kaler and Melanie Beres.
- *Netnography: Doing Ethnographic Research Online* (2010), by Robert Kozinets.
- *Improvising Theory: Process and Temporality in Ethnographic Fieldwork* (2007), by Allaine Cerwonka and Liisa Malkki.
- *The SAGE Handbook of Qualitative Research* (2005), edited by Norman Denzin and Yvonna Lincoln. 3rd edn.
- *The SAGE Handbook of Fieldwork* (2005), edited by Dick Hobbs and Richard Wright.
- *Fieldwork* (2005), edited by Christopher Pole. 4 vols.
- *Recording Oral History: A Guide for the Humanities and Social Sciences* (2005), by Valerie Raleigh Yow. 2nd edn.
- *Being Here and Being There: Fieldwork Encounters and Ethnographic Discoveries* (2004), edited by Elijah Anderson et al.
- *Dialogue with the Past: Engaging Students and Meeting Standards through Oral History* (2004), by Glen Whitman.
- *Qualitative Research Methods for the Social Sciences* (2003), by Bruce Berg. 5th edn.

Ethnographic Fieldwork: An Anthropological Reader, Second Edition. Edited by Antonius C. G. M. Robben and Jeffrey A. Sluka.
Editorial material and organization © 2012 John Wiley & Sons, Inc.
Published 2012 by John Wiley & Sons, Inc.

- *Participant Observation: A Guide for Fieldworkers* (2002), by Kathleen and Billie DeWalt.
- *Qualitative Research Methods* (2002), edited by Darin Weinberg.
- *Handbook of Ethnography* (2001), edited by Paul Atkinson et al.
- *Ethnography* (2001), edited by Alan Bryman. 4 vols.
- *The American Tradition in Qualitative Research* (2001), edited by Norman Denzin and Yvonna Lincoln. 4 vols.
- *Reflexive Methodology: New Vistas for Qualitative Research* (2000), by Mats Alvesson and Kaj Sköldberg.
- *Virtual Ethnography* (2000), by Christine Hine.
- *Qualitative Research* (1999), edited by Alan Bryman and Robert Burgess. 4 vols.
- *Ethnographer's Toolkit* (1999), edited by Jean Schensul and Margaret LeCompte. 7 vols.
- *Doing Ethnographic Research: Fieldwork Settings* (1998), edited by Scott Grills.
- *Basics of Qualitative Research: Techniques and Procedures for Developing Grounded Theory* (1998), by Anselm Strauss and Juliet Corbin. 2nd edn.
- *Feminist Dilemmas in Fieldwork* (1996), edited by Diane Wolf.
- *The World Observed: Reflections on the Fieldwork Process* (1996), edited by Bruce Jackson and Edward Ives.
- *Journeys Through Ethnography: Realistic Accounts of Fieldwork* (1996), edited by Annette Lareau and Jeffrey Shultz.
- *Co-operative Inquiry: Research into the Human Condition* (1996), by John Heron.
- *Ethnography: Principles in Practice* (1995), by Martyn Hammersley and Paul Atkinson. 2nd edn.
- *The Active Interview* (1995), by James Holstein and Jaber Gubrium.
- *Interpreting the Field: Accounts of Ethnography* (1993), edited by Dick Hobbs and Tim May.
- *Ethnography: Step-by-Step* (1992), by David Fetterman.
- *Participant-Observation: A Methodology for Human Studies* (1989), by Danny Jorgensen.
- *Systematic Fieldwork* (1987), by Oswald Werner and G. Mark Schoepfle. 2 vols.
- *The Politics and Ethics of Fieldwork* (1986), by Maurice Punch.
- *Interpreting Life Histories: An Anthropological Inquiry* (1985), by Lawrence C. Watson and Maria-Barbara Watson-Franke.
- *Social Researching: Politics, Problems, Practice* (1984), edited by Colin Bell and Helen Roberts.
- *In the Field: An Introduction to Field Research* (1984), by Robert Burgess.
- *Learning from the Field: A Guide from Experience* (1984), by William Foote Whyte.
- *Qualitative Methodology* (1983), edited by John Van Maanen.
- *Ethnographic Research* (1982), by Marion Dobbert.
- *People Studying People: The Human Element in Fieldwork* (1980), by Robert Georges and Michael Jones.
- *Fieldwork Experience: Qualitative Approaches to Social Research* (1980), edited by William Shaffir, Robert Stebbins, and Allan Turowetz.

- *The Fieldworker and the Field: Problems and Challenges in Sociological Investigation* (1979), edited by M. Srinivas, A. Shah, and E. Ramaswamy.
- *Doing Sociological Research* (1977), edited by Colin Bell and Howard Newby.
- *Introduction to Qualitative Research Methods: A Phenomenological Approach to the Social Sciences* (1975), by Robert Bogden and Steven Taylor.
- *Participant Observation: Theory and Practice* (1975), by Jürgen Friedrichs and Hartmut Lüdtke.
- *Research on Deviance* (1972), edited by Jack Douglas.
- *The Research Adventure: Promise and Problems in Fieldwork* (1972), by Myron Glazer.
- *Field Research: Strategies for a Natural Sociology* (1972), edited by Leonard Schatzman and Anselm Strauss.
- *Issues in Participant Observation: A Text and Reader* (1969), edited by George McCall and Jerry Simmons.
- *Hustlers, Beats, and Others* (1967), by Ned Polsky.
- *Sociologists at Work: Essays on the Craft of Social Research* (1964), edited by Phillip Hammond.
- *Reflections on Community Studies* (1964), edited by Arthur Vidich, Joseph Bensman, and Maurice Stein.

Appendix 2: Edited Cultural Anthropology Volumes on Fieldwork Experiences (chronological; oldest first)

- *In the Company of Man: Twenty Portraits of Anthropological Informants* (1960), edited by Joseph Casagrande.
- *Anthropologists in the Field* (1967), edited by D. Jongmans and P. Gutkind.
- *Stress and Response in Fieldwork* (1969), edited by Frances Henry and Satish Saberwal.
- *Marginal Natives: Anthropologists at Work* (1970), edited by Morris Freilich.
- *Women in the Field: Anthropological Experiences* (1970), edited by Peggy Golde.
- *Being an Anthropologist: Fieldwork in Eleven Cultures* (1970), edited by George Spindler.
- *Crossing Cultural Boundaries: The Anthropological Experience* (1972), edited by Solon Kimball and James Watson.
- *Encounter and Experience: Personal Accounts of Fieldwork* (1975), edited by André Béteille and T. N. Madan.
- *Anthropologists at Home in North America: Methods and Issues in the Study of One's Own Society* (1981), edited by Donald Messerschmidt.
- *Observers Observed: Essays on Ethnographic Fieldwork* (1983), edited by George Stocking.
- *Doing Fieldwork: Eight Personal Accounts of Social Research* (1989), edited by John Perry.
- *The Humbled Anthropologist: Tales from the Pacific* (1990), edited by Philip DeVita.

Ethnographic Fieldwork: An Anthropological Reader, Second Edition. Edited by
Antonius C. G. M. Robben and Jeffrey A. Sluka.
Editorial material and organization © 2012 John Wiley & Sons, Inc.
Published 2012 by John Wiley & Sons, Inc.

- *Experiencing Fieldwork: An Inside View of Qualitative Research* (1991), edited by William Shaffir and Robert Stebbins.
- *The Naked Anthropologist: Tales From Around the World* (1992), edited by Philip DeVita.
- *Fieldwork Under Fire: Contemporary Studies of Violence and Survival* (1995), edited by Carolyn Nordstrom and Antonius Robben.
- *Bridges to Humanity: Narratives on Anthropology and Friendship* (1995), edited by Frank Salamone and Bruce Grindal.
- *Being There: Fieldwork in Anthropology* (1995), edited by C. Watson.
- *In the Field: Readings on the Field Research Experience* (1996), edited by Carolyn Smith and William Kornblum.
- *Out in the Field: Reflections of Lesbian and Gay Anthropologists* (1996), edited by Ellen Lewin and William Leap.
- *Feminist Dilemmas in Fieldwork* (1996), edited by Diane Wolf.
- *Fieldwork Revisited: Changing Contexts of Ethnographic Practice in the Era of Globalization* (1997), special issue of *Anthropology and Humanism* 22:1, edited by Joel Robbins and Sandra Bamford.
- *Anthropological Journeys: Reflections on Fieldwork* (1998), edited by Meenakshi Thapan.
- *Being There: Fieldwork in Anthropology* (1999), edited by C. W. Watson.
- *Constructing the Field: Ethnographic Fieldwork in the Contemporary World* (2000), edited by Vered Amit.
- *Stumbling Toward Truth: Anthropologists at Work* (2000), edited by Philip DeVita.
- *Fieldwork Dilemmas: Anthropologists in Postsocialist States* (2000), edited by Hermine De Soto and Nora Dudwick.
- *Anthropologists in a Wider World: Essays on Field Research* (2000), edited by Paul Dresch, Wendy James, and David Parkin.
- *Anthropologists in the Field: Case Studies in Participant Observation* (2004), edited by Lynne Hume and Jane Mulcock.
- *Locating the Field: Space, Place and Context in Anthropology* (2006), edited by Simon Coleman and Peter Collins.
- *Engaged Observer: Anthropology, Advocacy, and Activism* (2006), edited by Victoria Sanford and Asale Angel-Ajani.
- *The Shadow Side of Fieldwork: Exploring the Blurred Borders between Ethnography and Life* (2007), edited by Athena McLean and Annette Leibing.
- *Knowing How to Know: Fieldwork and the Ethnographic Present* (2008), edited by Narmala Halstead, Eric Hirsch, and Judith Okeley.
- *Taking Sides: Ethics, Politics, and Fieldwork in Anthropology* (2009), edited by Heidi Armbruster and Anna Laerke.
- *Women Fielding Danger: Negotiating Ethnographic Identities in Field Research* (2009), edited by Martha Huggins and Marie-Louise Glebbeek.
- *Emotions in the Field: The Psychology and Anthropology of Fieldwork Experience* (2010), edited by James Davies and Dimitrina Spencer.
- *Centralizing Fieldwork: Critical Perspectives from Primatology, Biological and Social Anthropology* (2010), edited by Jeremy McClancy and Agustin Fuentes.

- *Anthropological Fieldwork: A Relational Process* (2010), edited by Dimitri Spencer and James Davies.
- *Between Art and Anthropology: Contemporary Ethnographic Practice* (2010), edited by Arnd Schneider and Christopher Wright.
- *Fieldwork Identities in the Caribbean* (2010), edited by Erin Taylor.
- *Anthropologists in the Securityscape: Ethics, Practices, and Professional Identity* (2011), edited by Robert Albro et al.

Appendix 3: Reflexive Accounts of Fieldwork and Ethnographies Which Include Accounts of Fieldwork (chronological; oldest first)

- *Greener Fields: Experiences among the American Indians* (1953), by Alice Marriott.
- *Hindus of the Himalayas* (1963), by Gerald Berreman.
- *The Savage and the Innocent* (1965), by David Maybury-Lewis.
- *Stranger and Friend: The Way of an Anthropologist* (1966), by Hortense Powdermaker.
- *The High Valley* (1966), by Kenneth Read.
- *Never in Anger: Portrait of an Eskimo Family* (1970), by Jean Briggs.
- *Doing Fieldwork: Warnings and Advice* (1971), by Rosalie Wax.
- *Down among the Wild Men: The Narrative Journal of Fifteen Years Pursuing the Old Stone Age Aborigines of Australia's Western Desert* (1972), by John Greenway.
- *Studying the Yanomamö* (1974), by Napoleon Chagnon.
- *When the Spider Danced: Notes from an African Village* (1975), by Alexander Alland, Jr.
- *African Odyssey: An Anthropological Adventure* (1976), by Mariam Slater.
- *An Asian Anthropologist in the South: Field Experiences with Blacks, Indians and Whites* (1977), by Choong Soon Kim.
- *Reflections on Fieldwork in Morocco* (1977), by Paul Rabinow.
- *The Headman and I: Ambiguity and Ambivalence in the Fieldworking Experience* (1978), by Jean-Paul Dumont.
- *The Bamboo Fire: An Anthropologist in New Guinea* (1978), by William Mitchell.
- *Tuhami: Portrait of a Moroccan* (1980), by Vincent Crapanzano.
- *The Innocent Anthropologist: Notes from a Mud Hut* (1983), by Nigel Barley.

Ethnographic Fieldwork: An Anthropological Reader, Second Edition. Edited by
Antonius C. G. M. Robben and Jeffrey A. Sluka.
Editorial material and organization © 2012 John Wiley & Sons, Inc.
Published 2012 by John Wiley & Sons, Inc.

- *Assault on Paradise: Social Change in a Brazilian Village* (1983), by Conrad Kottak.
- *Inis Beag Revisited: The Anthropologist as Observant Participator* (1983), by John Messenger.
- *A Plague of Caterpillars: A Return to the African Bush* (1986), by Nigel Barley.
- *Return to the High Valley: Coming Full Circle* (1986), by Kenneth Read.
- *In Sorcery's Shadow: A Memoir of Apprenticeship Among the Songhay of Niger* (1987), by Paul Stoller and Cheryl Olkes.
- *Hearts and Minds, Water and Fish: Popular Support for the IRA and INLA in a Northern Irish Ghetto* (1989), by Jeffrey Sluka.
- *Nest in the Wind: Adventures in Anthropology on a Tropical Island* (1989), by Martha Ward.
- *First Fieldwork: The Misadventures of an Anthropologist* (1990), by Barbara Anderson.
- *Road through the Rain Forest: Living Anthropology in Highland Papua New Guinea* (1990), by David Hayano.
- *Fighting for Faith and Nation: Dialogues with Sikh Militants* (1996), by Cynthia Mahmood.
- *Mad Dogs, Englishmen, and the Errant Anthropologist: Fieldwork in Malaysia* (1996), by Douglas Raybeck.
- *The Vulnerable Observer: Anthropology that Breaks Your Heart* (1997), by Ruth Behar.
- *Being There: The Necessity of Fieldwork* (1998), by Daniel Bradburd.
- *Around the World in Thirty Years: Life as a Cultural Anthropologist* (1999), by Barbara Anderson.
- *An Anthropologist in Japan: Glimpses of Life in the Field* (1999), by Joy Hendry.
- *The Politics of Fieldwork: Research in an American Concentration Camp* (2001), by Lane Hirabayashi.
- *Dark Shamans: Kanaima and the Poetics of Violent Death* (2002), by Neil Whitehead.
- *Doing Fieldwork in Japan* (2003), by Theodore Bestor, Patricia Steinhoff, and Victoria Lyon Bester.
- *The Ethnographic I: A Methodological Novel about Autoethnography* (2004), by Carolyn Ellis.
- *Journeys to the Edge: In the Footsteps of an Anthropologist* (2006), by Peter Gardner.
- *Improvising Theory: Process and Temporality in Ethnographic Fieldwork* (2007), by Allaine Cerwonka and Liisa Malkki.
- *Fieldwork Connections: The Fabric of Ethnographic Collaboration in China and America* (2007), by Strevan Harrell, Ma Lunzy, and Bami Ayi.
- *Objects and Objections of Ethnography* (2010), by James Siegel.

Appendix 4: Leading Cultural Anthropology Fieldwork Methods Texts (chronological; oldest first)

- *Notes and Queries on Anthropology* (1951), Royal Anthropological Institute of Great Britain and Northern Ireland. 6th edn.
- *Method and Perspective in Anthropology: Essays in Honor of Wilson D. Wallis* (1954), by Robert F. Spencer.
- *Methods in Social Anthropology: Selected Essays* (1958), by A. R. Radcliffe-Brown.
- *Human Organization Research: Field Relations and Techniques* (1960), edited by Richard Adams and Jack Preiss.
- *The Anthropology of Music* (1964), by Alan Merriam.
- *The Craft of Social Anthropology* (1967), edited by A. L. Epstein.
- *Field Methods in the Study of Culture* (1967), by Thomas Williams.
- *A Handbook of Method in Cultural Anthropology* (1970), edited by Raoul Narroll and Ronald Cohen.
- *Crossing Cultural Boundaries: The Anthropological Experience* (1972), edited by Solon Kimball and James Watson.
- *Handbook of Social and Cultural Anthropology* (1973), edited by John Honigmann.
- *Methods and Styles in the Study of Culture* (1974), by Robert Edgerton and L. Langness.
- *Ethnographic Film* (1976), by Karl Heider.
- *Anthropological Research: The Structure of Inquiry* (1978), by Perti Pelto and Gretel Pelto. 2nd edn.
- *The Craft of Community Study: Fieldwork Dialogues* (1979), by Solon Kimball and William Partridge.
- *The Ethnographic Interview* (1979), by James Spradley.

Ethnographic Fieldwork: An Anthropological Reader, Second Edition. Edited by Antonius C. G. M. Robben and Jeffrey A. Sluka.
Editorial material and organization © 2012 John Wiley & Sons, Inc.
Published 2012 by John Wiley & Sons, Inc.

- *The Professional Stranger: An Informal Introduction to Ethnography* (1980), by Michael Agar.
- *Participant Observation* (1980), by James Spradley.
- *Speaking of Ethnography* (1986), by Michael Agar.
- *Systematic Fieldwork* (1987), by Oswald Werner and G. Mark Schoepfle. 2 vols.
- *The Varieties of Sensory Experience: A Sourcebook in the Anthropology of the Senses* (1991), edited by David Howes.
- *Field Projects in Anthropology: A Student Handbook* (1992), edited by Julia Crane and Michael Angrosino.
- *Ethnomusicology: An Introduction* (1992), edited by Helen Myers.
- *Cross-Cultural Filmmaking: A Handbook for Making Documentary and Ethnographic Films and Videos* (1997), by Ilisa Barbash and Lucien Taylor.
- *Field Ethnography: A Manual for Doing Cultural Anthropology* (1997), by Paul Kutsche.
- *Handbook of Methods in Cultural Anthropology* (1998), edited by H. Russell Bernard.
- *Doing Cultural Anthropology: Projects for Ethnographic Data Collection* (2002), edited by Michael Angrosino.
- *Projects in Ethnographic Research* (2005), by Michael Angrosino.
- *Research Methods in Anthropology: Qualitative and Quantitative Approaches* (2005), by H. Russell Bernard. 4th edn.
- *Finding Culture in Talk: A Collection of Methods* (2005), by Naomi Quinn.
- *Fieldwork Is Not What It Used to Be: Learning Anthropology's Method in a Time of Transition* (2009), edited by James Faubion and George Marcus.
- *Ethnography: Step-by-Step* (2009), by David Fetterman.
- *Ethnographic Practice in the Present* (2009), edited by Marit Melhuus, Jon Mitchell, and Helena Wulff.
- *Doing Sensory Ethnography* (2009), by Sarah Pink.
- *Participant Observation: A Guide for Fieldworkers* (2010), by Kathleen DeWalt.
- *Being Ethnographic: A Guide to the Theory and Practice of Ethnography* (2010), by Raymond Madden.
- *Ethnography Lessons: A Primer* (2010), by Harry Wolcott.
- *Anthropological Practice: Fieldwork and the Ethnographic Method* (2011), by Judith Okeley.

Appendix 5: Early and Classic Anthropological Writings on Fieldwork, including Diaries and Letters (chronological; oldest first)

- Bronislaw Malinowski, "Introduction: The Subject, Method and Scope of This Inquiry," in *Argonauts of the Western Pacific* (1922), and his posthumously published *A Diary in the Strict Sense of the Term* (1967).
- On Franz Boas's diary, see Rohner 1969.
- Paul Radin, *The Method and Theory of Ethnology* (1933).
- Audrey Richards, "The Development of Field Work Methods in Social Anthropology" (1939).
- Claude Lévi-Strauss, *Tristes Tropiques* (1955).
- Ralph Piddington, "Methods of Field Work" (1957).
- On Lowie's fieldwork, see his *Robert E. Lowie, Ethnologist: A Personal Record* (1959).
- E. E. Evans-Pritchard, "Some Reminiscences and Reflections on Fieldwork" (1973).
- On Ruth Benedict's fieldwork, see Mead 1959 and 1977.
- On the fieldwork correspondence of Robert Redfield and Sol Tax, see Rubinstein 1991.

Ethnographic Fieldwork: An Anthropological Reader, Second Edition. Edited by Antonius C. G. M. Robben and Jeffrey A. Sluka.
Editorial material and organization © 2012 John Wiley & Sons, Inc.
Published 2012 by John Wiley & Sons, Inc.

Index

Ethnographic Fieldwork: An Anthropological Reader, Second Edition. Edited by
Antonius C. G. M. Robben and Jeffrey A. Sluka.
Editorial material and organization © 2012 John Wiley & Sons, Inc.
Published 2012 by John Wiley & Sons, Inc.